American Defense Policy

American Defense Policy

NINTH EDITION

Edited by Miriam Krieger, Lynne Chandler Garcia, John Riley, and Will Atkins

Assistant Editors
Seth Cannon, Jason Egger, and Noah Fisher

Johns Hopkins University Press
Baltimore

This work was created in the performance of a Cooperative Research and Development Agreement with the Department of the Air Force. The Government of the United States has certain rights to use this work.

The ideas expressed in this text do not represent the USAFA, US Air Force, Department of Defense, or the US government. This work has been cleared by Public Affairs: PA# USAFA-DF-2020-248-251.

Johns Hopkins University Press
2715 North Charles Street
Baltimore, Maryland 21218-4363
www.press.jhu.edu

Library of Congress Cataloging-in-Publication Data

Names: Krieger, Miriam, 1982– editor. | Chandler Garcia, Lynne M., 1973– editor. | Riley, John H., 1970– editor. |
    Atkins, Will, 1980– editor.
Title: American defense policy / edited by Miriam Krieger, Lynne Chandler Garcia, John Riley, and Will Atkins.
Description: Ninth edition. | Baltimore : Johns Hopkins University Press, 2021. | Includes bibliographical references
    and index.
Identifiers: LCCN 2020047104 | ISBN 9781421441474 (hardcover) | ISBN 9781421441481 (paperback) |
    ISBN 9781421441498 (ebook)
Subjects: LCSH: United States—Military policy.
Classification: LCC UA23 .A626 2021 | DDC 355/.033073—dc23
LC record available at https://lccn.loc.gov/2020047104

A catalog record for this book is available from the British Library.

Special discounts are available for bulk purchases of this book. For more information, please contact Special Sales at specialsales@jh.edu.

Johns Hopkins University Press uses environmentally friendly book materials, including recycled text paper that is composed of at least 30 percent post-consumer waste, whenever possible.

TO ERVIN J. ROKKE

whose long career of service to the nation
includes leading our department
and the USAFA faculty

Contents

Foreword

DAVID KILCULLEN

It is no exaggeration to say that the global environment and the role of the United States in international affairs—indeed, the very way in which Americans see themselves and are seen by others within the world strategic landscape—have shifted fundamentally since the last edition of *American Defense Policy* appeared in June 2005. The new edition of this seminal textbook is thus timely and relevant for any defense policy professional or student of strategy attempting to understand today's complex strategic terrain.

The World in 2005

When the previous edition appeared, the policy framework for American strategists and planners was the Global War on Terrorism (GWOT), then in its early stages. In 2005, the United States and its allies and coalition partners faced a fast-growing and multifarious sectarian insurgency in Iraq. They were struggling to extricate themselves from a morass of their own making in the Middle East and confronting an adaptive terrorist threat that was morphing worldwide—spreading through South and Southeast Asia, Africa, Europe and Australasia—even as the occupation of Iraq appeared to have no end in sight. Indeed, stabilizing and then leaving Iraq was so central to US defense policy in this period that an incoming secretary of defense could describe his top three priorities as "Iraq, Iraq and Iraq."[1]

In Afghanistan, still at this time seen as the "good war"—or rather, the more successful theater in the two-front counterinsurgency war in which the United States now found itself—the government of Hamid Karzai still seemed relatively robust. But Karzai was facing rising public unrest and criticism for incompetent governance, nepotism, and corruption and confronting a spike in insurgent activity across the majority-Pashtun south and east of the country.[2] The Taliban, emerging from their eclipse of 2002–2004, were beginning to reassert themselves, infiltrating the high mountain passes of the Hindu Kush from sanctuaries in Pakistan, contesting government authority in the countryside, and intimidating rural populations even as Afghanistan's cities and its northern and western regions remained relatively untouched by the growing guerrilla war in the villages.

American policy at this time was directed at deterring Pakistan from its increasingly obvious sponsorship of cross-border infiltration into Afghanistan, combating the regional terrorist (as distinct from local guerrilla) threat, encouraging greater NATO participation in the war, and broadening the alliance's mission in order to free US assets for the main effort in Iraq. NATO allies for the most part still saw the Afghan campaign as a postwar reconstruction and stabilization effort rather than an active theater of counterinsurgency warfare, a concept that, in 2005, was yet to be formally adopted by the Pentagon.[3]

The Iraq "surge" of 2007–2009, the precipitate withdrawal in 2010 that enabled the rise of Islamic State less than four years later, the time- and resource-limited Afghan surge of 2009, the Arab Spring uprisings that destabilized the Middle East and North Africa (MENA) region after 2011, and the horrific wars that followed in Libya, Syria, and Yemen, all lay in the future.

Obviously enough, given that they involved land-based irregular enemies who lacked air or maritime capabilities, Iraq and Afghanistan were mostly ground wars, with the Army and Marines shouldering the principal combat burden and suffering the vast majority of casualties. Air assets were committed to intelligence, surveillance, and reconnaissance (ISR), air interdiction, and close air support (CAS) missions, giving airpower a key—though not always fully exploited—role, while rotary-wing battlefield aviation once again proved to be a critical combat multiplier in irregular warfare.[4] Over time, the level of effort expected of high-end aircraft, designed for strategic bombing or air superiority missions but increasingly used for CAS in low-threat but high-tempo environments, would impose severe wear on aircraft fleets and force revisions to logistic and maintenance norms, as well as to acquisition policies. The crucial role of Joint Terminal Attack Controllers (JTACs) in Iraq and Afghanistan was starting to be recognized, as conflicts in Africa—a true "air theater," with its enormous distances and low force densities, where JTACs would come into their own—were beginning to emerge.[5] Remotely piloted aircraft such as the MQ-1 Predator had proven themselves in the ISR role, while the MQ-9 Reaper was entering service as a multi-role combat platform, and truly autonomous air combat vehicles were in development.[6] These were the harbingers of a new wave of autonomous systems and artificial intelligence (AI) that were to transform the technology available to allies and adversaries alike in coming years.

Maritime forces focused at this time on security force assistance (SFA) for partners threatened by seaborne terrorism, guarded sea lanes, and provided specialists such as Naval Construction Battalions (Seabees), riverine forces, counter–improvised explosive device (IED) teams, and individual reinforcements to support the GWOT. The US Navy—at this time, the world's largest navy, which happened also to include the world's second largest air force and its premier expeditionary ground force—was engaged across all theaters. Carrier aviation played a critical role in CAS for Iraq and Afghanistan, and amphibious and littoral operations were important in the early stages of both conflicts. Naval Special Warfare units were at the forefront of counterterrorism pursuit and direct action.[7] But overall, coalition navies found themselves less heavily committed to Iraq and Afghanistan than air forces; this gave naval planners and policy-makers greater freedom to look beyond the immediate irregular conflict and consider the rising threat of nation-state adversaries. Unsurprisingly, therefore, the US Navy sounded the alarm about China's anti-access/area denial (A2/AD) capabilities and growing maritime ambitions.

Indeed, away from center stage, where the GWOT still held the spotlight in US defense policy, parts of the defense establishment—notably the Navy leadership, the Office of Net Assessments, forward-thinking USAF air and space power theorists, and intelligence community analysts—were warning of the threat from an increasingly militaristic and aggressive Communist China and a resurgent Russian Federation. But policy-makers worried more about terrorism than state adversaries. With limited bandwidth and an almost daily series of crises emanating from Iraq, the most important resource of all—strategic attention—was overwhelmingly devoted to the MENA theater. More broadly, terrorism was still the key driver of US defense policy, military strategy, and force posture.

Of the potential peer adversaries, Russia, at this time, was still seen as broadly pro-Western in orientation, on its way to becoming a "normal" country within the US-dominated rules-based world order, albeit one with authoritarian tendencies that made Moscow a problematic partner in the counterterrorism fight. The Russian military had shown significant improvement in tactical skill and operational effectiveness since its debacles of the 1990s in Dagestan and Chechnya and a series of "frozen" conflicts across former Soviet space. But logistics, command and control (C2), and interservice coordination remained Russian weaknesses, a fact tragically underlined in September 2004, when Chechen terrorists murdered 334 people, including many elementary-school children in a horrific three-day siege, made even worse by an incompetent rescue attempt, in the town of Beslan in the Russian republic of North Ossetia.[8] Coming on top of previous jihadist attacks in Moscow and elsewhere, Beslan suggested to some strategists that Russian counterterror efforts were worthy of Western support. Russia's invasion of Georgia in August 2008, the New Look reforms that radically transformed Russian forces after that war, the failed US-Russia "reset," the resurgence of Russian activity across the Middle East and Africa, and the open breach with the West triggered by Russia's seizure of Crimea, semi-covert invasion of Ukraine, and alleged interference in the 2016 presidential election were all still in the future.

For its part, Communist China's military, in 2005, was described in the Pentagon's annual military power assessment as focused primarily on Taiwan, with amphibious and naval exercises growing in scale and scope and the People's Liberation Army (PLA) continuing "to deploy its most advanced systems to the military regions directly opposite Taiwan" even as guided-missile destroyers, advanced submarines, and improved amphibious armored vehicles represented "significant improvements from the older, less capable hardware that [remained] the bulk of China's inventory."[9] Beijing's newly announced notion of "peaceful rise" and the PLA's emphasis on operations in the country's immediate periphery and on "local wars under conditions of informationalization" encouraged a US view of China as a regional power focused on Taiwan, albeit one with wider ambitions.

The South China Sea was not seen as a key Chinese focus in 2005, nor were the PLA's island-building activities or its militarization and weaponization of that region on the radar for Pentagon policy-makers. The 2005 assessment mentioned the South China Sea once, in passing, noting somewhat dismissively that while the "PLA Navy occasionally patrols as far as the Spratly Islands, its limited organic air defense capability leaves surface ships vulnerable to attack from hostile air and naval forces. The PLA Navy Air Force and PLA Air Force currently lack the operational range to support PLA Navy operations."[10] The rapid rise of PLA air, surface, subsurface, space, and cyber capabilities—along with the modernization and expansion of strategic rocket forces, the emergence of a formidable A2/AD bubble in the region, and the development of antiship ballistic missiles able to kill aircraft carriers across most of the western Pacific—had yet to intrude on policy-makers' attention.

Iran and North Korea, two regimes referred to in President George W. Bush's 2002 State of the Union speech as forming an "Axis of Evil" with Saddam Hussein's Iraq, were treated at this time as important but regional threats.[11] Tehran and Pyongyang both had well-recognized nuclear ambitions, and the risk of rogue regimes channeling weapons of mass destruction to terrorists was clearly identified (indeed, arguably somewhat overplayed) by US policy-makers of the period.[12] Likewise, the role of Pakistan's A. Q. Khan network in facilitating rogue-nation nuclear programs was well known. What was perhaps less thoroughly understood was the transformative impact of the twin invasions of Afghanistan and Iraq on Iranian and North Korean strategic thinking.

With US forces now present on both its eastern and western borders, Iran felt encircled. At the same time, the fall of Saddam Hussein had toppled Tehran's rival for regional dominance and leadership of the Muslim world, offering opportunities for Iranian influence in majority-Shia Iraq. Likewise, the presence of coalition troops on its flanks gave Iran the strategically advantageous position of interior lines, allowing it to switch assets between fronts as it sought to disrupt the coalition's stabilization efforts. Realizing that a clear-cut US victory in either Iraq or Afghanistan would free resources for regime change in Iran—and noting influential American neoconservatives calling for such a move—Tehran adopted the strategic goal of keeping coalition forces bogged down in an unstable Iraq and Afghanistan, while ramping up its atomic weapons program to create a credible strategic deterrent for any attempted regime-change operation.[13] The result, over the next decade, was increasing Iranian influence in Iraq, a deepening relationship with Pakistan and the Taliban, closer cooperation with Beijing, and a rising regional nuclear threat, directed principally at Israel and secondarily at the Kingdom of Saudi Arabia—now Iran's main rival in a post-Saddam Middle East.

Nuclear capability also proved prominent in Pyongyang's reaction to the removal of Saddam. North Korean leaders saw Saddam's ineffectual weapons of mass destruction programs—in particular, his lack of an active nuclear program—as one cause of the coalition victory over Iraqi regular forces, even as the regime's interference with UN weapons inspectors provided the pretext for invasion. The lesson was clear: Saddam's weakness had been provocative, and to avoid the same fate, Pyongyang needed to use the window of opportunity afforded by Washington's preoccupation with Iraq to accelerate its nuclear program and improve ballistic missile capabilities until the cost of regime change became unacceptably high for the United States.[14] Raising the strategic stakes for the regime's adversaries would deter interference while North Korea modernized its conventional armed forces and used the missile threat, along with nonconventional means such as cybercrime, drug trafficking, and covert operations, to coerce its neighbors.

The United States in 2005 still enjoyed virtually uncontested mastery of space. Indeed, at this time US defense policy did not recognize space as an active warfighting domain, precisely because US dominance in that domain was so strong, though the risk of such a development in the future was contemplated. US military space programs—primarily for ISR, navigation, and targeting—continued, as did NASA's Shuttle program, while the United States dominated satellite navigation worldwide through the Global Positioning System satellite constellation and its willingness to allow commercial and foreign usage of that system. Rival systems such as Europe's Galileo and Russia's GLONASS were unable to match the US global footprint, while China's BeiDou system was in its infancy. The explosion in satellite navigation worldwide, prompted by the emergence of smartphones and other GPS-enabled handheld devices, was still in the future: the first-generation iPhone, which was to revolutionize handheld digital technology, create an entire new industry, and redefine the relationship between humans and data, would not be launched until January 2007.[15] In this context US dependence on GPS for everything from missile guidance systems to aircraft navigational aids and maritime communications was not yet seen as a dangerous vulnerability, though it soon would be.

On the nonmilitary front, climate change was beginning to be seen as a national security issue in 2005, even as its effects remained disputed, and key strategic impacts such as the appearance of year-round ice-free shipping lanes in the Arctic and their implications for naval and airpower had yet to become clear. US dependence on imported petroleum remained profound, yet was taken as a given by many strategists, and the role of hydrocarbons in the global economy was seen as an enduring basis for American engagement in the Middle East. The shale revolution, triggered by advances in hydraulic fracturing and horizontal drilling, which was to bring a profound transformation in US strategic interests in that region (lessening dependence on imported hydrocarbons, reducing financial transfers to countries whose actions ran counter to American interests, and cutting American greenhouse emissions through use of natural gas) was still a few years in the future, though all the relevant technologies had long been in place. The breakthrough event—the "gas rush" triggered by the successful extraction of shale gas at scale by Range Resources in the Marcellus Shale region—would occur in 2006.[16]

On a far less positive note, the 2008 Global Financial Crisis, which would be triggered by the collapse of lending institutions in the US subprime mortgage market and exposed the associated collateralized debt obligations, also still lay ahead. When it hit, in September 2008, it ushered in the so-called Great Recession with effects not only in the United States but worldwide—indeed, the Arab Spring uprisings can be seen in part as a delayed effect of worldwide economic disruption of 2008–2010, along with the associated spike in food prices and pressure on governments (including many in the MENA region) whose legitimacy in the eyes of their populations rested on economic performance rather than democratic accountability.[17] Countries such as Tunisia, Bahrain, Egypt, Yemen, Libya, and Syria all suffered major disruption, rebellion, or civil war during this period in ways that emphasized the tight linkage between global shocks, economic performance, human security challenges, and the potential for domestic unrest or interstate conflict—a linkage that manifest itself even more intensely in 2020.

The Environment in 2019

By 2019, almost all these features of the defense policy environment were dramatically different. The first key change was the end of the GWOT as an overarching framework for American defense policy. With the exception of a small training and special operations forces (SOF) component, the US and its coalition partners had pulled almost all ground troops out of Iraq. The territorial defeat of Islamic State's "caliphate" during the campaign of 2017–2019 had enabled troop withdrawals from Iraq and Syria, with the government in Baghdad experiencing political instability but no longer threatened with military defeat. The United States was no longer losing large numbers of Americans killed and wounded every month, spending hundreds of billions of dollars a year, and maintaining large permanent occupation forces in the Middle East. But the region remained chaotic, violent, and unstable, suffering the aftereffects of the ill-judged decision to invade Iraq in the first place and of the subsequent Arab Spring conflicts (including wars in Libya, Syria, and Yemen) that enabled the rise of ISIS. The coalition reintervention of 2014–2019 looked very different from the wars of 2003–2010, however.

With a preference for SOF rather than large conventional ground forces, no attempt to occupy territory or administer populations, and heavy use of precision airpower to enable maneuver by partner ground forces advised and assisted by small numbers of SOF and JTACs, the interventions in Iraq and Syria were far lighter in footprint. They succeeded in regaining territory from ISIS for minimal cost in allied lives and resources, but—like other SOF-centric light-footprint campaigns—could not, by definition, address the issues that had triggered the conflict and might make it flare again. The killing of ISIS leader Abu Bakr al-Baghdadi in October 2019 offered President Donald Trump an opportunity to declare victory and leave, but most defense policy analysts considered the anti-ISIS campaign as an incomplete victory at best, in that it merely pushed the Islamic State back below the threshold of conventional conflict into guerrilla mode, with thousands of fighters still active in Iraq and Syria, and the ISIS remnant well-funded, reorganizing, and aggressively ambitious.[18]

In Afghanistan, the Taliban had taken the war to the cities, with a series of major urban attacks beginning with the battle of Kunduz in September–October 2015. The conflict had spread to the northern and western parts of the country and expanded in scale and lethality.[19] Five years after the end of the large-scale counterinsurgency intervention in December 2014, the US and coalition footprint was small, emphasizing SOF, trainers, and support for the Afghan air force. Pakistan's importance in American defense policy had diminished as large-scale intervention ended, reducing Pakistan's spoiler role, and US and coalition assistance to Pakistan had diminished accordingly.[20] China increasingly filled the role of major ally for Pakistan and was fast becoming a key investor in Afghanistan. The Taliban were engaged in peace talks with the United States, though still refusing to deal directly with Kabul and unwilling to budge from their long-standing demand that all Western forces leave the country. Al-Qaeda remained active in Afghanistan and Pakistan, while ISIS, which hated the Taliban as much as the Kabul government, was killing thousands of Afghans.[21]

All this meant that the threat of transnational terrorism—the driver for the GWOT framework that shaped almost all aspects of US defense policy in 2005—was worse in 2019 by most measures. After almost twenty years of the war on terrorism, terrorist groups were larger and more active, controlled more territory and population worldwide (including extensive areas in Africa), and were able to mount attacks in most parts of the world, including the United States, Europe, and Australasia. To be sure, there had been no subsequent spectacular attack on the scale of 9/11, but the massive military interventions after 2001 had, if anything, worsened the problem they sought to solve, creating multiple generations of accidental guerrillas. The switch from large conventional wars of occupation and counterinsurgency toward light-footprint, air-enabled campaigns making extensive use of drones and SOF offered the possibility of a permanent worldwide campaign to disrupt terrorism, but at a more sustainable cost for Washington. Whether this was the best policy, as distinct from a merely feasible approach, was rarely debated in US policy circles.

In any case, by 2019 far less attention was being paid to terrorism, due to the reemergence of state threats as a central focus in US defense policy. As noted, the rise of Russia and China as military competitors occurred in part because of Western tunnel vision on terrorism and the extended effort to dig out of Iraq and Afghanistan. This absorbed so much attention in Washington, DC, and allied capitals and soaked up so many resources that it gave rival powers a free hand to modernize their forces and expand their influence in countries and regions that had been neglected or alienated by the United States and its allies after they had become bogged down in Iraq and Afghanistan during the GWOT.

Russia by 2019 was clearly once again a principal US adversary. In Eastern Europe and among Baltic and Scandinavian nations concerns about Russian interference, destabilization of neighbors, and political and economic bullying had led to renewed focus on resistance warfare, total people's defense, protection of critical infrastructure (including cyber infrastructure), and deterrence through national resilience.[22] NATO, as an alliance, was emphasizing the Atlantic Treaty's Article 3 requirements for resilience and whole-of-nation preparedness, even as the United States under President Trump was signaling only conditional commitment to Article 5 collective defense obligations, while demanding greater spending commitments from allies in return for continued US extended deterrence.[23] A protracted, painful Brexit had made the United Kingdom grip NATO more tightly than ever, though European unity looked increasingly tenuous, and trade and tariff disputes emphasized transatlantic differences. And Turkey's authoritarian domestic politics and neo-Ottoman foreign policy—expressed in interventions in Syria, weapons deals with Russia, tensions with Greece, and an increasingly assertive stance in North Africa—created another source of conflict within NATO.

President Trump—like President Barack Obama before him—was elected with the goal of improving ("resetting") relations with Russia and seeking ways to work together on common interests. But allegations of attempted Russian interference in the 2016 presidential election exacerbated existing acrimony and toxic partisanship in the United States, and made it politically impossible for the president to pursue this policy in office. American policy toward Russia became harsher and more robust across a range of issues from nuclear policy, to arming Ukraine, to oil and gas, to forward deployment of US troops in Poland and expanded exercises in Baltic and Scandinavian countries.[24] More broadly, the persistent US fantasy of Russia becoming a "normal" country—that is, one that cheerfully accepted secondary status within a US-led international order—was dead and buried by 2019.

Russia's intervention in Syria—which was arguably decisive in winning the Syrian Civil War for Bashar al-Assad—was one reason for this, and an active Russian military presence in the Middle East seemed likely to be a permanent feature of the region, along with expanded Russian naval activity in the Mediterranean. Less overt interventions in Africa, increased air and maritime activity in the Pacific and Indian Oceans, and expanded presence in Latin America also emphasized the return of Russia as a rival to Western democracies, and one with global aspirations.[25] The collapse of the

Intermediate Nuclear Forces treaty, Russia's move to acquire hypersonic missiles, and the modernization of both strategic rocket forces and battlefield nuclear weapons reemphasized a risk that had never gone away, though it had been less prominent in defense policy during the GWOT.[26] Russian naval and aerospace modernization, despite much fanfare from the Kremlin, had been patchy, with high-profile failures, though Russian ground forces and SOF were increasingly professionalized, having acquired small numbers of high-end capabilities such as autonomous ground systems, advanced armored vehicles, and drones.[27] Russia's ability to exploit the warming Arctic through specialized rapid-deployment Arctic brigades and a nuclear-powered icebreaker fleet gave it the edge in many parts of the high North, even as the effects of climate change on the polar icecap became increasingly evident.[28]

Iran and North Korea, the two surviving members of the "Axis of Evil," had significantly improved their strategic positions since 2005. US withdrawal from Iraq (and the pro-Iranian orientation of the post-occupation government of Nuri al-Maliki) allowed Iran to fill the gap and gain increasing influence in Iraqi economic, political, and defense policy. The ISIS blitzkrieg of 2014–2015 allowed Iran to capitalize on its political influence with military presence, sponsoring and training dozens of militias that played a key role in the defeat of ISIS and then became enforcers and enablers of Shia dominance. Qasem Soleimani, head of the Quds Force covert action arm of the Iranian Revolutionary Guard Corps (IRGC), was anything but covert during this period, playing a public role as the face of Iranian assistance and advice to Iraqi leaders.[29] Soleimani was also active in Syria, where the IRGC stiffened Bashar al-Assad's forces, provided resources and troops to enable Assad to recapture rebel territory, and stabilized his regime with help from Russia and from Iran's Lebanese proxy Hezbollah.[30]

Far from pushing back on expanded IRGC influence in Iraq and Syria, US policy under President Obama had focused almost exclusively on the issue of Iranian nuclear weapons—toward which the regime in Tehran had made significant progress since 2005. While some covert actions did occur—including alleged first use of offensive cyberwarfare against a state adversary to disable Iran's uranium-refining centrifuge program via the Stuxnet virus—the main US effort was diplomatic.[31] The Joint Comprehensive Plan of Action (JCPOA) of 2015 was seen within the Obama administration as a policy triumph, in that Iran formally agreed to limit its nuclear program for a decade in return for lifting of sanctions. The JCPOA was widely panned in the region, however, as enabling IRGC sponsorship of terrorism and helping Iran further expand its influence. One effect of this—and an outcome that would have been considered extraordinarily unlikely in 2005—was an emerging de facto partnership among Israel, Saudi Arabia, and several Arabian Gulf states, all of which increasingly saw Iran as a common threat. The war in Yemen, started by Saudi Arabia and a coalition of Gulf States in 2015 in response to Iranian sponsorship of the Ansar Allah (Houthi) militia, was another outcome, as Arab governments that saw Washington as unreliable took increasingly independent action.

The Trump administration quickly reversed this after 2017. The president repudiated the JCPOA, reimposed sanctions, and capitalized on regional fears of Tehran to cement the informal Israeli-Arab alignment into peace agreements between Israel, Bahrain, and the United Arab Emirates. While occasionally using force—including killing Qasem Soleimani in January 2020—Washington preferred economic rather than military tools in its Iran policy, emphasizing sanctions and trade restrictions rather than reacting militarily to Iranian provocations, such as the downing of a US drone and attacks on shipping in the Gulf.

This emphasis on economic rather than military tools was true also of US policy toward Pyongyang. North Korea's nuclear program, abetted by US distraction in Iraq and Afghanistan and Chinese chairmanship of the Six-Party Talks with Pyongyang, had made great strides since 2005, and the incoming Trump administration faced a sharp escalation of tension on the Korean Peninsula in 2017, with a series of atomic warhead tests, the detonation of an alleged thermonuclear device, and a string of ballistic missile launches, which by 2018 had given North Korea the ability to target the entire west coast of the United States, along with cities as far inland as Denver. After initially responding with harsh rhetoric, heightened military posture, and enhanced missile defenses, Washington settled on a policy of economic and political cooption, resulting in a broad (though creatively vague) agreement to denuclearize the peninsula, and two summit meetings between Kim Jong Un and President Trump. While cooling tensions in the short term, these summits allowed the Kim dynasty to attain a stature and legitimacy that had previously eluded them, cementing the success of Pyongyang's "regime-change deterrence through nuclear weapons" policy.

Perhaps the greatest shift in the strategic environment since 2005, however, was the transformation of Communist China's economic and military status and hence its role in international affairs. By 2019, in contrast to the Pentagon's dismissive assessment of 2005, Chinese island construction in the South China Sea had resulted in an extensive network of militarized artificial islands, including seven major offshore bases—complete with missiles, radar, airstrips, ports, and barracks—in the disputed Spratly Islands and several more in the Paracel Islands farther north, as well as dozens of smaller outposts and hundreds of other structures.[32] This permanent Chinese presence in disputed waters, supported by amphibious landing ships, patrolling aircraft, surface and subsurface maritime assets, an air defense interdiction zone, and an extensive ground garrison, represented a major transformation since 2005, but it was far from the only one.

By 2019 the Pentagon assessed that the Chinese Navy (PLAN) had overtaken the USN to become both "the largest navy in the world [and] an increasingly modern and flexible force that has focused on replacing previous generations of platforms with limited capabilities in favor of larger, modern multi-role combatants. As of 2019, the PLAN is largely composed of modern multi-role platforms featuring advanced anti-ship, anti-air, and anti-submarine weapons and sensors."[33] With two aircraft carriers in the water, two more under construction, a modern fleet of surface combatants, and a growing submarine arm that included both attack submarines and nuclear missile boats, the PLAN's blue-water assets—complemented by its naval base in Djibouti and construction of bases in Sri Lanka, Cambodia, Pakistan, and elsewhere—increasingly gave it global rather than regional reach.

With Beijing's stated objective of becoming a "world-class" military by midcentury, American analysts now saw China attempting to equal or surpass the US military in all domains by 2049. As the Pentagon report for 2019 (published in 2020) noted, China was already ahead of the United States in key areas including shipbuilding, land-based conventional ballistic and cruise missiles, and integrated air defense.[34] China's nuclear arsenal was rapidly expanding (albeit off a much lower base than that of the United States or Russia) while its military space programs were growing, as Beijing increasingly treated space as a warfighting domain. This had significant implications for US defense policy both in the space domain itself (as reflected in the creation of the US Space Force in the same year) and in other domains. China's completion of the Bei-Dou satellite constellation, for example, created a fully global rival to GPS, so that reliance on GPS by American and allied forces (along with its centrality to a host of civilian and commercial activities) now represented a clear vulnerability.[35] Likewise, in the cyber domain, as in technology and manufacturing more broadly, China's centrality to the global supply-chain ecosystem was unmistakable. At the same time, Chinese commercial penetration into Europe, Australia, Latin America, Africa, and the Middle East expanded exponentially and became increasingly tied to a mercantilist global policy through Beijing's economic development Belt and Road Initiative.

President Trump's most marked impact on American defense policy, from the moment of his election, was an overt and publicly stated recognition of this threat, and thus a shift in orientation toward a policy that saw Communist China as the greatest and most enduring geopolitical challenge to US strategic primacy over the next several decades. This reorientation—which, unlike almost any other policy pursued by the president, found agreement from many of his opponents—brought a broader recognition that Sino-American competition would be the defining feature of the twenty-first century global security environment. This in turn made China policy increasingly central to all aspects of American national policy, including but by no means limited to defense policy. The contrast to 2005—or even 2015—could not have been greater. And all this, of course, was still before the appearance of the novel coronavirus in the Chinese city of Wuhan and the rapid global spread of the associated COVID-19 pandemic.

The Crisis of 2020

Beginning in early 2020, the pandemic up-ended virtually every aspect of the global system. Massive cuts in global trade, transport, consumer demand, and manufacturing capacity led to huge drops in GDP—and unprecedented job losses—across most of the developed world in the first three quarters of 2020. In many ways this pattern, though triggered by a public health crisis, mimicked the Global Financial Crisis twelve years earlier: lockdowns designed to slow the spread of the disease triggered an economic crisis, quickly followed by a human security crisis for populations affected, then in turn by internal unrest, rioting, and protests, and a spike in international tension. Internal uprisings and revolutions along the lines of the Arab Spring conflicts that followed the Great Recession were yet to appear in most countries by the end of 2020 (though the United States, as discussed below, may prove to be an important exception). But at the level of international security, governments worldwide—threatened with internal unrest and criticism from their populations—sought to turn attention outward to external threats. Tensions spiked with a rapid succession of crises between China and India, China and Taiwan, Greece and Turkey, the United States and Venezuela, the United States and Russia, Egypt and Ethiopia, Turkey and Iraq, and internally in Venezuela, Belarus, and of course the United States.

In terms of Sino-American relations, the COVID crisis of 2020 exacerbated a preexisting "tech war" between Washington and Beijing, as each sought to control 5G communications technology, key commodities such as rare earths that feed the tech industry, silicon chip manufacturing, and the role of tech companies in social media and payment platforms.[36] The pandemic forced a broad public realization of just how dependent the United States—and every other country in the world—had become on Chinese manufacturing, including but not limited to critical supplies such as active pharmaceutical ingredients, personal protective equipment, small electrical goods, and handheld mobile computing technologies. Coming on top of a two-year trade war and against the backdrop of military rivalry noted earlier, all this reinforced the perception of a new cold war between the United States and China. Russia and Iran were increasingly partnering with China on military and economic matters, and although Russian and Chinese interests were often misaligned—as in the case of weapons sales to India—they increasingly made common cause against the United States.

On the military front, one of the more obvious implications of the pandemic was its impact on maritime and air forces. The aircraft carrier USS *Theodore Roosevelt* was effectively disabled for several weeks following a COVID outbreak on board, while France's only aircraft carrier, the *Charles de Gaulle*, suffered a similar effect. Aircraft deployments to Guam and other forward bases were also heavily affected, with crew and airframe rotations delayed or canceled and bases locked down. Major exercises were canceled or postponed, and both training and operational tempo were affected. Evidence is scant for the origin of the coronavirus in any military biowarfare program, despite persistent conspiracy theories to this effect. Still, for a country such as China, with one of the most active bioweapons and bioengineering programs on the planet and a strategy focused on finding ways to offset American conventional superiority, the implications were clear: if this level of global military disruption could be achieved through the accidental release of a non-weaponized pathogen, what might be done with a tailored bioweapon?[37]

More broadly, the long emergency—in terms of public health, economic disruption, internal security risk, and international tensions—triggered by the pandemic seemed likely to last for years at best, with potential longer-term disruptive effects on the international environment that could last a decade or more in some countries. In effect, it represented a reset in many areas of defense policy.

Future Defense Policy

Looking to the future, the crisis of 2020—coming on top of the enormous changes in the environment between 2005 and 2019—is thus likely to have substantial and enduring effects on the context for American defense policy going forward. Many of the fiscal assumptions that underpinned the record-high defense budgets of recent years will need to be revised. Domestic instability in the United States—whether through large-scale street violence, arson, rioting, and looting or through targeted domestic terrorism of one form or another—is likely to increase markedly following what is expected to be the most violently contested US presidential election in living memory. A focus on resilience at home, domestic security, defense of critical infrastructure, and (potentially) military assistance to civilian authorities would represent a major reorientation for the US defense establishment, which has been overwhelmingly oriented toward expeditionary operations for decades.

The potential for grey-zone operations against the United States—what might be called "liminal warfare," neither clandestine nor fully overt, but ambiguous, hybrid, and unconventional—by state adversaries cannot be ruled out under these circumstances. Sabotage, subversion, manipulation of protest movements, special operations targeting vulnerable points on the extended frontier of US presence overseas, or more direct challenges using conventional forces are all more likely risks. Economic warfare, through supply-chain manipulation, aggressive trade disruption, or dumping or currency manipulation are also likely to be elements of a potential future threat. China, Russia, and Iran (not necessarily in that order) are the most likely potential sponsors of such activity, but North Korea (with its track record of offensive cyber-intrusion, hacking, and use of criminal networks to advance regime objective overseas) as well as a range of non-state terrorist or extremist groups, are also possible sources of such disruption. Domestic instability, even without these external threats, is likely to remain a problem, so that resilience at home, critical infrastructure protection, public safety, and territorial defense are likely to increase in relative importance for policy-makers.

Climate—particularly in relation to wildfire management, drought mitigation, and operations in the high Arctic—is likely to play a more prominent part in defense policy, but perhaps not as expected in recent years. Rather than making efforts to reduce greenhouse emissions (as in the US Navy's Great Green Fleet initiative of the mid-2010s), defense policy is likely to focus on active support to broader government efforts to manage or mitigate the effects of a changing climate in the here and now.[38] Enhancing naval and air assets' ability to compete in the Arctic against peer or near-peer competitors and improving mountain and cold-weather operations capabilities for ground forces are key concerns for several allies and will also become more important for the United States as the high North continues to warm. And conflicts over water resources, climate-induced migration, and urban overstretch—all features of a warming planet—will likely need greater attention from strategists and policy-makers.

In stark contrast to 2005, US forces operate now in a highly contested space and cyber environment. Cyber-kinetic operations—that is, a blending of phys-

ical and cyber-operations in which kinetic actions are directed at an enemy's data, while actions in cyberspace may have direct lethal effects—are increasingly common for both state and non-state adversaries, with the cyber domain emerging as an adjunct maneuver space for military operations. The need to operate independently of GPS, or in an intermittent or contested communications environment, is increasingly pressing and will need policy attention as well as adjustments to acquisitions and warfighting doctrine. AI and autonomous systems will continue to transform the options open to both US forces and adversaries, with implications at the strategic as well as the tactical level.

At the grand-strategic level, US policy-makers face a future in which the US-led international rules-based order, as it existed since the end of the Cold War, is likely to give way to a period of intense multipolar great-power competition, rising frequently to crises, in which the risk of major war is greater than at any time so far in this century. The future of the alliance system—principally NATO, but also the ANZUS treaty with Australia and New Zealand and the bilateral security arrangements with Japan, the Republic of Korea, and other major non-NATO allies—is currently in flux, as allies face an increasingly divided, inward-looking, and transactional partner in the United States.

Under these circumstances, if the US defense establishment is to succeed in preserving the nation's security and furthering its interests into the future, American defense policy-makers will need to think creatively and argue persuasively for policies that are both effective and affordable. Each of the chapters that follow in this volume contributes something to that policy debate, while helping frame future challenges in the context of current thinking. Even in these times of rapid change, this book will therefore remain essential reading.

NOTES

1. Robert M. Gates, *Duty: Memoirs of a Secretary at War* (New York: Knopf Doubleday, 2014), Kindle ed., locations 461ff.

2. See Nasreen Ghufran, "Afghanistan in 2005: The Challenges of Reconstruction," *Asian Survey* 46, no. 1 (2006): 85–94.

3. Timo Noetzel Timo and Benjamin Schreer, *The German Army and Counterinsurgency in Afghanistan: The Need for Strategy* (Berlin: Stiftung Wissenschaft und Politik, 2008), https://www.swp-berlin.org/fileadmin/contents/products/comments/2008C01_ntz_srr_ks.pdf.

4. For an account of the rotary-wing role, see Ed Darack, *The Final Mission of Extortion 17: Special Ops, Helicopter Support, SEAL Team Six, and the Deadliest Day of the U.S. War in Afghanistan* (Washington, DC: Smithsonian Books, 2017).

5. See Steve Call, *Danger Close: Tactical Air Controllers in Afghanistan and Iraq* (College Station, TX: Williams-Ford Texas A&M University Military History Series Book 113, 2010).

6. US Air Force, "'Reaper' Moniker Given to MQ-9 Unmanned Aerial Vehicle," September 14, 2006, https://web.archive

.org/web/20110914055555/http://www.af.mil/news/story.asp?storyID=123027012.

7. See Committee on the Role of Naval Forces in the Global War on Terror *The Role of Naval Forces in the Global War on Terror: Abbreviated Version* (Washington, DC: National Academies Press, 2007), https://www.nap.edu/read/11918/chapter/1.

8. See John B. Dunlop and Donald N. Jensen, *The 2002 Dubrovka and 2004 Beslan Hostage Crises: A Critique of Russian Counter-Terrorism*, Soviet and Post-Soviet Politics and Society Series, Volume 26 (Stuttgart: Ibidem-Verlag, 2006).

9. US Department of Defense, *Annual Report to Congress: The Military Power of the People's Republic of China, 2005* (Washington DC: Office of the Secretary of Defense, 2005), 3–5.

10. US Department of Defense, *Annual Report to Congress*, 2005, 33–34.

11. "President Delivers State of the Union Address," White House, January 29, 2002, https://georgewbush-whitehouse.archives.gov/news/releases/2002/01/20020129-11.html.

12. For a critical assessment of this approach, see Ron Suskind, *The One Percent Doctrine: Deep Inside America's Pursuit of Its Enemies Since 9/11* (New York: Simon and Schuster, 2007).

13. For a series of Iranian intelligence community reports relating to Iran's reaction to the Iraq and Afghanistan invasions, see "The Iran Cables," The Intercept, 2019, https://theintercept.com/series/iran-cables/.

14. See Brandon K. Gauthier, "How Kim Jong Il Reacted to the 2003 Invasion of Iraq," *North Korea News*, March 20, 2013, https://www.nknews.org/2013/03/how-kim-jong-il-reacted-to-the-2003-invasion-of-iraq/.

15. Peter Cohen, "Macworld Expo Keynote Live Update: Introducing the iPhone," Macworld, January 9, 2007, https://www.macworld.com/article/1054764/liveupdate.html.

16. Tom Wilber, *Under the Surface: Fracking, Fortunes and the Fate of the Marcellus Shale* (Ithaca, NY: Cornell University Press, 2012), 70–92.

17. See Rami Zurayk, "Use Your Loaf: Why Food Prices Were Crucial in the Arab Spring," *The Guardian*, July 16, 2011, https://www.theguardian.com/lifeandstyle/2011/jul/17/bread-food-arab-spring; "The Economics of the Arab Spring," *Financial Times* (April 24, 2011), https://www.ft.com/content/9565ebac-f0d0-11e0-aec8-00144feab49a.

18. Lara Seligman, "Baghdadi Is Dead, but ISIS Remains Emboldened since Trump's Drawdown," *Foreign Policy*, October 27, 2019, https://foreignpolicy.com/2019/10/27/isis-islamic-state-leader-baghdadi-killed/.

19. See Anthony H. Cordesman, *The State of the Fighting in the Afghan War in Mid-2019* (Washington, DC: Center for Strategic and International Studies, August 13, 2019), https://www.csis.org/analysis/state-fighting-afghan-war-mid-2019.

20. See Memphis Barker, "US Military Confirms $300m Cut in Aid to Pakistan," *The Guardian*, September 2, 2018, https://www.theguardian.com/world/2018/sep/02/us-military-confirms-300m-cut-in-aid-to-pakistan.

21. Center for Strategic and International Studies, *Islamic State–Khorasan (IS-K)*, 2019, https://csis-website-prod.s3.amazonaws.com/s3fs-public/181113_IS-K_Backgrounder.pdf?LgtpuuPVxjdGU6g_idQlIH4cI1ILgZ0t.

22. See Stephen J. Flanagan, Jan Osburg, Anika Binnendijk, Marta Kepe, and Andrew Radin, *Deterring Russian Aggression in the Baltic States through Resilience and Resistance* (Santa Monica, CA: RAND Corporation, 2019), https://www.rand.org/pubs/research_reports/RR2779.html; John Friburg, "SOCEUR and Resistance Operating Concept (ROC)," *SOF News*, July 19, 2019, https://sof.news/uw/resistance-operating-concept/.

23. NATO, *Resilience and Article 3*, updated March 2020, https://www.nato.int/cps/en/natohq/topics_132722.htm.

24. For a summary, see Jen Kerns, "President Trump Is Tougher on Russia in 18 Months than Obama in Eight Years," *The Hill*, July 16, 2018, https://thehill.com/opinion/white-house/397212-president-trump-is-tougher-on-russia-in-18-months-than-obama-in-eight.

25. Paul Stronski and Richard Sokolsky, *The Return of Global Russia: An Analytical Framework* (Washington DC: Carnegie Endowment for International Peace, 2017), https://carnegieendowment.org/2017/12/14/return-of-global-russia-analytical-framework-pub-75003.

26. "INF Nuclear Treaty: Russia Follows US in Suspending Pact," BBC, February 2, 2019, at https://www.bbc.com/news/world-europe-47101429. See also Missile Defense Project, "Missiles of Russia," *Missile Threat*, Center for Strategic and International Studies, June 14, 2018, last modified August 24, 2020, https://missilethreat.csis.org/country/russia/.

27. Tyler Rogoway, "Russia's Accident-Plagued Aircraft Carrier Is on Fire," The War Zone, December 12, 2019, https://www.thedrive.com/the-war-zone/31451/russias-accident-plagued-lone-aircraft-carrier-is-on-fire.

28. Nurlan Aliyev, "Russia's Military Capabilities in the Arctic," *Diplomaatia*, June 25, 2019, https://icds.ee/en/russias-military-capabilities-in-the-arctic/.

29. "Iran's Qasem Soleimani Is Guiding Iraqi Forces in Fight against ISIS," NBC News, March 7, 2015, https://www.nbcnews.com/storyline/isis-terror/iranian-gen-qasem-soleimani-guiding-iraqi-forces-fight-against-isis-n321496.

30. Jonathan Saul and Parisa Hafezi, "Iran Boosts Military Support in Syria to Bolster Assad," Reuters, February 20, 2014, at https://www.reuters.com/article/us-syria-crisis-iran-idUSBREA1K09U20140221.

31. Paul Scharre, *Army of None: Autonomous Weapons and the Future of War* (New York: W. W. Norton, 2018).

32. Jin Wu, Simon Scarr, and Weiyi Cai, "Concrete and Coral: Tracking Expansion in the South China Sea," Reuters, May 24, 2018, https://fingfx.thomsonreuters.com/gfx/rngs/CHINA-SOUTHCHINASEA-BUILDING/010070760H9/index.html.

33. US Department of Defense, *Annual Report to Congress: Military and Security Developments Involving the People's Republic of China, 2020* (Washington, DC: Office of the Secretary of Defense, 2020), vii.

34. US Department of Defense, *Annual Report to Congress*, 2020, i–ii.

35. Namrata Goswami, "The Economic and Military Impact of China's BeiDou Navigation System," *The Diplomat*, July 1, 2020, https://thediplomat.com/2020/07/the-economic-and-military-impact-of-chinas-beidou-navigation-system/.

36. See Anja Manuel and Kathleen Hicks, "Can China's Military Win the Tech War?" *Foreign Affairs*, July 29, 2020, https://www.foreignaffairs.com/articles/united-states/2020-07-29/can-chinas-military-win-tech-war.

37. For a speculative assessment, see Chris O'Connor, "Contagion: COVID-19's Impact on the Operational Environment (Part 6)—Intentional Pandemics," *Mad Scientist* blog, May 7,

2020, https://madsciblog.tradoc.army.mil/234-contagion-covid
-19s-impact-on-the-operational-environment-part-6-intentional
-pandemics/?doing_wp_cron=1600824397.980097055435
1806640625.

38. Noah Schachtman, "How the Navy's Incompetence
Sank the 'Green Fleet,'" *Wired*, July 17, 2012, https://www.wir
ed.com/2012/07/green-fleet/.

39. Paul T. Ringenbach, *Battling Tradition: Robert F. Mc-
Dermott and Shaping the US Air Force Academy,* (New York:
Imprint Publications, 2006), 108.

40. Wesley W. Posvar and John C. Ries, eds., *American Defense Policy* (Baltimore, MD: Johns Hopkins Press, 1965), ix.

41. Posvar and Ries, *American Defense Policy*, ix.

42. Joe Gould, "Congress Adopts Defense Bill that Creates Space Force," DefenseNews.com, December 17, 2019,
https://www.defensenews.com/congress/2019/12/17/congress
-adopts-defense-bill-that-creates-space-force/.

43. "Trump Created Space Force. Here's What It Will Actually Do," NPR, December 21, 2019, https://www.npr.org/2019
/12/21/790492010/trump-created-the-space-force-heres-what-it
-will-do.

44. Clint Ensign, *Inscriptions of a Nation: Collected Quotes
from Washington Monuments* (Washington, DC: Congressional
Quarterly, 1994).

Preface

BRIGADIER GENERAL USAF (RET) CHERYL A. KEARNEY

In 1965, the first edition of *American Defense Policy* (*ADP*) was published to fill an intellectual gap identified by the Department of Political Science faculty at the United States Air Force Academy (USAFA). The newest of the military academies, USAFA was created in 1954 to educate and train future Air Force officers, and the faculty, composed of all military officers at the time, were selected as role models, mentors, and educators for these future officers. Brigadier General Robert Francis McDermott, the first permanent Dean of the Faculty, noted the scattered curriculum efforts to ensure future officers understood all aspects of defense. He directed the creation of a senior-level core course, "Defense Policy," to educate cadets on the intricacies and challenges facing future leaders involved in the nation's security.[39] However, there was no systematic and rigorous review of literature pertaining to US defense policy that could serve as a textbook for this course. Thus began the creative journey of *American Defense Policy*, a series that would further the discipline of defense studies and provide a continuing legacy of dialogue surrounding American defense policy by policy-makers, military professionals, educators, and practitioners.

In his inaugural edition of *ADP*, Colonel Wesley Posvar, the first Permanent Professor and Political Science Department Head, describes American defense policy as "a field of study that treats the function of preserving the national security in response to the dictates of the times."[40] The dictates of our time require an appreciation of the complexities and ambiguities of the domestic and international environments of the twenty-first century. Traditional models of analysis consisting of means and ends evaluations may be insufficient to understand the implications and consequences of the steady march forward of emerging threats and disruptive technology. Whether one is concerned with great-power politics, near-peer competitors, alliances, international organizations, cyberwarfare, nuclear weapons, civil-military relations, special forces, emerging technologies, multilateralism, or grand strategy—these topics are addressed in this single volume.

As lead editor of inaugural edition of *ADP*, Colonel Posvar described his editorial team's efforts as "an attempt to organize American defense policy into a coherent field of study."[41] Each successive edition has built on this model, and the seven editions since that first cornerstone volume have captured defense policy at the height and end of the Cold War, through the reforms and interventions of the 1990s, to the unfolding of the Global War on Terror. This ninth edition constitutes an additional contribution to this field of study as the twenty-first century enters its third decade with extraordinary ambiguity and complexity in an anarchic international political system.

American Defense Policy was last published in 2005 and focused on the emergence of the Department of Homeland Security and its implications for national security. At that time the United States was embroiled in Iraq, the Taliban was reemerging in Afghanistan, and the US economy was faltering under the auspices of a new administration. Now we are at a similar inflection point. The National Defense Authorization Act for Fiscal Year 2020 created the Space Force, the sixth branch of the Armed Forces of the United States and the first new military service in over seventy-plus years since the United States Air Force was created in 1947.[42] President Donald Trump stated, "Space is the world's newest war-fighting domain. . . . Amid grave threats to our national security, American superiority in space is absolutely vital."[43] This volume analyzes this new domain while at the same time including older domains such as nuclear warfare and counterinsurgency. As such, *ADP 9* provides breadth and depth of insights concerning American defense policy.

The selection of articles for this edition follows the roots of *American Defense Policy* by searching for the best literature to examine theories, processes, content, and outcomes in the contemporary environment. At the same time, *ADP 9* also branches out in new directions. It is a blend of classic pieces that speak to timeless defense policy issues as well as contemporary and new articles that address emerging challenges. As defense policy rapidly evolves, so too must this volume bridge that which is constant and that which is in flux. Such an effort may necessitate more contemporary— and hence more transient—snapshots of the rapidly changing environment alongside timeless pieces. This reflects *ADP*'s commitment to keep future volumes reflective of and relevant to the challenges of current day.

As the editors share in their afterword, every article selected was carefully considered to fit within the traditional *ADP* framework, which deftly pairs the old with the new. Yet there is also an acknowledgment that the nature, context, and character of American defense policy has rapidly changed over the past decade. The broader theme of turbulence, domestically and internationally, unites the articles in this volume as the United States endeavors to wind down its longest war and deals with the emerging COVID-19 pandemic.

This edited volume is organized into three parts, with an introduction to each part summarizing the key arguments of every article. Part I sets the foundation by examining the theoretical and strategic challenges that shape contemporary American defense policy. Part II examines the process and instruments of American defense policy, arguing that as perceptions about the military have shifted over the past decade, the only constant is change. Part III examines the new battlefield, the shifting force structure, and emerging disruptive technologies such as artificial intelligence and automation that may drastically change defense policy paradigms. In some cases, original articles were written for this volume to address specific areas of interest such as American values and defense policy in Part I, the evolving nature of the military profession in Part II, and the use of drones on the modern battlefield in Part III.

We hope this edition of *American Defense Policy* provides thought-provoking ideas and concepts as the United States moves forward into an uncertain future filled with the rise of peer competitors, the continuing evolution of non-state actors, and pandemics, as well as the benefits, constraints, and likely unforeseen consequences of an increasingly technologically sophisticated world. The twenty-first century is an information and instantaneous communications era in which knowledge and understanding may just be the keys to a more secure future. James Madison once remarked that "knowledge will forever govern ignorance; a people who mean to be their own governors must arm themselves with the power that knowledge gives."[44] It is our sincere hope that this edition adds knowledge and insights to our understanding of American defense policy as we continue this fragile experiment of democracy.

Brigadier General USAF (Ret) Cheryl A. Kearney, PhD
Professor Emeritus, USAFA
Former Permanent Professor and Department Head
Political Science Department, USAFA

Introduction

The Changing Character of War

GENERAL (RET) JOSEPH F. DUNFORD, JR.

The previous edition of *American Defense Policy*, published in 2005, offered enduring observations during an era when national security focused nearly exclusively on counterterrorism efforts overseas. However, over the past two decades, the strategic landscape has changed dramatically. While the fundamental *nature* of war has not changed, a rapidly accelerating pace of change and advances in modern technology, coupled with shifts in the nature of geopolitical competition, have altered the *character* of war in the twenty-first century. As defense challenges become increasingly diverse and complex, so too must defense policy adapt and expand to meet the dangers of today and counter the threats of tomorrow.

No doubt, things have changed during my forty years in uniform, but the change itself is not remarkable. Rather, it is the pace at which change is occurring. A brief anecdote may highlight this observation most effectively: when I was a lieutenant, I used the same cold-weather gear that my dad used in Korea in 1950, twenty-seven years earlier—and I don't mean the same kind of gear; I mean we went to the warehouse and dug out the very same gear. The radios we used would have been familiar to those who fought in Vietnam and the jeeps to World War II veterans. And despite incremental development in weapons and the dawn of the nuclear age, I think a lieutenant from World War II or Korea would have been very comfortable in the exercises I participated in as a lieutenant.

Fast forward to a platoon I observed in 2008 during a visit to Afghanistan. The platoon commander and his eighty marines were forty miles from the nearest platoon on their left, forty miles from the nearest platoon on their right, and about an hour by helicopter from the battalion command post. To give you some perspective, my appreciation of time and space when I was a lieutenant was that a rifle company defended on a 1,500-meter frontage and attacked on a 300-meter frontage. The marines I visited were wearing protective equipment and driving vehicles that would have been unrecognizable to infantry marines or soldiers just five years earlier. The platoon could receive and transmit voice, data, and imagery from a satellite and was supported by the High Mobility Artillery Rocket System (HIMARS), which can put precision fires out to over sixty kilometers. When I was a lieutenant, we relied on the 105mm howitzer, which had a max ef-

fective range of about 11,000 meters, and we didn't use the word "precision" in describing the 105.

The total effect was a unit wildly different in appearance, capability, and mission from what I saw as a lieutenant, and more importantly, from the platoons that existed even three years before, when the previous volume of *ADP* was published. Today, similar changes can be seen across the joint force, changes that have profound implications at the operational and strategic level, as well as the tactical. This pace of change continues to accelerate, putting new tools in the hands of our defense establishment but equally arming adversaries with new technology and new avenues for competition.

So, while the nature of war—the violent clash of political will—has not changed, we should expect that any future conflict is going to be transregional, rapidly crossing the boundaries of geographic combatant commands; all-domain, simultaneously involving combinations of land, sea, air, space, and cyberspace operational domains; and multifunctional, including conventional operations, special operations, ballistic missiles, and strike, cyber, and space capabilities. Moreover, contemporary and future warfare is deeply interconnected. Any future conflict on the Korean Peninsula will look nothing like the Korean War my father fought. Instead, it will involve every service and domain, touch multiple combatant commands communicating at lightning speed across continents and oceans, use technology that links the smallest units to strategic-level decision-makers, and likely incorporate a myriad of challenges barely visible on the horizon: artificial intelligence, space capabilities, quantum computing, hypersonics, and further developments we cannot yet imagine.

Just as the pace of change accelerates, so does our scope of responsibility. As a global power, the United States does not get to choose our fights, and we should expect no credit tomorrow for the peace we secured yesterday. The recent resurgence of great-power competition with Russia and China along with the challenges associated with North Korea and Iran demand that we prepare for a potential conflict even as we constantly face daily competition in a military dimension that falls short of traditional armed conflict.

However, this great-power resurgence has not lessened our obligations to current conflicts. We are a nation that thinks and acts globally, and as such we do not have the luxury of choosing between a force that can fight non-state actors, such as the Islamic State of Iraq and Syria (ISIS) and al Qaeda, and one that can deter and defeat adversaries possessing a full array of military capabilities. We are already seeing new functional and technological capabilities fielded by both state and non-state actors who will continually look for ways to harness those capabilities to exploit our vulnerabilities.

The United States also cannot afford to choose between meeting today's operational requirements and making the investments necessary for tomorrow. Over the past two decades, requirements on the force have been heavy—operations tempo is not decreasing, and the wear and tear on both the people and equipment of the joint force are profound. There are perilously few easy decisions in the world of defense resourcing, and policymakers are unlikely to receive a peace dividend that will allow for focused reinvestment in our forces.

This changing character of war means we must be sharper and more creative in crafting defense policy than ever before. Historically, defense decision-makers had the opportunity to recover if we got it wrong: leading into World War II, the United States had three years to evolve doctrine, build industrial capacity, build an army, develop leaders, and practice interoperability. In current and future conflicts, we are unlikely to have that same opportunity because our scope of responsibility has expanded and the pace of change has so greatly accelerated.

It is clear that adapting to the evolving character of war in the twenty-first century is going to require significant changes to our planning, organization, and command and control constructs—and we are already behind in so many ways. The service members and policymakers today are serving during a particularly dynamic period, one that Henry Kissinger has called the most volatile and complex security environment since World War II. In my career, I can't remember a time when the pace of change and scope of effort are even close to what we're seeing today, and I believe that makes our ability to anticipate change all the more important. My horizon for us to innovate and adapt our defense policy is not ten, fifteen, or twenty years from now; it is actually, and perhaps unfortunately, only three to five years from now. That is how urgently I believe we need to make fundamental changes to how we do business in defense and security policy.

This is the context the ninth edition of *American Defense Policy* captures: an accelerating pace of change, an ever-expanding scope of effort and spectrum of conflict, and a force that must both meet the operational needs of today and invest in the capabilities of tomorrow. It is no easy task, but I have great confidence in the next generation of leaders and decision-makers to educate themselves, make the changes necessary, and lead in the same manner that has allowed us to be successful over the past hundred years of war.

Acknowledgments

A project of this magnitude requires the assistance and cooperation of many people. The editors begin by offering a very special thanks to the Chairs of the Department of Political Science at the Air Force Academy: Cheryl Kearney and Paul Bolt. Their leadership, guidance, and support during one of the most exceptional academic years in our history is deeply appreciated.

In addition, the Eisenhower Center for Space and Defense Studies played an important role in supporting the development of this text. Under the umbrella of the Department of Political Science, the Eisenhower Center focuses on the advancement and dissemination of knowledge relevant to USAFA's National Security outcome. For *American Defense Policy*, the center tapped a vast network of scholars and practitioners in national security studies to suggest seminal articles as well as fresh topics tailored to the theme of turbulence in defense policy for this ninth edition.

Further, we wish to thank the Center for Character and Leadership Development and Scowcroft Professor Damon Coletta, for organizing discussions that yielded insightful feedback on both the content and structure of the text. Additionally, we owe thanks to the many individuals who made the Academy Assembly (the longest-running strategic studies undergraduate academic conference in the nation) possible, as their efforts contributed both ideas and authors to this project.

The assistant editors, Seth Cannon, Jason Egger, and Noah Fisher, were phenomenal members of this team. A lion's share of the copyediting fell on their shoulders and without complaint they did everything that was asked of them. To that end, so many members of our department contributed. In particular, Matt Van Hook's willingness to review this text with an eye to our American Government and National Security curricula was critically important.

Finally, we would like to thank our families, especially Kevin, Luis, Dawne, and Katrina. Their love and support made this possible.

Part I

Values and Interests for American Defense Policy

Introduction

LYNNE CHANDLER GARCIA

Defense policy is at a critical juncture as China and Russia challenge America's primacy, non-state actors continue to threaten security, and a host of other issues plague the globe. Space could be the next frontier for battle, climate change makes water and fertile land new points of conflict, while the potential consequences of cyber technology and artificial intelligence are not yet realized. In the midst of all these challenges, alliances are shifting in structure and form as nations rethink their allegiance to international organizations and agreements. Part I begins this ninth volume of *American Defense Policy* by looking at these challenges from a theoretical and strategic perspective. This section asks readers to consider US defense policy at a time when security challenges exist across numerous domains of warfare. To what extent are great-power theories guiding policy-making when a nation is simultaneously challenged for primacy by small war considerations such as criminal networks or terrorist threats? How well can existing theories about the international order incorporate technological change? In times of uncertainty, how does the United States conceptualize the battlespace and create strategies for every contingency? Part I provides the overview and background needed to understand American defense policy. Divided into four chapters, this section examines the theories and strategies that shape the United States' approach to security policy. It analyzes the values and principles that provide the foundation for policies. An overview of grand strategy and critiques of internationalism provide understanding of America's place in the world. Finally, this section investigates both allied and adversarial relationships as the United States determines how best to invest resources toward its national interest.

Chapter 1 sets the context for the rest of the volume by examining the foundations and theories that shape America's approach to defense policy. As the nature of war evolves, how do theories of international relations and studies of conflict correspondingly adjust? Does the morality of just wars change, and do traditional values fluctuate in importance? How do policy-makers think about causes of war and the responsibilities incumbent upon a hegemon? As the country considers its role, policy-makers must reflect on the values that provide the foundations for defense policy. The chapter begins by exploring how US history and traditional values influence the ways in which the United States defines its national interest. This leads to an exploration of understanding just war theory in a modern age. Then the chapter looks at how power theories shape US status on the international stage before concluding by challenging international relations theorists to think critically about the impact of technology and innovation.

Jeff Black begins this discussion through an exegesis of foundational documents in search of the founding principles of American defense policy. The American political system, he argues, aims at achieving the protection of rights and the pursuit of happiness. Principled defense policy helps achieve this goal. The principles of justice, necessity, and interest guided the Founding Fathers as they lay the foundations for defense policy, but as Black argues, the principles varied in importance among our nation's documents. Interest plays the decisive role in the Declaration of Independence; Publius's interpretation of the Constitution centers on necessity; and Washington's Farewell Address begins with justice before concluding with interest. On these three principles, the Founding Fathers designed the foundation of defense policy focused on the greatest human good.

Reflecting upon the values embodied in the United States' foundational documents leads to a consideration of the morality and ethics of war. Seth Lazar provides an overview of just war theory from the traditionalist and the revisionist camps, comparing and contrasting the views of each. The tradition of just war theory—the justifications of why and how wars are fought—has a long history stemming from Greek philosophy to modern times. Using Walzer's *Just and Unjust Wars* as the starting point for traditionalist theories, he first analyzes the methodological disputes that separate traditionalists from revisionists. He then addresses *jus ad bellum* as well as *jus in bello* through an examination of the principles of armed conflict. He concludes that although the study of just war theory is in the midst of turbulent times, ideas of legitimate defense and authority, proportionality, and necessity are not "morally rootless."

Lazar's conclusion leads to an inquiry into power and the United States' historical and contemporary role within the international community. Great-power theories based in realism illustrate the debate between advocates of security versus power within an international order. Dale Copeland asks if these systemic theories of great power and peace are still relevant for today, and he provocatively answers "yes," but for different reasons than in the past. In an age of catastrophic threats such thermonuclear combat, Copeland argues that the possibility of total war of unlimited scope is still frighteningly real. Neither classic realism, with an emphasis on balance of power, nor neorealism, with an emphasis on bargaining models, can explain why actors might inadvertently slip into a total war. To fill this deficit, Copeland integrates offensive and defensive realism into what he calls a "dynamic realist" viewpoint that takes into account factors that affect assessments of risk and long-term power positions. He builds a new approach for great-power theory by explaining the potential threat of war as countries rise and decline in power.

Francis Fukuyama then assesses the state of democracy over the past thirty years, which he views as an up and down trend. Identity politics are on the rise as groups on both the left and the right vie for recognition, respect, and dignity in a global society. The internet and social media have facilitated the fragmentation of society into siloed identity groups, but at the same time, these technologies have provided individuals much greater access to information and have broken down traditional hierarchies and social enclaves based on class, race, and gender. Fukuyama notes that democratic transitions have also been a mixed bag of failures and successes. While the 2003 US overthrow of Saddam Hussein in Iraq failed to create a democracy, other nations have experienced forward movement toward democracy. Overall, the past thirty years have moved US policy from an optimistic view of unrestricted capitalism and interventionism to a more cautious view of the neoliberalism with a healthy dose of realism.

This leads to the last article in the chapter, which speaks to how international relations theory addresses technology and innovation. Daniel Drezner points out that although technology is often considered an independent variable that affects military and economic power, causal relationships are not simple. Drezner classifies nuclear weapons as "prestige" technology because it has high fixed costs and public-sector dominance, while he categorizes the internet as "general purpose" technology because it has low fixed costs and private-sector dominance. Comparing these, Drezner finds that nuclear technology stimulates cooperation as states seek to prevent a nuclear war. Conversely, the advance of the internet has created quarrelsome international relationships as norms surrounding cybersecurity have come under fire. He concludes that technological innovations will impact international relations through the various norms that surround a particular technology.

Chapter 2 discusses the importance of grand strategy in setting the parameters for American defense pol-

icy. The chapter examines the future of grand strategy as the liberal order is stretched and American hegemony is challenged by rising great powers. Since the end of the Cold War, the United States has served as the liberal hegemon, setting the tone and security norms for the world. As times change, how do fluctuating power dynamics challenge US hegemony? What strategies should the United States consider to maintain power and promote stability? Where and how should the country invest its resources to best maintain the security of the homeland and the globe? This chapter begins with grand strategy, defining the term and providing its theoretical underpinnings, and then questioning the future of American grand strategy in the post–Cold War environment. It then frames the debate between liberal and conservative internationalism by exploring the benefits of multilateralism and cooperative security versus limited government and nationalism as leaders of foreign policy struggle to determine the United States' path in maintaining the world order.

Colin Dueck's article provides a primer for grand strategy. As the United States faces a multitude of challenges and threats, grand strategy helps a nation determine how to use its resources to best serve the nation's interests. Dueck likens it to a "road map" that matches resources to interests and policy needs. After explaining how and why grand strategy can change, Dueck concludes with a discussion of strategic adjustment in the light of international pressures and cultural constraints.

Matching resources to national needs leads to the last article in this chapter by Hal Brands and Eric Edelman, who worry that the United States is trending toward strategic insolvency. They analyze the numerous threats to the country's military primacy and outline options for restoring defense capabilities. With the myriad security challenges facing the United States, Brands and Edelman call for a significant investment in defense. Although they concede that this investment will not be cheap, they argue that it is necessary in order to support US grand strategy.

G. John Ikenberry then argues that the coronavirus has exposed a crisis in the Western liberal world order. Problems of modernity including pandemics, climate change, nuclear proliferation, and numerous other issues related to science, technology, and industrialism need world leadership that is united in its commitment to democracy, rule of law, and human rights. Ikenberry fears that the United States is turning away from multilateralism to a focus on great-power competition, which he sees as a grave mistake. Instead, he advocates for a return to a liberal coalition as envisioned by Franklin D. Roosevelt. The pandemic, he argues, is an opportunity for the United States and other liberal democracies to reform a coherent and functional global coalition.

Henry Nau's contribution provides a counter to Ikenberry in his conservative approach to internationalism. Whereas liberal internationalism favors global institutions and collective security, conservative internationalism upholds strong state governments and national defense forces. Nau supports diplomacy as a primary policy instrument but cautions that diplomacy must be armed to in order to ensure compliance with agreements. Nau argues for nationalism, based on limited government and national sovereignty—a type of policy that does not reject globalism but puts "America First."

Chapter 3 looks at defense policy from the viewpoint of engaging allies and participating in international organizations (IOs). From coalition support in Afghanistan to US basing agreements across the world, international alliances have proven to be a vital part of US defense policy. At the same time, alliances and IOs pose their share of issues. Divergent ideas on strategies, quarrels over burden sharing, and maintaining nationalism through international cooperation all pose challenges to the solvency of alliances. What is the future of the liberal international order, and what is the United States' role in this order? Can the United States maintain its world leadership role without the support of its allies? What responsibilities does the United States have to its allies and IOs, and are other members paying their fair share? As Winston Churchill famously said, "There is only one thing worse than fighting with allies, and that is fighting without them." While multilateralism and participating in IOs are challenging, the articles in this chapter contend that benefits generally outweigh the costs.

Michael Wesley begins this study with an excerpted chapter that is the introduction to a larger volume concerning US alliances in Europe and Asia with a focus on alliance dynamics and management. There, Wesley examines the structures that reinforce alliance systems among Asian and European countries. He sets the context that includes the waning of the United States' unipolar moment, the economic rise of countries such as China, and security challenges ranging from prolonged involvement in the Middle East to Russia's attacks on neighboring nations. Within this context, US allies face a paradox: new global challenges demonstrate the indispensability of the United States as a partner, whereas a decline in US primacy creates doubt concerning US capability. Alliance maintenance requires nations to consider the strategic costs and benefits of supporting a US initiative such as the invasion of Iraq. Wesley demonstrates that each US ally will consider both domestic and international consequences as multilateral and bilateral relationships evolve.

Economists Mancur Olson, Jr., and Richard Zechhauser then tackle the costs of participating in an alliance. Writing in the 1960s, the authors were responding to US accusations that other NATO members were not paying their share of the burden—a challenge that is still relevant in the year 2020. Using economic modeling, the authors demonstrate that larger nations do indeed bear a disproportionate share of the burden, but it is actually in a large country's national interest to continue contributing to collective security long after it is no longer in the national interest of a small country. Thus, they argue that the United States should not try to persuade other nations to be "fair" but should instead look to institutional changes that would better distribute marginal costs among nations.

Michael Barnett and Martha Finnemore round out the chapter with their discussion of IOs. They argue that US alliances, intended to provide extended deterrence, are weakening due to the increasing capabilities of US rivals and seemingly growing US isolationism. They contend that IOs can help fill this gap. Barnett and Finnemore explain the purpose and legitimacy of IOs as bureaucracies that can promote cooperation and the liberal order. At the same time, the authors point out that the power and authority granted to these organizations can come at a price.

Chapter 4 provides the complement to the previous chapter by looking at how US defense policy copes with adversarial relationships. Although the post–Cold War liberal order has witnessed remarkable successes, numerous challenges threaten the security of the United States and its allies. As September 11 demonstrated, terrorism poses a significant threat to the homeland; emerging nuclear powers such as North Korea and Iran are destabilizing forces; and China and Russia as great powers have the potential to upend the United States' role as the hegemon. In addition, weapons of mass destruction (such as nuclear, biological, and chemical weapons), organized crime, environmental warfare, and cyberattacks are among an increasing list of security threats. In turbulent times, how does defense policy meet all of the various threats to the nation? How should policy-makers classify threats when a nation can be both a valued trading partner and a security threat at the same time? What is in the United States' national interest?

Michael Mazarr's article begins this study of adversaries by pointing out that it is essential for security policy to understand who the enemy is, but defining who is an enemy is increasingly ambiguous. When war is declared, nations become enemies; when not at war these same nations are often "rivals" or "competitors." The challenge, Mazarr argues, is how to define nations that engage in hostile acts while still formally at peace. As rivals and competitors engage in politically or economically provocative actions, the United States will need to be careful to assess these acts in an objective manner lest the categorization of "enemy" becomes too commonplace.

Robert Gilpin turns to Thucydides and his concept of hegemonic war as a method to understand modern power dynamics. Through his analysis of the war between Sparta and Athens, Thucydides demonstrates that wars of hegemony emerge from social, economic, or technical revolution. Gilpin questions whether hegemonic war theory is still applicable in a nuclear age. As Thucydides points out, once begun, war unleashes unanticipated forces. This still applies in a nuclear age as a minor skirmish could escalate into nuclear war. At the same time, the threat of nuclear war has elevated the avoidance of such war to the highest priority among superpowers. He concludes that time will tell if hegemonic war theory holds true in the nuclear age.

Joseph Nye, Jr.'s, classic article concerning national interest centers on maintaining the United States' dominant global role as stabilizer, protector of the international commons, and maintainer of international laws and institutions. Nye argues that understanding the US national interest remains vitally important for foreign policy, but that that understanding must be reimagined in an information age. He advises policy-makers to categorize threats with those of the highest priority, such as Russia, receiving the greatest attention, while lower priorities such as humanitarian crises receiving great scrutiny before committing US resources. Prioritization will help the United States protect its national interest in the face of emerging threats and new technologies.

T. X. Hammes finishes this discussion on the adversary by surveying the many new technologies that are providing both large powers and small terrorist groups with increasingly lethal capabilities. Emerging technologies, he argues, are changing the strategic environment for state versus non-state conflicts. While small insurgent and terrorist groups are not likely to employ cutting-edge technology, commercial manufacturing of technology such as drones is changing small group tactics. Hammes concludes with advice for countering insurgents, terrorists, and criminal networks in a technology-driven era.

Chapter 1

Theories and Values

Necessity, Justice, Interest, and the Founding Principles of American Defense Policy

JEFF J. S. BLACK

Ancient Political thinkers incessantly talked about morals and virtue, those of our time talk only of business and money.

—Jean-Jacques Rousseau,
Discourse on the Sciences and the Arts (1750)

"War," Carl von Clausewitz tells us, "is a mere continuation of politics with other means."[1] The military may offer politicians distinctive means, but using military means does not introduce into politics a new, distinctive goal. Rather, military means aim at the same goal as politics itself. "The political object is the goal," Clausewitz explains, "war is the means of reaching it, and means can never be considered in isolation from their goal."[2] But the goal of politics, Aristotle claims in *Nicomachean Ethics*, is the greatest human good—if such a good exists.[3] So war policy—or as we euphemistically call it today, "defense policy"—tells politicians how to use distinctive military means to pursue their political goal: their vision of the greatest human good. A defense policy may contain principles of its own, guiding the use of military means, but these principles will be founded on more fundamental principles derived from a vision of the highest good for human beings.

This article examines three documents spanning a twenty-year period, 1776–1796, to seek in them the founding principles of American defense policy. The Declaration of Independence, the Constitution, and George Washington's Farewell Address were all composed while the American people, whether as citizens of newly independent states or of a newly constituted United States, were starting to think about how they should use their military means. A close reading of these three documents shows that early American thinking about defense policy was guided by ideas about necessity, or what they simply must do; justice, or what they ought to do; and interest, or what it would benefit them to do. In the Declaration, the Constitution, and the Farewell Address these three ideas are related in a way that points back to a distinctively American vision of the highest human good. To think clearly about defense policy, not just for the United States but in every case, we must think clearly about these three ideas, how they are related, and how defense policy emerges from the most fundamental political goals. In defense policy, claims about interest must underlie claims about justice and necessity, and therefore American defense policy in particular depends on a particularly American understanding of the highest human good.

The Declaration of Independence

The Declaration mentions necessity four times: three times while arguing for separation from Britain and once while arguing that the British king is a tyrant. The first of these mentions comes in the document's striking first sentence:

> When in the Course of human events, it becomes necessary for one people to dissolve the political bands which have connected them with another, and to assume among the powers of the earth, the separate and equal station to which the Laws of Nature and of Nature's God entitle them, a decent respect to the opinions of mankind requires that they should declare the causes which impel them to the separation.[4]

This sentence announces that American independence is necessary. It is the effect of causes that impel the American people. It is also just, something to which the American people are entitled. And the American people must declare its causes to all mankind, not only to the British people from whom they are separating.[5] The rest of the Declaration must defend these claims.

What sort of causes make the separation of one people from another necessary? By far the longest part of the Declaration tries to answer this question. "We hold these truths to be self-evident,"[6] it explains, and then it lists four truths: that before governments are established, all human beings are equal; that they all possess unalienable rights, including to life, to liberty, and to the pursuit of happiness; that governments are necessary to secure these rights, and just if they have the consent of the governed;[7] and that all peoples have the right to change their government if it fails to secure these rights. The beauty of these truths outshines the Declaration's cautious assertion of their self-evidence as principles. If to "hold" a truth to be self-evident means to choose to see it as self-evident, then holding a truth to be self-evident might be a sign that it is not self-evident at all. Really self-evident truths do not need to be held as such.[8] This is not to suggest that the

Declaration's principles are false. Instead, there is an argument for these principles, known to the authors of the Declaration and to the political theorists of the time. It begins by observing that there is no evident inequality among human beings sufficient to convince one to surrender one's life, liberty, or property to another.[9] All attempts to deprive human beings of these goods necessarily seem unjust as a result. All human beings must effectively be equal, then, and possess unalienable rights to these goods.[10] And since no human being has enough force by herself to secure these rights, some way of organizing human beings is necessary to secure them. These are governments to which we justly consent if they secure our rights and against which we justly rebel if they do not. So to hold the Declaration's four truths to be self-evident means to argue from necessity to justice. If human beings necessarily reject claims to rule based on inequalities, it is just to regard them as political equals. If they necessarily resist attempts to take their lives, liberty, or property, it is just to say they have rights to these goods. If they necessarily rebel against governments that deprive them of these rights, they have a right or even a duty to rebel. The idea of justice is a consequence of the idea of necessity in the Declaration: the American people are entitled to independence because they must separate from Britain.

On the basis of these principles, the Declaration finds the necessary cause of separation. "Prudence, indeed, will dictate," it continues, "that Governments long established should not be changed for light and transient causes; and accordingly all experience hath shown, that mankind are more disposed to suffer, while evils are sufferable, than to right themselves by abolishing the forms to which they are accustomed."[11] Prudence leads human beings to endure partial or temporary failures to secure their rights, then, because the price of rebellion is high. More than such failures is needed to make separation necessary. But in the case of the American colonies, "a long train of abuses and usurpations" proves that the failure is not temporary, and the goal of "absolute Despotism" proves that the failure is not partial. So the Declaration mentions necessity a second time. "Such has been the patient sufferance of these Colonies; and such is now the necessity which constrains them to alter their former Systems of Government."[12] Necessity again leads to justice: the lasting and total failure of the British crown to secure the Americans' rights activates the Americans' right to separate from Britain. But notice how the prudent calculation of interest has slipped in between the necessary cause and the just effect. Unjust governments are tolerable so long as the cost of rights violated is less than the cost of rebellion.

The rest of the Declaration, excepting its last paragraph, tries to show that the American people can tolerate no more. First it points to the length of the "train of abuses and usurpations" and to the colonies' repeated petitions for redress;[13] then it points to absolute despotism as the goal of the British crown. Nowhere does the Declaration reckon the probable costs of separation. We do not need to weigh the many facts the Declaration submits "to a candid world,"[14] though if all these facts are true, they more than justify separation.[15] Perhaps the Declaration's lengthy and detailed recitation of British abuses is meant less to prove that the American people can tolerate no more and more to influence the prudent calculation of their interest. Perhaps its authors felt it necessary to show the high cost of toleration, because they expected the cost of separation to be very high indeed.

Notice also that some of the abuses listed by the Declaration bear directly on defense policy. The British king "has kept among us, in times of peace, Standing Armies, without the Consent of our legislatures,"[16] "quartering large bodies of armed troops among us,"[17] in order "to render the Military independent of and superior to the Civil power."[18] If standing armies kept during peace, without legislative consent, and a superior and independent military are signs of absolute despotism—as means of controlling civilians by force—then a legitimate government will limit standing armies and establish civilian control of the military.

Having shown that the British crown aims entirely to deprive the American colonists of their inalienable rights, the Declaration mentions necessity one last time in its conclusion. The American colonies must "acquiesce in the necessity" that requires their separation and hold the British people "as we hold the rest of mankind, Enemies in War, in Peace Friends."[19] So they declare

> That these United Colonies are, and of Right ought to be FREE AND INDEPENDENT STATES; that they are Absolved from all Allegiance to the British Crown, and that all political connection between them and the State of Great Britain, is and ought to be totally dissolved; and that as Free and Independent States, they have full power to levy War, conclude Peace, contract Alliances, establish Commerce, and do all other Acts and Things which Independent States may of right do.[20]

The "Laws of Nature and Nature's God" include truths that we hold to be self-evident, truths that make it necessary, just, and prudent that the American people be independent. And once they are independent, it becomes necessary that the American people have a defense policy.

But what about the third claim of the Declaration's first sentence? Why must the American people declare the causes that impel them to their separation? A "decent respect to the opinions of mankind" requires such a declaration only if the causes it mentions can improve these opinions. That is, the Declaration is required only if the causes of the American people's separation from Britain are universal—if these causes apply, at least in principle, to every people. Mankind ought not to be mistaken about what sort of causes make the separation of peoples necessary, just, and prudent, lest some people mistakenly rebel when they ought to obey, and others obey when they ought to rebel. The American people must make the causes of their separation as clear as possible.

But this educational goal points to a puzzle. If the Declaration must show as clearly as possible why separation is necessary, why does it also argue that separation is just? Truly necessary causes, like the causes of the laws of universal gravitation, do not fail to produce their effects.[21] So if the causes found in the Declaration have the same kind of necessity, and this necessity is the basis for justice, then there can be no peoples who are entitled to independence but choose to obey, nor peoples who are not entitled to independence but choose to rebel. The fact of independence and the right to independence will always go together, since they are both necessary effects of the same cause. So since it is impossible to be mistaken about independence, there is no need to make the causes of American independence clear to other peoples. And if justice always follows necessity, then once necessity is present, claims about justice add nothing at all.

Yet clearly there could be other peoples who groan under tyranny's yoke. There were such peoples at the time of the Declaration, even under its authors' very noses. Surely "all experience hath shown" not just that "mankind . . . are disposed to suffer, while evils are sufferable,"[22] but also that human beings often are compelled or even choose to suffer evils that they ought to regard as insufferable. Not every people is as prudent as the Americans. This possibility suggests that the kind of necessity invoked by the Declaration is not unconditional. Thrown stones do not require a declaration of their right to fall back to earth, in accordance with the law of gravity. Rather, the necessity of separation must be conditional. Its full expression must take the form "if this is to be so, then this is necessary." If we are to survive, the colonists might have reasoned, then we must defend our rights; and if we are to defend our rights, then we must declare independence. The ultimate condition of such necessities, however, is not itself necessary. Rather, it relies on an idea of justice unsupported by necessity. If we are to survive, the colonists might have reasoned, then we must declare independence. And we ought to survive—but we might not.

So while the Declaration's claims of necessity are impressive and seem to ground its claims of justice, these claims ultimately depend on a prior idea of justice that is not grounded in necessity. Much of the argument of the Declaration can seem circular as a result: independence is just because it is necessary, but necessary because it is just. This circularity is typical of the reliance on necessity in defense policy, American or otherwise. To argue that some policy is necessary is to argue that the consequences of not following the policy are unacceptable, either as a matter of justice or as a matter of interest. The Declaration implies that the only way out of this circle is to weigh the costs and benefits of every policy—even those that seem to depend on principles of justice—in a prudent calculation of interest.

The Declaration of Independence is the founding text of American defense policy because it necessitates and justifies this policy. On the strength of the Declaration, the peoples of the American states first acquire the need, the right, and the power to "levy War, conclude Peace, [and] contract Alliances."[23] The Declaration also founds American defense policy by sketching some of its principles. Legitimate American governments will limit standing armies during peace, house their few troops in barracks or abroad, and establish civilian control. And the Declaration implies that independence from Britain does not require war with the British government or people. None of the American states born through the Declaration are obligated by it to be aggressive toward Britain or toward any other state. The announcement that the new states will hold all mankind "Enemies in War, in Peace Friends"[24] could even be taken to exclude aggression altogether—so that American war policy becomes a defense policy. But given that the principles of the Declaration are universal, and its necessities conditional, we must wonder whether it can be just, or even necessary, for the American states to assist the independence of other peoples whose rights are not secured by their governments. It would be hard to square such an obligation to assist with a military policy that is exclusively defensive.

Lastly, the Declaration of Independence offers to students of defense policy an early American articulation of the ideas of necessity, justice, and interest—ideas at work in all reasoning about defense policy. On its face, the Declaration asserts that American independence is necessary, and therefore just, and therefore in the American interest. But difficulties in its argument point to the opposite series of inferences as the Declaration's deeper meaning: independence is in America's interest, and therefore just, and therefore necessary.

The Constitution

By listing "to provide for the common defense"[25] among its goals, the Preamble to the Constitution identifies it as a second important source of founding principles for American defense policy. Article IV, section 4 partly specifies the kind of defense it envisions: there the United States collectively "guarantee to every State in this Union a Republican Form of Government" and undertake to "protect each of them against Invasion; and . . . against domestic Violence."[26] Aggressive war is not ruled out, nor is it even mentioned. The means to the common defense are specified in Articles I and II. Article I grants Congress the power "to make all Laws . . . necessary and proper" to "provide for the common Defence."[27] In particular, sections 11 through 17 of this article assign to Congress powers including

1. to "declare War";[28]
2. to appropriate funds for the establishment and maintenance of an army and navy,[29] and to make the rules that govern and regulate these military forces;
3. to provide for "organizing, arming, and disciplining" a militia, to provide for summoning it "to execute the laws of the Union, suppress Insurrections, and repel Invasions," and to provide for governing it when so summoned;[30]
4. and to exercise "exclusive Legislation in all Cases whatsoever" over "all Places purchased"—with the consent of the state legislature of the place—to serve as locations for "Forts, Magazines, Arsenals, dock-Yards, and other needful Buildings."[31]

By contrast, Article II, section 2, contains a single, curt provision for the common defense: "The President shall be Commander in Chief of the Army and Navy of the United States, and of the Militia of the several States, when called into the actual service of the United States."[32]

The Constitution's statements on defense policy are largely straightforward applications of the principles sketched in the Declaration of Independence. Since peacetime standing armies, kept without legislative consent, are among the abuses inflicted on the American colonists by the British Crown, the Constitution assigns the power to "raise and support" armies to Congress, limits appropriations for their support to two years—requiring the legislature to revisit support for long-standing armies—and assigns to the militia significant roles in domestic policing and repelling invasions.[33] Since quartering large bodies of troops with civilians is an abuse, Congress has the power to request sites for military installations from the states, and to exercise authority over these installations. And since a superior and independent military is a sign of despotism, the Constitution asserts civilian superiority by establishing the civilian president as Commander in Chief of all national military forces, and asserts military dependence by dividing

authority over the national military between Congress and the president.[34] The Constitution goes beyond the principles of the Declaration in one major respect, however. By denying to the states, "without the Consent of Congress," the power to "keep Troops, or Ships of War in time of Peace . . . or engage in War, unless actually invaded, or in such imminent Danger as will not admit of delay,"[35] Article I, section 10 makes clear that a "more perfect Union"[36] is one in which defense policy is a matter, not for the collective action of the states, but for the unified action of the national government.

The Constitution is explicit about the allocation of authority over defense policy between the states and the national government and between the legislative and executive branches of the national government. But it is nearly silent about the intentions behind these allocations and the kind of defense policy they are meant to support. The Constitution's Preamble lists to "establish Justice" among its goals,[37] but the document says nothing about the roles necessity, justice, and interest should play in American defense policy. For interpretations of these aspects of the Constitution's meaning, we must turn to the writings of Publius and Brutus, a defender and a critic of the Constitution during the Federalist—anti-Federalist debates over its ratification. Since Publius—the pen name for Alexander Hamilton, John Jay, and James Madison—wrote first,[38] it is best to begin with the collection of their writings known as the *Federalist Papers*.

The *Federalist Papers*

The *Federalist Papers* are traditionally divided into four series: on the advantages of a more perfect union (numbers 1–14), on the weaknesses of the existing confederation under the Articles of Confederation (numbers 15–22), on the powers that a national government should exercise (numbers 23–36), and on the conformity of the proposed Constitution with the principles of republicanism and good government (numbers 37–83).[39] But to follow Publius's predictions of American defense policy, we will divide the *Federalist Papers* into five groups: on how to judge the Constitution (number 1), on the international situation of the American colonies (numbers 2–8), on the colonies' domestic character and its international implications (numbers 9–14), on the powers necessary for the common defense (numbers 22–29), and on the insufficiency of the Articles of Confederation (number 43). Publius argues throughout these papers that to adopt the proposed Constitution is not just a matter of interest, but also a matter of necessity, because the American international situation is precarious, the American domestic character is expansionist, and the requirements of common defense are uncompromising. We will see whether

Publius's more explicit version of the Declaration's argument from interest to justice to necessity suffers from the same difficulties.

Hamilton begins Federalist 1 by arguing on the basis of interest. "It has been frequently remarked," he proclaims, "that it seems to have been reserved to the people of this country to decide, by their conduct and example, the important question, whether societies of men are really capable or not, of establishing good government from reflection and choice, or whether they are forever destined to depend, for their political constitutions, on accident and force."[40] Though Hamilton does not stand by the truth of this remark, he stands by its implications. All previous governments, even the one announced by the Declaration of Independence and constituted by the Articles of Confederation, have come about by "accident and force," that is, by necessity. But one example of a government founded by "reflection and choice" would prove that this kind of foundation is possible for human beings. It is up to the American people to prove this possibility. Despite their "full experience of the insufficiency of the existing federal government" under the Articles,[41] they now face the free choice to adopt or reject the proposed Constitution, according to their interest.[42] By "adding the inducements of philanthropy to those of patriotism,"[43] Hamilton gives to the Constitution and to the debate over its ratification something like the educational task of the Declaration of Independence. Through these texts the Americans can set an example for the world of an enlightened people choosing their interest, free from the constraints of necessity.

But Publius moves quickly to undermine this argument based on the free choice of interest. Hamilton uses the rest of Federalist 1 to describe the domestic obstacles to a free choice of the Constitution; and Federalists 2 through 5, written by John Jay, describe an international situation that constrains this choice. In Federalist 2, Jay insists that the greatness of the American people depends on the preservation of the union.[44] In Federalist 3, he explains why: only a union, rather than a confederacy, can secure the American people from foreign arms and influence. The separate states, each conducting its own foreign policy as a member of a confederacy, will be more likely to fall victim to particular passions or interests; by contrast, a union acting as a whole will have better leaders and will follow a wiser policy. So a union will offer foreign nations fewer just causes for war than a confederacy will and will settle the disputes it does cause more reasonably.[45] So far, Jay's argument follows familiar Federalist lines, about how an extended republic will dampen local passions and interests and put more national characters at the head of government. But he quickly gives it another basis. "Besides," Jay adds, "it is well known that acknowledgements, explanations, and compensa-

tions are often accepted as satisfactory from a strong united nation, which would be rejected as unsatisfactory if offered by a state or confederacy of little consideration or power."[46] Union might make the states more just in their international relations, but it will also make them stronger, which will make their international relations seem more just to other states. Not only justice but also strength makes the just causes for war fewer.

In Federalist 4 Jay grants that foreign nations might also have unjust causes for war with the United States: causes such as their national interest, or in the case of monarchies, personal motives like glory, revenge, ambition, and private interest.[47] He also grants that commerce can be a zero-sum game, in which one nation's success comes at the expense of its neighbors and competitors. "From these and like considerations," he allows, "which might, if consistent with prudence, be more amplified and detailed, it is easy to see that jealousies and uneasinesses may gradually slide into the minds and cabinets of other nations, and that we are not to expect they should regard our advancement in union, in power, and in consequence by land and by sea, with an eye of indifference and composure."[48] Jay thus adds fear to the list of causes of unjust war between nations. But he postpones the conclusion that by its greater power when compared with a confederacy, an American union could provoke fear and invite war.

Instead he insists that a strong union will be better than a confederacy at deterring unjust wars, too. A union offers "the best possible state of defense,"[49] because in the place of three or four, or even thirteen distinct militias, each with its own chain of command and plan of discipline, a union makes possible a single militia corps with a unified discipline and command.[50] A union will also make it possible to develop a powerful navy. If the American people are wise and choose to unite, Jay predicts, "the time may come when the fleets of America may engage attention."[51] Not until Federalist 5 does Jay allude to the consequences of his argument thus far. If the American states were to form one or several confederacies, rather than a union, he admits, then if one of those states or confederacies were to become more powerful than its neighbors, "that moment would those neighbors behold her with envy and with fear. Both those passions would lead them to countenance, if not to promote whatever might promise to diminish her importance; and would also restrain them from measures calculated to advance, or even to secure her prosperity."[52] Power necessarily causes fear and envy, even between allied states; and fear and envy are causes of war. The claim Jay makes about relations between states in a confederacy, or between several confederacies of states, applies with equal force to relations between neighboring nations, and so to relations between an American union and its neighbors. Whatever its other advantages, American strength will invite war.

Here Hamilton takes over Publius's pen, and makes the implications of Jay's argument more explicit in Federalists 6 through 8. If the states were to reject union in favor of confederacy, Hamilton argues in Federalist 6, they would end up warring with one another, because "men are ambitious, vindictive, and rapacious."[53] Treaties of alliance and ties of friendship cannot be expected to withstand the many causes of hostility among nations: those causes that have "a general and almost constant operation upon the collective bodies of society," like "the love of power, or the desire of preeminence and dominion" on the part of strong nations, and "the jealousy of power, or the desire of equality and safety" on the part of the weak; and those causes "which take their origin entirely in private passions; in the attachment, enmities, interests, hopes, and fears, of leading individuals in the communities of which they are members."[54] Like Jay, Hamilton distinguishes between public and private causes of war. But unlike Jay, he does not claim that a strong union will be less likely to offer just causes for war than a confederacy of separate states. Strong states love power and desire dominion. Also unlike Jay, Hamilton does not claim that a union will suppress private passions and interests and produce a more just foreign policy. Hamilton considers the argument that commercial republics like the American states are intrinsically pacific: that they "will be governed by mutual interest, and will cultivate a spirit of mutual amity and concord" because "the spirit of commerce has a tendency to soften the manners of men, and to extinguish those inflammable humours which have so often kindled into wars."[55] But in his view both human nature and historical evidence argue the contrary. All human beings seek to increase their relative power, the strong by becoming stronger, and the weak by making the strong weaker. Thus the "rival ships and competitions of commerce between commercial nations" are no less causes of hostility than the other collective and individual passions.[56] Hamilton ends Federalist 6 by quoting "an intelligent writer" with approval: "NEIGHBOURING NATIONS . . . are naturally ENEMIES of each other, unless their common weakness forces them to league in a CONFEDERATE REPUBLIC, and their constitution prevents the differences that neighbourhood occasions, extinguishing that secret jealousy, which disposes all states to aggrandize themselves at the expense of their neighbours."[57]

In Federalist 8 Hamilton applies this reasoning about the American international situation to standing armies. Despite their expense, standing armies are useful to states with close neighbors, because they make sudden conquests difficult and prevent the rapid desolation of their territories.[58] In commercial societies, where most citizens are incapable of serving as soldiers

in case of need, standing armies must be formed of professional soldiers to be effective.[59] And large standing armies formed of professional soldiers elevate the status of the soldier at the expense of the citizen, producing over time an independent and superior military.[60] But geographically isolated states need not fear sudden conquests, nor rapid desolation. So they have no need for standing armies. And since ratifying the Constitution will not change the geographic situation of the American states, it cannot make standing armies necessary. "If we are wise enough to preserve the union," Hamilton writes, "we may for ages enjoy an advantage similar to that of an insulated situation. Europe is at a great distance from us. Her colonies in our vicinity will be likely to continue too much disproportioned in strength, to be able to give us any dangerous annoyance. Extensive military establishments cannot, in this position, be necessary to our security."[61] Standing armies will become necessary to the American states only if these states reject the Constitution, form one or more confederacies instead, and become rivals. Standing armies are unnecessary to a more perfect union.

With this conclusion, Publius completes the first part of his interpretation of the Constitution's implications for defense policy. Right after claiming that the American people can choose to establish good government by "reflection and choice," rather than accept the dictates of "accident and force," he begins to constrain this choice. Surveying the international situation of the American states, he argues that a union will offer fewer just and unjust causes of war to foreign nations than any other arrangement—though he also admits that a strong union will provoke fear and incite war and perhaps even pursue power and desire war. One day, American navies may be especially fearsome and powerful. Considering the likely consequences of choosing confederacy over union, he lists several universal causes that necessarily make neighboring states enemies. Then he argues that the American states will not need standing armies under the Constitution, because only neighboring states need such armies, whereas isolated states do not. A great deal depends, then, on whether and for how long the United States can expect to remain isolated. As soon as these states have neighbors, their strength will provoke fear and incite war, and extensive military establishments will become necessary.

The next part of Publius's interpretation of the Constitution concerns the domestic character of the American colonies. Federalist 10, written by James Madison, begins the argument with a principle drawn from the Declaration of Independence.[62] Considering whether factions in an American union can be controlled by giving each citizen the same opinions, passions, and interests, Madison judges this policy to be impracticable.

The free exercise of reason causes differences in opinions, he argues, and self-love added to reason adds differences in passions to these differences in opinions. Both kinds of differences produce differences in interests. Moreover, "The diversity in the faculties of men, from which the rights of property originate, is not less an insuperable obstacle to an uniformity of interests. The protection of these faculties, is the first object of government. From the protection of different and unequal faculties of acquiring property, the possession of different degrees and kinds of property immediately results; and from the influence of these on the sentiments and views of the respective proprietors, ensues a division of the society into different interests and parties."[63]

The defenders of pure democracy, Madison continues, are mistaken to think that a perfect equality of political rights must lead to a perfect identity of possessions, opinions, and passions.[64] He thus assigns a narrowly political meaning to the Declaration's self-evident truth of human equality. While it is true that one human being will not submit to another because they are unequal, Madison admits, it does not follow that human beings should be equal in every respect. To the contrary, it follows from another of the Declaration's self-evident truths, that human beings have unalienable rights, that human beings will be unequal in many respects. The rights to life, liberty, and the pursuit of happiness, coupled with the "diversity in the faculties of men" to acquire property, will yield inequalities in property—inequalities a legitimate government is bound to protect, because its legitimacy depends on the security of these rights. The first object of government, Madison insists—and the object, we might add, whose achievement makes government legitimate according to the Declaration—is to protect the inequalities that justly result from unequal human abilities.[65]

When Hamilton takes over as Publius for Federalist 11, he draws the conclusion from Madison's beginning. The adventurous commercial spirit of the American people, Hamilton supposes, is already making the European maritime powers uneasy. The European powers already foresee that the Americans will infringe on their carrying trade and contest their naval superiority.[66] Concurring with Jay's vision, Hamilton thus calls on the American people to support the Constitution for the sake of establishing a national navy. Under an efficient national government, a navy would soon become so powerful that it could decide any naval contest by taking a side, even if it could not win every such contest singlehandedly. The American navy could, for example, decide European naval campaigns in the West Indies by guaranteeing the supplies of one of the adversaries. And this degree of naval power would let the Americans bargain for commercial privileges from a position of strength. "By steady adherence to the union," Hamilton promises, "we may hope, ere long, to become the arbiter of Europe in America; and to be able to incline the balance of European competitions in this part of the world, as our interest may dictate."[67] Repeating Jay's claim about the importance of strength, Hamilton adds: "The rights of neutrality will only be respected, when they are defended by an adequate power. A nation, despicable by its weakness, forfeits even the privilege of being neutral."[68] The nation needs a powerful navy, even if her ambitions go no farther than neutrality in European conflicts.

If the American people reject the Constitution, by contrast, Europe will succeed in restricting the American carrying trade, and the American states will be confined to a passive maritime commerce. "That unequalled spirit of enterprise," Hamilton continues, "which signalizes the genius of the American merchants and navigators, and which is in itself an inexhaustible mine of national wealth, would be stifled and lost; and poverty and disgrace would overspread a country, which, with wisdom, might make herself the admiration and envy of the world."[69] The unlimited individual pursuit of property eventually requires foreign commerce, and foreign commerce eventually requires naval power. So the unlimited individual pursuit of property necessarily leads to the national pursuit of greatness. "The necessity of naval power to external or maritime commerce, and the conduciveness of that species of commerce to the prosperity of a navy, are points too manifest to require a particular elucidation," Hamilton remarks. "They, by a kind of reaction, mutually beneficial, promote each other."[70]

Hamilton ends Federalist 11 with a vision of America's future that goes well beyond Jay's vision of a navy "of respectable weight": "Let Americans disdain to be the instruments of European greatness! Let the Thirteen States, bound together in a strict and indissoluble union, concur in erecting one great American system, superior to the control of all transatlantic force or influence, and able to dictate the terms of the connection between the old and the new world!"[71] This "great American system" is a hemispheric naval hegemony that can do much more than "incline the balance of European competitions" in the new world.[72] It is founded on the necessity to protect American maritime commerce, which is founded in turn on the necessity to protect the unequal outcomes of the unequal abilities of individual Americans to acquire property. Putting Hamilton's and Madison's arguments together makes the legitimacy of American government depend on its acquisition of a navy with hemispheric dominance.[73] But this conclusion has grave implications for Publius's earlier discussion of America's international situation. As a land power, the United States could "for ages enjoy an advantage similar to that of an insulated situation," making extensive military establishments unnecessary to their security.[74] But as a naval power, the United States are already provoking fear in the European great powers, and encroaching on their neighborhoods. By the argument of the first group of Federalist Papers, this fear will generate more causes for war,[75] and require more extensive naval establishments to carry out these wars, with unknown consequences for civilian control of the military.[76]

The last group of relevant Federalists is written by Hamilton, and treats the Constitution's provisions to "provide for the common defence." In Federalist 22, he surveys the shortcomings of the Articles of Confederation in this respect. The power to raise armies under the Articles, for example, is "merely a power of making requisitions upon the states for quotas of men."[77] That is, it is no power at all. The Revolutionary War made it clear that requisitions made the common defense less vigorous and less economical, by generating a market for soldiers in which the states were compelled to outbid one another to meet their quotas, and soldiers were encouraged to postpone or shorten their enlistment in the hopes of higher compensation in the future.[78] Such a market made insufficient numbers of troops available for emergencies. Worse, the numbers that were available fluctuated, ruining discipline and threatening public safety with the possibility that armies would have to be disbanded.

So to provide adequately for the common defense, Hamilton continues in Federalist 23, the union under the Constitution must be empowered to raise, provide for, govern, and direct a national army and a national navy. "These powers ought to exist without limitation," he insists, "because it is impossible to foresee or to define the extent and variety of national exigencies, and the correspondent extent and variety of the means which may be necessary to satisfy them. The circumstances that endanger the safety of nations are infinite; and for this reason, no constitutional shackles can wisely be imposed on the power to which the care of it is committed. This power ought to be co-extensive with all the possible combinations of such circumstances; and ought to be under the direction of the same councils which are appointed to preside over the common defence."[79]

An unlimited national power to provide for the common defense follows from the infinite circumstances that endanger the safety of nations, Hamilton explains, by means of a self-evident truth, a truth that "cannot be made plainer by argument or reasoning":[80] namely, the axiom that "the *means* ought to be proportioned to the *end*; the persons from whose agency the attainment of any *end* is expected, ought to possess the *means* by which it is attained."[81] Notice Hamilton's explicit reliance on the logic of conditional necessity implicit in the Declaration of Independence. If the circumstances that endanger the common defense are infinite, then the means to provide for it are infinite—he asserts this as a matter of fact. But if the national government ought to provide for the common defense, then it must possess unlimited power to do so—he presents this as a necessary inference from a moral premise. Hamilton does not try to prove his assertion that dangerous circumstances are infinite. Instead, he challenges his readers to prove the contrary. If they cannot, he concludes, then by necessary inference "there can be no limitation of that authority, which is to provide for the defence and protection of the community, in any matter essential to its efficacy; that is, in any matter essential to the *formation, direction,* or *support* of the national forces."[82]

On the basis of this argument for the unlimited power of the national government—an argument on which both he and Madison would rely repeatedly in the remaining *Federalist Papers*[83]—Hamilton devotes the next six Federalists to the constitutional provisions for the common defense. In Federalist 24 he replies to the objection that the Constitution does not adequately prohibit standing armies. The legislative branch, Hamilton notes, not the executive branch, possesses the whole power of raising armies under the Constitution. The proposed legislative branch is representative, democratic, and popular. Moreover, its appropriations for an army are limited to two years, which provides "a great and real security against military establishments without evident necessity."[84] But the security situation of the United States makes all other restraints upon legislative discretion over military establishments either improper to impose or, "from the necessities of society," unlikely to be observed.[85] Even though the American states are protected by oceans, they have British dominions on one frontier, Spanish colonies on another, and Native American settlements on a third. Since the United States are a threat to all three, they will likely cooperate to oppose American interests. Worse, "improvements in the art of navigation have, as to the facility of communication, rendered distant nations, in a great measure, neighbours."[86] Two of these new neighbors of the United States, with respect to communication at least, are among the principal maritime powers of Europe: Britain and Spain. Also, the American states need small garrisons on their western frontier. These could be manned by militia, but "in times of profound peace" they "would not long, if at all, submit to be dragged from their occupations and families, to perform that disagreeable duty."[87] Persuading or compelling the militia to garrison the frontier would cause increased private expenses, loss of labor, and interruptions of business for those who served. "It would be as burthensome and injurious to the public, as ruinous to private citizens,"[88] because the private interests of citizens of a commercial republic conflict with their public duties as militia. So a small standing army is necessary to provide these garrisons: a "permanent corps in the pay of the government."[89] If, as seems likely, Britain and Spain were to increase their military presence in North America and cooperate with the Native Americans against the United States, these garrisons would need to be larger. Finally, to secure the Atlantic coast, a navy is necessary, which means dockyards, arsenals, fortifications, and "probably" additional garrisons—at least until the fleet is strong enough to defend its own ports. These facts show, according to Hamilton, "the impropriety of a constitutional interdiction" of standing armies "and the necessity of leaving the matter to the discretion and prudence of the legislature."[90]

Given Hamilton's vision of America's future greatness and his judgment of its security situation, it should not surprise us that a Federalist paper insisting that the Constitution protects sufficiently against standing armies turns out to imply that the United States will soon require a standing army. But Federalist 24 also implicitly criticizes the militia. Hamilton makes this criticism explicit in Federalist 25, writing against the view that standing armies are unnecessary because "the militia of the country is its natural bulwark, and would at all times be equal to the national defense."[91] To the contrary: not only is the commercial spirit of the American citizen opposed to his service in the militia, but the militia is insufficiently expert and professional to succeed in modern warfare. "The steady operations of war against a regular and disciplined army, can only be successfully conducted by a force of the same kind," Hamilton judges. "War, like most other things, is a science to be acquired and perfected by diligence, by perseverance, by time, and by practice."[92] This strengthens Hamilton's argument against using militia to garrison the frontier, but it also implies that the Constitution was wrong to rely on the militia to "repel Invasions,"[93] at least by professional soldiers. State constitutional provisions in favor of the militia are also harmful, because they are ignored out of necessity: "Nations pay little regard to rules and maxims, calculated in their very nature to run counter to the necessities of society. Wise politicians will be cautious about fettering the government with restrictions, that cannot be observed; because they know, that every breach of the fundamental laws, though dictated by necessity, impairs that sacred reverence, which ought to be maintained in the breast of rulers toward the constitution of a country, and forms a precedent for other breaches, where the same plea of necessity does not exist at all, or is less urgent and palpable."[94] If a constitution is to be revered as a necessary law, its laws must conform as closely as possible to necessity. Unnecessary laws are disregarded, first out of necessity, then out of convenience—and the constitution is no longer revered. The proposed Constitution meets the test of

necessity by permitting standing armies to the extent necessary for guards and garrisons, by acknowledging that national exigencies are unlimited, and by conferring an unrestrained authority to provide for the national defense, a power equal to every possible contingency, to the national government.

The Federalist interpretation of the Constitution finds in it three founding principles for defense policy. First, Publius surveys the international situation of the American states and concludes that a more perfect union will offer fewer causes for war out of bad policy, but more causes for war to the extent it becomes powerful and encroaches on its powerful neighbors.[95] Second, Publius analyzes the domestic spirit of the American people and concludes that their pursuit of property will eventually require an extensive international carrying trade, with a navy to protect it. Such a navy will in effect make the United States the neighbor of the foremost European naval powers. Third, Publius considers the Constitution's provisions for the common defense and concludes approvingly that they are consistent with necessity: they permit a small standing army of professional soldiers,[96] an extensive naval establishment, and an unlimited power in the national government to meet an infinite range of military challenges.[97]

Madison concludes the Federalists relevant to American defense policy. While surveying the necessity and propriety of the proposed powers of the national government in Federalist 43, Madison addresses a question "of a very delicate nature." By what right can the Constitution supersede the Articles of Confederation, without the unanimous consent of the states party to the Articles?[98] Madison's answer returns once again to the principles of the Declaration of Independence: "The first question is answered at once by recurring to the absolute necessity of the case; to the great principle of self-preservation; to the transcendent law of nature and of nature's God, which declares that the safety and happiness of society, are the objects at which all political institutions aim, and to which all such institutions must be sacrificed."[99] Just as the right to life, the "great principle of self-preservation," grounds the "absolute necessity" of independence, so too this principle grounds the absolute necessity that the American people abandon the Articles of Confederation for the proposed Constitution.

But despite Madison's reliance on the Declaration, the Federalist interpretation of the Constitution diverges considerably from the principles of defense policy sketched in that text. The Declaration implies that the American states will hold all of mankind "Enemies in War, in Peace Friends," that they will prohibit or limit standing armies during peace and keep troops out of private homes, and that they will prevent their militaries from becoming superior or independent. Of these principles, only the bar on quartering troops in private homes—later codified as the Third Amendment[100]—survives Publius's reasoning untouched. Publius expects the powerful states of the world to regard the United States as an enemy, even during peacetime. He implies that the United States will regard its powerful neighbors as enemies in return. He refuses to rule out offensive wars against them.[101] He argues that standing armies are necessary and should not be subject to additional constitutional limits. He envisions a future naval establishment so considerable as to raise worries about civilian control. And in place of the Declaration's ambiguity about whether the American states must assist other peoples seeking independence, Publius substitutes the certainty that the Constitution requires an expanding naval power to protect expanding American commercial interests.

The idea of necessity drives these changes, because it drives Publius's reading of the Constitution. Although the *Federalist Papers* begin with the claim that "reflection and choice" should determine whether the Constitution is adopted, not "accident and force," the papers relevant to defense policy end by claiming that it is an "absolute necessity," grounded on the right to life, that the Constitution be put before the American people. Although the Articles of Confederation and the Constitution seem at first to be fundamental laws equally consistent with the principles of the Declaration of Independence,[102] by the time Publius is done, only the Constitution fits the bill. Reasoning on the basis of necessity, as we have said, involves characteristic difficulties. "Necessity, especially in politics," Hamilton himself admits, "often occasions false hopes, false reasonings, and a system of measures correspondingly erroneous."[103] Apparently absolute necessities are really conditional on moral claims about justice—claims that must be weighed by the prudent calculation of interest.

Brutus and the Anti-Federalists

Given how far Publius's interpretation of the Constitution diverges from the principles of the Declaration of Independence, the fierce objections of anti-Federalist writers to the Constitution's ratification should not surprise. In particular, we should expect an anti-Federalist objection to Publius's reasoning from interest to justice to necessity, one that denies that the self-evident truths of the Declaration necessarily lead to exchanging the Articles of Confederation for a Constitution that founds an expansionist commercial republic. But the essays of Brutus, the anti-Federalist writer with the most to say about the principles of American defense policy, do not go very far in making this objection. In the relevant essays (VII–X), Brutus criticizes Publius's reasoning, but he does not offer an interpretation of the Declaration's principles different enough from Publius's to allow him to draw wholly different conclusions. We will see that other anti-Federalist writers go farther than Brutus does in this respect—but that none of them goes far enough.

In Essay VII Brutus examines Hamilton's reasoning in Federalist 23. He does not take issue with Hamilton's conditional necessity: if the national government is charged with procuring the common defense, then it must be granted the powers to do so. Brutus even adds that some threats to national safety will exceed the resources available to repel them. But he rejects the claim of fact that underlies Hamilton's conditional necessity: that if the threats to national safety are unlimited, the means to repel them must be unlimited too. Instead, "Every nation may form a rational judgment, what force will be competent to protect and defend it, against any enemy with which it is probable it may have to contend. In extraordinary attack, every country must rely upon the spirit and special exertions of its inhabitants—and these extraordinary efforts will always very much depend upon the happiness and good order the people experience from a wise and prudent administration of their internal government. The [American] states are as capable of making a just estimate on this head, as perhaps any nation in the world."[104] By insisting that every state, whether small or large, can make a rational estimate of its security situation, Brutus rejects Jay's argument in Federalist 3 that a union of states will have a more prudent defense policy than one or a few confederations.[105] He gives an example of such an estimate later in the same essay, contesting Hamilton's judgment of the American security situation in Federalist 24. Brutus lists the same adversaries as Hamilton—the British dominions, the Spanish colonies, and the Native American settlements—but he rates them differently. The Native Americans are strong enough only to threaten the frontiers, not the interiors of the states. The European colonies are weak without support from their mother countries, and this support must be transported across the Atlantic, while the American states can defend themselves on their home soil, with all its resources.[106] "For defence against any assault," Brutus concludes, "which there is any probability will be made upon us, we may easily form an estimate."[107] So for ordinary threats to national safety, limited powers are sufficient to repel them. For extraordinary threats, each American state, like any state, must rely on "the spirit and special exertions of its inhabitants." While a national government charged with procuring the common defense must be granted the means to do so, and the threats to the common defense are unlimited, most threats are predictable, and in the American case the means necessary to repel them are limited. Brutus rules out that the American states might wage offensive war,[108] and he does not foresee naval engagements on the high seas in defense of American international trade.

Brutus also rejects Publius's argument that standing armies are necessary. In Essay VIII he instead reasserts the Declaration's principle that standing armies are a sign of despotic government. Brutus quotes approvingly from a speech in the British House of Commons, asserting that a large standing army threatens liberty because it forms a body distinct from the people, one governed by military rather than by civilian laws, with the habit of "blind obedience" and "entire submission" to the orders of its commanders.[109] If the reasoning of this speech is just, Brutus concludes, "it follows, that keeping up a standing army, would be in the highest degree dangerous to the liberty and happiness of the community—and if so, the general government ought not to have authority to do it,"[110] not even with the consent of the national legislature. After this renewed call for a more explicit constitutional prohibition on standing armies, Brutus returns in Essay X to Hamilton's argument in Federalist 24 that the American security situation requires a standing army. It has not and cannot be demonstrated, he insists, that in order to give the national government sufficient power to raise the troops it needs, it is necessary to give it an unlimited power to raise and keep armies. If the probable threats to the American states can be known, as Brutus thinks they can, then a limited power to meet these threats is enough for the national government. And this power need not include maintaining a standing army in times of peace. Brutus proposes an amendment to the Constitution that would prohibit standing armies; permit troops to be raised for guards, garrisons, and to repel attack or invasion; and require the consent of two-thirds of Congress to raise troops during peacetime.[111] This amendment should grant the national government sufficient power to repel ordinary threats. As for extraordinary threats, Brutus's mention of "the spirit and special exertions" of the American people indicates that to repel them, the American states will rely on their militias.[112]

Militias are exempt from some of the disadvantages of professional standing armies. Militia members come from the body of the people; they obey both military and civilian law; and their habit of obedience to their commanders is less ingrained than in a professional military. They represent less of a danger to civilian superiority, by this reasoning, than do professional militaries.[113] But Brutus's confidence that a militia will be sufficient to repel extraordinary foreign threats has a different basis. "The preservation of internal peace and good order, and the due administration of law and justice," he writes in Essay VII,

ought to be the first care of every government.— The happiness of a people depends infinitely more

on this than it does upon all that glory and respect which nations acquire by the most brilliant martial achievements—and I believe history will furnish but few examples of nations who have duly attended to these, who have been subdued by foreign invaders. If a proper respect and submission to laws prevailed over all orders of men in our country; and if a spirit of public and private justice, œconomy and industry influenced the people, we need not be under any apprehensions but what they would be ready to repel any invasion that might be made on the country. And more than this, I would not wish from them—A defensive war is the only one I think justifiable—I do not make these observations to prove, that a government ought not to be authorised to provide for the protection and defence of a country against external enemies, but to shew that this is not the most important, much less the only object of their care.[114]

To secure the common defense, government does not need an unlimited power to raise troops in the case of necessity. Instead, it needs to guarantee public and private justice, moderation, and industry. History shows, according to Brutus, that most nations that care more for these virtues than for military greatness can rely on their militias to repel invasions—even extraordinary ones. In interpreting the Constitution, Publius makes the error made by almost all European governments, which are "framed, and administered with a view to arms, and war, as that in which their chief glory consists."[115] He misunderstands the end of government, which is "to save men's lives, not to destroy them."[116]

Brutus's optimism about the power of militias seems unreasonable, given the power of modern military technology and professionalism. No nation today can rely solely on a militia of happy citizens to repel foreign invasion. But Brutus prompts us to ask whether Publius's interpretation of the Constitution conceals under the guise of necessity a longing for military glory that is not necessary to the American people, and perhaps also not in their interest. While Brutus couples his concern for virtue with a concern for "œconomy and industry," and exposes himself to the Federalist reply that commercial expansion requires military expansion, other anti-Federalist writers go further, expressing doubts about the American commercial spirit. In his survey of anti-Federalist political theory, *What the Anti-Federalists Were For*, Herbert J. Storing cites several examples of these doubts. Charles Turner claims that commerce causes luxury, which undermines republican virtue: "As people become more luxurious, they become more incapacitated of governing themselves."[117] "You are not to inquire how your trade may be increased," Patrick Henry warns, "nor how you are to become a great and powerful people, but how your liberties can be secured; for liberty ought to be the direct end of your Government."[118] And Cato argues that the government proposed in the Constitution itself threatens the liberties of the American people, precisely because of its commercial character:

> It is alledged that the opinions and manners of the people of America, are capable to resist and prevent an extension of prerogative or oppression; but you must recollect that opinion and manners are mutable, and may not always be a permanent obstruction against the encroachments of government; that the progress of a commercial society begets luxury, the parent of inequality, the foe to virtue, and the enemy to restraint; and that ambition and voluptuousness aided by flattery, will teach magistrates, where limits are not explicitly fixed to have separate and distinct interests from the people, besides it will not be denied that government assimilates the manners and opinions of the community to it. Therefore, a general presumption that rulers will govern well is not a sufficient security.[119]

Agrippa even raises the possibility that commerce between the states could be a fully satisfactory and less corrupting alternative to international commerce, and could serve as a ground of friendship rather than rivalry between the states. "All the states have local advantages," he writes, "and in a considerable degree separate interests. They are, therefore, in a situation to supply each other's wants. . . . The most friendly intercourse may therefore be established between them. A diversity of produce, wants and interests produces commerce, and commerce, where there is a common, equal, and moderate authority to preside, produces friendship."[120]

Brutus's version of the anti-Federalist critique of the Constitution fails fully to counter the Federalist interpretation, because he offers no alternative to Publius's argument that the principles of the Declaration of Independence dictate an expanding commercial republic with a powerful navy. Other anti-Federalist writers venture different claims about the goal of the American republic, but none of these claims yields as sustained a critique as Brutus's. But Publius's argument suffers from its own difficulties: it seems to be based on the idea of necessity, but the meaning of necessity is ultimately determined by the prudent calculation of interest. So the anti-Federalists' arguments fall short not because the Federalist argument is unproblematic, but because the anti-Federalists do not sufficiently develop an alternative account of the American people's interests.[121] To the extent that they accept Publius's premises, they must struggle to reject Publius's conclusions. The American people might not want military greatness, Publius could say to the anti-Federalists, but if

they want to acquire and keep unlimited property, they will have military greatness thrust upon them.[122]

Yet the anti-Federalists can claim greater fidelity to the principles of the Declaration of Independence. "There are certain rights which mankind possesses," Brutus argues in Essay IX, "over which government ought not to have any controul, because it is not necessary [it] should, in order to attain the end of its institution"[123]—namely, the greatest good of individuals, rather than the greatness of the state. So "there are certain things which rulers should absolutely be prohibited from doing, because, if they do them, they would work an injury, not a benefit, to the people."[124] After enough such injuries, a prudent people will exercise its right to change its rulers. "These principles seem to be the evident dictates of common sense"— they might even be self-evident—"and what ought to give sanction to them in the minds of every American," Brutus concludes, "[is that] they are the great principles of the late revolution."[125]

Soon after the Constitution's ratification, the first ten amendments were passed, adding a Bill of Rights that addressed many of the anti-Federalists' concerns. The Second Amendment calls "a well-regulated Militia . . . necessary to the security of a free State";[126] the Third Amendment prohibits quartering troops in private homes in peacetime without the owner's consent.[127] But none of these amendments imposes further limits on the power of the national government to raise and keep standing armies. So by the beginning of 1792, the principles of American defense policy were ambiguous. The Declaration of Independence had sketched several of these principles: no aggressive war, no standing armies during peace without legislative consent, no quartering troops in private homes, and no superior or independent military. These principles were largely codified in the Constitution. But the successful Federalist interpretation of the Constitution gave these principles a meaning that diverged from the spirit of the Declaration: no quartering troops in private homes, certainly, but perhaps small standing armies, perhaps considerable naval establishments, perhaps even offensive wars. It would fall to George Washington to resolve this ambiguity.

Washington's Farewell Address

The main aim of Washington's Farewell Address, which was published in September 1796, is to explain his decision to retire from public life at the end of his second presidential term, rather than stand for election for a third.[128] But Washington goes well beyond this aim by also offering at some length "the disinterested warnings of a parting friend, who can possibly have no personal motive to biass his counsel."[129] Two events during his second term prompted these warnings, events that fueled partisan conflicts between the Federalists and the Democratic-Republicans—the latter the political party that took up many anti-Federalist positions after the Constitution was ratified. The first event was the Neutrality Proclamation of 1793, made into law by the Neutrality Act of 1794. When war broke out between Britain and France during the French Revolution, Washington proclaimed that the United States would remain neutral. He did so despite the Constitution, which grants Congress the power to declare war, and so presumably the power to declare neutrality; despite a 1778 treaty with France, which required American assistance should war break out with Britain, in return for French assistance in the Revolutionary War; and despite popular feeling, which almost two decades after the revolution was still pro-French and anti-British. The second event was the Whiskey Rebellion of 1794, in which citizens of Western Pennsylvania refused to pay a national tax on whiskey production, requiring Washington to call forth the militias of Maryland, New Jersey, Pennsylvania, and Virginia, and to lead them in a display of force to bring the rebellion to a peaceful end. Washington's conduct in both events was unpopular, especially among Democratic-Republicans. This conduct required some explanation from Washington, which his Farewell Address aimed also to provide.[130]

Washington begins the Address by dealing briefly with the question of a third term. He wanted to retire at the end of his first term, he writes, but the "perplexed and critical posture of our affairs with foreign nations" in 1792 made retirement impossible. In 1796, by contrast, "the present circumstances of our country" permit his retirement. By dealing in this way with the question of a third term, Washington gives the "disinterested warnings" that follow a tone reminiscent of Federalist 1. Four years ago, his continuation as president was a matter of necessity, but it is so no longer. Now the readers of the Farewell Address will hear his warnings as recommendations of "reflection and choice," rather than of "accident and force."[131]

Washington's first warning sounds another Federalist note, concerning the preservation of the union. The people of the United States are happy now, he writes, because of their liberty. They will become worthy of imitation by other nations only if they can preserve this liberty and use it prudently.[132] But Washington worries that the happiness of the American people will not last. Now Americans know that national unity is the foundation of their liberty, prosperity, safety, peace, and tranquility.[133] Now they agree with the Federalists that a unified national government can procure these goods better than could the states, individually or in confederation. But external enemies will try to undermine Americans' attachment to their union. So the American people must not contribute to these ef-

forts by "characterizing parties by *geographical discriminations*,"[134] lest they come to believe that different parts of the nation have different interests, especially in foreign affairs. To the contrary, Washington insists, every part of the nation has the same economic interest: to preserve the union.[135] Connections with foreign powers cannot serve the interests of the parts so well as the union can.[136] Without the union, "foreign alliances, attachments, and intrigues" would only intensify the rivalries of individual states or of their confederations.[137] Union spares the states "the necessity of those overgrown military establishments," standing armies, "which under any form of government are inauspicious to liberty, and which are to be regarded as particularly hostile to republican liberty."[138] Washington turns the anti-Federalist opposition to standing armies to his advantage, as an argument for the preservation of the union. He says nothing about the Federalist argument that standing armies should not be prohibited by the Constitution because they may be necessary to the union.

"The basis of our political systems," Washington continues—writing of the state governments as well as the national—"is the right of the people to make and to alter their constitutions of government."[139] He follows this nod to the principles of the Declaration of Independence with a warning. "The very idea of the power and the right of the people to establish government presupposes the duty of every individual to obey the established government."[140] He defines the right to rebel against an illegitimate government, because it does not secure our inalienable rights, through a contrast with the duty to obey legitimate governments that do. Without this duty, the right to rebel would be no right at all. Washington implies that the revolutionary and founding period is ended, and a legitimate government is at last in place. The principles of the Declaration still hold, but now the Constitution is sacred and binding. Attempts now to assert the right to rebel, as in the Whiskey Rebellion, are no longer in Americans' interest, nor just, nor necessary. But that Americans are still making such attempts implies that not every American now knows that national unity is the foundation of his or her liberty, prosperity, safety, peace, and tranquility.

After these warnings against immediate threats, foreign and domestic, Washington takes "a more comprehensive view" of the dangers to the union. Regarding domestic dangers, he warns "against the baneful effects of the spirit of party, generally."[141] Party spirit "opens the door to foreign influence and corruption, which find facilitated access to the government itself through the channels of party passions. Thus the policy and will of one country are subjected to the policy and will of another."[142] Foreign influence threatens the United States not only if the states dissolve the union to go it alone or to form confederacies; it threatens the states even if they remain united. Public servants must hold themselves Americans first, and party members second.

Washington also warns against irreligion and immorality, arguing that religion and morality are necessary supports of political prosperity. "Let it simply be asked where is the security for property, for reputation, for life, if the sense of religious obligation *desert* the oaths, which are the instruments of investigation in Courts of Justice? And let us with caution indulge the supposition, that morality can be maintained without religion. Whatever may be conceded to the influence of refined education on minds of peculiar structure, reason and experience both forbid us to expect that National morality can prevail in exclusion of religious principle."[143] A few rare human beings, he concedes, can find a secular basis for morality. But this is impossible for a whole people. On the national level, without a religious reason to tell the truth and keep one's promises, justice cannot be done. If justice is not done, then inalienable rights to life, liberty, and the pursuit of happiness cannot be secured. And if such rights are not secured, then a prudent people will eventually exercise its right to replace its government. "Tis substantially true," Washington concludes, "that virtue or morality is a necessary spring of popular government."[144] But religion is not necessary to understand this truth. He calls for the promotion "as an object of primary importance, [of] Institutions for the general diffusion of knowledge"—schools, rather than churches. "In proportion as the structure of a government gives force to public opinion"—that is, to the extent that a government is democratic—"it is essential that public opinion should be enlightened."[145] Washington envisions a widespread secular education teaching the necessity of religion and morality as the supports of political prosperity. Prudence teaches that establishing justice is in the American people's interest.

Washington's last warning about domestic dangers concerns public credit. Debt is a promise by a debtor to pay a creditor, and it is no less important that the American nation keep its promises in this respect than that individual Americans do. So public credit—the trustworthiness of the nation when it contracts a debt—must be protected, by using it sparingly and discharging debts whenever possible. Otherwise, credit will not be available when the nation really needs it—for example, to prepare for and repel danger.[146] Washington thus calls on the nation to be moderate in its spending. But this call implies the need for individual moderation in spending, too—since statesmen conduct public business with the habits they acquire in their private business, and since one of the causes of immoderate public spending is the need to protect international trade as a source of immoderate private acquisitions.

In this subtle way Washington does more than Brutus to weaken the Federalist connection between the right to unequal and unlimited acquisition and the need for an extensive naval establishment.

Since war is the main cause of public spending and the main reason for public debt, peace is necessary if the nation is to maintain its credit. So Washington extends his argument about the American interest in justice from the domestic sphere to the international:

> Observe good faith and justice tow[ard]s all Nations. Cultivate peace and harmony with all. Religion and morality enjoin this conduct; and can it be that good policy does not equally enjoin it? It will be worthy of a free, enlightened, and, at no distant period, a great Nation, to give to mankind the magnanimous and too novel example of a People always guided by an exalted justice and benevolence. Who can doubt that in the course of time and things the fruits of such a plan would richly repay any temporary advantages w[hi]ch might be lost by a steady adherence to it?[147]

A defense policy guided by the idea of justice, Washington implies by his rhetorical questions, may involve temporary disadvantages in the short run, but will be the best policy in the long run. Even better, justice will help to make the United States great and to set an example for the rest of mankind. Justice is in the nation's interest, internationally as well as domestically. But in practice this means that "permanent, inveterate antipathies against particular Nations and passionate attachments for others should be excluded; and . . . in place of them just and amicable feelings towards all should be cultivated."[148] Lasting antipathies lead nations away from their duties and their interests—and sometimes even cost them their liberty—while passionate attachments create the illusion of a common interest and encourage unnecessary participation in others' wars. Both kinds of disorder are particularly dangerous to weak nations in their relations with strong ones. "The attachment of a small or weak, towards a great and powerful Nation," as in the case of the United States and France, "dooms the former to be a satellite of the latter."[149] Washington does not say whether strong nations can form lasting antipathies or passionate attachments to weak ones, nor whether these disorders can harm a strong nation that suffers from them.

The "equal and impartial hand"[150] Washington recommends in defense policy extends also to commercial policy. It is "folly in one Nation to look for disinterested favors from another,"[151] because such favors always cost the nation that accepts them a portion of its independence. The flip side of the policy of keeping promises is a policy of not making promises too costly to keep. But Washington does not advocate limiting America's international commercial connections. "The Great rule of conduct for us, in regard to foreign Nations is in extending our commercial relations to have with them as little *political* connection as possible. So far as we have already formed engagements let them be fulfilled, with perfect good faith. Here let us stop."[152] In particular, the United States should take care not to involve itself in European controversies that have nothing to do with American interests. It should instead take advantage of its "detached and distant situation"[153] to become stronger, until it is strong enough to "defy material injury from external annoyance."[154] Then its neutrality will be respected by belligerent nations—because they will be unable to do anything about it—and "we may choose peace or war, as our interest guided by our justice shall Counsel."[155] Washington's recommended defense policy is not just to avoid lasting antipathies and passionate attachments, but also "to steer clear of permanent Alliances, with any portion of the foreign world"[156]—though existing obligations should be fulfilled, as keeping promises is the best policy. "Taking care always to keep ourselves, by suitable establishments, on a respectably defensive posture, we may safely trust to temporary alliances"—not to the militia—"for extraordinary emergencies."[157]

This final warning clearly has implications for the Neutrality Proclamation and Act. Washington concludes his Farewell Address by making them explicit. In the war between Britain and France, "I was well satisfied that our Country, under all the circumstances of the case, had a right to take, and was bound in duty and interest, to take a Neutral position."[158] These circumstances, it is worth remembering, included a treaty of mutual assistance with France.[159] "The duty of holding a Neutral conduct may be inferred," Washington continues, "without any thing more, from the obligation which justice and humanity impose on every Nation, in cases in which it is free to act, to maintain inviolate the relations of Peace and amity towards other Nations."[160] Only in cases of absolute necessity, when a nation is not free to act, can the duty of neutrality be ignored. But, to repeat the lesson of the Declaration of Independence, there are no cases of absolute necessity in defense policy. However just neutrality may be, Washington's final word is that neutrality is also in America's interest: "to gain time to our country to settle and mature its yet recent institutions, and to progress without interruption, to that degree of strength and consistency, which is necessary to give it, humanly speaking, the command of its own fortunes."[161]

Like the Declaration of Independence and the Constitution as interpreted by the Federalists and the anti-Federalists, Washington's Farewell Address sketches several principles of American defense policy. Standing

armies are not necessary to the United States, or at least not as necessary as they are to the states divided, so they need not jeopardize civilian control. Permanent military alliances and preferential commercial relationships are to be avoided, either simply or for so long as the United States are relatively weak; instead, they should deal on an equal footing with all nations, in trade and in war. Offensive wars are not ruled out, but neither are they required. And most importantly, justice and interest generally agree in requiring American neutrality—unless necessity, which is to say, interest, dictates otherwise.

These principles of defense policy are rooted in the domestic policies Washington recommends. He calls for moderation of party passions, which unchecked lead American politicians to put regional or foreign interests above those of the United States as a whole. He calls for moderation in public spending, which unchecked will destroy American credit and make wars difficult to wage. And he calls for public religion, morality, and virtue as necessary supports of the political prosperity of a democracy.

Beneath Washington's warnings and appeals we find the connections between necessity, justice, and interest now familiar to us from the Declaration and the Federalist interpretation of the Constitution. Unlike those documents, the Farewell Address is careful not to found any policy on an assertion of absolute necessity. Every time Washington refers to necessity, he has a conditional necessity in mind. But Washington does stress the justice of the policies he recommends, and the coincidence of justice as he understands it with the United States' interest. By moving the focus from necessity to justice, Washington resolves the ambiguity introduced into the foundations of American defense policy by Publius's ambitious interpretation of the Constitution's sober codification of the Declaration's principles. He veils the immoderate implications of the Federalist interpretation, moderating them without ruling them out. In so doing, America's great first president, later reputed to be incapable of a lie,[162] gives American defense policy its characteristic, salutary rhetoric.

Conclusion

A close reading of the Declaration of Independence, the Constitution as interpreted by Publius and Brutus, and Washington's Farewell Address reveals a characteristic pattern in the connections between the ideas of necessity, justice, and interest in the principles of American defense policy. The Declaration argues from necessity to justice, though interest plays the decisive role in its argument. The Constitution as Publius interprets it begins with interest, but then argues from necessity, with few references to justice. Brutus objects to the Constitution on exactly these grounds—namely, that it does not meet the standard of justice set by the Declaration of Independence. Finally, the Farewell Address begins with justice and argues that it agrees fully with interest with few references to necessity. In each case, these attempts from the American founding to think through the principles of defense policy show that interest is the foundation of this thinking and that principles follow from interest either immediately, or though the mediation of conditional necessities, or through the mediation of claims about justice disguised as absolute necessities. In each case, the interest at the foundation of American defense policy is a vision of the greatest human good aimed at by the American political system: the protection of inalienable rights to life, liberty, and the pursuit of happiness through property.

Does a defense policy with this foundation require the American people to assist other peoples in their struggles to defend their inalienable rights? On its own the Declaration could be read to say yes, though the Farewell Address claims that even in such cases, American neutrality is consistent with justice. Must a defense policy founded on inalienable rights involve expanding commercial relations, defended by an expanding military establishment, one so large it could eventually threaten civilian superiority? The Constitution as Publius and Brutus read it argues yes, though the Farewell Address downplays and moderates this possibility. Does such a defense policy permit offensive American wars? The Declaration and the Farewell Address rule this out, whereas the Constitution as Publius reads it does not.

Among human beings at least, a defense policy in which ideas of necessity and justice do not ultimately depend on ideas of interest may be too much to hope for. It is hard to say that nations, to say nothing of individuals, can face absolute necessities, or that they should always do what justice demands, even if the heavens should fall. The liberal world order established after 1945 did much to loosen the connection between an expansionist commercial policy and an expansionist military policy. It remains to be seen whether the ongoing dismantling of this world order will tighten this connection again, in accordance with Publius's predictions. Anyone who wishes for a different kind of American defense policy, one founded on a different understanding of American interests, must begin by supplying the American political system with a different vision of its highest good.

NOTES

Thanks to the staff and resident fellows of the Stockdale Center for Ethical Leadership and the faculty of the Department of Leadership, Ethics, and Law for comments on an earlier draft of the Declaration of Independence section of this chapter. Thanks also to an anonymous reviewer for comments on an earlier draft of the whole chapter. The remaining errors are all mine.

1. This is my own translation of "Der Krieg ist eine bloße Fortsetzung der Politik mit anderen Mitteln," the title of section 24 of book 1, chapter 1 of *On War*. See Carl von Clausewitz, *On War*, ed. and trans. Michael Howard and Peter Paret (Princeton, NJ: Princeton University Press, 1976), 87. The German text of *Vom Kriege* is from the Bibliotheca Augustana website, at https://www.hs-augsburg.de/~harsch/germanica/Chronologie/19Jh/Clausewitz/cla_kri1.html#1, retrieved January 4, 2020. In my interpretation of Clausewitz's meaning, I follow Eliot A. Cohen in *Supreme Command: Soldiers, Statesmen, and Leadership in Wartime* (New York: Random House, 2002), 7–8.

2. I have modified Howard and Paret's translation of the last sentence, which in German reads, "die politische Absicht ist der Zweck, der Krieg ist das Mittel, und niemals kann das Mittel ohne Zweck gedacht werden." See Clausewitz, *On War*, 87.

3. Aristotle writes:

> If, therefore, there is some end of our actions that we wish for on account of itself, the rest being things we wish for on account of this end, and if we do not choose all things on account of something else—for in this way the process will go on infinitely such that the longing involved is empty and pointless—clearly this would be the good, that is, the best. . . . If this is so, then one must try to grasp, in outline at least, whatever it is and to which of the science or capacities it belongs. But it might be held to belong to the most authoritative and most architectonic one, and such appears to be the political art. (Aristotle, *Aristotle's Nicomachean Ethics*, trans. Robert C. Bartlett and Susan D. Collins [Chicago: University of Chicago Press, 2011], 2)

Aristotle's repeated hedging of his claims—"if . . . if . . . if . . . it might be held . . . such appears to be"—lead the reader to wonder what the status of politics, and therefore of defense policy, would be if there is no highest human good.

4. The Declaration of Independence, in Alexander Hamilton, John Jay, and James Madison, *The Federalist*, Gideon Edition, ed. George W. Carey and James McClellan (Indianapolis, IN: Liberty Fund, 2001), 495.

5. This is not to disagree with Pauline Maier's conclusion that more pains were taken for the Declaration to reach a domestic than an international audience, so that "the Declaration of Independence was designed first and foremost for domestic consumption." See Pauline Maier, *American Scripture: Making the Declaration of Independence* (New York: Alfred A. Knopf, 1997), 131. The addressees and the audience of a document can be different, and it could matter very much to a domestic audience that the Declaration be addressed to the peoples of mankind.

6. Declaration, 495.

7. If human beings must withhold their consent from governments that fail to secure their rights, must they also consent to governments that do secure them? The Declaration is not clear how much of a government's legitimacy comes from securing rights, and how much from popular consent. The argument that it is enough to withdraw one's consent from a government to make it illegitimate exploits this lack of clarity.

8. Consider Hamilton's discussion of self-evidence in Federalist 23, 113.

9. The "pursuit of happiness" seems to be Jefferson's version of what Locke calls "Estates." As Locke puts it in section 123 of the *Second Treatise of Government*, the goal of political society and government for those who consent to them is "the mutual *Preservation* of their Lives, Liberties, and Estates, which I call by the general Name, *Property*" (John Locke, *Two Treatises of Government*, ed. Peter Laslett [Cambridge, UK: Cambridge University Press, 1988], 350). For the likely presence of the phrase "pursuit of happiness" in Jefferson's first draft of the Declaration, see Carl L. Becker, *The Declaration of Independence: A Study in the History of Political Ideas* (New York: Random House, 1922), 142. For Jefferson's and the founding generation's familiarity with Locke's political theory and Newton's scientific theory more generally, see Becker, *Declaration of Independence*, 24–79.

10. For different examples of this reasoning, consider the first paragraph of part 1 of René Descartes, *Discourse on the Method*, ed. and trans. George Heffernan (Notre Dame, IN: University of Notre Dame Press, 1994), 15; chapters 13 and 14 of Thomas Hobbes, *Leviathan*, ed. Edwin Curley (Indianapolis, IN: Hackett Publishing Company, 1994), 74–88; chapter 2 of Locke's *Second Treatise*, 269–78; part 1, book 1, chapters 2 and 3 of Charles de Secondat, Baron de Montesquieu, *The Spirit of the Laws*, ed. and trans. Anne M. Cohler, Basia Carolyn Miller, and Harold Samuel Stone (Cambridge, UK: Cambridge University Press, 1989), 6–9; and Book 1, chapters 1–6 of Jean-Jacques Rousseau, *On the Social Contract*, in *The Collected Writings of Rousseau*, vol. 4, ed. Roger D. Masters and Christopher Kelly, trans. Judith R. Bush, Roger D. Masters, and Christopher Kelly (Hanover, NH: University Press of New England, 1994), 131–39.

11. Declaration, 495–96.

12. Declaration, 496.

13. Declaration, 497.

14. Declaration, 496.

15. If the British king really has declared the American colonies "out of his Protection" and waged war against them, for example, then according to the political theory of Locke, the colonies already are independent from Britain. See Declaration, 497, and sections 207, 210 and 242 of Locke, *Second Treatise*, 403–5, 427.

16. Declaration, 496.

17. Declaration, 497.

18. Declaration, 496–97.

19. Declaration, 498.

20. Declaration, 498.

21. For a discussion of how Newtonian physics, in addition to Lockean political theory, provides the context for the Declaration, see Becker, *Declaration of Independence*, 40–53.

22. Declaration, 495–96.

23. Declaration, 498.

24. Declaration, 498.

25. The Constitution of the United States, in Alexander Hamilton, John Jay, and James Madison, *The Federalist*, Gideon Edition, ed. George W. Carey and James McClellan (Indianapolis, IN: Liberty Fund, 2001), 526.

26. Constitution, 537–38.

27. Constitution, 530.

28. Constitution, 530.

29. Congress's power to appropriate funds for the army in particular is prominently limited: "no Appropriation of Money to that Use shall be for a longer Term than two Years" (Constitution, 531). No similar limit is placed by the Constitution on congressional appropriations for a navy. The two-year limit on use of appropriations for the army has been very narrowly interpreted.

30. Constitution, 531.

31. Constitution, 531.

32. Constitution, 534.

33. Constitution, 531.

34. This, at least, is the idea. For an argument that "the United States Constitution . . . does *not* provide for civilian control" over the military, see Samuel P. Huntington, *The Soldier and the State: The Theory and Politics of Civil-Military Relations* (Cambridge, MA: Harvard University Press, 1957), 163–92; emphasis added.

35. Constitution, 532.

36. Constitution, 526.

37. Constitution, 526.

38. The Federalists of concern here, numbers 1 through 43, appeared between late October 1787 and late January 1788 in periodicals in New York. The Brutus essays of concern, numbers VII through X, appeared in the same form, in the same state, at the same time: between early and late January 1788. Several of the latter's essays respond to arguments made in the former's. The identity of Brutus is uncertain. See Herbert J. Storing, with Murray Dry, *What the Anti-Federalists Were For* (Chicago: University of Chicago Press, 1981), 103.

39. See George W. Carey and James McClellan, "Reader's Guide to *The Federalist*," in *The Federalist*, lvii–lxxxiv.

40. Federalist 1, 1.

41. Federalist 1, 1.

42. If they adopt the Constitution, they will give the needed example to mankind. But wouldn't rejecting the Constitution also give mankind the example of a people "establishing good government from reflection and choice"? Hamilton would say no—not because in that case the government is not chosen, but because the chosen government is not good. But this makes it clear that the difference between "accident and force" and "reflection and choice" is not Hamilton's main concern. His main concern is with replacing the bad government under the Articles of Confederation with a good government under the Constitution.

43. Federalist 1, 1.

44. Federalist 2, 9.

45. Federalist 3, 9–12.

46. Federalist 3, 12.

47. Federalist 4, 13.

48. Federalist 4, 14.

49. Federalist 4, 14.

50. Federalist 4, 15.

51. Federalist 4, 15.

52. Federalist 5, 18–19.

53. Federalist 6, 21.

54. Federalist 6, 21.

55. Federalist 6, 23.

56. Federalist 6, 21.

57. Federalist 6, 26.

58. Federalist 8, 32.

59. Federalist 8, 32.

60. Federalist 8, 35.

61. Federalist 8, 36.

62. Madison does something similar in Federalist 41, 208–9, where he bases Hamilton's principle that the national government should have unlimited means to provide for the common defense on the Declaration's self-evident truth that human beings have a right to life.

63. Federalist 10, 43.

64. Federalist 10, 46.

65. For the connection between inequalities of possessions, the invention of money, and the unlimited increase of these inequalities, consider sections 46–51 of Locke's *Second Treatise*, 299–302.

66. Federalist 11, 49.

67. Federalist 11, 51.

68. Federalist 11, 51.

69. Federalist 11, 51.

70. Federalist 11, 53; compare Federalist 34, 164.

71. Federalist 11, 54–55.

72. Compare Federalist 11, 51.

73. In contrast to Hamilton's, Madison's vision of how American power will expand involved the addition of new states; see Federalist 14, 65. It is worth considering whether this kind of expansion must also make extensive military establishments more necessary, and bring the American states into the neighborhood of the European great powers.

74. Recall Federalist 8, 36.

75. In Federalist 15, 73, while arguing that the national government must operate directly on the American people, rather than indirectly on them through their state governments, Hamilton asserts: "Power controled or abridged is almost always the rival and enemy of that power by which it is controled or abridged." To the extent that American naval power controls or abridges European naval power, then, the European states will very likely become the rivals and enemies of the American states.

76. Hamilton says nothing about whether extensive naval establishments can threaten civilian control. But Madison thinks they cannot. "The batteries most capable of repelling foreign enterprises on our safety," he writes in Federalist 41, 212, "are happily such as never can be turned by a perfidious government against our liberties." He does not explain why he thinks this, however.

77. Federalist 22, 105.

78. Federalist 22, 105–6.

79. Federalist 23, 113.

80. Do the truths the Declaration of Independence holds as self-evident meet Hamilton's standard?

81. Federalist 23, 113.

82. Federalist 23, 113.

83. See, for example, Hamilton's argument for the national government's power to tax in Federalist 31, 151, and Federalist 34, 163. Madison uses Hamilton's argument to claim for the national government an unlimited power to deal with emergencies in Federalist 36, 178.

84. Federalist 24, 118.

85. Federalist 24, 120; compare Federalist 25, 126.

86. Federalist 24, 120.

87. Federalist 24, 120.

88. Federalist 24, 121.

89. Federalist 24, 120.

90. Federalist 24, 121.

91. Federalist 25, 125.

92. Federalist 25, 125.

93. Constitution, 531.

94. Federalist 25, 126; compare Federalist 24, 120.

95. Hamilton refuses to rule out offensive American wars: "tying up the hands of government from offensive war, founded upon reasons of state" would be a "novel and absurd experiment in politics" (Federalist 34, 164). And he insists that the United States will provoke jealousy and attempts at subversion from foreign powers (Federalist 59, 309). Perhaps such attempts are reasons for offensive war.

96. Hamilton expects the American states to have a small army "for a long time to come," though for reasons of limited resources, not for reasons of principle (Federalist 28, 139). Madison finds it impossible for the national military and marine forces to become larger than the combined state militias, numbering 3 million, and later calculates the maximum size of a standing army to be one 25th of the number of citizens able to bear arms, or less than "twenty-five or thirty thousand men" for "a militia amounting to near half a million of citizens" (Federalist 45, 240, Federalist 46, 247). He also expects periods of war to "bear a small proportion" to periods of peace for the United States (Federalist 45, 241).

97. Publius understands this power to be vested chiefly in the legislative branch. He has very little to say about the role played by the president as Commander in Chief in providing for the common defense.

98. Recall that the Constitution is to be ratified by conventions of the people of each state, rather than by each state government as a sovereign power. See Constitution, 539.

99. Federalist 43, 229.

100. Constitution, 541.

101. Consider Federalist 34, 164.

102. In *The Articles of Confederation* (1959) Merrill Jensen calls the Articles of Confederation "the constitutional expression of [an evolving democratic movement], and the embodiment in governmental form of the Declaration of Independence" (quoted in Carey and McClellan, Editors' Introduction, *The Federalist*, xxvi, n. 14).

103. Federalist 35, 169.

104. Herbert J. Storing, ed., *The Anti-Federalist: Writings by the Opponents of the Constitution* (Chicago: University of Chicago Press, 1985), 148.

105. Recall Federalist 3, 9–12.

106. Patrick Henry also judges it unlikely that the European powers pose a threat, and is willing to rely on "the American spirit" to meet this threat should it arise. See Storing, *The Anti-Federalist*, 301.

107. Storing, *The Anti-Federalist*, 148–49.

108. Storing reports the anti-Federalist position that wars might be necessary, but they should be strictly defensive. He compares Hamilton's scorn for "the novel and absurd experiment" of ruling out "offensive war founded upon reasons of state" (*What the Anti-Federalists Were For*, 31; recall Federalist 34, 164).

109. Storing, *The Anti-Federalist*, 152. Compare the similar opinion of standing armies held by the Impartial Examiner, writing on February 27, 1788 (Storing, *The Anti-Federalist*, 284).

110. Storing, *The Anti-Federalist*, 155.
111. The full text of Brutus's proposed amendment reads:

As standing armies in time of peace are dangerous to liberty, and have often been the means of overturning the best constitutions of government, no standing army, or troops of any description whatsoever, shall be raised or kept up by the legislature, except so many as shall be necessary for guards to the arsenals of the United States, or for garrisons of such posts on the frontiers, as it shall be deemed absolutely necessary to hold, to secure the inhabitants, and facilitate the trade with the Indians: unless the United States are threatened with an attack or invasion from some foreign power, in which case the legislature shall be authorised to raise an army to be prepared to repel the attack; provided that no troops whatsoever shall be raised in times of peace, without the assent of two thirds of the members, composing both houses of the legislature. (Storing, *The Anti-Federalist*, 161)

112. The Impartial Examiner also expects to rely on a numerous militia to repel sudden attacks (February 27, 1788, in Storing, *The Anti-Federalist*, 285).
113. Storing points out that some anti-Federalists, like the Federal Republican, saw standing armies as a threat to civic virtue as well as to civilian superiority (*What the Anti-Federalists Were For*, 20).
114. Storing, *The Anti-Federalist*, 146.
115. Storing, *The Anti-Federalist*, 146.
116. Storing, *The Anti-Federalist*, 146.
117. See Storing, *What the Anti-Federalists Were For*, 20.
118. As Storing explains, in the eyes of the Anti-Federalists, "The stress placed by Federalists on national defense and a vigorous commercial policy often seemed to mask a radical shift in direction from the protection of individual liberty to the pursuit of national riches and glory" (*What the Anti-Federalists Were For*, 30–31).
119. The quotation is from Cato V, in Storing, *What the Anti-Federalists Were For*, 34. According to Storing, the anti-Federalists judged that "the Federalist solution not only failed to provide for the moral qualities that are necessary to the maintenance of republican government; it tended to undermine them. Will not the constitutional regime, the Anti-Federalists asked, with its emphasis on private, self-seeking, commercial activities, release and foster a certain type of human being who will be likely to destroy that very regime?" (Storing, *What the Anti-Federalists Were For*, 73).
120. See Storing, *What the Anti-Federalists Were For*, 24–25.
121. In Storing's view, the anti-Federalists made "no attempt to articulate an alternative, [and offered] no account of the virtue of the agrarian way of life. There was some hankering after a simple, subsistence agricultural life, but the Anti-Federalists were irrevocably committed to a commercial order, as indeed American agriculture had always been. The Federalists drew out the implications of the commitment." Thus, "the basic problem of the Anti-Federalists was that they accepted the need and desirability of the modern commercial world, while attempting to resist certain of its tendencies with rather half-hearted appeals to civic virtue" (*What the Anti-Federalists Were For*, 46).

122. An author who does develop at length an alternative to the commercial republic, though not for the United States in particular, is Jean-Jacques Rousseau. Interested readers should begin with his *Discourse on the Sciences and the Arts*, or *First Discourse*, in *The Collected Writings of Rousseau*, vol. 2, ed. Roger D. Masters and Christopher Kelly, trans. Judith R. Bush, Roger D. Masters, and Christopher Kelly (Hanover, NH: University Press of New England, 1992), 1–22. For an introduction to this text, see Jeff J. S. Black, "The *Discourse on the Sciences and the Arts*," in *The Rousseauian Mind*, ed. Eve Grace and Christopher Kelly (New York: Routledge, 2019), 155–64. For a more thorough treatment of its argument, see Jeff J. S. Black, *Rousseau's Critique of Science: A Commentary on the Discourse on the Sciences and the Arts* (Lanham, MD: Rowman & Littlefield, 2009).
123. Storing, *The Anti-Federalist*, 153.
124. Storing, *The Anti-Federalist*, 153.
125. Storing, *The Anti-Federalist*, 153.
126. Constitution, 540.
127. Constitution, 541.
128. The Twenty-Second Amendment, limiting presidents to two terms, was not ratified until 1951; see Constitution, 548.
129. George Washington, The Farewell Address, in *George Washington: Writings* (New York: Library of America, 1997), 964.
130. For a concise account of the events of Washington's second term and the partisan strife they fueled, see Sidney M. Milkis and Michael Nelson, *The American Presidency: Origins and Development, 1776–2018*, 8th ed. (Los Angeles, CA: SAGE Publications, 2019), especially 96–108.
131. Recall Federalist 1, 1.
132. Washington, Farewell Address, 964.
133. Washington, Farewell Address, 964.
134. Washington, Farewell Address, 967; emphasis added.
135. Washington, Farewell Address, 965.
136. Washington, Farewell Address, 966.
137. Washington, Farewell Address, 966.
138. Washington, Farewell Address, 966.
139. Washington, Farewell Address, 968.
140. Washington, Farewell Address, 968.
141. Washington, Farewell Address, 969.
142. Washington, Farewell Address, 970.
143. Washington, Farewell Address, 971; emphasis added.
144. Washington, Farewell Address, 971.
145. Washington, Farewell Address, 972.
146. Washington, Farewell Address, 972.
147. Washington, Farewell Address, 972.
148. Washington, Farewell Address, 973.
149. Washington, Farewell Address, 974.
150. Washington, Farewell Address, 975.
151. Washington, Farewell Address, 976.
152. Washington, Farewell Address, 974.
153. Washington, Farewell Address, 974.
154. Washington, Farewell Address, 975.
155. Washington, Farewell Address, 975.
156. Washington, Farewell Address, 975.
157. Washington, Farewell Address, 975.
158. Washington, Farewell Address, 976.
159. The provisions of the treaty need interpretation. Article I requires France and the United States to provide one another mutual aid should war break out between France and

Great Britain, but is limited to "the continuance of the present war between the United States and England"—that is, the Revolutionary War. Article IV calls for concurrence between the United States and France, but allows this concurrence to depend on the "circumstances" and "particular situation" of each nation. Article XI sets down a mutual guarantee between the United States and France to protect one another's territories as they stand at the end of the Revolutionary War. And Article XII specifies that this guarantee will "have its full force and effect" the moment a future war breaks out between Britain and France. See *A Century of Lawmaking for a New Nation: U.S. Congressional Documents and Debates, 1774–1875*, 6–11,

https://memory.loc.gov/cgi-bin/ampage?collId=llsl&fileName=008/llsl008.db&recNum=19, retrieved January 4, 2020.

160. Washington, Farewell Address, 977.

161. Washington, Farewell Address, 977.

162. According to the Mount Vernon website, the story about George Washington and the cherry tree was invented by Washington's biographer, Mason Locke Weems, for the fifth edition of *The Life of Washington*, published in 1806. See "George Washington and the Cherry Tree Myth," MountVernon.org, https://www.mountvernon.org/library/digitalhistory/digital-encyclopedia/article/cherry-tree-myth/, retrieved January 4, 2020.

Just War Theory
Revisionists Versus Traditionalists

SETH LAZAR

Traditionalists and Revisionists

Since the publication of Michael Walzer's *Just and Unjust Wars*, in 1977, a "traditionalist" stance has dominated thinking about the morality of war in universities, military academies, and international legal circles. Its central commitment is to provide moral foundations for international law as it applies to armed conflict: States (and only states) may go to war only for national defense, defense of other states, or to intervene to avert "crimes that shock the moral conscience of mankind" (Walzer 2006b [1977], p. 107). Civilians may not be targeted in war, but all combatants, whatever they are fighting for, are morally permitted to target one another, even when doing so foreseeably harms some civilians (as long as it does not do so excessively).

Over the last two decades, this traditionalist theory of just war has been subjected to exacting scrutiny, as for the first time sustained analytical attention has been brought to bear on the ethics of war. Analytical philosophers have overturned almost all the conclusions of traditionalist theory; its continued popularity outside philosophy departments is now matched by its contentiousness within them. Many of these skeptics are "revisionists." They have (a) challenged the permissibility of national defense, and the moral standing of states more generally; (b) argued for expanded per-

missions for military intervention; (c) questioned civilian immunity; and (d) argued that combatants fighting for wrongful aims cannot do anything right, besides lay down their weapons.

This article is about the revisionist critique of traditionalist just war theory, and the traditionalist response. I begin with some methodological notes before turning to the ethical evaluation of first wars as a whole, then individual actions within war.

The Methodology of Just War Theory

In this section I identify some methodological disputes that underpin the substantive debate between revisionists and traditionalists. For each dispute I note that, although revisionists typically fall on one side and traditionalists on the other, this need not be the case. And for each I indicate which side presently has the better of the argument.

The first split is between philosophers who make institutions their focus and those who concentrate on acts. Institutionalists tend either to look to the long-term effects of the laws of war (Mavrodes 1975, Dill & Shue 2012, Shue 2013, Waldron 2016), or to see them as the basis of an actual or hypothetical contract between either states or their citizens (Benbaji 2008, 2011, 2014, Statman 2014). Non-institutionalists think that

Seth Lazar, "Just War Theory: Revisionists Versus Traditionalists," *Annual Review of Political Science* 20, no. 1 (2017): 37–54. Republished with permission of *Annual Review of Political Science*; permission conveyed through Copyright Clearance Center, Inc.

The author is not aware of any affiliations, memberships, funding, or financial holdings that might be perceived as affecting the objectivity of this review.

acts can be right or wrong independent of how they relate to existing or hypothetical institutions. They typically focus on the individual rights that the act threatens, and on its consequences (as contrasted with the long-run consequences of an institutional rule).

As I illustrate below, it is hard to see how some acts permitted by the laws of war could be non-institutionally justified. This is most obviously true for harms inflicted in the pursuit of an unjust cause. So it is unsurprising that most traditionalists are institutionalists, and most revisionists are not. But one can advance non-institutionalist arguments for traditionalist conclusions (e.g., Lazar 2015), and one could defend revisionism on institutionalist grounds—for example, Ryan (2016) advocates pacifism in virtue of moral criticism of the military-industrial complex.

Most revisionists, however, are *moral* revisionists only. They reject traditionalists' attempts to morally vindicate the laws of armed conflict, but they agree with traditionalists that we could not secure widespread agreement on any more restrictive changes to the laws of war, and any attempts to change them would undermine the laws' authority, with disastrous results.[1] One might infer that, if traditionalists and revisionists agree on what the laws of war should be, the dispute between them is merely ersatz. But this would be a mistake. Imagine you lived in a society in which physical assault was so widespread that the only way to limit the number of fatalities was to legally permit any assault that did not rise to the level of murder. Imagine that enough people benefit thereby that it is impossible to change the law to prohibit assault. Indeed, any attempts to do so would undermine the authority of the law, leading to an increase in murder rates. In such a society, we might well agree that the existing law should be retained, because it is the best we can do and at least reduces the amount of wrongful death. But would that settle the question of whether *you* should commit an assault? Clearly it would not.

So, even if traditionalists and revisionists reluctantly agree about preserving the existing laws of war, important questions remain to be settled. Do those laws reflect our moral reasons? Or do they merely set minimum standards that we should, in our own conduct, seek to exceed?

The next divide is more in-house. Most contemporary moral and political philosophers use something like Rawls's method of seeking reflective equilibrium. On this approach, we develop moral arguments by making our considered judgments about the permissibility of actions in particular cases, and trying to identify the underlying principles that unify them. We then take those principles and test their application to other cases. If the principles generate conclusions that conflict with our considered judgments about those cases, then we must revise either the principles or our

judgments. As our project evolves, and we revise our principles in light of our judgments and our judgments in light of our principles, we approach reflective equilibrium.

What kinds of cases should test our principles in the ethics of war? We can think of realistic scenarios, paying attention to international affairs and military history. Or, more clinically, we can construct hypothetical cases to isolate variables and test their independent impact on our judgments. Revisionists often use very abstract cases (e.g., McMahan 1994, Rodin 2002). Traditionalists take them to task for this, lamenting their tone-deaf ignorance of the realities of war (Walzer 2006b [1977], Dill & Shue 2012). Some philosophers buck these trends—there are revisionists who draw deeply on military history (e.g., Fabre 2012) and traditionalists who use far-fetched hypotheticals (Lazar 2013).

Abstraction has some advantages. It avoids awkward disputes over historical details and background political assumptions. Discussing the principle of proportionality by thinking about, say, the NATO campaign in Kosovo might well invite serious debate over how many civilians were actually killed in the campaign. Any examples involving Israel or Gaza are likely to inflame political passions.

But abstraction also has costs. Our intuitions about far-fetched cases might be unreliable. It is perhaps morally dubious to invoke sanitized hypothetical examples when we could instead draw on the harrowing experience of real victims of war. And in abstracting away from the distinctive nature of war, we often lose morally relevant information. Philosophers' cases usually presuppose omniscience, for example, rather than condescending to the radical uncertainty that bedevils all decisions about and within war. They make no concessions for fear or trauma, and underemphasize crucial aspects of the phenomenology of war, such as combatants' attachments to their comrades-in-arms.

We should avoid dogmatism; many different approaches can illuminate the morality of war. But I think that highly artificial hypotheticals should be used carefully, ensuring that any conclusions they support are tenable when applied to the messy reality of war; and that one's intuitive judgments are the starting point for investigation, rather than its end.

One reason for the preponderance of highly abstract hypotheticals in recent just war theory is that many revisionists are reductivists. They think that all justified killing, in war or outside of it, is justified at root by precisely the same properties. In their most extreme moments, they argue that wars are justified if and only if they are composed exclusively of justified acts of individual self- and other-defense (Rodin 2002, McMahan 2004). Nonreductivists think, in a nutshell, that there is something different about killing in war.

Wars have some distinctive properties that are relevant to the morality of killing. Typical examples include the sheer scale of the fighting, the widespread indifference to moral constraints that war often involves, the political and territorial goods at stake, the "fog of war," the existence of institutions such as international law, and the fact that the conflict is fought by organized groups.

As before, we can advance nonreductivist arguments for revisionist conclusions (Bazargan 2013) and reductivist arguments for traditionalism (Steinhoff 2008, Lazar 2015). But the predominant dialectic has been the other way. I cannot settle the debate between reductivists and nonreductivists here. Reductivist considerations are crucial—people have fundamental rights to life and liberty that they don't simply lose once they enter a state of war. But it is oddly dogmatic to confine our normative palette to these reasons alone. The laws of war matter morally. The institutions at stake matter morally. The collective character of military action matters. An exclusively reductivist account of the morality of war would be incomplete.

Just war theorists further divide in their attitudes toward the apparently collective nature of warfare. Some are all-out individualists: They think that only individuals act in war, not collectives (they are descriptive individualists), and they think that only individuals matter in war (they are evaluative individualists).[2] By contrast, Walzer's *Just and Unjust Wars* was evaluatively collectivist—pointing to something quasi-transcendental about the survival of political communities to justify intentionally attacking civilians in "supreme emergencies," for example (Walzer 2006b [1977], p. 247). Its implicit descriptive collectivism was made explicit in Walzer's later work (2006a). His first critics argued that applying a thoroughgoing descriptive and evaluative individualism to war entailed revisionist conclusions (Luban 1980b, McMahan 1994, Rodin 2002). Many philosophers then sought to defend traditionalism by rejecting either descriptive (Kutz 2005, Walzer 2006b [1977], Lazar 2012b) or evaluative individualism (Zohar 1993). Again, of course some individualists defend traditionalism (Emerton & Handfield 2009), and some collectivists are revisionists (Bazargan 2013).

Of all the divides that separate most traditionalists from most revisionists, this one is potentially the most consequential, while being the hardest to settle. War can provide useful test cases for thinking about collective action and the value of collectives; but we really need to develop our theory of collective action and value first, then apply it to war. My view on this question, then, is even more provisional than my verdict on the other disputes. I think that collectives can be valuable independently of how they contribute to their members' well-being, for the prosaic reason that not only individual well-being has value. Groups can in-

stantiate other goods—justice or solidarity, for example (Temkin 1993). I am not, ultimately, sure whether descriptive collectivism is true. It may be possible to reduce any putatively collective act to the acts of the collective's members. But doing so is often alarmingly circuitous, and does not, I think, alter the moral stakes. Some normative constraints apply primarily to what we do together, and they continue to apply regardless of how we decompose our group acts into individual acts. For example, when fighting a war, we must ensure that the overall harm that we inflict, together, is kept to the minimum feasible (Lazar 2012b).

The archetypal traditionalist, then, is a nonreductivist collectivist who uses realistic cases. The archetypal revisionist is an individualist reductivist who uses cases involving meteors and mind control. Simplifying a little, we might unify the former positions under the heading of political philosophy approaches to just war theory and group the latter together as moral philosophy approaches. There are, of course, political arguments for revisionism and moral arguments for traditionalism. But we can attribute much of the recent success of revisionist just war theory to the preponderance of moral philosophers in the field.

Jus ad Bellum

Just war theorists have traditionally divided their enquiry into thinking about the resort to war, *jus ad bellum*, and conduct in war, *jus in bello*. My approach is an extension of this. *Jus ad bellum* concerns the morality of the war as a whole. This obviously governs permissible resort, but it also determines whether the war can permissibly be continued. *Jus in bello* concerns the morality of particular actions within war. I address *jus ad bellum* first, then *jus in bello*.

The great suffering and destruction wrought by war can be justified only if fighting serves some great end. Just war theorists typically argue that going to war is impermissible unless it is aimed at a "just cause." And the cataclysm of war is so severe that the list of candidate just causes is short. Traditionalist just war theory recognizes only two: national defense (of one's own state or an ally's) and humanitarian intervention to avert the very gravest mass atrocities. Importantly, the right of national defense is assumed to apply to most actual states with all their flaws, not solely to (for example) ideal liberal democracies. Only states actively engaged in the kind of mass atrocities that can warrant humanitarian intervention lack rights of national defense.

Forty years ago, Walzer's *Just and Unjust Wars* offered three arguments to justify the state's right to national defense (2006b [1977], p. 58). First, states protect their citizens' basic human rights to life and liberty. Second, they protect a common cultural life made by their citizens over time. Third, they are the objects of a kind of organic social contract through which people have given up particular freedoms for the sake of a better outcome for all. Walzer construed this, too, as the object of a basic human right.[3]

These arguments for sovereignty are double-edged. They help justify wars of national defense but also raise the bar for justifying humanitarian intervention. Intervening militarily in the affairs of another state obviously threatens its political sovereignty and territorial integrity. Hence, Walzer wanted to tightly constrain military interventions in other states. They could be permitted, he argued, only to avert the very gravest of crimes.

Revisionists lacerated Walzer's arguments for traditionalist positions on national defense and humanitarian intervention. They highlighted and challenged his implicit evaluative collectivism (Doppelt 1978, Beitz 1980, Luban 1980a), noting that, far from protecting individual rights, states are often the preeminent threat to those rights. They also argued that the prosperity of the "common life" often means oppression for cultural minorities (Caney 2005). Even setting this point aside, is the common life of a state really threatened by war? And is it really worth killing for? They were equally skeptical about the organic social contract idea. Is it much more than a metaphor (Wasserstrom 1978, Luban 1980b)? Rodin (2002), in particular, developed a comprehensive argument that the traditionalist stance on when states may go to war in national defense could not be grounded in the defense of individual rights.

By undermining states' rights to national defense, revisionists also made humanitarian intervention easier to justify. Sometimes these arguments were directly linked: If states cannot protect their citizens' security, they lack the right to sovereignty which military intervention might otherwise undermine (Shue 1997). Caney (2005) concluded that military intervention is permissible just in case it improves the net satisfaction of basic human rights. Others defended, at least in principle, "redistributive" wars, fought against the global rich to redress the suffering of the global poor (Luban 1980b, Fabre 2012, Lippert-Rasmussen 2013, Øverland 2013).

Revisionists exposed the holes in Walzer's traditionalist arguments, but many philosophers have been reluctant to endorse the radical implications of their critique. In particular, if states' rights to national defense are grounded in individual rights, then national defense is impermissible against "lesser aggressors"—those who wage war for purely political and territorial reasons, who will threaten life and liberty only if their target state uses lethal force against them (think, for example, of the United States and its allies invading Iraq, or of the Falklands/Malvinas war). Moreover, if military intervention is permissible whenever it will secure a net gain in human rights satisfaction, then states lack rights of national defense against, for example, wars to spread democracy and other good liberal institutions. Indeed, on the individualist view, it is hard to see how any state short of an ideal Rawlsian liberal democracy would have rights of national defense (Kutz 2014). We have, then, two options: either endorse these radical implications or seek out alternative foundations for familiar rights of national defense (Emerton & Handfield 2014).

Some revisionists have argued that the defense of individual rights *is* sufficient to justify ordinary rights of national defense. They emphasize the importance of deterrence and the impossibility of knowing, in cases of lesser aggression, whether the aggression will remain bloodless (Fabre 2014). Others think that we must take people's political interests into account when justifying war. People have an interest in having at least a home-grown, if not a democratically elected, government. Perhaps these interests are not important enough for their defense to justify killing in isolated cases. But when enough people are threatened, perhaps the total interests at stake can justify the death and destruction of war (Hurka 2007, Frowe 2014).

These arguments in favor of national defense also limit the scope of humanitarian intervention. We can justify further limits if we recall the very limited conditions in which military intervention can succeed—for example, stopping an ongoing atrocity is considerably easier than improving a state's political institutions. Perhaps redistributive war could, in principle, be justified. But because any attempt to rescue the global poor by using force against the rich would obviously make life worse for the very people it aims to help, it is a moral nonstarter. That said, as the result of climate change, resource wars might become more practically salient in our more radically straitened future.

Walzer's defense of traditionalist positions came up short, but revisionists' early radicalism has since been much reined in. The most pressing challenge that remains, in my view, is to give a richer account of people's political *and territorial* interests, to explain just why we have an interest in being subject to home-grown government, even if it is not democratic; and why it matters to the average Turkish citizen, for example, that Russian aircraft remain outside their airspace. In each case, we must explain why these interests are worth killing for.

International law is written by and for states. Unsurprisingly, it has a statist bias. Only states have rights of national defense. It is much harder for non-state actors to acquire, for example, the rights to kill and to prisoner-of-war status than it is for the uniformed members of a state's armed forces. Together, these positions reflect a long-standing commitment in the just war tradition to the principle of "legitimate authority," according to which only sovereigns have the right to go to war.

Revisionists have argued that if war is justified by the protection of individual rights, then why should only sovereigns/governments be allowed to kill defensively? We are not obliged to await institutional support when using necessary lethal force in ordinary cases of self- and other-defense. So we should either disregard the requirement of legitimate authority or see it as one that non-state actors can, in fact, fulfill (Fabre 2008, Finlay 2010, Schwenkenbecher 2013).

Revisionists are, I think, right about defense of life and liberty. We are self-authorizing when those rights are at stake. But not all justified wars involve defending life and liberty alone. As we saw above, we cannot sustain ordinary rights of national defense without appealing to people's political interests in having a democratic, or at least home-grown, government. But these very interests are set back when states go to war without authorization from their polity. So a modicum of statism is appropriate: States are better able to secure the authorization of their people before going to war (either by explicit vote or by a standing constitutional license). Having this authorization makes it easier to justify the state's going to war. Non-state actors, and nondemocratic states, fare worse on this score than do democratic states.

With legitimate authority as with just cause, revisionists have shown the flaws of existing arguments for traditionalist conclusions. But, again, the appropriate response is not to jettison those conclusions but to seek better arguments. Perhaps legitimate authority as it was conceived in historical just war theory is unimportant; undoubtedly the statism of international law is overdone. But when a subset of a group fights on behalf of the group as a whole, then it clearly matters that they be authorized to do so. States, especially democratic states, are better able to secure that authorization than non-state actors.

The other key conditions of historical just war theory are right intention, reasonable prospects of success, imminent threat, proportionality, and necessity. Right intention now receives almost no attention—for good reason: It belongs to an age when princes rather than governments went to war, and just war theory's primary concern was to guide the princes' confessors. Revisionist just war theory has advanced our understanding of the other four conditions in two ways. First, it has undermined the canonical view that each of them is a necessary condition for *ad bellum* justice. In fact, only proportionality and necessity are truly necessary. Wars can be *ad bellum* just even if they lack reasonable prospects of success and even if the threat that they seek to avert is not imminent. Second, and relatedly, imminence and reasonable prospects of suc-

cess are not really distinct conditions for justification (Hurka 2005, 2007, McMahan 2016); they are staging-posts on the way to judgments of proportionality and necessity.

The necessity constraint prohibits the unnecessary infliction of harm (here I draw on Lazar 2012b). Harm is almost always bad (the exception may be where it is deserved), so it can be permissible only if it enables us to realize some countervailing good or avert some evil. If we could achieve the same good or avert the same evil by inflicting less harm, then the surplus harm is unnecessary, and so unjustified. Obviously, in actual wars, we cannot know how much harm we will inflict or, indeed, how much good fighting will do. We must therefore factor this uncertainty into our calculations of necessity. The simplest way to do this is to discount possible outcomes by their probability of occurring, so that we can weigh the *expected* harm inflicted against the *expected* good done. If we have two alternatives, A and B, and A will realize the same expected good as B but inflict less expected harm, then B involves unnecessary expected harm and so is impermissible. If the expected harm from A is less than that from B, but so is the expected good, then we need to decide whether the reduction in expected harm is morally important enough to require us to bear that much additional risk to the pursuit of our objective. If it is, then B involves inflicting unnecessary expected harm.

Proportionality and necessity are superficially distinct. A war might be necessary, because there is no other means to achieve its end, and yet disproportionate, because the end is not valuable enough to justify the means. To work out proportionality, we need to ask whether the evil averted is great enough to justify the evil inflicted. This means comparing going to war with what would happen if we allowed the threat to eventuate. That comparison is substantively identical to the comparisons between different means for achieving our ends involved in applying the necessity constraint. Applying the necessity constraint means comparing *all* of the options that have some prospect of averting the threat, to ensure that the chosen one does not involve inflicting unnecessary harm. Applying the proportionality constraint means comparing our best military option with what would happen if we did not avert the threat. Both could be subsumed into a broader criterion, which simply compares all our options in this way.

If a war lacks adequate prospects of success, then it is unlikely to be proportionate. Going to war involves inflicting great evils. If it is unlikely to achieve any good, then it is most likely ruled out. But this is a defeasible presumption: The costs of defeat might be great enough that even a very small chance of success is enough to make fighting proportionate.

If the threat is not imminent, then there are probably less harmful means to safety than the resort to war. Again, this presumption is defeasible. Sometimes delay will make defeat much more likely. Hence, Walzer (2006b [1977], p. 80) argued for the permissibility of preemptive attacks, such as Israel's in the Six-Day War. It is much harder to justify a "preventive" war, fought to avert a threat that is in the future, than to justify fighting a more proximate threat. The more distant the threat, the more likely it is that it can be neutralized by some means other than fighting. In practice, retaining the imminence requirement is a sensible way to minimize abuses by states looking for excuses to go to war (Buchanan & Keohane 2004). But this is a pragmatic concession to predictably wrongful state practice, rather than a deliverance of moral theory.

To work out proportionality and necessity, we need to ask what matters in war, and how it matters. What are the salient goods and bads? Obviously the goods involved in the just cause—the protection of life and liberty, and people's political interests—are vital. And the most obvious bads are the death and destruction to which fighting will inevitably lead. Crucially, we also need to consider *all* the goods and bads that will arise because of the war—including those that will follow the active phase of the conflict. Recent misadventures by the United States and its allies in the Middle East underscore how central to a war's justification is the realization of a worthy peace when the fighting is done (Bass 2004, Coady 2008, May 2012).

Knowing the goods and bads realized by war is not enough. We also need to know how to weigh them. The simplest approach would be to weigh all lives, for example, equally. But this is not plausible. Lives matter in two ways: first, because they add value to the world; second, because they are protected by rights (Lazar 2015). Ending a life is almost always bad, but it only sometimes amounts to a rights violation. And rights-violating killing is much harder to justify than its counterpart. Walzer (2006b [1977]) argued that all soldiers lose their right to life; many revisionists have replied that, even if this is true for those fighting for unjust ends, it is false for just combatants. But everybody thinks that *some* soldiers are unprotected by a right to life. And that clearly matters to the proportionality of the war.

We need also to consider our own standing in relation to lives taken. Many think that, when working out proportionality and necessity, deaths inflicted by the enemy side in a war should not count equally with the deaths we impose (though see Rodin 2014). Some think this is because we have stronger obligations not to do harm than we have to prevent harms done by others (e.g., McMahan 2010b). We might also think that the lives of those with whom we share special relationships should bear greater weight in our deliberations. This seems relatively obvious at the small scale, where deep personal relationships are concerned. But it also seems plausible when weighing the lives of comrades-in-arms and of compatriots (Kamm 2004, Hurka 2005, Lazar 2013).

Jus in Bello

Underpinning the law of armed conflict are three fundamental principles (see figure 1):

The Geneva Conventions

On discrimination (Article 48, first additional protocol to the Geneva Conventions): "In order to ensure respect for and protection of the noncombatant population and noncombatant objects, the Parties to the conflict shall at all times distinguish between the noncombatant population and combatants and between noncombatant objects and military objectives and accordingly shall direct their operations only against military objectives."

On proportionality [Article 51(4b), first additional protocol to the Geneva Conventions]: "[A]n attack which may be expected to cause incidental loss of noncombatant life, injury to noncombatants, damage to noncombatant objects, or a combination thereof, which would be excessive in relation to the concrete and direct military advantage anticipated."

On necessity (from Article 57, first additional protocol to the Geneva Conventions): "With respect to attacks, the following precautions shall be taken: (a) those who plan or decide upon an attack shall. . . (ii) take all feasible precautions in the choice of means and methods of attack with a view to avoiding, and in any event to minimizing, incidental loss of noncombatant life, injury to noncombatants and damage to noncombatant objects; . . . 3. When a choice is possible between several military objectives for obtaining a similar military advantage, the objective to be selected shall be that the attack on which may be expected to cause the least danger to noncombatant lives and to noncombatant objects."

Figure 1. The Geneva Convention

- Discrimination: Intentionally attacking noncombatants is impermissible.
- Proportionality: Unintentionally harming noncombatants is permissible only if the harms are proportionate to the goals the attack is intended to achieve.
- Necessity: Unintentionally harming noncombatants is permissible only if the least harmful means feasible are chosen.

These principles presuppose that the victims of war fall into two classes—combatants and noncombatants. Combatants may be killed almost without constraint.[4] Noncombatants enjoy substantial protections. Combatants are members of the armed forces of a group at war, as well as those who directly participate in hostilities, including those who have a continuous combat function. Noncombatants are not combatants. The boundaries are vague. What counts as direct participation in hostilities? When is one's combat function continuous? These are hard questions, and I do not answer them here.

Both international law and traditionalist just war theory assume that any combatant who adheres to these three principles fights permissibly, regardless of what she is fighting for.[5] This is the "moral equality of combatants," also known as the "symmetry thesis" and, as I refer to it below, "combatant equality."

Discrimination and combatant equality are the most controversial tenets in the traditionalist just war theory canon. (I discuss the principles of proportionality and necessity more briefly at the end of this section.) Walzer (2006b [1977]) argued that people have fundamental rights to life and liberty, grounded in their moral status. Attacking people in war can be justified only if those rights are either overridden or somehow lost. He argued that they could be overridden only in exceptional cases of "supreme emergency"—if attacking noncombatants were the only way to avert Nazi domination of Europe, for example. In the ordinary circumstances of warfare, an attack is permissible only if each of the victims has "through some act of his own . . . surrendered or lost his rights" (Walzer 2006b [1977], p. 135). In general, "a legitimate act of war is one that does not violate the rights of the people against whom it is directed" (p. 135).

Walzer (2006b [1977]) then argued that all combatants, and only combatants, lose their rights to life and liberty (p. 136). First, because they threaten the lives of others, they lose their own right to life (p. 142). Second, by joining the armed forces, a combatant has "allowed himself to be made into a dangerous man" (p. 145) and thus surrenders his rights. Noncombatants neither threaten others nor make themselves dangerous, so they retain their rights and may not be attacked. Discrimination follows directly—and combatant equality follows too: If all combatants lose their rights not to be killed, then a combatant fighting for an unjust cause does no wrong by killing just combatants.

Walzer's arguments for discrimination and combatant equality have been refuted by revisionist just war theorists. Even if we accepted Walzer's versions of discrimination, proportionality, and necessity, combatant equality would still be false, since unintended noncombatant deaths can be justified only if the goal fought for is worth those deaths. Unjust combatants fighting in pursuit of an unjust cause achieve nothing that can counterbalance the violated rights of their victims (McMahan 1994, Rodin 2002, Hurka 2005). When the Islamic State of Iraq and the Levant (ISIL) attacks Syrian and Iraqi towns, its intended goals cannot justify any unintended harm to noncombatants.

This is enough to refute the tenet of combatant equality. But Walzer's critics went further. Accepting his premise that, barring supreme emergencies, intentional killing in war must be justified by the target's lack of rights to life and liberty,[6] they disputed his account of how those rights can be lost. In particular, they have shown that posing a threat is neither sufficient nor necessary for one to be liable to be killed (McMahan 1994). Those who threaten others' lives in self-defense, or in defense of others, do not themselves forfeit their right to life. The combatants of the Kurdish Peshmerga, heroically fighting to rescue Yazidi Christians from ISIL's genocidal attacks, do not lose their rights against their Manichean adversaries. Nor are they like boxers or gladiators, who waive their right not to be attacked.

Nor is posing a threat necessary for one to lose one's right to life. Revisionists argue that what really grounds liability is *responsibility* for a *wrongful* threat. The commander-in-chief, for example, might be responsible for threats without posing them. The same is true for a terrorist leader. Combatants fighting for unjust causes are responsible for wrongful threats: They are liable to be killed. Just combatants are not responsible for wrongful threats: They are not liable. Only just combatants can kill legitimately. Combatant equality is false.

We must also reconsider the principle of discrimination (McMahan 1994, Arneson 2006, Fabre 2012, Frowe 2014). In many states, noncombatants play an important role in the resort to military force. In modern industrialized countries, as much as 25% of the population works in war-related industries (Downes 2006, pp. 157–58; see also Gross 2010, p. 159, Valentino et al. 2010, p. 351). We provide the belligerents with crucial financial and other services; we support and sustain the combatants who do the fighting; we pay our taxes, and in democracies we vote, providing the economic and political resources without which war would be impossible. Our contributions to the state's capacity give it the strength and support to concentrate on war. If the state's war is unjust, then many noncombatants are responsible for contributing to wrongful threats. They are therefore permissible targets.

This is a troubling conclusion. But if we insist that noncombatants are simply not responsible *enough* to be liable to be killed in war, then we will probably find that many unjust combatants also are not responsible enough to lose their rights (McMahan 1994). Whether through fear, disgust, principle, or ineptitude, many combatants are wholly ineffective in war, and contribute little or nothing to threats posed by their side (Marshall 1978, Grossman 1995). Many contribute no more to unjustified threats than do noncombatants. They also lack the *mens rea* that might make liability appropriate in the absence of a significant causal contribution. They are simply unlucky. The loss of their right to life is not a fitting response to their conduct.

If we insist that intentional killing in war is permissible only in supreme emergencies or when one's targets have lost their right to life, and if, as seems plausible, many unjust noncombatants and combatants are equally responsible for wrongful threats, then we face a dilemma. If the degree of responsibility required for liability to be killed is high, then noncombatants are protected in war; but so are many combatants—we would have to endorse a kind of near-pacifism. But if we lower the amount of responsibility required to lose one's right to life, to ensure that we can fight otherwise justified wars, then we also license much weaker protections for noncombatants than are currently provided by international law. If we care at all about the fit between one's behavior and the loss of one's right to life, then we must surely agree that many unjust combatants have done nothing that warrants their becoming liable to be killed. But if we don't care about fit, then we cannot deny that, in modern states, most adults contribute in some way to their government's capacity to wage unjust wars, and so are potentially liable. This is the "responsibility dilemma" for just war theory (Lazar 2010).[7]

As with the *jus ad bellum*, we find that Walzer's account of the *jus in bello* derived plausible conclusions from implausible premises. But the revisionists' counterarguments are not compelling enough to warrant jettisoning traditionalist conclusions without first seeking to provide them with firmer foundations.

Philosophers have pursued three paths in response to this dilemma. In the first camp are the all-out revisionists. Their task is to explain why killing apparently non-liable unjust combatants is permissible, without either undermining noncombatant immunity or reopening the door to combatant equality. They do this by insisting that all and only unjust combatants are liable to be killed. Sometimes this clearly involves ap-

plying a double standard—talking up the responsibilities of combatants, talking down those of noncombatants (e.g., McMahan 2011). But they have also advanced new arguments to this end. McMahan (2011), for example, has argued that unjust combatants can be liable to be killed simply by virtue of being responsible for making just combatants reasonably believe that they are liable on ordinary grounds. Others have abandoned Walzer's individualist focus and argued that unjust combatants are liable because they are complicit in wrongdoing, even if they do not causally contribute to it (Kamm 2004, Bazargan 2013).

These arguments are troubling. Whether we retain or lose our rights should depend only on what we ourselves do. The complicity-based argument comes too close to making mere membership, even *identity*, a basis for losing one's right to life. This is a chilling result. What's more, if combatants are complicit in the wrongdoing of their comrades-in-arms, then surely many noncombatants are also complicit in the wrongful actions of their military.

As to McMahan's (2011) argument: Perhaps *culpable* responsibility for others' false beliefs is relevant to permissible harm. It might be permissible for a policeman to kill a prankster who pretends to be a suicide bomber. But that is because the prankster is at fault. Philosophers typically agree that many unjust combatants are not culpable for the injustice of their war (McMahan 1994, Lazar 2010). Blameless responsibility for others' beliefs surely cannot make one a permissible target—although if it did, then that would resurrect combatant equality again, since most just combatants are also blamelessly responsible for unjust combatants' reasonable belief that they are liable to be killed.

The second approach is moderate traditionalist. It endorses a moderate form of combatant equality, according to which combatants are much more equal than the revisionists allow but not exactly equivalent. In most wars, many just combatants fight impermissibly, and many unjust combatants fight permissibly. Still, unjust combatants whose actions contribute only to the advancement of their side's unjust cause cannot fight permissibly, no matter how scrupulously they observe the principles of discrimination, proportionality, and necessity. That said, they always fight *less* wrongfully when they observe those principles.

The shortest route to moderate combatant equality starts by accepting that liability to be killed requires some fit between one's behavior and the severity of that fate. This is lacking for almost all noncombatants. They simply don't do anything that can warrant losing their right to life. This helps explain why killing noncombatants is so seriously wrong. But it also means that many unjust combatants retain their rights. The next step is to defend a principle I call "moral distinction": Killing noncombatants is worse than killing combatants. This is obviously true if the combatants are liable and the noncombatants are not; the challenge is to show that killing non-liable noncombatants is worse than killing non-liable combatants. If that is true, then it can be permissible to intentionally kill non-liable unjust combatants in war while non-liable unjust noncombatants remain impermissible targets.

Of course, even if killing combatants is better than killing noncombatants, that does not mean it is permissible. The third stage of the argument is to show that, since intentionally killing non-liable unjust combatants is not the most seriously wrongful kind of killing, it can be permissible even in ordinary wars. This allows us to deny pacifism, but it also supports the position of moderate combatant equality. If killing non-liable combatants is not the worst kind of killing, then it is easier to justify the use of lethal force against just combatants by unjust combatants.

We can argue for the moral distinction principle by explaining either why killing non-liable unjust combatants is not the worst kind of killing or why killing non-liable noncombatants is especially seriously wrongful. On the first point, the revisionist arguments just considered can be mobilized. In particular, although I deny that one can lose the right to life merely by virtue of membership in the armed forces, perhaps one does have a special reason to bear cost to avert wrongdoing by members of groups to which one belongs, which somewhat lowers the barrier against permissible harm.

Additionally, many just combatants in many wars fight justly only through their good luck. They simply obey orders. Everything within their control could have been held constant, and they could have been fighting unjustly. I think that when combatants conform to others' rights only by accident, they have weaker grounds for complaint against being harmed than do noncombatants who more robustly respect the rights of others (Pettit 2015).

Further, when combatants kill other combatants, they typically believe that their cause is just and that killing combatants is an acceptable means to further it. I argue elsewhere that killing people when you know that doing so is wrong is more seriously objectionable than when you reasonably believe you are acting permissibly (Lazar 2015). Knowingly violating someone's rights involves a special kind of disrespect for their moral standing.

Last, although combatants do not strictly consent to be killed by their adversaries, they do give their opponents a limited waiver of their rights. The role of the armed forces is to protect their noncombatant population from the ravages of war. This means, in part, drawing fire away from that population. They implicitly say to their adversaries, "You ought to cease fighting entirely. But if you are going to fight, then fight *us*." This is a very limited and conditional waiver of their rights against harm. But it does make harming those combatants somewhat less objectionable than harming noncombatants, who do not waive their rights even to this limited degree.

Just as we can show that killing innocent combatants is not the worst kind of killing, we can also show that killing innocent civilians is especially objectionable (Lazar 2015). First, although killing civilians can sometimes be necessary in war (Lazar 2014), it is typically wholly wanton.

Second, killing civilians typically involves an especially objectionable mode of harmful agency—their suffering is used as a means to compel their compatriots and leaders to end their war. Combatants, by contrast, are typically killed in order to avert the threat that they themselves pose. They are not used in the same way. Of course, at the strategic level, all the suffering of war is used as a means to coerce the enemy leadership. But the killing takes place at the tactical level, where there is a robust difference between anti-civilian and anti-combatant violence.

Third, because civilians are so rarely liable to be killed, attacking them involves a much bigger risk of violating their rights than does attacking combatants. Killing people in a more reckless way is worse than doing so when it is quite likely that they are liable. More precisely, killing an innocent person is more seriously wrongful the more likely it was that she was not liable to be killed (Lazar 2015).

Fourth, civilians are typically more vulnerable and defenseless than soldiers. The notions that we have special duties to protect the vulnerable, and that harming the defenseless is especially objectionable, are as fundamental as the idea that we ought not to harm the innocent. Of course, sometimes soldiers are vulnerable and defenseless, and this explains why harming them is sometimes harder to justify (think, for example, of the "Highway of Death" in Iraq in 1991).

We have established that killing non-liable noncombatants is worse than killing non-liable combatants. We can sustain a deep opposition to anti-civilian violence and hold that killing non-liable combatants is sometimes permissible. As a result, I think that unjust combatants who fight to defend their own territory, their co-citizens, and their comrades-in-arms can sometimes fight permissibly (Kamm 2004, 2005, Hurka 2005, Steinhoff 2008, Lazar 2013). This does not license them to make attacks that serve their unjust goals, but it does mean that combatant equality is closer to the truth than the revisionists believe.

Some traditionalists seek a more robust vindication of combatant equality. Three institutionalist arguments are especially prominent. The first is contractualist

(Benbaji 2008, 2011). On this view, the existing laws of war constitute a fair and optimal agreement among states and their populations, which allows all to sustain disciplined armies, necessary for national defense and international stability. Combatants waive their rights not to be killed, in order to allow themselves to go to war without having to analyze the merits on every occasion.

Although international law is clearly morally important—if you fight within international law, then you cannot be equated to a common murderer, even if your cause is unjust—I think Benbaji's (2008, 2011) view is too narrowly statist, and it cannot explain how combatants pursuing an unjust goal can proportionately kill non-liable noncombatants. If their ends are evil, they cannot justify any of the evil that they do.

The second argument appeals to the authority of domestic law. Just as we have an obligation to obey the laws of our state, so combatants are obliged to obey their state's orders to fight (for discussion, see Estlund 2007, Renzo 2013, Ryan 2016). Again, although I agree that this is a genuine moral reason, it is not weighty enough to license otherwise wrongful killing.

The third argument grounds combatant equality in its long-term results, arguing that the existing laws of war limit the suffering caused by war (Dill & Shue 2012, Shue 2013, Waldron 2016). Because combatants and their leaders almost always believe their cause to be just, requiring unjust combatants to lay down their arms would be wholly ineffective, and the additional permissions for just combatants would be abused by all sides. The existing laws of war are a necessary compromise with harsh reality.

As already noted, this argument is certainly plausible, but leaves important gaps. Of course the laws of war should be sensitive to predictable noncompliance, but that doesn't tell us what we ought to do in war. And we cannot premise that question on the assumption that we will predictably act impermissibly (Lazar & Valentini 2017). We need to know both what the laws of war should be and what we ought to do, faced with different situations in war.

Endorsing moral distinction brings us close to vindicating international law. But it does not take us the whole way. Discrimination prohibits intentional attacks on civilians; proportionality licenses unintended but foreseen harms; moral distinction gives no special role to intentions. To justify current international law, we need to go further. Doing so takes us into one of the oldest debates in normative ethics, concerning the "doctrine of double effect" (see Quinn 1989, Rickless 1997, McIntyre 2001, Delaney 2006, Thomson 2008, Tadros 2015).

We can defend this principle in two stages. First, we have to show that mental states in general can be relevant to the permissibility of our actions (Christopher 1998). Many philosophers deny even this (e.g., Thomson 1986, Kamm 1993). Second, we need a coherent account of which mental states matter for permissibility, an account that sets intentions in context. My own view is that intentions do matter to permissibility, because intending to harm someone evinces greater disrespect for that person than merely foreseeing that one's actions will harm him. But the difference between intended and merely foreseen harm is not categorical. I cannot see why we would, for example, absolutely prohibit intentionally violating someone's rights, while having a relatively permissive stance toward merely foreseen violations of rights. The difference is one of degree, not of kind.

I therefore think that the absolute prohibition on targeting civilians in international law is not directly grounded in our first-order moral reasons. However, here as elsewhere, hard cases make bad law: It is better to have an exceptionless principle at the heart of international law than to reflect the moral truth, lest the latter course lead to a serious increase in wrongful attacks on civilians. As it is formulated in international law, the discrimination principle is relatively clear and easy to apply (notwithstanding the difficulty of determining what counts as directly participating in hostilities). It is not a mere rule of thumb, since it is underpinned by the fact that killing civilians is worse than killing soldiers and the fact that intentional killing is worse than merely foreseen killing. But given these differences in degree, discrimination translates them into a difference in kind for the sake of minimizing wrongful killing.

Proportionality and necessity raise a number of other interesting questions, which I lack the space to address in depth. One issue that has been prominent in recent years is whether, when calculating proportionality, to discount the lives of civilians used as "involuntary human shields" by the enemy. Pro-Israeli commentators have argued that Hamas's putative responsibility for using civilians as cover diminishes the responsibility of the Israeli Defense Force (IDF) for their deaths (Walzer 2009). And they have argued that allowing Hamas to abuse the IDF's moral restraint creates perverse incentives for future conflicts (Keinon 2014; for a philosophical version of the point, see Smilansky 2010). Setting aside the disputed question of whether Hamas did in fact use civilians in this way, the moral arguments merit further consideration. My own view is that they don't stand up.

First, according to this argument, civilians' rights are diminished in weight by those who use them, without their consent, as cover. This should be cause for concern. We ordinarily think that we should lose or forfeit our rights against harm only through our own actions. Further, even if Hamas is responsible for using the civilians as cover, that does not diminish the IDF's responsibility for the resulting deaths—responsibility is not zero sum. Last, using these civilians as a means to deter future abuses of the IDF's moral restraint is even more objectionable than harming them as a side effect.

With respect to necessity, the most potent recent debate has touched on similar themes. International law requires combatants to "take all feasible precautions in the choice of means and methods of attack with a view to avoiding, and in any event to minimizing, incidental loss of civilian life, injury to civilians and damage to civilian objects" (Article 57, first additional protocol to the Geneva Conventions). This principle has deep moral foundations, which recent just war theory has helped bring to light (see especially Walzer 2006b [1977], p. 155, McMahan 2010b, Lazar 2012b, Luban 2014). Combatants are required to bear significant costs to reduce the risk to civilians. But how much cost? Working that out means attending to all the arguments for moral distinction, but also acknowledging soldiers' special obligation to protect noncombatants, and their duty to protect one another.

Conclusion

The last two decades have been turbulent for just war theory. For the first time, it has received the kind of sustained philosophical analysis that other areas of moral and political philosophy have enjoyed for much longer. The first fruits of that analysis were revisionist, throwing into question the hard-won consensus at the heart of international law and practice. But as the debate has evolved, the more radical revisionist conclusions have been shown to depend mostly on a limited conceptual palette. Grounding our account of the ethics of war in our intuitions about small-scale cases of self-defense is like grounding our theory of distributive justice in the principles appropriate to shipwrecked castaways dividing up cowrie shells on a desert island. Undoubtedly we can learn something about the morality of war from those highly simplified interpersonal cases. But we must also think about war itself. Once we expand our focus, we quickly find that the core of the law of armed conflict—its commitments concerning national defense, legitimate authority, proportionality and necessity *ad bellum* and *in bello*, and discrimination—may not precisely mirror our more fundamental moral reasons, but nor is it the morally rootless product of power and compromise.

NOTES

This article draws on all my work in just war theory, so the acknowledgments would be as long as the bibliography if I thanked everyone. But I owe particular gratitude to Henry Shue,

Jeff McMahan, and David Rodin, whose guidance was so crucial when I first approached these topics, and whose work has so much informed my own.

1. On the relationship between the morality of war and the law of war, see the broadly traditionalist arguments of Shue (2008, 2010, 2013) and Lazar (2012a); the morally but not legally revisionist arguments of McMahan (2008, 2010a); and the morally and legally revisionist arguments of Rodin (2011). For a book-length treatment of the topic, see Haque (2017).

2. Taylor (1995) provides a useful starting point for considering evaluative collectivism, as do List & Pettit (2011) for descriptive collectivism.

3. Walzer's work focuses on the importance of political sovereignty but says little about territorial rights. To date, little has been written about the role of territory in just cause (though see Stilz 2014).

4. Other principles prohibit harming combatants in particular ways—for example, with poisonous gas.

5. Article 43 of the first additional protocol of the Geneva Conventions states explicitly that "combatants . . . have the right to participate directly in hostilities." The Preamble, meanwhile, makes clear that these principles apply "without any adverse distinction based on the nature or origin of the armed conflict or on the causes espoused by or attributed to the Parties to the conflict."

6. The views in this and the next paragraph are widely shared. Some of the most significant sources are Rodin (2002), McPherson (2004), Arneson (2006), McMahan (2009), Fabre (2012), and Frowe (2014).

7. Some philosophers are happier than I am to skirt close to those extremes. Frowe (2014) endorses the responsibility view's troubling implications for the discrimination principle. Others (Rodin 2014, May 2015) endorse a form of contingent pacifism.

REFERENCES

Arneson RJ. 2006. Just warfare theory and noncombatant immunity. *Cornell Int. Law J.* 39:663–88

Bass GJ. 2004. Jus post bellum. *Philos. Public Aff.* 32/4: 384–412

Bazargan S. 2013. Complicitous liability in war. *Philos. Stud.* 165(1):177–95

Beitz CR. 1980. Nonintervention and communal integrity. *Philos. Public Aff.* 9:385–91

Benbaji Y. 2008. A defense of the traditional war convention. *Ethics* 118(3):464–95

Benbaji Y. 2011. The moral power of soldiers to undertake the duty of obedience. *Ethics* 122(1):43–73

Benbaji Y. 2014. Distributive justice, human rights, and territorial integrity: a contractarian account of the crime of aggression. See Fabre & Lazar 2014, pp. 159–84

Buchanan A, Keohane RO. 2004. The preventive use of force: a cosmopolitan institutional proposal. *Ethics Int. Aff.* 18(1):1–22

Caney S. 2005. *Justice Beyond Borders: A Global Political Theory.* Oxford, UK: Oxford Univ. Press

Christopher R. 1998. Self-defense and defense of others. *Philos. Public Aff.* 27(2):123–41

Coady T. 2008. *Morality and Political Violence.* Cambridge, UK: Cambridge Univ. Press

Delaney NF. 2006. Two cheers for "closeness": terror, targeting and double effect. *Philos. Stud.* 137(3):335–67

Dill J, Shue H. 2012. Limiting the killing in war: military necessity and the St. Petersburg assumption. *Ethics Int. Aff.* 26(3):311–33

Doppelt G. 1978. Walzer's theory of morality in international relations. *Philos. Public Aff.* 8(1):3–26

Downes A. 2006. Desperate times, desperate measures: the causes of civilian victimization in war. *Int. Secur.* 30(4):152–95

Emerton P, Handfield T. 2009. Order and affray: defensive privileges in warfare. *Philos. Public Aff.* 37(4):382–414

Emerton P, Handfield T. 2014. Understanding the political defensive privilege. See Fabre & Lazar 2014, pp. 40–65

Estlund D. 2007. On following orders in an unjust war. *J. Polit. Philos.* 15(2):213–34

Fabre C. 2008. Cosmopolitanism, just war theory and legitimate authority. *Int. Aff.* 84(5):963–76

Fabre C. 2012. *Cosmopolitan War.* Oxford, UK: Oxford Univ. Press

Fabre C. 2014. Cosmopolitanism and wars of self-defence. See Fabre & Lazar 2014, pp. 90–114

Fabre C, Lazar S, eds. 2014. *The Morality of Defensive War.* Oxford, UK: Oxford Univ. Press

Finlay CJ. 2010. Legitimacy and non-state political violence. *J. Polit. Philos.* 18(3):287–312

Frowe H. 2014. *Defensive Killing.* Oxford, UK: Oxford Univ. Press

Gross M. 2010. *Moral Dilemmas of Modern War: Torture, Assassination and Blackmail in an Age of Asymmetric Conflict.* Cambridge, UK: Cambridge Univ. Press

Grossman D. 1995. *On Killing: The Psychological Cost of Learning to Kill in War and Society.* London: Back Bay Books

Haque AA. 2017. *Law and Morality at War.* Oxford, UK: Oxford Univ. Press. In press

Hurka T. 2005. Proportionality in the morality of war. *Philos. Public Aff.* 33(1):34–66

Hurka T. 2007. Liability and just cause. *Ethics Int. Aff.* 21(2):199–218

Kamm FM. 1993. *Morality, Mortality.* New York: Oxford Univ. Press

Kamm FM. 2004. Failures of just war theory: terror, harm, and justice. *Ethics* 114(4):650–92

Kamm FM. 2005. Terror and collateral damage: are they permissible? *J. Ethics* 9(3):381–401

Keinon H. 2014. PM: Terrorists watching whether world gives immunity for attacks from schools, homes. *Jerusalem Post* Aug. 6

Kutz C. 2005. The difference uniforms make: collective violence in criminal law and war. *Philos. Public Aff.* 33(2):148–80

Kutz C. 2014. Democracy, defence, and the threat of intervention. See Fabre & Lazar 2014, pp. 229–46

Lazar S. 2010. The responsibility dilemma for *Killing in War*: a review essay. *Philos. Public Aff.* 38(2):180–213

Lazar S. 2012a. Morality and law of war. In *Companion to Philosophy of Law*, ed. A Marmor, pp. 364–79. New York: Routledge

Lazar S. 2012b. Necessity in self-defense and war. *Philos. Public Aff.* 40(1):3–44

Lazar S. 2013. Associative duties and the ethics of killing in war. *J. Pract. Ethics* 1(1):3–48

Lazar S. 2014. Necessity and non-combatant immunity. *Rev. Int. Stud.* 40(1):53–76

Lazar S. 2015. *Sparing Civilians.* Oxford, UK: Oxford Univ. Press

Lazar S, Frowe H, eds. 2016. *The Oxford Handbook of Ethics of War.* New York: Oxford Univ. Press

Lazar S, Valentini L. 2017. Proxy battles in just war theory: jus in bello, the site of justice, and feasibility constraints. In *Oxford Studies in Political Philosophy* III, ed. P Vallentyne, D Sobel, S Wall. Oxford, UK: Oxford Univ. Press. In press

Lippert-Rasmussen. 2013. Global injustice and redistributive wars. *Law Ethics Philos.* 1(1):65–86

List C, Pettit P. 2011. *Group Agency: The Possibility, Design, and Status of Corporate Agents.* Oxford, UK: Oxford Univ. Press

Luban D. 1980a. The romance of the nation-state. *Philos. Public Aff.* 9(4):392–97

Luban D. 1980b. Just war and human rights. *Philos. Public Aff.* 9(2):160–81

Luban D. 2014. Risk taking and force protection. In *Reading Walzer*, ed. Y Benbaji, N Sussman, pp. 230–56. New York: Routledge

Marshall SLA. 1978. *Men against Fire: The Problem of Battle Command in Future War.* Gloucester, UK: Peter Smith

Mavrodes GI. 1975. Conventions and the morality of war. *Philos. Public Aff.* 4(2):117–31

May L. 2012. *After War Ends: A Philosophical Perspective.* Cambridge and New York: Cambridge Univ. Press

May L. 2015. *Contingent Pacifism: Revisiting Just War Theory.* New York: Cambridge Univ. Press

McIntyre A. 2001. Doing away with double effect. *Ethics* 111(2):219–55

McMahan J. 1994. Innocence, self-defense and killing in war. *J. Polit. Philos.* 2(3):193–221

McMahan J. 2004. War as self-defense. *Ethics Int. Aff.* 18(1):75–80

McMahan J. 2008. The morality of war and the law of war. In *Just and Unjust Warriors: The Moral and Legal Status of Soldiers*, ed. D Rodin, H Shue, pp. 19–43. Oxford, UK: Oxford Univ. Press

McMahan J. 2009. *Killing in War.* Oxford, UK: Oxford Univ. Press

McMahan J. 2010a. Laws of war. In *The Philosophy of International Law*, ed. S Besson, J Tasioulas, pp. 493–510. New York: Oxford Univ. Press

McMahan J. 2010b. The just distribution of harm between combatants and noncombatants. *Philos. Public Aff.* 38(4):342–79

McMahan J. 2011. Who is morally liable to be killed in war? *Analysis* 71(3):544–59

McMahan J. 2016. Proportionality and necessity. See Lazar & Frowe 2016

McPherson L. 2004. Innocence and responsibility in war. *Can. J. Philos.* 34(4):485–506

Øverland G. 2013. 602 and one dead: on contribution to global poverty and liability to defensive force. *Eur. J. Philos.* 21(2):279–99

Pettit P. 2015. *The Robust Demands of the Good.* Oxford, UK: Oxford Univ. Press

Quinn WS. 1989. Actions, intentions, and consequences: the doctrine of double effect. *Philos. Public Aff.* 18(4):334–51

Renzo M. 2013. Democratic authority and the duty to fight unjust wars. *Analysis* 73(4):668–76

Rickless SC. 1997. The doctrine of doing and allowing. *Philos. Rev.* 106(4):555–75

Rodin D. 2002. *War and Self-Defense*. Oxford, UK: Clarendon

Rodin D. 2011. Morality and law in war. In *The Changing Character of War*, ed. S Scheipers, H Strachan, pp. 446–63. Oxford, UK: Oxford Univ. Press

Rodin D. 2014. The myth of national self-defence. See Fabre & Lazar 2014, pp. 69–89

Ryan C. 2016. Pacifism. See Lazar & Frowe 2016

Schwenkenbecher A. 2013. Rethinking legitimate authority. In *Routledge Handbook of Ethics and War: Just War Theory in the 21st Century*, ed. F Allhoff, N Evans, A Henschke, pp. 161–70. New York: Routledge

Shue H. 1997. Eroding sovereignty: the advance of principle. In *The Morality of Nationalism*, ed. R McKim, J McMahan, pp. 340–59. Oxford, UK: Oxford Univ. Press

Shue H. 2008. Do we need a morality of war? In *Just and Unjust Warriors: The Moral and Legal Status of Soldiers*, ed. D Rodin, H Shue, pp. 87–111. Oxford, UK: Oxford Univ. Press

Shue H. 2010. Laws of war. In *The Philosophy of International Law*, ed. S Besson, pp. 511–30. New York: Oxford Univ. Press

Shue H. 2013. Laws of war, morality, and international politics: compliance, stringency, and limits. *Leiden J. Int. Law* 26(2):271–92

Smilansky S. 2010. When does morality win? *Ratio* 23(1): 102–10

Statman D. 2014. Fabre's crusade for justice: why we should not join. *Law Philos.* 33(3):337–60

Steinhoff U. 2008. Jeff McMahan on the moral inequality of combatants. *J. Polit. Philos.* 16(2):220–26

Stilz A. 2014. Territorial rights and national defence. See Fabre & Lazar 2014, pp. 203–28

Tadros V. 2015. Wrongful intentions without closeness. *Philos. Public Aff.* 43(1):52–74

Taylor C. 1995. Irreducibly social goods. In *Philosophical Arguments*, pp. 127–45. Cambridge, MA: Harvard Univ. Press

Temkin LS. 1993. *Inequality*. Oxford, UK: Oxford Univ. Press

Thomson JJ. 1986. *Rights, Restitution, and Risk: Essays in Moral Theory*. Cambridge, MA: Harvard Univ. Press

Thomson JJ. 2008. Turning the trolley. *Philos. Public Aff.* 36(4):359–74

Valentino B, Huth P, Croco S. 2010. Bear any burden? How democracies minimize the costs of war. *J. Polit.* 72(2):528–44

Waldron J. 2016. Deep morality and the laws of war. See Lazar & Frowe 2016

Walzer M. 2006a. Terrorism and just war. *Philosophia* 34(1): 3–12

Walzer M. 2006b (1977). *Just and Unjust Wars: A Moral Argument with Historical Illustrations*. New York: Basic Books. 5th ed.

Walzer M. 2009. Responsibility and proportionality in state and nonstate wars. *Parameters* Spring: 40–52.

Wasserstrom R. 1978. Book review: *Just and Unjust Wars: A Moral Argument with Historical Illustrations*. Harvard Law Rev. 92(2):536–45.

Zohar NJ. 1993. Collective war and individualistic ethics: against the conscription of "self-defense." *Polit. Theory* 21(4): 606–22.

Systematic Theory and the Future of Great Power War and Peace

DALE C. COPELAND

This [article] is animated by a simple question: Are the core systemic theories of great power war and peace still relevant in the modern age of intercontinental missiles and the threat of thermonuclear war? Put somewhat differently, could one seriously imagine either China or the United States choosing to launch a major war against the other, as great powers did as recently as 1914, 1939, and 1941? If our initial reaction is to answer "no" to both versions of the question, it might seem clear that causes-of-war scholarship needs a fundamental refocus of its efforts—away from its traditional emphasis on great power war toward issues of regional conflicts, civil strife, or perhaps great power coercion short of war (e.g., economic sanctions). It does seem self-evident that neither Beijing nor Washington would see any "value" in deliberately initiating a full-scale conflict against the other.[1] But if the experience of the Cold War has taught us anything, it is that great powers in the nuclear age can still get frighteningly close to total war through escalating suspicions, military mobilizations, and events such as the 1962 Cuban Missile Crisis. Indeed, a fundamental goal of US

Dale C. Copeland, "Systematic Theory and the Future of Great Power War and Peace," in *The Oxford Handbook of International Security*, ed. Alexandra Gheciu and William C. Wohlforth (New York: Oxford University Press, 2018). © 2018 Oxford University Press; reproduced with permission of the Licensor through PLSclear.

policy-makers for the past three decades, both Democratic and Republican, has been the avoidance of a new
cold war with China, precisely because of the risks of
an unintended escalation to great power war that accompany such intense rivalries.

To show that our theories of war are still relevant
to the modern era, therefore, it is imperative that we
demonstrate that they can explain why states shift
from cooperation toward hard-line policies that increase the likelihood of either a cold war competition
or an actual crisis that could spiral to nuclear war. Unfortunately, few of our most well-known systemic
theories of war, including classical realism, power transition theory, neorealism, and the bargaining model of
war, are presently set up to do this.[2] Almost invariably,
these theories are built around the logical premise that
actors either initiate war or they do not, depending on
certain specified conditions. Such a premise may help
to create a foundation for explaining why states might
"choose" war over peace—usually within the larger
paradigm of "rational choice" theory. But they typically are not equipped to explain why leaders might
engage in actions that knowingly increase the risk of a
slide into an inadvertent war, that is, a war that, prior
to the action taken (e.g., crisis initiation), no actor
would ever want to see come about.[3]

The purpose of this [article] is to help correct this
oversight by discussing theories that are already set up
to explain behavior that increases the likelihood of spiraling into war, and also to suggest ways that other
theories might be adjusted to achieve this necessary
goal. In this sense, the [article's] objective is not to argue that some theories are better than others simply
because they capture the problem of inadvertent spiraling. Rather, it is to show that all theories of great
power war are relevant in the modern age, must be attuned to this problem, and adjusted accordingly, even
if deductive or formal theorizing is made much more
complicated in the process.

Theories of Great Power War and the Nuclear Question

The problem of building useful theories of great power
war in the nuclear age was identified more than half a
century ago by Thomas Schelling. Schelling's argument
was straightforward: given that states cannot actually
use nuclear weapons in the traditional Clausewitzian
sense—to grab and hold territory to advance national
political objectives—they are at best only devices to coerce others into offering concessions they would not
otherwise make (Schelling 1966).[4] Yet how they do this
is unique. Great powers with nuclear weapons are in the
ultimate Chicken game. They both might like to get the
other to "swerve" by conceding on a particular foreign
policy issue or territorial interest. Yet if they had to

choose, both sides would greatly prefer continued peace
or even a humiliating swerve to actual thermonuclear
war.[5] For Schelling, this means that states, to get what
they want, can only "manipulate the risk" of a slide into
nuclear war by pulling the other onto the slippery slope
to war and hoping it swerves first. In a world where no
state is rational to initiate nuclear war, it might still be
rational for each side to use the risk of an inadvertent
nuclear war to achieve its foreign policy ends. The Berlin
and Cuban crises of 1961–62, as Schelling suggests, can
be seen in this light. Needless to say, there are few leaders
that would want to use this tool of statecraft on an ongoing basis (sometimes when one rocks the boat, it does
go over).[6] And because cold wars increase the chance of
crises breaking out, leaders are also disinclined to fall
into such intense rivalries if they can avoid them.

Any theory of great power war worth its salt, therefore, must be able to explain why great powers that
have been peacefully cooperating for some time—the
United States and China since 1985, for example—
would ever take actions that might lead to a cold war
or to crises that raise the prospect of an undesired slide
into nuclear conflict. Surprisingly, however, there are
very few such theories in the field of International Relations. Consider some of the most prominent theories
of great power politics and war, and how they fare in
a world of nuclear weapons.

Classical Realism

Classical realists argue that systems where states exist
in a "balance of power," with all great powers essentially equal in relative power, are likely to be peaceful.[7]
Great power wars occur only when one state becomes
significantly superior in military power and can thus
contemplate a bid to take over the system. Multiple
systems make this more difficult, since smaller great
powers can use alliances to deter superior actors by
raising the costs of war and the risks of defeat. But such
actors, as Germany showed twice in the twentieth
century, may still decide to take on the system because
of their superiority in military power (Morgenthau
1978; Gluck 1962). Yet such a theory, as it stands, has
little predictive power in a world of nuclear second-
strike capability. Even a state with overwhelming "nuclear superiority" in the number of weapons and
launch vehicles—such as the United States in the 1950s
and today—would be extremely unlikely to launch a
war against another nuclear power. It would take only
a few retaliatory strikes by the other to make "victory"
meaningless and war thus irrational.[8]

Power Transition Theory

The same problem hangs over classical realism's main
challenger, power transition theory (or hegemonic sta-

bility theory). It argues that the presence of one hegemonically dominant state keeps the peace, while the rise of the second-ranked great power to essential equality with the former hegemony leads to war. The rising actor initiates war at this point of "power transition" because it now has incentives to alter the system through war to get the goodies (status, territory, economic concessions) that it has been historically denied.[9]

Power transition theory has a fundamental logical flaw at its heart: actors still rising in power always have an incentive to avoid war so they can fight later if necessary at less cost and risk. This means that any "power transition" point of military equality has no magical causal power to drive rising states into an initiation of war (Copeland 2000: 13–14).[10] The theory, however, makes even less sense when the equality of power is measured in terms of nuclear weapons. A China that grew to equality with the United States in nuclear throw-weight might believe the Chicken game was now between equal Mac trucks, rather than (as previously) a Mac truck and a VW bug. But thermonuclear war is still thermonuclear war, and no great power would willingly choose it just to gain goodies it believes it deserves. To be sure, such a state might be more willing to engage in Schellingesque "rocking the boat" to play upon the other's unwillingness to risk drowning in a nuclear sea. Yet as with classical realism, we cannot understand the triggers for such risk-taking behavior without theorizing the causal mechanisms linking changes in the distribution of power with the willingness of actors to assume increased risks of inadvertent war through hard-line policies.[11] Otherwise, power transition theory has little practical value in today's world, even if the logical flaw that argues that rising powers initiate conflicts is corrected.

Neorealism

Neorealist theories of great power war are similarly limited by their failure to deal with inadvertent war. Kenneth Waltz (1979, 1989) and John Mearsheimer (2001) have argued that bipolar systems are more stable than multipolar systems, mainly because the level of uncertainty is greater in the latter than the former, leading some actors to initiate wars that they think they can win quickly and easily. Yet surprisingly, both theorists are also famous for arguing that nuclear weapons provide the ultimate deterrent, making wars between nuclear great powers very unlikely, essentially regardless of the polarity of the system. Aside from the fact that the Cold War is their only example of bipolar stability—meaning any "peace" from 1945 to 1990 was clearly overdetermined by the presence of nuclear weapons[12]—the Waltz-Mearsheimer neorealist logic cannot explain variations in the probability of great

power war across time by invoking a constant such as polarity. Why did dangerous nuclear crises that risked nuclear war occur in the early 1960s, but were few and far between after 1965 and especially after 1985?

One might argue that Mearsheimer's theory does have an extra variable drawn from classical realism and deterrence theory—the relative equality or inequality of the military power balance—to explain changes in the propensity of war within multipolarity or bipolarity. Yet because he seeks to explain only why states might choose to initiate war, not why they might decide to engage in hard-line policies that increase the risk of inadvertent war, he has no theoretical explanation for why great powers might consciously accept the risks that cold wars and nuclear crises entail in the modern world—or why they might indeed moderate their policies to avoid these risks. Mearsheimer's "offensive" version of neorealism might seem to suggest that because states are forced to assume the worst about the other's intentions, they will be continually engaging in assertive behavior to expand their spheres, even at the risk of actual great power war. But this constant—the worst-case assumption—cannot explain why for decades states such as the United States and China after 1985 would be so prudently cautious in their diplomatic relations.[13]

More to the point, a theory based on a worst-case assumption cannot explain the conditions under which either side might decide to initiate behaviors that would indeed get them into a cold war or worse. Mearsheimer might invoke the costs of nuclear war as a cost parameter keeping the two moderate in behavior.[14] But costs and risks are two separate variables—one involves "given" expenses after war occurs, the other the probability that war occurs at all. Without a theory to explain the willingness to get out on the slippery slope to a nuclear war, therefore, offensive neorealism is only a theory of sphere consolidation and low-level incremental expansion, not a theory that helps us explain the conditions for great power war and peace.

Bargaining Model of War

We will see in a moment that the defensive realist strand of neorealism, when combined with a dynamic view of relative power, does help us overcome the limitations of the offensive realist position. But for now it is worth investigating the value of perhaps the most influential theory of international conflict for the last two decades, namely, the bargaining model of war.

The original formulation of the model (Fearon 1995) identified two main ways that a "rationalist" war between powerful actors could come about: information asymmetries and commitment problems.[15] In the first mechanism, if two great powers have private information about their own willingness to pay the costs of war, they might initiate a crisis or small-scale war against a third party, thinking the other great power lacks the resolve to fight to defend its interests. If costly signals through mobilization and public statements of resolve fail to overcome the information asymmetry, both sides may fail to make sufficient concessions for a deal that both sides prefer to war, leading one of the states to initiate actual great power war. In the second mechanism, one state fears the other's future intentions, either in the short term or long term. The other may be unable to credibly promise not to attack later because it has an incentive to hide its true desires. This may lead the first state to attack now because it believes the other is preparing for immediate attack (preemptive war) or because it believes the other is growing in military power and will attack later once it has reached a point of military advantage (preventive war). Either way, the inability of states to commit to being nice later can lead actors fearing a diminution of their military position to attack now for fear of the future.

Fearon's bargaining model of war has had an enormous impact on the studies of both coercion through crisis and war itself.[16] The model helps us establish the conditions under which states will or will not reach a bargain that both might otherwise prefer [rather than] have to fight a war. Yet when it comes to the study of great power war in the nuclear era, it suffers from the same problem previously discussed. In pretty well every formalization of the bargaining model logic, states are assumed to simply choose war as better than the next best alternative, namely, either the status quo (if the actor forgoes a "crisis stage" and simply attacks) or "backing down" (within any crisis that might arise).[17] Such a theoretical move is driven by the focus of uncertainty about the other's current intentions or resolve, with the presumption that if a state believes the other is Chicken, it will push forward, but if it believes the other has Prisoners' Dilemma or Stag Hunt payoffs and thus will indeed choose war over backing down, then making a deal is preferred.[18] But in the nuclear age, direct great power conflict is and always remains a Chicken game, since no state would rationally choose to initiate a war that would lead to thermonuclear destruction. As Schelling stresses, no state can credibly claim to prefer war to giving up a small part of its sphere or to the loss of a neutral third party. But it can still credibly communicate its willingness to risk an uncontrollable slide into general war that it knows it neither prefers to the status quo nor to making concessions.[19]

This means that bargaining approaches to war, if they are going to be relevant to modern great power politics, must build into their logics the exogenous risks of inadvertent spiraling to war that rise as both a function of overall hostility levels (as when states shift from relative peace to cold war) and the intensity of any crises that arise within an ongoing rivalry. More specifically, they must work from the assumption that states make their calculations based on their probabilistic assessments of the risks of action versus the risks of non-action, that is, of becoming more hard-line versus staying more soft-line.

Defensive Realism

This is where the insights of defensive realism have proved particularly helpful. Defensive realists stress the tragic reality of security dilemmas: the inability of one state to increase its security through things such as arms buildups and alliances without simultaneously diminishing the security of other states, either because such actions can suggest that the first state may be preparing for war or because they improve its relative ability to fight and win in a war. Other states can be expected to respond with similar measures, measures that end up reducing the security of the state that starts the ball rolling. Actors can thus find themselves in a spiral of increasing hostility and mistrust that puts both sides on a "hair-trigger" and increases the chances that dangerous crises may occur that lead to actual war (Jervis 1976, 1978; Glaser 1997, 2010; Booth and Wheeler 2008; Kydd 2005; Van Evera 1999). For this reason, defensive realists reject the worst-case assumption of offensive realists, arguing that such an assumption will lead to overly hard-line policies by both parties and a reduction, not "maximization," of the security of the players (Glaser 2010).

Defensive realism has proved particularly useful in explaining why states that have been relatively peaceful with each other—or even allies, as the United States and Russia had been during the Second World War—might fall into a spiral of arms racing and hostile posturing that greatly increases the risks of great power war. The main problem with defensive realism is a simple one: it assumes that the leaders are not aware of the risks of spiraling prior to the spiral, and that "if only" they had been aware, or had understood that the other was also seeking security, they would not have upped the ante through hard-line policies that trigger the spiral. Yet a properly defined rationalist logic must assume that leaders do indeed understand the problem of security dilemmas, and that they know they can trigger undesired escalation by their own policies. If we start with this assumption, the puzzle of great power politics becomes this: Why do actors ever switch from moderate policies that keep the risks of spiraling low to hard-line actions that knowingly increase those risks? If the "crash" in nuclear Chicken is so unacceptable, why do actors ever engage in actions that increase the risk of one?[20]

There is a deeper issue lurking behind this question. Scholars and policy officials have understood for decades that any great power stand-off in the nuclear era is similar to the 1950s game of teenagers driving toward each other at breakneck speeds, hoping to get the other to swerve first. Yet International Relations (IR) theorists rarely ask the prior question: Why do actors decide to "get on the road" in the first place? Why not use moderation and quiet bargaining to avoid putting one's reputation on the line, and thus being forced into playing such a dangerous game?[21] If great power leaders are aware of the perils of security-dilemma spiraling, as they clearly are,[22] we must turn to an investigation of exogenous factors that change leaders' calculation, leading them to accept the increased risks of spiraling and inadvertent war. If the life of great powers is about trade-offs, then their willingness to "up the ante" in the nuclear age will be a function of the kinds of things that force leaders to make choices they would otherwise not want to make.

Dynamic Neorealism

My own scholarly efforts to grapple with the above problems have led me to seek to integrate the insights of offensive realism and defensive realism into a more dynamic neorealist view of international politics. This dynamic neorealist position stresses the factors external to a state that can change its assessment of its long-term power position and security, and thus its willingness to accept the risks of spiraling. Declining power has been a major reason for large-scale wars between great powers in the pre-nuclear era.[23] Yet leaders of nuclear great powers also worry about relative decline. They know that they face difficult least-of-many-evils decisions to deal with it. If they continue with moderate policies in an effort to avoid spiraling, they know that the state may become more vulnerable to attack later on or be subject to efforts by growing adversaries to whittle down the state's sphere of influence. Yet if they switch to more hard-line policies in order to avert decline, they might increase the probability of an inadvertent slide into war through a spiral of hostility and mistrust (Copeland 2000: chap. 2 and 2015: 8–12, 42–44, 430–31). What factors will drive an actor's decision to shift to increasingly hard-line behavior, despite knowledge of the risks of triggering a security-dilemma spiral? By focusing our attention on these factors, within a logic that accepts that great power decision-making is all about trade-offs, we can begin to build a theoretical foundation that can predict when great powers, even in the nuclear age, will adopt policies that lead to cold wars and dangerous crises such as occurred in 1961 and 1962.

The first most obvious factor is a leader's assessment of the depth and inevitability of any decline currently taking place. If decline is seen as a short-term downward "blip" on an otherwise optimistic growth trajectory, then it is highly unlikely that a state would

risk setting off a cold war spiral, let alone initiate a full-blown nuclear crisis. China since 1990 has occasionally experienced temporary economic problems. But because its overall trends have been so positive, it has been very reluctant to do anything that might spark a return to cold war politics. A state anticipating steep decline if it remains cooperative, on the other hand, is much more likely to turn to containment to prevent this decline, notwithstanding the greater probability of great power war. This was the US situation in 1945 coming out of the Second World War. Harry Truman understood that continuing the wartime cooperation with the Soviet Union would only allow it to develop its now larger territorial base of power in Eurasia. He thus decided to end economic lend-lease aid, restrict reparation payments from western Germany, and expand on Roosevelt's policy of projecting US air power from bases surrounding the Soviet Union. He was well aware by mid-1945 that such policies would spark a cold war, but he adopted them as better than allowing the Soviets to grow unimpeded.[24]

Fortunately the United States has been in a more favorable situation over the last three decades than it faced in 1945. China may be closing the GNP gap, but there is no reason to think it will inevitably overtake America in total economic or technological power. And when one considers per capita GNP, it is clear that the United States will remain supreme for a long time to come (Brooks and Wohlforth 2015–16). This means that while Washington might "pivot" to Asia to signal its commitment to Asian allies, it has no need to embark on a Trumanesque containment of China, especially given the downside risks that a new cold war would entail (Copeland 2000: 240–45, 2015: 436–44).

A key related factor is a state's expectations of the future commercial environment, and how any actions it undertakes to shore up its position might shape the other's expectations of future trade. Trade between great powers and their spheres is a major source of economic growth for the actors. If they expect other great powers will continue this trade into the future, they will have reason to maintain relatively moderate policies. This will avoid pushing the other into restrictive commercial policies that destroy current trade benefits. It will also reduce the chance that the states might invoke a "trade-security spiral," whereby actions by one great power to contain the other's economic growth lead the second actor to build up its military strength and control over its commercial sphere, which only leads the first actor to increase its economic restrictions out of fear of the other's long-term intentions (Copeland 2015: 10–12, 39–49, 429–39).

The dramatic changes in the US-Japanese relationship from 1920 to 1941 illustrate the importance of the trade dimension in great power politics. In the 1920s, when trade relations were positive, Tokyo and Washington enjoyed a period of cooperation and peace. After 1929 and especially after 1940, trade fell dramatically, pushing the Japanese government into territorial policies that only heightened Washington's desire to tighten the economic screws. The result of course was the Pacific War. Severe economic restrictions during the Cold War also greatly exacerbated the level of hostility between the United States and Russia. Fortunately, the American and Chinese governments seemed to have learned from these dangerous periods of history, and have acted to avoid any trade-security spiraling sparked by such things as third-party instability in the Middle East or territorial questions in Central Asia or the South China Seas (Copeland 2015: chaps. 4–6, 442–44).

A third important parameter is a declining state's estimate of the likelihood of a rising state doing damage to its sphere later on, or actually launching a major war against it (Copeland 2000: 38–39). As the bargaining model correctly points out, rising states have great difficulty in credibly signaling their commitment to be peaceful in the future, once they have more power. In the pre-1945 era, this problem of uncertainty was particularly severe, since declining actors could indeed imagine that the rising state might think it was worth its while to launch an all-out war after it had gained preeminence. German civilian and military leaders in 1914 and 1939, for example, unanimously agreed that the rising Russian state might very well expand westward if it grew to a dominant position. The presence of nuclear weapons and secure second-strike capability greatly reduces this concern. But the fear that the rising state, if its base is allowed to grow, will increase its efforts to whittle down the dominant state's sphere to further its economic or power projection capability is still a real one. This of course has been a primary issue shaping talk of a "rising China threat" for the last two decades of US foreign policy.

The question of whether or not a rising state will embark on aggressive policies later reveals the value of including domestic- and individual-level variables as a complement to the systemic forces discussed so far. In a pure systemic set-up, we might assume that the declining actor is so uncertain about what type of actor it will face later, once the rising state has peaked in power, that its estimate of its likelihood of being aggressive is only a function of how big it will likely become. In the real world, of course, states in decline will not rely solely on any estimate of the depth of decline, but will also ask the question: What kind of state is the riser likely to be in 15 or 20 years, after it has become much more powerful?[25] In particular, any argument that incorporates security-dilemma insights must ask whether the other's expected future type will make it more or less likely to engage in the kinds of risky be-

haviors that can cause an action-reaction spiral to inadvertent war. Ideologically extreme states such as Stalinist Russia in the early 1950s or revolutionary Iran in the 1980s will clearly make declining states much more worried about the future. China's move away from Maoist extremism toward capitalist-based integration has predictably reduced fears that a growing China will shift to territorial expansionism down the road. Set against the clear risks of war associated with hard-line containment, both Republican and Democratic administrations have understandably maintained cooperative policies that serve to further bind China to the globalized world system.

Reformulating Systemic Theory

We have seen so far that systemic theory can still be relevant in the nuclear age, as long as it incorporates within its deductive logic actor awareness of military and trade-based security dilemmas and the concomitant risks of spirals to inadvertent war. If we start from the assumption that leaders are conscious of the difficult trade-offs in international politics, we can see why they usually prefer to maintain moderate politics (to avoid spiraling) but occasionally feel obliged to switch to hard-line policies to maintain their power positions in the face of what would otherwise be significant decline. Yet we have seen that most of the key systemic theories of great power war have not yet incorporated the risks of inadvertent war into their core causal logics. This section of the [article] will suggest a few ways to help these theories make this move, and thus reestablish their relevance in the contemporary age.

Classical realist theories of war can be improved by assuming that when nuclear states are significantly dominant in relative military power, they will be more likely to accept the risks of inadvertent spiraling to great power war.[26] The prediction here is that nuclear great powers will still be wary of setting off an uncontrollable escalation to war, but that when they are significantly superior, they will think it easier to "rock the boat" to get the other side to swerve. The Mac truck and the VW Bug in nuclear Chicken both fear the DD outcome, but the driver of the Mac truck might reasonably think the other will chicken out first as a crisis escalates.[27] Classical realists have implicitly done this when explaining such things as the US willingness to escalate the Cuban crisis of 1962; American naval and nuclear superiority put the balance of power in Washington's favor, explaining why the Americans would pull both sides out further on the slippery slope to nuclear war.[28] By more explicitly theorizing the role of security-dilemma spiraling, such realists would make their own theory more applicable to contemporary relations with China. Still, because of its static nature, the classical realist argument has trouble explaining why nuclear states would ever get on the road to play Chicken in the first place, either by initiating a cold war or a nuclear crisis. Bringing in power trends and the problem of decline would help correct this problem.

Power transition theory, as we have seen, suffers from the logical flaw of assuming that rising states seek war at points of power equality, even though they are still on an upward power trajectory. But we can correct this concern by bringing in the classical realist point that in any snapshot of time, the more relative power a state has, the more it is willing to take risks of escalation to war. When a rising power is weak, it will be cautious. If over many years it has built up its power so that it is closer to equality, it will be more willing to defend its interests when they are threatened. In the nuclear age, this means that power transition theory could argue that a now-equal great power might see itself no longer as a Bug but as a near-equal Mac truck, and that it "won't be pushed around anymore." Note, however, that its greater willingness to accept the risks of inadvertent war is not a function of its rising power trend—that trend will make it want to buy time for further growth, all things being equal—but rather the result of the new snapshot of relative power (see note 10 above). Power transition theory can thus be seen as ultimately grounded in classical realist thinking: taking snapshots of the distribution of power over time, it predicts that the more relative military power a state has, the more it will be willing to risk war. Yet when we bring trend lines back in, we see that a formerly inferior state will still be cautious if equal but still rising in power, because it knows that war later is better than war now. The true initiators of great power conflict will thus logically be states anticipating decline, either because of long-term internal problems or expectations that trade will increasingly be restricted and will not be restored.[29]

The neorealist theories of war must also explicitly incorporate defensive realist insights on spiraling if they are to remain relevant. In the end, as we saw earlier, Mearsheimer's offensive realism uses a classical realist logic about power differentials to argue that in either bipolar or multipolar systems, it is superior states that are the ones mostly likely to initiate war, with near-equal states being deterred by the balance of power. Once the risk of inadvertent war is built into the logic, a reformulated neorealism would mirror the predictions of the adjusted classical realist argument: dominant great powers will risk inadvertent nuclear war more readily than states that are only equal or in fact inferior in military power. Yet even with this reformulation, neorealism could not explain why actors, even dominant ones, would be moderate in behavior

for long periods of time, and then suddenly shift to hard-line policies that increase the chances of nuclear war. Neorealism is still too static, focusing as it does on snapshots of relative power. Declining power trends must be incorporated to explain the conditions under which strong powers might decide to accept the risks associated with cold war and nuclear crisis.[30]

The future task for the bargaining model of war is to set its insights within a framework that recognizes the ever-present problem of security-dilemma spiraling. The easiest way to do this is to formalize the idea that initiating a crisis, as opposed to simply starting a war, entails a series of "stages" or "moments" on a slippery slope, each one of which is associated with a higher exogenous probability that both actors will fall into the abyss of nuclear war. The probability of inadvertent war can be expected to increase for a variety of reasons: trigger-happy commanders, accidents that lead to incentives to preempt, or the over-commitment of reputations as regional nuclear skirmishes break out. Assuming that leaders understand the Schelling logic, and will manipulate the growing exogenous risk of war to get the other to back down, bargaining theory can then show under what conditions states might decide to keep playing nuclear Chicken in order to force a "negotiated deal" that both prefer to continued crisis (as opposed to "war" itself, as is assumed in almost every recent version of the bargaining model).

Work by Branislav Slantchev (2013) sets a standard for other bargaining theorists when it comes to understanding "crisis bargaining" through manipulation of risk. But even once the general bargaining model of war has been corrected to account for the risk of nuclear war in a crisis, it must still deal with the question of why great powers would ever get out on the road to nuclear Chicken in the first place. Can bargaining theory predict when and under what conditions China and the United States might leave behind the economic and political cooperation of the past 30 years and embark on a new round of cold war politics? Here bargaining theory is limited by its focus on the mechanisms of bargaining itself, and its bracketing of the underlying propelling forces might push states to use coercion during periods of peaceful cooperation. Dynamic theories focusing on the security concerns of declining actors can supplement bargaining models by revealing the different parameters that can make a moderate state start to lean to more hard-line actions, including cold war containment, military arms racing, and the occasional initiation of nuclear crises.

Conclusion

This [article] has shown that theories of great power war will have little relevance to the modern nuclear age unless they incorporate within their deductive logics the importance of security-dilemma spiraling and the ongoing risk of inadvertent war. Given the existential concerns associated with cold wars and crises, it seems clear that most nuclear great powers will want to avoid heated confrontations by maintaining moderate policies, most of the time. The puzzle of conflict for the present day can thus be boiled down to this: Why would a United States or a China ever embark on policies that knowingly could lead to a new cold war, let alone initiate a nuclear crisis of the kind we saw in 1961–62? The defensive realist insight into the tragic reality of spiraling and inadvertent war brings us part of the way to an answer. But to go further, we need theories that show us under what conditions states shift from peaceful cooperation to harder-line policies that consciously increase the risks of things "getting out of hand." Parameters that capture the intensity of a state's decline, its expectations of future trade, and the likelihood of a rising state doing damage later are all useful starting points for future research. Clearly much more theoretical work must be done before we can offer great power leaders the kind of advice that will help states maintain their security while keeping the risk of nuclear war to a bare minimum. But in an age when any future "world war" would likely be our last, there can be no denying of the importance of such scholarly efforts.

NOTES

1. Even pessimists about the world's ability to avoid nuclear war—see Dan Deudney in the *Oxford Handbook of International Security* (2018)—assume that the main danger lies not in the choices of great powers vis-à-vis each other, but rather in their interactions with smaller state and non-state actors in the system.

2. Due to space, I focus only on theories emphasizing systemic factors as causes of war. Unit-level arguments stressing the role of domestic politics and leader psychology have an advantage over systemic theories in explaining how nuclear war might occur, given their emphasis on the potentially self-defeating or irrational side of human decision-making. At the end of the [article], I will briefly mention how unit-level and systemic theories can be integrated into a fuller explanation of war and conflict.

3. On this definition, see George (1991: xi, 545). On the risks of inadvertent nuclear war during a crisis, see Schelling (1966); Frei (1983); Betts (1987); Jervis (1989); Blair (1993).

4. Nuclear weapons also serve important deterrence functions, of course.

5. In the traditional set-up of the Chicken game, cooperation or "CC" gives both payers a utility payoff of 3, getting the other to swerve is worth 4, swerving yourself is 2, and the "crash" of "DD" has a payoff of 1 (such that each player's preferences are DC > CC > CD > DD). A nuclear Chicken game has the same ordering of preferences, but might be better represented by a mutual DD payoff of –100 or –200 each, to remind the United States of the truly horrific nature of the crash.

6. And Escher and Fuhrmann (2017) show just how rarely this tool is employed historically.

7. For more on the various forms of realism discussed in this [article], see Adam Quinn, in *Oxford Handbook of International Security* (2018).

8. So-called neoclassical realists might be able to solve the problem by incorporating unit-level pathologies that lead to errors in crisis decision-making. Unfortunately, such realists have not yet built a theory of great power war that incorporates the risk of inadvertent nuclear war through irrational missteps and domestic pressures. See the edited volume by Lobell et al. (2009), as well as Ripsman et al. (2016).

9. See in particular Organski and Kugler (1980); Gilpin (1981); Kugler and Organski (1989); Tammen et al. (2000).

10. There is a common conceptual confusion that seems to provide power transition theory with some empirical support. When previously weak states have narrowed the gap in relative conventional power, they sometimes start to act more assertively (Germany after 1895, for example). Yet this is only because the differential of relative power is now more equal, which allows the formerly weaker state to advance its interests—not because the state with a rising power trajectory is destined to become more aggressive. In short, power transition theory fails to separate the causal effects of *snapshots* in the distribution of power from the effects of *dynamic trends* in any distribution. As I discuss later, power transition theorists are closer to classical realists than they think. Classical realists, using a series of snapshots of the power balance, can explain why states that were significantly inferior become increasingly assertive as they become more equal—they are relatively less deterred over time. The dynamics of the power balance, however, must still be taken into account: if these states are still on an upward power trajectory, they have strong incentives not to push too hard, and especially to avoid war until their power has peaked (Germany after 1913, given the newly rising Russian state).

11. Compare this to Kugler and Organski (1989: 185–90), who adamantly deny that the theory needs to be adjusted in any way to accommodate the reality of nuclear weapons.

12. See Copeland (1996) for an examination of three other (clearly unstable) cases of bipolarity: Sparta-Athens and Rome-Carthage in the ancient world and the French-Hapsburgs of the early sixteenth century.

13. Offensive realism, when it comes to the US-Chinese relationship, thus turns into a normative theory: Washington and China *should* be more hard-line and expansionist than they have been, if they want to respond rationally to the pressures of the anarchic system. The main problem, of course, is that holding to a worst-case assumption in a nuclear realm is a highly *irrational* way to behave (and US and Chinese leaders fortunately know this).

14. This would be consistent with Mearsheimer's claim that high conventional costs of war can deter expansionism (2001: 37).

15. A third possibility, wars due to the indivisibility of a particular good, is unlikely, precisely because states can use side payments to overcome the problem.

16. A small representative sample would include Goemans (2000); Powell (2002, 2006); Wagner (2007); Ramsay (2004); Slantchev (2013); Schultz (2001); Kydd (2005); Reiter (2003, 2009). My own thinking about war has been strongly influ-

enced by Fearon's work, notwithstanding my concerns for its limitations (Copeland 2000: 45–9, 2015: 12–13, 39–41).

17. The two are often combined by bringing in a small third party that one state attacks out of the blue, which leads to a crisis when the other major state countermobilizes, leading to a crisis that may or may not be resolved without war.

18. See references in note 16. Two notable exceptions of bargaining scholars that do incorporate into their logics the autonomous or exogenous risks of spiraling as a crisis proceeds are Powell (1990) and Slantchev (2013). However, they do not examine why rational actors would ever get themselves into a crisis in the first place, knowing that it might force them to take risky escalatory steps

19. Schelling (1966). In other words, the question of "resolve" in nuclear scenarios is not about "willingness to pay the costs of war"—the traditional bargaining model assumption—but rather the willingness to risk a war no state could possibly prefer to a negotiated peace.

20. See Copeland (2015: 12–13, 42–46, 430–31, and 2000: chap. 2).

21. Bargaining-model theorists that do incorporate the importance of exogenous increases in the risk of inadvertent war into their analyses, such as Powell (1990) and Slantchev (2013), invariably start with the fact of a crisis itself. They do not consider why the actors put themselves on the road to Chicken by choosing the hard-line actions that force a competition of prestige and reputation.

22. Snyder and Diesing (1977), for example, found that in 13 of 16 major crisis cases, leaders were highly conscious that their own actions might cause events to get out of hand.

23. Copeland 2000, 2015; Weisiger 2013. For further discussion and references regarding the preventive motive for war, see Levy (1987, 2008).

24. Copeland 2000, chap. 6; Copeland 2015, chap. 6.

25. See Copeland (2000: 38–39, 238–40, 2015: 46–47, 435–36, 445–46), which builds on some of the insights of Stephen Walt's (1996) balance-of-threat theory

26. In my own work, I build this point in as an additional parameter that shapes the willingness of a declining state to shift to more hard-line policies (see Copeland, 2000, 38–39).

27. China has felt the sense of its inferiority since it backed away from its hard-line stance over Taiwan in the 1995–96 stand-off in the East China Sea. Its subsequent efforts to build its military power in the region can be seen as a way to create a more "equal" Chicken scenario in any future Taiwan crisis, increasing the chance that Washington will be the one to swerve.

28. See Betts (1987).

29. We can thus predict that China, as long as it is still on an upward trajectory, will be relatively cautious about pushing too hard for territorial changes in Asia, whether over its border with India or in the East and South China Seas. China's "new and improved" snapshot level of relative power does give it more incentive to defend its interests in the region, but its upward trend line gives it an incentive not to provoke a superior but relatively declining United States. It is a shift to preventive containment by a declining America that is more likely to set off a spiral to cold war or a nuclear crisis in Sino-American relations. See Copeland (2015: 436–44; 2000: 240–45).

30. Fortunately, because of China's huge population, it will always have a much smaller per capita income than the United States, even if it overtakes America in total GNP (Brooks and Wohlforth, 2015–16; Copeland 2000: 242). This means that leaders in Washington can rationally continue to allow China to "catch up" in relative power rather than having to switch to the kind of hard-line preventive containment employed against the Soviet Union after 1945. The benefits of such a switch (maintaining US dominance) would not be worth the considerable risks (a new cold war and the attending chance of another 1962-type nuclear crisis).

REFERENCES

Betts, Richard K. 1987. *Nuclear Blackmail and Nuclear Balance.* Washington, DC: Brookings.

Blair, Bruce G. 1993. *The Logic of Accidental Nuclear War.* Washington, DC: Brookings.

Booth, Ken, and Nicholas J. Wheeler. 2008. *The Security Dilemma: Fear, Cooperation, and Trust in World Politics.* New York: Palgrave.

Brooks, Stephen G., and William C. Wohlforth. 2015–16. "The Rise and Fall of the Great Powers of the Twenty First Century: China's Rise and the Fate of Americas Global Position." *International Security* 40(3): 7–53.

Copeland, Dale. 1996. "Neorealism and the Myth of Bipolar Stability: Toward a Dynamic Realist Theory of Major War." *Security Studies* 5 (3): 29–89.

Copeland, Dale. 2000. *The Origins of Major War.* Ithaca, NY: Cornell University Press.

Copeland, Dale. 2015. *Economic Interdependence and War.* Princeton, NJ: Princeton University Press.

Fearon, James D. 1992. "Threats to Use Force." PhD dissertation, Department of Political Science, University of California, Berkeley.

Fearon, James D. 1995. "Rationalist Explanations for War." *International Organization* 49(3): 577–92.

Frei, Daniel. 1983. *Risks of Unintentional Nuclear War.* New York: UN Institute for Disarmament Research.

George, Alexander L. (ed.). 1991. *Avoiding War: Problems of Crisis Management.* Boulder, CO: Westview.

Gilpin, Robert. 1981. *War and Change in World Politics.* Cambridge: Cambridge University Press.

Glaser, Charles. 1997. "The Security Dilemma Revisited." *World Politics* 50(1): 171–201.

Glaser, Charles. 2010. *Rationalist Theory of International Politics.* Princeton, NJ: Princeton University Press.

Goemans, H. E. 2000. *War and Punishment: The Causes of War Termination and the First World War.* Princeton, NJ: Princeton University Press.

Gulick, Edward V. 1962. *Europe's Classical Balance of Power.* New York: Norton.

Jervis, Robert. 1976. *Perception and Misperception in International Politics.* Princeton, NJ: Princeton University Press.

Jervis, Robert. 1978. "Cooperation under the Security Dilemma." *World Politics* 30(2): 167–214.

Jervis, Robert. 1989. *The Meaning* of *the Nuclear Revolution.* Ithaca, NJ: Cornell University Press.

Kugler, Jacek, and A. F. K. Organski. 1989. "The Power Transition: A Retrospective and Prospective Evaluation." In

Manus I. Midlarksy (ed.), *Handbook of War Studies*. Boston, MA: Unwin Hyman.

Kydd, Andrew. 2005. *Trust and Mistrust in International Politics*. Princeton, NJ: Princeton University Press.

Levy, Jack S. 1987. "Declining Power and the Preventive Motivation for War." *World Politics* 40(1): 82–107.

Levy, Jack S. 2008. "Preventive War and Democratic Politics." *International Studies Quarterly* 52(1): 1–24.

Lobell, Steven E., Norrin M. Ripsman, and Jeffrey W. Taliaferro (eds.). 2009. *Neoclassical Realism, the State, and Foreign Policy*. Cambridge: Cambridge University Press.

Mearsheimer, John. J. 2001. *The Tragedy of Great Power Politics*. New York: Norton.

Morgenthau, Hans J. 1978. *Politics Among Nations*, 5th rev. ed. New York: Alfred A. Knopf.

Organski, A. F. K., and Jacek Kugler. 1980. *The War Ledger*. Chicago: University of Chicago Press.

Powell, Robert. 1990. *Nuclear Deterrence Theory*. Cambridge: Cambridge University Press.

Powell, Robert. 2002. "Bargaining Theory and International Conflict." *Annual Review of Political Science* 5(1): 1–30.

Powell, Robert. 2006. "War as a Commitment Problem." *International Organization* 60(1): 169–203.

Ramsay, Kristopher W. 2004. "Politics at the Water's Edge: Crisis Bargaining and Electoral Competition." *Journal of Conflict Resolution* 48(3): 459–86.

Reiter, Dan. 2003. "Exploring the Bargaining Model of War." *Perspectives on Politics* 1(1): 27–43.

Reiter, Dan. 2009. *How Wars End*. Princeton, NJ: Princeton University Press.

Ripsman, Norrin M., Jeffrey W. Taliaferro, and Steven E. Lobell. 2016. *Neoclassical Realist Theory of International Politics*. Oxford: Oxford University Press.

Schelling, Thomas C. 1966. *Arms and Influence*. New Haven, CT: Yale University Press.

Schultz, Kenneth. 2001. *Democracy and Coercive Diplomacy*. Cambridge: Cambridge University Press.

Sechser, Todd S., and Matthew Fuhrmann. 2017. *Nuclear Weapons and Coercion*. Cambridge: Cambridge University Press.

Slantchev, Branislav. 2013. *Military Threats: The Cost of Coercion and the Price of Peace*. Cambridge: Cambridge University Press.

Snyder, Glenn, and Paul Diesing. 1977. *Conflict Among Nations*. Princeton, NJ: Princeton University Press.

Tammen, Ronald, et al. 2000. *Power Transitions: Strategies for the 21st Century*. New York: Chatham House.

Van Evera, Stephen. 1999. *Causes of War: Power and the Roots of Conflict*. Ithaca, NY: Cornell University Press.

Wagner, R. Harrison. 2007. *War and the State*. Ann Arbor: University of Michigan Press.

Walt, Stephen M. 1996. *Revolution and War*. Ithaca, NY: Cornell University Press.

Waltz, Kenneth. 1979. *Theory of International Politics*. New York: Random House.

Waltz, Kenneth. 1989. "The Origins of War in Neorealist Theory." In Robert I. Rotberg and Theodore K. Rabb (eds.), *The Origins and Prevention of Major War*. Cambridge: Cambridge University Press.

Weisiger, Alex. 2013. *Logics of War: Explanations for Limited and Unlimited Conflicts*. Ithaca, NY: Cornell University Press.

Technological Change and International Relations

DANIEL W. DREZNER

Technology's relationship with international relations in 2019 would appear to be transformative. Innovation has had salutary economic effects, increasing labor productivity and reducing extreme poverty across the globe. At the same time, new technologies have also created new threats. The destructive power of modern militaries would dwarf those of a century ago. Innovation also generates societal churn; anxiety about these changes has midwifed movements ranging from the Islamic State to #MeToo. Some technologies have led to radical shifts in the distribution of power among states, as countries like China and India have played catch-up to the advanced industrialized economies. The relationship between states and non-state actors has also been transformed, as anyone familiar with WikiLeaks or Facebook would acknowledge. A more interconnected world has also highlighted vulnerabilities in the system, including exposure to pandemics such as Ebola. The speed of cross-border interactions has made diplomacy-by-tweet a thing. Despite a surge in protectionism from the G-20 economies, globalization continues apace. Technological change continues to lower the costs of cross-border exchange faster than governments can raise barriers.

As we mark the centenary of the academic study of International Relations in this issue, however, it is worth noting that almost every political effect of technology described in the previous paragraph would

Daniel W. Drezner, "Technological Change and International Relations," *International Relations* 33, no. 2 (March 2019): 286–303. Copyright © 2019 by SAGE; reprinted by Permission of SAGE Publications, Ltd.; permission conveyed through Copyright Clearance Center, Inc.

have applied with equal force in 1919. The First World War had just proven the awesome destructive capabilities of the machine gun and chemical weapons. A critical cause of that war was Germany's ability to catch up technologically to Great Britain, and German concerns with Russia's imminent catch-up. Non-state actors like the Suffragette movement, Second International, and Red Cross exploited new technologies to build transnational movements. Lowered transportation costs gave rise to the Spanish flu, the most deadly pandemic of the twentieth century. August 1914 was characterized by a flurry of rapid diplomatic and military signaling following the June assassination of Archduke Ferdinand. And in the run-up to the First World War, most European governments had raised tariffs in an effort to reduce economic interdependence. That did not stop trade from increasing; the spread of railroads and steamships overwhelmed protectionist barriers.[1] Perhaps the relationship between technological change and international relations might not be as transformative as technology enthusiasts believe.

Much IR scholarship treats technology as an exogenous shock, an independent variable that affects the contours of world politics through shifts in the distribution of military or economic power. There are two significant problems with this assumption, however. First, the causal arrow can also run in the other direction. Changes in the international system can also have pronounced effects on the pace of technological change. Second, not all kinds of technological change are created equal. Indeed, the development of nuclear weapons and the internet has had wildly different effects on the international system.

This article reflects on the role of technology has played in the last century of international relations. The economics of technological change are overwhelmingly positive, which can lull social scientists into a straightforward rationalist account of how great powers think about it. The international politics are far more fraught. Any technological change is also an exercise in redistribution. It can create new winners and losers, alter actor preferences, and allow the strategic construction of new norms. The nature of the technology itself, and the degree to which the public sector drives innovation, generates differential effects on international relations. To examine these dynamics, special emphasis is placed on two important innovations of the last century for international relations: nuclear weapons and the internet.

Rationalist Accounts of Technological Change . . . and Their Discontents

The salience of technology to world politics is often reduced to the simple equation that for sovereign actors, more technological innovation equals more power and plenty. Economists stress the unique importance of technological change to economic growth. Most econometric studies find that technological innovation is responsible for anywhere between 60 and 85 percent of economic growth in the developed world.[2] The diffusion of technology to less advanced economies is equally important. According to one recent literature review, foreign sources of technology are responsible for approximately 90 percent of productivity growth in most countries.[3] Regardless of where countries lie on the distribution of power or economic development, their primary engine of economic growth comes through technology. And it is through economic growth that states can convert plenty into power.

Because of technology's manifest salience to maximizing wealth and security, many scholars adopt a rationalist take on how actors will promote innovation. This is most evident in the economics literature, which focuses on domestic economic variables to explain the variation in technological innovation. Factors such as the availability and sophistication of capital markets, size of the market, or allocation of entrepreneurial ability are considered to be the causal drivers. This is true even when economists consider the role of states. The economic historian David Landes, in explaining why China did not maintain its technological edge over Europe, argued "China lacked a free market and institutionalized property rights" and that "the Chinese state was always stepping in to interfere with private enterprise."[4]

Politics plays a minor role in these narratives. In part, this is because economists often view noneconomic factors as epiphenomenal in their causal stories. For example, Gregory Clark has argued that institutions are unimportant in determining the pace of technological innovation. Eventually, once a state hits upon the correct institutional formula for promoting innovation, that institutional form will be adopted by all governments interested in promoting economic growth.[5] Clark's assumption is that once the correct institutions are seized upon, other actors will effortlessly switch to them.

Neorealists offer a causal logic that echoes economists. To them, the anarchy of the international system forces all great powers to exploit technological change or suffer the risk of not surviving. Kenneth Waltz and his acolytes posit that the self-help nature of the international system requires states to adapt to new technologies or face threats to their survival as they lag behind other states in relative capabilities.[6] For neorealists, the equation is simple: anarchy forces the rapid diffusion of technology across the world. Emily Goldman notes that "most neorealists posit few barriers to diffusion, short of the need for adequate resources and information."[7] Both neorealists and neoclassical economists agree that the incentives to acquire new technologies dominate all other factors.

This is not how most political scientists think about institutional change. There are several problems with frictionless theories of technological innovation and diffusion. The most obvious is that they ignore the ways that international relations is an independent variable affecting the pace of technological innovation. Consider, for example, Joseph Schumpeter's five canonical categories of innovation: invention, innovation in production processes, finding new markets, discovering new sources of supply, and developing new modes of economic organization.[8] They are only partially about technology itself; they are also about how societies respond to new opportunities presented by technological change. Three of Schumpeter's category of innovations are mediated through international relations to some degree.

Some economic historians acknowledge the role of international relations as an independent variable affecting the pace of innovation. They reference the distribution of power to explain why the Industrial Revolution originated in Europe rather than China. Both economic and military historians cite the anarchical politics of post-Westphalian Europe as a key permissive condition, in contrast to China's regional hegemony in East Asia. Joel Mokyr noted:

> The West was politically fragmented between more or less autonomous units that competed for survival, wealth, and power. . . . The struggle for survival guaranteed that in the long run rulers could not afford to be hostile to changes that increased the economic power of the realm because of the real danger that an innovation or innovator would emigrate to benefit a rival.

Paul Kennedy similarly observed, "The warlike rivalries among [Western Europe's] various kingdoms and city-states stimulated a constant search for military improvements."[9]

The inference to draw is that there is a "sweet spot" among the possible distributions of power that incentivizes states to invest in technological innovation. According to this logic, unipolarity depresses the rate of technological innovation. The hegemon feels so secure that it has little incentive to invest in disruptive innovations. Other states see the gap between themselves and the hegemon as too great to be overcome, blunting efforts to innovate. Similarly, a distribution consisting only of small states facing the threat of extinction would be too focused on the short term to bother with technological investments that pay out in the far future. Multipolarity, on the other hand, would generate the right mix of security and insecurity to spur more rapid innovations.

This is the logic that multiple scholars have used to explain why the Industrial Revolution originated in Great Britain.[10] Because it was an island, the country possessed a greater degree of security than the continental European states. At the same time, Great Britain was a part of the European state system. To maintain its relative position, it had an incentive to invest in science and technology as well.

Other IR approaches privilege the domestic politics of leaders and laggards as the key explanatory variable. Both long-cycle and power-transition theorists stress the domestic conditions of an aspiring hegemonic power as determining its relative rise. Countries acquire hegemonic status because they create fertile conditions to develop a cluster of technologies in leading sectors. Acemoglu and Robinson, for example, argue that innovation is more likely to occur in governments with inclusive selectorates. More authoritarian governments are warier of innovations that could upset the domestic status quo. This is why, for example, Tsarist Russia proved to be a reluctant adopter during the Industrial Revolution. More open polities, such as Great Britain and the United States, emerged as technological hegemons.[11]

Radical innovations in one sector generate spillover effects for the entire lead economy. This, in turn, leads to diffusion of growth and technological change across the global economy. Over time, however, these "technological hegemons" fail to maintain the rate of innovations, a phenomenon that Joel Mokyr labeled Cardwell's Law: "no nation has been (technologically) very creative for more than a historically short period."[12]

The reasons proffered for stagnation within the hegemonic actor are often political in nature. The most prominent political economy argument is that innovation represents a threat to those with a vested interest in the status quo. Schumpeter's aphorism about "creative destruction" is commonly understood today as meaning that the value added of new technologies dramatically outweighs the costs. This does not change the fact that innovation can also lead to massive redistributions of wealth. Those who stand to lose have an incentive to lobby the state to prevent relative losses. For Mancur Olson, the paradox of political stability leads to an accrual of rent-seeking that blunts technological dynamism. For Robert Gilpin, the domestic politics of a complacent hegemon lent itself to promote consumption rather than investment in the necessary public goods for innovation. For Paul Kennedy, hegemons suffered the wages of "imperial overstretch," diverting scarce capital from needed investments in technology. For Daron Acemoglu, the technological leader has to play the thankless role of "cutthroat capitalist" to promote innovation, which in turn subsidizes the more generous social safety nets of supporter states.[13] Eventually, the cost of this public goods provision ceases to be politically popular in the hegemonic state.

These explanations are not mutually exclusive, but they lead to the same outcome: a period of technological catch-up for challengers to the hegemon. Indeed, according to some economists, technologically backward countries have an advantage in catching up, as they can exploit their relative backwardness to leapfrog over technological dead-ends.[14] This period of stagnation and catch-up also triggers a period of geopolitical strife until a new hegemon emerges.[15]

The long-cycle and diffusion literatures have different causal mechanisms than the decentralization argument. Mark Z. Taylor is likely correct when he argues that a synthesis of the two is most apt: "countries for which external threats are relatively greater than domestic tensions should have higher national innovation rates than countries for which domestic tensions outweigh external threats."[16]

These explanations for how international politics can drive technological change are essentially rationalist in nature. Other research, however, suggests that the role of prestige has been neglected as an explanatory factor in driving large-scale investments in science and technology.[17] Prestige is a positional good; one only benefits from it by outperforming other actors in a designated social setting. Historically, many of the social settings designated as the most important have been in the field of science and technology. This can lead actors to direct investments in technology projects that might have limited military or economic value but generate great prestige.

The most obvious example from the past century of prestige investments in technology would be the massive sums allocated for manned space programs by the Cold War superpowers. The USSR's 1957 launch of Sputnik and 1961 manned orbit of Earth had a pronounced effect on the United States and its prestige. These acts caused policy-makers to worry that the United States was falling behind the Soviet Union in science and technology. Equally important, policy-makers were concerned about the perception that the United States was falling behind. In October 1961, the US Information Agency commissioned surveys of European audiences on this question, and they found a strong majority of Europeans believed the USSR to be winning the space race. Washington expended considerable resources to catch up and overtake the Soviet Union. According to one estimate the US Apollo program accounted for 2.2 percent of all federal government spending at its peak, more than twice the level of the Manhattan Project.[18]

These kinds of prestige-based investments in science and technology continue to affect twenty-first-century investments in research and development. China's first

manned space flight in 2003 triggered frenzied reactions from peer competitors, including a pledge by the United States to return to the moon and send a manned mission to Mars. Other countries with significant budget constraints nonetheless signaled interest in investing in outer space research. China's landing of a probe on the dark side of the moon in January 2019 generated similar responses.

The rationalist story of why states invest in technological innovation makes intuitive sense. But such a narrative is at best incomplete and at worst an incorrect description of how international politics affects technological change. The distribution of power, the nature of domestic institutions in leading economies, and the allure of prestige goods all drive innovation in ways different from the strictly rationalist account.

Varieties of Technological Change in World Politics

Talking about technological change in the abstract runs the risk of treating all innovations similarly. Whether one uses an economic or military lens of evaluation, not all technologies are created equal. Even though military necessity was a driver of both inventions, for example, nuclear weapons have had very different effects on world politics than the internet.

There are two criteria that help to parse how to think about the effect of different technologies on world politics. The first is the magnitude of fixed-cost investments necessary to develop or adopt a new innovation. Most inventions require significant fixed costs, but as a technology becomes more standardized, the investments necessary to develop them can decline.

That said, some technologies, even after standardization, still require considerable investments. This may be because the economic costs of production are high. In other cases, the disruptive effects of an innovation on political organizations or societal institutions are significant enough to make the costs of adaptation equally high. For example, the French navy pioneered several key technologies in the latter half of the nineteenth century, including shell guns and steel-hulled warships. Because it was unable to incorporate the organizational implications of those innovations, however, France found itself overtaken by other navies in the adoption of these technologies.[19]

The larger the fixed costs for acquiring innovations, the greater the barriers to entry for any actor attempting to acquire a new technology. The lower the fixed-cost investments, the greater the number of expected actors who will be able to develop and consume the technology in question.

The other dimension is whether the primary innovator of a new technology caters to the public sector or the private sector. Most significant innovations qualify

Table 1. A Typology of Technological Innovations

	Public-sector dominance	Private-sector dominance
High fixed costs	Prestige tech	Strategic tech
Low fixed costs	Public tech	General purpose tech

as "general purpose" technologies that both the security and civilian sectors can exploit. Some technological innovations, however, have limited civilian applications. Nuclear fission, for example, proved extremely useful for military technology. As a source of civilian energy, however, its profitability is circumscribed, particularly during periods of low hydrocarbon prices. The principal sources of innovation in nuclear technology have come from the state sector. The internet is a different story. While originally developed due to ample amounts of government funding, the data flows from its commercial applications have far outstripped its official purposes. Most online innovation has come from the private sector.

This creates a simple 2 × 2 of the different kinds of technological innovations (see figure 1).[20] Those inventions that have high fixed costs but significant civilian applications are strategic tech. Technologies with large fixed costs possess increasing-returns dynamics. This invites considerable amounts of great-power intervention to promote national champions and avoid dependence on foreign technologies, akin to strategic trade theory. The civilian aircraft sector fits nicely within this quadrant, as does the current development of 5G networks.

Technologies that have large fixed costs and limited civilian applications fall under the prestige tech category. Only states have the incentive to develop these technologies. Some of these technologies, such as nuclear weapons, provide obvious utility to governments. All of the technologies in this box, however, function as prestige goods because of their cost. Supersonic transport planes like the Concorde would also fall squarely into this category, as would manned space exploration.

Technologies with low fixed costs but limited private-sector opportunities would be considered public tech. This label is apt because if the barriers to entry are low but private-sector interest is minimal, then the innovation is likely to possess strong public goods qualities. The private sector has less of an incentive to develop technologies that are both nonrival and nonexcludable.[21] If the technology offers considerable social benefits, however, then one could envision governments having an incentive to make the necessary investments. Public health innovations, like vaccines, would fall under this category.

Finally, those innovations with lower fixed costs and significant private-sector possibilities fall under the category of general purpose tech. These goods may have been developed with public-sector purposes in mind, but the commercial applications are so manifest that private-sector activity drives the direction of the technology. The most obvious current example of this kind of technology is the diffusion of drones—although the development of artificial intelligence could eventually fall under this category as well.[22]

This typology is useful in considering how quickly certain technologies will diffuse from invention to standardization, and how great powers are likely to react to new innovations that can affect world politics. The more that a technology approaches the general purpose category, the more quickly it will diffuse across the globe. The lower the fixed costs—whether material, organizational, or societal in nature—the more rapidly a technology should diffuse from leader to laggards. Therefore, general purpose tech should diffuse the quickest, whereas prestige tech should have the most limited degree of proliferation.

Public policy also plays a critical role in determining the degree of diffusion. States have multiple domestic and international incentives to regulate the diffusion of new innovations. Governments on the technological frontier will be more likely to advocate for strong intellectual property rights. In theory, this should incentivize further innovations. The knock-on effect of such a policy is to limit the diffusion of technology across borders.[23] Similarly, governments are also likely to restrict access to technologies that have significant effects on military capabilities. This applies to nuclear weapons; there is an entire regime complex devoted to limiting the proliferation of that technology.

How Technology Affects International Relations

The rest of this article will focus on two prominent technologies of the past century: nuclear weapons and the internet. This is not because they are typical, but rather because they represent most-different forms of technological change. Nuclear weapons qualify as prestige tech, while internet applications primarily fall within general purpose tech. Exploring the effects of these two significant innovations on different dimensions of international relations theory should offer some fruitful reflections.

There are a limited number of components to international relations theory. Different theories stress different elements, but paradigms ranging from realism to poststructuralism have to cope with concepts like power, interest, and norms. Technological change has affected each of these dimensions of world politics. This section considers how the innovation of nuclear weapons and the internet have altered perceptions of each of these concepts.

Power

Nuclear weapons have existed since 1945, but as a form of prestige tech their diffusion has been restricted to fewer than ten actors. Despite this limited diffusion, international relations theorists have concluded that their development has had system-transforming effects. Thomas Schelling noted in the mid-1960s, "Our era is epitomized by words like 'the first time in human history' and by the abdication of what was 'permanent.' "[24] Once all the great powers became nuclear-armed nations, a large strain of international relations scholarship was dedicated to thinking about how nuclear weapons altered the dynamics of world politics.

This is most pronounced within the realist paradigm. Kenneth Waltz's structural realism was predicated on the notion that the structure of anarchy has been a constant in global affairs for centuries. Nonetheless, as the Cold War was ending, he concluded in multiple articles that nuclear weapons had altered the nature of the international system:

> Never since the Treaty of Westphalia in 1648, which conventionally marks the beginning of modern history, have great powers enjoyed a longer period of peace than we have known since the Second World War. One can scarcely believe that the presence of nuclear weapons does not greatly help to explain this happy condition.[25]

How did nuclear weapons affect international politics so profoundly? This innovation transformed power politics by disconnecting the power to destroy with other capabilities previously thought to be necessary for great-power status. Once a country possesses a perceived second-strike capability—either through hardened defenses or uncertainty about the location of their nuclear stockpiles—they possess the power to deter. There is no correlation, however, between nuclear deterrence and conventional measures of military power. As Waltz notes, "Nuclear weapons purify deterrent strategies by removing elements of defense and warfighting." Schelling is even more stark on this point: "Nuclear weapons make it possible to do monstrous violence to the enemy without first achieving victory."[26] At the same time, because nuclear weapons accomplish nothing but destruction, their utility in other arenas of world politics is limited. The power of nuclear weapons is not terribly fungible, even when compared with other dimensions of military power.

A paradoxical effect of the development of nuclear weapons is that it disconnects measurements of state power from other areas of technological innovation. Although the barriers to entry in the nuclear club are high, technologically backward states have been able to surmount it. Maoist China became a nuclear-capable state when it was one of the poorest countries on Earth. Neither a fractious Pakistan nor an autarkic North Korea were thought to be on the technological frontier, and yet these countries were able to develop nuclear warheads and the ballistic missile technology necessary to deliver these weapons. Once a state possesses nuclear weapons, however, it is afforded a different place in the power hierarchy than otherwise would be the case. This is true even in instances in which a state lags behind in other areas. As Waltz notes, "So long as a country can retaliate after being struck, or appears to be able to do so, its nuclear forces cannot be made obsolete by an adversary's technological advances."[27] This explains how Russia is viewed as one of the great powers in the twenty-first century despite controlling less than 4 percent of the global economy. This is why Iran and North Korea have occupied so much great-power attention for the last few decades.

While nuclear warheads are prestige tech, the internet and its myriad applications are general purpose tech. The commercialization of cyberspace generated two initial strands of scholarly thought about its effect on power. The first was that the internet altered the balance of power between states and non-state actors. In terms of communication speed, the internet was not much faster than the telegraph. What made the internet different was its low cost and resultant ease of access. Cyberspace's low barriers to entry dramatically lowered the transaction costs of non-state actors to organize. Furthermore, the internet's creators viewed state efforts to disrupt or prevent online activism with profound skepticism. The decentralized architecture of the internet ostensibly made it impossible for states to regulate. John Perry Barlow famously told *Time* magazine in 1993, "The Net interprets censorship as damage and routes around it." The use of social media and other online applications in color revolutions and the Arab Spring lent credence to this argument.

The second strand of thought was that the internet empowered liberal democracies over other regime types in world politics. Cyberspace originated with the United States and appeared to prize openness. It was viewed as enhancing all facets of America's soft power. The explosion of content in cyberspace demonstrated the vibrancy of American culture, as well as the US commitment to liberal values of open discourse. Its development was also a credit to prior US policies and would also augment American soft power.[28] Cyberspace's norm of openness also made it logical that democracies would benefit the most. Helen Milner argued that the nature of a country's democratic institutions determined how quickly it adopted online technologies. Writing in 2006, she concluded that democracies were far more likely to facilitate the spread of online tech than authoritarian regimes.[29]

Recent scholarship and recent events offer a more muddled picture. States learned how to be able to regulate the internet to serve their national interest with relative rapidity. On issues ranging from content regulation to copyright to privacy, great-power governments were able to get their way in cyberspace.[30] Domestically, authoritarian regimes moved quickly down the learning curve in permitting internet access while still being able to regulate the flow of information.[31] Initial scholarship underestimated the ways in which top-down bureaucracies could harness online data to exercise greater control over civil society. These actions have not eliminated the ability of non-state actors to influence world politics. But greater state capacity has likely redirected where non-state actors have had their greatest influence. WikiLeaks, for example, has focused its energies on Western democracies far more than authoritarian great powers such as Russia or China.

Furthermore, in recent years, authoritarian states have become more adept at exploiting online technologies to attack liberal democracies. North Korea responded to the release of a film satirizing Kim Jong Un by hacking into Sony Pictures and publishing embarrassing emails from its executives. The fallout cost Sony tens of millions of dollars. China exploited its cyber-capabilities to steal billions in intellectual property from the Western democracies. Russia's use of troll farms, sophisticated hacking, and disinformation campaigns to influence elections in the West is well known. Over time, revisionist actors have become adept at using these techniques to counteract the soft power of the West.

The prestige tech of nuclear weapons augmented the power of those actors who developed them, widening power inequalities between nuclear-armed states and nonnuclear states. The general purpose tech of cyberspace initially benefited liberal democratic actors more than others. Over time, however, its diffusion and exploitation by revisionist actors had a leveling effect on the balance of power.

Interests

An ongoing scholarly debate is whether actors view the international system as a zero-sum or non-zero-sum game. This difference in preferences is at the root of differences between realist and liberal theories of international politics. How states reacted to the development of nuclear and online technologies offer a useful guide into how technologies can alter or reveal changes in state preferences.

What is striking about the effect of nuclear weapons on world politics is that it falsified the notion that world politics was a zero-sum enterprise. Scholars of the nuclear age agree that the United States held an overwhelming superiority in nuclear weapons in their first decade of existence. The United States had demonstrated no compunction about using atomic weapons to hasten the end of the Second World War. If, as realists claim, world politics is a strictly zero-sum game, then the United States should have used its weapons in the 1950s to launch a preemptive strike against the Soviet Union. Given its advantages in the arms race at that time, Washington would have secured itself a relative advantage in any ensuing conflict. At a minimum, it should have been willing to use its nuclear stockpile to secure victory in the Korean War.

Of course, the use of nuclear weapons in the 1950s is a non-event. While the United States had internal debates about deploying atomic weapons in the Korean War, in the end policy-makers ruled out any first use.[32] The question of a preemptive strike on the Soviet Union was barely discussed. President Dwight D. Eisenhower recognized that nuclear preemption was a viable option. In his diary, however, he rejected the notion as contravening US traditions and procedures.[33]

It is also striking to see how the emergence of nuclear weapons triggered a surprisingly strong regime complex devoted to arms control and nonproliferation. Beginning with the 1963 Limited Nuclear Test Ban Treaty, the United States and Russia agreed to a welter of arms control agreements limiting their nuclear stockpiles by warhead yield, type of delivery vehicle, and related systems. The rest of the world agreed to the Nuclear Non-Proliferation Treaty (NPT) in 1970, and then permanently extended it in 1995. The International Atomic Energy Agency was created to enforce the NPT. In recent decades, an array of supporting and reinforcing agreements, including the Proliferation Security Initiative and the Nuclear Safety Summits, has also emerged. This kind of regime complex does not resemble the zero-sum description that is often ascribed to security issues. It would appear that the destructive power of nuclear weapons triggered higher levels of international cooperation than would otherwise have been expected. Indeed, the regime complex for nuclear weapons is far more robust than the one for conventional weaponry.

As general purpose tech, the internet was expected to jumpstart increases in labor productivity and economic growth. It would therefore be unsurprising to expect a more cooperative, non-zero-sum approach to its regulation. Intriguingly, this has not been the case. A quick survey of negotiations over different aspects of Internet regulation shows that national preferences and bargaining cleavages mirrored offline policy disputes.[34] The United States and the European Union have consistently been at loggerheads over questions of competition policy and privacy rights. As China and Russia have embraced the authoritarian uses of online activity, debates over internet governance have become far more contentious.

There are several possible explanations for this failure of online innovations to alter national preferences significantly. Since cyberspace's effect is as much on state-society relations as interstate relations, national governments prioritize domestic political considerations in the articulation of policy preferences. While all states are interested in the commercial opportunities afforded by online commerce, the past two decades demonstrate that national and internal security considerations will have priority. It is therefore unsurprising that issues like content regulation have no international agreement.

Another possible explanation is that the internet's anticipated productivity boom has not come to pass. The one economic trend associated with the development of online technologies has been the emergence of natural monopolies. Firms like Facebook, Google, and Weibo profit from considerable network externalities, achieving dominance in their particular fields. The cumulative macroeconomic effect of this kind of corporate concentration is to drag down economic growth.[35] To date, the actual effects of the internet on economic growth in the developed world have been far less than advertised.[36]

The effect of both prestige tech and general purpose tech on actor interests in world politics is indeterminate. The destructive power of nuclear weapons led to more cooperation than a zero-sum set of preferences would have predicted. Cooperation on nuclear weapons is a data point for liberals, demonstrating that complex interdependence can lead to cooperation in unlikely areas.[37] At the same time, the positive-sum nature of online innovation has not necessarily led to more cooperation in cyberspace. Conflict in cyberspace is a data point for realists, suggesting that greater interdependence breeds greater conflict.[38]

Norms

Technology has been hypothesized to have a direct effect on the spread of norms in the international system. In discussing the phenomenon of norm cascades, Martha Finnemore and Kathryn Sikkink explicitly tied the pace and scope of norm acceptance to technological change:

> Changes in communication and transportation technologies and increasing global interdependence have led to increased connectedness and, in a way, are leading to the homogenization of global norms. . . . The speed of normative change has accelerated substantially in the later part of the twentieth century.[39]

This hypothesis would seem to hold with even greater force in the twenty-first century. Norms regarding violence against women and gay marriage, for example, spread more quickly than similar twentieth-century norms.

Technological innovation has certainly facilitated the spread of norms. A more complex question is the role that norms play in the promulgation and use of new technologies. Almost by definition, new technologies emerge in environments that lack indigenous norms. The effect of a new technology on the social world is inherently uncertain. This uncertainty can make it difficult to envision which norms, rules, and codes of conduct are appropriate. New innovations might try to copy norms and practices from adjacent technologies, but whether those norms will apply with equal force to a new technological arena is an open question. Attempting to analogize old norms to new areas can lead to significant misperceptions.[40] As Finnemore and Sikkink noted, the promulgation of new norms is a strategic act.

This dynamic has been on display in the evolution of norms regarding nuclear weapons and cyberspace. Initially, the invention of the atomic bomb did not alter US military doctrine. Indeed, its use in August 1945 demonstrates that U.S. decision-makers did not view these weapons differently from other forms of ordinance. As Nina Tannenwald notes, "The atomic bombings were simply an extension of strategic bombing during a war that had substantially elevated the scale of destruction, flattening great cities in Europe and Japan."[41]

As the destructive power of these weapons became manifestly clear, however, a "nuclear taboo" emerged against the first use of these weapons.[42] This was materially harmful to the United States. In the 1950s, there were internal policy debates about using nuclear forces in the Korean War. More generally, the Soviet Union's conventional military superiority in Central Europe necessitated a US doctrine of first-use in case of a Warsaw Pact attack on North Atlantic Treaty Organization (NATO) forces.

The Eisenhower administration engaged in vigorous rhetorical efforts to make nuclear threats normatively acceptable in world politics. US officials found themselves on the losing side of the argument, even though there is suggestive evidence that nuclear threats are effective in international relations.[43] Beginning with the United Nations construction of the "weapons of mass destruction" category, this technology was perceived as being radically different from other forms of ordinance. This was true even though conventional strategic bombing had incurred a much greater loss of life in the Second World War. A welter of non-state actors pushed the taboo rhetoric, aided by a Soviet Union that at the time was disadvantaged in the nuclear arms race. Continued innovations in nuclear weapons technology only reinforced the taboo. As their theoretical destructive power increased, the use of these weapons became less and less conceivable. By the end of Eisenhower's second term, he acknowledged that "the new thermonuclear weapons are tremendously powerful; however, they are not . . . as powerful as is world opinion today in obliging the United States to follow certain lines of policy."[44]

By the end of the Cold War, the taboo had been internalized by all the great powers. As Tannenwald notes, "The taboo was no longer simply a 'constraint' but had itself become a foreign policy goal for a 'civilized' state."[45] This can be seen in debates about the use of low-yield tactical nuclear weapons. Even though these weapons could have been viewed as being useful during armed conflicts like the gulf wars, their actual use was eventually ruled out.[46]

Norms are not set in stone, and recent research has focused on the myriad tactics and strategies that can be deployed to alter or constrain a particular norm.[47] This parallels efforts by the two largest nuclear states to gain some degree of tactical flexibility within the nuclear taboo. This century has seen the end of the ABM and INF treaties, weakening the overall arms control regime. Russia has recently altered its nuclear doctrine to lower the threshold for the use of low-yield weapons. In response, the United States has also changed its doctrine to "enhance the flexibility and range of its tailored deterrence options . . . for the preservation of credible deterrence against regional aggression."[48] Whether this shift in doctrine leads to a shift in norms is unclear. Nonetheless, nuclear weapons are unique as a technology that defines great-power relations even though they have not been used in more than 70 years.

As with nuclear weapons, the norms environment surrounding cyberspace has evolved over time. On governance issues, for example, the initial debates surrounding how to run the internet echoed the norm of multistakeholderism, familiar to academic researchers that created the architecture of cyberspace.[49] By the late 1990s, what emerged was a multi-stakeholder model built on public-private partnerships. As Jeffrey Lantis and Daniel Bloomberg characterized it, "The goal was to establish a decentralized network for cyberspace that would be 'democratic' and treat the views of major corporations, governments, civil society, and even academics as equally important to help establish standards for the Internet activity."[50]

While multistakeholderism explained the norms governing early internet governance, the norms governing cybersecurity looked very different from the outset. Security concerns about cyberspace emerged even before the internet became general purpose tech. As early as 1991, a US National Research Council study warned, "Tomorrow's terrorist may be able to do more damage with a keyboard than with a bomb."[51] From the early days of trying to theorize about cyber-

security, researchers and defense strategists imported wholesale the norms of deterrence from nuclear doctrine.[52] According to this logic, the prospect of catastrophic cyberattacks required states to communicate the likelihood of retaliation.

Over time, however, initial governance and cybersecurity norms have come under severe challenge. As the internet diffused, countries such as Russia and China began to lobby for governance norms to shift from multistakeholderism to multilateralism. To that end, they lobbied for control over internet governance to be shifted from the Internet Corporation for Assigned Names and Numbers (ICANN) to the International Telecommunications Union (ITU), a more conventional international governmental organization. This led to a series of contentious ITU conferences in Dubai and Busan in the 2010s. At these meetings, the United States and Western allies functioned as "antipreneurs," creating powerful points of resistance to changing overall internet governance.[53]

On cybersecurity, the deepening of online activity could have strengthened the deterrence norm. As the internet diffused across the globe, the developments of cloud computing, social media, and smartphones meant that more aspects of daily life became intertwined with the online world. The greater degree of interconnectedness also meant that cyberattacks had the potential to pose a greater threat to economic growth and national security.

In recent years, however, it has become clear that the deterrence analogy has numerous flaws. The scope of cyberattacks has not been even remotely as significant as those involving nuclear weapons. Empirical research into actual cyberattacks reveals minimal negative feedback on bilateral interstate relationships.[54] Furthermore, the question of attribution dominates questions about cyberattacks. Cyberspace is a complex entity involving an array of state actors and networked non-state actors. The success of groups like WikiLeaks, Anonymous, and LulzSec, with varying degrees of great-power ties, confirms that this security environment resembles espionage far more than nuclear security. As Tim Stevens notes, "The conditions pertaining in cyberspace are such that it has been difficult to transfer the procedures and techniques of Cold War deterrence to this domain."[55]

The United States, in response to the failures of deterrence, has tried a different normative approach. In 2010, the US Deputy Secretary of Defense noted that "if there are to be international norms of behavior in cyberspace, they may have to follow a different model [than nuclear arms control], such as that of public health or law enforcement."[56] Joseph Nye argues that crime is the superior analogy to Cold War images of deterrence.[57] NATO's development of the Tallinn Manual, as well as the US use of legal norms to threaten prosecution of Chinese hackers, appears to be yielding more success at the promulgation of norms than the nuclear deterrence norms.

Finally, the proliferation of social media has also altered diplomatic norms. The progenitors of the modern internet have been aware of this possibility for decades. In 1985, researchers warned that online discourse was different from other forms of communication because of its "propensity to evoke emotion in the recipient . . . and the likelihood that the recipient will then fire off a response that exacerbates the situation." The analysts concluded, "These media are quite different from any other means of communication. Many of the old rules do not apply."[58] This accurately captures the early twenty-first century, in which great-power rivals troll each other on Twitter.[59]

The evolution of norms within technologically innovative areas has varied in different area of tech. With nuclear weapons, the emergence of a strong taboo against their use suggests a standard constructivist model of norms being deepened and internalized. With cyberspace, however, the initial set of norms imported from other arenas has not worked terribly well. As a result, cyber norms continue to be in flux.

Conclusion

This article has considered how technological innovation has affected international relations and vice versa. Contrary to strictly rationalist accounts, culture and prestige also affect patterns of innovation and diffusion. Technology is not merely an independent variable in international relations theory. There are reciprocal effects.

Regardless of the kind of tech, significant innovations augment the power of the actors that harness those inventions. Whether that power advantage persists depends on the quality of the technology itself. General purpose tech has a greater leveling effect than prestige tech. Technology's effects on national interests are contradictory. The prestige tech of nuclear weapons engendered surprising levels of cooperation, while cyberspace has triggered surprising levels of conflict. Prestige tech created norms that only grew more powerful over time. General purpose tech, on the other hand, developed a far more contentious normative environment. The pace of innovation within general purpose tech might be so accelerated that norm creation and norm maintenance become more difficult.

Concerns about technology's ability to create new threats are hardly a new phenomenon. On the other hand, technologies that look uncontrollable when they first emerge, look sedate with time. In 2019, the notion of diplomacy-by-tweet seems strange; a decade from now, it might seem as quaint as diplomatic cables. It might be more accurate to say that innovation can create temporary uncertainties in world politics. Over time, human beings adapt.

NOTES

1. Kevin O'Rourke and Jeffrey Williamson, *Globalization and History* (Cambridge, MA: The MIT Press, 1999).

2. Elhanan Helpman, *The Mystery of Economic Growth* (Cambridge, MA: Harvard University Press, 2004).

3. Wolfgang Keller, "International Technology Diffusion," *Journal of Economic Literature*, 42(3), 2004, pp. 752–82.

4. David Landes, "Why Europe and the West? Why Not China?" *Journal of Economic Perspectives*, 20(3), 2006, pp. 3–22.

5. Gregory Clark, *A Farewell to Alms: A Brief Economic History of the World* (Princeton, NJ: Princeton University Press, 2007).

6. Kenneth Waltz, *Theory of International Politics* (Reading, MA: Addison-Wesley, 1979).

7. Emily Goldman, "Cultural Foundations of Military Diffusion," *Review of International Studies*, 32(1), 2006, pp. 69–91.

8. Joseph Schumpeter, *Capitalism, Socialism, and Democracy* (New York: Harper & Brothers, 1942).

9. Joel Mokyr, *The Lever of Riches: Technological Creativity and Economic Progress* (New York: Oxford University Press, 1990), p. 206; Paul Kennedy, *The Rise and Fall of the Great Powers* (New York: Vintage Press, 1987), p. 2.

10. Mokyr, *Lever of Riches*.

11. Daron Acemoglu and James Robinson, *Why Nations Fail: The Origins of Power, Prosperity, and Poverty* (New York: Broadway Business, 2013).

12. Mokyr, *Lever of Riches*, p. 207.

13. Mancur Olson, *The Rise and Decline of Nations* (New Haven, CT: Yale University Press, 1982); Robert Gilpin, *War and Change in World Politics* (New York: Cambridge University Press, 1981); Kennedy, *Rise and Fall of the Great Powers;* Daron Acemoglu, James A. Robinson, and Thierry Verdier, "Asymmetric Growth and Institutions in an Interdependent World," *Journal of Political Economy*, 125(5), 2017, pp. 1245–305.

14. Alexander Gerschenkron, *Economic Backwardness in Historical Perspective* (Cambridge, MA: Belknap Press, 1962); Mark Z. Taylor, "Toward an International Relations Theory of National Innovation Rates," *Security Studies*, 21(1), 2012, pp. 113–52.

15. Daniel W. Drezner, "State Structure, Technological Leadership and the Maintenance of Hegemony," *Review of International Studies*, 27(1), 2001, pp. 3–25.

16. Taylor, "Toward an International Relations Theory."

17. Lilach Gilady, *The Price of Prestige: Conspicuous Consumption in International Relations* (Chicago, IL: University of Chicago Press, 2018).

18. Paul Musgrave and Daniel Nexon, "Defending Hierarchy from the Moon to the Indian Ocean: Symbolic Capital and Political Dominance in Early Modern China and the Cold War," *International Organization*, 72(3), 2018, pp. 591–626.

19. Michael Horowitz, *The Diffusion of Military Power* (Princeton, NJ: Princeton University Press, 2010).

20. See also Horowitz, *The Diffusion of Military Power*, p. 33.

21. Olson, *Rise and Decline of Nations*. One possibility is if firms bundle innovations with public goods qualities with products that do confer excludable benefits to them. Both web

browsers and social media sites would fall under this category, in which network externality effects are far more powerful than the free-riding effects from traditional public goods.

22. On drones, see Sarah Kreps, *Drones: What Everyone Needs to Know* (New York: Oxford University Press, 2016); on AI, see Michael Horowitz, "Artificial Intelligence, International Competition, and the Balance of Power," *Texas National Security Review*, 1(3), 2018, pp. 37–57.

23. Susan Sell, *Power and Ideas* (Albany, NY: SUNY Press, 1998).

24. Thomas Schelling, *Arms and Influence* (New Haven, CT: Yale University Press, 1966), p. 18.

25. Kenneth Waltz, "Nuclear Myths and Political Realities," *American Political Science Review*, 84(3), 1990, pp. 731–45.

26. Waltz, "Nuclear Myths and Political Realities," p. 732; Schelling, *Arms and Influence*, p. 18.

27. Kenneth Waltz, "The Emerging Structure of International Politics," *International Security*, 18(2), 1993, pp. 44–79.

28. Joseph Nye, *The Future of Power* (New York: PublicAffairs, 2011).

29. Daniel W. Drezner, "The Global Governance of the Internet: Bringing the State Back In," *Political Science Quarterly*, 119(3), 2004, pp. 477–98.

30. Drezner, "The Global Governance of the Internet."

31. Bruce Bueno De Mesquita and George W. Downs, "Development and Democracy," *Foreign Affairs*, 84(5), 2005, pp. 77–86.

32. Nina Tannenwald, "The Nuclear Taboo: The United States and the Normative Basis of Nuclear Non-Use," *International Security*, 53(3), 1999, pp. 433–68.

33. David Alan Rosenberg and W. B. Moore, "'Smoking Radiating Ruin at the End of Two Hours': Documents on American Plans for Nuclear War with the Soviet Union, 1954–55," *International Security*, 6(3), 1982 [1981], pp. 3–38.

34. Drezner, "Global Governance of the Internet."

35. Jan De Loecker and Jan Eeckhout, "The Rise of Market Power and the Macroeconomic Implications" (NBER working paper 23687, August 2017), available at: http://www.janeeckhout.com/wp-content/uploads/RMP.pdf.

36. Robert Gordon, *The Rise and Fall of American Growth* (Princeton, NJ: Princeton University Press, 2016).

37. Robert Keohane and Joseph Nye, *Power and Interdependence* (Boston, MA: Longman, 1977).

38. Waltz, *Theory of International Politics*.

39. Martha Finnemore and Kathryn Sikkink, "International Norm Dynamics and Political Change," *International Organization*, 52(4), 1998, pp. 887–917.

40. Yuen Foong Khong, *Analogies at War* (Princeton, NJ: Princeton University Press, 1992).

41. Tannenwald, "The Nuclear Taboo," p. 442.

42. Much of this paragraph draws from Nina Tannenwald, "Stigmatizing the Bomb: Origins of the Nuclear Taboo," *International Security*, 29(4), 2005, pp. 5–49.

43. Robert Pape, *Bombing to Win* (Ithaca, NY: Cornell University Press, 1996).

44. Tannenwald, "Stigmatizing the Bomb," p. 27.

45. Tannenwald, "The Nuclear Taboo," p. 460.

46. Tannenwald, "The Nuclear Taboo," pp. 458–62.

47. Rebecca Sanders, "Norm Spoiling: Undermining the International Women's Rights Agenda," *International Affairs*, 94(2), 2018, pp. 271–91.

48. US Department of Defense, "2018 Nuclear Posture Review," available at: https://media .defense.gov/2018/Feb/02 /2001872886/-1/-1/1/2018-NUCLEAR-POSTURE-REVIEW -FINAL-REPORT.PDF (accessed 1 June 2018), p. xii. On Russia's changing nuclear doctrine, see Nikolai Sokov, "The Origins of and Prospects for Russian Nuclear Doctrine," *Nonproliferation Review*, 14(2), 2007, pp. 207–26; Nina Tannenwald, "How Strong Is the Nuclear Taboo Today?" *The Washington Quarterly*, 41(3), 2018, pp. 89–109.

49. Mark Raymond and Laura DeNardis, "Multistakeholderism: Anatomy of an Inchoate Global Institution," *International Theory*, 7(3), 2015, pp. 572–616.

50. Jeffrey Lantis and Daniel Bloomberg, "Changing the Code? Norm Contestation and U.S. Antipreneurism in Cyberspace," *International Relations*, 32(2), 2018, pp. 149–72.

51. Quoted in Eric Sterner, "Retaliatory Deterrence in Cyberspace," *Strategic Studies Quarterly*, 5(1), 2011, pp. 62–80.

52. Tim Stevens, "A Cyberwar of Ideas? Deterrence and Norms in Cyberspace," *Contemporary Security Policy*, 33(1), 2012, pp. 148–70; Joseph Nye, "Deterrence and Dissuasion in Cyberspace," *International Security*, 41(3), 2017 [2016], pp. 44–71.

53. Lantis and Bloomberg, "Changing the Code?"

54. See, for example, Brandon Valeriano and Ryan C Maness, "The Dynamics of Cyber Conflict Between Rival Antagonists, 2001–11," *Journal of Peace Research*, 51(3), 2014, pp. 347–60; Maness and Valeriano, "The Impact of Cyber Conflict on International Interactions," *Armed Forces & Society*, 42(2), 2016, pp. 301–23; Erik Gartzke, "The Myth of Cyberwar," *International Security*, 38(2), 2013, pp. 41–73.

55. Stevens, "A Cyberwar of Ideas?" p. 151.

56. William J. Lynn III, "Defending a New Domain: The Pentagon's Cyberstrategy," *Foreign Affairs*, 89(5), 2010, pp. 97–108.

57. Nye, "Deterrence and Dissuasion in Cyberspace," p. 45.

58. Norman Shapiro and Robert Anderson, *Toward an Ethics and Etiquette for Electronic Mail* (RAND report R-3283-NSF/RC, July 1985), available at: http://www.rand.org/pubs /reports /R3283/index1.html (accessed 15 June 2018).

59. Daniel W. Drezner, "How Trolling Could Become the New International Language of Diplomacy," *Washington Post*, 15 May 2015, available at: https://www.washingtonpost .com /opinions/how-trolling-could-become-the-new-international -language-of-diplomacy /2015/05/15/5b092014-f9a0-11e4-a13c -193b1241d51a_story.html?noredirect=on&utm_term =.b1d545 df30af.

Chapter 2

American Grand Strategy

Power, Culture, and Grand Strategy

COLIN DUECK

The following [article provides] a conceptual basis for understanding patterns of U.S. strategic adjustment. I examine some of the most important potential sources of change and continuity in American grand strategy. I begin by defining the term "grand strategy," and indicate the ways in which strategies can vary. Then I examine two potential explanations for changes in grand strategy: first, a domestic cultural explanation, and second, a power-based explanation, emphasizing international conditions. Finally, I outline an alternative "neoclassical realist" model of strategic adjustment, showing how cultural and power-based variables interrelate in the formation of strategic choice.

Grand Strategy

What exactly is "grand strategy"? The phrase was first used by British military theorist B. H. Liddell Hart to describe the "higher level" of wartime strategy above the strictly military, by which the nation's policymakers coordinate all of the resources at their disposal—military, economic, diplomatic—toward the political ends of any given war.[1] As such, grand strategy was considered by Liddell Hart to be an essentially political exercise, conducted by the highest state officials, and involving a broad range of policy instruments besides the military. Still, he thought of it as a wartime phenomenon.[2] In recent years, there has been renewed interest in the concept of grand strategy, but the definition of it has been stretched to include periods of peace as well as war. In this new conception, not only the means of grand strategy, but also the ends have been expanded to include a broad range of peacetime goals—political, economic, and diplomatic. Recent definitions of grand strategy include the following:

- Any broad-based policies that a state may adopt for the preservation and enhancement of its security.[3]
- A political-military "means-ends" chain, a state's theory about how it can best "cause" security for itself.[4]

- A state's overall plan for providing national security by keeping national resources and external commitments in balance.[5]
- The full package of domestic and international policies designed to increase national power and security.[6]

All of these definitions have certain key features in common, and point toward a new conception of grand strategy; that said, a number of them are rather broad. The danger with too general a definition of "grand strategy" is that it leaves the term without any distinct meaning or utility. If, for example, it is used to refer to the pursuit of all national ends in international relations by all available means, it is difficult to see what distinguishes grand strategy from foreign policy in general. In that case, the phrase is no longer of any particular use.[7] What precise limits can we bring to the definition of grand strategy?

First, like all strategy, grand strategy is (1) a calculated relationship of ends and means, (2) in the face of one or more potential opponents. The task of identifying and reconciling goals and resources—of making difficult trade-offs and setting priorities in the face of potential resistance—is the essence of strategy.[8] In a world of unlimited resources, without the possibility of conflict, there is no need for strategy. But in a world of scarce resources, in which leading actors may or may not cooperate, strategic decisions are inevitable. In this sense, not all foreign policy is "strategic." But insofar as international relations involve scarcity and potential conflict, it is a realm of strategic interaction.

Second, it seems reasonable to suggest that grand strategy only exists when there is the possibility of the use of force internationally.[9] This restriction conforms to common usage. Generally, we do not refer to any nation's grand strategy, on a given issue or in a given region, when there is absolutely no possibility of armed conflict. If strategy refers to the balancing of ends and means in the face of potential resistance, then grand strategy refers to the same balancing act on the part of states, in the face of potential armed conflict with other international entities: states, terrorists, and so on. This means that military policy instruments will always be central to grand strategy—not exclusively so, but centrally. Foreign aid, diplomatic activity, even trade policy ought, under certain circumstances, to be considered crucial elements in a nation's grand strategy. But they are elements of a grand strategy only insofar as they are meant to serve the overall pursuit of national goals in the face of potential armed conflict with potential opponents.

Having narrowed down our definition of grand strategy somewhat, let us specify what it still includes. It includes the pursuit of a wide variety of nonmilitary interests, ends, and objectives, whether political, economic, or ideological. It includes the use of nonmilitary means, subject to the restrictions already specified. It includes peacetime as well as wartime policy-making— in fact, this study will focus primarily on peacetime grand strategy. It thus conforms in many respects to calls for a more expansive definition of the subject.[10] Grand strategy is a branch of foreign policy, and grand strategic outcomes are a subset of foreign policy outcomes. This means that the actors, causes, and processes involved in strategic adjustment will be similar to those of foreign policy decision-making. But grand strategy is not synonymous with foreign policy in general.

Any grand strategy involves the identification and prioritization of (1) national interests, goals, and objectives; (2) potential threats to such interests; and (3) resources and/or means with which to meet these threats and protect these interests.[11] A grand strategy is both a conceptual road map, describing how to match identified resources to the promotion of identified interests, and a set of policy prescriptions. The road map addresses the crucial question of how to rank interests, assess threats, and adapt resources; its essence is the attempted reconciliation of ends and means.[12] The specific policy prescriptions follow from the road map. In the final analysis, any grand strategy must provide concrete guidelines on the use of policy instruments such as the form and level of defense spending; the nature and extent of strategic commitments abroad; the deployment of military forces abroad, peacefully or not; the use of foreign aid; the use of diplomacy with real or potential allies; and the diplomatic stance taken toward real or potential adversaries.

It might be asked whether or not most governments actually follow any sort of conscious, coherent, and intentional strategic "plan" over time. The United States, in particular, seems unlikely to do so, given its fragmented and decentralized political system.[13] The short answer is that, for our purposes, it does not really matter. Whether or not national governments actually design and follow through on any overarching grand strategy, they act as if they do. Whether or not a strategic plan literally exists, nations must make difficult choices on matters of defense spending, alliance diplomacy, and military intervention. Decisions regarding trade-offs between ends and means are inevitable, even if they are neither coherent nor coordinated. This is as true for the United States as for any other country. We cannot assume the existence of a premeditated strategic design on the part of any administration, but it is not unreasonable to speak of governments being forced to make strategic decisions, whenever political and military ends and means must be reconciled amidst the possibility of armed conflict.

How, then, should we define change in grand strategy? There are a number of strategic typologies already in existence. Edward Luttwak contrasts "expansionist" strategies with "status quo" strategies.[14] Charles Kupchan offers a slightly more refined typology, distinguishing between "compellent," "deterrent," and "accommodationist" strategies.[15] Alastair Iain Johnston points out that states can follow defensive ends by aggressive means, and vice versa; he therefore leaves political ends out of his typology, but creates three categories of grand strategy otherwise similar to those of Kupchan: "accommodationist," "defensive," and "expansionist."[16] It is not difficult to imagine a number of dimensions along which we might categorize grand strategies: conflictual as opposed to cooperative, realist as opposed to idealist, unilateral as opposed to multilateral, and so on.

While the typologies offered by Luttwak, Kupchan, and Johnston do provide useful guidelines, it seems unlikely that most states follow either a purely defensive-status quo, offensive-compellent, or accommodationist strategy.[17] Nor is it likely that these three broad categories capture the subtle changes that characterize shifts between strategies, even at times of great upheaval. Presumably, it is quite rare that American grand strategy moves from one of these three categories to another, even assuming that it can be fitted into these three strategic archetypes.

A more fruitful approach might be to simply ask whether the United States has expanded, contracted, or in any way significantly changed its overall strategic capabilities and commitments: a process known as "strategic adjustment."[18] Referring back to the policy instruments typically associated with strategic decision-making, we could measure such change along the following dimensions:

1. Is military spending raised or lowered?
2. Are alliance commitments extended or withdrawn?
3. Are military deployments overseas expanded or reduced?
4. Is foreign aid increased or decreased?

5. Does the state engage in significant new diplomatic initiatives, or does it disengage from existing diplomatic activities?
6. Does the state adopt a more aggressive and confrontational stance toward its adversaries, or does it adopt a less confrontational stance?

Note that the United States might expand its commitments in one area while reducing them in another: for example, by extending new alliance commitments while reducing defense spending. It is nevertheless useful to ask whether the nation has expanded or contracted its strategic commitments as a whole, while keeping in mind the possibility of variation within each of these six categories. It is also useful to distinguish between major change and minor change in US grand strategy. A massive shift in the extent of strategic commitments—as in the case of the adoption of containment—can be described as a first-order change. A less fundamental alteration—for example, Dwight D. Eisenhower's introduction of the "New Look"—can be described as a second-order change. Most strategic adjustments are of the second order. And of course, a great deal of minor tinkering goes on within the framework of any given strategic approach, without qualifying as either a first- or second-order alteration.

In sum, variation in American grand strategy will be defined as a significant overall change in the nature and levels of military spending, alliance commitments, foreign aid, diplomatic activism, and/or foreign policy stands toward potential adversaries. This gives us a concrete set of strategic outcomes that vary in a precise and observable manner. We now know what must be explained when we ask how and why grand strategy changes. What are some potential explanations for such change?

Explaining Strategic Adjustment

It is quite probable that both the causes and the processes of strategic adjustment differ from one country to the next. The concept of grand strategy can and has been fruitfully applied to a variety of countries.[19] Our main concern in this book, however, is with the sources of American grand strategy. What theories and approaches might be helpful in focusing specifically on the sources of strategic adjustment within the United States?

Whenever attempting to explain the grand strategy of any country, it is always useful to begin with its position in the international system. The international system is a good place to start because it constitutes a powerful, generalizable influence on any country's grand strategy.[20] The further we get with this sort of "structural" explanation, in terms of testing its causal power, the further we have gone in developing a theory that may have cross-national applications. The same may be said for cultural theories. An appropriate method, then, in developing a model of US strategic adjustment is to begin by considering the potential weight of broad, general causes, such as power and culture, and subsequently to focus in on those elements of the decision-making process that are distinctive to the United States. This ought to provide us with a model of strategic choice unique to the United States, but with potential applications to other countries.

I will therefore begin with those factors and theories that possess the broadest potential for explaining strategic adjustment in comparative terms: specifically, international pressures (structural realist theory), and culture (constructivist theory).[21]

Power and Culture: The Debate

One potential explanation for strategic adjustment would refer to international pressures, such as the global distribution of power. Alternatively, one could refer to country-specific strategic cultures. In international relations theory, realists refer primarily to international ("systemic" or "structural") pressures, while constructivists refer primarily to culture. Realist theories and cultural-constructivist theories are both leading candidates for explaining changes in grand strategy. Thus far, however, constructivists and realists have tended to talk past one another, dismissing each other's claims without a serious, competitive testing of alternative approaches.[22] How do culture and international pressures "fit" together, if at all, in causing strategic outcomes? What is their exact relationship? What are the limits on each type of explanation? These are the kinds of questions that have yet to be satisfactorily answered.

We can at least begin to answer these questions by framing several potential theories of strategic adjustment in a clear, competitive fashion, and then testing each of them against the evidence. Only then can we gain a sense of how much cultural, as opposed to international-structural or power-based, factors actually explain, and how they may interrelate.[23] What follows is a brief summary of three potential explanations of strategic choice: cultural, structural or power-based, and neoclassical realist.

Cultural Explanations

Cultural explanations of strategic adjustment start from the premise that international pressures are essentially indeterminate. For cultural theorists, such as Thomas Berger, Elizabeth Kier, and Edward Rhodes, international pressures—like the "national interest"—must be interpreted and represented subjectively, through a cultural process, in order to have any effect on strategic choice.[24] This cultural process operates as follows. In formulating grand strategy, as in foreign policy generally, leading officials are forced to rely upon preconceived beliefs and assumptions in order to interpret and act upon a mass of incoming information.[25] These beliefs and assumptions may be held either by individuals or by groups of policy-makers as a whole. "Culture," as a general term, simply refers to any set of interlocking values, beliefs, and assumptions that are held collectively by a given group and passed on through socialization.[26] In the context of grand strategy, then, the relevant cultural values and beliefs are those that relate to the legitimate and efficient conduct of political-military affairs, while the relevant cultural unit or group is the citizenry of a given nation-state, and particularly its foreign policy elite.[27] Consequently, cultural theorists of grand strategy posit the existence of an interlocking set of values and beliefs held by the politically interested people of each nation-state that relate to strategic affairs; a set of beliefs that can be referred to as a nation's "strategic culture."[28]

Cultural theorists go on to suggest that culture shapes strategic choice in several ways. First, culture influences the manner in which international events, pressures, and conditions are perceived.[29] Second, it provides a set of causal beliefs regarding the efficient pursuit of national interests.[30] Third, it helps determine the actual definition of those interests, by providing prescriptive foreign policy goals.[31] In this last sense, it should be noted, political-military culture is normative as well as descriptive, and constitutive as well as cognitive.[32] Strategic culture not only provides a set of analytical tools; it also meshes with a sense of national self-image, or sense of identity, which is itself a ground for action.[33] For example, one constitutive effect of political-military culture may be that policy-makers are held to certain norms, or rules of behavior, not for consequentialist reasons, but simply because the violation of such rules is viewed as illegitimate and inappropriate.[34] The seeming violation of accepted norms, or the abandonment of culturally prescribed national goals, is likely to trigger domestic opposition that is not only strong, but emotional, since such norms and/or goals are closely linked to a basic and constitutive sense of national identity.[35]

Perhaps the most striking characteristic of cultural explanations is their claim that strategic culture can prevent meaningful choices by rendering certain plausible strategic alternatives unacceptable or even unthinkable. Culture is said to delimit a set range of acceptable options, tactics, and policies as legitimate and/or efficacious; any alternatives that fall outside this range will not even be seriously considered.[36] Cultural scholars would further suggest that the influence of strategic culture is entrenched through formal and/or informal institutionalization.[37] Formally, a particular culture can be institutionalized within bureaucratic agencies. Informally, it can be institutionalized through regular discourse.[38] The informal process of institutionalization is the less direct of the two but arguably the more powerful. As the assumptions of a given strategic culture are iterated again and again, the language itself takes on real power. It becomes difficult to discuss or even conceive, much less to consider, strategic alternatives that are not culturally sanctioned. Strategic assumptions that might otherwise be open to debate are instead taken for granted. As a result of this process of institutionalization, political-military culture tends to persist, independent of material changes; consequently, policy-makers tend to resist strategic adjustment, and adhere to existing grand strategies, in spite of changing international conditions.[39]

In sum, cultural theorists suggest that any state's grand strategy is best explained by the existence of distinct strategic cultures rather than by international material pressures. Culture determines strategic behavior by shaping the preferences, perceptions, and beliefs of a given nation's citizens. It predisposes each state toward certain strategic choices, in keeping with unique, deep-rooted cultural assumptions, which necessarily vary from state to state. When culture is taken as a variable, then a change in strategic culture is said to explain variation in grand strategy. When culture is taken as a constant, then each nation's strategic culture is said to limit and influence policy choices, without directly "causing" strategic adjustment.[40]

Power-Based Explanations

A second approach to explaining strategic adjustment is to emphasize international pressures, by pointing to conditions like the international distribution of power. This is the approach taken by structural realists of various types. Realists suggest that patterns of strategic adjustment are ultimately shaped by material or "structural" pressures at the international level.[41] The realist premise is that because the international system is an anarchic system, in which violent conflict is always a possibility, states are forced to rely upon their own material capabilities—along with those of their allies—in order to survive. Consequently, international pressures are the primary cause of the strategic behavior of individual states.[42] Realists do not deny that each nation-state within the international system may have peculiar historical, cultural, and/or domestic political legacies, but they do insist that these domestic-level differences tend to be washed out by the pervasive pressures of international competition. As a result, realists suggest that all states tend eventually to act in the same manner: they pay close attention to their relative position in the international system, try to promote their own power and security, and act to check potential threats.

They become "undifferentiated" or alike in their strategic behavior, regardless of cultural differences, due to the overriding pressures of international competition.[43]

Realists, like cultural theorists, however, are often vague as to the exact causal significance of international as opposed to domestic-level pressures when attempting to explain patterns of strategic adjustment. For "structural" realists, the problem of causal under-specification is particularly severe; the leading structural realist of the last thirty years, Kenneth Waltz, has stated quite consistently that his theory cannot be used to explain foreign policy outcomes.[44] But many international relations theorists remain unconvinced that structural realism does not or cannot make foreign policy predictions.[45] In practice, structural realism both requires and implies a theory of state behavior. This is hardly an insuperable obstacle for realists. But it does mean that realist theories of foreign policy must fill in the blanks left by Waltz; they must specify how far and to what extent systemic or structural pressures actually determine the foreign policy behavior of individual states. And on this question, realists divide into several distinct camps.

"Offensive" realists, such as John Mearsheimer, maintain that international systemic pressures and constraints exert an all-powerful influence on grand strategy. According to offensive realists, the fiercely competitive nature of the international system forces states to adopt aggressive strategies, and to expand their relative power, whenever possible.[46] As states grow in relative capabilities, they adopt more expansive grand strategies. According to Mearsheimer, such expansion is not necessarily intentional. Pervasive uncertainty over the intentions of other states forces policy-makers to seek a margin of safety internationally. Powerful states therefore end up acting as if they sought dominion, even if self-consciously they only seek security. The key point for offensive realists is that powerful states adopt more expansive grand strategies, because they have both the opportunity and the incentive to do so.[47]

Offensive realists also provide clear predictions regarding the relationship between international material pressures, distinct national cultures, and strategic adjustment. According to the logic of offensive realism, culture is essentially epiphenomenal or irrelevant to strategic choice.[48] Distinct strategic cultures may exist, but they have little or no independent impact on grand strategy. International pressures not only determine strategic choice; they also override cultural concerns. Cultural rhetoric may be used to justify chosen strategies, but the actual explanation for those strategies lies in the international system.[49] Finally, cultural beliefs may change, and these new beliefs may be co-incident with the selection of new policies, but offensive realists suggest that, in such cases, both the new strategy—and the new cultural beliefs—can be best explained by referring to international pressures.

Offensive realism has the virtue of conceptual clarity and parsimony; it claims to explain a great deal by referring to only a few simple variables. But this parsimony comes at a very heavy price. By suggesting that domestic-level variables are essentially irrelevant to strategic choice, offensive realism rests upon a dubious theoretical assumption. It is precisely for this reason that Kenneth Waltz never made any such claim.[50] The fact is, as even many realists admit, that domestic-level motives and intentions vary from state to state, and that such intentions often have a dramatic and independent impact upon foreign policy behavior.[51] Simply put, some states maximize power; others do not.[52] In reality, the grand strategies of states are regularly and significantly influenced by domestic-level factors, including cultural assumptions. By arguing the opposite, offensive realists inadvertently demonstrate the limits of systemic influences on state behavior. Such pressures may be the most important cause of foreign policy behavior without being entirely determinate. The challenge, for realists, is to create an internally consistent and empirically plausible theory that preserves an appreciation for the importance of systemic pressures alongside an appreciation of their limits.[53]

A Neoclassical Realist Model of Strategic Adjustment

An alternative to both offensive realist and cultural theories of strategic adjustment can be found in neoclassical realism. In recent years, there has been a striking tendency among many realists to "layer in" domestic-level factors when explaining foreign policy behavior. Authors such as Thomas Christensen, Aaron Friedberg, Randall Schweller, Stephen Walt, William Wohlforth, and Fareed Zakaria have all produced research that is recognizably realist in inspiration, but that admits a certain causal significance to domestic-level variables.[54] Gideon Rose has identified this trend as a revival of classical realist assumptions, albeit with a greater concern for theoretical rigor—hence the term "neoclassical realism."[55] According to Rose, neoclassical realists are united by certain common assumptions. First, they seek to explain particular foreign policy behaviors and not simply broad international outcomes. Second, they take the international system—understood in material terms—as the most important long-term cause of changes in any nation's foreign policy behavior. This is what makes them "realists." Third, they layer domestic-level factors into their explanatory models in order to achieve greater predictive and empirical precision. Simply put, they tend to be sensitive to the cultural legacies and domestic politics of specific countries. This is what makes them "neoclassical."[56]

How would neoclassical realism explain changes in grand strategy? First, it would look to the international system as the single most important overall cause of strategic behavior. It would suggest that strategic adjustment is encouraged by changes in the international distribution of power and/or changes in the level of external threat faced by the state.[57] When a given state becomes more powerful, or when it faces greater threats from abroad, it tends to adopt a more costly and expansive grand strategy. Conversely, when a state becomes less powerful, or when it faces fewer foreign threats, it tends to adopt a less costly and less expansive grand strategy. At the same time, neoclassical realists would agree that there is generally some indeterminacy in international conditions, some range of strategic options that might plausibly serve the national interest, and that within this limited range, culture—along with other domestic factors—can have an impact upon strategic choice.[58] Neoclassical realists would agree, for example, with cultural theorists that country-specific cultural variables can influence the preferences and perceptions of a state's foreign policy-makers; that culture can predispose a state toward certain strategic choices rather than others; and that culture can delimit the range of acceptable alternatives in a given situation. In other words, from a neoclassical realist perspective, cultural factors can help to specify and explain the final choices made by foreign policy-makers.

What exactly is the process by which strategic culture influences strategic choice? A neoclassical realist theory would suggest that the process is twofold. First, foreign policy officials need domestic support for any new departure in grand strategy.[59] This is particularly true in a democracy like the United States. Changes in grand strategy are often costly, involving the extraction and mobilization of considerable national resources. Such changes must be politically feasible at home before they can be implemented; they must be viewed as legitimate. Officials that violate cultural preferences and expectations in formulating grand strategy risk their own political support, as well as the success of their chosen policies. Consequently, there are strong political incentives to frame strategic choices in terms that are culturally acceptable, and to modify grand strategy in accordance with cultural preferences, in order to maintain domestic political support for new strategic initiatives. In fact, political officials frequently anticipate such domestic cultural constraints beforehand, and adapt their policies to them, precisely to avoid political controversy.[60] In this way, through the need for domestic support, strategic culture can have an impact on strategic choice, even when state officials employ cultural symbols instrumentally. But the causal influence of culture is not necessarily limited to the need for domestic political support. Foreign policy officials themselves may actually share, or come to share,

or even shape the cultural preferences and perceptions held by their constituents. That is to say, to a greater extent than is generally recognized by international relations theorists, the cultural assumptions voiced by elite foreign policy officials may be internalized and genuine.[61] And if national cultural assumptions regarding grand strategy are either shared or shaped by elite officials, then the beliefs of those officials are a second means by which culture can act as an important influence on patterns of strategic choice.

When applied to the subject of grand strategy, a distinct contribution of neoclassical realist theory is that it provides us with a more precise and subtle understanding of the ways in which international and cultural variables typically interact to shape and determine patterns of strategic choice. Neoclassical realists would concede that cultural factors influence the manner in which states respond to systemic conditions. Strategic adjustment is neither easy nor automatic, particularly when international pressures run up against deeply held cultural beliefs. For this very reason, the existence of nationally distinct strategic cultures often creates significant "lags" or discontinuities between international changes and national responses.[62] At the same time, however, neoclassical realists would argue that it is ultimately international conditions that drive the process of both strategic adjustment and cultural change. That is to say, when national strategic cultures come under intense international pressure, in the end they adjust and adapt.[63] New state strategies are adopted and state officials respond to international pressures by reframing cultural arguments in order to minimize the appearance of discontinuity; those nations that refuse to adapt or respond to systemic conditions are punished in the international arena.[64] Culture is thus best understood as a supplement to, and not a substitute for, realist theories of strategic choice.[65] Strategic culture can certainly help to explain "deviations" from balancing behavior, but since the very concept of such deviations presumes some sort of appropriate or expected response to international conditions, it is only within a realist framework that such explanations make any sense.[66]

A neoclassical realist model of strategic adjustments promises to be useful in bridging domestic and international factors, and in better understanding patterns of adjustment under a variety of circumstances. It sets the parameters for strategic choice more convincingly than either a purely cultural or a purely power-based approach. But even this neoclassical realist model cannot claim to completely explain specific policy decisions at the most detailed level. It still leaves room for other factors, such as domestic politics, as well as for choice on the part of individual policy-makers.

NOTES

1. B. H. Liddell Hart, *Strategy* (New York: Praeger, 1954), p. 31.

2. Liddell Hart, *Strategy*, pp. 335–36.

3. Eric Nordlinger, *Isolationism Reconfigured* (Princeton, NJ: Princeton University Press, 1995), pp. 9–10.

4. Barry Posen, *The Sources of Military Doctrine: France, Britain and Germany Between the World Wars* (Ithaca, NY: Cornell University Press, 1985), p. 13.

5. Charles Kupchan, *Vulnerability of Empire* (Ithaca, NY: Cornell University Press, 1994), p. 3, n. 4.

6. Thomas Christensen, *Useful Adversaries: Grand Strategy, Domestic Mobilization, and Sino-American Conflict, 1947–1958* (Princeton, NJ: Princeton University Press, 1996), p. 7.

7. Robert Art, "A Defensible Defense: America's Grand Strategy After the Cold War," in Sean Lynn-Jones and Steven Miller, eds., *America's Strategic Choices: An International Security Reader* (Cambridge, MA: MIT Press, 1997), p. 79.

8. Samuel Huntington, "The Evolution of National Strategy," in Daniel Kaufman et al., eds., *U.S. National Security Strategy for the 1990s* (Baltimore: Johns Hopkins University Press, 1991), pp. 11–12.

9. Edward Luttwak, *Strategy: The Logic of War and Peace* (Cambridge, MA: Belknap Press of Harvard University Press, 1987), p. 180.

10. Paul Kennedy, ed., *Grand Strategies in War and Peace* (New Haven, CT: Yale University Press, 1991), pp. 2–4.

11. Art, "Defensible Defense," pp. 51–52.

12. Michael Desch, *When the Third World Matters: Latin America and United States Grand Strategy* (Baltimore: Johns Hopkins University Press, 1993), p. 2; John L. Gaddis, *Strategies of Containment* (New York: Oxford University Press, 1982), p. ix.

13. Huntington, "Evolution of National Strategy," p. 11; Luttwak, *Strategy*, p. 235

14. Luttwak, *Strategy*, p. 182.

15. Kupchan, *Vulnerability of Empire*, pp. 67–68.

16. Alastair Iain Johnston, *Cultural Realism: Strategic Culture and Grand Strategy in Chinese History* (Princeton, NJ: Princeton University Press, 1995), p. 115.

17. As these three authors themselves admit.

18. Peter Trubowitz and Edward Rhodes, "Explaining American Strategic Adjustment," in Peter Trubowitz, Emily Goldman, and Edward Rhodes, eds., *The Politics of Strategic Adjustment: Ideas, Institutions and Interests* (New York: Columbia University Press, 1999), pp. 3–25.

19. See, for example, Thomas Berger, *Cultures of Antimilitarism: National Security in Germany and Japan* (Baltimore: Johns Hopkins University Press, 1998); and Johnston, *Cultural Realism*.

20. Fareed Zakaria, "Realism and Domestic Politics," *International Security* 17, no. 1 (Summer 1992): 177–98.

21. I do not claim that the list of generalizable causes of strategic adjustment is exhausted by these two factors alone. There is, for example, a very worthwhile literature on sectional and sectoral economic interests as a crucial source of strategic choice. Their relative causal weight in the process of strategic adjustment is beyond the scope of this book. For a work that emphasizes the centrality of economic interests in the formation of US grand strategy, see Peter Trubowitz, *Defining the National Interest* (Chicago: University of Chicago Press, 1998).

22. A point made by Stephen Brooks and William Wohlforth in "Power, Globalization and the Cold War: Reevaluating a Landmark Case for Ideas," *International Security* 25, no. 3 (Winter 2000–2001): 6–7.

23. Michael Desch, "Culture Clash," *International Security* 23, no. 1 (Summer 1998): 141–70.

24. Berger, *Cultures of Antimilitarism*, p. 9; Johnston, *Cultural Realism*, pp. 1–4; Elizabeth Kier, *Imagining War: French and British Military Doctrines Between the Wars* (Princeton, NJ: Princeton University Press, 1997), pp. 3–5.

25. Robert Jervis, *Perception and Misperception in International Politics* (Princeton, NJ: Princeton University Press, 1976), pp. 32–57, 117–287; Jerel Rosati, "The Power of Human Cognition in the Study of World Politics," *International Studies Review* 2, no. 3 (Fall 2000): 56–57.

26. Berger, *Cultures of Antimilitarism*, p. 9; John Duffield, "Political Culture and State Behavior: Why Germany Confounds Neorealism," *International Organization* 53, no. 4 (Autumn 1999): 765–70; David Elkins and Richard Simeon, "A Cause in Search of Its Effects, or What Does Political Culture Explain?" *Comparative Politics* 11, no. 2 (1979): 127–29; Johnston, *Cultural Realism*, pp. 34–36; Peter Katzenstein, ed., *The Culture of National Security: Norms and Identity in World Politics* (New York: Columbia University Press, 1996), pp. 6–7; Richard Wilson, "The Many Voices of Political Culture," *World Politics* 52, no. 2 (January 2000): 246–73.

27. Kupchan, *Vulnerability of Empire*, p. 5; Albert Yee, "The Causal Effects of Ideas on Politics," *International Organization* 50, no. 1 (Winter 1996): 86–88.

28. It is of course possible to conceive of cultural factors as also operating at the international or systemic level, and a variety of constructivist authors such as Alexander Wendt have made the case for such a conception. I do not deny the potential contributions of such an approach, but in the current discussion I am primarily interested in culture as a unit or state-level variable.

29. Berger, *Cultures of Antimilitarism*, pp. 9, 12; Kier, *Imagining War*, pp. 3–5.

30. Judith Goldstein and Robert Keohane, eds., *Ideas and Foreign Policy: Beliefs, Institutions and Political Change* (Ithaca, NY: Cornell University Press, 1993), pp. 13–17.

31. Emanuel Adler, "Seizing the Middle Ground: Constructivism in World Politics," *European Journal of International Relations* 3, no. 3 (September 1997): 330, 337; Berger, *Cultures of Antimilitarism*, pp. 16–19; Kier, *Imagining War*, pp. 3–5.

32. Berger, *Cultures of Antimilitarism*, pp. 14–16; Katzenstein, *The Culture of National Security*, p. 17.

33. Michael Barnett, "Identity and Alliances in the Middle East," in Katzenstein, ed., *The Culture of National Security*, pp. 400–447; Mlada Bukovansky, "American Identity and Neutral Rights from Independence to the War of 1812," *International Organization* 51, no. 2 (Spring 1997): 217–18.

34. Richard Price and Nina Tannenwald, "Norms and Deterrence: The Nuclear and Chemical Weapons Taboo," in Katzenstein, ed., *The Culture of National Security*, pp. 114–52.

35. Berger, *Cultures of Antimilitarism*, p. 21.

36. Duffield, "Political Culture and State Behavior," p. 772; Elkins and Simeon, "A Cause in Search of Its Effects," p. 128; Johnston, *Cultural Realism*, p. 35.

37. Sheri Berman, "Ideas, Norms and Culture in Political Analysis," *Comparative Politics* 33, no. 2 (January 2001): 38; Goldstein and Keohane, *Ideas and Foreign Policy*, pp. 20–24.

38. Yee, "The Causal Effects of Ideas on Politics," pp. 95–101.

39. Johnston, *Cultural Realism*, pp. 1–40.

40. Johnston, *Cultural Realism*, pp. 61–154.

41. A good example of such an argument is in Posen, *Sources of Military Doctrine*, pp. 7–8, 239.

42. For a summary of core realist assumptions, see Michael Doyle, *Ways of War and Peace* (New York: W. W. Norton, 1997), pp. 41–201; and Robert Gilpin, "The Richness of the Political Theory of Realism," *International Organization* 38, no. 2 (Spring 1984): 287–304.

43. Kenneth Waltz, *Theory of International Politics* (Reading, MA: Addison-Wesley, 1979), pp. 74–77, 93–97, 127–28.

44. Kenneth Waltz, "International Politics Is Not Foreign Policy," *Security Studies* 6, no. 1 (Autumn 1996): 54–55; Waltz, *Theory of International Politics*, pp. 70–72, 116–28.

45. See especially Colin Elman, "Why Not Neorealist Theories of Foreign Policy?" *Security Studies* 6, no. 1 (Autumn 1996): 7–53.

46. Eric Labs, "Beyond Victory: Offensive Realism and the Expansion of War Aims," *Security Studies* 6, no. 4 (Summer 1997): 1–49; John Mearsheimer, *The Tragedy of Great Power Politics* (New York: W. W. Norton, 2001), pp. 21–22, 31–39.

47. Robert Gilpin, *War and Change in World Politics* (New York: Cambridge University Press, 1981), p. 23; Martin Wight, *Power Politics* (London: Leicester University Press, 1978), p. 144.

48. John Mearsheimer, "The False Promise of International Institutions," in Michael Brown, Sean Lynn-Jones, and Steven Miller, eds., *The Perils of Anarchy: Contemporary Realism and International Security* (Cambridge, MA: MIT Press, 1995), pp. 369–70.

49. Hans Morgenthau, *Politics Among Nations: The Struggle for Power and Peace* (New York: McGraw Hill, 1993), pp. 99–102.

50. Waltz, *Theory of International Politics*, pp. 70–73.

51. Raymond Aron, *Peace and War* (New York: Praeger, 1966), pp. 90–91; Charles Glaser, "The Security Dilemma Revisited," *World Politics* 50, no. 1 (October 1997): 171–201; Andrew Kydd, "Sheep in Sheep's Clothing: Why Security Seekers Do Not Fight Each Other," *Security Studies* 7, no. 1 (Autumn 1997): 114–55.

52. Randall Schweller, "Neorealism's Status Quo Bias: What Security Dilemma?" *Security Studies* 5, no. 3 (Spring 1996): 90–121; Arnold Wolfers, *Discord and Collaboration* (Baltimore: Johns Hopkins University Press, 1962), p. 156.

53. Another version of realism that claims to explain changes in grand strategy is "defensive realism." Defensive realists start from the premise that international pressures by themselves rarely force states into aggressive behavior; aggressive grand strategies are typically best explained by domestic political pathologies, such as the formation of rent-seeking cartels within a particular state. Defensive realists certainly do not make the mistake of overemphasizing systemic pressures, but there are

questions as to whether such an approach is really consistent with realism as a research program. For leading defensive realist works, see Jack Snyder, *Myths of Empire: Domestic Politics and International Ambition* (Ithaca, NY: Cornell University Press, 1991), and Stephen Van Evera, *Causes of War: Power and the Roots of Conflict* (Ithaca, NY: Cornell University Press, 1999). For a penetrating critique of defensive realism, see Zakaria, "Realism and Domestic Politics."

54. Christensen, *Useful Adversaries*; Aaron Friedberg, *In the Shadow of the Garrison State: America's Anti-Statism and its Cold War Grand Strategy* (Princeton, NJ: Princeton University Press, 2000); Randall Schweller, *Deadly Imbalances* (New York: Columbia University Press, 1998); Stephen Walt, *Revolution and War* (Ithaca, NY: Cornell University Press, 1996); William Wohlforth, *The Elusive Balance: Power and Perceptions during the Cold War* (Ithaca, NY: Cornell University Press, 1993); Fareed Zakaria, *From Wealth to Power: The Unusual Origins of America's World Role* (Princeton, NJ: Princeton University Press, 1998).

55. Gideon Rose, "Neoclassical Realism and Theories of Foreign Policy," *World Politics* 51, no. 1 (October 1998): 144–72.

56. Ibid., pp. 146–47, 154. See also Jeffrey Taliaferro, "Security Seeking Under Anarchy," *International Security* 25, no. 3 (Winter 2000/2001): 132–35, 142–43.

57. Christensen, *Useful Adversaries*, p. 15; Gilpin, *War and Change in World Politics*, p. 96; Posen, *The Sources of Military Doctrine*, pp. 7–8, 239.

58. Raymond Aron, *Peace and War* (New York: Praeger, 1966), pp. 90–91; Randall Schweller, "The Progressiveness of Neoclassical Realism," in Colin Elman and Miriam Fendius Elman, eds., *Progress in International Relations Theory* (Cambridge, MA: MIT Press, 2003), p. 336; Jennifer Sterling-Folker, "Realist Environment, Liberal Process, and Domestic-Level Variables," *International Studies Quarterly* 41, no. 1 (March 1997): 9, 16–23.

59. Christensen, *Useful Adversaries*, p. 11.

60. Alexander George, "Domestic Constraints on Regime Change in U.S. Foreign Policy: The Need for Policy Legitimacy," in John Ikenberry, ed., *American Foreign Policy: Theoretical Essays* (New York: Longman, 1999), pp. 336–60.

61. Kupchan, *Vulnerability of Empire*, pp. 61–63.

62. Desch, "Culture Clash," pp. 166–69.

63. Jeffrey Legro, *Cooperation Under Fire* (Ithaca, NY: Cornell University Press, 1995), p. 231.

64. Jeffrey Lantis, "The Moral Imperative of Force: The Evolution of German Strategic Culture," *Comparative Strategy* 21, no. 1 (January–March 2002): 21–46.

65. Desch, "Culture Clash," pp. 166–69; Kurt Jacobsen, "Much Ado About Ideas," *World Politics* 47, no. 2 (January 1995): 285.

66. Schweller, "The Progressiveness of Neoclassical Realism," pp. 340–41; Sterling-Folker, "Realist Environment, Liberal Process, and Domestic-Level Variables," p. 20.

Toward Strategic Solvency

The Crisis of American Military Primacy and the Search for Strategic Solvency

HAL BRANDS AND ERIC EDELMAN

America is hurtling toward strategic insolvency.[1] For two decades after the Cold War, Washington enjoyed essentially uncontested military dominance and a historically favorable global environment—all at a comparatively low military and financial price. Now, however, America confronts military and geopolitical challenges more numerous and severe than at any time in at least a quarter century—precisely as disinvestment in defense has left US military resources far scarcer than before. The result is a creeping crisis of American military primacy, as Washington's margin of superiority is diminished, and the gap between US commitments and capabilities grows. "Superpowers don't bluff," went a common Obama-era refrain—but today, America is being left with a strategy of bluff as its preeminence wanes and its military means come out of alignment with its geopolitical ends.

Foreign policy, Walter Lippmann wrote, entails "bringing into balance, with a comfortable surplus of power in reserve, the nation's commitments and the nation's power." If a statesman fails to preserve strategic solvency, if he fails to "bring his ends and means into balance," Lippmann added, "he will follow a course that leads to disaster."[2] America's current state of strategic insolvency is indeed fraught with peril. It will undermine US alliances by raising doubts about the credibility of American guarantees. It will weaken deterrence by tempting adversaries to think aggression may be successful or go unopposed. Should conflict actually erupt in key areas, the United States may be unable to uphold existing commitments or only be able to do so at prohibitive cost. Finally, as the shadows cast by US military power grow shorter, American diplomacy is likely to become less availing, and the global system less responsive to US influence. The US military remains far superior to any single competitor, but its power is becoming dangerously insufficient for the grand strategy and international order it supports.

Great powers facing strategic insolvency have three basic options. First, they can decrease commitments, thereby restoring equilibrium with diminished resources. Second, they can live with greater risk by gambling that their enemies will not test vulnerable commitments or by employing riskier approaches—

such as nuclear escalation—to sustain commitments on the cheap. Third, they can expand capabilities, thereby restoring strategic solvency. Today, this approach would probably require a concerted, long-term defense buildup comparable to the efforts of Presidents Jimmy Carter and Ronald Reagan near the end of the Cold War.[3]

Much contemporary commentary favors the first option—reducing commitments—and denounces the third as financially ruinous and perhaps impossible.[4] Yet significantly expanding American capabilities would not be nearly as economically onerous as it may seem. Compared to the alternatives, in fact, this approach represents the best option for sustaining American primacy and preventing a slide into strategic bankruptcy which will eventually be punished.

I

Since the Cold War, America has been committed to maintaining overwhelming military primacy. The idea, as George W. Bush declared, that America must possess "strengths beyond challenge" has been featured in every major US strategy document and reflected in concrete terms.[5] Since the early 1990s, for example, the United States has accounted for 35–45 percent of world defense spending and maintained peerless global power-projection capabilities.[6] Perhaps more important, US primacy was unrivaled in key strategic regions such as Europe, East Asia, and the Middle East. From thrashing Saddam Hussein's million-man Iraqi military during Operation Desert Storm (1991) to deploying two carrier strike groups off Taiwan during the third Taiwan Strait crisis (1995–1996) with impunity, Washington has been able to project military power superior to anything a regional rival could employ, even on its own geopolitical doorstep.

This military dominance has constituted the hard-power backbone of an ambitious global strategy. After the Cold War, US policy-makers committed to averting a return to the unstable multipolarity of earlier eras and to perpetuating the more favorable unipolar order. They committed to fostering a global environment in which liberal values and an open international econ-

Hal Brands and Eric Edelman, "Toward Strategic Solvency: The Crisis of American Military Primacy and the Search for Strategic Solvency," *Parameters* 46, no. 4 (Winter 2016–2017): 27–42, published by the US Army War College.

omy could flourish and in which international scourges such as rogue states, nuclear proliferation, and catastrophic terrorism would be suppressed. And because they saw military force as the *ultima ratio regum,* they understood the centrality of military preponderance.

Washington would need the military power to underwrite worldwide alliance commitments and preserve substantial overmatch versus any potential great-power rival. The United States must be able to answer the sharpest challenges to the international system, such as Saddam's invasion of Kuwait in 1990 or jihadist extremism today. Finally, because prevailing global norms reflect hard-power realities, America would need superiority to assure its own values remain ascendant. Saying US strategy and the international order required "strengths beyond challenge" was impolitic, but it was not inaccurate.[7]

American primacy, moreover, has been eminently affordable. At the height of the Cold War, the United States spent over 12 percent of gross domestic product (GDP) on defense; since the mid-1990s, the number has usually been 3–4 percent.[8] In a historically favorable international environment, Washington has enjoyed primacy—and its geopolitical fruits—on the cheap.

Until recently, US strategy also heeded the limits of how cheaply primacy could be had. The American military shrank significantly during the 1990s, but US officials understood that if Washington cut back too far, US primacy would erode to a point where it ceased to deliver its geopolitical benefits. Alliances would lose credibility, stability of key regions would be eroded, rivals would be emboldened, and international crises would go unaddressed. American primacy was thus like a reasonably priced insurance policy, requiring nontrivial expenditures—and protecting against far costlier outcomes.[9] Washington paid the premiums for two decades after the Cold War. But more recently American primacy and strategic solvency have been imperiled.

II

For most of the post–Cold War era, the international system was—by historical standards—remarkably benign. Dangers existed, and as the terrorist attacks on September 11, 2001, demonstrated, they could manifest with horrific effect. But for two decades after the Soviet collapse, the world was characterized by remarkably low levels of great-power competition, high levels of security in key theaters such as Europe and East Asia, and the comparative weakness of "rogue" actors—Iran, Iraq, North Korea, and al-Qaeda—which most aggressively challenged American power. Now, however, the strategic landscape is darkening due to four factors.

First, great-power military competition is back. The world's two leading authoritarian powers—China and Russia—are seeking regional hegemony, contesting global norms such as nonaggression and freedom of navigation, and developing the military punch to underwrite these ambitions. Notwithstanding severe economic and demographic problems, Russia has conducted major military modernization emphasizing nuclear weapons, high-end conventional capabilities, and rapid-deployment and special operations forces—and utilized many of these capabilities in Ukraine and Syria.[10] China, meanwhile, has carried out a buildup of historic proportions, with constant-dollar defense outlays rising from $26 billion in 1995 to $215 billion in 2015.[11] Ominously, these expenditures have funded power-projection and anti-access/area denial (A2/AD) tools necessary to threaten China's neighbors and complicate US intervention on their behalf. Washington has grown accustomed to having a generational military lead; Russian and Chinese modernization efforts are now creating a far more competitive environment.

Second, international outlaws are no longer so weak. North Korea's conventional forces have atrophied, but Pyongyang has amassed a growing nuclear arsenal and is developing intercontinental delivery capability.[12] Iran remains a nuclear threshold state, which continues to develop ballistic missiles and A2/AD capabilities while employing sectarian and proxy forces across the Middle East. The Islamic State is headed for defeat, but has displayed military capabilities unprecedented for any terrorist group and shown that counterterrorism will continue to place significant operational demands on US forces. Rogue actors have long preoccupied American planners, but the rogues are now more capable than at any time in decades.

Third, the democratization of technology has allowed more actors to contest American superiority in dangerous ways. The spread of antisatellite and cyber-warfare capabilities, the proliferation of man-portable air defense systems and ballistic missiles, and the increasing availability of key elements of the precision-strike complex have had a military-leveling effect by giving weaker actors capabilities formerly unique to technologically advanced states. Indeed, as these capabilities spread, fourth-generation systems, such as F-15s and F-16s, may provide decreasing utility against even non-great-power competitors, and far more fifth-generation capabilities may be needed to perpetuate American overmatch.

Finally, the number of challenges has multiplied. During the 1990s and early 2000s, Washington faced rogue states and jihadist extremism but not intense great-power rivalry. America faced conflicts in the Middle East, but East Asia and Europe were comparatively secure. Now, old threats still exist, but the more permissive conditions have vanished. The United States confronts rogue states, lethal jihadist organizations, and great-power competition; there are severe challenges in all three Eurasian theaters. The United States thus faces not just more significant but also more numerous challenges to its military dominance than it has for at least a quarter century.

III

One might expect the leader of a historically favorable international system to respond to such developments by increasing its relatively modest investments in maintaining the system. In recent years, however, Washington has markedly disinvested in defense. Constant-dollar defense spending fell by nearly one-fourth, from $768 billion in 2010 to $595 billion in 2015.[13] Defense spending as a share of GDP fell from 4.7 percent to 3.3 percent, with Congressional Budget Office projections showing military outlays falling to 2.6 percent by 2024—the lowest level since before World War II.[14]

Defense spending always declines after major wars, of course. Yet from 2010 onward, this pressure was compounded by the legacy of Bush-era budget deficits, the impact of the Great Recession (2007–9), and President Barack Obama's decision to transfer resources from national security to domestic priorities. These forces, in turn, were exacerbated by the terms of the Budget Control Act of 2011 and the sequester mechanism. Defense absorbed roughly 50 percent of these spending cuts, despite accounting for less than 20 percent of federal spending. By walling off most personnel costs and severely limiting flexibility in how cuts could be made, moreover, the sequester caused the Department of Defense to make reductions in blunt, nonstrategic fashion.[15]

This budgetary buzz saw has taken a toll. Readiness has suffered alarmingly, with all services struggling to conduct current counterterrorism operations while also preparing for the ever-growing danger of great-power war. "The services are very good at counterinsurgency," the House Armed Services Committee noted in 2016, "but they are not prepared to endure a long fight against higher order threats from near-peer competitors."[16] Modernization has also been compromised; the ability to develop and field promising future capabilities has been sharply constrained by budget caps and uncertainty. This problem will only get worse—in the 2020s, a "bow wave" of deferred investments in the nuclear triad and high-end conventional capabilities will come due.[17]

Finally, force structure has been sacrificed. The Army has fared worst—it is slated to decline to 450,000 personnel by 2018, or 30,000 personnel fewer than prior to 9/11.[18] But all the services are at or near post–World War II lows in end strength, and the US military

is significantly smaller than the 1990s-era "base force," which was designed as the "minimum force . . . below which the nation should not go if it was to remain a globally engaged superpower."[19] "Strategy wears a dollar sign," Bernard Brodie wrote, and Washington is paying for less capability relative to the threats it faces than at any time in decades.[20]

IV

Cumulatively, these developments have resulted in a creeping crisis of US military primacy. Washington still possesses vastly more military power than any challenger, particularly in global power-projection capabilities. Yet even this global primacy is declining. The United States faces a Russia with significant extra-regional power-projection capabilities as well as near-peer capabilities in areas such as strategic nuclear forces and cyberwarfare. China's military budget is now more than one-third of the US budget, and Beijing is developing its own advanced power-projection capabilities.[21] Perhaps more importantly, US global primacy is also increasingly irrelevant, because today's crucial geopolitical competitions are regional contests, and here the trends have been decidedly adverse.

In East Asia, China's two-decade military buildup has allowed Beijing to contest seriously US power projection within the first island chain. "The balance of power between the United States and China may be approaching a series of tipping points," RAND Corporation analysts observe.[22] The situation in Eastern Europe is worse. Here, unfavorable geography and aggressive Russian modernization have created significant Russian overmatch in the Baltic; US and North Atlantic Treaty Organization (NATO) forces are "outnumbered and outgunned" along NATO's eastern flank.[23] In the Middle East, the balance remains more favorable, but Iranian A2/AD and ballistic missile capabilities could significantly complicate US operations, while the reemergence of Russian military power has narrowed US freedom of action. In key areas across Eurasia, the US military edge has eroded.

This erosion, in turn, has profound implications for American strategy. For one thing, US forces will face far harder fights should conflict occur. War against Iran or North Korea would be daunting enough, given their asymmetrical capabilities. Even Iran, for instance, could use its ballistic missile capabilities to attack US bases and allies, employ swarming tactics and precision-guided munitions against US naval forces in the Persian Gulf, and activate Shi'ite militias and proxy forces, all as a way of inflicting higher costs on the United States.[24]

Conflict against Russia or China would be something else entirely. Fighting a near-peer competitor armed with high-end conventional weapons and precision-strike capabilities would subject the US military to an environment of enormous lethality, "the likes of which," Army Chief of Staff General Mark A. Milley has commented, it "has not experienced . . . since World War II."[25] American forces might still win—albeit on a longer time line and at a painfully high cost in lives—but they might not.

According to open-source analysis, US forces would have little chance of halting a determined Russian assault on the Baltic states. Facing severe disadvantages in tanks, ground-based fires, and airpower and air defenses, those forces would likely be destroyed in place. NATO would then face an agonizing dilemma—whether to mobilize its resources for a protracted war that would risk nuclear escalation or acquiesce to an alliance-destroying fait accompli.[26]

Similarly, whereas the United States would have dominated any plausible conflict with China in the 1990s, according to recent assessments the most likely conflicts would be nearer run things today. Consider a conflict over Taiwan. Beijing might not be able to defeat Washington in a long war, but it could establish air and maritime superiority early in a conflict and thereby impose unacceptable losses on US air and naval forces. The crucial tipping point in a Taiwan contingency could come as early as 2020 or even 2017; in the Spratly Islands, it could come within another decade.[27] As US superiority erodes, America runs a higher risk of being unable to meet its obligations.

In fact, Washington's ability to execute its standing global defense strategy is increasingly doubtful. After the Cold War, the United States adopted a two major regional contingency standard geared toward preventing an adversary in one region from undertaking opportunistic aggression to exploit US preoccupation in another. By 2012, budget cuts had already forced the Obama administration to shift to a 1.5 or 1.7 war standard premised on decisively defeating one opponent while "imposing unacceptable costs" on another.[28] Yet the US capacity to execute even this less ambitious strategy is under strain, just as the international environment raises questions about whether the strategy is ambitious enough.

This doubt has arisen because the Obama administration's 2012 defense strategy was announced prior to sequestration, and prior to Russian aggression in Ukraine in 2014—which raised the disturbing possibility that one of America's wars might be against a nuclear-armed great-power competitor. And beyond these issues, events in Europe and the Middle East since 2012 have raised doubts about whether a 1.7 war standard is sufficient given the possibility the Pentagon might confront conflicts in three strategic theaters—against Russia in Europe, Iran or an Islamic State–like actor in the Middle East, and China or North Korea in East Asia—on overlapping time frames. In sum, the United States is rapidly reaching, if it has not already reached, the point of strategic insolvency. And even beyond the aforementioned risks, this situation poses fundamental strategic challenges.

The cohesion of US alliances will likely suffer, as American allies lose confidence in Washington's ability to protect them. Adversaries, in turn, will become more likely to test US commitments, to gauge Washington's willingness to make good on increasingly tenuous promises, and to exploit its declining ability to respond decisively. Russian intimidation of the Baltic states, Iranian expansionism in the Middle East, and increasingly aggressive Chinese coercion of the Philippines and Japan illustrate these dynamics in action.

Finally, as US military power becomes less imposing, the United States will find its global influence less impressive. Norms, ideas, and international arrangements supported by Washington will lose strength and increasingly be challenged by actors empowered to imprint their own influence on global affairs. American grand strategy and the post–Cold War system have rested on American military overmatch; as that overmatch fades, US grand strategy and the order it supports will come under tremendous strain.

V

So how should America respond? One option is reducing commitments. If the United States cannot sustain its existing global strategy, then it could pare back global obligations until they are more commensurate with available capabilities.

The United States might, for instance, embrace a twenty-first-century Nixon Doctrine, by stating that it will protect Middle Eastern partners from conventional, state-based aggression, but that they must defend themselves against nontraditional threats such as the Islamic State.[29] Or, America could simply delegate Persian Gulf security to its Arab allies in the region. Most dramatically, if the United States were really serious about slashing commitments, it could dispense with the obligations most difficult to uphold—to Taiwan and the Baltic states, for instance. In short, America would reduce commitments proactively, rather than having their hollowness exposed by war.

There are historical precedents for this approach. The Nixon Doctrine and US withdrawal from Vietnam helped Washington retreat to a more defensible strategic perimeter in the 1970s following strategic overstretch in the decade prior. More significantly, beginning in the late nineteenth century, the United Kingdom gradually conducted an elegant global retreat by first relying upon rising regional powers such as the United States and Japan to maintain acceptable regional orders and later encouraging Washington to shoulder many of

London's global burdens after World War II. Graceful retrenchment, then, is not an impossibility.[30]

It is, however, extremely problematic today. This approach—particularly the more aggressive variants—would be enormously difficult to implement. The US commitment to the Baltic states is part of a larger commitment to NATO; shredding the former guarantee risks undermining the broader alliance. Even in Asia, where the United States has bilateral alliances, withdrawing the US commitment to Taipei could cause leaders in Manila, Seoul, or Tokyo to wonder if they might be abandoned next—and to hedge their strategic bets accordingly. Alliances hinge on the credibility of the patron's promises; revoking some guarantees without discrediting others is difficult.[31]

This dynamic underscores another liability—the likelihood of profound geopolitical instability. Retrenchment works best when the overstretched hegemon can hand off excessive responsibilities to some friendly power. But today, there is no liberal superpower waiting in the wings. Rather, the countries most sympathetic to America's view of the international order—Japan, the United Kingdom, and key European allies—confront graver long-term economic and demographic challenges than the United States. The countries most likely to gain influence following US retrenchment—Russia and China—have very different global visions.

In these circumstances, US retrenchment seems unlikely to succeed. Rather than simply forcing friendly local actors to do more to defend themselves and check revisionist powers, the outcome might easily be underbalancing—in which collective action problems, internal political divisions, or resource limitations prevent timely action against a potential aggressor—or bandwagoning, in which exposed countries buy a measure of safety by aligning with, rather than against, an aggressive power.[32] Meanwhile, although writing off Taiwan or Estonia might produce a near-term improvement of relations with Beijing or Moscow, the longer-term effect would be to remove a chief constraint on the aggressive behavior these powers have been increasingly manifesting. If Moscow and Beijing seem eager to bring their "near abroads" to heel now, just wait until the United States retracts its security perimeter.[33]

If more aggressive variants of retrenchment are thus deeply flawed, even more limited versions, such as a Middle Eastern Nixon Doctrine, have weaknesses. As Iran's military power continues to grow, and the recent removal of nuclear-related sanctions makes this seem likely, even the wealthy Persian Gulf kingdoms will have great difficulty dealing with Tehran's advanced and asymmetric capabilities without US assistance. In fact, without US leadership, the long-standing collective action problems between the Gulf countries are

likely to worsen. Moreover, the United States essentially tried a version of this approach by withdrawing from Iraq in late 2011. But as soon became clear, Iraq, a vital state in a key region, could not withstand challenges from nontraditional foes such as the Islamic State on its own. In fact, US retrenchment actually encouraged developments that left Iraq more vulnerable to collapse, such as the increasingly sectarian nature of Nuri al-Maliki's governance and the hollowing out of the Iraqi Security Forces.[34] Retrenchment, then, may narrow the gap between capabilities and commitments in the short run, but only by inviting greater global dangers and instability.

VI

If the United States is unwilling to spend significantly more on defense, but does not wish to invite the geopolitical instability associated with retrenchment, a second option is to live with greater risk. Living with greater risk could take two different, but not mutually exclusive, forms. First, the United States could accept higher risk with respect to its global commitments by wagering that even exposed commitments are unlikely to be tested because US adversaries are risk averse and are unwilling to start a war, even a potentially successful one, that might cause American intervention. In other words, the United States might not be able to defend Taiwan effectively, but the mere prospect of an invasion provoking a Sino-American war would stay Beijing's hand.

Second, the United States could bridge the capabilities-commitments gap through riskier strategies substituting escalation for additional resources. Most likely, this would entail relying more heavily on nuclear warfighting and the threat of nuclear retaliation to defend vulnerable allies in East Asia or Eastern Europe. Because US allies are already covered by the US extended nuclear deterrent, this approach would involve making more explicit nuclear threats and guarantees and integrating greater reliance on nuclear weapons into US plans. Similarly, this approach could entail the use, or the threat of use, of powerful nonnuclear capabilities such as strategic cyberattacks against critical enemy infrastructure for the same purpose—bolstering deterrence on the cheap by raising the costs an aggressor would expect to pay.[35]

Lest these approaches sound ridiculous, both have a distinguished pedigree. In the late 1940s, the United States could not credibly defend Western Europe from a Soviet invasion. But the Truman administration still undertook the security guarantees associated with NATO on the calculated gamble that Moscow was unlikely to risk global war by attacking US allies, particularly during the period of the US nuclear monopoly.[36] And in the 1950s, to control costs and address the continuing deficiency of US and allied conventional forces, the Eisenhower administration relied heavily on nuclear threats to deter aggression.[37] Throughout much of the Cold War, in fact, the United States compensated for conventional inferiority—particularly in Central Europe—by integrating early recourse to nuclear weapons into its war plans. Accepting greater risk would mean updating Cold War–era approaches for today's purposes.

Yet substituting risk for cost entails serious liabilities. Simply hoping exposed commitments will not be challenged might work—for a while. But this strategy carries enormous risk of those guarantees eventually being tested and found wanting, with devastating effects on America's reputation and credibility. Meanwhile, a strategy of bluff could weaken deterrence and reassurance on the installment plan as allies and adversaries perceive a shifting balance of power and understand US guarantees to be increasingly chimerical.

The second variant of this approach, embracing more escalatory approaches, lacks credibility. Consider threatening to employ strategic cyberattacks against an aggressor in a conflict over Taiwan or the Baltic states. Such threats are problematic, because as President Obama acknowledged in 2016, "open societies" such as the United States are "more vulnerable" to massive cyberattacks than authoritarian rivals such as Russia or China.[38] America may simply lack the escalation dominance needed to make a strategy of cyber-retaliation believable.

So too in the nuclear realm. Threats to punish Communist aggression with nuclear retaliation might have been credible in the 1950s, when China lacked nuclear weapons: Washington had a massive nuclear advantage over Moscow, and neither adversary could reliably target the US homeland. But today, both rivals possess secure second-strike capabilities and could inflict horrific damage on America should nuclear escalation occur. This approach thus risks leading the United States into a trap where, if its interests are challenged, it faces a choice between pursuing escalatory options carrying potentially unacceptable costs and acquiescing to aggression. Awareness of this dynamic may, in turn, make adversaries more likely to probe and push. Trading cost for risk may seem attractive in theory, but in practice the risks may prove far more dangerous than they initially seem.

VII

This leaves a final option—significantly increasing resources devoted to defense, thereby bringing capabilities back into alignment with commitments and strengthening the hard-power backbone of US strategy. Given current trends, this strategy would likely entail a sustained, multiyear buildup of a magnitude roughly similar to the Carter-Reagan buildup, when real defense spending increased by around 50 percent. This buildup would require permanently lifting the Budget Control Act caps to provide increased resources and budgetary stability. It would require not just procuring larger quantities of existing capabilities but also investing aggressively in future capabilities geared toward defeating great-power challengers as well as middle-tier problem countries such as Iran and North Korea. And crucially, greater resources would have to be coupled with developing innovative operational concepts, streamlining Defense procedures and acquisition processes, and maximizing the Pentagon's other efforts toward effectiveness and efficiency.

Recent proposals demonstrate the likely parameters of this approach. If the goal was to restore an authentic two major regional contingency capability, the United States might follow the recommendations issued in 2014 by the National Defense Panel, which call for a force consisting, at minimum, of 490,000 active-duty Army personnel and 182,000 marines, a Navy of between 323 and 346 ships (versus 274 today), and an Air Force of unspecified size but substantially larger than the end-strength envisioned in late Obama-era budgets.[39] If, more ambitiously, the United States sought a two-plus or even a three-war standard, a more significant buildup would be required.

One recent estimate issued by Senator John McCain calls for a three-theater force—a Navy of over 330 ships and nearly 900 frontline naval strike fighters, an Air Force of 60 combat squadrons and 1,500 combat aircraft, an Army of at least 490,000–500,000 active-duty soldiers, and a Marine Corps of at least 200,000 active-duty marines. Because McCain's budget reaches out only 5 years, these numbers would presumably grow further over time.[40] Another three-theater proposal by the American Enterprise Institute advocates a 10-year expansion to 600,000 active-duty Army soldiers, over 200,000 active-duty marines, a Navy of 346 ships, and an Air Force of unspecified but significantly increased end strength. The number of F-22s, for instance, would rise from 185 to 450.[41]

These proposals would require significant new investments. The McCain budget calls for $430 billion in new money over 5 years, culminating in a Fiscal Year 2022 budget of roughly $800 billion.[42] The American Enterprise Institute proposal, issued in late 2015, calls for $1.3 trillion in new money over 10 years.[43] All of these force constructs reflect a high-low mix designed to enable effective operations ranging from counterterrorism, to major conventional war against Iran or North Korea, to high-end combat against a great-power adversary. All the proposals include robust recapitalization of the US nuclear triad. And although these proposals differ on specifics, all are meant to enable a range of investments necessary to maintaining US primacy in a more competitive environment.

If the United States were to undertake a buildup of this magnitude, it could, for instance, invest in a more survivable, multi-brigade presence in Eastern Europe. America could significantly increase investments in capabilities—from additional Zumwalt-class destroyers and nuclear attack submarines, to stealthy fighters and penetrating long-range bombers, to vastly enhanced stocks of precision-guided and standoff munitions, to improved air and missile defenses necessary to retain air and sea control in high-end conflicts as well as to maintain the upper hand in fights with Iran and North Korea.[44] This approach would ease the tradeoffs between critical capabilities for today's fight, such as the A-10, and those critical for tomorrow's fight, such as the F-35. Crucially, this approach would also allow aggressive development and production of future technologies in areas from hypersonics to directed energy, which currently receive seed funding but cannot be adequately fielded without additional resources.[45] Finally, this approach, particularly the more aggressive, three-theater option, would permit the increased force structure necessary to cover a larger number of contingencies and reduce stress on the current force.

So how viable is this option? Critics offer four primary objections. The first critique deems this approach unnecessary, because the Pentagon can maintain US primacy at existing budget levels either by pursuing technological innovation and strategic offsets or by undertaking business and acquisition reforms. The second critique asserts a sustained, multiyear buildup will overtax the US economy, given persistent budget deficits and a debt-to-GDP ratio of 76 percent.[46] The third critique views this approach as self-defeating because it will spur arms races with American adversaries. The fourth critique holds this approach will incentivize continued free-riding by US allies and partners by forcing Washington to continue subsidizing their defense. All of these arguments have some logic, but none is persuasive.

The first argument—about innovation, offsets, and defense reform—is alluring but unsatisfying. To be sure, repurposing existing capabilities, developing high-end future capabilities to create significant dilemmas for competitors from Iran to China, and designing innovative operational concepts—essentially, what former Secretaries of Defense Chuck Hagel and Ashton Carter termed the Third Offset Strategy—are absolutely vital to restoring strategic solvency. Yet offsets and innovation cannot by themselves compensate for the lack of resources Washington faces in covering the range of plausible contingencies.

Moreover, any meaningful offset strategy is dependent on significantly greater resources. As senior Pentagon officials have acknowledged, right now the United States simply cannot field even promising technologies in numbers sufficient to have strategic impact. "We'll do the demo, we'll be very happy with the results, [but] we won't have the money to go on," Undersecretary of Defense Frank Kendall warned in 2016.[47] Offsets and innovation are necessary for sustaining American primacy, but they are hardly sufficient. Similarly, although virtually all experts consider defense reform essential, no one has identified a feasible reform program sufficient to close the capabilities-commitments gap.

The economic argument is also deceptive. Although a multiyear buildup would be very expensive, it would hardly be unmanageable. Even the most aggressive proposed buildups would push defense spending only to 4 percent of GDP. The United States has previously supported far higher relative defense burdens without compromising economic performance.[48] One cannot draw a perfect parallel with earlier eras, of course, because during the 1950s America enjoyed higher growth and lower levels of deficits and debt. But these factors do not make a major buildup economically impossible.

For one thing, defense spending increases can actually stimulate growth. As Martin Feldstein, a former chair of the Council of Economic Advisers, has noted, "Military procurement has the . . . advantage that almost all of the equipment and supplies that the military buys is made in the United States, creating demand and jobs here at home."[49] Moreover, defense spending simply does not drive federal spending or deficits to the extent often imagined. In fiscal year 2016, defense consumed 16 percent of federal spending; domestic entitlements consumed 49 percent.[50] As a result, the growth of federal debt is influenced far more by unconstrained entitlement spending and insufficient tax revenues than by defense outlays. Put differently, if Washington can make politically difficult decisions regarding tax increases and curbing entitlement growth, it can spend significantly more on defense while also getting its fiscal house in order. If, conversely, the United States is unwilling to confront such politically difficult decisions, then the deficit will explode, the debt-to-GDP ratio will skyrocket, and Social Security and Medicare/Medicaid will go bankrupt regardless of how much or how little the country spends on defense.

The third objection, regarding intensified competition with US rivals, is also problematic. It is hard to see how increased US defense spending could trigger an arms race with Russia or China, or Iran or North Korea, because these countries are already developing significant military capabilities aimed at the United States. China, for instance, has averaged double-digit annual defense spending increases for two decades.

Strenuous military competition is already underway; US adversaries are just the ones competing most seriously. Moreover, although increased US defense efforts, particularly if paired with additional forward presence in Eastern Europe or East Asia, might cause increased near-term tensions with Moscow or Beijing, over the longer term, failure to counter Russian and Chinese buildups and limit their opportunities for successful coercion might well prove more destabilizing.

To be sure, Russia and China, or even Iran and North Korea, are not powerless to respond to US capability enhancement, and there may come a time when Washington simply cannot preserve the desired level of overmatch at an acceptable cost. Yet in light of the significant internal challenges—political, economic, demographic, or all of the above—facing each of America's adversaries, the passing of US primacy is hardly inevitable.[51] Given how advantageous US primacy has proven over the decades, America's goal should be to push that point of unsustainability as far into the future as possible.

The fourth and final objection, regarding allied free riding and the need for a collective approach, can also be answered. US strategy has always been a concert strategy, and so this approach certainly requires enhanced allied efforts. Countries from Japan and Taiwan to Poland and the Baltic states will have to spend more on defense if their situation is not to become untenable. They will, in many cases, also have to adopt more cost-effective and realistic defense strategies.[52] But because the United States cannot simply make this decision for its allies, the question is which US approach will best encourage constructive changes. And although advocates of retrenchment often argue allies will only do more if the United States does less, the United States has been most successful at securing increased allied contributions when it, too, has been willing to do more.

In previous instances when NATO allies collectively increased military spending—during the early 1950s or under the long-term defense program of the Carter-Reagan years—they did so as part of a broader program in which Washington also significantly increased its contributions to European security.[53] Likewise, the United States elicited the best performance from the Iraqi military and government when the American commitment to Baghdad was greatest, during the surge of 2007–8. The performance declined rather than improved as the US commitment was subsequently reduced.[54] In sum, the United States may actually get the most out of its allies and partners when those countries are reassured of the American commitment and thus prepared to take risks of their own.

As the principal objections to increasing defense resources fall away, the advantages and logic become clearer. This approach recognizes, for instance, how beneficial US military primacy has been in shaping a relatively stable, prosperous, and congenial international order, and it makes the investments necessary to sustain as much of this order as possible. This approach provides the United States with greater ability to meet aggression from a range of enemies and rivals without resorting to dangerously escalatory strategies in the most operationally demanding scenarios. As a result, this approach is arguably best suited to avoid the use of force over the long term, by averting situations in which American adversaries from Iran and North Korea to Russia and China think aggression might pay. "Peace through strength" is not a meaningless catchphrase; it is good strategy. Closing the capabilities-commitments gap by dramatically increasing the former therefore represents the best available approach.

VIII

"Without superior aggregate military strength, in being and readily mobilizable, a policy of 'containment' . . . is no more than a policy of bluff."[55] This admonition, written by the authors of NSC-68 in 1950, reflected a dawning realization that insufficient military power endangered America's global commitments. The United States faces another crisis of strategic solvency today as gathering international threats combine with dwindling military resources to leave the American superpower in an increasingly overextended and perilous state.

America thus confronts a stark choice about how to proceed. *Of the options considered here, the best approach is to find the resources necessary to bring American forces back into line with the grand strategy they are meant to support.* Undertaking a sustained, major military buildup will not be cheap, but is not unaffordable for a wealthy superpower that has benefitted so much from military primacy and its geopolitical benefits. Indeed, the fundamental question regarding whether America can undertake this course is not an economic one. It is whether the country will politically prioritize the investments needed to sustain its primacy or allow itself to slip further into strategic insolvency with all the associated dangers for the United States and the global order.

NOTES

1. This article is derived from a longer report: Hal Brands and Eric Edelman, *Avoiding a Strategy of Bluff: The Crisis of American Military Primacy and the Search for Strategic Solvency* (Washington, DC: Center for Strategic and Budgetary Assessments [CSBA], 2017).

2. Walter Lippmann, *U.S. Foreign Policy: Shield of the Republic* (Boston: Little, Brown, 1943), 9–10.

3. In practice, these options are not mutually exclusive—one could conceivably pursue a hybrid approach. But here, we treat these options as distinct to better flesh out their respective risks and merits.

4. Michael J. Mazarr, "The Risks of Ignoring Strategic Insolvency," *Washington Quarterly* 35, no. 4 (Fall 2012): 7–22, doi:10.1080/0163660X.2012.725020.

5. George W. Bush, "Commencement Address at the United States Military Academy in West Point, New York," June 1, 2002; and Eric S. Edelman, "The Strange Career of the 1992 Defense Planning Guidance," in *In Uncertain Times: American Foreign Policy after the Berlin Wall and 9/11*, ed. Melvyn P. Leffler and Jeffrey W. Legro (Ithaca, NY: Cornell University Press, 2011), 63–77.

6. Military spending statistics are drawn from the Stockholm International Peace Research Institute (SIPRI) database, https://www.sipri.org/databases/milex.

7. On post–Cold War grand strategy, see Hal Brands, "The Pretty Successful Superpower," *American Interest* 12, no. 3 (January/February 2017): 6–17; and Hal Brands, *Making the Unipolar Moment: U.S. Foreign Policy and the Rise of the Post–Cold War Order* (Ithaca, NY: Cornell University Press, 2016).

8. John Lewis Gaddis, *Strategies of Containment: A Critical Appraisal of American National Security Policy during the Cold War* (New York: Oxford University Press, 2005), 393; and "Military Expenditure (percent of GDP)," World Bank, http://data.worldbank.org/indicator/MS.MIL .XPND.GD.ZS?locations=US&page=3. /databases/milex.

9. William S. Cohen, *Report of the Quadrennial Defense Review, May 1997* (Washington, DC: Department of Defense [DoD], 1997).

10. International Institute for Strategic Studies (IISS), *The Military Balance 2015* (London: IISS, 2015), 159–67; and Catrin Einhorn, Hannah Fairfield, and Tim Wallace, "Russia Rearms for a New Era," *New York Times*, December 24, 2015.

11. SIPRI database.

12. Barbara Staff and Ryan Browne, "Intel Officials: North Korea 'Probably' Has Miniaturized Nuke," CNN News, March 25, 2016; and David Albright, *Future Directions in the DPRK's Nuclear Weapons Program: Three Scenarios for 2020*, North Korea's Nuclear Futures Series (Washington, DC: US-Korea Institute at SAIS, 2015).

13. SIPRI database.

14. "Military Expenditure," World Bank; and Loren Thompson, "Pentagon Budget Headed Below 3% of GDP as Warfighting Edge Wanes," *Forbes*, February 2, 2015.

15. Robert Zarate, "FPI Analysis: Obama's FY2014 Defense Budget & The Sequestration Standoff," *Foreign Policy Initiative*, April 11, 2013; and Todd Harrison, *Analysis of the FY 2013 Defense Budget and Sequestration* (Washington, DC: CSBA, 2012).

16. Quoted in Dave Majumdar, "The Pentagon's Readiness Crisis: Why the 2017 Defense Bill Will Make Things Worse," *Buzz* (blog), *National Interest*, July 13, 2016.

17. Todd Harrison and Evan Braden Montgomery, *The Cost of U.S. Nuclear Forces: From BCA to Bow Wave and Beyond* (Washington, DC: CSBA, 2015).

18. Jim Tice, "Army Shrinks to Smallest Level Since before World War II," *Army Times*, May 7, 2016; and Tony Capaccio and Gopal Ratnam, "Hagel Seeks Smallest U.S. Army Since before 2001 Attack," Bloomberg, February 24, 2014.

19. Mark Gunzinger, *Shaping America's Future Military: Toward a New Force Planning Construct* (Washington, DC: CSBA, 2013), 2–3.

20. Bernard Brodie, *Strategy in the Missile Age* (Santa Monica, CA: RAND Corporation, 1959), 358.

21. On Chinese spending, see SIPRI database.

22. Eric Heginbotham et al., *The U.S.-China Military Scorecard: Forces, Geography, and the Evolving Balance of Power, 1996–2017* (Santa Monica, CA: RAND Corporation, 2015), 342.

23. Heginbotham et al., *U.S.-China Military Scorecard*.

24. Mark Gunzinger, *Outside-In: Operating from Range to Defeat Iran's Anti-Access and Area-Denial Threats* (Washington, DC: CSBA, 2011), 21–52.

25. Sydney J. Freedberg Jr., "Army $40B Short on Modernization vs. Russia, China: CSA Milley," *Breaking Defense*, October 3, 2016.

26. David A. Shlapak and Michael W. Johnson, *Reinforcing Deterrence on NATO's Eastern Flank* (Santa Monica, CA: RAND Corporation, 2016).

27. Heginbotham et al., *U.S.-China Military Scorecard*, xxx, 338, 342.

28. DoD, *Sustaining U.S. Global Leadership: Priorities for 21st Century Defense* (Washington, DC: DoD, 2012), 4.

29. Under the Nixon Doctrine, Washington would keep existing treaty commitments in Asia and defend allies against aggression by a nuclear power, but it would provide only military and economic assistance to allies and partners facing other threats, namely insurgencies.

30. See, generally, Paul K. MacDonald and Joseph M. Parent, "Graceful Decline? The Surprising Success of Great Power Retrenchment," *International Security* 35, no. 4 (Spring 2011): 7–44.

31. On credibility and reputation, see Alex Weisiger and Keren Yarhi-Milo, "Revisiting Reputation: How Past Actions Matter in International Politics," *International Organization* 69, no. 2 (Spring 2015): 473–95, doi:10.1017/S0020818314000393.

32. On these phenomena, see Randall L. Schweller, *Unanswered Threats: Political Constraints on the Balance of Power* (Princeton, NJ: Princeton University Press, 2008); and Randall L. Schweller, "Bandwagoning for Profit: Bringing the Revisionist State Back In," *International Security* 19, no. 1 (Summer 1994): 72–107, doi:10.2307/2539149.

33. Hal Brands, *The Limits of Offshore Balancing* (Carlisle Barracks, PA: Strategic Studies Institute, 2015), 49–52.

34. Rick Brennan, "Withdrawal Symptoms: The Bungling of the Iraq Exit," *Foreign Affairs* 93, no. 6 (November/December 2014): 25–34; and Dexter Filkins, "What We Left Behind," *New Yorker*, April 28, 2014.

35. To clarify, this would entail more than simply using cyber as part of a US conventional defense of Taiwan or the Baltic. Rather, it would entail using strategic cyberattacks against strategic targets—economic, military, or infrastructure—not directly associated with the aggression.

36. Marc Trachtenberg, *A Constructed Peace: The Making of the European Settlement, 1945–1963* (Princeton, NJ: Princeton University Press, 1999), 87–90.

37. H. W. Brands, "The Age of Vulnerability: Eisenhower and the National Insecurity State," *American Historical Review* 94, no. 4 (October 1989): 963–89, doi:10.2307/1906591.

38. Ron Synovitz, "Europe Bracing against Risk of Russian 'Influence Operations,'" Radio Free Europe/Radio Liberty, January 16, 2017.

39. National Defense Panel, *Ensuring a Strong U.S. Defense for the Future: The National Defense Panel Review of the 2014 Quadrennial Defense Review* (Washington, DC: United States Institute of Peace, 2014).

40. Senator John McCain, *Restoring American Power: Recommendations for the FY 2018–FY 2022 Defense Budget* (Washington, DC: Senate Armed Services Committee, 2017), 9–14.

41. Marilyn Ware Center for Security Studies, *To Rebuild America's Military* (Washington, DC: American Enterprise Institute, 2015), 25.

42. McCain, *Restoring American Power*, 20.

43. Thomas Donnelly, "Great Powers Don't Pivot," in *How Much Is Enough? Alternative Defense Strategies*, ed. Jacob Cohn, Ryan Boone, and Thomas Mahnken (Washington, DC: CSBA, 2016), 7; also Ware Center, *To Rebuild America's Military*, 70.

44. On the importance of these various capabilities, see Evan Braden Montgomery, "Contested Primacy in the Western Pacific: China's Rise and the Future of U.S. Power Projection," *International Security* 38, no. 4 (Spring 2014): 140–43, doi:10.1162/ISEC_a_00160; Timothy A. Walton, "Securing the Third Offset Strategy: Priorities for the Next Secretary of Defense," *Joint Force Quarterly* 82 (3rd Quarter 2016): 6–15; and Gunzinger, *Outside-In*.

45. Sydney J. Freedberg Jr., "Pentagon Can't Afford to Field 3rd Offset Tech under BCA: Frank Kendall," *Breaking Defense*, October 31, 2016.

46. On debt-to-GDP ratio, see Congressional Budget Office (CBO), *The Budget and Economic Outlook: 2016 to 2026* (Washington, DC: CBO, 2016), 3.

47. Freedberg, "Pentagon."

48. Ware Center, *To Rebuild America's Military*, 2.

49. Martin Feldstein, "Defense Spending Would Be Great Stimulus," *Wall Street Journal*, December 24, 2008.

50. "Policy Basics: Where Do Our Federal Tax Dollars Go?," Center on Budget and Policy Priorities, March 4, 2016, http://www.cbpp.org/research/federal-budget/policy-basics -where-do-our-federal-tax-dollars-go.

51. See, for instance, Robert D. Kaplan, "Eurasia's Coming Anarchy: The Risks of Chinese and Russian Weakness," *Foreign Affairs* 95, no. 2 (March/April 2016).

52. See Jim Thomas, John Stillion, and Iskander Rehman, *Hard ROC 2.0: Taiwan and Deterrence through Protraction* (Washington, DC: CSBA, 2014); and Hal Brands, *Dealing with Allies in Decline: Alliance Management and U.S. Strategy in an Era of Global Power Shifts* (Washington, DC: CSBA, 2017).

53. See Richard L. Kugler, *Laying the Foundations: The Evolution of NATO in the 1950s* (Santa Monica, CA: RAND Corporation, 1990).

54. Stephen Biddle, Michael E. O'Hanlon, and Kenneth M. Pollack, "How to Leave a Stable Iraq," *Foreign Affairs* 87, no. 5 (September/October 2008): 40–58; also Peter R. Mansoor, *Surge: My Journey with General David Petraeus and the Remaking of the Iraq War* (New Haven, CT: Yale University Press, 2013).

55. National Security Council, "NSC-68, United States Objectives and Programs for National Security," April 14, 1950, http://fas.org/irp/offdocs/nsc-hst/nsc-68.htm.

The Next Liberal Order
The Age of Contagion Demands More Internationalism, Not Less

G. JOHN IKENBERRY

When future historians think of the moment that marked the end of the liberal world order, they may point to the spring of 2020—the moment when the United States and its allies, facing the gravest public health threat and economic catastrophe of the postwar era, could not even agree on a simple communiqué of common cause. But the chaos of the coronavirus pandemic engulfing the world these days is only exposing and accelerating what was already happening for years. On public health, trade, human rights, and the environment, governments seem to have lost faith in the value of working together. Not since the 1930s has the world been this bereft of even the most rudimentary forms of cooperation.

The liberal world order is collapsing because its leading patrons, starting with the United States, have given up on it. US President Donald Trump, who declared in 2016 that "we will no longer surrender this country . . . to the false song of globalism," is actively undermining 75 years of American leadership.[1] Others in the US foreign policy establishment have likewise packed their bags and moved on to the next global era: that of great-power competition. Washington is settling in for a protracted struggle for dominance with China,

G. John Ikenberry, "The Next Liberal Order: The Age of Contagion Demands More Internationalism, Not Less," *Foreign Affairs* 99, no. 4 (2020): 133–42. Republished with permission of *Foreign Affairs*; permission conveyed through Copyright Clearance Center, Inc.

Russia, and other rival powers. This fractured world, the thinking goes, will offer little space for multilateralism and cooperation. Instead, US grand strategy will be defined by what international relations theorists call "the problems of anarchy": hegemonic struggles, power transitions, competition for security, spheres of influence, and reactionary nationalism.

But this future is not inevitable, and it is certainly not desirable. The United States may no longer be the world's sole superpower, but its influence has never been premised on power alone. It also depends on an ability to offer others a set of ideas and institutional frameworks for mutual gain. If the United States abandons that role prematurely, it will be smaller and weaker as a result. A return to great-power competition would destroy what is left of the global institutions that governments rely on for tackling common problems.[2] Liberal democracies would further descend into disunion and thereby lose their ability to shape global rules and norms. The world that would emerge on the other side would be less friendly to such Western values as openness, the rule of law, human rights, and liberal democracy.

In the short term, the new coronavirus (and the resulting economic and social wreckage) will accelerate the fragmentation and breakdown of global order, hastening the descent into nationalism, great-power rivalry, and strategic decoupling. But the pandemic also offers the United States an opportunity to reverse course and opt for a different path: a last-chance effort to reclaim the two-centuries-old liberal international project of building an order that is open, multilateral, and anchored in a coalition of leading liberal democracies.

For guidance, today's leaders should look to the example of US President Franklin Roosevelt. The collapse of the world economy and the rapid spread of fascism and totalitarianism in the 1930s showed that the fates of modern societies were tied to one another and that all were vulnerable to what Roosevelt, using a term that seems eerily prescient today, called "contagion." The United States, Roosevelt and his contemporaries concluded, could not simply hide within its borders; it would need to build a global infrastructure of institutions and partnerships. The liberal order they went on to build was less about the triumphant march of liberal democracy than about pragmatic, cooperative solutions to the global dangers arising from interdependence. Internationalism was not a project of tearing down borders and globalizing the world; it was about managing the growing complexities of economic and security interdependence in the pursuit of national well-being. Today's liberal democracies are the bankrupt heirs to this project, but with US leadership, they can still turn it around.

The Problems of Modernity

The rivalry between the United States and China will preoccupy the world for decades, and the problems of anarchy cannot be wished away. But for the United States and its partners, a far greater challenge lies in what might be called "the problems of modernity": the deep, worldwide transformations unleashed by the forces of science, technology, and industrialism, or what the sociologist Ernest Gellner once described as a "tidal wave" pushing and pulling modern societies into an increasingly complex and interconnected world system. Washington and its partners are threatened less by rival great powers than by emergent, interconnected, and cascading transnational dangers. Climate change, pandemic diseases, financial crises, failed states, nuclear proliferation—all reverberate far beyond any individual country. So do the effects of automation and global production chains on capitalist societies, the dangers of the coming revolution in artificial intelligence, and other, as-yet-unimagined upheavals.

The coronavirus is the poster child of these transnational dangers: it does not respect borders, and one cannot hide from it or defeat it in war. Countries facing a global outbreak are only as safe as the least safe among them. For better or worse, the United States and the rest of the world are in it together.

Past American leaders understood that the global problems of modernity called for a global solution and set about building a worldwide network of alliances and multilateral institutions. But for many observers, the result of these efforts—the liberal international order—has been a failure.[3] For some, it is tied to the neoliberal policies that produced financial crises and rising economic inequality; for others, it evokes disastrous military interventions and endless wars. The bet that China would integrate as a "responsible stakeholder" into a US-led liberal order is widely seen to have failed, too. Little wonder that the liberal vision has lost its appeal.

Liberal internationalists need to acknowledge these missteps and failures. Under the auspices of the liberal international order, the United States has intervened too much, regulated too little, and delivered less than it promised. But what do its detractors have to offer? Despite its faults, no other organizing principle currently under debate comes close to liberal internationalism in making the case for a decent and cooperative world order that encourages the enlightened pursuit of national interests. Ironically, the critics' complaints make sense only within a system that embraces self-determination, individual rights, economic security, and the rule of law—the very cornerstones of liberal internationalism. The current order may not have realized these principles across the board, but flaws and failures are inherent in all political orders. What is unique about the postwar liberal order is its capacity for self-correction. Even a deeply flawed liberal system provides the institutions through which it can be brought closer to its founding ideals.

However serious the liberal order's shortcomings may be, they pale in comparison to its achievements. Over seven decades, it has lifted more boats—manifest in economic growth and rising incomes—than any other order in world history. It has provided a framework for struggling industrial societies in Europe and elsewhere to transform themselves into modern social democracies. Japan and West Germany were integrated into a common security community and went on to fashion distinctive national identities as peaceful great powers. Western Europe subdued old hatreds and launched a grand project of union. European colonial rule in Africa and Asia largely came to an end. The G-7 system of cooperation among Japan, Europe, and North America fostered growth and managed a sequence of trade and financial crises. Beginning in the 1980s, countries across East Asia, Latin America, and eastern Europe opened up their political and economic systems and joined the broader order. The United States experienced its greatest successes as a world power, culminating in the peaceful end to the Cold War, and countries around the globe wanted more, not less, US leadership. This is not an order that one should eagerly escort off the stage.

To renew the spirit of liberal internationalism, its proponents should return to its core aim: creating an environment in which liberal democracies can cooperate for mutual gain, manage their shared vulnerabilities, and protect their way of life. In this system, rules and institutions facilitate cooperation among states. Properly regulated trade benefits all parties. Liberal democracies, in particular, have an incentive to work together—not only because their shared values reinforce trust but also because their status as open societies in an open system makes them more vulnerable to transnational threats. Gaining the benefits of interdependence while guarding against its dangers requires collective action.

The Roosevelt Resolution

This tradition of liberal internationalism is often traced to US President Woodrow Wilson, but the great revolution in liberal thinking actually occurred under Roosevelt in the 1930s. Wilson believed that modernity naturally favored liberal democracy, a view that, decades later, led some liberals to anticipate "the end of history." In contrast, Roosevelt and his contemporaries saw a world threatened by violence, depravity, and despotism. The forces of modernity were not on the side of liberalism; science, technology, and industry could be harnessed equally for good and evil. For Roosevelt, the order-building project was not an idealistic attempt to spread democracy but a desperate effort to save the democratic way of life—a bulwark against an impending global calamity. His liberalism was a liberalism for hard times. And it is this vision that speaks most directly to today.

Roosevelt's core impulse was to put the liberal democratic world on a more solid domestic footing. The idea was not just to establish peace but also to build an international order that would empower governments to deliver a better life for their citizens. As early as August 1941, when the United States had not yet entered World War II, Roosevelt and British Prime Minister Winston Churchill articulated this vision in the Atlantic Charter, writing that if the United States and other democracies vanquished the Nazi threat, a new international order would secure "improved labor standards, economic advancement and social security." In the words of a Chicago journalist writing at the time, the New Deal at home was to lead to a "New Deal for the world."

Roosevelt's vision arose from the belief that interdependence generated new vulnerabilities. Financial crises, protectionism, arms races, and war could each spread like a contagion. "Economic diseases are highly communicable," Roosevelt wrote in a letter to the Bretton Woods conference in 1944. "It follows, therefore, that the economic health of every country is a proper matter of concern to all its neighbors, near and distant." To manage such interdependence, Roosevelt and his contemporaries envisioned permanent multilateral governance institutions. The idea was not new: since the nineteenth century, liberal internationalists had championed peace congresses, arbitration councils, and, later on, the League of Nations. But Roosevelt's agenda was more ambitious. International agreements, institutions, and agencies would lie at the heart of the new order. On issue after issue—aviation, finance, agriculture, public health—multilateral institutions would provide a framework for international collaboration.

Another innovation was to redefine the concept of security. In the United States, the Great Depression and the New Deal brought into existence the notion of "social security," and the violence and destruction of World War II did the same for "national security." Both were more than terms of art. They reflected new ideas about the state's role in ensuring the health, welfare, and safety of its people. "You and I agree that security is our greatest need," Roosevelt told Americans in one of his fireside chats in 1938. "Therefore," he added, "I am determined to do all in my power to help you attain that security." Social security meant building a social safety net. National security meant shaping the external environment: planning ahead, coordinating policies with other states, and fostering alliances. From now on, national governments would need to do much more to accomplish the twin goals of social and national security—both at home and abroad.

What also made Roosevelt's internationalism unique was that it was tied to a system of security cooperation among the big liberal democracies. The collapse of the post-1919 order had convinced internationalists on both sides of the Atlantic that liberal capitalist democracies would need to come together as a community for their common defense. Free societies and security partnerships were two sides of the same political coin. Even before US President Harry Truman and his successors built on this template, Roosevelt-era internationalists envisaged a grouping of like-minded states with the United States as, in Roosevelt's words, "the great arsenal of democracy." With the rise of the Cold War, the United States and its fellow democracies formed alliances to check the Soviet threat. The United States took the lead in fashioning a world of international institutions, partnerships, client states, and regional orders—and it put itself at the center of it all.

Clubs and Shopping Malls

In the face of today's breakdown in world order, the United States and other liberal democracies must reclaim and update Roosevelt's legacy. As a start, this means learning the right lessons about the failures of the liberal international order in the past three decades. Ironically, it was the success of the US-led order that sowed the seeds of the current crisis. With the collapse of the Soviet Union, the last clear alternative to liberalism disappeared. As the liberal order grew from being one-half of a bipolar system to a truly global order, it began to fragment, in part because it no longer resembled a club. Indeed, today's liberal international order looks more like a sprawling shopping mall: states can wander in and pick and choose what institutions and regimes they want to join. Security cooperation, economic cooperation, and political cooperation have become unbundled, and their benefits can be obtained without buying into a suite of responsibilities, obligations, and shared values. These circumstances have allowed China and Russia to cooperate with the liberal system on an opportunistic, ad hoc basis. To name just one example, membership in the World Trade Organization has given China access to Western markets on favorable terms, but Beijing has not implemented significant measures to protect intellectual property rights, strengthen the rule of law, or level the playing field for foreign companies in its own economy.

To prevent this sort of behavior, the United States and other liberal democracies need to reconstitute themselves as a more coherent and functional coalition. The next US president should call a gathering of the world's liberal democracies, and in the spirit of the Atlantic Charter, these states should issue their own joint statement, outlining broad principles for strengthening liberal democracy and reforming global governance institutions. The United States could work with its G-7 partners to expand that group's activities and membership, adding countries such as Australia and South Korea. It could even turn the G-7 into a D-10, a sort of steering committee of the world's ten leading democracies that would guide the return to multilateralism and rebuild a global order that protects liberal principles. The leaders of this new group could begin by forging a set of common rules and norms for a restructured trading system. They could also establish an agenda for relaunching global cooperation on climate change and confer about preparing for the next viral pandemic. And they should better monitor and respond to China's efforts to use international organizations to advance its national economic champions and promote its authoritarian mode of governance.

This club of democracies would coexist with larger multilateral organizations, chief among them the United Nations, whose only entry requirement is to be a sovereign state, regardless of whether it is a democracy or a dictatorship. That inclusive approach has its merits, because in many realms of international relations—including arms control, environmental regulation, management of the global commons, and combating pandemic diseases—regime type is not relevant. But in the areas of security, human rights, and the political economy, today's liberal democracies have relevant interests and values that illiberal states do not. On these fronts, a more cohesive club of democracies, united by shared values, tied together through alliances, and oriented toward managing interdependence, could reclaim the liberal internationalist vision.

A key element of this effort will be to reconnect international cooperation with domestic well-being. Put simply, "liberal internationalism" should not be just another word for "globalization." Globalization is about reducing barriers and integrating economies and societies. Liberal internationalism, by contrast, is about managing interdependence. States once valued the liberal international order because its rules tamed the disruptive effects of open markets without eliminating the efficiency gains that came from them. In giving governments the space and tools they needed to stabilize their economies, the order's architects tried to reconcile free trade and free-market capitalism with social protections and economic security. The result was what the scholar John Ruggie has called the compromise of "embedded liberalism": unlike the economic nationalism of the 1930s, the new system would be multilateral in nature, and unlike the nineteenth-century visions of global free trade, it would give countries some leeway to stabilize their economies if necessary. But by the end of the 1990s, this compromise had begun to break down as borderless trade and investment overran national systems of social protection, and the order became widely seen as a platform for global capitalist and financial transactions.[4]

To counteract this perception, any new liberal international project must rebuild the bargains and promises that once allowed countries to reap the gains from trade while making good on their commitments to social welfare. Economic openness can last in liberal democracies only if its benefits are widely shared. Without sparking a new era of protectionism, liberal democracies need to work together to manage openness and closure, guided by liberal norms of multilateralism and nondiscrimination. "Democracies have a right to protect their social arrangements," the economist Dani Rodrik has written, "and, when this right clashes with the requirements of the global economy, it is the latter that should give way." If liberal democracies want to ensure that this right to protection does not trigger destructive trade wars, they should decide its exact reach collectively.

How, then, to deal with China and Russia? Both are geopolitical rivals of the United States, and both seek to undermine Western liberal democracies and the US-led liberal order more generally. Their revisionism has put blunt questions of military power and economic influence back on the diplomatic agenda. But on a deeper level, the threat emanating from these states—particularly from China—only gives more urgency to the liberal international agenda and its focus on the problems of modernity. The struggle between the United States and China is ultimately over which country offers a better road to progress. Chinese President Xi Jinping's great project is to define an alternative path, a model of capitalism without liberalism and democracy.[5] The jury is out on whether a totalitarian regime can pull this off, and there is reason to be skeptical. But in the meantime, the best way to respond to this challenge is for liberal democracies to work together to reform and rebuild their own model.

"Brace Up"

It would be a grave mistake for the United States to give up any attempt to rescue the liberal order and instead reorient its grand strategy entirely toward great-power competition. The United States would be forfeiting its unique ideas and capacity for leadership. It would become like China and Russia: just another big, powerful state operating in a world of anarchy, nothing more and nothing less. But in its geography, history, institutions, and convictions, the United States is different from all other great powers. Unlike Asian and European states, it is an ocean away from other great powers. In the twentieth century, it alone among the great powers articulated a vision of an open, post-imperial world system. More than any other state, it has seen its national interest advanced by promulgat-

ing multilateral rules and norms, which amplified and legitimized American power. Why throw all this away?

There simply is no other major state—rising, falling, or muddling through—that can galvanize the world around a vision of open, rules-based multilateral cooperation. China will be powerful, but it will tilt the world away from democratic values and the rule of law. The United States, for its part, needed the partnership of other liberal states even in earlier decades, when it was more capable. Now, as rival states grow more powerful, Washington needs these partnerships more than ever. If it continues to disengage from the world or engages in it only as a classic great power, the last vestiges of the liberal order will disappear.

And so it is left to the United States to lead the way in reclaiming the core premise of the liberal international project: building the international institutions and norms to protect societies from themselves, from one another, and from the violent storms of modernity. It is precisely at a moment of global crisis that great debates about world order open up and new possibilities emerge. This is such a moment, and the liberal democracies should regain their self-confidence and prepare for the future. As Virgil has Aeneas say to his shipwrecked companions, "Brace up, and save yourself for better times."

NOTES

1. See Julian Hattem, "Trump Warns against 'False Song of Globalism,'" *The Hill*, 2016.
2. See Michael J. Mazarr, "This Is Not a Great-Power Competition, *Foreign Affairs*, 2019).
3. See Fareed Zakaria, "The Self-Destruction of American Power," *Foreign Affairs*, 2019.
4. See Jeff D. Colgan and Robert O. Keohane, "The Liberal Order Is Rigged," *Foreign Affairs*, 2018.
5. See Branko Milanovic, "The Clash of Capitalisms," *Foreign Affairs*, 2019.

REFERENCES

Colgan, Jeff D., and Robert O. Keohane. 2018. "The Liberal Order Is Rigged," December 8. https://www.foreignaffairs.com/articles/world/2017-04-17/liberal-order-rigged.

Hattem, Julian. 2016. "Trump Warns against 'False Song of Globalism.'" *The Hill*, April 27. https://thehill.com/policy/national-security/277879-trump-warns-against-false-song-of-globalism.

Mazarr, Michael J. 2019. "This Is Not a Great-Power Competition," June 1. https://www.foreignaffairs.com/articles/2019-05-29/not-great-power-competition.

Milanovic, Branko. 2019. "The Clash of Capitalisms," December 13. https://www.foreignaffairs.com/articles/united-states/2019-12-10/clash-capitalisms.

Zakaria, Fareed. 2019. "The Self-Destruction of American Power," December 31. https://www.foreignaffairs.com/articles/2019-06-11/self-destruction-american-power.

Why "Conservative," Not Liberal, Internationalism?

HENRY R. NAU

As John Maynard Keynes famously wrote, "Practical men who believe themselves to be quite exempt from any intellectual influence, are usually the slaves of some academic scribbler of a few years back." That surely is the case for presidents and foreign policy. Republican presidents such as Teddy Roosevelt and Richard Nixon generally have employed a realist theory of world affairs, attempting to maintain a balance of power in order to preserve peace. Democratic presidents such as Woodrow Wilson and Franklin Roosevelt have preferred a liberal internationalist approach, intended to strengthen multilateral institutions in an attempt to replace the balance of power. A few presidents, like Andrew Jackson and perhaps Donald Trump today, practice what might be called a minimal realist or nationalist approach. And some presidents, like Thomas Jefferson and Ronald Reagan, are claimed to be liberal internationalists even though they rejected the strengthening of centralized institutions, either domestic or international.

For some reason (perhaps because most academics are liberals), academics have seldom written about a "conservative" internationalist tradition. There is no broad literature to define this tradition as there is for realism, liberal internationalism, and nationalism. For 50 years, I wondered why this was so, even after Ronald Reagan fashioned a foreign policy strategy that explicitly deviated from both realism and liberal internationalism and produced an outcome, the end of the Cold War, that rivaled the achievements of Nixon or Wilson. My book, *Conservative Internationalism*, sets out to fill this gap.[1]

What Is Conservative Internationalism?

First, conservative internationalism is "conservative," favoring limited central government and a robust private sector or civil society. In foreign affairs, that idea translates into a world of strong states not universal global institutions, and of independent national defenses and competitive markets not expert-dominated collective security and globalization. Thomas Jefferson's view of the world rivals Woodrow Wilson's vision. Wilson foresaw global institutions eventually replacing national sovereignty. Thomas Jefferson, when contemplating the new states that might emerge in the Louisiana Territory, called them "sister republics" and said, "Keep them in the union, if it be for their good, but separate them, if it be better."[2] For Jefferson, the priority was republicanism not union. Nations remain separate and sovereign, especially when it comes to defense, but share republican virtues of self-government and commerce. Wilson envisioned the League of Nations, Jefferson the democratic peace.

Second, conservative internationalism is "internationalist" in the sense that national security is not only about territorial defense and geopolitical balances, but also about the kind of "political" or "ideological" world in which defense is executed. Defending America is much easier in a world in which democracies proliferate than in one dominated by authoritarian powers. This fact is often overlooked by realists and nationalists who take the world "as it is," and warn against ideological aims which pursue the world as "we wish it to be." Yet, consider how much more difficult American defense would be if the world today was like the world in 1914 or 1941. In short, regime type matters, and increasing the number of democracies in the world—however slowly or incrementally—is a fundamental tenet of national security. As my colleague, Mike Barnett, once put it felicitously: "A community of Saddam Husseins is unlikely to father a secure environment, while a community of Mahatma Gandhis will encourage all to leave their homes unlocked."[3]

Third, conservative internationalism believes that diplomacy works best when it is "armed." This contention follows not because conservatives are militarist while liberals are cooperative, but because nondemocracies use force congenitally and, if democracies negotiate unarmed, nondemocracies will achieve their objectives by arms outside negotiations. As Frederick the Great once said, "Negotiations without arms are music without instruments."[4] For conservative internationalism, the use of military force does not disrupt diplomacy; it makes the adversary take negotiations seriously. By contrast, liberal internationalism sees force as a "last resort" after negotiations fail and then only with multilateral consent. When the Soviet Union deployed missiles in Eastern Europe in the 1970s and waged proxy wars in Africa and Central America,

Henry R. Nau, "Why 'Conservative,' Not Liberal, Internationalism?" *Orbis* 62, no. 1 (Winter 2018): 22–29. Republished with permission of Elsevier; permission conveyed through Copyright Clearance Center, Inc.

liberal internationalists prioritized arms control (SALT I and II). That made "détente," as Reagan saw it, "a one-way street."[5] The Soviet Union became serious and reduced arms through negotiations only after the United States and Western allies boosted defense spending, deployed their own missiles in Western Europe, and backstopped freedom fighters in proxy wars.

Fourth, conservative internationalism sets "priorities" and seeks "compromises," recognizing that the pursuit of freedom through armed diplomacy, however incremental, raises the stakes. It prioritizes freedom where freedom counts the most, namely on the borders of Europe and Asia where strong free nations and markets already exist. And it uses diplomacy to discipline the use of force. The objective is to lock in incremental gains in priority areas, not to seek to spread freedom everywhere at once. Reagan offered the Soviet Union off ramps as well as road blocks—an end to the arms race and participation in the information revolution—and he prioritized freedom in Central Europe, not in Lebanon or Afghanistan. He accepted compromises only after he was convinced that those compromises would lead to greater freedom.[6]

So, conservative internationalism means fighting for freedom incrementally by leveraging diplomacy with force to achieve a decentralized world of separate and sovereign nations that champion individual freedom and live together under limited government, the democratic peace. When it comes to the importance of regime type for national defense, both conservative and liberal internationalists part company with realism and nationalism. And on the need for force to leverage diplomacy and the end goal of strong nations not international institutions, conservative internationalism parts company with liberal internationalism.

Let us take a closer look at each of the four aspects of conservative internationalism.

What Is Conservative?

There are many ways to differentiate conservatives from liberals and most of them are politically charged. Some are just downright partisan.

The fairest way to start is with the proposition that both conservatives and liberals care about the American experiment; that is, they all support the quest for liberty and equality, freedom and justice.

As Louis Hartz wrote in *The Liberal Tradition in America*, all Americans are liberals.[7] He meant classical liberals who advocate individual liberty, as laid out in the Declaration of Independence, and "republican" institutions, as provided by the checks and balances of the Constitution. There are no pre-Enlightenment conservatives in America who believe in authoritarianism, monarchy, aristocracy, class, or clericalism. For that reason, America—unlike Europe—has never had

a significant fascist, communist, or even confessional (that is, religious) party.

Where American conservatives and liberals differ, however, is on the priority they give to liberty versus equality. When there is a trade-off, liberals are more willing to accept restraints on liberty to achieve greater equality; conservatives are more willing to accept greater inequality to preserve more liberty. Both views are justified and necessary because, as Aristotle told us long ago, there are two types of inequality: one, when equal people are treated unequally—that is the liberal concern—and two, when unequal people are treated equally—that is the conservative concern.

Logically, therefore, conservatives see the greatest threats to liberty primarily coming from centralized institutions that treat unequal people equally and prescribe one-size-fits-all solutions that restrict choice. They worry about the executive or administrative state—that is, an unconstitutional "fourth branch" of government made up of unaccountable bureaucrats, experts, and judges—and prefer to leave most decisions to local and civil society institutions where equal opportunity does not preclude natural inequalities based on differences in ambition, effort, and talent.

Liberals, on the other hand, see the greatest threats to liberty arising from a private sector that treats equal people unequally and restricts opportunity, leading to poverty, racial discrimination, and corporate monopolies. They favor an activist central state that regulates the private sector and redistributes resources, insuring greater justice in outcomes as well as opportunity.

These differences have existed since the beginning of the Republic. Alexander Hamilton and the Federalists worried about the unruly mobs that refused to pay their whiskey taxes (dispatching an army to suppress them). Thomas Jefferson and the Republicans worried about an oppressive government that passed the Alien and Sedition Acts (imprisoning Republican journalists for merely criticizing the government).

In a republic, this is a healthy competition that tracks threats to liberty from both the public and private sectors.

What Is Internationalist?

Domestic differences between conservatives and liberals lead to significant and healthy differences in foreign policy.

First, because of their greater faith in government and experts, liberals believe that persistent diplomacy in international institutions will eventually temper and narrow differences between authoritarian and democratic regimes. They are willing to concede equality to authoritarian states in international institutions in order to pull them toward the "liberal" international order. The idea, as John Ikenberry writes, is to capture authoritarian states in an "iron cage of multilateral rules, standards, safeguards and dispute resolution procedures"[8] and eventually to domesticate and indeed democratize their politics. What is needed in this process is time, patience, and the realization that history is on freedom's side.

Conservatives, by contrast, believe that ideological differences may be too great to allow diplomatic outcomes that favor freedom. Treating authoritarian states equally in international institutions may only legitimize these regimes. In December 1945, Secretary of State James Brynes warned President Harry Truman that ideological differences with the Soviet Union made UN agreements unlikely and potentially threatening to freedom in Central Europe.[9] Truman recognized fairly quickly that these differences would not be resolved by diplomatic compromises, but would need to be litigated through deterrence and a competition between two ways of life. That was the vision he laid out in the Truman Doctrine.

What Is Armed Diplomacy?

Conservative internationalism expects that, in this ideological competition, the role of force will be more important than liberal internationalism assumes. The reason is that authoritarian states use force at home to sustain their rule and are more likely than democratic states to use it abroad to advance their foreign policy interests.[10] In short, authoritarian states can be expected to use force while they negotiate.

Thus, conservative internationalism arms diplomacy during negotiations with authoritarian states.[11] The purpose is not to scuttle negotiations, but to counter uses of force by authoritarian states outside negotiations in order to get them to take seriously the discussions inside negotiations. By contrast, liberal internationalism seeks to avoid the use of force during diplomacy regarding it as a "last resort" to be deployed only after diplomacy and economic sanctions have failed and then, for many, only with multilateral consent. President Barack Obama and Secretary of State John Kerry differed on this issue in Syria.[12] As the civil war heated up in that country, Kerry repeatedly counseled Obama to intervene militarily to counter the gains that Bashar al-Assad and his Russian and Iranian backers were making on the ground. The objective, Kerry said, was not to overthrow Assad, but to encourage him and his backers to take the peace negotiations seriously. As long as they had the upper hand on the battlefield, Kerry pointed out, they had no incentive to negotiate. Obama steadfastly resisted these requests. He believed that the use of force during negotiations would simply increase distrust and lead to a slippery slope of escalating force. In fact, Obama predicted that Russia's intervention would end up in a quagmire.

Both arguments are logical. The slippery slope is a real issue; it exposes conservative internationalist thinking to overreach and liberal internationalist thinking to appeasement. To escape this trap, conservative internationalism sets priorities and seeks compromises.

Setting Priorities

Conservative internationalism does not "support the growth of democratic movements and institutions in every nation and culture, with the ultimate goal of ending tyranny in our world."[13] Rather, it cares about the plight of freedom (human rights, democracy, etc.) in some countries more than in others. Specifically, it defends and, to the extent possible, extends freedom on the major borders of existing free countries. In more remote regions where few democracies exist, it is concerned primarily with threats, not with democracy promotion.

This means a greater concern for democracy on the major frontiers of freedom in Europe and Asia than in the Middle East or Southwest Asia. Today, the ideological hotspots on these borders are Ukraine and Korea. In these conflicts, conservative internationalism recommends that the United States holds out for democracy over the long haul, as it did during the Cold War. This approach is both necessary and possible. It is necessary because the consequences of losing freedom on these borders are far greater than in Iraq or Afghanistan. Think of the difficulties for freedom in Europe caused already by Russia's interventions in Georgia, Ukraine, and Syria (refugees). And it is possible because the costs of fighting for freedom on these borders are less, given the strong presence nearby of democratic alliances and capitalist markets.

In remote regions such as the Middle East and Southwest Asia, conservative internationalism recommends that the United States downplay democracy promotion. Deal with threats, such as the Taliban and ISIS, but, except for training and advice, do not station large forces or spend massive sums of money in these regions to transplant democracy. Above all, do nothing to weaken existing democracies in these regions like Israel or India.

Compromise

Conservative internationalism uses military leverage to achieve compromises that incrementally favor freedom. This stance represents an important difference from realists who also seek compromise, but only to secure the status quo and from some neoconservatives who seek total victory and no compromise at all.

In short, while conservative internationalism arms diplomacy with force, it never uses force without follow-up diplomacy, that is, without simultaneously offering a compromise or diplomatic off ramp for adversaries. A key element of this strategy is to cash in military gains for compromise at the moment when those gains are most significant.

James K. Polk was a genius at combining force and diplomacy. He kept diplomatic envoys in play throughout the war with Mexico, initially to avoid war and then to find off ramps to end the war without a long occupation. He succeeded. After conquering the entire country, American troops left Mexico within six months. George H. W. Bush also successfully leveraged military force in the First Persian Gulf War to launch the Madrid Middle East Peace Conference and the Oslo Accords that followed indirectly from Madrid. His son, George W. Bush, however, missed similar opportunities to leverage military success in the Second Persian Gulf War. He did not take up in 2003 an Iranian offer to negotiate its nuclear program and waited until November 2007 to launch a wider Middle East Peace Initiative, four-and-a-half years after the invasion and after his military leverage had waned enough to require a second military surge in Iraq.

How do we know when a compromise favors freedom or the status quo? It is not always easy. But negotiations in Ukraine offer an example. A conservative internationalist compromise would uphold the right for Ukraine to join NATO and the European Union someday, just as the West upheld that right for a divided Germany during the Cold War. A realist compromise would call for a buffer or bridge state, a Ukraine neither east nor west but neutral or both.[14]

Conservative Internationalism Summed Up

Thus, an internationalism that expands freedom conservatively means in sum the following:

- Upholding the importance of regime type and not just territorial defense in national security policy
- Recognizing the need to use force during negotiations to get authoritarian states to take negotiations seriously
- Setting priorities and using gains from armed diplomacy to secure compromises that weaken or at least do not legitimate authoritarian states
- Aiming for a world of "sister republics" that remain separate and sovereign but share republican or democratic values and bind together through robust volunteer markets and civil society exchanges

In the end, conservative internationalism embraces the *goals* of liberal internationalism (reforming the international system, not settling for the status quo), the

means of realism (use force during negotiations, not as a last resort), and the *purpose* of nationalism (a world of sovereign, but free nations, not global international institutions).

NOTES

1. Henry R. Nau, *Conservative Internationalism: Armed Diplomacy under Jefferson, Polk, Truman, and Reagan* (Princeton, NJ: Princeton University Press, 2015). An internationalist literature that is more conservative and places greater emphasis on ideologies than power (realism) or institutions (liberal internationalism) has been growing in recent years. See John M. Owen IV, *The Clash of Ideas in World Politics* (Princeton, NJ: Princeton University Press, 2010); Mark L. Haas, *The Ideological Origins of Great Power Politics, 1789–1989* (Ithaca, NY: Cornell University Press, 2005); Paul D. Miller, *American Power and Liberal Order* (Washington, DC: Georgetown University Press, 2016); and Robert G. Kaufman, *Dangerous Doctrine* (Lexington: University Press of Kentucky, 2016).

2. Jefferson to Breckenridge, Aug. 12, 1803, in Paul Leicester Ford, ed., *The Writings of Thomas Jefferson*, Vol. VIII (New York: Putnam & Sons, 1906), pp. 243–244.

3. Michael N. Barnett, "Identity and Alliances in the Middle East," in Peter J. Katzenstein, ed., *The Culture of National Security* (New York: Columbia University Press, 1996), p. 407.

4. Quoted in William Fiddian Reddaway, *Frederick the Great and the Rise of Prussia* (New York: Putnam & Sons, 1904), p. 132.

5. Reagan used this phrase; President's News Conference, Jan. 29, 1981, http://www.preside.ncy.ucsb.edu/ws/?pid=44101.

6. Reagan did not reach this conclusion until spring 1988. See Mark L. Haas, "The United States and the End of the Cold War," *International Organization* 61, no. 1 (2007), pp. 145–179.

7. Louis Hartz, *The Liberal Tradition in America* (New York: Harcourt, Brace and World, 1955).

8. G. John Ikenberry, Thomas J. Knock, Anne-Marie Slaughter, and Tony Smith, *The Crisis of American Foreign Policy* (Princeton, NJ: Princeton University Press, 2009), p. 16.

9. See Marc Trachtenberg, *A Constructed Peace* (Princeton, NJ: Princeton University Press, 1999), p. 16.

10. The literature on the democratic peace supports this expectation.

11. Armed diplomacy here means three uses of military force during negotiations that go beyond economic sanctions, but stop short of outright military intervention. These include: buildup of defenses and their deployment, use of proxy forces, and trade-off of arms within negotiations.

12. For the details here, see an interview with President Obama by Jeffrey Goldberg, "The Obama Doctrine," *The Atlantic*, April 2016, http://www.the.atlantic.com/magazine/archive/2016/04/the-obama-doctrine/471525/.

13. George W. Bush, Inaugural Address, Jan. 20, 2005, http://www.npr.org/templates/story/story.php?storyId=4460172.

14. Henry Kissinger, "To Settle the Ukraine Issue, Start at the End," *The Washington Post*, Mar. 5, 2015.

Chapter 3

The International Environment—Allies

30 Years of World Politics
What Has Changed?

FRANCIS FUKUYAMA

What has changed in world politics over the thirty years since the *Journal of Democracy* published its inaugural issue in January 1990, and how has the *Journal* changed in response?

First, to get the obvious out of the way, we are now living in a political climate very different from the one that existed in 1990. The *Journal of Democracy* began publication just past the midpoint of what Samuel P. Huntington called the "third wave" of democratization. The Berlin Wall had just been torn down, and communist regimes had begun collapsing across Central and Eastern Europe—the most dramatic advance for democracy during the entire thirty-year period. Today, by contrast, we are living in what Larry Diamond labels a "democratic recession," with reason to worry that it could turn into a full-scale depression.[1] Authoritarian great powers such as Russia and the People's Republic of China are openly challenging the Western liberal-democratic model, even as populists and nationalists launch attacks on that model from within the West itself. These setbacks have occurred not only in peripheral democracies, but in the very countries that led the democratic revolution, the United States and Britain.

The pages of the *Journal* have reflected this shift, going from cautious optimism to a focus on the different routes to democratic transition, to skepticism about whether "transition" was an adequate concept to capture what was happening, and then to a far more defensive concern with new and emerging threats to democracy. In recent years, this analysis has gingerly begun to include the threats emanating from within what had been considered "consolidated" democracies, as well as the new forms of "sharp power" that authoritarian regimes are deploying to undermine liberal-democratic norms and regimes around the world.[2] Underlying these changes has been a reorientation of the major axis of political polarization. In the twentieth century, politics was characterized by an ideological divide between a left and a right defined largely in economic terms, with the former demanding greater socioeconomic equality and a redistributive state, while the latter favored individual freedom and strong economic growth. Today the axis is shifting toward a politics based on identity. As part of this change, both the left and the right are redefining their own objectives.[3]

The psychological basis of identity politics lies in the feelings of humans that they possess an inner worth or dignity which the society around them is failing to recognize. The underappreciated identity may be unique to an individual, but more often it flows from membership in a group, particularly one that has suffered some form of marginalization or disrespect. Identity is intimately linked to emotions of pride, anger, and resentment based on the kind of recognition that one receives (or does not receive). Although perceived economic injustices may stimulate the demand for recognition, this drive is distinct from the material motives that impel *homo economicus*, and can often lead to actions that run counter to economic self-interest conventionally understood. Thus, for example, many who voted "Leave" in the Brexit referendum understood that Britain might suffer economically after parting ways with the EU, but judged this a price worth paying to restore British national identity. While today's nationalists and Islamists mobilize around different issues, they hold in common a feeling that members of their groups have been marginalized, and both demand respect from global society.

This demand for dignity motivates populist voters in Hungary and Poland, who feel that their national identities are under threat from immigration and liberal social values, much as it motivates supporters of Brexit in Britain and of Donald Trump in the United States. But it also characterizes the Hindu-nationalist supporters of Narendra Modi in India, who want to base Indian national identity on Hinduism, or the militant Buddhists in Burma and Sri Lanka, who feel that their nations' religious identities are under threat.

The shift from economics to identity has also led to a reordering of left and right in the developed democracies. While the twentieth-century left, whether communist, socialist, or social-democratic, promoted the interests of the broad working class, today's left is more likely to champion specific identity groups such as racial minorities, immigrants, women, people with disabilities, sexual minorities, indigenous peoples, and so forth. An accompanying idea is that since each of

Francis Fukuyama, "30 Years of World Politics: What Has Changed?" *Journal of Democracy* 31, no. 1 (2020): 11–21. © 2020 National Endowment for Democracy and the Johns Hopkins University Press; reprinted with permission of Johns Hopkins University Press.

these groups was marginalized in specific ways, remedies need to be tailored to each group. Over time, these group identities have often come to be seen as essential characteristics of their members, defining them at the expense of their individual identities. This ideological shift has had political consequences: Rather than focusing on the old working class and its trade unions (the great majority of whose members tended to belong to the dominant ethnic or racial group), leftist parties in the United States and other developed democracies now see themselves as representing the interests of various minorities. An upshot of this drift away from the old working class has been the movement of voters belonging to that class away from traditional left-wing parties and toward newer populist forces.

A similar transformation has been occurring on the right. Twentieth-century conservative parties defended free markets and individual rights, often with the backing of business interests that supported free trade and welcomed immigrants. That old right is now being displaced by one that emphasizes a traditional kind of ethnically based national identity and worries that "our country" is being taken over by a cabal of immigrants, foreign competitors, and elites who are complicit in the theft. Hence Prime Minister Viktor Orbán speaks explicitly about Hungarian national identity being based on Hungarian ethnicity, and endorses an "illiberal democracy" in which democratic majorities do not necessarily feel themselves bound to respect universal human rights.

This emerging new type of conservatism also includes an international dimension that Russia has played a role in shaping.[4] It is based on a defense of traditional national values and culture, and on opposition to liberal values such as rights for sexual minorities and openness to immigration. There is a deep and growing connection between Russia and parts of the Christian right in the United States, based on common opposition to gay marriage and on Vladimir Putin's promotion of Russia as a Christian country. Russia in recent years has lent moral and financial support to European populists as well, including Marine Le Pen's National Rally (formerly the National Front) in France and Matteo Salvini's Lega in Italy.

When Putin first came to power in 2000 and started drifting away from the United States and Europe, he seemed to be in search of an ideology that would justify his opposition to Western policies. He experimented with ideas such as Vladislav Surkov's "sovereign democracy," but these never really caught on, and Putin now seems to have found a role as the mentor of populist conservatives across the democratic world. It is unclear how seriously Putin himself takes any of these ideas, but they suit his foreign-policy purposes by helping to weaken the elites in countries that he regards as rivals.

The sociology of polarization has also been changing. Jonathan Rodden has shown that the single most powerful correlate of populist voting both in the United States and in Europe is low population density.[5] The global economy has been concentrating work and opportunity in ever-larger cities. These tend to produce more liberal voters, while populists are spread out in second—or third—tier towns and villages and in rural areas. Such voters tend to be older and less mobile, with fewer years of formal schooling. Population density has come to reflect not just economic opportunity, but cultural values as well.

Technology: From Friend to Foe?

The second major shift that has occurred in the thirty years of the *Journal* concerns the role of technology. This is a development not unrelated to the rise of identity as the major axis of world politics. The 1990s saw the birth of the global internet, which was almost universally touted at that time as offering help and support to aspiring democrats worldwide. The internet's model for distributed computing and communications seemed bound to upend existing authoritarian hierarchies and to spread information—and thus power—to a much broader range of people. And so it did: The "color revolutions" in the post-communist world and uprisings such as those of the Arab Spring all took advantage of the ability of activists to organize spontaneously using new horizontal forms of communication.

Unfortunately, technological development did not stop there, and the internet's decentralization did not last. Network externalities and the rise of social media gave tremendous advantages to early movers such as Google and Facebook, which began to exercise monopolistic control over the internet. Authoritarian rulers in Beijing and Moscow understood the threat that a decentralized internet posed to them, and they learned how to reshape it for their own purposes. Today, the global internet has been bifurcated into a closed internet controlled by China and a more open internet operated by a handful of private companies in the United States. The Chinese internet is deliberately managed with the goal of supporting China's authoritarian government, while the Western internet has been operated to serve the interests of the private companies that control it. The latter are not in principle opposed to democracy, but their self-interest has allowed them to be used by antidemocratic actors who have discovered that conspiracy stories and fabricated information often are rewarded with more clicks than the truth receives. Among the hierarchies disrupted by the internet was the one formed by the "legacy media" in democratic countries—media organizations working in print, radio, and television that had over time developed journalistic standards for vetting and verifying information. The rise of Google and Facebook undermined the old media's business model, and today it is not clear what economic incentives there are to provide reliable news to broad democratic publics.

The tendency of the new identity politics in both its leftist and rightist varieties has been to fragment societies into ever smaller identity groups. In many ways, social media are perfectly suited to facilitate this decomposition of society. They permit like-minded individuals to find one another, not just in their own nations but around the world, while simultaneously shutting out criticism and disagreement. On the left, sexual politics and "intersectionality" have led to the proliferation of distinct and sometimes mutually hostile identities, while on the right we have discovered the existence of communities such as "incels" (involuntarily celibate males) and of new vocabularies and symbols by which white nationalists can identify one another. Promoting all this have been external actors such as Russia, which seems less interested in recommending its own political model than in heightening distrust and division within Western societies.

It would be wrong, however, to attribute growing social fragmentation simply to the rise of the internet or to Russian policy. The decline in the authority of traditional social institutions began before the year 1990 and has been growing ever since. These institutions consist not just of governments, but the full range of mediating social structures, including political parties, business corporations, labor unions, churches, families, media outlets, voluntary organizations, and the like. This phenomenon was first noted in the *Journal of Democracy* by Robert D. Putnam, who published his widely read "Bowling Alone" essay in these pages in 1995.[6] Survey data capture the decline as well, showing how trust in these institutions has fallen over time. While the declines vary by institution and by country, the overall shrinkage in trust is strikingly cross-national—it appears in place after place throughout the democratic world.[7]

This weakening of trust in mediating institutions is in part a byproduct of many of the good things that are happening around the world. Populations are better educated than they were a few decades ago, which inclines people to think for themselves and not simply to defer to traditional sources of authority. There is much more transparency in the operations of our social institutions than there used to be, not just because of the internet, but because modern publics demand it. For example, it is very unlikely that sexual predation by Catholic priests is a new phenomenon; nor is sexual assault by powerful men in large organizations something that arose only in the twenty-first century. These have become major issues because transparency norms have changed. More information is available today, and people are less willing to excuse abuses or to cover up damaging material for the sake of the greater good.

When Putnam noted that there had been a long-term decline in voluntary associations in the United States, critics pointed out that US society had also become much more diverse since the 1950s. Women and racial minorities had been entering workplaces and organizations from which they had previously been excluded. The "old-boy networks" that had been highly homogenous in racial, gender, and religious terms engendered high levels of trust, but at the expense of excluding important parts of the population. The decline of trust in institutions is thus in part a result of modern democratic societies having grown more inclusive and socially just.

The early apostles of the information revolution believed that it would act as a force for democracy partly because they understood that the new technologies would have a direct impact at the level of the individual. In the 1980s, the advent of the desktop personal computer vastly multiplied the number of people who could have computing power at their fingertips. The 1990s saw the rise of universal internet connections, while the 2000s put all this together in the portable and ubiquitous form of the smartphone.

More recent technological developments, however, have shifted power back in a more centralized direction. While artificial intelligence and machine learning can be embedded in personal devices—and in fact depend on the vast troves of information captured by such devices—individuals cannot easily master these technologies, as they did the personal computer. Indeed, the datasets that allow machines to learn are so big that only large companies, or in some cases large countries, can make full use of them. The kind of surveillance system being created today in China—which will link hundreds of millions of sensors to large-scale machine learning—is feasible primarily in authoritarian political systems.

Even in the most democratic societies, moreover, the emerging "internet of things" is gathering mind-boggling mountains of information whose uses will be even more opaque to individual users than is the case with today's internet. Large and technically adept organizations, whether governments or private companies, *can* exploit "big data," however—and are already beginning to do so. None of this is likely to bode well for democratic empowerment, though we are way too early in these developments to predict their political consequences.

It would be wrong to focus solely on threats to democracy posed by the internet and social media. There has been a big shift in legacy media as well. Their increasing ownership by oligarchs has supported the rise of populist nationalism: In a pattern pioneered by Italy's Silvio Berlusconi, oligarchs have purchased legacy-media outlets and then used their ownership to promote their political careers. Once in office, such oligarchs can use political influence to protect their personal business interests. In Ukraine, every major television channel is connected to one of the half-dozen oligarchs who dominate the economy; in Hungary, the mainstream media are now controlled by wealthy businessmen tied to Orbán's ruling Fidesz party.

Neoliberalism and Its Discontents

A number of other slow-moving changes have shifted the environment in which democracy exists. The first has to do with economics. The early 1990s marked the apogee of the free-market revolution that had been unleashed a decade before by Ronald Reagan and Margaret Thatcher.[8] In reaction to the stagflation of the 1970s, the intellectual framework within which elites thought about economic policy was revised by scholars such as Milton Friedman, Gary Becker, George Stigler, Robert Lucas, Jr., and others. These thinkers provided a high-brow intellectual framework that essentially endorsed Ronald Reagan's quip, "The nine most terrifying words in the English language are 'I'm from the government and I'm here to help.'" The once-dominant Keynesian economics had seen a helpful role for governments in countering business cycles. Keynesianism was replaced by strict monetarism and an effort to reduce government intervention across the board through tax cuts, deregulation, privatization, tariff reduction, and a relaxed attitude toward corporate scale—the famous "Washington Consensus."

This shift toward what today is derided as "neoliberalism" permitted the emergence of new global powers such as China and India, lifted hundreds of millions of people out of poverty, and unleashed powerful entrepreneurial forces in the United States and other countries. But it had several baleful consequences in the years after 1990. The first was exacerbating the income inequality that had been growing since the 1960s, with enormous wealth becoming concentrated in the hands of a very small elite across the world. The second was the financialization of wealth, and the destabilization of the financial sector as a consequence of its deregulation, leading to major financial crises in Latin America, East Asia, the United States, and the Eurozone. The subprime-lending crisis of 2008 and the euro crisis of 2010 did much to discredit the elites who had promoted the liberal international order, thereby setting the stage for populism's rise in the succeeding decade.

The 1991 collapse of the former Soviet Union had seemed to validate the views of the extreme free-market advocates. "Dizzy with success" (as Stalin would say), they forgot that in a well-functioning market economy the state continues to play vital roles by enforcing the rule of law, maintaining political stability, and regulating economic activity. The advice coming out of Western capitals in the early 1990s was to deregulate and privatize as rapidly as possible, even where state weakness was extreme. The results in such cases were economic chaos, deepening poverty, and the rise of a class

of oligarchs who had figured out how to game the rapidly evolving situation. These outcomes became associated in the minds of many in the region with democracy itself, paving the way for the rise of Putin and other strongmen in the following decade.

Every generation's mental framework is shaped by the collective experiences that mark its members' formative years. For people who lived through the Cold War and its finale, the word "socialism" had very negative connotations. For people born after 1990, it is neoliberalism and its associated policies of fiscal austerity, privatization, and free trade that have taken on a negative valence. The popularity of socialism among progressive members of the "millennial" generation in the United States and the hostility to the EU professed by young Central and East Europeans are byproducts of this kind of generational forgetting.

Ivan Krastev and Stephen Holmes have suggested that there was an even deeper issue here. The communist regimes of Central and Eastern Europe and the former Soviet Union pretended that they had solved the problem of nationalism, but in fact they had simply swept it under the rug. After 1945, none of these regimes had made investments in trying to persuade the postwar generation of the evils of nationalism, as the West Germans had done with their own young people. Indeed, for many in the region nationalism and national identity came to have positive meanings, since communist regimes had denied and tried to suppress them. As a result, after 1989–91, the former "captive nations" embraced the democratic part of liberal democracy, but not necessarily the liberal part—that is, the idea that diverse peoples can live peacefully together under "equal laws, equally applied." The result was the emergence of illiberal democracy in places such as Hungary and Poland.[9]

In the former Soviet Union, meanwhile, US economic policy had a negative effect on democratic prospects that has not been fully acknowledged to this day. But US policy mistakes harmed democracy's outlook in other respects as well. The years from 1991 to 2008 were an extraordinary period of US political and military hegemony, when Washington's military budget outpaced the total defense spending of the rest of the world combined, and the United States faced no "peer competitor" that could counterbalance US power. The relatively easy victory won by the US-led coalition in the 1991 Gulf War convinced US policymakers that they had a unique instrument for reshaping global politics. This led to a second enormous policy blunder, which was the 2003 invasion of Iraq. Fearing what turned out to be nonexistent Iraqi weapons of mass destruction, the George W. Bush administration toppled Saddam Hussein's dictatorship and pursued a broader "Freedom Agenda" that sought to remake the politics of the entire Middle East. This

move had a number of unanticipated long-term consequences: The invasion shifted the power balance in
the region in favor of the Islamic Republic of Iran and
its Shia allies; this led to continuing instability in Iraq
and the rise of a new terrorist group, the Islamic State;
and it put severe strains on the Western alliance while
also discrediting the British government, which had
chosen to stand with Washington. Finally, in the minds
of many around the world, the invasion and occupation of Iraq created an association between democracy
promotion and the unilateral use of US military power.

The Iraq invasion together with the prolonged war
in Afghanistan had a major impact on how the people
of the United States view their relationship with the
outside world. Despite their many differences, Barack
Obama and Donald Trump share a belief that the
United States should reduce its presence in the Middle
East and avoid intervention (particularly for humanitarian purposes) when US interests are not heavily engaged. All this has led to increased levels of cynicism
on the part of younger Americans concerning prospects
for successful democracy promotion.

Another long-term shift has lowered expectations
regarding democratic transitions. The combined experiences of the former communist world and the Middle
East have fortunately induced a greater degree of realism in US views of democracy promotion (Europeans
generally were much more skeptical to begin with). The
seemingly rapid transition to liberal democracy of
countries such as Hungary and Poland after the sudden collapse of communism was in retrospect a highly
contingent event from which many in the United States
drew the wrong lesson. In 2005, George W. Bush's second inaugural address asserted the universality of
democratic rights and aspirations, and dedicated the
United States to the task of ending tyranny around the
world—a task, Bush said, whose accomplishment
would also ensure US national security. Overlooked
amid the focus on ending tyranny was the sheer difficulty of building a sustainable liberal democracy amid
the wreckage that tyranny leaves behind.

Democracy and State Capacity

The difficulty of building democracy was driven home
in the most painful possible way by Iraq. Saddam Hussein's removal did not lead to joyous crowds celebrating their liberation (as in Central and Eastern Europe),
but rather to years of violence and chaos as the US occupation sought to rebuild an Iraqi state. The huge
literature on democratic transitions, much of it published in the *Journal of Democracy*, focused on democratic institutions such as elections, electoral rules, parties, legislatures, and the like, or to a lesser extent on
key building blocks of liberalism such as constitutions
and legal codes.

These institutions are designed to constrain power
even as they legitimize it—but they are predicated on
the raw fact that power exists in the first place, in the
form of a state deploying a monopoly of legitimate coercion throughout a given territory. In Iraq and Afghanistan, US foreign policy confronted the need to build
such states before it could even begin the task of building democracy. When it comes to the problem of state-
building, however, contemporary political science has
little to say that is useful. The irony is that even in Hungary and Poland, what had seemed in the early 2000s to
be successful transitions to consolidated liberal democracy have turned out to be much less than that.

As a result, US policy has become far more cautious—
and rightly so—about the ability of outside powers to
control what happens the day after the dictator de-
parts. The last instance of this type of intervention was
NATO's action in Libya in 2011; Obama drew from
this experience the lesson that he should avoid significant military action in Syria.

The transitions literature, following a shifting policy agenda, has moved from a heavy focus on democratic institutions to the question of state capacity, and,
as part of that, to reflections on the problem of corruption and what to do about it. Afghanistan and Iraq
are extreme examples of state weakness, but there was
a growing recognition that many developing countries
with stable governments nonetheless suffered from
weak state capacity and high levels of corruption. In
some cases, as in Russia, the corruption was organized
from the top and became the basis of state power. In
other cases, such as in Brazil and Mexico, corruption
has coexisted with functioning democratic institutions,
but has delegitimized elected leaders. As a consequence,
each of these two Latin American countries is now led
by a populist president (a rightist one in Brazil and a
leftist one in Mexico).

What needs further investigation is the relationship
between democracy, on the one hand, and the problem
of corruption and state capacity on the other: There is
a widespread but seldom stated assumption that the
solution to systemic corruption is more democracy, but
the empirical relationship between the two is far more
complicated.[10]

The recent rise of populism has led to a questioning of parts of the consensus that existed a generation
ago about democratic transitions. Back then, political
scientists talked about "consolidated democracy," usually measured by Huntington's classic "two-turnover"
test: If elections had led to power peacefully changing
hands once, and then again, democracy could be said
to have achieved consolidation. With the backsliding
that has lately occurred in the most consolidated democracies (including the United States and Britain), the
notion that democracy can never go backward once
it reaches a certain point looks quaint. *Journal of*

Democracy authors such as Steven Levitsky have argued that the lethal threat to modern democracies is not the military coup, but rather a steady, gradual erosion of norms and institutions of the sort that has been going on in Hungary since 2011. Many people see this process unfolding in the United States itself.[11]

It would be wrong to end this overview on a purely pessimistic note. Over the past century, democracy has gone through many ups and downs. The current crisis is not nearly as severe as the one that struck in the 1930s, when fascism took hold in the heart of Europe. And that crisis arguably was rivaled by the loss of confidence in democracy that beset the West during the manifold troubles of the 1970s. The spark that animated the transitions of 1989–91 is still alive in many parts of the world. In just the past few years, Ukraine, Algeria, Sudan, Nicaragua, Armenia, and Hong Kong have all seen the emergence of mass protests against authoritarian government, even if these did not always lead to successful democratic transitions. The Czech Republic, Georgia, Romania, Slovakia, and even Russia have seen popular pushback against corruption and oligarchic control of the democratic process.

Brexit has fractured the British political system in a way that guarantees no other EU country will soon follow the British path. It is not clear that British voters themselves, if they had a chance to redo their decision, would now make the same choice that they did back in June 2016. While Donald Trump has challenged many of America's check-and-balance institutions, they have largely held; the most important check, an electoral one, may be forthcoming in 2020. Over the long run, demographics do not seem to favor populism; young people continue to move out of rural areas and into big cities.

In order to get to the long run, however, we must first survive the short run. Today, there are two opposite trends in the world: The first is social fragmentation and its concomitant, the decline of the authority of mediating institutions, primarily in established democracies. The second is the rise of new centralized hierarchies in authoritarian states. Surviving the present means rebuilding the legitimate authority of the institutions of liberal democracy, while resisting those powers that aspire to make nondemocratic institutions central. The *Journal of Democracy* has done a superb job of analyzing all these phenomena over the past thirty years. Let us hope that it will continue to do so as the decades roll on, for its insights will surely be needed.

NOTES

1. Larry Diamond, *Ill Winds: Saving Democracy from Russian Rage, Chinese Ambition, and American Complacency* (New York: Penguin, 2019).

2. Christopher Walker, "What Is 'Sharp Power'?" *Journal of Democracy* 29 (July 2018): 9–23.

3. This issue is explored at greater length in my book *Identity: The Demand for Dignity and the Politics of Resentment* (New York: Farrar, Straus and Giroux, 2018).

4. Marc F. Plattner, "Illiberal Democracy and the Struggle on the Right," *Journal of Democracy* 30 (January 2019): 5–19.

5. Jonathan A. Rodden, *Why Cities Lose: The Deep Roots of the Urban-Rural Political Divide* (New York: Basic Books, 2019).

6. Robert D. Putnam, "Bowling Alone: America's Declining Social Capital," *Journal of Democracy* 6 (January 1995): 65–78.

7. See, for example, Moisés Naím, *The End of Power: From Boardrooms to Battlefields and Churches to States, Why Being in Charge Isn't What It Used to Be* (New York: Basic Books, 2013); and Robert D. Putnam, *Bowling Alone: The Collapse and Revival of American Community* (New York: Simon and Schuster, 2000).

8. For an account of this shift, see Binyamin Appelbaum, *The Economists' Hour: False Prophets, Free Markets, and the Fracture of Society* (New York: Little, Brown and Company, 2019).

9. Ivan Krastev and Stephen Holmes, "Explaining Eastern Europe: Imitation and Its Discontents," *Journal of Democracy* 29 (July 2018): 117–28.

10. Roberto Stefan Foa, "Modernization and Authoritarianism," *Journal of Democracy* 29 (July 2018): 129–40.

11. Steven Levitsky and Daniel Ziblatt, *How Democracies Die* (New York: Crown, 2018).

REFERENCES

Appelbaum, Binyamin. 2019. *The Economists' Hour: False Prophets, Free Markets, and the Fracture of Society.* New York: Little, Brown and Company.

Diamond, Larry. 2019. *Ill Winds: Saving Democracy from Russian Rage, Chinese Ambition, and American Complacency.* New York: Penguin.

Foa, Roberto Stefan. 2018. "Modernization and Authoritarianism." *Journal of Democracy.*

Fukuyama, Francis. 2018. *Identity: The Demand for Dignity and the Politics of Resentment.* New York: Farrar, Straus and Giroux.

Krastev, Ivan, and Holmes, Stephen. 2018. "Explaining Eastern Europe: Imitation and Its Discontents." *Journal of Democracy.*

Levitsky, Steven, and Ziblatt, Daniel. 2018. *How Democracies Die.* New York: Crown.

Naím, Moisés. 2000. *The End of Power: From Boardrooms to Battlefields and Churches to States, Why Being in Charge Isn't What It Used to Be.* New York: Basic Books.

Plattner, Marc. 2019. "Illiberal Democracy and the Struggle on the Right." *Journal of Democracy.*

Putnam, Robert. 1995. "Bowling Alone: America's Declining Social Capital." *Journal of Democracy.*

Putnam, Robert. 2000. *Bowling Alone: The Collapse and Revival of American Community.* New York: Simon and Schuster.

Rodden, Jonathan. 2019. *Why Cities Lose: The Deep Roots of the Urban-Rural Political Divide.* New York: Basic Books.

Walker, Christopher. 2018. "What Is 'Sharp Power'?" *Journal of Democracy.*

Global Allies in a Changing World

MICHAEL WESLEY

In October 2001, in response to the 9/11 terrorist attacks on the United States, US forces invaded Afghanistan, the country from which the attacks had been planned and coordinated. Operation Enduring Freedom, the invasion and subsequent stabilisation and state-building project in Afghanistan, saw the United States supported by the largest-ever coalition of its allies: 10 from Europe and two from Asia.[1] Over the next 13 years, US allies from Asia and Europe planned, fought and worked side by side in unprecedented numbers and intensity, battling a rising Taliban insurgency and supporting the consolidation of the Afghan Government and security forces. In the process, the North Atlantic Treaty Organization (NATO) in Europe and the San Francisco System in Asia became global allies, collaborating not only in Afghanistan but also in the stabilisation of Iraq, the setting up of the Proliferation Security Initiative to prevent transnational nuclear proliferation, and enforcing anti-piracy patrols in the Gulf of Aden. Japan, South Korea, Thailand, the Philippines, Australia, New Zealand and Pakistan were designated 'major non-NATO allies' and began attending issue-specific discussions among NATO members in Brussels.

A decade after the invasion of Afghanistan, in a speech to a joint sitting of the Australian parliament, US President Barack Obama proclaimed that 'the United States is turning our attention to the vast potential of the Asia Pacific region . . . the United States will play a larger and long-term role in shaping this region and its future'.[2] By mid-2012, the administration's resolve had been written into strategic policy: the United States would 'rebalance' its attention away from the Middle East towards the Asia-Pacific region, where 60 per cent of its naval, space and cyber assets would be positioned.[3] The American rebalance caused more than a ripple of disquiet among US allies in Europe. Many responded to the understandable implication that a rebalance towards Asia would mean a diminution of America's commitment to its security partnerships elsewhere. For many NATO members, the Chinese challenge to America's Pacific primacy was remote, whereas Russia's increasingly assertive and aggressive policies towards its near neighbours, Georgia, the Ukraine and NATO members in the Bal-

tic states, represented the most profound challenge to European security since the end of the Cold War. Ironically at the same time in Asia, many security elites expressed scepticism about the seriousness of the rebalance. They questioned whether the United States would really be able to disentangle its forces and attention from the ongoing instability in the Middle East and North Africa and, even if it could, whether it would have the resolve to face down an increasingly confident and demanding China in the western Pacific. These concerns are likely to continue given the US air campaign against the Islamic State of Iraq and Syria (ISIS), and its recent recommitment of forces to Europe in the aftermath of Russian aggression in Ukraine.

Thus, in the first decade of the 21st century, US allies in Europe and Asia had traced the full arc of their new condition of interdependence, first tasting the benefits of collaboration and solidarity, and then the anxieties of competing for US commitment, attention and resources. Never before had NATO and the San Francisco system been so mutually significant. In 1949, the United States reversed 150 years of eschewing alliances by agreeing to a multilateral pact to shore up postwar Europe against an antagonistic and expansive Soviet Union. At the time, Washington had categorically ruled out a similar commitment in Asia, and rebuffed attempts by anxious wartime partners, such as Australia, to be allowed inside the NATO tent, at least at a consultative level. Gradually, however, whether as a condition for a peace deal with a rehabilitated Japan, or under the threat of communist expansion into the Pacific, it reneged, signing a series of alliances with Japan, South Korea, Taiwan, the Philippines, Thailand, Australia and New Zealand from 1951. Unlike NATO, these would be bilateral (or trilateral, in the case of Australia, New Zealand, United States Security [ANZUS]), and their operative clauses in general much less compelling as security guarantees than NATO's Article 5.

For the next half-century, the two alliance systems operated in isolation. While some NATO members joined the United Nations' enforcement action in Korea in the 1950s, it was not a NATO operation. None of the San Francisco allies showed the slightest interest in supporting the Asian commitments of European powers, even though Britain contributed to the postcolonial sta-

Michael Wesley, "Global Allies in a Changing World," in *Global Allies: Comparing US Alliances in the 21st Century*, 1–14 (Canberra: Australian National University Press, 2017).

bilisation and defence of Malaya. The Vietnam War in the 1960s and 1970s mobilised the San Francisco allies minus Japan, but not a single NATO member. Iraq's invasion of Kuwait in 1990 saw US allies from Europe and Asia come together to support a UN enforcement operation, as in Korea, but the experience was brief and had little effect on the different worlds of the two alliance systems. NATO became consumed by its post–Cold War expansion and the wars of the former Yugoslavia, while the San Francisco system seemed in decline, with Taiwan's loss of its formal alliance with the United States in 1978, New Zealand's expulsion from ANZUS in 1986, and the closure of US bases in the Philippines in 1992. As the new century dawned, it was not an attack on any smaller ally, but on the superpower anchor of both alliance systems that brought about a new era of interdependence. Suddenly the rationale of both alliance systems had shifted from deterring and defeating state-based aggression to addressing state dysfunction and battling transnational violent extremism. The new reality in a unipolar world was that allies of the sole superpower had to anticipate, understand and integrate with their major ally's new strategic imperatives. As a wounded America rose in fury, its long-time allies faced a choice of rising with it or being cast aside. For the first time, the thoughts and actions of remote US allies on the other side of the world became of abiding importance.

The Global Allies Project brought together strategic scholars from eight countries allied to the United States to discuss challenges in alliance dynamics and management. The project is a response to a major lacuna in this new era of alliance interdependence. While today America's European and Asian allies are intimately aware of each other's thinking on terrorism and counterinsurgency, counterproliferation, piracy and sea-lane security, cyber threats and hybrid challenges, there has been remarkably little discussion of the challenges of alliance management among the allies of the United States. While there are large and inevitable differences between different alliances, there are also significant commonalities, including dilemmas of commitment, trust and risk management, the difficulties of managing American expectations and domestic political resistance, issues of defence spending and interoperability, and reconciling alliance commitments with other foreign policy interests. For 60 years, US allies have managed these issues in mutual isolation, and sometimes in competition with each other. The Global Allies Project seeks to add a crucial tile to the alliance interdependence puzzle, by systematically comparing the challenges and processes of alliance management across a range of long-standing US allies in Europe and Asia.

Rather than look backwards, however, the Global Allies Project looks toward the future of alliance management in Europe and Asia. While it is impossible to tell whether another 9/11 will happen to reinforce the interoperation of Asian and European allies of the United States, we believe there are structural forces at play that will reinforce the interdependence of the two alliance systems and that make the case for comparing alliance management dynamics an enduring one. It is the purpose of this essay to explore what some of these structural forces are. In the sections ahead, I examine the imperatives of alliance policy in an era of relative US power decline, of regional and global order challenges by revanchist powers, and of the changing balance of costs and benefits in alliance commitments. Rather than establish a framework for the detailed alliance-specific case studies that follow, this essay is intended to set the general scene against which those case studies can be read.

Declining Relatives

The perennial debates about the relative decline of American power serve to underline how central US primacy has been for the post–World War II global order. The unprecedented and probably never-to-be replicated post–World War II power lead that allowed the United States to craft a world order according to its preferences, convince a large number of other states of its legitimacy, and defend it against its opponents, has been eroding steadily over the past 70 years. The collapse of the Soviet Union led to two decades of unipolarity but, unlike after World War II, the United States was not able to craft a stable or enduring 'new world order' as its first post–Cold War president promised. Indeed, the past two decades have demonstrated the complexity and intractability of threats to world order and the limits of American power to craft durable solutions to them.

Perhaps the greatest challenge to American primacy has been the pervasive uncertainty within its own policy-making system about what US power can achieve and how and when it should be wielded. As the dust of the Soviet collapse settled, Washington was nonplussed at the seeming puniness of those challengers that arose in defiance of George H. W. Bush's new world order: a jumped-up Iraqi strongman; Serbian paramilitary thugs; an unhinged, jumpsuit-wearing North Korean dictator; and drug-addled Somali gangs. But, despite not even approaching the seriousness of the Cold War's crises, these new challenges would prove anything but routine matters for the sole superpower. American forces had little trouble in winning kinetic victories; what American power couldn't achieve was enduring solutions that were acceptable to liberal consciences or the liberal order. What these frustratingly enduring challenges produced was a rising tide of criticism within the US of how those in charge of US foreign policy were handling the sword and shield of the Republic.

And so, American foreign policy lurched between extremes of aggression and restraint as the 21st century began. The George W. Bush administration brought to power a critical mass of neoconservatives who believed that it was imperative to use the unipolar moment to reshape the world for another era of American dominance and liberal peace. American power could not only recast an infinitely pliable world, it could create new realities. Those who resisted would be crushed, those who objected would be cast aside; those who were onboard would benefit from the new reality. But the early swagger of the neoconservatives turned sour as global opinion turned against the projected invasion of Iraq, and as coalition troops in both Afghanistan and Iraq faced rising insurgencies. The 2008 presidential election campaign saw both Republican and Democratic contenders criticise the Bush administration's recklessness in its use of force, its rhetorical excesses, and its cavalier treatment of long-time allies and partners of the United States. Bush's successor, Barack Obama, replaced confrontation with conciliation with those seen to be resisting the liberal global order—the Muslim world, China, Russia, Iran—and became as hesitant to use force as his predecessor had been bellicose. Yet Obama's foreign policy registered few successes. Despite his search for a series of 'resets', Russia, China and Iran became more assertive and defiant and a series of Muslim states in the Middle East and Africa succumbed to an even more brutal jihadist insurgency. The candidates in the 2016 presidential election have united in distancing themselves from the Obama approach to the use—and particularly the non-use—of American power.

The backdrop to the oscillation of approaches to American power has been the slow vanishing of the unipolar era due to a combination of factors. One was the real demonstration of the limits of American power in Afghanistan and Iraq; unlike the Vietnam War, which was a proxy conflict against two Cold War opponents, these have been 21st-century insurgencies combining a millennial ideology, brittle structures of domestic order, deep sectarian divisions, and global support networks facilitated by new social media. The United States ran down its stocks of goodwill, public support, defence financing and tolerance for casualties, while the challenges of state dysfunction and Islamist insurgencies continue unabated. Meanwhile the global financial crisis mired the United States, Europe and Japan in debt, while dealing a major blow to the legitimacy of Western liberal dominance of the global economy. In the aftermath of the crisis, it became less and less controversial to observe the growing economic heft of emerging economies, particularly in Asia; on current trends, the United States will yield its century-long position as the world's largest economy during this decade. China is already the world's largest economy in purchasing power parity terms, the world's largest importer of minerals and energy, the world's largest exporter, the world's largest manufacturer, the world's largest trading nation, and the primary trading partner for 130 countries. In the meantime, its military spending has been increasing rapidly, leading some observers to argue that China represents a more profound threat to US primacy than the Soviet Union ever did.

At this time of relative decline, the United States faces some profound challenges to the liberal global order it founded. The Arab 'Spring' of 2009–11 did not bring about a spread of representative democracy in the Middle East but, rather, the collapse of political order amid a virulent fanatical insurgency, deepening sectarian divisions and the growing assertiveness of regional powers. The global financial crisis bequeathed a chronically weak and unstable global economy, in which the status quo powers in the international economic order are faced with mounting debt and pervasive weaknesses in their currencies, and more and more countries are looking to decidedly illiberal means of returning to stability and growth.[4] Meanwhile, three powers have begun new forms of military adventurism across the Eurasian landmass. Using the pretext of protecting ethnic Russian minorities outside its borders, Russia launched attacks on Georgia in 2008 and Ukraine in 2014, dismembering parts of both states' territories. In the aftermath of the invasions of Afghanistan and Iraq, Iran used the resulting chaos to extend its influence into Iraq, Syria, Lebanon and Yemen. Iranian forces are currently at war in Iraq, Syria and Yemen. In eastern Asia, China asserted territorial claims in the East China Sea and the South China Sea and across the line of control with India. Taken together, these actions represent a challenge to the territorial order across Asia, agreed in 1991 in Europe, 1915 in the Middle East and 1945 in East Asia. And each of these three revisionist powers, having closely watched US air and sea power in action since the end of the Cold War, has been patiently building up its anti-area access and denial (A2AD) capabilities—a development that has created an uncertainty of response in the United States and its allies. Finally, the world now faces new threats to the global information commons. The increasingly interconnected information and control systems of societies have proven extremely vulnerable to criminal and coercive attack; at the same time, the resort of major states to authoritarian control over their information systems threatens a possible Balkanisation of the global information network.

The combination of falling US relative power and rising systemic threats to that power creates a paradox of rising indispensability and falling credibility for the United States among its allies. On the one hand,

Washington is unsure whether a decisive show of resolve will only further illustrate the ineffectiveness of US power *à la* Iraq and Afghanistan; on the other, each case of perceived American hesitance is taken as more evidence of the recession of American primacy. Meanwhile, American allies face challenges to the liberal order with a growing sense that any effective response must involve the full complement of allied commitment and solidarity, but such are the expectations of allies in Europe, Asia and the Middle East that the American response will almost inevitably be found wanting in each theatre. While Stephen Walt is right to observe that hard balancing against the unipole is unlikely even under conditions of declining relative power, the dilemmas of alliance commitment and credibility are no less diminished.[5]

Shoring Up the Liberal Order

The frequency of US allies' and partners' recent exhortations on the need to defend the liberal order is a compelling sign that they are increasingly worried about its integrity. The states system seems to be under attack from above and below. In the Middle East and North Africa, jihadist insurgencies explicitly reject the borders drawn between Muslim societies. Their goal of a transnational caliphate, if successful, seeks to recast the postcolonial order across the Muslim world. In place of state territorial boundaries would be a single confessional divide between the society of believers and those of the unbelievers; across this divide would exist a state of perpetual war.

Empire states exist in the Caucasus and the Western Pacific that are determined to expand their boundaries, either through formal annexations of territory or through the creation of spheres of influence. President Vladimir Putin's Russia grieves the collapse of the Soviet Union and the loss of territory, in Europe and Central Asia, but especially in the Caucasus. Both Georgia and Ukraine made the fatal mistake of seeking to align their countries more with the West and less with Russia; such a challenge to the Russian sphere of influence was met by direct aggression and the annexation of strategically crucial territory. In the Western Pacific, China increasingly views the 'first island chain', stretching from Japan through the Ryukyus and Taiwan to the Philippines, as a scheme imposed on it by the Western postwar settlement, to hem China in through an archipelago controlled by states hostile to it and allied with the United States. Beijing is increasingly intent on overturning this postwar settlement, absorbing Taiwan, building sea control in the South China Sea, and nibbling away at the Ryukyus via its claims to the Senkaku/Diaoyu Islands. As in the Caucasus, it is a process of challenging the status quo through unilateral and unpredictable *faits accomplis*.

In both Europe and Asia, the United States and its allies face a real paradox of liberal order maintenance that makes their commitments to uphold the liberal order both conditional and unconditional. The conditionality of the liberal order arises from its commitment to certain values, such as democracy, the rule of law and free assembly and exchange, as well as its belief that the liberal order will not be complete until there is universal adherence to these claims. Real problems arise when the liberal order is dependent on illiberal regimes for its stability. In these cases, support for authoritarian allies is always conditional and unpredictable; the fate of Egypt's President Hosni Mubarak showed that long-term US support can be suddenly withdrawn when one's authoritarian nature is suddenly on stark display. The parallel unconditionality of the liberal order arises from its commitment to liberal values and their eventual universality. This means that an attack on these values anywhere is taken to be an attack on them everywhere, creating mounting demands on the United States and its allies to 'do something' when these values are under assault. Whether or not actual strategic interests are at stake becomes secondary and, once committed to, the draining defence of liberal values becomes very hard to walk away from.

Both the conditionality and the unconditionality of liberal-order maintenance create real opportunities for those challenging the order. For a start, by definition these are states that do not identify with the order or its maintenance; they are able to free ride on those aspects they can benefit from, while avoiding, resisting or undermining elements they find threatening. The conditionality of US support for authoritarian or problematic allies creates opportunities for new partnerships, such as those developing between China and Saudi Arabia or between Russia and Pakistan. The unconditionality of US and allied commitments to defending liberal values generates a perpetual state of strategic chaos, as the upholders of the liberal order perpetually disperse their forces and resources based on maps not of interests but of values. The fanatical jihadists in the Muslim world can dependably draw the 'Great Satan' and its allies into what they believe to be a millennial battle on their own turf simply through a growing catalogue of outrages.

Alliance Costs and Benefits

The long history of regarding alliances in accounting terms, weighing up the costs and risks against the benefits and assurances they provide, is deeply embedded in political logics and the public mind. Arguably, one of the main reasons for the longevity of US alliances has been that their benefits have been seen to vastly outweigh their costs. For much of their history, US alliances have been relatively costless for both America and its allies. While it has become commonplace for American defence policy-makers to complain of their allies' underspending on defence, there is little to suggest that America's alliance commitments contributed to higher US defence spending than would otherwise have been the case, while for much of their tenure, most US basing commitments in Asia and Europe have been financially supported by its smaller allies. For those smaller allies, there has rarely been any serious doubt that their alliances with the United States allowed them a level of security out of all proportion to their direct investments in the military and intelligence capabilities; or that an ending of their alliance with the United States would necessitate much greater defence expenditure to acquire the same level of protection.[6] Even when there were losses of blood and treasure in fighting alongside the United States in regional conflicts, smaller allies were aware that such exercises allowed their forces to maintain cutting-edge capabilities and their agencies access to inner realms of American intelligence and strategy.

An argument could be made that, for both America and its allies, there has been a convenient security-political trade-off to be made through their security relationships. Alliances in Asia and Europe provided the United States with political cover for its security commitments; the willingness of major powers to partner with US security commitments across the globe provided a sense of universal legitimacy to US strategic goals, both during the Cold War and after. For allies, the US guarantee provided security cover for their political alignments with the United States and the West; this meant that European states living under the shadow of the Iron Curtain and Asian states concerned about the spread of communist insurgencies could reassure themselves that they were safer as staunch members of the West than they would be if they tried to become neutral and avoid the confrontation. Nor has there been a strong sense, on the part of the United States or its smaller allies, that the alliance has acted as a significant constraint on their freedom of foreign policy initiative.[7]

The politics of alliance maintenance have been subtle and varied across the various allied states. The virtues of American strategic power tend to erode quickly among both American and allied publics soon after that power is deployed. Consequently, alliance maintenance has always been an exercise in 'two-level games' in which allied governments must try to maintain domestic political acceptance for a range of alliance commitments that are regarded as acceptable by US policy-makers.[8] Repeatedly, the two-level logic of alliance maintenance, in combination with the alliance accounting (or insurance) metaphor, has led to allies casting the alliance as the objective, rather than the means, of foreign and strategic policy. This meant that the United States was often joined in the exercise of

coercion not because allies particularly subscribed to the objectives of coercion with the same intensity as the United States, but because they believed, and could argue to their publics, that 'alliance maintenance' required such a commitment to be shown.

There are three dangers in this approach. The first is that the alliance becomes heavily politicised. Controversial or costly actions taken in coalition with the intention of investing in alliance maintenance will end up increasing opposition to the alliance among both American and allied publics. The second cost is for the United States, because the imperative of alliance maintenance will mean that it finds itself paired with coalition partners who are less interested in the actual strategic objectives at hand than they are in keeping their major ally happy. This has been a problem in both Iraq and Afghanistan, where US allies have made decisions to pull out of operations long before the situation has been regarded as stable enough to justify withdrawal. The third danger of this approach to alliances is a tendency for both the United States and its allies to turn situations into tests of alliance credibility. The best example of this was the response to the 9/11 attacks, which the George W Bush administration clearly signalled was a test of how much allies were committed to American security and American global-order preferences. The result was broad buy-in to the invasion of Afghanistan, a country in which no Asian or European ally had any strategic stake. A couple of years later, Bush raised the alliance commitment bar by setting his sights on an invasion of Iraq, based on highly tenuous connections to the 9/11 attacks and global security more broadly. In this case, the Bush administration was in effect asking its allies not only to place their alliance ties above their own nonexistent interests in Iraq, but also above their commitments to the rule of international law and the substantial opposition of their own populations. In the end, two European allies (Britain and Spain) and one Asian (Australian) joined the invasion, all three using the demonstration of their solidarity with Washington to gain significant concessions from a grateful Bush administration. Ultimately, perhaps reflecting some realism on the part of the Bush administration, there were few negative consequences for allies that did not join the Iraq invasion or its subsequent stabilisation phase.

There are signs that the relatively costless nature of alliances is starting to be questioned in both Europe and Asia. In the face of direct Russian and Chinese challenges to the status quo and to American primacy, both the United States and its respective allies are aware of difficult choices.[9] During the 2016 US presidential election campaign, Republican candidate Donald Trump committed to requiring US allies in Europe and Asia to pay more of the shared cost of their own security or risk the attenuation of those alliances. It remains to be seen whether the president will deliver on these pledges. Victor Cha observes that, in Asia, an alliance security dilemma has developed: whereas US-alliance-initiated regional efforts are portrayed as latent strategies for containing China, region-initiated attempts to engage China are seen as attempts to exclude the United States.[10] A similar situation may be emerging in Europe, where US initiatives aimed at deterring further Russian adventurism are being seen by some as only increasing Russian hostility, while European efforts to engage with Russia are seen by others to be weakening NATO. Beyond this, the utility of alliances is starting to be questioned. In Asia, every Chinese provocation is now taken as a litmus test of American resolve and alliance commitment, a situation that bears heavily on American policy-makers and cedes a great deal of initiative to Beijing. In Europe, there is a sense that NATO has been of little utility in dealing with three pressing challenges: the war in the Levant, Russian adventurism in the Caucasus, and the growing refugee crisis. It seems that alliances, so often seen as the ends of security policy, are now being found wanting as the means to greater security in more challenging security environments in both Europe and Asia.

Conclusion

Against this background, the comparison of alliance-management challenges faced by European and Asian allies of the United States unfolds as a rich exercise. While clearly acknowledging the differences between the two regions—the nature of treaty commitments, multilateralism versus bilateralism, strategic geography and levels of development—what has been truly fascinating has been the similarities between the two regions. Indeed, there have been more than a few points of convergence: the dilemmas of dealing with 'grey zone'/hybrid threats, the challenges of interoperability and the tension between regional and global focus for alliance action. But perhaps the most intriguing convergence has been in relation to alliance structures: whereas in Asia a system of bilateral alliances is slowly

plurilateralising as US allies develop security partnerships with each other, in Europe there has been an observable process of NATO allies quietly developing their own bilateral security relationships with the United States.

NOTES

1. Canada, although not in Europe, was a contributing NATO member; New Zealand, although no longer a member of ANZUS, had been designated a non-NATO ally by the administration of Bill Clinton in 1997.

2. 'Text of Obama's Speech to Parliament', *Sydney Morning Herald*, 17 Nov. 2011, www.smh.com. au/national/text-of-obamas-speech-to-parliament-20111117-1nkcw.html.

3. US Department of Defense, 'Sustaining U.S. Global Leadership: Priorities for 21st Century Defense' (Washington, DC: Department of Defense, January 2012), p. 2.

4. The rise of statist economic models is the most prominent and worrying of these; see Ian Bremmer, *The End of the Free Market: Who Wins the War Between States and Corporations?* (New York: Portfolio, 2010).

5. Stephen M. Walt, 'Alliances in a Unipolar World', *World Politics*, vol. 61, no. 1, Jan. 2009, pp. 86–120, doi.org/10.1017/S0043887109000045.

6. Of course, there have been arguments that US alliances have actually detracted from allies' security by making them more prominent targets of attack.

7. See, for example, Michael Beckley, 'The Myth of Entangling Alliances: Reassessing the Security Risks of U.S. Defense Pacts', *International Security*, vol. 39, no. 4, Spring 2015, pp. 7–48, doi.org/10.1162/ISEC_a_00197.

8. See Robert D. Putnam, 'Diplomacy and Domestic Politics: The Logic of Two-Level Games', *International Organization*, vol. 42, no. 3, Summer 1988, pp. 427–60, doi.org/10.1017/ S0020818300027697.

9. See, for example, Stefanie V. Hlatky and Jessica T. Darden, 'Cash or Combat? America's Asian Alliances During the War in Afghanistan', *Asian Security*, vol. 11, no. 1, Mar. 2015, pp. 31–51, doi.org/10.1080/14799855.2015.1006360; Tongfi Kim, 'The Role of Leaders in Intra-Alliance Bargaining', *Asian Security*, vol. 10, no. 1, Mar. 2014, pp. 47–69, doi.org/10.1080/14799855.2013. 874338.

10. Victor D. Cha, 'Complex Patchworks: U.S. Alliances as Part of Asia's Regional Architecture', *Asia Policy*, no. 11, Jan. 2011, pp. 27–50.

An Economic Theory of Alliances

MANCUR OLSON, JR., AND RICHARD ZECKHAUSER

I. Introduction

This article outlines a model that attempts to explain the workings of international organizations, and tests this model against the experience of some existing international institutions. Though the model is relevant to any international organization that independent nations establish to further their common interests, this article emphasizes the North Atlantic Treaty Organization, since it involves larger amounts of resources than any other international organization, yet illustrates the model most simply. The United Nations and the provision of foreign aid through the Development Assistance Committee are discussed more briefly.

There are some important respects in which many observers in the United States and in some other countries are disappointed in NATO and other ventures in international cooperation. For one thing, it is often argued that the United States and some of the other larger members are bearing a disproportionate share of the burden of the common defense of the NATO countries,[1] and it is at least true that the smaller members of NATO devote smaller percentages of their incomes to defense than do larger members.[2] There is also some concern about the fact that the NATO alliance has systematically failed to provide the number of divisions that the NATO nations themselves have proclaimed (rightly or wrongly) are necessary or optimal.[3] Similarly, many nations, especially smaller nations, have failed to fulfill their quotas for UN contributions with the result that the United States contribution rises to a degree that threatens the independence of the organization. The meager level of total support for the UN and the mean and haphazard state of its finances are also sources of concern.

Some suppose that the apparent disproportion in the support for international undertakings is due largely to an alleged American moral superiority, and that the poverty of international organizations is due to a want of responsibility on the part of some other nations. But before resorting to any such explanations, it would seem necessary to ask whether the different sized contributions of different countries could be explained in terms of their national interests. Why would

it be in the interest of some countries to contribute a larger proportion of their total resources to group undertakings than other countries? The European members of NATO are much nearer the front line than the United States, and they are less able to defend themselves alone. Thus, it might be supposed that they would have an interest in devoting larger proportions of their resources to NATO than does the United States, rather than the smaller proportions that they actually contribute. And why do the NATO nations fail to provide the level of forces that they have themselves described as appropriate, i.e., in their common interest? These questions cannot be answered without developing a logical explanation of how much a nation acting in its national interest will contribute to an international organization.

Any attempt to develop a theory of international organizations must begin with the purposes or functions of these organizations. One purpose that all such organizations must have is that of serving the *common* interests of member states. In the case of NATO, the proclaimed purpose of the alliance is to protect the member nations from aggression by a common enemy. Deterring aggression against any one of the members is supposed to be in the interest of all.[4] The analogy with a nation-state is obvious. Those goods and services, such as defense, that the government provides in the *common* interest of the citizenry, are usually called "public goods." An organization of states allied for defense similarly produces a public good, only in this case the "public"—the members of the organization—are states rather than individuals.

Indeed, almost all kinds of organizations provide public or collective goods. Individual interests normally can best be served by individual action, but when a group of individuals has some common objective or collective goal, then an organization can be useful. Such a common objective is a collective good, since it has one or both of the following properties: (1) if the common goal is achieved, everyone who shares this goal automatically benefits, or, in other words, nonpurchasers cannot feasibly be kept from consuming the good, and (2) if the good is available to any one person in a group, it is or can be made available to the other members of the group at little or no marginal

Mancur Olson, Jr., and Richard Zeckhauser, "An Economic Theory of Alliances," *The Review of Economics and Statistics* 48, no. 3 (August 1966): 266–79. © 1966 by the President and Fellows of Harvard College and the Massachusetts Institute of Technology.

Table 1. **Nato Statistics: An Empirical Test**

Country	Gross National Product 1964 (billions of dollars)	Rank	Defense Budget as Percentages of GNP	Rank	GNP per Capita	Rank
United States	569.03	1	9.0	1	$2,933	1
Germany	88.87	2	5.5	6	1,579	5
United Kingdom	79.46	3	7.0	3	1,471	8
France	73.40	4	6.7	4	1,506	6
Italy	43.63	5	4.1	10	855	11
Canada	38.14	6	4.4	8	1,981	2
Netherlands	15.00	7	4.9	7	1,235	10
Belgium	13.43	8	3.7	12	1,429	9
Denmark	7.73	9	3.3	13	1,636	3
Turkey	6.69	10	5.8	5	216	14
Norway	5.64	11	3.9	11	1,484	7
Greece	4.31	12	4.2	9	507	12
Portugal	2.88	13	7.7	2	316	13
Luxembourg	.53	14	1.7	14	1,636	4

Ranks

GNP	1	2	3	4	5	6	7	8	9	10	11	12	13	14
Defense Budget as % of GNP	1	6	3	4	10	8	7	12	13	5	11	9	2	14
GNP per Capita	1	5	8	6	11	2	10	9	3	14	7	12	13	4

Source: All data are taken from the Institute for Strategic Studies, *The Military Balance* 1965–1966 (London, November 1965).

cost.[5] Collective goods are thus the characteristic outputs not only of governments but of organizations in general.[6]

Since the benefits of any action an individual takes to provide a public or organizational good also go to others, individuals acting independently do not have an incentive to provide optimal amounts of such goods. Indeed, when the group interested in a public good is very large, and the share of the total benefit that goes to any single individual is very small, usually no individual has an incentive voluntarily to purchase any of the good, which is why states exact taxes and labor unions demand compulsory membership.[7] When—as in any organization representing a limited number of nation-states—the membership of an organization is relatively small, the individual members may have an incentive to make significant sacrifices to obtain the collective good, but they will tend to provide only suboptimal amounts of this good. There will also be a tendency for the "larger" members—those that place a higher absolute value on the public good—to bear a disproportionate share of the burden, as the model of alliances developed below will show.

II. The Model

When a nation decides how large a military force to provide in an alliance, it must consider the value it places upon collective defense and the other, nondefense, goods that must be sacrificed to obtain additional military forces. The value each nation in an alliance places upon the alliance collective good vis-à-vis other goods can be shown on a simple indifference map, such as is shown in figure 1. This is an ordinary indifference map cut off at the present income line and turned upside down. Defense capability is measured along the horizontal axis and valued positively. Defense spending is measured along the vertical axis and valued negatively. The cost curves are assumed to be linear for the sake of simplicity. If the nation depicted in figure 1 were not a part of any alliance, the amount of defense it would obtain (OB) could be found by drawing a cost curve coming out of the origin and finding the point (point A) where this cost curve is tangent to the "highest" (most southeasterly) indifference curve.

In an alliance, the amount a nation spends on defense will be affected by the amount its allies provide. By moving the cost curve down along the vertical axis

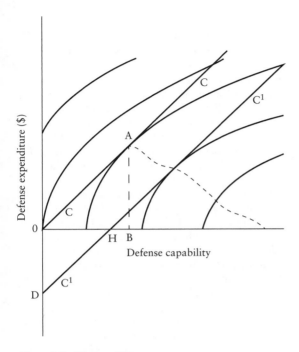

Figure 1. Indifference Map

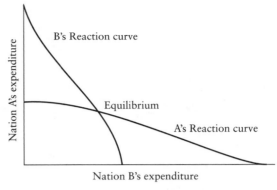

Figure 2. Reaction Curves

beneath the origin, we can represent the defense expenditure of allied nations as the distance between the origin and the juncture of the cost curve and the vertical axis. If a nation's allies spend OD on defense, and their cost functions are the same as its own, then it receives OH of defense without cost. This is directly equivalent to an increase in income of OD.[8] The more defense this nation's allies provide, the further the cost constraint moves to the southeast, and the less it spends on defense. By recording all the points of tangency of the total cost curve with the indifference curves, we can obtain this nation's reaction function. The reaction function indicates how much defense this nation will produce for all possible levels of defense expenditure by its allies. The amount of defense that this nation provides will in turn influence the defense output of its allies, whose reaction curves can be determined in the same way.

Figure 2 shows the reaction curves for a two-country model (which can easily be generalized to cover *N* countries).[9] The intersection point of the two reaction curves indicates how much of the alliance good each ally will supply in equilibrium.[10] The two reaction curves need not always intersect. If one nation has a very much larger demand for the alliance good than the other, its reaction curve may lie at every point outside that of the other, in which case it will provide all of the defense. The equilibrium output will then be the same as the isolation output of the country with the largest isolation output. Whether the reaction

curves intersect or not, the equilibrium output is necessarily determinate and stable unless defense is an inferior good, in which case there may be a number of equilibria, one or more of which may be unstable.[11]

In equilibrium, the defense expenditures of the two nations are such that the "larger" nation—the one that places the higher absolute value on the alliance good—will bear a disproportionately large share of the common burden. It will pay a share of the costs that is larger than its share of the benefits, and thus the distribution of costs will be quite different from that which a system of benefit taxation would bring about.[12] This becomes obvious when income effects—i.e., the influence that the amount of non-defense goods a nation has already forgone has on its desire to provide additional units of defense—are neglected.[13] This is shown in figure 3, which depicts the evaluation curves of two nations for alliance forces. The larger nation, called Big Atlantis, has the higher, steeper valuation curve, V_B, because it places a higher absolute value on defense than Little Atlantis, which has evaluation curve V_L. The OC curve shows the costs of providing defense capability to each nation, since both, by assumption, have the same costs. In isolation, Big Atlantis would buy B_i units of defense and Little Atlantis L_i, for at these points their respective valuation curves are parallel to their cost functions. If the two nations continued to provide these outputs in alliance each would enjoy B_i plus L_i units of defense. But then each nation values a marginal unit at less than its marginal cost. Big Atlantis will stop reducing its output of deterrence when the sum applied by the two nations together is B_i. When this amount (or any amount greater than L_i) is available, it is not in Little Atlantis' interest to supply any defense whatever. The two nations are therefore simultaneously in equilibrium *only* when Big Atlantis provides B_i of defense and Little Atlantis provides no defense whatever.

The disproportionality in the sharing of burdens is less extreme when income effects are taken into

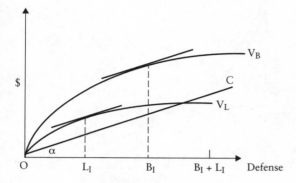

Figure 3. Evaluation Curves

account, but it is still important. This can be seen most easily by supposing that Big Atlantis and Little Atlantis are identical in every respect save that Big Atlantis is twice the size of Little Atlantis. Per capita incomes and individual tastes are the same in both countries, but the population and GNP of Big Atlantis are twice that of Little Atlantis. Now imagine also that Big Atlantis is providing twice as much alliance defense as Little Atlantis, as proportionality would require.[14] In equilibrium, the marginal rate of substitution of money for the alliance good (MRS) must equal marginal cost for each of these countries, i.e., $MRS_{Big} = MRS_{Little} =$ marginal cost (MC). But (since each country enjoys the same amount of the collective good) the MRS of Big Atlantis is double that of Little Atlantis, and (since the cost of an additional unit of defense is the same for each country) either Big Atlantis will want more defense or Little Atlantis will want less (or both will be true), and the common burden will come to be shared in a disproportionate way.

There is one important special case in which there will be no tendency toward disproportionality. That is when the indifference maps of the member nations are such that any perpendicular from the ordinate would intersect all indifference curves at points of equal slope. In this case, when the nation's cost constraint moves to the right as it gets more free defense, it would not reduce its own expenditure on defense. In other words, none of the increase in income that the nation receives in the form of defense is spent on goods other than defense. Defense in this situation is, strictly speaking, a "superior good," a good such that all of any increase in income is used to buy the good.[15]

This special case may sometimes be very important. During periods of all-out war or exceptional insecurity, it is likely that defense is (or is nearly) a superior good, and in such circumstances alliances will not have any tendency toward disproportionate burden sharing. The amount of allied military capability that Great Britain enjoyed in World War II increased from 1941 to 1944 as the United States mobilized, adding more and more

strength to the allied side. But the British war effort was maintained, if not increased, during this period.[16]

Although there is then one exception to the rule that alliance burdens are shared disproportionately, there is no equivalent exception to the rule that alliances provide suboptimal amounts of the collective good. The alliance output will always be suboptimal so long as the members of the alliance place a positive value on additional units of defense. This is because each of the alliance members contributes to the point where its MRS for the good equals the marginal cost of the good. In other words, the result of independent national maximization in an alliance, when the cost function is linear and the same for all members, is that $MRS_1 = MRS_2 = \ldots MRS_n = MC$. There could be an optimal quantity of the collective good only if the total value which all of the alliance members together placed on an additional unit of the good equaled marginal cost, i.e., only if $MRS_1 + MRS_2 + \ldots MRS_n = MC$. The individual nations in an alliance would have an incentive to keep providing additional alliance forces until the Pareto-optimal level is reached only if there were an arrangement such that the alliance members shared marginal costs in the same proportions in which they shared additional benefits (that is, in the same ratio as their marginal rates of substitution of money for the good). When there is such a marginal cost-sharing scheme, there need be no tendency toward disproportionality in the sharing of burdens.

III. Qualifications and Elaborations

One simplification assumed in the foregoing model was that the costs of defense were constant to scale and the same for all alliance members. Although military forces are composed of diverse types of equipment and manpower, and thus probably vary less both in cost from one country to another and with scale of output than many single products, it is still unlikely that costs are constant and uniform. For some special types of weapon systems there are undoubtedly striking economies of large scale production, and for conventional ground forces there are probably rising costs as larger proportions of a nation's population are called to arms. Because of this latter tendency, a small country can perhaps get a considerable amount of conventional capability with the first few percentiles of its national income. This tends to keep the military expenditures of small nations in an alliance above the very low level implied by our constant cost assumption. In any event, cross-country variations in marginal costs should not normally alter the basic conclusions deduced from the model. The differences in the amounts which member nations would be willing to pay for marginal units of an alliance good are typically so great that the cost differentials could hardly negate their effect. Even if there were very large differences in marginal costs among nations, there is no reason to assume that national cost functions would vary systematically with the valuation a country places on alliance forces.[17]

A nation's valuation of alliance forces obviously depends not only on its national income, but also on other factors. A nation on the enemy's border may value defense more than one some distance away. A nation that has a large area and long frontiers in relation to its resources may want a larger army than a compact country. On the other hand, if bomb and missile attacks are the main danger, a crowded country may wish to invest more in defense against attack by air. Similarly, a nation's attitudes or ideologies may partly determine its evaluation of defense. Many observers think that the uniformity and intensity of anti-communism is greater among the NATO countries with the highest per capita incomes, and these also happen to be the largest countries in the alliance. It also seems that many people in small and weak countries, both inside and outside of NATO, tend to be attracted to neutralist or pacifist ideologies. This pattern of attitudes may perhaps be partly explained by our model, for it suggests that small nations, which find that even large sacrifices on their part have little effect on the global balance, would often be attracted to neutral or passive foreign policies, and that large nations which know that their efforts can decisively influence world events in their own interest will continually need to emphasize the urgency of the struggle in which they are engaged. The popularity of pacific ideologies, the frequent adoption of neutralist policies in small and weak countries, and the activist attitudes and policies of the United States and the Soviet Union are at least consistent with our model.[18]

Whatever the reasons for the different evaluations different nations have for military capabilities in an alliance, the model here still applies. If two countries in an alliance had equal national incomes, but one was more concerned about the common enemy for geographic, ideological, historical, or other reasons, the more concerned nation would not only put a higher valuation on the alliance's military capacity, but would bear a share of the total alliance costs that was even greater than its share of the total benefits.[19] The model deals with the general case of differences in the absolute valuation that nations put upon additional units of an alliance good, whether these differences are due to differences in national income or to other reasons.[20]

Another assumption in the model developed in the foregoing section was that the military forces in an alliance provide only the collective benefit of alliance security, when in fact they also provide purely national, non-collective benefits to the nations that maintain them. When Portugal mobilizes additional forces to suppress the independence movement in Angola, a national goal unrelated to the purposes of NATO, she may at the same time be increasing the total strength of the alliance. Similarly, allied nations may be suspicious of one another, even as they cooperate in the achievement of common purposes, and may enlarge their military forces because of conceivable future conflicts with each other. In any situations in which the military forces of alliance members provide important non-collective benefits as well as alliance benefits, the degree of suboptimality and the importance of the disproportionality will decrease because the non-collective benefits give the member nations an incentive to maintain larger forces.

This fact leads to the paradoxical conclusion that *a decline in the amity, unity, and community of interest among allies need not necessarily reduce the effectiveness of an alliance,* because the decline in these alliance "virtues" produces a greater ratio of private to collective benefits. This suggests that alliances troubled by suspicions and disagreements may continue to work reasonably well. To be sure, the degree of coordination among the allies will decline, and this will reduce the efficiency of the alliance forces (in a sense leaving them on a poorer production function), but the alliance forces will be larger.

However important the non-collective benefits of alliances may be, there can be little doubt that above all alliances produce public goods. It is not easy to think of alliances that provide only private goods, though such alliances are perhaps conceivable. If nations simply trade sites for military bases, no common interests or public goods would necessarily be involved. An alliance might also be set up simply to provide insurance in the sense that two nations without any common purpose or common enemy would agree to defend each other in case of attack, but in which neither knew in advance which would suffer aggression. On the other hand, if these two nations thought (as they presumably would) that the fact of their alliance would make it less profitable for other nations to attack either of them, the alliance would provide a public good—a degree of deterrence that could deter an attack on either or both of these nations about as well as it could deter an attack on one alone. There is, moreover, no reason to describe a mere transaction in private goods as an alliance, and the word does not normally appear to be used in that way. A transaction in private goods would be quite as useful between enemies as between "allies," and would normally be completed by a single pair of actions or a single agreement which would not require the continuing consultation, cooperation, and organization characteristic of alliances.

Normally, an additional member can be added to an alliance without substantially subtracting from the amount of defense available to those already in the alliance, and any good that satisfies this criterion is by definition a public good.[21] Suppose two nations of the same size face a common enemy with an army larger than either of them provides by itself. They then form an alliance and maintain a level of military forces larger than either of them had before, but smaller than the sum of their two pre-alliance armies. After alliance both nations enjoy (1) more military security, and (2) lower defense costs, than they had before. This result comes about, not only because a military force can often deter attack by a common enemy against an additional nation without a substantial increase in cost, but also because an alliance may make a greater level of security economically feasible and desirable, and the gains from obtaining this extra security can leave both nations better off.[22]

Another defining characteristic that is sufficient (but not necessary) to distinguish a collective good is that the exclusion of those who do not share the cost of the good is impractical or impossible. Typically, once an alliance treaty has been signed, a member nation is legally bound to remain a member for the duration of the treaty. The decisions about how the common burden is to be shared are not, however, usually specified in the alliance treaty. This procedure works to the disadvantage of the larger countries. Often the smaller and weaker nations gain relatively more from the existence of an alliance than do the larger and stronger powers, and once an alliance treaty has been signed the larger powers are immediately deprived of their strongest bargaining weapon—the threat that they will not help to defend the recalcitrant smaller powers—in any negotiations about the sharing of the common burden. Even at the time an alliance treaty is negotiated exclusion may very well not be feasible, since most alliances imply an already existing danger or goal common to some group of states. That common danger or goal gives the nations that share it an incentive tacitly to treat each other as allies, whether or not they have all signed a formal agreement. A nation can only lose from having another nation with whom it shares a common interest succumb to an enemy, for that will strengthen the enemy's side at the expense of the first nation. It may well be that most alliances are never embodied in any formal agreement. Sometimes a nation may have a geopolitical position (e.g., behind an alliance member serving as a buffer state) such that it would be unusually difficult, if not impossible, to deny it the benefits of alliance protection. Then, if it regards alliance membership as a special burden, it may have an incentive to stay out of, or when legally possible to withdraw from, the alliance's formal organization.

This paper also made the simplifying assumption that no alliance member will take into account the reactions other members may have to the size of its alliance contribution. The mutual recognition of oligopolistic interdependence can be profoundly important in

small groups of firms, but in the NATO alliance at least, it seems to have been somewhat less important (except with respect to the infrastructure, which will be considered later). There are at least two important reasons why strategic bargaining interaction is often less important in alliances than in oligopolistic industries. First, alliances are often involved in situations that contain a strong element of irreversibility. Suppose that the United States were to threaten to cut its defense spending to nothing to get its allies to bear larger shares of the NATO burden. The Soviet Union, if it has the characteristics that American policy assumes, would then deprive the United States of its independence, in which case future defense savings would have little relevance. The United States' threat would have only a limited credibility in view of the irreversibility of this process. The second factor which limits strategic bargaining interaction among alliance members stems from an important difference between market and non-market groups. In an oligopolistic group of firms, any firm knows that its competitors would be better off if it were made bankrupt or otherwise driven out of the industry. Large firms thus sometimes engage in price wars or cut-throat competition to drive out the smaller members of an oligopolistic group. By contrast, non-market groups and organizations, such as alliances, usually strive instead for a larger membership, since they provide collective goods the supply of which should increase as the membership increases. Since an ally would typically lose from driving another member out of an alliance, a bargaining threat to that effect may not be credible. This will be especially true if the excluded nation would then fall to the common enemy and (as we argued before) thereby strengthen the enemy at the expense of the alliance.

Even when strategic interaction is important in alliances, the advantage paradoxically still rests in most cases with the smaller nations.[23] There are two reasons for this.[24] First, the large country loses more from withholding an alliance contribution than a small country does, since it values a given amount of alliance force more highly. In other words, it may be deterred by the very importance to itself of its own alliance contribution from carrying out any threat to end that contribution. Second, the large country has relatively less to gain than its small ally from driving a hard bargain. Even if the large nation were successful in the bargaining, it would expect only a relatively small addition to the alliance force from the small nation, but when the small nation succeeds in the bargaining, it can expect a large addition to the alliance force from the large nation. There is, accordingly, no reason to expect that there is any disparity of bargaining in favor of the larger ally that would negate the tendency toward disproportionality revealed by our model.

IV. Empirical Evidence

When other things are equal, the larger a nation is, the higher its valuation of the output of an alliance. Thus, if our model is correct, the larger members of an alliance should, on the average, devote larger percentages of their national incomes to defense than do the smaller nations. This prediction is tested against the recent data on the NATO nations in table 1. The following specific hypotheses are used to test the model's predictions:

H_1—In an alliance, there will be a significant positive correlation between the size of a member's national income and the percentage of its national income spent on defense. This hypothesis will be tested against [the null hypothesis]:

H_0—There will not be a significant positive correlation between the variables specified in H_1.

Since there is no assurance that the data are parametrically distributed, non-parametrical statistical tests must be used. The Spearman rank correlation coefficient for Gross National Product and defense budget as a percentage of GNP is .490. On a one-tailed test this value is significant at the .05 level.[25] We therefore reject the null hypothesis and accept H_1. There is a significant positive correlation indicating that the large nations in NATO bear a disproportionate share of the burden of the common defense. Moreover, this result holds even when the level of per capita income is held constant.[26]

Our model predicts that there are tendencies toward disproportionate burden sharing, not only in military alliances, but also in other international organizations, such as the United Nations. The test of this prediction is complicated in the case of the UN by the fact that the organization is supported primarily through assessments levied against individual members. These assessments are determined by a formula constructed by a committee of experts. The model would, however, suggest that the degree to which a member fulfills or oversubscribes its quota would be positively correlated with its size, and thus gives the following hypotheses:

H_2—In a voluntary organization with quota assessments that are not always satisfied, there will be a significant positive correlation between a member's GNP and the percentage of fulfillment or over-fulfillment of its quota.

H_0—There will not be a significant positive correlation between the variables in H_2.

The Spearman rank correlation coefficient between 1961 *GNP* and *percentage total UN contributions in 1961/normal assessment scale* was .404. This result is significant at the .01 level.[27] We thus accept H_2 and reject H_0, for, as the model predicted, the larger nations in the UN did a better job of living up to their normal assessments. The fact that members may lose prestige and membership rights if they fail to meet their assessments, i.e., that there are distinctly private benefits from contributions to the UN, makes this high correlation more striking.

The foreign aid that the industrialized democracies give to the underdeveloped countries is a collective good to these aid-giving nations, at least to the extent that they all value the development of the less developed areas. On the other hand, individual aid-giving nations often concentrate all of their aid on particular underdeveloped areas, such as past or present colonies, in which they have a special interest. To the extent that different aid-giving nations are interested in different underdeveloped areas, their aid allocations constitute private rather than collective goods. This tends to limit any tendencies toward suboptimality and disproportionality in the provision of foreign aid. We can test for any such disproportionalities with the aid of the following hypotheses:

H_3—Among a group of developed nations there will be a significant positive correlation between foreign aid expenditures as a percentage of national income and the size of the national income.

H_0—There will not be a significant positive correlation between the variables in H_3.

One set of data used to test these hypotheses revealed a correlation between *real national income and total grants and loans to underdeveloped countries as a percentage of national income in 1960* of .770.[28] This figure is significant at the .01 level. A different set of data for a different year (1962) showed a correlation between *GNP and total aid as a percentage of GNP* of .439.[29] With the small sample of only 12 nations, this value falls slightly short of the .05 level of significance (the borderline value is .506). Thus both sets of data yield correlation coefficients suggesting the expected positive relationship, but in one case the result is clearly statistically significant and in the other case it falls somewhat short of the .05 level of significance. We will take the most conservative course and await further research before finally accepting either H_3 or the null hypothesis. The most reasonable inference at the moment is that there is some tendency toward disproportionate burden sharing, but that the private, or purely national, benefits from foreign aid are probably also very important. This is, moreover, about what might be expected from the fact that the industrialized

Western nations express a common interest in the development of the poor nations generally, while at the same time many of these nations individually are interested primarily in particular underdeveloped areas with which they have special relationships.

Our model indicated that when the members of an organization share the costs of marginal units of an alliance good, just as they share in the benefits of additional units of that good, there is no tendency toward disproportionality or suboptimality. In other words, if each ally pays an appropriate percentage of the cost of any additional units of the alliance good, the results are quite different from when each ally pays the full cost of any amount of the alliance good that he provides. The costs of the NATO infrastructure (common supply depots, pipelines, etc.), unlike the costs of providing the main alliance forces, are shared according to percentages worked out in a negotiated agreement. Since each ally pays some percentage of the cost of any addition to the NATO infrastructure, we have here a marginal cost–sharing arrangement.

Thus our model suggests that the burdens of the NATO infrastructure should be borne quite differently from the rest of the NATO burden. There are other reasons for expecting that the infrastructure burden would be shared in a different way from the main NATO burdens. For one thing, the infrastructure facilities of NATO are all in continental European countries, and ultimately become the property of the host nation. Their construction also brings foreign exchange earnings to these countries, which for the most part are the smaller alliance members. In addition, infrastructure costs are very small in relation to the total burden of common defense, so a small nation may get prestige at a relatively low cost by offering to bear a larger percentage of the infrastructure cost. There are, in short, many private benefits for the smaller alliance members resulting from the infrastructure expenditures. Because of these private benefits, and more important because of the percentage sharing of marginal (and total) costs of the infrastructure, we would predict that the larger members of the alliance would bear a smaller share of the infrastructure burden than of the main alliance burdens.

This prediction suggests that the following hypotheses be tested:

H_4—In an alliance in which the marginal costs of certain activities are *not* shared (but fall instead upon those members who have an incentive to provide additional units of the alliance good by themselves), and in which the marginal costs of other activities are shared (so that each member pays a specified percentage of any costs of these activities), the *ratio* of a member's share of the

costs of the activities of the former type to his share of the costs of activities of the latter type will have a significant positive correlation with national income.

H_0—There will be no significant positive correlation between the variables in H_4.

To test these hypotheses we calculated the correlation coefficient between *national income* and *variable T* in table 2. The Spearman rank correlation coefficient between these variables is .582, which is significant at the .05 level. We therefore reject the null hypothesis and conclude that the larger members bear a larger proportion of the costs of the main NATO forces than they do of those NATO activities for which the costs of each unit are shared. The difference between the distribution of infrastructure costs and the distribution of alliance burdens generally is quite striking, as the tests of the following hypotheses indicate:

H_5—In the NATO alliance there is a significant negative correlation between national income and the percentage of national income devoted to infrastructure expenses.

H_0—There is no significant negative correlation between the variables in H_5.

The Spearman rank correlation coefficient between *national income* and *variable R* in table 2 is—.538, which is significant at the .05 level. Thus, not only is it the case that the larger nations pay a smaller share of the infrastructure costs than of other alliance costs; it is also true that there is a significant negative correlation between national income and the percentage of national income devoted to the NATO infrastructure, which is in vivid contrast to the positive correlation that prevails for other NATO burdens. This confirms the prediction that when there are marginal cost–sharing arrangements, there need no longer be any tendency for the larger nations to bear disproportionately large shares of the costs of international organizations. If it happens at the same time that the smaller nations get greater than average private benefits from their contributions, they may even contribute greater percentages of their national incomes than the larger members.[30]

IV. Conclusions and Recommendations

All of the empirical evidence tended to confirm the model. In the United Nations there appear to be systematic forces tending to make the small nations fail to meet their quotas and leading larger nations to assume larger shares of the costs. The larger industrialized nations, moreover, seem to bear disproportionate

Table 2. Nato Infrastructure

Country	National Income 1960[a] (billions of dollars) (1)	Infrastructure % Reconsidered in 1960[b] (2)	$R=(2)/(1)$ (3)	Military Budget 1960 (billions of dollars) (4)	$T=(4)/(2)$ (5)
United States	411.367	36.98	.0899	41.00	1.1087
Germany	51.268	13.77	.2686	2.072	.1504
United Kingdom	57.361	9.88	.1722	4.466	.4520
France	43.468	11.87	.2731	3.311	.2789
Italy	24.950	5.61	.2248	1.076	.1922
Canada	28.178	6.15	.2183	1,680	.2732
Netherlands	9.246	3.51	.3800	.450	.1282
Belgium	8.946	4.39	.4907	.395	.0900
Turkey	4.929	1.75	.3550	.244	.1394
Denmark	4.762	2.63	.5569	.153	.0582
Norway	3.455	2.19	.6338	.168	.0767
Greece	2.684	.87	.3242	.173	.1989
Portugal	2.083	.28	.1344	.093	.3321
Luxembourg	.386	.17	.4404	.007	.0412

Ranks

(1)	1	2	3	4	5	6	7	8	9	10	11	12	13	14
(3)	14	9	12	8	10	11	5	3	6	2	1	7	13	4
(5)	1	8	2	4	7	5	10	11	9	13	12	6	3	14

[a] United Nations, *Yearbook of National Accounts Statistics* (New York, 1964); *Balance of Payments Yearbook*, Vol. 15 (Washington, D.C.: International Monetary Fund, 1964).

[b] Charles Croot, "Coordination in the Sixties," reprinted from *NATO Letter* (August 1960).

shares of the burden of aid to the less developed countries. In NATO there is again a statistically significant positive correlation between the size of a member's national income and the percentage of its national income devoted to the common defense.

As our model indicated, this is in part because each ally gets only a fraction of the benefits of any collective good that is provided, but each pays the full cost of any additional amounts of the collective good. This means that individual members of an alliance or international organization have an incentive to stop providing the collective good long before the Pareto-optimal output for the group has been provided.[31] This is particularly true of the smaller members, who get smaller shares of the total benefits accruing from the good, and who find that they have little or no incentive to provide additional amounts of the collective good once the larger members have provided the amounts they want for themselves, with the result that the burdens are shared in a disproportionate way. The model indicated two special types of situations in which there need be no such tendency toward disproportionality. First, in cases of all-out war or extreme insecurity defense may be what was strictly defined as a "superior good," in which case a nation's output of a collective good will not be reduced when it receives more of this good from an ally. Second, institutional arrangements such that the members of an organization share marginal costs, just as they share the benefits of each unit of the good, tend to work against disproportionality in burden sharing, and it is a necessary condition of an efficient, Pareto-optimal output that the marginal costs be shared in the same proportions as the benefits of additional units. The NATO nations determine through negotiation what percentages of any infrastructure expenditure each member will pay, and this sharing of marginal costs has led the smaller members to bear a very much larger share of the infrastructure burden than they do of the other NATO burdens. The fact that the model predicts not only the distribution of the principal NATO burdens, but also the greatly differ-ent distribution of infrastructure costs, suggests that the results are in fact due to the processes described in the model, rather than to some other cause.

The model's implication that large nations tend to bear disproportionate shares of the burdens of inter-national organization, and the empirical evidence tend-ing to confirm the model, do *not* entail the conclusion that the small nations should be told they "ought" to bear a larger share of the common burdens. No moral conclusions can follow solely from any purely logical model of the kind developed here.[32] Indeed, our analy-sis suggests that moral suasion is inappropriate, since the different levels of contribution are not due to dif-ferent moral attitudes, and ineffective, since the less than proportionate contributions of the smaller na-tions are securely grounded in their national interests (just as the disproportionately large contributions of the larger countries are solidly grounded in their na-tional interests). Thus, American attempts to persuade other nations to bear "fair" shares of the burdens of common ventures are likely to be divisive and harm-ful even to American interests in the long run.

The model developed here suggests that the prob-lems of disproportionality and suboptimality in interna-tional organizations should be met instead through in-stitutional changes that alter the pattern of incentives. Since suboptimal provision is typical of international organizations, it is possible to design policy changes that would leave everyone better off, and which accord-ingly may have some chance of adoption. Appropriate marginal cost–sharing schemes, such as are now used to finance the NATO infrastructure, could solve the prob-lem of suboptimality in international organizations,[33] and might also reduce the degree of disproportionality. Substituting a union for an alliance or international organization would also tend to bring about optimality, for then the unified system as a whole has an incentive to behave in an optimal fashion, and the various parts of the union can be required to contribute the amounts their common interest requires. Even a union of smaller members of NATO, for example, could be helpful, and be in the interest of the United States. Such a union would give the people involved an incentive to contrib-ute more toward the goals they shared with their then more nearly equal partners. Whatever the disadvan-tages on other grounds of these policy possibilities, they at least have the merit that they help to make the na-tional interests of individual nations more nearly com-patible with the efficient attainment of the goals which groups of nations hold in common.

A final implication of our model is that alliances and international organizations, as presently orga-nized, will not work efficiently, or according to any common conception of fairness, however complete the agreement and community of interest among the mem-bers. Though there is obviously a point beyond which dissension and divergent purposes will ruin any organ-ization, it is also true that some differences of purpose may improve the working of an alliance, because they increase the private, non-collective benefits from the national contributions to the alliance, and this allevi-ates the suboptimality and disproportionality.[34] How much smaller would the military forces of the small members of NATO be if they did not have their pri-vate fears and quarrels? How much aid would the Eu-ropean nations give if they did not have private inter-ests in the development of their past or present colonies? How much would the smaller nations con-tribute to the UN if it were not a forum for the expres-sion of their purely national enmities and aspirations? The United States, at least, should perhaps not hope for too much unity in common ventures with other na-tions. It might prove extremely expensive.

NOTES

1. Hedley Bull, *Strategy and the Atlantic Alliance: A Cri-tique of United States Doctrine* (Princeton: Center of Interna-tional Studies, Princeton University, 1964), 42; Edward S. Mason, "The Equitable Sharing of Military and Economic Aid Burdens," *Proceedings of the Academy of Political Science*, XXVII (May 1963), 256–269, especially 264; John A. Pincus, *Sharing the Costs of Military Alliance and International Eco-nomic Aid* (Santa Monica, CA: The RAND Corporation, RM-3249-ISA, 1962), and *Economic Aid and International Cost Sharing* (Baltimore: Johns Hopkins University Press, 1965); and Bernard Brodie, "What Price Conventional Capabilities in Europe," *The Reporter*, XXVIII (May 23, 1963), 27.

2. See table 1.

3. "NATO was created as, and is still today officially pro-claimed to be, the shield that protects Western Europe from a Soviet attack on land. Yet it has never been clear how NATO could perform that function with the forces actually at its dis-posal or how it could have performed that function even with the much larger forces which its official spokesmen from time to time declared to be indispensable." Hans J. Morgenthau, "Fore-word," in Robert Osgood, *NATO: The Entangling Alliance* (Chicago: University of Chicago Press, 1962), vii. John Pincus speaks of "the relative willingness of countries to accept NATO force goals," and the fact that "the trouble comes in meeting those goals," *Economic Aid and International Cost Sharing*, 58.

4. "Peace is indivisible, and nuclear war even more so." Prime Minister Harold Wilson, as quoted in *The New York Times* (Dec. 17, 1964), 2.

5. See John G. Head, "Public Goods and Public Policy," *Public Finance*, XVII, No. 3 (1962), 197–219.

6. See Mancur Olson, Jr., *The Logic of Collective Action: Public Goods and the Theory of Groups* (Cambridge, MA: Harvard University Press, 1965), which treats organizations of individuals somewhat as this article treats organizations of nation-states.

7. Olson, *The Logic of Collective Action*, 5–52.

8. Free defense is not, however, the direct equivalent of an increase in income if the nation has already received so much defense that it would like to sell some if that were possible. This is what an ally would want to do if the OC curve had shifted so far to the right that it was no longer tangent to any indifference curve. In such a case, there is a corner solution and the nation provides none of the collective good itself.

9. The reaction curve is an *n*-dimensional surface in the *n*-nation alliance. This surface is symmetrical about all axes except the one for the reacting nation. The equilibrium is found at the point of joint intersection of these *n* surfaces. The symmetrical quality of these surfaces enables us to convert them into two-dimensional reaction curves relating the spending of one nation to the spending of all its allies.

10. The general model being developed here has several important advantages over Erik Lindahl's much different analysis of how two parties interested in a public good might interact, and over the very interesting modern versions of Lindahl's theory put forth by Leif Johanson and Richard Musgrave. For example, unlike Lindahl's model, it takes account of income effects, it shows that there are generally a multitude of Pareto-optimal outcomes, and it reveals the tendencies toward disproportionality and suboptimality.

11. To see this, suppose that A and B in figure 2 trade reaction curves. Then the equilibrium point given by the intersection point will be unstable, and there will be a tendency for one of the nations to provide all the defense. If one nation's reaction curve lies wholly outside that of the other, there will be a unique and stable equilibrium, whether or not defense is an inferior good.

12. The authors do not advocate benefit taxation, but believe that proportionality of benefits and costs provides a useful standard of comparison, particularly in alliances which nations join to further their national interests rather than to bring about any particular distribution of income among member nations. The equilibrium outputs are not consistent with any ordinary conceptions of ability-to-pay either. They would involve a very regressive sharing if the larger nation in an alliance had the lower per capita income.

13. Income effects are probably very important in practice, partly because it is usually very difficult for a government to increase taxes enough to bring military or other government spending far above the customary levels. Moreover, large increases in defense spending may lead to serious reductions in capital formation. There appears to be a remarkable constancy of the percentage of GNP that is made up by the sum of defense spending and capital formation. See Richard Zeckhauser, "Defense Spending, Capital Formation, and Economic Growth" (to be published).

14. It could be the case that even in isolation Big Atlantis would buy proportionately more defense than Little Atlantis. This would be the case if a nation's income elasticity of demand for the good were greater than one in the relevant range.

15. Apparently the literature has neglected goods of this kind, and not made clear that they are simply the logical converse of the much discussed inferior goods. When the phrase "superior good" has been used, it has usually been given an unsymmetrical and unclear meaning. We therefore distinguish the following classes of goods, realizing that the category to which a good belongs may depend on the level of income.

Class	Characteristic	Income elasticity of expenditure = E
Inferior good	Expenditure on the good decreases or is unchanged as income increases	$E \leq 0$
Inelastic good	Expenditure on the good increases, but by a smaller percentage than income increases	$0 < E < 1$
Elastic good	Expenditure on the good increases by a percentage that is as great or greater than the percentage by which income increases, but by a smaller absolute amount	$1 \leq E < Y_0/S_0$[a]
Superior good	Expenditure on the good increases by as much or more than income increases	$E > Y_0/S_0$

[a] S_0 is the expenditure on the good when income is Y_0.

In terms of an ordinary indifference map (rather than the inverted form used in this article) an inferior good is a good that has an income consumption line that (in the relevant range) approaches (or is parallel to) the axis along which income is measured, as the income constraint shifts outward. A superior good is a good with an income consumption line that (in the relevant range) approaches (or is parallel to) the axis along which the quantity of the good is measured, as the income constraint shifts outward. If there is an inferior good for an individual, there must be at least one superior good for that individual (saving is here considered a good) and all other goods in the aggregate must be superior. The converse is true for a superior good.

16. W. K. Hancock and M. M. Gowing, *British War Economy* (London: HMSO, 1949), 369–370; and Mancur Olson, Jr., *The Economics of the Wartime Shortage: A History of British Food Supplies in the Napoleonic War and World Wars I and II* (Durham, NC: Duke University Press, 1963), 117–131.

17. There could be pathological cost functions that would prevent any disproportionate burden sharing of the kind predicted by the model. If, for example, all of the nations had total cost curves with sharp kinks indicating abruptly rising costs after a certain point, they might all have an incentive to choose the defense outputs suggested by these kinks. These kinks would not, except by accident, be such as to lead the larger allies to bear a disproportionate share of the common burden.

18. One factor that might conceivably make small countries outside of an alliance spend little or nothing on defense is that they might think that the maximum force they could raise alone would not be sufficient to defeat any potential enemy, so that there would be no point in having any military forces at all. In an alliance, on the other hand, a small nation might suppose that its forces could provide the margin of victory and therefore increase its defense spending. The kink in the evaluation function that this argument implies is, however, made

much less likely by the fact that even a small military force may be quite valuable to a small, unaligned country, for it might increase the costs and risks to an aggressor enough to deter him from attacking a small (and therefore probably not very valuable) country. This seems to be one argument used to support the French nuclear force.

19. Benefits are of course defined in terms of the preferences of the two countries, which we here assume have been revealed.

20. The value which a nation puts upon alliance forces may also vary with alliance policies. An alliance must sometimes choose which of two or more alternative public goods to provide, and one public good may be more valuable to some alliance members and another more valuable to others. The NATO alliance, for example, provides conventional defense as well as nuclear protection, and there have been disagreements about the proper mix between these two goods. In such a case it is possible that some nations may supply additional forces in return for more influence on alliance policy, whereas other nations may make policy concessions in order to get other members to assume a greater share of alliance costs. Such trade-offs need not change the qualitative conclusions about disproportionate burden sharing. They might simply mean that a nation can bear part of its alliance burden by making policy concessions rather than by providing additional forces. When this happens, though, the allies that obtained the policy they wanted find they value the alliance good more than before, and the opposite is true for those who have relinquished some of their control over alliance policy. This in turn makes the former set of nations provide still more defense and the latter still less.

21. The number of people defended by a given military force can clearly increase without reducing the security per person. However, additional land area will normally require some additional military forces, if the area previously protected is to have the same degree of security as before, and if actual defensive conflict, rather than deterrence, is at issue. When the additional land area has no common border with the enemy, it can usually be defended without any significant extra cost. The extra cost to NATO of defending Belgium against a Soviet attack, once Germany and France are already defended, is negligible. Even when the extra land does have a common border with an enemy it is not always true that it costs much more to defend it. If the French had believed they had to defend Belgium as well as France in World Wars I and II, they might have fared better.

22. This suggests that the conventional view, that a good is a pure public good if it can be offered to additional consumers for free without any less being available to those already consuming the good, is somewhat too simple. For a good might be such that, if extra consumers enjoyed it, there would be a little less for those who had already been consuming it. Yet it might pay to let new consumers enjoy the present supply of the good at a zero price (or even less), if they would agree to share the costs of providing the additional amount of the good that it would be optimal to purchase once the additional consumers were involved.

23. Perhaps the bargaining advantage of the smaller, weaker nations should not be surprising. Schelling has found many other situations in which, for different reasons, weakness can be a source of bargaining strength. See Thomas C. Schelling, *The Strategy of Conflict* (Cambridge, MA: Harvard University Press, 1960), especially 22, 23, 37, 52, and 158.

24. These two reasons came to our attention through Klaus Knorr, "Notes on a Theory of Alliances," (unpublished manuscript, Center of International Studies, Princeton University, 23–24, and 28.

25. See Sidney Siegel, *Nonparametric Statistics* (New York: McGraw-Hill, 1956), 284. As a corroborative test, a different set of data for a different year (1960) was also used. With these data the Spearman rank correlation coefficient for Gross National Product *and* defense budget as a percentage of GNP was .635, a value significant at the .05 level on a one-tailed test. Once again Iceland was excluded; since she ranked fifteenth for both variables, her inclusion in either test would have improved the correlation. (Source: Stanford Research Institute, "The Economic Feasibility of Proposed Changes in NATO Strategy, 1962–1975" [Menlo Park, CA: Stanford Research Institute]).

26. This was done because of concern that the positive correlation in H_1 might be simply the result of a joint correlation of both national income and the percentage of defense spending with per capita income, for it happens that the larger NATO nations often have the higher per capita incomes. The effects of differences in per capita income were "held constant" with the aid of the Kendall partial rank correlation coefficient, which measures the relationship between two variables after the effects of a third, possibly related, variable have been removed. The Kendall partial rank correlation coefficient of *Gross National Product* and *defense budget as a percentage of GNP*, net of the effects of *per capita GNP*, is .445. To our knowledge there is no test for the significance of the Kendall partial rank correlation coefficient, but it is perhaps suggestive that this is virtually the same as the Kendall rank correlation coefficient (.384) that results when the effects of differences in per capita income are not partialled out. Moreover, there is no statistically significant relationship between *per capita GNP* and *defense budget as a percentage of GNP*; in fact, the correlation is slightly negative. Thus we concluded that the correlation between the size of an ally's national income and the percentage of its national income spent on defense cannot be explained in terms of any relationship of these two variables with per capita income.

27. The data were taken from Norman J. Padelford, "Financial Crisis and the Future of the United Nations," *World Politics*, XV (July 1963), 531–568. Our sample included 97 of the UN members cited, since separate GNP statistics were not given for the Ukraine or Byelorussia. We employed the Student's "t" distribution with conversion from the Spearman rank correlation coefficient to test the significance of the correlation (see Siegel, *Nonparametric Statistics*, 212).

28. The data were taken from Irving B. Kravis and Michael W. S. Davenport, "The Political Arithmetic of Burden Sharing," *Journal of Political Economy*, LXXI (Aug. 1963), 323 and 325. Though this article [Kravis and Davenport] does not explicitly rank the aid-giving nations by the percentage of their national incomes used for foreign aid, this ranking was none the less obtained from this article [Kravis and Davenport] by comparing the figures given for each nation's aid as a percentage of total aid with the figures given for each nation's national income as a percentage of the total income of the entire group of nations.

29. The data are those prepared by John Pincus and presented in his *Economic Aid and International Cost Sharing*, Tables 5-9 and 5-12, 135 and 140. Pincus has usefully discounted the value of the loans given as foreign aid at the interest rate prevailing in the donor country in computing the value of each nation's foreign aid.

30. Irving Kravis and Michael Davenport, in their previously cited article, appear at first sight to come to conclusions in direct opposition to our own, for they say, "All in all, there seems to be little basis for the feeling that the United States is bearing a disproportionate share of the costs of international cooperation." They examine the structure of contributions to the Universal Postal Union, the United Nations, the OECD, and the NATO infrastructure. Since each of these organizations usually shares marginal costs on a percentage basis, their results for these organizations are consistent with our predictions about the effects of marginal cost sharing and in accord with our findings about the NATO infrastructure. As we saw in note 28, Kravis and Davenport also examined the foreign aid given by a number of industrialized countries, but we found their aid figures confirmed the hypothesis suggested by our model in situations where marginal costs are not shared. That Kravis and Davenport's article is not actually in conflict with our own is evident not only because their data are generally consistent with our model, but also because they are concerned in large part with ethical or ability-to-pay considerations that are not relevant to it.

31. We do *not* argue that the output of every international institution *ought* to be increased. This is partly a question of personal values, and we feel that sometimes spending on some alliances and other international organizations might best be curtailed. The point in this article is rather that, *given* the values or preferences of the members of an international organization, they will tend to provide less of the collective good than would be Pareto-optimal in terms of those values.

32. We must strongly emphasize that we are *not* here questioning the fairness of the present distribution of the costs of any international undertaking. No statement about what distribution of costs ought to prevail can be made unless some (logically arbitrary) assumption is made about what income re-

distributions among participating nations would be desirable. Jacques van Ypersele de Strihou, in "Sharing the Burden of Defense Among Allies," an interesting PhD thesis available at Yale University (1967), has shown that, if the British rates of progression are used as a standard of fairness, it appears that the larger European members of NATO pay an unfairly large share of the common costs, that the United States (partly because of its high per capita income) pays about the right amount, and that the smaller NATO nations (because of the same general forces explained in this paper) pay an unfairly small amount.

33. A similar proposal has been suggested by Thomas Schelling. He suggests that each country's share of the alliance's expenditure be fixed and the overall total spending be left open. Thus a country whose share of the cost was ten percent would find that in return for spending this money it got not only the protection of the forces this money would buy, but also the forces created by those nations that paid the other 90 percent. See his *International Cost Sharing Arrangements*, Essays in International Finance, No. 24 (Princeton, NJ: International Finance Section, Princeton University Press, September 1955), 19.

34. Some other general reasons why alliances as presently organized will be inefficient, however complete the consensus among the members, are explained in our chapter in the forthcoming Universities-National Bureau of Economic Research volume on "The Economics of Defense." The model's implication that increased non-collective benefits improve the functioning of an alliance, and other implications of our model, have been tested by James A. Robinson and Philip M. Burgess of the Mershon Social Science Program at Ohio State University, through a most interesting gaming-simulation procedure. Their analysis of the data is not yet complete, but we are informed that the data generally appear to support the hypothesis that private, noncollective benefits can strengthen an alliance, and probably also other hypotheses suggested by our model.

The Power of Liberal International Organizations

MICHAEL BARNETT AND MARTHA FINNEMORE

International organizations are at the hub of most theoretical and historical discussions of global governance. Politicians, publics, and theorists alike believe that a globalizing world requires mechanisms to manage the growing complexity of cross-national interactions, and international organizations are the mechanism of choice. As a result of this vision, states have established more and more international organizations (IOs) to perform an increasingly varied array of tasks. IOs now manage conflicts, both international and civil. They promote economic growth and free trade, they work to avert environmental disasters, and they are ac-

tively involved in protecting human rights around the globe.

The reasons states turn to IOs and delegate critical tasks to them are not mysterious or controversial in most of the scholarly literature. The conventional wisdom is that states create and delegate to IOs because they provide essential functions. They provide public goods, collect information, establish credible commitments, monitor agreements, and generally help states overcome problems associated with collective action and enhance individual and collective welfare. This perspective generates important insights, but the statism

Michael Barnett and Martha Finnemore, "The Power of Liberal International Organizations," in *Power in Global Governance*, ed. Michael Barnett and Raymond Duvall, 161–84 (Cambridge: Cambridge University Press, 2005). © Cambridge University Press 2005; reproduced with permission of the Licensor through PLSclear.

and functionalism of this view also obscures important features of IOs, making it difficult to see the power they exercise in global governance. First, the functionalist treatment of IOs reduces them to technical accomplishments, slighting their political character and the political work they do. It also presumes that the only interesting or important functions that IOs might perform are those that facilitate cooperation and resolve problems of interdependent choice. However, IOs do much more. IOs also construct the social world in which cooperation and choice take place. They help define the interests that states and other actors come to hold and, we will argue here, do so in ways compatible with liberalism and a liberal global order. These are important exercises of power that the functionalist view neglects.

Second, the statism of many contemporary treatments of IOs treats them as mere tools of states and has difficulty seeing them as autonomous actors who might exercise power. Despite all their attention to international institutions, there is a tendency among many to treat IOs the way pluralists treat the state. IOs are mechanisms or arenas through which others (usually states) act. The regimes literature is particularly clear on this point. Regimes are "principles, norms, rules, and decision-making procedures." They are not purposive actors. IOs are thus passive structures; states are the agents that exercise power in this view. Yet IOs can, indeed, be autonomous actors with power to influence world events. IOs have autonomy because they have authority. When scholars using neoliberal institutionalism and principal-agent models think about authority, they imagine delegated authority. In this view, authority is a commodity over which states have property rights; it can be transferred to (or withdrawn from) an IO. This is a highly limited view of authority, both conceptually and substantively. Authority is not a commodity but an attribute generated from social relations. An actor cannot have authority in a vacuum; actors have authority because of the particular relations they have with others. The reason IOs have authority, we argue, is that the rationalization processes of modernity and spreading global liberalism constitute them in particular kinds of relations to others. IOs are bureaucracies, and Max Weber recognized that bureaucracy is a uniquely authoritative (and powerful) social form in modern societies because of its rational-legal (i.e., impersonal, technocratic) character. But IOs are also conferred authority because they pursue liberal social goals that are widely viewed as desirable and legitimate. IOs are thus powerful both because of their form (as rational-legal bureaucracies) and because of their (liberal) goals. This authority gives them a sphere of autonomy and a resource they can use to shape the behavior of others in both direct and indirect ways.

In this essay we offer an alternative framework for understanding the role of international organizations in global governance, one that provides a theoretical basis for expecting autonomous action by IOs, suggests new ways of understanding the various forms of IO power, and highlights the connections of IOs to global liberalism.[1] The first section briefly develops the argument that rationalization and liberalism constitute IOs as particular kinds of actors, ones that are able to help organize, regulate, and guide transnational interactions in ways that promote cooperation and liberal values. The second section argues that IOs can be usefully characterized as bureaucracies and are conferred authority for reasons owing to their rational-legal standing, their delegated tasks, their moral position, and their expertise. A focus on the authority of IOs generates three important insights: (1) it shows how authority provides the basis of IO autonomy; (2) it highlights how (often liberal) values and social purpose stand behind IOs' technocratic appearance, rules and routines; and (3) it shows how authority provides a resource that IOs use to exercise power in ways that directly shape behavior (compulsory power), indirectly shape behavior at a distance (institutional power), and contribute to the constitution of global governance (productive power). We conclude by considering several normative issues raised by our argument regarding IOs and global governance.

Liberal International Organizations

Our contemporary architecture of IOs can be understood as an expression of two central components of global culture—rationalization and liberalism. Max Weber introduced the concept of rationalization in order to describe the process whereby modes of action structured in terms of means and ends, often using impersonal rules and procedures, increasingly dominate the world. Weber clearly saw rationalization as a historical process that was increasingly defining all spheres of life, including the economy, culture, and the state. Liberal ideas have seen a similar, perhaps related, expansion across the globe. Liberal political ideas about the sanctity and autonomy of the individual and about democracy as the most desirable and "just" form of government have spread widely, as have liberal economic notions about the virtues of markets and capitalism as the best (and perhaps the only) means to "progress." These two cultural strands have constituted IOs in particular ways. Rationalization has given IOs their basic form (as bureaucracies) and liberalism has provided the social goals which IOs all now pursue (democracy, human rights, and material progress via free markets). We take up each of these in turn.

IOs are bureaucracies and the modern bureaucracy is, in many ways, exemplary of the rationalization process. It is defined by four central features (Beetham, 1996: 9–12). Modern bureaucracies exhibit *hierarchy*, for each official has a clearly defined sphere of competence within a division of labor and is answerable to superiors; *continuity*, where the office constitutes a full-time salary structure that offers the prospect of regular advancement; *impersonality*, where the work is conducted according to prescribed rules and operating procedures that eliminate arbitrary and politicized influences; and *expertise*, where officials are selected according to merit, are trained for their function, and control access to knowledge stored in files. The modern bureaucratic form is distinguished by the breaking down of problems into manageable and repetitive tasks that are the domain of a particular office, and then coordinated under a hierarchical command.

These are the very qualities and traits that led Max Weber (1978a) to characterize modern bureaucracies as more efficient than other systems of administration or organization and reflective of the rationalization processes that were unfolding:

> Bureaucracy exemplified "rationality" . . . because it involved control on the basis of knowledge; because it clearly defined spheres of competence; because it operated according to intellectually analyzable rules; because of the calculability of its operation; finally, because technically it was capable of the highest level of achievement. (Beetham, 1985: 69)

Bureaucracies, in Weber's view, are a grand achievement in that they depoliticize and depersonalize decision-making, and subject decisions to well-established rules. Decisions, therefore, are made on the basis of technical knowledge and the possession of information. Decision-making procedures informed by these qualities define a rationalized organization, one that can deliver precision, stability, discipline, and reliability.

Yet rationalization is not the only source of legitimacy for bureaucracies. We do not defer to bureaucracy and empower it simply because it is a bureaucracy. We defer because bureaucracies serve valued social goals. These rationalization processes are always linked to a broader collective purpose—to notions of "progress," development, justice, security, and the autonomy to develop self-fulfillment (Boli and Thomas, 1999: 38). Historically, bureaucracy has been linked to a variety of social visions. Communism was particularly adept at calling bureaucracy into service. Nationalist, theocratic, and authoritarian regimes of various kinds have all made use of bureaucracy and provided it with purposes of different kinds (Scott, 1998). But, internationally, liberalism has colored our attitudes toward the role of international organizations in global governance.

Liberalism has dominated thinking about IOs, both theoretically and in policy circles. Enthusiasm for international organizations as policy prescriptions flows directly from some of the most fundamental theoretical tenets of classical liberalism: a belief in progress and in the capacity of technological change and markets to transform the character of global politics in positive ways by creating ever-expanding material resources that can ameliorate social conflicts. IOs, in the liberal view, are both promoters and managers of these changes. They bring the benefits of progress to those in need and at the same time manage conflicts that may accompany these changes in a nonviolent, impartial, and rational way (see Keohane, 1990; Zacher and Matthews, 1995; Doyle, 1995). They also are valued because of the view that they help to bring about progress, nurturing development, security, justice, and individual autonomy (Boli and Thomas, 1999). Given these virtues, it is hardly surprising that liberals have been the most ardent and longstanding champions of IOs in policy circles (and the most attentive to IOs in the scholarship).[2]

As a historical matter, the creation of most international organizations has been part of a larger liberal project emanating from the West. In this view, international organizations are purveyors of progress, modernity, and peace. The first public international unions were created in the middle of the nineteenth century with an eye to spurring greater commercial ties and interdependence. The desire to introduce standardized weights and measures and to coordinate various communication and transportation lines were justified on the grounds that they would promote greater commerce and interdependence between states (Murphy, 1994). These functional associations would not only provide the technical and bureaucratic means to further economic liberalism; the growing interactions were also hypothesized to lead to more pacific relations between states (Russett and O'Neal, 2001; Mitrany, 1966). But IOs were evaluated not only on the grounds that they would promote greater and more profitable and peaceful interactions between states. There was also a liberal assumption that IOs would champion basic liberal values such as freedom, autonomy, and liberty against the lingering absolutism of the day (Iriye, 2002: 13). In other words, these "technical" activities were hardly apolitical and value-neutral and instead were serving cultural ends (Murphy, 1994; Boli and Thomas, 1999).

The next big push of IO-building came after World War I and is most closely associated with the liberal internationalism of Woodrow Wilson. He and other advocates of IOs saw them as able to sustain and promote basic liberal values such as national self-determination, group and minority rights, free trade, and democracy. These general ideas were clothed in notions of progress and order. As Martti Koskenniemi (2002) brilliantly chronicles, those who gathered at Versailles believed that the League of Nations and other international associations not only might help avoid a return to war but also could help civilize nations and bring about progress. In their view, the creation of more liberal states would help to produce a more stable international order. Liberalism, in essence, operated at two connected levels: a liberal domestic order would favor a liberal international order, and a liberal international order would favor a liberal domestic order (Iriye, 2002: chap. 2). This transnational liberal order would produce stability and progress. International organizations such as the League of Nations were designed not only to more rationally steer the world but also to produce a more liberal world that would be self-regulating in more desirable ways.

Despite Cold War tensions, the period after World War II saw an explosion of international organizations, most avowedly liberal in their character and missions. Many of those who were involved in the creation of these IOs were self-identified liberals, but realists, too, valued these international organizations as valuable tools for projecting US power and constructing a liberal international order (Murphy, 1994; Burley, 1993). The half-century of international organization activity between 1945 and 1989 reflects this conscious effort and was largely successful at achieving its goals. The economic institutions set up at Bretton Woods were heavily involved in promoting and sustaining an "embedded liberalism," attempting to guide the international economy away from the mercantilistic practices of the interwar period and toward a regulated but increasingly open international trade regime (Ruggie, 1982). The United Nations was pivotal to the epochal change from the era of empires to the era of sovereign states, helping to engineer a relatively peaceful decolonization process. The UN also assisted the birth of the human rights regime in this period, laying the groundwork for its extraordinary expansion since the end of the Cold War. IOs thus regulated the postwar world and helped to constitute a largely liberal world order.

With the end of the Cold War, major constraints on expanding liberalism disappeared and the relationship between IOs and construction of a liberal global order became unmistakable. In both their discourse and their activities, IOs revealed a liberal self-understanding and a liberal vision of the role they could and should play in the world. As they have for a century, advocates and staff of IOs hold that the world is being transformed by modernization processes, and that IOs are essential to manage the worst and guide the best of these processes. They also forward human rights and democracy as important principles for shaping and defining not only international but also domestic politics. While the state remains the cornerstone of international politics, many IOs attempt to promote the sanctity of the individual and give greater voice to various identity-based associations and collectivities. The liberal template is particularly noticeable when IOs attempt to "save failed states." Drawing from liberal models of the state, the architects and administrators of these rebuilding tasks nurture liberal practices. Good states have the rule of law and elections that result in changing governments and market economies, and international organizations of all kinds work hard to promote this model (Barnett, 1997). Through their activities and programs, many IOs articulate a notion of progress that is defined largely by liberal principles.

Yet liberalism is not of a piece, and, as IOs have attempted to spread and stabilize liberal values, they have confronted contradictions in liberalism and counterattacks from opponents. Contradictions and problems in the liberal vision are well known. Market economies tend not to produce equal distributions of wealth, thereby undermining equality and possibly human rights. Public bureaucracies, often called in by liberal polities to ameliorate the worst effects of markets, are not noted for their efficiency or accountability (Finnemore, 1996: 131–35). Democracy, understood as majority rule and competitive elections, might very well clash with liberal tenets of the rule of law and individual rights when they fail to elect upholders of either liberalism or democracy, producing "illiberal democracies" (Zakaria, 2003). Possible contradictions such as these within liberalism produce much of the politics we see within Western states, and as it spreads around the globe, exported in significant part by IOs, they have created similar tensions both within and among non-Western states as well.

One of the most consequential tensions in the Western (now global) liberal model that is currently fueling conflict around international organizations is the tension between free-market capitalism (liberal economics) and state autonomy (liberal self-determination norms). In the postwar "embedded liberal" compromise, as described by John Ruggie (1982), states were understood to have a legitimate role in protecting societies from the harshest features of free-wheeling capitalism, and were accorded substantial autonomy in devising social policies to protect their people from unwelcome features of global markets. International institutions as they operated in the postwar period respected, even celebrated, this buffering role of states as part of the rightful role political communities should play in the global order. Over time, and particularly since the 1980s, however, this buffering role for states has come under attack by pro-market forces of globalization, and international organizations have often been on the front lines of this dismantling of the embedded liberal compromise. The International Monetary Fund, World Bank, and the World Trade Organization have all consistently pushed for greater integration into world markets, even at the cost of domestic social compacts, as the only road to economic growth and prosperity (Stiglitz, 2002). Although international organizations are not alone in pushing the agenda from regulation to deregulation (nor are they even the most consequential actors), they are clearly among the most visible proponents. They have been central in legitimating this move and, as a consequence, have become lightning rods for political opponents of it, as events in Seattle, Prague, and Washington show.

Rationalization and liberalism have helped to constitute IOs. Certainly states are responsible for establishing them and delegating to them certain functions and tasks. States do this because they expect IOs to be a more effective governance mechanism, enabling them to get the best and avoid the worst of globalizing processes. But states create IOs in a specific historical and cultural context, one in which rationalization and liberalism figure prominently, and these two features have constituted IOs as particular kinds of subjects. IOs take the modern bureaucratic form because of modernity's belief that its organizing principles provide a more rationalized, precise, and efficient way to govern the world. And IOs are valued because of the liberal vision of "progress" they help realize for states and their citizens. As we will see in the next section, this combination has been particularly powerful. As bureaucracies pursuing valued goals, IO become authorities in modern life and are able to help create a liberal world that they are then particularly well suited to regulate.

The Authority of IOs

Dominant approaches to international organizations all produce an image of IOs as lacking agency and autonomy, even though they arrive at this conclusion through different theoretical channels. Utilitarian, economistic, and regime approaches deny agency or autonomy by treating IOs only as arenas for action by others, while more structural approaches like that of the institutionalists in sociology treat IOs as mere accretions of global culture, dutifully enacting their scripts. In neither case are IOs autonomous agents. The understanding we offer, of IOs as constituted by both rationalization processes and global liberalism, provides a different view. In this section we show how IOs have been constituted in very particular ways such that they are endowed with authority, ergo autonomy, precisely because they are rationalized, liberal actors.

By *authority* we mean the ability of one actor to deploy discursive and institutional resources in order to get other actors to defer judgment to them (Lincoln, 1994). Authority has several important characteristics that concern us here. First, authority is a social construction and is part of social relations. It cannot be understood and, indeed, does not exist apart from the social relations that constitute and legitimate it. Second, one of authority's most prominent features is the character of the social relations it entails: authority requires some level of consent from other actors. An actor may be powerful regardless of what others think, but she is only authoritative if others recognize her as such. Other levers of power may be seized or taken, but authority must be conferred. Third, when actors confer authority and defer to the authority's judgment, they grant a right to speak and to have those statements conferred credibility. There is always a range of opinions about any contentious political problem, but not all views receive equal weight or equal hearing. Authority helps an actor's voice be heard, recognized, and believed.

Fourth, this right to speak credibly is central to the way authority produces effects. Because individuals defer judgment to those who are conferred authority, they are likely to alter their behavior in ways that are consistent with the directions laid out by that authority. Authority involves more than the ability to get people to do what they otherwise would not; authority often consists of telling people what is the right thing to do. There is a persuasive and normative element in authority that is tightly linked to its legitimacy. The exercise of authority in reasonable and normatively acceptable ways bolsters its legitimacy. Conversely, it is because we believe in the legitimacy of authorities that we often follow their directives and think those directives are right and necessary, even when we do not like them. This does not imply that compliance is automatic, however. Actors might recognize an authority's judgment as legitimate but still follow an alternative course of actions for some other set of reasons. Indeed, sometimes there are alternative voices, each viewed as an authority, that are giving different judgments and instructions to actors.

IOs are conferred authority because they embody rational-legal principles that modernity values and are identified with liberal values that are viewed as legitimate and progressive. Bureaucracies, international and otherwise, contain authority that derives from their rational-legal character. This argument is most closely associated with Weber's claim that modern bureaucracies are conferred authority because they are organized along rational-legal principles that modernity highly values. In contrast to earlier forms of authority that were invested in a leader, legitimate modern authority is invested in legalities, procedures, and rules and thus rendered impersonal. This authority is "rational" in that it deploys socially recognized relevant knowledge to create rules that determine how goals will be pursued. The very fact that they embody rationality is what makes bureaucracies powerful and makes people willing to submit to this kind of authority. According to Weber (1978b: 299),

> In legal authority, submission does not rest upon the belief and devotion to charismatically gifted persons . . . or upon piety toward a personal lord and master who is defined by an ordered tradition. . . . Rather submission under legal authority is based upon an *impersonal* bond to the generally defined and functional "duty of office." The official duty— like the corresponding right to exercise authority: the "jurisdictional competency"—is fixed by *rationally established* norms, by enactments, decrees, and regulations in such a matter that the legitimacy of the authority becomes the legality of the general rule, which is purposely thought out, enacted, and announced with formal correctness.

It is because national and IO staff are perceived as performing "duties of office" and as implementing "rationally established norms" that they are viewed as possessing authority.

Yet this instrumental character of bureaucracy— their need to serve others—means that rational-legal authority, alone, is not sufficient to constitute it. Rational-legal authority gives international organizations their basic form (bureaucracy) and behavioral vocabulary (general, impersonal rule-making), but the form requires some substantive content. Bureaucracy must serve some social purpose (as Weber and others have noted). It is the values and people it serves that make bureaucracy, including international organizations, respected and authoritative. We identify three broad categories of such substantive authority that undergird international organizations and make them authoritative actors: delegation, morality, and expertise. Central to our analysis is that IOs are viewed as pursuing goods and ends that are culturally valued—and doing so through means that are viewed as technical, apolitical, and rational. Thus, international bureaucracies are hardly the value-neutral, technical instruments that they often present themselves as being, and instead are authorities that are invested with cultural content. In the case of IOs, that content has a strong liberal character. Delegation to IOs tends to happen within a distinctly liberal framework of participation, accountability, and transparency; and the moral purposes IOs draw on for legitimacy (for example, promoting human rights and democracy) are decidedly liberal.

At a rudimentary level the authority of international organizations is *delegated authority* from states (Sarooshi, 1999; Keohane and Nye, 2001; Abbott and Snidal, 1998). International organizations are authorities because states have put them in charge of certain tasks. The UN's authority to do peacekeeping comes from the mandate given to it by member states through the Security Council. The authority of the Office of the UN High Commissioner for Refugees derives from its statute created by member states. The European Commission's authority derives from the powers delegated to it by the European states. Member states delegate to the IMF the authority to act in certain domains regarding international financial matters. International organizations are thus authoritative because they represent the collective will of their members who are, themselves, legitimate authorities.

At first glance, this type of authority would not appear to provide any autonomy for international organizations at all and is fairly consistent with the functionalist view of international organizations. However, the delegation process is not so simple, nor is the kind of authority delegation confers. States often delegate to international organizations tasks which they cannot perform themselves and about which they have limited knowledge. Mandates to international organizations are often vague or broad, or contain conflicting directives. Consequently, mandates need to be interpreted and, even with oversight, the agenda, interests, experience, values, and expertise of IO staff heavily color any organization's response to delegated tasks. Thus, international organizations *must* be autonomous actors in some ways simply to fulfill their delegated tasks (Abbott and Snidal, 1998).

As in the case of rational-legal authority, though, delegation authorizes international organizations to act autonomously only to the extent that they appear to be serving others, in this case the delegators. Delegated authority is always authority on loan. To use it, international organizations must maintain the perception that they are faithful servants to their mandates and masters. However, serving their mandates may often conflict with serving particular desires of particular (often powerful) state masters, and sorting out these tensions can be a major activity for many international organizations. Whatever solution is worked out, though, international organizations must be presented as *not* autonomous, but instead as dutiful agents.

International organizations also can embody *moral authority*. IOs are often created to embody, serve, or protect some widely shared set of principles and use this status as a basis of authoritative action. The UN secretary-general, for example, often uses the organization's status as protector of world peace and human rights to induce deference from governments and citizens. The Office of the UN High Commissioner for Refugees similarly uses its moral duty to protect refugees as a basis for autonomous action on their behalf. In addition to such straightforward mandated moral authority, however, international organizations often traffic in another kind of moral appeal. IOs of all kinds often emphasize their neutrality, impartiality, and objectivity in ways that make essentially moral claims against particularistic self-serving states. Thus, we see the heads of international organizations expending considerable energy attempting to demonstrate that they are not doing the bidding of the great powers but instead are the representative of "the international community." The moral valence here is clear: international organizations are supposed to be more moral (ergo more authoritative) in battles with governments because they represent the community against self-seekers.

This aspect of moral authority also allows international organizations to present themselves as depoliticized and impartial. Obviously, defending moral claims is political and in some sense partisan, but to the extent that international organizations present themselves as champions of the shared values of the community against particularistic interests, they draw support for their actions. IOs defending peace and human rights, for example, can claim their actions are neutral and impartial because these are motherhood-and-apple-pie values that we all profess to love.

Finally, international organizations also contain *expert authority*. One important reason why states create bureaucracies is that states want important social tasks to be done by individuals with detailed, specialized knowledge about those tasks. Nuclear proliferation should be monitored by physicists and engineers who know about nuclear weapons; the HIV/AIDS epidemic should be handled by doctors and public health specialists who know about disease prevention. Specialized knowledge derived from training or experience persuades us to confer on experts, and the bureaucracies that house them, the power to make judgments and solve problems. Deployment of specialized knowledge is central to the very rational-legal authority which constitutes bureaucracy in the first place since what makes such authority rational is, at least in part, the use of socially recognized relevant knowledge to carry out tasks (Brint, 1994: 7).

Expertise thus makes international organizations authoritative, but it also shapes how these organizations will behave in important ways. Just as international organizations authorized by a moral principle must serve that principle and make their actions consistent with it to remain legitimate and authoritative, so too, when international organizations are authorized by expertise, they must serve that specialized knowledge and make their actions consistent with it. The IMF cannot propose any policies it chooses. It can only offer policies that are supported by the economic knowledge it deploys. In fact, the organization will not readily entertain policy options not supported by its expertise. Professional training, norms, and occupational cultures strongly shape the way experts view the world. They influence what problems are visible to staff and what range of solutions are entertained (Brint, 1994; Schein, 1996).

Like delegated and moral authority, expert authority also creates the appearance of depoliticization. By emphasizing the "objective" nature of their knowledge, international organizations are able to present themselves as technocrats whose advice is unaffected by partisan squabbles. Some kinds of expertise make this presentation easier than others. For instance, quantification vastly enhances the power of these claims of political neutrality and impartiality. Ironically, the more successful experts are at making numbers "speak for themselves" and yield clear policy prescriptions without interpretation from bureaucrats, the more powerful those policy prescriptions are. The greater the appearance of depoliticization, the greater the power of the expertise.

These four types of authority—rational-legal, delegated, moral, and expert—each contributes in different ways to making international organizations autonomous actors. However, in exercising each type, IOs must manage an important paradox. On the one hand, bureaucracies are always created to defend or promote values, and their promotion of (or embodiment of) widely held social values is what gives them authority and legitimacy. Bureaucracy is inevitably linked to a broader normative order that gives purpose and meaning to all social action, including that of bureaucrats (Zabusky, 1995; Herzfeld, 1993). On the other hand, bureaucracies often justify their power on the basis of their supposedly objective and rational character. In fact, however, such objectivity does not and probably cannot exist, but the myth of such objectivity is central to their legitimacy.

To reconcile contradictory demands of rational objectivity and service to social values, bureaucracies rely on self-effacement. They present themselves as embodying the values of the collectivity and as serving the interests of others—and not as powerful and commanding deference in their own right. To be authoritative, international organizations must be seen to serve some valued and legitimate social purpose, and, further, they must be seen to serve that purpose in an impartial and technocratic way. The power of international organizations, and bureaucracies generally, thus lies with their ability to present themselves as impersonal and neutral—as *not* exercising power but instead serving others (Fisher, 1997; Shore and Wright, 1997). The presentation and acceptance of these claims are critical to their legitimacy and authority. IOs work hard to preserve this appearance of neutrality and service to others. The need to appear as impartial servants is central to understanding IO behavior, particularly since in many situations there is no neutral or apolitical ground for international organizations to occupy.

IOs are constituted by both rationalization processes and liberalism, and, accordingly, their practices are reflections of these relations of social constitution. On the one hand, they try to act in impartial, technocratic ways as required by the rational-legal authority that constitutes them. On the other hand, their missions for which they were created require them to pursue and promote social goods that may be deeply politicized. It is this paradoxical blending of their technical form with deeply held values that generates authority and autonomy for IOs, but also creates contradictions and tensions to be managed. In the next section, we examine the way IOs use their authority and show how IOs are able not only to regulate directly and at a distance, but also to help constitute the world that needs to be regulated.

IOs, Authority, and Power

By recognizing that IOs have authority (i.e., that others defer to their judgment), we gain a new perspective on how IOs can exercise power. In this section we show how IOs are able to use their authority to regulate what already exists and thus exhibit compulsory and institutional power. We also show how IOs contribute to the social constitution of the world and thus play an important role in shaping subjectivities, fixing meaning, and weaving the liberal international order; in this way, they exhibit productive power.

Compulsory Power: Authority as a Normative Resource to Direct Behavior

Typically international relations scholars discount the ability of IOs to exercise power because they assume that the most meaningful and significant resources are material. Certainly there are times when IOs have this kind of power. Sometimes IOs do have material resources. They often have money, even guns, and can use these to influence the behavior of others. The World Bank can use its money to get small farmers to do what it wants. The UNHCR can use food and other resources to shape behavior of refugees. UN peacekeepers sometimes have guns (or can call upon those who do have guns) to coerce parties in conflicts. Such power over non-state actors is often overlooked by our state-centric discipline, but IOs also, on occasion, shape state behavior. For example, the IMF can coerce states into adopting policies they would not otherwise adopt because of its ability to deny funds or to categorize a country as not on the "right track." While IOs never have the material might to coerce the strongest states into actions they actively oppose, IOs do have material means to shape the behavior of many states on many occasions—a fact often overlooked by IR scholars.

IOs also can use normative resources to shape the behavior of state and non-state actors. In this instance of compulsory power, IOs use their normative (and sometimes material) resources to try and get other actors to alter their behavior. IOs are quite candid in their beliefs that one of their principal functions is to try to alter the behavior of states and non-state actors in order to make sure that they comply with existing normative and legal standards. Officials in international organizations often insist that part of their mission is to spread, inculcate, and enforce global values and norms. Although IOs often use techniques of teaching and persuasion that fall outside power, they also use various sorts of shaming techniques or material sanctions to get states and non-state actors to comply with existing or emergent international practices (Katzenstein, 1996; Finnemore, 1996; Legro, 1997). Armed with a notion of progress, an idea of how to create the better life, and some understanding of the conversion process, many high-ranking staff of IOs claim that their goal is to shape state action by establishing "best practices," by articulating and transmitting norms that define what constitutes acceptable and legitimate state behavior. The European Union, for example, is hard at work persuading members to reconfigure domestic institutions and practices in ways that harmonize with European and international standards. The Organization for Security and Cooperation in Europe is similarly engaged. The greater the material sanctions used to alter behavior, the more this activity looks like what Andrew Hurrell calls coercive socialization.

IOs, like all other actors using rhetoric to shape the behavior of others, can and do use a variety of techniques for this purpose. They may frame issues in particular ways, so that desired choices seem particularly compelling or manipulate incentives so that the sanctions and penalties associated with particular policies are excessively high. They may exploit emotions of decision-makers and publics, creating empathy for landmine victims, refugees, and genocide survivors. They may use information strategically, gathering some kinds of information but not others. They may manipulate audiences strategically, inviting or including only some kinds of participants in their bureaucratic process (for example, the economists and bankers "doing" development) but not others (peasants and informal laborers who are the objects of development).[3]

Normative resources are certainly not the only forces shaping the policies of the state and non-state actors with which IOs deal. Rhetoric and authority are frequently supported by material resources, sometimes (but not always) held by resource-rich states. But to overlook how states and organizational missionaries work in tandem is to overlook a fundamental way in which they are able to directly change behavior.

Institutional Power: Guiding Behavior at a Distance

IOs can also guide behavior in ways that are both indirect and unintended. IOs can structure situations and social understandings in ways that channel behavior toward some outcomes rather than others. There may be no overt conflict in this exercise of power. Indeed, part of the power exercised here is the creation of nondecisions when situations are structured such that actors perceive no choice to be made. Furthermore, power can operate indirectly. Power need not be a local phenomenon, and IOs often change behavior in ways that are historically and spatially distant. This is most obvious in instances when international organizations' rules and norms have lingering effects, when policies and rules established at one time have echoes long into the future. It is also apparent when behavior is not directly caused by the institution but when it is an "intervening variable" or operating in conjunction with other causes.

One example of this is the way international organizations can exercise power through their agenda-setting activities (Cox and Jacobson, 1971; Pollack, 2003). IO staff frequently have the formal and informal capacity to determine the agenda at fora, meetings, and conferences. This capacity gives them a substantial role in determining what is—and is not—discussed. Therefore, agenda-setting capacity gives IO staff considerable influence over what policies are passed and motions are carried. This sort of agenda-setting power is not hard to find. The UN secretary-general frequently structures the options for particular peacekeeping operations and, therefore, establishes the parameters and the directions of the debate in the Security Council. The UN secretary-general's decision to make humanitarian intervention a defining theme of his 1999 address to the General Assembly shaped subsequent discussions. EU officials are renowned for possessing this sort of influence. UNHCR staff shape the discussions at Executive Committee meetings. World Bank officials are directly involved in drawing up the agenda for meetings. In this significant way, IO staff can help to orient discussions and actions in some directions and away from others.

Another way in which IOs have institutional and indirect power over behavior is through classificatory practices. An elementary feature of bureaucracies is that they classify and organize information and knowledge. This classification process is a form of power because it "moves persons among social categories or . . . invent[s] and appl[ies] such categories" and, therefore, constitutes a way of "making, ordering, and knowing social worlds" (Handelman, 1995: 280; see also Starr, 1992). The ability to classify objects, to shift their very definition and identity, is one of bureaucra-

cy's greatest sources of power. This power is frequently treated by the objects of that power as accomplished through caprice and without regard to their circumstances, but is legitimated and justified by bureaucrats with reference to the rules and regulations of the bureaucracy. The IMF has a particular way of categorizing economies and determining whether they are on the "right track," defined in terms of their capital accounts, balance of payments, budget deficits, and reserves. To be categorized as not "on track" can have important consequences for the ability of a state to get external financing at reasonable rates, to get access to IMF funds, or to escape the IMF's conditionality demands. The world is filled with individuals who have either been forced or chosen to flee their homes, and the UNHCR operates with a classification scheme that distinguishes between refugees, migrants, internally displaced peoples, and other sorts of displaced peoples or those who cannot return home. The UNHCR's unwillingness to extend refugee status to groups or individuals can leave them on the margin or physically vulnerable (Harrell-Bond, 2002). Similarly, classification of a conflict as a "civil war" or "genocide" triggers one set of responses by international actors rather than another.

Productive Power: Constitution

Authorities not only regulate but also help to constitute the world. IOs are an important part of a broader process that is helping to constitute a liberal global order that is productive of particular kinds of actors and associated practices. This is consistent with the argument we made in the first section. To recall, we suggested that IOs are constituted by rationalization and liberalism and that they, in turn, are central to the diffusion and deepening of this rationalized and global liberal order. IOs, in this crucial respect, are involved not only in helping to regulate the social world (as neoliberal institutionalists claim), but also in constituting that world that needs to be regulated. IOs do constitutive work, helping to shape the underlying social relations that create categories of action, fix meanings, shape subjectivities, and define the good life. IOs are not alone in this process. International NGOs have played a crucial role. So, too, have resource-laden great powers. But IOs, because of their number and, crucially, because of their authority, are central actors in this process.

One important aspect of this power is that IOs are often the actors who help to constitute the problems that need to be solved. Problems do not simply exist out there as objective facts; they are defined as problems by some actor (often an IO) through a process of social construction (Edelman, 1988). Thus, coordination and cooperation problems are not part of some objective reality that stands outside experience but are subjectively defined and constituted within social experience—and authorities help create that subjective reality (Raz, 1990). Authorities are often the ones who help to determine whether a problem exists to be solved; they define the problem for others, offering judgments about what kind of problem it is. As authorities, IOs do much of this work in global governance. Development agencies, for instance, were very much involved in determining that "development" was an omnibus solution to a set of problems associated with the inability of countries to apply resources in efficient ways to further economic growth (Escobar, 1995). In this respect, authorities help to define problems in relationship to a category of actions and goals that they view as good and legitimate.

Not only do authorities, such as IOs, help identify problems, they also help solve problems by crafting particular solutions to them and persuading others to accept them. Often there are a great many ways in which a problem might be addressed. Identifying the particular solution to be pursued is extremely consequential and an important exercise of power. Once such a problem is identified and a solution is proposed, the next logical step is to identify a set of actors that should take responsibility for implementing the solution. Authorities such as IOs once again step into the breach. They are often viewed as qualified to manage these solutions to already identified problems and to coordinate the activities of others.

IOs thus use their rules to define problems, craft solutions, and assign responsibilities for action. Their rules may be contested at times. They may also conflict with other rules. But because authorities are frequently defined in terms of their expertise and knowledge, they are viewed as eminently qualified to render a judgment on these matters. They are oftentimes perceived as doing good, and, because their intentions are honorable and they are experts in their field, they are given the legitimate right to intervene (Fisher, 1997).

A good example of this process in action is offered by James Ferguson's (1994) analysis of development organizations in Lesotho. Development agencies have as their very *raison d'être* the production of (economic) development. Third World countries are in particular need of their assistance because they are lacking in both development and the expertise and resources to accelerate development. But development agencies have a readymade solution to the problem of development—more market mechanisms. If development is not occurring, then it is because the economy and polity are not organized properly. So, the development agencies propose various policies that are designed to institutionalize market mechanisms but also to teach producers how to respond efficiently and properly to market signals. In this way, they view their goals as transforming self-sufficient "peasants" into market-dependent "farmers." Although development officials see the introduction of the market as a technical solution to the problem of development, the consequence of this technical solution is deeply political because it completely upends social relations in the family, between producers and consumers, and between the village and the state apparatus. In this way, as development agencies attempt to bring about progress and development, they introduce particular solutions to particular problems that not only regulate what currently exists but also help to constitute new social relations that require regulation.

Another example comes from peacekeeping and peacebuilding activities. The second-generation peacekeeping operations that emerged after the end of the Cold War were designed to help states move from civil war to civil society. As the UN intervened in order to save failed states, it attempted to redeem the fallen by producing states modeled on the image of the Western state. Accordingly, peace operations were designed to create a particular kind of state, one that had working markets, was a working democracy, had the rule of law, and the like. In short, these were intended to be liberal, democratic states (Paris, 1997; Barnett, 1997). Many parts of the UN system were involved in this constitutive work (as were NGOs and INGOs, other IOs, and states), and the expectation was that liberal states would be self-regulating and would not require repeated intervention by the international community.

IOs thus help to make a more liberal and rationalized world. They help determine what is progress and what constitutes the good life, both for their own work and for the rest of us. Their notions of progress and the good life, though, are inextricably tied to liberal categories and ideas. They emphasize individual autonomy, democracy, and market economics as the preferred progressive forms of social organization, and remake social institutions which do not conform to these notions. In this important sense, IOs are constituting the world in ways that reflect the same global values that constitute them as social actors.

Conclusion

For much of the past half-century, international organizations have been praised and have benefited from the presumption that globalization requires IOs at the hub of any system of global governance. The reasons for this enthusiasm were many. Historically, traditional liberal sentiments favored international organizations as champions of community interests over self-seeking states, and as clearly preferable to the alternative mode of conflict resolution, war, which was so painfully evident in the first half of the twentieth century. Theoretically, neorealists and neoliberals might have disagreed about the conditions under which international organizations might be effective, but they agreed that they could do important work in furthering state interests where they were allowed to work. For both policy-makers and scholars, international organizations provided solutions to an array of policy problems, and challenges to their essential goodness were few and far between.[4]

This general enthusiasm has waned over the last decade. There is growing concern that the "progress" IOs bring comes at a steep price as individuals, peoples, and states all find it increasingly difficult to control their own fate. Consequently, there are subtle signs of a growing interest in reining in the reach of international organizations. Whereas once international law operated on the implied-power doctrine—international organizations can move into new areas of competence unless it is specifically denied by member states—over the past decade international courts have been increasingly likely to rely on the specialty (or attribution) doctrine—international organizations are limited to the powers specifically delegated to them (Klabbers, 2001: 231). Similarly, IOs are increasingly interested not in regulating but rather in deregulating—a development that mimics what has taken place at the state level (Klabbers, 2001: 238). Subsidiarity and the possibility of opting out, once a concern only in the EU, have become important principles for many areas of governance. Further, there is also a growing sense that formal, bureaucratic international organizations are too ossified and slow to respond efficiently in a globalizing world. Informal networks and similar decentralized, less bureaucratic forms of governance have become all the rage in many policy circles as an antidote to perceived bureaucratic sclerosis. Thus, there is a growing interest in protecting the local over the universal, an implicit recognition that bureaucracy's presumption that "one-size-fits-all" mentality can be highly inefficient. There is also a growing interest in using policy networks that use different architectures to address specific issues (Keohane and Nye, 2001; United Nations, 2000: chap. 2). There is a growing concern about whether IOs are truly promoting social justice, and whose vision of social justice they are promoting (Weber, 2000). There is a growing interest in IO accountability, transparency, and the democratic deficit. The more international organizations are pushed to the forefront of global governance, the more frequent are the catcalls and criticisms—and the more interested are social movements and states keen to question their actions, to limit their powers, and to search for alternatives.

These developments speak directly to the question of the authority and legitimacy of international organizations. They challenge whether states are likely to continue to delegate to international organizations at the same rate or with the same reflexiveness, whether international organizations will be able to claim the same degree of expert authority in relationship to other expert claims, and whether international organizations will be able to maintain the same level of moral authority. What this portends is a challenge to IO legitimacy on at least three dimensions. First, these developments threaten procedural legitimacy, which considers actions legitimate to the extent that they follow a decision process that is viewed as proper and right, which in this context means conforming to democratic principles. Increasingly, legitimate procedures involve transparency, democratic deliberation, and local participation. On all three counts, IO procedures have been found wanting. Second, they threaten substantive legitimacy, which involves not process but decision output and whether that output is consistent with the values of the broader political community. Refugee policies that violate refugee rights, development policies that impoverish people, and peacekeeping missions that fuel, rather than end, conflicts have all undermined the legitimacy of various international organizations. This legitimation problem is exacerbated by the simple fact that, increasingly, international organizations are involved in multifaceted governance projects that leave them accountable to different political constituencies at different moments, and those constituencies do not all agree on what constitutes substantive success. Finally, the legitimacy of international organizations is very much bound up with ongoing debates over who, exactly, are "the governed" in global governance. Are international organizations governing a community of states or are they governing a community of peoples? Much of the current dissatisfaction with global governance generally and international organizations specifically stems from champions of "the people" who believe their interests are being forgotten. This is certainly true in the protests against international financial institutions, but the issue is also central in the discussions within the EU, where opinion polls consistently show that publics believe the union is an elite project and are deeply skeptical about its virtues.

Neither international organizations nor the tensions that are inherent in their liberal mission are likely to disappear any time soon. This rather fatalistic observation we owe to Max Weber. One hundred years ago he observed that his Prussia was becoming bureaucratic. He welcomed this development, recognizing that it would enable an increasingly complex society to coordinate its activities in a more rational, objective, and peaceful manner. He was further heartened by the realization that the bureaucracy was helping to inculcate in his fellow citizens the very liberal, rational values that he prized. But his joy was quickly moderated by his concern that a bureaucratic world had its own perils, producing increasingly powerful and autonomous bureaucrats who can be "spiritless" and driven by rules, and who can apply those rules in ways that harm the very people whom they are expected to serve. For the remainder of his life, Weber feared that the very bureaucracy that was needed to keep a society democratic, prosperous, and healthy might also undermine society's well-being.

What Weber observed at the beginning of the past century at the domestic level, we observe at the beginning of the new century at the global level. States have built a metropolis of international and regional organizations that are intended to help them facilitate interdependence and manage its excesses. Without international organizations, states would be less likely and able to reap the fruits of commercial exchange, find nonviolent dispute mechanisms, or solve their environmental problems. But international organizations are not only helping states coordinate their activities, they also are shaping which activities the international community values and holds in high esteem. Beginning in the nineteenth century and continuing into the twenty-first century, international organizations have been disseminating the liberal values that are the foundations for a global liberal culture. But the very source of their power to do good might also be the source of their power to do harm, to run roughshod over the interests of states and citizens that they are supposed to further. We live in an age when international bureaucracies are necessary to manage globalization, and desirable because they can nurture a global liberal culture. But that will come at a cost.

NOTES

The authors would like to thank the participants at the conference on "Who Governs in Global Governance?" at the University of Wisconsin-Madison in April 2003, Tom Biersteker, and especially Bud Duvall for comments on the essay.

1. This essay draw heavily from Barnett and Finnemore (2004).

2. For instance, Harold Jacobson's opening sentence of his *Networks of Interdependence* (1979: 1) is: "This is an optimistic book, though I hope not an unrealistic one." He then proceeds to offer a succinct statement that captures most of the classic liberal themes linking progress, change, the prospect of harmony of interests, and the central role of IOs to that end. This positive view of international organizations has been reinforced in recent years by the emergence of an "analytic liberalism" which draws on microeconomics (economic "liberalism") to understand international politics. This view suggests that international organizations provide coordination that enables states to overcome collective problems, produce Pareto-improving outcomes, and perform various functions that enable states to overcome obstacles to cooperation. Implicit in this view are a number of assumptions about IOs, that they are welfare-improving for their members, as well as rational and impartial servants of their members. Given these assumptions, it is hardly surprising that contemporary liberal scholars draw heavily on economistic

and rationalist approaches to the study of organizations. These approaches come out of economics departments and business schools and are rooted in assumptions of instrumental rationality and utility maximization. The fundamental theoretical problem for this group, laid out first by Coase and more recently by Williamson, is why we have business firms. Within standard microeconomic logic, it should be much more efficient to conduct all transactions through markets rather than "hierarchies." Consequently, the fact that economic life is dominated by huge organizations (business firms) is, itself, an anomaly. The body of theory developed to explain this focuses on organizations as efficient solutions to contracting problems, incomplete information, and other market imperfections.

3. For a taxonomy of tools of persuasion, see Finnemore (2003: chap. 5).

4. As several observers have noted, there was automatic approval for almost any sort of "international project" to the extent that "anything international is good, as long as it is international." See Kennedy (1994), cited in Klabbers (2001: 225). The first quote is from Kennedy, the second from Klabbers.

REFERENCES

Abbott, Kenneth, and Duncan Snidal. 1998. "Why States Act Through Formal International Organizations," *Journal of Conflict Resolution* 42(1):3–32.

Barnett, Michael. 1997. "Bringing in the New World Order: Legitimacy, Liberalism, and the United Nations," *World Politics* 49(4):526–51.

Beetham, David. 1985. *Max Weber and the Theory of Modern Politics*. New York: Polity.

Beetham, David. 1996. *Bureaucracy*. Minneapolis: University of Minnesota Press.

Boli, John, and George M. Thomas. 1999. "INGOs and the Organization of World Culture." In J. Boli and G. M. Thomas (eds.), *Constructing World Culture: International Organizations Since 1875*, pp. 13–49. Stanford, CA: Stanford University Press.

Brint, Steven. 1994. *In an Age of Experts: The Changing Role of Professionals in Politics and Public Life*. Princeton, NJ: Princeton University Press.

Burley, Anne-Marie. 1993. "Regulating the World: Multilateralism, International Law, and the Projection of the New Deal Regulatory State." In J. Ruggie (ed.), *Multilateralism Matters: The Theory and Praxis of an Institutional Form*, pp. 125–56. New York: Columbia University Press.

Cox, Robert, and Harold Jacobson. 1971. *The Anatomy of Influence*. New Haven, CT: Yale University Press.

Doyle, Michael. 1995. "Liberalism and World Politics." In C. Kegley (ed.), *Controversies in International Relations Theory: Realism and the Neoliberal Challenge*, pp. 81–94. New York: St. Martin's Press.

Edelman, Murray. 1988. *Constructing the Political Spectacle*. Chicago: University of Chicago Press.

Escobar, Arturo. 1995. *Encountering Development: The Making and Unmaking of the Third World*. Princeton, NJ: Princeton University Press.

Ferguson, James. 1994. *The Anti-Politics Machine*. Minneapolis: University of Minnesota Press.

Finnemore, Martha. 1996. *National Interests in International Society*. Ithaca, NY: Cornell University Press.

Finnemore, Martha. 2003. *The Purpose of Intervention: Changing Beliefs About the Use of Force.* Ithaca, NY: Cornell University Press.

Fisher, William. 1997. "Doing Good? The Politics and Antipolitics of NGO Practices," *Annual Review of Anthropology* 26:439–64.

Handelman, Don. 1995. "Commentary on Heyman," *Current Anthropology* 36:280–1.

Harrell-Bond, Barbara. 2002. "Can Humanitarian Work with Refugees Be Humane?" *Human Rights Quarterly* 24:51–85.

Herzfeld, Michael. 1993. *The Social Production of Indifference.* Chicago: University of Chicago Press.

Iriye, Akira. 2002. *Global Community: The Role of International Organizations in the Making of the Contemporary World.* Berkeley: University of California Press.

Jacobson, Harold. 1979. *Networks of Interdependence: International Organizations and the Global Political System.* New York: Alfred A. Knopf.

Katzenstein, Peter (ed.). 1996. *The Culture of National Security.* New York: Columbia University Press.

Keohane, Robert O. 1990. "International Liberalism Reconsidered." In J. Dunn (ed.), *The Economic Limits to Modern Politics*, pp. 165–94. New York: Cambridge University Press.

Keohane, Robert, and Joseph Nye. 2001. "The Club Model of Multilateral Cooperation and Problems of Democratic Legitimacy." In R. Porter et al. (eds.), *Efficiency, Equity, and Legitimacy: The Multilateral Trading System at the Millennium*, pp. 264–94. Washington, DC: Brookings Institution Press.

Klabbers, Jan. 2001. "Changing Image of International Organizations." In J. Coicaud and V. Heiskanen (eds.), *The Legitimacy of International Organizations*, pp. 221–55. New York: United Nations University Press.

Koskenniemi, Martti. 2002. *The Gentle Civilizer of Nations: The Rise and Fall of International Law, 1870–1960.* New York: Cambridge University Press.

Legro, Jeff. 1997. "Which Norms Matter? Revisiting the 'Failure' of Internationalism," *International Organization* 51(1): 31–64.

Lincoln, Bruce. 1994. *Authority: Construction and Corrosion.* Chicago: University of Chicago Press.

Mitrany, David. 1966. *A Working Peace System.* Chicago: Quadrangle Books.

Murphy, Craig. 1994. *International Organizations and Industrial Change.* New York: Oxford University Press.

Paris, Roland. 1997. "Peacebuilding and the Limits of Liberal Internationalism," *International Security* 22(2):54–89.

Pollack, Mark A. 2003. *Engines of Integration.* New York: Oxford University Press.

Raz, Joseph. 1990. "Introduction." In J. Raz (ed.), *Authority*, pp. 6–11. New York: Cambridge University Press.

Ruggie, John Gerard. 1982. "International Regimes, Transactions, and Change: Embedded Liberalism in the Postwar Economic Order," *International Organization* 36(2): 379–415.

Russett, Bruce, and John O'Neal. 2001. *Triangulating Peace: Democracy, Interdependence, and International Organizations.* New York: Norton.

Sarooshi, Danesh. 1999. *The United Nations and the Development of Collective Security: The Delegation by the UN Security Council of Its Chapter VII Powers.* New York: Oxford University Press.

Schein, Edgar. 1996. "Culture: The Missing Concept in Organization Studies," *Administrative Studies Quarterly* 41:229–40.

Scott, James C. 1998. *Seeing Like a State: How Certain Schemes to Improve the Human Condition Have Failed.* New Haven: Yale University Press.

Shore, Cris, and Susan Wright. 1997. "Policy: A New Field of Anthropology." In Cris Shore and Susan Wright (eds.), *Anthropology of Social Policy: Critical Perspectives on Governance and Power*, pp. 3–41. New York: Routledge.

Starr, Paul. 1992. "Social Categories and Claims in the Liberal State." In M. Douglas and D. Hull (eds.), *How Classification Works: Nelson Goodman Among the Social Sciences*, pp. 154–79. Edinburgh: Edinburgh University Press.

Stiglitz, Joseph E. 2002. *Globalization and Its Discontents.* New York: W. W. Norton.

United Nations. 2000. *Millennium Report of the Secretary-General of the United Nations.* www.un.org/millennium/sg/report.

Weber, Max. 1978a. "Bureaucracy." In H. H. Gerth and C. W. Mills (eds.), *From Max Weber: Essays in Sociology.* New York: Oxford University Press.

Weber, Max. 1978b. "The Social Psychology of the World Religions." In H. H. Gerth and C. W. Mills (eds.), *From Max Weber: Essays in Sociology.* New York: Oxford University Press.

Weber, Steve. 2000. "International Organizations and the Pursuit of Justice in the World Economy," *Ethics and International Affairs* 14:99–118.

Zabusky, Stacia. 1995. *Launching Europe: An Ethnography of European Cooperation in Space Science.* Princeton, NJ: Princeton University Press.

Zacher, Mark, and Richard Matthews. 1995. "Liberal International Theory: Common Threads, Divergent Strands." In C. Kegley (ed.), *Controversies in International Relations Theory: Realism and the Neoliberal Challenge*, pp. 107–50. New York: St. Martin's Press.

Zakaria, Fareed. 2003. *The Future of Freedom: Illiberal Democracy at Home and Abroad.* New York: Norton.

Chapter 4

The International
Environment—Adversaries

The Growing Challenge of Defining an "Enemy"

MICHAEL J. MAZARR

The concept of an "enemy" is central to traditional understandings of national security. The purpose of national security policies and institutions is to defend a nation against enemies; an enemy is usually the "other" who helps to define a nation or other in-group;[1] support for enemies has been outlawed and punished by death. If a nation cannot clearly identify its enemies, it is far more difficult to have a coherent national security policy.

This essay argues that, given the evolving character of conflict, it is becoming much more challenging to distinguish between nations that ought to be considered outright enemies and those that are merely competitors, rivals, or not formally aligned. This development may become especially problematic for the United States, which has depended on unambiguous distinctions between friends and enemies in its traditional approaches to national security.

International Relations Theory: Competitors and Rivals

Theoretical accounts of international relations consider the drive for power, security, prosperity, and prestige among nations jostling for position in a partly orderly and partly chaotic international system. Conflicts and contests for supremacy are the rule, not the exception. As a result, international relations theory tends to employ terms other than "enemy" in describing most other actors in the international system. Nations may become enemies when war is declared, but more typically they are viewed as competitors or rivals.

Despite its widespread use in the theoretical literature, the term "competitor" is badly undertheorized and not well defined. A recent RAND study on the subject reviewed the available definitions of competition and competitors and proposed a new definition: competition is "the attempt to gain advantage, often relative to others believed to pose a challenge or threat, through the self-interested pursuit of contested goods such as power, security, wealth, influence, and status."[2] That two nations (or a nation and competing non-state groups) are competitors does *not* presume that they are trying to injure one another; they are engaged in a contest for material or nonmaterial gains, sometimes in absolute terms and sometimes relative to one another. But in theory, nations can compete without trying to harm one another through direct attack.

The term "rival," by contrast, has been the subject of an extensive literature. International relations scholars point to a number of factors as being necessary for a rivalry: it is typically "militarized," characterized over time by wars or militarized disputes,[3] though precisely how much it has to be characterized by military action is the subject of some dispute.[4] One leading scholar of rivalry, William Thompson, contends that states are rivals when by mutual threat perceptions they *believe themselves* to be so.[5] To be counted as rivals, a pair of states must generally regard one another as both "competitive" and "threatening."[6] The term "rival" therefore implies a greater degree of hostility than "competitor": rivals, in classic international relations, are countries that are often on the brink of war and tend to be actively seeking to undermine the power and sometimes the stability of the other countries involved in the rivalry.

From Rival to Enemy: Nations in Conflict

A critical message of international relations theory is that, given the perpetual contest for power, security, and other goods in world politics, we should expect countries, especially major powers, to be competitors as a standard practice. These competitions may be highly compartmentalized, as in US-European trade and economic competition, for example, or US competition with rising countries like India and Brazil for control of the global diplomatic agenda. In other cases, as with Russia and China today, competitions can be more generalized and comprehensive. In some cases, such as the Cold War, they can become zero-sum, with each nation or system predicated on the objective of undermining or transcending the other.

Even at their most confrontational, however, competitors typically do not rise to the level of an enemy or adversary. Those terms are usually reserved for countries actively seeking, through war or other usually violent means, to do severe damage to a nation, to the point of occupying or even destroying it. This distinction can become very blurry; today, for example, given that Russia and China each have doctrines of persistent competition, they may take on some characteristics of a classic competitor and wartime adversary at the same time.

Basic dictionary definitions offer some help in understanding the commonsense concept of an enemy.

Merriam-Webster defines an enemy as "one that is antagonistic to another," which hardly distinguishes the category from a rival.[7] Dictionary.com refers to "a person who feels hatred for, fosters harmful designs against, or engages in antagonistic activities against another; an adversary or opponent."[8] Both also point to a narrower conception: an enemy is some entity with which a country is formally and actively at war. But just what it means to be "at war" with someone or something takes many forms; historically, the term "enemy" has even been used to refer to specific hated or demonized groups said to pose an ethnic, religious, cultural, or other threat to the country. The Nazis defined Jews, gypsies, homosexuals, and selected other persecuted groups as the enemies of Germany in this way; ethnic wars in the Balkans in the 1990s also saw the widespread use of such demonization.

The concept of an enemy is not strongly defined in most academic treatments, which generally do not take the concept far beyond these commonsense notions. Carl Schmitt's binary conception of friend and enemy as the basis of politics—which has been severely criticized—nearly engages in a tautology in understanding an enemy as that foreign power which threatens a nation.[9] Broadly speaking, the implication is that an enemy is always a country or group that is posing an identifiable threat to a nation.

When forced to formally define an enemy in legislation—as the United Kingdom and United States did when passing Trading with the Enemy Acts in 1939 and 1917, respectively—states often begin by referring to the narrower conception of a foreign country (or any of its supporting individuals or corporations) that exists in a state of war with one's own.[10] Later modifications of the US version of this legislation broadened the definition to include any state designated as being an enemy during war or "any other period of national emergency declared by the president."[11] The act was later applied to the Soviet Union during the Cold War and gradually became a justification for economic and other forms of warfare even during peacetime.

Drawing on these various definitions, we can say that the concept of an enemy extends beyond formally declared war to any state or non-state group that is (1) hostile to the country and seeking to harm it, and (2) engaged in some form of active campaign or conflict to achieve that end. This wider conception already begins to blur the distinction between competitor and enemy, and now multiple developments in the twenty-first century—most notably, the degree of competitive behavior among major powers and the evolving character of conflict—are accelerating this blurring of categories and making it even more difficult to identify a true enemy.

An Increasingly Zero-Sum and Hostile Era

One trend complicating any conception of enemies is the return to an era of generalized hostility among major powers. Although a comparison to the Cold War misleads in many ways, it does accurately convey the reality of a time when major states—in this case the United States and both Russia and China, with Iran and North Korea playing similar if less dominant roles—view each other as bitter rivals engaged in a largely zero-sum standoff. The result is that, as during the Cold War, countries tend to view one other as "enemies" even in peacetime.

Hardening this perception is that according to widespread open-source reporting, the governments of Russia and China (as well as Iran and North Korea) view themselves as being already "at war" with the United States in geopolitical and ideological, if not military, terms.[12] This is partly the United States' fault, due to its support of "color revolutions" and repeated implications that it is seeking a version of regime change that would overturn the governments in these countries. One effect is that all four of these rivals have begun to actively undermine American power, influence, and credibility and in some cases—such as direct cyberattacks—to bring damage to the US homeland.

The question is how to characterize powers that engage in such hostile acts while remaining formally at peace. They certainly meet the criteria for competitors. Russia and China also meet the criteria for rivals in a classic sense: the United States has a history of open conflict with China and decades of clandestine and proxy conflict with both during the Cold War. It is not clear, however, if either of China or Russia should be described as an "enemy." It is one thing to identify a nation such as China as a competitor: the implication is of a constrained if vigorous contest for influence. But such competition does not imply a zero-sum struggle with existential overtones. Nor does it suggest that the countries involved in a competition will attack each other directly and violently. Those more extreme forms of conflict are typically reserved for enemy relationships—yet they may be increasingly characterizing major power relations.

At the same time, numerous third parties are caught in between the big players in this intensifying competition. Many of these in-between nations have adopted various forms of hedging or balancing as their primary strategy, rather than making a decisive and unconditional choice of one "side" or another. Some—including India, Vietnam, Indonesia, and Serbia—have long championed versions of nonalignment as essential to their identity on the world stage.

The result is a secondary version of the blurring boundary between competitor and enemy—namely, a similarly weakening distinction between friend and rival (or enemy). The United States is having to deal with a growing number of "frenemies" on the international stage. These include countries such as Pakistan, which has some goals aligned with those of the United States but whose own threat perceptions, identity, and national strategies cause it to take actions that Washington considers unjust and sometimes traitorous to a true partnership. Living in a world of such hedging and balancing powers—partly friends, sometime partners, occasional rivals and critics and even sponsors of hostile acts against the United States—is becoming the norm.

The Evolving Character of Conflict

A second major engine of the blurring definitions of an enemy is the gradual move away from classical, Napoleonic forms of military aggression to more limited and constrained forms of competition and conflict that nonetheless pose significant threats to homelands. The nuclear revolution and other developments have reduced the chances of encountering other states as "enemies" in the traditional sense—in major war, with armies clashing in grand combat. The result is that the most traditional concept of an "enemy" nation, as a neighboring or nearby country threatening one's territorial integrity, has lost much of its currency. At the same time, new technologies and operational concepts have provided competitors with the tools to perpetrate the kinds of damage that enemies do.

One of these means of aggression is economic sanctions, which have long been a tool of statecraft but have become more precise in recent years, in being employed against specific companies and even individuals in target countries. One leading assessment of such techniques refers to them as "war by other means."[13] They furnish states with an ability to manipulate the economic well-being of other nations from a great distance.

Information warfare tools typically referred to as "cyber weapons" provide a second category of adversarial aggression. These take multiple forms and have many degrees of seriousness. Some involve mere temporary disruption; others target critical infrastructure elements of other societies.[14] The effect of cyber aggression is potentially becoming even more pronounced in an era of more densely networked information economies, created by developments such as the Internet of Things (IoT). A recent RAND report describes these emerging capabilities as "virtual societal warfare"—capable of doing tremendous damage to target nations without a single soldier crossing a single frontier.[15]

A third category is more targeted violence against specific individuals or groups in other countries. Examples include Russian assassinations of political enemies, alleged Israeli killing of Iranian nuclear scientists, and US drone strikes against terrorist cells. Such tools are becoming more widespread. For instance, Benjamin Wittes and Gabriella Blum have chronicled the rise of such new technologies as insect-sized attack drones and engineered biological weapons. They conclude that "in a world that generates such a ferocious capacity for small groups to launch attacks, individuals and groups at all levels of society—and societies and states themselves—will face enormous vulnerability as a daily fact of life."[16]

The result is a context in which aggression becomes more gradual, persistent, and in some cases deniable.[17] Countries can attack one another's homeland in much more fundamental ways than before without ever declaring "war" or dispatching any "military" forces. And yet countries engaged in an escalating battle using tools such as economic sanctions or cyber warfare are much more than competitors or even rivals. They are, in every way that matters, enemies—but enemies in a strange, cloudy, often unacknowledged way, which constantly threatens to spill over into major war. And many third parties stand by, hesitant to take sides and unwilling to formally join these clandestine campaigns—and thus, in the eyes of many Americans, likely unwilling to clearly identify themselves as friends. The geopolitical context is becoming very murky indeed.

A Proliferation of Enemies

Together these trends are creating an increasingly dangerous situation in which competing and rivalrous nations have both the means and the ways of intruding into one another's societies and launching various forms of attack to disrupt and undermine one another's economic and political systems. More countries are beginning to seem like "enemies," in active confrontation with the United States. Fewer are appearing to be true "friends," unquestioningly aligning themselves with the United States and following its lead on most international issues. As it was during the Cold War, managing threat perceptions in such an era—avoiding extreme overreactions and assessing the behavior and hostility of others in a calm and objective way—is becoming a major test for US national security strategy.

NOTES

1. Shoon Kathleen Murray and Jonathan A. Cowden, "The Role of 'Enemy Images' and Ideology in Elite Belief Systems," *International Studies Quarterly* 43, no. 3 (September 1999), 455–81.

2. Michael J. Mazarr, Jonathan S. Blake, Abigail Casey, Tim McDonald, Stephanie Pezard, and Michael Spirtas, "Understanding the Emerging Era of International Competition: Theoretical and Historical Perspectives" (Santa Monica, CA: RAND Corporation, 2018), 5.

3. Paul F. Diehl and Gary Goertz, *War and Peace in International Rivalry* (Ann Arbor: University of Michigan Press, 2000), 19–25. See also D. Scott Bennett, "Security, Bargaining, and the End of Interstate Rivalry," *International Studies Quarterly* 40, no. 2 (1996): 157–83; Charles S. Gochman and Zeev Maoz, "Militarized Interstate Disputes, 1816–1976: Procedures, Patterns, and Insights," *Journal of Conflict Resolution* 28, no. 4 (1984): 585–616; Paul F. Diehl, "Contiguity and Military Escalation in Major Power Rivalries, 1816–1980," *Journal of Politics* 47, no. 4 (1985): 1203–11.

4. M. P. Colaresi, Karen Rasler, and William R. Thompson, *Strategic Rivalries in World Politics: Position, Space and Conflict Escalation* (Cambridge: Cambridge University Press, 2008), 22; William R. Thompson, "Identifying Rivals and Rivalries in World Politics," *International Studies Quarterly* 45, no. 4 (2001): 558–59.

5. Diehl and Goertz, *War and Peace*, 19–25.

6. Karen Rasler, William R. Thompson, and Sumit Ganguly, *How Rivalries End* (Philadelphia: University of Pennsylvania Press, 2013), 3.

7. Merriam-Webster, s.v. "enemy," accessed January 14, 2020, https://www.merriam-webster.com/dictionary/enemy.

8. Dictionary.com, s.v. "enemy," accessed January 14, 2020, https://www.dictionary.com/browse/enemy.

9. Carl Schmitt, *The Concept of the Political*, trans. George Schwab (Chicago: University of Chicago Press, 1996). See also Predrag Petrović, "Enemy as the Essence of the Political," *Western Balkans Security Observer* 13 (April–June 2009), https://www.libraryofsocialscience.com/assets/pdf/Petrovic-Enemy.pdf; Reinhard Mehring, "Carl Schmitt's Friend-Enemy Distinction Today," *Filozofija i Društvo* 28, no. 2 (2017): 304–317.

10. Clive Parry, "The Trading with the Enemy Act and the Definition of an Enemy," *Modern Law Review* 4, no. 3 (January 1941): 164.

11. "Trading with the Enemy Act of 1917," 40 U.S.C. § 411, https://www.govinfo.gov/content/pkg/USCODE-2011-title50/pdf/USCODE-2011-title50-app-tradingwi.pdf.

12. See for example Max Boot, "Russia's Been Waging War on the West for Years. We Just Haven't Noticed," *Washington Post*, March 15, 2018; Matt Field, "Pentagon Report: Russian Leaders Believe They Are Already at War with the United States," *Bulletin of the Atomic Scientists*, July 5, 2019.

13. Robert D. Blackwill and Jennifer M. Harris, *War by Other Means: Geoeconomics and Statecraft* (Cambridge, MA: Harvard University Press, 2017).

14. A very good recent treatment of recent cyber attacks is John P. Carlin and Garrett M. Graff, *Dawn of the Code War: America's Battle against Russia, China, and the Rising Global Cyber Threat* (New York: PublicAffairs, 2018).

15. Michael J. Mazarr, Ryan Michael Bauer, Abigail Casey, Sarah Heintz, and Luke J. Matthews, *The Emerging Risk of Virtual Societal Warfare: Social Manipulation in a Changing Information Environment* (Santa Monica, CA: RAND Corporation, 2019).

16. Benjamin Wittes and Gabriella Blum, *The Future of Violence: Robots and Germs, Hackers and Drones—Confronting A New Age of Threat* (New York: Basic Books, 2015).

17. See Michael J. Mazarr, "Rivalry's New Face," *Survival* 54, no. 4 (2012): 83–106.

The Theory of Hegemonic War

ROBERT GILPIN

In the introduction to his history of the great war between the Spartans and the Athenians, Thucydides wrote that he was addressing "those inquirers who desire an exact knowledge of the past as an aid to the interpretation of the future, which in the course of human things must resemble if it does not reflect it. . . . In fine, I have written my work, not as an essay which is to win the applause of the moment, but as a possession for all time."[1] Thucydides, assuming that the behavior and phenomena that he observed would repeat themselves throughout human history, intended to reveal the underlying and unalterable nature of what is today called "international relations."

In the language of contemporary social science, Thucydides believed that he had uncovered the general law of the dynamics of international relations. Although differences exist between Thucydides' conceptions of scientific law and methodology and those of present-day students of international relations, it is significant that Thucydides was the first to set forth the idea that the dynamic of international relations is provided by the differential growth of power among states. This fundamental idea—that the uneven growth of power among states is the driving force of international relations—can be identified as the theory of hegemonic war.

This essay argues that Thucydides' theory of hegemonic war constitutes one of the central organizing ideas for the study of international relations. The following pages examine and evaluate Thucydides' the-

Robert Gilpin, "The Theory of Hegemonic War," reprinted from *Journal of Interdisciplinary History* 18, no. 4 (1988): 591–613, with the permission of the editors of *The Journal of Interdisciplinary History* and The MIT Press, Cambridge, Massachusetts. © 1988 by the Massachusetts Institute of Technology and The Journal of Interdisciplinary History, Inc.

ory of hegemonic war and contemporary variations of that theory. To carry out this task, it is necessary to make Thucydides' ideas more systematic, expose his basic assumptions, and understand his analytical method. Subsequently, this article discusses whether or not Thucydides' conception of international relations has proved to be a "possession for all time." Does it help explain wars in the modern era? How, if at all, has it been modified by more modern scholarship? What is its relevance for the contemporary nuclear age?

Thucydides' Theory of Hegemonic War

The essential idea embodied in Thucydides' theory of hegemonic war is that fundamental changes in the international system are the basic determinants of such wars. The structure of the system or distribution of power among the states in the system can be stable or unstable. A stable system is one in which changes can take place if they do not threaten the vital interests of the dominant states and thereby cause a war among them. In his view, such a stable system has an unequivocal hierarchy of power and an unchallenged dominant or hegemonic power. An unstable system is one in which economic, technological, and other changes are eroding the international hierarchy and undermining the position of the hegemonic state. In this latter situation, untoward events and diplomatic crises can precipitate a hegemonic war among the states in the system. The outcome of such a war is a new international structure.

Three propositions are embedded in this brief summary of the theory. The first is that a hegemonic war is distinct from other categories of war; it is caused by broad changes in political, strategic, and economic affairs. The second is that the relations among individual states can be conceived as a system; the behavior of states is determined in large part by their strategic interaction. The third is that a hegemonic war threatens and transforms the structure of the international system; whether or not the participants in the conflict are initially aware of it, at stake is the hierarchy of power and relations among states in the system. Thucydides' conception and all subsequent formulations of the theory of hegemonic war emerge from these three propositions.

Such a structural theory of war can be contrasted with an escalation theory of war. According to this latter theory, as Waltz has argued in *Man, the State, and War*, war occurs because of the simple fact that there is nothing to stop it.[2] In the anarchy of the international system, statesmen make decisions and respond to the decisions of others. This action-reaction process in time can lead to situations in which statesmen deliberately provoke a war or lose control over events and eventually find themselves propelled into a war. In effect, one thing leads to another until war is the consequence of the interplay of foreign policies.

Most wars are the consequence of such an escalatory process. They are not causally related to structural features of the international system, but rather are due to the distrust and uncertainty that characterizes relations among states in what Waltz has called a self-help system.[3] Thus, the history of ancient times, which introduces Thucydides' history, is a tale of constant warring. However, the Peloponnesian War, he tells us, is different and worthy of special attention because of the massive accumulation of power in Hellas and its implications for the structure of the system. This great war and its underlying causes were the focus of his history.

Obviously, these two theories do not necessarily contradict one another; each can be used to explain different wars. But what interested Thucydides was a particular type of war, what he called a "great war" and what this article calls a "hegemonic war"—a war in which the overall structure of an international system is at issue. The structure of the international system at the outbreak of such a war is a necessary, but not a sufficient cause of the war. The theory of hegemonic war and international change that is examined below refers to those wars that arise from the specific structure of an international system and in turn transform that structure.

Assumptions of the Theory

Underlying Thucydides' view that he had discovered the basic mechanism of a great or hegemonic war was his conception of human nature. He believed that human nature was unchanging and therefore the events recounted in his history would be repeated in the future. Since human beings are driven by three fundamental passions—interest, pride, and, above all else, fear—they always seek to increase their wealth and power until other humans, driven by like passions, try to stop them. Although advances in political knowledge could contribute to an understanding of this process, they could not control or arrest it. Even advances in knowledge, technology, or economic development would not change the fundamental nature of human behavior or of international relations. On the contrary, increases in human power, wealth, and technology would serve only to intensify conflict among social groups and enhance the magnitude of war. Thucydides the realist, in contrast to Plato the idealist, believed that reason would not transform human beings, but would always remain the slave of human passions. Thus, uncontrollable passions would again and again generate great conflicts like the one witnessed in his history.

Methodology

One can understand Thucydides' argument and his belief that he had uncovered the underlying dynamics of international relations and the role of hegemonic war in international change only if one comprehends his conception of science and his view of what constituted explanation. Modern students of international relations and of social science tend to put forth theoretical physics as their model of analysis and explanation; they analyze phenomena in terms of causation and of models linking independent and dependent variables. In modern physics, meaningful propositions must, at least in principle, be falsifiable—that is, they must give rise to predictions that can be shown to be false.

Thucydides, by contrast, took as his model of analysis and explanation the method of Hippocrates, the great Greek physician.[4] Disease, the Hippocratic school argued, had to be understood as a consequence of the operation of natural forces and not as a manifestation of some supernatural influence. Through dispassionate observation of the symptoms and the course of a disease, one could understand its nature. Thus, one explained a disease by recognizing its characteristics and charting its development from its genesis through inevitable periods of crisis to its final resolution in recovery or death. What was central to this mode of explanation was the evolution of the symptoms and the manifestations of the disease rather than the search for the underlying causes sought by modern medicine.

Thucydides wrote his history to fulfill the same prognostic purpose, namely, to recognize that great wars were recurrent phenomena with characteristic manifestations. A great or hegemonic war, like a disease, displays discernible symptoms and follows an inevitable course. The initial phase is a relatively stable international system characterized by a hierarchical ordering of the states in the system. Over time the power of a subordinate state begins to grow disproportionately, and that rising state comes into conflict with the dominant or hegemonic state in the system. The ensuing struggle between these two states and their respective allies leads to a bipolarization of the system, to an inevitable crisis, and eventually to a hegemonic war. Finally, there is the resolution of the war in favor of one side and the establishment of a new international system that reflects the emergent distribution of power in the system.

The dialectical conception of political change implicit in his model was borrowed from contemporary Sophist thinkers. This method of analysis postulated a thesis, its contradiction, or antithesis, and a resolution in the form of a synthesis. In his history this dialectic approach can be discerned as follows:

1. The *thesis* is the hegemonic state, in this case, Sparta, which organizes the international system in terms of its political, economic, and strategic interests.
2. The *antithesis* or contradiction in the system is the growing power of the challenging state, Athens, whose expansion and efforts to transform the international system bring it into conflict with the hegemonic state.
3. The *synthesis* is the new international system that results from the inevitable clash between the dominant state and the rising challenger.

Similarly, Thucydides foresaw that throughout history new states like Sparta and challenging states like Athens would arise and the hegemonic cycle would repeat itself.

Conception of Systemic Change

Underlying this analysis and the originality of Thucydides' thought was his novel conception of classical Greece as constituting a system, the basic components of which were the great powers—Sparta and Athens. Foreshadowing later realist formulations of international relations, he believed that the structure of the system was provided by the distribution of power among states; the hierarchy of power among these states defined and maintained the system and determined the relative prestige of states, their spheres of influence, and their political relations. The hierarchy of power and related elements thus gave order and stability to the system.

Accordingly, international political change involved a transformation of the hierarchy of the states in the system and the patterns of relations dependent upon that hierarchy. Although minor changes could occur and lesser states could move up and down this hierarchy without necessarily disturbing the stability of the system, the positioning of the great powers was crucial. Thus, as he tells us, it was the increasing power of the second most powerful state in the system, Athens, that precipitated the conflict and brought about what I have elsewhere called "systemic change," that is, a change in the hierarchy or control of the international political system.[5]

Searching behind appearances for the reality of international relations, Thucydides believed that he had found the true causes of the Peloponnesian War, and by implication of systemic change, in the phenomenon of the uneven growth of power among the dominant states in the system. "The real cause," he concluded in the first chapter, "I consider to be the one which was formally most kept out of sight. The growth of the power of Athens, and the alarm which this inspired in Lacedaemon [Sparta], made war inevitable."[6] In a like fashion and in future ages, he reasoned, the differential growth of power in a state system would undermine the status quo and lead to hegemonic war between declining and rising powers.

In summary, according to Thucydides, a great or hegemonic war, like a disease, follows a discernible and recurrent course. The initial phase is a relatively stable international system characterized by a hierarchical ordering of states with a dominant or hegemonic power. Over time, the power of one subordinate state begins to grow disproportionately; as this development occurs, it comes into conflict with the hegemonic state. The struggle between these contenders for preeminence and their accumulating alliances leads to a bipolarization of the system. In the parlance of game theory, the system becomes a zero-sum situation in which one side's gain is by necessity the other side's loss. As this bipolarization occurs the system becomes increasingly unstable, and a small event can trigger a crisis and precipitate a major conflict; the resolution of that conflict will determine the new hegemon and the hierarchy of power in the system.

The Causes of Hegemonic War

Following this model, Thucydides began his history of the war between the Spartans and the Athenians by stating why, at its very inception, he believed that the war would be a great war and thus worthy of special attention. Contrasting the beginnings of the Peloponnesian War to the constant warring of the Greeks, he began in the introduction to analyze the unprecedented growth of power in Hellas from ancient times to the outbreak of the war. Although, as we have already noted, Thucydides did not think of causes in the modern or scientific sense of the term, his analysis of the factors that altered the distribution of power in ancient Greece, and ultimately accounted for the war, is remarkably modern.

The first set of factors to explain the rise of power in Athens and the expansion of the Athenian empire contained geographical and demographic elements. Because of the poverty of its soil, Attica (the region surrounding Athens) was not envied by any other peoples; it enjoyed freedom from conflict. As a consequence, "the most powerful victims of war or faction from the rest of Hellas took refuge with the Athenians as a safe retreat," became naturalized, and swelled the population.[7] With an increase in population Attica became too small to sustain its growing numbers, and Athens began to send out colonies to other parts of Greece. Athens itself turned to commerce to feed her expanding population and became the "workshop of ancient Greece," exporting manufactured products and commodities in exchange for grain. Thus, Athens began its imperial career from demographic pressure and economic necessity.

The second set of influences was economic and technological: the Greek, and especially the Athenian, mastery of naval power, which had facilitated the expansion of commerce among the Greek states and the establishment of the hegemony of Hellas in the Eastern Mediterranean. After the defeat of Troy, Thucydides tells us, Hellas attained "the quiet which must precede growth" as the Greeks turned to commerce and the acquisition of wealth. Although Athens and other seafaring cities grew "in revenue and in dominion," there was no great concentration of power in Hellas prior to the war with Persia: "There was no union of subject cities round a great state, no spontaneous combination of equals for confederate expeditions; what fighting there was consisted merely of local warfare between rival neighbors."[8] The technical innovation of naval power, the introduction into Greece of fortification techniques, and the rise of financial power associated with commerce, however, made possible an unprecedented concentration of military and economic power. These developments, by transforming the basis of military power, created the conditions for the forging of substantial alliances, a profound shift in the power balance, and the creation of large seaborne empires. In this novel environment, states interacted more intimately, and an interdependent international economic and political system took shape. These military, technological, and economic changes were to favor the growth of Athenian power.

The final factor leading to the war was political: the rise of the Athenian empire at the conclusion of the war with Persia. That war and its aftermath stimulated the growth of Athenian power at the same time that the war and its aftermath encouraged Sparta, the reigning hegemon and the leader of the Greeks in their war against the Persians, to retreat into isolation. With the rise of a wealthy commercial class in Athens, the traditional form of government—a hereditary monarchy—was overthrown, and a new governing elite representing the rising and enterprising commercial class was established; its interest lay with commerce and imperial expansion. While the Athenians grew in power through commerce and empire, the Spartans fell behind and found themselves increasingly encircled by the expanding power of the Athenians.

As a consequence of these developments, the Greeks anticipated the approach of a great war and began to choose sides. In time, the international system divided into two great blocs. "At the head of the one stood Athens, at the head of the other Lacedaemon, one the first naval, the other the first military power in Hellas."[9] The former—commercial, democratic, and expansionist—began to evoke alarm in the more conservative Spartans. In this increasingly bipolar and unstable world a series of diplomatic encounters, beginning at Epidamnus and culminating in the Megara Decree and the Spartan ultimatum, were to plunge the rival alliances into war. In order to prevent the dynamic and expanding Athenians from overturning the international balance of power and displacing them as the hegemonic state, the Spartans eventually delivered an ultimatum that forced Athens to declare war.

In brief, it was the combination of significant environmental changes and the contrasting natures of the Athenian and Spartan societies that precipitated the war. Although the underlying causes of the war can be traced to geographical, economic, and technological factors, the major determinant of the foreign policies of the two protagonists was the differing character of their domestic regimes. Athens was a democracy; its people were energetic, daring, and commercially disposed; its naval power, financial resources, and empire were expanding. Sparta, the traditional hegemon of the Hellenes, was a slavocracy; its foreign policy was conservative and attentive merely to the narrow interests of preserving its domestic status quo. Having little interest in commerce or overseas empire, it gradually declined relative to its rival. In future ages, in Thucydides' judgment, situations similar to that of Athens and Sparta would arise, and this fateful process would repeat itself eternally.

The Contribution of Thucydides' Model

Thucydides' history and the pattern that it reveals have fascinated students of international relations in all eras. Individuals of every political persuasion from realist to idealist to Marxist have claimed kinship to him. At critical moments scholars and statesmen have seen their own times reflected in his account of the conflict between democratic Athens and undemocratic Sparta. The American Civil War, World War I, and the Cold War between the United States and the Soviet Union have been cast in its light. In a similar vein, Mackinder and other political geographers have interpreted world history as the recurrent struggle between land power (Sparta, Rome, and Great Britain) and sea power (Athens, Carthage, and Germany) and have observed that a great or hegemonic war has taken place and transformed world affairs approximately every 100 years. The writings of Wright and Toynbee on general war are cast in a similar vein. The Marxist theory of intra-capitalist wars can be viewed as a subcategory of Thucydides' more general theory. More recently, a number of social scientists have revived the concept of hegemonic war. The "power transition theory" of Organski, Modelski's theory of long cycles and global war, and the present writer's book on international change are examples of elaborations of Thucydides' fundamental insights into the dynamics of international relations.[10] Although these variations and extensions of Thucydides' basic model raise many interesting issues, they are too numerous and complex to be discussed here. Instead, the emphasis will be on the contribution of Thucydides' theory, its applicability to modern history, and its continuing relevance for international relations.

The theory's fundamental contribution is the conception of hegemonic war itself and the importance of hegemonic wars for the dynamics of international relations. The expression "hegemonic war" may have been coined by Aron; certainly he has provided an excellent definition of what Thucydides called a great war. Describing World War I as a hegemonic war, Aron writes that such a war "is characterized less by its immediate causes or its explicit purposes than by its extent and the stakes involved. It affect[s] all the political units inside one system of relations between sovereign states. Let us call it, for want of a better term, a war of hegemony, hegemony being, if not the conscious motive, at any rate the inevitable consequence of the victory of at least one of the states or groups." Thus, the outcome of a hegemonic war, according to Aron, is the transformation of the structure of the system of interstate relations.[11]

In more precise terms, one can distinguish a hegemonic war in terms of its scale, the objectives at stake, and the means employed to achieve those objectives. A hegemonic war generally involves all of the states in the system; it is a world war. Whatever the immediate and conscious motives of the combatants, as Aron points out, the fundamental issues to be decided are the leadership and structure of the international system. Its outcome also profoundly affects the internal composition of societies because, as the behavior of Athens and Sparta revealed, the victor remolds the vanquished in its image. Such wars are at once political, economic, and ideological struggles. Because of the scope of the war and the importance of the issues to be decided, the means employed are usually unlimited. In Clausewitzian terms, they become pure conflicts or clashes of society rather than the pursuit of limited policy objectives.

Thus, in the Peloponnesian War the whole of Hellas became engaged in an internecine struggle to determine the economic and political future of the Greek world. Although the initial objectives of the two alliances were limited, the basic issue in the contest became the structure and leadership of the emerging international system and not merely the fate of particular city-states. Ideological disputes, that is, conflicting views over the organization of domestic societies, were also at the heart of the struggle; democratic Athens and aristocratic Sparta sought to reorder other societies in terms of their own political values and socioeconomic systems. As Thucydides tells us in his description of the leveling and decimation of Melos, there were no constraints on the means employed to reach their goals. The war released forces of which the protagonists had previously been unaware; it took a totally unanticipated course. As the Athenians had warned the Spartans in counseling them against war, "consider the vast influence of accident in war, before you are engaged in it."[12] Furthermore, neither rival anticipated that the war would leave both sides exhausted and thereby open the way to Macedonian imperialism.

The central idea embodied in the hegemonic theory is that there is incompatibility between crucial elements of the existing international system and the changing distribution of power among the states within the system. The elements of the system—the hierarchy of prestige, the division of territory, and the international economy—became less and less compatible with the shifting distribution of power among the major states in the system. The resolution of the disequilibrium between the superstructure of the system and the underlying distribution of power is found in the outbreak and intensification of what becomes a hegemonic war.

The theory does not necessarily concern itself with whether the declining or rising state is responsible for the war. In fact, identification of the initiator of a particular war is frequently impossible to ascertain and authorities seldom agree. When did the war actually begin? What actions precipitated it? Who committed the first hostile act? In the case of the Peloponnesian War, for example, historians differ over whether Athens or Sparta initiated the war. Whereas most regard the Megara decree issued by Athens as the precipitating cause of the war, one can just as easily argue that the decree was the first act of a war already begun by Sparta and its allies.

Nor does the theory address the question of the explicit consequences of the war. Both the declining and rising protagonists may suffer and a third party may be the ultimate victor. Frequently, the chief beneficiary is, in fact, a rising peripheral power not directly engaged in the conflict. In the case of the Peloponnesian War, the war paved the way for Macedonian imperialism to triumph over the Greeks. In brief, the theory makes no prediction regarding the consequences of the war. What the theory postulates instead is that the system is ripe for a fundamental transformation because of profound ongoing changes in the international distribution of power and the larger economic and technological environment. This is not to suggest that the historic change produced by the war must be in some sense progressive; it may, as happened in the Peloponnesian War, weaken and eventually bring an end to one of mankind's most glorious civilizations.

Underlying the outbreak of a hegemonic war is the idea that the basis of power and social order is undergoing a fundamental transformation. Halévy must have had something like this conception of political change in mind when, in analyzing the causes of World War I, he wrote that "it is thus apparent why all great convulsions in the history of the world, and more particularly in modern Europe, have been at the same time

wars and revolutions. The Thirty Years' War was at once a revolutionary crisis, a conflict, within Germany, between the rival parties of Protestants and Catholics, and an international war between the Holy Roman Empire, Sweden, and France."[13] Similarly, Halévy continues, the wars of the French Revolution and Napoleon as well as World War I must be seen as upheavals of the whole European social and political order.

The profound changes in political relations, economic organization, and military technology behind hegemonic war and the associated domestic upheavals undermine both the international and domestic status quo. These underlying transformations in power and social relations result in shifts in the nature and locus of power. They give rise to a search for a new basis of political and social order at both the domestic and international levels.

This conception of a hegemonic war as associated with a historic turning point in world history is exemplified by the Peloponnesian War. A basic change in the nature and hence in the location of economic and military power was taking place in Greece during the fifth century B.C. This changing economic and technological environment had differing implications for the fortunes of the two major protagonists. The Peloponnesian War would be the midwife for the birth of the new world. This great war, like other transforming wars, would embody significant long-term changes in Greece's economy, military affairs, and political organization.

Prior to and during the Persian wars, power and wealth in the Greek world were based on agriculture and land armies; Sparta was ascendant among the Greek city-states. Its political position had a secure economic foundation, and its military power was unchallenged. The growth in the importance of naval power and the accompanying rise of commerce following the wars transformed the basis of power. Moreover, the introduction into Greece of fortification technology and the erection of walls around Athens canceled much of the Spartan military advantage. In this new environment, naval power, commerce, and finance became increasingly important components of state power. Thus, whereas in the past the nature of power had favored the Spartans, the transformed environment favored Athens and other rising commercial and naval powers.

Athens rather than Sparta benefited from this new military and economic environment. Domestically, Athens had experienced political and social changes that enabled it to take advantage of the increased importance of sea power and commerce. Its entrenched landed aristocracy, which had been associated with the former dominance of agriculture and land armies, had been overthrown and replaced by a commercial elite whose interests lay with the development of naval power and imperial expansion. In an increasingly monetarized international economy, the Athenians had the financial resources to outfit a powerful navy and expand its dominion at the expense of the Spartans.

By contrast, the Spartans, largely for domestic economic and political reasons, were unable or unwilling to make the necessary adjustment to the new economic and technological environment. It was not merely because Sparta was land-locked, but also because the dominant interests of the society were committed to the maintenance of an agricultural system based on slave labor. Their foremost concern was to forestall a slave revolt, and they feared external influences that would stimulate the Helots to rebel. Such a rebellion had forced them to revert into isolation at the end of the Persian wars. It appears to have been the fear of another revolt that caused them eventually to challenge the Athenians. The Megara decree aroused the Spartans because the potential return of Megara to Athenian control would have opened up the Peloponnesus to Athenian influence and thereby enabled the Athenians to assist a Helot revolt. Thus, when Athenian expansionism threatened a vital interest of the Spartans, the latter decided that war was inevitable, and delivered an ultimatum to the Athenians.[14]

The differing abilities of the Athenians and the Spartans to adjust to the new economic and technological environment and the changed nature of power ultimately led to the war. The development of naval power and acquisition of the financial resources to purchase ships and hire sailors necessitated a profound reordering of domestic society. Whereas the Athenians had reformed themselves in order to take advantage of new opportunities for wealth and power, the Spartans would or could not liberalize due to a constellation of domestic interests and their fear of unleashing a rebellion of the Helots. The result was the uneven growth of power among these rivals that Thucydides viewed as the real cause of the war.

The critical point arrived when the Spartans began to believe that time was moving against them and in favor of the Athenians. A tipping-point or fundamental change in the Spartan perception of the balance of power had taken place. As certain contemporary historians assert, Athenian power may have reached its zenith by the outbreak of the war and had already begun to wane, but the reality of the situation is not particularly relevant, since the Spartans believed that Athens was growing stronger. The decision facing them had become when to commence the war rather than whether to commence it. Was it better to fight while the advantage still lay with them or at some future date when the advantage might have turned? As Howard has written, similar perceptions and fears of eroding power have preceded history's other hegemonic wars.[15]

The stability of the Greek international system following the Persian wars was based on an economic and technological environment favoring Spartan hegemony.

When agriculture and land armies became less vital to state power and commerce and navies became more important, the Spartans were unable to adjust. Therefore, the locus of wealth and power shifted to the Athenians. Although the Athenians lost the war when they failed to heed the prudent strategy laid down by Pericles, the basic point is not altered; the war for hegemony in Greece emerged from a profound social, economic, and technological revolution. Wars like this one are not merely contests between rival states but political watersheds that mark transitions from one historical epoch to the next.

Despite the insight that it provides in understanding and explaining the great wars of history, the theory of hegemonic war is a limited and incomplete theory. It cannot easily handle perceptions that affect behavior and predict who will initiate a hegemonic war. Nor can it forecast when a hegemonic war will occur and what the consequences will be. As in the case of the theory of biological evolution, it helps one understand and explain what has happened; but neither theory can make predictions that can be tested and thereby meet rigorous scientific standard of falsifiability. The theory of hegemonic war at best is a complement to other theories such as those of cognitive psychology and expected utility and must be integrated with them. It has, however, withstood the test of time better than any other generalization in the field of international relations and remains an important conceptual tool for understanding the dynamics of world politics.

Hegemonic War in the Modern International System

In the modern world, three hegemonic wars have successively transformed the international system. Each of these great struggles not only involved a contest for supremacy of two or more great powers, but also represented significant changes in economic relations, technological capacities, and political organization. The war arose from profound historical changes and the basic incongruity between new environmental forces and existing structures. Each was a world war involving almost all of the states in the system and, at least in retrospect, can be considered as having constituted a major turning point in human history. These long and intense conflicts altered the fundamental contours of both domestic societies and international relations.[16]

The first of the modern hegemonic wars was the Thirty Years' War (1619 to 1648). Although this war may be regarded as a series of separate wars that at various times involved Sweden, France, Spain, Poland, and other powers, in sum it involved all the major states of Europe. As Gutmann points out, the origins of the war were deeply embedded in the history of the previous century.[17] At issue was the organization of the

European state system as well as the internal economic and religious organization of domestic societies. Was Europe to be dominated and organized by Habsburg imperial power or autonomous nation-states? Was feudalism or commercial capitalism to be the dominant mode of organizing economic activities? Was Protestantism or Catholicism to be the prevalent religion? The clash over these political, economic, and ideological issues caused physical devastation and loss of life not seen in Western Europe since the Mongol invasions of earlier centuries.

Underlying the intensity and duration of the war was a profound change in the nature of power. Although the power of a state continued to be based primarily on the control of territory, technology and organization were becoming more important in military and political affairs. From classical times to the seventeenth century, military technology, tactics, and organization had hardly changed; the pike, the Greek phalanx, and heavy cavalry continued to characterize warfare. By the close of that century, however, mobile artillery, professional infantry in linear formations, and naval innovations had come to dominate the tactics of war. In conjunction with what has been called the Military Revolution, the modern bureaucratic state also came into existence. This development greatly enhanced the ability of rulers to mobilize and increase the efficient use of national resources. With these military and political innovations, the exercise of military power became an instrument of foreign policy; war was no longer "the [unrestrained] clash of societies" that was characteristic of warfare in the ancient and medieval worlds.[18]

The Thirty Years' War transformed the domestic and international political scene. The Habsburg bid for universal empire was defeated, and the nation-state became the dominant form of political organization in the modern world. In the Treaty of Westphalia (1648), the principle of national sovereignty and non-intervention was established as the governing norm of international relations; this political innovation ended the ideological conflict over the religious ordering of domestic societies. For the next century and a half, foreign policy was based on the concepts of national interest and the balance of power; as a result, the scale of European wars tended to be limited. The commercial revolution triumphed over feudalism, and the pluralistic European state system provided the necessary framework for the expansion of the global market system.[19] With their superior armaments and organization, the several states of Western Europe created overseas empires and subdued the other civilizations of the globe.

In the closing decade of the eighteenth century, a second great war or series of wars once again transformed international affairs and ushered in a new historical epoch. For nearly a century France and Great Britain, operating within the framework of the classical balance of power system, had been fighting a series of limited conflicts both in Europe and overseas to establish the primacy of one or the other. This "hundred years' war," to use Seeley's expression, culminated in the great or hegemonic wars of the French Revolution and Napoleon Bonaparte (1792 to 1815).[20] As in other hegemonic conflicts, profound political, economic, and ideological issues were joined: French or British hegemony of the European political system, mercantilistic or market principles as the organizing basis of the world economy, and revolutionary republicanism or more conservative political forms as the basis of domestic society. The ensuing conflagration engulfed the entire international political system, resulting in unprecedented violence and the opening of a new age of economic and political affairs.

During the second half of the eighteenth and the first decade of the nineteenth century, economic, technological, and other developments transformed the nature of power and undermined the relative stability of the previous system of limited warfare. At sea the British gained mastery of the new tactics and technology of naval power. On land the military genius of Napoleon brought to a culmination the revolution wrought by gunpowder as the new weaponry, tactics, and doctrine were integrated. The most significant innovations, however, were organizational, political, and sociological. The conception of the levée en masse and the nation at arms made it possible for the French to field mass armies and overwhelm their enemies. Under the banner of nationalism the era of peoples' wars had arrived. The new means of military organization had transformed the nature of European warfare.[21]

After twenty years of global warfare extending to the New World and the Middle East, the British and their allies defeated the French, and a new international order was established by the Treaty of Vienna (1815). On the continent of Europe, an equilibrium was created that was to last until the unification of German power in the middle of the century. British interests and naval power guaranteed that the principles of the market and laissez faire would govern global economic affairs. Underneath the surface of this Pax Britannica, new forces began to stir and gather strength as the decades passed. Following a century of relative peace, these changes in the economic, political, and technological environment would break forth in the modern world's third hegemonic war.

Like many other great wars, World War I commenced as a seemingly minor affair, even though its eventual scale and consequences were beyond the comprehension of contemporary statesmen. In a matter of a few weeks, the several bilateral conflicts of the European states and the cross-cutting alliances joined the Europeans in a global struggle of horrendous dimensions.

The British-German naval race, the French-German conflict over Alsace-Lorraine, and the German/Austrian-Russian rivalry in the Balkans drew almost all of the European states into the struggle that would determine the structure and leadership of the European and eventually of the global political system.

The scope, intensity, and duration of the war reflected the culmination of strengthening forces and novel forms of national power. The French under Napoleon had first unleashed the new religion of nationalism. During the ensuing decades of relative peace, the spread of nationalistic ideas tore at the traditional fabric of European society, undermined stable political structures, and set one people against another. The Industrial Revolution also had diffused from Great Britain to the Continent. War had become industrialized and fused with the passion of nationalism. An era of rapid economic change and social upheaval had also given rise to radical movements threatening revolution and challenging the domestic status quo of many states.[22] In this new environment of industrialized and nationalistic warfare, the political leaders lost control over the masses, and war reverted to what it had been in the premodern era: an unrestrained clash of societies. Nations threw men and machinery at one another causing massive carnage and social dislocations from which Europe found it difficult to recover. Only mutual exhaustion and the intervention of a non-European power—the United States—ended the destruction of total war.

The terrible devastation of the war brought to a close the European domination of world politics and resulted in a new attitude toward war. The democratization and industrialization of war had undermined the legitimacy of military force as a normal and legitimate instrument of foreign policy. In the Treaty of Versailles (1919), statesmen outlawed war, and the revolutionary concept of collective security was embodied in the charter of the League of Nations. States for the first time were legally forbidden to engage in war except in self-defense and were required to join together in the punishment of any aggressor. In contrast to the other great peace conferences and treaties of European diplomacy the settlement failed to reflect the new realities of the balance of power and thereby was unable to establish a new and stable European political order.[23] This failure laid the foundation for World War II, which should be seen as the continuation of the hegemonic struggle begun in 1914 with the breakdown of the European political order.

The postwar international order has been based on American-Soviet bipolarity and the concept of mutual deterrence. Peace has been maintained and war as a means of settling conflicts between the superpowers has been stayed by the nuclear threat and the possibility of mutual annihilation. Whether or not this system will also one day be undermined by historical developments and utterly destroyed by a hegemonic war fought with weapons of mass destruction is the fundamental question of our time.

The Nuclear Revolution and Hegemonic War

Although the theory of hegemonic war may be helpful in understanding the past, one must ask whether it is relevant to the contemporary world. Has it been superseded or somehow transcended by the nuclear revolution in warfare? Since no nation that enters a nuclear war can avoid its own destruction, does it make any sense to think in terms of great or hegemonic wars? Morgenthau was referring to this profound change in the nature of warfare and its political significance when he wrote that the "rational relationship between violence as a means of foreign policy and the ends of foreign policy has been destroyed by the possibility of all-out nuclear war."[24]

That a revolution in the nature of warfare has occurred cannot be denied. Nuclear weapons have indeed profoundly transformed the destructiveness and consequences of a great war. It is highly doubtful that a war between two nuclear powers could be limited and escalation into a full-scale war prevented. Nor is it likely that either protagonist could escape the terrible devastation of such a great war or find the consequences in any sense acceptable.[25] In the nuclear age, the primary purpose of nuclear forces should be to deter the use of nuclear weapons by one's opponent and thereby prevent the outbreak of hegemonic warfare.

It does not necessarily follow that this change in the nature of warfare, as important as it surely is, has also changed the nature of international relations. The fundamental characteristics of international affairs unfortunately have not been altered and, if anything, have been intensified by the nuclear revolution. International politics continues to be a self-help system. In the contemporary anarchy of international relations, distrust, uncertainty, and insecurity have caused states to arm themselves and to prepare for war as never before.

To be able to say that nuclear weapons have changed the nature of international relations and thus made impossible the outbreak of hegemonic war, a transformation of human consciousness itself would have to take place. Humankind would have to be willing to subordinate all other values and goals to the preservation of peace. To insure mutual survival, it would need to reject the anarchy of international relations and submit itself to the Leviathan of Thomas Hobbes. Little evidence exists to suggest that any nation is close to making this choice. Certainly in this world of unprecedented armaments of all types, no state is behaving as if nuclear weapons had changed its overall set of national priorities.

One cannot even rule out the possibility of a great or hegemonic war in the nuclear age. The theory of hegemonic war does not argue that statesmen "will" a great war; the great wars of history were seldom predicted, and their course has never been foreseen. As Thucydides argued in his discussion of the role of accident in war, once it has begun, war unleashes forces that are totally unanticipated by the protagonists. In the nuclear age there is no guarantee that a minor conflict between the superpowers or their allies will not set in motion untoward developments over which they would soon lose control. In brief, the fact that nuclear war would wreak unprecedented devastation on mankind has not prevented the world's nuclear powers from preparing for such a war, perhaps thereby making it more likely.

What nuclear weapons have accomplished is to elevate the avoidance of a total war to the highest level of foreign policy and the central concern of statesmen. Yet this goal, as important as it surely is, has joined, not supplanted, other values and interests for which societies in the past have been willing to fight. All of the nuclear states seek to avoid nuclear war at the same time that they are attempting to safeguard more traditional interests. The result has been, for the superpowers at least, the creation of a new basis of international order. In contrast to the balance-of-power system of early modern Europe, the Pax Britannica of the nineteenth century, or the ill-fated collective security system associated with the League of Nations, order in the nuclear age has been built on the foundation of mutual deterrence.

The long-term stability of this nuclear order is of crucial importance, and the threat to its existence over time certainly cannot be disregarded. Each superpower fears that the other might achieve a significant technological breakthrough and seek to exploit it. How else can one explain the hopes and anxieties raised by the Strategic Defense Initiative? In addition, with the proliferation of nuclear weapons to more and more states, there is a growing danger that these weapons might fall into the hands of desperate states or terrorist groups. The nuclear order is a function of deliberate policies and not, as some argue, an existential condition.

Historically, nations have consciously decided to go to war, but they have seldom, if ever, knowingly begun hegemonic wars. Statesmen try to make rational or cost/benefit calculations concerning their efforts to achieve national objectives, and it seems unlikely that any statesman would view the eventual gains from the great wars of history as commensurate with the eventual costs of those wars. It cannot be overstressed that, once a war, however limited, begins, it can release powerful forces unforeseen by the instigators of the war. The results of the Peloponnesian War, which was to devastate classical Greece, were not anticipated by the great powers of the day. Nor were the effects of World War I,

which ended the primacy of Europe over other civilizations, anticipated by European statesmen. In both cases, the war was triggered by the belief of each protagonist that it had no alternative but to fight while the advantage was still on its side. In neither case did the protagonists fight the war that they had wanted or expected.

The advent of nuclear weapons has not altered this fundamental condition. A nation still might start a war for fear that its relative strength will diminish with time, and an accident still might precipitate unprecedented devastation. It is not inconceivable that some state, perhaps an overpowered Israel, a frightened South Africa, or a declining superpower, might one day become so desperate that it resorts to nuclear blackmail in order to forestall its enemies. As in war itself, an accident during such a confrontation could unleash powerful and uncontrollable forces totally unanticipated by the protagonists. Although the potential violence and destructiveness of war have been changed by the advent of nuclear arms, there is unfortunately little to suggest that human nature has also been transformed.

Conclusion

One can hope that the fear of nuclear holocaust has chastened statesmen. Perhaps they have come to appreciate that a nuclear order based on mutual deterrence should be their highest priority. But against this expectation one must set the long history of human foibles and mankind's seeming inability to sustain peace for very long. Only time will tell whether the theory of hegemonic war holds true in the nuclear age. In the meanwhile, avoidance of a nuclear war has become imperative.

NOTES

1. Thucydides (trans. John H. Finley, Jr.), *The Peloponnesian War* (New York, 1951), 14–15.
2. Kenneth N. Waltz, *Man, the State, and War: A Theoretical Analysis* (New York, 1959).
3. Kenneth N. Waltz, *Theory of International Relations* (Reading, Mass., 1979).
4. W. Robert Connor, *Thucydides* (Princeton, 1984), 27.
5. Robert Gilpin, *War and Change in World Politics* (New York, 1981), 40.
6. Thucydides, *Peloponnesian War*, 15.
7. Thucydides, *Peloponnesian War*, 4.
8. Thucydides, *Peloponnesian War*, 9, 11.
9. Thucydides, *Peloponnesian War*, 12.
10. Halford J. Mackinder, "The Geographical Pivot of History," in Anthony J. Pearce (ed.), *Democratic Ideals and Reality* (New York, 1962), 1–2; Quincy Wright, *A Study of War* (Chicago, 1942); A[rnold]. Toynbee, *A Study of History* (London, 1961), Vols. 3–4; Vladimir Ilyich Lenin, *Imperialism: The Highest Stage of Capitalism* (New York, 1939). See, for example, A. F. K. Organski, *World Politics* (New York, 1968; 2nd ed.); Organski and Jacek Kugler, *The War Ledger*

(Chicago, 1980); George Modelski (ed.), *Exploring Long Cycles* (Boulder, 1987); Gilpin, *War and Change*.

11. Raymond Aron, "War and Industrial Society," in Leon Bramson and George W. Goethals (eds.), *War-Studies from Psychology, Sociology, Anthropology* (New York, 1964), 359.

12. Thucydides, *Peloponnesian War*, 45.

13. Eli Halévy (trans. R. G. Webb), *The Era of Tyrannies* (Garden City, N.Y., 1965), 212.

14. G. E. M. de Ste. Croix, *The Origins of the Peloponnesian War* (London, 1972).

15. Michael Howard, *The Causes of War* (Cambridge, Mass., 1983), 16.

16. Summary accounts of the wars and their backgrounds are contained in R. Ernest Dupuy and Trevor N. Dupuy, *The Encyclopedia of Military History from 3500 B.C. to the Present* (New York, 1984; 2nd rev. ed.), 522–546, 730–769, 915–990.

17. Myron P. Gutmann, "The Origins of the Thirty Years' War," *Journal of Interdisciplinary History*, XVIII (1988), 749–770.

18. Howard, *Causes*, 16; Michael Roberts, *The Military Revolution, 1560–1660* (Belfast, 1956); George Clark, *War and Society in the Seventeenth Century* (Cambridge, 1958).

19. Jean Baechler (trans. Barry Cooper), *The Origins of Capitalism* (Oxford, 1975), 73–86.

20. John R. Seeley, *The Expansion of England: Two Courses of Lectures* (Boston, 1905), 28–29.

21. See Gunther G. Rothenberg, "The Origins, Causes, and Extension of the Wars of the French Revolution and Napoleon," *Journal of Interdisciplinary History*, XVIII (1988), 771–793.

22. Robert E. Osgood and Robert W. Tucker, *Force, Order, and Justice* (Baltimore, 1967), 3–192; Halévy, *Era*, 209–247.

23. Howard, *Causes*, 163.

24. Hans J. Morgenthau in Michael Howard, Sidney Hook, H. Stuart Hughes, and Charles P. Snow, "Western Values and Total War," *Commentary*, XXXII (1961), 280.

25. Robert Jervis, *The Illogic of American Nuclear Strategy* (Ithaca, 1984), 19–46.

Redefining the National Interest

JOSEPH S. NYE, JR.

Confusion after Kosovo

NATO's military intervention in Kosovo dramatically raises a larger problem: how should the United States define its interests in today's world? After the collapse of the Soviet Union, what are the limits of America's concerns abroad? Can one define interests conventionally in the information age? The "national interest" is a slippery concept, used to describe as well as prescribe foreign policy. Hence the considerable debate about it. Some scholars have even regretted the waning of the very idea of a "national" interest today. Writing in these pages, Samuel P. Huntington argued recently that "without a sure sense of national identity, Americans have become unable to define their national interests, and as a result subnational commercial interests and transnational and nonnational ethnic interests have come to dominate foreign policy."

For almost five decades, the containment of Soviet power provided a North Star to guide American foreign policy. From a longer historical perspective, however, the Cold War was the anomalous period, and even it involved some bitter disputes over where our interests lay—during the Vietnam War, for example. Before World War II, confusion was more often the rule. For example, ethnic differences colored appraisals of

whether the United States should enter World War I. Peter Trubowitz's recent study of American definitions of national interests in the 1890s, 1930s, and 1980s concludes that "there is no single national interest. Analysts who assume that America has a discernible national interest whose defense should determine its relations with other nations are unable to explain the persistent failure to achieve domestic consensus on international objectives."

With all that said, it would be a mistake to discard the term. As the Commission on America's National Interests declared in 1996, "National interests are the fundamental building blocks in any discussion of foreign policy. . . . In fact, the concept is used regularly and widely by administration officials, members of Congress, and citizens at large." The commission goes on to identify five vital interests that most agree would justify the unilateral use of force. Not everyone would agree with this particular list. Economic and humanitarian interests are also widely thought important. Many experts argue that vital strategic concerns are more widely shared than other interests, and deserve priority because were we to fail to protect them, more Americans would be affected and in more profound ways. Leaders and experts are right to point out dangers to the public and to try to persuade it. Yet even "objective" threats are not always obvious. The connection between a particular event (Iraq's invasion of Kuwait or Serbia's rejection of the Rambouillet agreement) and an American interest may involve a long causal chain. Different people see different risks and dangers. And priorities vary: reasonable people can disagree, for example, about how much insurance to buy against remote threats and whether to do so before pursuing other values (such as human rights). In a democracy, such political struggles over the exact definition of national interests—and how to pursue them—are both inevitable and healthy. Foreign-policy experts can help clarify causation and trade-offs in particular cases, but experts alone cannot decide. Nor should they. The national interest is too important to leave solely to the geopoliticians. Elected officials must play the key role.

In a democracy, the national interest is simply the set of shared priorities regarding relations with the rest of the world. It is broader than strategic interests, though they are part of it. It can include values such as human rights and democracy, if the public feels that those values are so important to its identity that it is willing to pay a price to promote them.

The American people clearly think that their interests include certain values and their promotion abroad—such as opposition to ethnic cleansing in the Balkans. A democratic definition of the national interest does not accept the distinction between a morality-based and an interest-based foreign policy. Moral values are simply intangible interests. Leaders and experts may point out the costs of indulging these values. But if an informed public disagrees, experts cannot deny the legitimacy of public opinion. Polls show that the American people are neither isolationist nor eager to serve as the world's police. But finding a middle course is proving difficult and complex.

The Impact of the Information Age

Strategists advise that interests should be defined in relation to power—but how would one describe the distribution of power in the information age? Some think the end of the bipolar world left multipolarity in its stead. But that is not a very good description of a world in which one country, the United States, is so much more powerful than all the others. On the other hand, unipolarity is not a very good description either, because it exaggerates the degree to and ease with which the United States is able to get what it wants—witness Kosovo.

Instead, power today is distributed like a three-dimensional chess game. The top, military board is unipolar, with the United States far outstripping all other states. The middle, economic board is multipolar,

with the United States, Europe, and Japan accounting for two-thirds of world production. But the bottom—representing transnational relations that cross borders and lie outside the control of governments—has a more dispersed structure of power. This complexity makes policy-making today more difficult. It means playing on several boards at the same time. Moreover, although it is important not to ignore the continuing importance of military force for some purposes, it is equally important not to be misled into thinking that American power can always get its way in nonmilitary matters. The United States is a preponderant, but not a dominant, power.

Another distinction to keep in mind is that between "hard power" (a country's economic and military ability to buy and coerce) and "soft power" (the ability to attract through cultural and ideological appeal). It is important that half a million foreign students want to study in the United States each year, that Europeans and Asians want to watch American films and TV, and that American liberties are attractive in many parts of the world. Our values are significant sources of soft power. Both hard and soft power remain vital, but in the information age soft power is becoming more compelling than ever before.

Massive flows of cheap information have expanded the number of contacts across national borders. In a deregulated world, global markets and nongovernmental actors play a larger role. States are more easily penetrated today and less like the classic realist model of solid billiard balls bouncing off each other. As a result, political leaders are finding it more difficult to maintain a coherent set of priorities in foreign policy, and more difficult to articulate a single national interest.

Yet the United States, with its democratic society, is well placed to benefit from the rapidly developing information age. Although greater pluralism may diminish the coherence of government policies, our institutions are attractive and the openness of our society enhances credibility—a crucial resource in an information age. Thus the United States is well placed to make use of soft power. At the same time, the soft power that comes from being a "city on the hill" does not provide the coercive capability that hard power does. Alone, it does not support a very venturesome foreign policy.

Hence different aspects of the information age mean different things for America's national interests. On the one hand, a good case can be made that the information revolution will have long-term benefits for democracies. Democratic societies can create credible information because they are not threatened by it. Authoritarian states will have more trouble. Governments can limit their citizens' access to the internet and global markets, but they pay a high price if they do so. Singapore and China, for example, are currently wrestling with these problems. Moreover, transparency is becoming a key asset for countries seeking investments. Governments that want rapid development will have to give up some of the barriers to information flows.

On the other hand, some aspects of the information age are less benign. The free flow of broadcast information in open societies has always had an impact on public opinion and the formulation of foreign policy. But now the flow has increased in volume, and shortened news cycles have reduced the time for deliberation. By focusing on certain conflicts and human rights problems, the media pressure politicians to respond to some foreign problems and not others—for example, Somalia rather than southern Sudan in 1992. The so-called CNN effect makes it hard to keep items that might otherwise warrant a lower priority off the top of the public agenda. Now, with the added interactivity of groups on the internet, it will be harder than ever to maintain a consistent agenda.

Also problematic is the effect of transnational information flows on the stability of national communities. The Canadian media guru Marshall McLuhan once prophesied that communications technologies would turn the world into a global village. Instead of a single cosmopolitan community, however, they may have produced a congeries of global villages, each with all the parochial prejudices that the word implies, but with a greater awareness of global inequality. Transnational economic forces are disrupting traditional lifestyles, and this increases economic integration and communal disintegration at the same time. This is particularly true in the post-Soviet states and the old European-built empires of Africa. Political entrepreneurs use inexpensive information channels to mobilize the discontented on subnational tribal levels: some to the cause of repressive nationalism, and some to transnational ethnic and religious communities. This in turn leads to increased demands for self-determination, increased violence, and other violations of human rights—all in the presence of television cameras and the internet.

American Power and Priorities

William Perry and Ashton Carter have recently argued that we should rethink the way we understand risks to US security. At the top of their new hierarchy they put "A list" threats like that the Soviet Union once presented to our survival. The "B list" features imminent threats to US interests—but not to our survival—such as North Korea or Iraq. The "C list" includes important "contingencies that indirectly affect U.S. security but do not directly threaten U.S. interests": "the Kosovos, Bosnias, Somalias, Rwandas, and Haitis."

What is striking is how the "C list" has come to dominate today's foreign policy agenda. Carter and

Perry speculate that this is because of the disappearance of "A list" threats since the end of the Cold War. But another reason is that "C list" issues dominate media attention in the information age. Dramatic visual portrayals of immediate human conflict and suffering are far easier to convey to the public than "A list" abstractions like the possibility of a "Weimar Russia," the rise of a hegemonic China and the importance of our alliance with Japan, or the potential collapse of the international system of trade and investment. Yet if these larger, more abstract strategic issues were to turn out badly, they would have a far greater impact on the lives of most Americans.

How should Americans set priorities in such a world? We should start by understanding our power. On one hand, for reasons given above, American power is now less fungible and effective than it might first appear. On the other, the United States is likely to remain preponderant well into the next century. For a variety of reasons, the information revolution is likely to enhance rather than diminish American power.

As a wealthy status quo power, the United States has an interest in maintaining international order. Behind the abstractions about rising interdependence are changes that make it more difficult to isolate the United States from the effects of events in the rest of the world. More concretely, there are two simple reasons why Americans have a national interest in preventing disorder beyond our borders. First, events and actors out there can hurt us; and second, Americans want to influence distant governments and organizations on a variety of issues such as the proliferation of weapons of mass destruction, terrorism, drugs, shared resources, and the environment.

To do so, the United States cannot merely set a good example—it needs hard-power resources. Maintaining these will require an investment that Americans have recently been unwilling to make—witness the decline in the foreign affairs budget and the reluctance to take casualties. It is difficult to be a superpower on the cheap. Second, the United States has to recognize a basic proposition of public-goods theory: if the largest beneficiary of a public good (such as international order) does not provide disproportionate resources toward its maintenance, the smaller beneficiaries are unlikely to do so. This puts a different twist on Secretary of State Madeleine K. Albright's phrase that the United States is "the indispensable nation," and one less palatable to the public and to Congress.

Third, we should make sure that top priority is given to those aspects of the international system that, if not attended to properly, would have profound effects on the basic international order and therefore on the lives and welfare of Americans. Some analysts have suggested that we can learn something from the lesson of the United Kingdom in the nineteenth century, when it was also a preponderant but not dominating power. Three public goods that Britain attended to were maintaining the balance of power among the major states, promoting an open international economic system, and maintaining open international commons such as the freedom of the seas. All three translate relatively well to the current American case. In terms of the distribution of power, we need to continue to "shape the environment" (in the words of the Pentagon's *Quadrennial Defense Review*), and that is why we keep 100,000 troops based in Europe, another 100,000 in Asia, and some 20,000 near the Persian Gulf. Our role as a stabilizer and a reassurance against the rise of hostile hegemons in important regions has to remain a top priority, an "A list" issue.

Meanwhile, promoting an open international economic system is good not just for America's economic growth but for other countries' as well. In the long term, economic growth is likely to foster stable democratic middle-class societies around the world. To keep the global system open, the United States must resist protectionism at home and strengthen international monitoring institutions such as the World Trade Organization, the International Monetary Fund, and the Bank for International Settlements. In regard to international commons, the United States, like nineteenth-century Britain, has an interest in freedom of the seas, but also in the environment, in the preservation of endangered species, and in the uses of outer space and of the new cyberspace.

Beyond the nineteenth-century analogy, in today's world the United States has a general interest in developing and maintaining the international laws and institutions that deal not just with trade and the environment, but with arms proliferation, peacekeeping, human rights, and other concerns. Those who denigrate the importance of law and institutions forget that the United States is a status quo power. They also ignore the extent to which legitimacy is a power reality. True realists would not make such a mistake.

Finally, as a preponderant power, the United States can provide an important public good by acting as a mediator and convener. By helping to organize coalitions of the willing and by using its good offices to mediate conflicts in places like Northern Ireland, the Middle East, or the Aegean Sea, the United States can help to shape the world in ways that are beneficial to us as well as to other nations.

The C List

If we did not live in the information age, the foregoing strategy for prioritizing America's national interests might suffice. But the reality is that nonvital crises like Somalia, Bosnia, Haiti, and Kosovo continue to force their way to the foreground because of their ability to command massive media attention. Such crises raise moral concerns that the American people consistently include in their list of foreign policy interests. Policy experts may deplore such sympathies, but they are a democratic reality.

Some might object that a strategy based on "A list" issues does not take account of the ongoing erosion of Westphalian national sovereignty that is occurring today. It is true that old-fashioned state sovereignty is eroding—both de facto, through the penetration of national borders by transnational forces, and de jure, as seen in the imposition of sanctions against South Africa for apartheid, the development of an International Criminal Court, and the bombing of Yugoslavia over its policies in Kosovo. But the erosion of sovereignty is a long-term trend of decades and centuries, and it is a mixed blessing rather a clear good. Although the erosion may help advance human rights in repressive regimes by exposing them to international attention, it also portends considerable disorder. Recall that the seventeenth-century Peace of Westphalia created a system of sovereign states to curtail vicious civil wars over religion. Although it is true that sovereignty stands in the way of national self-determination, such self-determination is not the unequivocal moral good it first appears. In a world where there are some two hundred states but many thousands of often overlapping entities that might eventually make a claim to nationhood, blind promotion of a human rights policy of self-determination would have highly problematic consequences.

So what do we do about the humanitarian concerns and strong moral preferences that Americans want to see expressed in their foreign policy? Americans have rarely accepted pure realpolitik as a guiding principle, and human rights and the alleviation of humanitarian disasters have long been important aspects of our foreign policy. But foreign policy involves trying to accomplish varied objectives in a complex and recalcitrant world. This entails trade-offs. A human rights policy is not itself a foreign policy; it is an important *part* of a foreign policy. During the Cold War, this balancing act often meant tolerating human rights abuses by regimes that were crucial to balancing Soviet power—for example, in South Korea before its transition to democracy. Similar problems persist in the current period—witness our policy toward Saudi Arabia, or our efforts to balance human rights in China with our long-term strategic objectives.

In the information age, humanitarian concerns dominate attention to a greater degree than before, often at the cost of diverting attention from "A list" strategic issues. Since pictures are more powerful than words, arguments about trade-offs become emotional and difficult. Of course, acting on humanitarian values is often appropriate. Few Americans can look at television pictures of starving people or miserable refugees and not say that their country should do something about them. And the United States often does respond to such catastrophes. Sometimes this is quite easily done, such as hurricane relief to Central America or the early stages of famine relief in Somalia. But apparently simple cases like Somalia can turn out to be extremely difficult to resolve, and others, like Kosovo, are difficult from the start.

The problem with such hard cases is that the humanitarian interest that instigates the action often turns out to be a mile wide and an inch deep. The American public's impulse to help starving Somalis (whose food supply was being interrupted by various warlords) vanished in the face of televised pictures of dead US soldiers being dragged through the streets of Mogadishu. Such transience is sometimes attributed to popular reluctance to accept casualties. But that is too simple. Americans went into the Gulf War expecting and willing to accept casualties. As this suggests, Americans are reluctant to accept casualties in cases where their *only* foreign policy goals are unreciprocated humanitarian interests. Ironically, when opinion turns against such cases, this may not only divert attention and limit willingness to support "A list" interests but may also undermine support for action in other, more serious humanitarian crises. One of the direct effects of the Somalia disaster was America's failure (along with other countries') to support and reinforce the United Nations peacekeeping force in Rwanda that could have limited a true genocide in 1994.

There are no easy answers for such cases. We could not simply turn off the television or unplug our computers even if we wanted to. The "C list" cannot simply be ignored. But there are certain rules of prudence that may help the integration of such issues into the larger strategy for advancing the national interest. First, there are many degrees of humanitarian concern and many degrees of intervention to reflect them, such as condemnation, sanctions targeted on individuals, broad sanctions, and various uses of force. We should save violent options for the most egregious cases. When we do use force, it is worth remembering some principles of the "just war" doctrine: having a just cause in the eyes of others; discrimination in means so as to not unduly punish the innocent; proportionality of means to ends; and a high probability of good consequences (rather than wishful thinking).

We should generally avoid the use of force except in cases where our humanitarian interests are reinforced by the existence of other strong national interests. This was the case in the Gulf War, where the United States was concerned not only with the aggression against Kuwait, but also with energy supplies and regional allies. This was not the case in Somalia. In the former Yugoslavia (Bosnia and Kosovo), our interests combine both humanitarian values and the strategic concerns of European allies and NATO. We should try to involve other regional actors, preferably in the lead role when possible. In Africa after 1995, the United States offered to help with training, intelligence, logistics, and transportation if African countries provided the troops for a peacekeeping force. There were few takers. If African states are unwilling to do their part, we should be wary of going it alone. In Europe, we should welcome the idea of combined joint task forces that would be separable but not separate from NATO and encourage the Europeans to take the lead on such issues.

We should also be clearer about what are true cases of genocide. The American people have a real humanitarian interest in not letting another Holocaust occur. Yet we did just that in Rwanda in 1994. We therefore need to do more to organize prevention and response to real cases of genocide. Unfortunately, the Genocide Convention is written so loosely and the word is so abused for political purposes that there is danger of the term becoming trivialized. But a strict historical interpretation of the crime, based on the precedents of the Holocaust and Rwanda, can help to avoid such pitfalls.

Finally, Americans should be very wary about intervention in civil wars over self-determination. The principle is dangerously ambiguous; atrocities are often committed by activists on both sides and the precedents can have disastrous consequences.

How could these rules of prudence have helped in the case of Kosovo? At an earlier stage, they would have produced more caution. In December 1992, President George H. W. Bush issued a vague threat that Serbia should not attack ethnic Albanians in its Kosovo province while he remained silent on Bosnia. A year later, the Clinton administration reiterated the warning. The United States was saved from having to back up these threats by the Kosovar Albanians' pacifist leader, Ibrahim Rugova, who espoused a Gandhian response to Serbian oppression. After 1996, the rise of the militantly pro-independence Kosovo Liberation Army undermined Rugova's leadership. According to journalist Chris Hedges, the radicals of the KLA, who combine "hints of fascism on one side and whiffs of communism on the other," have been labeled a terrorist organization by US government officials. A KLA victory might well have involved atrocities and ethnic cleansing of the Serb minority in Kosovo. The KLA's refusal to sign the Rambouillet agreement in the first round of talks in February let the NATO alliance off the moral hook and should have been used as an opportunity to step back. Instead, the United States "fixed the problem" by pretending to believe the KLA's promise to accept autonomy within Yugoslavia. The United States then threatened to bomb Serbia. Milošević called the American bluff and initiated his planned ethnic cleansing of Kosovo.

At that point, new facts on the ground raised Kosovo from the "C list" to the "B list" of US foreign policy concerns. The scale and ferocity of Milošević's ethnic cleansing could not be ignored. European allies such as the United Kingdom, France, and even Germany joined the United States in calling for NATO action. If the United States had then pulled the rug out from under its pro-interventionist allies, it would have produced a NATO crisis on the scale of Suez in 1956. The humanitarian impact had grown immensely and was now reinforced by a strategic interest in the future of the American alliance with Europe. Skeptics argue that one should never pursue "sunk costs." By this argument, if Kosovo was not worth intervention before, it is not worth it now. But history is path-dependent, since choices, once made, eliminate certain options and create others. In calculating the costs and benefits of future actions, policy-makers must realistically assess the current situation, not the past. It does no good to lament the more prudent paths not taken at an earlier stage.

Kosovo illustrates how a "C list" issue can migrate to the "B list" of national interests that merit the use of force. Kosovo itself is not a vital American interest, and it only touches tangentially on an "A list" issue (the credibility of the NATO alliance). The "A list" also includes the future of Russia and of international laws and institutions such as the United Nations. NATO, Russia, and the United Nations must all figure in how we resolve the Kosovo crisis. And the rules of prudence must still be applied as we insist on the return of the refugees and the withdrawal of Serbian forces. If moral outrage or unilateralist temptations blind Americans to their other "A list" priorities, the United States may dangerously overreach itself and turn a just cause into a counterproductive crusade.

Prudence alone cannot determine the national interest in the information age. But better consequences will flow if American values and goals are related to American power, and interests are rationally pursued within prudent limits. Determining the national interest has always been contentious throughout US history. That is to be expected in a healthy democracy. But the debate about the American national interest in the information age should pay more attention to the peculiar nature of American power today; it should establish strategic priorities accordingly; and it should develop prudential rules that allow the United States to meld its strategic, economic, and humanitarian interests into an effective foreign policy.

Technology Converges; Non-State Actors Benefit

T. X. HAMMES

The fourth industrial revolution will provide insurgents and terrorists with capabilities that, until very recently, were the preserve of large, powerful, wealthy states. The convergence of new technologies will provide them access to relatively cheap, long-range, autonomous weapons. To define the problem this presents to the United States, this paper will first explore the technologies—powerful small warheads, autonomous drones, task-specific artificial intelligence, and advanced manufacturing—that are providing increased range, numbers, and lethality for dramatically lower cost today. It will close the technology discussion with a brief examination of biotechnology, which has enormous potential as a weapon but, fortunately, remains mostly beyond the reach of non-state actors today.

However, the most important point to remember is that while new technologies will make tactical operations against insurgents much more difficult, US failures against non-state actors have consistently been caused by strategic deficiencies not tactical ones. Therefore, following the discussion of emerging technologies, this essay will examine how changing political, social, and economic conditions are changing the strategic environment of state versus non-state conflicts. Then, tying the technology to these new strategic conditions, it will suggest ways in which non-state actors will exploit the new technologies and new conditions to defeat states. The paper will close with a discussion of what approaches have worked for the United States in the past and how they may be adapted to the new conditions.

Key Technologies

The starting point of the technology discussion must be the recent history of non-state actors' use of technology. In the 1980s, the author worked with ten dif-

T. X. Hammes, "Technology Converges; Non-State Actors Benefit," *Policy Analysis* 786 (January 27, 2016): 1–10.

ferent insurgent groups in different regions. Despite US efforts to encourage these groups to use cutting-edge technology, uniformly they refused. Further, if one studies their use of technology, one finds that non-state actors, with the exception of certain drug cartels, primarily use technology that is widely available in their societies. They seemed to do so for two reasons. First, they lacked confidence in cutting-edge technology—and since they were betting lives on it, they were reluctant to use it. They wanted to use technology they were comfortable with and confident in. For instance, when US forces were conducting security operations in Iraq from 2003 to 2008, the Iraqis used common household items such as cell phones, base station phones, and garage door openers to detonate their improvised explosive devices. They did so for good reason. Every neighborhood had a shop that sold and repaired these devices and so had the knowledge to modify them for use in weapons. As an added benefit, the use could spread easily across the insurgency.

In contrast, while commercial drones first began flying in the late 1990s, they did not show up in insurgent arsenals until 2014 for surveillance and 2016 for attack.[1] It was not until then that hobbyist and commercial drones were widespread in global society. Even then, ISIS required a focused effort to build and operate them. A special unit kept detailed records of operations to improve their effectiveness.[2] By 2018, insurgent drone use had spread to Afghanistan. And criminal elements have begun to use drones both for surveillance and to disrupt police operations.[3]

While it is a bit comforting to know non-state actors have not been at the leading edge of technology historically, we do have to expect insurgent and terrorist groups to use technology as it becomes widely available in civil society.

With that as a caveat, it's time to look at the new technologies that will present non-state actors with greatly enhanced capabilities in the immediate future. The fourth industrial revolution has already proliferated a series of technological advances that have created a generation of small, smart, and cheap weapons. Progress in small warheads, drones, task-specific artificial intelligence, advanced manufacturing, and cheap space capabilities have converged to provide insurgents with capabilities that used to be the preserve of large, technologically advanced states. This paper will first examine the technologies themselves, then look at how they empower non-state actors.

Small Warheads

While new explosives are increasing the power of warheads, the most effective use of small warheads is to adopt the concept of "bringing the detonator not the explosive." Rather than building a system to deliver a large warhead, this concept uses a small, smart drone to detonate the very large explosive potential present in society, such as commercial aircraft, fuel trucks, or fixed facilities with fuel, fertilizer, and other industrial chemical storage sites. This is not a theoretical approach. It has already been used repeatedly. From 2015 through 2017, Russian operatives or Ukrainian separatists used drones to drop simple thermite grenades in a series of attacks on Ukrainian government ammunition dumps that detonated hundreds of thousands of tons of explosives.[4]

A second approach for increasing the destructive power of a small warhead is the use of an explosively shaped penetrator (EFP). An EFP approximately 1 inch in diameter with as little as 1 ounce of high explosive can penetrate up to 1/2 inch of steel.[5] Such a device is small enough to be mounted on a wide variety of small drones to serve as the detonator. It could easily detonate the commercial fuel trucks that have been essential to US operations in Afghanistan and Iraq. It is also powerful enough that if fired into the hood of a motor vehicle, it will destroy the engine, resulting in a mobility kill. And they are capable of attacking moving vehicles. As early as 2013, hobbyists were using drones with GoPro cameras to film individual trucks and drivers in off-road races.[6] Simply mounting a small EFP next to the lens of the GoPro camera would allow the operator to fire the EFP where the camera is pointed. An operator can select a specific vehicle even in fast-moving traffic.

While EFPs have been used widely in Iraq, the insurgents were limited to placing ground IEDs and hoping the target passed over it. Drones allow the attacker to actively hunt selected targets even if they are behind blast walls. It is also possible to create warheads with multiple penetrators[7] and self-forging fins[8] to increase stand-off ranges and lethality.

Advanced Manufacturing

Advanced manufacturing will allow the production of tens of thousands of small, smart, but inexpensive drones. It combines additive manufacturing (a.k.a. 3D printing), robots, and artificial intelligence to massively increase the speed and quality of manufacturing. In the last decade, as 3D pioneers mastered various materials and techniques, they began to focus on speed of printing. Of particular importance in small-drone production is rapid printing of composite material. In April 2016, Carbon introduced a commercial 3D printer that was 100 times faster than previous printers. In addition to speed, the continuing massive investment in 3D printing has improved both quality and complexity of manufactured products while reducing prices. Prices have dropped to the point that weekend hobbyists are printing their own drones. A popular website even rates the top 10 3D printed drone kits for sale commercially.[9]

Drones

The dramatic increase in 3D printing speeds has major implications for warfare. In 2014, researchers at the University of Virginia successfully 3D-printed a drone in one day. By snapping in place an electric motor, two batteries, and an Android cell phone, they made an autonomous drone with a range of approximately 50 kilometers. It took about 31 hours to print and assemble the drone at a total cost (excluding the printer) of about $800.[10] While it could be controlled by a ground station, the GPS in the phone allowed the drone to fly a specified route autonomously. Such a system is vulnerable to GPS jamming but a number of new approaches are being developed that will allow drones to navigate in GPS-denied environments.[11]

Other programs allow a cell-phone camera to identify people and objects even under low light conditions.[12] Combining small warheads, GPS-independent navigation, and cell-phone target identification can create autonomous, inexpensive drones that can range for dozens of miles, then hunt and engage specific targets. Think of them as IEDs that hunt you.

Long-range air[13] and undersea autonomous drones[14] are also being produced today, and manufacturers are competing hard to reduce the price even as they dramatically increase range and payload. The Aerovel Flexrotor has a range of 1,500 miles, the Defiant Lab DX-3 over 900 miles,[15] and the Volans-I over 500 miles while carrying a 20-pound payload at sustained speeds of 150 miles per hour.[16] While not technically stealthy, the small size of these systems mean they have the radar signature of a small bird.[17] And, like most new technologies, these systems can be greatly improved for relatively little money. Thus naval and air forces will also be at risk from inexpensive, smart, long-range weapons. In particular, fixed facilities like air bases will be vulnerable.

Globally, state militaries are developing very high-capability drones. However, this paper will not discuss them since they remain beyond the reach of most insurgent and terrorist organizations—unless a state sponsor chooses to make them available.

Task-Specific Artificial Intelligence

There is a great deal of disagreement over when or even if general artificial intelligence will emerge. While an interesting discussion, it is irrelevant for the purposes of this paper. Much more important is the current state of limited or task-specific artificial intelligence. While the literature normally refers to this type of AI as "limited," "task-specific" is more accurate. It is better than any human at the specific task it is designed to do. Thus in its niche area, task-specific AI creates a distinct advantage for the nation that fields it first.

To create the AI necessary for truly autonomous attack drones, designers had to address two issues—navigation and target identification. Task-specific artificial intelligence has clearly mastered both. The Israeli Harop drone, initially fielded in 2005, uses GPS guidance to arrive in a target area and then shifts to visual, infrared, and electronic search modes to identify and attack a target.[18]

Striking the target is a separate problem. It requires the autonomous system to identify a specified target and then maneuver through obstacles to strike it. While this is a very challenging issue, commercial firms are already deploying autonomous air taxis and ground vehicles based on a range of ever more effective, precise, and inexpensive sensors, which have obvious applications in improving the hunting capability of autonomous drones. In fact, as of January 2019, commercial firms were offering 9 different models of drones that could autonomously follow and film an athlete, including mountain bikers riding trails.[19]

While western states continue to debate whether autonomous drones will be required to maintain a command and control link so the mission can be canceled or diverted, insurgents and terrorists will not accept that limitation. Doing so would increase the technical complexity of the systems as well as increase the vulnerability to enemy cyber or microwave defenses. Thus non-state actors are likely to treat a drone as a round of ammunition—fire and forget. By employing autonomous drones without a command link, they eliminate the possibility the drone can be defeated by electronic jamming of the command signal.

Current drones still remain vulnerable to GPS jamming. However, commercial drone developers are working to make their autonomous drones GPS-independent and hardening them against microwave signals. By shifting from GPS-dependent navigation to inertial plus visual navigation, delivery drones will be able to operate in the urban canyons where GPS signals are often blocked. And, if drone delivery systems are to succeed, the drones must also be immune to local high-power emissions from airport radars, high-power transmission lines, and other commercial sources. This will mitigate one of the most promising defenses against autonomous drones—electronic magnetic pulses generated by high-powered microwaves. As commercial drones become hardened to electronic interference, non-state actors will take advantage of that capability.

Cheap Space Capabilities

Given the very long range of new autonomous drones, a third major technical problem is locating the targets precisely. Years ago, Google Maps and Google Earth solved the problem of finding major installations like airfields, ports, and industrial and political facilities for insurgents. If one wants to know where the C-17s and larger commercial aircraft park at Bagram Air Base in Afghanistan, simply look it up on Google Maps. Shift to satellite mode and you have sufficient resolution to direct a smart drone to within a couple hundred feet of the target. Given Google Maps' global coverage, it provides a first rate intelligence source for anyone with an internet connection. Admittedly these images are dated, but it is a pretty safe assumption the big airplanes still park in the same place and thus a drone with visual target identification could fly to the parking apron and then select a target.

More recently, current imagery has become available to anyone with an internet connection and a credit card. Over the last two decades, the development of cube satellites and the infrastructure to launch them cheaply in large numbers have made space imagery commercially available.[20] Planet, a private company, uses its cube satellite network to take submeter resolution imagery of the entire planet *daily*, and it sells these images on line.[21] Planet can provide images based on visual or infrared cameras as well as synthetic aperture radar. Apple now provides the SpyMeSat, "the only mobile app to offer on-demand access to the latest commercial high resolution satellite imagery, and with the release of v3.1, the only mobile app offering users the ability to task high resolution commercial imaging satellites."[22] The bottom line is that multiple companies now or will soon offer near real-time imagery of anywhere on the planet. The days of hiding military movement on the surface are clearly drawing to a close.

Biotechnology

Synthetic biology and rapid advances in gene editing have truly frightening potential. Therefore, while the impact of biotechnology in state versus non-state conflicts is a bit farther out, readers need to understand it has by far the greatest destructive potential. Fortunately, it is very unlikely that non-state actors have the necessary skills and resources to use these advanced tools to create biological weapons. As noted earlier, non-state actors have rarely used cutting-edge technology. Thus any biological attack they generate is much more likely to use commercially available products. For decades, we have speculated that a terror cell could conduct a devastating economic attack on the United States by introducing hoof and mouth disease or mad cow disease into our livestock industry. By infecting an unknown number of animals and then reporting their infection to media outlets, a terror group could cause major economic damage by attacking the US cattle industry. In 2017, it generated almost $90 billion in meat and milk products.[23] Yet, to date, the biological terror attacks in the United States have been very minor, such as the 1984 Rajaneeshee poisoning of salad bars, the 2001 Amerithrax attacks on Capitol Hill, and the ricin letters mailed in 2003 and 2004.

While bioweapons have the most potential, the difficulty in producing them has so far prevented non-state actors from using them. However, states must carefully monitor progress in this area. Because while states will hesitate to use such a weapon due to potential infection of its own population as well as massive retaliation, nihilistic terrorist organizations are probably the most likely to consider loosening a contagious disease on the planet.

This brief examination of how non-state actors can exploit new technologies indicates the depth of the tactical problem. However, to understand the strategic problem, we must examine the emerging strategic conditions that will govern state versus non-state conflicts.

Drivers of Insurgency

Military institutions and the manner in which they employ violence depended on the economic, social and political conditions of their respective states.

Even as technology is providing weapons that exploit current western vulnerabilities, the fact remains that economic, social, and political conditions of the various entities in the conflict will determine how the technology is employed.[24] Emerging technologies will challenge every aspect of the current US operational approach to counterinsurgency. An even greater challenge is the fact that changes in the primary political driver of insurgency will make US counterinsurgency doctrine obsolete.

It is essential to understand that the primary causes driving post–World War II insurgencies have evolved. The initial major driver—anticolonialism—has obviously passed. Colonial powers were driven out. Unfortunately, their withdrawals led directly to the second major driver of insurgencies—conflicts over who would rule the state the colonists established and left behind. The National Union for the Total Independence of Angola (UNITA)'s long war with the Popular Movement for the Liberation of Angola (MPLA) over who would rule Angola is a clear example of this motivation. Despite its ethnic and tribal aspects as well as its 20-year duration, the conflict did not change the territorial borders of Angola.

Now a third driver is gaining prominence—the desire to change the old colonial borders. The colonial borders were drawn without any consideration of the historical ethnic, cultural, or religious networks on the ground. Today, we are seeing an increase in conflicts in regions where the colonial borders artificially divided much older cultures. The Balouch of Afghanistan, Pakistan, and Iran are prime examples. Their society was divided for the convenience of the British colonial government. This has left them as ignored and often persecuted minorities in each of the three existing countries. In response, they have conducted a decade-long insurgency in an attempt to establish a homeland. They join the Kurds of the Middle East in struggling against the colonial boundaries. The intra-state conflicts across the Sahel between Arab northern societies and southern African ones also illustrate the failure of colonial powers to create national identities. At the same time, subnational movements are redefining borders in other areas. The peoples of the old Yugoslavia, Sudan, and Somalia are still working through the process.

The third driver means insurgencies are increasingly transnational, trans-dimensional coalitions of the willing and opportunists. And they will be long. Each aspect creates significant problems for the United States.

Third-driver efforts to redraw political boundaries to align with social boundaries means most insurgencies will be transnational. This very fact stymies US counterinsurgency doctrine, which is based on working with the host nation. Afghanistan illustrates the problem. The insurgency is primarily Pashtun yet more Pashtuns live in Pakistan than Afghanistan. So there are really two host nations. Further complicating the problem is the fact the two host nations' strategic interests do not align. Pakistan feels it must maintain relations with the Taliban as a strategic hedge against India. Yet the Afghan government cannot accept continued Pakistani support for its primary enemy. The United States and its coalition partners have been unable to resolve this fundamental difference of strategic outlooks.

Today insurgencies are also trans-dimensional in that they operate in both the real and the cyber world. Driven by necessity, many non-state actors have learned to use the internet both to communicate and to recruit. Because boundaries are about identities, it is easier to use social media to involve ethnic diasporas. We have seen the impact of this in recruiting for the conflict in Syria as well as the continuing struggle in Somalia.

In addition, identity-based insurgencies reflect the societies they live in. Given the nonhierarchical nature of many postcolonial societies, they have tended to be coalitions rather than hierarchies. The Afghans, Kurds, Iraqis, Chechens, and Syrians were/are not unified insurgencies but rather coalitions of the willing and the opportunistic. This vastly complicates the counterinsurgent's task because there is no single political entity to either defeat or negotiate with.

Finally, identity-based insurgencies are likely to be very long. The counterinsurgent is not simply trying to build a functioning state to run an existing nation. He is trying to create a nation from a variety of other identities. In Europe and Asia, it took between 400 and 1,000 years to create nations with a common identity. Unfortunately, it also involved a great deal of warfare and often ethnic cleansing. Thus, we should anticipate identity-based insurgencies will be long—think decades not years.

The different drivers have dramatically changed the character of the insurgencies, their organizations, and their approaches to gaining power. But they have not changed the fact they will use force to achieve their goals.

Insurgent Strategy

While a number of insurgents have provided theories of insurgency (Mao, Che, Giap, et al.), there is no general insurgent strategy. However, there is a practical approach that has often worked to convince outside powers to quit fighting and go home. Successful insurgencies have focused on wearing down the political will of the outside power via a campaign of attrition. In the past, the attrition has been limited primarily to attacking the outsiders that have entered the insurgent's country. As will be discussed below, today's technology may open entirely new paths for the insurgents to attack the will of outside powers. Then, as always, the insurgents will have to win the internal civil war against the host nation government. Unfortunately, new technologies will provide new tools for that fight too.

Insurgent Tactical Options Created by 4IR Technologies

With insurgent strategy focused on destroying the will of outside policy-makers, insurgents have adopted tactics to maximize outside casualties while "proving" the government is making little or no progress in defeating them. They do not have to seize territory but only visibly continue the fight to prove the government is not succeeding. In the past, equipment limitations meant insurgents were usually limited to direct attacks on counterinsurgent forces and the population in the country. And, they often fought at a range and firepower disadvantage.

New technology is changing that. The arrival of commercial drones means insurgents can launch attacks from outside the range of most government surveillance and weapon systems. Unfortunately, current US approaches to fighting insurgents are extremely vulnerable to this type of attack. US forces travel into a theater via large aircraft and then operate from easily identified fortified bases, and move about in distinctive vehicles. In the last 18 years, both Arab and Afghan insurgents focused their attacks on the bases and communications links between them using IEDs and ambushes. They also constantly refined their suicide attacks against fixed positions and public gatherings. While coalition forces developed more effective tactics, techniques, and procedures to defend against this type of attack, doing so required the dedication of enormous resources and severely restricted coalition operations. Through decades of effort, the United States has developed very effective defenses against ground attacks by non-state actors. Physical barriers backed by armed personnel who are alerted by extensive surveillance systems have prevented hundreds of attacks from reaching the vulnerable interiors of US facilities. Despite these efforts, coalition forces have only significantly reduced the number of attacks when the mass of the population shifted allegiance to the government

These attacks became less of a problem with the withdrawal of major combat forces from Iraq and Afghanistan. Since then US involvement has focused on advising and providing fire support. The majority of US forces operate from fortified bases. Those that move off base do so in armored vehicles or by air. The combination has dramatically reduced US casualties. Since 2015, more service people have died in peacetime training than combat.[25]

However, each node within the US system, whether US forces are actively fighting the insurgents or are in an advisory role, is vulnerable to attack by autonomous drones. Airfields are the most vulnerable. The very large perimeter and vulnerability of key elements of the system from radars to fuel farms to the aircraft themselves will make these a prime target for insurgent or terrorist attacks. Using Google Maps, insurgents can see the entire layout of airfields that US forces use. Shifting to the satellite image, one can locate the parking apron for C-17s and other large aircraft at Bagram Airfield, Afghanistan. Clearly, if a C-17 or large commercial aircraft is damaged or destroyed on the ground, the United States will discontinue airlift into the attacked airfield—and perhaps all airfields in the theater until the threat can be addressed.

Unfortunately, neither the United States nor any other nation has created truly effective defenses against drones. And insurgents recognize the value of attacking aircraft on the ground. While the Russians claim to have defeated all 23 drone attacks against their main air base in Syria,[26] other reports show images of damaged Russian aircraft.[27] Further, it is essential to note most of the Russian success came from using electronic warfare to defeat the drones' very crude control systems or jam the signal from the pilot. As noted, autonomous drones do not have a link to a pilot and can be hardened against high-energy microwaves. Soon they will not be susceptible to GPS jamming either.

Another major component of US counterinsurgency operations is fixed outposts. While much smaller than airfields, they are also very numerous. They range from major support facilities with stores of fuel, lubricants, and ammunition to individual platoon outposts and police checkpoints. How can the government protect the thousands of military, police, and government outposts across a nation from drone attack? Consolidating bases would reduce the problem but also dramatically curtail the contact between the population and the government. And of course the capability to direct air attacks means the use of public meetings, or "shuras," a key element of US counterinsurgency doctrine, becomes a much more difficult and hazardous problem. This threat can further reduce the critical contact between the government and the people.

Perhaps the most difficult to protect from cheap, fast drones are the ground convoys and patrols that are an essential part of counterinsurgency operations. Insurgents in both Iraq and Afghanistan have severely restricted ground movement of coalition forces through the use of improvised explosive devices. Despite enormous effort by coalition forces hunting IEDs and the networks that produce them, government forces have been unable to neutralize this threat. The addition of fast, small drones will complicate the problem immensely. If a cheap commercial drone can autonomously identify and track a runner in motion, it can identify and fly into a vehicle or a patrol. The IEDs will now be actively hunting both moving and stationary government assets.

As early as January 2017, ISIS was conducting at least one drone mission a day over coalition forces.[28] To increase the impact of their attacks, they released numerous videos of their drones attacking coalition forces.[29] One even showed a complex attack with a drone dispersing the personnel at a checkpoint to clear the way for a suicide car bomb attack.[30] Clearly the sophistication of the attacks will continue to improve. And as 3D printing of drones becomes more widespread, we should expect to see a significant increase in the number of drones employed.

In addition, very long-range drones like the Flexrotor, Volans-I, and DX-3 will become widely available. Well-funded insurgent or terrorist groups will inevitably arm one or more. They can then reach out of theater to threaten US forces in transit. Drawing a 1,500-mile-range ring around ISIS or Taliban territory gives an idea of how deeply these systems can strike into America's logistics pipeline.

A more sophisticated group could blackmail other nations to refuse US transit rights. Recent events at Heathrow and Gatwick demonstrated the difficulty of preventing drones from entering airspace around an airfield. And a small drone can easily carry enough explosives to damage a 777 or an A380 parked at a gate on a major airfield—with accurate placement it could ignite a secondary explosion from the fuel on board. Thus an insurgent or terror group could offer a state like Germany or Kuwait a choice: terminate US support flights passing through your nations or face attacks on your air transportation industry. A single successful attack will result in billions worth of economic damage if the nation refuses the insurgent demands.

In short, the emergence of large numbers of autonomous armed drones will require the United States to rethink its entire concept of counterinsurgency operations.

Terrorist Options

If terrorists adapt drones, they effectively neutralize 95% of all anti-terror physical barriers. The last few decades have taught security forces that layered protection against a ground attack is essential. Governments, businesses, and even private individuals have invested in walls, barriers, vehicle mazes, ditches, barbed wire, and other physical obstacles, all backed up by armed guards. For the most part, standoff distance and defense in depth have prevented attacks against fixed facilities.

Fortunately, today's commercial drones carry relatively small payloads so they will not cause great damage by themselves. Unfortunately, a precisely delivered small payload can be used in a couple of creative ways. First, it can serve as a detonator for the explosive power that is present in any modern society—fuel depots, fertilizer storage facilities, key elements of the power grid, and chemical plants. In 1947, the *SS Grandcamp* caught fire, which resulted in the detonation of 2,200 tons (a 2-kiloton equivalent) of ammonium nitrate fertilizer that killed over 500 people and flattened the Port of Texas City.[31] The 1984 Union Carbide disaster in Bhopal, India, released tons of methyl isocyanate that resulted in thousands dead and hundreds of thousands injured.[32] These two accidents clearly demonstrate the massive level of destructive power embedded in the commercial sector. New technologies will provide terrorists with the ability to precisely deliver the detonator to set off the explosive energy spread across modern society.

For high visibility attacks, terrorists have consistently attacked aircraft. Today's airport security has made that very difficult. However, a small drone bypasses virtually all current airport defenses and can deliver high explosive or incendiary devices directly to an aircraft parked at a gate. For a terrorist group intent on doing maximum economic damage to the global economy, simultaneous attacks on key international air hubs will fit the bill. By selecting airports in nations that lack global reach for counterattacking, the terrorists can also reduce the risk to themselves. Using 5–10 small drones at each target airfield, terrorists can be relatively certain of hitting at least one target. Of course, they would video the attack and release the video on line immediately. The financial impact of striking multiple key nodes in the global air system will be enormous. Today air cargo accounts for 35% of global trade by value—not including the value of transporting passengers.[33] If multiple nodes are struck at once, air operations will have to cease while risk assessment and mitigation are conducted. Given the current state of defense against drones, it is likely the shutdown will endure for weeks if not months as governments try to solve this exceptionally difficult security issue.

A second approach is to use precision to strike just key government officials or uniformed security forces. This has three effects. It shows the people the terrorists are only fighting the government and not the people; it separates the security forces from the people as they build barriers between themselves and the populations; and it shows the government cannot even protect itself, much less the population. And of course, precision drones can be used for high-profile attacks or assassinations. Drones have already been flown very close to two national leaders—German Chancellor Angela Merkel and Venezuelan President Nicolas Maduro.

Criminal Organizations

While not strictly speaking a form of insurgency, crime has also become a major driver of instability in many nations. Criminal organizations across the globe are challenging governments for control of territory. They emerge in numerous forms from gangs to drug cartels to transnational criminal networks that deal in commodities from guns to drugs to people. With the exception of first-generation street gangs, these criminal organizations have a common motivation—profit.[34] While some commentators dismiss this as a law enforcement problem, criminal organizations have demonstrated the ability both to ally with insurgents (Colombia) or effectively seize and rule territory within a state (Mexico). These cases demonstrate how criminals can impact the security of the United States.

As commercial drone usage expands, criminals have been quick to see the possibilities. In 2017, Australian police arrested members of a drug gang that were using drones to warn them if police were in the area.[35] In May 2018, reports emerged that criminals had used a swarm of drones to disrupt an FBI hostage rescue operation by repeatedly buzzing the FBI surveillance team.[36] Numerous drones have been intercepted smuggling drugs, phones, or money over prison walls as well as smuggling drugs across international boundaries. As drone capabilities increase, we can expect to see increased usage by criminals with a focus on smuggling, surveillance, and intelligence operations. And we have to assume criminals will soon be using suicide drones for attacks on opponents.

How Can the United States Respond?

In short, the drivers of insurgency, terror, and criminal activity are not going away. Their widespread distribution means it is inevitable these conflicts will destabilize important allies or impinge on world energy supplies. The United States may also have to respond when a party or parties to a conflict provides sanctuaries for terrorists targeting the United States or its allies.

To do so, we have to develop a strategic approach to each separate problem—insurgency, terror, and crime.

Unfortunately, the very phrases "counterinsurgency or counterterror strategy" confuse methods or ways of fighting with a complete strategy. Neither is a strategy. They are merely one approach in a range of possible ways in the ends, ways, and means formulation of strategy.

Population-centric counterinsurgency, as documented in *FM 324 Counterinsurgency*, is only one possible approach to such a campaign. A disturbingly large portion of the discussion within the United States government simply accepts *FM 324*'s recommended best practices and believes that, if applied as package, they create a strategy. Yet by nature, best practices in counterinsurgency are essentially tactical or, at the most, operational-level efforts.

In fact, there is no general counterinsurgency or counterterror strategy just as there is no anti-submarine or anti-aircraft strategy. One doesn't develop a strategy against an operational technique. Each conflict requires the development of a case-specific strategy that includes assumptions, coherent ends-ways-means, priorities, sequencing of events, and a theory of victory. And it must be flexible enough to respond to the changes that are an inevitable part of any conflict.

Rather than unquestioningly accepting that "counterinsurgency or counterterror strategy" is the correct solution to a conflict, planners must start by first understanding the specific conflict. Since it will be impossible to know everything necessary to develop a strategy, they must next think through and clearly state their assumptions about that specific conflict. With this level of understanding, they will be ready to start the difficult process of developing coherent ends, ways, and means, prioritizing and sequencing their actions, and developing a theory of victory. Only then will they have a strategy that is appropriate for the actual conflict.

What Has Worked for the United States as an Expeditionary Power?

In considering the various counterinsurgency approaches, the most important question for the United States is what works best for an expeditionary power. When discussing the future of US counterinsurgency, it is absolutely essential to differentiate between those approaches that work for domestic campaigns and those that work for expeditionary campaigns. Unfortunately, *FM 324 Counterinsurgency* drew most of its best practices from the domestic counterinsurgency efforts of the British in Malaya and North Ireland and the French in Algeria. In all three cases, the counterinsurgent was also the government. Thus, they could make the government legitimate by removing any person or organization that was hurting that legitimacy.

It is much more difficult for an outside power to force the host country to make the necessary political changes. As the United States experienced in Vietnam, Iraq, and Afghanistan and the Soviets in Afghanistan, an outside power cannot force the government to be legitimate. Even removing illegitimate leaders and replacing them with those picked by the expeditionary power failed for the United States in Vietnam and for the Soviets in Afghanistan.

That said, the United States has been successful at expeditionary counterinsurgency. US efforts to assist the Philippines in 1950s and again since 2001, Thailand from the 1950s to the 1970s, El Salvador in the 1980s, and Colombia against its insurgents in the 1990s and 2000s have all been successful. In each case, the United States used an indirect approach rather than a direct approach. The indirect approach meant that US personnel provided advice and support to host-nation forces as those nations fought. While this support at times even included tactical leadership, the focus was always on assisting the host nation and not on US elements engaging the enemy. In addition, these efforts were kept relatively small. This had two major benefits. First, it kept the US presence from distorting the local political and economic reality too badly. Second, it prevented impatient Americans from attempting to do the job themselves because they simply lacked the resources to do so.

Based on our historical record, America should only provide advice and assistance to the host nation or nations in a counterinsurgency campaign. As insurgents employ larger numbers of more effective, longer-range precision weapons, the United States will have to modify its approach to even this mission. It will want to minimize the presence of US government personnel in the country and adopt a more austere, expeditionary footprint. In particular, while continuing to pursue technological approaches to defeating drones, it must fall back on ancient methods. Overhead protection— even something as simple as dirt—can defeat the vast majority of drones. All US government facilities will require overhead protection of key nodes or sources of explosive energy like fuel tanks, large vehicles, etc. The second approach is to strive to blend into the population. Rather than moving about in high profile armored vehicles, whether military or armored Chevy Suburbans, US personnel should travel in local vehicles without ostentatious security.

A further major benefit of keeping any supporting effort small is that it extends the timeline. By remaining small, the effort remains below the interest level of the vast majority of Americans and thus can be sustained for the very long timelines of a nation-building effort. Just as important, if despite our assistance, the government fails to reform and achieve popular support, the United States needs to admit it cannot fix another country and withdraw. By keeping the effort small, it allows us to do so without a major loss of international credibility.

Does the United States Need a Counterinsurgency Capability?

The high cost and lack of success in Iraq and Afghanistan mean hostility to counterinsurgency as a concept is rising. Yet, the capability has enduring relevance. Nor is it only relevant in the event of some distant future conflict. It is an essential element of national security today. One of the critical issues facing today's Pentagon is designing and building the appropriate force structure in the resource constrained, post-Afghanistan period. The United States must balance the risk of not being prepared in some mission areas against the ongoing cost of maintaining readiness across the spectrum of conflict. If the counterinsurgency skeptics prevail, then the United States may choose to severely reduce or eliminate the capabilities necessary for fighting an insurgency. In short, the Pentagon could choose the same route that left the nation intellectually unprepared for the conflicts in Iraq and Afghanistan. It failed to anticipate the insurgencies that were almost inevitable and when it did accept the insurgencies were happening, responded very slowly.

Rather than arguing about the effectiveness or ineffectiveness of a nonexistent strategy, we need to be discussing if the United States needs to maintain counterinsurgency capabilities in its national security tool kit. If so, what should such capabilities focus on? Is there an approach or approaches that have been successful for expeditionary forces in insurgencies? How do we modify them to the new capabilities that insurgents are already using? Answers to these questions are an essential part of answering the larger question concerning future US force structure.

Counterterrorism Strategy

As US strategic documents from the National Security Strategy to the US Director of National Intelligence assessments have noted, terrorist groups remain a threat to the United States. However, the sheer magnitude of the problem prohibits the United States from "fixing" the dozens of countries that are both the source and target of terror groups. There is an emerging understanding that, like many wicked problems, terror cannot be fixed but only managed. Thus the United States continues to conduct operations globally to reduce terrorists' capabilities to strike. Sometimes referred to as "mowing the grass," this ongoing campaign recognizes it is only an attempt to manage a problem beyond our capability to solve.

Unfortunately, the capabilities emerging from the fourth industrial revolution make it inevitable that terrorists will be able to conduct more effective attacks on US facilities and personnel overseas and even in the United States. Thus resilience will become a much greater part of the US counterterror approach. The American people must understand that some attacks will get through and that the United States will NOT launch a multi-decade, multi-trillion-dollar effort to fix the country that was the source of the attacks. Rather the United States will continue to work to preempt attacks and improve its resilience but will have to accept that terrorists will occasionally succeed.

Dealing with Crime

Profit-seeking criminals will be happy to exploit new technology but will use it mostly to avoid contact with the police. Contact, potential conflict, and confinement greatly increase the cost of doing business. Dealing with these groups should be based on police methods—adapted as necessary to deal with increasing criminal capability. Unfortunately, this is likely to result in further movement of policing to a paramilitary basis, which historically has not boded well for the people of the nation.

In contrast, those criminals who choose to carve territory out of a state to prevent state interference in their business have really moved into the realm of insurgency. They are seizing political control of a region. Dealing with these groups will require more of a counterinsurgency concept like that described above.

Conclusion

The converging technologies of the fourth industrial revolution are shifting the military balance between states and non-state actors in favor of the non-state actors. Insurgents, terrorists, and criminals now have access to capabilities formerly reserved for major powers. The United States will have to adapt accordingly. But the most important point to remember is that our failures since World War II have not been the result of an inability to solve tactical problems but rather the consistent failure to match US strategy to the particular situation. Therefore the critical piece is to truly understand the problem and adopt a strategy that solves the problem confronting the United States. Then we can adapt at the tactical and technical levels to deal with the new problems presented by emerging technology.

NOTES

1. Kate Conger, "How Consumer Drones Wind Up in the Hands of ISIS Fighters," *TechCrunch*, October 13, 2016, https://techcrunch.com/2016/10/13/how-consumer-drones-wind-up-in-the-hands-of-isis-fighters/.

2. Eric Schmitt, "Papers Offer a Peek at ISIS' Drones, Lethal and Largely Off-the-Shelf," *New York Times*, January 31, 2017, https://www.nytimes.com/2017/01/31/world/middleeast/isis-drone-documents.html.

3. Jonathan Vanian, "Criminals Used a Fleet of Drones to Disrupt an FBI Hostage Operation," *Fortune*, May 4, 2018, http://fortune.com/go/tech/drone-fbi-hostage-criminals/.

4. Kyle Mizokami, "Another Ukrainian Ammo Dump Goes Up in Massive Explosion," *Popular Mechanics*, September 27, 2017, https://www.popularmechanics.com/military/weapons/news/a28412/ukrainian-ammo-dump-explosion/.

5. "EFP Charge Demonstration Video," *ISSEE*, https://www.youtube.com/watch?v=G0ZOPFiuOL8.

6. XP2 Quadcopter Off Road Racing Demo Reel-Aerial Video and Photography, YouTube, July 3, 2013, https://www.youtube.com/watch?feature=player_embedded&v=QRrSriR5b6s.

7. Richard Fong et al., "Multiple Explosively Formed Penetrator (MEFP) Warhead Technology Development," 2004, www.dtic.mil/get-tr-doc/pdf?AD=ADA432897.

8. Jian-qing Liu et al., "Formation of Explosively Formed Penetrator with Fins and Its Flight Characteristics," *Defence Technology*, June 2014, Vol 10, Iss 2, 119–123, https://www.sciencedirect.com/science/article/pii/S2214914714000348.

9. "Top 10 3D Printed Drones," *3Dnatives*, December 10, 2018, https://www.3dnatives.com/en/top-3d-printed-drones-101220185/.

10. Jordan Golson, "A Military-Grade Drone That Can Be Printed Anywhere," *Wired*, September 16, 2014, http://www.wired.com/2014/09/military-grade-drone-can-printed-anywhere.

11. Riley Bauer, Shannon Nollet, and Dr. Saad Biaz, "A Novel Approach to Non-GPS Navigation Using Infrasound. Technical Paper #CSEE14-03," September 11, 2014, www.eng.auburn.edu/files/acad_depts/csse/csse_technical_reports/csse14-03.pdf.

12. Hillary Grigonis, "Google Designed an Object-Recognition Program That Won't Need the Internet," *Digital Trends*, June 15, 2017, https://www.digitaltrends.com/mobile/google-mobilenets-open-source/.

13. "US Government Makes Aerovel's Flexrotor ITAR-Free," *Aerovel News Release*, November 24, 2014, http://aerovel.com/aerovel-flexrotor-itar-free/.

14. Mark Thompson, "The Navy's Amazing Ocean-Powered Underwater Drone," *Time*, December 22, 2013, http://swampland.time.com/2013/12/22/navy-underwater-drone/.

15. "Flexrotor Specification," http://aerovel.com/flexrotor/; and "Defiant Labs Launches Next Gen Drone: DX-3," Defiant Lab Press release, February 10, 2017, https://news.usaonline.us/press-releases/Defiant-Labs-Launches-Next-Gen-Drone-DX-3-86383.

16. Lora Kolodny and Darren Weaver, "These Drones Can Haul a 20-Pound Load for 500 Miles and Land on a Moving Target," CNBC, May 26, 2018, https://www.cnbc.com/2018/05/26/volans-i-drones-can-haul-cargo-for-500-miles-and-land-on-a-moving-ship.html.

17. Tyler Rogoway, "Meet Israel's 'Suicide Squad' of Self-Sacrificing Drones," *The Warzone*, August 8, 2016, http://www.thedrive.com/the-war-zone/4760/meet-israels-suicide-squad-of-self-sacrificing-drones.

18. "Harop Loitering Munitions UCAV System," *Air Force Technology*, accessed October 22, 2020, www.airforce-technology.com/projects/haroploiteringmuniti/.

19. Jesse Wong, "9 Best Drones That Follow You [Crystal Clear Video] 2019," *Drone Guru*, January 11, 2019, http://www.droneguru.net/8-best-drones-that-follow-you-follow-drones/.

20. "What Are Small Sats and Cube Sats?" *NASA*, February 26, 2015, https://www.nasa.gov/content/what-are-smallsats-and-cubesats.

21. Nathan Hurst, "How Daily Images of the Entire Earth Will Change the Way We Look at It," Smithsonian.com, March 13, 2017, http://www.smithsonianmag.com/innovation/how-daily-images-entire-earth-will-change-way-we-look-it-180962467/#J24AmE8xz2EVa3j8.99.

22. SpyMeSat, https://spymesat.com/.

23. "Overview of U.S. Livestock, Poultry, and Aquaculture Production in 2017," U.S. Department of Agriculture, https://www.aphis.usda.gov/animal_health/nahms/downloads/Demographics2017.pdf.

24. Epigraph from Carl von Clausewitz, *On War*, edited and translated by Michael Howard and Peter Paret, Princeton University Press, Princeton, NJ, 1976, 6.

25. Erika I. Ritchie, "Training Kills More Troops Than War. Here's What's Being Done About It," Military.com, May 14, 2018, https://www.military.com/daily-news/2018/05/14/training-kills-more-troops-war-heres-whats-being-done-about-it.html.

26. "Rise in Drone Attacks on Russian Airbase in Syria: Monitor," France24, August 24, 2018, https://www.france24.com/en/20180824-rise-drone-attacks-russian-airbase-syria-monitor.

27. Tom Demerly, "Defining Asymmetrical Warfare: Extremists Use Retail Drones to Attack Russian Air Base in Syria," *The Aviationist*, January 8, 2018, https://theaviationist.com/2018/01/08/defining-asymmetrical-warfare-extremists-use-retail-drones-to-attack-russian-air-base-in-syria/.

28. Ben Watson, "The Drones of ISIS," *DefenseOne*, January 12, 2017, https://www.defenseone.com/technology/2017/01/drones-isis/134542/.

29. ISIS drone attack videos, *YouTube*, https://www.youtube.com/results?search_query=isis+drone+attack+video.

30. "ISIS 'Industrial Revolution of Terrorism'", June 2, 2017, https://www.youtube.com/watch?v=0vY7i_eR06M.

31. "1947 Texas City Disaster," accessed October 22, 2020, http://www.texascity-library.org/page/history.1947.home.

32. "Bhopal Disaster," *Encyclopaedia Britannica*, January 17, 2019, https://www.britannica.com/event/Bhopal-disaster.

33. "Air Cargo Matters," *IATA*, https://www.iata.org/what wedo/cargo/sustainability/Pages/benefits.aspx.

34. John P. Sullivan and Robert J. Bunker, "Drug Cartels, Street Gangs, and Warlords," *Small Wars and Insurgencies*, March 17, 2008, http://www.academia.edu/36483305/Drug _Cartels_Street_Gangs_and_Warlords.

35. Ray Downs, "Australian Drug Gang Suspected of Using Drone to Monitor Police," UPI, June 30, 2017, https://www .upi.com/Top_News/World-News/2017/06/30/Australian -drug-gang-suspected-of-using-drone-to-monitor-police/29114 98801791/.

36. Jason Murdock, "'Drone Swarm' Used by Criminals to Disrupt an FBI Hostage Rescue Operation," *Newsweek*, May 4, 2018, https://www.newsweek.com/drone-swarm-used -criminals-disrupt-fbi-hostage-rescue-operation-910431.

Part II

Evolution and Revolution in Defense Policy, Process, and Institutions

Introduction

MIRIAM KRIEGER

The study of American defense policy has long been a juxtaposition of continuity and change. In this edition of *American Defense Policy*, that truism holds. The overarching theme of turbulence—the changing character of war and the accelerating pace of change—drives scholars and policy-makers to constantly assess to what extent the status quo is an analog for challenges on the horizon. Part I outlined many of the consistent themes and theories that underpin defense policy and strategy, updating our current understandings of concepts such as great-power politics and alliance dynamics for the contemporary international environment. Part III, in contrast, reflects a world of change in the modern battlefield driven by new technologies and evolving missions, which in turn may aggregate to tectonic shifts in defense policy.

The concepts discussed in part II—that of American defense policy, process, and institutions—usually fit somewhere in the middle ground of this change dynamic, with key issues such as civil-military relations and the profession of arms remaining reliably static, and minor progress being made on the mechanics of defense policy, such as budgeting, organizing, and equipping for American defense. However, this edition of *American Defense Policy* catches us in a time of volatility across even the traditionally quiet fields of civil-military relations. Fundamental questions are being asked about the American military force: its relationship to both society and civilian oversight bodies, its nature and composition, and its ability to meet the challenges that confront the United States today as well as those that are emerging. Not since the establishment of the all-volunteer force nearly fifty years ago have such fundamental questions arisen in the realm of defense policy, questions driven by many of the transformations captured in this edition: an exhausting two decades of war against an enemy that refuses to conform to military expectations, advances in space and cyber technology and their associated vulnerabilities, and the evolution of hybrid and grey-zone conflicts deliberately designed to keep military forces "on the bench."

The authors in part II all seek to unravel both what is the same and what is different in the fabric of identity and process in American defense policy, at times providing more questions than answers. The section flows as follows: first, chapter 5 dives into the currents of civil-military relations, incorporating updated analyses of the classic civil-military concepts and debates; chapter 6 moves into the broader profession of arms, describing fundamental changes in force structure and identity; and chapter 7 updates the tools of American defense policy with a discussion of budget, acquisitions, and the role of National Guard and reserve forces.

In Chapter 5, Gordon Adams starts the conversation on civil-military relations with the perennial issue of institutional imbalance in the making of American foreign policy. Drawing from his book, *Mission Creep*, Adams begins with the premise that the military apparatus in the form of the Department of Defense has acquired overwhelming influence in foreign policy-making, squeezing out its civilian counterparts in the Department of State and beyond. He attributes this to a variety of factors, including size, funding, and coherence of the institutions; their differing constituencies in Congress, society, and industry; organizational culture; and planning capacity. The sum of these factors yields a civil-military imbalance that pervades American policy-making, from threat identification, through planning and strategy, to resource allotment and, ultimately, ownership and execution. Implicit in Adams's account is the notion that as the international environment gets increasingly complex and "threats" with nonmilitary dimensions emerge (climate change, refugee flows, and ungoverned spaces to name a few), the disproportionate power the military possesses in setting agendas and planning responses induces risk—and sometimes failure. This militarization of American foreign policy has profound impact, and, as Adams argues, "not examining and correcting this imbalance poses serious risks for the long-term success of American statecraft."

If there is an imbalance in the institutions of statecraft, so too is there an imbalance in the execution of civilian control. In a particularly unique piece, Senator John McCain offers a personal viewpoint as a senior statesman, longtime leader of the Senate Armed Services Committee, and decorated veteran in his own right. His argument is simple: Congress has abdicated its constitutional role as a democratic check on an increasingly powerful executive, particularly in the realm of national security where thoughtful deliberation and a long view are critical. Citing historical and personal examples, McCain articulates the unique role of bipartisan cooperation in the legislature in informing defense policy and strategy and suggests that Congress's failure in "deliberating and debating the strategy to address the global challenges and opportunities we face is one of the great tragedies of our modern political system."

Closing out the perspective of the rising military influence in civil-military relations, Jessica Blankshain offers a contemporary piece assessing the role of the military in the Donald Trump administration. The purpose of including this piece is not to present a critique of current civilian control but to demonstrate contemporary civil-military relations as a clear culmination of the trends over the preceding decades. As the military has accrued increasing foreign policy cachet and unquestioning public support, American presidents have staffed greater proportions of their nonmilitary executive positions with retired general and flag officers. The Trump administration elevated this to a new level, and Blankshain explores the twin concerns of an increasingly uniform-wearing cadre of advisors. The first, focused on policy-making, worries that the military perspective will dominate foreign policy decisions to the exclusion of alternative perspectives or that every challenge will become a problem for the military to solve, further extending an already hollow force. The second concerns the risk of increasing politicization of the American military eroding its nonpartisan ethic, either in actuality or in the eyes of the society it serves. The article wraps up with a warning about a slow-moving crisis in civil-military relations with unknown consequences.

With the extraordinary power of the defense institution, increasing influence of military members, and Congress sitting on the sidelines, the ethical obligations of those who serve become an important and provocative issue. Writing from the Army War College, Don Snider picks up this question of moral agency in the military with a deep dive into the appropriateness of dissent from civil authority. In what is more than just a treatise on the bounds of civilian control, Snider engages the ideas of disobedience and loyalty along a spectrum that includes public resignation. His discussion of the professional ethic and the "moral workspace" of the profession of arms is a necessary cornerstone piece for contemporary and future military leaders and the perfect way to close this chapter on the troubling state of civil-military relations.

Fueling this changing relationship between civilian and military instructions are foundational shifts in the profession of arms itself. It is therefore no accident that chapter 6 kicks off with a profound exploration of the evolving nature of the military profession. Christopher Miller leverages his military and academic experience to push the boundaries of the profession of arms, asking if scholars and practitioners of defense are even using the right terminology when they conceptualize war and peace, soldier and civilian, combatant and noncombatant, battlefield and home front. In a world where uniformed military often support civil society

endeavors, civilian contractors and industry partners operate at the tip of the spear, and competition and conflict occur in every domain, medium, and location—including the bank accounts and ballot boxes of the American heartland—Miller suggests that our outdated understandings of these basic concepts threaten the cohesiveness and efficacy of the profession of arms.

Jeffrey Donnithorne takes up Miller's thesis, contributing a revolutionary analysis of the role service culture plays in the development of defense policy. His premise is that despite progress in operational capability as a Joint Force, the identity of the military remains at the service level. These individual service identities in turn drive defense priorities, perception of threats, mission flexibility, and reactions to input from civilian control bodies. Breaking down the fundamentals of identity into *who*, *what*, *when*, *where*, and *why* for each service yields insights into their institutional behavior and lends predictive power as to *how* each may adapt to the changing battlespace described throughout this edition. In addition to the helpful portraits Donnithorne paints of service identities, he leaves us with a prediction for the future identity of the new Space Force based on the same methodology.

One of the most monumental changes in defense policy made in recent years is captured by Megan MacKenzie in her article on women in combat. In December 2015, Secretary of Defense Ash Carter announced the end of the military's ban on women in combat and the opening of combat units across all military branches to women. MacKenzie charts the history of women in combat roles, then captures—and counters—the primary objections to further inclusiveness on the eve of full integration. From physical capability to unit cohesiveness, MacKenzie outlines the arguments against women in combat units and offers the compelling argument that spurred this monumental change: that success in overcoming the myriad challenges inherent in contemporary warfare requires diversity and that the overall level of talent in the armed forces will increase if gender is no longer a limiting factor. The full implications of this enormous (and enormously controversial) policy change have yet to be fully felt; but, as women begin to graduate from the military's most arduous courses and lead troops in combat, questions about Selective Service, military capability, and American society's tolerance for war remain. We will look to the next edition of *American Defense Policy* to provide updates and answers on the full integration of women in combat units.

The integration of women in the US military was no doubt a milestone for defense policy, but it is not the only diversity challenge the armed forces—and indeed the country—currently face. As this volume came together, the United States was rocked by protests and demonstrations confronting racial injustice and discrimination that spilled well beyond civilian domestic issues. The editors considered how this monumental movement connected to defense policy and ultimately selected two pieces that speak to its importance. First, Bishop Garrison argues that racial inequality undercuts national security and defense policy in interconnected ways, reducing military effectiveness and undermining the beacon of American exceptionalism. Second, a short collection of speeches point to the civil-military implications of American troops being positioned in opposition to protestors, as well as internal failures to integrate and promote non-white servicemembers within the services. Though racial integration officially occurred in the armed forces many decades ago, these pieces indicate it is far from complete.

Of course, the expansion of US military forces has not been limited to toppling gender barriers or seeking racial equality. Though military contractors are not a new phenomenon, the quantity, quality, and scope of contracted missions have grown exponentially in the decades of war against terrorist organizations across Africa, the Middle East, and Asia. Deborah Avant and Renée de Nevers tackle the evolving role of military contractors and their increasing indispensability to the American way of war. They begin with the startling fact that more than half of US personnel deployed to Iraq and Afghanistan have been contractors and proceed to trace the benefits and risks associated with legal, societal, and governmental differences between the uniformed military and vast swath of private military and security contractors. In keeping with the theme of an ever-widening array of requirements for military force, contractors may provide instant expertise, surge capacity, and moral deniability not possible in the uniformed military. The consequences for defense policy are profound: increasingly able to purchase capability and capacity, the American way of war is irrevocably reliant on contracted forces to do everything from laundry services to armed security. However, as Avant and Nevers conclude, for all the benefits of expertise they provide, contracted services may also create a sticky melee in which war is both easier and less accountable than ever before.

The changing landscape of force structure in American defense policy also includes new concern with the quality of the force. This worry is primarily expressed in terms of talent management and talent retention, a topic raised by Tim Kane in his piece capturing the exodus of the best and brightest from the Army. Part of a larger book, *Bleeding Talent*, and his follow-on work on reforming the All-Volunteer Force, the economist describes two types of bleeding: external, when promising young officers leave the force because outdated personnel systems force untenable choices due simply to bureaucratic inflexibility, and internal, where military members with specific talents are mismatched to jobs that do not capitalize on their skills and billets that need them go unfilled. Kane's research in *Bleeding Talent* has helped inform a transformation in personnel policy across the Department of Defense, as policy leaders endeavor to shift from "personnel management" to "talent management" to retain and maximize the quality workforce they recruit.

In the intellectual space between Kane's recruitment and retention dynamics lie the policies for educating and developing future leaders of the defense policy enterprise. Daniel McCauley's article on developing twenty-first century strategic leaders explores the necessity to change the skillset (and hence education) of senior leaders and thinkers based on the rapidly evolving information space. As military operations enter the information age, uncertainty, task unfamiliarity, and disagreement are increasing. McCauley argues that leaders cannot be trained to respond to nonattributable cyber hacks nor taught how to build foreign bureaucracies; rather, they need mental agility and the critical thinking skills to act across functions, domains, and organizations and lead in the myriad unforeseen challenges inherent in the current and future battlespace.

Having discussed the evolutions and revolutions in the foundations of civil-military relations and the profession of arms, part II moves to chapter 7's treatment of the complicated and often unglamorous processes of defense policy. James Miller and Michael O'Hanlon begin with a snapshot of the trade-offs of contemporary defense spending. Acknowledging that US defense spending is huge—roughly three times that of China, the world's second largest military power—these experienced practitioners argue that it is still not enough to meet the variety and difficulty of the challenges of hegemony. Like all things budget related, their prescription is controversial: focus on quality over quantity and on modernization and readiness over force size and structure. They prioritize repairing the readiness gap that has grown after nearly two decades at war, then turning the focus to a force that can win in great-power competition. The challenge, they say, is to maintain a force that is "modernized for greater lethality, and made more resilient and survivable against the kinds of cyber, anti-satellite, and other asymmetric attacks future adversaries would be sure to employ." Doing so is no easy task even given today's high-dollar defense authorizations.

Keeping in the vein of defense spending, Sue Payton and Sally Baron address how these budgets are spent, charting the evolutions in defense acquisitions principles, policy, and process. The tools and platforms the defense establishment invests in are foundational to its ability to deter, fight, and win the nation's wars. Thus, the procurement process is the proverbial "sausage factory" for American security and success. Given the enormous growth of defense spending over the previous decades, the onus and urgency for meaningful acquisitions reform have increased commensurately. Beginning with a brief history on reform efforts dating from the landmark 1986 Packard Commission, the authors build a case that the defense acquisition process is fundamentally flawed, and suggest that "much has been done to study the problem, identify candidate solutions, and execute reforms, only to return to the conclusion that more reform is needed." Their hopes for meaningful reform short of organizational transformation are slim—a dismal prediction for such a crucial, if understudied, area of defense policy.

In echoes of Donnithorne's argument about service culture driving policy, Michael McInerney, Lin Conway, Brandon Smith, and Joseph Lupa, Jr., make their case for fundamental revisions in the logic of defense acquisitions. As much as the American armed forces have increasingly come to train, learn, operate, and fight as a single joint force, the authors suggest that basic incentives in the acquisitions process hamstring operational effectiveness. Services, as the force providers, drive decision-making on where, when, and in what to invest their precious defense dollars, and, in seeking the platforms and systems that reify their unique identities, they are often unresponsive to the needs of combatant commanders fighting today's conflicts. Their conclusion—to empower the chairman of the Joint Chiefs and secretary of defense—is controversial to say the least, but indicative of the problem-solving leaps policy-makers must consider in crafting policy for the twenty-first century.

Michael Gambone rounds out chapter 7 and the whole of part II with a discussion of the changing role of Guard and reserve forces. Tracing their origin from a Cold War hypothetical of sequential backfill for active duty units to the major changes wrought by the Global War on Terror, Gambone hones in on a profound transformation in defense policy: the shift from a strategic to an operational reserve force. Although the "total force" concept barely passed the stress test of two decades of war, it not only saved the all-volunteer force from resorting to a draft, but also catapulted itself (if temporarily) into budgetary and operational relevance on par with the active military component. More interestingly, it was this link to the traditional citizen-soldier that spurred numerous policy changes to better care for the career and family stability, deployment time, and mental health of both the active and reserve components.

In its entirety, part II leaves the reader with an impression that there is more revolution than evolution in the fundamental fabric of defense policy, process, and institutions. The demands on military structure, budgets, and identity levied by two decades of war, new technologies and strategies, and the rapidly changing battlespace have resulted in fundamental questions on issues once thought to be largely solved. New thinking on relationships, processes, personnel, equipment, defense spending and acquisitions, and culture and identity all seek to mitigate or solve the myriad challenges facing the American defense establishment. Perhaps Christopher Miller best articulates the task facing defense policy when he observes that "we must summon the will to think beyond war, boots, and bombs to understand and respond to the fundamentals of future consequential contests—small or large, visible or invisible—that *will* find us, whether or not we choose to find them."

Chapter 5

Evolution and Revolution in Civil-Military Relations

The Institutional Imbalance of American Statecraft

GORDON ADAMS

It is important . . . that the habits of thinking in a free country should inspire caution in those entrusted with its administration, to confine themselves within their respective constitutional spheres, avoiding in the exercise of the powers of one department to encroach upon another. The spirit of encroachment tends to consolidate the powers of all the departments in one, and thus to create, whatever the form of government, a real despotism.

—President George Washington,
Farewell Address, 1796

Over the past seventy years, the Defense Department and the military services have increasingly become "full service" institutions, with broad and deep involvement in strategic planning, diplomacy, public diplomacy, economic development and reconstruction, and many other areas of policy (Adams and Murray 2014). Today, DoD is simply larger, better financed, and has a much broader array of capabilities than the civilian foreign policy institutions, principally the State Department and USAID. The evolution of US strategic purposes in the Cold War, rooted in a military confrontation with the Soviet Union, played an important role in the emergence of a serious imbalance between the military and the civilian institutions of American statecraft. But the imbalance is not purely a result of the larger size and budgetary endowment of the Defense Department; it also grows out of cultural and institutional weaknesses and realities internal to the civilian foreign policy institutions.

This [essay] argues that the imbalance between the military and civilian institutions of American statecraft is the result of a combination of factors. One is the difference in sheer size and in the coherence of the two sets of institutions. A second is the measurable difference in the constituencies in the Congress, the economy, and American society that support the institutions and their missions. A third is the distinct differences in the organizational culture of the military and that of diplomacy and foreign assistance. A fourth is the difference between the two when it comes to planning capacity for strategy and resources. These multiple differences have in turn affected the way the two sets of institutions are dealt with in the White House and in the Congress.

There is little research focusing on this institutional imbalance and virtually no analytical writing on the evolution of the civilian institutions or the consequences of this trend for civilian foreign policy institutional evolution and capacity.[1] This is a critical research gap. Merely reassigning programs and authorities from one set of institutions to the other will fail, unless these deeper organizational and cultural differences are understood.

Institutional and Structural Size and Coherence

The disparity in size and institutional coherence between the military and civilian institutions is a significant source of the imbalance and the trend toward the militarization of American statecraft. At nearly $600 billion a year in fiscal year 2013, the defense budget is twelve times the size of the budget available to the civilian foreign policy institutions. The Defense Department work force is more than a hundred times as large as that of the State Department and USAID. DoD employs over 1.5 million active duty forces, another million in the Reserves and National Guard, and nearly 770,000 civilians, nearly 28 percent of the federal civil service (Office of Personnel Management 2012; US Department of Defense 2012b).[2] At 68,000, the Special Operations forces of the Pentagon are larger than the personnel of the civilian foreign policy agencies. The State Department, by contrast, employs roughly 19,000 Foreign Service officers and civil servants, while USAID's total employment is slightly over 2,000.[3] The Defense Department's overseas presence also dwarfs that of State/USAID. DoD has more than 660 overseas bases and permanent installations in 40 countries, while the State Department/USAID have 250 embassies, consulates, and missions spread across 196 countries (US Department of Defense 2012a). In 2008, for example, for every single USAID employee deployed overseas, there were 23 State Department employees, and 600 DoD military and civilian personnel (Adams et al. 2010).[4]

Gordon Adams, "The Institutional Imbalance of American Statecraft," in *Mission Creep: The Militarization of US Foreign Policy?* ed. Gordon Adams and Shoon Murray, chapter 2 (Washington, DC: Georgetown University Press, 2014), 22–46. Reprinted with permission; © Georgetown University Press, 2014.

In sheer size and capabilities, the US military not only dwarfs the civilian foreign policy institutions; it is exponentially more significantly endowed than the military forces of any other country, making it a powerful tool for US policy officials. It is the world's only truly global military force: it could, if needed, deploy to any country, fly in any airspace, sail to any port. It has the only global logistics, infrastructure, transportation, communications, and intelligence. Neither the civilian institutions, nor any other country, have equivalent capacity, resources, flexibility, or readiness.[5]

The capability "gap" alone is a critical source of the institutional imbalance. But it is reinforced by a significant difference in institutional coherence, one rarely mentioned in research and writing on foreign policy institutions. Despite decades of analysis of the divisions, differences, and conflicts among the military services and much scholarly and policy attention to the difficulties the secretary of defense has imposing central discipline on the defense bureaucracy, DoD has had significantly greater institutional unity and coherence than the civilian foreign policy institutions. Huntington's observation is astute: "a group which is structurally united possesses great advantages in dealing with a group which is structurally disunited" (Huntington 1957, 87).

This disparity in institutional coherence began in the 1940s and has grown over time. The secretary of defense and the Defense Department can think, plan, strategize and speak with a significantly more unified voice in national security policy deliberations than the civilian institutions. When the DoD was created, the military services retained considerable autonomy over resource and force planning and there was at best only a limited capacity in the Office of the Secretary to control strategic or resource planning across the services (Hitch 1965). Nonetheless all significant military capabilities were grouped under one institutional roof, an important first step, and the secretary could begin to play a role as the single voice on defense policy.

Faced with the reality that greater organizational unity was needed, the central authority of the secretary and the chairman of the Joint Chiefs of Staff was strengthened in 1958. The true revolution in central authority, however, was the arrival of Secretary of Defense Robert McNamara, whose reforms constituted a quantum leap in centralized management of the military services and the empowerment of his office. The Planning, Programming and Budgeting System (PPBS) McNamara created cemented a central role for the secretary in defense planning, budgeting, and management. It allowed the secretary greater access to and control over force and budget planning with respect to all military capabilities.[6] Today, for all the internal institutional politics of the Defense Department, the secretary is its most important voice and leader and the

chairman of the Joint Chiefs of Staff is the first among equals among the military service chiefs (Locher 2004).

By contrast, the secretary of state does not have the same broad authority over all the civilian institutions involved in US foreign policy. She does not have the capacity to carry out coherent strategic, program, or budgetary planning for all of the institutions that play a foreign policy role. Nor does she have substantive authority over all the nonmilitary ways in which the United States engages overseas: trade, finance, diplomacy, economic and security assistance, or exchanges. This is one of the most important and fundamental sources of the institutional imbalance between the military and civilian institutions. While the military instrument was being unified after World War II, US civilian engagement underwent an institutional "diaspora" that grew directly out of the way the civilian foreign policy institutions and programs evolved after World War II and reflects the institutional culture of the State Department itself.

Before World War II, US foreign relations had essentially two features: diplomacy toward other nations and US involvement in international trade and financial matters—missions that were already divided between the State Department and the Treasury Department.[7] However, the agenda of US global engagement broadened substantially after the war. The trade and financial missions expanded as the US emerged as the dominant global economy and new institutions like the International Monetary Fund (IMF), the International Bank for Reconstruction and Development, and the General Agreement on Tariffs and Trade were created, largely under American leadership. The responsibility for US involvement in the expanded set of international financial institutions, however, remained largely with the Treasury Department, while leadership in trade negotiations was removed from State in the 1960s and ultimately given to the White House when the Office of the US Trade Representative (USTR) was created in 1962.

Beyond finance and trade, other new missions became part of American foreign policy, including foreign economic assistance, security assistance, public diplomacy, and arms control negotiations. None of these missions had much precedent in US foreign operations and none had a clear institutional home. As each mission began to grow it was housed, fully or in part, in some other institution than the State Department, which did not assert strong claims for leadership in these areas of policy that had not been elements of traditional US diplomacy.

The institutional diaspora that occurred—with other or even new agencies being responsible for planning, budgeting, and implementing these missions—has been a major obstacle to the ability of the State Department to oversee and direct the civilian elements of overseas US engagement, and an important source of State's declining role relative to DoD. The patchwork quilt of departments and agencies has weakened the coherence of US foreign relations, sapped the secretary of state's influence in interagency discussions, and hamstrung the secretary's ability to make a coherent, strategic case for foreign affairs budgets to the Congress.

State has always been the home of the elite Foreign Service, whose members represent the United States, negotiate on its behalf, report back to Washington, DC, and advise the president on foreign policy matters. Rather than expand the State Department's mission to accommodate the growing agenda of US statecraft, the Foreign Service resisted this evolution, reflecting cultural characteristics discussed below.[8]

In the realm of economic assistance, the Marshall Plan (European Recovery Program) was the first such decision. Although it was designed at the State Department, it was soon lodged in an independent institutional home as the Economic Cooperation Administration.[9] Over time, responsibility for US international economic engagement was distributed to several institutions, each with its own agenda, budget, and relationship with the Congress. The Export-Import Bank, supporting the financing of US exports, remained an independent agency. The US Agency for International Development, created in 1961, was intentionally separated from State, so as to focus on long-term development and be (ostensibly) free of direct ties to near-term US policy objectives. The Peace Corps was created in 1961, similarly free of a formal connection to US foreign policy goals as shaped at State.

The Treasury Department's role in such assistance also expanded over the years. To its IMF and World Bank responsibilities, it has added budgetary and planning control over the US role in the regional development banks (the Inter-American, African, Asian Development Banks and Funds, and the European Bank for Reconstruction and Development). Treasury was also given responsibility for US debt forgiveness to low-income countries (HIPC, for Heavily Indebted Poor Countries) and directly administers its own technical assistance program providing advice on financial and budgetary practices to developing countries and the former Soviet Union.

This diaspora of foreign economic assistance programs has continued to the present day. President George W. Bush created two innovative foreign assistance programs: the Millennium Challenge Corporation (MCC) and the President's Emergency Program for AIDS Relief (PEPFAR). The former was established as a separate institution by statute, while the latter was located at the State Department, but is headed by a coordinator who has substantial budgetary and planning autonomy, including the coordination of HIV/AIDS programs in other federal agencies.[10]

With regard to economic assistance programs, State has direct responsibility and control over Economic Support Funds (ESF) and economic assistance to Central Europe and the former Soviet Union countries. ESF, a roughly $5 billion program, provides economic assistance closely linked to US foreign policy objectives and only secondarily to development objectives. State, however, lacks the internal capacity to implement programs with economic goals, which is not a core competence of the Foreign Service. Hence, to add to the institutional complexity, State has the policy lead over ESF decisions with respect to countries and overall funding levels, but implementation is largely the responsibility of USAID.

The management of security assistance programs is even more complex.[11] State has direct authority over budgets and country selection for the traditional security assistance portfolio, namely Foreign Military Financing (FMF), Foreign Military Sales (FMS), and International Military Education and Training (IMET).

However, lacking military expertise and appropriate personnel, State shares responsibility for the development of security assistance programs with the combatant commands and the military services, while implementation is the responsibility of a DoD agency—the Defense Security Cooperation Agency (DSCA)—and the military services. In addition, as noted below, DoD has also developed its own direct portfolio of security cooperation programs.

Authority over US public diplomacy (exchange programs, overseas cultural centers, and international broadcasting) has also been dispersed over the years. Some public diplomacy programs and activities (such as exchanges) have been inside State, then outside, then back inside. From 1953 to 1999, the United States Information Agency (USIA) had responsibility for public diplomacy including the Voice of America. In 1999, it was absorbed into the State Department in a reversal of the diaspora trend. However, at the same time, international broadcasting operations (largely the Voice of America) were spun off from USIA and merged into yet another independent agency—the Broadcasting Board of Governors—whose responsibilities now also include funding and oversight of surrogate broadcasting (see Carlson 2014).[12]

As noted, the Defense Department itself has been part of this foreign policy diaspora. Its global deployments and operations overlap substantially with State Department and even USAID operations, including such missions as development assistance, governance advice, diplomacy, and public diplomacy. Nor is DoD the only federal agency with an expanding international agenda and presence. As the array of issues on the US foreign policy agenda has grown, most of the other federal agencies have created international programs and operate out of US embassies abroad. This trend has included a sizable contingent from the Department of Justice and FBI dealing with international crime and terrorism, growing activity by the Department of Health and Human Services and the Centers for Disease Control and Prevention, and an expanding overseas presence from the Department of Homeland Security.[13]

The secretary of state has no authoritative oversight responsibility or internal capacity to coordinate this broad inventory of international funding, programs, and policies among the civilian agencies. In 2005, a State Department office to coordinate budget planning for foreign assistance programs was created. It has authority only over State and USAID programs, and even that relationship is an uneasy one (Adams and Williams 2010, 32–65).

The reality of this institutional diaspora makes it virtually impossible for the secretary of state to provide the same kind of strategic direction to US civilian engagement, build integrated programs, or manage budgetary trade-offs among agencies and policy priorities the secretary of defense can provide at DoD. She cannot coordinate these instruments and programs abroad, deploy or redeploy capabilities, or respond quickly to crisis and opportunity. While diplomats suggest that coordination works better in the field than it does in Washington, making integration work in the field depends greatly on the ability of the ambassador to coordinate at the mission level (Marks 2014). This ability is not routinely found in every embassy, nor has such coordination been successfully transplanted back to Washington, DC. Over time, this has led to a weakening of the civilian side of the institutional balance with DoD.

This institutional weakness is exacerbated by internal structural realities at State that make coordination of policy and programs even more challenging. The regional bureaus are at the apex of the department, in terms of prestige, influence, and institutional authority, but uneven structural changes over decades have left the department somewhat fractured internally. Functional bureaus and offices, intended to deal with policy and program issues that cut across regions, are undervalued in an institution driven by regional and country bureaus and offices. The leadership role played at State by the Foreign Service has led to an undervaluing of the department's sizable civil service staff, who are frequently the actual managers of State Department programs. Repeated efforts to reform the human resources and structural challenges inside State have generally fallen short of changing this reality. These internal challenges further weakened the capacity of the State Department to balance the capabilities of DoD.[14]

Constituencies

The budgets and capabilities of US government organizations are substantially strengthened by their linkages within American society, its economy, and its political culture. The network that exists between an agency and the society, economy, and politics of the country can create a constituency that reinforces the agency's mission and capabilities. The linkages can be both direct, between the agency and its stakeholders, and indirect, through the Congress. The differences between the military and civilian institutions along this dimension are one of the most significant sources of the institutional imbalance and mission creep at DoD. The military and civilian agencies are at opposite extremes with respect to their domestic networks and constituency inside the United States.[15]

The Defense Department and the military services have a significant domestic presence, providing an ample local, regional, and congressional constituency, which the civilian foreign policy agencies do not have.[16] The Department of Defense, its contractors, and its supporters in the Congress are not reluctant to mobilize this national constituency on behalf of their needs.[17] As noted, employment in the Defense Department is a large proportion of total US government employment. In addition, there are over a million National Guard and military reservists, more than 2 million military retirees (plus their spouses and dependents), and over 20 million military veterans.

This directly employed and retiree population is based at more than 2,500 defense installations—bases, offices, depots, and headquarters—scattered across the country, with some kind of economic impact in every location. While the number of defense installations has shrunk since the mid-1980s, as the military has shrunk and bases have been closed, the military presence is notable in Alabama, Alaska, Arizona, California, Hawaii, Missouri, New Jersey, Texas, and Virginia, in particular. Moreover, this same constituency is organized into active-duty, veterans, and retiree organizations with strong grass roots and a presence in Washington such as the Military Officers Association of America, the Reserve Officers Association, the National Guard Association, the Navy League, the Association of the US Army, and the Air Force Association.

Contracting is another vehicle for constituency development. Over time, the impact of defense spending on US economic activity has declined, with the share of defense spending in the gross domestic product falling from an average of 9.4 percent in the 1950s to 3.8 percent in the first decade of the 21st Century.[18] Nevertheless, defense funds that buy weapons, other products, and services constitute more than 40 percent of the defense budget in any given year, a market of more than $300 billion. DoD buys 75 percent of all goods and services purchased by the federal government. While the prime contracting firms doing business with DoD have become more geographically concentrated, the local economic impact of these firms can be significant.[19] Dollars for prime contracts continue to flow into the economies of such states as California,

Virginia, Texas, Maryland, and Connecticut, among others.[20] Moreover, this economic impact expands as the prime contractors subcontract work out to the thousands of technology and parts suppliers and vendors supplying metal parts, materials, wiring, electronics, communications, information, and other gear and services, reaching widely into the broader economy.

This broad constituency for DoD and the military is actively engaged in the business and politics of defense budgets and policy.[21] Contractors mobilize local work forces and communities and encourage them to engage in direct grassroots lobbying aimed at the appropriate members of Congress. The industrial community serving the defense market is also organized into national-level organizations such as the Aerospace Industries Association, the Electronics Industries Association, and the National Defense Industrial Association.

When it comes to constituency development there could hardly be a more striking contrast than with the civilian foreign policy agencies. Few of the civilian foreign policy institutions have as direct a penetration into American society and the economy. The much smaller federal employment base of these institutions is largely concentrated in the Washington, DC, area (roughly 13,000 State Department employees, for example) or deployed overseas. Aside from a finance center in South Carolina and twenty-five passport offices in major cities, State Department and USAID installations are not scattered widely across the country.

The local and national constituency for diplomacy outside of Washington, DC, is relatively small, concentrated in groups and national organizations with an interest in foreign affairs: World Affairs Councils, the Chicago Council on Global Affairs, the Pacific Council on International Policy, the Council on Foreign Relations in New York, for example. There are few "trade associations" linked to diplomacy, the most prominent being the relatively new (1995) US Global Leadership Campaign, founded with the explicit purpose of supporting the budget for all civilian foreign policy agencies, whose members include corporations, as well as retired military officers and diplomats and former senior policy officials.

USAID and the other foreign economic assistance organizations have their own constituency, albeit a small one. The bulk of foreign economic assistance dollars are spent in the United States, buying goods and services and paying consultants and contractors. The funding is small, however, less than a tenth of what DoD spends annually, with a relatively small footprint in the American economy. The bulk of development assistance consultants and contractors, for example, are in the Washington, DC, area or overseas. These firms, and the nongovernmental organizations that support foreign assistance, are smaller and less geographically dispersed than DoD contractors. There are several national-level organizations based in Washington, DC, supporting USAID, principally Interaction (1984), a coalition of 165 American and international nonprofits, consulting groups, and nongovernmental organizations, many with grassroots membership, who support the agency and advocate for foreign assistance dollars. These organizations have generally supported the autonomy of USAID and the other foreign assistance agencies, which reinforces the institutional diaspora of the civilian institutions.

The same can be said for the foreign policy agencies responsible for trade, investment, and financial programs and policies. This constituency is more elite than grassroots, but includes, for example, the major exporting companies in energy and commercial aircraft; foreign investors in technology, hotels, and tourism; and oil and engineering infrastructure firms that use and support the funding for the Export-Import Bank, Overseas Private Investment Corporation, and Trade and Development Agency. Exporting firms support an open trade policy and trade negotiations, and are also organized into such associations as the National Foreign Trade Council (1914) with three hundred corporate members. While these businesses clearly constitute a constituency for overseas engagement, their work also reinforces the institutional diaspora on the civilian side of the government.

In sum, defense programs, budgets, and policies have a substantial constituency inside the United States, consistent with the size and geographic dispersal of the defense institutions, bases, and DoD's contractors. The civilian foreign policy and foreign assistance agencies do not have the same domestic constituency, making it more difficult to win public and congressional support for institutional needs and foreign policy programs.

Organizational Culture

Institutional resources, coherence, and constituency are major sources of the institutional imbalance. Differences in organizational culture, which are rarely included in research on foreign policy institutions, also play an important role.[22] Institutional culture means their different values, customs and operating norms, and the behavioral consequences of the training and operational experience they provide for their employees.[23] There are important differences between the military and civilian institutional cultures, particularly DoD and the State Department, that make an important contribution to the institutional balance, the way the agencies participate in the interagency policy process, and the militarization of statecraft. One analyst of the cultural differences put it this way:

These two cultures are as alien as life forms from two competing planets, the warrior from Mars and the diplomats from Venus. Similar in many respects—professionalism, dedication and competence—Martians and Venutians often have an antagonistic relationship. They are generally polar opposites in character, in approach to problem solving, and in worldview. (Rife 1998, 3)[24]

The uniformed military is at the center of the DoD culture. While generalizations are risky, the culture of the military services and the military personnel system value hierarchy, discipline, and organization. As Colonel Rife described it, the military culture values "competence, efficiency, achievement . . . [people who are] mission/task oriented . . . 'give me a mission and get out of my way' types."[25]

The military system rewards personnel who are organized and disciplined, and prepared to range across multiple tasks. Military training focuses on strategy, warfighting skills, and technical know-how. At the outset, there is relatively little attention to a specific country or region where combat might take place. The core military skill is prevailing over adversaries, at sea, in the air, or on land. The military career process assigns its officers across a broad variety of job categories, including combat command, program management, resource planning, policy-making, even relations on Capitol Hill, valuing the experience obtained in each assignment. It provides systematic, career-long training opportunities. A career military officer might rise through onboard posts in the Navy, company-regiment-battalion responsibilities in the Army, or air wing positions in the Air Force, followed by a base management slot or a program acquisition position, as they move up the promotion ladder. Senior officers might be detailed to defense strategy and policy offices, the Joint Staff, and such external responsibilities as the National Security Council, or to the office of a member of Congress.

As a result, in the senior military ranks, one finds officers with this combination of experiences. They might have worn both uniforms and civilian dress, know how the equipment works, understand the planning and budget processes, what their counterparts in the other services and the Pentagon civilians do, and how the senior appointed officials and members of Congress do their jobs. They arrive at the senior level with a sense of discipline and hierarchy and a "can do" attitude. Once a decision is made on doctrine, programs, policies, or budgets, military members and the military system are organized, responsive, and ready to execute.

In addition, the Department of Defense is organized to execute across a wide spectrum of activities. Its 2.2 million military and civilian personnel function as a virtual government, with functions ranging across the entire spectrum of public sector activities, from program management, to strategic planning, to administration, to finance and accounting, to field and hospital medicine, to education and training, to basic and applied research. For almost every aspect of governmental responsibility and many functions in society, there is likely to be an equivalent somewhere in DoD.

The diplomatic culture at the State Department is a sharp contrast. To cite, again, the perceptive analysis by Colonel Rife, the diplomatic community, whose core culture is that of the Foreign Service, is from Venus. The diplomatic culture values competence, intellectual ability, and individual achievement; they "believe in intuition and psychology. Planning is not a core value to most Venutians. . . . They prefer a more fluid approach that is event driven" (Rife 1998, 7). Diplomats are more "feeling" than "thinking" oriented. They see the world in terms of "endless possibilities," and prefer to keep decisions open to evolve with events (Rife 1998, 11). Rife quotes Ambassador Robert Beecroft, summing it up: "The military wants a roadmap before they start the journey, the foreign service officer gets in the car, starts driving, and then says, 'OK—who has the compass?'" (Rife 1998, 13). There is no judgment implied here; the cultures are simply different. But in response to the challenges of the first decade of the 21st century, this difference has been important in the way the military and civilian institutions respond. They also make a difference in the way in which the two sets of institutions have developed internally.

While similarly hierarchical in structure, the Foreign Service culture emphasizes skills in negotiation, political analysis, and report writing in comparatively narrow stovepipes of responsibility. The culture and training tend not to include skills in program management, strategic planning, or administration.[26] Organizationally, these latter functions are largely carried out by State Department civil servants. Training programs for the Foreign Service focus on culture and language, reporting and negotiation, and policy analysis. Training of this kind takes place only at the start of a career or with a change in country, with little or no further training opportunities or requirements as a Foreign Service career develops.[27] Career paths take place along fairly circumscribed stovepipes, usually called "cones"—management, consular, political, economic, and public diplomacy. The political cone has the most prestige, taking a career Foreign Service Officer overseas with regularity, an ambassadorship being the ultimate rank. Career paths based solely in the United States are less valued, as are interagency assignments (to USAID, for example), management, and strategic and resource planning. Such assignments are unlikely to be career enhancing.[28]

Foreign Service Officers who are part of USAID have greater management responsibilities, but their professional orientation is largely external to the United States. They, and the other civilian foreign assistance professionals, receive greater management training, as they are directly involved in shaping and implementing assistance programs overseas or are overseeing private contractors, who are implementing programs. Training and mobility in the foreign assistance culture, however, focus on activities in countries and regions outside the United States, and on the technical dimensions of economic assistance—agriculture, water supply, education, humanitarian aid, economic planning, or governance. International knowledge—of other governments and international organizations—takes precedence in career advancement over an understanding of domestic policy-making, budgeting, or US political processes. And as with the traditional diplomatic corps, foreign assistance career paths are oriented toward overseas missions.

The diaspora of foreign assistance agencies away from State is reinforced by another cultural feature of the development community. The dominant value of "economic development" is powerful, leading to a resistance to linking development work with other foreign policy and national security strategy goals being pursued by the State Department. Development professionals are often wary of the link between their work and the broader foreign policy goals of the United States. Development, itself, separate from other strategic goals, is viewed as a long-term US interest, rather than focusing on assistance to countries of strategic importance in the pursuit of more immediate political or security needs.[29] This aspect of foreign assistance culture can make it difficult to persuade policy officials at State, the White House, or Congress that foreign assistance investments pay appreciable dividends for US national security. It tends to sideline development professionals in the policy process, and poses problems for obtaining foreign assistance funding.

These marked differences in personnel and in organizational culture have real consequences for the balance between the military and civilian institutions. Senior-level policy-makers tend to see the military institutions as organized, disciplined, and capable of taking on a task they will perform efficiently and effectively. In the interagency process, diplomatic institutions are seen as important for negotiating and advising policy, but not for planning and management, or program delivery. Inside the State Department, planning and management are not a central value, reinforcing this disparity in the way the institutions are viewed. As Derek Reveron has put it:

> Military leaders typically command more attention than civilian leaders do, and they see themselves as policy actors. . . . In addition to influence, military leaders also command more capabilities than leaders from other government departments and are consistently viewed by presidential administrations as capable of "getting the job done." (Reveron 2010, 42)

Strategic and Budgetary Planning

The cultural difference between the military and civilian institutions is apparent when it comes to strategic thinking, planning, and budgeting. Here, the culture of the State Department contributes noticeably to the imbalance in the department's impact on national security policy-making and implementation. As noted above, the Department of Defense gained considerable institutional coherence with the introduction of the Planning, Programming, and Budgeting System (PPBS) in the 1960s.[30] Although the PPBS system was initially resisted by the services, in reality it fit well within a culture where combat and campaign planning was already the norm.[31] The addition in the early 1990s of a statutory requirement for a quadrennial review of strategy was not a stretch for an institution already steeped in planning culture.[32]

Strategic thinking and planning for forces and resources became a norm for the military and the Defense Department during the Cold War. The adversary was clearly defined and his military capabilities known. The objective was military "containment" of the Soviet Union, with a force that could deter, defend, and prevail if conflict occurred. However overstated that threat might be, the technological and military requirements could be defined. The first and most significant PPBS exercise was to shape and project US strategic nuclear forces, across services, in response to a defined requirement (Gordon, McNichol, and Jack 2009).

The strategy and planning exercise for the military and DoD necessarily focused on the long term: deterrence and containment were long-term strategic goals and recruiting, training, and equipping the force—DoD "outputs"—took much longer than one or two years to deliver.[33] While the effectiveness of PPBS has been debated (and it was eroded by the decision to plan funding for the wars in Iraq and Afghanistan outside the PPBS process), the basic DoD commitment to a multiyear, structured planning process and culture remains largely intact.[34] Even if predictions turn out to be wrong, the simple act of forecasting forces the military to focus on the relationship between means and ends over time.

Moreover, despite the criticisms of DoD management (especially financial management), the outputs and even many of the outcomes of military planning can largely be measured.[35] DoD can measure the forces, equipment, and training funded by the defense budget. Force size and organization, equipment acquired, training provided, sailing, flying, driving days and hours, and readiness can all be quantified. The cost, quantity, and performance of equipment can be evaluated, and become a subject of frequent political argument as a result. Even the outcome of military operations can be observed and, to some degree, measured, as well as disputed.[36]

The unique strategic and resource planning process at DoD gives defense plans an unusual degree of transparency, clarity, and consistency, and facilitates the justification of these plans, and the budgets that support them, to OMB and the Congress. It provides major political "heft" to the defense budget request that the civilian foreign policy agencies lack.[37] They do not have an equivalent planning culture or process. The requirement for an overall report from the White House on national security strategy is relatively recent (1986).[38] There is no statutory requirement for a State Department strategic plan equivalent to the QDR.[39] In 2009, for the first time, Secretary of State Hillary Clinton undertook a top-down strategic planning process, the Quadrennial Diplomacy and Development Review (QDDR), modeled after the Defense Department's QDR, covering both State and USAID. This first effort was not the same as the QDR or linked to a PPBS-type process, however. The secretary provided no strategic guidance at the start of the QDDR and the focus of the effort was on "capabilities," not foreign policy goals. The QDDR process was ad hoc, not institutionalized in the two agencies. And the outcome was some restructuring of processes and offices at State and USAID, but not a set of planning guidelines that might influence resource planning in either agency.

Strategic and resource planning at State has been an institutional challenge for decades. The output of diplomacy does not lend itself to the same kind of measurement as the outputs of the Defense Department. International events and diplomatic relations are notoriously difficult to forecast. The secretary's span of control over other civilian foreign affairs agencies is limited. The Foreign Service culture has not encouraged training in strategic planning, program management, or budgeting. Budgets in the foreign policy world are, as a result, planned year by year, not over a longer term.

Until 2005, the department did not have a formal budget office or process at the level of the secretary of state. Budgets for State Department personnel and administration were prepared by the under secretary of state for management, while foreign assistance budgets were prepared separately by relevant regional and functional bureaus. There was no review process at State for the budgets of other foreign affairs agencies. In 2005, building on a small staff for the secretary,

Condoleezza Rice created the position of director of foreign assistance (known as "F") to coordinate budget planning for foreign assistance programs. While F is clearly a step toward a more institutionalized planning process, its authority and range of coverage are limited. F does not have statutory standing; it oversees foreign assistance programs, but not State Department operations and management; and it has responsibility only for State and USAID programs, not those of other agencies involved in foreign assistance.[40]

Measuring the outputs and outcomes of civilian foreign policy is also uneven and more difficult than for the military. Some outputs can be measured—diplomats trained, dollars provided for particular countries. Some diplomacy output measures would be trivial; the number of demarches, cables, and diplomatic facilities tells us little about the success or failure of statecraft. Even significant outputs—treaties, for example—take years to negotiate and the outcome of those treaties may take even longer to observe, often in non-events, such as the nonproliferation of nuclear weapons.

Much of the outcome of diplomacy is difficult to measure or is disputed: maintenance of good relations, promotion of national interests, effectiveness and longevity of international organizations. Does the apparent failure of economic assistance over decades to Egypt constitute a negative performance outcome or is it a consequence of events over which the United States has no control? Is a decade of peace with Israel the appropriate performance measurement for the assistance program to Egypt? Does the deferral of the North Korean nuclear program as a result of the 1994 Agreed Framework constitute success, or did the North Koreans simply end-run the terms of the agreement, thereby making it a performance failure? Was negotiating the Kyoto Protocol on climate change a success, while deferring its ratification by the Senate a failure? The goals of diplomacy are often so broad—democracy and economic freedom in the Muslim world, or strengthened alliances and partnerships—that the outcome is difficult to measure, especially in the near term. Moreover, because many other countries and international organizations, as well as international events, will affect these goals and events, it is often difficult to draw causal links between US diplomatic activity and the outcomes.

Outputs are more numerically measurable with respect to foreign economic assistance—dollars spent, wells drilled, schools and health clinics built. Outcomes—development itself—are also measurable, but establishing a link with bilateral US assistance programs is often problematic, making it challenging to justify the funding to the Congress. US foreign assistance agencies regularly cite success stories. But was South Korea's economic growth the result of US aid, or of decades of foreign investment and internal savings? Is the slow development of African economies due to assistance failures or a more complex mixture of internal culture, health, infrastructure, education, commodity prices, debt, and weak or corrupt governance?

The civilian foreign policy agencies are still a long way from having the strategic and resource planning processes available to the Defense Department. The civilian agencies' planning processes are poorly institutionalized, their strategic and resource planning staffs are small, and they lack coherence as a group of institutions. Outputs and outcomes are more intractable. As a result, defense agencies can prepare, present, and defend an apparently more credible, long-term strategy and plan and display results more persuasively than the civilian institutions. This reality exacerbates the funding gap and incentivizes policy-makers to call on the military institutions to execute additional missions, and thus advance the process of militarizing US foreign policy.

The Impact of the Imbalance on the White House and Congress

The imbalance between DoD and the civilian foreign policy institutions clearly has an impact on how the two sets of institutions are dealt with in the White House, both in crisis and in longer-term planning. DoD and the military bring to the table significant assets: an institutional capacity to act quickly, a constituency of public support, a "can-do" operational culture, long-term strategic and planning capabilities, and the capacity to measure and demonstrate results. The civilian foreign policy institutions are hampered by fewer resources, internal and interagency coordination challenges, a small public constituency, a culture of negotiation, deliberation, and deferral, a much smaller operational capability, an absence of strategic planning, and difficulty demonstrating results.

While both sets of institutions and cultures have value in the policy process, the White House generally likes to act quickly and with impact. Some secretaries of state, such as Henry Kissinger, command personal influence that can outweigh the institutional imbalance.[41] But the ability to deliver plays an important role in shaping how a national security issue is defined and which agency is asked to execute policy.

The White House offices are also organized in a way that both recognizes and perpetuates DoD's influence. The National Security Council is organized with a specific office dedicated to defense issues, but more than one for the diplomatic, regional, and assistance issues. Functional offices at the NSC operate on an interagency basis, with both DoD and State participating. At the NSC Principals Committee meetings, there are two military participants—the Office of the Secretary of Defense and the Joint Chiefs of Staff. The secretary of state participates, but a representative from USAID is not usually at the table, unless specifically invited.[42]

On the resource side, the White House Office of Management and Budget is deeply involved in the DoD planning process, well before the defense budget arrives at the White House, through a process known as the "joint review." This process, which is unique to DoD, permits OMB budget examiners to meet with military service budget offices as they prepare the initial stage of the PPBS process—programming—in the preparation of the services' Program Objective Memorandums (POMs). Once the services have reported their POMs to the secretary of defense, OMB participates directly in the DoD meetings that prepare the program and budget decisions at the Pentagon. OMB also conducts its own internal review of DoD budget issues, so that by the time DoD transmits its budget numbers formally to OMB, there are no surprises for the White House, and the few remaining issues can be resolved at a senior, even presidential level.

OMB does not conduct a joint review with State/USAID or the other civilian foreign policy agencies, although it may be invited to some of the hearings State's Office of the Director of Foreign Assistance (F) conducts to review its budgets. OMB is the only executive branch organization where the budgets of all of the foreign affairs agencies come together, but it provides minimal strategic or program integration of those requests.[43]

The consequence of this disparity in capabilities and treatment is that the views, preferences, and operational capabilities of the military weigh heavily in the White House decision-making process. The Defense Department can deliver capability; the State Department faces a greater challenge.

The civilian/military institutional imbalance is reflected in the Congress, as well. The authorizing committees for the two sets of institutions are strikingly different in composition and impact in the congressional process (Cushman 2014).[44] The Armed Services Committees in the two chambers legislate authorities and programs for the Defense Department every year, hold high-visibility hearings, and over the years have played a significant role in legislating what scholars call "structural" provisions with respect to the defense institutions.[45] In particular, these committees legislate the authorities that have expanded the military's role into missions beyond deterrence and combat.[46]

In contrast, the House and Senate Foreign Affairs/Relations committees, while prestigious, have significantly less legislative impact. On the foreign assistance side, in particular, while the committees have been able to pass legislation authorizing specific new foreign assistance programs, such as the Support for East European Democracy (SEED) and the Freedom Support Act (FSA, for the former Soviet Union states), the foreign relations authorizers have not passed a bill authorizing US foreign assistance programs overall since 1986, leaving it to the Appropriations Committees to waive the need for authorization to provide appropriated funds.[47]

As for its treatment of budgets, the congressional process tends to fund the military budget request fully while diplomatic and foreign assistance budget requests are often a residual category in the budget process. The congressional budget committees set ceilings for budget "functions." The "function" for national defense consists largely of the Department of Defense (plus nuclear weapons programs at the Department of Energy), while the International Affairs function covers the many budgets in the foreign policy institutional diaspora. From 1990 to 2002, when overall discretionary spending was limited by statutory caps, there were also subcaps (1991–93 and again for 1996–99) that provided a specific funding level for "national defense." "International affairs" funds, on the other hand, were included in the overall cap for "non-defense discretionary" spending. This disparity of treatment meant that defense would generally be fully funded, while international affairs funds had to be weighed against the budget requests for domestic agencies. Given the weak constituency for foreign affairs, the Budget Committee has typically reduced international affairs funds below the administration's budget request, using the excess funds to support domestic programs, at little political cost to legislators.

Once the Budget Committee has set the overall funding ceilings, the budgets for the two sets of agencies arrive at the Appropriations Committee, where DoD also fares better than the civilian agencies. Allocations by the Appropriations Committee chair to the appropriations subcommittees generally provide full funding for defense, while the allocations for international affairs are frequently below the requested level, even below the level set in the Budget Committee. Both DoD and the foreign affairs agencies have dedicated appropriations subcommittees.[48] The impact of the ample constituency for defense is seen in the appropriations process, through "earmarks" and member requests for programs with local impacts. Civilian foreign policy agencies do not have comparable constituency support. Reinforced by the general congressional skepticism about State Department and USAID planning and management capabilities, diplomacy and foreign assistance programs have never been popular in Congress.

The civil/military institutional imbalance in the executive branch is reflected and sometimes magnified in the Congress. The military organization, with plans, heft, and coherence, and a large budget request with a significant domestic constituency, stands in sharp contrast to a dispersed set of agencies with less funding and the absence of a domestic constituency.

Conclusion

Over time, the Defense Department and the military services have been asked to develop the capability to provide a growing number of missions and functions that are not core to military combat or deterrence. This has led to a growing imbalance in the resources and capabilities of the major institutions of American statecraft. As this [essay] demonstrates, this imbalance and the reliance on the military is not a new trend, nor is it solely the result of a national security strategy that focused on a military confrontation with the Soviet Union or the unintended consequences of the decision to invade Iraq. This [essay] argues that the trend has its origins in the way the institutions of American statecraft have developed, their size, coherence, constituencies, and culture. History plays an important role. The Cold War clearly emphasized the capabilities of the Defense Department and incentivized its growth. But DoD and the services also benefited from the reality that they became a large, institutionalized presence inside the United States, creating a strong constituency for their programs and budgets. History also played a role in the evolving weaknesses of the civilian institutions, especially a series of decisions that dispersed responsibility for civilian foreign policy across a variety of agencies and programs the State Department does not coordinate or plan.

Culture has also played a significant role in the imbalance and the militarization process. The military provides a focused, planned, coordinated, "can-do" opportunity to the White House. The State Department culture is slower and less operationally driven. The impact of this difference was strikingly apparent in the invasions and occupations of Iraq and Afghanistan (see Reveron 2014). State and USAID were both blocked from the task, and slow to rise to the challenge, leaving the responsibility with the military.

It is not obvious how this trend might be reversed. The weaknesses of the State Department and USAID can become a self-fulfilling prophecy; each slow response, lack of capacity or resources, or absence of a long-term plan further reinforces the sense policymakers have that the civilian institutions are not capable of providing the strategic leadership and operational capabilities they require. This, in turn, reinforces the policy-makers' tendency to call upon DoD for rapid response and planning, exacerbating the disparity in resources and capabilities. Removing these capabilities from DoD and returning them or grafting them on to the State Department, without cultural and institutional changes at State, runs the risk of failure.

However, not examining and correcting this imbalance poses serious risks for the long-term success of American statecraft.

NOTES

1. Glain (2011) deals largely with the strategic perspectives of senior policymakers. Reveron (2010) focuses on security cooperation policies and programs, but not on the institutional trends in depth. Priest (2003) deals with the diplomatic activities of regional commanders, but not the broader institutional relationships.

2. In addition, DoD contracting for services, alone, employed the equivalent of 767,000 workers as of 2009 (Government Accountability Office 2011, 13).

3. The State Department also employs over 30,000 non-Americans overseas, known as "Foreign Service Nationals." There are no data available on DoD employment of non-Americans overseas or on the number of State/USAID services contracting personnel, though that is likely to be small.

4. The military/civilian number would be 356, if one subtracted active-duty personnel then in Iraq, Afghanistan, and counterterror operations. All figures derived from the US Office of Personnel Management, with the exception of military personnel taken from DoD's Statistical Information Analysis Division, available at siadapp.dmdc.osd.mil/personnel/MILITARY/miltop.htm. Reveron (2010, 4, 87) notes that the Combatant Command for Africa, AFRICOM, has 1,200 people on its staff; the State Department's Africa Bureau has 80; the military has 2,000 people deployed in East Africa; State/USAID have only a few hundred. And, he notes, the Navy has more construction personnel than the entire Foreign Service. Owens underlines the impact of this disparity: "Unfortunately, the power of a theater combatant commander, which exceeds that of just about every civilian in government except the president and secretary of defense, makes it tempting for him to go beyond implementing policy to presuming to make it" (Owens 2011, 74).

5. As Owens puts it: "Of course, when it comes to the influence of the military, the fact is that the size, budget, available manpower, and attitude of the American defense establishment enable the military to take on challenges that are not within the capacity of other government agencies" (Owens 2011, 79).

6. On the origins and development of the PPBS system, see Enthoven and Smith (2005), Hitch (1965), and Gordon, Mc-Nichol, and Jack (2009).

7. In addition to these major functions, trade policy responsibility was scattered between Treasury and Commerce, while the Export-Import Bank for trade promotion was created in 1934 largely to ensure that US exports to the Soviet Union would be guaranteed.

8. Much of the following discussion is drawn from Adams and Williams (2010, 8–92).

9. Economist Tom Schelling described this decision as "a Congressional vote of 'no confidence' in the executive talents of the State Department" (Schelling 1968, 7).

10. Suggestive of the dilemmas created by the "diaspora," USAID implements the MCC "threshold" country agreements, but not its larger "compacts," and also implements a number of global health programs, beyond those it executes for PEPFAR.

11. This and the later discussion of security assistance programs draw substantially on Adams and Williams (2011) and Serafino (2011).

12. Surrogate radios provide news-like services prepared by nationals of the serviced countries, such as Radio Free Europe/Radio Liberty, Radio Sawa, Radio Free Asia, and Radio and Television Marti.

13. For an early inventory of the international efforts of other federal agencies, see US Senate (1998).

14. There have been a number of reform studies focusing on the State Department. The most recent include Stimson Center/American Academy of Diplomacy (2008), Advisory Committee on Transformational Diplomacy (2008), and the HELP Commission (2007). For incisive discussions of the department's internal issues, see Rubin (1985) and Schake (2012).

15. This is an important, if commonly underestimated, source of the difference in civil-military relations when the US is compared with other countries, most of which have parliamentary systems of government, with substantially more disciplined legislative bodies. A disciplined party majority translated into government can provide considerable autonomy for defense and foreign policy decisions in a country like the United Kingdom, compared with the more dispersed political authority characteristic of the American system.

16. The terms frequently used to describe this relationship—"military industrial complex," or "iron triangle"—capture some of the essence of the relationship, though they may ascribe more effective control over policy and resources at all times than is the case.

17. There is substantial literature on the politics of defense lobbying, going back to the well-known Eisenhower farewell address, warning of the consequences of this relationship. See Adams (1981), among many such studies. William Olson (2012) notes: "Power in Washington is a function of manpower and money. . . . DOD has developed into the largest lobbying organization in the country, working Congress and the Executive Branch not so much with finesse as with sheer weight of numbers." For a discussion of the role of constituencies in national security budget decision making, see Adams and Williams (2010, 221–44).

18. "National Defense" (budget function 050) as a proportion of US GDP, from US Department of Defense (2012b Table 7, 264–66).

19. Major prime contractors like Boeing continue to be important employers in St. Louis, Missouri; Long Beach, California (both former McDonnell Douglas facilities); and Seattle, Washington. Lockheed Martin is economically important to Georgia and Texas, while General Dynamics is significant to the local economy of eastern Connecticut and San Diego, California, among others.

20. See www.statemaster.com/graph/mil_def_con_exp-military-defense-contracts-expenditures for state-by-state data.

21. See, for example, the major 2012 campaign against allowing automatic cuts (sequester) to impact the defense budget, led by the Aerospace Industries Association at www.aia-aerospace.org/.

22. On the role of institutional culture in the national security agencies, see George and Rishikof (2011).

23. George and Rishikof define organizational culture as "a system of shared meaning or values that the organization's

membership holds and that distinguish it from other groups" (George and Rishikof 2011, 4). Huntington describes the impact of cultural differences on the institutional balance having been established during World War II, when the civilian institutions left the economic aspects of the war to the military, out of disinterest: "This was due primarily to the lack of interest in the nonmilitary aspects of the war by the civilian branches of the government, and the absence of civilian institutions equipped to perform these functions. As a result, the War Department assumed the job of mobilization planning. The civilians imposed a civilian war function on a military agency. In this sense, the national mobilization planning of the War Department in the thirties was a forerunner of the vast civilian abdication of function which was to take place during and after World War II" (Huntington 1957, 309).

24. The Myers-Briggs data is based on interviews done by Ted Strickler (1985).

25. On the Myers-Briggs Type Inventory, he reports, military personnel are 30 percent introverted, sensing, thinking, and judging, as opposed to 6 percent of the US population as a whole (Rife 1998, 10).

26. Schake writes: "State has a terrible reputation on Capitol Hill for pulling rabbits out of its budgetary hat instead of carefully costing and tracking programs in ways that would build congressional confidence in its ability to manage larger budgets" (Schake 2012, 11). Ted Strickler, who retired from the Foreign Service, writes: "While recognizing the need for true management skills in senior leadership positions, the Foreign Service has never been able to take the necessary actions to insure that these skills are developed and tested throughout an officer's career. . . . [T]he Foreign Service fills its senior managerial positions with ambassadors . . . based on the assumption that success in managing policy will equate to success in managing resources. . . . Management functions are viewed with considerable disdain by most FSO's" (Strickler 1985, 43–44, 52).

27. Strickler calls this an "aversion to formal training as an important part of career development" (Strickler 1985, 51).

28. There is little interest in changing this culture, according to Schake: "The Foreign Service is content to replicate itself rather than evolve, and has been permitted to" (Schake 2012, 36).

29. This orientation is reflected in the proposal to establish an independent cabinet-level department for economic development. See Modernizing Foreign Assistance Network (2008).

30. For a detailed description of the PPBS process (now known as PPBES with the addition of "Execution" to the name), see Keehan and Land (2010).

31. For a discussion of the early years of PPBS and the services' reactions, see Gordon, McNichol, and Jack (2009), and Hitch (1965).

32. For the most recent QDR, the fifth since the requirement was created, see US Department of Defense (2014).

33. A ready division for the Army, air wing for the Air Force, or battle group for the Navy takes years to assemble, has a long, predictable, and measurable cycle between preparation, deployment, downtime, and new preparation, and has costs over that time that can be predicted with reasonable accuracy. Military hardware takes a long time to develop (well over ten years for major equipment) and production can run for many years.

34. See, for example, Business Executives for National Security (2001, 20–21), based on two papers by Tom Davis, "Framing the Problem of PPBS" and "Changing PPBS," unpublished, 2000.

35. See, for example, Government Accountability Office (2012).

36. This is not always the case. The Cold War military was designed to deter attack, defend the nation and its allies, and prevail in conflicts. These desired outcomes were a nonevent in the Cold War—success meant no Soviet attack, or no expansion of Soviet influence. Proving the negative, however, is not simple; other factors such as internal weakness or lack of intention could explain the absence of Soviet military action and the outcome.

37. Other agencies have tried, with mixed success, to emulate the PPBS system, notably the Departments of Energy and Homeland Security. See, for example, US Department of Energy (2003).

38. The first and probably most comprehensive such strategy document was NSC 68, "United States Objectives and Programs for National Security" (US National Security Council 1950). President Nixon and Henry Kissinger undertook a similar effort known as NSSM 3 in 1970.

39. In 1993, the Government Performance and Results Act required all federal agencies to develop a strategic plan. State and USAID drafted several plans consistent with this requirement. However, it sets no priorities and has not been integrated into any overall program or resource planning at State. The last such report, covering the years 2007–12, was released in May 2007. See US Department of State (2007).

40. In the 1960s, economist Thomas Schelling examined the applicability of PPBS to foreign policy programs and budgeting. He urged that recipient countries be the focus of such a planning effort, but argued that the diaspora of organizations and the difficulties of measuring outputs and outcomes would make such an effort difficult (Schelling, 1968, 26–36).

41. One might argue that Henry Kissinger was such a secretary of state, but his influence stemmed from his relationship with the president as national security advisor, rather than representing the strength of the State Department.

42. For a detailed discussion of NSS structure and practices, see Whittaker, Smith, and McKune (2011).

43. For the difference in OMB treatment of the defense and foreign policy agencies, see Adams 2011.

44. The literature on Congress and foreign and national security policymaking is relatively thin and somewhat dated. See Lindsay and Ripley 1993; McCormick 1993; and Deering 1993. Though dated, the general conclusions and analyses of these three pieces continue to reflect congressional realities.

45. One of the most significant such structural legislative actions was the passage of the Goldwater-Nichols Act in 1986, which made the chairman of the Joint Chiefs of Staff the principal military adviser to the president, enhanced the role of the combatant commanders, and required "joint" service as a prerequisite for promotion to flag officer. See Locher (2004).

46. The authorities that allowed the military to engage in development-oriented reconstruction and governance assistance in Iraq and Afghanistan (the Commander's Emergency Response Program, CERP), to educate foreign militaries' counterterrorism personnel (Counter Terrorism Fellowship Program),

to reimburse other countries for material support to US counter-terrorism operations (Coalition Support Funds), to provide global security sector assistance jointly with State (Global Security Contingency Fund) and to provide counterterrorism assistance to countries around the globe (the Section 1206 program) were all legislated by the Armed Services committees. See Adams and Williams (2011) and Serafino (2011).

47. The two foreign relations/affairs committees did pass legislation in 2008 authorizing the State Department's office of the Coordinator for Reconstruction and Stabilization and the creation of a civilian corps for reconstruction operations, but the program has been weakly funded, limiting its activities. See Serafino (2012).

48. Until 2005–07, State operations (personnel and administration) and foreign assistance funds were divided between two appropriations subcommittees, forcing a trade-off between State's operating funds and the funds for Commerce and Justice. This division was ended in 2005 and 2007, when State operations were folded into the existing Foreign Operations subcommittee, creating a single subcommittee for State and Foreign Operations. Defense budgets are considered in three subcommittees, but two of them—Defense Appropriations, and Military Construction and Veterans Affairs—focus almost entirely on defense-related funding. The third—Energy and Water—covers the budget for nuclear weapons programs of the National Nuclear Security Administration (NNSA—Department of Energy), which generally has significant political support.

REFERENCES

Adams, Gordon. 1981. *The Iron Triangle: The Politics of Defense Contracting.* New Brunswick, NJ: Transaction Press.

———. 2011. "The Office of Management and Budget: The President's Policy Tool." In *The National Security Enterprise: Navigating the Labyrinth,* edited by George Roger George and Harvey Rishikof, 55–78. Washington, DC: Georgetown University Press.

Adams, Gordon, and Shoon Murray. 2014. "An Introduction to Mission Creep." In *Mission Creep: The Militarization of US Foreign Policy?* Edited by Gordon Adams and Shoon Murray, 3–12. Washington, DC: Georgetown University Press.

Adams, Gordon, and Cindy Williams. 2010. *Buying National Security: How America Plans and Pays for Its Global Role and Safety at Home.* New York: Routledge.

Adams, Gordon, Cindy Williams, Rebecca Williams, and Trice Kabundi. 2010. "Buying National Security: The Lopsided Toolkit." *The Will and the Wallet: Budgeting for Foreign Affairs and Diplomacy Blog,* February 26. The Stimson Center. http://thewillandthewallet.squarespace.com/blog/2010/2/26/buying-national-security-the-lop sided-toolkit.html.

Advisory Committee on Transformational Diplomacy. 2008. *Final Report of the State Department in 2025 Working Group.* Washington, DC: Department of State

Business Executives for National Security. 2001. *Call to Action.* Washington, DC: Tooth-to-Tail Commission.

Carlson, Brian D. 2014 "Who Tells America's Story Abroad? State's Diplomacy or DoD's Strategic Communication?" In *Mission Creep: The Militarization of US Foreign Policy?* Edited by Gordon Adams and Shoon Murray, 145–65. Washington, DC: Georgetown University Press.

Cushman, Charles B., Jr. 2014. "Congress and the Politics of Defense and Foreign Policy Making: Big Barriers to Balance." In *Mission Creep: The Militarization of US Foreign Policy?* Edited by Gordon Adams and Shoon Murray, 74–94. Washington, DC: Georgetown University Press.

Deering, Christopher. 1993. "Decision Making in the Armed Services Committees." In *Congress Resurgent: Foreign and Defense Policy on Capitol Hill,* edited by Randall Ripley and James Lindsay, 155–82. Ann Arbor: University of Michigan Press.

Enthoven, Alain C., and K. Wayne Smith. 2005 [1971]. *How Much Is Enough? Shaping the Defense Program 1961–1969.* Santa Monica, CA: Rand Corporation.

Glain, Stephen. 2011. *State vs. Defense: The Battle to Define America's Empire.* New York: Crown.

Gordon, Vance, Dave McNichol, and Bryan Jack. 2009. "Revolution, Counter-Revolution, and Evolution: A Brief History of the PPBS." Unpublished manuscript.

Government Accountability Office. 2011. *Defense Acquisitions: Further Action Needed to Better Implement Requirements for Conducting Inventory of Service Contract Activities.* GAO 11-192, January. Washington, DC: Government Printing Office.

———. 2012. "DOD Financial Management: Improvements Needed in Prompt Payment Monitoring and Reporting." Letter to Sen. Carl Levin. GAO-12-662R, June 26. Washington, DC: Government Printing Office.

HELP Commission. 2007. *The HELP Commission Report on Foreign Assistance Reform.* HELP Commission. Washington, DC: Government Printing Office.

Hitch, Charles J. 1965. "Decision-Making for Defense." Gaither Memorial Lectures, April 5–9, University of California.

Huntington, Samuel. 1957. *The Soldier and the State: The Theory and Politics of Civil-Military Relations.* Cambridge, MA: Belknap Press of Harvard University Press.

Keehan, Mark P., and Gerry Land. 2010. "Teaching Note: Planning, Programming, Budgeting, and Execution (PPBE) Process." February. Washington, DC: Defense Acquisition University. https://learn.test.dau.mil/CourseWare/802510/1/M8/JobAids /PPBE.pdf.

Lindsay, James M., and Randall B. Ripley. 1993. "How Congress Influences Foreign and Defense Policy." In *Congress Resurgent: Foreign and Defense Policy on Capitol Hill,* edited by James M. Lindsay and Randall B. Ripley, 17–35. Ann Arbor: University of Michigan Press.

Locher, James. 2004. *Victory on the Potomac: The Goldwater-Nichols Act Unifies the Pentagon.* College Station: Texas A & M University Press.

Marks, Edward. 2014. "The State Department: No Longer the Gate Keeper." In *Mission Creep: The Militarization of US Foreign Policy?* edited by Gordon Adams and Shoon Murray, 235–54. Washington, DC: Georgetown University Press.

McCormick, James. 1993. "Decision Making in the Foreign Affairs and Foreign Relations Committees." In *Congress Resurgent: Foreign and Defense Policy on Capitol Hill,* edited by Randall Ripley and James Lindsay, 115–54. Ann Arbor: University of Michigan.

Modernizing Foreign Assistance Network. 2008. *New Day, New Way: US Foreign Assistance for the 21st Century.* Washington, DC: Center for Global Development.

Office of Personnel Management. 2012. "Total Government Employment Since 1962." http://www.opm.gov/policy-data-oversight/data-analysis-documentation/federal-employment-reports/historical-tables/total-government-employment-since-1962.

Olson, William J. 2012. "The Slow Motion Coup: Militarization and the Implications of Eisenhower's Prescience." *Small Wars Journal*, August 11. http://smallwarsjournal.com/jrnl/art/the-slow-motion-coup-militarization-and-the-implications-of-eisenhower%E2%80%99s-prescience.

Owens, Mackubin Thomas. 2011. *US Civil-Military Relations after 9/11: Renegotiating the Civil-Military Bargain.* New York: Continuum.

Priest, Dana. 2000. 2003. *The Mission: Waging War and Keeping Peace with America's Military.* New York: W. W. Norton.

Reveron, Derek S. 2010. *Exporting Security: International Cooperation, Security Cooperation, and the Changing Face of the US Military.* Washington, DC: Georgetown University Press.

Rife, Lt. Col. Rickey L. 1998. "Defense Is from Mars; State Is from Venus." Army War College Strategy Research Project. Carlisle, PA: Army War College.

Rubin, Barry. 1985. *Secrets of State: The State Department and the Struggle over US Foreign Policy.* New York: Oxford University Press.

Schake, Kori. 2012. *State of Disrepair: Fixing the Culture and Practices of the State Department.* Palo Alto, CA: Hoover Institution Press.

Schelling, Tom. 1968. "PPBS and Foreign Affairs." *Public Interest* 11, Spring.

Serafino, Nina M. 2011. *Security Assistance Reform: "Section 1206" Background and Issues for Congress.* Report RS22855, February 11. Washington, DC: Congressional Research Service.

———. 2012. *Peacekeeping, Stabilization and Conflict Transitions: Background and Congressional Action on the Civilian Response/Reserve Corps and Other Civilian Stabilization and Reconstruction Capabilities.* RL32862, October 2. Washington, DC: Congressional Research Service.

Stimson Center/American Academy of Diplomacy. 2008. *A Foreign Affairs Budget for the Future.* Washington, DC: Stimson Center.

Strickler, Ted. 1985. "The US Foreign Service: A Fit of Crisis or a Crisis of Fit." Research Report, March. Washington, DC: National War College.

US Department of Defense. 2012a. *Base Structure Report, Fiscal Year 2012 Baseline.* Washington, DC: Office of the Deputy Under Secretary of Defense. http://www.acq.osd.mil/ie/download/bsr/BSR2012Baseline.pdf.

———. 2012b. *National Defense Budget Estimates for FY 2013.* March. Washington, DC: Office of the Under Secretary of Defense. http://comptroller.defense.gov/defbudget/fy2013/FY13_Green_Book.pdf.

———. 2014. "Quadrennial Defense Review (QDR)." Washington, DC: Department of Defense.

US Department of Energy. 2003. *Audit Report: National Nuclear Security Administration's Planning, Programming, Budgeting, and Evaluation Process.* DOE/IG 1604, August. Washington, DC: Office of the Inspector General, Office of Audit Services.

US Department of State. 2007. "FY 2007–2012 Department of State and USAID Strategic Plan." https://2009-2017.state.gov/s/d/rm/rls/dosstrat/2007/html/index.htm.

US National Security Council. 1950. "United States Objectives and Programs for National Security." NSC 68. Washington, DC. http://www.fas.org/irp/offdocs/nsc-hst/nsc-68.htm.

US Senate. 1998. Budget Committee. *International Affairs: Activities of Domestic Agencies: Statement of Benjamin F. Nelson, Director, International Relations and Trade Issues, National Security and International Affairs Division, General Accounting Office.* GAO/ T-NSIAD-98-174, June 4. Washington, DC: Government Printing Office.

Whittaker, Alan G., Frederick C. Smith, and Elizabeth McKune. 2011. *The National Security Policy Process: The National Security Council and Interagency System.* Research Report, August 15. Washington, DC: Industrial College of the Armed Forces, National Defense University. http://www.ndu.edu/icaf/outreach/publications/nspp/docs/icaf-nsc-policy-process-report-08-2011.pdf.

Restoring the Vision

Overcoming Gridlock to Reassert Congress's Role in Deliberating National Security

JOHN MCCAIN

In recent years, Congress's role in shaping American national security strategy has diminished due to partisan gridlock from both parties. It's time to reassert our status as a coequal branch of government and do our part to ensure our national security.

One of the early strokes of genius by the architects of the American system was entrusting to Congress the sacred duty of supporting and providing for our military. The founding fathers did so to guard against an all-powerful executive and protect the foundations of

John McCain, "Restoring the Vision: Overcoming Gridlock to Reassert Congress's Role in Deliberating National Security," *Texas National Security Review* (November 2017).

individual liberty. However, two centuries of democratic governance, separation of powers, and dedication to the propositions of our founding revealed their true brilliance and foresight.

As America has realized the limitless potential of its ideals, its citizens, and its destiny, the US military has been transformed from a potential threat to liberty to the indispensable guardian of it—at home and around the world. Today, the challenge for Congress is navigating how to fulfill its constitutional duties in accordance with America's global responsibilities.

Through the years, as the country grew into its role as a world power, the obligation of Congress to ensure America lived up to the hopes and dreams of the founders only became more important. The post–World War II global order relies fundamentally on American leadership. The role of Congress, therefore, is not only to serve as the legislature of our great nation, but also—as a co-equal branch of government for the most powerful country in the world—to help maintain the stability and prosperity of the liberal order. We cannot take this charge seriously enough.

That is why the diminished role of Congress in deliberating and debating the strategy to address the global challenges and opportunities we face is one of the great tragedies of our modern political system.

Congress has a fairly straightforward set of constitutional roles and responsibilities: raising and supporting armies; providing and maintaining a Navy; providing advice and consent on treaties and nominations; controlling the purse strings; conducting oversight of executive branch departments and agencies; and exercising checks and balances as a co-equal branch of government.

Yet, Congress has a more fundamental role in shaping American national security strategy than conventional constitutional wisdom would dictate. Unfortunately, we have allowed these important duties to wither away.

The legislature, and in particular the Senate, is intended to be a deliberative body—one that is capable of providing a thoughtful, reasoned, and measured approach to matters of national import. In the national security sphere, the benefits of this deliberative approach are clear. Where the executive branch is consumed with the urgency of day-to-day events, the legislature can take time for precious debate and careful consideration of both current problems and future potentialities. Free from the paralysis of dealing with crisis management, Congress should be able to provide the strategic thinking that national security demands.

Practically speaking, the process for Congress's role starts with a sober assessment of national security threats. It then proceeds with spirited debate about the requirements necessary to meet those threats, followed by the authorization of policies and appropriation of resources to support those requirements. Finally, it provides vigorous oversight of those policies and resources. At its best, this is how Congress can—and has—functioned.

In recent years, however, Congress has become only a shadow of the deliberative body it was intended to be. Political polarization has led to partisan gridlock. No matter which party is in power, the majority seems intent on imposing its will, while the minority seems solely interested in preventing any accomplishments. As we lurch from one self-created crisis to another, we are proving incapable of not only addressing the country's most difficult problems but also fulfilling our most basic legislative duties. "Compromise" has become a dirty word and working across the aisle a political liability. But these very principles were meant to define our legislative process.

Over time, regular order—the set of processes, rules, customs, and protocols by which Congress is supposed to govern itself and do business on behalf of the American people—has totally broken down. This has led to a paralysis that has rendered the institution largely incapable of exercising its unique responsibility to thoughtfully consider broader strategic questions. In doing so, Congress has diminished its role and, ultimately, disempowered itself.

This has wrought havoc, most crucially, on our country's national security policies. Nowhere is this more apparent than our defense budget. For years, US military spending has been senselessly constrained by sequestration—perhaps the single greatest legislative failure that I have seen. Never intended to become law at all, sequestration was meant to be a threat so grave that it would force bipartisan agreement to reduce the deficit. But bipartisanship proved too difficult for Congress, and the result was that arbitrary spending caps and sequestration became the law of the land.

There is broad agreement on both sides of the aisle that defense has been woefully underfunded since the spending caps and sequestration came into effect. Even still, Congress has not been able to muster the political will to find a permanent solution to the problem. Instead, we have fallen into the habit of funding our government through short-term budget deals that we all know have a harmful impact on our military. Congress has all but given up on the appropriations process, and we regularly threaten the possibility of government shutdown. If we cannot fund the government, we are failing to fulfill even the most basic constitutional duties in a reliable and proper way—and, in doing so, we are ceding power to the executive and further weakening our own branch of government.

I am proud to say that the Senate Armed Services Committee has long been one of the rare exceptions to the breakdown of regular order. For more than 50 consecutive years, Congress has enacted the National Defense Authorization Act in a bipartisan manner, and presidents of both parties have signed those bills into law.

Unfortunately, even the bipartisanship surrounding the defense authorization bill has proven fragile. In recent years, we have struggled to reach agreement on a process to debate and vote on amendments under an open process on the floor of the Senate—undercutting one of its central purposes. While in the end a large majority of senators from both parties vote for the legislation each year, it is disappointing that we can no longer find a way to openly debate matters of such consequence to our military and our national security.

It is essential that we find a way to restore Congress's unique role in providing the deliberative, strategic approach that is so needed in our national security decision-making—especially in today's increasingly dangerous and unstable world. To do so, we should look to our own past. At several key moments in recent history, Congress has demonstrated the courage and moral fortitude to do the hard work of thoughtful deliberation and strategic thinking to enact visionary reforms, policy changes, or shifts in national security strategy.

There are a few episodes that stand out during my time in Washington. The first demonstrates the ability of a small group of members of Congress with strong personal convictions to change the trajectory of national security—despite determined opposition from a president. In the late 1970s, President Jimmy Carter was considering withdrawing all US troops from the Korean Peninsula in an effort to negotiate with the Chinese and the Soviets to prevent another war. As a Navy liaison in the Senate at the time, I escorted a bipartisan delegation of senators, including Henry "Scoop" Jackson and William Cohen, on a visit to South Korea. That on-the-ground experience led these leaders to conclude that troop withdrawal would aggravate rather than alleviate the security situation.

Upon our return to Washington, the senators went to the White House and worked hard to convince the president that a troop withdrawal would not be the right course of action. These senators were highly regarded for their national security experience and expertise. While one of them might not have made a difference, the bipartisan group was able to change his mind and, in doing so, change the course of history. The results of withdrawing troops from South Korea would have been disastrous for our interests and those of our allies in the region.

The second episode demonstrates the value of careful study, oversight, and reform—even when faced with bureaucratic opposition from the executive branch. The Goldwater-Nichols Defense Reorganization Act was the most consequential reform of the Department of Defense since its creation. Passed in 1986, my last year in the House of Representatives before I came to the Senate, this legislation was the result of years of hard work by the Armed Services Committee.

Goldwater-Nichols came about in response to a series of military failures—the Vietnam War, the failed hostage rescue in Iran, and difficulties during the invasion of Grenada. After years of meticulous deliberation and study, the committee identified the root causes of these failures and enacted sweeping organizational reforms to fix the problems, increase efficiency, reduce waste, and encourage a more unified force. On the whole, those reforms have served our country well.

The third episode demonstrates the power of shifting the paradigm during a crisis—in the face of strong path dependency from the administration. In 2006, the situation in Iraq was rapidly spiraling out of control. Those dark days saw slow progress, rising casualties, and dwindling public support for the war. The Bush administration continued to pursue the same strategy in the face of mounting evidence of its catastrophic failure. In Congress, we knew a new approach was urgently needed to turn the tide. As the representatives of the people, we understood that a mood of defeatism was rising, as critics who would have preferred failure called for unconditional troop withdrawal.

Together with a group of highly regarded national security experts, Congress demanded a change in strategy. The intellectual contributions of thought leaders were central to crafting the troop surge strategy, and Congress played an important role in building public support—in part through high-profile hearings like the one that allowed Gen. David Petraeus and Ambassador Ryan Crocker to make the case against accepting defeat. In 2007, President George W. Bush finally changed course and adopted a strategy that could lead to victory, working tirelessly to earn public support for the surge. While the gains made after the surge have since been squandered, we should not underestimate how the change in strategy turned the tide.

It is time to get back to this way of doing business. To be sure, Congress is not perfect—least of all, its members. We have all made our fair share of mistakes and have gotten the details wrong on more than one occasion.

Even so, we owe it to those who put our system in place to become the deliberative body we were intended to be. When it comes to asserting our role in national security, we owe it also to the men and women serving in our armed forces who put their lives at risk every day to keep our nation free.

By reinvigorating the processes, rules, protocols, and customs of Congress, we can get back to fulfilling our unique role in national security decision-making.

Through deliberation, debate, and regular order, we can overcome our current polarized, paralyzed moment—just as the founding fathers intended us to. By doing so, we can reassert our status as a coequal branch of government and do our part to ensure our national security.

Only then can we—imperfectly—help our country move forward, secure our interests, defend our values, and protect the world order that has brought peace and prosperity to so many.

Trump's Generals
Mattis, McMaster, and Kelly

JESSICA BLANKSHAIN

In the weeks and months leading up to President Donald Trump's inauguration, many national security analysts—both academics and practitioners—expressed concern over the number of retired general officers the new president planned to appoint to senior positions.[1] Trump's original appointees included retired Marine four-star James Mattis as secretary of defense, retired Marine four-star John Kelly as secretary of homeland security, and retired Army three-star Michael Flynn as national security advisor. Of primary concern was that having so many senior individuals with close ties to the military would undermine civilian control (or at the very least, perceptions of civilian control). More specifically, many feared that the prominence of military voices around a president inexperienced in foreign affairs and the armed forces would lead to a further militarization of US foreign policy.[2] These concerns were revived when, a month into the new administration, Trump appointed Lt. Gen. H. R. McMaster, an active-duty Army officer, to replace Flynn as national security advisor.[3] In July 2017, when the president moved Kelly from the Department of Homeland Security to a traditionally more political role as White House chief of staff, the conversation broadened to more explicitly include the risks of politicizing the military.[4] These fears, however, were balanced by hope that seasoned national security professionals like Mattis, McMaster, and Kelly would be the "grown-ups in the room," steering the new, inexperienced president toward better decisions and bringing stability to an erratic and impulsive administration.[5]

These appointment-related concerns about civil-military relations in the era of Trump can be grouped into two broad categories: concerns related to policy-making within government, and those about the rela-tionship between the military and the society it serves. The perceived risk to policy-making is that Trump's appointment of, and deference to, senior officials with strong, recent ties to the military would give the military too much influence in foreign policy, harming perceptions of civilian control. This strand of concerns has both a relational component—the prospect of normalizing the privileging of military over civilian views—and a policy content component—a further "militarization" of American foreign policy. Militarization, in this context, does not necessarily mean starting more wars, or using military force more often. Evidence suggests that in general, those with military experience are less likely to want to initiate conflict, but are more likely to use overwhelming force once a conflict has started.[6] Rather, it reflects a concern that the military perspective will dominate a wide range of foreign policy decisions to the exclusion of alternative perspectives, or that every issue will become a problem for the military to solve, whether that is through traditional use of force or not.[7]

The other area of apprehension—the relationship between the military and society—centers on the risk that Trump's use of the military as a political prop would drag it into the political arena, harming its respected status with the American public. Normalizing the use of those connected to the military as political actors risks creating an environment where criticism of the military is completely off limits for some segments of society, while trust in the military is equally as unthinkable in others.[8]

Just over one year into the Trump administration, what evidence have observers seen to support or refute these concerns?

It is too early for definitive answers, but the evidence thus far suggests that the disquiet over both sets

Jessica Blankshain, "Trump's Generals: Mattis, McMaster, and Kelly," in "Policy Roundtable: Civil-Military Relations Now and Tomorrow," chaired by Celeste Ward Gventer, special issue, *Texas National Security Review*, March 27, 2018.

All views are the author's own and do not represent the views of the United States Government, Department of Defense, Department of the Navy, or US Naval War College.

of issues was well founded. Trump's generals, as he likes to call them, do seem to be extremely influential in policy-making, and the administration has done little to distance these senior officials from their military backgrounds. Some observers have suggested that the generals have been a moderating influence on the president, steering Trump toward better foreign policy decisions.[9] In a *Texas National Security Review* roundtable, Emma Ashford and Joshua R. Itzkowitz Shifrinson argue that the Trump administration's first year, including its first *National Security Strategy* (NSS), was far more in keeping with status-quo American foreign policy than the president's rhetoric would have suggested.[10] But if this is true, it suggests that civilian control may in fact be eroding, at least insofar as enacted policy and strategic documents have been inconsistent with the stated political preferences of the president. Since active or former military officers were so instrumental in policy-making, including the drafting of the NSS, it appears that it is their preferred policies that won the day. Meanwhile, evidence of politicization of the military abounds, although it is difficult to measure how enduring an erosion of social and political norms might be in such a short time span.

While the active and retired military officers in the administration are often discussed as a whole, when it comes to considering the implications for civil-military relations discussed above, it will be helpful to consider each of the most prominent players separately. The three most important generals throughout the full first year of the administration have been Mattis, McMaster, and Kelly. Despite their similarities, these three individuals hold three very different positions that one would expect to have different impacts on civil-military relations. It is useful to examine how each of these individuals has either confirmed or refuted the early anxieties about their appointments. While all three concerns apply to each appointment, each of their positions underscores a different one in particular. In the case of the secretary of defense, the question of civilian political preferences prevailing over military ones, "relational control," is most at play. Militarization of foreign policy is more of a factor in the case of the national security advisor, while politicization of the military, or at least of one particular former general, is most strongly visible in the case of the White House chief of staff. While McMaster is set to depart the administration in early April, it is still important to consider the impact of his time as national security advisor, and what it might mean for the future of American civil-military relations.

Mattis: Ceding Civilian Control

James Mattis's appointment as secretary of defense was one of the first nominations announced by the new ad-

ministration. The decision was much discussed in particular because the 1947 legislation that created the modern national security establishment, as well as the position of secretary of defense, included a provision that the person filling that position must not have been a member of the military within the previous ten years.[11] America has a long tradition of fearing a large standing army.[12] When the post–World War II drawdown was limited by the onset of the Cold War, the prospect of maintaining a substantial, permanent force for the foreseeable future raised hackles on the Hill and beyond. Congress viewed a civilian secretary of defense—without recent, close ties to the military—as one of the keys to maintaining civilian control in such an environment. Congress passed a one-time exception to the ten-year rule for George Marshall in 1950, and changed the limit to seven years in 2008.[13] Congress similarly granted a waiver to allow Mattis, who had been retired for fewer than five years, to serve as secretary of defense.

Most analysts who worry about a secretary of defense who is too closely tied to the military focus on the question of civilian control. As Peter Feaver points out, this is partially about symbolism: "The secretary of defense is the person in government who embodies civilian control 24-7. . . . That it is a civilian face, wearing civilian clothes, receiving salutes and courtesies from uniformed personnel, is a powerful visible symbol of civilian control."[14] But there are also concerns about what such an appointment would mean for the military's influence over policy. As a Cabinet-level political appointee, the secretary is supposed to be the president's representative, overseeing the Department of Defense and the military, working to further administration policy objectives, and ensuring compliance with administration directives. A defense secretary who is too closely linked to the military might be susceptible to serving the military's interests more than the president's interests.

One can already see indications that the president is happy to defer to Mattis's military expertise. To begin with, Trump backed down from his campaign-trail support for "enhanced interrogation" after learning that Mattis didn't support it.[15] By most accounts, Mattis (with support from McMaster) convinced the president to support an increased troop presence in Afghanistan, despite the president's campaigning against protracted military interventions around the world.[16] The answer from the Pentagon, populated by many senior officers who have enormous personal and professional investment in that conflict, was to keep American troops there.

Feaver raises an additional concern:

[I]f recently retired as a four-star, that means the individual has reached the pinnacle of their individual service and so has developed exceptionally strong service loyalties and ties. It will be harder for such a person to then move into an honest broker position that is supposed to be above service rivalry.[17]

In Mattis's case, there is some early evidence that this phenomenon has not, in fact, occurred. The public version of the *2018 National Defense Strategy* represented Mattis's first chance to make a public statement of his priorities for the Department of Defense. In it, he emphasizes preparing for a future of great-power rivalry—a priority that has been pushed by the Air Force and the Navy in recent years—over counterinsurgency and counterterrorism missions in the Middle East, both of which have been led primarily by the Army and the Marine Corps.

Of course, Mattis's appointment did not only rouse concerns. In the current administration, the possibility that he would stand up to the president and prevent him from enacting some of his more radical policies seemed to be precisely why many outside observers critical of the new president were optimistic about Mattis's appointment. Conservative columnist Jennifer Rubin recently wrote a column celebrating Mattis's service in this respect:

> The country should be immensely grateful that Secretary of Defense Jim Mattis is there—not only because he is a steady hand and speed bump on President Trump's rash decisions, but because every week he demonstrates how one can serve without degrading one's self in this administration.[18]

Perceptions of Mattis's pushback on presidential directives may be more important than the actual substance of his influence. It has been suggested that Mattis has explicitly resisted some of the president's policy changes, such as the proposed ban on transgender troops. But these tales of pushback have, at times, been exaggerated or misleading. For example, some claimed that Mattis went against the president's order on the transgender ban, when Mattis was in fact drafting a memo implementing the policy.[19] Other reports suggested that the Department of Defense was refusing to enact a presidential order when it was, in fact, simply complying with court orders.[20] Still others have asserted that Mattis's close relationship with the current service chiefs, and especially with the Chairman of the Joint Chiefs of Staff, Marine General Joseph Dunford, has allowed them to take liberties in resisting the president's agenda that they wouldn't otherwise take.

Philip Carter names this new stance "respectful disobedience," and uses the label to describe what he sees as senior military pushback with respect to the transgender troop ban and the president's statements after the deadly rally and counterprotest in Charlottesville, VA. Carter argues:

> It's clear that military leaders have found a formula for saluting their commander in chief while keeping his worst excesses at bay. In this, they are probably aided by a secretary of defense and White House chief of staff who have literally worn their shoes. . . . [Mattis and Kelly] almost certainly provide cover for senior military leaders behind closed doors, where they can explain to the president why the generals are behaving a certain way.[21]

An interesting question is what this "disobedience" will mean for long-term civil-military norms if Mattis's pushback on the administration is seen as military insubordination in a way that it wouldn't be with a truly civilian secretary of defense.

On the surface, Mattis's performance thus far would seem to be reassuring for those concerned about his appointment. He has proven more capable of separating himself from the politics of the administration than perhaps any other official serving in it. Mattis also appears to have been a moderating force on a range of policy issues, from torture to openly transgender service members. But the idea that the president's deference to senior military leaders, even recently retired ones, is saving the country is precisely what concerns many scholars of civil-military relations. Through no fault of his own—simply by doing the job he was asked to do—Mattis may subtly undermine long-standing civil-military norms, precisely as feared.

McMaster: Militarization of Foreign Policy

H. R. McMaster presented a different set of concerns. Much of the discussion in civil-military relations circles surrounding his appointment as national security advisor centered on the fact that he was still an active-duty Army officer. While he was certainly not the first active-duty officer to hold the position—he joins John Poindexter and Colin Powell—these individuals have been the exception, not the rule.[22] There are many reasons to regard this kind of appointment with caution. First, being national security advisor requires a military officer to stray "outside their lane," advising the president on issues far afield from their core military expertise. The national security advisor is supposed to help the president integrate all levers of American power—economics, information, diplomacy, and law enforcement—most of which are well outside the core experience and education of a senior military officer.

Second, making an active-duty officer a visible representative of administration policy potentially turns that officer from a defender of the Constitution to a defender of a political administration. This phenomenon was underscored when McMaster authored (with Gary Cohn, now former Director of the National Economic Council) a *Wall Street Journal* op-ed in support of

Trump's America First foreign policy.[23] This would be an unremarkable thing for a national security advisor to do, but it is quite uncommon for an active-duty military officer to publicly argue in support of a broad administration policy of this nature. Moreover, the symbolism to the rest of the world matters—the primary source of advice to the president on overall national security is coming from someone wearing a uniform.

In many analyses of the administration's *2017 National Security Strategy*, observers have noted that they could see a tension between Trump's "America First" approach and the more traditional approach of McMaster and the National Security Council senior director for strategy, Nadia Schadlow. Kori Schake, writing of the strategy, applauded Schadlow and McMaster "for pulling the president's well-known views that far into reasonable territory."[24] McMaster also reportedly clashed with then-White House strategist Steve Bannon over Afghanistan policy, siding with Mattis on keeping troops in that country. One wonders whether the president would have been inclined to listen to civilians in either position arguing for a 16-year war that shows no signs of ending, particularly when the president campaigned against it, as Bannon and even Attorney General Jeff Sessions were eager to remind him.[25] Whatever the content of McMaster's views, it seems clear that he was working an agenda that was not wholly consistent with the stated aims of the president.

It is very difficult to judge whether H. R. McMaster contributed to the militarization of foreign policy, as it isn't always clear what the "military" view of a policy would be. But he does seem to have been instrumental in pushing the president to send additional troops to Afghanistan, and in keeping the administration on high alert with respect to North Korea. While some level of politicization is inherent in the position, it isn't clear that this has bled over to the military more generally in McMaster's case. McMaster's imminent replacement by John Bolton will remove this visible source of military influence from the White House (although it should be noted that the current deputy national security advisor is Ricky Waddell, an Army Reserve two-star general). But McMaster's tenure as national security advisor may yet have long-lasting impacts on civil-military norms. Much will depend on what McMaster chooses to do in retirement—whether he speaks publicly about his time in the White House, and whether he remains a political figure.

John Kelly: Politicization of the Military

Whatever concerns may exist about Mattis and McMaster, they are modest compared to those surrounding White House Chief of Staff John Kelly. When he was appointed as secretary of homeland security, the most significant issue from a civil-military relations point of view was not the appointment itself but that Kelly would be the third recently retired general, two of them Marines, serving at high levels in the administration. This risked limiting the views the president was exposed to and creating the perception that a military junta was running the show.

When he was appointed chief of staff, however, the potential for politicization of the military seemed a far greater danger. In his new role, it would be difficult for Gen. Kelly (as most would continue to call him) to avoid identification with the administration's policy agenda and political actions. Furthermore, the justification for putting Kelly in such a position was less clear than the rationale for putting him, a recent commander of Southern Command, in charge of the Department of Homeland Security. The chief of staff is an explicitly political position with no clear need for military expertise. While many hoped Kelly's military background would allow him to bring order to a chaotic White House, chiefs of staff are more often selected for their political acumen.

Kelly has entered the political arena to a far greater degree than the other two generals discussed above have, thus raising much greater concerns about civil-military relations. Since becoming chief of staff, he has made multiple statements that effectively widened the civil-military divide, further separating the military from, and elevating it over, the civilian public it is intended to serve. For example, when Kelly took the podium in the White House briefing room to defend the president's handling of a phone call to the wife of an American soldier killed in Niger, he said,

> We don't look down upon those of you who that haven't served. In fact, in a way we're a little bit sorry because you'll have never have experienced the wonderful joy you get in your heart when you do the kinds of things our service men and women do—not for any other reason than they love this country. So just think of that.[26]

At the same press conference, Kelly only took questions from reporters with a connection to a gold star family. The next day, when a reporter asked press secretary Sarah Sanders about Kelly's accusations against a member of Congress, Sanders responded, "If you want to go after Gen. Kelly, that's up to you, but I think that if you want to get into a debate with a four-star Marine general, I think that that's something highly inappropriate."[27] This is precisely the type of statement that worries scholars of American civil-military relations—the assertion that as a recently retired four-star general, the president's chief of staff is above reproach. This is particularly worrisome when that military credibility is attached to a particular administration.

Kelly has also made controversial comments on topics unrelated to the military. When asked about the debate over Confederate monuments, Kelly argued that "the lack of an ability to compromise led to the Civil War."[28] This led many to ask what, exactly, Kelly believed the two sides should have compromised about. Kelly also drew criticism based on a discussion of why the number of registered Deferred Action for Childhood Arrivals (known as DACA) participants was lower than the number eligible: "The difference between 690 and 1.8 million were the people that some would say were too afraid to sign up, others would say were too lazy to get off their asses, but they didn't sign up."[29] Kelly had already established himself as an immigration hard-liner during his time at the Department of Homeland Security, but this indelicate statement certainly underscored those views.[30]

Most recently, Kelly was criticized for protecting White House staff secretary Rob Porter when credible allegations that Porter had abused two ex-wives prevented him from obtaining a security clearance. Kelly reportedly offered to resign over the incident, but, as of the writing of this piece, had not been asked to do so.[31] The incident rekindled discussions of the Marine Corps' handling of domestic violence, sexual assault, and harassment cases, with some arguing that Kelly was a product and perpetuator of a Marine Corps culture that protects abusers.[32]

In these ways, Kelly seems to have gone above and beyond the initial concerns about his role as chief of staff. It was always going to be a difficult role for a retired military officer, but Kelly has become more involved in White House politics and scandals than anyone initially predicted. If he, and the administration, continue to use his military service as a political shield, the broader military may eventually find itself dragged into the fray as well.

Conclusion

It seems clear that "Trump's Generals"—Mattis, McMaster, and Kelly—have had a significant influence on this administration's policy-making, as one would expect from any secretary of defense, national security advisor, and chief of staff. But what role do their positions as retired or active military officers play in that influence? The picture is unclear. All three seem to have held considerable sway in the administration, in large part due to their military credentials. Mattis and McMaster have clearly been able to pursue policy preferences in a way that civilians may not have, although we cannot know for certain what policies civilians in these roles would have advocated. In that sense, concerns about military influence over policy, if not fully realized, are not to be fully dismissed either. Both McMaster and Kelly have entered the political arena, the

latter to a much greater degree. Has this politicized the military? It has certainly politicized those two individuals. What larger effect this might have is not yet clear.

Kori Schake has suggested a potential upside to the politicization, and public failings of, military officers. In a tweet about Mike Flynn, Schake argued that Flynn was "making fast progress getting Americans to take military leaders off pedestals and treat as regular citizens when politically active."[33] The military, like any other large group, contains individuals of all types, some of whom will act dishonestly, commit crimes, or hold controversial political views. While this may decrease public respect for the military from its recent lofty heights, if accompanied by a decrease in unquestioning deference, the change might not be all bad.

The first year of the Trump administration does not seem to have changed the public's generally high regard for the US military. In October 2016, a Pew Research Center survey found that 79 percent of US adults reported having "a great deal" or "a fair amount" of confidence in the military "to act in the best interests of the public." This was compared to 27 percent having similar confidence in elected officials.[34] A January 2018 poll by NPR/PBS News Hour/Marist found that "the only institution that Americans have overwhelming faith in is the military—87 percent say they have a great deal or quite a lot of confidence in the military." This was compared to 51 percent reporting the same levels of confidence in the courts, 43 percent in the presidency, and 25 percent in Congress.[35] The polls are not directly comparable, but they do suggest that confidence in the military has not declined in the first year of the Trump administration, and may even have increased.

While a first-year assessment is useful, two of the primary concerns associated with these appointments—the normalization of civilian policy-makers deferring to military experts and the increased politicization of the military—are about trust relationships and societal norms, things that change slowly over time. We have certainly seen evidence of shifts and cracks, but it is too soon to tell whether these will lead to seismic changes. With respect to the concern about militarization, policy can shift more quickly than norms, but it is difficult to determine what "militarization" really means. We will need more studies on how military policy preferences and world views differ from those of civilians, and how much these differences remain when a military officer retires.

The somewhat peculiar character of this administration, which has already challenged American political norms of all varieties, makes judging the impact of any short-term trends in civil-military relations especially difficult. After all, concerns about the health of the civil-military relationship were alive and well in other recent administrations, from Bill Clinton to Barack Obama, but never resulted in catastrophe. Still, it is important that scholars and observers continue to keep a close eye on the role men and women in (or recently out of) uniform play in policy-making, and on their relationship with society more broadly. The effects of the president's approach to staffing his administration, and relating to the military, may last long beyond the tenure of any particular appointee. A true crisis in civil-military relations may be slow to develop. But if it arrives, it will be extremely difficult to reverse.

NOTES

1. See, for example, Mark Landler and Helene Cooper, "Trump's Focus on Generals for Top Jobs Stirs Worries Over Military's Sway," *New York Times*, Nov. 21, 2016, https://www.nytimes.com/2016/11/21/us/politics/donald-trump-national-security-military.html; Carol Giacomo, "Why Donald Trump Shouldn't Fill the Cabinet with Generals," *New York Times*, Nov. 30, 2016, https://www.nytimes.com/2016/11/30/opinion/why-donald-trump-shouldnt-fill-the-cabinet-with-generals.html; David A. Graham, "All the President Elect's Generals," *The Atlantic*, Dec. 8, 2016, https://www.theatlantic.com/politics/archive/2016/12/all-the-president-elects-generals/509873/.

2. See, for example, Bryan Bender, "Is Trump Hiring Too Many Generals?" *Politico*, Dec. 2, 2016, https://www.politico.com/story/2016/12/trump-transition-generals-232148.

3. David Barno and Nora Bensahel, "An Active-Duty National Security Advisor: Myths and Concerns," *War on the Rocks*, Feb. 28, 2017, https://warontherocks.com/2017/02/an-active-duty-national-security-advisor-myths-and-concerns/.

4. Elliot Kaufman, "Against John Kelly as White House Chief of Staff," *National Review*, Aug. 1, 2017, https://www.nationalreview.com/2017/08/john-kelly-wrong-man-white-house-chief-staff-civilian-control-military/.

5. Jonathan Stevenson, "The Generals Can't Save Us from Trump," *New York Times*, July 28, 2017, https://www.nytimes.com/2017/07/28/opinion/sunday/mattis-mcmaster-foreign-policy-trump.html.

6. Christopher Gelpi and Peter D. Feaver, "Speak Softly and Carry a Big Stick? Veterans in the Political Elite and the American Use of Force," *American Political Science Review* 96, no. 4 (December 2002): 779–793.

7. See, for example, Rosa Brooks, *How Everything Became War and the Military Became Everything: Tales from the Pentagon* (New York: Simon and Schuster, 2017).

8. For evidence of the effect of partisanship and ideology on confidence in the military, see David T. Burbach, "Partisan Dimensions of Confidence in the US Military, 1973–2016," *Armed Forces & Society* (January 2018), http://journals.sagepub.com/doi/abs/10.1177/0095327X17747205?journalCode=afsa.

9. See, for example, James Kitfield, "Trump's Generals Are Trying to Save the World. Starting with the White House," *Politico*, Aug. 4, 2017, https://www.politico.com/magazine/story/2017/08/04/donald-trump-generals-mattis-mcmaster-kelly-flynn-215455.

10. Emma Ashford and Joshua R. Itzkowitz Shifrinson, "Trump's National Security Strategy: A Critic's Dream," *Texas National Security Review*, Dec. 21, 2017, https://tnsr.org/roundtable/policy-roundtable-make-trumps-national-security-strategy/#essay2.

11. National Security Act of 1947, p. 500, http://legisworks.org/congress/80/publaw-253.pdf.

12. See the *Federalist Papers*, especially 8 and 24–29, available at https://www.congress.gov/resources/display/content/The+Federalist+Papers; and *Anti-Federalist Papers*, especially 23–25, http://resources.utulsa.edu/law/classes/rice/Constitutional/AntiFederalist/antifed.htm.

13. Peter Feaver, "Mattis' Appointment Would Require Special Approval from Congress," interview by Michel Martin, *All Things Considered*, NPR, Dec. 3, 2016, https://www.npr.org/2016/12/03/504274577/mattis-appointment-would-require-special-approval-from-congress.

14. Peter Feaver, "A General to Be Secretary of Defense? A Good Choice for Civil-Military Relations," *Foreign Policy*, Dec. 2, 2016, http://foreignpolicy.com/2016/12/02/a-general-to-be-secretary-of-defense-a-good-choice-for-civil-military-relations/.

15. Sheri Fink and Helene Cooper, "Inside Trump Defense Secretary Pick's Efforts to Halt Torture," *New York Times*, Jan 2, 2017, https://www.nytimes.com/2017/01/02/us/politics/james-mattis-defense-secretary-trump.html.

16. Michael R. Gordon, Eric Schmitt, and Maggie Haberman, "Trump Settles on Afghan Strategy Expected to Raise Troop Levels," *New York Times*, Aug. 20, 2017, https://www.nytimes.com/2017/08/20/world/asia/trump-afghanistan-strategy-mattis.html.

17. Feaver, "A General to Be Secretary of Defense?"

18. Jennifer Rubin, "Distinguished Person of the Week: He Deftly Defies Trump," *Washington Post*, Feb. 11, 2018, https://www.washingtonpost.com/blogs/right-turn/wp/2018/02/11/distinguished-person-of-the-week-he-deftly-defies-trump/.

19. Fred Barbash and Derek Hawkins, "Mattis Hailed as 'Hero' for 'Defying' Trump on Transgender Policy. But Did He?" *Washington Post*, Aug. 30, 2017, https://www.washingtonpost.com/news/morning-mix/wp/2017/08/30/mattis-hailed-as-hero-for-defying-trump-on-transgender-policy-but-did-he/.

20. Dan Lamothe and Ann Marimow, "In Defiance of Trump Ban, Pentagon Releases Detailed Policy for Recruiting Transgender Troops," *Chicago Tribune*, Dec. 20, 2017, http://www.chicagotribune.com/news/nationworld/politics/ct-pentagon-recruiting-transgender-policy-20171220-story.html.

21. Philip Carter, "The Pentagon's Response to Trump's Transgender Troop Ban Reflects Leaders' New Posture of Respectful Disobedience," *Slate*, Dec. 12, 2017.

22. David Barno and Nora Bensahel, "An Active-Duty National Security Advisor: Myths and Concerns," *War on the Rocks*, Feb. 28, 2017, https://warontherocks.com/2017/02/an-active-duty-national-security-advisor-myths-and-concerns/.

23. H. R. McMaster and Gary D. Cohn, "America First Doesn't Mean America Alone," *Wall Street Journal*, May 30, 2017, https://www.wsj.com/articles/america-first-doesnt-mean-america-alone-1496187426; discussed in Carter "U.S. Military Chiefs Respond to Trump's Decisions with Respectful Disobedience."

24. See, for example, Kori Schake, "How to Grade Trump's National Security Strategy on a Curve," *Foreign Policy*, Dec. 19, 2017, http://foreignpolicy.com/2017/12/19/how-to-grade-trumps-national-security-strategy-on-a-curve/.

25. Philip Rucker and Robert Costa, "'It's a Hard Problem': Inside Trump's Decision to Send More Troops to Afghanistan," *Washington Post*, Aug. 21, 2017, https://www.washingtonpost.com/politics/its-a-hard-problem-inside-trumps-decision-to-send-more-troops-to-afghanistan/2017/08/21/14dcb126-868b-11e7-a94f-3139abce39f5_story.html?utm_term=.a9ebe72f93ad.

26. Transcript, John F. Kelly remarks in the White House briefing room, *New York Times*, Oct. 19, 2017, https://www.nytimes.com/2017/10/19/us/politics/statement-kelly-gold-star.html.

27. Callum Borchers, "The White House's 'Highly Inappropriate' Response to a Fact-Check Reveals an Authoritarian Mindset," *Washington Post*, Oct. 20 2017, https://www.washingtonpost.com/news/the-fix/wp/2017/10/20/white-house-to-media-its-highly-inappropriate-to-question-john-kelly-because-hes-a-4-star-general/.

28. Maggie Astor, "John Kelly Pins Civil War on a 'Lack of Ability to Compromise,'" *Washington Post*, Oct. 31, 2017, https://www.nytimes.com/2017/10/31/us/john-kelly-civil-war.html.

29. Miriam Valverde, "In Context: John Kelly's Remarks on 'Lazy' Immigrants and DACA," *Politifact*, Feb. 7, 2018, http://www.politifact.com/truth-o-meter/article/2018/feb/07/context-john-kellys-remarks-lazy-immigrants-daca/.

30. Jonathan Blitzer, "Evaluating John Kelly's Record at Homeland Security," *The New Yorker*, Aug. 1, 2017, https://www.newyorker.com/news/news-desk/evaluating-john-kellys-record-at-homeland-security.

31. Maggie Haberman, Julie Hirschfeld Davis, and Michael S. Schmidt. "Kelly Says He's Willing to Resign as Abuse Scandal Roils the White House," *New York Times*, Feb. 9, 2018, https://www.nytimes.com/2018/02/09/us/politics/trump-porter-abuse.html.

32. Don Christensen, "John Kelly and the 'Good Soldier' Defense," *The Atlantic*, Feb. 26, 2018, https://www.theatlantic.com/politics/archive/2018/02/john-kelly-rob-porter/554177/; Joanne Lipman, "Surprised John Kelly Would Overlook Abuse? The Military that Bred Him is Rife with It," *USA Today*, Feb. 13, 2018, https://www.usatoday.com/story/opinion/2018/02/13/john-kelly-rob-porter-donald-trump-overlooking-abuse-military-culture-column/328994002/.

33. Kori Schake (@Kori Schake), "Flynn making fast progress getting Americans to take military leaders off pedestals and treat as regular citizens when politically active," Twitter, Dec. 5, 2016, https://twitter.com/KoriSchake/status/805949423050059780.

34. Brian Kennedy, "Most Americans Trust the Military and Scientists to Act in the Public's Interest," Pew Research Center, Oct. 18 2016, http://www.pewresearch.org/fact-tank/2016/10/18/most-americans-trust-the-military-and-scientists-to-act-in-the-publics-interest/.

35. Domenico Montanaro, "Here's Just How Little Confidence Americans Have in Political Institutions," *All Things Considered*, NPR, Jan. 17, 2018, https://www.npr.org/2018/01/17/578422668/heres-just-how-little-confidence-americans-have-in-political-institutions.

Dissent, Resignation, and the Moral Agency of Senior Military Professionals

DON M. SNIDER

I am delighted to participate with my colleagues Peter Fever, Richard Kohn, and James Dubik in this forum on a timely and important subject, that of the appropriateness of principled resignation by senior military leaders. That said, as will be clear, we do not agree. This fact all the more boosts my delight to be able to present a particular view.

To do that I will proceed in three steps. First, I will point out what we do agree on, the historical precedents for the currently perceived norm of "no principled resignations allowed, period." Then I will present two related arguments to establish my position that in very rare cases they are to be allowed, indeed even perhaps obligatory. In the first argument, I will draw very clear distinctions between modern military professions and military bureaucracies, their characteristics, and the expected behavior of each. Second, I

will look carefully at the content and motivation of the means of social control of each institution—their ethics—for understanding of the moral obligations of their leaders. And, as we shall see, there is a small space for loyal dissent by senior military leaders, even principled resignation.

Our Starting Point

I agree with my colleagues in this forum on the start point for our diverging views—it is the fact established in history that senior military leaders in our services simply have not resigned their position as a form of dissent to civilian decisions. In his influential study of every use of American forces since the end of World War II, Richard Betts stated in 1977, "There is also a myth that high-military figures have extraordinary in-

Don M. Snider, "Dissent, Resignation, and the Moral Agency of Senior Military Professionals," *Armed Forces & Society* 43, no. 1 (2017): 5–16. Republished with permission of Sage Publications Inc.; permission conveyed through Copyright Clearance Center, Inc.

fluences and prevent their superiors from over ruling them because of a unique tendency to resign and attack their administrations. But the evidence does not support the theory." He continued, "Chiefs have been fired, not reappointed when it was expected they would be, or carried along with short appointments, but none in the post-war period has ever resigned" (Betts, 1977, p. 7). In the second edition of his book published some 14 years later, having found no contradictory evidence in the intervening period, he concluded, "So my point in the first edition stands" (Betts, 1991, p. xii).

So the historic fact is established, and not just by Betts; others including members of this forum have arrived at the same conclusion (Kohn, 2009; Feaver, 2015). But the reasons why senior military leaders have never resigned in protest are much less clear. Those offered vary widely. One is that resignation is very personally expensive to the senior leader involved—they forfeit their retirement pay and all other emoluments to which they would be eligible for their decades of service, not a trivial amount by any means given the socialized medical care they will receive for life, and so on. Researchers of this mind go on to state,

> Quitting [resignation in protest] is viewed by many as the ultimate means of expressing opposition to official policy or slight. Despite its seeming attractiveness as a way of making an emphatic point, there are complications and principals involved which make it a rarely exercised alternative. (Matthews, 1990, p. 12)

Another reason offered is that over time the positive became normative, meaning the tradition of "no resignations" was gradually accepted as the right thing to do and as such was incorporated into the evolving ethos of our military services. As just one example, General Maxwell Taylor wrote for the Army's premier professional journal in 1980, "A Do-It-Yourself Professional Code." In it Taylor notes,

> In the absence of authoritative means to identify an unjust war in time to avoid participation, an officer has little choice but to assume the rightness of a governmental decision involving the country in war. Having made this assumption, he is honor-bound to carry out all legal orders and do his best to bring the war to a prompt and successful conclusion. (Taylor, 1980, p. 13)

This is a splendid example of one way that military professions create their expert knowledge and pass it on as authoritative to succeeding generations of leaders—the role of the respected senior professional and mentor. And in this case, one who like his peers at the time allowed little room for principled resignation.

We can also see in the content of Taylor's admonitions another likely reason why the positive became normative—the immense influence of Samuel Huntington and his theories of civil-military relations on our services in the post–World War II era, and particularly on the US Army (Coffman, 1991). Huntington's central contribution of civilian control of the military as best manifested by "objective" means granted the military the autonomy needed to be a profession in return for their neutrality on matters of politics and policy, areas which he believed were beyond the competency of military leaders (Huntington, 1957). In his words, then, the military was to be controlled so as to be only "a tool of the state." Thus, he posited a clear distinction between the spheres of responsibility and action by the civilian leaders in contrast to those of the military leaders—civilians to set policy and strategy with the advice of the military and the military then were to execute faithfully such policy with little interference from civilian leaders. Eliot Cohen has subsequently shown that such "bright lines" between policy and strategy and their execution in wartime have seldom existed, nor should they in his view (Cohen, 2002). Yet, when published this theoretical ideal of American civil-military relations strongly appealed to our armed services. Such ideas and arrangements seemed to match the experiences of those leading our massed, conscripted armies of World War II; and they were taught in the postwar military schools even though the same leaders were then fighting the suffocating "centralization and over control" of bureaucracy within the occupational Army in Europe (Davidson, 1961).

However influential, Huntington's ideas have not all stood the test of time (Nielsen & Snider, 2009). And this returns us to the issue at hand, principled resignation, or as some call it, resignation in protest, because it is my contention that two misconceptions in Huntington's theory of objective control still fuel our divergence on the appropriateness of this particular practice of dissent.

My Position I—Military Professions and Their Essential Character

Huntington's view of the character of our post–World War II military institutions was ambivalent as to whether they were bureaucracy or profession, a distinction he never resolved. His view of military professions was derived from his own historical research and held that they were "more narrowly defined, more intensively and exclusively pursued, and more clearly isolated from other human activity than most occupations. . . . The military function is performed by a public bureaucratized professional expert in the management of violence and responsible for the military security of the state." Thus, notwithstanding an unresolved conception of whether the military was to be a military profession or a hierarchical government bureaucracy, he posited that "loyalty and obedience" were the two cardinal virtues of military institutions. To him, such normative responses were simply owed to the state through its civilian leaders via our Constitutional arrangements and were most applicable for his theory of the military as a "tool of the state."

With respect to the essential character of American military institutions, Huntington failed to recognize what is now known, particularly from the sociology of professions, that they do not have a single character, but rather are of a dual character—that of government bureaucracy and military profession. Thus, there exists a constant, often ferocious, internal tension between them with uniformed leadership determining at any time and location which culture and behavior are predominant (Snider, 2015). Absent strong leadership, the default position is that of government bureaucracy as mandated in the Constitutional provision for executive departments. This is clearly not what is needed for the security of the Republic in the 21st century nor desired by its polity who would prefer that their military services be both effective and ethical. So, what problems does this dual character cause?

Unlike government bureaucracies that deal in routine, often repetitive, nonexpert work, a profession is "a relatively high status occupation whose members develop and apply expert knowledge as human expertise to solve problems in a particular field of endeavor" (Burk, 2005, p. 41). There are five aspects of a profession that are inferred in this definition: (1) professions provide a unique and vital service to the society served, one it cannot provide itself, (2) they do so by the application of expert knowledge and practice, (3) because of their effective and ethical application of their expertise, they earn the trust of the society, (4) professions self-regulate; they police the practices of their members to ensure it is effective and applied only by following the profession's ethic. This includes the responsibility to educate and certify professionals, ensuring only the most proficient members actually apply their expertise on behalf of the client, and (5) professions are therefore granted significant autonomy in their practice on behalf of the society.

Traditionally, the law, medicine, and theology were considered professions within Western democracies. More recently, the military, accountancy, architecture, and a few other service vocations have been accorded the status of professions by the societies they serve. Let me expand a bit on these characteristics as they apply in particular to military professions and their civil-military relations including the norms applicable to dissent by senior leaders.

First, the service provided by military professions—providing for the "common defense"—is obviously vital to the flourishing of the protected society. Yet, such work is clearly beyond the ability of the members of most societies to provide for themselves. Thus, *a deeply moral and mutual relationship of trust* is created between the profession, its individual members as "professionals," and the society served. Simply stated, the society perishes if their profession fails to provide for the common defense. The military profession, which exists only to serve and protect the society which created it, is thus morally obligated as a "social trustee" type of profession to use its military expertise only in accordance with the values held by that society, values which also so strongly inform the profession's ethic. And, these social values do evolve over time—recent examples are the inclusion of openly serving gay soldiers and civilians and allowing women to serve in combat roles.

Second, unlike bureaucracies in the purest sense, professions create and work with expert knowledge developed into human expertise, performing uniquely expert work. Such work is not often the routine or repetitive work of a bureaucracy. A professional's expertise is most often applied within new, often unexpected, situations. Military professionals require years of study and practice before they are capable of such expert work, either as individuals or as a unit. Effectiveness, rather than strict efficiency, is the key to the work of professionals—the sick want a cure, the sinner wants restoration, the accused and the victim want justice, and the defenseless want security. Although the professional must always aim for both effectiveness and efficiency, effectiveness is what counts most to their client.

Third, when a profession's work is done effectively and ethically, the institution and its individual members are granted significant autonomy. Members of professions are trusted to perform their expert work without close supervision. The professional's actual work is *the continuous exercise of discretionary judgments*, acted upon and followed up by the professional for effectiveness (Army Doctrinal Reference Publication 1, 2015). Think of an Air Force doctor doing surgery during an air evacuation, a junior Army leader conducting security operations in a combat zone, or a Defense Department civilian scientist doing research in a government laboratory. All have trained for years, all are surrounded by immensely expensive technology, and all are granted extensive autonomy in the execution of their own discretionary judgments and actions. Each is working as a professional, within a military profession.

The word "discretionary" in the definition above was carefully chosen by Army leaders as they established for the first time ever official doctrine on what it means for that institution to actually be a profession with a culture and behavior that overmatch its original, founding character of a government bureaucracy. Obviously, such discretion increases as leaders rise in rank and responsibility. But the point is that at all levels military professionals are not to act as compliance-based, rule-following, job holders in a big government bureaucracy. Rather, discretionary judgments based on expert knowledge and its effective and ethical applications are the coin of the realm in military professions and in their trust relationship with the society they protect, and so it is with their senior leaders—the stewards of the profession.

Stated another way, such discretion is to be informed by the professional ideology of service that goes beyond serving others' choices. Rather, it claims a devotion to a transcendent value. Moral philosophers call this the moral or common good; in our military profession, we call it the security of the Republic, or in Constitutional language "the common defense." According to one scholar of professions,

> This transcendent value infuses the profession's specialization with a larger and putatively higher goal which may reach beyond those they are supposed to serve. Each body of professional knowledge and skill is attached to such a value. . . . It is because they claim to be a secular priesthood that serves such transcendent and self-evidently desirable values that professionals can claim independence of judgment and freedom of action rather than mere faithful service. (Freidson, 2001, p. 122)

Contrast now, if you will, this doctrine with Huntington's idea that "loyalty and obedience are to be the cardinal virtues" within the military. If so, what is left to discretion? For that let's turn next to a discussion of the content and power of the profession's means of self-control, its ethic. So the question I will address next is loyalty and obedience to whom and for what reason. As we shall see, it is not as straightforward as Huntington would make it seem.

My Position II—The Power of a Professional Ethic and the Senior Leaders' Responsibility to It

His second idea that fuels current debate is Huntington's weak understanding of the content and power of the ethic that informs the behavior of professions as institutions, and their members including their leaders. In this area, more recent research has established new understandings about competitive military professions and their ethics, particularly those of the US Army (Abbott, 2002; Cook, 2002; Mattox, 2005; Pfaff, 2005).

The new understanding is that professions earn and maintain the trust of their clients through their effective and ethical application of their expertise on behalf of the society they serve. Thus, *it is the society served* that will determine whether the profession has earned the high status of a noble occupation and the autonomy that goes along with it. It is not true as Huntington implied that once a profession, always a profession. Simply stated, modern professions die (Abbott, 1988). And in my own experiences, this includes military ones.

I served in the US Army in 1970–1971 in Vietnam when it was not a military profession in any sense of the sociological, or military, construct. Modern professions do die, and in the case of the US Army at the end of the Vietnam War that means having morphed into its alternative character of big government bureaucracy with very limited military effectiveness, utterly untrusted and "spat upon" by the society it served. The professional culture had died and within it, also its ethic. The institution was then controlled more like an untrusted government bureaucracy than a profession. Its professional renewal with a new all-volunteer force and a re-professionalized noncommissioned corps was accompanied by more detailed, top-down policy guidance from both civilian and military leaders covering everything from organization to individual training, greatly restricting previously granted autonomy (Kitfield, 1995; Millett and Maslowski, 1994; Powell, 1995) This continued until the Army once again proved itself as a military profession by contributing greatly to the successful outcome of the Cold War and then decimating Saddam's forces in Kuwait in 1990. My point, contra Huntington, is simply that the behavior of a single military institution can vary widely over time between its two organizational characters; and, military professions do on occasion die.

One major reason for this is that, again unlike government bureaucracies, the means of social control within professions is their ethic. It controls and guides the actions of the institution, the individual professionals, and the effectiveness of their work. A professional ethic is the evolved set of laws and moral values and beliefs deeply embedded within the core of the profession's culture, which binds individual members together in common purpose to do the right thing for the right reason in the right way. The ethic sets the conditions for the creation and maintenance of a motivational, meritocratic culture for all who volunteer to serve. The ethic provides a set of standards which individual professionals willingly impose on each other to keep trust both internally and externally with their client. Hence, an actively *self-policed ethic* is a necessity for any military profession; non-policing bystanders are simply not professionals. This is of special importance for a military profession given the lethality inherent in its expertise.

A profession's ethic also serves powerfully to motivate members of the profession (Snider, 2014). Today, businesses and bureaucracies motivate their workers primarily through extrinsic factors such as salary, benefits, and promotions. In contrast, *professionals themselves place the greatest value on the intrinsic satisfactions inherent in the service they render to society*, and they value those more than the remunerations society extends them. This is why service and sacrifice within a profession is a *calling*—something far more important and satisfying to the professional than just a job. And that also is why the inspirational power of our service's ethic produces more effective units via transformational leadership than does the obligatory ethic of loyalty and obedience within a government bureaucracy.

Concluding Arguments

Turning now to the issue at hand, acts of dissent including resignation by senior military leaders at the nexus of American civil-military relations, I should be clear that I am only discussing relationships in which the military partner is a professional in the context I have been describing. The behavior of military bureaucrats is no longer being discussed here.

Now, I want to recall from Huntington that the responsibilities of the military leader to the state are 3-fold: (1) the representative function (to represent the claims of military security within the state machinery), (2) the advisory function (judgments on alternative courses of state action from the military point of view), and (3) the executive function (to implement state decisions with respect to military security even if it runs violently counter to his military judgment).

Note that the representational and advisory functions are by many understood to be the same, and most often in practice they are. But what we are discussing here in this forum is the possibility of those few instances when, in the discretionary judgment of the senior steward of a military profession, they must of necessity diverge and by what cause. In other words, are the steward's duties from his or her oath to "support and defend" the Constitution, and their fiduciary responsibilities to the profession, its expert knowledge, and its ethical use, always the same? This is the critical question it seems to me. Might there be rare exceptions when their Constitutional duties to "advise" and then "execute" civilian orders clash with their professional responsibilities to "represent the profession" and the effective, ethical application of its expertise—that which they alone hold as a fiduciary trust for the American people.

Professor Martin Cook, the holder of the Stockdale Chair of Ethics at the Naval War College has noted that these two obligations might diverge on occasion. He states, the challenge is:

how to understand professionalism so that two equal values, somewhat in tension with each other,

are preserved: the unquestioned subordination of military officers to Constitutionally legitimate civilian leadership; and the equally important role of the officer corps in providing professional military advice, unalloyed with extraneous political or cultural considerations. (Cook, 2004, p. 55)

As Cook believes, part of that judgment must rest on the idea that professionals are obligated not only to serve the client (in this case, ultimately, the state and its polity) but also obligated to have "their own highly developed internal sense of the proper application of the professional knowledge" (Cook, 2004). In other words, dissent without insubordination to civilian authority can rightly be based on loyalty to the profession's expert knowledge and its appropriate application. If this were not the case, there would be no need for military professions—the Republic's security could be provided by businesses and bureaucracies.

In a more recent paper, Cook helpfully notes two examples of parallel cases from other professions where the scope and limits of a professional's moral autonomy will cause acts of dissent: (1) physicians must refuse to provide medical services that are "not medically indicated" regardless of how strenuously the patient may ask for it, and (2) lawyers will not violate disclosure rules even if the information disclosed is detrimental to their case because the integrity of our adversarial justice system rests on the "fair fight" (Cook, 2015).

Professor James Burk, currently the President and Chair of the Inter-University Seminar on Armed Forces & Society, has expressed a similar view in more detail. In a challenge to Huntington's functionalist assertion that loyalty and obedience are the cardinal military virtues, James Burk contends that

military professionals require autonomy, to include moral autonomy, to be competent actors held responsible for what they do. By autonomy, I mean the ability to govern or control one's actions with some degree of freedom. Autonomous action is a condition for responsible obedience and the opposite of blind obedience. . . . [There is a] conceptual space within which military professionals exercise moral discretion. The map includes a definition of responsible obedience and disobedience. But it also includes two types of actions that do not fit the classic definitions of these alternatives. They each exhibit a defect in which discretion is used either to do what is morally wrong or to do what was explicitly not authorized. Nevertheless, they are not simply forms of disobedience. They are "protected" actions, protected because the discretion to commit them preserves the autonomy on which the moral responsibility of the military profession depends. (Burk, 2010, pp. 162–163)

As I have argued several times, my own view has long agreed with the theme of those just referenced (Snider, 2008). I believe there is that narrow moral space wherein the exercise of discretionary professional judgment can lead to loyal dissent. Such acts by the stewards of military professions can fall in the "protected space" that all professionals' actions occupy, a space that may indeed require acts of dissent or disobedience if in Burks's words "the moral responsibility of the profession is to be preserved."

In fact, below are several quite plausible instances in which I believe such an act of dissent should be given serious consideration. All of these situations have occurred during my decades of service to the Republic and, it seems to me, are of such moral gravity and of such grave implications for our national security that senior military professionals might exercise their discretionary judgment to consider a principled resignation:

- Civilian leaders indicate they will pursue the zero nuclear option, idealistically denuclearizing US Armed Forces while allies and adversaries remain nuclear capable;
- Civilian leaders direct the planning of a war of aggression;
- Civilian leaders direct the planning of a war the execution of which is clearly not going to achieve strategic purposes, wasting the lives of military and civilians alike (e.g., as in the lack of Phase IV planning for the invasion of Iraq in 2002).
- Civilian leaders refuse to resource the armed forces for probable future conflict (e.g., as in the well-known case of a future Task Force Smith).

So, with plausible cases such as these, I believe Huntington's conceptions of loyalty and obedience simply cannot be understood to mean in every case they are to overrule a senior leader's professional judgment. That is the behavior of bureaucracy, not of profession.

Some of my colleagues have argued that this moral space to dissent is so small that it vanishes on closer inspection and application (Golby, 2015). I respectfully disagree. Neither do I agree with other colleagues who argue that a Constitutional or political "crisis" will inevitably ensue from a military leader's resignation in protest, thereby causing grave damage to the democratic institutions and processes of our Republic. I have seen a president resign, another forced not to run for reelection, a president and his brother presidential candidate be assassinated, the firings of two secretaries of defenses, more than one service secretary and many four-star military leaders . . . and the Republic with its venerable democratic institutions still stands! So, are we to believe that the resignation in protest of one senior military professional would be more stressful than these instances? Not convincing; not at all.

Rather, I believe that the office which Army professionals enter when taking their oath is not a physical workspace; it is a moral workspace. And because of the nature of their fiduciary trust as stewards of the American people's military professions, senior military leaders can never relinquish their individual moral agency within that trust. Thus, it may in rare cases require them to act with public dissent which, of course, can include a principled resignation in protest. Without the ability to exercise such authoritative discretionary judgment, which distinguishes professions from all other occupations, they "would become little more than servants in a cafeteria . . . doing whatever is demanded of them, and seeking above all else to please." (Freidson, 1994, p. 211).

NOTES

An accompanying podcast for this article is available at http://journals.sagepub.com/doi/suppl/10.1177/0095327X16657322.

REFERENCES

Abbott, A. (1988). *The system of professions: An essay on the division of labor*. Chicago, IL: University of Chicago Press.

Abbott, A. (2002). The army and the theory of professions. In D. M. Snider & G. Watkins (Eds.), *The future of the army profession* (pp. 523–536). New York, NY: McGraw-Hill.

Army Doctrinal Reference Publication 1. (2015). *The army profession*. Washington, DC: Headquarters Department of the Army.

Betts, R. (1977). *Soldiers, statesmen and Cold War crises* (1st ed.). Cambridge, MA: Harvard University Press.

Betts, R. (1991). *Soldiers, statesmen and Cold War crises*. New York, NY: Columbia University Press.

Burk, J. (2005). Expertise, jurisdiction, and legitimacy of the military profession. In D. M. Snider & L. J. Matthews (Eds.), *The future of the army profession* (2nd ed., pp. 39–60). New York, NY: McGraw-Hill.

Burk, J. (2010). Responsible obedience and discretion to do what is wrong. In S. C. Nielsen & D. M. Snider (Eds.), *American civil-military relations: The soldier and the state in a new era* (pp. 149–171). Baltimore, MD: Johns Hopkins University Press.

Coffman, E. (1991). The long shadow of the soldier and the state. *Journal of Military History*, 55, 69–82.

Cohen, E. (2002). *Supreme command*. New York, NY: The Free Press.

Cook, M. (2002). Army professionalism: Service to what ends? *The future of the army profession*. New York, NY: McGraw-Hill.

Cook, M. (2004). *The moral warrior: Ethics and service in the U.S. Military*. Albany: State University of New York Press.

Cook, M. (2015). Unpublished paper presented at US Army Command and Staff College Ethics Conference, Ft Leavenworth, KS. Copy in possession of author.

Davidson, G. (1961, December). Decentralization—A key to command effectiveness. *Army Information Digest*, 13–16.

Feaver, P. (2015). The irony of civil-military relations. *Strategic Studies Quarterly, 9*, 3–15.

Freidson, E. (1994). *Professionalism reborn: Theory, prophecy and policy.* Chicago, IL: University of Chicago Press.

Freidson, E. (2001). *Professionalism: The third logic.* Chicago, IL: University of Chicago Press.

Golby, J. (2015). Beyond the resignation debate: A new framework for civil-military dialogue. *Strategic Studies Quarterly, 9*, 18–46.

Huntington, S. (1957). *The soldier and the state.* Cambridge, MA: Belknap Press of Harvard University.

Kitfield, J. (1995). *Prodigal soldiers: How the generation of officers born of Vietnam revolutionized the American style of war.* New York, NY: Simon and Schuster.

Kohn, R. (2009). Building trust: Civil-military behaviors for effective national security. In S. C. Nielsen & D. M. Snider (Eds.), *American civil-military relations: The soldier and the state in a new era* (pp. 264–289). Baltimore, MD: Johns Hopkins University Press.

Matthews, L. (1990, January). Resignation in protest. *Army Magazine*, pp. 12–21.

Mattox, J. (2005). The moral foundation of army officership. In D. Snider & L. Matthews (Eds.), *The future of the army profession* (2nd ed., pp. 293–312). New York, NY: McGraw-Hill.

Millett, A., & Maslowski, P. (1994). *For the common defense: A military history of the United States of America.* New York, NY: The Free Press.

Nielsen, S. C., & Snider, D. M. (Eds.). (2009). *American civil-military relations: The soldier and the state in a new era.* Baltimore, MD: Johns Hopkins University Press.

Pfaff, T. (2005). The officer as leader of character: leadership, character, and ethical decision-making. In D. Snider & L. Matthews (Eds.), *The future of the army profession* (2nd ed., pp. 153–160). New York, NY: McGraw-Hill.

Powell, C. (1995). *My American journey.* New York, NY: Random House.

Snider, D. M. (2008). Dissent and strategic leadership of the military professions. *ORBIS, 52*, 256–277.

Snider, D. M. (2014). Renewing the motivational power of the army's professional ethic *Parameters, 44*, 7–11.

Snider, D. M. (2015). American military professions and their ethics. In G. Lucas (Ed.), *Routledge handbook of military ethics* (pp. 15–31). London, England: Routledge.

Taylor, M. (1980, December). A do-it-yourself professional code. *Parameters, 10*(4), 10–15.

Chapter 6

The Changing Profession of Arms

Redefinitions and Transformations in the Profession of Arms

CHRISTOPHER D. MILLER

The difficulty lies, not in the new ideas, but in escaping from the old ones, which ramify, for those brought up as most of us have been, into every corner of our minds.

—John Maynard Keynes, *The General Theory of Employment, Interest, and Money*

American military professionals, like their counterparts worldwide, seek to maintain capability, capacity, and relevance in order to fulfill their historic role as protectors of territories and people and principal arbiters of victory and defeat in violent confrontations. Yet the past several decades of technological advancements and societal trends have increasingly assaulted time-honored foundational assumptions about the military ethos, the boundaries between civilian and military occupations, the habits of civil-military relations, and the organization for national security. As the very words we use to describe war and peace, battlefields and weapons, and warriors themselves are being stretched to the breaking point, it is important to ask if it is time to retire the idea of the *profession of arms* in favor of the less evocative but more useful concept of the *military profession*. Doing so may allow us to develop a common perspective among military members and the society they serve that focuses beyond the *tools* of war, toward its *ends*: beyond the "management of violence" to the "mastery of lethal competition."

This essay sets out to formulate the questions that will guide those forthcoming investigations. It starts by examining the concept of the profession of arms and then turns to the changing conduct of war in the twenty-first century. Subtly and without heralds, we have crossed a Rubicon, and modern conflict has become fundamentally different—however, we have yet to sort out the effects of the ever-smaller gap between politics and war on the stability of the international system. What constitutes the boundary between politics and war and what defines moderation in these new competitive spaces? Turning to military expertise, what are the consequences of changing the location and timelines of war on the men and women who fight it? As conflict expands more definitively into new domains and effectively both shrinks the time and transforms the human face society has come to associate with war, the role and identity of the military professional is being morphed, stretched, and challenged. What should

we value and honor in the twenty-first-century warrior? These questions in themselves suggest that a reorientation of the profession of arms is taking place, but our understanding of this change has not kept pace; given the tectonic changes in technology, society, and the execution of war, is it still appropriate to define our military as mere warriors who are members of the profession of arms that manage violence? Are they not something more?

Meaningful Definitions in the Profession of Arms

Nowhere is the turbulence of contemporary international relations more relevant than for the American profession of arms, whose membership has varied over time and whose history includes a record of tactical and operational success that predates nearly all living Americans. Fortified by a sense of insulation from likely military threat to American territory and lacking the fearful urgency of the early Cold War, contemporary Americans understandably have a propensity to view the use of military force as mostly expeditionary and elective—despite clear evidence that technology increasingly makes geography less of a barrier to foreseeable physical and virtually-inflicted harm, and threats to US interests, allies, and homeland continue to multiply.[1] This underlying sense of sanctuary, combined with habits of proactive power projection in response to crises and to bolster allies, strongly shapes civilian leaders' and the public's instinctive views of the role of military force.

Elsewhere in this volume, Jeffrey Donnithorne (chapter 6) explores the nature of professions in general, how service organizational cultures evolved, and the ways they manifest in the Department of Defense. There are many competing definitions of "a profession," all of which have value for understanding the broad and significant concept, and all of which, to one degree or another, identify relatively exclusive possession and regulated use of specialized knowledge as requisite for a profession to be so called. Older views tend to prescribe specific milestones as necessary for a profession to exist, such as associations and journals. More recent observers, such as sociologist James Burk, have written that a profession can be defined more functionally as "a relatively 'high status' occupation whose members apply abstract knowledge to solve problems in a particular field of endeavor."[2] The Air Force and Army have recently defined professions specific to each service, with nuances involving certification and type of service and a distinction made between the institution and the organizational bureaucracy that constitutes its personnel.[3] One of the earliest writers to specifically address the military profession, Samuel Huntington, asserted that "the distinguishing characteristics of a profession as a special type of vocation are its expertise, responsibility, and corporateness."[4] Not all would agree that there is such a thing as a universal military profession; instead of being guided by the universal ethos of a profession, performance in the military setting depends on individual judgment and organizational proficiency.[5]

Setting aside these very real definitional questions, however, it is most relevant in the context of this discussion to recognize that occupational groups are generally accorded "professional" status not by autonomous decree, but by the society to whom they provide essential and distinctive functions. Their claim to a particular jurisdiction and the degree of autonomy they are granted to operate within that jurisdiction depend on their expertise and their legitimacy in developing, extending, and employing it to achieve the outcomes society values.[6] Moreover, jurisdictional boundaries are not fixed,[7] and in the case of the American military, they can be redrawn both within the larger military profession and outside it: in evolutionary practice and competition between the services themselves, by executive decision of the secretary of defense, or by law when Congress acts. When considering the future of the profession of arms and when considering national security writ large, it is important to recognize that the military possesses neither formal nor informal *exclusive* jurisdiction. In this regard, it operates within what Andrew Abbot calls an "interdependent system" of professions.[8]

As a profession, the American military remains very highly regarded by the public, as reported by successive years of reputable opinion polling.[9] From the early 1900s, there was a general recognition that the officer corps possessed a necessary, specialized expertise. James Burk notes that the military's professional progression can be "reduced to slogan form by saying the Army has moved from the management of war early in the century to the management of defense (a wider concern) during the Cold War to the management of peace (an even wider concern)" during the Global War on Terror.[10] From the early years of counterterror operations to the present day, the public narrative has arguably been a dialectic involving ideal ends—seen as infeasible—and very real ongoing costs in blood and treasure, which have been seen as increasingly unbearable. The last two decades of military operations in Afghanistan, Iraq, and Syria have arguably not been seen as "managing peace," but neither have they been perceived as waging war to a definitive conclusion. Thus, no slogan as crisp as "managing peace" has yet emerged for the future military profession. On the contrary, the degree of sacrifice associated with multiple, frequent deployments and the tactical mastery exhibited by American military forces have served as a basis for the American military today to be given professional status. Such recognition implicitly recognizes its central role in preservation of a technologically complex, politically tumultuous, geographically vast, and economically dynamic nation. It competes for resources, prestige, the ability to self-police and to determine its own standards and membership, based on its ability to deliver that societal good. It does so as part of a complex, disparately resourced and supervised national security enterprise charged with mastering the extraordinary demands a complex, connected global society inevitably imposes on it. Where jurisdictional boundaries are drawn and how well they are navigated within the military is important to joint war-fighting effectiveness in the classical sense; where boundaries are drawn within the larger national security enterprise is equally, if not more important in countering evolving national security threats.

War and its core constituents, the risking and taking of life, have had such a powerful imprint on military ethos and public imagination that any change is likely to be extraordinarily difficult. Matters of technology, acquisition, resources, doctrine, or strategy are always pressing, often critically important, and routinely draw great attention from all involved in government decision-making. Yet it is arguably far more important to reconsider the way we think about and perpetuate military ethos, often encapsulated in the phrase "profession of arms," so as to ensure that the profession's ethos actually prepares it to reliably master tomorrow's contests. An honest examination of fundamental, mostly unspoken, assumptions about war and warriors, and the link between them, is perennially necessary and now long overdue. Such an examination should encompass what society values, how traditional military virtues and attributes should be manifest in the future, and by whom, how defense professionals and elected leaders holistically understand and communicate about threats to national security and prioritize people, energy, and resources to address those threats; and it should examine and recognize disconnects in the language that describes human conflict, including the civil-military communications that remain central to success and failure. Accordingly, failure to grapple with deeply held assumptions and evolve the national security enterprise—its ethos, organization, or both—is likely to be devastating.

At its core, understanding the modern profession of arms is not an exercise in sociology; it is an exercise in clarity of thought and alignment with the world as it is becoming, not the world that has been. If we do not understand the battle itself, who fights it on our behalf, the tools and partners they fight with, the values they bring to the fight and the enemies they fight against, we cannot expect to succeed. Looking inward is difficult but it is the sine qua non for a viable military profession.

The Twenty-First Century *Is* Different

"War" is a short word with a long history. It is still used as a definitive marker for a phenomenon that has actually mutated into something far more ambiguous. This mutation is critical because as concepts of war change, so too should understanding of the profession of arms and a service member's role in the military. Conflict today—whether or not recognizable as war—must be understood to encompass the real harm that can be invited by, inflicted through, or suffered by the complex physical and virtual connections between societies. The future of conflict will only occasionally involve what militaries like to call "war." Combat may look like it has for centuries—identifiable combatants using lethal force, ranging in magnitude from knives to nuclear weapons, exposing themselves and others to risk of life and limb, enduring and inflicting privation and sacrifice in order to achieve victory, however it is defined. Yet we are actually living in the sum of ancient and modern worlds, where attacks can be as horrific as a beheading, as instantly destructive as a thermonuclear blast, or as subtle as insertion of lines of malign code in essential war-fighting or national infrastructure systems. The former attacks demand and would be likely to receive immediate response. For the latter, the members and organizations that compose the profession of arms may lack the mission, tools, or awareness to repel them until after substantial damage is inevitable in the fabric of the society they are charged to defend. Thus for twenty-first-century militaries, the range of actions required to succeed in managing those future conflicts is an "and," not an "or," conundrum. Violent death is not going away, but it is no longer the clear harbinger of very real lethal intent.

The fate of nations in this century will also, and increasingly, depend on nonlethal actions of varying visibilities, magnitudes, and objects, whose consequences are less direct and predictable than traditional combat, but which could be equally—if differently—devastating. Future conflict will increasingly traverse lines on the map through tangible and less-tangible domains and involve groups of widely varying and incommensurate sizes. War was once fought solely on land or sea, analogous to a chessboard; potentially lethal conflict is pursued today on a multilevel chessboard, for mental as well as physical terrain, with new kinds of chess pieces, between adversaries who may or may not be able to see each other. As Mike Mazarr points out in chapter 4 of this volume, blurring of categories makes it increasingly difficult to define entities that are "enemies."

In the world of land armies, castles, and moats, a prince would surrender when the inhabitants of his fortification were starved, killed, or in revolt and unwilling to fight. In today's world, "If you can win the internet, you can win silly feuds, elections, and deadly serious battles alike. You can even warp how people see themselves and the world around them."[11] In short, the desired effect of militaries and politicians at war, since time immemorial, has been to convince the enemy to yield; whether by force of arms or by altering the enemy's view of the world and willingness to fight, the effect is the same.

The difficulty of adapting to this new kind of conflict environment is illustrated by the oft-heard Clausewitzian truism that "the nature of war is constant; only the character of war changes."[12] In venerating the nature of war as a constant, the unstated assumption is that warriors remain responsible for conducting it and that the only challenge is anticipating and mastering changes in its character. In other words, with the right resources, technology, training, strategy, operational plan, and partners, "war" can be identified, prepared for, initiated, prosecuted, concluded, and won at some level—by military forces. However, as we shall discuss below, this comforting thought is misleading. It is analogous to saying that water doesn't change, thus implicitly equating the effects of years of drip-by-drip erosion with the impact of a tsunami on a city—and expecting the same kinds of people to deal with the full range of problems that "water" presents.

The United States retains allies, interests, and commitments across the globe that it continues to support, defend, and honor as it has for decades. Simultaneously, the panoply of real threats to US territory and population is significant and growing. It includes the familiar—such as conventional and direct nuclear attack—and the less familiar, such as attack on space-based commercial or military infrastructure; electromagnetic pulse; cyberattack on the electrical grid; compromise and functional destruction of self-driving transportation; genetically targeted biological attack; misinformation directed against educated, politically empowered citizens; and exfiltration of immense volumes of scientific, technical, and personal data. All of these less-familiar threats share a common characteristic in that they are, or were recently thought to be, highly improbable. They do not draw the same urgency and public understanding as insurgencies, terrorism, civil wars, and preparation for potential state-on-state warfare. As Thomas Schelling wrote in 1962, however, "There is a tendency in our planning to confuse the unfamiliar with the improbable. The contingency we have not considered seriously looks strange; what looks strange is thought improbable; what is improbable need not be considered seriously."[13] We have recent experience, with the COVID-19 pandemic, of a stressor on the US population and economy, and the rapid adoption of tech-enabled virtual work illustrates both agility and the potential vulnerability associated with reliance on such systems. Neither of these phenomena was unanticipated before the opening months of 2020; their magnitude and interaction, however, came as a surprise. Emerging threats look strange only because of the lenses we use to examine them.

This is perhaps so because millennia of history have shaped a pervasive Western assumption that the activity known as war, when it involves military force, is about attacking and defending lines on the ground. Human experience of war has shaped our language and public discourse around sacrifice, physical action, proximate conflict, comradeship strengthened by shared risk and privation, and stakes that clearly and compellingly involve life and death. Such powerful shared assumptions, particularly in the United States, are both compelling and confining when it comes to comprehending evolving conflict modalities. On a practical level, that same experience has been systematically codified in various "principles of war" that proceed directly from the demands of waging physical combat, such as mass, maneuver, simplicity, surprise, and others.

For example, the nominal course of an armed conflict is codified in US joint doctrine, which states that each phase is a "definitive stage or period during a joint operation in which a large portion of the forces and capabilities are involved in similar or mutually supporting activities for a common purpose."[14] These notional phases include shaping, deterring, seizing initiative, dominating, stabilizing, and enabling civil authority.[15] While not necessarily present or sequential in any given conflict, they reflect assumptions that military action will largely focus on physical control of territory and lines of communication because these things have historically been prerequisites for maintaining the security of people and nations or the objectives for acquisitive powers desiring to accumulate greater resources.

Regardless of the causes of armed conflicts—whether religious, ethnic, ideological, resource, or miscalculation—the idea that peace and war are two somewhat mutually exclusive sides of a coin has been a consistent thread throughout the history of warfare, shaping the way states have organized, trained, equipped, and conceived of using their military forces. The dichotomy has shaped models of civil-military relations, and it is embedded in language—from the US Constitution to common discourse to the writings of military theorists. Carl von Clausewitz made two telling assertions: "War is not a mere act of policy but a true political instrument, a continuation of political activity by other means,"[16] and "the end for which a soldier is recruited, clothed, armed, and trained, the whole object of his sleeping, eating, drinking, and marching *is simply that he should fight at the right place and at the right time*."[17]

This binary mental model, in which peace and war are clearly delineated, is gradually being supplemented by terms such as "gray zone," "hybrid warfare," "cyber warfare," and the like. In an alternative mental model, modern conflict is more like a matrix of parallel and perpendicular beams of light passing through a misty three-dimensional battlespace, where the beams represent *interests*—possessed by states, organizations, alliances, and even individuals—and the intersection of beams represents the *interaction* of those interests. When they intersect in such a way that they reinforce each other, there is coexistence and cooperation; but where they collide, the result can be constructive competition, adversarial conflict, or combat in one or more domains for some period of time. The interests are continuously variable, changing the position and size of the nodes of intersection where they collide or cohere. Major war can flare at any of these nodes when conflicting interests are vital or perceived to be so; conversely, conflict and competition at these intersections may exist chronically, never escalating to something as easily identifiable as "war." Depending on the domain, geography, and other factors, any conflict may be more or less visible to the people and nations involved.

The location and timeline of war have changed. Sharply contrasting with World War I a century ago, where logistical preparations and operations plans were concrete, pervasive, and time-consuming and battle was joined with great violence on now-hallowed, distant physical battlefields, modern conflict is capable of occurring in the silicon of sensors and data stores that shape human perception and can develop in microseconds to minutes, not months. An attack on a nation's infrastructure might have required a lengthy physical deployment and days or months of combat operations in years past, but is now conceivably achieved through far quicker cyber action; as General Paul Nakasone, commander of US Cyber Command, testified in 2019, "Our adversaries in cyberspace are acting and taking risks in seeking to gain advantage without escalating to armed conflict; they are conducting campaigns to gain cumulative advantage (these include theft of intellectual property and personal information, malign influence and election interference, efforts to circumvent sanctions, and probes and positioning to threaten critical infrastructure)."[18] Stanley Hoffmann, writing in 1965, addressed the stability of systems in an international conflict by asserting that "when one major actor's decision to discard [moderation] coincides with or brings about a revolution in the technology of conflict or a change in the basic structure of the world (or both), the system is particularly unstable."[19] In this case, technology appears to have changed the temporal, as well as the strategic, stability of the system.

Future conflict is also going to be different because public awareness of events is rapid, but understanding of the instability of national and international systems is not robust. Unlike tanks massed on a border or bombers overhead, which are within common imagination, few people know which spacefaring nations and industries provide their personal phones with satellite navigation and timing signals, earth-sensing for weather and precision agriculture applications, or communications for everything from power distribution to on-demand logistics to daily news and information. From their generally military origin and application to commercial development and deployment, these systems have grown to have tremendous impact on daily life.[20]

These evolutions are one of the reasons for the fraying of elements of post–World War II international consensus. Wherever their interests intersect, global actors (nations and others) have always engaged in politics, cooperation, competition, and conflict. Combatants prepare for and conduct wars when other elements of national power fail to achieve their objectives. The stakes have expanded beyond control of territory, however, and the international system has become less stable because it is increasingly difficult to ascertain what constitutes the boundary between politics and "war" and what defines moderation in these new competitive spaces.

Military Expertise and Values

Just as the foundational definitions of war versus peace and the geography and timelines of conflict have adjusted or frayed, so too has the role and identity of the military professional. The traditional uniformed managers of violence have taken on increasingly nonviolent roles in contemporary conflict—as nation-builders, government advisors, and emergency responders. And conversely, new players have assumed the mantle of defending society from harm: hackers and cyber operators, remote controllers of aircraft and satellites, data analysts and political affairs specialists, uniformed and civilian, all only marginally connected to the prototypical notion of "arms" and yet inextricably members of a profession that defends the nation. In some respects, this is not a new dynamic; militaries over millennia have been divided by combatant and support roles, often referred to as "tip of the spear" and "rear echelon" troops. The reality has also been that not all combatants fight and not all support personnel are immune from enemy action, so the distinction has been more rhetorical than real depending on the war, the kind of fighting force, and the era. Yet what has changed recently is crucially important: with the rise of remotely piloted aircraft and the increasing likelihood that conflict in space and cyberspace will result in real harm to platforms and societies, "warriors" in these areas no longer inherently incur physical risk but can inflict direct or indirect physical harm, with or without classical violence. As Morris Janowitz foreshadowed, technology has indeed affected this traditional combatant/noncombatant categorization, with long-term implications for the idea of the "profession of arms."

Writing in the decade following the Second World War, during the early years of the Cold War and about a force still largely made up of conscripts, Samuel Huntington closely associated the profession of arms with *management of violence*. His definition of the military professional was centered on the experienced military officer, whose special expertise was developed with long experience and specific military education; it explicitly excluded the lower officer and enlisted ranks whose skills were technical, not managerial, and who applied rather than managed force. All of his elaborations of core military expertise were oriented toward discharging a distinctive responsibility, "the military security of his client, society."[21] Huntington also famously proposed what he called an "objective control" model for civil-military relations, in which the military gains a greater degree of autonomy in exchange for remaining explicitly apolitical with regard to civilian society and partisan politics.[22] The conceptual clarity and deconflicted prerogatives associated with this model remain powerfully attractive and have generally been reflected in words and actions on both sides of the civil-military relationship, despite much evidence that reality is far more complicated.

Shortly after Huntington wrote in 1957, Morris Janowitz advanced an alternative view, still firmly anchored in the Cold War's underlying tension between fear of nuclear Armageddon and the reality of continued use of conventional arms, that the "use of force in international relations has been so altered that it seems appropriate to speak of constabulary forces, rather than of military forces . . . continuously prepared to act, committed to the minimum use of force, [seeking] viable international relations, rather than victory, because [they have] incorporated a protective military posture."[23] Janowitz predicted that military and civilian technologies and functions would become increasingly intermingled, with consequences for the nature of that force, noting that "the effectiveness of the military establishment depends on maintaining a proper balance between military technologists, heroic leaders, and military managers."[24] Samuel Moskos, in turn, noted the postmodern military's "genetic self-image is that of a specialist in violence" while positing the ascendance of soldier-scholars and soldier-statesmen to deal with post–Cold War substate military challenges.[25] Of these three, Janowitz may have been most prescient in describing the trends that have resulted in today's American military composition, missions, and organization.

More recent scholars have described nuances of civil-military relations and the military's behavior as a bureaucratic actor with greater precision and more current empirical data. Paula Thornhill articulated a contrast in concepts of military organization and identity when she noted that the American military faces a dichotomy between a historically validated, force-employment-focused "overseas" paradigm and an emerging "guardian" paradigm. This echoes in some respects Huntington's and Janowitz's models, with their differing emphases on where, how, and under what circumstances force is an appropriate tool for militaries and the composition of the force wielding it.[26] Peter Feaver cogently portrayed the military's ability to either support or undermine civilian leaders within the context of a principal-agent relationship, as well as the range of consequences that actions within that context can have for civil-military relations.[27]

Despite the validity and accuracy of competing analyses of the military profession's nature and its role in society, Huntington's description of the military professional's unique expertise in "management of violence" has arguably had the most powerfully sustained influence on the core identity of the American military professional.[28] This conception reflects solidification of a long trajectory in the evolution of the military as a professional endeavor, what Sir John Winthrop Hackett called "the ordered application of force in the resolution of a social or political problem, under an unlimited liability."[29]

Because the ancient lexicon of discord—words like "war," "arms," "force," "military," "violence," "death," "battlefield," and many others—has retained all of its resonance while losing some of its relevance, it is becoming dangerously incomplete and misleading in describing modern military professionals or the kinds of battles they can be required to fight. Powerful emotions associated with tangible, lethal violence reinforce increasingly outdated stereotypes of all meaningful conflict as violent, episodic, and valorous, which in turn substantially shape and often circumscribe military, popular, and prevailing elite approaches to modern conflict and constrain the breadth and utility of civil-military dialog.

From the bugles of the traditional battlefield to the cacophony that is modern social media, this visceral drumbeat about war and warriors has been audible for millennia. Whether it rings clear in the words of Shakespeare's *Henry V* as he exalts the bond of shared bloodshed,[30] is seen in the market success of myriad war movies, is written in the language of national defense policy documents, or appears in the contemporary, omnipresent "thank you for your service," there remains a rhythmic undertone of soldiers standing in the breach as defenders of society. It resounds over time, powerful and seemingly immutable.

The underlying assumption that the uniformed military is about what Don Snider has called the "killing and dying business"[31] is reflected in the articulated values of the US military services and visible in every artifact associated with the services, from uniform insignia to the words used in evaluations and decorations to the precedence of those decorations themselves. An instructive example of this is the creation of the Distinguished Warfare Medal (DWM), announced by Secretary of Defense Leon Panetta in February 2013. In Panetta's words, "The medal provides distinct, departmentwide recognition for . . . extraordinary achievements that directly impact on combat operations, but that do not involve acts of valor or physical risk that combat entails."[32] This medal, which was the first new combat decoration since the Bronze Star was created in 1944, would have ranked below Distinguished Service and Flying Cross awards; but it was rescinded by Panetta's successor, Secretary Chuck Hagel, a mere two months later in a memo that recognized the evolving nature of warfare while doubling down on warrior tradition:

> The character of modern warfare has changed and will continue to evolve. Technological advancements have led to remarkable military accomplishments that have direct bearing on battlefield success even though they entail less direct physical risk to our force. Extraordinary achievements of our Service men and women under these circumstances deserve distinct recognition. . . .
>
> Utilizing a distinguishing device [on noncombat decorations] to recognize impacts on combat operations *reserves our existing combat medals* for those Service members who incur the physical risk and hardship of combat, perform valorous acts, are wounded in combat, or as a result of combat give their last full measure for our Nation.[33]

One inference that can be drawn from this decision is that the military services place a higher value on risk and sacrifice than they do on battlefield effect, again reinforcing the supremacy of the warrior ethos—the armed and armored knight—implicit in Huntington's description of the military profession. This tension between "valor and value" is made clearer by two examples. First, consider that for remotely piloted aircraft operators, after rescission of the DWM, the Air Force elected to approve an "R" (remote) device to be attached to peacetime decorations to recognize the "direct impact Remotely Piloted Aircraft aircrews have on the battlefield."[34] While significant, and despite the fact that RPA crewmembers routinely employ lethal force and risk moral injury similarly, if not more acutely, than combatants in a battle where the risks of dying and killing are more symmetrical, this is not a combat decoration. Second, the creation of the US Space Force in late 2019 implies that, for the first time, members of an entire US military service will have no real path to winning a traditional, recognized combat decoration, despite being responsible for launching, operating, and actively defending immensely valuable space systems that themselves provide vital systemic information and services to the United States and allied militaries, governments, and populations. Alignment of recognition with the magnitude of nontraditional warriors' value to national security remains, for now, an open question.

Past Operational and Tactical Excellence Does Not Guarantee Strategic Success

Emerging from the Second World War's unconditional victories against the Axis powers, the American military establishment was reinforced in its belief in the value of industrial, logistical, and operational mass; the efficacy of firepower; the importance of maneuver; and the criticality of superior technology. These touchstones, bound together with sufficient training and professional leadership, were seen as fully sufficient to take and hold territory and compel an adversary to yield. Conscripted citizen-soldiers, led by a standing cadre of officers and noncommissioned officers, brought skill, courage, persistence, and the full panoply of traditional warrior values to bear in bloody struggle that, apart from the technologies used to prosecute it, resembled the campaigns of Nelson, Napoleon, or Alexander the Great. The ethos of the modern US military is seen and revisited partly through unit campaign streamers, unit designations, and shared heritage that would have been novel in detail but not in kind to those ancient warriors.

The emergence of oppositional blocs and the proliferation of atomic weapons rapidly imposed strong disincentives for the kind of mass warfare that characterized the World Wars. Even the Korean conflict—as bloody and protracted as it was—reflected the sharply different calculus of a world where weapons of mass destruction existed in the hands of opposing nations. Thus, the US military increasingly adapted to the existence of this ceiling on violence over time. Doctrine, force structure, training, operational concepts, and publicly articulated strategies favored deterrence and minimized risk of inadvertent escalation beyond the nuclear threshold; US military actions were calibrated to

maximize the value of possession of nuclear weapons but avoid their use.

Throughout the post–Cold War decades, American military operations achieved an enviable record of battlefield success in conventional operations and counterinsurgencies alike, leveraging highly trained military personnel, extraordinarily effective weapon systems, and an unprecedented fidelity and volume of combat-relevant intelligence information. In many respects, the modern American military has done—and has been seen to do—everything that civilian leaders and citizens expected of it in the face of geopolitically difficult conflicts. Yet this record of success on the battlefield—which adds natural momentum to the desire to do the same kinds of things better—does not necessarily presage victory in future conflicts. Rather than dissecting and assessing all of the counterinsurgencies and conventional military operations over the last half-century, engaging in a thought experiment encompassing a hundred years of history (1945–2045) may better serve to underscore the complexity of future national security problems and illuminate the challenge of anticipating and mitigating complex, novel threats.

In the 1940s, tens of thousands of Allied aircraft attacked Axis targets in order to destroy transportation and other infrastructure. Over a period of years, tens of thousands of airmen perished, along with greater numbers of combatants and noncombatants in the places that were targeted. The success of the effort was uneven and the cost, in lives and suffering, immense. No nation wished to repeat such horrors or to suffer air attack of any kind. Thus, in the 1950s and 1960s, when a nuclear-armed Soviet Union threatened North America with long-range bombers, the United States and Canada allied to create NORAD (North American Aerospace Defense), a bi-national military structure to provide long-range detection of attacking aircraft and air defense of their territory. NORAD built a vast radar network, deployed more than a thousand air defense fighters and hundreds of surface-to-air missiles, and later developed the ability to detect ballistic missiles as they came into the Soviet arsenal. While imperfect even when fielded, this classical military response to a tangible challenge sufficed to defend territory and population for its time. In short, a physical threat emerged, a military response ensued, and a national security objective was achieved.

By 2045, it is reasonable to assume industry will be in the process of successfully fielding a North American network of autonomous, mostly electrically powered vehicles. Projections vary for how widespread autonomous vehicles will be, but the long-haul trucking industry is likely to be the leading edge of the transition. Compared to defending rail lines, highways, power plants, and the like against kinetic attack, the dynamics of ensuring an autonomous, electrically powered transportation network remains capable of carrying the commerce required to sustain life and enable prosperity are entirely different. Intellectual property rights and commercial incentives will largely determine the design of the autonomous vehicles and supporting systems of the future. The military has no clear responsibility or authority to mandate, develop, or fund their resiliency against cyberattacks on electrical power or the software and sensors of the vehicles themselves. Economic disincentives will make it less likely they will be designed with backup means of operation, and future generations will not naturally develop the skills to navigate or control vehicles. In March 2020, the congressionally chartered Cyber Solarium Commission highlighted the need to build collective understanding, national will, and mechanisms to increase resilience of transportation and other critical digital systems against adversary attack, but the magnitude of the tasks is immense.[35]

What is crystal clear, however, is that we can no longer defend against World War II–style effects on modern infrastructure with *an after-the-fact, uniformed military defense based on lines on a map.* Defending something as critical as the North American transportation network fifty years ago was nearly *exclusively* a military function; defending it fifty years hence may be *barely* a military function. This raises the question of whether "fighting and winning America's wars," as shorthand for the purpose of US military services' existence, retains the same explanatory power it has had in the past. Tactical success—even operational success—as valued in the battles of the past simply does not guarantee strategic success in the future, because the battlespace is different. Put another way, war is very often not what it used to be. Ensuring future national security will demand overcoming instinct and inertia: the *instinct* to think of war as primarily physical, discontinuous, and military; and the *inertia* of having very successfully waged it for the last century using people, weapons, and organizations whose ethos dates back to the days before Thucydides.

Thus, even as the US military grapples with the technology and nature of future conflict in an era of renewed great-power competition, it must also rethink the essence of the American profession of arms, the ways citizens relate to those who defend them, and perhaps the organizations intended to maintain national security. Physical courage will be required in the future, just as it has in the past. Moral courage, along with the training and education to understand new faces of old ethical issues, will be equally important in continuous conflict beyond line of sight, in space, or in cyberspace. Military functions have already stretched to include vital roles that do not involve "arms" in the classical sense of the word—and potential adversaries see contemporary American lines of political oversight, resourcing, professional jurisdiction, organizational ethos, and legal authority for the military and nonmilitary national security organizations not just as traditional markers of organizational power or control, but as seams in our national security architecture they can exploit.

Reorienting the Profession of Arms

The pace and precise direction of the reorientation described above is unclear. However, the December 2019 creation of the United States Space Force[36] can be considered a warning shot across tradition's bow, marking three important and telling shifts: the loss of jurisdiction by one service due to a perception that national needs could be better met by a distinct organization; the creation of a military service whose primary tools of the trade are not "arms" in any classic sense; and the legitimization of an entire service whose members will not, in any significant way, be routinely called upon to risk their lives in order to fully and honorably fulfill the functions the nation has asked of them. These three things arguably make the Space Force fundamentally different from all traditional services—and from "noncombatant" functions in those services—and this difference has implications for recruiting and accession, personal development, recognition, and longevity of service, which are only now coming into partial focus. Members of the new Space Force should logically profess the same values their comrades in other services do—honor, courage, loyalty, commitment, integrity, service, duty, excellence—yet in order to allow the Space Force to prevail in its operational environment, the way many of these values will manifest in practice will be very different. The Space Force will be an important test case for American society's ability to understand, value, and appropriately support those new members of the armed forces.

Foreseeable real conflict with real consequences in space and cyberspace makes it increasingly clear that the warrior ethos and mental models that have made American forces successful in combat to date must be questioned and expanded to cover the full range of future threats to national security. Ironically, the term "profession of arms" has gained currency and popular use within the military services even as the threats to national security that do not necessarily involve arms in the classical sense have proliferated. The term itself contains a reinforcement of Huntington's construct by elevating the tool—the arms—to a defining characteristic of the profession, leading some to propose that the military profession should be recrafted as a "profession of effects" in order to focus military and civilian attention on desired outcomes rather than the tools of the trade.[37] This is not likely to gain traction in the face of tradition, but the concept has merit.

More fundamentally, an expansion of the warfighting ethos to better account for the inherent "team of teams" nature of any modern national security approach would also require a tectonic shift in the language used to talk about it. Words as basic as "war," "combat," "victory," "battlefield," and "warrior" have deep historical meaning but caricature the modern dynamic underlying them. Alternative words such as "conflict," "contest," "advantage," "battlespace," and "guardian" might shift the organizational culture of the military toward focus on effects rather than arms; but this, too is a challenging prospect. The same emotion that makes civilian leaders and commanders extraordinarily careful about sending soldiers, sailors, airmen, and marines "into harm's way" *should make them equally solicitous* before they send those same professionals in to be "on point for the nation."

To succeed in the complex future outlined above, the American profession of arms must realize a much fuller measure of the diversity and inclusion it has been pursuing for decades. These include racial integration efforts in the mid-1900s, the more complete incorporation of women into the services in the late 1900s and into combat roles in the early 2000s, and incremental removal of barriers to service based on sexual orientation and other previously barred categories. While ensuring equitable opportunities and advancement for all service members regardless of demographic is still a "work in progress," the military now faces an even more difficult challenge with greater implications for its existing organizational culture and unspoken assumptions: the full integration, inclusion, and leveraging of service members whose cognitive styles and physical attributes may not fit classical stereotypes but whose contributions to the multidomain, physical, and nonphysical competitive environment in which the military operates are increasingly essential. In practical terms, this will require military leaders, civilian policymakers, and society to consider cost and benefit, for example, of recruiting the prototypical hacker or the brilliant engineer into the military itself and whether deployability and appearance are relevant to an all-domain force or only to those whose inherent function requires them to fight forward. This is a new variant of the military/civilian total force calculus that has existed for decades, but it is important to resolve.

It is worth taking a brief and final look at the implied social contract fulfilled by the profession of arms. For most of American history, "who" bore responsibility for protecting citizens was very tangible: the individual, a local law enforcement entity, and the military. In today's world, where the Department of Defense shares responsibility with the Department of Homeland Security for some aspects of that protection, and large portions of American infrastructure are the sole responsibility of their owners, we would only benefit from greater clarity on the question of "*who* defends us." Against *what* does each entity defend us? *When and where* do our military professionals fight, given that conflict is omnipresent, not always violent, and sometimes inside our own shoreline? Finally, *why* they fight is complex yet critical; how do we define an ethos that is powerful enough and flexible enough to guide a soldier's decision to kill or a cyber operator's decision to deny a city or a country its power? Regardless how difficult it may be to answer these questions, any blurring in language and responsibility that exists is worthy and important to bring into focus.

For all of the reasons outlined above, changing the prevailing culture of the profession of arms is likely to be extraordinarily challenging. Yet if the profession cannot grow to visibly master the demands of new forms of conflict and to work at scale and speed with a much wider spectrum of civilian national security entities to mitigate the threats they pose, it will inevitably fail, be reorganized further, or both. Before the creation of the Space Force in 2019, the last fundamental reorganization of the US defense establishment occurred in 1947. The National Guard has transformed from strategic reserve during the Cold War to an operational reserve over the last two decades. As with the Space Force, some have called for creation of a Cyber Force in response to perceived deficits in existing US government capabilities.[38] All of these organizational changes, as well-advised and useful as they may have been, have scarcely altered the defense establishment's underlying assumptions. It is not inconceivable that space and cyber professionals, if not fully incorporated in every aspect of military ethos, might eventually be seen as better aligned with nonmilitary national security organizations.

War *is* changing. *What we do not describe accurately, we cannot fight competently*. And as "war" changes, the profession of arms must change with it. The tangibility and immediacy of any particular battle and the magnitude of its impact on national security bear no necessary relation to one another. We still and will always need modern professionals to manage violence expertly, using force ethically to kill in combat when called upon. In recent decades, we have demanded our military professionals take on less obvious, but still potentially lethal, competition on land and sea, in air, space and the cyber domain. Yet it is not enough to merely continue adding brushstrokes of better weapons and tactics to the ancient and aging canvas of military conflict. Rather, we must summon the will to think beyond war, boots, and bombs to understand and respond to the fundamentals of future consequential contests—small or large, visible or invisible—that *will* find us, whether or not we choose to find them. Perhaps it is time to retire the *profession of arms* in favor of the less evocative but more useful concept of the *military profession*, so that we can develop warriors beyond "management of violence" to "mastery of lethal competition." There's a difference. Our ability to accept and act on that distinction may mean the difference between national success and failure in future conflict.

NOTES

1. Robert K. Knake, "Top Conflicts to Watch in 2020: A Cyberattack on U.S. Critical Infrastructure," *Council on Foreign Relations* blog, January 17, 2020, https://www.cfr.org /blog/top-conflicts-watch-2020-cyberattack-us-critical -infrastructure.

2. James Burk, "Expertise, Jurisdiction, and Legitimacy of the Military Profession," in *The Future of the Army Profession*, 2nd ed. (Boston: McGraw-Hill, 2005), 41.

3. The US Air Force defines the Air Force profession of arms as "a vocation comprised of experts in the design, generation, support and application of global vigilance, global reach and global power serving under civilian authority, entrusted to defend the Constitution and accountable to the American people" ("Strategic Roadmap: United States Air Force Profession of Arms," https://www.airman.af.mil/Portals/17/001%20 Home%20Page/008%20-%20StrategicRoadmap /StrategicRoadmap.pdf?ver=2016-03-07-154949-547). The US Army's definition is similar: "The Army profession is a trusted vocation of Soldiers and Army civilians whose collective expertise is the ethical design, generation, support, and application of landpower; serving under civilian authority; and entrusted to defend the Constitution and the rights and interests of the American people" (Army Doctrine Publication 6-22, C1, November 25, 2019, https://armypubs.army.mil/epubs/DR_pubs /DR_a/pdf/web/ARN20039_ADP%206-22%20C1%20 FINAL%20WEB.pdf).

4. Samuel B. Huntington, *The Soldier and the State: The Theory and Politics of Civil-Military Relations* (Cambridge: Harvard University Press, 1957), 8.

5. Tony Ingesson, "When the Military Profession Isn't," in *Redefining the Modern Military: The Intersection of Profession and Ethics*, ed. Nathan K. Finney and Tyrell O. Mayfield (Annapolis, MD: Naval Institute Press, 2018), 83–84.

6. Ingesson, "When the Military Profession Isn't," 48.

7. Andrew Abbott, *The System of Professions: An Essay on the Division of Expert Labor* (Chicago: University of Chicago Press, 1988), 33.

8. Abbott, *The System of Professions*, 86.

9. "Confidence in Institutions," Gallup, accessed May 28, 2020, https://news.gallup.com/poll/1597/confidence-institutions .aspx.

10. Burk, "Expertise," 50.

11. P. W. Singer and Emerson T. Brooking, *Like War: The Weaponization of Social Media* (Boston: Houghton Mifflin Harcourt, 2018), 179–180.

12. See, for example, a recent statement by chairman of the Joint Chiefs of Staff, Gen Joseph Dunford in Jim Garamone, "National Military Strategy Addresses Changing Character of War," Defense.gov, July 12, 2019, https://www.defense .gov/explore/story/Article/1903478/national-military-strategy -addresses-changing-character-of-war/.

13. Thomas Schelling, introduction to *Pearl Harbor: Warning and Decision*, ed. Roberta Wohlstetter (Stanford, CA: Stanford University Press, 1962), vii.

14. US Department of Defense, *Joint Publication 3-0, Joint Operations* (Washington, DC: US Department of Defense 2017), xvii.

15. US Department of Defense, *Joint Publication 3-0*, V-8.

16. Carl von Clausewitz, *On War*, trans. Michael Howard and Peter Paret (Princeton, NJ: Princeton University Press, 1976), 87.

17. Clausewitz, *On War*, 95; emphasis added.

18. *Hearing to Review Testimony on United States Special Operations Command and United States Cyber Command in review of the Defense Authorization Request for Fiscal Year 2020 and the Future Years Defense Program, before the Committee on Armed Services, Subcommittee on Personnel*, 116th Congress, Feb. 14, 2019, statement of Gen Paul M. Nakasone, Commander, United States Cyber Command, Washington, DC, p. 5, https://www.armed-services.senate.gov/imo/media /doc/Nakasone_02-14-19.pdf.

19. Stanley Hoffmann, *The State of War: Essays on the Theory and Practice of International Politics* (New York: Praeger, 1965), 92–93.

20. Robert S. Wilson et al., "The Value of Space" (Washington, DC: The Aerospace Corporation, 2020), https:// aerospace.org/sites/default/files/2020-05/Gleason-Wilson _ValueOfSpace_20200511.pdf, 1, 15.

21. Huntington, *The Soldier and the State*, 15.

22. Huntington, *The Soldier and the State*, 189–192. The nuances of civil-military relations are beyond the scope of this discussion, but Huntington's model of objective control arguably coexists today with Morris Janowitz's competing view of subjective control—which could be paraphrased as the full participation of military members in all aspects of civilian political and social life such that they the military is controlled through its complete identification with, rather than structural separation from, civil society. We see this in the National Guard and militias of the several states, where the civilian, military, and federalized guardsman roles are far less distinct than those of full-time, active-duty federal military personnel.

23. Morris Janowitz, *The Professional Soldier: A Social and Political Portrait*, rev. ed. (Glencoe, IL: Free Press 1971), 418.

24. Janowitz, *The Professional Soldier*, 424.

25. Charles Moskos, "Toward a Postmodern Military: The United States as a Paradigm," in *The Postmodern Military: Armed Forces after the Cold War*, ed. Charles Moskos, John Williams, and David Segal (New York: Oxford University Press, 2000), 19.

26. Paula G. Thornhill, *The Crisis Within: America's Military and the Struggle Between the Overseas and Guardian Paradigms* (Santa Monica, CA: RAND Corporation, 2016), 46–49, https://www.rand.org/pubs/research_reports/RR1420.html.

27. Peter Feaver, *Armed Servants: Agency, Oversight and Civil-Military Relations* (Cambridge, MA: Harvard University Press, 2003), 298–302.

28. Peter Feaver, "The Civil-Military Problematique: Huntington, Janowitz, and the Question of Civilian Control," *Armed Forces & Society* 23, no. 2 (Winter 1996): 158.

29. General Sir John Winthrop Hackett, "Harmon Memorial Lecture in Military History #13" (Colorado Springs: US Air Force Academy, 1970), 1–2.

30. Norman Augustine and Kenneth Adelman, *Shakespeare in Charge: The Bard's Guide to Leading and Succeeding on the Business Stage* (New York: Hyperion Miramax, 2001), 12–13.

31. Don M. Snider, "Once Again, the Challenge to the U.S. Army during a Defense Reduction: To Remain a Military Profession," Professional Military Ethics Monograph (Carlisle, PA: US Army War College, 2012).

32. Department of Defense, News Release, February 13, 2013, https://archive.defense.gov/news/newsarticle.aspx?id=119290.

33. Secretary of Defense Chuck Hagel, Memorandum for Acting Under Secretary of Defense (Personnel and Readiness) and the Chairman of the Joint Chiefs of Staff), Subject: Distinguished Warfare Medal (DWM), Washington, DC, April 15, 2013, https://archive.defense.gov/pubs/PR%20and%20CJCS%20Memo%20DWM.pdf; emphasis added.

34. 432nd Wing/432nd Air Expeditionary Wing Public Affairs, "Air Force Awards First Remote Device: Dominant Persistent Attack Aircrew Recognized," July 18, 2018, https://

www.creech.af.mil/News/Article-Display/Article/1572571/air-force-awards-first-remote-device-dominant-persistent-attack-aircrew-recogni/.

35. United States Cyberspace Solarium Commission, *Final Report* (Washington, DC, Cyberspace Solarium Commission, March 2020), 17, 81, https://drive.google.com/file/d/1ryMCIL_dZ30QyjFqFkkf10MxIXJGT4yv/view.

36. "About the US Space Force Fact Sheet," United States Space Force, accessed May 11, 2019, https://www.spaceforce.mil/About-Us/Fact-Sheet.

37. James G. Stavridis, Ervin J. Rokke, and Terry Pierce, "Crafting and Managing Effects: The Evolution of the Profession of Arms," *Joint Forces Quarterly* 81 (2nd quarter 2016): 4–9.

38. James Stavridis, "The U.S. Needs a Cyber Force More than a Space Force," Bloomberg Opinion, August 14, 2018, https://www-bloomberg-com.cdn.ampproject.org/c/s/www.bloomberg.com/amp/view/articles/2018-08-14/u-s-needs-a-space-force-and-a-cyber-force.

Identity Politics

How Service Cultures Influence the Evolving Profession of Arms

JEFFREY DONNITHORNE

From the beginning of man's recorded history physical force, or the threat of it, has always been freely applied to the resolution of social problems. This phenomenon seems to persist as a fundamental element in the social pattern.

General Sir John Hackett, *The Profession of Arms*

Scholars of military strategy insist that the nature of war endures, while its character evolves.[1] The same pattern holds true for the profession whose craft is war. "The function of the profession of arms," argues General Sir John Hackett, "is the ordered application of force in the resolution of a social problem."[2] Hackett's spare definition holds true across the millennia of military history. Like the professions of medicine or law, the profession of arms claims a canon of expert knowledge, a coherent membership, tailored education, a suite of supporting institutions, defined career pathways, and an avowed service to society.[3] Its nature and function reliably endure. The character of the profession of arms, however, must evolve with the character of war itself. In his contribution to this volume, "Redefinitions and Transformations of the Profession of Arms," Lieutenant General (Ret) Christopher Miller describes the stressing conditions that prompt new thinking about the profession of arms for the future.

Pushing those ideas further, this essay considers what that new thinking might look like and how it might vary across the United States military services.

The Evolving Character of War

Military professionals strive to bring order, stability, and peace to a world that is changing faster than our ability to make sense of it.[4] Our inherited assumptions about warfare, the warrior ethos, and the profession of arms are all under challenge, as today's empirical patterns stretch the conceptual boundaries of old categories and definitions. We are left with more ambiguity than clarity, and today's military professionals inherit more questions than answers. Addressing the basic framework of what, when, where, who, and why helps to characterize these rapid evolutions. The platforms for coercion and risk-taking are converting from analog to digital (what); temporal distinctions between war and peace have blurred into persistent ambiguous competition (when); the terrain of adversarial access expands daily (where); distinctions between combatants and noncombatants erode in a world of pervasive societal exposure (who); yet warfare remains a coercive application of power to bend another group to one's will—the *why* remains largely unchanged. The following discussion highlights these trends further.

The information age accelerated into the networked age, where ever more of our human experience is captured, digitized, networked, and exposed. When daily life is digitally mediated, potential vectors for malign interference increase exponentially. Life in the networked age brings untold opportunity, but connections do something for us and *to* us. We are coding a world of pervasive exposure, infected with zero-day exploits lying in wait. Our bodies, homes, identities, perceptions, infrastructure, and political systems have become the new terrain of coercion. In this saturated battlespace, hackers, scammers, and defenders pursue code supremacy: the power to define reality in the digital age. In such a world, what does it mean for a warrior class to bear societal risk to defend the American way of life?

Historically, war and peace were meaningful categories, distinguishable from one another empirically and temporally. Nations once at peace declared war, fought violently, sued for peace, and negotiated settlements. Like night and day, there was war, and there was peace. Today, the clock seems frozen at twilight, with shadows of conflict that are neither war nor peace as classically understood. While competition between nations has always been persistent, new networked opportunities for access and coercive leverage bring adversaries within range as never before. With fraying distinctions between war and peace, how does the profession of arms define the proper jurisdiction of its expertise?

The jurisdiction is under threat both conceptually and geographically. Military history reveals that groups perpetually seek new and clever corridors of access to coerce their neighbors. From land to sea, into air, space, cyberspace, and the electromagnetic spectrum, groups maneuver to impose their will on others. The steady expansion of these access corridors defines the expanding contours of a complex battlespace. As more of the human experience migrates onto a digitally connected grid, we create new strategic chokepoints and wrap the battlespace more tightly around civil society. In such a world, how does the profession of arms partition the *experience* of war? How can war be sequestered to the professionals when the contested terrain has been atomized across society?

The atomized terrain of coercion erodes distinctions between combatants and noncombatants, as once understood. When leverage against neighbors was exclusively physical, men-at-arms threatened or destroyed what others held dear through violent means. Those entrusted with the ordered application of violence were held in high esteem, as they bore risk of physical, psychological, and moral injuries on behalf of others. Naturally, a warrior ethos developed around this shared sacrificial experience, uplifted by martial virtues: courage, valor, sacrifice, honor, loyalty, and self-

lessness, among others. In the era described above, however, where distinctions between war and peace are blurred, where the battlespace is entangled in the daily life of citizens, and where contests may be decided through bits not bombs, what kind of ethos will prevail? Who is a warrior, by what standard, and sustained by what virtues?

War remains a clash of wills to address social and political problems—its nature endures. Its character, however, appears to be evolving rapidly, and with it the profession of arms. Today's military professionals must make sense of a fast-changing corpus of expert knowledge. At the same time, they must reform the practices through which their expertise protects and serves society.

This essay offers a new perspective on how the US military services will likely navigate these changes. It begins by explaining why the burden of change falls largely on these military services—the Army, Navy, Air Force, Space Force, and Marine Corps—as the dominant organizations within the United States national security establishment.[5] The argument holds that each service will diagnose and address the ambiguity in the strategic environment differently, based on each service's beliefs about its strategic core: *why* it exists, *what* resources it needs, *where* it operates, *when* it is optimized for maximum effect, and *who* its individual members understand themselves to be. The essay focuses primarily on the four long-standing services in the Department of Defense, as performing this analysis on the newly created Space Force would be premature. Still, it will consider the cultural implications of establishing the Space Force, then conclude with summary insights.

A Service-Centric Approach to Change

Over the past several decades, the US military has undoubtedly become more "joint" in its thinking, planning, and employing. Due in part to the altered incentives imposed by the Goldwater-Nichols Act of 1986, combined with nearly 20 years of active combat operations in the Middle East, the Department of Defense (DoD) now plans and employs force more jointly than ever. Soldiers, sailors, airmen, and marines are accustomed to working in deployed environments with members of other services. The joint staffs, whether in the Pentagon or at combatant command headquarters, are increasingly filled with the services' most talented and upwardly mobile personnel. Officers rising through the ranks must complete joint professional military education at regular intervals, with a goal of ach ing joint acculturation across the senior ra combined weight of these initiatives shaped a modern military force that and even appreciates the respec other services.

Despite these meaningful gains, however, thinking jointly reaches a natural limit for the services and their members. Two core realities create this limit. First, the military services retain legal authority in Title 10 of the United States Code for three major verbs of military life: organize, train, and equip.[7] These responsibilities of organizing, training, and equipping are the budget-driven foundation of all military operations. This seemingly straightforward work, owned and dominated by the services, consumes the focus of senior military and civilian leaders in the Pentagon. The combatant commands fight the wars of today, but the services recruit, acquire, organize, train, and prepare forces for the uncertain conflicts of the future.

The second core reality that drives service-centric thinking is a simple but critical technicality: no one actually joins the "United States Military" per se. Military personnel enter and develop through one of the *services*, with all of its particular traditions, customs, uniforms, ranks, incentives, and cultural assumptions. The services are the colorful meaning-makers, answering elemental questions of daily life: What will I wear? What will I be called? Where will I live? What will I do? What gear will I use? When, where, and for how long will I deploy? Who promotes me? Who hires and fires me? Who pays me? The services determine the facts of daily life for real people.

Furthermore, the combatant commands fighting today's wars do not grow their own joint personnel; no one actually wears purple.[8] The joint commands fight with the equipment, personnel, and ideas grown by the services. The services provide the raw material of military force, and each does so through its own logic of power and purpose. At its core, the Army is a force of *ultimate occupation*—fueled by the conviction that wars are ultimately decided by a "man on the scene with a gun."[9] The Navy wields power through *forward projection*; its carriers and ships maneuver steel acres of sovereign US firepower across the world, when and where strategic logic dictates. The Marine Corps delivers the power of *responsive intervention*; whenever the call, whatever the task, "Send in the Marines!" is a cherished refrain.[10] Lastly, the Air Force offers power through *strategic interdiction*; airmen hold key targets at risk across the globe, with rapid destructive power that none other can provide. These ... of power are not just the conceptual ingredients ... operations; they are the services' heuristic ... for how to pursue advantage in the future. ... builds on existing works that posit the ... cultural agents, shaped by the in... nal nature and political nur... a unique strategic culture, ...acteristics of its opera- ...ith the political char- ...ory. This combina-

tion creates unique "diagnostic and choice propensities" for each service as it makes sense of the world and its place within it.[12] The bulk of the discussion is focused on these service-level approaches: How will each service's culture condition its approach to the shifting demands of its profession?

The following discussion addresses five questions that shape each service's approach to change. The first considers *why* each service exists and evaluates the security of its professional jurisdiction. A service's sense of organizational security—or vulnerability—conditions a particular posture toward change. The second question focuses on the *what*—the significance of physical assets within the service. How strongly does each service feel about its kit, and why? During a period of rapid technological change, each service's approach to its gear enables and constrains its professional evolution. The third question probes the role of physical geography in each service's mindset—the *where* of strategy. Military history is a story of explorer-strategists pursuing new corridors of access to gain leverage against neighbors. These physical boundaries between operational domains tend to define the professional boundaries between services. Operational geography underwrites each service's sense of power and purpose.

The fourth question asks *when*. What is each service's relevant operational time scale? Each service clicks along to its own metronome for common pacing. In an age of accelerated change, a service's relative sense of fast and slow is a key ingredient in managing change. Finally, the fifth question asks *who*. To what organizational level does the identity of service members tend to gravitate? Some services elevate *national* loyalties, for example, while others privilege the primacy of the service. These different reference points create further variation among the services in their professional evolution.

Why: The Security of Professional Jurisdictions

Why does each service exist, and how does its understanding of mission and purpose shape its posture toward change? In a crowded marketplace of expert labor, professional organizations seek stable jurisdictions within which to practice.[13] The military services are no exception. Each service thrives when its professional jurisdiction is clearly defined, with a mission and purpose that serve the nation and align with the service's preferred self-conception. A service's sense of organizational security casts a long shadow over its approach to strategy and change.

The Army rarely wrestles with its sense of why. Land armies have been essential to defending political communities across the millennia. If you want to secure your borders and defend your interests, you have an army. And if you want to reject colonial subjugation and stake a claim to a new nation, you need an army to fight and make it so. Today's US Army proudly traces its heritage to George Washington's scrappy Continental Army—the resilient underdog that beat back the dominant imperial power of its day. The Army sees itself as so closely aligned with the birth and development of the United States that its reason for being speaks for itself. A former chief of staff of the Army—the senior-most four-star general leading the service—once commented, "There has always been an Army. . . . We don't have to justify the need or relevancy of an Army. America requires an Army. The other services have to justify themselves in terms of their platforms or weapon systems. . . . There will always be an Army."[14] While the shape, size, and means of the Army evolve over time, its existential *why* remains constant and confers a robust sense of organizational security. This deep sense of enduring purpose gives the Army a profound conservatism in its approach to change.

The Navy likewise has no difficulty defending its purpose for the nation. Its settled sense of self benefits from a national debate 230 years ago, when Alexander Hamilton, James Madison, and John Jay served as its leading advocates. An important thread in *The Federalist Papers* connected a blue-water seafaring navy with national prestige and power. In Federalist 11, Hamilton argued that even a small US Navy could affect the European balance of power by its friendship or neutrality, but "a nation, despicable by its weakness, forfeits even the privilege of being neutral."[15] In view of the powerful British and French fleets marauding the Atlantic corridor, Edward Rutledge of South Carolina concurred: "We must hold our country by courtesy, unless we have a navy."[16] When the US Constitution was later signed, it provided for a national navy, and the US Navy has generally been on firm bureaucratic ground ever since. If anything, the Navy is *so* secure in its purpose that it can feel entitled to autonomy. Life at sea is sufficiently unknowable to land-dwellers, the thinking goes, that matters of naval operations and strategy must be fully entrusted to sailors alone, with minimal interference from unsalted amateurs. To change the Navy generally requires the advocacy of a trusted insider.

Unlike the Army and Navy, the Air Force does not enjoy the settled confidence of a clear jurisdiction. For the Air Force, the mere existence of the air domain is *not* sufficient justification to have an independent service that owns (in a bureaucratic sense) the domain. Instead, the Air Force had to argue its way into existence with prophecy, logic, and evidence. As military aviation developed in the early decades of the twentieth century, the existing services found novel utility in exploiting the air domain to support existing models of battlefield operations. The Army clearly valued the

third dimension for observation, reconnaissance, and even aerial bombardment of fielded forces. The Navy and Marine Corps likewise developed aerial tactics for supporting maritime fleet operations. But a separate tribe of air-minded enthusiasts, largely within the Army's aviation units, began to argue for a separate service and to conceive of the air domain in fundamentally different ways. These ambitious secessionists believed air power changed the face of warfare; the air domain, they believed, offered new war-winning approaches that the other services would not be inclined to pursue.

The Air Force's quest for organizational independence—achieved in 1947—continues to echo across the service. The viability of the Air Force's founding argument either motivates or haunts the service, depending on the particular tranche of evidence that supports or challenges its existential hypothesis. Since its creation, moreover, the Air Force has sought to lead the search for new domains of coercive access. The service has added space and cyberspace to its core portfolio, and it espouses a culture of innovation, novel thinking, and a propensity for going "over, not through" conventional problems.[17] While fostering a truly innovative culture is as difficult for the Air Force as it is for any large organization, the Air Force's self-styled narrative welcomes change, as newness is at the heart of the service's core contribution. Whereas the Army and Navy offer the nation an enduring *sameness* of purpose over time, the Air Force sees its role as offering perpetually new thinking and novel capabilities.

The Marine Corps has historically felt the least organizationally secure of the services. Unlike the other three services, the Marine Corps is not defined by a single domain, but offers an integrated, all-domain striking force. In a sense, it offers at reduced scale what the entire joint force offers in full. Consequently, if an outsider merely scanned the balance sheet of the DoD, the Marine Corps could appear unnecessarily duplicative of the other services. "In terms of cold, mechanical logic," observed Lieutenant General Victor Krulak, "the United States does not *need* a Marine Corps. However, for good reasons which completely transcend cold logic, the United States *wants* a Marine Corps."[18] Absent a rational need, the Marines have to be wanted; the corps is therefore passionate about being—*and being seen as*—useful to the nation.

The Marines' fight for secure organizational terrain is a natural by-product of their founding charter. Created within the Department of the Navy, but chartered to perform army-like functions, the Marine Corps was bureaucratically wedged between the Army and Navy—and loved by neither. A favorite Marine legend, in fact, recounts the end of the Revolutionary War, when all the kit that supposedly remained was a corps of mules and two battalions of marines. The Army and

Navy flipped a coin to divide them up; the Army won and chose the mules.[19]

Despite this apparent lack of esteem from either the Army or Navy, marines were an essential component of a navy ship in the eighteenth and early nineteenth centuries. Marines served as boarding parties, assault forces, sharpshooters, and martial guards to protect the ship's officers from a potentially unruly ship's company. But important evolutions within the Navy forced a reckoning for the corps. As the Navy professionalized in the late nineteenth century, the presence of marines on ships fostered a "penal colony" atmosphere of suspicious supervision.[20] At the same time, the Navy was moving from sails and wood to steam and steel, and these changes in ship architecture spurred new duties for those onboard. These evolutions in naval equipment, operations, and culture eroded the rational basis for stationing marines on Navy ships. The Navy asked to remove marines from their surface fleet, putting at risk the very purpose of the corps. Amid a flurry of presidential and congressional activity, the tension climaxed in 1909 and ultimately yielded legislation that protected the original Marine Corps' mission afloat—even though that purpose had become largely outdated. This contest to define the proper place of the Marine Corps was one of many—the corps claims it has survived fifteen attempts on its life—that define its history and confer a constructive paranoia on the service.[21]

Across its history, the Marine Corps has survived organizationally by doing any and every job asked of it, while maintaining an emotional connection with the American people—and their representatives in Congress. This approach makes the Marine Corps "paradoxically committed to *both* tradition and change."[22] In pursuit of organizational survival, the corps heralds its tradition of service to the American people, while scrambling to pursue the operational changes necessary to maintain a viable mission.

In view of these service-level variations in organizational security, how might the services vary in their approach to changes in the profession of arms? In general, this dimension of organizational security tends to keep the Army and Navy content with their historic status quo, while the Air Force and Marine Corps are more readily postured to evolve and change to maintain organizational viability. While all of the services will no doubt evolve to meet new security demands, the Army and Navy are more likely to evolve their *means*—designing new approaches to enduring tasks.[23] The Air Force and Marine Corps will likely be more entrepreneurial in their approach, conceptualizing new opportunities, strategies, and mission concepts that are not yet part of their core portfolio. Airmen and marines are incentivized to pursue not only new means, but new ways and new ends as well.

What: The Significance of Physical Assets

The military services are responsible for organizing, training, and *equipping* combat-ready forces. This task of equipping the American military is massive in scope, with implications that extend across the DoD, the US government, the industrial base, international alliances, and the global economy. The services obligate hundreds of billions of dollars annually, investing in material capabilities to achieve coercive leverage. Life in the Pentagon is ordered by the gravitational force of the defense budget; planning, programming, budgeting, and executing taxpayer dollars consume the lives of service staff officers.

Physical means define an essential element of strategy, as means must co-evolve with ends. What we have determines what we can do, and what we *want* to do informs what we should buy. Each service's strategic culture conditions a strong preference for the kind of physical assets that give form its preferred warfighting concept. Each expends limited resources on the things it believes will most likely confer advantage. What a service buys reflects both identity and values, making tangible its theories of advantage for the future. In short, a service's approach to physical assets is a proxy for its truest sense of purpose and identity.

For the Air Force, its existence is predicated on designing, building, and operating sophisticated technologies that overcome the force of gravity. The Air Force is no force at all without its aircraft, satellites, ballistic missiles, and other machines. The service prospers through its technological marvels, giving the Air Force an acute focus on the *quality* of its machine fleet. In his study of service personalities, defense analyst Carl Builder suggested of the Air Force that "to be outnumbered may be tolerable, but to be outflown is not. The way to get the American flier's attention is to confront him with a superior machine."[24] The Air Force's pursuit of better, higher, and faster comports with the service's self-conception as the service of *new*: fresh thinkers, pioneers of new domains, and strategist-hackers with sleek technology who find new ways to win.

But is higher quality always the better buying option? Given budget constraints, functional suitability, or portfolio diversification, when might less sophisticated machines be the better acquisition choice for the Air Force? These questions surfaced in a 2019 debate on acquiring new air superiority fighters. The service is clearly betting on the fifth-generation multi-role F-35 Joint Strike Fighter as the bulk-buy fighter aircraft for the future. As a complement to the F-35 acquisition, some Pentagon analysts have argued for a hedging strategy: buying upgraded versions of the fourth-generation F-15 Eagle.[25] The F-15, in all its variants, has been an indisputably capable fighter aircraft for nearly forty years. Defense contractor Boeing continues to upgrade versions of the F-15, often for foreign military sales, and an internal Pentagon analysis argued that buying new models of this proven aircraft would be a smart addition to the Air Force fighter portfolio. The intensity of the debate highlights the countercultural nature of stepping back a generation in fighter technology: Why, the Air Force wonders, would we double-down on the past instead of committing to the technologies of the future?

The Navy's principal focus centers on the number of ships in its seafaring fleet—and how big those ships must be. Naval strategy hinges on *position*. Control of the seas, whether for conventional battle or to ensure freedom of commercial navigation, requires the right ships at the right place at the right time. Position demands numbers, so the total number of ships in the US Navy is a convenient short-hand for its capability. During the Reagan administration, for example, Secretary of the Navy John Lehman fixed his sights on a 600-ship Navy as the force required to defeat the Soviet Navy and preserve world order.[26] Fast-forwarding to late 2019, acting Secretary of the Navy Thomas Modly laid down a marker for the Navy to reach 355 ships within a decade.[27] Reduced to a soundbite, the number is the strategy.

But if quantity matters to the Navy, the *quality* of those ships ranks a close second. The Navy arranges its fleet around major capital ships, from its first six frigates of the eighteenth century, to the battleships of the nineteenth and early twentieth centuries, to the aircraft carriers of today. A consistent belief that "bigger is better" runs throughout the Navy's history, with various alternatives for smaller or more diverse fleets sparking heated resistance from the service core.

For the Army, the basic task of equipping a force so large and diverse is a herculean effort. As a massive organization tasked to perform a wide array of missions, the US Army must be varied and subspecialized in its structure. The core of the Army lives in its three main combat arms branches—the infantry, field artillery, and armor—but over two dozen other branches complement these three.[28] Furthermore, the Army organizes forces under both state and federal control, across various degrees of readiness, from active duty through guard and reserve forces. The Army is therefore the largest and most fragmented of the services, driving a strong imperative to coordinate, synchronize, and standardize.

This enormous Army machine, distributed globally across its component pieces, tends to prioritize sufficiency, standardization, and interoperability in its approach to physical assets. Whatever the Army buys, it must get *enough* to serve its entire force, in a standardized plug-and-play model, as a component piece of the tightly coupled Army machine. Any signature Army acquisition project is a complex undertaking of meeting diverse distributed needs, at enterprise scale, in an integrated way with Army doctrine, organization, and existing equipment.[29]

The Marine Corps focuses far more on marines themselves than the gear they employ. "For the Marine Corps," writes historian Allan Millett, "the first priority in defining the Corps has always been its people, not its functions or its technology."[30] When it comes to physical assets, the corps boasts a proud history of being scrappy, creative, frugal, and effective with its gear. Marines see themselves as faithful stewards of the national trust. If the American people will trust the Marine Corps enough to keep it alive, the corps will honor that trust by husbanding its tax dollars effectively and creatively. This principle has been central to the corps from its earliest days. Funded through the Navy Department, but requiring weapons and gear like the Army, the early Marine Corps fought creatively for every resource. Without a separate budget or cabinet-level representation, the corps relied on the secretary of the Navy for advocacy. In practice, this often meant that marines received second-hand goods or manufacturing defects from the Army. Consequently, marines cared religiously for the gear they *did* receive. Commandant of the Marine Corps Archibald Henderson, who led the corps for thirty-nine years (1820–1859), wasted nothing and "set the tune in establishing institutional frugality as a Marine Corps principle."[31] Future commandants extended Henderson's legacy, as Lieutenant General John Lejeune made it a point as commandant (1920–1929) to return a portion of the Marine Corps' appropriation back to the US Treasury each year. In short, the Marine Corps generally cares less about the exact specifications of the gear it acquires—as long as it gets *something* to do its mission.

The one piece of kit that marines do care about passionately is the rifle. Complete with a creed that venerates the role of the rifle in the hands of a marine, the corps believes, preaches, and lives the dictum that *every marine is a rifleman*. The most important resource on the Marine equipment ledger is the low-tech but highly effective coupling of a marine and his rifle. The marine infantryman, equipped with his rifle, is the venerated icon of the Marine Corps and the critical resource for the corps' success.[32]

For all of the services, the rapid pace of technological change has and will continue to stress the ponderously long acquisition timelines within the DoD. Technology is changing quickly, but the DoD buys things slowly, painfully, and inefficiently.[33] Additionally, the gear the services buy reflects their hypotheses about how to achieve coercive leverage in future conflicts. But the shifting landscape of armed conflict casts a veil of uncertainty over how militaries will be used in the future. If military assets are the union of technological capability and a theory of future victory—both of which are steeped in uncertainty—a coherent strategy of military acquisition will be especially difficult to derive.

This dynamic may be especially stressing for the Air Force and Navy, whose investment choices get pooled in large material assets (i.e., ships and planes) with long timelines for research, development, production, and testing. Staying current with new technology to build and buy highly technical systems at scale will be a significant challenge. The Air Force has recognized this tension and is experimenting with new approaches to fielding fighter aircraft in the twenty-first century. The Air Force's assistant secretary for acquisition, technology, and logistics, Dr. Will Roper, has outlined a vision for the "Digital Century Series" of fighter aircraft. Roper plans to use agile software development, open architecture systems, and digital engineering to build digital prototypes of future aircraft that can be virtually tested, e-flown, and debugged hundreds of times before ever committing to bending metal.[34] While the concept will no doubt be challenging to execute, the vision reflects the changing demands and opportunities of a new era.

Where: The Geographic Determinants of Strategy

Military services operate in, from, and through specific domains—for the purpose of setting conditions that (should) lead to better political outcomes. A sense of geography is central to military strategy. Geography strongly conditions the political outcomes that military force strives to affect. And geography enables and constrains the kinds of effects that militaries deliver. The four services approach geography differently, however, because where one operates affects how one thinks. Each service brings a set of assumptions and geographic preoccupations to its operational tasks.

Geography plays an enduring role in military strategy, but the conditions of the networked age challenge traditional ideas of territoriality. New layers of strategic geography overlay the core grid of land, sea, and sky. The domain of outer space is no longer just a functional extension of the air for communication, navigation, and reconnaissance assets, but has taken on greater strategic significance. Now considered a warfighting domain, space is an arena in which states actively compete for advantage. Additionally, the domain of cyber is metastasizing aggressively, as the physical world converts to data, shrinking and connecting the globe in real-time. Finally, faster weapons such as hypersonic missiles destabilize familiar rhythms of detection and response.[35] Hypersonic weapons, ripping through the atmosphere at speeds of Mach 5, on nonballistic trajectories, put acute pressure on decisionmakers whose time to react collapses to nearly zero. These evolutions in territoriality and time-distance

frameworks will challenge the services in different ways, depending on their baseline sense of operational geography.

For the Army and Navy, lines on the map are a defining reality. The Army is a map-driven service that brings order out of chaos by drawing clarifying lines. For a massive land force that must live in its battlespace and synchronize its maneuver, lines mean things: the forward edge of the battle area (FEBA) and the forward line of troops (FLOT), as well as phase lines for synchronizing maneuver and deconfliction lines that divide terrain between units are among the defining features of Army operations. The Army defines places based on grid coordinates and gives names to prominent terrain features based on demarcated elevations on published maps. Maps and their associated signs and symbols—lines, grids, terrain features, and boundaries—form the common layer of abstraction that unifies positioning, maneuvering, and employing of fielded forces on real terrain.

Even in new eras of prominence for space and cyberspace, the Army will likely remain committed to the irreducible demands of life on the ground. At least in the near term, Army soldiers are likely to view space and cyber as enabling domains that assist Army units in their core responsibility to shoot, move, and communicate on land. To the extent that the Army pursues positional advantage in the shifting terrain of cyberspace, the dominant metaphor of physical territoriality will likely serve as the unifying abstraction for defining cyberspace. One might expect that Army-led efforts will appropriate a "lines on the map" approach to making sense of cyber terrain and coordinating effects within it.

The Navy likewise defines reality with maps—though sailors insist on properly calling them *charts*. The Navy operates under the tyranny of oceanic distance. With 70 percent of the world's surface covered in water, 80 percent of the world's population living on or near a coastline, and 90 percent of global commerce moving by water, the Navy wields the distributed tentacles of American power globally and persistently.[36] The Navy must patrol thousands of square miles, but it cannot adjust the position of its ships at a greater rate than 20–30 knots. Imagine if a single precinct of the New York Police Department had responsibility for all five boroughs of the city—but had no police cars and could patrol only by foot. Distances are large, reaction times are slow, so *presence* is key.

Naval power therefore follows a logic of position, defined by strategic chokepoints of conspicuous land-sea conjunction. While most oceanic traffic crosses a vast undefined (and not easily governed) commons, corridors of predictable passage become especially important. The Straits of Gibraltar, Hormuz, Malacca, Bosporus, and Dardanelles, for example, are natural bottlenecks of human relations, where critical volumes of activity—commercial, military, and otherwise—must squeeze through thin nautical corridors. Patrolling and controlling these straits confers positional advantage; you don't have to be everywhere if you can be where it counts. For the Navy, geography is radically asymmetrical. Controlling what matters is what matters.

Like the Army, the Navy is unlikely to be distracted by new conceptions of territoriality or virtual geography. The tightly coupled relationship between humankind and the sea means that controlling the oceanic commons is an enduring mission. Strategic chokepoints remain. Straits such as Malacca and Hormuz are not shrinking or swelling just because space and cyberspace grow in importance. Physical goods, whether raw or finished, still need transport, and the sea still offers the most cost effective way of doing so. The Navy will certainly find enabling advantages from space, cyberspace, and the electromagnetic spectrum—and will pursue them as such. The Navy's approach to these domains should include a keen eye toward position, chokepoints, and presence, as these attributes of naval power offer ready templates for making sense of the alternative geographies in other domains.

True to its hybrid charter between land and sea, the Marine Corps' sense of geography reflects a liminal sense of place. Marines dominate littoral spaces, classically understood as the coastal boundary zones between land and sea. The Marine Corps deploys afloat on one domain, with a mission of achieving a beachhead of presence on another. *Transitioning power between domains* is therefore one of the signature missions of the Marine Corps. Marines operate in and across the major domains of land, sea, air, and cyberspace, with a common organizational model, unity of command, singularity of purpose, and a unifying warrior culture. For these reasons, geographic thinking in the Marine Corps may be the most holistic, balanced, and proportional of the four services. Domain or geographic boundaries are less constraining or defining for the corps, as their mission is to operate across domains with an effective transition of presence from one domain to another.

The Marine Corps could be well-positioned to innovate new approaches to multidomain conflict in the years ahead. All of the services are wrestling, individually and collectively, to define joint concepts that will harmonize military effects across multiple domains. As a multidomain service whose signature mission is to transition power between domains, the Marines may be the right pioneer-strategists to characterize the conceptual littorals between space and cyberspace or between cyberspace and the physical domains of air, land, and sea. The services' evolution in jointness has given each service better language ability across domains, but

the Marines may be the closest to *thinking* across domains. This could give the Marine Corps a cognitive advantage in making sense of an all-domain future battlespace.

Lastly, the Air Force's sense of geography is the most fluid of the services. It prizes its ability to go *over, not through* conventional problems. For the Air Force, geography is merely a planning factor, rarely a limiting constraint. With bases positioned around the world and concentrations of various aircraft surrounding key contested areas, airmen routinely pull off a precise rendezvous of far-flung assets in space and time. A mission to drop bombs in the Pacific may originate with US-based bombers, refueled by airborne tankers rejoining from still a third continent, supported by in-theater fighter escorts from yet another region, all synchronized and informed by satellites in various Earth-circling orbits. Time and distance are just variables to be solved with good planning and sound math; rarely are they immovable obstacles.

Curiously, the Air Force's domination of air and space confers a keen sense of thinking in the *third* dimension, but not necessarily agility in thinking in *three* dimensions. Airmen looking down on the Earth's surface from above do not necessarily or intuitively appreciate the two-dimensional realities that so strongly determine operations and tactics on land and sea. For airmen, borders and boundaries are more to be crossed than reified. Developing an intuitive feel for terrain, as both enabler and constraint, is an uncommon and hard-earned skill among airmen whose natural mode of thinking and operating is more nonlinear.

The Air Force's sense of geography is nearly unbounded in scope. The service prides itself as the nation's pioneer-strategists, exploring and exploiting new domains for coercive access. Air, space, cyberspace, the electromagnetic spectrum, information, and the cognitive domain all represent physical or conceptual domains the Air Force seeks to control for advantage. Looking to the future, the Air Force will likely continue its flexible and dynamic approach to operational geography. In fact, the service's pursuit of multidomain operations is ultimately a bid to shrink the globe even further and redefine operational geography. As an integrator of joint capabilities, the operational goal for airmen is to have global situational awareness, with the ability to bring military effects to bear on any situation on demand. In pursuing this vision, airmen reveal their strategic propensity for mastering a fluid all-domain geography in which physical terrain is more footnote than reality.

When: Timeliness Is Relative

The variable of time dominates strategy. Time is the universal resource that all parties have and spend at the same rate. A military, state, or business that competes favorably in time transforms a commodity into a comparative advantage. John Boyd, the Air Force colonel and maverick genius behind the design of the F-15 and F-16 (among other things), famously outlined his elegant model of competing in time: the OODA loop of observe, orient, decide, and act.[37] In military parlance, strategists and tacticians seek to dominate the enemy's OODA loop, by spinning through our OODA cycles faster or better than they do. But not all OODA loops are created equal. OODA loops are scalable, with applications ranging from fighter aircraft making split-second decisions in a dogfight to issues of grand strategy in which states compete against other strong powers for decades. The US military services have their own baseline OODA loops as well, an operational circadian rhythm that gives the service metronomic stability and a shared sense of pace. In an age of accelerated change, each service's general approach to time and timing influences the rate at which it co-evolves with the environment.

At one end of the spectrum, the Navy holds the longest view of operational time. Naval power operates through a logic of presence and persistence. The mission of the US Navy is to be forward, at sea or in foreign ports, showing the artful mix of the flag and the guns in whatever proportion the situation requires. As *The Armed Forces Officer* guide explains, "The Navy culture is a *deployment* culture; deployments form the rhythm of Navy life for the Sailors and for their families."[38] Being deployed at sea is the operational expectation of the Navy; life ashore at home port is the aberrant state. The tactical pace of Navy operations is likewise patient, almost leisurely, given the physics of turning thousand-foot ships and the time-distance challenges of covering millions of square miles at a clip of 25–30 knots. From force planning to strategy to operations and tactics, the Navy's body clock ticks at a long and patient interval. The acceleration of the present age is unlikely to force a false sense of urgency on the Navy, which will hold fast to its steady course of naval strategy and the inherent patience it requires.

The Army also thinks on long time horizons, but for the opposite reason: that is, being permanently deployed should *not* be the default position of the Army. Deploying the US Army in force represents a massive logistical undertaking and should be reserved for serious commitments of the national will. When the big Army machine goes somewhere, it does not go lightly, quietly, or especially quickly. And if getting the Army into a hotspot is difficult, getting the Army *out* of that spot may be even tougher. The Army is the nation's long-term heavyweight force, tasked to occupy territory and finish the task. And since wars are typically much easier to start than finish, the Army inherits complex political tasks that defy easy completion. "If the

nation loses a war, the Army gets blamed," lamented one senior Army officer. "*No one will blame the other services for losing our nation's wars.* If the Air Force screws it up, it just means the Army has to finish it."[39] At its best, the Army therefore plans with sober judgment about the utility of force and beginning a conflict with the end in sight, because while all the services contribute, the Army *commits*. Looking to the future, one can expect the Army to resist reactive engagements in the world's frozen conflicts, while seeking to recharacterize war and peace as distinct categories with meaningful differences—despite the current blurring between the two.

The Marine Corps operates on a highly responsive time scale as the nation's first responders for urgent military crises. Marine leaders consistently trumpet the corps as "this nation's force in readiness . . . a small, highly mobile, efficient, combat-ready striking force, which could be deployed rapidly as this nation's 'first strike' capability."[40] Indeed, the rallying cry of "first to fight" is enshrined in the Marine Corps hymn, hailing the corps' timely interventions from the halls of Montezuma to the shores of Tripoli. The Marine Corps postures itself as a quick reaction force, ready to move into the world's messiest hotspots to bring quick resolution or establish a beachhead of American presence for later reinforcement. But the corps, like the Army, does not have its own strategic lift capability. Marines need a ride to the fight, so the responsiveness of Marine Corps forces typically depends on the current position of the Navy ships on which the marines are embarked or the availability of Air Force transports to carry them to the fight. In its planning, posture, and attitude, the Marine Corps operates on a short time cycle; in its execution, the Marines operate as fast as the other services can get them to the fight. Fueled by an existential urgency, the future Marine Corps may look for creative ways to remain "first to fight," whether through new prepositioning schemas, deployment modalities, or conceiving of cyberspace as a new quick-reaction battlespace.

The Air Force flies at the fastest end of the time-scale spectrum. Airmen understand their no-fail contribution to the nation as holding targets at risk, anytime, anywhere. In fact, the 2005 version of the Air Force mission statement (which has since been updated) began: "Deliver sovereign options for the defense of the United States of America."[41] In releasing the new mission statement, the Air Force secretary and chief of staff explained, "Our task is to provide the president, the combatant commanders, and our nation with an array of options . . . options that are not limited by the tyranny of distance, the urgency of time, or the strength of our enemy's defenses. With one hand the Air Force can deliver humanitarian assistance to the farthest reaches of the globe, while with the other hand we can destroy a target anywhere in the world."[42] The Air Force's sense of timing is therefore the most immediate, urgent, and responsive of all the services. Through the speed, range, and flexibility of its air and space assets, its airmen collapse geography and time to deliver beans or bombs anywhere, anytime.

This eagerness to deliver timely options to decision-makers shrinks the default time horizon of airmen in their operational art and strategy. Unlike Army leaders who are more likely to ask *tell me how this ends*, the more natural question for airmen is *what can we deliver—and how soon?* Its deliveries are not always explosive, of course, as moving gear, people, and aid is a critical element of strategic air power. This default mode of thinking gives the Air Force a well-developed sense of targeting, coercion, and creating effects. While these sensibilities yield good theories of combat, operations, or even campaigning, they do not typically sum to a long-view theory of *war* as a political instrument.[43]

The age of acceleration only fuels the Air Force's drive to collapse geography and time. As a technical service with a passion for going fast and delivering options, the Air Force of the future will likely chase an ever-smaller OODA loop down to the idealized state of an OODA point—a mythic place where complete information and a diverse arsenal of coercive options are united by perfect anticipatory decisions. The operational time-scale for airmen of the future will be faster than ever.

Who: The Locus of Personal Identity

Most of this essay has treated the services as anthropomorphic characters with unique meta-personalities, shaped by each service's operational nature and political nurture. In this section, the level of analysis shifts down to the individual people within those services. A military service is co-constituted with its members; the service is the sum of the people within it, as well as an emergent force that shapes the worldview of the people who compose it. Each service uses internal narratives, telling meaningful stories of what makes the service unique: accepted legends of why it exists, the resources it requires, and where and when it prefers to operate. In doing so, each service confers upon its members a salient identity, defining who they are as members of that proud organization. As a culminating element of the service's strategic culture, these identity frames tend to differ from one service to the next. The services accentuate different elements of their task and purpose, resulting in different levels of salient identity that predominate across the members of those services.

This focus on personal identity within the services is especially relevant for a discussion of the future of the profession of arms. Being a "professional" is in fact one of the overlapping identities that compete for

prominence in the minds of US military personnel. As the services wrestle organizationally and strategically with adapting to the future of the profession of arms, the individuals in those services will likewise need to grapple with what it means to be a *member* of the profession of arms. These two layers of sense-making are occurring simultaneously and interdependently, as individual understandings of the profession shape service-level adaptations, and vice-versa. For each service, the baseline significance of being a member of the profession of arms forms the starting point for identity-based adjustments in the future.

Of all the services, the Army most prominently espouses its role as the national steward of the profession of arms, focusing less on the organizational *Army* per se. While the other three services are more apt to advocate for their interests and herald their glories, the Army often deflects its organizational loyalty toward the loftier ideals of the nation and the enduring profession of arms. In describing the tenets of the Army's professional ethic, for example, a senior Army officer put "[an embrace of] national service" and "loyalty to the Constitution" in the two highest spots on the list.[44] Similarly, the Army's extensive project on "The Future of the Army Profession," published in 2005, listed four dimensions of the Army officer's identity: warrior, member of profession, servant of country, and leader of character.[45] Notably, none of these identities calls out the Army organizationally; instead, they point to higher callings of national service and professional legacy.

Given the Army's avowed dedication to being a national steward of the profession of arms, one can expect the Army to take a cautiously conservative stance on the extent to which changing strategic conditions require new conceptions about the profession itself. The Army is more likely to nurture the historical continuity of its role, rather than quibbling over a series of potential discontinuities, none of which threatens to change the identity of an Army officer as warrior, member of profession, servant of country, or leader of character. In pondering changes to the future of the profession, one can expect the Army to think carefully and change slowly.

Life in the Marine Corps fosters a different salient identity than life in the Army. While both institutions boast a warrior culture, the Marine Corps tends to focus on *the corps* as the defining identity for all its members. Being a marine means forging a new identity—a new self-conception that supersedes all competing claims. While members of the other three services tend to speak of being *in* the Army, Navy, or Air Force, members of the Marine Corps declare an identity: they *are* marines. This identity transformation begins immediately. From their first moments at Marine Corps basic training, recruits are physically and emotionally stripped of personally identifiable traits such as haircuts, personal space, or even proper names—they must identify themselves only as "this recruit." In a process once described as an "egoectomy," recruits forcibly extract their self-centered persona and replace it with a new Marine identity.[46] Once recruits become marines, they inherit the full heritage of the corps and are expected to sustain the elite warrior spirit that defines it.

This dominant Marine identity unifies the corps. The other three services tend to have pronounced subcultures and internal hierarchies of prestige, but Marines resist such internal distinctions within an already prestigious outfit. Other than aviator wings, dive qualification badges, and airborne badges, marines do not wear job specialty insignia on their uniforms, nor do they display unit patches for division, regimental, or battalion affiliations.[47] Even the statutory and institutional divide between officer and enlisted ranks is minimized in the Marine Corps, as all marines are marines, stewards of a common legacy.

This salience of the Marine identity above all others tends to unite the professional and organizational adjustments that Marines will make in the future. While the Marine Corps implicitly sees itself as part of the profession of arms, life in the corps tends to foster a much stronger affiliation with the Marine Corps itself, and not with an impersonal service-agnostic membership in a larger profession. For example, in his 2019 *Commandant's Planning Guidance to the Marine Corps*, the commandant of the Marine Corps, General David Berger, offered this opening epigram: "I believe in my soul that Marines are different. Our identity is firmly rooted in our warrior ethos. This is the force that will always adapt and overcome no matter what the circumstances are. We fight and win in any clime and place."[48] In his thoughtful, far-sighted articulation of planning guidance for the corps, General Berger offered a series of compelling adjustments that Marines would need to make in coming years. Nowhere does the document explicitly mention the profession of arms, however, or the Marine Corps' institutional role in stewarding it as such. For the Marine Corps, adapting to the future will most likely be a series of internal organizational adaptations—in concert with its maritime partner, the US Navy—that will perpetuate the corps' ability to be first to fight and ready to win.

With both national and service-level identities, the Navy appears to be a hybrid of the characteristics just described. The Navy takes great pride in its unique *national* role of promoting US interests abroad and protecting the commercial interests of the nation. From the dawn of the republic, Navy captains served as a deployed cadre of American diplomats and ambassadors, negotiating positions of advantage for the growing republic. Similarly, the Navy nurtures a unique obligation to defend the economic and commercial prosperity of the nation—an obligation highlighted by none of the other military services. One of the earliest nineteenth-century textbooks at the United States Naval Academy, for example, reminded future Navy officers of this important purpose: "To maintain the unvarnished honor of the government and of the nation and, at the same time, *promote its commercial interests in peace*, is an obligation upon the Naval Officer equal with his obligation to defend his ship to the last moment in the hour of battle."[49]

The uniqueness of naval power for the nation gives the Navy a national sense of purpose along with a pronounced service-level identity. In fact, some particularly strong voices argue that the Navy should be understood not merely as a separate service but as a *separate profession*. Former Secretary of the Navy John Lehman, for example, criticized service-unification initiatives, to include the Goldwater-Nichols Act of 1986, as a failure to recognize that the Army and Navy are "very, very different professions."[50] According to Lehman, the institutional separation between the War Department and Navy Department between 1798 and 1949 was a distinction rooted in the Constitution, reflecting elemental differences in their founding charters. The Constitution gives Congress power to "raise and support armies" for two-year periods, but a more enduring and expansive authority to "provide and maintain a navy."[51] The Navy thus operates under different Constitutional authority, the thinking goes, creating a form of national power that is not subordinate to general military power, but alongside it—stewarded by its own body of *professionals*.

It is difficult to appraise the extent to which this thread of unique professionalism holds sway among Navy sailors today. Looking forward, as the future of the profession of arms is considered, debated, and challenged, the Navy may well rekindle a renewed sense of independence in its professional obligations. While the Navy is unlikely to reject the prevailing currents of jointness—the services have come too far for outright resistance—the Navy may still pursue pockets of autonomous uniqueness in making sense of the ambiguous future. The Navy may not join close ranks with the Army as stewards of the national profession of arms; instead, it may advance a complementary identity as stewards of the adjacent profession of naval power. This raises the intriguing possibility that future debates about the profession of arms may spur two distinct threads, with the Army and Navy leading two different conversations.

Lastly, the Air Force fosters still a different sense of self among its airmen. The Air Force does so many different things for the nation that it struggles to find the unifying narrative that brings all airmen under a common mission, legacy, or identity.[52] In a service where structures and operations are often built around machines, the loyalties of airmen naturally migrate toward these machines. Given the visceral experiences afforded by the human-machine union, airmen commonly identify themselves with their primary aircraft, weapons system, or functional occupation. Familiar introductions include, "I'm a Predator pilot," or "She's a C-130 crew chief," or "He's a cyber guy." This identity dynamic tends to dilute common bonds of task and purpose across the service and to give rise to a "fractionated confederation of sub-cultures rather than a cohesive military service."[53] The Air Force finds it difficult to craft a collective narrative among such diverse clans and tribes, with each subgroup defined largely by the machine it operates.

This technological identification has important implications for the service's adaptation to the future of the profession of arms. The Air Force of course understands, and even expresses, its role in stewarding the historic profession of arms. But the daily practice of life inside the service's culture does not prioritize that identity frame. Instead, an *occupational* rather than a professional or institutional orientation tends to prevail among airmen.[54] This occupational orientation shifts the locus of identity to the task, the machine, or the function—and away from broader concerns of professional identity, responsibility, and stewardship on behalf of society. Consequently, the Air Force may be least likely to wrestle with the ways in which current trends put stress on the historic profession of arms. Airmen feed on change, discovering new platforms and machines that produce coercive leverage against competitors. The burden felt by airmen is not to maintain deep continuities with the past, but to stay ahead of the future.

Making Room for a Fifth: The Cultural Implications of a New Space Force

A major development in evolving the profession of arms is the addition of a new military service. In December 2019, Congress passed the National Defense Authorization Act for Fiscal Year 2020, which establishes the Space Force as an independent military service within the Department of the Air Force. This final analysis section offers prospective ideas on how the operational nature and political nurture of this fledgling Space Force may define the service's founding culture. As both civilian and military leaders think carefully about the kind of force they want to create, they should consider how these founding moments establish cultural precedents that will long endure.

This essay views the origins of a service's strategic culture as the contingent interaction of its operational nature and political nurture. The general characteristics of the service's operating domain tend to shape particular disciplines of mind and action. These physi-

cal characteristics work together with the human elements of political intrigue, military history, and organizational behavior to shape a service's prevailing sense of preferred ends, ways, and means. Looking ahead to the new Space Force, how will these two key elements combine, and what will the broader implications be across the DoD?

The physical characteristics of the space domain will exert a powerful influence on the culture of the new Space Force. The shape of that influence may depend, however, on the scope of the mandate given to the service and the technological requirements of that mandate. In short, the culture of the Space Force may hinge on whether it follows Johannes Kepler or Captain Kirk: maintaining predictable orbits or boldly going where no one has gone before. Some commentators frame the choice as a brown-water space force versus a blue-water one.[55] Extending the maritime analogy, a brown-water force controls close-in territorial spaces, while a blue-water force moves beyond the littorals into the ungoverned commons. Will the new service double-down on the status quo in brown-water space or expand into more ambitious blue-water space-guardian roles? Will it focus largely on strengthening current missions such as reconnaissance, navigation, and communication, or will it be more like a Coast Guard in space, focused not only on homeland defense but also exploration, law enforcement, search and rescue, freedom of navigation, and rule-based commerce?

Current technologies do not yet permit a blue-water space force to begin operating in the blue immediately—Kepler still reigns at present. Limitations in propulsion systems, affordable launch and recovery, and human life-support systems (among other things) prevent the Space Force from operating immediately as an empowered galactic coast guard. These technological limits, however, do not have to function as limits to the chartered mission of the Space Force. Congress can charter a force that reflects current capabilities, or it can charter an aspirational force that demands new technologies for the future. Either choice is defensible, but each has implications. If the Space Force receives a Keplerian mandate to mature and defend what is *already done* in space, that decision will have cascading effects on the culture. It will foster cultural norms of predictability, situational awareness, and orbital mastery. Dedicated space professionals will look for new and clever ways to dominate low-earth and geosynchronous orbits with dynamic constellations of better satellites, launched faster and more cheaply than ever before. These are worthy objectives and may be the prudent strategy for the new Space Force.

Conversely, an aggressively aspirational charter for the Space Force would likewise shape the culture for decades. The aspirational charter may fuel technological breakthroughs that would never be funded otherwise.

It would foster cultural norms of creativity, exploration, innovation, and cross-sector collaboration with commercial partners. Such a charter could also be problematic—it could be *so* aspirational that it fuels a perpetual "say-do gap," with ambitious space pioneers promising game-changing capabilities that are *almost* here but perpetually remain three to five years away. A too-ambitious culture could create credibility gaps that would undermine its effectiveness as part of the joint force; establishing trust as part of the joint force should be of paramount concern to the new service.

The political circumstances that create a new military service also cast a long shadow over its strategic culture. New organizations must solve problems of both external adaptation and internal integration; as they solve these problems well enough to stay alive, early provisional solutions become reified as *the way things are done around here.*[56] The founding context of the Space Force appears to be unique among the services. While the 1947 secession of the Air Force from the Army looks like a close analog, a key difference suggests otherwise. Most prominently, the case for an independent Air Force was largely made from *within*, argued with logic and battle-tested evidence by air-minded secessionists with a mature sense of what independent airpower could do *differently* for the nation. Since its founding, the Air Force has felt pressure to confirm the hypothesis of its origin story, making good on its promise to use airpower decisively for the nation. This pressure to perform has been a feature of Air Force strategic culture ever since.

Creating an independent space force, however, has been spurred largely by *external* agents. While some space professionals have certainly been in the conversation, they have not been the leading provocateurs. Instead, various high-level commissions, key committee leaders in Congress, Vice President Mike Pence, and President Donald Trump have been the prominent agenda setters for the new Space Force. The president, vice president, and Congress forced the national conversation—even if some of it happened on late-night comedy talk shows—and pushed the DoD to draft a legislative proposal, over the initial objections of the secretary of the Air Force and chief of staff of the Air Force.[57] The Space Force now exists as the visible offspring of a highly publicized presidential directive. As such, the force will face significant and rapid pressure to prove its value and confirm the prudence of creating it. Even in its early months and years, while still preoccupied with finding office space, choosing uniform colors, and hiring administrative assistants, the Space Force will be expected to prove its independent value to the DoD and the nation. It will be expected to do things in and through space that the Air Force would not have done or been able to do. Given its external presidential origins, this performance pressure will likely be even more acute than the Air Force faced. Unless bold space leaders provide extraordinary top cover to the middle ranks, the Space Force will find it difficult to carve out experimental spaces to innovate, fail forward, learn, and try again. Failure of almost any sort may be politically untenable. These validation pressures could become defining—though uncomfortable—elements of the Space Force's strategic culture.

The cultural implications of the Space Force will not be limited to that force alone. Creating a new military service forces a renegotiation of professional jurisdictions among the existing services as well. The organizational structure of the DoD makes a statutory distinction between force development (the organizing, training, and equipping done by the services) and force employment (the operational warfighting done by the combatant commands). As an interim step in strengthening US capabilities in space, the unified combatant command of US Space Command was reestablished in a White House Rose Garden ceremony on August 29, 2019.[58] US Space Command brings together space capabilities under a common warfighting commander to achieve unified effort in that domain. Reestablishing this combatant command after its seventeen-year hibernation was a responsible and important step—and a far less contentious one than creating a new service. Within the defense ecosystem, force employment finds easy agreement; force development does not.

The services dominate the defense establishment, controlling huge budgets, career incentives, and professional identities. Combatant commands come and go, formed and disbanded as geopolitical conditions evolve over time. The services, however, are practically permanent. With a Space Force now created, all of the services must redraw the conceptual boundaries of their professional jurisdiction. In effect, the services must renegotiate peace treaties as they carve up the finite terrain of national security expertise: "I work over here; you work over there; here are our borderlands, and this is how we will work together." The four current services all rely heavily on space for their operations, and all of them have some amount of space equipment on their ledger. Making these capabilities available for unified employment under US Space Command was not especially controversial. But in the future, if the Space Force lays claim to *ownership*—not just employment—of all or most space-based assets, new rounds of heated interservice negotiation will ensue. The four existing services—especially the Air Force—will likely want to retain independent space capabilities to meet service-specific needs. Moving from a posture of independent execution to dependent reliance on another service breeds suspicion and frustration. The non-space-owning Air Force will likely chafe at that dependency.

Lastly, senior leaders in the Air Force and Space Force must proactively manage the interpersonal relationships between the sibling services to maintain trust. Members of the Space Force, who were airmen yesterday, see themselves differently today. Someone else now controls the dynamics of daily life: what to wear, where to live, what to do, what to buy, when to deploy, and who gets promoted and why. In defining its new identity, the Space Force may find the Air Force to be a useful foil—the repressive motherland of fighter pilots that never really appreciated their talents and potential. Defining oneself in contrast to an *other* can bring helpful clarity to an organization, but it can also create seams of distrust. To organize into groups is to create an "us" and a "them," invoking the "fundamental constraint in the empathetic bandwidth of the human mind."[59] To be effective in its joint warfighting mission, the Space Force must do everything possible to set a culture of trust-building collaboration, keeping "the point at which everyone else sucks" at distant remove.[60]

The space domain matters greatly for today's joint force and the global economy. Creating a new military service to control that domain is a strategic move—one that does something *for* the nation and *to* it. As Congress and other defense leaders nurture the infancy of the new Space Force, close attention to these cultural implications may help the decision pay long-lasting dividends at a reasonable price.

Conclusion

The words of General Sir John Hackett opened this discussion, affirming society's perpetual need to defend itself by force. In closing, Hackett's *organizational* insights on societal defense now ring true: "What is best for his service will always be sought by the serving officer, and if he believes that in seeking the best for his service he is rendering the best service he can to his country, it is easy to see why. He may have to be restrained. He can scarcely be blamed."[61] The preceding analysis strongly endorses Hackett's view on the primacy of service-oriented thinking in the minds of military officers.

This essay's contribution to *American Defense Policy* has advanced four main propositions. First, the profession of arms in the United States is evolving in its character, while its nature steadfastly endures. War remains a political instrument, "an act of force to compel our enemy to do our will," while the character of that compellence and the particular expressions of force evolve over time.[62] New stressing conditions in the character of warfare fracture today's inherited assumptions. Traditional categories, definitions, and distinctions blur, throwing into confusion what it means to defend the American way of life in an accelerated networked age. The geography, timing, technology, and

pervasiveness of coercive competition are changing faster than our ability to make sense of them.

The second proposition of this argument is that the military services within the Department of Defense serve as the principal sense-making agents in adapting to the future demands of the profession of arms. The services represent the appropriate level of analysis; focusing broadly on "the military" overlooks core differences between the services, while looking narrowly at specific platforms, subgroups, or individuals admits endless variation. The services control hundreds of billions of dollars annually; they design, acquire, train, and field the weapon systems used in battle; and they hold sway over the dominant incentives of daily life for their hundreds of thousands of members. Moreover, the services exhibit lifelike qualities, with vivid personalities and enduring beliefs shaped by their operational environments and unique histories. The services, in fact, are co-constituted with their personnel: soldiers make up the Army, but the Army makes the soldiers. An aggregate service personality bears down on its members, exerting a powerful normalizing influence on individual minds and actions; those individuals in turn become cultural carriers, animating the hive mind of service personality. To understand how the United States military might respond to a given impulse, a specific analysis of the services and their strategic cultures is the right place to begin.

The third main proposition of the essay—the one explored at greatest length—is that each of the services will approach the evolving profession of arms uniquely, informed by its particular sense of jurisdiction, resources, geography, timing, and identity. In each of these areas, the services' strategic cultures give them "diagnostic and choice propensities," baseline scripts for making sense of ambiguity—one of the signature features of the current geopolitical environment.[63] The present age of accelerated change cloaks more of the defense environment in ambiguity and uncertainty. These conditions suggest that long-proven strategic cultures will be more prominent than ever, providing reliable waypoints to navigate uncertain terrain.

The fourth and final proposition of the chapter is largely speculative in character but firm in precedent: with the new Space Force created by Congress, civilian and military leaders must pay careful attention to its early cultural foundations. The scope of the Space Force's nascent charter, the external political pressures to prove its value quickly, and the consequent renegotiation of professional jurisdictions in the DoD will combine to establish *the way things are around here* for decades. "Founding moments loom large" for major bureaucratic organizations such as military services.[64] Legislative, executive, and military leaders must be savvy organizational designers, paying close attention to the interaction of operational nature and political nurture thrust upon the infant Space Force.

The profession of arms in the United States continues to be a deep reservoir of moral strength. Our nation's military members take pride in being *professionals*, committed to the mastery of expert practice, employed on behalf of the American people, under the direction of properly constituted authority. Despite the accelerating evolution of that expertise, the steadfast and sacrificial commitment of American military professionals remains an unchanging and irreplaceable good for the nation.

NOTES

1. Colin Gray, "War: Continuity in Change, Change in Continuity," *Parameters* 40, no. 2 (Summer 2010): 5–13.

2. General Sir John Hackett, *The Profession of Arms* (New York: Macmillan, 1983), 9.

3. Hackett, *Profession of Arms*, 9.

4. Joi Ito and Jeff Howe, *Whiplash: How to Survive our Faster Future* (New York: Grand Central Publishing, 2016), 19.

5. Some readers may reasonably question my omitting the fifth armed service in the United States, the US Coast Guard. The Coast Guard is unquestionably an important, historic, and honorable institution that serves the nation with great valor and sacrifice. But given the Coast Guard's hybrid nature—part of the Department of Homeland Security in peacetime, but transferred to Department of Defense leadership in wartime—it sits at the margins of the argument presented in this essay. The weight of analysis here is on the services that reside permanently inside the DoD. Additionally, as this volume goes to press, the new Space Force has been established as the sixth armed service (the fifth in full-time DoD service). While the Space Force is too young for a complete analysis, the cultural implications of the new service are addressed at the end of the essay.

6. Chairman of the Joint Chiefs of Staff Instruction (CJCSI) 1800.01E, *Officer Professional Military Education Policy (OPMEP)*, May 29, 2015, https://www.jcs.mil/Portals/36 /Documents/Doctrine/education/cjcsi1800_01e.pdf?ver=2017 -12-29-142206-877.

7. Title 10, USC.

8. Purple is the color associated with the Joint Staff and has become a shorthand reference to all things joint.

9. J. C. Wylie, *Military Strategy: A General Theory of Power Control* (Annapolis, MD: Naval Institute Press, 1989), 72.

10. This phrase has classic resonance in the Corps and is highlighted as the Marine raison d'être in the 2019 edition of the *Commandant's Planning Guidance to the Marine Corps*. See General Daniel Berger, *Commandant's Planning Guidance: 38th Commandant of the Marine Corps*, July 17, 2019, http:// www.marines.mil/Portals/1/Publications/Commandant's%20 Planning%20Guidance_2019.pdf?ver=2019-07-17-090732 -937.

11. For a more complete description of this approach to service strategic culture, see Jeffrey Donnithorne, *Four Guardians: A Principled-Agent View of American Civil-Military Relations* (Baltimore, MD: Johns Hopkins University Press, 2018), 29–31.

12. Alexander George, "The Causal Nexus between Cognitive Beliefs and Decision-Making Behavior: The 'Operational Code' Belief System," in *Psychological Models in International Politics*, ed. Lawrence S. Falkowski (Boulder, CO: Westview Press, 1979), 101.

13. Andrew D. Abbott, *The System of Professions: An Essay on the Division of Expert Labor* (Chicago: University of Chicago Press, 1988).

14. Stephen K. Scroggs, *Army Relations with Congress: Thick Armor, Dull Sword, Slow Horse* (Westport, CT: Praeger, 2000), 123.

15. Alexander Hamilton, James Madison, and John Jay, *The Federalist: A Commentary on the Constitution of the United States*, ed. Henry Cabot Lodge (New York: G. P. Putnam's Sons, 1888), 63.

16. Rutledge quoted in Jonathan Elliot, ed., *The Debates in the Several State Conventions on the Adoption of the Federal Constitution* (Philadelphia: J. B. Lippincott, 1881), 4:299.

17. Paula G. Thornhill, *"Over Not Through": The Search for a Strong, Unified Culture for America's Airmen* (Santa Monica, CA: RAND Corporation, 2012).

18. Victor H. Krulak, *First to Fight: An Inside View of the U.S. Marine Corps* (Annapolis, MD: Naval Institute Press, 1984), xv.

19. J. Robert Moskin, *The U.S. Marine Corps Story*, 3rd rev. ed. (Boston: Little, Brown, 1992), 24.

20. Allan R. Millett, *Semper Fidelis: The History of the United States Marine Corps* (New York: Macmillan, 1980), 122.

21. Krulak, *First to Fight*, 13.

22. James A. Warren, *American Spartans: The US Marines: A Combat History from Iwo Jima to Iraq* (New York: Free Press, 2005), 9.

23. The Army has recently made notable strides to evolve forward, establishing Army Futures Command in 2018, led by a four-star general and headquartered in civilian office space in Austin, Texas—the heart of start-up country. See, for example, Joe Lacdan, "Establishment of Army Futures Command Marks a Culture Shift," August 27, 2018, https://www.army .mil/article/210371/establishment_of_army_futures_command _marks_a_culture_shift.

24. Carl H. Builder, *The Masks of War: American Military Styles in Strategy and Analysis* (Baltimore, MD: Johns Hopkins University Press, 1989), 22.

25. See, for example, Rick Berger, "F-15X vs. F-35: The Air Force Debate that Is Dominating the Headlines," *National Interest*, June 11, 2019, https://nationalinterest.org/blog/buzz/f-15x -vsf-35-air-force-debate-dominating-headlines-62112. John A. Tirpak, "'Lockheed Fatigue,' Need for Affordable Mix Drove F-15EX Decision," *Air Force Magazine*, March 23, 2019, https://www.airforcemag.com/Lockheed-Fatigue-Need-for -Affordable-Tactical-Mix-Drove-F-15EX-Decision/.

26. Kenneth Hagan, *This People's Navy: The Making of American Sea Power* (New York: The Free Press, 1991), 383.

27. Megan Eckstein, "Acting SECNAV Modly Puts a Ten-Year Clock on Reaching 355 Ship Navy," USNI News, December 10, 2019, https://news.usni.org/2019/12/10/acting-secnav -modly-puts-a-ten-year-clock-on-reaching-355-ship-navy.

28. For the historic list of the Army's basic and special branches compiled by the US Army Center of Military History, see https://history.army.mil/html/faq/branches.html.

29. For a compelling example of this, see Thomas L. Mc-Naugher, *The M16 Controversies: Military Organizations and Weapons Acquisition* (Westport, CT: Praeger, 1984).

30. Millett, *Semper Fidelis*, 611.

31. Krulak, *First to Fight*, 141, 143.

32. Warren, *American Spartan*, 11.

33. For an explanation of why this is so, see Payton and Baron in this volume.

34. Will Roper, "Opinion: Let's Ensure Tech Innovation Gets to the Military," *Wired*, November 1, 2019, https://www.wired.com/story/opinion-lets-ensure-tech-innovation-gets-to-the-military/.

35. For a basic overview of hypersonic weapons, see Missile Defense Advocacy Alliance, "Hypersonic Weapon Basics," May 30, 2018, https://missiledefenseadvocacy.org/missile-threat-and-proliferation/missile-basics/hypersonic-missiles/#_edn1.

36. The Navy is fond of quoting the 70-80-90 rule as the geopolitical pretext for a global navy. See, for example, The Honorable Roy Mabus, Secretary of the Navy, "27th Annual Emerging Issues Forum: Investing in Generation Z," February 7, 2012, https://www.navy.mil/navydata/people/secnav/Mabus/Speech/emergingissuesfinal.pdf.

37. Grant T. Hammond, *The Mind of War: John Boyd and American Security* (Washington, DC: Smithsonian Institution Press, 2001), 4–5.

38. Department of Defense, *The Armed Forces Officer* (Washington, DC: US Department of Defense, 2006), 86.

39. Scroggs, *Army Relations with Congress*, 121; emphasis added.

40. Paul Starobin and Robert Leavitt, "Shaping the National Military Command Structure: Command Responsibilities for the Persian Gulf," Case 85-628 (Cambridge, MA: Kennedy School of Government Case Program, Harvard University, 1985), 26.

41. Master Sgt. Mitch Gettle, "Air Force Releases New Mission Statement," December 8, 2005, https://www.af.mil/News/Article-Display/Article/132526/air-force-releases-new-mission-statement/.

42. Gettle, "Air Force Releases New Mission Statement."

43. This proposition derives from arguments in Michael Sherry, *The Rise of American Air Power: The Creation of Armageddon* (New Haven, CT: Yale University Press, 1987), 251–52.

44. Matthew Moten, *The Army Officers' Professional Ethic—Past, Present, and Future* (Carlisle, PA: US Army War College, Strategic Studies Institute, 2010), 14.

45. Don M. Snider, "The U.S. Army as a Profession," in *The Future of the Army Profession*, ed. Don M. Snider and Lloyd J. Matthews (Boston: McGraw-Hill, 2005), 13–21.

46. Krulak, *First to Fight*, 161.

47. Thomas G. Mahnken, *Technology and the American Way of War* (New York: Columbia University Press, 2008), 7–8.

48. General Daniel Berger, *Commandant's Planning Guidance: 38th Commandant of the Marine Corps*, July 17, 2019, http://www.marines.mil/Portals/1/Publications/Commandant's%20Planning%20Guidance_2019.pdf?ver=2019-07-17-090732-937.

49. Peter Karsten, *The Naval Aristocracy: The Golden Age of Annapolis and the Emergence of Modern American Navalism* (New York: Free Press, 1972), 35; emphasis added.

50. John Lehman, former secretary of the Navy, in discussion with the author, February 2013.

51. US Const., art. I, § 8.

52. Thornhill, "*Over Not Through.*"

53. James Smith, "Air Force Culture and Cohesion: Building an Air and Space Force for the Twenty-First Century," *Airpower Journal* 12, no. 3 (Fall 1998): 46.

54. Smith, "Air Force Culture and Cohesion," 48.

55. For a useful overview of the space force discussion, see David Montgomery, "Trump's Excellent Space Force Adventure," *Washington Post*, December 3, 2019, https://www.washingtonpost.com/magazine/2019/12/03/trumps-proposal-space-force-was-widely-mocked-could-it-be-stroke-stable-genius-that-makes-america-safe-again/.

56. Edgar H. Schein, *Organizational Culture and Leadership*, 3rd ed. (San Francisco: Jossey-Bass, 1989).

57. Montgomery, "Trump's Excellent Space Force Adventure." See also "Commanding Space: The Story Behind the Space Force," Center for Strategic and International Studies, April 11, 2019, https://aerospace.csis.org/commanding-space/.

58. U.S. Space Command Public Affairs, "U.S. Space Command Recognizes Establishment," September 9, 2019, https://www.spacecom.mil/MEDIA/NEWS-ARTICLES/Article/1955528/us-space-command-recognizes-establishment/.

59. General Stanley McChrystal, *Team of Teams: New Rules of Engagement for a Complex World* (New York: Penguin Random House, 2015), 127.

60. McChrystal, *Team of Teams*, 126.

61. Hackett, "The Military in Service of the State," 523.

62. Carl Von Clausewitz, *On War* (Princeton, NJ: Princeton University Press, 1984), 75.

63. George, "The Causal Nexus," 101.

64. Amy B. Zegart, *Flawed by Design: The Evolution of the CIA, JCS, and NSC* (Stanford, CA: Stanford University Press, 1999), 7.

Let Women Fight
Ending the US Military's Female Combat Ban

MEGAN H. MACKENZIE

Today, 214,098 women serve in the US military, representing 14.6 percent of total service members. Around 280,000 women have worn American uniforms in Afghanistan and Iraq, where 144 have died and over 600 have been injured. Hundreds of female soldiers have received a Combat Action Badge, awarded for actively engaging with a hostile enemy. Two women, Sergeant Leigh Ann Hester and Specialist Monica Lin Brown, have been awarded Silver Stars—one of the highest military decorations awarded for valor in combat—for their service in Afghanistan and Iraq.

Yet the US military, at least officially, still bans women from serving in direct combat positions. As irregular warfare has become increasingly common in the last few decades, the difference on the ground between the frontline and support roles is no longer clear. Numerous policy changes have also eroded the division between combat and noncombat positions. More and more military officials recognize the contributions made by female soldiers, and politicians, veterans, and military experts have all begun actively lobbying Washington to drop the ban. But Congress has not budged.

Proponents of the policy, who include Duncan Hunter (R-Calif), former chair of the House Armed Services Committee, and former Senator Rick Santorum (R-Pa.), rely on three central arguments: that women cannot meet the physical requirements necessary to fight, that they simply don't belong in combat, and that their inclusion in fighting units would disrupt those units' cohesion and battle readiness. Yet these arguments do not stand up to current data on women's performance in combat or their impact on troop dynamics. Banning women from combat does not ensure military effectiveness. It only perpetuates counterproductive gender stereotypes and biases. It is time for the US military to get over its hang-ups and acknowledge women's rightful place on the battlefield.

Women in a Man's World

Women have long served in various auxiliary military roles during wars. Further, the 1948 Women's Armed Services Integration Act created a permanent corps of women in all the military departments. This was considered a step forward at the time, but it is also the origin of the current combat ban. The act limited women's number to 2 percent of total service members and formally excluded them from combat duties. The exclusion policy was reinforced in 1981, when the US Supreme Court ruled that the all-male draft did not constitute gender-based discrimination since it was intended to increase combat troops and women were already restricted from combat.

Despite this restriction, the share of women in the US armed forces increased in the 1980s and 1990s, from 8.5 percent to 11.1 percent, as a result of the transition to an all-volunteer force in 1973 and high demand for troops. Today, the Air Force is the most open service for women. Women have been flying in combat aircraft since 1993, and they now make up 70 of the 3,700 fighter pilots in the service.

In the rest of the military, restrictions on women have also been slipping for some time, albeit more slowly, due to an increase in female enlistment and the public's growing sensitivity to equal labor rights. In January 1994, a memorandum from then–Secretary of Defense Les Aspin rescinded the "risk rule" barring women from any positions that could expose them to direct combat, hostile fire, or capture; the rule was replaced by the "direct ground combat assignment rule," which more narrowly tailored the restriction to frontline combat positions.

Recent policy changes have also blurred the distinction between combat and support roles. In 2003, the army began reorganizing units and increasing the number of brigades within each division. Under this system, forward support companies, which provide logistical support, transportation, and maintenance to battalions, are now grouped together on the same bases as combat units. Since women are permitted to serve in such support units, a major barrier designed to keep them away from combat has almost vanished.

The assignment of women to combat-related tasks has further undermined the strength of the ban. Beginning in 2003, for example, so-called Lioness teams were deployed to assist combat units in Iraq searching women for weapons and explosives. Drawing from this model, the military created several other female-only units in 2009, including "female engagement teams." In their first year of operation, these teams conducted over 70 short-term search-and-engagement missions in Afghanistan. Paying lip service to the exclusion policy, the military specified that these units could not contribute to hunt-and-kill foot patrols and should stay at combat bases only temporarily. In practice, however, this meant that female soldiers were required to leave their combat bases for one night every six weeks before immediately returning. Not only did this practice put women at risk with unnecessary travel in an insecure environment, it also exemplifies the waste and hardship that the preservation of the formal ban imposes on the military.

Meanwhile, the US military is finding different ways to recognize the fact that women now fight in the country's wars. Members of forward support companies and female engagement teams now receive combat pay, also known as "hostile fire" or "imminent danger" pay, acknowledging the threats women regularly face. And 78 percent of the deaths of female US service members in Iraq were categorized as hostile, yet another sign of how American women in uniform regularly put their lives at risk.

In light of all these changes, in 2011 the Military Leadership Diversity Commission recommended that the Department of Defense remove all combat restrictions on women. Although the total number of jobs closed to women is now relatively low, at 7.3 percent, the commission found that "exclusion from these occupations has a considerable influence on advancement to higher positions" and that eliminating the exclusion is essential "to create a level playing field for all service members who meet the qualifications." Echoing this sentiment, Senator Kirsten Gillibrand (D-N.Y.) introduced the Gender Equality in Combat Act in 2012, which seeks the termination of the ground combat exclusion policy. In addition, Command Sergeant Major Jane Baldwin and Colonel Ellen Haring, both of the Army Reserve, filed a lawsuit in May against the secretary of defense and the Army's secretary, assistant secretary, and deputy chief of staff claiming that the exclusion policy violates their constitutional rights.

Responding to growing scrutiny, the Pentagon's press secretary, George Little, announced on February 9, 2012, that the Department of Defense would continue to remove restrictions on women's roles. Since then, the military has made a slew of policy revisions and commissioned a series of reviews. In May 2012, for example, the army opened up more than 14,000 combat-related jobs to women. Much of this increase, however, came from officially recognizing the combat-related nature of the jobs conducted by medics and intelligence officers, among others, positions that are already open to women. More substantially, the Marine Corps announced in April 2012 that for the first time, women can enroll and train, but not yet serve, as infantry combat officers. The Army has also opened six new combat-related occupational specialties to women. In June 2012, Cicely Verstein became the first woman to serve in one of these newly opened combat support roles when she enlisted as a Bradley Fighting Vehicle systems maintainer. Women such as Verstein can now operate with combat arms units in select positions, yet they are still technically restricted from infantry and special operations roles.

Although the ban still exists on paper, the military is finding various ways to lift it in practice, and so the complete repeal of the policy would not constitute a radical change in operational terms. But it would be an acknowledgment of the contributions that women are already making to US military operations. As Anu Bhagwati, a former Marine captain and now executive director of the Service Women's Action Network, explained in a BBC News interview, "Women are being shot at, are being killed overseas, are being attached to all of these combat arms units. . . . The [combat exclusion] policy has to catch up to reality." Indeed, all soldiers, female as well as male, have been given extensive combat training since 2003, when the army altered its basic training procedures in response to the growth of irregular warfare in Afghanistan and Iraq. The main obstacle that remains for women who want to serve their country is an outmoded set of biased assumptions about their capabilities and place in society.

Why Women Can Keep Up

The argument that women are not physically fit for combat is perhaps the most publicized and well-researched justification for their exclusion from fighting units. In her 2000 book, *The Kinder, Gentler Military*, the journalist Stephanie Gutmann summarized the position this way: "When butts drop onto seats, and feet grope for foot pedals, and girls of five feet one (not an uncommon height in the ranks) put on great bowl-like Kevlar helmets over a full head of long hair done up in a French braid, there are problems of fit—and those picayune fit problems ripple outward, eventually affecting performance, morale, and readiness."

This argument continues to receive a significant amount of attention in the United States, despite the fact that other militaries across the world have found that with proper training and necessary adaptations, women can complete the same physical tasks as men. In the 1970s, the Canadian military conducted trials that tested women's physical, psychological, and social capacity for combat roles. The results informed the final decision of the Canadian Human Rights Tribunal to remove Canada's female combat exclusion. After similar tests, Denmark also lifted its combat ban in the late 1980s.

The physical fitness argument, which tends to focus on differences between average male and female bodies, is also undermined by the fact that women who join the military tend to be more fit than the average American. Additional training and conditioning further decrease the gap between female and male service members, and evidence indicates that women usually benefit substantially from fitness-training programs. More to the point, performance is not necessarily determined by gender; it is determined by other attributes and by an individual's determination to reach physical prowess. To put it bluntly, there are physically fit, tough women who are suitable for combat, and weak, feeble men who are not.

The US armed services would do a better job recognizing this were it not for the fact that, as critics have pointed out, the military's physical standards were created to measure male fitness, not job effectiveness. As Matthew Brown, a US Army colonel and director of the Arizona Army National Guard, found in a US Army War College study, "There is no conclusive evidence that all military members, regardless of occupational specialty, unit assignment, age or gender, should acquire the same level of physical fitness." The US General Accounting Office (now the Government Accountability Office) also admitted in a 1998 report that physical fitness tests are not necessarily a useful gauge of operational effectiveness, explaining, "Fitness testing is not aimed at assessing the capability to perform specific missions or military jobs." To be sure, men and women have different types of bodies, but growing research points to the limitations of having a single male-centered standard for fitness and equipment. Recently, for example, the Army has moved to design body armor for women rather than force them to continue wearing equipment that restricts their movement and cuts into their legs because it was designed for men. With proper training and equipment, women can contribute to missions just as well as men.

Breaking Up the Band of Brothers

Even though the physical argument does not hold up to scrutiny, many in the military establishment continue to instinctively oppose the idea of women serving in combat roles. In a 1993 *New York Times* article, General Merrill McPeak, former chief of staff of the Air Force, admitted that he had "a culturally based hang-up." "I can't get over this image of old men ordering young women into combat," he said. "I have a gut-based hang-up there. And it doesn't make a lot of sense in every way. I apologize for it." This belief had earlier been spelled out in the 1992 report of the Presidential Commission on the Assignment of Women in the Armed Forces, which was established by George H. W. Bush to review the combat exclu-

sion. The commission identified several factors related to having women serve in combat roles that could negatively impact troop dynamics, including the "real or perceived inability of women to carry their weight without male assistance, a 'zero privacy' environment on the battlefield, interference with male bonding, cultural values and the desire of men to protect women, inappropriate male/female relationships, and pregnancy—particularly when perceived as a way to escape from combat duty."

While campaigning for the Republican presidential nomination this year, Santorum, the former senator, echoed these concerns, arguing that "instead of focus[ing] on the mission, [male soldiers] may be more concerned about protecting . . . a [female soldier] in a vulnerable position." Others fear that men will not be able to restrain themselves sexually if forced to fight and work in close proximity to women. The conservative Independent Women's Forum strongly supports the ban because of the "power of the sex drive when young women and men, under considerable stress, are mixed together in close quarters."

Even as these false assumptions about the inherent nature of men and women persist, many in the military and the general public have changed their minds. In 2010, Admiral Mike Mullen, then chairman of the US Joint Chiefs of Staff, said, "I know what the law says and I know what it requires, but I'd be hard pressed to say that any woman who serves in Afghanistan today or who's served in Iraq over the last few years did so without facing the same risks as their male counterparts." Similarly, Bhagwati contends that "as proven by ten years of leading troops in combat in Iraq and Afghanistan, there are women that are physically and mentally qualified to succeed . . . and lead infantry platoons." Meanwhile, a 2011 survey conducted by ABC News and the *Washington Post* found that 73 percent of Americans support allowing women in combat.

Despite such shifts in opinion, defenders of the status quo argue that lifting the ban would disrupt male bonding and unit cohesion, which is thought to build soldiers' confidence and thereby increase combat readiness and effectiveness. In 2007, Kingsley Browne, a former US Supreme Court clerk and the author of *Co-ed Combat: The New Evidence That Women Shouldn't Fight the Nation's Wars*, argued that "men fight for many reasons, but probably the most powerful one is the bonding—'male bonding'—with their comrades. . . . Perhaps for very fundamental reasons, women do not evoke in men the same feelings of comradeship and 'followership' that men do." These comments betray the widely held fear that women would feminize and therefore reduce the fighting potential of the military. The Israeli military historian Martin van Creveld has echoed this sentiment, writing, "As women enter them, the armed forces in question will become both less willing to fight and less capable of doing so."

And as Anita Blair, former assistant secretary of the Navy, warned, "The objective for many who advocate a greater female influence in the armed services is not so much to conquer the military as conquer manhood: they aim to make the most quintessentially masculine of our institutions more feminine." By such lights, women fundamentally threaten the unified masculine identity of the military and could never properly fill combat roles because they are inherently incapable of embodying the manly qualities of a soldier.

This argument is intuitive and plausible. It is also dead wrong. It assumes that a key objective of the military is enhancing masculinity rather than national security and that unit bonding leads to better task performance. In fact, a 1995 study conducted by the US Army Research Institute for the Behavioral and Social Sciences found that "the relation between cohesiveness and performance is due primarily to the 'commitment to the task' component of cohesiveness, and not the 'interpersonal attraction' or 'group pride' components of cohesiveness." Similarly, a 2006 study in *Armed Forces and Society*, written by the scholars Robert MacCoun, Elizabeth Kier, and Aaron Belkin, concluded that "all of the evidence indicates that military performance depends on whether service members are committed to the same professional goals, not on whether they like one another."

There is significant evidence that not only male bonding but any sort of closeness can actually hinder group performance. In a 1998 study on demographics and leadership, the group management experts Andrew Kakabadse and Nada Kakabadse found that "excessive cohesion may create a harmful insularity from external forces," and they linked high cohesion to "high conformity, high commitment to prior courses of actions, [and a] lack of openness." In her analysis of gender integration in the military, Erin Solaro, a researcher and journalist who was embedded with combat troops in Afghanistan and Iraq, pointed out that male bonding often depended on the exclusion or denigration of women and concluded that "cohesion is not the same as combat effectiveness, and indeed can undercut it. Supposedly 'cohesive' units can also kill their officers, mutiny, evade combat, and surrender as groups."

The mechanisms for achieving troop cohesion can also be problematic. In addition to denigrating women, illegal activities, including war crimes, have sometimes been used as a means for soldiers to "let off steam" and foster group unity. In sum, there is very little basis on which to link group cohesion to national security.

Strength in Diversity

Over the last century, the military has been strengthened when attitudes have been challenged and changed.

Despite claims in the 1940s that mixed-race units would be ineffective and that white and black service members would not be able to trust one another, for example, integration proceeded without any major hiccups. A 2011 study of the impacts of racial integration on combat effectiveness during the Korean War found that integration "resulted in improvements in cohesion, leadership and command, fighting spirit, personnel resources and sustainment that increased the combat effectiveness." Initial research indicates that mixed-gender units could provide similar benefits.

Leora Rosen, a former senior analyst at the National Institute of Justice, found that when women were accepted into mixed-gender units, the groups' effectiveness actually increased. Similarly, a 1993 RAND Corporation paper summarizing research on sexual orientation and the US military's personnel policy found that diversity "can enhance the quality of group problem-solving and decision-making, and it broadens the group's collective array of skills and knowledge." These conclusions are supported by a 1993 report by the General Accounting Office, which found that "members of gender-integrated units develop brother-sister bonds rather than sexual ones. . . . Experience has shown that actual integration diminishes prejudice and fosters group cohesiveness more effectively than any other factor." The same report also found that gender homogeneity was not perceived by soldiers to be a requirement for effective unit operations.

It should come as no surprise that elements of the military want uniformity in the ranks. The integration of new groups always ruffles feathers. But the US military has been ahead of the curve in terms of the inclusion of most minority groups. It was the first federal organization to integrate African Americans. And with the repeal of the "don't ask, don't tell" (DADT) policy, the military now has more progressive policies toward gay employees than many other US agencies. In fact, DADT was repealed despite the fact that there are no federal laws preventing employment discrimination on the basis of sexual orientation.

In September 2012, one year after the repeal of DADT, a study published by the Palm Center found that the change "has had no overall negative impact on military readiness or its component dimensions, including cohesion, recruitment, retention, assaults, harassment or morale." The research also found that overall, DADT's "repeal has enhanced the military's ability to pursue its mission." Previous claims about the negative impact that gay service members might have on troop cohesion mirror those currently used to support the female combat exclusion.

Unlike the military's treatment of other groups, its current policies toward women are much more conservative than those of other federal and state government bodies. Women who choose military service confront not only restricted career options but also a higher chance of harassment, discrimination, and sexual violence than in almost any other profession. The weak record on addressing these issues gives the impression that the military is an unwelcome place and an unsafe career choice for women. In an interview with National Public Radio in 2011, Sergeant Kayla Williams, who served in Iraq, explicitly linked the combat exclusion and harassment: "I believe that the combat exclusion actually exacerbates gender tensions and problems within the military because the fact that women can't be in combat arms jobs allows us to be portrayed as less than fully soldiers." Fully integrating women could therefore begin to address two major issues for the US military: enhancing diversity and equality and also weakening the masculine culture that may contribute to harassment.

Unsubstantiated claims about the distracting nature of women, the perils of feminine qualities, and the inherent manliness of war hardly provide a solid foundation on which to construct policy. Presumably, some levels of racism and homophobia also persist within the military, yet it would be absurd, not to mention unconstitutional, for the US government to officially sanction such prejudices. The US military should ensure that it is as effective as possible, but it must not bend to biases, bigotry, and false stereotypes.

Just as when African Americans were fully integrated into the military and DADT was repealed, lifting the combat ban on women would not threaten national security or the cohesiveness of military units; rather, it would bring formal policies in line with current practices and allow the armed forces to overcome their misogynistic past. In a modern military, women should have the right to fight.

The Fight against Racial Injustice in America and Its Necessary Connection to National Security

BISHOP GARRISON

The United States once again finds itself at a crossroads. Stricken by heartache and disbelief over the continued loss of innocent Black lives at the hands of authorities, citizens have marched through the streets; they have in one collective voice begun to demand action. Communities are desperate to see change reflected in a variety of aspects of their daily lives—the businesses we invest in, the conversations we have among friends and loved ones, even the entertainment we consume. In the months following the George Floyd tragedy, early efforts for change appear to be taking root in a variety of forms, allowing hope for a more diverse future blossom for many for the first time in years. It is a moment that has given rise to an opportunity to finally address the underlying issues of systemic racism and inequality in our society. Hope may shine bright, however, it is not without darkness.

The United States remains imperfect as it strives for the "shining city" standard. The militarization of policing remains an issue to be resolved; the country continues a scattered, uncoordinated, pandemic response hurtling toward 200,000 deaths; and socio-economic disparities and inequality are rampant in our society. These are not individual circumstances to be addressed through siloed policies, but instead a group of collective crises whose outcomes will create long-term damage to the United States' global persona. Each of these circumstances has fundamental connections not only to national security, but also to unequal outcomes for communities of color.

It has become increasingly difficult to understand how we can continue to debate global national security and foreign policy issues—from nuclear nonproliferation to great-power competition to interventionism in fragile states—when a significant segment of our population feels unsafe in their own neighborhoods, and, at times, even in their own homes. The latest instance of police violence in the shooting of Jacob Blake, mere months following the death of George Floyd, and the subsequent demonstrations that have resulted in death and destruction reignite this debate.

Nefarious actors have coopted peaceful protests in an attempt to breed chaos and elicit real terror in the community. They wish to have those who advocate for change seen simply as violent actors. At the same time, the social media giant Facebook has uncovered a renewed plot by international actors aimed at interference in yet another election cycle. Both actions have disproportionately targeted communities of color.[1]

These domestic issues are continuing to cause an upheaval that has already begun to affect how the United States engages in issues of diplomacy. For example, when the nation attempted to address the antidemocratic actions of the Chinese government with respect to ongoing demonstrations in Hong Kong, Hua Chunying, the spokeswoman of China's Foreign Ministry responded with the words, "I can't breathe," the final words of George Floyd prior to his death.[2] The domestic issue of racial injustice and its relation to security can no longer be ignored.

There continues to be a disconnect between the image that the United States strives to project to the world and the realities that are unfolding in cities across the country. In that stark contrast, we see how inequality undermines our diplomatic and security goals.

Racial inequality undercuts the nation's international status, actions, and aims in three interconnected ways. First, as we speak of diplomacy, a lack of equality within our own society diminishes our message. Advocating for the advancement of human rights while the world watches in horror at autocratic responses by authorities to protests against police brutality translates, at best, into a hypocritical hollow message. Second, the military will not be the effective fighting force that the United States requires if it fails to diversify the leadership in its armed forces and policy communities. Study after study indicates that a diverse work environment produces better outcomes and happier, more successful teams. If subordinates do not see proper representation in their officer corps, which is almost 80 percent White,[3] as well as the potential to move forward in their own careers, they will find other industries with a greater appreciation for their talent. Third, a defense policy is a reflection of its society. If that society remains fractured, then, overtime, its security will reflect those schisms. That is to say, if society speaks of security, defense, and diplomacy, whose interests are ultimately reflected in that question? If the United States remains hyper-partisan and divided, then who is security for? If Americans increasingly answer the question differently, then the military's ability to protect the homeland and project power abroad will certainly diminish.

Still, the national security apparatus cannot take a tactical pause. Its mission is vital to the ongoing safety of American citizens and interests. Thus, the introspection it will take to forge a path forward must occur in concert with the ongoing fulfillment of that mission. The community must constantly pursue its national security objectives while finding new avenues for critical engagement in topics not previously considered. How can this community identify strategic threats while at the same time giving due consideration to this emerging connection between domestic racial injustice and security interests? To properly address this long-overlooked issue, a paradigm shift is in order. Not only must the study, scholarship, and practice of racial in-

justice be fully respected and embraced by the national security and foreign policy communities, but also both the root causes of and potential methods to address systemic racism must be viewed as a pivotal policy practice area akin to defense, security cooperation, or any other functional area. Leaders must consider the intersection of racial injustice and national security as a key policy concern for US stability and the nation's global image moving forward.

There are three basic pillars that should be leveraged to help guide the development of policy goals and discussion concerning racial injustice and national security: empathy, representation, and unification.

Defining the Nexus: The Three Pillars

There are many ways to define, specifically, what principles make up a nation's security. Since its inception, the United States has lived by basic freedoms and principles that continue to shape its society today; the vast majority of these are enshrined in the text of the Constitution, its amendments, and legal interpretations throughout history. The priorities of the national security apparatus, however, are controlled by the executive. While the aforementioned freedoms may produce legal parameters and bedrock traditions, it is the *National Security Strategy* that provides the framework for how the whole of the national security community engages the many threats facing the nation.[4] Its priorities shift from administration to administration, but broadly speaking, these documents, in their various iterations, focus on what that executive believes will be necessary to protect the United States and its interests.

Empathy is a necessary pillar of any security strategy. How can a military force smartly and safely work with locals in a combat zone to conduct operations and maintain order without understanding what the population has experienced? How can a diplomatic corps engage in meaningful dialogue and negotiations without understanding their counterpart's interests and role in the global community? And how can allied nations maintain confidence in their relationships if a distress call is answered only when it is beneficial for the strategic partner to do so? It is through a lens of empathy, or an ability to understand, translate, and share the feelings of others, that our discussions of domestic and international security should be shaped and defined. According to Joshua Baker, lecturer in History, Politics, and International Relations at the University of Leicester,

The nexus between empathy and the security dilemma is a productive site for scholarship on emotions and IR [international relations] as empathy has occupied an implicit yet important place in security dilemma thinking for decades. John Herz, who first coined the term "security dilemma" (1950), was the first to theorize that if leaders could attempt to understand their adversaries by putting "oneself in the other fellow's place," and consider that they too may be motivated by fear as opposed to aggression, then this may hold the key to the de-escalation of conflicts.[5]

If empathy is an ability to understand another's position, then it would follow that a diversity of backgrounds, experiences, and thought within an organization can be key, if not critical, to mission success. As stated in a 2020 *Harvard Business Review* article, "Diversity, equity, and inclusion attempt to level the playing field to allow the best ideas to flourish, connect talented individuals from underrepresented backgrounds with opportunities that those in the majority often have unfair access to, and empower the best organizations to thrive."[6] To ensure proper diversity throughout an organizational structure, leaders must engage in thoughtful representation for as many constituencies as possible.

Next, an effective US foreign policy requires that those diverse and marginalized voices see their own life experiences reflected in their leadership. Representation ensures that those diverse and otherwise marginalized voices are properly heard and included in organizational activity. Moreover, these voices provide a depth of understanding of substantive content that is shaped by their own personal perspective. This principle again emphasizes the importance of empathy within any system. If there is no clear desire to understand their needs, marginalized communities are often overlooked and their voices go unheard, exacerbating the societal conflicts the nation continues to experience. It is the desire to understand that will allow the space necessary for proper representation. And proper representation creates the teams that develop thoughtful policies and dialogue designed to reduce domestic stresses and addressing racial injustice.

The importance of representation at all levels throughout an organization cannot be understated. It is important for subordinates to see organizational diversity reflected in both frontline and senior leadership. A more diverse workforce helps to create a healthier work environment that will lead to more quality solutions for complex issues. Further, if the nation maintains the will to engage with issues of racial injustice, it will require the acumen and experience of a diverse group of experts to develop solutions to the issues. Recently, the new chief of staff of the Air Force, General Charles Brown, spoke about a discussion with his son and wife that moved him to speak out on the racism and lack of diversity he has experienced in his own career.[7] As a former commander of the Pacific Air Forces, General Brown explained that he was not sure

how to respond to the death of Michael Brown in Ferguson, Missouri, in 2014.[8] Pressed by his son, General Brown found the words to engage an issue that few, if any, senior military leaders had ever dared to broach publicly. General Brown ultimately decided to release a video shortly before his confirmation as chief of staff in which he discusses the "immense expectations" to respond, given both his new position and current public discourse.[9]

As events unfolded, other services saw the necessity of speaking up about racial injustice and the moment in which the nation found itself. Chief Master Sergeant of the Air Force Kaleth Wright spoke candidly about his experiences of often being the only person of color in the room.[10] As Chief Master Sergeant Wright recalled in an interview on preparing for his remarks in the wake of the tragedy of George Floyd's death, he said to himself, "Who am I? . . . I am George Floyd. . . . It got to a point where I just felt like, man, enough is enough."[11] Even as the Donald Trump Administration denied the existence of systemic racism in the country, military leaders continued to strike a much different tone. After initially calling protests of racial injustice a "battlespace," Secretary of Defense Mark Esper revised his views and his language when briefing the Pentagon press corps: "Racism is real, in America, and we must do our very best to recognize it, to confront it, and to eradicate it."[12] In addition, then Chief of Staff of the Air Force David Goldfein joined Chief Master Sergeant Wright in a video to speak of his outrage over the issue, while Chief of Staff of the Army James McConville, Sergeant Major of the Army Michael Grinston, US Space Force Commander General John Raymond, Chief Master Sergeant of the US Space Force Roger Towberman, and Chief of Naval Operations Admiral Mike Gilday all released their own statements and videos expressing their outrage over and disgust with racism and George Floyd's death.[13] The collective uniformed leadership of the military views the challenge not only as a serious issue, but as a threat to the comradery and collaborative team environment military leaders are constantly seeking to cultivate.

In their opinion piece, former Under Secretary for Policy at the Department of Defense Michèle Flournoy and former Senior Policy Advisor at the Department of Homeland Security Camille Stewart surmise that the need for the nation's most diverse workforce lies heavily in the national security community. As they state, "Nowhere will a qualified team of advisers with a diversity of lived experience and expertise be more important at every level than in the national security realm."[14] This premise is in line with the aforementioned discussion of why diversity is of such great importance in the national security sector both generally and given the moment the United States currently faces.

Finally, it is unification—the process of being made whole—that will help the nation address these historic divides. The national security community can help lead the way in achieving solidarity, safety, and providing a new paradigm for diversity, inclusion, and equity by looking to a historically diverse team of thoughtful experts who can recommend policies aimed at maintaining order, protecting rights, and creating opportunities for growth for all. Providing scholarships and educational programs for the study of national security and foreign policy in socioeconomically depressed areas, supporting grassroots and local elected leaders in the development of new policing strategies, and creating programs geared toward fighting radicalization through community engagement are just a few examples of how government at every level can help create solutions geared towards the eradication of the intolerance and injustice.

Recommendations

While the national security and foreign policy community has identified the need for greater diversity, they can also lead this pivotal societal conversation through action and dialogue. Committing to a more diverse workforce is a good step toward addressing the persistent problems that have plagued the nation in whole, but developing policies at the nexus of domestic and national security interests will be key to creating permanent relief. The first step should be a complete review of the militarization of policy and policing. The federal government must work with state and local officials to determine both how to best review current systems and procedures and how to plot a course going forward that keeps communities and law enforcement officials safe, thereby rebuilding trust and relationships between the police and the communities they serve. Any programs or initiatives to reallocate funding should be crafted thoughtfully, with both elected and community leadership and law enforcement working alongside each other, so as to address root causes of criminal activity and not superficial or stereotypical concerns of what criminal nature might be.

Second, a larger effort to reestablish the definition of American values both home and abroad must take place. In recent years, the United States has withdrawn from several traditional seats of strategic and policy leadership from a variety of security concerns, while simultaneously redefining long-held relationships with several of its allies. These actions have taken place while civil unrest over the loss of innocent Black life continues to send shockwaves through public discourse, and this reality not only hampers the nation's ability to engage in thoughtful diplomacy, but also decreases its moral authority when dealing with bad actors who place the human rights and lives of those who

are governed below the interests of the government itself. To say the least, it is difficult to hold a nation accountable for infringing on its citizens' right to protest when global news is littered with footage of US federal authorities clashing with protesters night after night or a law enforcement official kneeling on a suspect's neck. If the United States is to regain international prominence and our traditional seat at the table, the United States must unequivocally declare once again its values to the world and demonstrate them through active participation in the global community. Isolationism will do nothing but ensure that the United States stands cold and alone in a chaotic time.

Finally, the nation must find a way to reduce the hyper-partisanship that has engulfed the country for more than a decade. Although citizens view a variety of issues, ranging from immigration policy to climate change, nuclear modernization, and a host of other concerns, along partisan lines and there may have been different opinions about how these issues should be addressed, there was little disagreement that national security and foreign policy were issues that remained above the political fray. Even today, the only bill that is regularly introduced, debated, amended, and passed is the National Defense Authorization Act. It has often been said that "politics end at the water's edge," meaning our diplomatic relations are focused on what is in the best interest for the American people and not a segment of it. There has to be an effort to overcome our political differences and find common ground in issues not only of international security concern, but also domestic issues as well, that help to ensure our infrastructure is sound and address underlying issues of inequality that can create the aforementioned domestic challenges in the first place. Provisions for free or subsidized childcare, education, and healthcare, for instance, could go a long way toward helping to remove some of the long-standing barriers to opportunity for communities of color and socioeconomically stressed populations. There are no "silver bullets" or sure-fire solutions to these challenges. However, it is clear that the national security apparatus, including the military, will continue to miss out on recruiting diverse talent if many of these domestic issues are not addressed. Instead, the likelihood of tensions causing unrest will persist and cause greater problems in the near future.

Conclusion

Ultimately, the promise of the United States is directly connected to the country's image on the international stage and its ability to engage in thoughtful diplomatic action as well as project power. For far too long the trials and tribulations facing Black, Indigenous, and People of Color have been treated as lesser issues of political interest by many in the national security community. American society must realize that the protests we are witnessing are not a temporal inflection point but a product of a modern culture that has collectively ignored systemic racial injustice. This injustice must be addressed at every level of government, and, in the process, it must be recognized that taking action accordingly—or not doing so—will have an impact on our national security. When the national security community fails to address not only its own shortcomings and broader domestic concerns, but also both in relation to each other, it does so at the risk of the long-term safety and stability of our country and its standing in the global community. A nation cannot maintain itself or achieve its true potential without collaborative efforts and tangible connection between domestic concerns and international interests. Unfortunately, now after years of failing to address these domestic concerns, we see the consequences in our fractured political discourse and civil upheaval.

NOTES

1. Donie O'Sullivan, "After FBI Tip, Facebook Says It Uncovered Russian Meddling," CNN Business, September 1, 2020, https://www.cnn.com/2020/09/01/tech/russian-troll-group-facebook-campaign/index.html.

2. Adela Suliman, Ed Flanagan, and Justin Solomon, "China Jeers as George Floyd Protests Sweep U.S," NBC News, June 1, 2020, https://www.nbcnews.com/news/world/china-jeers-george-floyd-protests-sweep-u-s-while-some-n1220186.

3. Council on Foreign Relations, "Demographics of the U.S. Military," July 13, 2020, https://www.cfr.org/backgrounder/demographics-us-military.

4. Historical Office, Office of the Secretary of Defense, National Security Strategy, n.d., as of September 12, 2020, https://history.defense.gov/Historical-Sources/National-Security-Strategy/.

5. Joshua Baker, "The Empathic Foundations of Security Dilemma De-Escalation," *Political Psychology* 40, no. 6 (2019): 1251–66.

6. Ruchika Tulshyan, "Do Your Employees Know Why You Believe in Diversity?" *Harvard Business Review* (online), June 30, 2020, https://hbr.org/2020/06/do-your-employees-know-why-you-believe-in-diversity.

7. Dan Lamothe, "The New Air Force Chief Wasn't Sure How to Address George Floyd's Killing. Then He Talked to His Son," *Washington Post*, August 19, 2020, https://www.washingtonpost.com/national-security/the-new-air-force-chief-wasnt-sure-how-to-address-george-floyds-killing-then-he-talked-to-his-son/2020/08/19/f7c63e24-de3c-11ea-b4af-72895e22941d_story.html.

8. Lamothe, "The New Air Force Chief Wasn't Sure How to Address George Floyd's Killing."

9. Lamothe, "The New Air Force Chief Wasn't Sure How to Address George Floyd's Killing."

10. The full text of Chief Master Sergeant Wright's remarks can be found following this article.

11. Stephen Losey, "Retiring CMSAF Wright Talks Candidly about the Future of the Air Force, His George Floyd Post and the 'Enlisted Jesus' Memes," *Air Force Times*, August 10, 2020, https://www.airforcetimes.com/news/your-air-force/2020/08/10/retiring-cmsaf-wright-talks-candidly-about-the-future-of-the-air-force-his-george-floyd-post-and-the-enlisted-jesus-memes/.

12. Marcus Weisgerber, Kevin Baron, and Bradley Peniston, "Service Chiefs Acknowledge Racism in the Ranks, Pledge Dialogue, Change," *Defense One News*, June 3, 2020, https://www.defenseone.com/threats/2020/06/military-brass-acknowledge-racism-ranks-pledge-dialogue-change/165896/.

13. Weisgerber, Baron, and Peniston, "Service Chiefs Acknowledge Racism in the Ranks."

14. Michèle A. Flournoy and Camille Stewart, "Opinion: Where We Need the Most Diverse Team of Advisors for US Safety," CNN, September 3, 2020, https://www.cnn.com/2020/09/02/opinions/diversity-in-national-security-us-flournoy-stewart/index.html.

Diversity, Equity, and Justice in American Defense Policy

EDITORS OF *AMERICAN DEFENSE POLICY* (9TH ED.)

During the production of this volume, our country was shocked by the circumstances surrounding the deaths of Breonna Taylor, George Floyd, Jacob Blake, and so many other African Americans. As protests against police violence filled the streets of many major cities across the United States, and the predictable backlash ensued, it felt like the country was experiencing a pivotal moment. However, what was the connection, if any, to American defense policy?

The events on June 1, 2020, at Lafayette Square helped illuminate the first answer. Insofar as the military is an imperfect reflection of American society, it cannot extricate itself from the debates surrounding race, equality, and justice; rather, it is inextricably—perhaps to its leadership's chagrin—intertwined in the collective search for answers.

After days of protests, the White House activated the National Guard, which was called in to clear the federal property. Shortly thereafter, President Donald Trump and an entourage of his staff walked across the square to Saint John's Church for a photo opportunity. Included in this group was Chairman of the Joint Chiefs of Staff General Mark Milley. His participation sparked debate on the status of civil-military relations during a contentious time in American politics. In his commencement speech to the National Defense University one week later, General Milley stated that his participation was a mistake and commented on the status of race relations and political cleavages within the nation:

The United States military faces many challenges. Abroad, China and Russia are increasing their military capabilities and taking assertive actions to exert global influence and challenge the existing international order. North Korea threatens our regional Allies and potentially our homeland with the development of nuclear and ballistic missile capabilities. Iran is the world's largest state sponsor of terrorism, and they have taken advantage of instability to expand their malign influence and challenge the interests of the United States and our Allies and partners in the Middle East. And violent extremism remains a generational, trans-regional struggle requiring sustained political, fiscal, and military solutions.

The international order born from the ashes of the Second World War is under assault. The world has enjoyed unprecedented economic development and relative peace and stability since more than 150 million people were killed in the conduct of Great Power War in the 31 years between 1914 and 1945. Twice before in history that I'm aware of—from 1648 to 1750 and 1815 to 1914—there was an international order established on the continent of Europe. Both lasted about 100 years. We are now in the 75th year of the current order and it is under stress. We are in the return of great power competition and we need to remain in competition and prevent the return of great power war.

Our contribution as a military to that end state is a highly capable, agile, and ready Joint Force. We have taken significant steps to increase investment in current readiness in order to deter and defend against today's threats, while modernizing our force through innovative concept development, advanced technology, and new capabilities for the security challenges of tomorrow. We are, indeed, leading the Joint Force in dynamic and uncertain times. The recent medical crisis has cost over 100,000 American lives, and it has stressed our health system, our economy, and the social fabric of our communities. All of these challenges and many more will exist in the national security framework under which you, each of you, will operate as senior officers.

But we have also seen over the last two and a half weeks an especially intense and trying time for America. I am outraged by the senseless and brutal killing of George Floyd. His death amplified the pain, the frustration, and the fear that so many of our fellow Americans live with day in, day out. The protests that have ensued not only speak to his killing, but also to the centuries of injustice toward African Americans. What we are seeing is the long shadow of our original sin in Jamestown 401 years ago, liberated by the Civil War, but not equal in the eyes of the law until 100 years later in 1965. We are still struggling with racism, and we have much work to do. Racism and discrimination, structural preferences, patterns of mistreatment, and unspoken and unconscious bias have no place in America and they have no place in our Armed Forces.

We must, we can, and we will do better.

And we should all be proud that the vast majority of protests have been peaceful. Peaceful protest means that American freedom is working. And I'm also proud of the response of our National Guard forces, who provided excellent support to local and state law enforcement under the control of state governors in more than 30 states across the country. We never introduced federal troops on the streets of America as a result of the combined efforts of the Guard and law enforcement at quelling the violence and de-escalating very, very tense situations. We all know that our system in the United States is imperfect, full of passionate debate, and continually evolving, and we in the military will continue to protect the rights and freedoms of all the American people.

The foundational value that underpins American rights embedded in the Constitution is that all people, no matter who you are, are born free and equal, and I want to address this value in the context of our military.

Our military has a mixed record on equality. We fought World War II with a racially-segregated military. The Tuskegee Airmen are just one example of courageous men who fought for freedoms they themselves did not enjoy at home. Racial segregation of the armed forces ended in 1948, and today the military has come to reflect the diversity of our nation—the strength of our nation.

In recent decades, millions of Soldiers, Sailors, Airmen, Marines, and Coast Guardsmen have been part of cohesive teams consisting of people of different races, genders, religions, and orientations working to accomplish their mission in peace and war, all over the globe. Our troops demonstrate every day their ability to thrive as a result of their diversity. The diversity of America is one of the core strengths of our nation, and therefore, it is a core strength of our military.

And while the military sets an example for civil society through our inclusiveness, we too have not come far enough. We all need to do better. For example, although the United States military has a higher proportion of African Americans serving in our ranks than in society at large, only 7% of our flag and general officers are African American. The Navy and Marine Corps have no African Americans serving above the 2-star level, and the Army has just one African American 4-star.

The United States Air Force will soon swear in our first African American Service chief—an achievement long overdue. We cannot afford to marginalize large portions of our potential talent pool or alienate certain demographic groups. No—we need all the talent that American society can muster. Our responsibility as military leaders is to ensure that each and every one of our service members is treated fairly, with dignity and respect, and each of them is given equal opportunity to excel.

So what can we do? We will collectively take a hard look at how we recruit, retain, and promote talent within our Services. We must ensure that diverse candidates have equal opportunity to branch into the career fields and serve in key positions most likely to produce our future senior leaders. And we must ensure fairness and equity at all key gateway selection boards, including promotion, command, and war college. We must take advantage of the diversity committees, councils, and offices in each of the Services to identify best practices in talent management and act on them.

Mentorship also plays a vital role. All of us in the military must engage in more meaningful mentoring today. So, how do you do that? As senior leaders we reach down into the pool of rising stars among our troops from all walks of life and put into action what you've learned in your career. None of us got to where we are by ourselves. We all have had a helping hand. Take an active interest in providing the next generation of leaders the tools they need to succeed. And be inclusive. Make a commitment to seek out and surround yourselves with those who don't look like you, think like you, and who come from different backgrounds.

Specifically, reach out to junior officers and enlisted members whose background is different than yours and mentor them. It may be uncomfortable at first, but you will help them grow into future leaders, and they will help you grow to be a better leader yourself. Equality and opportunity [are] a matter of readiness. [They are] the basis of cohesion. We fight wars as teams and we cannot tolerate anything that divides us.

Let me conclude with two simple pieces of advice, based on 40 years in uniform, that you may find useful as many of you will surely go on to be flag officers. First is always maintain a keen sense of situational awareness. As senior leaders, everything you do will be closely watched. And I am not immune.

As many of you saw, the result of the photograph of me at Lafayette Square last week sparked a national debate about the role of the military in civil society. I should not have been there. My presence in that moment and in that environment created a perception of the military involved in domestic politics. As a commissioned uniformed officer, it was a mistake that I have learned from, and I sincerely hope we all can learn from it. We who wear the cloth of our nation come from the people of our nation, and we must hold dear the principle of an apolitical military that is so deeply rooted in the very essence of our republic. And this is not easy. It takes time, and work, and effort, but it may be the most important thing each and every one of us does every single day.

And, my second piece of advice is very simple: embrace the Constitution; keep it close to your heart. It is our North Star; it is our map to a better future. Though we are not a perfect union, believe in the United States, believe in our country, believe in your troops, and believe in our purpose. Few other nations have been able to change for the greater good, and that is because of the rights and values embedded in our Constitution. The freedoms guaranteed to us in the Constitution allow people to demand change, just as the peaceful protestors are doing all across the country. That is why we serve in the military.

On day one, you and I, we all swore an oath to support and defend the Constitution, and its essential American principle: that all men and women are born free and equal. That is the foundation of our military ethos—who we are as service members and as an institution. All of us in uniform are willing to die for the idea, the idea that is America. And so we must also be willing to live for that idea. Freedom of speech, freedom of the press, freedom to peacefully assemble, freedom to vote, and freedom to believe as you wish and your religion: These are essential freedoms that are the cornerstone of our country. Americans have spilled their blood to protect them in the past and they continue to be worth fighting for.

This we will defend.[1]

General Milley's statement that "equality and opportunity [are] a matter of readiness" struck a chord with us. As professors Orlando Richard and Carliss Miller argue, "Diversity is associated with better creative problem solving, innovation, and improved decision making."[2] Similarly, a Congressional Research Service report argues that "a more diverse force has the potential to be more efficient and flexible, able to meet a broader set of challenges."[3] US Army strategist Colonel Joe Funderburke would agree, arguing that "diversity creates a synergy of different perspectives. This is particularly useful when trying to find solutions to perplexing and wicked problems such as the ones the national-security profession encounters daily."[4] More generally, the Congressional Research Service report indicates that a "broadly representative military force is more likely to uphold national values and to be loyal to the government—and country—that raised it."[5]

Questions of diversity, equity, and justice in the US military are as foundational to the country's defense as any weapon system or debate over grand strategy. The United States will be able to defend successfully its role in the world and the values for which it abides only if the armed forces take stock of where it has led and failed to lead on these first-order principles. This analysis, however, has been found lacking in certain areas. A recent report by the Government Accountability Office (GAO) on racial disparity in military justice finds that "the Department of Defense (DOD) has taken *some* steps to study disparities but has not comprehensively evaluated the causes of racial disparities in the military justice system," despite Black servicemembers being twice as likely to be tried in courts-martial than their White counterparts.[6] Such disparities accumulate, and when paired with high-visibility events such as the death of George Floyd, they result in public outcries by our nation's highest military leaders.

In response, we turn to a social media post, written by only the second African American to hold the position of Chief Master Sergeant of the Air Force, Kaleth Wright:

Like me, acknowledge your right to be upset about what's happening to our nation. But you must then find a way to move beyond the rage and do what you think is right for the country, for your community, for your sons, daughters, friends and colleagues . . . for every Black man in this country who could end up like George Floyd. Part of my group's solution involves helping to bridge the communication and understanding gap between law enforcement and young Black men. You decide what works best for you, where you can have the most meaningful impact and most importantly, what you can stay committed to. . . . We didn't get here overnight so don't expect things to change tomorrow. . . . We are in this for the long haul. Vote, protest peacefully, reach out to your local and state officials, to your Air Force leadership and become active in your communities. . . . We need all hands on deck.

If you don't do anything else, I encourage everyone to fight, not just for freedom, justice and equality but to fight for understanding. You might think you know what it's like to grow up, exist, survive and even thrive in this country as a Black person . . . but let me tell you, regardless of how many Black friends you have, or how Black your neighborhood was, or if your spouse or in-laws are Black . . . you don't know.

You don't know the anxiety, the despair, the heartache, the fear, the rage and the disappointment that comes with living in this country, OUR country every single day. So, take the time to talk to someone—your brand new Airmen, your [Non-Commissioned Officer in Charge] or your Flight Commander—about their experiences so that you have a better understanding of who they are, where they come from and what drives them. Frankly, you owe this to every Airmen, but I'm asking you specifically to pay attention to the Black Airmen in your ranks during this trying time. Don't misunderstand me, they don't need, nor do they want any special treatment . . . but they deserve to be treated fairly and equally, both by our United States Air Force and these United States of America. . . . This begins with you, and I am asking, no fighting, for your understanding.

Like you, I don't have all of the answers, but I am committed to seeing a better future for this nation. A future where Black men must no longer suffer needlessly at the hands of White police officers, and where Black Airmen have the same chance to succeed as their White counterparts. Trust me, I understand this is a difficult topic to talk about . . .

Difficult . . . not impossible.

Difficult . . . but necessary.

Who am I . . .

I am Kaleth. I am a Black Man who happens to be the Chief Master Sergeant of the Air Force and I am committed to making this better.[7]

NOTES

1. Mark Milley, "National Defense University 2020 Class Graduation Address," *American Rhetoric*, June 11, 2020, https://www.americanrhetoric.com/speeches/markmilleynationaldefenseuniversitygraduationremarks.htm.
2. Orlando C. Richard and Carliss D. Miller, "Considering Diversity as a Source of Competitive Advantage in Organizations," in *The Oxford Handbook of Diversity and Work*,

ed. Quinetta M. Roberson (New York: Oxford University Press, 2012), p. 240.
3. K. N. Kamarck, *Diversity, Inclusion, and Equal Opportunity in the Armed Services: Background and Issues for Congress*, CRS Report R44321 (Washington, DC: Congressional Research Service, 2017), 4.
4. Joe Funderburke, "Diversity: Our National-Security Advantage," *Foreign Policy*, September 25, 2014, https://foreignpolicy.com/2014/09/25/diversity-our-national-security-advantage/.
5. Kamarck, *Diversity, Inclusion, and Equal Opportunity in the Armed Services*.
6. US Government Accountability Office, "DOD and the Coast Guard Need to Improve Their Capabilities to Assess Racial Disparities," Publication No. GAO-20-648T (Washington, DC: GAO, June 2020), https://www.gao.gov/assets/710/707582.pdf; emphasis added.
7. Kaleth Wright, open letter, June 1, 2020, *Facebook*, https://www.facebook.com/CMSAFOfficial/posts/1372637459591835.

Military Contractors and the American Way of War

DEBORAH D. AVANT AND RENÉE DE NEVERS

More than one-half of the personnel the United States has deployed in Iraq and Afghanistan since 2003 have been contractors. Part of the global private military and security industry, contractors are deeply intertwined with the American military and US foreign policy.[1] Whatever one chooses to call them—mercenaries, contractors, or private military and security companies (PMSCs)—they have a different relationship to the US government, the American public, and domestic and international law than do military personnel. These differences pose both benefits and risks to the effectiveness, accountability, and values represented in American actions abroad.

In the best case, American use of PMSCs can provide or enhance forces for global governance. PMSCs can recruit from around the world to quickly mobilize expertise as needed. If their employees are instilled with professional values and skills and engaged in a way that is responsive to the demands of the US public, the international community, and local concerns, these forces could contribute to managing a global demand for security that US forces alone cannot meet. In the worst case, PMSCs can provide a means for pursuing agendas that do not have the support of American, international, or local publics. They may

siphon off US dollars for practices that are wasteful, are antithetical to US interests, or undermine global stability. Thus far, the use of PMSCs has produced mixed results: it has increased effectiveness somewhat, but often at the expense of accountability and with dubious attention to the values the United States and the international community hold dear. Moving forward in a way that maximizes the benefits of contractors and minimizes their risks will require careful management of the uncomfortable trade-offs these forces pose.

The degree to which the United States relies on private security vendors has become clear during the hostilities in Iraq and Afghanistan, as contractors have provided logistical support for US and coalition troops. Less well known is that as US forces were stretched thin by the lawlessness resulting from the fall of Saddam Hussein in 2003, the first "surge" involved private personnel mobilized to protect expatriates working in the country and train the Iraqi police force and army; and a private Iraqi force was hired to guard government facilities and oil fields.[2] Retired military or police from all over the world, employed by a wide array of PMSCs, worked for the US government (and others) throughout the country.

Deborah D. Avant and Renée de Nevers, "Military Contractors and the American Way of War," *Daedalus* 140, no. 3 (Summer 2011): 88–99. © 2011 by the American Academy of Arts and Sciences. (daed_a_00100)

Although precise figures are difficult to determine, by 2008, the number of personnel in Iraq under contract with the US government roughly equaled or was greater than the number of US troops on the ground.[3] In September 2009, two months prior to the Barack Obama administration's announcement of the troop surge in Afghanistan, contractors made up an estimated 62 percent of the US presence in that country.[4] The use of contractors in these conflicts represents a dramatic expansion in the US military's reliance on PMSCs. During the 1991 Gulf conflict, the ratio of troops to contractors was roughly ten to one; in 2007, the ratio of troops to contractors in Iraq was roughly one to one.[5] In Afghanistan in 2010, there were roughly 1.43 contractors for every American soldier.[6] The Commission on Wartime Contracting (CWC), established by Congress in 2008, estimates conservatively that at least $177 billion has been obligated in contracts and grants to support US operations in Afghanistan and Iraq since 2001.[7]

PMSCs offer a wide range of services, including tasks associated with military operations, policing, and the gray area between the two that is an increasingly large part of twenty-first century conflict. Common services include support for weapon systems and equipment, military advice and training, logistical support, site security (armed and unarmed), crime prevention, police training, and intelligence.[8] While some firms specialize in a specific area, others provide an array of services, and a few offer the entire range. The CWC divides the services provided by contractors into three categories: logistics, security, and reconstruction.[9]

Logistics services include the supply of food, laundry, fuel, and base facility construction. Kellogg Brown and Root (KBR) held the US Army's logistics civil augmentation contract (LOGCAP) in the early years of the Iraq and Afghanistan conflicts. In June 2007, the new contract (LOGCAP IV) was awarded to three companies: DynCorp International LLC, Fluor Intercontinental, Inc., and KBR. In Iraq alone, the LOGCAP contract paid out $22 billion between 2003 and 2007.[10]

Security services include guarding people, buildings, and convoys. Many security contractors are armed; in carrying out their duties, they routinely shoot and are shot at.[11] The Congressional Budget Office estimated that in 2008, 30,000 to 35,000 of the contractors working in Iraq were armed; in early 2010, private security contractors numbered roughly 11,000.[12] Blackwater (now Xe) employees, recruited to support both the military and the US State Department, have received the most notoriety for their security work in Iraq and, more recently, in Afghanistan. Working under the State Department's Worldwide Personal Protective Services (WPPS) contract in Iraq, Blackwater personnel carried weapons, had their own helicopters, and defended against insurgents in ways hard to distinguish from military actions.[13] They were later joined by newer companies such as Triple Canopy, Crescent Security Group, and Custer Battles.[14]

Reconstruction services incorporate everything from building physical infrastructure (for roads, communication, water, and power) to strengthening institutions (for example, by training government employees, including military, police, and justice personnel at the national, provincial, and local levels; supporting civil society groups; and promoting rule of law and democratization). A wide range of PMSCs, along with other contractors, have delivered these services. DynCorp, an old company with roots in technical support and an increasing presence in policing and police training, has trained Iraqi police, constructed police and prison facilities, and built capacity for a justice system.[15] Three companies that provided training for the new Iraqi Army early in the conflict are Vinnell Corporation, a company with a long history of providing military training in Saudi Arabia; MPRI, a firm that gained prominence by training Croatian and then Bosnian troops in the 1990s; and USIS, which was established as the result of an Office of Management Personnel privatization effort in 1994.[16] Parsons Corporation, another older firm with a long record in the building of infrastructure, has worked on many large infrastructure projects. Myriad others have delivered various capacity-building services.[17]

Though their use in Iraq and Afghanistan dominates the discussion of contractors in the US context, PMSCs are important players in all aspects of the US military and US foreign policy.[18] Contractors working for the Departments of Defense (DoD) and State contribute significantly to US foreign policy projects aimed at enhancing development and security in a number of states; they also support US troops and diplomats. Their tasks cover all three categories noted above. Consider, for instance, the contractor support for US foreign assistance policies in Africa and Latin America.

In Africa, the United States has relied on the private sector to support missions such as military training and peacekeeping operations. These programs fall within AFRICOM, the US military command for Africa established in 2007, and the State Department's Africa Peacekeeping program (AFRICAP), which is similar in structure to the army's LOGCAP contract. In 2008, AFRICAP's stated objectives were to enhance regional peace and stability in Africa through training programs in peacekeeping and conflict management and prevention for African armed forces, as well as through logistics and construction activities in support of peacekeeping and training missions.[19] AFRICOM's stated purposes are "to build strong military-to-military partnerships," to help African countries better address the threats they face by improving African military capacity, and to bolster peace and security there.[20] Since its inception, AFRICOM has awarded contracts for training, air transport, information technology, and public diplomacy to companies such as DynCorp, which is training Liberia's armed forces, and PAE, a company specializing in infrastructure, mission support, and disaster relief.[21]

US foreign policy in Latin America, dominated since at least 2000 by antinarcotics and counterterrorism efforts, also relies heavily on contractors.[22] Plan Colombia, the central element of a counterdrug initiative focused on the Andean region, has sought to reduce drug production in Colombia and strengthen Colombian security forces to better secure the state against threats posed by terrorists, drug traffickers, and paramilitary groups. The program has failed to slow drug production there, but military and police training conducted by both US troops and civilian contractors has led to security improvements.[23] Roughly half of the military aid to Colombia is spent on private contractors funded by the DoD and the State Department. Like Plan Colombia, the 2007 Mérida Initiative, a US-Mexico assistance agreement, seeks to disrupt drug-trafficking activities by providing equipment and training to Mexican security forces.[24]

PMSCs are incorporated in many countries and employ a mix of US citizens, local citizens, and "third country nationals" (recruits from neither the United States nor the host state). That combination changes over time and from contingency to contingency. For example, an April 30, 2008, census by the US Army Central Command found that the 190,200 contractors in Iraq included about 20 percent (38,700) US citizens, 37 percent (70,500) Iraqis, and 43 percent (81,006) third country nationals.[25] In March 2010, the total number of contractors had dropped to 95,461, 26 percent of which were US citizens, 56 percent third country nationals, and 18 percent Iraqis.[26] The number of locals working as private security contractors (as opposed to logistics or reconstruction contractors) in Iraq has been relatively low: about 10 percent of private security contractors in 2010 were Iraqi. In Afghanistan, the DoD has relied more heavily on locals. The total number of contractors in March 2010 was 112,092, 14 percent of which were US citizens, 16 percent third country nationals, and 70 percent Afghans. Also, the numbers of locals who work in private security are higher than those who provide other services. About 93 percent of the private security contractors in 2010 were Afghans.[27]

When the United States hires PMSCs to train militaries abroad, the contractor may take a small team of US personnel (as MPRI did in Croatia), or it may recruit an international team (as DynCorp did in Liberia). Companies providing logistics support abroad often rely on locals or third country nationals to cut costs. Hiring locals or third country nationals can also avoid a variety of political restrictions and diminish visibility when the United States is undertaking more controversial missions. For instance, Congress restricted the number of American contractors the United States could use under Plan Colombia to three hundred (raised to four hundred in 2001); PMSCs bypassed this restriction by hiring personnel from Peru, Guatemala, and other Latin American countries.[28]

In addition to nationality, personnel hired by PMSCs vary in their employment backgrounds. PMSCs that offer military training primarily hire former military officers. Those that offer armed security services hire a broader range of military veterans. Those that offer police training often hire former police officers. As the number of companies and the range of services they offer have expanded to meet market demand, companies have hired employees with more diverse experience.

Contracting for military and security services has raised questions about the effectiveness of using force, political accountability for the use of force, and the social values to which force adheres. Some concerns vary according to which service is provided, while others apply more generally across different tasks.

Military *effectiveness* rests on a range of components, including skill of personnel, quality of materiel, and military responsiveness to contextual or external constraints. A critical component noted in recent research is integration: that is, the degree to which military plans follow from overarching state goals and to which activities are internally consistent and mutually reinforcing.[29]

Contracting can influence both the military's effectiveness and its broader mission. For example, when US goals change, as they did after the Cold War's end, contracting enhances the military's ability to integrate forces with (new) political goals. Speed and flexibility are the hallmark benefits of contracting, and contractors can quickly provide tools or skills for new missions that regular military forces may lack—or cannot identify rapidly within their ranks. Using a contract with MPRI, for instance, the Africa Crisis Response Initiative (ACRI) military training courses for French-speaking African countries were staffed with employees who spoke French. The US military was also able to mobilize civilian police forces, first for Haiti in 1994, and then for contingencies in the Balkans, via contracts with DynCorp.

Different concerns regarding effectiveness emerge with contracting for logistics, security, and reconstruction services. Logistics services are fundamental to the military's ability to operate. Without personnel to provide logistics services, the US military simply cannot go to war. Contracting for logistics also requires strong oversight. Early in the Iraq conflict, serious concerns were raised about adequate staffing for logistics contracts. General Charles S. Mahan, Jr., then the Army's top logistics officer, complained of troops receiving inadequate support because of problems deploying contractors.[30] After the Coalition Provisional Authority appointed him the new Head of Contracting Authority in February 2004, Brigadier General Stephen Seay hired more acquisition staff, enabling overburdened contracting officers to do their jobs more effectively.[31] More recently, military personnel have expressed general satisfaction with the quality of logistics services.[32] Many worries over logistics contracting in Iraq and Afghanistan have focused on lack of oversight (particularly inadequate numbers of contract officers), along with waste and fraud.[33] But logistics contracts require fewer skills specific to military personnel, and logistics contractors do not need to work as closely with military personnel on the ground as do security and reconstruction contractors.

The activities of contractors who provide security services are most similar to those performed by soldiers. Many are armed and, in carrying out their duties, pose deadly risks to those working around them. Periodic tensions between contractors and regular forces—aggravated by disparities in pay and responsibilities—have raised the issue of whether these two types of forces can work together effectively. A recent survey of DoD personnel and their perceptions of private security contractors suggests that combining these forces in conflict zones is problematic. Lower-ranking and younger personnel in particular claim that pay disparities between military personnel and contractors are detrimental to the morale of their units in Iraq.[34] However, many security services tasks do not require close interaction with military personnel. Roughly one-third of military personnel surveyed in Iraq, for example, had no firsthand experience with private security contractors.[35] These tasks are also frequently less crucial to the performance of military units than are logistics services.

Nonetheless, the behavior of contracted security personnel matters to the overall US mission. The hazards of questionable behavior were demonstrated most vividly in the September 2007 Blackwater shootout in Nisoor Square. Both Iraqis and Americans, however, had consistently reported this type of behavior long before that dramatic incident. Private forces have tended to focus on the strict terms of their contracts (protecting particular people or facilities) rather than on the overarching goals of the United States (effectively countering the insurgency). Some of the tactics developed to protect clients, such as driving fast through intersections and rapid resort to force, alienated the local population in ways that undermined the broader counterinsurgency strategy. Similar problems persist in Afghanistan. Among military personnel who had experience with security contractors, approximately 20 percent reported firsthand knowledge of PMSC failure to coordinate with military forces "some-

times"; another 15 percent of this population witnessed such coordination problems "often."[36]

In today's conflicts, reconstruction tasks—particularly training—are often more crucial for achieving the goals of the war effort than either logistics or security services. Often, reconstruction tasks must be coordinated so that police training and justice reform, for instance, complement one another, and so that civilian leaders understand the military they are expected to oversee. Contractors who provide reconstruction services must not only deliver quality work but coordinate that delivery with other contractors, the US military, and other government agencies. Thus, these services are among the most crucial for US goals *and* the most challenging to coordinate. Moreover, concerns have been raised about the military's ability to ensure that these tasks are carried out effectively when they have been outsourced. Notably, DynCorp's training of the Afghan National Police and Army is widely regarded as a failure, but the DoD has been unable to move the training contract to a different company because of DynCorp's legal protest regarding contract competition.[37] Yet these jobs are less important to the functioning of military units than logistics support, and they pose less deadly risk than security operations do. Problems with integration of activities—or unity of effort—were among the most significant challenges to reconstruction, as noted by the CWC's 2009 interim report.[38]

Thus, the overall picture of how contractors shape effectiveness is complicated. Clearly, contractors can quickly deploy skilled personnel, and the majority of contractors are good at what they do. But the United States does not have the capacity to oversee these contracts successfully, and this failure has led to waste, fraud, and particularly with regard to security contracts, abuse. Furthermore, the level of integration needed for the most effective delivery of services has lagged in Iraq and Afghanistan.

How does contracting for military and security services affect the United States' capacity to take political accountability for forces? Mobilization via contract operates differently than military enlistment, with consequences for the relationship between the force and civilians—the political elite and the public included. The US experience in Iraq suggests that forces raised via contract operate much more opaquely than military forces. Largely because of this reduced transparency, Congress has struggled to exercise constitutional authorization and oversight. Furthermore, the public has less information about the deployment of contractors. Though evidence suggests that the public is just as concerned about the deaths of contractors as it is about military deaths, statistics on the former are much less likely to be known.[39]

Using contractors speeds policy response but limits input into the policy process. As the insurgency grew in Iraq, for example, the United States mobilized 150,000 to 170,000 private forces to support the mission there, all with little or no congressional or public knowledge—let alone consent. President Bush was not required to appeal to Congress or the public for these additional forces, which doubled the US presence in Iraq. As evidence from the reaction to the request for a mere 20,000 troops for the 2007 surge suggests, the president may well not have been allowed to deploy additional personnel if he had been required to obtain permission. Because the use of PMSCs garners little attention, their employment reduces public arousal, debate, commitment, and response to the use of force.

How contracted forces relate to civilian leaders is an important question. Some claim contracted forces can be more responsive (given the potential for losing their contracts) than the military bureaucracy. Flexibility in how contracts are written can accelerate mobilization in ways that military organizations often cannot deliver. Certainly, contractors are designed to deliver whatever the client wants. They are thus much less prone to standard operating procedures or organizational bias that can inhibit responsiveness in military organizations.

Not at all apparent, however, is the US government's capacity to oversee contracts in a manner sufficient to generate responsiveness. Even as DoD contract transactions *increased* by 328 percent between 2000 and 2009, the staff responsible for reviewing contractor purchasing at the Defense Contract Management Agency *declined* from seventy in 2002 to fourteen in 2009.[40] Contracting in individual service branches faced similar problems. The dearth of contract officers makes it difficult to effectively oversee contracts at home, but concerns about adequate oversight are even more pressing when PMSCs are operating abroad. The relevant contracting officer is often not even in theater. Inadequate contract staffing and oversight have been important complaints in both Iraq and Afghanistan and have been tied to numerous problems—from poor performance to waste, fraud, and abuse. Though the risks of poor oversight vary according to task, difficulties in overseeing contractors have been common to all three areas of contract services. The challenge of overseeing expeditionary operations may undermine companies' responsiveness to contractual obligations.

Overall, then, the use of contractors has skirted accountability, making half of US mobilization largely invisible to Congress and the public; as a result, it has masked the number of conflict-related casualties.[41] Though one could argue that contractors are more responsive to political leaders, this likelihood can only be the case once political leaders know what contractors are doing—and evidence shows that this has not been the case in Iraq and Afghanistan.

A final point of evaluation is to look at whether contractors allow the exercise of force in a way that is consistent with the larger *values*, culture, and expectations of the society they represent. Over the course of the Cold War and in its aftermath, military professionalism within advanced industrial states increasingly enshrined principles drawn from theories of democracy (civilian control of the military and abidance by the rule of law), liberalism (respect for human rights), and the laws of war.[42] Though marginal differences exist, the values that govern US military personnel are largely shared with their Western partners. The ease of mobilization that contracting offers is viewed by some as consistent with the United States' evolving concerns with global security and global governance. But in practice, the use of PMSCs has not fit well within the normative and legal frameworks that underpin global security.

Two factors strain the impact of contracting on the values represented by military forces. First, precisely which professional norms inform the PMSC industry remains unclear. Americans employed by PMSCs have a range of military and law enforcement backgrounds—some distinguished and others less so. However, the industry increasingly recruits from a global market. As recruiting and subcontracting have become more transnational, personnel are from countries as diverse as the United Kingdom, Nepal, Fiji, South Africa, El Salvador, Colombia, and India. These geographic differences bring an even more diverse array of professional norms. Concerns about lax industry vetting of employees have raised the question of whether PMSCs are increasingly hiring employees with less distinguished service records.[43] Finally, many PMSCs also hire local personnel. In addition to lower costs, these forces bring many benefits: local knowledge and ties that can aid companies' effectiveness. However, they also bring local values that may not be consistent with democracy, liberalism, or the laws of war. For instance, evidence suggests that local companies hired by the United States to provide convoy security in Afghanistan funneled money to Taliban forces or were otherwise engaged in corrupt practices that promise to undermine US goals and the values it seeks to support in Afghanistan.[44]

Even if all contractors were well-socialized military or police professionals, they nonetheless operate in a different environment—vis-à-vis both the law and command and control—than troops do. Commanders are less likely to notice or to punish offenses committed by contractors than offenses committed by troops. Over time, a lack of punishment can be expected to lead to more lax behavior; indeed, many have claimed that this outcome is the case in Iraq and Afghanistan. Though reliable, systematic evidence is not yet available, a wealth of anecdotal evidence lends credibility to this conclusion.[45] Military officers have expressed their concern that the "culture of impunity" surrounding PMSCs has become a real problem.[46]

The increasing US reliance on contractors suggests that national military forces are unsuited to meet the foreign policy goals that US leaders consider vital to national security. It may also reflect the degree to which leaders believe public support does not exist for the kind of foreign policy they deem necessary. The fact that leaders can turn to contractors has allowed them to pursue their goals nonetheless.

While potentially beneficial to effectiveness, the availability of contractors has also permitted leaders to avoid reconciling foreign policy with national values and institutions. Enhancing effectiveness in this way has undermined the accountability of US forces. Even as the United States works to make the use of contractors more efficient and effective, part of the attraction is that private forces are accountable to leaders, not publics or their representatives, thereby allowing elected representatives to pursue a global mission without first convincing the electorate to make the sacrifices required.

Efforts to make contractors more broadly accountable, though, can undermine the flexibility that makes them effective. For instance, spelling out more clearly in each contract the limits of action can address congressional concerns and enhance accountability, but it diminishes the flexibility that PMSC personnel can deliver on the ground. Furthermore, contractors are even more important to the State Department than they are to the DoD. Attempts to rein in contractor numbers, then, would further fuel questions about the appropriate balance between civilian and military activities in US foreign policy initiatives. Although interagency efforts have sought to ensure that US assistance in Africa, for example, extends beyond military training, the budgetary and personnel imbalance between the DoD and the State Department makes such a realignment of programs unlikely to occur in the near future.[47]

Finally, efforts to implement professional and legal standards for contractors promise to improve behavior but may also limit reliance on local residents in a way that could increase costs and inhibit the input of local knowledge. To the extent that US standards are perceived as national rather than global, they may omit a large portion of the global industry. The effort now under way to coordinate regulatory and legal mechanisms and create global standards of behavior for personnel and companies in the PMSC industry is a promising development, but its implementation will require a good deal of cooperation between the United States, other governments, NGOs, journalists, industry groups, and additional stakeholders.[48]

Reliance on contractors has generated tensions between the effectiveness of forces, their accountability, and the degree to which they represent US values.

These tensions, though not insurmountable, are not easily resolved. They require persistent management by US leaders in cooperation not only with the American public but also with other governments and the variety of additional stakeholders that have an interest in how contractors behave. Thus, while contracting is likely to remain, it is also likely to continue to generate unease in US foreign policy.

NOTES

1. The contemporary "total force concept" explicitly includes contractor personnel. For general overviews of the private military and security industry, see Peter Singer, *Corporate Warriors: The Rise of the Privatized Military Industry* (Ithaca, N.Y.: Cornell University Press, 2003); Deborah D. Avant, *The Market for Force: The Consequences of Privatizing Security* (New York: Cambridge University Press, 2005). For a discussion of the role of contractors in US foreign policy more generally, see Allison Stanger, *One Nation Under Contract: The Outsourcing of American Power and the Future of Foreign Policy* (New Haven, Conn.: Yale University Press, 2009).

2. David Isenberg, "A Government in Search of Cover: Private Military Companies in Iraq," in *From Mercenaries to Market: The Rise and Regulation of Private Military Companies*, ed. Simon Chesterman and Chia Lehnardt (New York: Oxford University Press, 2007), 83

3. Determining exact numbers is difficult because the Department of Defense (DoD) did not begin to collect reliable information on the contractors it employed until 2007. Furthermore, contractors were hired by many other government agencies in addition to the DoD; Moshe Schwartz, "Department of Defense Contractors in Iraq and Afghanistan: Background and Analysis" (Washington, D.C.: Congressional Research Service, December 14, 2009), 4.

4. In Afghanistan's case, this percentage represents a drop in the ratio of contractors to uniformed personnel, from a high of 69 percent contractors in December 2008; Schwartz, "Department of Defense Contractors in Iraq and Afghanistan," 5–13.

5. This ratio was at least 2.5 times higher than the ratio during any other major US conflict; Congressional Budget Office, "Contractors' Support of U.S. Operations in Iraq" (Washington, D.C.: CBO, August 2008), http://www.cbo.gov/ftpdocs/96xx/doc9688/08-12-IraqContractors.pdf.

6. T. X. Hammes, "Private Contractors in Conflict Zones: The Good, the Bad, and the Strategic Impact," *Strategic Forum* no. 260 (Washington, D.C.: Institute for National Strategic Studies, October 2010).

7. Commission on Wartime Contracting, "At What Risk? Correcting Over-Reliance on Contracting in Contingency Operations" (Washington, D.C.: CWC, February 2011), 1.

8. Avant, *The Market for Force.*

9. Commission on Wartime Contracting, "At What Cost? Contingency Contracting in Iraq and Afghanistan" (Washington, D.C.: CWC, June 2009).

10. Congressional Budget Office, "Contractors' Support of U.S. Operations in Iraq."

11. Congressional Budget Office, "Contractors' Support of U.S. Operations in Iraq."

12. Schwartz, "Department of Defense Contractors in Iraq and Afghanistan," 6.

13. Dana Priest, "Private Guards Repel Attack on U.S. Headquarters," *The Washington Post*, April 6, 2004.

14. See descriptions of these companies in Steve Fainaru, *Big Boy Rules: America's Mercenaries Fighting in Iraq* (Philadelphia: Da Capo Press, 2008); T. Christian Miller, *Blood Money: Wasted Billions, Lost Lives, and Corporate Greed in Iraq* (New York: Little, Brown, 2006); and Tom Ricks, *Fiasco: The American Military Adventure in Iraq* (New York: Penguin, 2006).

15. See DynCorp International, webpage, n.d., http://www.dyn-intl.com/history.aspx.

16. See the discussion of Vinnell Corporation in Avant, *The Market for Force*, 18, 114, and 148. MPRI stands for Military Professional Resources Incorporated; the company is now a part of L-3 Communications. For a discussion of its role in the Balkans, see Avant, *The Market for Force*, chap. 3. For the history of USIS (US Investigations Services), see USIS, website, n.d., http://www.usis.com/Fact-Sheet.aspx.

17. See Parsons, website, n.d., http://www.parsons.com/pages/default.aspx.

18. Stanger, *One Nation Under Contract*.

19. Office of Logistics Management, *AFRICAP Program Re-Compete* (Washington, D.C.: U.S. Government Printing Office, February 6, 2008), https://www.fbo.gov/index?s=opportunity&mode=form&tab=core&id=4fbad7bde428a5595aca7bfe3cdbco2d&_cview=1.

20. Government Accountability Office, "Actions Needed to Address Stakeholder Concerns, Improve Interagency Collaboration, and Determine Full Costs Associated with the U.S. Africa Command," GAO Report #GAO-09-181 (Washington, D.C.: GAO, February 2009).

21. See Pae Group, website, n.d., http://www.paegroup.com.

22. Connie Veillette, Clare Ribando, and Mark Sullivan, "U.S. Foreign Assistance to Latin America and the Caribbean," Congressional Research Service Report #RL32487 (Washington, D.C.: CRS, January 3, 2006), 2.

23. Government Accountability Office, "Plan Colombia: Drug Reduction Goals Were Not Fully Met, but Security Has Improved," GAO Report #GAO-09-71 (Washington, D.C.: GAO, October 2008), 15.

24. Clare Ribando, "Mérida Initiative for Mexico and Central America: Funding and Policy Issues" (Washington, D.C.: Congressional Research Service, April 19, 2010), 1–3.

25. Congressional Budget Office, "Contractors' Support of U.S. Operations in Iraq."

26. Schwartz, "Department of Defense Contractors in Iraq and Afghanistan," 9.

27. Schwartz, "Department of Defense Contractors in Iraq and Afghanistan," 12; Moshe Schwartz, "The Department of Defense's Use of Private Security Contractors in Iraq and Afghanistan: Background, Analysis, and Options for Congress" (Washington, D.C.: Congressional Research Service, February 21, 2011), 10.

28. Lora Lumpe, "U.S. Foreign Military Training: Global Reach, Global Power, and Oversight Issues," *Foreign Policy in Focus* Special Report, May 2002, 11–12.

29. Risa Brooks and Elizabeth Stanley-Mitchell, eds., *Creating Military Power: The Sources of Military Effectiveness* (Stanford, Calif.: Stanford University Press, 2007).

30. This complaint was aired in a draft of what became Gregory Fontenot, E. J. Degen, and David Tohn, *On Point: The United States Army in Operation Iraqi Freedom* (Fort Leavenworth, Tex.: Combat Institute Press, 2004). In the final version of the document, however, the discussion of the difficulty with logistics did not mention contractors. General Mahan's complaints were also reported by Anthony Bianco and Stephanie Anderson Forest, "Outsourcing War," *Business Week*, September 15, 2003; and David Wood, "Some of Army's Civilian Contractors Are No-Shows in Iraq," Newhouse News Service, July 31, 2003.

31. Office of the Special Inspector General for Iraq Reconstruction, *Hard Lessons: The Iraq Reconstruction Experience* (Washington, D.C.: U.S. Government Printing Office, 2009), 172–173. Another example of the negative consequences of poor oversight is seen in the contractor abuses at Abu Ghraib prison; see Steve Schooner, "Contractor Atrocities at Abu Ghraib: Compromised Accountability in a Streamlined, Outsourced Government," *Stanford Law and Policy Review* 16 (2005): 549–572.

32. On troop satisfaction, see Commission on Wartime Contracting, "At What Cost?" 45.

33. Commission on Wartime Contracting, "At What Cost?" 39–59.

34. Sarah Cotton, Ulrich Petersohn, Molly Dunigan, Q. Burkhart, Meghan Zander-Cotugno, Edward O'Connell, and Michael Webber, *Hired Guns: Views About Armed Contractors in Operation Iraqi Freedom* (Santa Monica, Calif.: RAND Corporation, 2010), Figure S1.

35. Cotton et al., *Hired Guns*, Figure S1.

36. Cotton et al., *Hired Guns*, Figure S1.

37. Christine Spolar, "Military Training of Afghan National Police Mired in Contract Dispute," The Huffington Post Investigative Fund, February 22, 2010, http://huffpostfund.org/stories/2010/02/military-training-afghan-national-police-mired-contract-dispute.

38. Commission on Wartime Contracting, "At What Cost?" 3.

39. Deborah D. Avant and Lee Sigelman, "Private Security and Democracy: Lessons from the US in Iraq," *Security Studies* 19 (2) (2010).

40. Commission on Wartime Contracting in Iraq and Afghanistan, "Defense Agencies Must Improve Their Oversight of Contractor Business Systems to Reduce Waste, Fraud, and Abuse," CWC Special Report 1, September 21, 2009, http://www.wartimecontracting.gov/index.php/reports. See also, Jacques S. Gansler et al., *Urgent Reform Required: Army Expeditionary Contracting* (Washington, D.C.: Commission on Army Acquisition and Program Management in Expeditionary Operations, October 31, 2007), 4.

41. T. Christian Miller, "Contractors in Iraq Are Hidden Casualties of War," ProPublica, October 6, 2009, http://www.propublica.org/feature/kbr-contractor-struggles-after-iraq-injuries-1006.

42. See Charles C. Moskos, John Allen Williams, and David R. Segal, *The Postmodern Military: Armed Forces after the Cold War* (New York: Oxford University Press, 2000).

43. Senate Committee on Armed Services, *Inquiry into the Role and Oversight of Private Security Contractors in Afghanistan*, 111th Cong., 2nd sess., September 28, 2010, http://info.publicintelligence.net/SASC-PSC-Report.pdf.

44. Dexter Filkins, "Convoy Guards in Afghanistan Face an Inquiry: U.S. Suspects Bribes to Taliban Forces," *The New York Times*, June 7, 2010.

45. See, for instance, Fainaru, *Big Boy Rules*.

46. Schwartz, "The Department of Defense's Use of Private Security Contractors in Iraq and Afghanistan," 19. There are international efforts to establish standards for PMSCs, codes of conduct for personnel, and standards for the legal responsibilities of companies and individuals that may begin to address some of these concerns. See International Committee of the Red Cross and the Swiss Federal Department of Foreign Affairs, "The Montreux Document on Private Military and Security Companies" (Montreux, Switzerland: ICRC, September 17, 2008); Swiss Directorate of Political Affairs, "International Code of Conduct for Private Security Service Providers" (Bern, Switzerland: Federal Department of Foreign Affairs, November 9, 2010).

47. Government Accountability Office, "Actions Needed to Address Stakeholder Concerns, Improve Interagency Collaboration, and Determine Full Costs Associated with the U.S. Africa Command."

48. See International Commission of the Red Cross and the Swiss Federal Department of Foreign Affairs, "The Montreux Document on Private Military and Security Companies"; Swiss Directorate of Political Affairs, "International Code of Conduct for Private Security Service Providers."

Exodus

TIM KANE

> The increasing mechanization and complexity of defense forces make technical skills and a wide background of experience vastly more important than ever before. . . . But at this time when we must still maintain large forces under arms and alerted throughout the world, it is difficult to attract and retain volunteers, both enlisted and commissioned.
>
> —President Dwight D. Eisenhower, Special Message to the Congress, January 13, 1955

The Army knew it had a problem after a few years of occupying Iraq, and it wasn't long before the public knew it too. On April 10, 2006, a headline in the *New York Times* announced: "Young Officers Leaving Army at a High Rate" and noted that the retention rate for West Point graduates had collapsed.[1] This was a recurrent problem that the Pentagon had struggled with since at least the end of World War II, although the shift to an all-volunteer force in the 1970s and consequent improvement in the quality of life had, it was thought, solved the problem.

Higher-than-normal attrition rates wouldn't matter so much if it weren't the young Mitchells, Nimitzes, and Eisenhowers quitting, but in the modern military the cream of the crop tend to leave fastest. A series of official Army research reports published in 2010 by Major David Lyle and fellow West Point faculty members Casey Wardynski and Michael Colarusso showed higher attrition rates among the Army's best junior officers: "[P]rospects for the Officer Corps future have been darkened by an ever-diminishing return on this investment, as evidenced by plummeting company-grade officer retention rates. Significantly, this leakage includes a large share of high-performing officers." They noted that the captain-retention situation had been becoming "untenable"[2] even before the 9/11 attacks in 2001.

Captains in particular were the source of anxiety for Army planners, since they were choosing to resign just as their initial commitments were up, leaving behind a smaller class of midcareer officers than was needed. The numbers of officers in each cohort was essentially set in stone because Army policy generally "grows its own" from lieutenant to general, and does not allow anybody to join the middle of the ranks. As for the cause of the exodus, which also included captains commissioned through the Reserve Officers' Training Corps (ROTC) at universities, the *Times* pointed to the "end of a burst of patriotic fervor" and the ongoing "burden of deployments" to both Iraq and Afghanistan.

What I'll try to show in this chapter is how severe the exodus was (and still is), but also that the larger problem of bleeding talent cuts deeper than retention of junior officers. We'll look at a number of surveys—including one I conducted for this book—to understand the motivations of departing officers as well as retained officers. These surveys also provide recommendations for a personnel system that can improve the military. I'll also explain what makes these survey results scientifically valid, which is the knee-jerk objection to studies critical of the status quo, especially surveys of active duty attitudes the generals prefer to pretend aren't representative. In the end, the exodus is a symptom of a larger problem, one that might even seem to be lessening as the wars draw down. The reality is that bad human-resource policies damage the military from the first day an officer pins on bars and long after that officer resigns.

Captains and Colonels

Matt Kapinos was one of half a dozen cadet regimental commanders in the class of 2001 and graduated near the top of his class at West Point. For that class in particular, the attacks of 9/11 will forever hold a special meaning. No American will ever think back on that year and forget what happened, much less anyone in the military. Like the infamous attacks on Pearl Harbor in 1941, the al Qaeda–master-minded suicide hijackings that destroyed the Twin Towers and a full wing of the Pentagon marked 2001 as a year of war.

Lieutenant Kapinos was assigned to the Eighty-Second Airborne, the unit led by Jack Gavin in World War II. In early 2003, he was leading a platoon of 40 men in Afghanistan. After a brief rotation home where he was reunited with his young wife, the newly promoted Captain Kapinos was commanding a company of nearly 200 soldiers in Iraq. Andrew Tilghman described Kapinos's story in an excellent essay called the "Army's Other Crisis," which was published in the *Washington Monthly* in 2007:

> In Afghanistan, [Kapinos] had suggested that instead of merely conducting nighttime raids, his men should camp in small villages to help local leaders root out insurgents and their sympathizers. His commanders repeatedly rejected the idea. In Iraq, he was full of similarly innovative proposals, but felt his commanders disregarded his input. "After a while, you just stop asking," he said.
> . . . Kapinos, however, is no longer in the Army. Fifteen days after his initial five-year service agreement expired, he left military life entirely. When I met him, it was near the downtown campus of the Georgetown University Law Center, where he was taking a break from classes on corporate income tax law. Tall and fit, with close-cropped sandy brown hair and a green cable-knit sweater, he resembled both the lawyer he is preparing to be and the Army captain he once was. "I was a true believer at West Point. When Afghanistan kicked off, I don't want to say I bought the propaganda, but I wanted to change the world," he said. "I thought I was going to be a four-star general."[3]

Tilghman argued that the strain of the Iraq War, visibly depreciating the military's equipment, was at the same time invisibly depreciating its human capital. Looking back on that story after five years (and a relatively successful conclusion to the Iraq War), I wonder if something may have been missed by Tilghman and others in the media. Captains are only half of the story, the superficial half; these are young warriors in harm's way with young spouses and toddlers back home. The more nuanced and more important other half of story is about the colonels.

Getting a great first assignment after commissioning is essential in climbing the ladder, especially given the nature of Army promotions. When merit is all but erased from formal metrics, soldiers need to check exactly the right boxes—get the right jobs, go to the right professional schools on time, earn "distinguished graduate" from those schools—to prove themselves. And getting into the infantry, armor, or other combat-arms branches is considered important. If one is "going infantry," the ideal path is to get light but not too light. Specialized units such as the US Navy SEALs or the Army's Delta Force might be too far off the beaten path (too light), whereas mechanized infantry might be a shade too heavy.

Like Kapinos, Dick Hewitt graduated near the top of the class from West Point. And also like Kapinos, his first assignment was with the legendary Eighty-Second Airborne Division at Fort Bragg, North Carolina. Hewitt, like Kapinos, also decided to leave the Army a few years after the 9/11 attacks. But here's the difference: Hewitt had served a full 20-year career. He had checked all the right boxes, even getting tapped to command a battalion when he was just a major. So when Hewitt decided to leave, it was not because the Army had a minor morale problem causing retention heartburn, but rather it was because of a deeper and more nuanced institutional dysfunction.

"I can still remember how he first impressed all of us during a platoon attack exercise that he commanded one night," remembers Brigadier General Wayne Grigsby about the time they met at the infantry officer basic school (IOBC).[4] "His charisma, his intellect, the way he carried himself, the way he commanded his soldiers, his physical prowess, the way he worked with his peers—I have never seen a finer leader in my 28 years of service and 50 months in combat. I thought I'd be working for Dick by now and was sure he was going to be wearing two or three stars, easy." Although the path to general is a narrow one, Hewitt did everything the Army asked and more to stay out front, getting all the right jobs and impressing peers and subordinates along the way. So what happened that got him put onto the Personnel Command (PERSCOM) black list?

In the summer of 1980, Hewitt was a freshman at West Point. He graduated with the class of 1984 during the height of the Cold War, and was promoted to captain exactly four years later, just like everyone else in his year group. Hewitt's second assignment was a one-year tour of duty as the battalion maintenance officer for the 1–5 Infantry Mechanized, Second Infantry Division. A year later, Hewitt was given a company command at Fort Ord, California. Next, he was sent to the University of Chicago's Graduate School of Business, followed by a two-year assignment as a professor of economics back at West Point's famous Sosh department. At some point, he was selected a year before his peers for promotion to major. After a year of advanced military training at the Command and General Staff College (CGSC) at Fort Leavenworth, Kansas, Hewitt was sent "home" to Fort Bragg where he checked all the boxes: one year on division staff, one year as battalion ops officer, and so on. This is where his story gets interesting.

At that moment, Major Hewitt was a prime candidate to serve as a general officer someday, maybe even lead the Army if he played his cards right. He had been tapped for promotion to lieutenant colonel (known as "major P" for "promotable"), and now awaited the outcome of the Army's boards—formal committees of senior officers who rank-order officers in the zone for battalion command openings in the coming year. This is a cohort of lieutenant colonels and a few major Ps all across the Army. In November 1999 a personnel officer visited Bragg and told Hewitt that he was a "fifty-fifty" for one of the openings, which actually meant it was a sure thing. The officer was the chief of the section that doled out jobs for PERSCOM, then located in the Hoffman building in Washington, DC. In reality, Hewitt was again at the top of the list. Of all the battalion command positions the Army awards each year, the top ones are given to tactical officers. Hewitt was one of those, and he was a year younger than others in the year group. Once the list was announced in early 2000, buzz around the Army and congratulations rolled in.

The next step for the selected officers—there were 16 that year for light/airborne/air-assault infantry commands—was to submit a list of their preferences to PERSCOM. The staff at the Hoffman Building would sort through the preferences in order to produce an optimized match, a process known as "slating." Hewitt submitted his preferences, ranking the 16 options from first to last with a remote tour of duty in South Korea ranked last. He told the officers at Hoffman over the phone that the Korea job in particular would be hard on his family. With two preschool sons and another little one on the way, the separation required by the Korea assignment might be more than the family could bear. "It will not be well received in my house," he bluntly told the assignments officer. Now it was in the hands of the planners at PERSCOM

to slate the officers and issue orders through the acquiring commanders.

As you might guess, a few weeks passed, and then Hewitt received a phone call. It was Major General Dees, calling from South Korea. "Congratulations, Dick. Welcome to the team."

Hewitt said all the right things on the phone that day and even accepted the first month of command training at Fort Benning in Georgia before realizing the outcome just wasn't acceptable. He had two conversations with senior officers after slating to see if there was any flexibility in the process to change the assignment—maybe he could trade with someone?—and was told it was a done decision.

In a move that sent tremors through the Army, Hewitt called the planners at the Hoffman Building and declined command. The staffer on the other end of the phone was surprised and calmly warned: "Do you understand that this means your record will be marked 'declination with prejudice'?" He offered Hewitt 24 hours to think it over. Not necessary, Hewitt answered. In his mind, it was a choice between career suicide and tearing apart his young family.

Even though he seemed destined for high rank, that one clash with the inflexible Army personnel system essentially ended his career after 15 flawless years. Hewitt committed no crime, disappointed no commander, and lost the faith of none of his troops. In fact, his career was flying high when he made the mistake of asking for a one-year reprieve from the fast track.

Today, Hewitt is a successful entrepreneur. He presides over a small, thriving financial firm in Carmel, California. "I can control my own destiny and work with partners I trust." His partner is Jerry Lidzinski, a 1995 graduate of the Air Force Academy. Hewitt made a vow after retiring from the Army never to work for someone else, where he was not in control.

The story of Hewitt's departure from the Army has two footnotes.

First, in early 2000 he received a phone call from the Pentagon. The chief of staff of the Army, General Eric Shinseki, was having a bad year because, among other things, dozens of officers had declined battalion command. Hewitt wasn't alone. In armor, engineers, infantry, and aviation, all the branches were suffering from high rates of dissatisfaction with the command slating. So Hewitt and others like him were invited to the Pentagon to give feedback to the vice chief, General Jack Keene. Questions were asked, data collected, and the day ended.

As Hewitt changed into civilian clothes for his flight home, another officer asked what assignment he had turned down.

"Korea."

"Funny," said the other officer. "My wife is from Korea. I would have loved that job."

The irony here is painful.

Second, consider what the Army did with Hewitt afterward. In mid-2000, Hewitt had only one year left at Bragg, then three years before he could retire with the standard 20-year military pension. He had an MBA from one of the top schools in the nation, so it was a no-brainer for the dean of West Point, Dan Kauffman, to bring him to campus as the director of the economics program. While at West Point, Hewitt impressed the superintendent, General William Lennox, who asked him to stay for another four or more years as permanent faculty. Hewitt agreed. Lennox sent a letter to Hoffman asking for them to "rebranch" Hewitt in strategic plans, making official what was already the unofficial end of his infantry career. The commandant of cadets, Leo Brooks, sent a letter of support, as did the dean.

At that time in 2004, the folks at PERSCOM understood fully that Hewitt had no further obligation to stay in uniform, and that if he was not allowed to rebranch, he could simply retire. But in their records, his file was stamped with a bright red "declination with prejudice." So the story ends this way: Hewitt's wife received a letter from PERSCOM while he was teaching classes at the academy, so she called him during his free hour and read him the jargon-filled letter over the phone. It explained that the needs of Army prevented his rebranching.

"What does that mean?" she asked.

"It means we're retiring," he said.

In May 2004, at the age of 42, Lieutenant Colonel Dick Hewitt left the Army, driving out the same gates at West Point that he had entered more than two decades before. The last five years that concluded Hewitt's career are what I refer to as "internal bleeding."

The Retention Crisis

All cadets who graduate from the US Military Academy commit to serve a minimum of 5 years as a military officer, after which they can resign their commissions or continue on, presumably toward the full 20-year career. Retirement is available to everyone who serves 20 years or more, which means half of one's monthly pay for the rest of one's life, plus full benefits. A few cadets agree to longer commitments (2–5 additional years) in exchange for graduate school or flight training.

When the US Military Academy (USMA) class of 1999 reached its 5-year mark in 2004, 72 percent of the graduates chose to stay in uniform, and 28 percent resigned. This net retention rate sends a signal about the overall health of the junior officer corps, and 2004 was an early warning sign compared to the normal range of 75–80 percent. A year later, the retention rate

dropped again to slightly less than 66 percent, the highest departure rate in 16 years. Not since the end of the Cold War had so many young officers left the service after their initial commitment. In the late 1990s, junior officers were being asked to leave, but by 2005 the military was begging them to stay.

While all branches of the military experienced challenges, only the Army was in crisis. According to a March 2007 story in *USA Today*, the retention rate of West Point graduates was "as much as 30 percentage points lower than the rates for graduates of the Navy and Air Force academies."[5] A common complaint was that the elitist academy graduates were the problem, not the Army per se, since ROTC and Officer Candidates School (OCS) officers remained at high rates, but that's a myth. Retention problems afflicted ROTC *scholarship* officers even more than West Point graduates. The 2010 Strategic Studies Institute monograph by Colonel Casey Wardynski, Major David Lyle, and Michael Colarusso (the Wardynski monograph) analyzed the retention of officers in the 1996 cohort by commissioning source. While it is true that the percentage of West Pointers in the class of 1996 drops dramatically at the 5-year point (from 90 to 60 percent), it must also be said that OCS officers started the year at 70 percent. And while the USMA rate declined steadily to 41 percent at the 8-year mark, this mirrored the ROTC officers who had 3-year scholarships, and was higher than the 35 percent 8-year retention of 4-year ROTC scholarship officers.[6]

I faced similar skepticism about West Point elitism after presenting my survey of 250 West Point grads— but the Wardynski monograph made it clear that the exodus was as real as it was widespread. But the puzzle as to why remained. As author Wardynski asked: "How did the [the Army] move from a senior captain surplus, then to shortage, then to crisis in the decade following the end of the Cold War?"[7] A report by the Government Accountability Office (GAO) in January 2007 provided even more details:

> The Army, which continues to be heavily involved in combat operations in Iraq and Afghanistan, faces many retention challenges. For example, the Army is experiencing a shortfall of mid-level officers, such as majors, because it commissioned fewer officers 10 years ago due to a post–Cold War force reduction. It projects a shortage of 3,000 or more officers annually through FY 2013. While the Army is implementing and considering initiatives to improve officer retention, the initiatives are not integrated and will not affect officer retention until at least 2009 or are unfunded. As with its accession shortfalls, the Army does not have an integrated strategic plan to address its retention shortfalls.[8]

There were many reasons for the crisis, but the explanation that seems most obvious is the ongoing wars in the Middle East. As Tilghman wrote, the exodus was sending "alarming warnings about the strain that the Iraq War has placed on the military."[9] Remember that late 2006 to early 2007 was the lowest point in the war. The George W. Bush administration was starting to admit what troops on the ground had been saying all along: the strategy in Iraq was not working. In the words of Colonel Jeff Peterson, now a permanent member of West Point's faculty: "We were losing in Baghdad in 2006. We were *losing*. The enemy was winning. It had to change."[10]

Relying on a volunteer force is challenging, especially when the economy is strong (meaning demand for talent is high), but even more so during a conflict that the public dislikes. That's all the more reason to think carefully about the intertwining issues. Peterson wasn't saying that the war or the volunteer force was the source of retention and recruiting woes. He was simply commenting on the nature of fighting an insurgency. Peterson, like almost all officers, supports the all-volunteer force and he also disagrees with characterizations of the personnel system as being in crisis. The news media, however, found the war explanation too convenient.

Here's the catch. None of the war explanations can explain why retention problems *preceded* the 9/11 attacks. In a 2002 RAND report, James Hosek and Beth Asch "identified a roughly 5 percent decline in officer annual continuation rates among those [officers] in their midcareer." The authors argued that the number is deceptively small, but "small declines in annual continuation rates can translate into dramatic declines in manpower over a several-year period. Therefore, this decline must be taken seriously."[11] Likewise, Wardynski et al. argued that declining retention has been a problem since 1983 and that "by 2001 the captain retention situation was becoming untenable."[12] In fact, the Army has been plagued with talent bleeding for decades, and its personnel practices have never been reformed to address the problem.[13,14] President Harry Truman appointed a committee to consider the problem in 1949, and the secretary of defense asked the Brookings Institution's Harold Moulton to do the same in 1950. Two more task forces were commissioned early in the Dwight D. Eisenhower administration, calling attention to an annual retention rate of enlistees of just 20 percent. Then in 1954, after the Korea hostilities stopped, the Senate Armed Services Committee called attention to the "critical and delicate" problem of the officer brain drain. Arthur Coumbe, a military historian, attributes the severity of the competency weaknesses in the officer corps to the centralization of command and control in the 1960s. Regardless, retention rates simply collapsed late during the Vietnam conflict, down to 34 percent for OCS officers in 1969 and 11 percent for ROTC officers in 1970. All this goes to show that the current crisis has a long precedent.[15]

RAND Corporation's Hosek produced another study in 2006 that examined the "unprecedented strains on the all volunteer force" to identify the causes behind the most recent exodus.[16] The study was comprehensive in scope, reviewing published literature and surveys of military personnel conducted by the Defense Manpower Data Center (DMDC), as well as original focus groups of active-duty service members. What Hosek found was the deployments alone were a positive, not a negative, factor in retaining soldiers. Service members valued deployments as an opportunity to participate in an activity and mission that they believed in and that also enhanced their career prospects; however, the frequency and duration of deployments were weighing negatively on soldiers. "High op tempo" is the phrase used to describe the high demands on soldiers' time—long hours of work every day with few days truly off. Wartime means there is immense stress placed on soldiers, but also on their families, with troops facing mental fatigue or worse from multiple deployments.

Now, half a decade after the crisis broke into the public's consciousness, the matter may seem resolved. Already history. The war is over, so we can forget about how hard it was, right? That would be an error.

Bleeding talent still happens every day in the Army, Marines, Air Force, Navy, and Coast Guard. It happens in peacetime as well as wartime. The talent that was lost and mismanaged during the Iraq War will have consequences for decades to come, and the unresolved dysfunction in the personnel system is likely to get worse if the armed forces use force-shaping techniques based on seniority instead of merit. A potential drawdown in the years ahead must draw lessons from what caused the mid-war manpower malfunction.

The West Point Survey

In 2010, I conducted a survey of the West Point graduates from the classes of 1989, 1991, 1995, 2000, 2001, and 2004, and highlights were featured in the *Atlantic* magazine in early 2011. Before the article appeared, I was able to brief the survey's results to officers and key policy-makers in Washington, DC, during the fall of 2010. I incorporated feedback from those sessions into a second part of the survey.

An email solicitation to each member of class was sent from a fellow graduate who serves as the class scribe. The initial survey (Part One) was conducted from late August through mid-September of 2010 using an online survey tool. A total of 250 individuals completed the survey. Of those respondents 78 (31 percent) were on active duty. A follow-up survey (Part Two) was created based on their comments and feedback, sent to the initial 250 respondents in mid-September, and completed by 126 of them by the October deadline.[17]

Survey—Part One

The first question asks: "Do the best officers leave the military early rather than serving a full career?" The survey did not define "best" or "early" in an effort to ensure that respondents would not bracket the question in terms of external criteria (e.g., I might have framed it as the "most entrepreneurial leaders," while other scholars might frame it in terms of effectiveness, inspiration, management excellence, and so on. I thought a neutral framing was the least biased). Only 7 percent of respondents believed that most of the best officers stay in the military. Among the active-duty respondents, only 17 percent believed that most of the best officers are staying in the military. Younger graduates were more negative than older. It must be said that the 45 percent of responses held that "about half the best leave," and another 45 percent held that "MOST of the best leave, some stay."

One respondent wrote in the optional comments box: "Good leaders, those with entrepreneurial tendencies, are crushed by the military in spirit and in deed. I think this type of leader is attracted to the military, and during their [sic] personal growth stage, do well. But they soon 'outsmart' the norm and become frustrated by the confines of their senior leaderships' boundaries." Another wrote, "The best junior officers have spent 8 years doing more work for the same pay as their peers who contribute only the bare minimum. There is no system to reward the best officers prior to the BZ [i.e., 'below the zone' or one year early] Major board at 8 years of service." These were comments made before the respondents saw other questions about entrepreneurial values and personnel-specific questions.

The second question asked respondents to compare military and civilian promotions systems on a 1–10 scale of merit versus seniority. The results were significant by any technical metric, with a plurality giving the private sector a three and the US military an eight. This view holds, albeit less strongly, when the sample is limited to active-duty officers. Younger cohorts tend to view the military as less of a meritocracy, but all respondents give the private sector similar scores on average.

Attitudes were consistent in the comments, along the lines of: "In the civilian world, my performance is all that matters. There are no year groups. For the most part, a promotion is based on talent, not seniority. The year group system is one of the most asinine things the Army uses." Other comments pointed to the biased na-

ture of top-down evaluations that skewed promotions to meritorious behavior aimed not at productivity or mission, but at supporting the immediate rater in the chain of command. A final factor was that promotions had become less meritorious once the seniority system cracked under such low retention rates, meaning officers were pulled up to captain and major faster than the norm out of a need for warm bodies more than as a reward for their competence. In short, the top-down structure had no native capacity to handle scarcity, which is exactly what markets do.

Next, the survey asked respondents to grade, on an A–F scale, various aspects of the military in terms of fostering "innovative and entrepreneurial" leadership. As a benchmark, the raw talent (recruitment) received 55 percent As and Bs, the fourth highest. The other aspects can be understood in terms of this ratio as either improving or degrading the initial entrepreneurial talent. In general, formal training programs received average marks, including everything from service academies and war colleges to initial through senior officer training. Even doctrine received good marks. The weakest factors were all in the personnel system: evaluations (with an AB/DF ratio of 0.6), job assignments (0.5), promotions (0.4), and compensation (0.3). For example, only 8 out of 250 respondents gave the job-assignment system an A grade, compared to 39 who gave it an F. While these various personnel systems may serve other Army missions, they are perceived as failing to promote entrepreneurial leadership.

An active-duty colonel recommended that I add a question to assess the culture of innovation at the unit level, in contrast to the larger organization. Brilliant idea, and he was right. More than two-thirds of respondents agreed (18 percent agreeing strongly) with the statement: "Creative thinking and new ideas are (were) valued in your military units." This is a powerful finding that Army culture and Army soldiers are innovative and entrepreneurial, which is exactly what the talent paradox was claiming. One respondent summarized the dilemma with some additional color: "For the most part, creative thinking is valued, but there is only so much leeway given the crushing hand of the Army regulatory system and the constant turnover of leadership at all levels."

The last question on the survey is the most direct exploration of why soldiers had left the military. Since this question speaks so directly to the subject of this [essay], I'll present the full results in table 1.

Four reasons stand out as the most frequently cited by officers in explaining why they left the ranks. High op tempo during war, other life goals, and family income all play a role. But even then—during wartime—the top reason this panel cited for leaving the military is frustration with military bureaucracy, with 82 percent agreeing and 50 percent agreeing strongly.

Table 1. What Were The Reasons You Left the Military? Agree or Disagree If They Were Important Reasons for Your Decision

	Strongly Agree (%)	Agree (%)	Disagree (%)	Strongly Disagree (%)
Frustration with military bureaucracy	50	32	16	2
Family	57	24	15	5
Other life goals	35	45	15	5
Higher potential income	45	35	14	4
Frequent deployments	31	32	30	4
Limited opportunity in military	17	40	32	10
Pace of military promotions	22	31	39	7
Weak role models/commanders	24	22	35	19
Higher education	20	25	45	9
Better leadership opportunity	7	25	53	14
Retirement age (20 years+)	5	6	44	44
Medical discharge	2	4	25	68

Survey—Part Two

The nice way to introduce this section is this: Part Two of the survey was developed in response to feedback based on private presentations of the initial results. A more honest introduction would say: The initial impact of my West Point survey was tremendous, including some very high-level briefings at the Pentagon; however, there was some very aggressive pushback. Incredibly, one full colonel reacted to my presentation of the results of Part One by saying that the findings were unimportant. To paraphrase, he said: "Sure, you've described the personnel system, which has pluses and minuses like any system. But your results don't claim any harm to national security, and I think you're overinterpreting your poll results." I decided a few weeks later to extend the survey with Part Two. An email message was sent directly to the initial 250 respondents, and 126 of those individuals engaged in the follow-up.

The questions in Part Two were very direct, but I felt they had to leave no room for misinterpretation. [. . .] Only one-fifth of active-duty respondents (18 percent) think the military does a good job matching talents with jobs, and the same number thinks the Army is weeding out the weakest leaders. The final option asks whether the personnel system should be radically reformed, something we asked as a contrast with common calls for incremental change, and 55 percent of respondents agree.

It was seen that 78 percent of all respondents (and 78 percent of active-duty respondents) agree that *the current exit rate of the best officers harms national se-*

curity, while 65 percent (68 percent among active duty) agree that *it leads to a less competent general officer corps.* Typical responses in conversations about military retention are that high turnover is normal in the contemporary US economy and that high attrition rates are normal in the "up or out" military rank structure. While turnover may be high, turnover of *top* talent is the issue under scrutiny in this survey.

I also asked a new question about the causes of attrition. Recall the question in Part One was directed in a very personal way ("What were the reasons *you* left the military?" rather than "What are the top reasons *some* officers leave the military?"), which runs the risk of getting feedback that dodges self-criticism. Although anonymity was promised to all respondents, I decided to ask a more general question using the language: "Many of the best officers who leave the service would stay if . . ." Of the respondents 90 percent agreed that the best officers would be more likely to stay if "the military was more of a meritocracy." There was overwhelming support for other core principles as well, including if "job assignments were matched with a market mechanism instead of central planning" (87 percent), if "the military had a more entrepreneurial personnel system" (88 percent), and if "pay was based on performance instead of time in service" (70 percent). A few other options had far less support, so personnel flexibility really did seem to dominate the perceived causes of high attrition, but I offered one catch-all option just to confirm the departing officers weren't simply headed for the exits no matter what. Only 30.6 percent of respondents agreed that many of the best officers would leave "regardless of reforms to the personnel system."

The Dregs Who Remain

On January 4, 2011, the *Atlantic* published the findings in the essay "Why Our Best Officers Are Leaving," a modified version of the first chapter of this [original] book. Within hours, the essay went viral among US Army officers worldwide and then troops from all the services. It was reprinted in the influential "Early Bird" daily clippings distributed around the Pentagon. Within a few days, many military blogs had their own reactions,[18,19] each with dozens of comments. Nothing I'd ever written had caught fire like this, and I received hundreds of letters, including a long, carefully typed letter from a World War II veteran who lamented that nothing had changed since his time. One email from Iraq stands out in my mind, as it represents the level of frustration that apparently my essay had given voice to:

I read your article in the Atlantic Monthly and could have cried tears of joy. I am a prior enlisted 1LT and have 11 years in service. I was a Distinguished Military Graduate through the ROTC, quantified top 10% in every military course I attended and deployed to Iraq for a total of 39 months. I have chosen to leave the Army due to [sic] their inability to assess talent. The only way to affect change is to publicize a need for it and circumvent the obdurate system.

Respectfully,
Name Withheld

Questioning the Survey's Validity

The *Defense Media Network* published a major story on the survey by Eric Tegler on February 25, 2011.[20] Tegler requested an interview with US Army Human Resources Command and with Army headquarters, but those were declined; however, he was able to interview Colonel Thomas Collins, chief spokesman for Army Public Affairs. Collins, speaking for the Army, questioned the survey's validity and dismissed the idea of a more flexible assignments system. "I'm not sure that a survey of only 250 people is enough to make such a sweeping judgment. Personally, I simply don't believe the best are leaving." Collins also claimed that the "battle-tested force" serving in Iraq and Afghanistan proves my underlying premise wrong.

Questioning the validity of the survey is a powerful point, and seems to be about the only serious objection I face, so let me be clear. According to the fourth edition of the textbook *Survey Research Methods* by Floyd J. Fowler Jr., the goal of a sample survey is to accurately describe the underlying population. As Fowler notes, there are a handful of ways that a survey can produce flawed results. *Margin of error* is what the lay public assumes is the big issue. *Sample quality* is another concern. But the biggest factor is *question design*.

I chose for my sample to target officers who were produced from only one commissioning source: the United States Military Academy, including classmates who were on and off active duty. Critics imply this is a biased source, but subsequent surveys that include officers from other commissioning sources have confirmed my findings.

Furthermore, I narrowed the target population to officers who served during a period of time that was generally consistent and relevant, graduating between the years 1989–2004. Why not older graduates? Mixing attitudes of officers who served in the 1970s or 1980s with those serving today would mix apples and oranges. If the sample included older officers, critics would no doubt say their experiences were irrelevant to today's military.

What about sheer size? Two hundred and fifty people may seem unrepresentative, but it's actually in the same ballpark of national surveys that use three or four hundred respondents to measure the attitudes of the entire nation. My West Point survey had a maximum *margin of error* of 6.2 percent at 95 percent confidence. So when 93 percent of Army officers in my survey say that most of the best officers leave the military, statistics says the lowest the number could be for the full population is "only" 87 percent of all Army officers agreeing.[21]

Let's turn now to *question design*. Solid statistical bona fides are no seal of approval. Surveys that report a small margin of error are easily corrupted with poorly designed questions or by flawed sample recruitment. For example, a widely reported Zogby poll was found to use deeply flawed question design, but not until after it garnered massive media attention questioning the US military effort in the Middle East. In early 2006, Zogby asked an anonymous sample of deployed US troops about the war in Iraq, which the media cited widely with the headline "72 Percent of Troops Say It's Time to Leave Iraq."[22] The actual survey question asked how long the United States should *stay*, not *leave*, but three of the four answers were phrased in terms of when to *withdraw*, and then those responses were summed up as a majority opinion. The only other option: stay indefinitely.

The design of my questions was intentionally neutral in the sense that each question either offered a balanced response set (with an equal number of positive and negative response options) or a mix of positive and negative statements that an individual could agree with. No one, in fact, has suggested the questions were designed poorly. What is most telling is that defenders of the status quo who objected to my survey have put forth no facts or studies claiming attitudes of the soldiers or commanders are different. There has been no counterpoint. Instead, what has emerged is a chorus of support from voices including, to my surprise, Secretary of Defense Robert Gates.

Falk-Rogers

Other studies of service members' attitudes seem to support or echo my West Point study. In its 2011 annual survey, the Center for Army Leadership at Fort Leavenworth reported numerous frustrations among Army leaders, a group that included officers, warrant officers, and senior noncommissioned officers (NCOs).[23] Only 38 percent agreed that "the Army is headed in the right direction," which was unchanged from 2006. Of those who thought it was heading in the wrong direction, the second most-cited reason (by 58 percent of the subset) was the Army's inability to retain quality leaders. About one-fourth (24 percent) of Army leaders believe that honest mistakes are held against them in their unit/organization, while one-third (30 percent) believe that their unit/organization *promotes* a zero-defect mentality (emphasis added).

In March 2011, a pair of graduate students at Harvard's John F. Kennedy School published a survey that was very similar to mine. Sasha Rogers and Sayce Falk (a Marine veteran who served in Iraq) reached out to former junior military officers from the Army, Navy, Marines, and Air Force who had left the service between 2001 and 2010. They recruited their sample with the goal of including a proportional number of ROTC and OCS officers, and did so by reaching out through ROTC university alumni networks, graduate-school military organizations, and other veterans groups. While this approach assured a diversity of recently active junior officers (all respondents were O-2 through O-4), the lack of active-duty participants might have tainted the results. To counter such potential bias, Falk and Rogers also surveyed a group of 30 active-duty junior officers across the services. The executive summary states:

> Fully 80% of our respondents reported that the best officers they knew had left the military before serving a full career. Yet some factors widely portrayed as driving young officers from service were less important to our junior officer cohort than we anticipated. For instance, only 9% of respondents indicated that deployment cycles and operational tempo were their most important reason for leaving. In the same vein, nearly 75% ranked compensation and financial reasons as their least important consideration.

What does matter? Two factors emerged as areas of surprising consensus among former officers: organizational inflexibility, primarily manifested in the personnel system, and a lack of commitment to innovation within the military services.[24]

Specifically, Falk and Rogers found that "the number one reported reason for separation among our respondents was limited ability to control their own careers." The active-duty component was no more forgiving of the personnel system, with a majority agreeing that the personnel system does not do a good job of "matching talent to jobs (75%) or weeding out the weakest leaders (82%)."[25]

Another surprising feature of the Falk-Rogers study was the confirmation that deployments and high op tempo were not decisive factors. As the authors put it:

> [L]ess than 7% indicated that deployment strain was their most important reason for leaving. This tends to reinforce the argument that deployment, even with combat, is not a primary driver of attrition among junior officers. Nearly three-fourths of the junior officers we surveyed commissioned during or after 2001, suggesting that not only did they understand they would deploy and see combat, but in fact that was precisely *why* they joined.[26]

Reaction

The Army's initial reaction to the exodus was slow. Bleeding talent had been the norm for decades, and furthermore the Army was in the middle of two very difficult wars. As Falk and Rogers point out: "By 2007, the Army was predicting a total shortfall of over three thousand officers, particularly in the crucial senior captain and major range."[27]

Once it realized the problem, the Pentagon reacted like a bureaucracy typically does: It threw money at the problem using generic one-size-fits-all cash bonuses, offered to any officer who would stay, while the management system itself remained unchanged. The aforementioned studies demonstrate that this was bandaging the wound rather than addressing the underlying causes of the problem. "Although it now appears as if the Army has righted its ship when it comes to retaining the right number of officers, it did so largely by filling shortages via across-the-board promotions to field-grade officer rank,"[28] wrote Falk and Rogers. "Less than 85% of available billets at those ranks were filled by officers with the requisite rank and time in service—a critical shortfall, by the Army's own definition—and today's senior lieutenants and junior captains spend less time than ever before in critical development positions such as company command."[29]

The money throwing took the form of a 2007–2008 program called CSRB, which stands for "critical skills retention bonus." It offered lump-sum payments ranging from $25,000 to $35,000 in exchange for three additional years of service commitment. Wardynski and colleagues called it "counter to the sound market principles that should underpin any retention policy."[30] CSRB cost the taxpayers half a billion dollars, with scant evidence that it improved retention. The flaw with such programs is that most of the recipients were planning to stay in uniform anyway.

By addressing its quantity problem—not enough captains—the Army's cure had a side effect in terms of exacerbating its quality problem. It suspended forced distribution ratings for lieutenants and captains in 2004 because by identifying its weakest young officers, it would risk losing them. But by keeping them, and in a sense hiding them from future commanders and themselves, the effect on peer officers was lower morale and thus retention of the best and brightest. Wardynski warned: "By promoting and advancing officers who previously would have been culled from the service, however, the Army only accelerated talent flight."[31] Despite the governing federal legislation known as DOPMA (Defense Officer Personnel Management Act), which in theory constrains the percentage of promotions (80 percent to major, 70 percent to lieutenant colonel, and 50 percent to colonel), all four branches were over-promoting during the last decade. The Air Force promoted 90 percent of its officers to major, the Army promoted 94 percent, the Marines 87 percent, and the Navy promoted 84 percent to its equivalent rank of lieutenant commander.[32]

Fortunately, the Army instituted another program with a longer-term focus called OCSP, or the Officer Career Satisfaction Program. It was designed by economists and officers at the Office of Economic and Manpower Analysis at West Point, and in short allows graduating cadets from the academy and ROTC an opportunity to increase their branch-selection order in exchange for an additional three years of service. OCSP also gives cadets the option to add 3 years of service commitment in exchange for a post-of-choice or a guaranteed graduate school option. This cost the Army zero dollars, and has resulted in raising the 8-year retention rate from 47 percent to 69 percent, an addition of nearly 18,000 motivated man-years from its application to the classes of 2006–2009. Analysts from the Office of Economic and Manpower Analysis (OEMA) recognized that the most sensitive decision point for a junior officer is at the 5-year point. If junior officers can be encouraged to stay at least 8 or 9 years, then the likelihood of their serving a full 20-year career is much higher. To be sure, using economically inspired incentives was controversial, but we now know that they worked.

Losing Security

Doug Webster is a senior executive at Cisco. In the spring of 1991, he was a college senior on Yale's track team and one of the few Ivy League members of ROTC. After graduation, most of his classmates would head to Wall Street or graduate school, but Webster was waiting for his orders from the Air Force. And waiting. And still waiting. To the Air Force, Webster was at the bottom of the totem pole. The Cold War had just ended, and the Air Force had more people than it could use. So as graduation came and went, the US Air Force's Military Personnel Command (MPC, now renamed Air Force Personnel Command, or AFPC) told Webster that his orders were to wait for a few months until they found him a job. He still owed his four years, but they wouldn't let him start.

So Webster did what any enterprising Yale track star with academic honors would do: He took a temp job selling men's clothing at a department store for the summer as he waited to be called for active duty. And then the fall. And then the winter. Eventually, 51 weeks after waiting, just one week shy of authorized limit, the Air Force commissioned Webster and sent him to Goodfellow Air Force Base in Texas for back-to-back programs in military intelligence. Within four years, Lieutenant Webster was lauded as the top intelligence collector of 1994 in the military by the CIA at its Langley headquarters. By then it was the spring of 1995, and Webster realized he wanted more challenges than the military was going to let him have. The Cold War drawdown and subsequent force-shaping, conducted using cash incentives for early retirement that many of the most impressive senior officers were taking, on top of a narrow career path made the Air Force look increasingly less interesting. It wasn't hard for Webster to decide that he wanted out, too.[33]

In the early 1990s, computer security was in its infancy. Each branch of the military was wrestling with the issue: How can we protect our secrets from foreign hackers? The new technology was beyond the expertise of senior and midlevel officers, so junior officers fresh from ROTC programs at engineering schools were tasked with developing solutions. One of Webster's friends at Yale was another Air Force lieutenant, named Scott Waddell, a computer programmer who was assigned to the nascent US Air Force Information Warfare Center. After building a program that worked wonders for the Air Force, the Navy, the Army, and a handful of other government agencies started adopting the technology. But Waddell and his team were constrained. They were only captains and NCOs, non-pilots besides, in a service that was a virtual caste system. It didn't take long for them to realize that they could build an even better technology and deploy it more widely in a private start-up company. And that's how Wheelgroup was born.

Wheelgroup is an exodus case study. In 1995, 10 individuals cofounded the firm. All of them were recently minted veterans. They built a new technology from scratch, free of the architecture that the military regulations had imposed, and called it NetRanger, one of the first intrusion-detection software products that are now known as "firewalls."

Within two years they were on the cover of *Fortune* magazine. A year later, Cisco decided to augment its internet security business from scratch, and it knew it needed to acquire the best young firm. Naturally, it tapped Wheelgroup. So in less than 36 months, the founders went from making $4,000 a month to making a $124-million-dollar merger with arguably the internet's most important company. Not bad.

Some might contend that security technology is better developed in the private sector, that the Pentagon is better suited to buying its technology from the free market, just like it buys its fighter jets from Boeing and General Dynamics. But that's a dodge. The question is why the Air Force couldn't promote its Wheelgroup team members to lieutenant colonels to develop this technology inside the organization? For a few million dollars a year of flexible treatment, who knows what it could have achieved?

More Questions Than Answers

To be fair, the military is not the only organization that loses good people. Even the best private-sector firms lose good people, and the more famous they are for producing leaders—say, General Electric or Procter & Gamble—the more likely their best managers are to be headhunted away. But here's the difference: Once the military lets an officer out, it can never get him or her back in. By law. Senior officers can only be promoted from within. If IBM had been run that way, it could have never hired Lou Gerstner.

The larger question is why the Army does not allow itself to promote talent early, to pay specialized talent appropriately, and to match talent with jobs effectively. Why not make Dick Hewitt a colonel at 15 years of service? Why not pay officers with cyberwarfare talents a massive skills bonus? Why not loosen the organizational reins a bit and give the "volunteers" more control of their own careers? Why not let officers take sabbaticals into the "real world" the way other professions do? In short, what is the rationale for the system?

NOTES

1. Thom Shanker, "Young Officers Leaving Army at a High Rate," *New York Times*, April 10, 2006, http://www.nytimes.com/2006/04/10/washington/10army.html.
2. Casey Wardynski, David S. Lyle, and Michael J. Colarusso, "Towards a U.S. Army Officer Corps Strategy for Success: Retaining Talent," The Official Homepage of The United States Army, January 28, 2010, http://www.army.mil/article/33628/.
3. Andrew Tilghman, "The Army's Other Crisis: Why the Best and Brightest Young Officers Are Leaving," *Washington Monthly*, December 2007, http://www.washingtonmonthly.com/features/2007/0712.tilghman.html.
4. Wayne Grigsby, personal interview with the author, February 2010.
5. Tom Vanden Brook, "Officer Shortage Looming in the Army," *USA Today*, March 12, 2007, http://www.usatoday.com/news/washington/2007–03-12-officer-shortage_N.htm.
6. Wardynski, Lyle, and Colarusso, "Towards a U.S. Army Officer."
7. Wardynski, Lyle, and Colarusso, "Towards a U.S. Army Officer."
8. United States Government Accountability Office, "Military Personnel: Strategic Plan Needed to Address Army's Emerging Officer Accession and Retention Challenges," Report to the Committee on Armed Services, House of Representative, January 2007.
9. Tilghman, "The Army's Other Crisis."
10. Jeff Peterson, interview with the author, Spring 2010.
11. James R. Hosek and Beth J. Asch, "Changing Air Force Compensation: A Consideration of Some Options," in the 9th Quadrennial Review of Military Compensation, 2002, http://prhome.defense.gov/rfm/mpp/qrmc/Vol4/v4c4.pdf.
12. Wardynski, Lyle, and Colarusso, "Towards a U.S. Army Officer," 11.
13. According Arthur Coumbe: "Officer attrition is a problem that has intermittently afflicted the Officer Corps since the conclusion of World War II. Over this period, the Army has frequently struggled to retain not only the requisite number of officers but 'talented' officers as well. The retention of junior officers has posed a particularly difficult challenge." See Arthur T. Coumbe, *Army Officer Development: Historical Context* (Carlisle, PA: Strategic Studies Institute, April 2010).
14. David McCormick describes poorly executed demobilizations after World War II, Korea, and Vietnam in his book about the post–Cold War "downsizing [that] has compromised the army's institutional health." He writes: "The quality of the officer corps in each case suffered as the army lost some its brightest young officers." *The Downsized Warrior: America's Army in Transition* (New York: NYU Press, 2008), 7.
15. Coumbe, *Army Officer Development*.
16. James Hosek, "Deployment, Stress, and Intention to Stay in the Military" (Santa Monica, CA: RAND Corporation, 2006), http://www.rand.org/content/dam/rand/pubs/research_briefs/2006/ RAND_RB9150.pdf.
17. The full results of the survey were published in a paper on the Social Science Research Network (SSRN) and are abridged in [the original] volume's appendix. Note that in most cases, percentages are reported as whole numbers, which may not total 100 percent because of rounding. Percentages for each result are calculated based on the number of responses to

individual questions. See Tim J. Kane, "The Entrepreneurial Army: A Survey of West Point Graduates," Social Science Research Network, January 4, 2011, http://papers.ssrn.com/sol3/papers.cfm?abstract_id=1734594.

18. "Why Our Best Officers Are Leaving," *Small Wars Journal Blog*, January 5, 2011, https://smallwarsjournal.com/blog/why-our-best-officers-are-leaving.

19. UltimaRatioReg, "Why Our Best Officers Are Leaving?" *US Naval Institute Blog*, January 7, 2011, http://blog.usni.org/2011/01/07/why-our-best-officers-are-leaving/.

20. See Eric Tegler, "The Officer Market," February 25, 2011, http:// www.defensemedianetwork.com/stories/the-officer-market/.

21. A related statistic that Fowler's textbook spends much more time on is the response rate, which is the percentage of people who actually respond to one's survey request. If I ask 100 people a question, and only 10 answer, are the results valid? On the other hand, one could inflate the response rate by taking a survey of 3 people, getting 3 responses, and declaring a perfect rate. My sample frame was a list of roughly 3,100 individual email addresses. I do not know how many of those received, opened, and read the email, but let's assume all of them did. This yields a response rate of just under 8 percent. In theory, a low response rate can yield biased results. But the relationship between response rate and actual survey error isn't linear. The potential for bias decreases exponentially with each extra respondent. Recent studies by Allyson Holbrook of the University of Illinois and her colleagues challenge the empirical effect of lower response rates. For example, a 2007 study of Holbrook's reviewed 81 national surveys with response rates varying from 5 to 54 percent, and reported that lower rate surveys were marginally less accurate. See Allyson Holbrook, Jon Krosnick, and Alison Pfent, "The Causes and Consequences of Response Rates in Surveys by the News Media and Government Contractor Survey Research Firms," in *Advances in Telephone Survey Methodology*, edited by James M. Lepkowski, N. Clyde Tucker, J. Michael Brick, Edith D. De Leeuw, Lilli Japec, Paul J. Lavrakas, Michael W. Link, and Roberta L. Sangster (New York: Wiley, 2007). Following numerous such studies, the American Association for Public Opinion Research (AAPOR) stated that response rates "do not necessarily differentiate reliably between accurate and inaccurate data." See "Response Rate—An Overview," http://www.aapor.org/Response_Rates_An_Overview1.htm (accessed January 23, 2012).

Perhaps the 8-percent respondent sample in my survey included a large number of disgruntled ex-officers with an axe to grind? That's possible. This is especially possible given that the survey was voluntary. However, I took the precaution of using neutral language in the solicitation message that invited participants to the survey. Also, the demographics of the respondents matched the larger population, particularly the fact that the proportion of active-duty respondents was one-third of the sample, which is higher than if we had just randomly selected graduates or even the larger officer population.

22. Charles Levinson, "As War Grows Longer, Troops' Patience Is Shorter," *Christian Science Monitor*, May 2006, reprinted at http://seattletimes.nwsource.com/html/ nationworld/2002898832_troops30.html.

23. Regarding the survey statistics: "Approximately 22,500 Army leaders participated, with a response rate of 16.1%. This participation provides an overall sampling error of approximately +/- 0.6%. Essentially, this means that 95 times out of 100 the percentage reported will be within 1% of the true percentage (of perceptions)."

24. Sayce Falk and Sasha Rogers, "Junior Military Officer Retention: Challenges & Opportunities," Policy Analysis Exercise, John F. Kennedy School of Government, Harvard University, March 2011.

25. Falk and Rogers, "Junior Military Officer Retention," 15.

26. Falk and Rogers, "Junior Military Officer Retention," 27; emphasis in the original.

27. Falk and Rogers, "Junior Military Officer Retention," 4.

28. Falk and Rogers, "Junior Military Officer Retention," 4.

29. Falk and Rogers, "Junior Military Officer Retention," 4.

30. Wardynski, Lyle, and Colarusso, "Towards a U.S. Army Officer."

31. Wardynski, Lyle, and Colarusso, "Towards a U.S. Army Officer."

32. See Jim Tice, "Army Scaling Back Officer Promotion Rates," *ArmyTimes*, January 23, 2012, http://www.armytimes.com/news/2012/01/army-scaling-back-officer-promotion-013012w/ and various GAO studies, notably "Strategic Plan Needed to Address Army's Emerging Officer Accession and Retention Challenges," GAO-07–224, January 19, 2007, http://www.gao.gov/new.items/d07224.pdf.

33. Doug Webster, personal interview with the author, Summer 2011.

Rediscovering the Art of Strategic Thinking
Developing 21st-Century Strategic Leaders

DANIEL H. MCCAULEY

At a time when global instability and uncertainty are undeniable, the demand for astute American global strategic leadership is greater than ever. Unfortunately, tactical superficiality and parochial policies of convenience are undermining joint strategic leader development and the ability to operate effectively around the world.[1] Tactical supremacy and the lack of a peer competitor have contributed to strategic thinking becoming a lost art. This critical shortfall has been recognized for a number of years. General Anthony Zinni, USMC (Ret), and Tony Koltz stated in their 2009 book, *Leading the Charge*, that leaders today have no vision and consequently have "lost the ability to look and plan ahead."[2] Trapped within rigid bureaucracies, today's joint strategic leaders immerse themselves in current operations, reacting to, rather than shaping, future events.

This strategic leadership shortfall is not unique to the military establishment. A 2014 leadership study conducted by the Palladium Group surveyed more than 1,200 companies in 74 countries. In this study, although more than 96 percent of the "respondents identified strategic leadership as an organizational 'must-have' and a key to future success," over 50 percent of the respondents "stated that the quality of their organization's strategic leadership was unsatisfactory."[3] Fully two-thirds of the respondents serving in an organizational capacity as board member, chief executive officer, or managing director "did not believe that their current leadership development approach was providing the necessary skills to successfully execute their strategy."[4]

Obviously, there is a recognized strategic leadership gap across multiple disciplines, but how to remedy that shortfall has eluded both trainers and educators. The only certainty is that strategic leader development remains entrenched within the same development processes that are falling well short of the desired outcome. In an attempt to change this legacy thinking, General Martin Dempsey, USA, during his last 2 years as Chairman of the Joint Chiefs, issued white papers on mission command, the profession of arms, and joint education, as well as a memorandum on desired leader attributes. Each of these documents highlighted this shortfall in strategic leadership in some form.[5] The then-Chairman's direction, however, failed to change the approach to leader development in any meaningful way. Instead of designing a strategic leadership program to meet the demands of the 21st century, the military community continues to embrace the outdated practices of the past.

To rediscover the art of strategic thinking and planning, joint strategic leader development must disconnect itself from the paradigm of the past in which outcomes are known, risk is certain and manageable, and linear thinking is the norm. In its place, a developmental paradigm that embraces the discomforts of ambiguity, uncertainty, and complexity must be adopted. Modifying the training adage that the joint force must train the way it will fight, joint strategic leader development must reflect the realities of the global environment within which strategic decision-making occurs. Specifically, the joint force must develop strategic thinking competencies that will prepare strategic leaders for the ambiguities, uncertainties, and complexities of the 21st-century global security environment.

Strategic Leadership

Why are the Chairman and so many others focused on leadership? There are a number of reasons. First, local and regional trends, which were once somewhat isolated and constant, are interacting with global trends to accelerate rates of change. This increased acceleration leaves little decision-making time for cumbersome bureaucracies; rather, the environment demands timely strategic decisions at the field level. Second, the accelerated rates of change in local, regional, and global environments have increased uncertainty at all levels, paralyzing decision-makers looking for risk-free strategies or plans. Third, as the world appears to grow smaller due to advanced communications and transportation systems, complexity actually increases because of the expanded numbers of stakeholders in today's interconnected global systems. Fourth, global interdependencies—economic, social, religious, and military, among others—demand that local or regional issues be viewed in a depth and breadth not previously undertaken.[6] Joint strategic leaders are reluctant to embrace security issues in their broader context even when the interrelated global security environment requires a long-term approach to do so.

Daniel H. McCauley, "Rediscovering the Art of Strategic Thinking," *Joint Force Quarterly* 81 (April 2016): 26–33.

Finally, in a review of the lessons learned over the past 13 years of war, various organizations and studies assessed strategic thinking and strategic leadership as lacking during national strategic decision-making.[7]

These five reasons demand that joint officers develop a level of understanding not previously required from a national security perspective or demanded of them individually. This newly required depth and breadth of understanding entail the development of a perspective that encompasses longer periods of time—not only the present and near future, but also the distant past as well as the distant future. By drawing on an understanding of the past, joint strategic leaders can build a realistic vision that pulls joint organizations through the challenges of the present while positioning the nation for future success. Without a vision of the future, the joint force is at a distinct disadvantage, as it will be caught unaware of developing trends, policies, and potential adversaries.

Strategic leader responsibilities generally encompass multiple organizations and echelons diverse in missions and responsibilities.[8] The interdependencies and interactions of the global environment have cre-

ated a skills mismatch for joint strategic leaders over the past few decades. The current challenge is how to address the multitude of global challenges, given the limited range of individual and staff expertise and experiences. Considering figure 1, one can get a sense of the skill requirements necessary in the industrial age. Generally, the degree of certainty of any given issue and the degree of agreement among experts for a solution (as indicated by the x and y axes) were fairly high. As such, knowledge—usually in the form of domain-specific experts—was foundational in developing an understanding of the issue. In most cases, both the tasks and the environment were familiar; thus, the need for different thinking methodologies (meta-knowledge) and cultural understanding (humanistic knowledge) was relatively small in comparison to foundational knowledge. If a problem was encountered, an expert was called in to "solve" it.[9]

Figure 2 illustrates the transposition of skills needed in the information age. Again, generally speaking, the strategic operating environment has expanded to include regions in which the United States has little or no expertise, with tasks becoming increasingly unfamiliar.

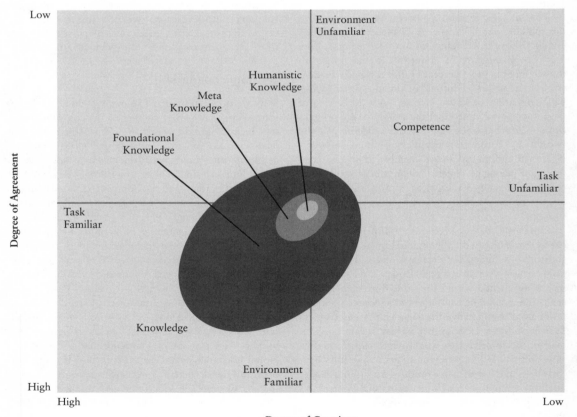

Figure 1. **Industrial Age Skills**

As the degrees of certainty and expert agreement have decreased, the need for domain-specific foundational knowledge has significantly diminished. In the information age, meta- and humanistic knowledge come to the fore as the need to address the dynamics of integrated domains and multiple cultural perspectives increases. Specific foundational knowledge is decreased proportionally because collaborative approaches can potentially develop multiple solutions needed to address the complexities of integrated security domains.

Joint Leadership

Given the skills required of strategic leaders in the information age, it is necessary to undertake a short review of Service and joint leadership development and doctrine to identify the current strategic leadership shortfall. As expected, the Services do an excellent job describing leadership at multiple command levels. For example, Army Doctrine Publication 6-22, *Army Leadership*,[10] and the Air Force's Core Doctrine, Vol. II, *Leadership*,[11] provide definitions, purpose, competencies, and attributes required by leaders for conducting

warfighting. Service leadership clearly formed the bedrock of American tactical and operational successes for many decades.

In his white paper titled *America's Military: A Profession of Arms*, General Dempsey further amplified this symbiosis between battlefield success and leadership, stating that the foundation of the military profession is leadership.[12] Unfortunately, unlike the focus the Services place on leadership, the joint community falls short. In lieu of leadership, joint doctrine relies on operational concepts, functions, and processes. For example, Joint Publication (JP) 1, *Doctrine for the Armed Forces of the United States*, does a very good job describing command and control within joint organizations.[13] However, it fails to describe the leadership differences that emerge as leadership and decision-making transition from the joint task force (JTF) or component level to the combatant command, Joint Staff, and interagency levels. JP 1 does provide a short description of the profession of arms, listing character traits, competencies, and values, but these are relegated to an appendix not quite two-and-a-half pages in length.[14]

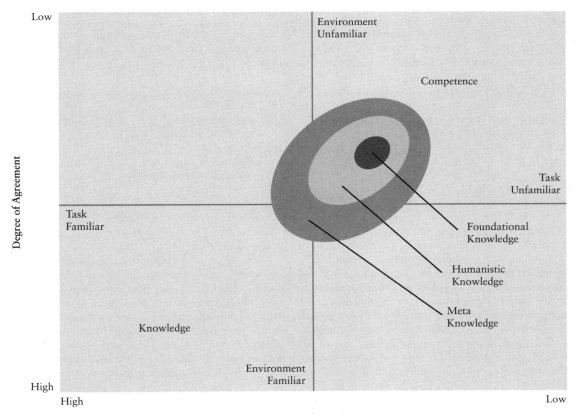

Figure 2. Information Age Skills

Recognizing this shortfall in joint doctrine and leader development, General Dempsey provided new guidance for the joint community based on a review of the past 13 years of war. In 2013, he laid out six desired attributes for leaders in a memorandum for Service chiefs, combatant commanders, the National Guard bureau chief, and the directors of the Joint Staff. These attributes assist the joint force in developing "agile and adaptive leaders with the requisite values, strategic vision, and critical thinking skills to keep pace with the changing strategic environment."[15] Coupled with the character, values, and competencies listed in JP 1, a leadership framework begins to emerge.[16]

Examining this framework, two issues become readily evident. First, the definition of joint leadership is missing. Second, the competencies as described in joint doctrine focus primarily on the tactical and low operational levels of war and fail to address strategic leadership in any form. Unfortunately, each of these missing pieces reinforces a tactical perspective of leadership at all echelons. Joint doctrine appears to assume that Service leadership development is adequate for strategic leadership despite recent evidence to the contrary.

As General Dempsey and others have noted, the required leadership skills can vary broadly depending on the level of operations. For example, most joint officers are familiar with their Services' roles and missions, having spent the majority of their careers in the tactical environment. This familiarity generally includes the types of organizations (for example, JTFs and components) and processes (for example, troop-leading procedures and the air-tasking cycle). At this level, complexity is limited because most interaction is at the individual or small group level, with decision-making measured in seconds, minutes, hours, or a few days.

The operational level of leadership expands complexity to include multiple organizations and the proliferation of the number and types of processes and products used. Reflecting this increased complexity, combatant commands operate at a different speed of decision-making to incorporate increased stakeholder views and desires. Combatant command regional and functional strategies and plans are complicated further by the needs of the individuals and organizations at the tactical level. The strategic level of leadership expands complexity to include the defense enterprise decision-makers, such as the Secretary of Defense and Chairman. At this level, specific processes reduce in number, but the numbers of stakeholders, including allies and partners, increase across a broader range of domains, such as the economic and domestic domains. Decision-making can lengthen to months, years, or even decades. Finally, at the national strategic level, decision-makers such as the President must deal with global complexity that involves decisions spanning the time range of each of the lower levels—seconds, days, months, and years.

Wherever one resides in an organization—whether at the tactical, operational, or strategic level, or some level in between—different leadership paradigms exist. To meet strategic leadership demands, the joint community must develop strategic thinking competencies. Strategic thinking is a cognitive process used to design and sustain an organization's competitive advantage.[17] It is a holistic method that leverages hindsight, insight, and foresight, and precedes strategy or plan development. Strategic thinking relies on an intuitive, visual, and creative process that explores the global security environment to synthesize emerging patterns, issues, connections, and opportunities.[18] Developing strategic thinking skills or competencies fills the strategic leadership shortfall while incorporating the desired leadership attributes identified by General Dempsey. Joint leader development thus becomes the vehicle that transitions the outdated military educational paradigm of the industrial age into one that serves the realities of the current information-age environment.

Strategic Thinking Competencies

To reacquire the lost art of strategic thinking, seven competencies have emerged as vital for strategic leaders:

- critical thinking
- creative thinking
- contextual thinking
- conceptual thinking
- cultural thinking
- collaborative thinking
- communicative thinking.[19]

Cultivating these strategic thinking competencies can provide current and future strategic leaders with the skills necessary to develop and execute strategies and plans successfully.

The first competency, critical thinking, provides joint strategic leaders with a depth and breadth of understanding that leverage hindsight, insight, and foresight. Insight represents the ability to analyze a thing and break it apart to see how its individual components are related and work together. By breaking a thing down into its component parts, elements and relationships not usually visible or understood are exposed. To gain an appreciation of a system's current state, the past, including the environmental dynamics responsible for system creation, must be understood. The continued interplay of these dynamics provides additional system insights and aids in the development of foresight. Trend extrapolation provides strategic leaders with a temporal bridge between the past and present to the future. This extrapolation of both environmental change and constants aids joint strategic leaders in developing an understanding of what may lie ahead and in anticipating future events and subsequent plan development.[20] Understanding the possible, plausible, and probable futures of a system aids strategic leaders in shaping the current conditions into those that are more preferable.

When applying critical thinking to the global security environment, the sheer volume of information and potential actors is overwhelming. Two key tools of critical thinking that facilitate joint strategic leader understanding and enhance their organizational principles are systems thinking and visual thinking. *Systems thinking* is an approach that promotes understanding of events and behavior through the identification and understanding of underlying structures.[21] Viewed as systems, these structures are an organized set of elements interconnected in a way that achieves the stated purpose. Systems, therefore, have three components: elements, relationships, and purpose. System elements can be either tangible or intangible, although tangible elements are naturally more readily identifiable. System relationships or interconnections hold the elements together and represent the physical flow governing a system's processes. A system's purpose is not easily discerned because the formal stated function is often different from its actual purpose. So the best way to deduce the system's purpose is to observe it for a while.[22]

Visual thinking engages the unconscious mind[23] and is vital in problem-solving and modeling systems, especially ill-structured problems.[24] Visual thinking al-

lows for the processing of enormous amounts of information across multiple dimensions,[25] adds clarity to communication, more fully engages group members, and enhances memory.[26] Visual thinking assists joint strategic leaders by increasing their ability to recognize patterns and similarities and to see formal and informal relationships.

An example of critical thinking that leverages systems and visual thinking is the international security challenge the United States faces with Iran. Critical thinking requires the strategic leader to undertake a historical analysis of the two countries to develop an understanding of the current grievances between them. A systems map, leveraging visual thinking, helps to illustrate the current US national security system and how Iran is undermining it (figure 3). National security interests and the intensity of those interests, along with key leverage elements, could be identified using a systems map. In addition, possible strategies or approaches to limiting Iranian influence are more easily identified, together with the associated first-, second-, and third-order effects. Systems and visual thinking enhance joint strategic leader critical thinking by portraying system complexity and interrelationships in ways that simple narratives or discussion cannot.

Solving globally complex security problems is the raison d'état of joint strategic leaders; unfortunately, finding enduring solutions is frustratingly elusive. Why is that? Typically, the same assumptions that created the problem continue to frame any potential approaches to solving it. As assumptions are the personal or organizational perceptual bedrock used to develop and sustain views of reality, the second strategic thinking

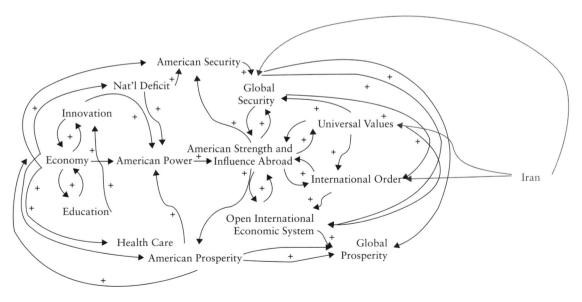

Figure 3. **Critical Thinking**

competency, creative thinking, is needed to overcome this flawed perception. Creative thinking forces joint strategic leaders to challenge underlying assumptions, look for system patterns, view relationships and actors in new ways, take more risks, and leverage opportunities. Creative thinking uses the critical thinking tools of systems thinking and visual thinking to expose preexisting paradigms and develop new paradigms for developing and integrating new perspectives. Joint strategic leaders who can represent problems in as many ways as possible will ultimately achieve higher rates of success.

Systems and visual thinking tools enable joint strategic leaders to develop different perspectives of an opposing system. For example, creating a depiction of the Iranian sociopolitical system might provide the strategic leader with new insights into why current policies or operations are not creating the desired results. Systems and visualization tools are particularly effective for gaining insights into complex, adaptive systems (figure 4). Creative thinking leverages primarily critical and collaborative thinking.

The third strategic thinking competency is contextual thinking. Contextual thinking leverages the skilled judgment of the joint strategic leader by analyzing an environmental fact or situation as an individual part of a complex continuum rather than the outcome of a specific cause or influence. Contextual thinking assists strategic leaders in the development of a better understanding of the nature of social interactions and the effects on cognitive processing. In complex problems, when context is missing, meaning is lost. In the global strategic security environment, the multiple solutions, methods, criteria, and perspectives surrounding the ill-structuredness of the security issue must be conveyed, not eliminated. Joint strategic leaders must then learn to sift through layers of context to identify those that are most relevant and important when solving problems.[27]

For example, in a typical military context, there is often a failure to differentiate between the strategic, operational, and tactical levels of war when discussing an issue. As we know, stakeholders and problems change depending on perspective. There are a number of questions that can be used to help frame context. What is the history of the issue? What was the strategic political and social context? Who were the actors? What was the central issue? What were the surrounding issues? Contextual thinking frames a point of com-

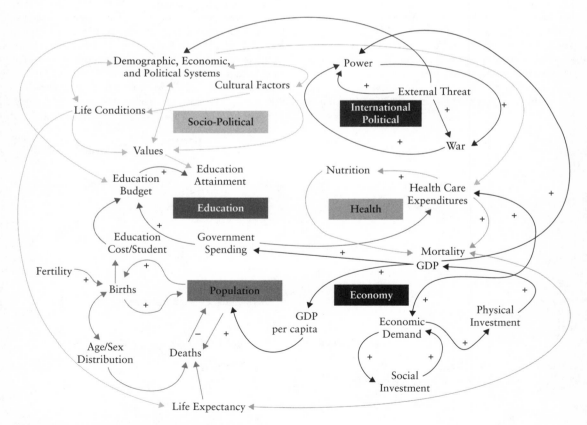

Figure 4. **Creative Thinking: Iranian Systems Map**

mon understanding for all stakeholders and participants. It leverages critical, creative, and conceptual thinking.

The fourth strategic thinking competency, conceptual thinking, is used by joint strategic leaders to understand a situation or problem by integrating issues and factors into a conceptual framework. Concepts, and the resulting maps, are the basis for human understanding and reasoning. Therefore, concepts are a form of knowledge structure that facilitates understanding.[28] Purposeful models help strategic leaders structure the exploration of a problem situation and are the most common means of initiating a comparison stage of problem-solving or understanding.[29]

When dealing with complex problems, conceptual thinking helps joint strategic leaders illustrate interrelationships, facilitating much-needed discourse. Complex systems must be conceptually simplified to make them understandable.[30] Conceptual thinking requires joint strategic leaders to be open to new ways of viewing the world, with a willingness to explore issues through alternative disciplines. Conceptual thinkers can effectively translate abstract thoughts to unfamiliar audiences. Conceptual thinking leverages critical, creative, contextual, and communicative thinking competencies.

The fifth strategic thinking competency is collaborative thinking, which creates synergy, improves performance, and motivates people to learn, develop, share, and adapt to changes. Collaborative thinking assists joint strategic leaders in developing synergy from stakeholders by openly sharing knowledge and experience, while acknowledging and affirming the same in others. Mutual sharing, respect, diversity, and equal participation that occur through high-order social learning, thinking, and communicating characterize collaborative groups.[31] Collaborative communication is the foundation of effective engagement, peak performance, and innovative outcomes; more importantly, it helps to develop and achieve common goals across national and institutional boundaries.

In today's global security environment, the joint force cannot claim expertise across the globe. Rather, joint strategic leaders must integrate stakeholders' deep understanding of their environments to find a heightened level of perception and new ways to think about issues. Collaborative thinking directly enhances critical and creative thinking and is influenced by cultural and communicative thinking competencies.

Cultural thinking, the sixth strategic thinking competency, is used to understand the interconnected world, incongruence of national borders, and synthesis of perspectives across a broad spectrum of cultures. Cultural thinking enables joint strategic leaders to understand a wider range of views and the beliefs, norms, values, and rituals associated with the global security environment. Enabled by information technology, the post–Cold War security environment collapsed into an intrinsically connected economic, cultural, and security global village. This interconnected world requires joint strategic leaders to understand that today's security environment is not only multipolar but also exhibits characteristics of cross-pollinated perspectives, ideologies, goals, and capabilities.

Within this global village, the costs of individual action have been intensified, with potentially substantial implications for the international security community. This new security reality has created a different ideological context that calls for international security responsibilities that go beyond individuals and nation-states.[32] Joint strategic leaders regularly face tough ethical challenges because of various cultural factors. The greater the complexity of the environment within which the joint force is operating, the greater potential there is for ethical problems or misunderstandings to exist. As joint strategic leaders become ethically attuned, they must learn to view the world through a variety of lenses, developing a personal sense of right and wrong, and to interpret the influences that affect individual and group behavior.[33] Cultural thinking leverages critical, collaborative, and communicative thinking.

The last strategic thinking competency is communicative thinking. Communicative thinking is used by joint strategic leaders to understand the various means and modes of communicating, as well as the challenges associated with communicating complex issues among individuals, organizations, societies, cultures, and nations. A strategic leader must be able to build a desired, shared vision for the organization and communicate that vision internally and externally to various audiences. Joint strategic leaders must conceptualize complex issues and processes, simplify them, and inspire people around them. In today's multicultural world, strategic leaders must be able to communicate across cultures as easily as they can communicate internally.

Joint strategic leaders must understand the cultural nuances of communication and be capable of communicating using multiple modes and methods, including blogs, tweets, written and oral reports, videos, storyboards, PowerPoint presentations, and formal and informal sessions. They must also be aware that communication occurs continuously and that it can occur nonverbally and through inactivity. Joint strategic leaders must understand that communication is a filtered, continuous, and active process and cannot be undone.[34] Communicative thinking leverages critical, collaborative, and cultural thinking competencies.

Recommendations and Conclusion

In the slower moving world of the industrial age, joint strategic leaders could plod their way through familiar tasks and concepts, developing solutions to a level of certainty most experts could agree on. In the fast-moving interconnected global security environment of today, however, strategic leaders do not have the luxury of time, task familiarity, or certainty. As a result, strategic leader competencies are needed more than ever. The difference between strategic leadership and "regular" leadership is that a strategic leader's responsibilities are far broader and deeper in scope. These responsibilities typically cross not only functions and domains, but also often encompass multiple organizations that have diverse roles and responsibilities.

As officers transition from the tactical to the operational to the strategic level, new skills and competencies are needed, and that is where strategic leadership comes into play. With unmatched tactical and operational skills, US joint doctrine should not be changed to deemphasize this critical operational leadership focus. Rather, doctrine must be expanded to include strategic leadership to address the competencies needed for strategy and policy development. Given this understanding of the leadership environment, and lacking a current joint definition of *strategic leadership*, the following definition is proposed:

> The interactive process of leveraging unique stakeholder capabilities in the pursuit of common and enduring national, partner, and alliance security needs by identifying and communicating the goals and objectives of cooperative and willing stakeholders, and influencing their attainment.

As Zinni and Koltz state in their book, the joint force needs officers who possess the requisite strategic thinking competencies demanded by both the current and the future global security environments.[35] Current joint doctrine focuses on the low operational and tactical levels of war, and is insufficient for the development of joint strategic leaders.

Joint officer development must change the paradigm of the past 50 years or so to acknowledge the new skills required as the world continues the transition from the industrial age to the information age. As the chairman and others have identified, strategic leadership is a necessity for operating in the 21st-century security environment. This framework provides an approach to fill the leadership development shortfall in joint officer development, education, and doctrine.

NOTES

1. Jason Katz, "America's Lack of Leadership Is Feeding Global Instability," *Congress Blog*, September 18, 2014, available at <http:// thehill.com/blogs/congress-blog/foreign-policy /217930-americas-lack-of-leadership-is-feeding-global-insta bility>.

2. Tony Zinni and Tony Koltz, *Leading the Charge: Leadership Lessons from the Battlefield to the Boardroom* (New York: Palgrave Macmillan, 2009), 28.

3. James Creelman et al., *2014 Global State of Strategy and Leadership Survey Report* (New York: Palladium Group, Inc., 2014), 8, 18.

4. Creelman, *2014 Global State*, 9.

5. Martin E. Dempsey, *America's Military—A Profession of Arms*, White Paper (Washington, DC: The Joint Staff, 2012); *Mission Command*, White Paper (Washington, DC: The Joint Staff, 2012); *Joint Education*, White Paper (Washington, DC: The Joint Staff, 2012); *Desired Leader Attributes for Joint Force 2020*, Memorandum (Washington, DC: The Joint Staff, 2013).

6. Richard L. Hughes, Katherine M. Beatty, and David Dinwiddie, *Becoming a Strategic Leader: Your Role in Your Organization's Enduring Success*, 2nd ed. (San Francisco: Jossey-Bass, 2014), 11.

7. Linda Robinson et al., *Improving Strategic Competence: Lessons from Thirteen Years of War* (Santa Monica, CA: RAND, 2014), xi–xii.

8. Richard L. Hughes and Katherine L. Beatty, *Becoming a Strategic Leader: Your Role in Your Organization's Enduring Success*, 1st ed. (San Francisco: Jossey-Bass, 2005), 11.

9. Sarah W. Fraser and Trisha Greenhalgh, "Complexity Science: Coping with Complexity: Educating for Capability," *The British Medical Journal* 323 (2001): 799.

10. Army Doctrine Publication 6-22, *Army Leadership* (Fort Eustis, VA: Training and Doctrine Command, 2012).

11. Air Force Core Doctrine, Vol. II, *Leadership* (Maxwell Air Force Base, AL: USAF Doctrine Center, 2012).

12. Dempsey, *America's Military*, 1–6.

13. Joint Publication (JP) 1, *Doctrine for the Armed Forces of the United States* (Washington, DC: The Joint Staff, March 25, 2013), V-1–V-20.

14. JP 1, B-1–B-3.

15. Dempsey, *Desired Leader Attributes*, 1–2.

16. JP 1, B-1–B-3.

17. T. Irene Sanders, *Strategic Thinking and the New Science: Planning in the Midst of Chaos Complexity and Change* (New York: The Free Press, 1998), 162.

18. Hughes and Beatty, *Becoming a Strategic Leader*, 43–51.

19. Daniel H. McCauley, "An Institution for the Profession of Arms and Thought," *Campaigning*, Fall 2014, 7.

20. Edward Cornish, *Futuring: The Exploration of the Future* (Bethesda, MD: World Future Society, 2004), 1–8.

21. Peter M. Senge, *The Fifth Discipline: The Art and Practice of the Learning Organization* (New York: Doubleday, 1990), 6, 186.

22. Donella H. Meadows, *Thinking in Systems: A Primer* (White River Junction, VT: Sustainability Institute, 2008), 11–17.

23. Michel Marie Deza and Elena Deza, *Encyclopedia of Distances* (New York: Springer, 2009).

24. David H. Jonassen, *Learning to Solve Problems: An Instructional Design Guide* (New York: Routledge, 2011), 1–3.

25. Tony Buzan, *The Mindmap Book: How to Use Radiant Thinking to Maximize Your Brain's Untapped Potential* (London: Penguin Group, 1993).

26. Tom Wujec, "3 Ways the Brain Creates Meaning," TED Talk, February 2009, available at www.ted.com/talks/tom _wujec_on_3_ways_the_brain_creates_ meaning?language=en.

27. Jonassen, *Learning to Solve Problems*, 209.

28. Jonassen, *Learning to Solve Problems*, 210.

29. Peter Checkland, "Soft Systems Methodology: A Thirty-Year Retrospective," *Systems Research and Behavioral Science* 17, supplement 1 (November 2000), S11–S58.

30. Jonassen, *Learning to Solve Problems*, 29–31.

31. Timothy Stagich, *Collaborative Leadership and Global Transformation: Developing Collaborative Leaders and High Synergy Organizations* (Miami Beach: Global Leadership Resource, 2001), 1–18.

32. Elizabeth Filippouli, "Cultural Understanding and Global Thinking in Business," *Huffington Post*, March 6, 2014.

33. Robert Rosen et al., *Global Literacies: Lessons on Business Leadership and National Cultures* (New York: Simon & Schuster, 2000), 32–53.

34. Hughes, Beatty, and Dinwiddie, *Becoming a Strategic Leader*, 145–191.

35. Zinni and Koltz, *Leading the Charge*, 24–25.

Chapter 7

Resource Allocation and Force Structure for a Complex World

Quality over Quantity

US Military Strategy and Spending in the Trump Years

JAMES N. MILLER AND MICHAEL O'HANLON

Introduction

The Trump administration, with the bipartisan support of Congress, has achieved large increases in defense spending in recent years. The 2020 national defense budget of some $750 billion is much larger than the Cold War average of some $575 billion or President Obama's last budget of just over $600 billion.

Our view is that after two decades of war, a decade of budgetary irregularities in Washington, and nearly ten years of gradual decline in the military top line, there is no doubt that the Pentagon can make good use of these funds. Former Defense Secretary Jim Mattis's National Defense Strategy sensibly calls on the Department of Defense (DoD) to reinvigorate its capabilities vis-à-vis China and Russia, including addressing dangerous vulnerabilities in cyberspace and outer space, while still managing today's wars in the Middle East as well as the potential for a near-term crisis on the Korean Peninsula. That is a daunting set of tasks.

While we do not doubt that the Pentagon *can* make good use of a $750 billion national defense budget in 2020, we are very concerned *whether* it will do so. Each of the services continues to clamor for more force structure: more ships for the Navy, more tactical aircraft squadrons for the Air Force, and more troops for the Army. While growth in some key areas such as unmanned systems, cyber and space resilience, and precision-guided munitions is warranted, it makes no sense under a strategy focused on China and Russia to grow the force overall. The nation's fiscal plight, with a 2019 federal budget deficit approaching $1 trillion, reinforces the expectation, as evidenced in the Trump administration's own budget projections for 2021 and beyond, that real defense spending will not grow further and might well shrink. For that reason as well, tough choices are necessary.

We conclude in this essay that the central choice for policymakers and candidates running for election in 2020 is clear. Increased military spending largely serves three possible objectives: better modernization for the future, upgraded unit-by-unit readiness for today, and increased force size and structure. Of these, the last is the least important to the US military for the foreseeable future, and by draining away resources needed elsewhere, increasing force size is actually counterproductive. The focus should be on quality over quantity.

The US armed forces need to innovate and invest in breakthrough capabilities and to improve immediate readiness, but they can do so at their current overall size. Investing in modernization and readiness rather than growth, paired with more clever and efficient management of the military, can allow today's US military of roughly 1.3 million active-duty troops, just over 900,000 reservists, and almost 750,000 full-time civilians to do the job. By giving up most plans for expansion, the military services can ensure that modernization and readiness get the resources they crucially require.

Background: Is US Defense Spending High or Low?

First, some broad perspective is in order. Is American military spending today high or low? How one answers this question sets the political and budgetary context for more detailed debates over strategy, modernization, and force structure.

Today's US national defense budget is certainly large by some measures. It exceeds the Cold War average for the United States of about $575 billion as expressed in 2020 dollars. The US national defense budget, which does not include budgets for the Department of Veterans Affairs or the Department of Homeland Security (but does include Department of Energy nuclear weapons expenses as well as most intelligence accounts and war costs), constitutes nearly 40 percent of global military spending. The United States' allies and close friends account for another third or so of the global total, meaning that the Western alliance system wields the preponderance of global military resources even in the context of China's rise and Russia's revanchism.

Individual parts of the defense budget are reasonably healthy, too. Military compensation compares well with civilian jobs requiring comparable skills and experience across the preponderance of military specialties. Weapons procurement budgets exceed $100 billion a year; the so-called procurement holiday of the 1990s and early 2000s is definitively over. Research and development budgets in 2019 are also robust. Funds for training are proportionate to the size of the force, akin to Reagan-era levels as well in terms of flight hours, steaming days, major ground exercises, and the like.

The same is true of maintenance budgets. The problem with the latter accounts in recent years has been unpredictability and delay more than inadequate resources.

But at the same time, US defense spending is hardly huge or unaffordable. Relative to the size of the economy, it is down to about 3.5 percent of GDP, after having reached nearly 5 percent in the latter George W. Bush and early Obama years. During the Cold War, it varied roughly between 5 percent and 10 percent of GDP, by way of comparison. Also, today's US military is modest in size. Its 1.3 million active-duty uniformed personnel are far fewer than the Cold War force that exceeded 2 million during its latter decades. It is also smaller than China's and not much bigger than the Indian or North Korean militaries. In short, it is a reasonably expensive but affordable military that relies on sustaining a qualitative edge over adversaries to maintain its combat punch and to protect US interests across the globe.

US military spending may well be, as President Obama noted in his 2016 State of the Union address, roughly equal to the next eight highest-spending countries combined.[1] But defense budgets do not always dictate combat outcomes or ensure effective deterrence. Chinese precision missiles or Russian advanced air defenses, advanced submarines, cyberattacks, anti-satellite weapons, and other such capabilities—whether operated by Beijing and Moscow or sold to other parties—can cause asymmetric, disproportionate effects.[2] New technologies offer promise for US armed forces, but also new ways for adversaries to challenge or hurt the United States. As such, it is essential for DoD to have enough resources to pursue a qualitative military advantage over potential adversaries through a robust and well-directed modernization program.

So yes, US military spending is large. Indeed, it is now roughly three times that of China, the world's number-two military power—after having been nearly ten times as great at the turn of the twenty-first century. That may sound like a comfortable advantage. It is not, especially when the correct strategic goal for the United States military is not primarily to defeat China or Russia in combat but to deter China and Russia in the first place, by being able to deny the objectives of any aggression and impose unacceptable costs.

As a result of military modernization and reform efforts this century, China now possesses advanced weapons systems including the DF-21 and DF-26 anti-ship ballistic missiles with homing warheads, other precision-strike options that could be used against American and allied bases in the region, quiet submarines that could approach US Seventh Fleet ships undetected, and potent threats against American cyber, space, and communications systems that have previously provided the United States with unalloyed asymmetric advantages.[3] Russia, for its part, is in a position to move up to several hundred thousand forces within its own borders quickly, such that they could threaten NATO members Estonia, Latvia, and Lithuania—at a time when those three Baltic nations combined have aggregate military strength of just some 30,000, and when the United States plus other NATO allies have only about 5,000 troops in the general vicinity under normal peacetime conditions.[4]

One might ask why the United States should shoulder so much of the burden of deterring Russia and China. Shouldn't our allies do more? While some of the United States' allies have stepped up to the plate in terms of defense spending (for example, South Korea at about 2.4 percent in 2018, Australia and the United Kingdom at 2 percent, and France at 2.3 percent of GDP), many have not kept their military spending levels as high as they had promised, and they have not always spent their resources well. So, without a doubt, the United States must continue to press allies to spend more for their own defense. However, even if allied defense budgets rise, the reality is that there is no substitute for the skill and scale of the US military. Thus, the United States must take a lead role in deterring China and Russia from coercion or aggression.

Finally, one might ask, is DoD so wasteful that it could actually preserve or improve combat power with far fewer budgetary resources, if only they could audit their own expenses? While it is true that DoD is inefficient, much of the waste is marbled into muscle—difficult to excise without painstaking and patient work, lest major combat capabilities be damaged along the way. For example, the military health care enterprise is probably too large and expensive. But access to high-quality health care is a crucial military benefit that helps attract and retain such a high-quality all-volunteer force. And most proposals for health care reform would, once implemented, save at most a few billion dollars a year—important savings, yet modest relative to the overall size of the nation's military budget and defense needs.

Or take base closures. After five generally successful rounds of base closures and realignments since the late 1980s, the DoD still has 20 percent more infrastructure than its current force posture requires. More base closures are needed—at least one if not two more rounds. A future round will likely yield eventual savings of $2 billion to $3 billion a year, as did the first four rounds.[5] That's real money, but not huge money relative to a $700-billion-plus budget. Also, net savings would not accrue for half a decade, so like many defense reforms, base closures are more a question of smart long-term planning than a near-term budgetary fix.

The Mattis Agenda: "Sharpening the American Military's Competitive Edge" for Great-Power Competition

There is much to like about the overall direction that former Secretary of Defense Jim Mattis had taken and Secretary Mark Esper has since sustained at the Pentagon. Although we have often been critics of Trump administration foreign policy, there is a clarity and cogency to longer-term defense strategy, reflected most vividly in Mattis's National Defense Strategy of early 2018, entitled "Sharpening the American Military's Competitive Edge." That document prioritized great-power competition over the forever wars of the Middle East and South Asia. The shift toward focusing on China's rise, with economic and diplomatic as well as military tools, had begun in the Obama administration, with the so-called pivot or rebalance to Asia starting in 2011. The changes intensified after Russia's annexation of Crimea and aggression against eastern Ukraine in 2014, as well as the promulgation of a "third offset" modernization agenda. But Mattis brought even greater mission clarity—and more budgetary resources—to DoD. No one wants war with Russia or China. However, to prevent it, intensified efforts to shore up the United States' deterrence of these two powers, especially for possible crises or conflicts in Eastern Europe and the western Pacific region, are entirely warranted.

All that said, the Mattis revolution is incomplete at best, and now it appears to be imperiled by a recent shift in political and budgetary winds. President Trump increased the US national defense budget substantially in his first three years in office. But the 2020 national defense budget of $750 billion may well prove to be the peak level of the buildup. It is worth noting that former Secretary Mattis, former Joint Chiefs Chairman General Joseph Dunford, and most recently the independent congressionally mandated National Defense Strategy Commission had all advocated ongoing real growth of at least 3 percent a year into the indefinite future. Based on Trump administration budget projections and other political realities, they seem unlikely to get their wish.

The Democratic takeover of the House of Representatives, and the persistent presence of Tea Party Republicans in the Congress as well, do not augur well for large increases in defense spending. After all, a federal budget deficit approaching $1 trillion is a national security concern, too. There is a real threat to long-term economic power and thus national security when publicly held debt approaches the size of GDP, as will likely happen in the 2020s. Given the realities of US domestic politics, it is hard to believe that meaningful deficit reduction will happen without a broad sense of shared national sacrifice. Moreover, a boom-

and-bust approach to defense spending results in billions being wasted through inefficiency. Stable and predictable defense budgets help US taxpayers as well as the United States' global credibility.

The Mattis agenda could suffer serious harm and the nation could face growing risks if the defense budget is slashed. Yet never-ending real (inflation-adjusted) growth, while affordable, may be neither necessary nor sensible given the rising US debt. What to do?

The Path Ahead: Quality over Quantity, Modernization and Readiness over Force Size and Force Structure

Fortunately, there is a lodestar that Pentagon officials can refer to in order to guide their difficult work—and it is consistent, we believe, with Mattis's central priorities and with the nation's strategic needs. Put bluntly, the military should not grow significantly in size, as all of the services currently intend. Prioritization should instead be given to longer-term innovation and modernization, as well as unit-by-unit readiness, of the current force.

So far, if there has been one central flaw in much-needed boosts in defense spending, it is that rapidly increasing resources have allowed the Army, Air Force, Navy, Marine Corps, and defense agencies to have it all. The budgets of the services have not yet demonstrated the clarity and focus of Mattis's strategic vision. Desires for a larger force have been tacked onto more crucial matters of military innovation, as well as repairs to readiness after two decades of war and one decade of bipartisan budgetary dysfunction in Washington.

The Army now wants to grow its active-duty force from some 480,000 soldiers to at least 500,000 and perhaps 540,000. The Navy wants to increase the size of its fleet from some 285 ships to 355 (in fairness, that latter goal dates back to the latter Obama years). The Air Force came out with a plan in the fall of 2018 to increase its own force structure from 312 operational squadrons (of all types of aircraft combined, and including the Guard and Reserve) to 386.

To be sure, there are good reasons for the services to want larger forces. Our soldiers, sailors, marines, and airmen are often fatigued and stressed from extended deployments. And we have been asking a lot of their equipment as well. The two tragic Navy ship collisions of 2017, higher accident rates in recent training exercises, personnel shortages for military specialties such as pilots, and serious readiness challenges in certain categories of equipment such as Marine Corps helicopters have been the results.

The solution, however, is not a larger force, but a more consistently funded, more efficiently operated, and more modern one. For all of the military's problems, readiness is strained and not broken, and many of its fundamentals are sound.

In fact, many key elements of US military readiness today are often fairly good. Start with weaponry. Most equipment is in fairly good shape. For example, Army equipment on average has mission-capable rates today exceeding 90 percent, a historically high level. That said, some types of weapons, such as many aircraft, are aging fairly substantially. And maintenance schedules have been badly disrupted due to Washington's budgetary shenanigans.

Training was also disrupted by sequestration and continuing resolutions rather than proper budgets in recent years, as well as by wartime demands since 2001, but it is recovering.[6] The Army is again resourcing a sustainable level of training with brigade rotations to the national training centers (almost twenty such rotations a year, roughly the correct sustainable number for a total force of some sixty brigade combat teams). The Navy is also operating at a pace adequate to put crews and ships through major training cycles every two to three years now, depending on ship type. The Marine Corps is putting twelve infantry battalions a year through large training exercises, out of an overall number roughly twice that large in the whole force. And the Air Force is funding various components of its readiness programs at 80 to 98 percent of preferred resource levels.[7]

A third element of readiness, people, may be the most crucial of all. Today, recruiting and retention statistics are generally good, with the partial exception of recent trends in Army recruiting. Today's all-volunteer force is generally highly educated and experienced.[8] For example, typical scores of new recruits on the armed forces qualification test have improved considerably over time relative to the population at large. They are now significantly better than in the Reagan years or the immediate pre-9/11 period (two useful benchmarks for comparison). Mean time in service, a reflection of the experience of the force (albeit an imperfect gauge of overall quality), now averages about eighty months in the enlisted ranks. In other words, the typical enlisted soldier, sailor, marine, airman, or airwoman has been in uniform more than six years. That is not quite as good as in the 1990s when averages were eighty-five to ninety months, but better than the seventy-five-month period that typified the Reagan years or the lower figures of the 1970s.[9] To consider one service, albeit the one least affected by the wars of this century, Navy reenlistment rates have been about 25 percent higher over the last fifteen years than during the Reagan years (and almost twice as high as during the "hollow force" years of the late 1970s); attrition rates of those leaving the service before finishing a planned tour are also at historic lows.[10]

To the extent that there are problems, better management and care of the force can make a big differ-

ence. Congress needs to help by providing budgets on time and predictably, avoiding the twin scourges of sequestration and continuing resolutions that deliver resources too late and haphazardly.

And the military services, with support from civilian leadership, need to do things differently too. The Army is overworked partly because it maintains deployments of several thousand soldiers in South Korea and Poland through frequent rotations of multiple units, rather than permanent stationing of individual brigades in these locations (the Mexico border deployment of late adds to the strain). The Air Force could consider similar changes in how it maintains key units in parts of the Middle East. Several fighter squadrons could, for example, be based in Persian Gulf states rather than rotated through. The Navy still focuses too rigidly on maintaining a permanent presence in the broader Persian Gulf and western Pacific regions. More flexible and unpredictable deployments can ease strain on the force without giving adversaries any solace. The Navy can also consider crew swaps while ships remain at sea, rather than bringing crews and ships home from deployment together every six to eight months, as is now the norm.

So growing the military falls into the "nice to have, but not essential" category. We do not oppose it, so much as we argue that if something has to give, plans to increase the size of the military should be that something. Readiness should be fixed primarily by proper, timely resourcing of individual units, equipment maintenance schedules, and the like—as well as timely replacement of aging equipment.

That leads directly to the question of modernization. It is absolutely essential for today's and tomorrow's force. That is not because the US military is obsolescent. Rather, the pace of innovation in key areas of military technology and the way in which vulnerabilities in our existing military could be exploited by Russia or China require it. If we fail to make the US military more modern, resilient, lethal, and survivable, the perception could grow that relative American combat power is fading—or that the American military has developed systemic vulnerabilities that an enemy could exploit to produce catastrophic failure. Deterrence could weaken. War could result. And we could quite credibly even lose such a war.

The period of 2020–2040 seems likely to see even more change in the technologies and the character of warfare than have recent decades. For the period 2000–2020, revolutionary technological change probably occurred only in various aspects of computers and robotics. For the next two decades, those areas will remain fast-moving, and they will be joined by various breakthroughs in artificial intelligence and the use of big data. The battlefield implications in domains such as swarms of robotic systems usable as both sensors and weapons may truly come of age. In addition, progress in laser weapons, reusable rockets, hypersonic missiles, unmanned submarines, biological pathogens, and nanomaterials may wind up being made very fast. The sum total may or may not add up to a revolution. But the potential cannot be dismissed.[11]

The rise of China and the return of Russia supercharge the competition and raise the strategic stakes. The marriage of rapid technological progress with hegemonic change could prove especially potent. The return of great-power competition during an era of rapid progress in science and technology could reward innovators and expose vulnerabilities, much more than has been the case in the twenty-first century to date.

Some areas of military technology—most types of sensors, most types of major vehicles, most underlying technologies for nuclear and chemical weapons—seem unlikely to change dramatically. But perhaps even without such developments, a true military revolution of sorts will occur due to other advances in other technological domains. The key question, as always, will be how these technology trends interact synergistically with each other and how military organizations as well as political leaders innovate to employ them on the battlefield.

Not every modernization program is equally important, of course. Some should be rethought. The US tactical aircraft modernization agenda is a prime example. In fiscal year 2019, the Pentagon requested and Congress approved about $1.9 billion for additional F/A-18 aircraft—a venerable plane that would likely not survive long against either Chinese or Russian air defenses. With a defense strategy appropriately oriented toward China and Russia, it is very difficult to make the case for buying more non-stealthy "fourth-generation" aircraft such as the F/A-18. Additional questions relate to the balance between manned and unmanned systems and between relatively short-range fighters and longer-range bombers. All told, the United States should be shifting its resource priorities away from fourth-generation and toward fifth-generation fighters, and over time away from manned to unmanned aerial vehicles, as well as to longer-range systems. During the transition period, a portfolio of capabilities including upgrades to existing aircraft (not more fourth-generation aircraft), greater innovation and deployment of new unmanned aircraft of various ranges, more long-range stealth bombers, and fewer numbers of US F-35s than currently planned (and more sales to allies and partners, who are already "forward deployed") makes more sense.

There are other programs to reassess, and perhaps scale back or delay, in order to make room for more survivable systems—for example, reducing procurement of surface ships in favor of attack submarines and unmanned undersea vehicles for the Navy. On balance, in broad brush and in overall resource requirements, the Mattis agenda for modernization makes sense. It is important to prioritize and preserve it.

Conclusion

Today's already excellent American military is big enough to meet the reasonable requirements of ongoing commitments and great-power competition—provided, that is, that it improves further. It needs to repair readiness. Most of all, it must be modernized for greater lethality and made more resilient and survivable against the kinds of cyber, anti-satellite, and other asymmetric attacks future adversaries would be sure to employ.

We need to keep our eye focused clearly on the ball and our resource allocations focused clearly on the strategy. We need a more modern and ready force, not a larger one.

NOTES

1. Barack Obama, "Remarks of President Barack Obama—State of the Union Address As Delivered," Washington, DC, January 12, 2016), https://www.whitehouse.gov/the-press-office/2016/01/12/remarks-president-barack-obama-%E2%80%93-prepared-delivery-state-union-address.

2. Jennifer H. Svan, "USAFE Chief: Russian Air Defenses No. 1 Concern," *Stars and Stripes*, December 11, 2015, 2.

3. See, for example, Eric Heginbotham, Michael Nixon, Forrest E. Morgan, Jacob L. Heim, Jeff Hagen, Sheng Li, Jeffrey Engstrom, Martin C. Libicki, Paul DeLuca, David A. Shlapak, David R. Frelinger, Burgess Laird, Kyle Brady, and Lyle J. Morris, *The U.S.-China Military Scorecard* (Santa Monica, CA: RAND Corporation, 2015), https://www.rand.org/content/dam/rand/pubs/research_reports/RR300/RR392/RAND_RR392.pdf; "Annual Report to Congress: Military and Security Developments Involving the People's Republic of China 2018" (Washington, DC: Office of the Secretary of Defense, May 2018), https://media.defense.gov/2018/Aug/16/2001955282/-1/-1/1/2018-CHINA-MILITARY-POWER-REPORT.PDF.

4. General Sir Richard Shirreff, *War with Russia: An Urgent Warning from Senior Military Command* (New York: Quercus, 2016); David A. Shlapak and Michael Johnson, *Reinforcing Deterrent on NATO's Eastern Flank: Wargaming the Defense of the Baltics* (Santa Monica, CA: RAND Corporation, 2016), https://www.rand.org/pubs/research_reports/RR1253.html.

5. Statement of Robert F. Hale, under secretary of defense for financial management and comptroller, Brookings Institution, Washington, DC, January 7, 2013.

6. For an excellent and thorough discussion of this issue, see Robert F. Hale, "Budgetary Turmoil at the Department of Defense from 2010 to 2014: A Personal and Professional Journey," (Washington, DC: Brookings Institution, August 2015), http://www.brookings.edu/research/papers/2015/08/budget-turmoil-defense-department-hale.

7. "United States Department of Defense Fiscal Year 2016 Budget Request, Overview," (Washington, DC: Department of Defense, February 2015), 3-1–3-15, https://comptroller.defense.gov/Budget-Materials/Budget2016/. These figures were essentially unchanged in the FY 2017 budget proposal.

8. For a similar view, though one also sharing our concerns about various challenges and problems, see Mackenzie Eaglen, *State of the U.S. Military: A Defense Primer* (Washington, DC: American Enterprise Institute, October 2015), 22–25,

https://www.aei.org/publication/state-of-the-us-military-a
-defense-primer. For a paper expressing some concerns about
trends in the academic aptitude of Marine Corps officers, however, see Matthew F. Cancian and Michael W. Klein, "Military
Officer Quality in the All-Volunteer Force" (Washington, DC:
Brookings Institution, July 2015), http://www.brookings.edu
/~/media/research/files/papers/2015/07/20-military-officer
-quality/military-officer-quality-in-the-all-volunteer-force.pdf.

9. "Population Representation in the Military Services,
2014" (Washington, DC: Department of Defense, 2014), https://
www.cna.org/pop-rep/2014/appendixd/d_08.html.

10. "Attrition and Reenlistment of First-Term Sailors"
(Alexandria, VA: Center for Naval Analyses, 2015).

11. For more on the development of military technology
over the past two decades, see Michael O'Hanlon, "A Retrospective on the So-Called Revolution in Military Affairs,
2000–2020" (Washington, DC: Brookings Institution, September 2018), https://www.brookings.edu/research/a-retrospective
-on-the-so-called-revolution-in-military-affairs-2000-2020/.
For more on likely future developments in military technology
over the coming decades, see Michael O'Hanlon, "Forecasting
Change in Military Technology, 2020–2040" (Washington,
DC: Brookings Institution, September 2018), https://www
.brookings.edu/research/forecasting-change-in-military
-technology-2020-2040/.

Acquisition and Policy-Making

Echoes from the Past; Visions for the Future

SUE PAYTON AND SALLY BARON

More than thirty-three years have passed since the Blue Ribbon Commission on Defense Management, more widely known as the Packard Commission, issued its final report—*A Quest for Excellence*—to President Ronald Reagan in June 1986.[1] The report was a landmark document in the area of defense acquisitions, outlining both challenges and keys to success in this critical defense enterprise. This article begins from that turning point in 1986 and asks a number of questions about how defense acquisition has changed and improved. How far have we come in the last thirty-five years? Are we more efficient than we were in the late twentieth century? How do we learn from our failures? How do we leverage our successes? This article addresses how policy affects acquisition processes and, in turn, how acquisition processes shape defense policy. In it, we argue that the Packard Commission's findings remain relevant for today's defense acquisition. Beginning with a case study featuring the B-2 Radar Modernization Project (RMP), we argue that many of the failures of the modern acquisition process lie within organizational processes and personnel management. After reviewing these issues within the B-2 RMP, we return to four of the key recommendations from the Packard Commission that are still critical for acquisition processes today.

The Packard Commission Report

The 1980s were a time of military reinforcement and restructuring in response to threats from the Soviet Union, and military spending increased quickly. Following bizarre and shocking reports of overspending by defense contractors, President Reagan enacted a task force—

including the finest minds in both government and industry—to examine the defense acquisition process.[2] This committee, led by David Packard, co-founder of Hewlett-Packard and former deputy secretary of defense, along with future secretaries of defense and a future director of the CIA, was comprised by an astute blend of experience from the uniformed as well as civilian Department of Defense (DoD) and industry and served as a clear turning point in acquisition history. From April 1985 to June 1986, they honed in on the key problems facing DoD management and acquisition, as well as the paths for solutions. Their research concluded that

> DoD must displace systems and structures that measure quality by regulatory compliance and solve problems by executive fiat. Excellence in defense management cannot be achieved by numerous management layers, large staffs, and countless regulations in place today. It depends, as the Commission has observed, on reducing all of these by adhering closely to basic, common sense principles: giving a few capable people the authority and responsibility to do their job, maintaining short lines of communication, holding people accountable for results.[3]

The 1986 Blue Ribbon Panel nailed it; moreover, their conclusions hold even today. While DoD has made some strides in improving and streamlining acquisition, policy-makers have discovered that most, if not all, of the problems they identified still exist in some form. And while some issues have improved, many have gotten worse. Since the 1980s, for a variety of reasons, these streamlining principles have been lost, and many DoD staffs have grown rather than remaining lean as the panel recommended. Above all, the Packard Commission asserts the value of "giving a few capable people the authority and responsibility to do their jobs," a common sense principle. Unfortunately, this has not happened, and bureaucratic growth in many government agencies continues.[4]

According to a multitude of post–Packard Commission acquisition reform studies, including those by the Air Force Studies Board, and the Government Accountability Office (GAO) and RAND findings on the failures of the defense acquisition system and the large major defense acquisition programs (MDAPs),[5] the root causes of performance shortfalls and cost and schedule overruns are multifaceted and complex. Failures are due primarily to overly optimistic initial cost estimates and resistance to initially allocating the full funding; unrealistic schedule baselines; enormously complex weapon system performance requirements; and the inability to attract and retain a professional acquisition workforce. A case study involving the B-2 RMP illustrates each of these failures.

B-2 RMP Case Study

The B-2 stealth bomber remains one of the world's most feared warplanes, having performed superbly over Kosovo, Afghanistan, and Iraq, and it is still in critical demand with the reemergence of Chinese and Russian threats. While the thirty-year-old bomber is legendary, it is also an example of a weapon system acquisition that struggled through cost and schedule nightmares and continues to be beleaguered with slow and costly life-cycle upgrades. In 2008, the future of this aircraft was in jeopardy if its AN/APQ-181 radar operating frequency band was not upgraded. Without immediate replacement of this all-weather, low probability of intercept (LPI) phased array radar system with precision targeting modes and terrain-following radar, the B-2 mission was at risk.

The nadir of this struggle took place when the Federal Communications Commission (FCC) inadvertently allocated the B-2 radar's electromagnetic spectrum to the commercial satellite industry. Put bluntly, this was a big mistake, done totally outside the authority of DoD and the Air Force, and it left the Air Force financially responsible and accountable to solve the problem within a short deadline. Facing intense pressure to move into production and without a sound business case, the Air Force initiated the B-2 Radar Modernization Program (B-2 RMP) Low Rate Initial Production (LRIP) program.[6]

When the Air Force Review Board (AFRB) met, many believed that the decision to begin LRIP was a foregone conclusion and the meeting would end quickly with a rubber stamp approval by the Air Force service acquisition executive (SAE) accepting the cost, schedule, and performance baselines as briefed. After all, the B-2 was one of the most powerful, survivable airborne systems on the planet and arguably the most exquisite aircraft ever developed and flown. As the review board progressed, however, it became obvious that the business case would not close.

During the most critical and expensive phase, the period when the test phase of the program was being conducted concurrently with radar development, the schedule to complete showed no float time (i.e., the time a task can be delayed without the entire project being delayed). This was a huge red flag. Additionally, the cost curve provided by the finance briefer disclosed an extremely low funding level, resulting in a 60 percent confidence level for success. Simply put, if ten things went wrong, there was only enough money to fix six of them. Schedule and funding issues coupled with a noncompetitive award to the only contractor with data rights were additional red flags. But the urgent need for continued operation of the B-2 mission created intense pressure to deviate from sound acquisition processes and just move on with the program, hoping for success.

Instead of approving the acquisition plan as briefed, the SAE, with no fear of reprisals from higher ranking stakeholders, disapproved the LRIP phase of the program, refused to move forward with the B-2 RMP without an addition of 20 percent funding to the program, and shockingly ended the AFRB immediately. After the stunning revelation that the program could not continue without additional funds and SAE approval, the required funds were taken from other areas of the Air Force budget and added to the B-2 RMP budget.

Without the increase in funding demanded during the AFRB, and the superb B-2 acquisition team and leadership skills of Colonel Mark C. Williams, B-2 system program director, and his predecessor, Colonel Kevin Harms, the B-2 RMP would have likely resulted in a Nunn-McCurdy Breach,[7] and it would have been added to the extensive list of "failed" DoD MDAP programs.[8] Instead, the $1.2 billion B-2 RMP was successfully completed, meeting cost, schedule, and performance requirements by the thinnest of margins.

The B-2 RMP illustrates three critical points of failure in the modern acquisition process: budgeting, personnel management, and the rewards system. Each is reviewed below, and collectively they underline the Packard Commission's recommendation to "enhance the quality of the acquisition personnel" and empower key decision-makers with the authority to do their job well.

A System Budgeted to Fail

Since the SAEs and senior acquisition leaders have little authority over requirements and even less control over funding allocations, in order to start healthy programs, protect the reputation of the acquisition workforce, and increase the probability of success for their programs, their only option is to "just say no." This is an untenable position. Who wants to be the one to put a thumbs-down on such an important system? Who wants the title of holding up the world's most feared flying weapon system?

The success of the B-2 RMP is the anomaly that proves the rule. In this case, the SAE was willing to shock the system and demand realistic upfront budgeting and timelines. The SAE was joined by an exceptional leadership team who overcame significant cost and schedule breaches that plagued far too many DoD weapon systems, such as the Air Force space-based infrared system (SBIR), the Army's Future Combat System (FCS), the Marines' presidential helicopter, and the Navy's long-range anti-ship missile (LRASM) and F-35 joint strike fighter just to name a few.[9] Too many programs are started without well-understood and documented requirements, adequate funding, realistic schedules, and with flawed acquisition strategies. Put simply: they are set up to fail.

This is not the way to manage people and programs. Retaining excellent acquisition professionals requires that they are in a system that actually works, is designed to facilitate program managers' success, and does not place the workforce in a constant threat for survival.

The classic studies of threat rigidity illustrate that individuals, groups, and organizations do not perform well under high-anxiety circumstances.[10] Too little funding, loss of funding, and the realization that a program for which one is responsible will fail are threats to an individual and can result in anxiety that inhibits his or her ability to solve problems. At the group level, cohesion, leadership and control are upset. The group may seek consensus, but also restrict the flow of information, which in the case of a DoD project is counterproductive. At the organizational level, Barry Staw and colleagues identified resource scarcity as one threat, in that it can often cause the organization to become rigid and revert to comfortable behaviors and reliance on prior knowledge. In such a case, the organization tends to move away from new and creative solutions to threat-induced problems. In the case of the B-2 RMP, a significantly inadequate budget (scarce resources) should have caused the program to fail.

The Failed Personnel System

For the B-2 RMP, personnel saved the day. This point supports the Packard Commission's findings and "Formula for Action," especially regarding the need to attract and retain the very best defense acquisition workforce. Of all the root causes for failure of acquisition programs, it is the personnel issue that is the most vital to solve, especially as the United States returns to an era of great-power competition. Most critically, the US acquisition process has lost technical competency and empowered leadership.

One of the great casualties of personnel reduction of the post–Cold War era was the severe decrease in the technical engineering talent in the acquisition workforce. No service suffered more than the Air Force, which, prior to the mid-1990s "was widely recognized as being a premier technical acquisition enterprise."[11]

During the early stages of the post–Cold War period, the Air Force implemented the total system performance responsibility (TSPR) acquisition methodology and thereby reduced the technical civil service and uniformed acquisition workforce by thousands. Instead, the Air Force relied on defense contractors to own the technical responsibility for program success or failure and be rewarded based on performance. This TSPR methodology, when implemented in the extreme, resulted in Air Force personnel acquiring fewer technical and leadership roles and being relegated to oversight positions, gathering status information from the contractors rather than directing the technical decisions of many programs.[12]

Additionally, one of the key changes in DoD acquisition management, as a result of the Packard Commission recommendations and Goldwater-Nichols Act of 1986,[13] was the establishment of a Senate-confirmed presidential appointee called the under secretary of defense for acquisition and logistics (USD/AT&L) as the defense acquisition executive (DAE). Similarly appointed and confirmed counterpart SAEs were established in the services. Under these presidential appointees, responsibility for acquisition moved from the uniformed military to civilians. For MDAPs, the law shifted acquisition authority away from the services up to secretary of defense and Joint Staff levels, which removed decision-making from actual combat domain expertise even further. Congress felt that there was too much service rivalry and duplication of effort and not enough support for the needs of the joint warfighter. The act put more authority to define requirements in the hands of the Joint Chiefs of Staff and combatant commanders, thereby placing civilians in the Office of the Secretary of Defense in charge of major weapon systems acquisitions as the locus of control shifted out of the hands of service chiefs and secretaries.

Then, as now, finding highly qualified senior executives with business experience in industry willing to take large pay cuts, divest stocks, and comply with onerous government post-employment restrictions is challenging.

The Packard Commission addressed this issue as "costly to the government's ability to recruit presidential appointees and costly in financial sacrifices to a number of honest and dedicated public officials."[14] From 2000 to 2016, the Senate-confirmed Air Force SAE position was either vacant or filled by a civilian in an "acting" role 46 percent of the time.[15] In 2009, although asked to continue into the Barack Obama administration, the George W. Bush–appointed SAE resigned due to increasingly stringent post-employment restrictions mandated by the new administration. At least three people who interviewed for the position in 2009 refused to consider the position after a full understanding of the post-employment restrictions. This meant that the Senate-confirmed Air Force SAE position was vacant or had a lower ranking civilian in an "acting" role for four years and ten months until February 2014.

The Senate-confirmed SAE is equivalent to a four-star general in rank and possesses equivalent decision-making authority. A key finding of the 2016 Air Force study "Owning the Technical Baseline for Acquisition Programs in the U.S. Air Force" was that "prolonged vacancies of the Air Force SAE position have, over time, eroded the necessary senior leadership and hierarchical support for program executive officers (PEOs) and program managers (PMs), particularly when making potentially controversial decisions about mission-critical defense programs."[16] In October 2013, Paul Francis, managing director of acquisition and sourcing management in GAO, echoed the same concern about the necessity of having in place senior acquisition leaders who can withstand the pressure of many high-ranking stakeholders with conflicting demands when it comes to major weapon systems decisions. He made the case that acquisition failures result from pressures that create incentives for senior acquisition leaders to deviate from sound acquisition processes and initiate programs without a sound business case.[17] Francis contends that "the process of acquiring new weapons is (1) shaped by its different participants and (2) far more complex than just buying equipment to counter a threat. Buying new weapon systems is not just about meeting a military need. It is unfortunately more about defining the importance of certain hierarchical roles and functions, achieving policy decisions, justifying budget levels and shares, advancing service reputations, advancing the authority of oversight organizations, allocating defense spending in localities, funding certain segments of the industrial base and advancing individual careers."[18] All these collective interests "create incentives for pushing programs and encouraging undue optimism, parochialism and compromises of good judgement."[19] When acquisition leadership succumbs to pressures imposed by a multitude of competing interests and overly optimistic cost baselines it sets the stage for program management failures and billions of dollars of cost overruns.

The Upside-Down Reward System

Returning to the B-2 RMP example, the SAE possessed the rank to make the difficult decision to just say no. The non-career civilian appointee was not dependent on a senior ranking military officer for rewards and promotions. When an entire organization is out-ranked by competing organizations 46 percent of the time, as is the case when the SAE post is vacant, bad decisions will be made. This happens particularly due to pressure from those competing and higher-ranked organizations seeking to save budget dollars for other programs or desiring "gold-plated" performance. Absence of an empowered executive authority also exacerbates the burden of onerous regulations.

Elon Musk famously stated, "There is a fundamental problem with regulators. If a regulator agrees to change a rule and something bad happens, they could easily lose their career. Whereas if they change a rule and something good happens, they don't even get a reward."[20] Akin to what Musk argues, in DoD there are no rewards for taking risk. This is a long-standing, deeply ingrained characteristic of the federal government. Even innovators who have been vital to the success of US defense have been punished along the way. The US military is still the most powerful defense force in the world, and it must stay that way. Though this article focuses on defense reform efforts since 1986, we also recognize that there were reform efforts prior to that. Since the 1986 *Quest for Excellence*, technology has changed immensely, but human nature has not. Our findings include what we have observed over the past three decades.

First, in keeping with the axioms and countless studies of human behavior, it bears repeating that human beings respond to rewards, and the current reward system is upside-down. DoD rewards program managers who grow large staffs and large programs. For example, we interviewed a retired colonel who told us that he visited the Pentagon to report on his budget. The auditor asked him how much more money and people his program would need for the next fiscal year. He responded that the program was "fat," and he could manage it with half the resources. The auditor looked up from his desk in shock and told him that in thirty-five years at the Pentagon, no one had ever asked for fewer resources. Although anecdotal, this is not at all surprising and is in keeping with human nature. Consistent with Maslow's hierarchy of needs, people seek status and survival. DoD has made it clear that the measure of merit for promotion and reward in defense acquisition is the number of people in one's organization and the millions allocated to the budget program element. However, as the *Quest for Excellence* observed, the metrics for rewards and promotions should be based instead on successfully delivering high performing systems under budget and ahead of schedule.

The Packard Commission cautioned against offering rewards for anything but productivity, noting that "DoD must displace systems and structures that measure quality by regulatory compliance and solve problems by executive fiat. Excellence in defense management cannot be achieved by numerous management layers, large staffs, and countless regulations in place today."[21] Notwithstanding this caution, the situation has not changed for many federal employees. As a result, quality employees become frustrated as they see quality projects go unrewarded. Acquisition personnel waste countless hours briefing OSD staff on bureaucratic milestone accomplishments, as if risk is managed solely by meeting inch-stones on the way to milestones. Many of the best and brightest engineers and program managers head off to different careers and are especially attracted to commercial technology companies where the business model embraces rapid decisions and rewards innovation and productivity. As Jeff Bezos stated at the 2019 Reagan National Defense Forum, "Innovative people will flee organizations that cannot make decisions rapidly and take risks."[22] A sobering finding of the 2016 Air Force study "Owning the Technical Baseline for Acquisition Programs in the U.S. Air Force" was that in 1995 there were more than 6,500 Air Force officers in the technical developmental engineering and acquisition fields, with 60 percent possessing master's degrees. The Air Force had ten engineers for every program manager. In 2015, there were only 4,000 officers in the technical developmental engineering and acquisition fields, and only four engineers for every program manager.[23] The number of engineers is going down and the number of managers is going up—a perfect recipe for a fat, inefficient organization.

Thankfully, there is some reason for optimism. The Air Force now has two program offices and multiple special access programs (SAPs) focused on these metrics. Big Safari and the Rapid Capabilities Office are structured to move rapidly with lean and trusted technical staffs. SAPs operate similarly to the B-2 development program with lean program teams and less onerous oversight from OSD and Congress. These program offices do not violate any federal regulations, but they do have high-ranking top cover, authority, and accountability vested in the program manager and are trusted with some of the Air Force's and US Special Operations Command's (SOCOM's) highest priority programs, such as the B-21 next-generation stealth bomber.

A Formula for Action amid Today's Warfighting Challenges

The B-2 case study illustrates many of the warfighting challenges of today. Since the Cold War ended, American defense policy has focused on many diverse strategies to counter a large number of security challenges. American military dominance has eroded due to the emergence of the new battlefields of space and cyberspace, new disruptive technologies, and the reemergence of near-peer adversaries. We can conceive of American defense policy as a set of rules established to safeguard national interests, and the national defense strategy (NDS) as the specific defense game plan to achieve those goals. Seen that way, the 2018 NDS (the first new NDS in a decade) is a brilliant attempt to document the critical steps necessary to maintain DoD's "enduring mission to provide combat-credible military forces needed to deter war and protect the security of our nation."[24] For the first time in decades, the NDS recognizes that the "central challenge to U.S. prosperity and security is the reemergence of long-term, strategic competition of revisionist powers represented by China and Russia who want to shape a world consistent with their authoritarian model—gaining veto authority over other nation's economic, diplomatic and security decisions."[25] The military options now require the means to counter terrorism overseas and at home, conventional weapon systems in anti-access/area denial (A2/AD) environments, and countermeasures to protect and defend our nation in all domains—ground, sea, air, space, and cyberspace.

An immense challenge to executing the game plan presented in the 2018 NDS is the ability of the defense acquisition system to deliver the innovation necessary to "deter war and protect the security of our nation."[26] A deeper dive into the 2018 NDS reveals echoes of the Packard Commission report: a call for an agile acquisition system and business processes that must be able to rapidly respond with innovative technologies and war-winning capabilities to counter the multitude of threats to our nation and our allies.

Among the three lines of effort listed in the NDS is "build a more lethal force."[27] Here we find the strategy for building a superior acquisition system and developing a personnel system that produces a highly qualified and innovative workforce. Within this line of effort, the NDS requires the US military to "modernize key capabilities," because "we cannot expect success fighting tomorrow's conflicts with yesterday's weapons and equipment."[28] The NDS goes on to state that the military will make "targeted, disciplined increases in personnel and platforms"[29] to meet defense policy needs. This will require new processes of acquisition and incorporating commercial technology and products into the Defense Department's arsenal.

The NDS also calls on the Defense Department to recruit, develop, and retain a talented and creative workforce. Warfighters must be able to "integrate new capabilities, adapt warfighting approaches, and change business practices to achieve mission success."[30] Cultivating workforce talent includes ensuring that acquisition personnel possess the technical knowledge to make sound decisions and are capable of taking risks on innovative systems.

We believe that there is little hope in achieving the goals of the 2018 NDS using the post–Cold War defense acquisition system, with its three distinct decision bureaucracies overseeing requirements, funding, and acquisition management, while diffusing authority and accountability for weapon system success across so many fiefdoms. It is a miracle any capability ever becomes operational. The 2018 NDS accurately describes an acquisition business process that is "centered on exacting thoroughness and minimizing risk above all else."[31] Clearly, countering the number and level of the urgent threats to our nation and the speed at which we must respond cannot be achieved using an untailored, "unresponsive process that is over-optimized for exceptional performance at the expense of providing timely decisions, policies, and capabilities to the warfighter."[32] Instead, we advocate returning to the Packard Commission of 1986 to find the strategy for successful acquisitions processes.

Listed below are the Packard Commission findings, described as their "Formula for Action." Though all these findings are important, we focus on A, E, F, and H.

A. Streamline acquisition and organizational procedures
B. Use technology to reduce cost
C. Balance cost and performance
D. Stabilize programs
E. Expand the use of commercial products
F. Increase the use of competition
G. Clarify the need for technical data rights
H. Enhance the quality of acquisition personnel
I. Improve the capability for industrial mobilization

Streamline Acquisition and Organizational Procedures

How can DoD become streamlined and win the great-power contests when its organization is motivated to do the opposite? In December 2019, Secretary of the Air Force Barbara Barrett spoke at the Reagan National Defense Forum, in Simi Valley, California. She discussed the emergence of "near-peer" space adversaries who are approaching the once-unapproachable US military technologies and becoming even more advanced. The good news—if there could be any good news on this front—is that near-peer competition sends a "Sputnik-like" wake-up call for all hands on deck to rapidly counter the threats and advance US capability to deter aggression.[33]

The late 1950s and early 1960s were a time of fear for the United States. The Soviet Union was ahead in space technology and proved it with the 1957 successful launch and orbit of the very first satellite: Sputnik. The United States responded a short year later with Explorer I in 1958. Today most DoD built satellites take five to ten years to buy and launch. So how did the United States respond so quickly back then? Motivation and leadership from the highest levels of the government were the key ingredients.

In 1958, Representative Sam Rayburn and Vice President Richard Nixon signed the National Aeronautics and Space Act encouraging the fledgling NASA to go fast. Accordingly, NASA was "to acquire (by purchase, lease, condemnation, or otherwise), construct, improve, repair, operate, and maintain laboratories, research and testing sites and facilities, aeronautical and space vehicles, quarters and related accommodations for employees and dependents of employees of the Administration, and such other real and personal property (including patents), or any interest therein, as the Administration deems necessary."[34] Emphasizing the urgency of the task, the Other Transaction Authority (OTA), which was part of the 1958 act, allowed government workers to do everything that was needed to get the job done. The focus was the product, not the process.

The government leaders who understand our space and cyberspace threats have turned to congressionally approved accelerated acquisition authorities, such as the use of newly enhanced OTAs and Section 804 "middle-tier acquisition authority" to counter these urgent threats. The standard DoD 5000 processes are routinely seen as hindering, rather than facilitating, rapid results. The newly enhanced OTA is one of the most disruptive, long-standing but little used acquisition authority available to development programs. This alternative acquisition approach to the conventional Federal Acquisition Regulation–based mechanisms of contracts, grants, and cooperative agreements can be far more flexible and timely because an OTA is not subject to the same onerous regulations, policies, and statutes as conventional contracts. It is designed to attract nontraditional companies that have no understanding, capability, or desire to comply with standard FAR provisions but offer innovation and the ability to rapidly prototype dual-use commercial technology to augment DoD capabilities. "In total, DoD OTA obligations have increased 352 percent in the last three years . . . and AF OTA obligations have grown 9,982 percent since 2015." The total DoD potential value of OTAs rose from less than $2 billion in 2014 to over $26 billion in 2018.[35]

As of July 2019, DoD was executing 89 MDAPs, primarily using the DoD 5000 acquisition process.[36] Several of these MDAPs are being managed under Section 804, which gives DoD authority to conduct what lawmakers tout as a faster, specially tailored requirements and acquisition process that DoD can use for technologies that are mature enough to be rapidly prototyped or fielded within two to five years. A second provision (Section 806) lets the DoD secretary waive virtually any acquisition law or regulation if it is deemed that a particular weapons system is vital to national security.[37]

Rear Admiral David Small, the program executive officer (PEO) for Navy integrated warfare systems, welcomed the change, as this type of accelerated acquisition pushes authority to the program managers and "unburdens them from a lot of documentation, especially with acquisition and requirements documentation. It reduces the numbers of meetings and bandwidth and the number of people required allowing for small empowered teams to achieve success."[38] The Navy has a set of high-priority MDAPs under review as candidates for Section 804 accelerated acquisition, but realizes that typically slow funding allocations must be better synchronized to keep pace with the more streamlined processes.

Air Force leaders claim that they have already saved billions of dollars and taken years out of program schedules—including major satellite procurements such as the Next Generation Overhead Persistent Infrared (OPIR) program, which is critical to countering space threats and is slated to cost over $11 billion in the next five years.[39] While Air Force acquisition leadership was eager to start the program under Section 804, in order to take years out of the schedule to launch, the funding required from Air Force budget authorities was $632 million short and in 2019 required "significant reprogramming requests of Congress to keep the program on schedule."[40] There is great concern that "the Air Force rushed the program using 804 authorities but didn't have enough funds to support that schedule, stirring concerns that maybe this program is too complex and too expensive to be handled as a rapid prototyping project."[41] While we have great hope that newly employed authorities such as Section 804 and OTAs with provisions to award production contracts become the default methods for acquiring our future weapon systems, starting programs with adequate funding is the first principle of success.

Additionally, we expect pushback. As new streamlined processes prove successful in DoD, established bureaucrats will probably wait patiently for programs managed under accelerated authorities such as Section 804 and OTAs to fail, as indeed some may. However, innovation studies have illustrated that failing early and cheaply will increase learning and therefore success.[42] We know that returning to the DoD 5000 will not increase innovation and success.

Finally, Congress needs to allow DoD to do its job. Back in 1986, the Packard Commission stated it well: "Congress must resist its inveterate tendency to legislate management practices and organizational details for DoD. Excellence in defense management will not come from legislative efforts to control and arrange the minutest aspects of DoD's operations. Congress can more usefully contribute by concentrating on larger, often neglected issues of overall defense posture and military performance."[43] In DoD and related government agencies, increased congressional oversight has caused growth. In politics (as physics) for every action there is an equal and opposite reaction. For every report Congress requires, DoD staff must grow to "feed the beast." If Congress requires routine reporting, then the organization must have the staff to provide it. We have seen cases in which congressional members help select industry partners based on congressional districts. This simply must stop as it is not the way to engineer programs. As programs grow, accountability becomes diffused.[44] And programs always grow. As discussed earlier, DoD personnel are motivated to have large staffs and large budgets; not surprisingly, that's what happens. The Packard Commission's first finding for streamlining is as relevant today as it was in 1986. As an organization grows, productivity suffers when the support staff begins to micromanage program oversight activities with a multitude of procedures.

Expand the Use of Commercial Products

Eight years after the Packard Commission's report was published, committee member William Perry was named secretary of defense. During his first weeks in office he distributed "A New Way of Doing Business"[45] (best known as the 1994 "Perry Memo") based on his experience in industry, government, and academia. Perry was determined to enact change that would enable the policies recommended in *A Quest for Excellence*. In this memo, Perry outlined measures by which DoD would make acquisition more efficient, including a paradigm shift from the use of "milspecs" to embracing superior products in the commercial sector when available. Secretary Perry had long observed the government using inefficient and outdated methodologies, which included the government building custom products at huge costs when superior off-the-shelf products already existed in the commercial sector.

Government-built systems can never emulate the infinite market effects of a capitalist economy. One of the most stunning examples of this dichotomy is the computer market. In the mid-twentieth century, the integrated circuit (IC), later known as a "chip," was expensive. In 1965, the visionary Gordon Moore published a paper in which he asserted that chip density would double about every two years.[46] This prediction became widely known as Moore's Law. With that and the expansion of the commercial market, including home computers, small companies had access to millions of customers, needing billions of chips. Personal computers became remarkably inexpensive due to the economies of scale that a large customer base offered. Market forces pushed and pulled, and research and development in both the public and the private sectors were and still are expanding computing power beyond what many could have ever imagined.

From the mid- to late-twentieth century, DoD and other agencies tried to out-perform the private sector by attempting to produce government-purposed hardware and software, but commercial companies simply left them in the dust. We recall DoD attempting to build government-unique workstations, when Apple, Hewlett Packard, Dell and others simply zoomed past with faster, better, and cheaper products. Today, the government would not dream of building a laptop—they are far too inexpensive off the shelf—but there was a time when it did. DoD, however, must proceed with caution as today much technology (hardware and software) comes from near-peer adversaries. Once again, we return to the issue of trust. Acquisition professionals must do their homework and understand their contractors and suppliers. Identifying innovative but trusted suppliers will require hard work and diligent acquisition professionals.

Consider high-resolution satellite imagery. At one time, this remarkable capability and superior products were highly classified, but today it is common technology. Several commercial companies have successfully produced multispectral imagery cheaply and in as high a resolution as the US government will allow.[47] Though US commercial companies are limited to 0.25-meter resolution, they are technically capable of higher resolution. When foreign commercial companies have this technology, it is unlikely that the federal government will have much control over these companies. The United States will have to play catch-up and approve higher resolution.

In sum, acquisition professionals must ask themselves, in 2020, what other products are faster, better, and cheaper off the shelf?

Increase Competition

The United States is the most technologically advanced and strongest country in the world due primarily to competition. Competition keeps companies sharp and tenacious. Since the Cold War ended, dozens of defense companies, once offering exceptional competition for MDAPs, have merged into five or six large corporations, devastating the ability of DoD and the intelli-

gence community to benefit from competition. As Nobel economist Oliver Williamson observed, a large number of competitors at the outset often evolves into a smaller number,[48] but, if a genuine free market exists, new competitors will emerge. A second reason for the lack of competition, especially as weapon systems need upgrades, is the negative impact of closed architectures and proprietary systems. Ironically, in several cases, DoD has made its defense industrial partners weaker by standing them up every time they fail or overrun because DoD is held hostage to closed systems or lack of data rights.

How can DoD move forward? Mandatory requirements for open systems and vigilance in continuously enforcing openness is paramount. All interfaces must be published and available to all vendors to prevent new programs from being held hostage to costly vendor lock. Prototyping and experimentation with new technologies that allow closed legacy systems to become more open to timely insertion of enhanced technology in order to counter emerging threats must be funded and implemented. Competition will not increase as long as big prime defense industrial base leaders are given special treatment and continually rewarded during failures. Age-old ties with the Pentagon keep competition at bay. It is easier to continue to do what has always been done than to change direction and risk being blamed for failure. Newer, superior products wait in the wings while foreign countries snap them up.

Rewind more than a century back. In 1905, the Wright brothers tried to sell their Wright Flyer to the War Department. The airplane was 100 percent privately funded; the Wrights had done all the development on their own, costing the taxpayer nothing. Although the War Department had discussed and even experimented with a heavier-than-air flying machine, Major General G. L. Gillespie told the Wrights that the department was not interested in their invention.[49] By his response it appears that he barely read their proposal, misinterpreting it as a request for grant money. The brothers, in debt from years of research and development expense, looked overseas for buyers, and found them in Germany and Great Britain.[50]

Around the same time, a lesser known innovator, Vice Admiral Charles "Swede" Momsen was working on innovations of his own. As a young officer, he attempted to make submarine duty safer after witnessing the deaths of all sailors aboard a submarine that sank in relatively shallow water. Momsen tried to convince the Navy there was a way to rescue sailors from a sunken submarine. After he retired, he concluded:

> In the military career I chose it becomes clear very early on, perhaps for good reason, the best way to get ahead is to stay with the pack. I guess in my

career I steered a course a bit too much my own. It's happened in other services too. When an officer with initiative and imagination leaves the middle of the road, he's bound to have trouble. His superiors get set in their ways, indifferent or even hostile to new ideas. Sometimes it's just because they didn't think of it themselves. Often when I presented a new proposal, I was made to feel like a felon committing a crime, and ended up not only having to defend the idea, but myself for daring to bring it up. But it did happen—too rarely, maybe—to have someone up the line say, "That sounds good. Let's do it." I'd like to think that situation has much improved.[51]

Momsen was ultimately rewarded for his inventions such as the diving bell, but he clearly states his frustrations with the Naval hierarchy. Prior to the success of his inventions, he was not well-supported. Without appropriate funding and staff, he often had to be his own test subject for his experiments, among using other innovative methods for saving funds.

These examples give pause, even now. Who is the twenty-first century Gillespie who sent the Wright Brothers overseas? What is DoD sending overseas today that would win wars and save lives? The trend in 2018 gives slight room for optimism as the growth of defense contract obligations was at that time more evenly distributed between small, medium, and other large vendors.[52] But are we moving too slowly? Is DoD overlooking critical new technologies? Time will tell.

Enhance the Quality of Acquisition Personnel

The original Packard Commission emphasized the need to attract and retain the very best defense acquisition workforce. Yet, since its report was published, DoD has failed to achieve much success in this task. Of all the causes for acquisition failures, this personnel issue is, we believe, the most important to address. In his contribution to this volume, Tim Kane outlines several case studies and reasons why DoD has trouble retaining talent.

One encouraging step to improve talent management and enable tailored and agile development of Air Force officers was announced by Secretary of the Air Force Barbara Barrett in October of 2019. Effective in March of 2020, officers with highly technical expertise will no longer compete for promotions with air operations, special warfare, nuclear and missile operations, space operations, and information warfare officers. Instead, technical personnel such as chemists, physicists, nuclear engineers, developmental engineers, and acquisition managers will compete in a line of the Air Force dedicated to promoting technical officers. "Now rather than competing for promotion

against 40 different career fields with varied job requirements, officers will compete against officers . . . that have similar progression milestones, experiences and mission area focus. The new categories will allow each career field the freedom and agility to better tailor officer development to meet job demands without compromising competitive position at a promotion board."[53]

We are encouraged by the efforts of the Air Force to change the seventy-year promotion board status quo process. The new promotion structure, long overdue, holds great promise in retaining acquisition experts through rewards of higher promotion rates and indicating to the workforce that they are valued members of the Air Force. To be sure, some excellent people stay despite being rewarded badly, but others get frustrated and seek careers elsewhere.

Conclusion

For decades, American defense policy has defined high-level goals that include protecting our country and our allies through the use of strategic deterrence and partner building, as well as combatting human rights abuses around the world. Long-standing weapon systems such as the B-2 are examples of how MDAPs have implemented American defense policy. There is no doubt about the success of the most powerful military in the world in the quest to successfully conduct and meet the goals of defense policy. The issues described in this article concern how DoD can more rapidly, effectively, efficiently, and affordably provide for the defense of the United States and our allies. There is not a single silver bullet that solves this complex problem in a short-term timeline. The nine items outlined in the Packard Commission's "Formula for Action" recognized the complex set of solutions needed and are as relevant today as they were in 1986.

It is imperative to start with a laser focus on recruiting and retaining a highly capable technical acquisition workforce. Without a highly valued and rewarded acquisition brain-trust to design systems to counter the multidomain threats against us, we will fail. Given a quality workforce with authority and streamlined processes supported by their senior leaders, we must then be able to rapidly out-innovate our adversaries. We have already out-innovated, but we need to get these innovative products to the warfighter. To do this, we must attract commercial companies, defense contractors, academia, government labs, and program leaders, together with the actual warfighter, to rapidly design technological solutions and experiments, not relying on the outdated multiyear requirements definition timeline. This is an all-hands-on-deck moment and the best of America is needed to protect and defend the United States and our allies. Innovation must be done with regard for the economy of scale that commercial products provide. Acquisition professionals must be knowledgeable of the technical marketplace and thorough in their market searches. The technology sought should not only counter the threats we face but also reduce the cost that those capabilities require.

To embolden competition, experimentation using streamlined digital engineering,[54] model-based system engineering,[55] and high-fidelity prototyping must be done using open standards and architectures with published interfaces so that multiple providers can continuously compete to replace outdated, underperforming, or high-cost hardware and software. Program managers and designers must ensure that the use of proprietary software and components be allowed only at points in the architecture that can be easily replaced. Special programs should be established and funded to experiment with the latest cyber-secure technologies that allow currently closed systems to be freed from vendor lock.

Finally, we must learn to rebuild trust between Congress, DoD, and industry teams. We must accentuate the positive and focus on those successful examples of acquisition management that engender trust and drive down the cost of success. In his classic writings on transaction costs, Oliver Williamson asserts that trust in and between organizations in the market reduces transaction costs.[56] Others who have studied Japanese car manufacturing have written about supply chains and the just-in-time supply philosophy. This philosophy requires trusting suppliers and ensuring suppliers are trustworthy. As many have noted, trust is often easy to acquire, but once violated is extremely difficult to retain.[57] The Pentagon has decades-old ties with several large defense contractors, and trust is vital.

Here is the dilemma: with extremely complicated systems, it is impossible for any one person to understand all parts of it. Herbert Simon called this situation "bounded rationality."[58] That is, organizational actors are rational, but bounded by what they can understand. Therefore, in order to succeed, DoD must incentivize industry partners to develop and continuously validate trusted, secure supply chains.[59] Supply chains must be subject to a rigorous but rapid system of checks and balances enforced in every program.

As DoD begins the early stages of critical new defense programs, DoD senior executives and Congress would be wise to review and finally implement the nine findings of the Packard Commission. DoD must provide streamlined acquisition processes and authorities that allow our acquisition experts to be successful. These processes must ensure that the program manager be granted authority for program management decision-making, have stable funding and well-defined mission profiles, and then be held accountable and rewarded for success by senior executives who must provide top cover and withstand the pressure that will always exist from multiple shareholders with competing goals and motives.

NOTES

1. David Packard, Chairman, et al., *A Quest for Excellence: Final Report to the President by the President's Blue Ribbon Commission on Defense Management* (Washington, DC: Government Printing Office, 1986).

2. Fred Hiatt "Now, the $600 Toilet Seat," *Washington Post*, February 5, 1985, https://www.washingtonpost.com/archive/politics/1985/02/05/now-the-600-toilet-seat/917c98b4-c2fc-40a5-808b-87ff4e5884c8/.

3. Packard, *A Quest for Excellence*, xiii.

4. See, for example, Robert J. Kohler, "Commentary: The Essential Revolution of the NRO: A Second Opinion," *SpaceNews*, December 16, 2014, https://spacenews.com/38719the-essential-revolution-of-the-nro-a-second-opinion/.

5. This is an acquisition program that is designated by the under secretary of defense for acquisition and sustainment or estimated to expend a total of more than $365 million in Research Development, Test & Evaluation or more than $2.19 billion in procurement (in fiscal year 2000 constant dollars).

6. Bill Sweetman, "Spectrum Squeeze to K.O. B-2 Bombers Radar?," *Defense Industry Daily*, March 24, 2009, https://www.defenseindustrydaily.com/Spectrum-Squeeze-to-KO-B-2-Bombers-Radar-05348/.

7. When a program's cost growth exceeds the statutory thresholds, it is said to have a Nunn-McCurdy breach. A critical breach occurs when the cost increases 25 percent or more over the current baseline estimate or 50 percent or more over the original baseline estimate.

8. Col. (Ret) Mark C. Williams, B-2 System Program Director, Fighters & Bombers Directorate, Aeronautical Systems Center, interview by authors, November 26, 2019.

9. Eric Tegler, "How the F-35 Got to Be Such a Mess," *Popular Mechanics*, July 27, 2018, https://www.popularmechanics.com/military/a21957/wtf-35/; Christopher J. Niemi, "The F-22 Acquisition Program Consequences for the US Air Force's Fighter Fleet," *Air & Space Power Journal* 26, no. 6 (December 2012): 53–82.

10. Barry M. Staw, Lance E. Sandelands, and Jane E. Dutton, "Threat Rigidity in Organizational Behavior: A Multilevel Analysis," *Administrative Science Quarterly* 26, no. 4 (December 1981): 501–24.

11. Gary E. Christle, Dan Davis, and Gene Porter, "CNA Independent Assessment: Air Force Acquisition" (Alexandria, VA: Center for Naval Analyses, 2009), 1.

12. Henry A. Obering, Chair, Lawrence J. Delaney, Vice Chair, Donald R. Eberschloe, Millard S. Firebaugh, Michael D. Griffin, Gary A. Kyle, Thomas L. Maxwell, Sue C. Payton, Richard T. Roca, William J. Strickland, Deborah L. Westphal, Rebecca Winston, *Owning the Technical Baseline for Acquisition Programs in the U.S. Air Force* (Washington, DC: National Academies Press, 2016), 1–2.

13. Robert Goldich, "Goldwater-Nichols Act," Encyclopedia.com, accessed December 3, 2019, https://www.encyclopedia.com/history/encyclopedias-almanacs-transcripts-and-maps/goldwater-nichols-act.

14. Packard, *A Quest for Excellence*, 131–32.

15. Obering, *Technical Baseline*, 25, figure 3.1.

16. Obering, *Technical Baseline*, 25, figure 3.1.

17. *Defense Acquisitions: Where Should Reform Aim Next? Testimony before the Committee on Armed Services*, 113th Cong. 2 (2013) (statement of Paul L. Francis, Managing Director Acquisition and Sourcing Management).

18. *Defense Acquisitions*, 7.

19. *Defense Acquisitions*, 8.

20. Ashlee Vance, *Elon Musk: Tesla, SpaceX, and the Quest for a Fantastic Future* (New York: HarperCollins, 2015), 242.

21. Packard, *A Quest for Excellence*, 52.

22. Jeff Bezos, "Reagan National Defense Forum: Conversation with Jeff Bezos," interview by Roger Zakheim, *Ricochet*, December 22, 2019, audio, 26:35, https://ricochet.com/podcast/reaganism/reagan-national-defense-forum-conversation-with-jeff-bezos/.

23. Obering, *Technical Baseline*, 33, figure 3.3.

24. Department of Defense, *Summary of the 2018 National Defense Strategy of the United States of America* (Washington, DC: Department of Defense, 2018), 1.

25. Department of Defense, *National Defense Strategy*, 2.

26. Department of Defense, *National Defense Strategy*, 1.

27. Department of Defense, *National Defense Strategy*, 5.

28. Department of Defense, *National Defense Strategy*, 6.

29. Department of Defense, *National Defense Strategy*, 6

30. Department of Defense, *National Defense Strategy*, 7.

31. Department of Defense, *National Defense Strategy*, 10.

32. Department of Defense, *National Defense Strategy*, 10.

33. Barbara Barrett, "Next Steps in Space: Launching America's Sixth Military Branch," Reagan National Defense Forum Panel, December 6, 2019.

34. National Aeronautics and Space Act of 1958, Pub. L. No. 85-568, 72 Stat. 426–438 (1958).

35. Rhys McCormick, *Defense Acquisition Trends: Topline DoD Trends* (Washington, DC: Center for Strategic and International Studies, 2019), 6–7.

36. Department of Defense, *Major Defense Acquisition Programs (MDAP) and Major Automated Information Systems (MAIS) List* (Washington, DC: Department of Defense, July 1, 2019).

37. Jared Serbu, "Navy Will Use New Legal Authorities to Speed Up Top Acquisition Priorities," *Federal News Network*, January 18, 2019, https://federalnewsnetwork.com/navy/2019/01/navy-will-use-new-legal-authorities-to-speed-up-top-acquisition-priorities/.

38. Serbu, "Navy Will Use New Legal Authorities."

39. Sandra Erwin, "Congress Worries Authorities It Gave DoD Might Backfire," *Spacenews*, May 23, 2019, https://spacenews.com/congress-worries-authorities-it-gave-dod-might-backfire/.

40. Erwin, "Congress Worries."

41. Erwin, "Congress Worries."

42. Robert I. Sutton, *Weird Ideas That Work: 11 1/2 Practices for Promoting, Managing, and Sustaining Innovation* (New York: Free Press, 2002).

43. Packard, *A Quest for Excellence*, 16.

44. Sally J. F. Baron, "Inaction Speaks Louder than Words: The Problems of Passivity," *Business Horizons* 56, no. 3 (May 2013): 301–11.

45. William J. Perry, "Specifications and Standards—A New Way of Doing Business," official memorandum (Washington, DC: Department of Defense, 1994).

46. Gordon E. Moore, "Cramming More Components onto Integrated Circuits," *Electronics* 38, no. 8 (April 1965): 114–17.

47. Walter Scott, "Op-Ed: U.S. Satellite Imaging Regulations Must Be Modernized," *Spacenews*, August 29, 2016, https://spacenews.com/op-ed-u-s-satellite-imaging-regulations-must-be-modernized/.

48. Oliver E. Williamson, *Markets and Hierarchies* (New York: Free Press, 1975).

49. Orville Wright and Wilbur Wright, *Miracle at Kitty Hawk: The Letters of Wilbur and Orville Wright*, ed. Fred C. Kelly (New York: Da Capo Press, 2002).

50. Wright and Wright, *Miracle*.

51. Peter Maas, *The Terrible Hours: The Man Behind the Greatest Submarine Rescue in History* (New York: Harper Collins, 1999), 258.

52. McCormick, *Defense Acquisition Trends*, 1.

53. Secretary of the Air Force Public Affairs, "Air Force Formalizes Officer Developmental Categories, Effective March O-5 Board," U.S. Air Force, October 21, 2019, https://www.af.mil/News/Article-Display/Article/1993911/air-force-formalizes-officer-developmental-categories-effective-march-o-5-board/.

54. Department of Defense, *Digital Engineering Strategy* (Washington, DC: Office of the Deputy Assistant Secretary of Defense for Systems Engineering, 2018), https://fas.org/man/eprint/digeng-2018.pdf.

55. Model-Based System Engineering Expert, "Free, Open Source & Commercial MBSE+SysML Tools," *MBSE Tool Reviews*, Pivotpoint Technology Corp., December 15, 2020, https://mbsetoolreviews.com/.

56. Williamson, *Markets*.

57. Roderick M. Kramer, "Trust and Distrust in Organizations: Emerging Perspectives, Enduring Questions," *Annual Review of Psychology* 50 (February 1999): 569–98.

58. Herbert Simon, "Bounded Rationality," in *Utility and Probability*, ed. John Eatwell, Murray Milgate, and Peter Newman (London: Palgrave Macmillan, 1990).

59. Brian Aoaeh, "Commentary: Modern Autonomous Supply Chains Need an Easy Way to Enable Trust and Security," Freightwaves, October 30, 2019, https://www.freightwaves.com/news/commentary-modern-autonomous-supply-chains-need-an-easy-way-to-enable-trust-and-security.

The Case for Joint Force Acquisition Reform

MICHAEL E. MCINERNEY, CONWAY LIN, BRANDON D. SMITH, AND JOSEPH S. LUPA

In the past two years, Congress has enacted new reforms to enable rapid acquisition of technologies for military use. If successful, these reforms may end up delivering war-fighting capability more quickly and cheaply, but they will not solve the fundamental flaw in defense acquisitions. While efficiency is a worthy goal, the bedrock value of acquisitions must be to deliver a joint force with the capability and capacity to effectively meet the demands of combatant commanders.

The Goldwater-Nichols Department of Defense Reorganization Act of 1986 revolutionized how America goes to war by imposing jointness on the command structure of the US military. Goldwater-Nichols turned the military Services into force providers responsible for organizing, manning, training, and equipping units that are then employed by war-fighting combatant commanders as a joint force.

This dynamic leaves the Services fundamentally in control of the acquisition process, creating a classic "principal-agent" problem characterized by misaligned incentives. As agents, the Services should act on behalf of their principals, developing forces tailored to the needs of the combatant commanders. History has demonstrated repeatedly, however, that the services are too often motivated by parochial incentives, which do not always align with those of the combatant commanders. The result has been the consistent development of materiel solutions that are not optimized for joint war-fighting. To improve joint interoperability and war-fighting capability, Congress should reform the Defense Acquisition System (DAS) to empower combatant commanders and the Chairman of the Joint Chiefs of Staff with early, direct, and proactive influence over materiel systems development.

Acquisition System vs. Acquisition Process

For decades, critiques of the DAS have plowed the same infertile ground. Dozens of failed efforts to reform the system have diagnosed the inefficiency of the acquisition process and then suggested additional regulations, authorities, and oversight as the cure. For example, in his March 1973 statement before the US House Committee on Armed Services, Comptroller General of the United States Elmer B. Staats identified that "overly ambitious performance requirements combined with low initial cost predictions [and] optimistic risk estimates . . . lead almost inevitably to engineering changes, schedule slippages, and cost increases."[1] Yet 43 years later, in the 2016 National Defense Authorization Act, Congress articulated the need for a new round of acquisition reforms in parallel language, noting that "both the Department of Defense [DOD] and Congress are complicit in pursuing acquisition strategies that downplay technical risk and underestimate cost . . . resulting in an acquisition process that is not agile enough, too risk averse, and takes too long to deliver."[2]

Why do problems with the DAS persist despite decades of attempted reforms? One reason these reform efforts fall short is that their respective analyses tend to concentrate on ways for DOD to more quickly and cheaply purchase equipment.[3] While efficiency and timeliness of acquisitions are obviously important concerns, the myopic focus on these two goals obscures the fact that the biggest defense acquisition problems often have nothing to do with how cost-effectively materiel is purchased.

Stories of money wasted during development of ambitious acquisition programs like the F-35 fighter or the Marine Corps' Expeditionary Fighting Vehicle excite the media and may infuriate taxpayers. What the war-fighter finds more troubling, however, is when the Services continue to champion fruitless acquisition programs like the Army's Future Combat System (FCS) for years while underinvesting in capabilities demanded by combatant commanders to support ongoing operations around the globe. Without fixing that issue, efforts to improve the acquisition process may inject some efficiency into the system but will not lead to a more integrated and capable joint force.

To understand this point, it is important to first sketch out the bigger picture of how materiel development and acquisition works. The DAS—colloquially known as "Big A" acquisitions—is actually three interconnected subprocesses within DOD. First, the Joint Capabilities Integration and Development System (JCIDS) is the subprocess that identifies capability gaps and generates requirements. Think of JCIDS as the way that DOD decides what to buy. Second, the Planning,

Michael E. McInerney, Conway Lin, Brandon D. Smith, and Joseph S. Lupa, "The Case for Joint Force Acquisition Reform," *Joint Force Quarterly* 90, no. 3 (July 2018): 36–40.

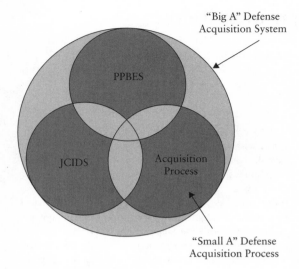

"Big A" Defense
Acquisition System

"Small A" Defense
Acquisition Process

Figure 1. The Acquisition System

Programming, Budgeting, and Execution (PPBE) system is the subprocess that matches available resources against these requirements to produce a spending plan and a budget. The PPBE is the way that DOD decides how much it can afford to buy and when. Finally, the Acquisition Process—called "Small A" acquisitions—guides how those budgeted resources are spent to develop and procure materiel capabilities. The main concerns in this process are cost and schedule—in other words, how to efficiently buy the equipment. This article purposely does not focus on the Small A subprocess, as it is downstream of the root problem in the Big A system (figure 1).

To be successful, the DAS must buy the right amount of the right things at the right time. If decisions regarding what, when, and how much are wrong, it does not matter how efficiently money is spent—the wrong equipment is procured.[4] For that reason, and because the Acquisition Process has been studied exhaustively, this article proposes modest reforms to JCIDS and PPBE in order to make the DAS more accommodating of combatant commander needs.

Misalignment of Incentives

The 2006 Defense Acquisition Performance Assessment Report, led by Lieutenant General Ronald Kadish, found that "combatant commanders participate but do not play a leading role in defining capability shortfalls."[5] Often, this leads to the Services generating and validating requirements that are not linked to what combatant commanders really need.[6] Despite almost 17 years of war in Iraq and Afghanistan, criticisms persist that the Services place too much focus on winning conventional wars, leaving combatant com-

manders perpetually short of the systems needed to (1) conduct intelligence, surveillance, and reconnaissance; (2) deploy joint capabilities globally into contested environments; (3) conduct sustainment; (4) command and control widely dispersed joint forces; and (5) fight the asymmetric wars we currently confront and that we predict for the future.[7]

Former Secretary of Defense Robert Gates called this "next-war-itis"—the tendency of the Services to overly focus on creating exquisite and expensive systems to dominate possible future battlefields rather than on providing combatant commanders with good-enough interoperable capabilities that they need right now.[8] Every program emanating from a "Center of Excellence," which focuses on closing a Service-peculiar capability gap without due regard for what value the capability provides the joint force war-fighter, highlights the danger of misaligned incentives in the DAS. When producers deliver a product that their customer does not want or need, it really is not relevant how efficiently that product is produced.

Goldwater-Nichols charged combatant commanders with employment of joint war-fighting forces around the globe. It therefore follows that combatant commanders have an incentive to pursue materiel solutions that increase joint capability and prioritize characteristics such as interoperability, deployability, sharing of advanced technologies, minimal duplication of programs with similar capabilities across Services, joint logistical and maintenance support, and compatible software. Meanwhile, although the Services are charged with training and equipping the joint force on behalf of the combatant commander, in practice the Services are actually heavily incentivized and motivated by budget pressures to act in their own respective best interests: dominance of war-fighting capabilities within their domains of land, sea, air, space, and cyberspace.[9]

Additionally, even if the Services pursue a joint vision, there are conflicting time-based incentives for the principal and agent. The combatant command focus is on the near-term problems of crisis response, current operations, and showing progress along lines of effort in the five-year Theater Campaign Plan. The Services are fundamentally focused on long-term problems like preserving budget share over time and managing the life cycle of programs in the Future Years Defense Program and beyond. Therefore, the principal prioritizes short-term thinking, while the agent has a strong disincentive to resource near-term demands at the expense of long-term requirements.

To align efforts, the Services must have more incentive to see the problem from the perspective of the combatant commanders. In the social sciences and in economics, this tension between the incentives of combatant commanders and the Services is classically defined, as noted earlier, as the *principal-agent problem.* In this construct, combatant commanders are collectively the principal due to their responsibilities to employ forces in joint operations, while the Services are the agents that generate these forces. Normally, an effective principal-agent relationship requires that the agent is compelled to act on behalf of the principal. However, in defense materiel acquisition, a principal-agent problem arises due to a misalignment of the incentives between combatant commanders and the Services.

The result of incentive misalignment is that programmed funding only haphazardly follows joint priorities. The Chairman of the Joint Chiefs of Staff issues the National Military Strategy, which lists his strategic priorities, and the Secretary of Defense issues the Defense Planning Guidance to influence the Services' Program Objective Memoranda. Once the memoranda are complete, the Secretary proposes changes through Resource Management Decisions. However, this process on average results in a change of less than two percent in the Service budgets from year to year.[10] In other words, this review ends up being largely a rubber stamp of the Service budgets. Since each Service essentially controls its own budget, it remains stovepiped, focusing on Service requirements ahead of the needs of combatant commanders.

The Chairman's Program Assessment and the Chairman's Program Review theoretically offer additional points for joint input, but evidence over many years and several chairmen confirms that these tools have little measurable impact on budgets. In fact, "Each Service's share of the defense budget . . . with a standard deviation of less than 1.8 percent over a 40-year period" has remained consistent. Despite "massive strategic or technological changes over four decades" and the transition from "Cold War to peace dividend to sustained irregular warfare during the war on terror" or even "during the so-called revolution in military affairs and Donald Rumsfeld's efforts at transformation," Service shares of the defense budget have remained steady. In the end, "if major external factors cannot change Service shares, there must be powerful internal forces at work."[11] In other words, no one outside the services has any significant impact on Service budgets.

Examples of how the misalignment of priorities affect materiel development are numerous. Greg Milner's book *Pinpoint* highlights an episode from the 1970s in which Air Force leadership underfunded, neglected, and eventually tried to kill the Global Positioning System, known at the time as the 621B Program. Milner notes that "the Air Force gets to build for space, but the Marine Corps, Army, and Navy are much more reliant on actual space services [for navigation] than the Air Force itself is. The budget for space is in the Air Force, but in terms of the number of customers and users, they're all in the other Services."[12] This telling historical example demonstrates how a critical joint warfighting capability was neglected because the Service with the least need for the capability happened to control the budget.

A more recent example is the reluctance of the Army to procure the Mine-Resistant Ambush Protected (MRAP) vehicle. To reduce casualties from improvised explosive devices in Iraq and Afghanistan, US Central Command was demanding a blast-resistant vehicle to replace the overburdened and under-armored high-mobility multipurpose wheeled vehicle. At the time, the Army had spent the previous decade championing its $160 billion FCS program, a family of high-tech systems envisioned to fight a near-peer competitor in major ground combat. Rather than divert money away from FCS to pay for the MRAP, Army leadership insisted that "everything we're doing in Future Combat System has a direct relationship to what Soldiers in combat need today."[13] Despite these assurances, the first vehicles were not scheduled to be fielded for another 10 years.[14] Months later, Secretary of Defense Robert Gates personally killed off the FCS and diverted the money to meet US Central Command's need. Simply put, a combatant commander desperately needed a capability to fight an ongoing war, yet the Service strongly resisted due to the long-term monetary impact on other acquisition programs that it rated as a higher priority. While it is difficult to go into much detail here on current capability gaps, a conversation with requirements managers at any combatant command will reveal that these problems persist.

Achieving Joint-Focused Defense Acquisitions

Alignment of combatant commanders' desire for joint capability with the acquisition actions of the Services can be achieved by addressing how requirements and funding are handled in DOD. Some might argue that combatant commanders already have sufficient input in these processes. For example, they submit an integrated priority list (IPL) consisting of their highest priority joint war-fighting capability gaps to the Joint Staff annually. The Joint Staff analyzes these gaps and recommends solutions to the Joint Requirements Oversight Council (JROC), a board consisting of the Service chiefs and chaired by the Vice Chairman of the Joint Chiefs. In previous years, the combatant commanders were also members of this council; however, the 2017 National Defense Authorization Act reduced their role from full members "when matters related to the area of responsibility or functions of that command are under consideration" to advisors whose input the "council shall seek and consider."[15]

Despite the joint purview and powerful membership of the JROC, the impact of the IPL on Service budgets is negligible. Of over 250 issues submitted by combatant commands in a recent year, the council only recommended for the Services to "invest additional resources" for four issues. Even then, the Services are not bound to implement these recommendations, and the chairman of the Joint Chiefs of Staff lacks the authority to direct procurement of any materiel capabilities.[16] Additionally, although the Chairman does publish the Chairman's Program Recommendation each year, this input is not directive and only affects Service budgets on the margins.[17]

To be effective, reforms must align Service and combatant command incentives in the JCIDS and PPBE. This will not be easy, as it will affect Service equities and may require congressional action, but the cost of failure in both blood and treasure is high.

Our recommended solution requires revamping how the IPL is handled to ensure that combatant commander needs drive the "front end" of the requirement process. Combatant commanders continue to submit their highest priority capability gaps and capacity shortfalls in the IPL. Additionally, the commands should coordinate a list of common high-demand gaps and shortfalls that span all commands. To reduce staff churn and institutionalize longer range thinking, this process should take place no more than once every two years.

These submissions would be developed by the Joint Staff Functional Capability Board and validated by the JROC with combatant commands serving as voting members. To put teeth into this effort, the resulting recommendation would nominate the list of gaps and shortfalls to the Secretary of Defense for endorsement.

Next, the Services would have the opportunity to bid on these gaps and shortfalls by proposing programs to address these needs. For example, if strategic power projection is a high-priority gap, the Air Force could present a plan to purchase additional airframes, while the Navy might present a requirement for a new high-speed transport vessel. The JROC would then vote on these proposals, with the winning proposals passed to the Office of the Secretary of Defense for final endorsement and resourcing decisions.

To react to these requirements, the Secretary of Defense would need to provide more flexibility in how Service procurement budgets are allocated. One way would be to designate a percentage of the overall acquisition budget, separate from the Service base budgets, to support this new process. With this budget flexibility, the Secretary would direct the corresponding base procurement budget share to the winning bidder's base budget. Once the Service receives the money, it manages these programs the same as every other acquisition program. This aligns incentives because reacting to combatant command needs would add budget share rather than cut into limited resources.

Services would retain control over a majority of their procurement budget for long-term service needs under this plan. The major change is the opportunity to secure additional base budget resources by satisfying combatant command requirements. The incentive not to shift money away from these programs would be the simple fact that failing to deliver on these programs would influence later rounds of bidding. This plan places the JROC at the center of joint force development, aligns combatant command and Service incentives more closely, and leaves civilian control of the military and its finances with the Secretary of Defense and ultimately with Congress.

Although Goldwater-Nichols imposed jointness on the US military, it failed to fundamentally change the incentives that had long driven the Services to competition and self-interest rather than cooperation. To get the Services to act on behalf of the combatant commanders—working together to develop forces tailored for joint warfighting—the DAS must be reformed to empower combatant commanders and the chairman of the Joint Chiefs of Staff with direct, proactive control over requirements and funding.

NOTES

1. Robert N. Charette, "The More Things Change . . . A Sampling of Viewpoints about Problems in Defense Acquisitions over the Last 25 Years," *IEEE Spectrum*, November 1, 2008, available at <http://spectrum.ieee.org/aerospace/aviation/the-more-things-change>.

2. Moshe Schwartz, *Acquisition Reform in House- and Senate-Passed Versions of the FY2016 National Defense Authorization Act (H.R. 1735)*, R44096 (Washington, DC: Congressional Research Service, July 2, 2015).

3. Ronald T. Kadish et al., *Defense Acquisition Performance Assessment Report* (Washington, DC: Office of the Deputy Secretary of Defense, January 2006), 17, available at <www.dtic.mil/dtic/tr/fulltext/u2/a459941.pdf>.

4. Mary Maureen Brown, Robert M. Flowe, and Sean Patrick Hamel, "The Acquisition of Joint Programs: The Implications of Interdependencies," *CrossTalk* 20, no. 5 (May 2007), 23. The authors present evidence that "joint" acquisition programs are, in general, less efficient than single Service programs, though they do not identify a cause. Even if correct, we contend that it is still preferable to pursue less efficient joint programs if they result in a more effective joint warfighting force.

5. Kadish et al., Defense Acquisition Performance, 36.

6. Leslie Lewis, Roger Allen Brown, and John Y. Schrader, Improving the Army Planning, Programming, Budgeting, and Execution System (PPBES) (Santa Monica, CA: RAND, 1999), available at <www.dtic.mil/dtic/tr/full-text/u2/a370563.pdf>.

7. Christopher J. Lamb, Matthew J. Schmidt, and Berit G. Fitzsimmons, "MRAPs, Irregular Warfare, and Pentagon Reform," Joint Force Quarterly 55 (4th Quarter 2009), 77; and

Del C. Kostka, "Moving Toward a Joint Acquisition Process to Support ISR," Joint Force Quarterly 55 (4th Quarter 2009), 70.

8. Robert Gates, speech, United States Military Academy, West Point, NY, February 25, 2011, available at <http://archive .defense.gov/Speeches/Speech.aspx?SpeechID=1539>.

9. Jim Cooper and Russell Rumbaugh, "Real Acquisition Reform," Joint Force Quarterly 55 (4th Quarter 2009): 63–64.

10. Cooper and Rumbaugh, "Real Acquisition Reform," 61.

11. Cooper and Rumbaugh, "Real Acquisition Reform," 63.

12. Greg Milner, Pinpoint: How GPS Is Changing Technology, Culture, and Our Minds (New York: Norton, 2016), 45.

13. Sandra I. Erwin, "Immunizing Weapons Against Next-War-itis," National Defense, July 1, 2008, available at <www .nationaldefensemagazine.org/articles/2008/7/1/2008july-immu nizing-weapons-against-nextwaritis>.

14. Erwin, "Immunizing Weapons."

15. US Senate, National Defense Authorization Act for Fiscal Year 2017, Public Law 114–328, 114th Cong., December 23, 2016, 130 Stat. 2360 § 925, available at <www.congress.gov /114/plaws/publ328/PLAW-114publ328.pdf>.

16. Defense Acquisition University (DAU), Joint Program Management Handbook (Fort Belvoir, VA: DAU Press, July 2004).

17. Cooper and Rumbaugh, "Real Acquisition Reform," 61.

Conflated Reality

Reserve and Active Duty Components in American Wars

MICHAEL D. GAMBONE

Introduction

The separate roles for the reserve component (RC) and active duty component (AC) have their origins in the US Constitution; however, their relationship is often ill defined. Fighting wars in Afghanistan, Iraq, as well as the Global War on Terror (GWOT), have left the American ranks thin and in need of members of the reserves and the National Guard to plug the holes. Without much public debate, this move has transformed reserve units to strategic ones. This essay considers the consequences of this shift by examining the costs to the reserve units and the sustainability of this model in the near future.

By tradition and practice, the National Guard and reserves are a large and integral part of the American military. In 2018, almost a million personnel—approximately 45 percent of US forces—served in all US military reserve components.[1] More importantly, the reserve components have been direct participants in contemporary overseas contingency operations. By 2010, half of all Army reserve units saw combat.[2] At the time of this writing, National Guard and reserve forces have suffered approximately one-fifth of the total casualties in current US military conflicts.[3]

Reserve component forces provide two main contributions to the US force structure. The first is simple combat muscle. In 2000, the Army National Guard fielded a total of forty-six brigades or their equivalents.[4] Although this number has declined since the September 11 attacks, Army National Guard brigades comprise approximately half of the branch's combat power.[5] These units have been regularly deployed abroad to fight alongside active duty units engaged against insurgents in Iraq and Afghanistan.[6] For their part, Air National Guard pilots made significant contributions to the war, flying almost one-third of fighter and attack aircraft in 2007.[7]

A second critical role involves logistics, upon which modern, technologically advanced militaries depend. In 2017, Army Reserve units provided 82 percent of civil affairs, 56 percent of transportation, and 50 percent of medical support units.[8] Similarly, Air Force reserve components are responsible for aerial refueling, tactical reconnaissance, military airlift, and command and control. Air National Guard pilots handled approximately one-quarter of remotely piloted aircraft sorties in 2010.[9]

Once deployed, reserve components are also critical agents of "soft power," or, as General David Petraeus once described it, "non-kinetic operations."[10] By virtue of their expertise in infrastructure, these units are intimately involved with restoring power grids, roads, bridges, and homes, all of which are important to developing popular support. In another sense, through the work of civil affairs, intelligence collection, and military police, reserve units allow a more precise application of American power, one theoretically better versed in the local language and customs of a region, while incorporating a range of nonlethal options.

Until the September 11 attacks, the US military rarely conceived of reserve components as a strategic force. The First Gulf War and a number of subsequent peacekeeping and peace-enforcement missions tested some of the basic assumptions and practical problems of deployment. However, it was not until the September 11 attacks and the GWOT that Defense Department leadership fully understood the significant challenges involved in transforming the reserves and National Guard into integral components of the US military.

This essay discusses the evolution of reserve components from their role as a basic building block of local defense to a contemporary strategic asset. It tracks the early origins of the American militia, a force that underwent a gradual series of reforms as the nation moved from a small republic on the periphery of world affairs to a global superpower. It then highlights military deployments that followed the September 11 terrorist attacks to assess the strains placed upon the reserves as assumptions formed by decades of planning were tested by the hard realities of war.

The Force of History

The American military has been heavily reliant on part-time service members for most of its history. From the founding of the original colonies through the American Revolution, the common defense was almost completely dependent on local volunteers. While regiments of continental regulars and French troops joined American armies as the revolution progressed, the backbone of the revolutionaries' military was the militia. When the war ended, the value of the blue and buff of the Continental Line was largely discarded, and entrenched tradition reasserted itself. In 1784, Congress demobilized the regular Army to the point that it contained only eighty men.[11]

Regardless of its lack of uniformity, the eighteenth- and nineteenth-century militia system was useful because it provided a cushion against mass conscription for standing armies. For most of the nineteenth century, American wars rarely required more than 3 percent of the country's total resident population serving in the active military.[12] When war required large-scale mobilization, it was treated as an expedient—a necessary evil.

Although the system proved problematic at best during subsequent American conflicts, meaningful military reforms awaited the twentieth century. These involved coordinating and consolidating American military forces under federal control. The Dick Act (1903), a second Militia Act (1908), and the National Defense Act of 1916 allowed for the finishing touches on a renovated, twentieth-century US military establishment.[13]

World War I tested the new system as a whole. The United States was able to deploy millions of newly raised forces to France under the able leadership of General John J. Pershing. Although the American Expeditionary Force witnessed significant shortcomings in training and equipment, it arrived at a critical juncture in the war and proved decisive to German defeat.

The massive requirements of global force projection during World War II completely reversed this trend. National Guard and reserve units were assimilated into the massive mobilization that eventually included 16 million citizens who volunteered or were conscripted to fight the "Good War." Many reserve units, such as the Pennsylvania 28th Infantry Division and Oklahoma's 45th "Thunderbird" Division served with distinction. Moreover, the Reserve Officer Training Corps was significantly expanded and provided thousands of junior leaders critical to lead this massive military establishment.

Reserve components were also fundamental to US military readiness in the early stages of the Cold War. Although a peacetime draft continued after 1945 and the newly created Defense Department maintained substantial conventional forces—1.5 million total in 1947—the National Guard and reserves were a critical part of US strategic reserves.[14] The outbreak of hostilities in Korea highlighted this dependence in the frantic mobilization of American forces that followed after North Korean forces crossed the 38th Parallel in June 1950. By the end of the conflict, approximately one-fifth of personnel who served during the Korean conflict came from the reserve components.[15]

The relatively large numbers of reservists committed to service during Korea proved highly unpopular. Consequently, when the United States military began to escalate operations in Southeast Asia, the decision to leave the reserves home was more political than practical. Throughout the Vietnam War, the Defense Department deliberately relied on a force structure built on active duty units, increasing numbers of draftees, and a profligate use of firepower to bolster American combat operations.

With the end of both the draft and the Vietnam War, the Pentagon embarked on a new round of reforms that addressed the transition to an all-volunteer force and an increasing reliance on reservists. Army Chief of Staff Creighton Abrams introduced the "total force" concept that incorporated the National Guard and reserve directly into the US defense structure. Abrams's original plan designated the reserves as part of strategic forces available for gradual commitment to large-scale conflicts, with a conventional war in Western Europe as the main expected battlefield. Function followed this intent, with the National Guard comprising half the Army's combat units. Combat support—transport, engineers, civil affairs, military police—was consigned almost entirely to the reserves.[16]

The "total force" concept was never tested during the Cold War, although it was partially implemented during Desert Shield/Desert Storm in 1990 and 1991. One in four US soldiers deployed to the Middle East at the time was a reservist. Most of these individuals performed combat support missions. The handful of Army National Guard combat brigades mobilized to fight were not deployed by the time Desert Storm commenced in January 1991, largely because they were not ready for the fight.[17] As the 1990s progressed, the reserve components provided increasing numbers of personnel for peacekeeping and peace enforcement, disaster aid, humanitarian relief, post-conflict reconstruction, and other missions categorized under the contemporary label of Military Operations Other than War (MOOTW).[18]

The Impact of 9/11

Although operational tempo increased in the 1990s, it did not place a heavy burden on the reserves. Until 2002, roughly one of the thirty-eight Army National Guard Brigade Combat Teams was deployed in any given year, usually as part of peacekeeping duties in the Balkans or the Middle East.[19] However, this situation markedly changed in the aftermath of the September 2001 terrorist attacks on the United States. Immediately afterward, the Pentagon embarked upon a period of sustained military deployments that recalled past wars, but on a far larger scale and longer duration. The total number of annual duty days served by reserve components skyrocketed from 12.7 million prior to September 11 to 62.8 million just two years later.[20] Initially, reservists provided extra security at airports and other transportation hubs around the country. In the wake of Operation Enduring Freedom (2001) and Operation Iraqi Freedom (2003), more and more reserve and National Guard formations made their way into combat zones to support coalition efforts.

These deployments went against a number of initial assumptions made by the White House and senior Defense Department leadership. In the early stages of the war, Secretary of Defense Donald Rumsfeld embraced an operational concept that would keep US ground forces at a minimum. Emphasizing the utility of advanced guided weapon systems used in concert with local forces, the argument went that there would be no need for a large military footprint in the opening days of the GWOT. The early, remarkably rapid success of rapid decisive operations (RDOs) in Afghanistan appeared to support this school of thought.

The same assumptions about "shock and awe," as RDO was popularly known, reappeared during war planning for Operation Iraqi Freedom (OIF). When General Tommy Franks began the Iraqi invasion, he had a fraction of the forces—128,000 troops under Operational Plan (OPLAN) 1003V—available during Operation Desert Storm a decade earlier.[21] This strategy proved to be unsustainable in the long run. American and coalition ground forces were inadequate to prevent the breakdown of civil order, the ensuing insurgency, and subsequent stability operations. Within a year of the beginning of Operation Iraqi Freedom in 2003, three-quarters of the Army's combat brigades were deployed abroad, and more were needed for ongoing operations.[22] Overall, the Army was the most heavily deployed branch, comprising 58 percent of total personnel overseas between 2001 and 2015.[23]

As active duty regulars began to run out, the National Guard and reserves plugged the gap. Only four years after planes struck the Pentagon and World Trade Center, 150,289 of 558,000 Americans serving in the reserve components were on active duty, the largest number since the Korean War.[24] Again, the Army National Guard and reserves provided the largest contingent, 38 percent of total individuals deployed by the branch. The Air Force (25 percent), Marine Corps (10 percent), and Navy (9 percent) offered considerably smaller contributions.[25]

In a manner reminiscent of the 1950 Korea mobilization, there was a definite haphazard quality to post–September 11 reserve deployments. As will be discussed below, mission-critical equipment was embarrassingly deficient. Too many units departed for combat assignments without pre-deployment training or complete personnel rosters. Time was also in very short supply for many reservists. In the rush to mobilize, members of the Michigan Army National Guard shipped out for Iraq with only forty eight hours' notice.[26]

There were also a number of important departures from the 1950 model. Tours of duty were markedly longer. By 2007, Army National Guard and reserve deployments lasted sixteen to eighteen months. In order to reach adequate readiness levels, units routinely conducted four months of pre-deployment training followed by a year on the ground in country.[27] Many units also deployed for multiple tours, particularly those with key military specialties. In 2004, while approximately one-third of the guard and reserve were on active duty, 45 percent of reserve officers in military police, intelligence, and fixed-wing aviation had deployed. A further 55 percent of enlisted personnel in law enforcement, motor vehicle operation, and security forces received call-up notices during the same period.[28] Units with such critical skillsets subsequently experienced repeated deployments. The Maryland Army National Guard's 115th Military Police Battalion was called up three times in a two-year period, for example.[29]

Counting the Costs

The premise that a reservist could serve for one weekend a month and two weeks during summer annual training—thirty-nine days each year—is simply obsolete in the current military environment. In practice, the actual number varies from this pre-2001 Cold War standard to as many as 150 days each year.[30] Today, it is not uncommon for routine monthly drill "weekends" to start on a Thursday and continue into the following week.

In fundamental terms, the need for force readiness drives concurrent institutional demands for both time and resources. During the last decade and a half, the

Pentagon has attempted to apply many of the hard lessons following the September 11 attacks, particularly with respect to reserve components. In testimony before the Senate in 2018, Army Reserve commander Lieutenant General Charles D. Luckey noted that the goal was to have 30 percent of his component maintaining a high level of readiness to shorten the amount of time necessary for deployment.[31] In fact, Luckey's testimony was simply punctuating a process that has been ongoing for almost a generation. Significant increases in operational tempo have created a trickle-down effect throughout the force structure. Each of the separate branches has argued for new funding to cover pay, equipment modernization, training, and a host of new expenses necessary for sustained overseas contingency operations. According to research done by John Nagl, outlays for reserve component personnel increased by 50 percent between 2001 and 2010. Spending for maintenance (33 percent) and procurement (157 percent) also rose substantially.[32]

Unfortunately, this generosity in funding levels was a short-lived phenomenon. National politics and a rapidly escalating national debt eventually intruded upon the brief period of reserve component recovery and modernization. Between the 2008 Iraq drawdown and the emergence of the Islamic State of Iraq and Syria (ISIS) in 2014, Congress embarked upon a significant period of military budget cuts aimed at reducing an annual federal deficit that exceeded $1.1 trillion in 2012.[33] That year, according to the Budget Control Act, Congress agreed to a debt ceiling deal that resulted in substantial reductions in military spending. "Sequestration," as it came to be known, reduced discretionary outlays for aircraft, vehicles, ships, and a host of other items. Overall, it projected a 10 percent cut in defense spending by 2014.[34]

The ebb and flow of defense spending priorities is not the only reason readiness standards fluctuated wildly throughout the GWOT. The mass deployments following September 11 produced a systemic shock to the reserves. Many units were unprepared for long-term operations outside the United States, while others were tasked with missions outside their conventional training. Circumstances sometimes dictated tactical choices. In 2004 and 2005, for example, most Army National Guard brigade combat teams in Iraq and Afghanistan were engaged in counterinsurgency missions regardless of their training, specialization, or readiness.[35] It was not uncommon for field artillery units to leave their guns and conduct patrols as infantry. Where units were not trained in their new missions, they simply adapted and improvised in place.

Equipment and personnel shortages plagued the reserves components. Prior to September 11, many units commonly lacked either the quantity or quality of items available to regular forces. This was especially true with respect to transportation, weapon systems, and communications gear. It was common for Army National Guard combat units to have only two-thirds to three-quarters of the materiel and personnel necessary for their assigned missions. This lack of readiness reached an embarrassing moment in 2004 when Secretary of Defense Donald Rumsfeld visited troops at Camp Buehring, Kuwait, as they marshaled for movement into Iraq. Members of the Tennessee and Idaho Army National Guard challenged the secretary on "shortages and antiquated equipment" as well as "hillbilly armor" scavenged from garbage dumps to upgrade vehicles.[36] Rumsfeld's response of "You go to war with the Army you have, not the Army you might want or wish to have at a later time," while technically accurate, betrayed an incredible tone deafness to the core problem.[37]

In the first years of the GWOT, the Army National Guard simply cannibalized equipment to meet its escalating deployment demands. According to the Government Accountability Office (GAO), in 2005, the Guard transferred 101,000 items from nondeploying units to formations going overseas. This process included generators, armored Humvees, night-vision devices, and other mission-critical items.[38] Unfortunately, much of what these units took to Iraq and Afghanistan remained behind when they returned home. According to a GAO study, 64,000 pieces of equipment stayed in combat zones for follow-on forces. The National Guard could not account for half of it. Military police reservists alone left over 600 Humvees and other armored vehicles before returning to their home stations.[39] The practice significantly disrupted recovery efforts when units returned to the United States after completing their deployments.

Changes to military manpower policies also had significant consequences. The common practice of "cross leveling," or shifting tens of thousands of personnel out of their parent units to fill deploying formations, also had a long-term and profoundly negative impact on the reserves. In a move that hearkened back to Defense Department practice during the Vietnam War, key leaders or individuals with critical military occupational specialties found themselves reassigned to units bound for combat. Between 2001 and 2004 alone, over 74,000 personnel were affected by this policy.[40]

As the war ground on, overall readiness eroded across the board. In 2007, a congressionally chartered independent Commission on the National Guard and Reserves examined the issue and unearthed serious deficiencies. Some conclusions were basic. The commission reported that cross leveling, while sufficient to meet immediate needs, had "degraded unit cohesion" within the Guard. Moreover, the commission observed that "while the operational tempo of all the reserve components has increased substantially, resourcing has not kept pace."[41] Other systemic trends were more disturbing. The commission noted a steady decrease in prior active duty personnel in the reserves as well as recruitment and retention difficulties that were "highly problematic."[42] Although the report found that increased budgets could alleviate attrition to people and equipment in principle, the commission added the important caveat: "DOD historic budget data show that Army plans for projected funding increases for the Army National Guard are not reliably carried through."[43]

The Army National Guard experience was not unique within the US military. The other services have struggled with the impact of multiple, long-term deployments on personnel and equipment. This is true of Army and Marine Corps ground forces as well as the surface and subsurface fleets employed by the US Navy.[44]

Other branches attempted to address readiness difficulties by improvising. The Air Force approached the problem through institutional reorganization. In Wyoming, Nebraska, Virginia, and Georgia the Air Force created the hybrid "Reserve/Active-Associate Wing Model," designed to pool aircraft and personnel to meet new missions and responsibilities.[45] The 170th Group from the Nebraska Air National Guard currently serves as part of the Air Force's 55th Wing, the largest in Air Combat Command. The unit operates seven different types of planes, from the E-4B command-and-control platform to variations of the RC-135 reconnaissance aircraft. It benefits from the combination of first-line equipment and active duty and reserve talent. However, its improved utility has correspondingly resulted in increased operational tempo and deployments. One study commented on the "extraordinary turnover" caused by repeated overseas deployments.[46]

The GWOT has had a significantly negative impact on the reserve components' aging physical infrastructure. Across the country, it is easy to find armories in use that date back to the nineteenth century. Although a surge in construction during the Cold War produced modernized facilities, some of these are now more than sixty years old and badly in need of routine maintenance and essential updates.[47] They suffer from faulty heating and air conditioning, a lack of storage space, bad plumbing, outdated electrical power systems, and poor internet access. Moreover, almost fifty years after women began joining the "total force" military in significant numbers, many armories still rely on improvised female bathrooms.[48]

Federal appropriations have not come close to meeting actual need. According to the 2014 Army National Guard Readiness Center Transformation Plan, the Defense Department needed to spend $1.4 billion a year over twenty years to remedy fundamental infrastructure problems. Real expenditures fell far short of basic necessities. In fiscal year 2015, the National Guard received $155 million for construction projects. Subsequent years were equally parsimonious: $167 million in FY 2019 and $174 million in FY 2020.[49]

When counting the costs of the GWOT to reserve components, it is important to consider the human element. As noted above, the reserve components brought specific talents necessary to conduct effective stabilization operations. However, individuals with specialties in military police, civil affairs, and other related fields were in high demand, participated in multiple deployments, and suffered disproportionately higher rates of attrition.

Some of these problems were easier to identify than others. One is a surprising unemployment rate experienced by reservists. Federal law dedicated to ensuring employment security, the Uniformed Services Employment and Reemployment Rights Act (USERRA) of 1994, is a modern update of the original G. I. Bill and predated the surge in overseas contingency operations.[50] Its basic provisions seemed relatively straightforward. Deploying service members could expect to have their original jobs back once they returned home. Being able to count upon civilian careers left behind was an obvious boon to part-time reservists. This specific protection reinforced the basic contract between the government and its citizen-soldiers.

As overseas contingency operations surged, the implementation of USERRA was more problematic. In 2011, the National Guard Bureau estimated that 20 percent of returning reservists were unemployed, twice the rate for all veterans after 2001.[51] As it evolved, the GWOT proved especially disruptive to workers and employers alike. One difficulty was scale. Between 2001 and 2014, 815,000 reservists were called up, separating them for months if not years from their civilian jobs.[52] Multiple deployments, particularly in the early years of the war, were onerous for both individuals and their parent companies.

The economic impact of reserve duty varied according the location and the individual. Ten states—California, Texas, Pennsylvania, Florida, New York, Ohio, Georgia, Virginia, Illinois, and Alabama—bore the brunt of military mobilization, as did their respective workforces.[53] The economic disruptions created by military service almost certainly contributed to unemployment insecurity during the Great Recession of 2007–2009.

Individuals coming home experienced additional difficulties. Besides the loss of work, many returning reservists also discovered that they had fallen behind with respect to job training or found their experience obsolescent after multiple deployments.[54] Some specific sectors were affected more than others. A 2014 study, for example, noted that male reservists were overrepresented among first responders, specifically police, fire, and emergency medical services. As a result, hundreds of police and fire departments across the country were saddled with extra workloads that could only be partially covered with overtime pay and temporary hires. Consequently, mobilization affected both the reservists, who lost valuable training, experience, and seniority, and their local communities, which had to adapt to lengthening emergency response times.[55]

Reserve component mobilization proved expensive for businesses as well. Companies complying with USERRA had to absorb the increased costs of overtime, temporary replacements, and ongoing pension benefits in some cases. A number of companies simply cut their losses through a variety of machinations designed to avoid federal law. In the first two years of the war, 5,690 veterans lost their jobs after returning home or were fired before deploying.[56]

Federal authorities offered what were at best incomplete or inadequate solutions to these issues. Although the USERRA protected service members against discrimination, it was limited in scope and applicability. Passed in an era before the September 11 attacks, the law protected employment for activated reservists for up to five years. Lawmakers never anticipated multiple or multiyear deployments that went beyond this limit. Other provisions of the USERRA simply shifted costs from businesses to the reservist. For example, while the law mandated that deployed individuals could keep their employer health insurance and pension plans, it made them responsible for payments, a difficult prospect for reservists on a military pay scale.[57]

Most returning reservists did not contest the loss of jobs or increased personal expenses. According to one estimate, as many as two-thirds of veterans did not bother to follow official channels for redress.[58] However, many did file complaints with the Department of Labor. In 2004, approximately 1,500 did so. Seven years later, the number of complaints was almost identical.[59] Individuals could file complaints with the Veterans' Employment and Training Service in the Department of Labor. Additionally, federal employees serving in the reserves could use the same process or present themselves before the Merits System Protection Board, which handles appeals from federal civil servants.[60] To circumvent federal intervention, many businesses simply required new hires to sign pre-employment agreements to take any disputes to binding arbitration.[61] This tactic has withstood subsequent challenges in federal courts.

National Guard and reserve families suffered other meaningful costs as a result of overseas contingency operations. A RAND study noted that divorce rates in the National Guard rose sharply after 9/11, jumping 1 percent from 2001 to 2003. The problem was more pronounced in the reserves, where divorces more than doubled from just fewer than 2 percent to 5.5 per-

cent.[62] Although divorce rates leveled off in the mid-2000s, the problem persists in specific branches. According to a 2015 Defense Department study, the divorce rate in the Army Reserve remained high at 4.9 percent while in the Air National Guard and Air Force Reserve, it was just slightly above pre-September 11th percentages at 2.2 percent.[63]

The economics of reserve component service has also placed considerable strain on families. The disparity between civilian and military pay and benefits shocked more than a few spouses tasked with making ends meet during deployments. Regular expenses—mortgages, utilities, and groceries—became increasingly harder to meet. New costs, such as phone cards, which became instrumental in communicating with deployed servicemembers, placed unexpectedly substantial burdens on monthly budgets.[64]

For the uninitiated, both the military bureaucracy and its benefits system, which covers a spectrum from medical insurance to military public schooling, could be both perplexing and incredibly frustrating. Many spouses struggled to navigate the new doctors, facilities, and protocols that came with the military health-care system. Moreover, returning servicemembers were met with unwelcome surprises as they transitioned from military back to civilian benefits packages provided by their employers. Many reservists who successfully completed their deployments and returned to their old jobs discovered that they had to reapply for their civilian health insurance plans. When they did so, a number of companies took the opportunity to raise rates or deny them coverage based on preexisting conditions.[65]

Other social changes impacted reserve families. Unlike the active duty component, reservists do not enjoy the informal safety net within the military community that offers experienced advice or basic information to help navigate home life during deployments. This situation often left the parent who remained in the United States to struggle with the daily responsibilities of two people—doctor's visits, shopping, commuting to practices, to name a few—without a support structure.[66] Inevitably, increasing burdens and subsequent stress traveled down to the children of reservists. According to recent research, these strains affected educational progress and also resulted in increasing behavioral problems.[67]

Their deployed parents suffered as well. According to a 2010 study of approximately 10,000 reserve component members published in the *Journal of Traumatic Stress*, returning reservists and National Guardsmen experienced higher rates of post-traumatic stress disorder (PTSD) and depression than active duty personnel.[68] This was especially true among the senior enlisted: "NCOs [non-commissioned officers], similar to officers, generally have a substantial responsibility for the well-being of junior enlisted service members, yet often lack the influence over policy and resources available to officers."[69] While this circumstance is not unusual for NCOs in any part of the military, the factor that stood out in the 2016 study was the influence of civilian life on PTSD rates. Incidence rates for PTSD among reservists and the National Guard were much higher—more than double—among individuals reporting civilian trauma prior to enlistment.[70] These experiences were likely higher among reservists drawn from police, fire, and emergency medical services, some of the most deployed parts of the reserves. Overall, it appears that rather than provide a cushion against the costs of war, civilian experience may be a feature of reserve service that may actually worsen the pathologies affecting veterans.

The Dilemma of Future Sustainability

Although military operations began winding down in the second decade of the new century, they continue to significantly impact the reserves and National Guard. Without question, the United States' "Forever War" has changed the public's perception of military service, particularly among potential recruits. A June 2006 youth poll indicated that only 14 percent of young men expressed an interest in joining the military, down 33 percent from the previous year. Surveys also recorded a significant decline—from 70 percent in 2001 to 40 percent in 2002—in parents likely to recommend military service to their children.[71]

Maintaining current recruit quality has subsequently become somewhat difficult. A 2015 Congressional Research Service study noted that the individual military branches generally were able to sustain two metrics of recruit quality: 90 percent possessing a high school diploma and 60 percent scoring above average on the Armed Forces Qualification Test (AFQT).[72] However, in 2013 and 2014, the components that consistently struggled the most to achieve these baselines were the Army National Guard and Army Reserves, the two components most heavily deployed after September 11.[73] During the same time period, active duty forces have maintained a higher retention rate than the Guard and reserve, something that has hurt the reserve components, which draw approximately 10 percent of their personnel from former regulars.[74]

Explanations for the decline vary. Diminishing interest in military service may be correlated to a relatively strong economy and labor market. Once the dislocations of the Great Recession passed, unemployment dropped to record lows.[75] Until the COVID-19 pandemic and severe economic disruptions that followed it, the military had to compete with a comparatively more attractive civilian sector.

To alleviate the recruiting problem, the Defense Department significantly increased spending on reenlistment incentives. The Army National Guard paid out $27 million for bonuses in 2004. Two years later, the amount increased an order of magnitude to $308 million.[76]

Other structural changes also helped to offset the actual need for recruits. After peaking in 2011, active duty military headcount has since declined from approximately 1.5 million to 1.3 million in 2018.[77] Army (476,000), Navy (327,000), Marine Corps (185,000), and Air Force (325,000) staffing now stands at a historic low.[78] With the exception of the Marine Corps, all the active services branches are smaller than they were before the start of the Korean War.[79]

Military retention offers a separate set of challenges that varies according to each military branch. Matched against the specific annuals goals set by the military, active duty forces have posted high retention rates in recent years. In FY 2014, for example, the lowest reenlistment rate for first term enlisted service members was 94.6 percent in the Navy, which retained 7,799 of the 8,248 goal for that year. The Marine Corps (96 percent), Army (114.4 percent) and Air Force (128.4 percent) posted impressive numbers during the same period.[80]

Reserve component retention was a somewhat different story. The Air National Guard, the Air Force Reserve, and the Marine Corps Reserve all consistently stayed at or below their attrition ceilings between 2013 and 2014. The Army National Guard missed its goal of 16.3 percent attrition in 2013, but achieved it the following year after raising the cap to 19.1 percent. The Army Reserve exceeded its attrition level in both years.[81]

The service branches have attempted to address this trend with a number of measures. The reserve components introduced hundreds of new recruiters and increased funding for enlistment and reenlistment bonuses. At the same time, the Army National Guard and Army Reserves cut their 2018–2024 annual recruiting goals by half, from 4,000 soldiers to 2,000.[82]

In many respects, the Guard and reserves are learning to make do with less. This applies to recruiting. It also pertains to future training and readiness. There was a point in the years immediately after the September 11 attacks that the Defense Department attempted to align reserve component training with the active duty military. Since the 2008 Status of Forces Agreement with Iraq and the general drawdown of forces in Afghanistan, that effort has atrophied. The contemporary Guard and reserve have largely reverted back to the twentieth-century standard of localized training conducted by individual units. For example, although the Army National Guard is organized into brigade combat teams like their active duty counterparts, they almost never train as a collective whole. Today, access to advanced training is rare, especially as contingency operations wind down. Tennessee's 278th Armored Brigade Combat Team, for example, visited the National

Training Center (NTC) in 2004 and did not return again for fourteen years. Ten years after the Iraq Status of Forces Agreement, a 2018 *Army Times* story noted that the Pentagon had dispatched National Guard brigades to both the National Training Center and the Joint Readiness Training Center for the first time.[83]

The lack of training opportunities on par with active duty forces has had a profound impact, particularly for high-demand military specialties. While individual reservists are expected to have the same training as active duty units, this is rarely the case. Army civil affairs soldiers, 82 percent of whom were reservists in 2017, should have the benefit of language classes, airborne qualifications, and other related training that normally takes years to complete. However, for these particular reservists, this training is compacted into eleven weeks at the JFK Special Warfare Center and does not include language training or airborne school.[84]

The COVID-19 Inflection Point

The 2020 pandemic renewed focus on the domestic missions of the National Guard and reserves. As the number of Americans affected by the disease rapidly escalated in March and April, state governors called up National Guard units to bolster health services that were beginning to break under the surge of new patients. To supplement civilian medical facilities, they constructed field hospitals in California, Connecticut, New York, and Kentucky, among many other locations.[85] The Iowa and Nebraska Guard transported critical supplies to hospitals, distributed food to people in need, and expedited shipment of test kits to labs.[86] Units in Michigan, Nevada, and New Hampshire helped officials conduct COVID-19 testing. In Wisconsin, the National Guard assisted the local government in maintaining polling stations during their August primary voting.[87]

Pandemic service has come at a cost for the National Guard and reserves. Despite establishing protocols to mitigate risk, once units began to assemble, many personnel tested positive for COVID-19 and had to enter quarantine or, in the worst case, be hospitalized for treatment.[88] Units deployed in response to widescale protests and civil unrest suffered the same outcome. Members of the Washington, DC, Army National Guard reported positive tests among its membership in June 2020.[89]

Moreover, as reserve components attempt to accomplish a variety of missions during the pandemic, they have not escaped the politically charged atmosphere present throughout the United States. In a July 2020 testimony before the House Committee on Natural Resources, Army National Guard Major Adam DeMarco, who had served earlier on a combat deployment to Iraq, contradicted official statements that tear gas was not used during operations against protests in Lafayette Park and noted further that "from my observation, those demonstrators—our fellow American citizens—were engaged in the peaceful expression of their First Amendment rights. Yet they were subjected to an unprovoked escalation and excessive use of force." As the late Representative John Lewis said, "When you see something that is not right, not just, not fair, you have a moral obligation to say something, to do something."[90]

Conclusions

The modern history of US reserve components is characterized by cycles of stagnation, progress, and predictable regression. In the wake of the Vietnam War, the Defense Department created the "total force" more as a concept than a practical option for US national security. In principle, it made sense. The reserve and National Guard occupied an important place as a strategic reserve for a hypothetical European war against the Soviet Union. Planning followed the logic that the next major conflict would allow for the gradual and sequential mobilization of reserve components from the continental United States to the battlefield. According to the theory of operations, both combat and combat support units would enter into a force structure as fully integrated components of the whole.

In practice, these principles were difficult to implement. The GWOT proved to be a formidable stress test of the "total force" concept. Overseas contingency operations exercised their own war of attrition on equipment, personnel, and the military community as a whole. In the long term, these strains continue to be illustrated not only in the wear and tear on aging armories, but more importantly on retention rates, particularly in the Army National Guard.

Faced with ongoing challenges, the reserve components have done what the American military has always done during difficult times: they adapt. Whether in the form of "hillbilly armor" or hybrid formations in the Air National Guard, reservists have used their initiative to accomplish tactical missions and maintain long-term operational effectiveness. These efforts have been accompanied by institutional reforms to training, procurement, and unit deployment cycles. By 2011, the mid-point in US overseas contingency operations, it appeared as if the reserve components had reached a positive tipping point.

However, these adaptations were dependent on consistent support and funding from civilian leadership. By the second Barack Obama administration, the US government rediscovered parsimony, which in turn forced the defense establishment into a period of retrenchment, which adversely affected hard-won progress. In the ripple effect of hard calculations that followed, the reserve components lost much of the in-

stitutional traction they had gained in the years following September 11.

Despite these reversals, the National Guard and reserves are better off compared to pre-2001 standards in
terms of training and overall experience. A 2007 Defense Department task force was prescient when it observed: "If the Department believes that the Global
War on Terror is a generations-long conflict, the Army
should examine the balance of its 'total force' structure
if it wishes to move toward meeting the policy objectives of the Secretary."[91] The same could be said of all
the service branches as they assess future reforms to the
"total force."

Old habits and institutional inertia are difficult, but
not impossible obstacles to overcome. Defense spending is again on the increase as the United States con-
templates new twenty-first-century missions. As the
United States emerges "from a period of strategic atrophy," as one 2018 Defense Department publication
put it, policy-makers will once again consider the role
of the reserve components.[92] Moreover, as it retools
doctrine for the part-time military, the Pentagon would
be well advised to consider the long-term impact of deployments on individual health and civilian employment as well as the attrition suffered by military families. In this way, it can promote American national
security while it also preserves a crucial link to the
country as a whole. The COVID-19 pandemic continues to emphasize the latter mission in particular.

NOTES

1. Lawrence Kapp, *Defense Primer: Reserve Forces*, CRS
7-5700 (Washington, DC: Congressional Research Service,
December 12, 2018), 2.

2. John A. Nagle and Travis Sharp, "Operational for
What? The Future of the Guard and Reserves," *Joint Forces
Quarterly* 59 (2010): 22.

3. Stewart Smith, "The True Cost of War since September 11th, 2001," The Balance Careers, July 9, 2019. https://
www.thebalancecareers.com/the-cost-of-war-3356924. See also
Department of Defense, Casualty Status as of 10 a.m. EDT,
August 20, 2019, https://www.defense.gov/Newsroom/Casu
alty-Status/

4. Army National Guard Divisions, Globalsecurity.org,
https://www.globalsecurity.org/military/agency/army/division
-arng.htm (accessed July 18, 2019).

5. Congressional Budget Office, *The Military's Force Structure: A Primer* (Washington, DC: CBO, 2016), 2, 17. In 2016,
the active Army had thirty combat brigades, while the Army
National Guard contributed twenty-six.

6. Max Boot, "The Struggle to Transform the Military,"
Foreign Affairs 84 (March–April 2005): 107.

7. Lieutenant Colonel Kevin S. Dailey, "Air National
Guard Structure for the Twenty-First Century: The Multimis-
sion Framework for Total Force Integration," Air War College
Maxwell Paper No. 43 (Maxwell Air Force Base, AL, May
2008), 4, 7.

8. US Army Reserve, *America's Army Reserve at a Glance*
(2017), 9. https://www.usar.army.mil/AtAGlance/.

9. Nagle and Sharp, "Operational for What?" 24.

10. David H. Petraeus, "Multinational Force-Iraq Commander's Counterinsurgency Guidance," *Military Review* 88
(September–October 2008): 2.

11. Allan R. Millett and Peter Maslowski, *For the Common Defense: A Military History of the United States of
America* (New York: Free Press, 1994), 91.

12. Molly Clever and David R. Segal, "After Conscription:
The United States and the All-Volunteer Force," *Security and
Peace* 30 (January 2012): 9–10. Clever and Segal note that the
Civil War (3 percent) and World War I (3 percent approached
this threshold, while Korea involved slightly more than 2 per-
cent of the population and Vietnam less than 2 percent).

13. Alan R. Millett and Peter Maslowski, *For the Com-
mon Defense: A Military History of the United States of
America* (New York: Free Press, 1994), 330. See also Walter
Millis, *Arms and Men: A Study in American Military History*
(New Brunswick, NJ: Rutgers University Press, 1984), 179–80.

14. In 1939, there were 334,473 active duty US military
personnel. See Department of Defense, Directorate of Information Operations and Support, *Selected Manpower Statistics: Fiscal Year 1997* (Washington, DC: Government Printing
Office, 1998), 51.

15. During Korea, the Defense Department activated
857,877 reservists in total. See Lawrence Kapp and Barbara
Salazar Torreon, *Reserve Component Personnel Issues: Questions and Answers*, RL30802 (Washington, DC: Congressional
Research Service, October 2018), 7.

16. Lawrence J. Korb, "Fixing the Mix: How to Update the
Army's Reserves," *Foreign Affairs* 83 (March–April 2004): 2–7.

17. GlobalSecurity.org, "Reserve Component," https://www
.globalsecurity.org/military/library/report/call/call_92-2_hiso
.htm (accessed September 12, 2019).

18. Clever and Segal, "After Conscription," 12. See also
John L. Romjue, *American Army Doctrine for the Post–Cold
War* (Washington, DC: Center of Military History, 1997).

19. Congressional Budget Office, "Statement of J. Michael
Gilmore, Assistant Director of National Security: Issues that Af-
fect the Readiness of the Army National Guard and Reserve,"
(Washington, DC: CBO, May 16, 2007), 1.

20. Dailey, "Air National Guard Structure for the Twenty-
First Century," 2.

21. Michael D. Gambone, *Small Wars: Low-Intensity
Threats and the American Response since Vietnam* (Knoxville:
University of Tennessee Press, 2013), 240–61.

22. Korb, "Fixing the Mix," 4.

23. Jennie W. Wenger, Caolionn O'Connell, and Linda Cottrell, *Examination of Recent Deployment Experience across the
Services and Components* (Santa Monica, CA: RAND Corporation, 2018), 3.

24. Sharon Otterman, "Iraq: Troop Reinforcements," Council on Foreign Relations, February 2, 2005, https://www.cfr.org
/backgrounder/iraq-troop-reinforcements.

25. Wenger, O'Connell, and Cottrell, *Examination of Recent Deployment Experience*, 3.

26. Korb, "Fixing the Mix," 5.

27. Department of Defense, Office of the Secretary of Defense, Defense Science Board, *Final Report of the Defense Science
Board Task Force on Deployment of Members of the National*

Guard and Reserve in the Global War on Terrorism (Washington, DC: Department of Defense, 2007), 9.

28. US Congressional Budget Office, *The Effects of Reserve Call-Ups on Civilian Employers* (Washington, DC: CBO, May 2005), 9.

29. Korb, "Fixing the Mix," 5.

30. Michael Wickman, "Always Ready, Always There? National Guard Readiness in the Contemporary Operational Environment," Modern War Institute, April 26, 2019, https://mwi.usma.edu/always-ready-always-national-guard-readiness-contemporary-operational-environment/.

31. Lieutenant General Charles D. Luckey, "The Posture of the United States Army Reserve, America's Global Operational Reserve Force," Testimony before the Senate Appropriations Committee—Defense Hearing, April 17, 2018.

32. Nagl and Sharp, "Operational for What?" 26.

33. Congressional Research Service, *The Defense Budget and Budget Control Act: Frequently Asked Questions*, R44039 (Washington, DC: CRS, September 30, 2019), 1.

34. Congressional Research Service, *The Defense Budget and Budget Control Act*, 5; Rhys McCormick, Andrew P. Hunter, and Gregory Sanders, *Measuring the Impact of Sequestration and the Drawdown on the Defense Industrial Base* (New York: Center for Strategic and International Studies, December 2017), 1–10.

35. Sydney J. Freedberg, "National Guard Commanders Rise in Revolt against Active Army; MG Rossi Questions Guard Combat Role," Breaking Defense, March 11, 2014, https://breakingdefense.com/2014/03/national-guard-commanders-rise-in-revolt-against-active-army-mg-ross-questions-guard-combat-role/.

36. Eric Schmitt, "Troops' Queries Leave Rumsfeld on the Defensive: Lack of Equipment," *New York Times*, December 9, 2004, A1.

37. Schmitt, "Troops' Queries."

38. Government Accountability Office, *Reserve Forces: Army National Guard's Role, Organization, and Equipment Need to be Reexamined*, GAO-06-170T (Washington, DC: GAO, 2005), 4.

39. GAO, *Reserve Forces*, 14.

40. GAO, *Reserve Forces*, 10.

41. Michael Waterhouse and JoAnne O'Bryant, *National Guard Personnel and Deployments: Fact Sheet*, RS22451 (Washington, DC: Congressional Research Service, January 2008); Commission on the National Guard and Reserves, *Second Report to Congress, March 1, 2007* (Arlington, VA: Commission of the National Guard and Reserves, 2007), ix–x.

42. Commission on the National Guard and Reserves, *Second Report to Congress, March 1, 2007*, ix.

43. Commission on the National Guard and Reserves, *Second Report to Congress, March 1, 2007*, ix.

44. Government Accountability Office, *Navy Readiness: Action Needed to Address Costly Maintenance Delays Facing the Attack Submarine Fleet*, GAO-19-229 (Washington, DC: GAO, November 2018); Government Accountability Office, *Navy Readiness: Action Needed to Address Persistent Maintenance, Training, and Other Challenges Facing Fleet*, GAO-17-7987T (Washington, DC: GAO, September 2017).

45. Dailey, "Air National Guard Structure," 13–17.

46. Dailey, "Air National Guard Structure," 21.

47. According to the Army National Guard, 47 percent of its armories are at least fifty years old. See Army National Guard,

"ARNG 4.0: Focused Readiness," n.d., https://www.army.nationalguard.mil/Resources/Focused-Readiness/ (accessed 15 September 2019).

48. Adam Stone, "Building Problem," *National Guard Association of the United States Magazine*, July 11, 2019, https://www.ngaus.org/about-ngaus/newsroom/building-problem.

49. Stone, "Building Problem."

50. United States Department of Justice, Uniformed Services Employment and Reemployment Rights Act of 1994, https://www.justice.gov/crt-military/uniformed-services-employment-and-reemployment-rights-act-1994.

51. Alexandra Zavis, "National Guard Soldiers and Airmen Face Unemployment Crisis," *Los Angeles Times*, November 23, 2012, https://www.latimes.com/world/la-xpm-2012-nov-23-la-me-national-guard-employment-20121124-story.html.

52. Christopher J. Coyne, Abigail R. Hall, Patrick A. McLaughlin, and Ann Zerkle, "A Hidden Cost of War: The Impact of Mobilizing Reserve Troops on Emergency Response Times," *Public Choice* 161 (December 2014): 289–90.

53. CBO, *The Effects of Reserve Call-Ups on Civilian Employers*, 5.

54. Laura Werber Castaneda, Margaret C. Harrell, Danielle M. Varda, et al. *Deployment Experiences of Guard and Reserve Families: Implications for Support and Retention* (Santa Monica, CA: RAND Corporation, 2008), 87.

55. Coyne et al., "A Hidden Cost of War," 290; CBO, *The Effects of Reserve Call-Ups on Civilian Employers*, 6–7.

56. Timothy W. Maier, "Pink Slips Greet Returning Soldiers," *Insight on the News* 20 (January 6, 2004): 26.

57. CBO, *The Effects of Reserve Call-Ups on Civilian Employers*, 13, 16–17.

58. Alexandra Zavis, "Betrayed? Citizen Soldiers Lose Jobs: U.S. Government Biggest Offender," *Los Angeles Times*, May 5, 2013, https://www.latimes.com/local/la-xpm-2013-may-05-la-me-citizen-soldiers-20130506-story.html.

59. CBO, *The Effects of Reserve Call-Ups on Civilian Employers*, 15; Zavis, "Betrayed?"

60. Maier, "Pink Slips Greet Returning Soldiers," 26.

61. Libby Denkmann, "Fired after Military Deployment, Reservist Seeks His Day in Court," The American Homefront Project, October 20, 2017, https://americanhomefront.wunc.org/post/fired-after-military-deployment-reservist-seeks-his-day-court.

62. Benjamin R. Karney and John S. Crown, *Families under Stress: An Assessment of Data, Theory, and Research on Marriage and Divorce in the Military* (Santa Monica, CA: RAND Corporation, 2007), 118, 128–29.

63. US Department of Defense, Office of the Deputy Assistant Secretary of Defense for Military Community and Family Policy, *2015 Demographics: Profile of the Military Community* (Washington, DC: Department of Defense, 2015), 98. Military divorce rates were comparable to the US national rate. According to the Centers for Disease Control and Prevention, civilian rates were 3.2 percent in 2014 and 3.1 percent in 2015. Centers for Disease Control and Prevention, National Center for Health Statistics, Marriage and Divorce, *National Marriage and Divorce Rate Trends, 2000–2107*, https://www.cdc.gov/nchs/fastats/marriage-divorce.htm

64. Castaneda et al., *Deployment Experiences of Guard and Reserve Families*, 67, 85.

65. Castaneda et al., *Deployment Experiences of Guard and Reserve Families*, 68.

66. Castaneda et al. *Deployment Experiences of Guard and Reserve Families*, 79.

67. Coyne et al., "A Hidden Cost of War," 291; Katrin Cunitz, Claudia Dölitzsch, Marcus Kösters, et al., "Parental Military Deployment as Risk Factor for Children's Mental Health: A Meta-Analytical Review," *Child and Adolescent Psychiatry and Mental Health* 13, no. 26 (June 2019): 1–10, https://doi.org/10.1186/s13034-019-0287-y; Sharon Pexton, Jacqui Farrants, and William Yule, "The Impact of Fathers' Military Deployment on Child Adjustment. The Support Needs of Primary School Children and Their Families Separated during Active Military Service: A Pilot Study," *Clinical Child Psychology and Psychiatry* 23, no. 1 (2018): 110–24.

68. Keith D. Renshaw, "Deployment Experiences and Postdeployment PTSD Symptoms in National Guard/Reserve Service Members Serving in Operations Enduring Freedom and Iraqi Freedom," *Journal of Traumatic Stress* 23 (December 2010): 815–18.

69. David S. Fick, Gregory S. Cohen, Laura A. Sampson, et al. "Incidence of and Risk for Posttraumatic Stress Disorder and Depression in a Representative Sample of U.S. Reserve and National Guard," *Annals of Epidemiology* 26 (March 2016): 195.

70. Fisk et al., "Incidence of and Risk for Posttraumatic Stress Disorder and Depression," 194.

71. Defense Science Board, *Final Report of the Defense Science Board Task Force*, 13. A more recent Harvard Youth Poll indicated that interest in military service remains low. According to a 2018 poll, 82.7 percent of males and 88.1 percent of females said they would "definitely not" or "likely not" enlist. See Yashaar Hafizka, "Harvard Youth Poll: Decreasing Interest in Community and Military Service," *Harvard Political Review*, April 25, 2018, https://harvardpolitics.com/united-states/harvard-youth-poll-decreasing-interest-in-community-and-military-service/.

72. Congressional Research Service, *Recruiting and Retention: An Overview of FY2013 and FY2014 Results for Active and Reserve Component Enlisted Personnel*, RL32965 (Washington, DC: CRS, June 26, 2015), 1.

73. CRS, *Recruiting and Retention*, 7–8.

74. Todd South, "Retention, More Recruiters and Lower Goals Are Putting Guard, Reserve on Track to Fill Ranks," *Army Times*, April 11, 2019, https://www.armytimes.com/news/your-army/2019/04/11/retention-more-recruiters-and-lower-goals-are-putting-guard-reserve-on-track-to-fill-the-ranks/.

75. At the time of this writing, the US unemployment rate was 3.6 percent. See Bureau of Labor, Labor Force Statistics from Current Population Survey, https://www.bls.gov/cps/ (accessed June 15, 2019).

76. Defense Science Board, *Final Report of the Defense Science Board Task Force*, 12.

77. CRS, *Recruiting and Retention*, 3–5, 11.

78. Katherine Blakeley, *Military Personnel* (Washington, DC: Center for Strategic and Budget Assessments, August 15, 2017), https://csbaonline.org/reports/military-personnel.

79. Millett and Maslowski, *For the Common Defense*, 656. The respective strengths of each branch in 1950 were: Army (593,000), Air Force (411,000), Navy (382,000), and Marine Corps (74,000).

80. CRS, *Recruiting and Retention*, 14.

81. CRS, *Recruiting and Retention*, 15. The Army Reserve attrition goal was 17.2 percent in FY 2013. The actual percentage was 18.1. In FY 2014, the goal was 16.4 percent, and the actual attrition percentage was 18.6.

82. South, "Retention, More Recruiters and Lower Goals."

83. Meghann Myers, "Only a Third of Army's BCTs are Ready to Deploy," *Army Times*, May 21, 2018, https://www.armytimes.com/news/your-army/2018/05/21/only-a-third-of-the-armys-bcts-are-ready-to-deploy-heres-how-the-service-plans-to-fix-that/.

84. David Harrell, "The Army Reserve's Troubling Little Secret: Cheap, Inadequate Training," United States Military Academy: Modern War Institute, September 7, 2017, https://mwi.usma.edu/army-reserves-troubling-little-secret-cheap-inadequate-training/.

85. Michael R. Sisak, "Many Field Hospitals Went Largely Unused, Will Be Shutdown," *Military Times*, April 29, 2020, https://www.militarytimes.com/news/coronavirus/2020/04/29/many-field-hospitals-went-largely-unused-will-be-shut-down/.

86. Steve Liewer, "In Nebraska and Iowa, Coronavirus Is National Guard's Biggest Emergency Response in Years," *Omaha World-Herald*, May 30, 2020, https://omaha.com/local/in-nebraska-and-iowa-coronavirus-is-national-guards-biggest-emergency-response-in-years/article_4d7d66cf-8aab-51d2-b9f9-b12629cd6270.html.

87. Vaughn R. Larson, "Wisconsin National Guard Supports Election across State," National Guard, August 12, 2020, https://www.nationalguard.mil/News/Article/2309782/wisconsin-national-guard-supports-election-across-state/.

88. Rachel McDevitt, "Members of Pennsylvania National Guard Test Positive for COVID-19," WITF, April 10, 2020, https://www.witf.org/2020/04/10/members-of-pennsylvania-national-guard-test-positive-for-covid-19/.

89. Ali Idrees, "D.C. National Guard Responding to Protests Test Positive for Coronavirus," Reuters, June 9, 2020, https://www.reuters.com/article/us-health-coronavirus-usa-military/d-c-national-guard-responding-to-protests-test-positive-for-coronavirus-idUSKBN23G2Z8.

90. Written Statement of Adam DeMarco, "Unanswered Questions About the U.S. Park Police's June 1 Attack on Peaceful Protestors at Lafayette Square," Hearing Before the Committee on Natural Resources, U.S. House of Representatives, July 28, 2020, 5.

91. Defense Science Board, *Final Report of the Defense Science Board Task Force*, vii, 27.

92. Department of Defense, *Summary of the 2018 National Defense Strategy of the United States of America: Sharpening the American Military's Competitive Edge* (Washington, DC: Department of Defense, 2018), 1.

Contemporary Issues in American Defense Policy

Introduction

JOHN RILEY

Part III examines how purpose and process translates into American defense policy. Organized into three chapters, part III investigates how the new battlefield, shifting force structure, and emerging disruptive technologies are impacting American policies. This introduction begins by examining the overarching themes running throughout the chapters and then turns to the thesis of each essay.

Taken as a whole, part III suggests that American defense policy is undergoing tremendous turbulence; the first quarter of the twenty-first century is providing a stress test that America is finding difficult to pass. The threats fall into three overlapping categories. First, the threat from terrorism persists. In some ways though, the threat of a terrorist attack on the United States has started to feel almost mundane—terrorism is an evil that can be held at bay with surgical strikes or nighttime raids—and this will continue to be an accepted view until the next cataclysmic attack. Second, history has returned. Great-power competition is in fashion again as China has risen to a peer competitor status and Russia continues to move against Western interests in Ukraine and the Middle East. Third, we are reminded of nature's principle role in defining what it means to be secure. At the time of this writing, the United States was undergoing a pandemic that has killed over 500,000 of its citizens and threatens to devastate its economy. The world's focus is rightly on COVID-19, but other potentially more devastating Black Swans or Grey Rhinos (see Epilogue) loom over the horizon as climate change goes largely unabated.

The United States is trying to adapt, but as it extracts itself from the quicksand of Afghanistan, it is still struggling with how to define what victory would have looked like, or perhaps what a reasonable standard should be in a next counterinsurgency. All the while, the United States relies increasingly on special operations forces (SOF) throughout the globe to tamp down on threats of every size and shape.

These events are also occurring in a world where the cyber and space domains raise unprecedented challenges to homeland security. The 2016 presidential election demonstrated the United States' vulnerability to foreign interference via rudimentary cyber tools, and it served as a proof of concept for those looking to undermine the American public's confidence in its institutions. As Thomas Rid and Ben Buchanan argue in chapter 8, the United States' technical infrastructure of voting machines and information databases are acutely at risk—cyber-hacking competitions are literally turning them into video games—and thereby putting the entire American democratic system into peril. The space domain highlights a different but equally dangerous set of vulnerabilities for American defense.

In many ways, space operations are the backbone of US military strength, but the susceptibility of those assets to both cyber and physical intercepts are well known. The solution was to launch a US Space Force with an aim to "dominate." The success of this decision will be measured not just by whether this was a smart administrative move—a bureaucratic end-run-around the US Air Force, which were perceived by some as not being able (or perhaps willing) to achieve the undefined task of dominating space. Rather, success will be more of a function of whether the United States can now meet the challenge it has created for itself.

That is, by declaring its intent to dominate, the United States has admitted either its unwillingness or inability to lead the international community in the global common and thereby inadvertently legitimized any future adversaries' attempts to exploit US vulnerabilities in space. By intent or otherwise, the United States has declared that space will no longer be a domain that will only support land, air, and sea operations; space will be a battlefield subject to those operations as well. This is a self-inflected wound, and only over time will we know its lethality.

Finally, game-changing technologies—from artificial intelligence to hypersonic weapons—present themselves as silver bullets that could either slay the US hegemon or ensure its ascendency for the decades to come. This realm of near possibilities is equally tantalizing and frustrating. Quantum computing is a perfect case in point. If quibits become reality, then projects that might have taken traditional supercomputers a year to complete would be solved in minutes, and mainstay tools, such as encryption, might immediately become obsolete. On the other hand, quantum computing might be remembered as fondly as the "successful" achievement of cold fusion.

In some ways, these challenges are not new. Separating the signal from the ground noise has always been the task of the policy-maker. Stakes are high now, but they are not higher than those raised by nuclear annihilation during the Cold War. Moreover, it would take the most anachronistic eye to see any point in modern US history as being easily guided or under control.

Rather, what this section's collection of essays suggest is that the United States is not well positioned to pass this stress test. Humility is needed if it is going to learn the lessons from Iraq and Afghanistan. Reassessment of how, when, and why America uses its SOF and its remotely piloted aircraft is required. Strategic leadership is needed if arms control and nuclear proliferation regimes are going to persist. Perhaps most importantly, adaptability and resiliency will become one of the country's most important assets. As the essays in this section make clear, having access to a path-breaking technology is important, but it is hardly determinative of military success. Will the United States follow the atrophied British Empire that relegated the aircraft carrier to little more than a naval scouting ship, or will it follow its own standard forged during World War II and make transformative changes?

Regarding the specific contributions to this volume, part III begins with an examination of the threats to homeland security. Everett Carl Dolman opens chapter 8 with an exceptionally provocative argument that the United States and China are on a collision course for war—and may in fact already be at war over outer space. Drawing upon hegemonic stability theory (see chapter 4), Dolman argues that the US empire, and perhaps its hegemonic status, are in jeopardy. The ascendant China has challenged the United States in the "one incompatible, uncompromising realm . . . outer space." The solution is for the United States to seize "effective control of space and do so in a way that [is] perceived as tough, nonarbitrary, and efficient." Akin to the British patrolling the high seas, America ought to dominate the lower earth orbit and a new regime will emerge. The essay frames the logic (without the endorsement) of a US space force and serves as an intellectual foundation for proponents and critics to respond.

Moving from outer space to what was traditionally the United States' principle strategic concern, nuclear weapons, James Smith examines the impact low-yield nuclear weapons (LYNWs) are making on the increasingly daunting challenge of maintaining strategic stability. After tracing the American and Soviet effort to deter each other's advance, Smith problematizes the destabilizing effect that LYNWs play in the modern hyper-complex—and in many critical areas poorly understood—international environment. One consequence of the proliferation of LYNWs is that the traditional strategy of strategic stability might have to be set aside for a novel approach that is modeled on continuous change. Shifting to a "dynamic stability" approach would recognize that "it may become necessary to destabilize one area in order to stabilize a more

timely or important challenge, with a plan already in place for longer-term stabilization of the destabilized area."

Thomas Rid and Ben Buchanan examine perhaps the greatest threat that the cyber domain poses to US national security: the subversion of American democracy. "The stakes could not be higher: liberal democracy has become a juicy target of ever more sophisticated Computer Network Attacks (CNAs)—and CNAs have become a preferred semi-covert action tool of the early 21st century." Moreover, America's cybersecurity is not up to the task. There are plenty of soft targets, and cybersecurity "disappoints in practice, policy, and scholarship." This is a "reckoning," and unless dramatic changes are made to the US infrastructure and private-public information sharing is increased, American liberal democracy may perish.

The chapter ends with Lawrence Freedman asking what the lessons of history can tell us about the likelihood of a surprise cyberattack. Freedman observes that although surprise attacks have been the "melodramas that drive much of the narrative of real and imagined events," the reality is that they often have proven ineffective. Surprise attacks often fail (e.g., Iraq invasion of Kuwait) or they have not translated into decisive blows. Returning to the question of a massive cyberattack against the United States, the question is not whether this is possible or even probable. More importantly, what would follow?

Chapter 9 turns to the changes in the US force structure as it makes contact with a dynamic battlespace. Austin Long's opening essay on SOF makes is clear that the nadir of the 1980s has been reversed and that SOF are now the ubiquitous tool favored by policy-makers who are often looking to avoid the political costs associated with conventional forces. SOF have become "generalized specialists" that link the strategic, operational, and tactical levels of warfare in a unique way that gives them a market advantage. As Long argues, however, SOF are hardly a panacea, and policy-makers and analysts have to recognize their limitations in both direct and indirect actions. The danger is not simply the misuse of SOF, but the creation of a frustrated customer as policy-makers hold unrealistic expectations of what SOF can achieve.

Flying next to SOF, both literally and figuratively, are unmanned aerial systems (UAS). Like SOF, UAS are a politically expedient tool that affords US forces global reach without running the risk of incurring immediate causalities. At the same time, there is probably no other tool in the American arsenal that is subject to greater potential misuse.

Michael Kreuzer reviews the increasingly large types of UAS and their varied uses on the battlefield. As Kreuzer notes, in air warfare, no issue encapsulates the debate over whether technology is fundamentally changing the characteristic of war then UAS. From the US perspective, UAS that are matched with the nation's global satellite infrastructure and precision munitions become a strategic resource that allows the United States to carry out five core missions (air and space superiority; intelligence, surveillance, and reconnaissance; rapid global mobility; global strike; and command and control). For non-state actors, commercial off-the-shelf technology "make quadcopters and home-made medium-range UASs the IEDs of the sky or the insurgent's cruise missile." However, as the United States sought to stand up its Iraqi coalitional partner, US officials underestimated the organizational and cultural challenges associated with the adoption of advanced technologies. There is the danger that the technological tool can undermine the strategic objectives.

John Nagl grounds the ongoing American quagmire in the Middle East and Afghanistan with lessons offered by Clausewitz and Napoleon: the critical role the public plays in supporting or defeating an insurgency. That is, approaches to conventional warfighting that seek to annihilate the enemy are poorly situated to defeat an insurgency. Rather, the focus ought to be on separating the revolutionaries from the people and bolstering the legitimacy of the counterinsurgency. Minimum force should therefore be the guiding principle of any counterinsurgency; the people should feel that the government seeks to protect them—"not destroy them."

What, then, are the lessons we should learn from the war in Afghanistan? Hew Strachan asks whether we are reliving the 1980s when the "US Army had opted not to learn its lessons, but to treat the experience as an aberration," and the British took a similar stance toward their experiences in Northern Ireland. After nineteen plus years of painful experiences fighting counterinsurgencies, there is a yearning to fight the next war within the realm of one's own core competencies. For the Americans and British this translated into returning to preparation for war against a peer competitor. With the United States' endless war coming to a close, the temptation will be to discount the largely horrific experience. However, if the country is willing to learn from Afghanistan, it must recognize the importance that coalitional forces played in the war and that its coalitional partners' experiences might offer the most important lessons.

David Sacko concludes the chapter by asking what victory in modern irregular warfare (IW) looks like. Rejecting the likelihood that direct action will translate into a short-term victory in IW, Sacko draws upon all the works of this chapter and suggests a very novel perspective. That is, victory will be possible only when a whole-of-US government approach engages in persistent engagement; systematic efforts to shape individual expectations with the ultimate aim to integrate

them into the international system, and not seek to burn it down. In turn, maintenance of the international liberal order is contingent on the United States not walking away from its obligations in nontraditional wars. Broadly stated, American success is therefore determined by how well it can foster this symbiotic relationship.

Concluding this edition, each of the essays in chapter 10 speak to a radically different near future. Michael Horowitz's essay examines artificial intelligence (AI), perhaps the ultimate enabling technology, and its impact on international competition and the balance of power. Advancing his adoption capacity theory, Horowitz predicts that the "relative financial and organizational requirements for adopting a military innovation influence the rate of diffusion of that innovation and its impact on the balance of power."

In the case of AI, it is still too early to tell what its full impact may be. Horowitz's article, however, does suggest several principles that should guide American defense policy. First, AI represents a major strategic opportunity for many capital-rich countries that have "commercial incentives for AI developments and the dual-use character of AI applications." AI may also fundamentally change the character of war by doing things such as increasing the speed in which countries fight and influencing the force structure they are able to employ on the battlefield. Third, and perhaps most important, if the United States is to effectively implement AI, it must overcome the constraints of an organizational cultural that resists paradigmatic change. Examples of the Air Force's continued emphasis on manned pilots or the military's failure to fund the X-47B drone suggest that US military's cultural barrier to incorporate organizationally disruptive technologies into its overall force structure may prove to be fatally prohibitive.

Mauro Gilli also examines the complexity of modern warfare and he takes up the issue of diffusion of military technology. Debunking the long-held assumption of the "advantage of backwardness," Gilli makes a detailed and compelling argument that modern military technology does not diffuse downward easily or inexpensively. That is, countries "cannot simply free ride on the research and development of the most advanced states." Modern military technology, such as stealth, has become exponentially complicated and countries must first develop the industrial and scientific capabilities before attempting to become "first-tier weapons manufacturers." China's expensive and frustrating efforts to replicate the US F-22A/Raptor jet fighter are hopeful signs that the United States' military technical dominance may continue for the foreseeable future.

The disruptive effects of technological innovation are also felt in the nuclear and cyber realms. Keir Lieber and Daryl Press argue that the technological revolution in conventional warfare potentially lay waste to two fundamental assumptions guiding US nuclear deterrence and usage: that nuclear arsenals reliably deter attacks via retaliation, and that nuclear weapons produce mass slaughter. That is, the precision and speed of conventional weapons, combined with the relatively small size of a country's nuclear arsenal, has dramatically increased an adversary's ability to launch a conventional military strike or counterforce attack and destroy its opponent's nuclear weapons. Moreover, as nuclear proliferation continues, the United States may increasingly find itself in a conflict with an adversary that would be willing to engage in "coercive nuclear escalation" to avoid a conventional loss. Taken together, these two arguments suggest that advances in conventional military technology may undermine US efforts to maintain its nuclear deterrent and simultaneously lead its adversaries to nuclear escalation to avoid defeat.

Adding to the danger, nuclear weapons are increasingly vulnerable to cyber attacks. Erik Gartzke and Jon Lindsay demonstrate that there is an unappreciated danger that the "warfighting advantages of cyber operations become dangerous liabilities for nuclear deterrence." It is not that cyber capabilities can be weapons of mass destruction—an overhyped possibility; rather, a "catalytic instability" arises when the cyber domain interacts with the nuclear. The nuclear deterrent relies on transparency and clear communication while cyber operations rely on deception. Therefore, a cyber attack on a country's nuclear command, control, and communications could create a dynamic whereby the attacker knows it has gained an advantage (which it cannot reveal without comprising its future cyber capabilities), "while the adversary will continue to believe it wields a deterrent that may no longer exist." A fog of war during the decision-making processes could emerge whereby the target may press for an advantage without the capabilities it thinks it possess, or the target state might recognize its compromised position. In the latter scenario, the target may escalate out of fear of being further compromised. The presence of these "unknown unknowns" could lead to a cyber-nuclear escalatory spiral.

Finally, John Allen and Bruce Jones argue that climate change might be the defining existential crisis of our time, and their short essay maps the security consequences for the United States and the international community. On the one hand, several challenges stem from the immediate consequences of climate change, such as the likely proliferation of intrastate violence, migration and refugee crises, and rising sea levels. An equally daunting challenge is set at the feet of the great powers. If China and India continue to industrialize in the same manner that the West did, then the world will likely lock in a 4-degree rise in temperature, a disastrous scenario. Will Russia and Saudi Arabia transition their economies onto a footing that does not depend on the extraction of fossil fuels? For American defense policy, the challenge is clear: "If the United States fails to lead, it risks squandering its moral standing and its leadership at a critical time in the international order—with serious, perhaps severe, costs."

Chapter 8

Homeland Defense: Threats from All Sides

New Frontiers, Old Realities

EVERETT CARL DOLMAN

The coming war with China will be fought for control of outer space. Although its effects will be widely felt, the conflict itself will not be visible to those looking up into the night sky. It will not be televised. Most will not even be aware it is occurring. It may already have begun.

And yet, this new kind of war will not be so different that it will be unrecognizable. The principles of war and the logic of competition remain as they have always been. Only the context has changed. When we have this mind-set and apply the tenets of traditional realist and geopolitical theories that have survived millennia in their basic forms, the unavoidable conclusion is that the United States and the People's Republic of China (PRC) are on a collision course for war.

The following offers an interpretation of the neoclassical geopolitical context that shapes the potential for conflict between the United States and China, places that discussion within a broader theory of strategy, tactics, and war, and assesses the potential for a twenty-first-century Great Wall in low-Earth orbit.

Neoclassical Geopolitics

Almost 2,500 years ago, Thucydides foresaw the inevitability of a disastrous Peloponnesian war due to "the rising power of Athens and the fear it caused in Sparta."[1] Indeed, whenever an extant international order is challenged by a rising power, the reigning hegemonic authority is obligated to respond. Such conditions are relatively rare in history, but when they occur, the resulting war is not for minor spoils or border modifications, but for leadership of a new world order. It is a great war, a hegemonic war.[2] This is the context in which the world now exists. The relatively stable global hegemony of the United States since 1945, punctuated by limited wars and shifting balances of opposition, is directly challenged by the rising power of the PRC—and the fear it is generating in the United States is palpable. Such determinist theory is quickly countered by those who find its implications abhorrent. Inevitability is a crass and unsubtle divination. Because a thing has always happened does not mean that it always will. Nor does the reverse necessarily hold. Because something has never happened does not mean

that it cannot be so. The realist paradigm of power politics does not have to hold sway. The cruelly consistent narrative of history need not be eternally retold. Nothing is inevitable, counter the idealists. The world can be made different; the world today *is* different.

The power of possibility is tantalizing, but the brusque strength of probability, for a decision-maker, usually holds sway. The past foreshadows the future—and the calculation of probability over time, combined with risk, is more persuasive than platitudes. If an event is likely, its influence is plain, and its outcome perceptible, then preparations must be made to mitigate its effects. If an event is unlikely, even if its impact is serious, actions to mitigate it are often deferred to the future—even though this form of political gambling tends to magnify the deleterious effects of the event when it eventually comes to pass. If the state's sovereignty is at risk, however—no matter how unlikely the event—it must be dealt with directly. The well-understood—if not everywhere accepted—logic of raison d'état calculations is fully in accord with classical geopolitical dictums dating back at least as far in their theoretical lineages.

The resurrection of geopolitics as a valid body of military theory is in full swing. By applying the tenets and dicta of geopolitics to the current age with a focus on space activities, I hope to contribute to its revival. That classic geopolitical thought should require resurrection means that it has gone through a period of disfavor and decline, a history that will require further examination. For now it is enough to assert that geopolitics collapsed of its own weight, from the misuse and abuse that followers subjected it to by taking its less-defensible precepts to their extreme ends. Just as neoliberalism, neorealism, and neo-Marxism seek to return to founding theories for their inspiration and avoid the perversions and misapplications of often well-meaning but logically off-track followers, so too does neo-geopolitics seek a reaffirmation of basic principles and an explanation for the misuse of them in history.

Geopolitics looks to geographic or Earth-centered physical and spatial characteristics for its explanatory power.[3] The unit of analysis is the state. Its location, size, resources, and population are placed in the context of political ideology, sociocultural values, and technology to assess the dominant forms of war in a given time. The manipulation of this knowledge is called *geostrategy*—a state-dominant assessment of the geospatial bases of power in plans or strategies for continuing military, economic, diplomatic, and sociocultural advantage.

Geopolitics as a unified body of theory was not apparent until the later nineteenth century, but its inherited lineage is clear in retrospect. To the extent that the strong do what they will and the weak suffer what they must, as Thucydides had the imperial Athenians tell the neutral Melians in his celebrated dialogue on state power and pride, realpolitik has always focused on manipulating the extant balance of power for its persuasiveness.[4] Although it is conceptually separate from geopolitics, in both meaningful theory and practice, the two schools of thought are logically inseparable.

Geopolitics describes the sources—the what—of state power; *geostrategy* explains the how. Neither provides the underlying rationale, the why. That requires a broader theoretical perspective. The one that dominated the architects of geopolitical thought clusters under the rubric of realism.

If state power, expressed in terms of capacity for violence, is the ultima ratio of international relations,[5] then geopolitical theory is extremely useful. Thucydides and Machiavelli perceived the self-interest of states coincident with that of humanity: a hierarchy of fear, interest, and honor.[6] The state that does not protect itself will be overcome; that which does not grow will wither and die. Cardinal Richelieu summed it up in the phrase "raison d'état."

In an environment of relative scarcity, the interests of states overlap, and conflict can be expected. Prudent leaders will recognize the geographically advantageous positions and capacities that enhance state power and will attempt to control those positions—or at a minimum deny control of those positions to an opponent—to ensure the continued health and growth of the state. A study of such capacities, incorporated into a plan for continuing advantage, is called *geostrategy*.

For example, Alfred Thayer Mahan argued that in the modern era, great power required the possession of a navy capable of projecting influence globally.[7] It was time, he asserted near the end of the nineteenth century, for the United States to develop a maritime force equal to its economic clout, throw off its cloak of isolationism, and take its rightful place at the forefront of nation-states. Mahan was an American nationalist, to be sure, but his theories applied to any state in a similar position. Great power leads to great responsibility, he reasoned, and America was abrogating its obligations by failing to lead.

The first truly global geostrategist, Halford Mackinder, described a cyclical clash of land and sea powers through history, a view that coincides with other prominent theories of recurring rivalries, such as the interplay of offensive or defensive technologies or capacities for maneuver or mass that tend to dominate the battlespace in a given era. Sea power, Mackinder argued, in ascendance with the development of reliable oceangoing shipping after 1500, was by the beginning of the twentieth century ceding maneuver dominance to mass-force land power as the technology of the railroad created relatively fast and inexpensive internal lines of supply and communication.[8]

As technology developed, the details of geostrategic theory morphed toward actionable decisions, but the essential logic persisted. Similar arguments were made for air and missile power and are currently in vogue for space power. As we work through the ramifications of an *astropolitik* approach, several conclusions are readily apparent:[9]

- Classical geopolitics provides the most enduring realist explanations for change in the international system.
- Many classical geopolitical theories prove readily adaptable to the realm of outer space.
- These theories, tailored for sea, rail, air, and missile power, can be viewed as segments of an evolutionary process. Space power is their logical and apparent heir.
- The special terrain of outer space dictates tactics and strategies for efficient exploitation of space resources.
- Space is a national power base today—an optimum deployment of space assets is essential on the current terrestrial and future space-based battlefield.

US *and* PRC or US *versus* PRC?

At first glance, geopolitical forces may seem to be in dynamic balance. The United States is the overwhelming sea and air power, offensively oriented and favoring maneuver and precision strike for advantage in war. The PRC is potentially the greatest land power the world has ever known, defensively established and reliant on masses of infantry as its core strength. Neither has a globally significant advantage vis-à-vis the other. There is no plausible near-term scenario in which the United States could invade and sustain an occupation of the Chinese mainland. Likewise, the United States is currently impervious to any invasion and occupation by Chinese forces. Neither state's sovereignty appears in doubt because of actions by the other. At the level of grand strategy, neither maneuver nor mass, neither offense nor defense, has a transformational advantage. From this perspective, war, inevitable though it might be, is not imminent.

Less-venerable theories of conflict and cooperation are more favorable toward long-term peace.[10] Economically, the United States and the PRC are tightly bound. Chinese markets are opening, and the productivity of PRC manufacturing has allowed the United States to move into a post-industrial economy. Trade is increasing substantially, and China holds much of America's foreign debt, to the point that neither state benefits fiscally by engaging in a conflict that will sever (or even just weaken) these ties. Culturally and historically, the Chinese and American people are inclined toward mutual admiration and respect. Despite the political differences between Chinese communism and Western liberal democratic capitalism, both sides value human connections and government rapprochement. An appreciation of American technological innovation and Chinese work and spiritual ethics imbues the still-developing relationship. Both sides seem willing to engage diplomatically and sustain a world system in which each nation-state has its place and its independence.

In every sphere but one, it seems, the two great powers are building toward peace. In every sphere of competition, with one exception, there is room for negotiation and mutually beneficial outcomes. That one incompatible, uncompromising realm is outer space.

Western Action versus Eastern Timing

The essential strategic view that confounds cooperation in space is paradox. The Western mind sees transparency and openness as the surest way to peace. When one state can effectively monitor another, fears of surprise attack are mitigated, and the tendency to overestimate a potential opponent's capacities and intentions is minimized. With transparency, the security dilemma is obviated, and cooperation is possible.[11]

But transparency as a confidence-building measure is a purely Western mode of thought. To an Eastern strategist, letting an opponent know precisely one's strengths and weaknesses merely invites attack. The key to stability in this view is uncertainty—not knowing how strong or how weak an opponent is and never, under any circumstances, revealing one's own strengths or weaknesses. The more sure the knowledge, the more crafty the countervailing plan, and the more likely its success.

The essential disconnect between West and East in the conduct of war is in the difference between action and timing.[12] The Western strategist too often seeks to force change through positive steps. Analyses focus on the likely response to specific activities and assessments of whether more or less force is necessary to accomplish change. The future is constructed wholly through the effort and interplay of action.

To the Eastern strategist, proper war-making is a matter of timing. Balance of force is not a single calculation but a continuing one. Power is a function of capa-

bilities, position, and morale—just as it is in the West—but it is also a result of numerous immutable and sometimes unknowable forces. Structure dominates agency. Rather than force a change through positive actions, the Eastern strategist bides time until the moment to strike is ripe. Indeed, the gardening analogy is a strong one in Chinese military writings. No matter how much effort one puts into growing a crop—learning how to garden, preparing the soil, tending the plants—there is no benefit in harvesting too early or too late.

My interaction with Chinese strategists and generals anecdotally confirms such biases. When someone suggests long-term planning is advantageous, these officials are liable to chuckle and say, "I do not know what will happen tomorrow, how can I know what will happen in years or decades?" The Eastern strategist studies, prepares, and waits. Through careful study and reflection, the strategist learns about the opponent's forces and his or her own, as well as the terrain, technologies, and sociopolitical contexts that shift in time. Through preparation and training, military forces required by the strategist are available when needed. Awaiting the proper moment for action guarantees success.

Western hubris and Eastern inscrutability thus dominate security relations between those regions. When Douglas MacArthur famously stated that there is no substitute for victory, he was affirming an agent-centered dictum.[13] His meaning was clear. Those who prevail in war need make no excuses for the manner in which the battles were fought. History is written by the victor. Alternatively, when Sun Tsu claimed that the apex of skill is to win without fighting, he did not refer to a passive or inactive strategy.[14] He averred that following the study-prepare-and-wait model leads to a position where the outcome is obvious to all parties, and a capable opponent will choose to negotiate the best terms rather than fight to a foregone and disastrous conclusion.

Geopolitical analysis has the capacity to accept the logic of both East and West. Rather than choose one over the other, the geostrategist perceives them holistically and seeks a third way that links the two without diminishing the power of either.

Strategy and the Space Domain

Within military strategy are operational categories of violence or force that are separated by domain.[15] This is more than an economizing or efficiency categorization of force. It is recognition that strategies for each realm are unique and have individual requirements for tactical proficiency. It is also the operational concept that links the logic of strategy with the grammar of tactics.

A military strategist understands the requirements of organizing, training, and equipping for war. This is the unique purpose of military power. As such, the top military strategist prepares overall force structures and establishes a plan for their continuing health and proficiency. Dividing the domains of war into land, sea, and air is useful for assigning service authority (for the United States, to the Army, Navy, and Air Force, respectively). Today space is widely recognized as a separate domain, and some state militaries have separate services for it—Russian Rocket Forces, for example. To the extent that these domains are merely convenient delineations, strategy applies equally across all, even though tactical expertise may be quite diverse in different realms. As such, how forces are divided is merely a preference, subordinate to an overall theory of war. To have a separate strategy for each domain, the unique purposes of each must be discerned. To have a strategy for space—that is, a theory of space war—the strategist must distinguish the unique roles and missions of the space domain. If nothing is unique, then a distinction does not add value.

Moreover, the distinct realms or domains of land, sea, air, and space (and perhaps cyberspace) need to be more than physically and conceptually separable. They must be of complementary value—otherwise they should be subordinate to another domain—and nested within the proper role of military power. Typically, domains are separable by physical characteristics or platform operations. In the former case, ground territory is the domain of land power, oceans and waterways define sea power, and the aerodynamic properties of the skies or orbital characteristics of the heavens define air and space power. In the latter, if it walks or moves on the earth, it is land power and properly under the control of the Army; if it floats or operates in the water, it is the Navy's responsibility; and if it flies through the air or space it is—for the United States—properly controlled by the Air Force. This causes problematic overlap when assigning domain responsibility, however. Can the Navy use aircraft to patrol the oceans? Who should own and operate a submarine-launched ballistic missile which begins in the ocean but travels through the air and space and targets a city on the earth? Does the source or origination define the authority in the submarine case (sea power), or should the target be the discriminator (land power)? Taken to an extreme, all sea, air, and space operations begin on the land; should navies and air-space forces exclusively engage in support activities for the army? This, too, creates more problems than it solves. If I discriminate by target, am I conducting economic warfare when I destroy a factory, regardless of the means? If I bomb a school with an airplane, am I conducting educational warfare?[16] That is absurd. Fortunately, the model for power discrimination has already been defined; as with military force as a means of state power, domain authority is best understood as a function of purpose. When defined this way, the conundrums above disappear.

The military purpose of land power is to take and hold territory. This is understood as control and is the mission properly assigned to armies. The military purpose of sea power is to control the sea. Navies do this. The military purpose of air power is to control the air. Fittingly, the military purpose of space power is to control space. Following the primary dictum of classical geopolitics, if one cannot achieve or sustain control, then it is vital that one's potential adversary cannot achieve or sustain control. This is called *contestation*. Land forces should thus be organized, trained, and equipped to control and contest the ground, naval forces the seas, and air forces the sky; critically, if space is a separate war-fighting domain, then space forces must be prepared and capable of controlling and contesting space.

Control provides the capacity to use the domain to create effects. In other words, what one does with land, sea, air, or space power is entirely dependent on the capacity to operate from or through the land, sea, air, or space. In the airpower case, the capacity to bomb, move supplies, or do observation with aircraft requires that one can get into the air and then to the target. As with land power, however, gaining control so that the domain can be used does not necessarily mean constant or pervasive application of military force throughout the domain. In an uncontested environment, access is based entirely on the capacity to get and use the resources necessary to move from one point to another and the extent to which legal rules are followed to deconflict operating in congested areas (e.g., airport flight control regimes). However, the continuing presence of an uncontested domain has historically been due to the existence of a military or police capacity held in reserve to ensure rules are obeyed and that unauthorized inhibiting of movement through the domain is punished. This is the current case for the global sea and air commons. The US Navy is the primary agent to ensure that the current 12-mile extension of national sovereignty into the oceans is not exceeded (as with its actions against Libya in the Gulf of Sidra), that vital narrows in sea lanes of commerce are not blocked (e.g., the Strait of Hormuz), and that non-state criminal activity is prevented or punished (such as the ongoing efforts against Somali pirates in the Indian Ocean). However, without the ability to apply force on and in the seas, to board and inspect suspicious or rules-defying vessels, to escort and defend innocent passage, and more, the US Navy cannot defend or deter on the seas without violating other states' sovereignty or relying on non-naval assets for deterrence and punishment.

In space, no state has yet attempted to gain general control of a discernible location, and nations capable of operating in space have for the most part done so in accordance with legal or treaty obligations. This is the model that air followed in its initial development (and probably sea access, at some time in prehistory).

Until World War I, the air was not contested. Unfettered access was a function of desire, technology, aerodynamics, weather, law, and money. Such is the case with space today. No state has yet acted militarily to contest any other state's use of space (that we know of). The geostationary belt is regulated by international agreement, and various rules limit the placement of weapons of mass destruction in space. Registration and liability rules have been crafted and widely accepted, and the effects available from spacecraft and the use of space are generally available to all—and yet the exploitation of space is still suboptimal.[17] No US Navy equivalent is lurking ready to ensure that rogue states cannot extend their sovereign territory beyond generally accepted limits of air-powered flight or to stop illegal activities if and when they occur. Military activities create debris and other navigational hazards, yet there is no equivalent of a minesweeper to clear out unwanted military detritus. And if some state or organization should desire to contest or control space, denying the fruits thereof to another state, there is simply no defense against such an action—there is only deterrence through the threat of asymmetric, Earth-centered retaliation.

Contestation is the ability to block or deny access to a domain. Critically, contestation does not give the capacity to use a domain; it only inhibits. This is why, to a military strategist, *control* is a vital concept. Control may be general or limited to specific times and places, but without the ability to get into the domain and operate there, the strategist cannot use the domain to create effects. Thus for every military domain, control is possible only from within the domain. This is obvious when the domain is contested, but control also must be exercised in an uncontested domain when illegal or harmful activities are occurring there.

A military must control a domain to be able to use it. To maintain control, a military planner must be able to contest the littoral areas of those domains that are adjacent to it. For example, a military requires an army or land force to gain control and then use contested territory. This is the much-vaunted concept of "boots on the ground": to the extent a military needs territorial control, it requires boots on the ground (or wheels, tracks, etc.). To the extent a military desires air control over enemy territory in order to bomb targets there, boots on enemy ground may be immaterial. Let us call this the "wings in the air" dictum and make another one for "oars in the water." To use the domain, I must be able to operate in the domain.

The land force that is occupying or controlling territory will not be able to maximize use of the domain if the air space above it is not controlled by friendly forces. The land force must therefore try to block access to opposing air forces or accept the free flight of enemy aircraft over its positions. The latter may be a necessity if the means to contest the air are not available, but it is an undesirable operational condition. For this reason, land forces generally have antiaircraft artillery and missiles. Land forces also properly construct coastal defenses to prevent seaborne attacks and invasion. Since the purpose of these actions is to contest the littorals of the land domain, they are properly assigned to and integrated into army operations and doctrine. For their part, navies maintain land forces—marines and shore police—to contest beaches and protect ports. Navies also have significant antiaircraft capabilities on their ships and maintain fleets of aircraft to contest the antishipping efforts of opponents. Air forces must secure bases as well and contest the antiair efforts of armies and navies. Space forces likewise should have the capacity to deny ground-, sea-, and air-based anti-satellite weapons from space.

In some instances, a state may not need or desire domain control or contestation. A land-locked state will see no need to develop a naval force for sea control and likely will not acquire specialized sea-contestation capability. Most states will attempt to acquire air-contestation capabilities, such as advanced surface-to-air missiles, but many will not be able to afford air control assets. Their military strategies will develop with an understanding that effects delivered from or through the air, such as close air support or aerial resupply, are not likely to be available in a time of conflict or crisis.

If space is a military domain, then it should follow the same logic. A state that relies on military support from space—the effects it achieves from having assets in space—must plan to gain at least limited or temporary control of space in times of conflict. And, as is obvious from the description of analogous domains above, control is possible only from within the domain. If the state is unwilling to put weapons into space, then it cannot hope to ensure effects from space when another state attempts to contest its position. Its logical recourse is to wean itself quickly from space support, enhancement, and enablement, and move to a pre-space military force structure. It must then stop wasting procurement money, production, and personnel on military space. If the military might be forced to fight without assured space support, then it should train to do so. The most efficient military in a space-denied environment will be the one that does not require the use of space at all. Of course, if a military force is proficient in fighting without space, why should it spend scarce resources to organize, train, and equip itself to fight any other way? It is the height of folly for a commander to rely on a capacity that may or may not be available when needed. With the military force preparing to fight without space, government funding for military space support will be scaled back and ultimately cut. Without a military presence to protect fragile space assets and ensure treaty compliance in space, along with drastic reductions in the space industry as military contracts end, commercial space development will be severely curtailed. Developing ground-, sea-, and air-based anti-space weapons would be prudent for such a military so that an opponent cannot use space freely against it, but to waste capital and effort on a nice-to-have capacity in space that is not needed to conduct operations on the earth would be ludicrous. Following this logic, denying oneself the capacity to put military force in space is tantamount to giving up on the military (and probably civil) value of space.

To be sure, the cost to weaponize space effectively will be immense. It is a cost that America, or any other state, needs to undertake if it wants a military force structure that relies on space support and enablement to operate as it does now and will increasingly do so in the future. Weaponizing space will have benefits for the military that may not be readily apparent.

Where will we get the money for this space weapons capacity? It will not come from school budgets or foreign aid programs. It will not come at the expense of health care reform or corporate bailouts. It will come at the expense of conventional military capabilities on the land and sea and in the air. There will be fewer aircraft carriers and high-dollar fighter aircraft and bombers. If the United States deploys space weapons capable of targeting the earth, relatively slow-moving ships and aircraft will become conceptually obsolete, instantly vulnerable to space weapons. As we scrounge money for space lasers and exotic kinetic-kill satellites, the systems these space weapons make defenseless will be scrapped. More funding will come from current ballistic and antiballistic missile development and deployment, as global ballistic missile defense from space is more cost-effective and practically effective than comprehensive ground- or sea-based systems. And most importantly, it will come from personnel reductions—from ground troops currently occupying foreign territory. In this way, the United States will retain its ability to use force to influence states around the world, but it will atrophy the capacity to occupy their territory and threaten their sovereignty directly. The era of US hegemony will be extended, but the possibility of US global empire will be reduced.

Maybe. The future is not determined or even determinable. I have argued elsewhere the practicality of controlling space. I will not add to that argument here. I have also pointed out that the theory animating these conclusions is precise and well-developed, but the real world is too complex to mirror theory. The political will necessary to weaponize space and follow up with a regime capable of ensuring commercial and cooperative development of space is not yet evident, and such a pure, realist *astropolitik* vision is thus not currently viable. But support for the common or collective good

that could come from a properly weaponized space force may change that. Space weapons have some potential missions that could help generate the will to pay for and use them. These missions do not detract from the primary purpose of the weapons but complement the goal of space control. For example, nuclear-powered space-based lasers could, in theory, clean up debris from high-traffic orbits—good target practice for their operators. Assured access to space provided by a robust space control force could pave the way for clean, permanent nuclear and toxic waste disposal, as such items currently stored on Earth could be sent into the sun. Space-based solar power generation could provide the world with cheap, abundant energy that would deemphasize the value and authority of current oil-producing states and fundamentally change the geopolitical landscape of the Earth. These scenarios are far more likely with the monitoring and protection provided by a space-based military or police power.

These scenarios are an even more difficult dilemma for those who oppose weapons in general and space weapons in particular. Ramifications for the most critical current function of the Army, Navy, and Marines—pacification, occupation, and control of foreign territory—are profound. With the downsizing of traditional weapons programs to accommodate heightened space expenditures, the ability to do all three would wane significantly. At a time when many are calling for *increased* capability to pacify and police foreign lands, in light of the no-end-in-sight deployments of US peacekeeping forces around the world, space weapons proponents must advocate *reduction* of these capabilities in favor of a system that will have no direct potential to pacify and police.

Hence, the argument that the unilateral deployment of space weapons will precipitate a disastrous arms race is further eroded. To be sure, space weapons are offensive by their very nature. They deter violence by the omnipresent threat of precise, measured, and unstoppable retaliation. But they offer no advantage in the mission of territorial occupation. As such, they are far less intimidating to the international environment than any combination of conventional weapons employed in their stead. Which would be more threatening to a state that opposes American hegemony: a dozen lasers in space with pinpoint accuracy or (perhaps for about the same price) a dozen infantry divisions massed on its border? A state employing offensive deterrence through space weapons can punish a transgressor state, but it is in a poor position to challenge that state's sovereignty. A transgressor state is less likely to succumb to the security dilemma if it perceives that its national survival is not at risk. Moreover, the tremendous expense of space weapons would inhibit their indiscriminate use. Over time, the world of sovereign states may recognize that the United States could not and would not use space weapons to threaten another country's internal self-determination. The United States still would challenge any attempts to intervene militarily in the politics of others, and it would have severely restricted its own capacity to do the latter. Judicious and nonarbitrary use of a weaponized space eventually could be seen as a net positive—an effective global police force that punishes criminal acts but does not threaten to engage in an imperial manner.

A Twenty-First-Century Great Wall in Space

Slightly over three years ago, China successfully engaged one of its own satellites in space.[18] This was extraordinarily provocative. The United States simply has no defense against such a weapon system, and China's antisatellite test was intended to remind the world of this weakness. Moreover, its use of a standard medium-range ballistic missile (which the PRC produces in mass) to propel the kill vehicle indicates a potential antisatellite weapons capability sufficient to target the entire US low-Earth-orbit inventory. Current efforts to place ground-based missile interceptors in strategic locations would be useless, regardless of deployment, as these are designed to engage incoming ballistic missiles in the mid or terminal phase of flight. The Chinese missile achieves orbital altitude just minutes after launch, so the only possible defense against it—which would have the added advantage of ensuring any destructive debris from a successful engagement would land on Chinese soil—would be from a network of antiballistic missile satellites operating in Earth orbit.

Just such a space-based antimissile capability, envisioned for years and technically feasible since the late 1980s, has long been the optimum solution for military planners. Yet, such a system has been annually tabled due to high cost estimates and fears of encouraging other states to develop anti-space weapons. The latter concern is now overcome by events. But the cost issue remains.

With the global war on terrorism and major terrestrial deployments drawing the lion's share of attention and budget, shifting funds from immediate operational requirements to long-term security is a tall order. The *timing* of the Chinese antisatellite test coincides perfectly with their perception that the United States is ill positioned to respond with force, and they are probably right.

China's ultimate goal appears to be to assert its regional supremacy and achieve co-equal (if not dominant) status as a global power. Control of space is a critical step in that direction. Without its eyes and ears in space to provide warning and real-time intelligence, the United States would be in a painfully awkward situation should the PRC put direct military pressure on Taiwan. To those who argue that China is as eager to avoid a damaging war in space as any other space-faring state, especially given its increasing integration into the world economy and dependence on foreign trade for its continuing prosperity: do not discount the capacities of its authoritarian leadership. This is the same regime that embraces the deprivations of government-induced cyclical poverty to spare its populace the moral decadence of capitalist luxury.

As with the famous Great Wall running across northern China, built for the dual purpose of inhibiting nomadic incursions and creating a magnificent public work to legitimize the government and inspire its domestic population, a significant military presence in low-Earth orbit has a parallel value for the PRC today. Its increasing capacity in space is extremely popular domestically (in addition, providing an enhanced reputation for China's capacity to develop high-technology products and services) and helps to diminish internal dissent by legitimizing the communist government. The massive government-led effort to build a dominating space presence is tantamount to the expenditures of states to create huge public works that were so important to past regimes (and modern ones as well; for example, the interstate highway system of the Eisenhower administration). Ultimately, however, the primary purpose of a controlling or at least lockdown contestation of space access would have the same general effect as the original Great Wall in keeping foreign influences out of the Middle Kingdom. For China, the past has always been prologue.

To be sure, China's increasing space emphasis and its cultural antipathy to military transparency suggest a serious attempt at seizing control of space is in the works. A lingering fear is the sudden introduction of an unknown capability (call it "Technology X") that would allow a hostile state to place multiple weapons into orbit quickly and cheaply. The advantages gained from controlling the high ground of space would accrue to it as surely as to any other state, while the concomitant loss of military power from the denial of space to America's already space-dependent military forces could usher in a significant reordering of the international system. The longer the United States dithers on its military responsibilities, the more likely a potential opponent could seize low-Earth orbit before it is able to respond.

And in such circumstances, the United States certainly would respond. Conversely, if the United States were to weaponize space, it is not at all sure that any other state or group of states would find it rational to counter in kind. The entry cost to provide the necessary infrastructure is still too high—hundreds of billions of dollars, at minimum. The years of investment needed to achieve a comparable counterforce capability—essentially from scratch—would provide more than ample time for the United States to entrench itself in space and readily counter preliminary efforts to displace it. The tremendous effort in time and resources would be worse than wasted. Most states, if not all, would opt not to counter US deployments *directly*. They might oppose American interests with asymmetric balancing, depending on how aggressively it uses its new power, but the likelihood of a hemorrhaging arms race in space should the United States deploy weapons first—at least for the next few years—is remote.

This reasoning does not dispute the fact that US deployment of weapons in outer space would represent the addition of a potent new military capacity, one that would assist in extending the current period of American hegemony well into the future. Clearly this would be threatening, and America must expect severe condemnation and increased competition in peripheral areas. But such an outcome is less threatening than another, particularly illiberal authoritarian state doing so. Although there is obvious opposition to the current international balance of power, the majority of states seem to regard it as at least tolerable. A continuation of the status quo is thus minimally acceptable, even to states working toward its demise. As long as the United States does not employ its power arbitrarily, the situation would be accommodated initially and grudgingly accepted over time.

Mirror-imaging does not apply here. An attempt by China to dominate space would be part of an effort to break the sea-air dominance of the United States in preparation for a new international order with the weaponizing state at the top. Such an action would challenge the status quo rather than seek to perpetuate it. This would be disconcerting to nations that accept the current international order—including the venerable institutions of trade, finance, and law that operate within it. Simultaneously, it would be intolerable to the United States. As leader of the current system, the United States could do no less than engage in a perhaps ruinous space arms race, save graciously deciding to step aside and accept a diminished world status.[19]

Seizing the initiative and securing low-Earth orbit now, while the United States is dominant in space infrastructure, would do much to stabilize the international system and prevent an arms race in space. The enhanced ability to deny any attempt by another nation to place military assets in space and to readily engage and destroy terrestrial antisatellite capacity would make the possibility of large-scale space war or military space races *less* likely, not more. So long as the controlling state demonstrates a capacity and a will to use force to defend its position, in effect expending a small amount of violence as needed to prevent a greater

conflagration in the future, the likelihood of a future war *in* space is remote.

Moreover, if the United States were willing to deploy and use a military space force that maintained effective control of space and did so in a way that was perceived as tough, nonarbitrary, and efficient, such an action would serve to discourage competing states from fielding opposing systems. It could also set the stage for a new space regime, one that encourages space commerce and development. Should the United States use its advantage to police the heavens and allow unhindered peaceful use of space by any and all nations for economic and scientific development, over time its control of low-Earth orbit could be viewed as a global asset and a public good. In much the same way the British maintained control of the high seas in the nineteenth century, enforcing international norms against slavery while protecting innocent passage and property rights, the United States could prepare outer space for a long-overdue burst of economic expansion.

There is reasonable historic support for the notion that the most peaceful and prosperous periods in modern history coincide with the appearance of a strong, liberal hegemon.[20] America has been essentially unchallenged in its naval dominance over the last 60 years and in global air supremacy for the last 15 or more. Today, there is more international commerce on the oceans and in the air than ever. Ships and aircraft of all nations worry more about running into bad weather than about being commandeered by a military vessel or set upon by pirates. Search and rescue is a far more common task for the Navy than forced embargo, and the transfer of humanitarian aid is a regular mission. The legacy of American military domination of the sea and air has been positive, and the same should be expected for space.

Conclusion

Geopolitics is in ascendance because it provides practical blueprints for action to those who perceive the world in realist terms. Halford Mackinder confirmed the primary tenet of geostrategy. To dominate the battlespace, it is necessary to control the most vital positions. If the most vital positions cannot be controlled, then they must be contested. The opponent cannot have uninhibited access. This simple dictum, known by every strategist and tactician but articulated so clearly by Mackinder, is the essence of the geostrategist's logic. Control is desirable, contestation is imperative. This dictum applies to every medium and theater of war.

To be sure, America *will* maintain the capacity to influence decisions and events beyond its borders, with military force if necessary. Whether that capacity comes from space as well as the other military domains is undetermined. But the operational deployment of space weapons would increase that capacity by providing for nearly instantaneous force projection worldwide. This force would be precise, unstoppable, and deadly. The United States will maintain its position of hegemony as well as its security, and the world will not be threatened by the specter of a future American empire.

There will always be arguments for testing the resilience of systems against the worst case. If they can cope with the most severe threats, then lesser cases should be manageable. The worst case may depend on the aggressor being foolish and futile, but stupidity is one of the hardest things for any intelligence agency to predict. At the same time, when planning an offensive, every effort must be made to make the first blows count. The key point, however, is that even with surprise and maximum effort, these first blows are unlikely to be decisive on their own, especially against an opponent with any reserves of strength. This depth is why states must look beyond surprise attacks to what follows, to the second and third blows, and also to those much further down the line, perhaps delivered by irregulars who have taken over the struggle after the defeat of the regulars. The surprises of war do not just come at the start.

NOTES

1. Robert Strassler, ed., *The Landmark Thucydides: A Comprehensive Guide to the Peloponnesian War*, trans. by Richard Crawley (New York: Free Press, 1996), 16.

2. See Robert Gilpin, *War and Change in World Politics* (Cambridge: Cambridge University Press, 1981), for a full treatment.

3. I draw on definitions by Geoffrey Parker, *Western Geopolitical Thought in the Twentieth Century* (New York: St. Martin's, 1986), for this analysis.

4. Strassler, *Landmark Thucydides*, 352.

5. The position of neorealist founding father Kenneth Waltz, *Theory of International Relations* (New York: McGraw-Hill, 1979).

6. Jack Donnelly, *Realism and International Relations* (Cambridge: Cambridge University Press, 2000), 43–44.

7. Alfred Thayer Mahan, *The Influence of Seapower upon History: 1660–1783* (Boston: Little-Brown, 1890).

8. Halford Mackinder, *Democratic Ideals and Reality: A Study in the Politics of Reconstruction* (New York: Henry Holt, 1919).

9. These hypotheses are extracted from Everett Dolman, *Astropolitik: Classical Geopolitics in the Space Age* (London: Frank Cass, 2002).

10. Less so, at least in terms of longevity. These include cooperation-producing economic theories of interdependence, functionalism, and neofunctionalism, and variants of the so-called democratic peace theory to include the Kantian peace and capitalist peace theory.

11. On the original security dilemma, see Robert Jervis, "Cooperation under the Security Dilemma," *World Politics* 30, no. 2 (January 1978): 167–74.

12. This argument is heavily indebted to Francois Jullien, *A Treatise on Efficacy: Between Western and Chinese Thinking* (Honolulu: University of Hawaii Press, 2004).

13. MacArthur was defending his conduct in Korea. For a counter opinion and critique, see Everett Dolman, *Pure Strategy: Power and Principle in the Space and Information Age* (London: Frank Cass, 2004), 6–7. For a positive account, see Theodore and Donna Kinni, *No Substitute for Victory: Lessons in Leadership from Douglas MacArthur* (Upper Saddle River, NJ: FT Press, 2005).

14. Sun Tzu, *The Art of War*, trans. by Ralph Sawyer (Boulder, CO: Westview Press, 1994), 177.

15. This section is distilled from a much fuller discussion of the roles of strategy, operations, and tactics in Dolman, *Pure Strategy*.

16. An argument adapted from an economic assertion made by David Baldwin, *Economic Statecraft* (Princeton, NJ: Princeton University Press, 1985), 6–15.

17. John Hickman and Everett Dolman, "Resurrecting the Space Age: A State-Centered Commentary on the Outer Space Regime," *Comparative Strategy* 21, no. 1 (2002): 1–19.

18. For an apologist stance, see Li Jiuquan, "Legality and Legitimacy: China's ASAT Test," *China Security* 5, no. 1 (Winter 2009): 43–52.

19. Following the logic of hegemonic stability theory (HST) as generally outlined by Duncan Snidal, "The Limits of Hegemonic Stability Theory," *International Organization* 39, no. 4 (Autumn 1985): 579–613.

20. Immanuel Wallerstein, "The Rise and Future Demise of the World Capitalist System: Concepts for Comparative Analysis," *Comparative Studies in Society and History* 16 (1974): 387–415.

Strategic Stability

The Low-Yield Nuclear Weapon Challenge

JAMES M. SMITH

Half a century ago, this author completed a mandatory course in American defense policy at the Air Force Academy. That course was built on the second edition of *American Defense Policy* (*ADP*), which focused on limited war.[1] In the wake of the Cuban Missile Crisis, and as the United States and the Soviet Union approached a state of strategic balance characterized by assured destruction, attention shifted from general, strategic nuclear war to other forms of conflict ranging from limited nuclear war to insurgency. That foundation served as a prelude to the evolving environment that students of that time would face to today. This essay is written in the hope that it, and the remainder of this book, will well serve today's students on their way forward across the next several decades.

The "strategic stability" concept and components have been central to US nuclear policy and strategy throughout the Cold War and beyond. First-strike stability, crisis stability, arms-race stability, arms control stability, and more, are core concepts within the policy community and are part of the effort to ensure effective deterrence and avoid nuclear conflict. The bilateral nuclear balance between the United States and the Russia is framed in those terms. The term "strategic stability" is less visible in the operational community, where weapons and particularly delivery systems and doctrine are the primary focus, rather than these stability concepts and the role they played in shaping those systems and doctrinal development. For example, during the simulations that the Air Force ran to inform decisions on numbers and systems recommendations leading into the New Strategic Arms Reductions Treaty (New START) negotiations, "strategic stability" was never actually mentioned. But its core concepts drove considerations on the Air Force inputs to the negotiation process. So policy-makers have sought broader stability while practitioners have focused on effective implementation of operational doctrine toward deterrence—and stability—effects. The combined results have been apparently effective in ensuring adequate deterrence and stability to navigate the Cold War and its aftermath without resort to nuclear war.

The reality has never been simple, as stability was viewed differently not only at various levels of government, but also by nations. During the Cold War, for example, the United States focused primarily on the nuclear balance while the Soviet Union looked beyond just the nuclear dimension to add other elements of the overall relationship. In short, from the beginning, strategic stability was more complex than it appeared, and that complexity has now been magnified greatly by post–Cold War changes in both the nuclear and broader strategic environments.

Reflecting back on strategic stability in light of today's developing international strategic environment, Thomas Schelling (who was the author of six excerpted readings in that second edition of *ADP*) stated:

> I was brought up on the "stability of mutual deterrence" half a century ago, and it was not all that difficult to understand. . . . Now we are in a different world, a world so much more complex than the world of the East-West Cold War. It took 12 years to begin to comprehend the "stability" issue after 1945, but once we got it we thought we understood it. Now the world is so much changed, so much more complicated, so multivariate, so unpredictable, involving so many nations and cultures and languages in nuclear relationships, many of them asymmetric, that it is even difficult to know how many meanings there are for "strategic stability," or how many different kinds of such stability there may be among so many different international relationships, or what "stable deterrence" is supposed to deter in a world of proliferated weapons.[2]

In the face of that compounding complexity, and facing the myriad strategic challenges that the United States faces today—including and beyond those addressed by Schelling—it is ever more important to examine those challenges both individually and together in the effort to enhance stability. Effective deterrence and stability remain the primary objectives and highest purpose of American defense policy, framing and founding the career paths of defense policy students and practitioners going forward.

This essay examines strategic stability as challenged by the destabilizing influences of low-yield nuclear weapons (LYNW), a central capability enhancement as advocated by the 2018 Nuclear Posture Review (NPR) to meet the challenges presented by similar Russian weapon systems and doctrine. It first develops basic concepts of deterrence and stability as applied across the Cold War. It then traces the core role of strategic stability in the 2010 Obama NPR, extends that development into the very different roles and concepts of the

2018 Trump NPR, and presents a sampling of the contemporary stability and deterrence challenges presented to the strategic community, including LYNW. Second, the essay reviews the LYNW challenge as it has progressed from "tactical nuclear weapons," to "theater nuclear weapons," to "nonstrategic nuclear weapons," and on to "low-yield nuclear weapons" across and beyond the Cold War. It specifically examines LYNW in US policy and strategy from the George W. Bush to the Donald Trump administrations as framed by the Russian challenge of "escalate to de-escalate" strategies as well as in response to theater war challenges from China, North Korea, and Iran. Third, given destabilizing challenges from LYNW—among other sources—the essay suggests the usefulness of the seemingly paradoxical notion of "dynamic stability" as a central approach for strategic policy today. This approach could lead to destabilizing one level or aspect of the relationship in order to stabilize another, higher priority area at least temporarily. Or it could lead to less stability of one nuclear power in order to enhance stability of another. This is the reality of the deterrence and stability challenge to today's strategists.

Deterrence and Stability

We begin with Schelling's central concept of the "stability of mutual deterrence," or deterrence stability. "Deterrence" can be characterized as involving "operations [that] convince adversaries not to take actions that threaten US vital interests by means of decisive influence over their decision-making. Decisive influence is achieved by credibly threatening to deny benefits and/or impose costs while encouraging restraint by convincing the actor that restraint will result in an acceptable outcome."[3]

Deterrence convinces an adversary *not* to take an action that we deem threatening to our vital interests through fear that either they cannot achieve their objective (denial) or they will suffer unacceptable consequences (punishment), and that their restraint will not materially harm them. Note that deterrence is a psychological effect on the adversary's decision calculus. It is a perception in their mind(s), not an objective fact. The numbers and capabilities of a delivery system or the destructive power of a warhead may help to form that perception, but many other factors also contribute to the creation of the psychological effect of restraint. "Decisive influence" over decision-making requires specific messaging tailored to those specific decision-makers and their decision calculus. And "mutual deterrence" means that in an adversarial relationship, both sides are creating deterrence perceptions in the minds of each other—neither side sees a win or an acceptable outcome in attacking the other—with restraint as the selected outcome for both sides.

Stability, then, can be seen as that state of mutually accepted restraint. Like deterrence, it is not an objective reality, but a perception of relative balance. For example, "first-strike stability" is usually put forward as the heart of strategic stability. This means that neither side sees a positive outcome from initiating a nuclear attack—seeking to disarm or defeat the adversary with a disarming, debilitating preemptive nuclear attack. Surveillance and warning systems, hardened silos and mobile launchers, secure second-strike capabilities—all help ensure this type and level of stability. However, management of the overall relationship—diplomatic, economic, and societal in addition to these military measures—is perhaps most responsible for encouraging this restraint. Thus, first-strike stability, crisis stability (not letting a crisis situation escalate to general war), arms race stability (controlling and limiting arms buildups and technological advances to prevent either side from gaining a decisive first-strike advantage), all are factored into the overall relationship to maintain relative restraint.

During the Cold War and its aftermath there were numerous challenges to stability. There were crises in the relationship that might have involved nuclear weapons—from Cuba to Berlin to the Middle East and beyond—but these were ultimately managed and defused without nuclear employment. There were also the ongoing issues of arms buildups and technological advances. The United States created a stockpile of over 30,000 nuclear weapons at one point, and the Soviet Union eventually topped 40,000 weapons, and there were ongoing advances in weapons, delivery, and associated capabilities throughout the entire period. All created destabilizing pressures that had to be mitigated within the strategic relationship.

Perhaps the strongest stabilizing mechanism for the United States and the Soviet Union was arms control. For example, in the late 1960s, with the memory of the Cuban Missile Crisis still fresh, with the US nuclear inventory at its peak and the Soviet inventory reaching over 30,000 weapons, with technological advances looming toward heavier missiles and multiple independently targetable reentry vehicles (MIRV), and with the development of first-generation antiballistic missile defenses (ABM), both the United States and the Soviets felt that they must work to enhance stability. Early surveillance systems could monitor launchers, but they could not necessarily detect MIRVed warheads, and ABM technologies were too new in their development for a full understanding of their potential effectiveness.

The Strategic Arms Limitations Talks (SALT) began toward a treaty that could at least temporarily address these destabilizing factors. The SALT I Treaty (1972) was the first bilateral US-Soviet strategic arms control agreement. It capped the number of strategic ballistic missile launchers, prevented conversion of existing launchers to accommodate heavy missiles, and allowed the substitution of additional submarine-launched ballistic missile tubes for the elimination of the same number of land-based launchers. The two sides were not limited to equal numbers or types of launchers, but the "essential equivalence" of effective capabilities was accepted as stabilizing. On the strategic defenses side, the concurrent ABM Treaty did limit both sides to no more than two sites—one to protect the capital and one launcher site; later reduced to one site—and a maximum of 100 launchers and 100 missiles, as well as limiting the deployment locations of ABM radars. Many saw the ABM Treaty as the cornerstone of strategic arms control as future development of fully effective ballistic missile defense would basically destroy first-strike—and strategic—stability.[4] Subsequent bilateral strategic arms control treaties (SALT II, the Intermediate Nuclear Forces Treaty [INF], START I, START II, the Strategic Offensive Reductions Treaty [SORT], and the New START) and the high-level discussions, transparency, and confidence-building processes associated with nuclear weapons diplomacy continued this practice of formalized stability assurances.

The US-Russia relationship remains at the center of deterrence and stability considerations today. The strategic arms control process was an essentially bilateral process, with the US side subsuming Great Britain and France as nuclear states into one player, and from a US perspective, the Soviet Union/Russia and nuclear China forming the other side. The treaties, which implemented verification measures, and strategic diplomacy affected only the United States and the Soviet Union/Russia, but the other three initial nuclear powers were seen as non-destabilizing partners in the overall resulting relationship. Ideological affinities and relatively small nuclear stockpiles largely maintained that bipolarity even with French military independence from NATO and the Sino-Soviet split from the 1960s. China's emergence as a global power and a more consequential nuclear power have now modified this to at least a three-player, multipolar challenge. So today, with only one remaining US-Russia strategic nuclear treaty still in effect—the New START Treaty (2010), scheduled for expiration in early 2021—and with China joining the strategic tier, the strategic stability challenge is complex.

The Obama administration sought a major adjustment in strategic policy and stability. First, the president in his Prague declaration sought to reduce the role of nuclear weapons in US policy as an initial step toward advancing a deliberate, cautious disarmament agenda. Note that his corollary to the call for a nuclear-free world was a pledge for continuing an effective deterrence until global conditions would warrant that disarmament. The first steps on that path were outlined in the 2010 Nuclear Posture Review (NPR). The hope was that Russia and China could each accept basic nuclear deterrence relationships with the United States, and that each could then initiate bilateral strategic stability dialogues with the United States. Strategic stability, with a more cooperative cast, was to replace the more adversarial focus on deterrence as the organizing concept for major power relations.[5] The administration also conducted a further review and was prepared to enter into negotiations with Russia for a New START follow-on treaty reducing deployed strategic warheads well below the 1,550 limit of New START. However, both Russia and China rejected the call for enhanced strategic cooperation, and by 2016 US-Russia relations had reverted to an almost Cold War coolness, with a NATO-Russia confrontation over Ukraine and with both sides pursuing active nuclear-force modernization programs. With China, relations also hit snags, and China's force modernization and build-up programs continued.[6]

The 2010 NPR did not just address Russia and China. A main point was the issuance of negative security assurances to those states that were Nuclear Non-Proliferation Treaty (NPT) signatories and were in compliance with NPT requirements. The United States would not use nuclear weapons against nonnuclear states that had signed and abided by the NPT. This assurance directly excluded rising regional states with nuclear ambitions, specifically North Korea and Iran. The United States now acknowledged facing potential and rising regional nuclear powers in addition to traditional strategic challengers.[7]

The hopeful tone that began the Obama administration was replaced with skepticism and caution by the Trump administration. The 2017 National Security Strategy (NSS) and particularly the 2018 National Defense Strategy (NDS) took as their departure point the *"reemergence of long-term, strategic competition"* with "revisionist powers" China and Russia.[8] It also singled out North Korea and Iran as destabilizing regional "rogue" regimes, and it noted that under pressures from these revisionist powers and rogue regimes every domain is contested and thus unstable. And it also highlighted the instability being driven by "rapid technological advancements and the changing character of war": "advanced computing, big data analytics, artificial intelligence, autonomy, robotics, directed energy, hypersonics, and biotechnology."[9] The 2018 NDS then provided broad guidance for a strategy that prioritizes addressing the China and Russia challenges while also deterring and countering regional challengers, specifically calling out North Korea and Iran. The strategy called for modernized nuclear capabilities as well as "dynamic force employment" to bring new strategic pressures and expand deterrent effects, including through allies and partners.

The 2018 Nuclear Posture Review guides implementation of the NDS at the nuclear force level. The

NPR continues the full modernization of the strategic nuclear triad—sea- and land-based intercontinental ballistic missile (ICBM) systems, new bombers equipped with both bombs and stand-off nuclear-tipped air-launched cruise missiles, and an upgraded nuclear force command and control system—as well as continued upgrade of nonstrategic nuclear capabilities including the B-61-12 gravity bomb modernization and F-35 dual-capable (conventional and nuclear) fighter-bomber delivery system. The NPR also proposes enhanced low-yield "non-strategic" nuclear capabilities including a down-loaded, primary only W76-2 warhead submarine-launched ballistic missile (SLBM) option, and a new nuclear-tipped sea-launched cruise missile (SLCM) as replacements for the retired Tomahawk system. The emphasis on expanded low-yield, nonstrategic nuclear systems is designed to add force employment options in response to Russian strategy developments while also adding capabilities and strategy options to address regional challenges.[10] Nonstrategic nuclear weapons and strategies have been a potentially destabilizing factor in US-Soviet/Russia strategic stability since early in the Cold War. That factor and today's new low-yield nuclear weapons developments are the subject of the next section of this essay.[11]

The strategic stability picture is, thus, complex as viewed from 2020. One complicating factor is that the definition of "strategic" is in question. "Strategic" in a military sense used to mean simply "nuclear." Today we see discussions of "nonnuclear strategic" systems, "nonstrategic nuclear" systems, and "cross-domain strategic" issues, with "strategic" now indicating the highest, gravest level of national interest, threat, or warfare. The nuclear and the existential, or at least vital, are no longer exclusively linked. Further complicating the picture is that a range of emerging and developing technologies with potentially strategic effects are now at play. These include the "advanced computing, big data analytics, artificial intelligence, autonomy, robotics, directed energy, hypersonics, and biotechnology" cited above, but that list is not necessarily complete, or enduring.

Finally for this analysis, perhaps the defining characteristic of the contemporary strategic security environment is the proliferation of players of strategic concern. We have progressed from the NPT core P-5 group of nuclear powers (the United States, the Soviet Union/Russia, the United Kingdom, France, and China) to add Israel as a presumptive nuclear state and India, Pakistan, and North Korea as nuclear weapons states. South Africa also developed a small number of atomic weapons that they subsequently dismantled to become the only nuclear state to voluntarily disarm. Iran has existing pre-bomb nuclear materials programs, while several other states developed nuclear weapons programs to one degree or another before abandoning those efforts.[12] For the United States to-day, the most direct concern is with Russia, China, North Korea, and Iran, which are singled out as strategic competitors and/or adversaries in the recent national security guidance. India and Pakistan are also of major concern as nuclear conflict in South Asia would have broad and disastrous consequences on a global scale.

For this essay, the consequences of proliferation for the United States include a general, global instability given the broader threat of nuclear weapon employment. More significantly, the regionalization of the nuclear threat beyond Russia and to a traditionally much lower degree China presents major challenges. Moreover, significant complexity is added by the different strategic personalities and decision sets that now comprise deterrence and stability for the United States. The United States now faces the enduring (and resurgent) global threat from Russian strategic systems and the US-Russia strategic relationship. It also faces the enduring challenge of Russia's threat to Europe and the accompanying extended deterrence, alliance maintenance, and assurance challenges, now in a new form. Plus it now must address a regionally aggressive China with extra-regional strategic challenges as well, with that challenge set involving bilateral and alliance deterrence and extended deterrence dimensions. And it simultaneously faces a North Korea deterrence and extended deterrence challenge in that same Northeast Asia region, as well as an emerging Middle East deterrence challenge that also involves a NATO/Europe dimension plus concerns for and about a nuclear Israel. Traditional deterrent-force silo-based ICBMs in the central United States and relatively large-yield, MIRVed SLBM warheads at sea provide some answers to some of these challenges. B61 bombs and NATO/US dual-capable fighter-bombers provide some additional options and answers. However, the military challenges and target sets differ. The adversary strategies, strengths, and weaknesses vary. And the adversary decision-makers, along with their deterrence perception calculus sets, alliance partner requirements, and regional realities, all vary even given different adversaries in the same region. The deterrence and stability challenge today is indeed complex, and a range of capabilities and strategies is needed for the United States. A sampling of these issues and challenges is now addressed in detail by examining the issue set of nonstrategic, low-yield nuclear weapons and their operational contexts today.

Low-Yield Nuclear Weapons

Tactical, theater, or nonstrategic nuclear weapons have been a central fixture of US and Soviet/Russian nuclear strategies since very early in the Cold War through to today. As noted, the United States produced over 30,000 nuclear weapons during the Cold War; approximately 15,000 of those were designed for strategic delivery, with the remaining almost 20,000 consisting of tactical nuclear weapons.[13] The Soviet side produced almost 45,000 nuclear weapons at that time; about 12,000 were strategic, and the other approximately 33,000 were tactical.[14] These tactical nuclear weapons were central to each side's strategy, especially in Europe, and both the United States and Russia still have actively deployed "tactical" nuclear forces today.

After World War II and the Western military drawdowns, the Soviet Union enjoyed a very large advantage in conventional force numbers, tanks, and artillery tubes. Initial NATO strategy in the face of that opposition was "Massive Retaliation," or the threat of meeting a Soviet conventional attack with US strategic nuclear attacks on Russia. As Soviet strategic capabilities allowed targeting of the United States, NATO adopted a strategy of Flexible Response in which NATO depended on a combined US-NATO conventional force augmented by tactical nuclear weapons to halt and defeat a Soviet attack in Europe. These weapons were small, relatively low-yield nuclear weapons—gravity bombs, artillery shells, demolition devices, short-range missile warheads, some under "dual-key" arrangements to be employed by NATO allies—and were intended to fill the conventional forces deficit in facing the superior Soviet/Warsaw Pact forces. And although they were nuclear devices, these weapons were treated in strategy and doctrine as war-fighting weapons—basically as enhanced conventional weapons. The term "tactical" implied this war-fighting, enhanced conventional status. Over time, the United States developed nuclear weapons as small as bazooka shells, hand grenades, and land mines. The Soviet side also developed and deployed tactical nuclear battlefield weapons.

NATO strategy, of necessity, held that these tactical nuclear weapons could be employed in a first-use escalation to tactical nuclear conflict to stem, or hopefully halt, the mass conventional attack and initiate an effective intra-war deterrent outcome. This was, in effect, an "escalate to deescalate" strategy, and nuclear first use (at the tactical level) was a central component of the strategy. This tactical nuclear use was an intentional but limited escalation, with the small numbers and sizes of the initial use as well as the targeting of Soviet/Warsaw Pact forces on European—not Russian—soil in the early stages meant to create a firebreak rather than automatically escalate to strategic nuclear conflict. But that danger remained. The "dual-key" nature of the employment of some of these weapons required an employment decision by both the United States as supplier of the weapon and by the government of the state whose forces would employ the weapon. There were also mechanisms for NATO preapproval of the employment of nuclear weapons.

These early battlefield nuclear weapons, particularly artillery and short-range missile systems, were "tactical nuclear weapons" designed and designated for use with and multipliers of conventional force. Longer-range, somewhat more powerful nuclear systems were under development by both sides during this period as well. Of concern was the Soviet deployment of the intermediate-range SS-20, a three-warhead mobile system that could target NATO European member capitals from Russian soil. This system ensured that what could earlier be considered a tactical employment or even exchange would now have immediate strategic consequences. A Soviet employment would be a strike from the Russian homeland (strategic attack), and a NATO retaliation or counterforce strike would be an attack on that Russian homeland (strategic attack), even if launched from the NATO theater, not from United States territory. These systems, and the intermediate-range Pershing II and ground-launched cruise missile (GLCM) systems later developed by the United States and deployed to NATO, which could reach many targets in Russia from launch in Western Europe, constituted a new category of "theater nuclear weapons." These theater nuclear weapons systems raised very serious concerns about the effectiveness of any "tactical nuclear" firebreak and were seen as almost certain to lead to uncontrolled escalation to strategic nuclear conflict.[15]

Once again, the two sides brought the stabilizing mechanism of arms control into play, and the 1987 INF treaty addressed this destabilizing situation. Under INF the United States withdrew the Pershing II and GLCM systems from Europe and then destroyed those missiles under Russian monitoring while Russia withdrew its intermediate systems and destroyed those missiles under US monitoring. This was the first on-site inspection and verification in US-Soviet/Russia arms control, and on-site inspection then became the cornerstone of the START, SORT, and New START treaties. After INF and the fall of the Soviet Union, a series of nontreaty, unilateral but at least partially reciprocated Presidential Nuclear Initiatives (PNI) by the American and Russian presidents led to the removal of at least 85 percent of US tactical nuclear weapons from Europe by 1993, as well as the withdrawal of Russian tactical nuclear weapons to Russian territory.[16] Approximately 200 forward-deployed US B-61 nuclear gravity bombs designated for employment by a small number of US and allied dual-capable aircraft (DCA) remain deployed in NATO today. President Jimmy Carter ordered the withdrawal of US nuclear gravity bombs for US dual-use aircraft delivery from South Korea to the United States. President George H. W. Bush directed the withdrawal of tactical nuclear weapons (other than the Tomahawk land-attack missile [TLAM] and nuclear warhead) from US Navy ships under a PNI. And the retirement of the TLAM nuclear system was directed by President Barack Obama; this left the

Europe-based B61s as the only forward-deployed US nuclear weapons system today.

The B61 is referred to as a "nonstrategic nuclear weapon" (NSNW). The bomb can be carried by either a strategic bomber or a tactical DCA fighter-bomber and can be designated for a wide range of targets depending on the range of the delivery system at the theater or strategic levels. In this case, the term "nonstrategic" indicates that this nuclear weapon is not limited by strategic arms control treaties such as New START. New START limits apply only to nuclear weapons deployed on strategic launch platforms; B61s deployed on B-1 bombers count as strategic weapons; B61s deployed on DCA do not. They are "nonstrategic." Neither New START nor any previous strategic arms control agreements addressed tactical nuclear systems. Even as a nonstrategic weapon, the B61 has not lately had true "tactical" status. As the Cold War wound down, the 1990 London Summit charged the alliance "to adopt a new NATO strategy making nuclear forces truly weapons of last resort."[17] The "New Strategic Concept" adopted at Rome the following year declared that "the fundamental purpose of the nuclear forces of the Allies is political" and went on to describe a solely deterrent role.[18] Note that in addition to the B61 gravity bombs, the NATO nuclear forces include the UK nuclear force and at least one alliance-designated US SLBM submarine backed up by the entire US strategic force; the B61 has been lumped into that strategic structure since at least 1990/1991. NATO has continued an active debate on whether to retain the B61 in Europe well into the second decade of this century.[19]

Today's renewed strategic competition between the United States/NATO and a revisionist Russia has caused the United States (and the NATO allies) to reexamine the theater nuclear situation. Russia since at least 2008—in its more assertive foreign policy, in its more coercive public attention to its strategic forces and modernization and expansion programs, in the earlier and more prominent role of nuclear weapons in its military exercises, and in its aggressive approach to key neighbors—has adopted a revised strategy. This strategy includes a nuclear doctrine often called "escalate to deescalate," or sometimes simply "escalate to win."[20] Remember that NATO, when facing a superior Soviet conventional force early in the Cold War, adopted a nuclear "first-use" and "escalate to deescalate" strategy. Today Russia finds itself facing a superior conventional NATO, and it is exercising, teaching, and refining a nuclear "first-use," "escalate to deescalate," and staged escalation strategy. As NATO addresses that situation, particularly in the Baltics and given its own inability to match possible Russian moves at the lowest end of the nuclear spectrum, the current B61 inventory alone is seen as an insufficient deterrent.[21]

In response, the Trump administration is proposing a series of nuclear force adaptations to emphasize and acquire more low-yield nuclear weapons options. The LYNW has been an enduring feature of the US nuclear inventory. The B61 has long had multiple "dial a yield" options. The new B61-12 variant (which will replace the older B61 bombs in NATO) includes that adjustable yield feature, including very low-yield options that, along with greater precision significantly, enhances the weapon's military utility and effectiveness. President George W. Bush sought, in the first Nuclear Posture Review, a ground-penetrating low-yield nuclear capability in response to emerging threats in North Korea and Iran.[22] Congress declined to fund the development of this new robust nuclear earth penetrator warhead.[23] The Trump NPR, as outlined above, seeks LYNW options to address both Russian and regional challenges.

In addition to the B61-12, the United States has begun to download the W76 SLBM warhead, creating a much lower-yield W76-2 warhead. A few tubes per boat will carry these new systems for enhanced deterrence against the Russia escalation challenge and other new challenges.[24] This combination of the B61 modification and the W76-2 is a near-term, low-cost package intended to provide initial LYNW options. In addition, the Air Force is currently developing a new air-launched cruise missile, popularly known as the long-range stand-off weapon (LRSO), which can provide low-yield options, and the Navy is exploring a replacement for the TLAM as a sea-launched option. Note that other than the B61, none of these systems would have to be deployed on NATO territory to challenge a Russian incident or crisis. This eases the potential for the kind of political opposition that was seen when the United States deployed the INF systems in Western Europe as an element of NATO strategy.[25]

Thus, these systems provide some technical and strategic answers to the Russian "escalate to deescalate" challenge. However, like INF and beyond, they blur the distinction between theater and strategic conflict. They represent capabilities that easily can cross lines into home territories and up to higher levels of conflict. They create very real difficulties for escalation management, let alone dominance, and they raise the bar very high for intra-war deterrence effectiveness. The United States thought that by limiting numbers, yields, and targets, it could clearly signal limited intent and create real possibilities for a firebreak/intra-war deterrent success at times during the Cold War. Russia seems to be adopting similar practices today. However, observers must remember the blurring effects of the INF systems deployed by both sides. Today, when written into an exercise or a regional strategy, LYNWs must be seen as a signal that the United States, and NATO in this context, are ready to consider LYNWs a deliberate escalation or counterescalation mechanism. A very long series of high-level discussions, deliberate nuclear diplomacy, confidence-building experiences, and stability enhancements would be needed to begin to hope to limit the escalation probability of a US-Russia LYNW exchange. Those discussions, diplomacy, and experiences do not currently exist other than in the New START context, and the future of that agreement remains in doubt as of this writing. Some semiofficial discussions of nuclear issues do exist with Russia, but they do not now address how to successfully signal, convey restraint, and build the likelihood of success in an LYNW intra-war deterrent effort.

Further, the United States and Russia have by far the longest and most advanced experience with nuclear diplomacy and strategic stability. US-Russia direct engagements on nuclear weapons issues began in the 1950s, and the two sides also have the experience of nuclear weapons summits since the 1960s. They have shared on-site inspection experience since the 1980s. These steps take time, deep engagement, mutual understanding, and an amount of trust and transparency that is not currently being widely renewed.[26] And no such foundation for nuclear cooperation or progress exists with China, North Korea, or Iran.

The United States and China did not have diplomatic relations until the 1970s, and we have never undertaken high-level nuclear discussions or bilateral nuclear diplomacy. There has been a productive semiofficial dialogue series between the United States and China the last several years, including retired senior military and diplomatic officials on both sides, as well as mid-level current defense and diplomatic personnel and think tank and university experts. These dialogues have advanced understanding and brought some limited areas of agreement and increased clarity on areas of continuing disagreement. However, the Chinese side has continually declined to elevate these discussions to the official level, and the United States is now backing off from its interest in continuing at the unofficial level.[27] These dialogues have indicated some growing understanding of major strategic issues and positions between the two sides; however, there are still many pitfalls and opportunities for misunderstanding and misinterpretation, and there remains a potential for regional crises that could escalate to involve nuclear forces, even up to the strategic level. Note that China has not to this point developed Western-style NSNWs, but does deploy theater-range nuclear systems that could be employed in a conflict with escalation potential. China, like Russia, is developing an "integrated strategic deterrence" concept that coordinates conventional, theater nuclear, and strategic nuclear systems. China continues to present at least as many questions as answers, and tailoring US strategic deterrence, regional deterrence, and crisis responses presents a continuing challenge.

Effective deterrence requires an effective capability set, but capability—weapons—alone does not and cannot ensure effectiveness. Effectiveness is more dependent on credibility, creating the perception of effectiveness around those weapons. And both capability and credibility, as well as any messaging/signaling associated with that set, require clear communication of the deterrent message to its intended audiences. That communication must be tailored to convey the intended message to the deterrence target; the signal/message must be translated to create the intended perception to that specific strategic personality/decision-maker. Further, that communication must also convey tailored messaging to allies and regional partners, to interested third parties, to the global community, and to the American public. There is a tendency to think of deterrence in terms of $D=C$ (usually stated in terms of capability, as for example "400 minuteman missiles is certain to deter"). $D=C^3$ is the correct equation incorporating capability, credibility, and (tailored) communication. Effective cross-cultural communication to strategic and regional deterrence targets is essential. We have some basis for that with Russia, a small foundation but more questions with regard to China, and little understanding for communication with North Korea or Iran.[28]

The current strategic environment is characterized by new and enhanced strategic nuclear systems, expanded and expanding regional nuclear dimensions, emerging nonnuclear strategic domains and systems, and new nuclear states and arenas, strategic personalities and cultures, asymmetric forces, and stakes. Strategic deterrence depends on effective strategies and activities at these various levels, in these various domains, against these diverse systems, and within these multiple decision sets. Effective deterrence, and certainly stable deterrence, is a much more complex quest today. This must be seen as a time for caution going forward with LYNW development and planning.

Dynamic Stability

The United States deterrence challenge today is clearly complex. At the strategic level, Russian and American recapitalization of their traditional strategic nuclear forces is ongoing to extend the current relative balance. Yet missile defense advances on the US side and new systems development on the Russian side present new and increasing challenges. The United States also faces strategic challenges from China and North Korea, with similar and different challenges on those fronts. And there is also the question of the meaning of "strategic," with new domains such as space and cyber presenting new challenges, and new technologies rising to this level as well (e.g., hypersonics for one). Plus there are dual deterrence issues that combine the conventional and nuclear spheres (the United States has kept nuclear responses on the table as options against biological weapons attacks, in declaratory policy terms at least through the Obama administration).

At the regional nuclear level, perhaps more accurately referred to as "theater strategic," the deterrence challenge is present in multiple regions, and sometimes with multiple deterrence target states in the same region. Force sizing, deployment, tailoring, and flexibility are all critical factors. And systems such as LYNWs create linkages between this level and the strategic level. There was a perceived deterrence deficit relative to Russia at the regional level, and LYNWs were the start of one answer to address that deficit; they were seen as enhancing regional deterrence, yet those weapons and their employment strategy may tend to destabilize strategic US-Russia and possibly US-China relations. Depending on numbers, employment strategy, and presentation, these weapons regionalize strategic conflict for one deterrence target state and raise regional conflict to the strategic level for another state. Both weapon characteristics and employment strategies, as perceived, are central factors in the relative success or failure at the regional level. Real or perceived strategy objectives such as "regime replacement" are primary drivers here. And integrated strategic deterrence doctrines meld conventional through LYNW/regional nuclear systems to strategic nuclear systems into a single continuum.

If we were to chart this current deterrence challenge starting at the strategic level, we would have multiple columns representing different challengers and domains. Those columns would soon be replaced by helixes with multiple strands for different weapons/deterrence categories. Levels would have to be added to address the regional/theater challenges, with more strands linking levels/categories and sometimes crossing over to a neighboring helix. LYNWs are one of those inputs that cross columns, levels, strands. This picture has already exceeded my ability to visualize, and it still does not include all of the components of the challenge. How could a major strategic power such as the United States begin to enhance its deterrence effectiveness in all of these sectors and levels?

One could compartmentalize and address targets or factors individually to enhance one deterrence challenge at a time. But the degree of overlap and linkage confounds that exercise. One could take a single adversary/deterrence target and address comprehensive deterrence across levels and dimensions for that one target. But targets like Russia or China differ on several levels and dimensions, with multiple interactive relationships. Enhancing one level might degrade another. Similarly, one could address a single region to enhance regional deterrence. But a region such as Northeast Asia presents a very complex challenge on its own, which is further complicated by its internal and external linkages and responses. Framing the challenges and the interactive factors is at least the first step to addressing this challenge.[29]

The best answer today may be to address the US deterrence challenge as a dynamic system, charting the components and their influences and linkages. One could then at least conceptualize key elements and effects, planning enhancements in a given area in full knowledge of their given consequences. It may become necessary to destabilize one area in order to stabilize a more timely or important challenge, with a plan already in place for longer-term stabilization of the destabilized area.

This approach is one of dynamic stability. The two terms are contradictory; a dynamic system is not stable and is tending away from stability, but insolating one area from forces of change can cause larger and longer-term damage to the whole. Change and continuous challenge are needed today and the foreseeable future. Strategists who think in broader, dynamic terms are needed. The United States needs strategists who see the big picture in the context of the past, the present, and the future and who can chart the interactions and forces of change, not just describe a single isolated point in time. We face a dynamic, complex deterrence challenge. We face a dynamic strategic security challenge. "Dynamic stability" is one answer; it may be an imperative.

NOTES

1. Mark E. Smith III and Claude J. Johns Jr., eds., *American Defense Policy, Second Edition* (Baltimore: Johns Hopkins University Press, 1965).

2. Thomas C. Schelling, Foreword, in *Strategic Stability: Contending Interpretations*, ed. Elbridge A. Colby and Michael S. Gerson (Carlisle, PA: Strategic Studies Institute, February 2013), v, vii–viii.

3. Department of Defense, *Deterrence Operations Joint Operating Concept*, Version 2.0 (Washington, DC: Department of Defense, December 2006), 8.

4. See Jeffrey A. Larsen and James M. Smith, *Historical Dictionary of Arms Control and Disarmament* (Lanham, MD: Scarecrow Press, 2005) for SALT and ABM Treaty details.

5. *Nuclear Posture Review Report, 2010* (Washington, DC: Department of Defense, 2010).

6. See Brad Roberts, *The Case for U.S. Nuclear Weapons in the 21st Century* (Stanford, CA: Stanford University Press, 2016) and Brad Roberts, "Strategic Stability under Obama and Trump," *Survival* 59, no. 40 (2017): 47–74. Roberts was a central voice in the 2010 NPR and early Obama nuclear policy in his role as deputy assistant secretary of defense for nuclear and missile defense policy.

7. *Nuclear Posture Review Report, 2010.*

8. *Summary of the 2018 National Defense Strategy of the United States of America* (Washington, DC: Department of Defense, 2018), 2; emphasis in the original; and *National Security Strategy of the United States of America* (Washington, DC: White House, December 2017).

9. *2018 National Defense Strategy*, 3.

10. *Nuclear Posture Review 2018* (Washington, DC: Department of Defense, February 2018). On low-yield, nonstrategic nuclear options also see Elbridge Colby, "Defining Strategic Stability: Reconciling Stability and Deterrence," in *Strategic Stability: Contending Interpretations*, ed. Elbridge A. Colby and Michael S. Gerson (Carlisle, PA: Strategic Studies Institute, February 2013), 65–70, for an early statement of the argument for these capabilities. Colby served as deputy assistant secretary of defense for strategy and force development and was a central voice in the 2018 National Defense Strategy early in the Trump administration.

11. There were also missile defense reviews in addition to the nuclear posture reviews early in the Obama and Trump administrations. Both supported a phased BMD deployment in NATO as well as deliberately limited but increasingly capable BMD system deployments in the United States. The 2019 report also provided a foundation for further BMD development and expansion. The NATO system is seen as destabilizing by Russia despite US assurances that its target is Iran. The US system is seen as destabilizing by China despite US assurances that its target is North Korea. See *Ballistic Missile Defense Review Report, February 2010* (Washington, DC: Department of Defense, 2010); and *2019 Missile Defense Review* (Washington, DC: Department of Defense, 2019).

12. See, for example, Kurt M. Campbell, Robert J. Einhorn, and Mitchell B. Reiss, eds., *The Nuclear Tipping Point* (Washington, DC: Brookings, 2004); Etel Solingen, *Nuclear Logics* (Princeton, NJ: Princeton University Press, 2007); and James J. Wirtz and Peter R. Lavoy, eds., *Over the Horizon Proliferation Threats* (Stanford, CA: Stanford University Press, 2012) as a sampling of quality sources on nuclear program decisions and cases.

13. Jeffrey Larsen, Introduction, in *Controlling Non-Strategic Nuclear Weapons*, ed. Jeffrey A. Larsen and Kurt J. Klingenberger (Colorado Springs, CO: Institute for National Security Studies, US Air Force Academy, July 2001), 5.

14. Rose Gottemoeller, Foreword, in *Controlling Non-Strategic Nuclear Weapons*, ed. Jeffrey A. Larsen and Kurt J. Klingenberger (Colorado Springs, CO: Institute for National Security Studies, US Air Force Academy, July 2001), xi. Ambassador Gottemoeller served as chief negotiator for the New START Treaty.

15. See Maynard Glitman, *The Last Battle of the Cold War* (New York: Palgrave Macmillan, 2006).

16. Glitman, *The Last Battle of the Cold War*. See also Maynard Glitman, "U.S. Sub-Strategic Nuclear Forces and NATO," in *Controlling Non-Strategic Nuclear Weapons*, ed. Jeffrey A. Larsen and Kurt J. Klingenberger (Colorado Springs, CO: Institute for National Security Studies, US Air Force Academy, July 2001), 65. Ambassador Glitman served as chief negotiator for the INF Treaty.

17. "1990 London Declaration," in *Controlling Non-Strategic Nuclear Weapons*, ed. Jeffrey A. Larsen and Kurt J. Klingenberger (Colorado Springs, CO: Institute for National Security Studies, US Air Force Academy, July 2001), 270.

18. Quoted in Stanley Sloan, "NATO Nuclear Strategy Beyond the Cold War," in *Controlling Non-Strategic Nuclear Weapons*, ed. Jeffrey A. Larsen and Kurt J. Klingenberger (Colorado Springs, CO: Institute for National Security Studies, US Air Force Academy July 2001), 46.

19. See a variety of views from this debate in Tom Nichols, Douglas Stuart, and Jeffrey D. McCausland, eds., *Tactical Nuclear Weapons and NATO* (Carlisle, PA: Strategic Studies Institute, April 2012); and Stefanie Von Hlatky and Andreas Wenger, eds., *The Future of Extended Deterrence* (Washington, DC: Georgetown University Press, 2015).

20. See David Johnson, *Russia's Conventional Precision Strike Capabilities, Regional Crises, and Nuclear Thresholds*, Livermore Papers on Global Security No. 3 (Livermore, CA: Center for Global Security Research, Lawrence Livermore National Laboratory, February 2018).

21. *Nuclear Posture Review 2018*.

22. See James Wirtz and Jeffrey Larsen, eds., *Nuclear Transformation: The New US Nuclear Doctrine* (New York: Palgrave Macmillan, 2005) for open-source details and analysis of the 2002 NPR.

23. See Jonathan Medalia, "'Bunker Busters': Robust Nuclear Earth Penetrator Issues, FY2005–FY2007," Congressional Research Service, February 21, 2006 update.

24. Department of State, "Strengthening Deterrence and Reducing Nuclear Risks: The Supplemental Low-Yield U.S. Submarine Launched Warhead," *Arms Control and International Security Papers* 1, no. 4 (April 24, 2020): 4.

25. See Matthew Kroenig, *A Strategy for Deterring Russian Nuclear De-Escalation Strikes* (Washington, DC: Atlantic Council, April 2018). Kroenig presents a view of the issues and response that is compatible with the 2018 NPR. He also calls for NATO land-based LYNW missile systems deployment to solidify US/NATO solidarity.

26. Even with the long experience between the United States and Russia, significant differences endure. For example, Americans compartmentalize and take a narrow view of strategic issues. Russia takes a much broader view and incorporates several other, nonstrategic and nonmilitary factors into its strategic decision calculus. See for example Michael J. Deane, "Soviet Assessment of the Correlation of World Forces—Implications for American Foreign Policy," *Orbis* 20, no. 3 (Fall 1976): 625–36, which first introduced this author to this important factor.

27. See Lewis A. Dunn, ed., *Building Toward a Stable and Cooperative Long-Term U.S.-China Strategic Relationship* (Honolulu: Pacific Forum, SAIC, and CACDA, December 31, 2012), for an example of the focus and content of one of these dialogues.

28. See, for example, Kerry M. Kartchner and Michael S. Gerson, "Escalation to Limited Nuclear War in the 21st Century," in *On Limited Nuclear War in the 21st Century*, ed. Jeffrey A. Larsen and Kerry M. Kartchner (Stanford, CA: Stanford University Press, 2014), 144–71, for a detailed discussion of escalation control and dominance in the face of new actors and multiple strategic personalities.

29. There are a few suggestions for strategies or strategy frameworks to begin to address this problem. See for example John K. Warden, *Limited Nuclear War: The 21st Century Challenge for the United States*, Livermore Papers on Global Security No. 4 (Livermore, CA: Center for Global Security Research, Lawrence Livermore National Laboratory, July 2018).

Hacking Democracy

THOMAS RID AND BEN BUCHANAN

Introduction

Cybersecurity—the practice and the debate—is more than a quarter century old. Early on, military concepts dominated, with the US Air Force and the RAND Corporation among the earliest adopters.[1] The context for this pioneering work was command-and-control warfare. By the mid-1990s the declared goal was winning in network-centric warfare, taking advantage of a new "revolution in military affairs," and achieving "information dominance." The utopian goal of turn-of-the-century military visionaries was striking: to win a war before it even started. Meanwhile, for twenty-five years, the corresponding dystopian vision of an "electronic Pearl Harbor" formed a counterpoint in the early cyberwar debate. The vision of winning swiftly by high-tech cyberattack dialectically nourished the fear of perishing in one.[2] Perhaps no idea was more critical at the extreme ends of the spectrum of computer network attack—and defeat—than the commonly accepted view that the internet, like airpower, affords advantage to the offense over the defense.[3] Whoever acts first, wins.

Then came the year 2016. Cybersecurity turned into the central issue of the US general election, gaining further in profile during the transition period and early 2017. Information operations helped mar the presidential ambitions of the losing Democratic candidate and undermined the legitimacy of the winning Republican president. Both of these assessments are highly charged and animate a debate that is more political than technical—this deeply politicized state of the art illustrates that cybersecurity has been elevated to a public profile and significance never seen before in its quarter-century history. Yet, despite it all, almost no serious commentators were ready to see the much-feared electronic Pearl Harbor in Russia's election interference, let alone a "cyberwar"; these military monikers were flawed. 2016 showed that the quarter-century-old debate was littered with broken ideas.

Cybersecurity was not and still is not ready for prime time. The field disappoints in practice, policy, and scholarship. Cybersecurity is under-delivering on the defense, because, even decades later, soft targets are still soft, and fruits are still hanging low aplenty.

Cybersecurity is under-delivering in the public debate because facts are too often poorly shared, and major incidents are not revealed, with too many public commentators still struggling to distinguish firm forensics from flimsy. Finally, cybersecurity is under-delivering in theory, because twenty-five years after the first seminal works, core concepts are still wobbly and contested too easily. These flaws are not just impairing hacking victims, news stories, or research articles—this triple deficiency is subverting democracy itself. 2016 has brought the collective information security vulnerabilities of the American democratic process into sharp relief. The stakes could not be higher: liberal democracy has become a juicy target of ever more sophisticated Computer Network Attacks (CNAs)—and CNAs have become a preferred semi-covert action tool of the early 21st century.

In this article we take stock. We do so by asking three questions. The first is a conceptual one: what kind of internet-enabled offensive operations have proven to be most dangerous for liberal democracies? The second question is a historical one: how have these types of political computer network operations evolved, and what proved to be their most significant mechanisms of hacking democracy as they evolved? The third question is practical: what can be done to fix the problem as we move forward?

The well-established adage that the internet is "offense-dominant" is accurate, but for a widely misunderstood reason. The common, yet flawed, technical argument is that the architecture of the internet means that the offense dominates in computer network operations. This argument has become gospel in the cybersecurity debate. The offense has indeed often dominated in computer network operations thus far, but this dominance has been a result of flaws in the broader cybersecurity field, not just in specific technologies. The offense dominated in the 2016 election interference, in the 2012 Saudi Aramco incident, and in the 2007 Estonia case because of the field's triple deficiency, not because of long-suspected technical characteristics inherent in the architecture of the internet. To focus only on the technical, or only on the political, is to take too narrow a view.

The re-emergence of active measures fueled by hacking and leaking exacerbated this already existing

Thomas Rid and Ben Buchanan, "Hacking Democracy," *SAIS Review of International Affairs* 38, no. 1 (2018): 3–16. © 2018 Johns Hopkins University Press; reprinted with permission of Johns Hopkins University Press.

trend. Active measures are intelligence operations designed to shape decisions and opinions of adversaries. Sometimes active measures exploit technical weaknesses, but more fundamentally these operations exploit fissures in political systems, societies, and communities, including in the cybersecurity research community. The oft-repeated claim that "cyberspace is offense dominant" both admits failure in the past and concedes defeat in the future, thus conceding weakness and limiting ambitions in theory and in operations. Instead, we argue that the cult of the online offensive is contingent, that it can be reversed through better cybersecurity practice, policy, and theory. Upon closer examination it becomes clear that open societies have already begun to harden their defenses against computer network operations and have mechanisms to continue this buildup into the future.

This paper is structured as follows. In four sections, we will briefly outline democracy's main potential weak points against cyber operations. The first weak point is the cybersecurity debate itself. The more direct political targets then fall into three sets: institutions, infrastructure, and intelligence. Within these sets, this paper will first present the most visible type of offensive activity and work toward the most clandestine and hard-to-examine form of operation. As the analysis moves from overt to covert, the challenges for researchers and investigators fast increase in scholarship, government, and industry.

A Fractured Field

The field of cybersecurity has been shaped by major incidents over the decades. These advances and attention have often fed into the policy discussion. Perhaps the first major case, thirty years ago, was the Morris worm, a highly infectious piece of malicious software. Later, in late 1996, Department of Defense investigators discovered *Moonlight Maze*, the first major state-on-state espionage campaign; "MM," as it came to be known, arguably never stopped.[4] Slammer, the uncontrolled computer worm that found its way into a nuclear power plant, made its mark fourteen years ago.[5] The first *Sofacy*/APT28 samples date back to 2004, but were identified publicly only years later. *Titan Rain*, the first large Chinese espionage campaign, was revealed in 2005, but had already been under way for several years by then.[6] The infamous "Denial of Service" attacks on Estonia, which were christened *Web War One* by *Wired* magazine,[7] occurred one decade ago roughly concurrently with the development of Stuxnet,[8] a potent Israeli-United States sabotage attack against Iran's nuclear enrichment facilities. Five years ago, in the summer of 2012, Saudi Aramco experienced what may still be one of the most devastating publicly known computer network intrusions, which incapacitated 30,000 workstations in the world's largest oil company.[9]

In February 2013, Mandiant published a landmark attribution report, "APT1." The document contributed to changing the notion that digital intruders could easily cover their tracks, and therefore attracted a great deal of attention.[10] Since 2013, both the pace of major incidents increased, as did their often-public investigations. In May 2014, the FBI filed its first indictment of adversarial hackers, of five Chinese People's Liberation Army intelligence operators.[11] Later in 2014, North Korea's high-profile hack of Sony Pictures Entertainment revealed what was then the politically most famous cybersecurity incident to date.[12] This increase in the volume of operations and their visibility is the result of a number of factors. In particular, it is likely that the publicity that followed Stuxnet as well as the National Security Agency (NSA) leaks led a number of countries to make investments in offensive capabilities—the leaks, counterintuitively, also showed that the West's advanced technical intelligence agencies have superb attribution capabilities and apparently better operational security than their Russian or Chinese counterparts.[13]

Meanwhile, the policy debate struggled to keep pace with incidents, especially after 2013.[14] Conferences like Defcon, Blackhat, RSA, or Infosec Europe have mushroomed from niche meetings into gargantuan conventions. A host of smaller annual conferences serves an ever more finely branched community of researchers, such as Kaspersky's Security Analyst Summit, BSides, Code Blue, ShmooCon, Troopers, S4, the new OffensiveCon, or the Chaos Computer Club conferences—the last with a more notable anti-establishment tinge. Graduate programs in cybersecurity are proliferating. Major news outlets have designated cybersecurity reporters, and the press coverage of major incidents has improved significantly.

Yet at closer examination, the community is disintegrating rather than consolidating. Entire subfields and sub-debates have emerged, for example the debates on vulnerabilities and exploits, on civil society targeting, on industrial control system security, on digital forensics and incident response—"DFIR" in jargon—or on threat intelligence and "threat hunting," as well as on privacy, encryption, and bulk collection and surveillance. The overlaps between these subfields are shrinking rather than growing, foreshadowing less fruitful dialogue even within the field. One example is the highly contentious issue of applying the Wassenaar export control (a multilateral agreement regulating the export of weapons) to hacking tools. This cacophony makes it harder for elected officials and policy-makers to grasp important trends. Developments such as the emergence of politically motivated wiping attacks (deleting or destroying sensitive or key data), including a large number of undisclosed wiping incidents, have been lingering at the shadowy fringes of the debate for too long.

The fissures in the debate are not just inconvenient for newcomers, journalists, and policy-makers. The cracks in the field also make it easier for adversaries to exploit the cybersecurity debate itself. Just as journalists added value to the DNC leaks by sifting dumps and pulling out the gems, so did cybersecurity experts add value to the Shadow Brokers' recent dumps of NSA hacking tools by sifting files, testing them, and pulling out shiny objects—thus enabling the desired operational effect against the US government in the first place. The Shadow Brokers' operation was likely designed with this dynamic in mind. It cleverly distracted the cybersecurity community from larger political questions while weaponizing the community's collective sleuthing abilities.

Scholarship on cybersecurity faces unique and particularly difficult challenges. In recent years, every large international relations journal has published articles on cybersecurity. Yet some of the debate's most influential texts are conceptual in nature, for example, the landmark 1993 piece "Cyberwar is Coming!"[15] the 1995 article "What is Information Warfare?"[16] or the 2013 retort "Cyber War Will Not Take Place."[17] Too many scholars find this old and tired debate about cyberwar to be irresistible—an especially glaring shortcoming considering the proliferation of incidents and the rich empirical material available today.

University-based academics, no matter their discipline, face an additional unique challenge in this field: most cutting-edge work requires access to insights and data from operations and incidents. Some of the most valuable sources for research, as a consequence, are either in the intelligence community (IC) or, more likely, in the vibrant private sector market for incident response, digital forensics, and threat intelligence. Yet most PhD students, post-docs, junior faculty, and even senior scholars have little or no access to these communities. The dearth of scholarship that effectively utilizes leaked NSA and Government Communications Headquarters (GCHQ) documents is an illustration of this problem. Insightful research that takes advantage of some of the more technical leaks is all too rare. The mirror image of this problem is reflected in the private sector, where a wide range of companies share reports under the so-called Traffic Light Protocol (TLP), a trust-based industry classification system. The number of TLP-coded reports is today reaching well into the five digits. Yet too few scholars have seen, let alone taken advantage of, these rich data sources.

Not even the name of the field is settled. The information security community still rolls its collective eyes at the vintage cringe-worthy "cyber"—which has quickly become a noun, especially in policy and military circles—although most use the moniker at the same time. "Imagine a stranger renamed your profession 'poop-mining'—and you had to start using the term yourself. This is how I feel about 'cyber,'" wrote Matthew Green, a prominent professor of cryptography at Johns Hopkins University, in May 2017.[18] His note received than 2,300 approvals on Twitter. To a non-specialist, "cyber" can feel at once ephemeral and intimidating.

Institutions

The main targets of computer network operations against democracy are institutions, not computer networks. Institutions are based on trust; they work because people trust them to work. That trust is one of the top targets of 21st-century digital active measures. It is also one of the easiest targets. Undermining institutions that serve key democratic functions is a blow against democracy itself.

Two broader categories of institutions are being targeted. Political institutions comprise the first and most prominent type of target. These organizations, such as political committees or campaigns, offer a soft and large target surface. In many respects, election cycles are the most vulnerable moment for liberal democracies, akin to the period during which a lobster sheds its protective shell, and for a while remains covered in a soft, vulnerable shell, marking it out as particularly easy and attractive prey. Espionage during this vulnerable period is not new. Probably the most notable early examples of computer hacking assisting in this espionage effort come from the 2008 election cycle, in which Chinese operatives reportedly targeted both the Obama and McCain campaigns.[19] Even in 2016, the Democratic campaign was not targeted by only Russian actors. But while a democracy should attempt to thwart this kind of intrusion, the theft of documents does not pose the same kind of threat as more active operations.

Four points deserve attention, in light of the 2016 activities. First, the Russian operations targeted voters directly. Cold War active measures were mostly directed against politicians and journalists and reached the wider public only indirectly. By the early 2010s, social media introduced a new platform that allowed remote operators to reach voters directly, via ads, trolls, and personal messages. The Robert Mueller indictment brought forward against the Internet Research Agency on February 18, 2018, brought a number of case studies to wider public attention. Second, and related, the 2016 operations took place at a substantial scale. They played out in traditional mass media and on social media, reaching millions of people. The operators published tens of thousands of individual documents in more than eighty individual leaks. Most (although not all) active measures throughout the Cold War tended to be far smaller and narrower. Russian intelligence agencies successfully used the scalability of innovative hack-leak-amplify activities to their advantage.

Third, the 2016 influence operations were poorly disguised, perhaps even semi-overt by design. Not only was it obvious that a hacking-aided influence campaign was going on, but it was reasonably apparent which foreign power was conducting it. As early as mid-June 2016, a range of outside experts squarely placed the blame of the budding leaking operation on Russia, following the initial hacking attribution of the cybersecurity firm CrowdStrike.[20] Politically there may have been partisan incentives to call the evidence into question. Technically and historically, however, the evidence of a Russian hand was inescapable early on.[21] Fourth, the operation almost certainly worked better and longer than anticipated—independent of whether the active measures actually affected the vote or not. Candidate Donald Trump cited foreign hacking favorably on numerous occasions during the campaign.[22] He repeatedly cited hacked documents, professed his "love" for WikiLeaks,[23] and encouraged Russian computer network intrusions to recover Hillary Clinton's emails of interest. Taunted and provoked, Trump himself worsened damage to the legitimacy of his own presidency, both before and after the election. Moreover, after Trump was sworn in as President of the United States, he continued to call the evidence of Russian election interference into question, thus inadvertently straining the credibility of America's intelligence and law enforcement community, thus providing incentives and cover for follow-on active measures.

The other category of democratic institutions at exceptional risk of nation-state hacking is civil society groups, particularly those agitating for human rights or democratic policies. Activist movements often find themselves in at least partially threatening situations. Governments, often including their own domestic government, perceive grassroots activists to be threats to stability and order. Most non-democratic regimes target, with some semi-regularity, citizen activists. One of the clearest example of this campaign comes from the United Arab Emirates. Ahmad Mansoor, a noted activist there and a member of Human Rights Watch, found himself in the crosshairs of a conglomerate run by a leading member of the ruling family. Investigation by cybersecurity researchers revealed that—in addition to old-fashioned tools of repression like arrest, theft, and beating—Mansoor was the victim of more new-fangled hacking.

The spyware that targeted Mansoor was in place for more than a year before researchers found it. It was intrusive, gaining deep insight into his digital life and his organizing activities. The intimidating effects were real, even after the hacking operation was eventually thwarted. "It was as bad as someone encroaching in

your living room, a total invasion of privacy, and you begin to learn that maybe you shouldn't trust anyone anymore," Mansoor said.[24]

The story, thus far, has no happy ending. The hacking effort against Mansoor garnered some media attention, and great notice within the cybersecurity community. The technical mechanics of it, including the use of significant hacking tools, indicate that Mansoor was a priority target. But the publicity did little to help him. On a later trip to the United Arab Emirates, he was arrested again and remains detained. Mansoor was not alone. Invoices from the company Hacking Team, which carries out or enables a great deal of government-sponsored hacking operations, show an extensive relationship with the United Arab Emirates. The Emirates, as of 2015, appear to be the company's second biggest customer. They have paid more than $630,000 for hacking operations targeting more than a thousand people. It is yet another reminder of how significant and scalable the hacking threat can be.

It is not just the United Arab Emirates that has used hacking tools against civil society. China, Mexico, Ethiopia, Morocco, and others are doing so as well.[25] Their targets vary, and some are more directly connected to movements for representative governments than others, but the overall trend is clear: hacking is a tool not just for non-democratic foreign governments to target mature liberal democracies, but for non-democratic governments to nip domestic threats to their regime in the bud.

Infrastructure

Another form of political targeting is directed not at the trust in institutions, but at the underlying technical infrastructure. This form of hacking goes one level deeper and interferes either with the integrity of key data or with machines. While such operations can certainly also have an effect on trust—an attack on infrastructure can also be an attack on institutions—at its core it is something more direct than the last category of operations.

Some theorized attacks on infrastructure have been demonstrated in practice by researchers. Foremost amongst these are the myriad of ways in which voting infrastructure could be targeted.[26] The range of possible attack vectors is significant and can be illustrated by tracing the path a typical American voter takes in order to participate in an election. A citizen's first formal step of political engagement upon reaching adulthood is to register to vote. In doing so, they input their personal—and often private, sensitive, or identifying—data into a computer system. The maintenance and security of these computer systems varies enormously, but it is clear both that they are significant targets and that hackers have had success in breaching them and copying out the data within. These registration data-bases are ripe targets for compromise. There are numerous examples of hackers penetrating the registration systems and databases of American states and other entities. The total number of records affected often numbers well into the millions, sometimes into the hundreds of millions.[27]

On Election Day, in-person voters check in at their assigned polling places. Election workers typically verify the voter's registration in a poll book, which contains a list of all the voters eligible to vote at that place. Some states, such as Ohio, have digitized these books.[28] Digital records are more efficient, but can get hacked. One possible vector of attack is to manipulate the poll books in a given area, perhaps by removing five percent of the voters of a given party—a so-called data integrity attack. If voters of a particular political affiliation, gender, race, or age were disproportionately turned away, this could quickly fuel claims that the election was subject to illicit manipulation.

Next, the voter actually marks and casts their ballot. Unfortunately, the cybersecurity of voting machines is both important and flawed. Voting machine security is uneven. A series of audits turned up a wide range of problems in many of the major voting machines used in the United States. Due to a lack of funding, a sizable portion of voting machines is more than a decade old and depends upon outdated security models. Notorious examples abound, such as Wi-Fi-connected systems that used a default password of "abcde,"[29] or the system that researchers were able to reconfigure in order to play popular video games like Pac Man. In 2017, the hacker conference DEF CON vividly highlighted the state of affairs with their "Voting Machine Hacking Village," in which attendees worked together to quickly and successfully demonstrate a substantial number of security flaws.

Before a Communist Party election, Josef Stalin famously said, "I consider it completely unimportant who in the party will vote, or how; but what is extraordinarily important is this—who will count the votes, and how."[30] This quote suggests a fourth step in the voter's journey, and another opportunity for hackers: tabulation. Many of the vulnerabilities with machines can permit the manipulation of vote-counting functions.[31] In more centralized systems, the computers at the core of the voting infrastructure are ripe targets. In Ukraine in 2014, hackers launched a wiping campaign against these vital machines just three days before the election.[32]

After vote tabulation, citizens find out the result of the election. Here, too, there is the possibility for trouble and worries of illegitimacy. No example is more prominent than the Bush-Gore controversy in 2000, in which major networks first called Florida for Al Gore, then retracted the claim amidst a vote count that came down to the wire. The uncertainty lasted into the next month before the United States Supreme Court awarded the state to George W. Bush. The case might provide inspiration for digital saboteurs.

Intelligence

Intelligence agencies are fundamental to protecting democracy. The NSA in particular takes on a direct role in engaging with and thwarting their foreign counterparts, including attempts to target democratic institutions and infrastructure. For this and other reasons, the US intelligence community and its allies find themselves in the line of fire. The most striking post–Cold War case of a counter-IC active measure is known as Shadow Brokers. First visible in a series of August 2016 messages, the operators behind various Shadow Brokers' social media and developer accounts began posting evidence that they had obtained classified NSA tools (referring to the NSA in infosec-jargon as "Equation Group"). The messages escalated throughout the next twelve months, revealing more and more about NSA activities. The group revealed some of the agency's most potent penetration tools. This included one, ETERNALBLUE, which United States government operators had used for years; one source called the exploit "fishing with dynamite."[33]

The Shadow Brokers' move to publish the pilfered tools had a triple effect. First, it thrust secret NSA operations back into the media spotlight. The NSA faced questions about how these powerful tools got out of its secure confines, and whether it was right to retain such vulnerabilities in the first place, as others could have exploited them as well. Major companies, such as Microsoft, sharply criticized the NSA in this regard.[34] Even a hawkish former director of both the NSA and the CIA, Michael Hayden, said, "If American espionage cannot protect the special tools that it possesses, it doesn't matter that they are good people working for good purposes under good oversight. If they cannot protect the tools, I just can't mount the argument to defend that they should have them."[35] Secondly, the leaks made it either technically impossible or politically much more difficult for NSA to use the published tools.[36] The disclosure, highly likely an adversarial intelligence operation, sabotaged NSA's collection capabilities. Third, the leaks enabled others to use NSA's insights for their own purposes. Others, less worried about getting caught, could use the publicized tools as blueprints for developing their own similar capabilities. The most prominent example of this is an attack, known as *WannaCry*, which occurred in May 2017. Likely conducted by North Korea, this attack rapidly spread to hundreds of thousands of computers around the world. Most prominently, this included many computers operated by Britain's National Health Service. The attack code served as a broken form of ransom-ware, encrypting the machine's files until a payment was made; in a sign of incompetence, an inadvertent start to the operation, or a desire to make noise and not money, the payment and decryption mechanism appeared broken.

A little more than a month later, Russian military intelligence launched a comparable attack that caused "billions" of dollars of damage to the world economy.[37] The operation, named *NotPetya*, limited its targets to users of a Ukrainian tax reporting software; but the attack spread quickly within the networks of a significant number of international companies. Though *NotPetya* spread using a variety of mechanisms, including credential theft, it in part took advantage of the same software vulnerabilities the NSA had exploited, again generating embarrassing and damaging publicity for the American intelligence agency. In effect, *NotPetya* served as a double sabotage tool: it crippled Ukraine and embarrassed the United States.[38] One minister of the Russian Federation directly challenged US intelligence at the Munich Security Conference 2018 by bringing up *NotPetya*'s ETERNALBLUE reuse as an example of US government malpractice.

The likely goal of the Shadow Brokers operation was weakening Five Eyes (Australia, Canada, New Zealand, the United Kingdom, and the United States) intelligence. The NSA is the most potent signals intelligence agency of any liberal democracy, and its work has enabled many advance threat warnings to NATO allies, against terrorism as well as against ongoing espionage campaigns—weakening the West's wider intelligence community is therefore weakening the capacity of democracies to self-defend.

The technical intelligence community in the West especially faces another new problem: the loss of their near-complete monopoly on technical intelligence and classified information. A range of private sector companies are now competing with signals intelligence organizations not just for talent, but in collection and analysis as well. But in this newfound competition also lies a great opportunity for the defense of democracy from new threats.

In the early 2010s, more and more companies started to "publish" restricted reports under the so-called Traffic Light Protocol. The traffic light protocol is an industry-wide, trust-based convention that governs the sharing of confidential information, both orally and in writing. The protocol is usually abbreviated as TLP. The protocol works as follows: TLP:WHITE means the document is public; TLP:GREEN means recipients can share the file with peers; TLP:AMBER means recipients can share within their own organization; and TLP:RED means recipients cannot share with any parties outside of the exchange or meeting in which the information was originally disclosed. The US and UK governments,

and many others besides, have endorsed the system and sometimes use it themselves. TLP reports usually have a classification header, like a government document would have.

The private sector is taking the lead in intelligence because firms often have greater access to information and data through their products and services. This rise of private sector intelligence comes with a range of risks. One is imperfect quality assurance and vetting for reports and analysis. Another one is the rising number of proprietary, for-profit reports that never get published as TLP:WHITE at all, and thus remain out of view. But TLP reports have one major advantage over classified government documents: they can be shared more easily, and data, as well as insights, sometimes permeate out into the semi-public and public debate. Indeed, sometimes private sector reports may be used as a vehicle to publish previously classified information on high-profile cases.

Despite these challenges, the overall trend is a positive one: after decades of a predominantly military frame of mind, epitomized in the tired notion of "cyberwarfare" and "offense domination," the field of cybersecurity is beginning to right itself back to where it always belonged, which is at the intersection of public and private intelligence.

Ever growing numbers of operators in the wider information security community have cut their teeth in intelligence. These individuals tend to be more comfortable talking about collection rather than about coercion, about interception rather than intervention. The notion that political aspects pollute a pure technical analysis has, thankfully, less and less currency. More and more terms of art from the study and the history of intelligence find their way into the cybersecurity lexicon, for example, "active measures," "active and passive collection," "operational security," "all-source in investigations," "attribution," "estimative language," "assessment," "analysis of competing hypotheses," "aperture of analysis." The paradigm is shifting from a military mindset to an intelligence-led philosophy of information security—indeed the quiet rise of the term "infosec" over "cyber" highlights this trend. It is this area of public-private partnership, thus far mostly out of public view, where great opportunities to defend democracy have emerged.

Conclusion

The cybersecurity debate, and the wider infosec community, face a moment of reckoning. 2017 has exposed that one of the greatest vulnerabilities of liberal democracy in the 21st century is the information security of the wider political system, from personal email authentication to government routers, from boutique malware attacks to old-school infiltration, from voting machine compromise to shrewd forgeries, from hacking the grid to brazen active measures against the NSA as well as everyday voters.

The offense has indeed dominated for decades, not as a result of technical defects, but as a result of man-made defaults. It is still too easy not to use two-factor authentication; it is still too easy to hide bots at scale on some social media platforms; it is still too easy to breach networks and stay undetected for months; it is still too easy to lure journalists with a scoop on a flimsy intelligence story. Geeks and wonks face mirroring temptations: overestimating what they understand, underestimating what they don't understand, dismissing the silly mannerism and alien jargons of the other side, and secretly sneering at the inevitable mistakes of those who try to cross the divide. This is not a trite, smartass observation from two smug academics: 2016 has brought to the fore that adversaries are again getting better at driving wedges into the divisions that divide us. "Us" as liberal, open democracies. But also, "us" as a community of professionals dealing with information security. Spotting useful idiots is easy after all—just ask, "Am I still willing to adjust my view in response to new insights or new evidence and admit that I was wrong?"

NOTES

1. These early adopters derived the term for "cybernetics." See Thomas Rid, *Rise of the Machines* (New York: W. W. Norton, 2016).
2. These terms and the transition into this stark tension is best articulated by Richard Clarke and Robert Knake, *Cyberwar* (New York: HarperCollins, 2010).
3. For further discussion of offense dominance and its central role in international relations scholarship, see Robert Jervis, "Cooperation under the Security Dilemma," *World Politics* 30, no. 2, 1978. For an analysis of sources arguing the offense dominance of the internet, see Ben Buchanan, *The Cybersecurity Dilemma* (New York: Oxford University Press, 2017), chap. 5.
4. For full discussion, see Rid, *Rise of the Machines*. See also Juan Andres Guerrero-Saade, Costin Raiu, Daniel Morre, and Thomas Rid, "Penguin's Moonlit Maze: The Dawn of Nation-State Digital Espionage," London: Kaspersky Lab, April 3, 2017.
5. Kevin Poulsen, "Slammer Worm Crashed Ohio Nuke Plant Network," *Security Focus*, August 19, 2003.
6. For discussion of this case, see Joel Brenner, *America the Vulnerable* (New York: Penguin, 2011).
7. Joshua Davis, "Hackers Take Down the Most Wired Country in Europe," *Wired*, August 21, 2007.
8. For the best history, see Kim Zetter, *Countdown to Zero Day* (New York: Crown, 2014).
9. Christopher Bronk and Eneken Tikk-Ringas, "The Cyber Attack on Saudi Aramco," *Survival* 55, no. 2, 2013.
10. "APT1," Alexandria, VA: Mandiant, February 18, 2013.
11. Ellen Nakashima, "Indictment of PLA Hackers Is Part of Broad U.S. Strategy to Curb Chinese Cyberspying," *The Washington Post*, May 22, 2014.

12. Michael Schmidt, Nicole Perlroth, and Matthew Goldstein, "F.B.I. Says Little Doubt North Korea Hit Sony," *The New York Times*, January 7, 2015.
13. Thomas Rid and Ben Buchanan, "Attributing Cyber Attacks," *Journal of Strategic Studies* 39, no. 1, 2015.
14. Adam Segal calls this fateful moment "year zero" for cybersecurity. For a full discussion, see Adam Segal, *The Hacked World Order* (New York: Public Affairs, 2016).
15. John Arquilla and David Ronfeldt, "Cyberwar Is Coming!" (Santa Monica, CA: RAND Corporation, 1993).
16. Martin C. Libicki, *What Is Information Warfare?* (Washington, DC: National Defense University, 1995).
17. Thomas Rid, *Cyber War Will Not Take Place* (Oxford/New York: Oxford University Press, 2013).
18. See @matthew_d_green, May 19, 2017, https://web.archive.org/web/20170724110256 /https:// twitter.com/matthew _d_green/status/865666772241862656
19. Ryan Naraine, "Newsweek: Obama, McCain Campaigns Hacked by 'Foreign Entity,' " *Newsweek*, November 5, 2008.
20. Dmitri Alperovitch, "Bears in the Midst: Intrusion into the Democratic National Committee," *CrowdStrike*, 2016.
21. See Thomas Rid, "All Signs Point to Russia Being Behind DNC Hack," *Motherboard/Vice*, July 25, 2016.
22. Ashley Parker and David Sanger, "Donald Trump Calls on Russia to Find Hillary Clinton's Missing Emails," *The New York Times*, July 27, 2016.
23. Patrick Healy, David Sanger, and Maggie Haberman, "Donald Trump Finds Improbable Ally in Wikileaks," *The New York Times*, October 12, 2016.
24. Nicole Perlroth, "Governments Turn to Commercial Spyware to Intimidate Dissidents," *The New York Times*, May 29, 2016.
25. Perlroth, "Governments Turn to Commercial Spyware."
26. For a full discussion, see Ben Buchanan and Michael Sulmeyer, "Hacking Chads," Cambridge, MA: Harvard Kennedy School, Belfer Center for Science and International Affairs, October 2016.
27. Sometimes these systems have shockingly little security. For the biggest example, see Nick Corasaniti and Rachel Shorey, "Millions of Voter Records Posted, and Some Fear Hacker Field Day," *The New York Times*, December 30, 2015.
28. Karen Farkas, "Electronic Poll Books Will Be at Voting Locations across the State by November 2016," *Cleveland Plain Dealer*, August 28, 2015.
29. "Security Assessment of Winvote Voting Equipment for Department of Elections," Commonwealth Security and Risk Management: Virginia Information Technology Agency, 2015.
30. Boris Bazhanov, *Memoirs of the Former Secretary of Stalin* (Moscow: III Tysiacheletie, 2002).
31. For a series of audits, see "Source Code Review of the Sequoia Voting System," University of California, Berkeley: California Secretary of State, 2007; "Source Code Review of the Diebold Voting System," University of California, Berkeley: California Secretary of State, 2007; "Source Code Review of the Hart Intercivic Voting System," University of California, Berkeley: California Secretary of State, 2007.
32. Mark Clayton, "Ukraine Election Narrowly Avoided 'Wanton Destruction' from Hackers," *Christian Science Monitor*, June 17, 2014.

33. Ellen Nakashima and Craig Timberg, "NSA Officials Worried About the Day Its Potent Hacking Tool Would Get Loose. Then It Did.," *The Washington Post*, May 16, 2017.

34. "Ransomware Attack 'Like Having a Tomahawk Missile Stolen,' Says Microsoft Boss," *The Guardian*, May 14, 2017.

35. Ken Dilanian, "Can the CIA and NSA Be Trusted with Cyber Hacking Tools?" *NBC News*, June 30, 2017.

36. For two examples, see "ProjectSauron: Top Level Cyber-Espionage Platform Covertly Extracts Encrypted Government Comms," Kaspersky Lab, August 8, 2016; "Equation: The Death Star of Malware Galaxy," Kaspersky Lab, February 16,

2015. See also Ben Buchanan, "The Legend of Sophistication in Cyber Operations," Cambridge, MA: Harvard Kennedy School, Belfer Center for Science and International Affairs, January 2017.

37. "Statement from the Press Secretary," White House, February 15, 2018, https://web.archive. org/web/20180315182022 /https://www.whitehouse.gov/briefings-statements/statement -press-secretary-25/.

38. Nicole Perlroth, Mark Scott, and Sheera Frenkel, "Cyberattack Hits Ukraine Then Spreads Internationally," *The New York Times*, June 27, 2017.

Beyond Surprise Attack

LAWRENCE FREEDMAN

A surprise attack, conceived with cunning, prepared with duplicity, and executed with ruthlessness, provides international history with its most melodramatic moments. A state believes itself to be at peace then suddenly finds itself at war, in agony and embarrassed that it failed to pick up the enemy plot and will now suffer the consequences of blows from which recovery will be hard. Melodramas along these lines play out not only in the worst-case scenarios of military planners and alarmist commentators but also in movies and novels. They offer a compelling narrative: the most powerful states are humiliated and the course of history altered as one power sees possibilities for action that its victim misses completely. It is also a credible narrative as surprise attacks have been regular occurrences throughout history. They make military sense as defeating a strong opponent is always going to be difficult unless the first blows really count. Maximizing operational secrecy is essential to maximizing operational success.

Surprise makes the most sense when battles are decisive. Otherwise, the effect will be to start a war—with all the pain, risk, and uncertainty—without ensuring victory. A decisive victory forces the enemy hand. An important legacy of the Napoleonic Wars was the conviction that such a victory depended on the effective elimination of the enemy army. At some point surprise could make the critical difference when two essentially symmetrical armies, relying on superior tactics, organization and armaments, faced each other. Catching an unprepared enemy with an early blow from which it could never really recover, even if it tried to fight on, should allow the whole business of war to be concluded quickly.

The Franco-Prussian War underscored the importance of early battlefield success. The Prussians were astonished when the French, having declared war, were slow to mobilize. They did not make the same mistake. The efficiency of their mobilization, along with the innovative tactics of Helmuth von Moltke, caught France unaware, leading to its defeat at the Battle of Sedan at the start of September 1870. Germany executed the ideal campaign, quick and truly decisive, spoiled only by the refusal of the French population to accept the verdict of battle until their unexpected resistance was crushed. Moltke showed how to surprise the enemy, and his successors in the German general staff took note: To win a war, mobilize early and strike hard and fast.

The German victory also led to speculation about how other powers might be caught out by a ruthless and resourceful enemy, including books imagining how other great powers might also suffer sudden and catastrophic defeats. An early example of this genre was *The Battle of Dorking*, written by a British Army officer. Appearing in 1871 just after von Moltke's victory, *Dorking* described a German invasion from across the channel in which telegraph cables were cut to prevent advance warning. The Royal Navy, which had allowed itself to become overextended because of colonial commitments, lost its warships to "fatal engines which sent our ships, one after the other, to the bottom." The drama concluded with a last stand on a ridge near Dorking in southern England, where a brave combination of regulars and reserves were let down by the army's miserable organization. And so, the accumulated prosperity and strength of centuries was lost in days. A once-proud nation was stripped of its colonies, "its trade gone, its factories silent, its harbours empty, a prey to pauperism and decay."[1]

Lawrence Freedman, "Beyond Surprise Attack," *Parameters* 47, no. 2 (Summer 2017): 7–14, published by the US Army War College.

As with so much writing about the future of war, this example essentially made a point about the present, in this case the need for army reform, a statement about what might happen if sensible measures were not taken urgently. Other books followed with similar themes about the dangers of spies or readying young men for the demands and sacrifices of war, or sometimes in counternarratives to the gloom, demonstrating how a brave nation could cope with all challenges. By the start of the twentieth century, writers were exploring the military possibilities opening up with new technologies such as heavier-than-air flying machines.[2] The imagination of the British novelist H. G. Wells even stretched to atom bombs.[3] A regular theme in all this literature was the importance of surprise and the first blow. The key to victory was seizing the initiative.

There were those, such as the Polish banker Ivan Bloch, who understood that even the cleverest plans might fail, that defenses might cope better than expected with dashing attacks, and that a defiant population might resist foreign occupation.[4] Still, the Germans opened the First World War with an ambitious offensive designed, once again, to defeat France quickly. But this time they failed. Instead of a decisive victory, they got caught up in a long attritional slog, in which they struggled to cope with the superior economic and demographic strengths of their enemies.

After 1918, alternative routes to a quick victory were sought. One possibility was to use tanks to wage a rapid offensive. But there was another alternative that dispensed with forcing an enemy land invasion. Instead of pressuring the enemy government to capitulate as a result of the annihilation of its army, it would have to surrender because of the demands of a desperate population unable to cope with a succession of massive air raids and being hit by high explosives, incendiaries, and poison gas. A new dystopian literature quickly developed, telling of the trials of ordinary people as they fled their burning cities or of the hopelessness of governments in the face of weapons they were unable to counter. The theme comes through in some of the titles: *The Poison War*, *The Black Death*, *Menace*, *Empty Victory*, *Invasion from the Air*, *War upon Women*, *Chaos*, and *Air Reprisal*.[5]

Air raids did not provide the opening shots of the Second World War, but they soon came, becoming regular and progressively more destructive. Although their effects were certainly terrible, they were not decisive.[6] The resilience of ordinary people and of modern societies had been underestimated. Only with the war's finale and the atom bombs dropped on Hiroshima and Nagasaki was the deadly promise of air power realized. Previous air raids had killed as many people, but this time the devastation required only single weapons and the impact was emphasized by the surrender of an already beleaguered Japan.

The prospect that the next war could soon "go nuclear" inevitably dominated strategic debates after 1945. But, the trauma of the two surprise attacks that brought the Soviet Union and then the United States into the Second World War shaped considerations of what that might mean. Pushing the logic of seizing the initiative to the extreme, Hitler launched Operation BARBAROSSA against Russia in June 1941 while the British were still fighting; the Japanese attacked the US Pacific Fleet at Pearl Harbor, despite failing to pacify China. Both efforts were enormous gambles, bold in their execution and complete in their surprise. Both offensives were characterized by arrogance, for their leaders were convinced their nations were superior in spirit and in discipline, but also in recklessness, taking on much larger powers before defeating the existing enemies.

Both gambles failed. The Soviet Union was rocked; at one point it looked like it would succumb, but it held on. Gradually, the size of the country, its harsh climate, reserves of strength, and Nazi mistakes turned the tide of war.[7] There was never much chance that Japan would conquer the United States—the objective was to get in the best position for what was assumed to be an inevitable war. The result was a terrible conflict with great suffering, ending with Japan under American occupation.[8]

The most important lesson was that getting in the first blow, however well designed and executed, did not guarantee victory. Yet for the victims of 1941, the basic lesson was that great power did not provide immunity from surprise attack. The United States and the Soviet Union won in the end, but their fights were long and painful, and the results were not preordained. The shock effect was substantial, and it left a legacy in the way both thought about war thereafter. In 1958, when experts from both superpowers met briefly to discuss their fears of surprise attacks, the Soviets were fixated on yet another large offensive set in motion by Germany, this time backed by the North Atlantic Treaty Organization (NATO), while the Americans were focused on another Pearl Harbor–type "bolt from the blue," this time with nuclear missiles.[9]

The impact of these shocks could be seen during the Cold War, especially in regard to nuclear strategy. In Washington the dominant fear was that Soviet leadership might become convinced that a well-crafted first strike would put it in a position where it need not fear retaliation. Starting numbers were irrelevant if the United States could be disarmed by a surprise Soviet attack directed against its bombers, intercontinental ballistic missiles, and missile-carrying submarines.[10] In the 1960s, the Pentagon set a test for the US nuclear arsenal: could it "assure destruction" of the Soviet Union? In other words, could America maintain "at all times a clear and unmistakable ability to inflict an unacceptable degree of damage upon any aggressor, or combination of aggressors—even after absorbing a surprise first strike"? This damage was quantified at 33–20 percent of the Soviet population and 75–50 percent of the Soviet industrial capacity. These criteria assumed a pain threshold well above the losses experienced in World War II, which were hardly willingly accepted. Then, the highest possible intelligence assessments about future Soviet capabilities were considered to see whether any extra capabilities were required to ensure that the assured destruction criteria could be met. The answer was not a lot was needed beyond existing plans.

This effort was not a prediction of the course of a future war, or of the American government's reaction to a complete failure of deterrence. The aim was to leave no doubt in the minds of Soviet leadership that aggression carried an unavoidable risk of nuclear devastation. An American response could not be guaranteed because the Soviet Union could also, even after absorbing a first strike, ensure similar levels of destruction of the United States. Hence "mutual assured destruction," naturally known as MAD, came to describe the standoff between the nuclear powers during the Cold War. How much the capability contributed to preventing a hot war remains a matter for conjecture. There were many reasons why political leaders would have been desperate to avoid a Third World War, but the possibility of mutual destruction was hardly irrelevant. It was not necessary to gaze for long into a crystal ball to see the awful devastation with which a future war might end.[11] Would the Germans and Japanese in 1941 have really been so ready to launch their wars if their crystal balls had shown them how bad things might turn out? The point of deterrence was to persuade a potential adversary not to bank on the first move being decisive, and to think through the consequences of an enemy still capable of fighting back.

Establishing there was no sure way to win a nuclear war did not end all fears. The Soviet Union kept building up its own arsenal, suggesting it had a different view of how deterrence might work, which might even include some plan for a nuclear victory. Even if MAD meant the nuclear arsenals neutralized each other, the Soviet strength in conventional capabilities provided them with other options for mischief. This capacity left plenty of scope for inventiveness when it came to imagining how Moscow might take an initiative that would catch Washington unaware and so allow stealing some geopolitical advantage. One scenario actively debated in the 1970s was the possibility of a sudden and vast Warsaw Pact offensive into West Germany that required little prior mobilization, and so, no practical warning to NATO about the attack.[12] This worst-case scenario assumed everything worked perfectly for the enemy while NATO was left flat-footed, over-

whelmed before it could even consider escalation to nuclear force.

Yet, even when contemporary wars have opened with surprise attacks, the results have not been encouraging. Israel's demolition of Egypt's air force on the first day of the Six-Day War (1967) is one example where the enemy was left helpless by a well-executed attack. Although, this war also demonstrates how conquering and occupying another's territory might also lead to persistent terrorism and insurgency. Two prime examples of surprise attacks that failed to deliver early victories are North Korea's move against South Korea in 1950 and Iraq's contest with Iran three decades later. The North might have succeeded if an international coalition had not managed to aid South Korea before it was completely overrun. Iraq found itself struggling to cope with Iran's counter-invasion in 1980 and became caught in a war lasting until 1988. Its resultant indebtedness to those who helped it fund its defense was one reason for its next surprise attack—Kuwait in August 1990. The occupation was easily accomplished, but it barely lasted six months. Kuwait was liberated under an American-led coalition in early 1991.

The most striking feature of modern wars is not how quickly they can be concluded but how long they last.[13] The United States achieved quick victories in Iraq and Afghanistan against regular forces but then got bogged down dealing with insurgencies. Russian aggression against Ukraine has left it bogged down in an inconclusive struggle. Syria has become an arena in which a whole series of regional conflicts are playing out without an identified route to anything resembling peace being identified. With civil wars, the typical conflict now lasts years, long after the economy, society, and political system have been broken, with the violence sustained by criminals as well as zealots, warlords, and neighboring states.

Major powers now often appear tentative and unsure. Even when, as with Russia, they seem to be taking bold steps, their objectives turn out to be limited. Grand victories are no longer in mind. Instead of audacious moves geared to a quick victory, a probing, patient alternative approach is even seen in China's disputes in the South China Sea.

Yet, none of this has erased concerns about surprise attacks. One reason is the recollection of al-Qaeda's attacks on New York and Washington on September 11, 2001, after which commentary soon turned again to Pearl Harbor. The lesson lay not in the revenge taken against al-Qaeda and its Taliban sponsors in Afghanistan but the shock of discovering the vulnerability of modern, open societies to malicious attack. The aim seemed simply to cause maximum pain, and that goal soon led to speculation about the many ways that pain might be inflicted. Scenarios in which small terrorist cells or even "lone wolves" could cause harm using basic weapons such as guns, knives, highly explosive materials, aircraft or motor vehicles turned into lethal weapons were constructed. Attacks of this sort could not bring a modern Western state to "its knees."[14] The surprise they achieved was essentially tactical in its effects. At most, strategically they were part of an ongoing and largely uncoordinated global insurgency. Despite the obvious differences in scale and impact, the outcome of a Taliban ambush in Kabul or of a shooting in Paris were part of a campaign that began before 9/11 and appears to be of indefinite duration.

All of this needs to be kept in mind when addressing claims that future surprise attacks will come out of cyberspace and have effects tantamount to defeat in war. As early as the 1990s, the growing dependence of vital services on digital networks led to warnings of an "electronic Pearl Harbor" directed against the critical infrastructure supporting energy, transport, banking, and so on.[15] Instead of trying to get quick victories by taking out enemy forces, why not instead take out the enemy society? While the technical issues are quite different from more classical forms of military attack, and the practice would be far less violent, there are similarities to the post-1918 claims about strategic air bombardment providing a more satisfactory route to victory than attritional fights between armies.[16] As with a nuclear first strike, the best case for the perpetrator requires confidence that preparations for an attack are not detected, that the appropriate networks are properly identified and could be attacked, and that the cyberattacks will work as planned. And then, as with Operation BARBAROSSA and Pearl Harbor, there is the question of what happens after the first blow. How would this turn into a lasting political gain? A cyberattack does not lead to territory being occupied. The victims would be expected to respond, even as they struggled to get the lights back on and systems working. An attack that produced drastic effects could be considered a casus belli, and classical military responses might be considered legitimate.[17]

The issue is not whether critical infrastructure can be vulnerable and lead to major upset if taken down. Hostile activity in the cyber domain, represented by a continuing offense-defense duel, is now constant and ubiquitous. It involves activists, terrorist and criminal organizations and poses constant trouble for those trying to preserve the integrity and the effectiveness of vital networks. The danger, however, is not so much of some one-off catastrophic surprise attack but a series of events in line with modern conflict, reflecting the blurring of the military and civilian spheres, efforts to weaken and subvert opponents without attacking them head on. These are wars with occasional military strikes and battles, often vicious but still short of being truly decisive. Cyberattacks represent another way to cause injury and irritation short of obvious acts of war, as well as serving as natural accompaniments to acts of war.

There is, therefore, a disconnect between the continuing search for a route to a decisive victory and the contemporary experience of warfare, which once started, is hard to stop. Even if enemy regulars are overwhelmed, the result is as likely to be insurgency, especially directed against foreign forces. This tends to be reflected in more recent future war fiction, such as *Ghost Fleet* by Peter Singer and August Cole. This story opens with a surprise attack of impressive complexity, cunning and duplicity, which almost succeeds but fails in the end.[18]

There will always be arguments for testing the resilience of systems against the worst case. If they can cope with the most severe threats, then lesser cases should be manageable. The worst case may depend on the aggressor being foolish and futile, but stupidity is one of the hardest things for any intelligence agency to predict. At the same time, when planning an offensive, every effort must be made to make the first blows count. The key point, however, is that even with surprise and maximum effort, these first blows are unlikely to be decisive on their own, especially against an opponent with any reserves of strength. This depth is why states must look beyond surprise attacks to what follows, to the second and third blows, and also to those much further down the line, perhaps delivered by irregulars who have taken over the struggle after the defeat of the regulars. The surprises of war do not just come at the start.

NOTES

1. George Chesney, "The Battle of Dorking: Reminiscences of a Volunteer," *Blackwood's Magazine* (May 1871), http://gutenberg.net.au/ebooks06/0602091h.html.

2. See the two novels about Robur, with his heavier-than-air flying machine, by Jules Verne, *The Clipper of the Clouds* (London: Sampson Low, 1887); and Jules Verne, *Master of the World* (London: Sampson Low, 1904).

3. H. G. Wells, *The World Set Free, a Story of Mankind* (London: Macmillan, 1914).

4. Ivan Stanislavovich Bloch, *Is War Now Impossible? Being an Abridgment of the War of the Future in Its Technical Economic and Political Relations* (London: Grant Richard, 1899).

5. I. F. Clarke, *Voices Prophesying War: Future Wars, 1763–3749* (Oxford: Oxford University Press, 1992), 169–70.

6. Richard J. Overy, *The Bombing War: Europe 1939–1945* (London: Allen Lane, 2013).

7. Christian Hartmann, *Operation Barbarossa: Nazi Germany's War in the East, 1941–1945* (Oxford: Oxford University Press, 2013).

8. Jeffrey Record, *A War It Was Always Going to Lose: Why Japan Attacked America in 1941* (Washington, DC: Potomac Books, 2011).

9. Jeremi Suri, "America's Search for a Technological Solution to the Arms Race: The Surprise Attack Conference of 1958

and a Challenge for 'Eisenhower Revisionists,'" *Diplomatic History* 21, no. 3 (Summer 1997).

10. Albert Wohlstetter, "The Delicate Balance of Terror," *Foreign Affairs* 37, no. 2 (January 1959).

11. Albert Carnesale et al., *Living with Nuclear Weapons* (Cambridge, MA: Harvard University Press, 1983).

12. A "standing start" attack was a theme in an influential report by Senators Sam Nunn and Dewey F. Bartlett, "NATO and the New Soviet Threat," US Senate, Armed Services Committee, 95th Congress, First Session (Washington DC: US Government Printing Office, 1977). See also Robert Close, *Europe without Defence? 48 Hours that Could Change the Face of the World* (Brussels: Editions Arts and Voyages, 1976).

13. Ann Hironaka, *Neverending Wars: The International Community, Weak States, and the Perpetuation of Civil War* (Cambridge, MA: Harvard University Press, 2005).

14. The most alarming prospect was a terrorist nuclear weapon. Graham Allison, *Nuclear Terrorism: The Ultimate Preventable Catastrophe* (New York: Times Books/Henry Holt, 2004).

15. The first to refer to the possibility of an "electronic Pearl Harbor" was Winn Schwartau, *Terminal Compromise* (Old Hickory, TN: Interpact Press, 1991), http://www.gutenberg.org/files/79/79.txt.

16. See John Arquilla, "The Computer Mouse that Roared: Cyberwar in the Twenty-First Century," *Brown Journal of World Affairs* 18, no. 1 (Fall/Winter 2011): 39–48.

17. George Lucas, *Ethics and Cyber Warfare: The Quest for Responsible Security in the Age of Digital Warfare* (New York: Oxford University Press, 2017).

18. P. W. Singer and August Cole, *Ghost Fleet: A Novel of the Next World War* (Boston: Houghton Mifflin, 2015).

Chapter 9

Unconventional Wars and Unconventional Forces

The Limits of Special Operations Forces

AUSTIN LONG

In the early 1980s, the future of US special operations forces (SOF) looked decidedly grim. The Vietnam-era boom in SOF had long since expired and the 1970s ended with the debacle of the attempted SOF-led rescue of US hostages in Iran. After two decades of rebuilding, SOF were much more capable on the eve of the September 11, 2001, attacks, but were still only used sparingly and in the shadows.[1]

Now, nearly two more decades later, the SOF pendulum has fully swung in the opposite direction of the nadir of the early 1980s. SOF are routinely deployed in a variety of missions globally, from direct action missions against terrorists to training and advising both conventional and unconventional allied forces (often termed the "indirect approach"). The US SOF community has expanded greatly in both size and missions and has become, along with remotely piloted aircraft (a.k.a. drones), the weapon of choice for small-footprint counterterrorism and counterinsurgency operations as well as the projection of discrete and discriminate force.[2]

Yet, despite the current enthusiasm, special operations are not a panacea for all security challenges. Policymakers and analysts must remain cognizant of the limits of SOFs while developing military strategy lest too much be asked of the force. This is particularly important as the security environment changes—a SOF-centric strategy might be appropriate for some challenges but inappropriate for others.

This article describes the limits of SOF and proceeds in four parts. The first describes some limitations common to all special operations. The second describes limitations on the direct approach for the employment of SOF (e.g., direct action and special reconnaissance), while the third describes limitations on the indirect approach (e.g., unconventional warfare and foreign internal defense). It concludes with recommendations to policymakers.

It is worth noting up front that while this article will necessarily focus on the shortcomings of special operations, it is not intended to denigrate the importance of special operations or SOF. Instead, it should be read as an attempt to manage expectations for the force so it can be employed effectively and efficiently. While it is currently unimaginable that SOF could re-turn to something like the dark days of the early 1980s, it is equally important to remember that the current prominence of SOF was equally unimaginable then. Remaining cognizant of the limits of SOF is crucial to preventing overreliance on the force, which could in turn lead to a significant reduction in willingness to support or employ SOF.

General Limitations of Special Operations

All special operations share some common limitations, the first being that special operations (and by extension SOF) almost never achieve decisive strategic success on their own. Special operations and SOF alone can often only achieve decisive tactical success. Occasionally, special operations can have some strategic effect on their own, particularly in terms of signaling commitment and capability through discrete operations. But absent other supporting elements—whether military, diplomatic, or economic—the achievement of decisive strategic effects by SOF is very rare.

For example, one of the most daring direct-action missions of World War II was the German seizure of the massive Belgian fortress of Eben Emael in May 1940. Yet the German elite paratroopers' capture of the fortress and nearby bridges would have been only a tactical success without prompt link-up with the advancing 18th Army. By linking up quickly with the 18th Army, the rapid capture of the fort enabled German conventional forces to cross into Belgium before British units could reinforce Belgian defenses, a key element of Allied plans. A well-orchestrated combination of special and conventional operations thus allowed a decisive tactical success to have a decisive strategic effect as well.[3]

In contrast, the British effort to seize the bridge at Arnhem during Operation MARKET GARDEN (the so-called bridge too far) was ineffective despite employment of a much larger force of paratroopers. While the intent of the operation was similar to that of Eben Emael, the British XXX Corps was unable to advance to Arnhem, leaving the British paratroopers stranded and eventually overrun. Without effective support from conventional forces, what should have been a tactical special operations success became a rout.[4]

Austin Long, "The Limits of Special Operations Forces," *PRISM* 6, no. 3 (2016): 35–47.

The Israeli raid on Green Island in July 1969 further underscores the importance of orchestrating elements of national power to enable SOF success to achieve strategic effect. Green Island was home to important Egyptian intelligence and early warning installations during the war of attrition between Israel and Egypt. While the island could have been attacked using conventional means, Israeli command decided to use SOF to demonstrate Egyptian vulnerabilities, even in highly fortified positions.

The Israeli raid was a tactical success, despite the high number of Israeli casualties. By following up the raid with airstrikes exploiting the newly created gap in Egyptian air defense as well as diplomatic messaging, the Israelis ensured the raid's success contributed significantly to the strategic objective of ending the war. Absent this support, the raid might even have been viewed as a strategic failure, given the amount of Israeli casualties.[5]

The raid that led to the killing of Osama bin Laden by US SOF in 2011 had a strategic effect in the sense that it was viewed as bringing some level of closure to the September 11, 2001, attacks. Like the raid on Green Island, it demonstrated to current and potential adversaries the capability of US special operations forces.[6] Yet this strategic effect was far from decisive, either in the Afghanistan-Pakistan region or in the global war on terror. The Israeli raid on Entebbe, Uganda, was similar in demonstrating the long reach of Israeli SOF, while also rescuing hostages that would otherwise have been a strategic bargaining chip for terrorists.[7]

This limitation is not just applicable to the direct approach. British SOF were remarkably successful in helping Oman decisively defeat an insurgency in the province of Dhofar in the 1970s. However, SOF tactical success in leading and advising Omani units was aided by diplomatic efforts, which brought Iranian troops and support into the conflict on the side of Oman. British intelligence launched a parallel effort to build and advise Oman's intelligence service. British advisers also helped Oman craft an economic policy to make the most of its valuable, but limited oil reserves. Absent this multidimensional support (and as noted below, Omani willingness to reform) the SOF tactical success would have been unlikely to produce such a decisive strategic victory.[8]

The US SOF mission in El Salvador in the 1980s was likewise enabled by extensive whole-of-government support. Economic assistance and advice helped sustain an economy battered by war while the US intelligence community provided important support in a variety of ways, including covert action. The US Ambassador was particularly crucial, as US support to El Salvador was controversial, and absent deft management could have been suspended entirely.[9]

In stark contrast, recent SOF tactical successes were not well supported in either direct or indirect action

in Yemen against al-Qaeda in the Arabian Peninsula (AQAP). Tactical successes did not yield strategic success as the government of Yemen collapsed into civil war, creating an opportunity for AQAP to fill the void created as US SOF withdrew from the country.[10] It remains to be seen if the Saudi-led coalition, which relies heavily on SOF, will have greater strategic success than its predecessor.[11]

The second common limit of SOF is the inherent high-risk nature of special operations. While this risk can be managed, it cannot be eliminated. This risk is only of moderate importance when policy-makers are heavily committed to achieving an outcome such as victory in a major war. Yet policy-makers often turn to SOF when seeking a limited liability military option—one just short of major war or intervention. In such situations, policy-maker commitment to the objective may be sufficient to deploy SOF, but insufficient to sustain that deployment after a negative event occurs as a result of required risk taking.

This environment produces a paradox, which limits SOF. If SOF are to continue being deployed in this environment, policy-makers must either eschew necessary risk taking or assume risk, knowing a sufficiently negative incident could end the deployment. The former choice means operations will be suboptimally effective, while the latter choice means a single negative event could end an entire SOF campaign (often with severe consequences for SOF careers).

The events in Mogadishu, Somalia, in the fall of 1993 highlight this paradox. Task Force Ranger had been committed precisely to achieve US objectives without employing a major military force. In conducting operations against Mohammed Farah Aidid and his militia forces, the task force commander, Major General William Garrison, assumed risk by necessity. A series of missions culminated in the events of 3–4 October, when an operation to capture senior supporters of Aidid encountered much greater resistance than anticipated. Despite an effective withdrawal by Major General Garrison against a vastly larger force, the operation still resulted in substantial and highly publicized American casualties. The task force was completely withdrawn soon after and Major General Garrison's career, exemplary to that point by all accounts, was effectively ended.[12]

Conversely, many indirect approach missions are suboptimally effective as SOF are prohibited or discouraged from taking risk. After 1969, military advisors to the CIA-sponsored Provincial Reconnaissance Unit (PRU) program in Vietnam, one of the only effective indigenous direct action capabilities, were no longer allowed to accompany the PRUs on missions. This restriction was not only imposed because of the physical risk to advisors, but also because of the political risk to individuals in Washington. The latter was particularly important as the US commitment to South Vietnam dwindled and allegations of US and South Vietnamese war crimes grew after the events in My Lai. Keeping US advisors at arm's length from an effective but ruthless military campaign (many PRU members were seeking revenge against the insurgency) became a political imperative. Unfortunately, the resultant negative impact on PRU morale and effectiveness was substantial.[13]

Similar restrictions were imposed on the US military advisory group in El Salvador in the 1980s. Paradoxically, by limiting US advisor participation in combat operations to limit political risk, it became very difficult to disprove allegations of human rights abuses by the Salvadoran military. Reducing risk thus limited the potential effectiveness of Salvadoran operations from both a military and political perspective.[14]

Limits on SOF in the Direct Approach

Beyond these general limitations, SOF face specific challenges when used in the direct approach (direct action and special reconnaissance). The first is related to one of the major applications of US and allied SOF in the 21st century—the targeting of insurgent and terrorist leadership. The theory behind such "high-value targeting" operations is that the loss of leaders will lead to the collapse or at least the serious degradation of the terrorist or insurgent leadership structure.

However, the effects of targeting leadership appear to vary widely and are highly dependent on the characteristics of the organization. Some organizations are highly dependent on a single charismatic leader or a handful of skilled organizers to provide organizational direction and cohesion. Others are much more institutionalized, with regularized procedures for replacing lost leaders—the latter being a common problem for any combat organization, whether insurgency or army.

For example, Sendero Luminoso (Shining Path) of Peru was highly dependent on its founder and leader, Abimael Guzman (aka Comrade Gonzalo). After organizing in the 1970s, Sendero Luminoso began a successful (and brutal) guerrilla campaign in the 1980s—at one point controlling much of south and central Peru. Yet following Guzman's capture in 1992, the organization began to splinter, a process accelerated by the capture of a handful of other key leaders, including Guzman's eventual replacement in 1999. Subsequent loss of leadership in the 2000s further weakened the organization. While the loss of leadership was not the only factor contributing to Sendero Luminoso's decline and near total defeat, it is clear the capture or killing of a small number of leaders by SOF (in this case from Peru's elite counterterrorism police unit) had a very large impact.[15]

In contrast, the capture of Abdullah Ocalan, the supreme leader of the Partiya Karkerên Kurdistanê (Kurdistan Worker's Party, or PKK), had only a modest effect on the survival of the organization. Ocalan's capture by Turkish SOF in Kenya did lead to a temporary PKK cease-fire with the government. However, unlike Sendero Luminoso, the PKK did not begin to lose cohesion after the capture of its supreme leader and has renewed its rebellion against the Turkish state on two occasions (roughly 2004–2012 and 2015 to present).[16]

Beyond targeting specific senior leaders, SOF can also be employed in a more comprehensive campaign against both senior and mid-level leaders and technical experts (such as bomb makers or financiers). Such campaigns are intended to remove key figures at all levels, eventually disrupting the organization by eliminating these individuals faster than they can be replaced. Such campaigns require substantially more resources, in terms of intelligence, surveillance, and reconnaissance assets, as well as units to take action against the targets.

The US and allied SOF campaigns against insurgents in Iraq and Afghanistan, including al-Qaeda in Iraq (AQI) and the Taliban in Afghanistan are examples of these sustained and well-resourced high-value targeting campaigns. In both cases, these campaigns have been remarkably successful at the tactical and operational level. Beginning with founder Abu Musab al-Zarqawi, the senior leaders of AQI have been killed on a number of occasions, with a replacement emerging each time.[17]

In Afghanistan, the coalition realized even greater tactical success against mid-level leaders. As journalist Graeme Smith notes:

A Canadian military intelligence officer looked back at his tour of duty [in Afghanistan] with satisfaction in the spring of 2008, believing that nearly all the middle ranks of the local insurgency had been killed or captured during his nine months in Kandahar. The elimination of those field commanders, he calculated, would leave the insurgents with little remaining capacity for the summer fighting season.[18]

Similarly, operations against AQI were sustained at a high level. This was enabled by the massing of intelligence and surveillance assets under a SOF task force, which then was resourced to undertake multiple actions per night.[19] As a report from the Joint Special Operations University notes, "Between 2006 and 2009 the task force maintained an operational tempo of 300 raids a month against AQI's networks in Iraq."[20]

The impact of these sustained tactical and operational successes were, however, decidedly mixed. Against some insurgent organizations these campaigns had significant effect. The Fallujah Shura Council in Iraq was a powerful insurgent umbrella organization in the early days of the war. However, it soon disintegrated following the loss of its key leader, Abdullah Janabi, and several mid-level commanders in 2004.[21]

In contrast, AQI and the Taliban were able to survive and continue fighting on a significant scale despite massive loss of leaders. As Graeme Smith recounts of the Canadian military intelligence officer's claim that the Taliban would have little fight left in Kandahar:

Sadly, he was proved wrong: the summer of 2008 was the deadliest period Kandahar has witnessed during the latest war. It could be argued that the violence might have been worse if certain Taliban commanders had not been killed, but so far attacks on insurgent commanders have shown no signs of weakening the insurgency.[22]

Similarly, despite over 1,000 raids against AQI leadership in three years, along with a surge of US conventional forces and the Sunni Awakening against AQI, in 2010 AQI was weakened but by no means crippled. Despite this weakening it was still able to launch multiple daily attacks across Iraq in January 2011;[23] and in March 2011, it was able to temporarily seize the provincial government buildings in Tikrit.[24]

Five years later, AQI's descendant, the Islamic State of Iraq and the Levant (ISIL), has seized substantial territory in Iraq and Syria. Though it is being degraded by a sustained air and military campaign, including SOF action against its leaders, it shows remarkable resilience as of this writing. Indeed, ISIL has been able to extend footholds into other countries, most notably Libya.[25]

The central limitation on these SOF campaigns is the nature of the adversary. AQI/ISIL and the Taliban are much more institutionalized organizations than Sendero Luminoso or the Fallujah Shura Council. Despite suffering massive leadership losses and tactical and operational setbacks, both organizations have remained coherent and combat-effective.

SOF reconnaissance operations for targeting also face similar limitations. In 2001, SOF targeting support linked US airpower to the indigenous ground forces of the Northern Alliance in Afghanistan. The result was devastating to the Taliban and its al-Qaeda allies.[26]

SOF reconnaissance linked to air power against North Vietnamese logistics in Laos produced a much less significant strategic effect. As part of a comprehensive campaign against the Ho Chi Minh Trail, SOF units conducted special reconnaissance missions to find and target US airpower against trucks transporting material down the trail. This was supplemented by SOF units placing sabotaged ammunition in insurgent caches they discovered. Yet despite tactical and operational success against logistics, the supply of material into South Vietnam was not strategically disrupted.[27]

As with direct action, the pivotal factor for SOF reconnaissance and airpower is the adversary. In 2001, many local Taliban abandoned the fight quickly, shocked by the efficacy of the US and allied offensive.[28]

The North Vietnamese and their insurgent brothers were more able to adapt to US airpower by distributing lessons learned and using deception and other means to neutralize SOF and airpower.[29] Crucially, the Vietnamese were able to maintain the will to fight despite massive losses through a combination of revolutionary ideology, social control mechanisms, and relentless self-criticism.[30]

Limits on SOF in the Indirect Approach

Whatever its limitations, one major advantage of the direct approach to using SOF is control. Policymakers have high confidence that, when directed, US SOF will execute missions as briefed. They will not shirk responsibilities nor seek to derive personal profit from operations in almost all cases.

The same cannot be said of many forces SOF support in the indirect approach, which is a major limitation. As Daniel Byman has described, US interests often diverge wildly from the interests of local allies in counterterrorism and counterinsurgency campaigns.[31] SOF efforts to work "by, with, and through" indigenous allies are constrained by the need to manage these divergences in interest.

Typically, indigenous partners come in two varieties: proxies (sometimes called "surrogates") and partners. Proxies are defined principally as sub-state actors (e.g., militias) having a direct relationship with the United States and only a limited (or nonexistent) relationship with the nation where they operate. Partners in contrast are an element of an existing nation-state's security apparatus.

Proxies offer the advantage of greater possibility of aligning US interests with those of the proxy. With loyalty principally to itself, the proxy force may be resolute and motivated as long as support from US SOF is central to achieving the proxy's goals. Good pay, combined with the lack of viable alternatives to US support, will typically produce very reliable and effective proxies.

Though reliable and effective, proxies are still not the equivalent of US SOF (or even regular military forces in some cases). For example, US and allied SOF, in conjunction with the CIA, supported a variety of proxy forces in Laos in the early 1960s. The proxies, in most cases drawn from ethnic minorities, had been neglected by the Laotian government and viewed US support as their principal alternative to continuing neglect. With proper training and advising from SOF, these proxies were very effective within certain constraints. As CIA historian (and former case officer in Laos) Thomas Ahern notes:

Whether firing a carbine or an M-l, nearly every Hmong volunteer needed only a few hours at the improvised firing range before the training team moved on to combat organization and tactics. The Hmong would not be mounting company or even platoon-size operations, at first, and [name redacted] trained them to operate in three-man fire teams. They immediately grasped the principle of fire-and-maneuver, in which one man or element fires from cover while the other advances, in a kind of leap-frog approach toward the enemy's position.... A Pathet Lao unit of reported battalion strength moved to within 2 miles of the training base, and the Hmong irregulars went into action within a week of the first weapons drop. The guerrillas ambushed the advancing Pathet Lao, and in the two days of combat that followed killed a reported 17 enemy. Never to be renowned for their fire discipline, the Hmong exhausted their ammunition supply during this action.[32]

This anecdote highlights both the strength of such motivated proxies—conducting an effective ambush within a week of being given the first modern weapons they had ever seen—as well as the limits—lack of fire discipline. For the next decade the proxies in Laos would perform well in ambush and other guerilla roles while never becoming particularly good infantry. Ahern concludes, "Motivated almost exclusively by the urge to protect their families, these irregulars, even with more training than time and resources allowed, would never be regular infantry capable of a frontal assault."[33]

Partnering with proxies also faces another substantial limitation, which is that in many cases SOF must manage a complex relationship between the proxy and the host nation. As the Laos example shows, many proxies are motivated precisely because they have a poor relationship with their own government. Whether the Hmong in Laos, or the Kurds in Iraq and Syria, the most motivated and loyal proxies are frequently drawn from groups with complex or adversarial relationships with their own government.[34]

This reality means proxies and host-nation governments can end up in conflict. This is allegedly what happened when the Kandahar Strike Force, a proxy, had a tense stand-off escalating into a gun battle with the Afghan police in 2009.[35] In South Vietnam, US forces faced a similar problem with ethnic minority proxies and attempted to create a stronger relationship with the government by including South Vietnamese SOF in their programs. This worked to a point; then one proxy force mutinied and massacred its Vietnamese SOF advisers.[36]

If proxies are potentially better aligned with the United States at the cost of friction with the host nation, partner forces are the opposite. As part of the host nation government, they have clear authority to use force and collect intelligence without risking conflict with other parts of the host-nation security force (in most cases). At the same time, the partner force is subject to all the frailties, divergent interests, and political problems of the host nation.

In rare instances, this is not a problem. The British SOF fighting insurgency in Oman were fortunate in having the British-educated Sultan Qaboos as a partner. After deposing his unenlightened father, Qaboos became the model of an enlightened despot, making reforms to both his security forces and the overall nature of government in his country based on advice from the British. The result was an enormously effective set of partners, ranging from the reformed regular armed forces of the Sultan to the irregular *firqat*, composed of defectors from the insurgency.[37]

Yet the example of Sultan Qaboos is as dramatically positive as it is rare. More typical is Iraq, where partner units for US SOF were often subject to a variety of political limitations. General Nomon Dakhil, commander of the Iraqi Ministry of Interior's elite Emergency Response Brigade, was widely viewed by US SOF as an outstanding partner. Yet when Dakhil became too aggressive in targeting Shia militia elements, he was arrested on corruption charges and his unit became substantially less effective.[38]

In addition to the inherent limitations of control, the other principal (and related) limitation of SOF in the indirect role is the need for patience to achieve results. Whether with proxy or partner forces, the time required to achieve strategic effects is often long. Even in the ideal case of Sultan Qaboos in Oman, success took five years—most efforts take much longer.

In a more typical case, US and allied SOF began partnering with Colombian SOF in the 1990s. It took more than a decade for this indirect approach to achieve strategic effects, ultimately helping bring the Fuerzas Armadas Revolucionarias de Colombia (FARC) insurgency to the edge of defeat and subsequent peace negotiations.[39] The SOF mission to the Philippines required 13 years to achieve significant strategic success.[40]

Conclusions

Patience and a willingness to tolerate a lack of control are not characteristics common to US policy-makers—unless they have no other choice. It is thus unsurprising that policy-makers have preferred the direct approach in many instances since 2001. Yet the limitations of the direct approach, principally its requirement for a significant commitment in terms of both political and physical capital, have often required policy-makers to accept the exigencies of the indirect approach.

As a result, policy-makers have simultaneously embraced SOF and become frustrated by their limitations.

As with covert action conducted by the CIA, presidents often become enamored and then disenchanted with SOF. The ability to create tactical and operational effects with limited commitment and liability often fails to yield sufficient strategic results.

The central insights for policy-makers regarding SOF were well captured by Colin Gray just before the post–September 11 resurgence in SOF. He noted, "SOF need an educated consumer, political and military patrons who appreciate what SOF should, and should not, be asked to do. . . . SOF need protection from the fantasies of political sponsors."[41] Without sufficiently educated policy-makers, SOF, regardless of approach, will not be able to realistically achieve policy-makers' goals.

Future policy-makers should be cognizant of the limitations of both SOF approaches. For the direct approach, the strategic effects are likely to be limited without additional supporting efforts. Direct action against terrorist and insurgent leadership can achieve tactical and operational effects, buying space and time for other efforts. But absent additional effort, direct action can only manage and limit strategic challenges, disrupting plots and degrading capabilities, not fully defeat them.

For the indirect approach, policy-makers must cultivate the rare virtue of patience. This will often require trying to get problems off the front pages of the newspaper (or digital equivalent). SOF support in Oman, the Philippines, and Colombia benefited from the fact that there was little attention paid to those operations. In contrast, the high visibility of the war in Syria and the political limitations on support to Syrian rebels ensured that patience—and success—were both unlikely.

NOTES

1. Colin Jackson and Austin Long, "The Fifth Service: The Rise of Special Operations Command" in Harvey Sapolsky, Benjamin Friedman, and Brendan Green, eds., *U.S. Military Innovation Since the Cold War: Creation Without Destruction* (New York: Routledge, 2009).

2. See Austin Long, "A New Wary Titan: US Defence Policy in an Era of Military Change, Asian Growth and European Austerity," in Jo Inge Bekkevold, Ian Bowers, and Michael Raska, eds., *Security, Strategy and Military Change in the 21st Century: Cross-Regional Perspectives* (New York: Routledge, 2015).

3. William McRaven, *Spec Ops: Case Studies in Operational Warfare: Theory and Practice* (New York: Presidio Press, 1996), chapter 2.

4. Cornelius Ryan, *A Bridge Too Far* (New York: Simon and Schuster, 1974).

5. Ze'ev Almog, *Flotilla 13: Israeli Naval Commandos in the Red Sea, 1976* (Annapolis, MD: Naval Institute Press, 2010).

6. Nick Rasmussen, "The Weight of One Mission: Recounting the Death of Usama bin Laden," May 2, 2016, available at <https://www.whitehouse.gov/blog/2016/05/02/weight-one-mission-recounting-death-usama-bin-laden-five-years-later>.

7. McRaven, *Spec Ops*, chapter 9.

8. James Worrall, *State Building and Counter Insurgency in Oman: Political Military and Diplomatic Relations at the End of Empire* (New York: I. B. Tauris & Co. Ltd., 2013).

9. BDM International, *Oral History of the Conflict in El Salvador, 1979–Present*, 6 vols., 1988. Available at the U.S. Army Military History Institute.

10. Dion Nissenbaum, "U.S. Confirms Military Withdrawal From Yemen," *Wall Street Journal*, March 22, 2015.

11. W. J. Hennigan and Brian Bennett, "Pentagon Sends Special Operations Team to Fight Al Qaeda in Yemen," *Los Angeles Times*, May 6, 2016.

12. Richard W. Stewart, "The United States Army in Somalia, 1992–1994" (Washington, DC: Center of Military History, 2002).

13. Thomas L. Ahern Jr., *CIA and Rural Pacification in South Vietnam* (Washington, DC: Center for the Study of Intelligence, 2001); and Andrew Finlayson, "A Retrospective on Counterinsurgency Operations: The Tay Ninh Provincial Reconnaissance Unit and Its Role in the Phoenix Program, 1969–70," *Studies in Intelligence* 51, no. 2 (2007).

14. BDM International, *Oral History of the Conflict in El Salvador*.

15. Michael L. Burgoyne, "Lessons from Peru's Fight Against Sendero Luminoso," *Military Review* (September–October 2010).

16. Miron Varouhakis, "Fiasco in Nairobi: Greek Intelligence and the Capture of PKK Leader Abdullah Ocalan in 1999," *Studies in Intelligence* 53, no. 1, (March 2009).

17. Tim Arango, "Top Qaeda Leaders in Iraq Reported Killed in Raid," *New York Times*, April 19, 2010.

18. Graeme Smith, "What Kandahar's Taliban Say," in *Decoding the New Taliban: Insights from the Afghan Field*, ed. Antonio Giustozzi (New York: Columbia University Press, 2009), pp. 193–194.

19. Michael T. Flynn et al., "Employing ISR: SOF Best Practices," *Joint Forces Quarterly* 50 (3rd Quarter, 2008).

20. Richard Shultz, *Military Innovation in War: It Takes a Learning Organization—A Case Study of Task Force 714 in Iraq* (Tampa, FL: Joint Special Operations University, 2016), p. 67.

21. Austin Long, "Whack-a-Mole or Coup de Grace? Institutionalization and Leadership Targeting in Iraq and Afghanistan," *Security Studies* 23, no. 3 (August 2014).

22. Smith, "What Kandahar's Taliban Say," p. 194.

23. John Leland, "Car Bombings Kill Dozens on Pilgrims' Route in Iraq," *New York Times*, January 20, 2011.

24. Tim Arango, "Iraqi Hostages Die in Attack on Leadership of Province," *New York Times*, March 29, 2011.

25. Hassan Hassan, "Washington's War on the Islamic State Is Only Making It Stronger," *Foreign Policy*, June 16, 2016, available at <http://foreignpolicy.com/2016/06/16/washingtons-war-on-the-islamic-state-is-only-making-it-stronger-syria-iraq-libya/>.

26. Charles Briscoe et al., *Weapon of Choice: U.S. Army Special Operations Forces in Afghanistan* (Fort Leavenworth, KS: Combat Studies Institute Press, 2003).

27. William Rosenau, *Special Operations Forces and Elusive Enemy Ground Targets: Lessons from Vietnam and the Persian Gulf War* (Santa Monica, CA: RAND, 2001).

28. Stephen Biddle, "Allies, Airpower, and Modern Warfare: The Afghan Model in Afghanistan and Iraq," *International Security* 30, no. 3 (Winter 2005/06).

29. Anderson et al., *Insurgent Organization and Operations: A Case Study of the Viet Cong in the Delta, 1964–1966* (Santa Monica, CA: RAND, 1967); and Rosenau, *Special Operations Forces.*

30. Jasen J. Castillo, *Endurance and War: The National Sources of Military Cohesion* (Stanford, CA: Stanford University Press, 2014).

31. Daniel Byman, "Friends Like These: Counterinsurgency and the War on Terrorism," *International Security* (Fall 2006).

32. Thomas Ahern, *Undercover Armies: CIA and Surrogate Warfare in Laos, 1961–1973* (Washington, DC: Center for the Study of Intelligence, 2006) p. 44.

33. Ahern, *Undercover Armies*, p. 51.

34. Zack Beauchamp, "America's Kurdish Problem: Today's Allies against ISIS Are Tomorrow's Headache," Vox.com, April 8, 2016, available at <http://www.vox.com/2016/4/8/11377314/america-kurds-problem>.

35. Dexter Filkins, Mark Mazzetti, and James Risen, "Brother of Afghan Leader Said to Be Paid by C.I.A.," *New York Times*, October 27, 2009.

36. 5th Special Forces Group Headquarters, *U.S. Army Special Forces Participation in the CIDG Program Vietnam, 1957–1970* (1970; reprinted by Radix Press, 1996).

37. See Austin Long et al., *Locals Rule: Historical Lessons for Creating Local Defense Forces for Afghanistan and Beyond* (Santa Monica, CA: RAND, 2012).

38. Tim Durango, Duraid Adnan, and Yasir Ghazi, "U.S. Loses Ally as Iraqi General Waits for Trial," *New York Times*, July 27, 2011.

39. Austin Long et al., "Building Special Operations Partnerships in Afghanistan and Beyond: Challenges and Best Practices from Afghanistan, Iraq, and Colombia" (Santa Monica, CA: RAND, 2015).

40. Sam LaGrone, "U.S. Officially Ends Special Operations Task Force in the Philippines, Some Advisors May Remain," *USNI News*, February 27, 2015, available at <https://news.usni.org/2015/02/27/u-s-officially-ends-special-operations-task-force-in-the-philippines-some-advisors-may-remain>.

41. Colin Gray, "Handfuls of Heroes on Desperate Ventures: When Do Special Operations Succeed?" *Parameters* (Spring 1999).

Unmanned Aircraft in Modern Conflicts

Diverging Paths and Key Lessons

MICHAEL P. KREUZER

The story of Western military operations from the end of the Cold War to date has been largely dominated by a debate over the nature of warfare and what future conflicts will look like. As the explosion of the information age has led to precision weapons, global communications and navigation, stealth technology, robotics, and the prospect of radically improved artificial intelligence systems, a debate rages between camps that proclaim a technology-driven revolution in military affairs has fundamentally changed the character of war, while a legacy of stalemate in "gray zone" conflicts has led many others to focus on the enduring political underpinnings of conflict and the vital importance of tactical maneuver to secure military victory in the context of a political struggle. In air warfare, no issue encapsulates this debate better, and likely no debate offers more passion, than the growing role and proliferation of unmanned aerial systems (UAS), or "drones."

The proliferation of unmanned aircraft technology and parallel innovations in the information and weapon systems environments has led to an increase in their use in unconventional military conflicts, in which they serve a number of air domain functions for major powers and non-state actors alike. Nation-states at the forefront of military technology, notably the United States and Israel among others, made significant strides through the late Cold War period and into the post–Cold War era developing medium- and high-altitude aircraft primarily for long-dwell surveillance missions, or smaller aircraft deployable with ground units for near-real-time battlefield surveillance in a rapidly shifting operating environment. The addition of precision munitions to these aircraft in the early 2000s made the UAS almost the ideal weapon for a counterterrorism conflict. One possible complication to this, however, is the ability to strike from a distance, with a minimal ground footprint, reliant on a silent and almost invisible (albeit large, complex, and time-consuming) human component might make overreliance on the tool too alluring.

As US counterterrorism operations continue, technology is advancing. At the high end, states with advanced air forces and technology stare down the potential for armed unmanned combat air vehicles (UCAVs) to supplement or some in cases supplant manned fighters. These advanced UASs will likely combine many of the innovations of the information age—stealth technology, encrypted data links, and algorithms—to enable a single aircraft to control a small swarm of UASs, which, in turn, will provide established powers advanced capabilities for air-to-air combat, electronic warfare, and other missions in a contested near-peer conflict. At the low end, commercial off-the-shelf technology combined with the ingenuity of insurgent combatants who drove the improvised explosive device (IED) campaign of Operation IRAQI FREEDOM stand poised to make quadcopters and homemade medium-range UASs the IEDs of the sky or the insurgent's cruise missile.

In between those extremes, the proliferation of advanced technology, the drive to keep up, and the challenges of organizational capacity pose a significant dilemma for states with limited air capabilities, and with it the prospect of falling farther behind in addressing the challenges of the twenty-first century. The United States and coalition forces have sought to develop partner forces in a "by, with, and through" partnership model to transfer military capabilities, but a failure of strategists to recognize the organizational challenges associated with advanced technology adoption has at times undercut the strategic objectives, leading to waste of money and time. The evolution of coalition UAS operations in Iraq, the adoption of UASs by the Islamic State of Iraq and Syria (ISIS) and other insurgent groups, and attempts to develop a modern Iraqi Air Force based on the US model combine to illustrate the potential, the perils, and the challenges of UAS proliferation in modern conflicts.

Terminology and Classifications

Beginning in about 2008, when public awareness of unmanned aircraft systems in modern conflicts first gained widespread notoriety, many commentators began speaking of drones as a singular innovation. Early discussion of UASs focused on the "three D's of drones"—dull, dirty, and dangerous mission sets—but by 2010 the drone was considered a silver bullet for airpower and a terror of the sky: an almost ubiquitous eye in the sky capable of readily identifying and targeting individual humans at will. In practice, the evolution of the most visible US drones, the MQ-1 Predator and MQ-9 Reaper, was deliberate but much more limited in scope than the public largely saw, and predominantly fell into the category of "dull" missions owing to their long mission times and the volume and variety of intelligence required to execute a precision strike. The significant growth of human capital in the intelligence and operations communities behind those aircraft represented as significant a shift in military posture as did the technology at the tip of the spear.[1]

Continuing innovation associated with the information revolution has enabled the development of significantly smaller unmanned aircraft than initially envisioned by conventional military forces in the 1980s and into the 1990s. This has led to the growth of un-

manned systems in a fourth role for drones beyond the "three D's," the "low detection" range of operations. This low detection range is found on the seam between operational and tactical airpower where smaller short-range systems can evade traditional detection and air defense systems, enabling non-state actors to surveil and engage in harassing attacks against conventional forces.

As with manned aircraft, unmanned aerial systems are not limited to a single class of "aircraft"; rather, they vary greatly in size, payload, flight profiles, cost, and characteristics. First, a distinction must be made between the aircraft itself, the unmanned aerial *vehicle* (UAV) or "drone," and the unmanned aerial *system*. The former gets the most attention as it represents the tip of the spear that is visible to combatants, while the latter includes the support infrastructure necessary to sustain the aircraft in flight. This includes launch and recovery systems, control network infrastructure, and support personnel (among other elements). Depending on the size and function of the aircraft in question, the system could simply include a pilot and a line-of-sight controller, as is the case with a basic commercial quadcopter, or it could include a global system of hundreds of personnel as pilots, analysts, and maintainers, linked by a global command-and-control system, as is the case with advanced US systems such as the MQ-9 Reaper.

A framework for categories of unmanned systems is required in order to understand both their use and proliferation in the modern operating environment, both for nation-states and non-state actors. One of the more recognized frameworks for UAV classifications is the US Department of Defense's categorization chart, defined in *Joint Publication 3-30*. Accordingly, unmanned aircraft are characterized and differentiated according to their weight, operating altitude, and airspeed, with Group 1 consisting of under twenty-pound aircraft, Group 2 being between twenty-one and fifty pounds and flying under 3,500 feet, Group 3 being aircraft that can fly up to 18,000 feet and having a gross weight under 1,320 pounds, and Groups 4 and 5 being larger aircraft distinguished by altitude (above or below 18,000 feet).[2] This scheme provides a useful means of evaluating the aircraft itself (the UAV) through its capabilities and payloads and, as such, is a solid starting point for evaluating the potential mission sets and threats posed by UAVs as their use expands more broadly.

This typology is problematic, however, as it focuses heavily on the vehicle itself, and not on the system or missions of the aircraft. The proliferation of UAVs cannot be decoupled from the deeper operating construct of the system behind them, the full UAS. The principle advantage to the UAV is that by removing the person from the cockpit, the aerial vehicle can be made smaller and less susceptible to the vulnerabilities associated with maneuverability or exposure to elements (bioweapons, radiological weapons, and so on), thereby making it ideal for the four key roles of modern drone operations: dull, dirty, dangerous, and minimal detection. As with all innovations, though, the unmanned aircraft comes with a number of trade-offs and new risk exposures, most prominently in the networks for control, the electronic systems onboard the aircraft, and the organizations and training required to execute operations from a distance.

For UAS operations, I add the qualifications "tactical," "advanced," or "strategic" to emphasize both the battlefield applications of the aircraft and the scope/scale of the people and equipment behind the UAV to better define the threat and vulnerabilities of the system. There is a long-standing debate within the US military community on what constitutes "strategic" versus "operational" versus "tactical" in defining weapon systems, with the Air Force emphasizing that the effects drive that definition, rather than the platform. Although that discussion is important in a number of circumstances, in the context of UAS operations it is vital to focus on the system as much if not more than on the aircraft itself, and I find these terms to be the best descriptors for the standard groups of UAVs identified in joint doctrine. A tactical UAS is what I am most comfortable describing as a "drone": it is either wholly purchased or purpose built through commercially available products and can be operated by a single controller. These drones range from basic quadcopters used by hobbyists to medium-range fixed-wing aircraft capable of delivering global positioning system (GPS)–guided bombs. Regardless of how threatening the aircraft and range may seem, these systems are vulnerable when their opponent is aware of the threat and possesses basic jamming capabilities, effectively neutralizing the threat either through active defense or deterrence and pushing the threat away to softer targets.

As the technology to make commercial-off-the-shelf drones remains cheap and proliferates globally, so too can the potential counters to unencrypted communication, the weak link of tactical UASs. As threat awareness of tactical UASs has risen, counter-UAS technology also has spread, decreasing their effectiveness against military targets. In response, the next evolution of adversary UASs will be toward what I refer to as "advanced" UASs, which are systems that have many of the same characteristics as tactical UASs but with additional military-grade features to harden them against counters and enable effective attack operations. These may include inertial navigation systems, optical navigation, or light detection and ranging that enable advanced UASs to overcome GPS-jamming for terminal control and potentially for weapons guidance.[3]

Add to that the global satellite infrastructure and precision munitions necessary for global near-real-time intelligence, surveillance, reconnaissance, and targeting, and an "advanced" UAS can be classified as a "strategic" UAS—the principle distinction being the nature of the targeting decision and the echelon of control of the UAS.

At the same time, these additional features come with a number of trade-offs in cost for equipment and operational security that will likely limit their battlefield proliferation. Actors still at the early stages of UAS development will need to make greater investments in supply chains to build UASs, and the loss of even a single UAS to an advanced adversary, such as the United States, may jeopardize the future of any program by exposing vulnerabilities to be exploited. This will likely drive these UASs to be larger and have higher payoff in terms of strategic impact, and also require launch and recovery space as well as training grounds. In this regard, the "poor man's air force" begins to look more like a developing nation's air force, with all the strengths and vulnerabilities that come with it.

UAS Mission Sets

From the early twenty-first century the US and allied air forces have in general stood at the forefront of airpower doctrine, including in their role as early adopters of the UAS mission set. The US Air Force defines five core missions of air power, and while these historically have applied to manned aircraft, each has seen increased potential and even expanded roles for unmanned aircraft. These five core missions are air and space superiority; intelligence, surveillance, and reconnaissance (ISR); rapid global mobility; global strike; and command and control.[4] At the high end of conflict and with technologically advanced states, air superiority and mobility are emerging mission sets for UASs, with advanced unmanned combat aerial vehicles and aerial refuelers, as well as resupply and search and rescue UASs being developed for both military and civilian purposes. For non-state actors and fledgling UAS forces, intelligence, aerial bombardment, and propaganda represent the main mission sets, similar to the early days of manned flight.

ISR

ISR is the oldest mission set of airpower, with observation balloons and kites predating the invention of the aircraft by centuries. Aviation in World War I began with aerial observation alongside rudimentary aerial bombardment of fielded forces. The US Department of Defense defines ISR as "an integrated operations and intelligence activity that synchronizes and integrates the planning and operation of sensors, assets, and processing, exploitation, and dissemination systems in direct support of current and future operations."[5] This definition applies most specifically to the integrated ISR model applied by US forces and their allies and to their common doctrine, which focuses on the process of collecting and integrating information from all sources to generate rapidly actionable intelligence for forces without specific emphasis on the platforms of collection. In contrast, insofar as this essay looks specifically to the acquisition and use of platforms by nations and non-state actors often with nascent intelligence collection capabilities, it is important to break the ISR construct down into its components and consider how each could apply to UASs largely in isolation.

In terms of ISR, "intelligence" is somewhat ambiguous. The US Department of Defense defines it as "1. The product resulting from the collection, processing, integration, evaluation, analysis, and interpretation of available information concerning foreign nations, hostile or potentially hostile forces or elements, or areas of actual or potential operations, [or] 2. The activities that result in the product."[6] *Intelligence* is thus both a product of ISR and a part of ISR. The best way to understand it is to think of the intelligence in ISR as intelligence amassed with traditional products and new collection from intelligence disciplines that does not neatly fit into the definitions of "surveillance" or "reconnaissance," such as human intelligence. Surveillance is the systematic observation of areas, places, or persons by any means available. This includes, but is not limited to, visual, signals, photographic, or other means. Reconnaissance, in contrast, is a single specific mission undertaken to obtain information about activities or resources or to secure data.

At the tactical level of ground operations, UASs can support military operations and militia movements by reconnaissance and surveillance. According to US Army *Doctrine Publication 2-0* intelligence supports critical offensive and defensive operations including movement to contact, attack, exploitation, pursuit, mobile defense, area defense, and retrograde.[7] All require regular updates to commanders to visualize terrain, determine threat strengths and disposition, and confirm or deny adversary courses of action. Specific intelligence tasks in this process include understanding terrain and how the enemy may apply it; developing situation templates; identifying obstacles, conditions, lanes, and bypass locations; identifying threats such as IEDs or mines and their potential locations; identifying potential enemy fields of fire; and generating awareness for the commander of how to conceal friendly courses of action and the composition and location of friendly forces.

Given an environment sufficiently permissive to operate Group 1 through 3 UASs, these systems can be ideally suited to provide significant tactical advantages to employing forces, particularly for regular surveillance of adversary locations and battlefield reconnaissance in depth. UAS operators, embedded with forward units facing a hostile adversary, can provide valuable insights for breaching operations, route clearance, and movement to contact, and they can point defense to secure a forward location from indirect fire or counterattack upon completion of an engagement operation. These operations can be skillfully undertaken through an integrated operations plan connected to a larger operational-level intelligence network or by a single operator and commander with basic knowledge of the battlefield. In the latter case, this might involve accessing a discrete tactical overwatch position—and using little more than the skills used by a hobbyist with a drone—to view activity over the next hill or fly full-motion video (FMV) missions ahead of an advancing column to scout for an awaiting ambush. With additional training and practice, a small team of operators and analysts can rapidly gain skills to routinely survey a wider area of the battlespace, noting changes over time and patterns of movement to increase the commander's situational awareness and plan operations.

At the far extreme of this tactical UAS is the integration of platforms in a larger system of intelligence collection and production through globally integrated ISR. The US Air Force defines globally integrated ISR as "cross-domain synchronization and integration of the planning and operation of ISR assets; sensors; processing, exploitation and dissemination systems; and, analysis and production capabilities across the globe to enable current and future operations."[8] This means using multiple sensors and platforms from multiple geographic commands at all levels of war and across all domains of war to gather intelligence and create products for customers at all levels. For UASs, this means the system includes pilots, sensor operators, and analysts both at forward operating locations and in "reachback" locations in the continental United States, collecting against requirements submitted by commanders at all levels and facilitating products ranging from near-real time video feed accessible in operations centers to detailed analysis of multiple products elapsed over time for planning and strike operations.[9]

While basic UAS operations can be conducted with a single operator or a small team providing battlefield intelligence to a tactical commander, globally integrated ISR requires the successful integration of two advanced military constructs. The first requirement is a professional military, led by a professionalized officer corps and a strong noncommissioned officer corps who embody the qualities of military expertise, corporateness, and the responsibility of service to the state.[10] This professional ethos is vital to integrating the second requirement, a culture of what the US Army refers to as "mission command," or what the Air Force refers to as "centralized control and decentralized execution." Both services exercise central authority to keep the focus on strategic objectives, while allowing lower-echelon personnel to gain tactical advantages through unilateral action under the higher echelon's intent. This tenet is central to the adoption in land operations of what Stephen Biddle referred to as the "modern system,"[11] and when applied to globally integrated ISR, it represents the fusion of the revolution in military affairs literature with the maneuverist literature to show how technological advancement and organizational capital must intersect to execute complex operations. To produce timely and accurate intelligence for multiple customers simultaneously requires delegation of significant power and control of ISR operations to junior operators—a process that can exist only in a highly professionalized, highly skilled, mission-oriented team, not in a rigid hierarchic organization.

Attack

Though the UAS had existed in the US inventory in ISR roles in various forms since the 1960s and prominently with the first unarmed Predator variant in the 1990s, UASs gained significant public attention beginning in the late 2000s when the armed Predator and Reaper increasingly became the weapons of choice in the US war on terrorism as the United States sought to dramatically scale back its ground footprint in Iraq and Afghanistan. "Surgical strikes" became a catch-phrase of the Barack Obama administration, defining his approach to counterterrorism in the public eye.[12] As small UASs proliferate, a common concern is the risk in democratization of aerial violence through armed UAVs, and likely without the surgical precision or professional restraint emphasized by the United States. To date, modern war zones that include civilian populated areas have seen booby-trapped crashed UASs, crude aerial bombardment from improvised grenade-laden aircraft, and UASs modified into flying bombs—in essence making them basic cruise missiles or as others have called them "kamikaze drones."

The most basic attack using commercial off-the-shelf drones is as old as insurgent warfare itself—reliance on explosive booby traps. With basic drones, the prospect of losing a UAS to a lost communication link, jamming, enemy fire, or other issues with malfunction heightens the chance that the aircraft wreckage will be captured and thus vulnerable to exploitation. The old rule for these circumstances holds true for UAVs as it did for US soldiers looking at capturing intelligence or souvenir hunting in previous conflicts: if you didn't place it in the battlefield, you don't pick it up. Downed UAVs have been found in multiple theaters over the past decade lined with TNT and other explosives, ready to detonate when tampered with. ISIS has exploited this tactic on multiple occasions as I shall discuss in greater detail later, but Houthi militias in Yemen, insurgents in Burma, and numerous other groups around the world have used similar tactics both to take advantage of the potential for a battlefield loss and likely in planned attacks.

A similar but potentially more devastating tactic against soft targets is to use explosive-laden UAVs in direct attacks, effectively as low-budget cruise missiles. Even before the prospect of low-cost UASs became a reality of modern warfare, observers of the technology anticipated the prospect that the information revolution would lead to an explosion in the proliferation of cruise missiles.[13] Though multiple international regimes served to limit mass proliferation of the most advanced cruise missile technologies by limiting the proliferation of key technologies, the armed UAS is today poised to serve as an alternative for many groups seeking a very basic missile capability that often has a low operational impact, but potentially large strategic impact through the use of information operations. This technology can work both ways, however, as Israeli UASs have also been used as defensive missiles to target air incendiary kites and balloons launched by Palestinian insurgent groups.[14]

The most fearsome advance from the perspective of those who see UAS proliferation as enabling a poor man's air force is the prospect of larger systems capable of aerial bombardment. This tactic also has been observed in recent battles, with the most notable being an attack on Russian facilities in January 2018. Pro-Syrian-regime forces captured one of these systems as part of a mini "swarm" attack on the Russian facility,[15] when ten similar drones targeted Hmeimim Air Base in Syria and three more targeted a Russian naval base in Tartus.[16] Russians reported no damage or casualties from the incident, but similar aircraft and munitions have been discovered on multiple occasions throughout Syria. Such aircraft use grenades or mortars as improvised bomblets, outfitted with tailfins that can be hand-manufactured using balsa wood or 3D-printed if the capability is available.

Less of an apparent threat, but potentially more costly to civil society, are attacks not of a kinetic and explosive nature, but through disruption of nonmilitary targets. The most famous case to date has been the Gatwick Airport incident, when a series of drone sightings caused the airport to be intermittently shut down between December 19 and 21, 2018. The incident affected over 110,000 passengers and 760 flights and resulted in several million dollars in lost revenue for airlines.[17] Absent protective measures, nuisance UAS incidents like these could threaten infrastructure and transit in the future and potentially become a military challenge should drone swarms impede airways and landing zones required for military operations.

Information Operations

Though ISIS and other insurgent groups throughout the world have had relatively low direct impact on the battlespace through UAS-directed attacks, the information power of their adoption of these weapons has yielded some dividends in terms of raising the cost of counterinsurgency through additional protective measures, recruitment support, and propaganda in multiple forms. As insurgency and counterinsurgency are ultimately a political struggle for control of territory and populations through sustaining insurgent capacity versus expanding the legitimacy of the government, information warfare can be a decisive phase of modern conflict, and the value and roles of UASs in this aspect of war must be a serious consideration for military planners.

Through their cyber caliphate and via other online channels hosting video footage of insurgent attacks, ISIS has released videos showing possible attacks from the perspective of unmanned bombers and has exploited much of the hype surrounding UASs to drive reactions through media reporting. In January 2017, ISIS released a video demonstrating a new, armed UAS launching bombing raids against Iraqi military positions during the initial phases of the recapture of Mosul.[18] In 2017, as ISIS was collapsing in the midst of assaults from both Syrian forces in the west and coalition and Iraqi forces in the east, ISIS released a video showing bombs being dropped on Syrian military positions likely in hopes of projecting strength in the midst of the onslaught.[19] Though it is unclear if the videos are authentic or carefully edited to make more traditional bombing attacks appear to have been launched from UASs, the reporting they produced and the exploitation by ISIS for numerous propaganda videos over the following months speak to the perception on their side of the success in demonstrating even a nascent capability.

UAS Diffusion

Although UAS technology has existed for decades, and although concerns surrounding the dangers of UAS proliferation have existed for nearly twenty years, UAS proliferation remains in a nascent state with few definitive conclusions to be drawn based on evidence to date. Despite that, the anecdotal evidence available combined with existing academic work on weapons proliferation allows us to look at some early projections for UAS diffusion, and some general trends can be observed that point to the likely trajectory of near-term UAS utilization. The low cost and ease of use associated with tactical UAS systems (Groups 1–3), combined with the nature of insurgent and terrorist tactics throughout the world, suggest that these aircraft, both armed and unarmed, will continue to proliferate widely and remain a valuable tool of insurgency for intelligence, attacks, and propaganda purposes. World powers with advanced aircraft technology and a strategic need to compete with other great powers will also see significant growth in advanced UASs, particularly UCAVs needed to fight for air supremacy in contested environments and long-loiter ISR/strike aircraft for stability and counterterrorism/counterinsurgency operations. Between these extremes, most countries will likely face significant challenges incorporating UASs into their military inventory and will be faced with a difficult dilemma: modernize their forces to enable them to take advantage of advanced UASs or compete with basic tactical UASs as their air forces fall farther behind.

To analyze UAS diffusion, I rely heavily on an adoption-capacity model, first proposed by Michael Horowitz.[20] This model examines the ability of a state or international organization to incorporate a major military innovation by looking at its financial intensity on one hand and its organizational capital on the other. Given that UASs run the gamut of innovation based on their size and mission, the diffusion of UASs will vary across this spectrum much as manned aircraft have.

Figure 1 estimates the relative cost and organizational capacity required for different subsets of UASs and implied rates of diffusion. The closer to the lower left of the graphic, the faster and more broadly the system will spread. The closer to the top right, the slower and more limited the spread of the system. In general, ISR requires a higher organizational capital requirement than basic strike, as the human capital and supporting intelligence infrastructure to yield information of interest from imagery, signals intelligence, and other airborne assets rise along with the technological capability of the asset. Tactical imagery, such as video derived from a Group-2 drone flying just beyond the horizon, is relatively simple for most ground commanders to understand and incorporate into planning without a long intelligence chain to make sense of what is being shown. As the distance from fielded forces grows, and as intelligence collection technology becomes more abstract to the average intelligence customer, the intelligence tail grows in complexity, and with it so does the level of trust put into intelligence networks to decipher the meaning of what is being observed. Adding a strike capacity to an aircraft can dramatically raise its cost, owing to the additional weight to be carried (and thus size and propulsion of the aircraft) and complexity of remote release systems, but the level of complexity backing a strike decision is ultimately at the discretion of the operator.

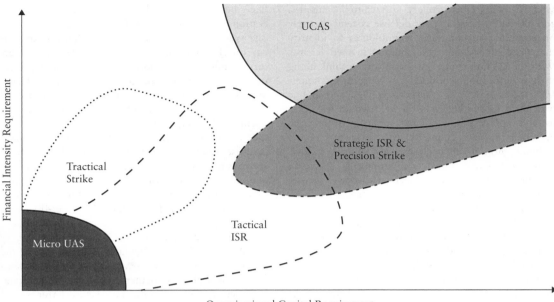

Figure 1. Notional Adoption-Capacity Model for UAS Diffusion

The most costly and expensive weapon systems will require the same advanced aviation technology as current fifth-generation fighters, supplemented by stealth and encrypted data links to support either swarming operations or control from a "mother ship." Further, these systems will likely require significant augmentation from either advanced air-to-air combat algorithms and/or artificial intelligence in order to react and fight in future air battles.[21] Nearly as costly, but more intense from an organizational side, advancements in ISR and precision-strike UASs will require continued investments to improve the intelligence capability and command-and-control of strike decisions to ensure the accuracy and value of those strikes, to maximize the second- and third-order effects of strikes, and to minimize the potential for collateral damage, which could result in strategic failure from a poor strike.

Attempts to export more advanced UASs to other states have shown the weak spot that exists at the center of the chart, in that many of those states have been unable to successfully employ them in the manner for which they were designed. This effectively makes these exported UASs large and expensive tactical UASs, if they fly at all. Coalition experiences in Iraq highlight the possibilities and perils of UAS proliferation to date and provide lessons for the future of gray-zone conflict, partner force development, and advanced UAS development.

Counter-UAS Diffusion

As military UAS technology spreads, so too will counter-UAS technology. In 2012, the US Defense Science Board released a key report titled "The Role of Autonomy in DoD Systems," primarily outlining how unmanned systems will be integrated into US forces but also anticipating the need to develop counter-UAS programs. The report noted that "while all vehicle sizes are possible, the threats from smaller platforms, particularly small UAVs, that can be launched covertly from the ground, may be an especially difficult threat to counter—even in the presence of U.S. air superiority,"[22] and it went on to identify significant harassment on the battlefield, low-intensity surveillance prior to hostile action, and asymmetric attack on the US homeland as the biggest potential threats. At the time, the report found little evidence that domestic governments were working to counter the homeland threat of UASs, but in the eight years since the original report was written, counter-UAS technology has expanded significantly. By 2018, a study published by Bard College's Center for the Study of the Drone outlined over 200 counter-UAS systems on the market or under development, and nearly twenty major events or points of interest where counter-UAS technology was employed to varying degrees of success.[23]

The chief counter to manned aircraft has traditionally been kinetic responses in the form of pursuit aircraft, anti-aircraft artillery, surface-to-air missiles, and ultimately integrated air defense systems that rely on combinations of these technologies to identify threat aircraft and apply the optimum layered defense. With the UAS, the initial response was to think along these lines and thus consider possible kinetic counter-UAS technology; it is intuitive, familiar, and in line with what most soldiers in the field would feel comfortable applying in a combat scenario. Among the most common early counter-UAS weapons was a basic shotgun, and this remains the easiest solution to low-flying quadcopters in austere environments. However, inability to identify/track objects at distances greater than approximately 100 meters and the challenges of accurately guessing the range of an unknown object against the empty sky make this a highly inaccurate choice, with the added hazard of the kinetic threat to people on the ground. Net guns with their ability to catch a drone in mesh mid-flight have also been popular for public discussion, but suffer from many of the same challenges as shotguns. Among the most accurate kinetic counter-quadcopter techniques is also one of the most low-tech: several states have shown that falcons can be trained to grab aircraft in mid-flight, making them effective living drone-hunters.

Recognizing that the control and electronic systems aboard the aircraft are the critical vulnerability of UASs, many nations and their militaries are turning instead to nonkinetic means to deny airspace access to UASs or, when necessary, bring them down. Among the first nonkinetic responses to gain public interest was the "zombie drone," a technique exploiting vulnerabilities in the software of common quadcopters that enables other drones to take control, potentially creating an army of drones.[24] The Israelis, facing significant domestic UAS threats, were among the first movers of UASs for military applications in the 1980s and have been an early adopter in counter-UAS nonkinetic technology. The Israeli company Rafael markets its Drone Dome protection system including 360-degree radar and radio frequency sensor to detect and identify a drone as small as .002 square meters from a range of 3.5 kilometers and neutralize it through reactive jamming.[25] This system played a critical role in ending the Gatwick Airport incident.[26] In 2019, the US Air Force unveiled the Tactical High Power Microwave Operational Responder (THOR), which was designed to protect bases from UAS swarms within four kilometers, and the Counter-Electronic High-Power Microwave Extended-Range Air Base Air Defense (CHIMERA), which is designed to hit targets at medium to long ranges. Both systems identify potential threats and then use short bursts of high-power microwaves to disable the UAV.[27]

As with other military operations, a multilayered, multi-sensor package for counter-UAS systems will likely be necessary for defenses in future military operations. Synergia's dronesafeguard, which represents one example of a layered system available on the private market, includes fixed and mobile radar detectors, acquisition and motion detectors, water projection, radio frequency disruptors, sacrificial collision drones, and zombie drone commandeers.[28] As awareness of the risks of UAS technology grows, integrated counter-UAS programs can continue to spread to both the public and private market, enabling significant dual-use technology advances. Future military vehicle convoys in gray-zone conflicts are likely to see at least one vehicle armed with a counter-UAS suite capable of defending the convoy in much the same way previous generations relied on advanced counter-IED technology.

Counter-UAS technology will likely trail advances in UAS technology, particularly with respect to the hardening of signals and GPS guidance. Further, a number of issues plagues counter-UAS technology, particularly detection effectiveness, interdiction hazards, and interdiction effectiveness in conflict zones. Counter-UAS systems are reliant on multiple sensor types, each with drawbacks depending on the environment and advance knowledge of potential threat aircraft. Electro-optical and radar sensors are commonly used for conventional aircraft detection, but the low altitudes at which many aircraft fly and the fact that many attacks come during nighttime hours can limit the effectiveness of both sensors. Acoustic sensors are also employed by a number of counter-UAS systems, but these rely largely on matching detected sounds to an internal database of known UAS sounds and thus might lag a dynamic UAS environment. A successful system will likely require a combination of multiple sensors to identify and verify potential threats, as well as advanced algorithms or artificial intelligence mechanisms to reduce the likelihood of false-positive and false-negative reporting necessary for a viable defense system.

Even if a system is able to identify and track an enemy UAS sufficiently, engagement itself can be hazardous. Kinetic engagement poses the challenge of downed UASs falling from the sky along with potentially spent munitions being used to bring down the aircraft and whatever explosive or otherwise hazardous material may be on the craft. In a military engagement away from civilian populations, this will likely be a secondary concern that can be mitigated through training, but populated areas represent a significant physical and information operations risk. Electronic warfare interdiction may be of limited utility against more advanced weapons system and may in many cases result in collateral electromagnetic spectral damage by jamming communications or flight equipment of friendly military positions or among the civilian population, again posing an information operations risk to mission success.

Real-World Experiences: Lessons from Iraq

As projections for diffusion of UASs indicate the possibility for rapid expansion of small systems for tactical mission sets is high, current military operations in Iraq and Afghanistan should provide the US military a number of early lessons for the prospects of "drone wars" and the intersection of theory and practice on this subject. The first and most obvious example of the use of UASs in small wars has been their use by the US military and coalition allies for ISR and strategic attack in passive environments, using strategic medium-altitude long endurance aircraft tied via satellite to both command-and-control and processing hubs around the world.

In the first fourteen months of the war against ISIS, the air campaign was a significant factor in destroying their capability to sustain control of their territory and set the conditions for Iraqi forces backed by US and coalition operators to gradually destroy ISIS's territorial control across Iraq and Northern Syria. This complex air-centric operation, costing an estimated $10 million dollars per day, featured aircraft flying coordinated missions out of Kuwait, Qatar, the United Arab Emirates, Jordan, and Turkey, sometimes controlled from the United States. It required days to months to gather sufficient intelligence to launch such strikes.[29] As airstrikes received the most visibility, the process behind the scenes readily evolved to meet the challenges of the new battlespace, often initiated by junior personnel innovating new strategies to rapidly process the sheer volume of data being collected daily from multiple platforms.[30]

As the conflict dragged on and US UAS exploits at the high end of conflict signaled a slow but steady reduction in ISIS's ability to counter, ISIS and other parties to the conflict sought out UAS technology, making this one of the first major drone insurgency conflicts. Meanwhile, as calls increased for "more airstrikes" and the desire to build up Iraqi forces to take on an increasing share of the war burden, the Operation INHERENT RESOLVE (OIR) coalition moved to develop an organic Iraqi ISR and strike capability, sometimes manned and sometimes with UASs.

ISIS and Non-State UAS Adoption

At the insurgent end of the spectrum, the proliferation of commercial off-the-shelf drone technology has provided adversaries a potential new weapon, both for kinetic operations and in the information realm. Beginning in 2016, Western media became aware of the emerging threat from small commercial off-the-shelf drones to US forces and allies. In early October 2016, a group of Kurdish forces in Northern Iraq shot down what appeared to be a small UAV like many others that had been spotted in recent months surveying their positions. When they went to investigate the UAS and exploit the aircraft, however, the plane blew up and killed two Kurdish forces.[31] In the battle for Mosul, over 300 drone missions were flown in the span of one month, with as many as 100 of them being armed strike operations.[32] In early 2018, the US Air Force noted that it had not been since the Korean War sixty-five years earlier that US forces had faced threats from enemy aircraft, but that today the proliferation of commercial quadcopters rendered forces vulnerable to munitions such as grenades dropped from $650 drones.[33]

ISIS and other non-state actors throughout Iraq and Syria have been at the forefront of exploiting small drones in the disorganized battlespace that has followed the collapse of their territorial holdings. Initially, they were used as surveillance platforms to collect intelligence on new Iraqi military posts in Northern Iraq as Iraqi forces slowly moved toward Mosul. One surveillance video, placed online through the "cyber Caliphate," was then followed by Katyusha rocket attacks on the outpost resulting in one US marine being killed—one of only seventeen US military members killed due to an adversary attack through mid-February 2020.[34] At the time, the precision accuracy of this missile was speculated to be attributable to the use of UAS for targeting purposes, a claim emphatically rejected by then-OIR commander Lieutenant General McFarland.[35]

Though the fear remains that UAS proliferation could result in an emerging capability for insurgents to build their own air force complete with a full ISR and attack capability, in practice the threat has been more limited than initially advertised. Even as American forces have regularly reported seeing UASs in the vicinity of American bases, no similar precision attacks aided by UASs have been noted to date. The Islamic State regularly posts propaganda videos showing the capability to employ armed drones in mock attacks on vehicle convoys and other scenarios, but outside of engagements against other non-state forces, propaganda appears to be the extent of this capability for the immediate future. In part this may be due to US forces expanding the use of anti-drone technology and investing more heavily in anti-drone technology, and in part this may be a function of the nature of the conflict. When the United States employed a heavy ground force and relied on regular ground movements to attack the Islamic State, they were vulnerable to small UASs; today, while operating from fixed locations in a supporting role, the Katyusha rocket remains the weapon of choice.

In this sense, the tactical UAS is more akin to an IED operating in the vertical dimension of war. It is a clear threat at the tactical level with the ability to cause strategic damage to advancing forces, but it is largely reliant on those forces advancing and in situations where they might lose visibility of the threat. But as with radio-controlled IEDs, investment in high-tech counter-solutions can offset this threat for many state actors willing to invest in the technology, training, and other elements necessary to execute an electronic warfare strategy. When the United States and allies executed a similar strategy to defeat a proliferation of radio-controlled IEDs in Iraq back in 2007, the response by insurgents was to regress to lower-tech command wire and victim-operated IEDs once more. Like rockets and mortars, this was a better investment at least given the strategy and the timing.

The United States and its allies were slow to react to the UAS threat and likely paid a short-term cost in the 2016–2019 timeframe as a result. Despite warnings of the perils of the democratization of drone technology dating to the beginning of the decade, it was not until the threat emerged on the battlefield that the United States invested heavily in counter-UAS technology. Moving forward, both UAS and counter-UAS will need to rapidly evolve as the technologies continue to evolve on both sides. Adversaries may continue to adopt small UASs to improve communication security, which could raise their costs and potentially expose their supply lines in much the way advanced IED networks came to be traceable during the 2007 Iraq War surge, but at the same time, UASs could once more become a more viable threat in the battlespace, evading both detection and visibility by opposing forces. Larger, medium-range UASs have also been observed in the battlefields of Syria, extending the range for operations and the payloads as well.[36] In the future, these aircraft could be used for reconnaissance and propaganda against coalition bases, flying at sufficient altitudes to image fixed targets, while overflying shorter-range counter-UAS systems. But again, with increased size and altitude come trade-offs: reduced target accuracy (think high-altitude unguided bombs), the need for airfields and training grounds for mission rehearsals, and crossing the threshold to where they are vulnerable to conventional radar detection. As with the early days of manned aviation, the future of unmanned aviation is dynamic, and actors must remain vigilant of advancements to stay ahead of the threat and effectively defeat a rapidly changing adversary force in the sky.

Partner-Force UAS

Between the two extremes sits the Iraqi air enterprise, and with it a significant data point on the nature and limits of UAS diffusion. That is, the Iraqi efforts may serve as a warning sign for policy-makers seeking to build basic partner-force UAS capacity, and it may be reassuring to those who fear rapid uncontrolled pro-

liferation of "killer robots" that there are very real organizational obstacles to implementing a complex new system of warfare. In 2005, when addressing soldiers returning to Fort Bragg, North Carolina, from operations in Iraq, President George W. Bush codified the US mission in Iraq in simple terms that have largely been a mantra for coalition forces ever since: "Our strategy can be summed up this way: As the Iraqis stand up, we will stand down."[37] Just over two years later, Iraq would begin procuring its own ISR aircraft, and with it the hopes of many that the Iraqis would be able to shortly begin collecting airborne intelligence to support their own operations and thus enable a gradual decline in US ISR operations in Iraq as demands elsewhere in the world rose.

The first assets acquired by the Iraqis were manned imagery-capable platforms such as the Cessna 208 and the King Air 350. In 2008 the Iraqi Air Force purchased three ISR-only C-208s and three AC-208s, capable of firing Hellfire missiles, in essence making these similar to manned, lower loiter time Predator systems. These aircraft were further supplemented in 2016 by two additional AC-208 aircraft in a purchase deemed by the US State Department as contributing "to the foreign policy and national security of the United States by helping to improve the security of a strategic partner."[38] As the thought process goes, the simplicity and reliability of the aircraft enable both cash-strapped nations to have a cheap air-to-ground alternative to the F-16 and the United States to have a partner capable of its own internal defense from the air.[39] At the higher end of the Iraqi ISR force is the King Air 350, which Iraq also began acquiring in 2007 with its initial order of five ISR variants.[40]

In late 2017, Iraq's ISR program expanded to include its first significant UAS platform, the Insitu Scan Eagle, with an initial purchase of six aircraft for just under $8 million.[41] Though the Scan Eagle is significantly smaller and less capable than the larger systems employed by the coalition, it and other Group-2 UAVs represent the largest growth in UAS proliferation around the world owing to their per-unit reduced cost, lack of need for significant airfield infrastructure to support (requiring instead a catapult launcher and "skyhook" arresting system), and seemingly more intuitive tactical operational perspective given its shorter range and FMV-dominant collection suite.[42] The United States had flown Scan Eagle in Iraq since 2005, and thus on the surface it appeared a logical platform to spearhead the Iraqi ISR force.

Iraq, like many other Gulf states, has also sought to purchase advanced UAS technology from the United States and coalition allies to give it a capability, on paper at least, similar to US attack capability through systems like the armed variant of the US MQ-1 as well as the MQ-9. Strict export controls, such as the Missile Control and Technology Regime, dramatically limited the willingness of the United States to consider transferring armed UAS technology to states that were not already members of such technology control regimes.[43] In May 2019, this policy changed to allow US corporations much greater flexibility to sell UAS technology,[44] but as of 2020 the United States has not sold its most advanced UASs to Iraq. Instead, in 2014 Iraq began investing in the Chinese equivalent of the early MQ-1, the CH-4. To date, the government of Iraq has acquired ten of these systems, but as of August 2019, only one was assessed to be operational and scarcely flew operational missions.[45]

In the case of both the Scan Eagle and CH-4, attempts by coalition forces to integrate these systems into the Iraqi military have been largely unproductive. As of the end of 2019, of the ten CH-4s operated by the Iraqi government, only one was considered to be mission capable. Of the ten Scan Eagles owned by the Iraqis, an inspector general report showed that only two sorties were flown in the spring of 2019 due to a "combination of Iraqi training in the United States, a lapse in maintenance contracts, and problems with signal interference."[46]

Challenges of Adopting Precision-Strike UAS

President Bush's pronouncement that "as the Iraqis stood up, we would stand down" was succinct and seemingly logical in its application, but the reality of this strategy has proved problematic at best and detrimental at worst. The challenge is twofold, stemming on one side from attempting to transfer a system of military operations designed for the strategic needs of expeditionary coalition forces and not the strategic needs of the domestic Iraqi government, and on the other an operating concept reliant on diffused operations between teams with a common sense of purpose in a very hierarchic and bureaucratic military structure. The Iraqi ISR enterprise in this regard represents a strong case study in the challenges of diffusing military tasks and technology to a force without the requisite organizational capacity to adopt such systems.

At the root of the problem is the strategic guidance of standing up Iraqi forces to take on the responsibilities of coalition forces in what naturally appears as a one-for-one tradeoff. The system employed by the United States and its allies for the past two decades of conflict has centered on precision munitions and strategic airpower, combined with a light ground footprint of Special Operations and light infantry units, to defeat adversary forces outside major military operations. These precision strike operations are executed through a complex network spanning the globe, consisting of tens of thousands of operators, analysts, and command-and-control functions operating in a reachback capacity while relying on advanced technology to increase battlespace awareness with a minimal ground footprint. This arrangement serves both to relieve the host nation of the pressures of a significant occupying force undercutting domestic perceptions of government sovereignty and to reduce the threat of coalition casualties, which could undercut support for the intervention by those countries' domestic audiences.

The tradeoff, however, is a large, expensive, complicated, and often time-consuming process of translating volumes of material from information and rumors about ground truth in the operating environment into actionable military targets. Figure 2 illustrates in a very simplified manner how this process works. Precise intelligence is produced to reach down to a near-real-time strike decision in the dynamic targeting cycle through the intelligence cycle of planning; collection; processing, exploitation, and dissemination (PED); analysis; and dissemination, all of which operate at all levels of war. The last step, full motion video watching a target followed by a precision strike, is the only part of the process most people outside of the kill chain see. The prior steps in the intelligence cycle are necessary to enable the high-fidelity intelligence to make the strike a reality, from national agencies building baseline Joint Intelligence Preparation of the Battlespace, through research and national- and/or theater-level assets, to refined collection at the operational and tactical level through organic assets and specialized collection methods. To make this work in practice involves not three distinct processes but an ongoing dialogue of many layers, while analysts from Washington, DC, and across the United States interact with operators in Nevada, the Gulf states, and on the ground in Iraq to ensure unity of effort in understanding the intelligence picture and executing operations.[47]

For their part, our partner forces see the end result and want that capability, as do most countries. It appears simple, and the prospect of having a capability with just the platform and missiles for this phase of the operation makes it seem within reach. For coalition forces, the apparent simplicity of this final phase of operations is seductive as well—just provide partner forces the platform and missiles, the coalition will provide the intel leading to that point, and the partner force will be able to pick up these operations for themselves, freeing our assets for other priorities. The US military's "strategy-to-task" framework for planning these complex operations, taking a desired end state and dividing it into lines of effort and discrete tasks to be performed, adds to the illusion that the military's "easy button" is to pass each discrete task to the partner force one by one. US Air Force doctrine in particular is largely built

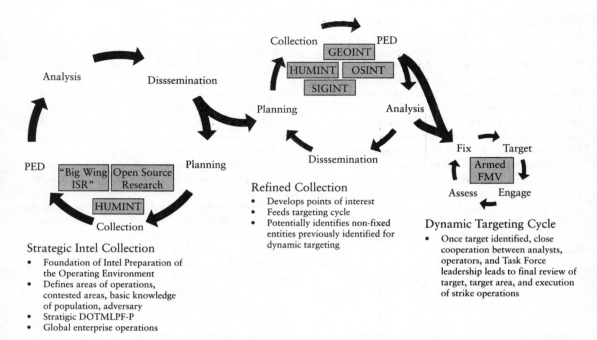

Figure 2. Interconnected Intelligence Cycles for Globally Integrated ISR & Strike

around this concept, which has proved vital to executing theater-wide air operations by synchronizing numerous tactical objectives. Air Force doctrine for foreign internal defense (FID), the operations most associated with counterterrorism/counterinsurgency in states such as Iraq, makes this model explicit. Through a strategy-to-task framework, planners can build a "FID plan with a concept of operations that includes estimated timelines with phased initiatives, goals, and objectives for US actions. The FID plan can be reconciled and adjusted in accordance with the HN's [host nation's] . . . strategy. The FID plan gives commanders a starting point for initiating appropriate actions"; these are to build a plan, identify tasks, identify which tasks the partner force can do, and pass those tasks to them over time.[48]

The first big challenge is that the strategic objectives of the partner force are ultimately distinct from the force enabler, in this case the United States and coalition partners. The coalition's primary goal is disruption, destruction, and suppression of the insurgent/terrorist force to the degree that the partner force can then reestablish sovereignty over its territory. The partner force, by contrast, has the goal of creating and expanding territorial control by the government for the purpose of building sovereignty. In this regard, military operations are at cross purposes. For the coalition, minimizing the ground footprint through air presence

and aerial targeting enables the mission. For the host nation, however, ground presence is a virtue and not a vice. National sovereignty is fundamentally focused on the ability to control territory free of outside interference and should be manifested through a ground presence ultimately executing government order through the law. Domestic reliance on a heavy militarized UAS presence is in effect tacit admission of no ability to control or even access territory, and thus its use undermines the goals of establishing sovereignty. But, by focusing first on building a military force that mirrors our own, the United States projects on them the need to pick up and run with US doctrine models when instead it should be focused on their strategic goals and how to enable them with their own doctrine.

If that alone were the main challenge to building an Iraqi air enterprise capable of executing precision-strike operations, there would be a number of plausible work-arounds. Building the capability would be largely incidental, a temporary measure incorporated by the Iraqi forces while the insurgency remained a viable option with the understanding that it would transition to more traditional law enforcement operations as time went on. The larger challenge is one of organizational capacity. The Iraqi military has no military tradition of strategic airborne ISR, no history or doctrine of aerial bombardment, and no sense of delegating command to lower echelons to carry out command intent at the tactical level. All of these issues render the prospect of passing a precision-strike capability to Iraq a generational change at least, with significant coalition involvement to change the entire culture of the Iraqi military.

For the United States, the growth of the airborne targeting enterprise has been a long evolution. Even excluding most of the first century of aerial warfare and starting the clock at Operation DESERT STORM and the first declaration of a precision-targeting revolution in military affairs,[49] through campaigns in Kosovo, Afghanistan, the second Iraq War (2003–2010), and right through the early phases of Operation INHERENT RESOLVE (2014–present), the US military's targeting process has shifted to involve more precision munitions, less emphasis on fixed targets, greater reliance on global information networks, and an increasingly versatile intelligence-targeting-operations infrastructure to adapt to the needs of the changing battlefield.[50] At the core of this system is the firm embrace of the concept of mission command, empowering agile and adaptive tactical leaders to execute commander's intent absent specific directive orders. In the US ISR system, a junior soldier or enlisted airman based in the continental United States can talk in real time with a junior officer UAS pilot in Nevada to discuss the merits of a strike halfway around the world, and that team can request and receive permission either to move the sensor or to initiate a strike decision through direct interaction with commanders, while all are watching a common feed.[51] Timeliness, professionalism, communication, and sense of mission at all levels are vital to facilitating this system of warfare.

The challenge for Western forces seeking to train and equip partner nations to fight domestic insurgents is a lack of a military culture in many of these regions capable of executing these operations. This isn't an intellectual challenge, but a challenge of military culture—partly derived from underlying Arab culture, and partly from a military designed under years of dictatorship and still uncertain of its country's future. As Atkine and Serrano maintain, decisions are made at the highest levels of government, information is hoarded because it represents power in society, equipment is not delegated to lower echelons, and combined arms operations are virtually nonexistent.[52] Too much knowledge, too much power, and too much decision-making authority at lower levels is historically viewed with paranoia in nonprofessionalized militaries. Absent the willingness to share information and delegate decision-making authority, precision aerial targeting loses its timeliness factor, in effect rendering it an expensive but operationally useless tool.

In practice, unlike the US model for UAS, the Iraqi model is top-heavy, linear, bureaucratic, and time-consuming. Human intelligence is maintained through the Iraqi National Intelligence Service, and held tight for the most part. What is reported goes to the highest levels of the Iraqi military to be looked at alongside what the regional military commanders are requesting for future operations to determine what should be tasked for ISR. When a mission is tasked, it is explicit on what is to be looked at and evaluated, likely without context for why the analyst is looking at the site and no ability to maneuver the platform to look at other potentially related sites (such as for a vehicle follow). The products are then transferred back to the Joint Operations Center, which in turn makes determinations on what to strike. On paper this looks like a simplification of the US system (figure 3), but in practice a lot less information is passed at all levels, and the time to go through it

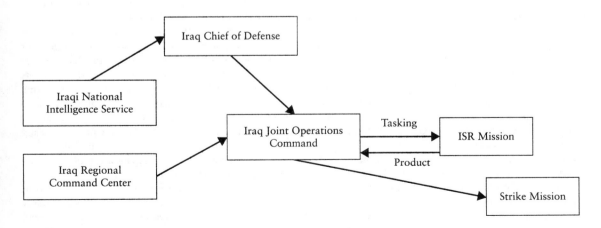

Figure 3. **Iraqi Strike Tasking Mode**

can take days to even weeks as opposed to near-real-time dialogue and constant information-sharing. This is not by any means a new observation, but the point is far-reaching in terms of its impact on broader strategy to implement a partner force development strategy that at its core is wholly reliant on a combined arms approach with an underlying foundation of trust and information-sharing. In critiquing partner-force training in 1999,

> joint commands are paper constructs that have little actual function. Leaders look at joint commands, joint exercises, combined arms, and integrated staffs very cautiously for all Arab armies are a double-edged sword. One edge points toward the external enemy and the other toward the capital. The land forces are at once a regime-maintenance force and threat at the same time. No Arab ruler will allow combined operations or training to become routine; the usual excuse is financial expense, but that is unconvincing given their frequent purchase of hardware whose maintenance costs they cannot afford. In fact, combined arms exercises and joint staffs create familiarity, soften rivalries, erase suspicions, and eliminate the fragmented, competing organizations that enable rulers to play off rivals against one another.[53]

In effect, current strategy puts the cart before the horse: focus on technical and tactical skills, and over time professionalism and combined arms execution will follow. Meanwhile, as significant doubts likely remain about the viability of democratic governance outside significant Western support, leaders both within the military and in the government are unlikely to abandon anytime soon the historical domestic checks on power and authority that have existed in the military culture for decades.

Ultimately, this partner force model as applied is effective primarily against fixed targets, within line-of-sight communications range, where sufficient time exists for the most senior leaders in country to approve of operations. These can then be struck by armed UASs, but they can similarly be struck either by fighter aircraft or by long-range artillery. Under the circumstances, the report of the inspector general for Operation INHERENT RESOLVE might be incomplete in observing that "a combination of Iraqi training in the United States, a lapse in maintenance contracts, and problems with signal interference resulted in only two sorties since March of this year [2019] by Iraq's fleet of more than 10 ScanEagle tactical UASs."[54] More likely, airborne ISR and aerial strike facilitated by UAS represents a mission set not aligned to the strategic needs of the Iraqi government

and cannot be executed in a timely manner by the Iraqi military. As Norvell B. De Atkine observed in 1999:

> Taking responsibility for a policy, operation, status, or training program rarely occurs. U.S. trainers can find it very frustrating when they repeatedly encounter Arab officers placing blame for unsuccessful operations or programs on the U.S. equipment or some other outside source. A high rate of non-operational U.S. equipment is blamed on a "lack of spare parts"—pointing a finger at an unresponsive U.S. supply system despite the fact that American trainers can document ample supplies arriving in country and disappearing in a malfunctioning supply system. (Such criticism was never caustic or personal and often so indirect and politely delivered that it wasn't until after a meeting that oblique references were understood.)[55]

The challenge could be an Arab problem as Atkine and Serrano imply, or it may be a broader path dependency issue for militaries in states with a history of factionalism and dictatorship, and thus nonprofessionalized army. Regardless of what shapes the underlying military culture, the case of Iraq is a reminder of the need to take that military culture into account and to assess organizational capacity for adoption of military innovations.

Conclusions

More than twenty years into the age of unmanned air warfare, a number of patterns are emerging that will likely shape the future evolution of both state and non-state weapons of war. Small UASs, made with commercial-off-the-shelf materials and other homemade solutions (including 3D printing) are a reality of the modern battlespace; they are significant tactical weapons similar to IEDs against an unprepared adversary and a potent terrorist threat to soft targets for both kinetic strikes and nuisance swarm attacks. At the high end, as the United States and other world powers experiment with UCAVs capable of supplementing fifth-generation fighters carrying out multiple air superiority missions, the future of air-to-air combat appears to be faster, powered by artificial intelligence, and fought increasingly through the electromagnetic spectrum and the ability to anticipate a rapidly evolving battlespace on many layers.

Trapped in between these extremes are numerous states that face instability at home and have already struggled to keep up with the growing military strength of major powers. While some have sought UASs as prestige weapons, large UASs may in the long run be a burden to these states rather than a force multiplier that allows them to skip generations of aviation technology. As coalitions seek to build up partnerships and enable states to tackle instability at home, the lessons of these early UAS wars should serve as a reminder. Organizational capital matters. Military culture plays a dominant role in dictating organizational capital, and we cannot take for granted the complexity below the surface of modern combat operations. The UAS like other weapon systems is ultimately a tool in a military system. The system must drive the tool, and not the other way around.

NOTES

1. Michael P. Kreuzer, *Drones and the Future of Air Warfare* (New York: Routledge, 2016).

2. Joint Chiefs of Staff, "Joint Publication 3-30, Command and Control of Joint Air Operations," July 25, 2019, https://www.jcs.mil/Portals/36/Documents/Doctrine/pubs/jp3_30.pdf.

3. Margaret Miller, "The Poor Man's Air Force: Unattributed Mid-Range Drone Attacks," College of William and Mary: The Project on International Peace and Security, April 2018, https://www.wm.edu/offices/global-research/projects/pips/_documents/pips/2017-2018/miller.margaret.pdf.

4. US Air Force, "Global Vigilance, Global Reach, Global Power for America," n.d., accessed February 20, 2020, https://www.af.mil/Portals/1/documents/newGV_GR_GP_PRINT.pdf.

5. Office of the Chairman of the Joint Chiefs of Staff, *DoD Dictionary of Military and Associated Terms*, January 2020, https://www.jcs.mil/Portals/36/Documents/Doctrine/pubs/dictionary.pdf, p 110.

6. Office of the Chairman of the Joint Chiefs of Staff, *DoD Dictionary*, 107.

7. Department of the Army Headquarters, "ADP 2-0, Intelligence," fas.org, July 2019, https://fas.org/irp/doddir/army/adp2_0.pdf.

8. US Air Force Doctrine Center, *Annex 2-0 Global Integrated ISR Operations*, January 29, 2015, https://www.doctrine.af.mil/Portals/61/documents/Annex_2-0/2-0-D01-ISR-Introduction.pdf.

9. Kreuzer, *Drones and the Future of Air Warfare.*

10. Samuel Huntington, *The Soldier and the State* (Cambridge, MA: Belknap Press, 1981 [1957]).

11. Stephen Biddle, *Military Power: Explaining Victory and Defeat in Modern Battle* (Princeton, NJ: Princeton University Press, 2006).

12. Steve Coll, "The Unblinking Stare: The Drone War in Pakistan," *New Yorker*, November 17, 2014, https://www.newyorker.com/magazine/2014/11/24/unblinking-stare.

13. Dennis M. Gormley, *Missile Contagion: Cruise Missile Proliferation and the Threat to International Security* (Annapolis: Naval Institute Press, 2010).

14. Jonathan Rupprecht, "Drone Sabotage on Saudi Pipeline Facility Raises Concerns," *Forbes*, May 15, 2019, https://www.forbes.com/sites/jonathanrupprecht/2019/05/15/drone-sabotage-on-saudi-pipeline-facility-raises-concerns/#66265ebe79dc.

15. Asia-Pacific Counter-IED Fusion Center, "Monthly IED Activity Report," US Army Pacific, January 31, 2018, https://www.usarpac.army.mil/apcied/Monthly/2018-01_IED_Report.pdf.

16. David, Reid, "A Swarm of Armed Drones Attacked a Russian Military Base in Syria," CNBC, January 11, 2018, https://www.cnbc.com/2018/01/11/swarm-of-armed-diy-drones-attacks-russian-military-base-in-syria.html.

17. "Gatwick Airport: Drones Ground Flights," BBC, December 20 2018, https://www.bbc.com/news/uk-england-sussex-46623754.

18. Charlie Moore, "ISIS Unveils a New Remote-Controlled Drone That They Film Dropping a Bomb in Mosul," *Daily Mail* (UK), January 23, 2017, https://www.dailymail.co.uk/news/article-4149622/ISIS-reveals-bombing-drone.html.

19. ISIS, "ISIS Drone Bombing Propaganda Video," Youtube, accessed February 21, 2020, https://www.youtube.com/watch?v=cz2jrmnm7ds.

20. Michael C. Horowitz, *The Diffusion of Military Power: Causes and Consequences for International Politics* (Princeton, NJ: Princeton University Press, 2010). See also his contribution to this volume: "Artificial Intelligence, International Competition, and the Balance of Power."

21. David J Blair and Nick Helms, "The Swarm, the Cloud, and the Importance of Getting There First," *Air and Space Power Journal* 27, no. 4 (July 2013): 14–38, https://apps.dtic.mil/dtic/tr/fulltext/u2/a618996.pdf.; Michael W. Barnes, "Nightfall: Machine Autonomy in Air-to-Air Combat," *Air and Space Power Journal* 28, no. 3 (May 2014): 48–75, https://www.airuniversity.af.edu/Portals/10/ASPJ/journals/Volume-28_Issue-3/F-Byrnes.pdf.

22. Defense Science Board, "The Role of Autonomy in DoD Systems," fas.org, July 2012, 13, https://fas.org/irp/agency/dod/dsb/autonomy.pdf.

23. Arthur Holland Michel, "Counter-Drone Systems," Bard College, February 2018, https://dronecenter.bard.edu/files/2018/02/CSD-Counter-Drone-Systems-Report.pdf.

24. Dana Liebelson, "Now There's a Zombie Drone That Hunts, Controls, and Kills Other Drones," *Mother Jones*, December 6, 2013, https://www.motherjones.com/politics/2013/12/zombie-drone-samy-kamkar-amazon-security/.

25. Rafael Advanced Defense Systems, "Drone Dome," Rafael, March 1, 2019, https://www.rafael.co.il/wp-content/uploads/2019/03/Drone-Dome-Updated-march-19-1.pdf.

26. Eytah Halon, "Israeli Anti-Drone Technology Brings an End to Gatwick Airport Chaos," *Jerusalem Post*, December 21, 2018, https://www.jpost.com/International/Israeli-anti-drone-technology-brings-an-end-to-Gatwick-Airport-chaos-575054.

27. Andrew Liptak, "The US Air Force Has a New Weapon Called THOR That Can Take Out Swarms of Drones," The Verge, June 21, 2019, https://www.theverge.com/2019/6/21/18701267/us-air-force-thor-new-weapon-drone-swarms.

28. Chenega, "Counter-UAV Solutions: Protection-in-depth," chenegaeurope.com, n.d., accessed February 21, 2020, https://www.chenegaeurope.com/media/1221/counteruav_ce.pdf.

29. David Martin, "Inside the Air War," *60 Minutes*, October 25 2015, https://www.cbsnews.com/news/inside-the-air-war-against-isis-60-minutes/.

30. Michael P. Kreuzer and Denis Dallaire, "Targeting the Islamic State: Activity-Based Intelligence and Modern Airpower,"

The Mitchell Institute for Aerospace Studies, April 14 2017, http://www.mitchellaerospacepower.org/single-post/2017/04/14/Targeting-the-Islamic-State-Activity-Based-Intelligence-and-Modern-Airpower.

31. Michael S. Schmidt and Eric Schmitt, "Pentagon Confronts a New Threat From ISIS: Exploding Drones," *New York Times*, October 11, 2016, https://www.nytimes.com/2016/10/12/world/middleeast/iraq-drones-isis.html.

32. Mark Pomerleau, "How $650 Drones Are Creating Problems in Iraq and Syria," C4ISR.net, January 5, 2018, https://www.c4isrnet.com/unmanned/uas/2018/01/05/how-650-drones-are-creating-problems-in-iraq-and-syria/.

33. Pomerleau, "How $650 Drones Are Creating Problems."

34. "U.S. Military Casualties—Operation Inherent Resolve (OIR) Military Deaths," Defense Casualty Analysis System, February 20, 2020, https://dcas.dmdc.osd.mil/dcas/pages/report_oir_deaths.xhtml.

35. Schmidt and Schmitt, "Pentagon Confronts a New Threat."

36. Margaret Miller, "The Poor Man's Air Force: Unattributed Mid-Range Drone Attacks," College of William and Mary: The Project on International Peace and Security, April 2018, https://www.wm.edu/offices/global-research/projects/pips/_documents/pips/2017-2018/miller.margaret.pdf.

37. George W. Bush, "Bush: 'As the Iraqis Stand Up, We Will Stand Down,'" CNN, June 29, 2005, https://edition.cnn.com/2005/POLITICS/06/28/bush.excerpts/.

38. Defense Security Cooperation Agency, "News Release: Republic of Iraq—AC-208 Aircraft," October 7, 2016, https://www.dsca.mil/major-arms-sales/republic-iraq-ac-208-aircraft.

39. Joseph Trevithick, "This Tiny Plane Is an F-16 for Cash-Strapped Air Forces," *War Is Boring*, December 5, 2014, https://warisboring.com/this-tiny-plane-is-an-f-16-for-cash-strapped-air-forces/

40. "Standing Up the IqAF: King Air 350s," *Defense Industry Daily*, September 24, 2014, https://www.defenseindustrydaily.com/standing-up-the-iqaf-king-air-350s-05101/.

41. John Lee, "US Firm Wins Drone Contract in Iraq," *Iraq Business News*, September 29, 2017, https://www.iraq-businessnews.com/2017/09/29/us-firm-wins-drone-contract-in-iraq/.

42. Dan Gettinger, "ScanEagle: A Small Drone Making a Big Impact," Bard College, January 6, 2014, https://dronecenter.bard.edu/scaneagle-drone/.

43. Michael C. Horowitz, "Drones Aren't Missiles, So Don't Regulate Them Like They Are," *Bulletin of the Atomic Scientists*, June 26, 2017, https://thebulletin.org/2017/06/drones-arent-missiles-so-dont-regulate-them-like-they-are/.

44. Office of Public Affairs, "U.S. Policy on the Export of Unmanned Aerial Systems," (Washington, DC: US Department of State, May 21, 2019), https://www.state.gov/u-s-policy-on-the-export-of-unmanned-aerial-systems/.

45. Janes 360, "Only One Iraqi CH-4 UAV Fully Operable," UAS Vision, August 9, 2019, https://www.uasvision.com/2019/08/09/only-one-iraqi-ch-4-uav-fully-operable/.

46. David Axe, "You Get What You Pay For with China's CH-4 Drones," *National Interest*, November 21, 2019, https://nationalinterest.org/blog/buzz/you-get-what-you-pay-chinas-ch-4-drones-97977.

47. Kreuzer, *Drones and the Future of Air Warfare*.

48. LeMay Center, "Annex 3-22 Foreign Internal Defense: Strategy-to-Task FID Planning," US Air Force Doctrine Center, February 1, 2020, https://www.doctrine.af.mil/Portals/61/documents/Annex_3-22/3-22-D38-FID-Strat-Task-Planning.pdf.

49. Eliot A. Cohen, "A Revolution in Warfare," *Foreign Affairs* 75, no. 2 (March 1996): 37–54, https://www.comw.org/rma/fulltext/9603cohen.pdf.

50. Kreuzer and Dallaire, "Targeting the Islamic State."

51. Michael C. Sirak, "ISR Revolution," *Air Force Magazine*, May 26, 2010, https://www.airforcemag.com/article/0610isr/.

52. Norvell B. De Atkine, "Why Arabs Lose Wars," *Middle East Quarterly* 6, no. 4 (December 1999), https://www.meforum.org/441/why-arabs-lose-wars; Lauren Serrano, "Arab Cultural Manifestations in the Iraqi Army," *Small Wars Journal* (November 1, 2019), https://smallwarsjournal.com/jrnl/art/arab-cultural-manifestations-iraqi-army.

53. De Atkine, "Why Arabs Lose Wars."

54. Operation INHERENT RESOLVE Lead Inspector General, "Report to the United States Congress, April 1 2019–June 30 2019" (Washington, DC: US Department of State, August 6, 2019), https://www.stateoig.gov/system/files/q3fy2019_leadig_oir_report.pdf, p. 46.

55. De Atkine, n.p.

The Hard Lessons of an Insurgency

JOHN A. NAGL

Low-intensity conflict has been more common throughout the history of warfare than has conflict between nations represented by armies on a "conventional" field of battle. Until relatively recently, however, those who took up arms against the state were referred to as bandits or criminals rather than as combatants in irregular warfare; it was only the rise of nationalism, and the corresponding growth of acceptance of individual liberty and responsibility, that provided a sort of legitimacy to violence directed against the state.[1]

The essential features of guerrilla warfare are avoiding the enemy's strength—his main fighting forces—while striking at outposts and logistical support from unexpected directions. This principle is now often described as "asymmetric," but it is as old as the word *guerrilla* itself. The term is derived from the Spanish term for "small war" and springs from the Spanish rebellion of 1808 against an occupying French army. The combined efforts of Wellington's 60,000 men, a small Spanish army, and the Spanish *guerrilleros* tied up more than 250,000 French troops and supported Henry IV's remark that "Spain is a country where small armies are beaten and large ones starve."[2] Henry's appreciation for the unpleasant fate that befell foreign armies invading Spain echoes the Roman experience there in the second century B.C.; Napoleon was not the first to be checked by Spanish guerrillas!

Henry focused on the country of Spain, but the combination of difficult, broken terrain and a proud people who refuse to bow before a foreign invader is one of the constants of guerrilla warfare. A more contemporary observer describes the essential nature of terrain in increasing the ability of guerrillas to defeat a conventional army, noting that such terrain includes

> swamps, mountains and forests where mobility is limited to movements on foot and in light vehicles. The fact that the partisan operates in such terrain will be to his advantage for in an environment of this nature the regular forces lose the use of their vehicles and artillery as well as the ability to mass superior numbers. In essence, the terrain reduces the better equipped, better trained, and better armed regular force to a level where the partisan is equal.[3]

The essential features of guerrilla warfare—the tactics of applying weakness against strength and the clever use of terrain to conceal guerrilla forces from the enemy's main body—have barely changed since the days of the Romans and Persians. What has changed, and made guerrilla warfare an altogether more potent form of conflict for the accomplishment of political goals, is the addition of revolutionary politics to the mix. The man who first wrote penetratingly on these changes fought at the same time as the campaigns that gave guerrilla warfare its name: Carl von Clausewitz.

Clausewitz and People's Wars

Carl von Clausewitz's *On War* is important for our purposes both because it places guerrilla warfare in the context of conventional warfare and because it has exerted considerable influence on Western armies attempting to defeat insurgency—often through the medium of Clausewitz's contemporary, Henri Jomini.[4]

Clausewitz fought against Napoleon and later wrote about the Corsican's remarkable success in revolutionizing war. In comparison to the set-piece battles of the eighteenth century, in which European armies fought by mutual consent and a single battle often decided a war, Napoleon's use of the French nation to support his campaigns constituted nothing less than a revolution in military affairs. In pre-Napoleonic European warfare, the role of the army, acting as the striking hand of the national sovereign, had so overshadowed the role of the people of a nation in supporting war that warfare had been called "the sport of kings" for centuries. Armies acted as the instruments of state power for national leaders who often personally led them into battle. Warfare involved governments and armies, arousing surprisingly little interest in the majority of the population, who often did not notice a change in rulers that resulted from battles won or lost.

Napoleon's decisive contribution was his discovery that armies and kings needed no longer fight in isolation from the people of their states. Building upon changes that had emerged during the French Revolution, Napoleon harnessed the power of the French people to make warfare a "remarkable trinity" composed of the people,

John A. Nagl, "The Hard Lessons of an Insurgency," in *Learning to Eat Soup with a Knife: Counterinsurgency Lessons from Malaya and Vietnam*, 15–33 (Chicago: University of Chicago Press, 2005). Republished with permission of University of Chicago Press—Books; permission conveyed through Copyright Clearance Center, Inc.

the army, and the government. Clausewitz described what Napoleon grasped almost instinctively: war is "a paradoxical trinity—composed of primordial violence, hatred, and enmity, which are to be regarded as a blind natural force; of the play of chance and probability within which the creative spirit is free to roam; and of its element of subordination, as an instrument of policy, which makes it subject to reason alone. The first of these three aspects mainly concerns the people; the second the commander and his army; the third the government."[5]

Another element has been added to warfare; the sport of kings has become the business of the people. Although the common people had always played an important role in warfare by providing the men, taxes, and foodstuffs with which the army was supplied, the rise in nationalism meant that people and armies were much more intimately linked. The people increased in relative importance, forming the raw material for a mass army; the new spirit of enraged nationalism often kept them fighting even when the national government or army had been conquered or ceased to exist. Clausewitz's "remarkable trinity" of the people, the army, and the government is an effective way to depict the evolution of the concept of "people's war" and will also be very useful in understanding why some armies are better than others at comprehending how to combat revolutionary war.

Absolute Victory: Jomini, Clausewitz, and the Propagation of an Idea

Clausewitz's interpretation of Napoleon's revolution in military affairs is neither the only nor the most influential interpretation. The ideas of Clausewitz's contemporary, Antoine-Henri Jomini, are important both in their own right and in their shaping of the influence of Clausewitz on history. Jomini was a Swiss banker who, like Clausewitz, was swept up in the events unleashed by the French Revolution. A bookish soldier, he took a position on Marshal Ney's staff and began to publish works on military history in 1803. The key principles of all of his years of writing (he lived another sixty-five years) were clearly laid out in Jomini's first book:

- Strategy is the key to warfare.
- All strategy is controlled by invariable scientific principles.
- These principles prescribe *offensive action* to *mass forces* against weaker enemy forces at some *decisive point* if strategy is to lead to victory.[6]

Jomini served in the Ulm, Jena, Eylau, Spanish, and Russian campaigns, earning some renown as a soldier but much more as the dominant military historian and theorist of his day. His most famous book, *A Summary of the Art of War*, was published in 1837; it maintained his emphasis on scientific principles of warfare and on massive battles of annihilation. Like Clausewitz, Jomini hungered for but never enjoyed the command of troops in battle. Jomini deserted Napoleon in 1813 to serve on the Russian General Staff; again, he never gained independent command. This lifelong position on the perimeter of power led Jomini to proclaim in his writing that the military commander should have absolute control of decisions in campaigns; his models were Frederick the Great and Napoleon. The principle they followed was the same one he advocated: mass your own armies to threaten a decisive point; then defeat a fraction of the enemy army with all of your own.

Jomini is important because of his prescription of the annihilation of the opponent's force as the best route to victory, a sentiment often and mistakenly attributed to Clausewitz. The Prussian was actually much too subtle to say that anything was always the best route to victory—except the accomplishment of the political objectives for which the war was being fought. That Jomini's most famous prescription is misattributed to Clausewitz, who disliked Jomini personally and thought his ideas rubbish, is more than ironic; as John Shy says in *Makers of Modern Strategy*, "If there can be such a thing as a joke in military history, surely this is it."[7] The question of how this ironic joke came about has much to do with the historical impact of Clausewitz versus Jomini and can be explained very simply. Soldiers—and most statesmen—are uncomfortable with ambiguity, with Clausewitzian "it depends" answers. They like checklists of simple principles that always apply, ideas such as "Annihilate the enemy's force in the field and you will win the war." Jomini had given his audience what it wanted; Michael Howard notes, "This was the kind of thing that appealed to practical soldiers."[8]

It was Moltke more than any other who popularized Jominian ideas and called them Clausewitzian; for instance, "Victory through the application of armed force is the decisive factor in war. . . . It is not the occupation of a slice of territory or the capture of a fortress but the destruction of the enemy forces which will decide the outcome of the war. This destruction thus constitutes the principal object of operations."[9] Moltke supported such statements with quotations from Clausewitz, but certainly by the end of his life Clausewitz had developed a much more nuanced view of warfare than always prescribing the destruction of the enemy forces. That was a Jominian idea, misattributed to Clausewitz by Moltke, who muddied the waters for future generations of strategists still unborn.

This misattribution is important not just because it confuses military historians, but also because the Jominian concept of victory through annihilation of the enemy forces influenced other thinkers about strategy as well as generations of practitioners. The belief that annihilating the enemy army was the certain route to victory was corrupted before World War I into the concept that offense was both practically and morally superior to defense in all cases, a concept Clausewitz would have abhorred but in the defense of which he was repeatedly quoted. When ideas that were decidedly non-Clausewitzian resulted in the bloody stalemate of World War I, he was again quoted out of context to justify the continuation of the slaughter for no possible political gain. This occurred despite the fact that, as Bernard Brodie points out, German Army chief of staff Schlieffen himself was "sufficiently a student of Clausewitz" to have absorbed the concept of the primacy of the political over the military, "for he is on record as having urged in writing that if the Plan should fail, as of course it did in 1914, Germany should at once seek a negotiated peace."[10] No matter. After the war, Clausewitz took the blame for the conduct of a war of annihilation of which he would most certainly have disapproved.

The importance of Jomini for a student of counterinsurgency learning is evident: Jomini emphasizes the destruction of the enemy army in the field, despite Clausewitz's understanding that the true power of armies in the wake of Napoleon rests in the people and their government.[11] Nonetheless, armies ever since have clung to what they continue to describe as "Clausewitzian" (actually Jominian) principles of destroying the enemy army as the key to victory.

Clausewitz was primarily concerned with understanding conventional war fought by national armies, albeit armies inspired by the then-revolutionary ideas and currents unleashed by the ideals of liberty, equality, fraternity, and love of *patrie*. However, the feelings, aspirations, and energies of the people that Napoleon harnessed for the benefit of the state in conventional warfare would play a dramatic role in modifying the nature of unconventional warfare as well. Clausewitz describes "the people in arms" as "smoldering embers," which

consume the basic foundations of the enemy forces. Since it needs time to be effective, a state of tension will develop while the two elements interact. This tension will either gradually relax, if the insurgency is suppressed in some places and slowly burns itself out in others, or else it will build up to a crisis: a general conflagration closes in on the enemy, driving him out of the country before he is faced with total destruction.[12]

His theoretical description would come to life more than a century later, half a world away from Prussia. The man who fanned the embers of the most populous nation in the world was the son of a Chinese peasant. His name was Mao Tse-Tung.

From Clausewitz to Mao: The Revolution Continues

However much we may seek it elsewhere, the basic text for ideas about revolutionary war is in the writings of Mao Tse-Tung.

—John Shy and Thomas W. Collier

Mao Tse-Tung was born in Hunan province in central China in 1893.[13] His father was a "middle peasant," a man who earned enough money to ensure that his family had enough to eat. Mao had a hard childhood; his father was strict but provided him with the comparative luxury of a high school education. Mao responded by reading everything he could and was a keen observer of the inability of the Chinese government to meet the needs of the peasants with whom he grew up. His service as a private soldier in a corrupt and inefficient army further increased his political awareness; Mao was "the Chinese version of an angry young man" when he began working in the library of the University of Peking in 1917.[14] He soon had contact with the precepts of communism and helped organize the Chinese Communist Party in Shanghai in 1921.

Mao described the China in which he grew up as "semi-colonial and feudal."[15] It was a country in which 400 million peasants "ate bitterness" throughout their difficult lives and had been exploited by Western nations for over a century. Griffith notes that "a potential revolutionary situation exists in any country where the government consistently fails in its obligation to ensure at least a minimally decent standard of life for the great majority of its citizens."[16] It would be hard to imagine a better case in support of Griffith's argument than Mao's China of the 1920s, though the very use of the word *government* is somewhat misleading; in fact, there were several rival governments in China, and the standard of living was probably improving—though not fast enough to suit Mao.

The Chinese Communist Party took advantage of the corruption and inefficiency of the government to recruit the proletariat for membership in trade unions. Mao was sent to his home province of Hunan to recruit in 1926; he was surprised by the groundswell of peasant support for the National Revolutionary Army in 1926. Mao fled to the Chingkang Mountains of southern Hunan province after leading four auxiliary regiments in the abortive Autumn Harvest Uprising of September 1927. Chu Teh, another survivor of the coup, joined Mao in 1928; after a series of defeats in attacks on Nationalist-held cities in 1930, they jointly decided that in China the revolution had to be based on the peasant rather than the urban proletariat. Douglas Blaufarb notes, "The problem confronted by Mao in China in 1927 was that of writing Hamlet with a midget prince of Denmark."[17] China was simply not industrialized enough for the urban workers to form a viable base for revolution. Griffith calls this shift in emphasis from urban workers to rural peasants "the single most vital decision in the history of the Chinese Communist Party."[18]

Chiang Kai-Shek, heartened by the Communist defeat at Changsha that had led to Mao's decision to focus on the peasants, announced a "Bandit Suppression Campaign" in October 1930. It failed miserably, as did three similar campaigns in following years. The Nationalist troops displayed the conduct that would prove to be their downfall: Chiang's "divisions flailed over the land like locusts, further alienating peasants, the ill-treated, illiterate soldiers frequently deserting to the Communists."[19] Only when Chiang Kai-Shek accepted the advice of his German adviser, General von Falkenhausen, who drew on the British lessons of the Boer War and advanced slowly and methodically through the Communist base areas with a force of some 500,000 supported by artillery and aircraft, did the Communists begin to feel the pressure of the counterinsurgency campaign.

The Communists broke through the Nationalist lines to begin the "Long March" of some 6,000 miles to a new base in Shensi province in October 1934. Over twelve months later, some 30,000 survivors of the 130,000 who began the march arrived in Shensi; Mao's wife died on the march. Costly as it was, the Long March demonstrated the will of the people to support the revolutionaries.[20] It also taught Mao a great deal about revolutionary warfare; it was while he was rebuilding Communist strength in Yenan after escaping yet another attack by Chiang Kai-Shek in 1936 that Mao wrote *Guerrilla Warfare*.

The continuing encroachment of Japan into China gave Mao's Communists the political issue they needed to mobilize the people behind their cause. Chiang's refusal to ally his forces with Mao's in a national front against the invader allowed Mao to "appropriate nationalism from the Nationalists and [make] it a powerful Communist weapon."[21] Chiang agreed to the creation of a united front only after literally being kidnapped by his own forces shortly before the Japanese invasion in 1937. The Japanese invasion was a blessing in disguise for Mao and the Communists: it "broke the hold of parochialism on the Chinese peasant. Before the Japanese invasion the Chinese peasant was indifferent to 'Chinese' politics, being wholly absorbed in local affairs. The war totally destroyed the rural society order and sensitized the Chinese peasantry to a new spectrum of possible

associations, identities, and purposes. Foremost among the new political concepts were those of 'China' and 'Chinese nationality.' "[22]

Mao turned the principles of guerrilla warfare he had used against the Nationalists to the struggle against the Japanese, simultaneously husbanding his own forces for the battle against Chiang's forces once the Japanese had been evicted. Both sides kept their eye on the real prize: the eventual total control of China. Mao's ideas on how to accomplish that task with his poorly armed, unprofessional band of Communist peasants would lead to the greatest revolution in military thought since the ideas of Clausewitz.

Mao's contribution to the theory of warfare is an even closer interlinking of the people, the army, and the government than that discovered by Napoleon and analyzed by Clausewitz. In fact, the people in and of themselves were the greatest weapon the Communists possessed, both in their struggle against the Japanese invaders and in the temporarily postponed fight against the Nationalists. In Mao's own words, "The richest source of power to wage war lies in the masses of the people."[23] This doctrine was largely one of necessity: it was essential that the army, without an established government to provide logistical support, retain the goodwill of the people in order to ensure its own survival. Hence Mao's insistence on "a unity of spirit" between troops and local inhabitants, which is evident in a code known as "The Three Rules and the Eight Remarks" which guided the activities of the Communist Eighth Route Army:[24]

Rules

1. All actions are subject to command.
2. Do not steal from the people.
3. Be neither selfish nor unjust.

Remarks

1. Replace the door when you leave the house.
2. Roll up the bedding on which you have slept.
3. Be courteous.
4. Be honest in your transactions.
5. Return what you borrow.
6. Replace what you break.
7. Do not bathe in the presence of women.
8. Do not without authority search those you arrest.

The implementation of such precepts allowed the army of the people to be truly an army of the people; it was strict adherence to these regulations that emphasized to the common people that the Communists were on their side and that the Nationalist armies were not much better than the Japanese. Full implementation would create an organized Chinese populace, aroused against the Japanese invaders (and later, the

Chinese Nationalists): "The Japanese aggressor, like a mad bull crashing into a ring of flames, will be surrounded by hundreds of millions of our people standing upright, the mere sound of their voices will strike terror into him, and he will be burned to death."[25]

This is a new conceptualization of the idea of "people's war," with even more emphasis on the decisive role of an aroused populace fighting against a conventional army weakened by corruption and inefficiency and crippled by the hatred of the local populace. The army and the government were now of the populace, living within it and emerging to strike at the enemy before fading back into the cover provided by the population.

It is nearly impossible to overstate the emphasis that Mao placed on ensuring the support of the people for the revolutionary war that he saw ahead. He returns to the point throughout his writing: "This question of the political mobilization of the army and the people is indeed of the greatest importance. We have dwelt on it at the risk of repetition precisely because victory is impossible without it. There are, of course, many other conditions indispensable to victory, but political mobilization is the most fundamental."[26]

Revolutionary war is protracted. Mao foresaw three phases through which the war of national liberation would pass: one of organization, consolidation, and preservation; one of progressive expansion; and the final decisive phase culminating in the destruction of the enemy. During the first phase, military operations would be limited and sporadic; the revolution would focus on training cadres, organizing the peasantry, and gathering its strength. The second phase exploits the gathering strength of the revolution to attack isolated enemy outposts and patrols with two motives: undermining the faith of the populace in the government while increasing the prestige of the revolutionaries and taking arms, ammunition, and equipment from government forces to serve as the "storehouse of the revolution." In the decisive third phase, the guerrilla fighters transform themselves into conventional military forces that confront and defeat the government in open battle. All phases can and should occur simultaneously; recruitment and training of cadres, consolidation of public support, and guerrilla operations will all be conducted in support of the decisive battles of phase III.

The patience and willingness to suffer over a long period in order to achieve ardently desired revolutionary goals have led one observer of the phenomenon to note, "Insurgents start with nothing but a cause and grow to strength, while the counter-insurgents start with everything but a cause and gradually decline in strength and grow to weakness."[27]

This is exactly what happened in the aftermath of the Japanese defeat in World War II. Chiang Kai-Shek's Nationalist forces, despite overwhelming material advantages and the logistical support of the United States, were defeated by those of Mao, buoyed by the support of the vast majority of the Chinese people. Admittedly, the Chinese Communist victory of 1949 reflected a conventional operation, but the guerrilla war against the Nationalists of 1930–1936, and that against the Japanese of 1937–1945, had set the stage. The impact of Mao's victory on the nations of the West would be hard to overstate: in the words of one observer, "The fall of the Chinese nationalist regime in 1949 to the Communists led by Mao, more than any other event, created a new Western consciousness of how protracted armed conflict, using guerrilla tactics and guided by a heterodox version of Marxism-Leninism, might achieve decisive revolutionary victory."[28] The revolution in military affairs that Mao unleashed would soon be adopted by disciples of the Chinese revolution taking advantage of the changes in the international system that occurred in the wake of World War II. These included the end of imperialism, the rise of modern media, the increase in portability and effectiveness of weaponry, and the rise of political awareness in the peoples of former colonies of the West.

Insurgency: A Special Kind of Revolutionary War

The reader will agree with us when we say that once barriers are torn down they are not so easily set up again.

—Carl von Clausewitz

John Shy and Thomas Collier begin their essay "Revolutionary War" in *Makers of Modern Strategy* (1986) by noting that the 1941 edition of the book did not have a chapter on the subject.[29] The reason for the increased importance of revolutionary warfare in the fifty years since the first edition is "the sudden decline in power and prestige of the traditional nation-state system. . . . The crumbling of European empires under colonial and even domestic assault, and the rapid appearance amidst the imperial ruins of new successor states, often weak, are the main reasons why we see this new dimension of military theory where none was apparent in 1941."[30]

Although the rise of nationalism and relative decline of imperial powers are certainly the primary reasons for the increased importance of revolutionary warfare after World War II, they are only part of the answer. Nationalism and the supranational philosophy of communism were important motivations for peoples seeking to form governments responsive to their own needs; these are the ends of a revolutionary strategy. The means changed as well. The proliferation of portable and extremely effective killing machines in the wake of World War II dramatically increased the amount of firepower available to groups wishing to overthrow governments and continues to be a substantial problem today.[31] Just as important is the increase in the ability of the media to get close to even the most distant conflicts and to transmit pictures and sounds to both the local population and the population of any foreign power intervening in a revolutionary conflict. T. E. Lawrence noted, "The printing press is the greatest weapon in the armory of the modern commander."[32] All of these factors, along with a growing disinclination in the national publics of major powers to accept casualties[33] or any evidence of oppression by their forces, have made the phenomenon of revolutionary warfare both more prevalent and far more important than it was when the Spanish guerrillas inflicted such punishment on French forces in the Peninsular campaign.

These changes in the ends of insurgency, that is, communist or nationalist (or both) domination of the government of a nation, and in the means, including more effective weaponry and the use of the media as an important weapon of the insurgent, changed the nature of revolutionary warfare as well. Clausewitz believed that people's war could serve only as a strategic defensive; changes in the ends and means of insurgency allowed revolutionary warfare to become not just an adjunct to conventional conflict but a strategically offensive form of warfare in its own right. The weapons of modern war in the hands of a politically aware and motivated populace appeared to create a new kind of war; even if the tactics had not changed since Alexander the Great, the means and ends had. As Robert Taber notes in the wonderfully titled *The War of the Flea*, "The specifically modern aspect of guerrilla warfare is in its use as a tool of political revolution—the single sure method by which an unarmed population can overcome mechanized armies, or failing to overcome them, can stalemate them and make them irrelevant."[34]

One of the advantages fleas enjoy in their attacks on much larger creatures is their autonomy. Similarly, nations composed of a large number of small, autonomous villages are hard to conquer, as each individual village will fight on individually after the defeat of the national army and will have to be individually subdued. Mao took advantage of this knowledge, gained from hard-won experience, to organize his Communists into a number of independent cells that could not be defeated en masse. The original revolutionaries proselytize to create small groups of believers in outlying villages, often through the threat of force: "power flows from the barrel of a gun." These groups in turn both create local armed forces to operate as guerrillas against the occupying power and further expand the reach of the organization. Over time, district committees are formed to control the various village cells, while larger military formations are created from the best of the local guerrilla forces.

Far from Communist insurgency's being a new kind of war, it is in fact merely an adaptation of Clausewitz's "remarkable trinity." Changes in weaponry (including the media) and especially in the increased role of the people as the logistical support; recruiting base; providers of intelligence, cover, and concealment; and armory of the army meant that enemy forces could no longer be defeated by mere defeat of the enemy army, as had previously been the case. Now defeating the army required that the people be defeated as well—or at least persuaded not to fight on behalf of, nor even support, the insurgents. In the words of a perceptive United States Army officer:

> When there are no economic and political foundations for the guerrilla movement, there will be no guerrilla movement. The bulk of any guerrilla movement joins out of belief in what it is doing; the hard core of leaders keeps going because of political beliefs. If the bulk of the band find they can live as decent human beings, do not have to rob to live, and can have land and homes, they will be poor guerrillas from then on. If the great mass of the population knows it will be protected by a strong, just government, it has no reason to cooperate with the guerrillas, and the system of intelligence and supply that sustains all guerrilla movements breaks down. Without popular support the mopping up of the hard-core die-hards is fairly easy.[35]

Counterinsurgency: Two Approaches

Revolutions are, by their very nature, hard to understand for those who live through them. Because revolutions in any field represent a dramatic shift in understanding of the way society is organized and in the precepts that have previously governed social behavior, it is not surprising that they result in questions about the best way to counter them. Napoleon's grasp of revolutionary warfare necessitated a coalition of Prussia, Russia, and Britain to defeat him; Mao's revolutionary warfare would also present major conceptual challenges to the nations of the West. The challenge posed by Mao would be even more difficult to confront because conventional military forces have always had difficulties in engaging guerrillas.

The difficult nature of guerrilla warfare led to two different approaches to countering insurgencies, exemplified by differing approaches to the problem of subduing the Welsh in the Norman era. The Norman King

William II (Rufus) waged a ruthless campaign against the Welsh under Gruffydd in 1097 in which William "intended to abolish and utterly destroy all of the people until there should be alive not so much as a dog. He had purposed also to cut down all of the woods and groves so that there might not be shelter nor defense for the men of Gwynedd henceforth."[36]

Another approach is presented in Gerald of Wales's *Description of Wales*, written in 1194. He offers instructions in more appropriate techniques for subduing the Welsh: "The prince who would wish to subdue this nation and govern it peaceably, must use this method. . . . Let him divide their strength and by bribes and promises endeavor to stir up one against the other. . . . In the autumn let not only the marshes, but also the interior part of the country be strongly fortified with castles, provisions and confidential families."[37]

These two different approaches—annihilating versus turning the loyalty of the people—are the foundation of the two approaches to counterinsurgency (COIN) to which armies have turned throughout history. The newest edition of the British army's *Counterinsurgency Manual* explains the advantages and disadvantages of each approach, demonstrating that the British have come a long way from the counterinsurgency principles of William Rufus:

A straightforward attritional approach is one option. Such strategies have been adopted and some have worked. Absolute repression was used by the Germans in response to guerrilla attacks during the Second World War. Saddam Hussein's use of chemical weapons against the Kurds and his campaign against the Marsh Arabs in Southern Iraq are contemporary examples of the use of attrition. . . . None of the attritional "solutions" described above is appropriate in a liberal democracy and it is considered that a "gloves off" approach to any insurgency problem has a strictly limited role to play in modern COIN operations.

Furthermore, the record of success for attrition in COIN operations is generally a poor one. Undue focus on military action clouds the key political realities, which can result in a military-dominated campaign plan that misses the real focus of an insurgency. An inability to match the insurgent's concept with an appropriate government one—likened by [Sir Robert] Thompson to trying to play chess whilst the enemy is actually playing poker—is conceptually flawed and will not achieve success. Having deployed conventionally trained troops and large amounts of firepower, the attritionalist commander generally feels compelled to use them. The head of the US Mission to South Vietnam, General

Harkins, claimed in September 1962 that what was required to defeat the Viet Cong within 3 years were "Three Ms"—men, money, and material. The result of this approach (normally to the delight of an insurgent) is an escalating and indiscriminate use of military firepower. The wider consequences of this approach, seen both in South Vietnam and elsewhere, will often be an upward spiral of civilian alienation.[38]

The two approaches to counterinsurgency in many ways resemble the two approaches often taken to conventional warfare, known as the direct and the indirect approach. A participant in the counterinsurgency effort in Vietnam explains:

In essence, military strategy generally boils down to a choice between direct and indirect methods. Direct methods imply the physical destruction of the enemy's means to make war as a preliminary to the imposition of one's physical will on the enemy, and are exemplified by the Franco-Prussian War and by the Western Front of the First World War. Indirect methods seek to attain the political objective of the war by avoidance of a frontal clash between opposing forces.[39]

The direct approach to defeating guerrillas and insurgents is well represented by Harry Summer's phrase "A war is a war is a war." The indirect approach can be clearly explained through reference to Mao's own concept that the revolutionaries are like fish that swim in the water of the people; defeating insurgents is then a matter of "separating the fish from the water."

The Direct Approach: A War Is a War Is a War

The central thesis of the direct approach to fighting a revolutionary war is that unconventional war is much like conventional war in the European setting; in the words of the American Army Colonel Harry Summers, "A war is a war is a war."[40] In order to defeat the enemy, it is only necessary to defeat his armed forces. This approach is based on a Jominian interpretation of the wars of Napoleon. Armies that resort to this method to defeat insurgents are not fighting the last war, but rather, fighting the last revolution in warfare: the Napoleonic nation in arms rather than Mao's armed nation. This is a standard military misinterpretation based on substantial experience in conventional warfare according to the European model.

Western armies often attempt to apply the same concept to the defeat of a people's army: the counterinsurgent army focuses on the defeat of the guerrilla fighters. The essence of Mao's theory of revolutionary warfare is that the warriors are part of the people, living among them during the day and striking at night; this makes difficult the determination of which are legitimate targets of a counterinsurgency campaign. One answer is the killing of all natives down to and including domestic animals as advocated by William Rufus.

The Indirect Approach: Separate the Fish from the Water

The other approach to defeating an insurgency is a function of a better understanding of Mao and a change in the perception of the nature of revolutionary warfare. While continuing to attack the armed elements of the insurgency, the indirect approach recognizes that it is essential also to attack the support of the people for the insurgents. The approach is well described in the following passage from Frank Kitson's *Low Intensity Operations*, which plays on Mao's description of a revolutionary army as relying on the people for support "like fish swimming in the water of the population:"

> In attempting to counter subversion it is necessary to take account of three separate elements. The first two constitute the target proper, that is to say the Party or Front and its cells and committees on the one hand, and the armed groups who are supporting them and being supported by them on the other. They may be said to constitute the head and the body of a fish. The third element is the population and this represents the water in which the fish swims. Fish vary from place to place in accordance with the water in which they are designed to live, and the same can be said of subversive organizations. If a fish has got to be destroyed it can be attacked directly by rod or net, providing it is in the sort of position which gives these methods a chance of success. But if rod and net cannot succeed by themselves it may be necessary to do something to the water which will force the fish into a position where it can be caught. Conceivably it might be necessary to kill the fish by polluting the water, but this is unlikely to be a desirable course of action.[41]

The indirect approach of defeating an insurgency by focusing on dividing the people from the insurgents, removing the support that they require to challenge the government effectively, is rather different from the direct approach and in the long term is usually more effective. Once the local and regular armed units are cut off from their sources of supply, personnel, and, most importantly, intelligence, they wither on the vine or are easily coerced to surrender or destroyed by the security forces with the aid of the local populace. Winning

that support is the critical battle in a counterinsurgency campaign—as Robert Thompson emphasizes in his Five Principles of Counterinsurgency.[42]

1. "The government must have a clear political aim: to establish and maintain a free, independent and united country which is politically and economically stable and viable."
2. "The government must function in accordance with law."
3. "The government must have an overall plan."
4. "The government must give priority to defeating the political subversion, not the guerillas."
5. "In the guerilla phase of an insurgency, a government must secure its base areas first."

Evaluating Counterinsurgency Doctrine and Practice

[These Five Principles of Counterinsurgency] are derived from an analysis of the objectives and techniques of insurgency as posited in this [essay] and are heavily informed by Robert Thompson's Five Principles of Counterinsurgency, themselves drawn from a study of the theory and practice of insurgency.

The first point of comparison, *victory*, may seem to be an unfair one, as the achievement of national objectives depends to a great extent on factors outside the control of the army conducting a counterinsurgency campaign, including geography, strength of the local government and of the insurgents, and degree of popular support for the campaign in the nation supporting the beleaguered government. Nonetheless, the ultimate determinant of the success or failure of counterinsurgency theory and practice is the attainment of national objectives; neglecting the explicit consideration of this characteristic would only relegate it to the realm of unstated but inescapable facts. It is better to confront it directly.

Although the achievement of national goals may not be determined entirely by the army's counterinsurgency doctrine and practice, the army as a powerful bureaucratic actor inevitably affects the definition of national *objectives* for the conflict. Whether these are capable of realization will to a large degree determine whether victory in the campaign is attained—and the army contributes materially to the determination of which tasks it can and cannot do, and how, and why.

As Thompson's Five Principles make clear, the achievement of these goals depends to a great extent on the creation of an effective local government that earns the support of the people; note that Thompson does not even mention the counterinsurgent army or armies. An army that subordinates all military action to the achievement of these political goals facilitates *unity of command* over all the organizations attempting to defeat the insurgency—and makes accomplishment of the objective more likely.

Question Set: Did the Army Develop a Successful Counterinsurgency Doctrine?

1. Victory: Did the doctrine adopted achieve national goals in the conflict?
2. Objective: Did the army contribute to the setting of realistic national goals in the conflict?
3. Unity of Command: Did the military accept subordination to political objectives?
4. Minimum Force: Did the military use the minimum amount of force necessary to accomplish the mission?
5. Mass: Did the military structure itself in an appropriate manner to deal with the threat at hand?

Similarly, Thompson's principles highlight the fact that the counterinsurgency forces must use force in support of the government's effort to establish legitimacy at the expense of the insurgents. Military operations that do not exercise *minimum force* instead diminish the support of the people for the government, which they feel should protect them—not destroy them. In a metaphor proposed by Brigadier Michael Addison, "economy of force" is the principle of war that states that a sledgehammer should not be used to crack a nut because the sledgehammer might be better employed elsewhere. The doctrine of "minimum force" forbids the use of a sledgehammer to protect the nut inside the shell.[43]

Finally, military forces that structure themselves for conventional warfare will not succeed in protecting and hence earning the support of the populace. It is essential that they use the principle of *mass* to protect the critical battleground over which the campaign is being fought: the people.

These five questions have the merit of being based on both the history and the theory of insurgency and guerrilla warfare. They also provide a critical perspective for comparison of learning during the conduct of counterinsurgency campaigns.

NOTES

1. John Ellis, *A Short History of Guerilla Warfare* (London: Ian Allen, 1975), 7. Though now somewhat dated, this remains a good short survey of the topic. The best single source is Robert B. Asprey's *War in the Shadows: The Guerrilla in History* (New York: William Morris, 1994).

2. Thomas E. Griess, ed., *The Wars of Napoleon* (West Point, NY: Avery Publishing Group, 1985), 100–101.

3. A. H. Sollom, "Nowhere Yet Everywhere," in Franklin Mark Osanka, ed., *Modern Guerrilla Warfare: Fighting Communist Guerrilla Movements, 1941–1961* (New York: The Free Press of Glencoe, 1962). The author, a United States Ma-

rine Corps lieutenant colonel, originally published this article in the *Marine Corps Gazette* of June 1958.

4. One good source is Peter Paret's "Clausewitz and the Nineteenth Century," in Michael Howard, ed., *The Theory and Practice of War* (London: Indiana University Press, 1965), 21–41. Perhaps the best book on Clausewitz and his ideas is Michael Howard's *Clausewitz* (Oxford: Oxford University Press, 1983).

5. Carl von Clausewitz, translated by Michael Howard and Peter Paret, *On War* (Princeton, NJ: Princeton University Press, 1984), 89.

6. John Shy, "Jomini," in Peter Paret, ed., *Makers of Modern Strategy from Machiavelli to the Nuclear Age* (Princeton, NJ: Princeton University Press, 1986), 146. Emphasis in original.

7. Shy, "Jomini," 177.

8. Michael Howard, "The Influence of Clausewitz," in Clausewitz, *On War*, 30.

9. Howard, "The Influence of Clausewitz."

10. Bernard Brodie, "The Continuing Relevance of *On War*," in Clausewitz, *On War*, 56.

11. This is the supreme irony of Harry Summer's modestly titled book, *On Strategy: A Critical Analysis of the Vietnam War* (Novato, CA: Presidio, 1982), which uses what Summers calls "Clausewitzian" principles of war to explain that the reason the U.S. Army lost the war in Vietnam is that it was not allowed to annihilate the opponent's force in the field—a clearly Jominian argument. In fact, by focusing on the Jominian concept of destroying the enemy army at all costs, the U.S. Army ignored the one absolute principle of Clausewitz: that war must always be subordinate to the political goals for which it is fought.

12. Clausewitz, *On War*, 479–480.

13. Epigraph from John Shy and Thomas W. Collier, "Revolutionary War," in Paret, *Makers of Modern Strategy*, 838–839.

14. Asprey, *War in the Shadows*, 246.

15. Mao Tse-Tung, translated by Samuel Griffith, *On Guerrilla Warfare* (London: Cassell, 1965), 14.

16. Mao, *On Guerrilla Warfare*, 8.

17. Douglas Blaufarb, *The Counterinsurgency Era: U.S. Doctrine and Performance* (New York: The Free Press, 1977), 3.

18. Mao, *On Guerrilla Warfare*, 16.

19. Asprey, *War in the Shadows*, 249.

20. Dick Wilson, *The Long March 1935: The Epic of Chinese Communism's Survival* (New York: Penguin, 1982).

21. J. A. Harrison, *China Since 1800* (New York: Harcourt Brace & World, 1967), 168, in Asprey, *War in the Shadows*, 252.

22. Chalmers Johnson, *Peasant Nationalism and Communist Power* (Stanford, CA: Stanford University Press, 1962), 5, in Blaufarb, *The Counterinsurgency Era*, 7.

23. Mao Tse-Tung, *Selected Military Writings of Mao Tse-Tung* (Peking: Foreign Language Press, 1966), 260.

24. Mao, *On Guerrilla Warfare*, 66–67.

25. Mao, *Selected Military Writings*, 260.

26. Mao, *Selected Military Writings*, 261.

27. Frank Kitson, *Low Intensity Operations: Subversion, Insurgency and Peacekeeping* (London: Faber & Faber, 1971), 29.

28. John Shy and Thomas W. Collier, "Revolutionary War," in Paret, *Makers of Modern Strategy*, 845. The story of American advice and assistance to Chiang Kai-Shek and the resistance of the Nationalist government to suggestions for

political and military reforms is well told in Barbara Tuchman, *Sand Against the Wind: Stillwell and the American Experience in China, 1911–1945* (London: Futura, 1985).

29. Epigraph from Clausewitz, *On War*, Book VIII, quoted in Howard, *The Theory and Practice of War*, 35.

30. Shy and Collier, "Revolutionary War," 816.

31. A fascinating if horrifying examination of this issue is John Ellis, *The Social History of the Machine Gun* (Baltimore, MD: Johns Hopkins University Press, 1987).

32. Asprey, *War in the Shadows*, 262.

33. For an examination of the modern phenomenon of casualty aversion, see Don M. Snider, John A. Nagl, and Tony Pfaff, *Army Professionalism, the Military Ethic, and Officership in the 21st Century* (Carlisle, PA: U.S. Army War College Strategic Studies Institute, 1999).

34. Robert Taber, *The War of the Flea: A Study of Guerrilla Warfare, Theory and Practice* (New York: Citadel Press, 1965), 131–132.

35. Frederick Wilkins, "Guerrilla Warfare," in Franklin Mark Osanka, ed., *Modern Guerrilla Warfare: Fighting Communist Guerrilla Movements, 1941–1961* (New York: The Free Press of Glencoe, 1962), 14. The author, a retired lieutenant colonel of the United States Army, first published this article in the *U.S. Naval Institute Proceedings* of March 1954.

36. A. Jones, trans., *The History of Gruffydd ap Cynan* (Manchester: Manchester University Press, 1910), 141, in El-

lis, *A Short History of Guerrilla Warfare*, 33. This is both the standard military response to insurgency and the typical response from the population that suffers from a scorched-earth counterinsurgency policy.

37. Gerald of Wales, translated by T. Wright, *The Historical Works of Geraldius Cambriensis* (London: H.G. Bohn, 1863), 511–512 and 517–518, in Ellis, *A Short History of Guerrilla Warfare*, 35.

38. British Army Code No 71596 (Part 2), *Army Field Manual*, Volume V, *Operations Other Than War*, Section B, *Counter Insurgency Operations*, Part 2, *The Conduct of Counter Insurgency Operations*, 2-1 through 2-2.

39. Robert J. O'Neill, *Vietnam Task: The 5th Battalion, Royal Australian Regiment* (Marrickville, Australia: Southwood Press, 1968), 185.

40. Harry Summers, "A War Is a War Is a War Is a War," in Loren B. Thompson, ed., *Low Intensity Conflict: The Pattern of Warfare in the Modern World* (Lexington, MA: Lexington Books, 1989).

41. Frank Kitson, *Low Intensity Operations: Subversion, Insurgency and Peacekeeping* (London: Faber & Faber, 1971), 49.

42. Robert F. Thompson, *Defeating Communist Insurgency: Experiences from Malaya and Vietnam* (London: Chatto & Windus, 1972), 50–60.

43. Brigadier (Ret) Michael Addison, private correspondence with the author, 11 February 1997.

Learning Lessons from Afghanistan

Two Imperatives

HEW STRACHAN

On October 7, 2001, the United States began bombing Taliban communications and air defenses (such as they were). So began a commitment to the security of Afghanistan that continues to this day. Operation ENDURING FREEDOM in Afghanistan was designed to use only a light footprint, leaving the bulk of the fighting to the mujahideen whom the United States had supported in their fight against the Soviet Union. In March 2002, after its quick success in toppling the Taliban, Washington turned its attention to Saddam Hussein. Between 2002 and 2009, Iraq, not Afghanistan, dominated American counsels. Here too initial operations were rewarded with quick success, largely characterized in terms of state-of-the-art conventional warfare. Signs of guerrilla warfare and irregular resistance were dismissed, and it was often junior commanders who detected the changing character of the

war they were fighting. The standard assumption of the late 1980s, shaped by the Cold War, persisted: an army that prepared for operations at scale against a peer enemy could adjust to "low-intensity war" against an enemy lacking in discipline, organization, and sophisticated weaponry.

By 2005, it had become clear the received wisdom was not working, and that its hold was preventing soldiers from fully understanding the sort of conflict in which they were engaged. The experience of Iraq prompted the US Army to reshape its doctrine for what it increasingly described as counterinsurgency campaigns. The Combined Arms Center at Fort Leavenworth began work in earnest in October 2005, when Lieutenant General David Petraeus took over its command after his second tour in Iraq. Petraeus turned to his West Point classmate, Conrad Crane, to oversee the

Hew Strachan, "Learning Lessons from Afghanistan: Two Imperatives," *Parameters* 49, no. 3 (2019): 5–10, published by the US Army War College.

development of new doctrine, or in some respects the recovery of old but neglected knowledge. Crane drew on inputs from both theaters of war, Afghanistan as well as Iraq, and on the US Marine Corps as well as the Army. Field Manual 3-24, also branded as Marine Corps Warfighting Publication 3-33.5, was ready by December 2006.

In 2007, Petraeus was back in Iraq, masterminding the surge. A war that the United States had been losing was turned around, at least for the time being. The success in Iraq in 2007 made counterinsurgency the most obvious lesson learned from the post-9/11 wars, and when the US Army returned its attention to a now much more dangerous situation in Afghanistan, it took the message of counterinsurgency with it. Field Manual 3-24 was itself commercially published, and a raft of books and articles on irregular war both preceded and followed its appearance.

In the United Kingdom, the epiphany was both slower and less dramatic. Britain thought it knew about "small wars" from its experience of imperial conquest and colonial settlement, and about counterinsurgency specifically from the "success" of its post-1945 withdrawal from the empire. That phase of its history ended, comparatively ignominiously, in the withdrawal from Aden in 1967 and with the decision to close British bases east of Suez in the following year. The 30-year conflict in Northern Ireland, which followed almost immediately, began badly: counterinsurgency principles applied in a colonial context had to be rethought for use closer to home. But the lessons of Northern Ireland proved a false friend when its units deployed to Iraq in 2003. Many officers had only seen the tail end of a campaign, which by then they were winning: conditions were much more favorable in the 1990s than they had been in the 1970s, and by then the army had the upper hand in intelligence, tactical know-how, and public support.

Basra was in every way a tougher operating environment than Belfast, the troop-to-population ratio was much less favorable, and language, religion, and culture all presented unfamiliar challenges. By 2006, humiliated in southern Iraq and confronting fierce fighting in southern Afghanistan, the British Army began to realize the need to revisit its background in counterinsurgency. However, it did so reluctantly and late. Only in October 2009 did the British Army publish an updated doctrine, and in the same year, the British Ministry of Defense produced Joint Doctrine Publication 3-40, on stabilization operations.

During the crisis years of the campaigns in Iraq and Afghanistan, especially 2006 to 2009, the soldiers of American and British armies, as they convened conferences and workshops that addressed these themes, referred with regret to their own absentmindedness and that of their predecessors. After the Vietnam War, the US Army had opted not to learn its lessons, but to treat the experience as an aberration, or so the prevailing narrative ran. Its doctrinal response, Field Manual 100-5, *Operations*, particularly in its 1982 edition, focused on the conventional level of war, and prepared American soldiers to defend the inner German border against the Soviet Union. The British narrative was not dissimilar. Those units who fought in Northern Ireland were "double-hatted," their principal strategic function being, as for their American allies, the defense of Western Europe against the Soviet Union.

In both cases, preparation for war against a peer competitor took priority over counterinsurgency. Economies of scale demanded flexibility. That seemed to be a reasonable expectation of two armies that were now regular and professional. If they could do the first, and implicitly harder, task, then—so the wisdom ran—they would be capable of dropping down a rung, to do the "lesser" work of small unit patrols, hearts and minds, and stabilization. The slowness of both armies' adaptation after 2002, five years for the Americans and seven for the British (longer than either of their individual experiences of the Second World War), suggested those assumptions were wrong. An army is a big beast, its training protocols are reinforced by its hierarchy, and it struggles to adapt quickly from one sort of war to another. For those thinking about lessons learned from 2005 to 2009, the conclusion was simple: do not do after these wars what they had done in the 1980s. They mocked the naivety of their predecessors of a quarter of a century before for their readiness to see war in only one dimension. Too much recent real war had proved "asymmetric" for conventional war to be the dominant paradigm, however much the latter might shape doctrine and theory. Experience was a more profound lesson, and their generation, that of the veterans of Al Anbar or Helmand, could not possibly forget that as those of the 1980s had done.

But many of them have forgotten, or at least they have to an extent that would surprise those reflecting on these issues a decade ago. In 2019, the debate is once again dominated by peer competitors (China for the United States and Russia for its European allies), counterinsurgency has dropped out of fashion, and some well-informed commentators have persuasively argued that its principles have been overstated. A military tendency to look not back, but forward, to look to the next war not to be captured by the last, has been reinforced by policy.

In 2009, Barack Obama embraced a strategy that used airpower (including drones) in conjunction with special forces and local proxies, rather than "boots on the ground." Armies conducting the counterinsurgency campaigns of the early twenty-first century incurred casualties, which made overseas interventions unpopular. So democratically accountable politicians have sought other ways to wage war. The new strategy, not unlike the old, has contained the problem for the time being. But it is too early to say whether it will produce lasting results. Soldiers argue presence on the ground, and in sufficient numbers to have effect, is the only way to implement a satisfactory and stable outcome. Moreover, the employment of drones and proxies raises legal, ethical, and political issues, which may not in the long run be compatible with the norms of democratic states.

So the North Atlantic Treaty Organization (NATO) and America's wider circle of allies are at an inflection point where it ill behooves them not to reflect on the lessons from Afghanistan and to incorporate them into their thinking for the future. This does not mean that wars like those fought in Afghanistan are necessarily a model for what will happen again. History does not repeat itself, but it certainly deepens understanding. For a start, allied forces are still in the country, although most of their publics seem unaware of the fact. Moreover, it would be rash to suggest that NATO is not going to find itself fighting another counterinsurgency in, say, the next 25 years. Lessons may be negative (that of Vietnam: "we certainly will not do that again") as much as positive (that of Malaya: "this is a model for how to win the support of the local population"). The absence of debate and discussion is the worst possible outcome. It can leave preconceptions unchallenged, and it throws away the wisdom garnered through hard work, suffering, and loss.

Neither the United States nor Britain has gone through the process of learning lessons from Afghanistan on a scale commensurate with the effort put into the war. In Washington, the political will has not been there, and in the Army, the views on counterinsurgency and its principal exponents have become too politicized, and in some respects personalized, for an avowedly apolitical army to collate them effectively. Thanks not least to the persistence of Raymond T. Odierno when, as the Army's Chief of Staff, a history of the US Army's role in the Iraq War was initiated. It provides a potentially rich foundation for the learning of lessons, but whether it will do so is yet to be seen. A similar project on Afghanistan will require a similar drive from the top.

Britain too has paid more attention to Iraq than Afghanistan. The British Army sidelined two internal studies on Iraq, before Prime Minister Gordon Brown commissioned a government enquiry on the war in 2009. Since the Chilcot report was published in 2016, the Ministry of Defense has tackled the lessons to be learned from with commendable seriousness. However, the delays and costs incurred by the inquiry have removed any impetus for something similar on Afghanistan. Unlike the United States, Britain has lost the appetite for official histories: there is no enthusiasm for one on Operation BANNER, the campaign in Northern Ireland, perhaps itself a reason for British officers applying the wrong lessons in Iraq. Nor has the Army revisited its counterinsurgency doctrine since 2009, thus forfeiting the opportunity to embody the lessons from the severe fighting in Helmand in 2009–13. The revision of Joint Doctrine Publication 3-40 on stabilization operations, begun in the immediate aftermath of Libya in 2011, has floundered.

The United States and Britain possess the two NATO armies with the clearest sense of continuity in counterinsurgency operations, however discontinuous their attention to the subject has been in practice. Afghanistan, unlike Iraq, was an alliance undertaking. Common approaches to the conduct of operations, as well as agreed and standardized procedures, are the bedrock of NATO cohesion. Its members' armed forces speak to each other in terms that they all understand. Policy differences provide volatility, but they are offset by military commonalities.

Counterinsurgency doctrine is a major exception to this generalization: NATO collectively does not have one, nor do most of its individual members. For the states of continental Europe, irregular and guerrilla warfare is linked historically to major war in ways that do not apply to Britain and the United States, who are both secured by the natural defenses provided by the sea. Such forms of war were the only option left to the states that were overrun and then occupied by Germany between 1940 and 1942. And the same might have applied during the Cold War if the Soviet Union had launched an invasion. Partisan war was an option to be exercised at home because conventional war was no longer possible: it was politically destabilizing and its conduct was ruthless. It bore little relationship to the idealized if somewhat fanciful ideas of counterinsurgency in the Anglophone world, applied at a distance in wars that could be characterized as "limited." For America's and Britain's partners in Afghanistan, overseas operations were associated with peacekeeping and policing, and were conducted under a resolution of the United Nations Security Council.

As the United States and the United Kingdom reembraced and rethought their counterinsurgency doctrines, they opened a divide between themselves and their European allies, which they struggled to comprehend. They could not understand why the Germans, Norwegians, or Poles did not also develop and adopt comparable solutions. In particular, they failed to understand how the other NATO member with a clear inheritance in counterinsurgency, France, interpreted the war in Afghanistan. France, like Britain, had conquered and pacified an empire in the nineteenth century, and then had lost it after 1945—in fighting that proved far more politically divisive and existentially defining than had Britain's campaigns in Malaya, Kenya, or Cyprus. Successful counterinsurgency itself carried revolutionary implications for France: it had done so after 1792 and 1870 within metropolitan France, and it redivided the "nation in arms," shattered in 1940, in Indochina and Algeria in the 1950s. Americans understood this experience through an atypical lens, David Galula's report for RAND, *Pacification in Algeria, 1956–58*, which became a core text at the operational level but was not set in its political context: the end of France's Fourth Republic and the establishment of the Fifth Republic.

Galula was not translated into French until 2009. Vincent Desportes, then responsible for defense doctrine, set out to link France's contribution to NATO in Afghanistan by drawing the attention of its soldiers to their colonial inheritance, citing the examples of Joseph-Simon Gallieni in Indochina and Madagascar and Louis-Hubert-Gonzalve Lyautey in Morocco. In reality, he might have done better to go even further back, to Thomas-Robert Bugeaud, Duke d'Isly in Algeria. The pattern of colonial conquest that he promoted put battle at its heart (as—it is worth pointing out—did Charles Callwell in his textbook, *Small Wars*, adopted by the British Army in 1896), not winning over the local population by "hearts and minds." Afghanistan was France's first major NATO operation following its decision to rejoin the military alliance, and so it saw it less as a commitment to a "small war" than as its reentry to the big league. As subsequent operations in Mali and elsewhere have shown, students of the American and British armies should not see France's approach to counterinsurgency and irregular war as more of the same or as corroboration of what they do.

Learning lessons from Afghanistan, therefore, has two imperatives. The first is that of the needs of coalition warfare. At its peak over 50 states contributed to the war in Afghanistan, making this probably the most impressive alliance effort in military history. That achievement has been overshadowed by the tokenism of many of the contingents sent into theater, by national caveats surrounding their employment, and by the part played by domestic politics in the timing of their withdrawals. The focus on these dysfunctionalities has been reinforced by Washington's constant reprimand, voiced as much by the Obama administration as by that of Donald Trump, that NATO member states are failing to contribute two percent of their gross domestic product to defense. The United States was reluctant to accept the support of its allies in the direct aftermath of 9/11, when NATO immediately invoked Article 5, and has been reluctant to give thanks for their readiness to serve outside NATO's core area, in a country in which none of them had a direct national interest, in war waged on behalf of the United States. If the United States anticipates fighting future wars with allies, it needs NATO collectively as well as individually to draw lessons from Afghanistan, and to do so in ways that reflect the full range of what the member states experienced.

The second imperative follows from the first. This search for lessons must not just be in pursuit of commonalities. Such an exercise is in danger of looking at and recognizing the experience of others through the prism of the United States, and so ignoring differences—like that of France—which may themselves be instructive. Just because the US Army may deem something not to have been "invented here" does not meant that it is therefore unworthy of consideration. After all, that too-ready dismissal of others' experiences and of their possible applicability was a major source of exactly the problems the US Army confronted from 2002 to 2004.

The challenge inherent in that statement should not be exaggerated. The overwhelming conclusion [drawn has been] the power the United States exercises over its allies.

The Regularity of Irregular War
Defining Victory in Persistently Engaged Wars

DAVID SACKO

In the conduct of modern Irregular Warfare (IW), the United States should take care not to conflate traditional conceptions of victory with the deceptively complex IW successful endings. This essay integrates insights from the IW literature and argues that victory in IW is predicated on the larger effort of maintaining a liberal world order, and that IW victory occurs only once the IW combatants come to value that system. This is a kind of victory that is achievable only through an approach to IW that is similar what US Cyber Command (USCYBERCOM) calls "Persistent Engagement." In the context of IW, Persistent Engagement entails a whole-of-government approach that provides constant pressure on malign non-state groups while simultaneously seeking to build the legitimacy of the host nation's government and win the support and trust of the population.

War and Irregular War

Borrowing heavily from Carl Von Clausewitz,[1] the Department of Defense (DoD) defines war as "socially sanctioned violence to achieve a political purpose."[2] Contingency operations, or "small wars," then, are those specific military actions against a US enemy military force (or operations during a national emergency declared by the president or Congress) that today truly constitute war.[3] The US military broadly understands such small wars as irregular conflict, distinguishing between two fundamental warfare types—traditional and irregular wars, each with different strategic objectives. Traditional war is a violent contest for control between states to compel an enemy to change politically. As such, victory normally means defeating an enemy's military forces, annihilating an adversary's war-making facility, and holding enemy territory by offensive, defensive, and stability operations orchestrated against enemy centers of gravity. Traditional warfare typically involves military operations against enemies engaging conventional and special operations forces (SOF) in the land, sea, air, space, and cyber domains. Traditional interstate war is a rare event (and constitutionally declared war by the United States is an extremely rare event). While US contingency operations in Iraq and Afghanistan early on had traditional characteristics, very quickly these conflicts became "untraditional," or in DoD parlance, "irregular."

DoD defines IW as a violent struggle between state and non-state actors for legitimacy and influence over the nation, rather than the state.[4] This type of warfare is irregular only in the sense to emphasize that the violent struggle is with a non-state actor rather than the traditional state opponent. Formally, DoD defines five principle IW operational modalities: counterterrorism (CT), unconventional warfare (UW), foreign internal defense (FID), counterinsurgency (COIN), and stability operations (SO).[5] Warfare, in a unified whole, incorporates both traditional and irregular aspects. For example, the US-Panama historical relationship had periods of what qualified as irregular war only to be punctuated by the traditional war in 1989 before returning to successful low-intensity irregular conflict. As Max Boot's *Invisible Armies*, a guerilla warfare history, points out, non-state armed groups have asymmetrically opposed larger conventionally effective state actors since the Mesopotamians asserted empire over other nations four millennia ago.[6] Clausewitz coined the term "small war" (now commonly referred to as guerilla warfare),[7] a term embraced by C. E. Callwell,[8] Mao Tse-Tung,[9] and the US Marine Corps;[10] David Galula,[11] John Nagl,[12] and David Kilcullen[13] refine the concept of one particular variant of small war, insurgency. Terminologically, the broadest manifestation of

the small war concept is, then, IW, or militarized conflict in which one combatant is a non-state armed group that applies violence, or the threat of violence, to achieve a political aim.

Understanding Victory for Irregular Warfare

Ultimately, the United States' strategic objective in IW is to affect people's thinking who are living within a state, rather than that state's external political and security interests and national values. In IW, a less powerful and capable non-state rival attempts to upset or nullify the military capabilities and benefits of the more powerful military, the US military, to achieve opposed political goals.[14] This rival employs asymmetric military capabilities to contest US power, influence, and will to increase its own legitimacy and influence over the relevant populations. For example, in Iraq and Afghanistan, the initial state opponent quickly succumbed but elements of that Baathist and Iraqi Shia or Taliban regime reorganized and reconfigured as insurgent, militia, terrorist, and criminal groups, with each modality petitioning the people of Iraq and Afghanistan for different modes of support and then thereby engaging the United States in different modes of IW.

IW victory, therefore, is not a question of a successful conventional military operation, but rather of a whole-of-government approach in which the military instrument of power sets conditions for victory within the opponent's political, military, economic, social, information, and infrastructure critical vulnerabilities. Simply put, victory in IW begins with the establishment and consolidation of a capable political regime within the host nation that is friendly, or at least potentially amiable, to US interests. Victory occurs when the transfer of operational capacity from the United States—which initially is the primary military option to degrade and destroy non-state violent opposition—to the friendly host nation regime that rises in legitimacy with the local populous. Victory does not necessarily entail the destruction of the enemy. Rather, victory in IW is dependent on creation of something new: the populous believes in the friendly regime's right to rule. As joint doctrine describes, "The goal is to enhance a local partner's legitimacy and influence over a population by addressing the causes of conflict and building the partner's capacity to provide security, good governance, and economic development."[15]

As compared to victory in a traditional war—the military accomplishing what Clausewitz terms the culminating point of victory—IW victory is the long, evolutionary influence of a critical mass of the population. Ultimately, both are aimed to achieve a political objective, but IW is fundamentally focused on the people rather than the elites and the regime. DoD's "Continuum of Operations" scheme illustrates this dual focus.

Traditional war operational plans (OPLANs) focus on reacting to the actions of state actors while IW operations focus on popular attitudes and reactions. DoD's primary model for developing OPLANs has six phases: Phase 0 (Shape), Phase I (Deter), Phase II (Seize the Initiative), Phase III (Dominate), Phase IV (Stabilize), and Phase V (Enable Civil Authority). Together, these imply conflict evolution through the culminating phase (Phase III) of major combat operations and a "post-conflict" period of stabilization and transition.[16] If conducted successfully, Phase 0, shaping the environment, will preclude the necessity for kinetic IW modes. This phase involves those joint interagency and multinational activities conducted on a routine basis to assure or solidify friendly relationships and alliances and/or deter potential adversaries. Promotion of the legitimacy of the state and its friendly relations with the United States is the fundamental goal. Phase IV and Phase V are the active IW modes. Phase IV's priority, stabilizing the environment, involves the reconstitution of infrastructure and the restoration of services. This phase concludes with the transfer of regional authority to a legitimate civil entity. In Phase V, legitimate civil authorities are enabled in their efforts to provide essential services to the populace. These activities include required coordination activities by US military forces with multinational, interagency, and nongovernmental organizations while promoting a favorable attitude to US policy.

Applying Persistent Engagement to Irregular Warfare

Irregular war's many phases are already a regular part of US defense policy, particularly in the conduct of the shaping operation necessary in Phase 0. Though not always kinetic, IW may involve direct threat to US personnel. In a whole-of-government approach, the United States needs to be always shaping operations (Phase 0), enabling stabilization (Phase IV) and enabling civil authority (Phase V). Related to this mindset is US-CYBERCOM's new Persistent Engagement doctrine.

Traditional US defense strategies, such as deterrence or compellence, assume a rational state opponent and a time horizon allowing deliberative action. For instance, in the face of a Soviet invasion of Afghanistan, the National Security Council met and proposed options to President Jimmy Carter, and then Carter ordered economic sanctions in restricting wheat sales to the Soviets and diplomatic actions in issuing a statement at the United Nations and boycotting the 1980 Moscow Olympics, in addition to military signaling by

putting forces on alert. Cyber (and IW) threats do not behave so linearly. Given the knowledge that states and bad cyber actors engage the US cybersphere in real time, an effective cyber strategy needs to be continuous and immediately reactive. Persistent Engagement seeks to counter the type of consistent daily malicious cyber activity not involving the type of armed threat necessitating a NSC meeting. To be effective, this doctrine must integrate informed daily rules of engagement that understand the threat and that it cannot be vanquished easily and that act to expose adversary intentions, capabilities, and vulnerabilities to counterattack and diminish that threat's capabilities. In essence, the new paradigm of persistence recognizes interconnectivity and proposes to punish (or reward) proactively and proportionally rather than reactively and aggressively—it recognizes that we are in a world of perpetual, but low-level, conflict. These points analogize to IW exactly. IW's primary goal is to influence foreign national support for US goals in the face of an alternative enemy narrative.

Countering this narrative requires what Persistent Engagement calls subtle, nuanced, and daily consistent competition. Both are whole-of-government approaches, and successful implementation for both requires the United States to do five things: (1) provide and maintain strong and sustained military and civilian leadership invested in proactive engagement; (2) field an organized, trained, and equipped force; (3) clearly signal to adversaries; (4) build the trust of international and domestic partners; and (5) develop and consistently work for a robust interagency process.[17] As posed, IW is the domain of several government agencies beginning with the US military and Joint Special Operations Command, the US State Department, and the US Agency for International Development, along with a myriad of other government agencies as well as international and local partners. There is no unifying interagency doctrine clearly identifying IW means and ends, nor is there consensus on the requirements for the type of personnel needed to field a long-term IW force.

IW phases are not as clear as traditional war phases for three reasons. First, IW campaigns are not small versions of traditional wars. A Persistent Engagement approach recognizes that IW is qualitatively different in that weaker actors exploit the vulnerabilities of the stronger actor by stretching the conflict over both time and space, which, in turn, requires a more reactive doctrine on the part of the stronger actor. While the quick and decisive war favors the strong, weak actors win an irregular war by slowly bleeding the stronger actor, exposing it as an illegitimate foreign force, and constantly moving back the moment of victory. Traditional war-planning phases are at best incongruent with IW and, more often, misleadingly dangerous. Though they may overlap, they are distinct, violent political processes, and, IW is much more common, whether it is violent or nonviolent in nature.

Second, traditional military-centered approaches to deterring, dominating, and pacifying adversaries prove to be only marginally successful in population-centric irregular conflicts. Again, Persistent Engagement's emphasis on countering attacks immediately at their origins or preventing the attack from ever occurring is a different mode. As John Nagl argues, pacifying states frequently use the military to punish in the hopes of deterring future insurrection.[18] However, the results are predictable. Throughout history, we see that weak actors are quick to recognize IW tactics as a viable counter to strong traditional militaries and strategies based on force-on-force benefits.[19] Consequently, pacification efforts may bring short-term relief, but they further legitimize the very raison d'être of the insurgency.

Third, the successful irregular conflict outcome will likely be determined by the success of Phase 0 and Phase I operations to properly shape, or win over, nonstate armed groups from directly opposing US interests. One of Persistent Engagement's crucial but difficult implementation requirements is building international as well as local partner trust. Shaping operations in IW need to be designed to positively affect the targeted population's perceptions of the cooperative local government first and the United States only in tertiary terms.[20] Such shaping operations may occur over several years, if not decades.

Persistent Engagement and US Defense Strategy

In IW, victory is not accomplished simply with the destruction of the enemy regime. The secondary, but perhaps more daunting task, lies in either convincing the local population to stop fighting or meeting irregular warfare's minimum threshold of creating regimes friendly to US interests—thus, leading to the question, what is an agreeable US interest? Moreover, why would the United States wish to support such ubiquitous operations that carry the high potential to produce enormous casualties and cost immense national wealth? In large part, the answer is derived from a larger US strategic objective.

During the Cold War, the United States integrated foreign and defense policy to contain the Soviet Union as the United States built global institutions protecting international commerce, liberal political institutions, and human rights. Premised on maintaining friendly regimes, US policy buttressed conventional (and strategic) deterrence (Phase I) with active irregular conflict support in the form of robust counterinsurgency, CT, UW, FID, and SO.

After 1991, President George H. W. Bush's "New World Order" attempted to consolidate the three points of democratization, marketization, and human rights throughout the international system. There were a few rogue conventional threats (notably Saddam Hussein's Baathist Iraq), but the primary impetus was to shape domestic regimes to be friendly to these US priorities. The United States sought to promote strong CT operations in response to an international Hezbollah, early al Qaeda operations, the Revolutionary Armed Forces of Colombia (FARC), and a host of other threats. This led to UW operations, stalwart FID, and a special operations footprint primarily in the developing world. Any public US casualties, however, were greeted with a great deal of popular skepticism, such as the eighteen military deaths and 84 casualties in Somalia (ostensibly involving COIN/special operations modes of IW) at the onset of the Clinton administration.

After 9/11, the United States defined its interests and stability in very different terms. The priority was to disrupt adversaries before they could strike at vital US interests, the homeland, and the international economy. Since the Global War on Terror (GWOT) was *fundamentally* an irregular one that featured conventional operations against Afghanistan and then Iraq for only brief periods, IW modes of CT, COIN, UW, FID, and SO predominated from 2001 through today. The primary operators, today, for the kinetic modes of IW are SOF. SOF are "units trained to operate in small teams, behind enemy lines, utilizing a wide range of organizational resources and special capabilities that are employed to provide innovative solutions to problematic circumstances."[21] Their mission set includes CT, COIN, counter–weapons of mass destruction (WMD), special reconnaissance, and direct action, along with the indirect (reliant on partner actor) UW, information operations (IO), military information support operations (MISO), psychological operations (PsyOps), civil affairs assistance (CA), security force assistance (SFA), and FID.

It is in this spirit, that Austin Long's "Limits of Special Operations Forces" (chapter 9) is particularly relevant. Long breaks down the utility of SOF and argues that although SOF possess a hard-earned subject-matter expertise and comparative advantage to project discrete and discriminant force for counterterrorism and counterintelligence, their actions are not appropriate for all modalities of IW. As Long demonstrates, SOF's high-risk missions can achieve tactical and operational successes, but these accomplishments do not achieve decisive strategic success without the strategic military, economic, or diplomatic support that comes from a whole-of-government approach.[22] Unfortunately, this has been lost on the United States during operations in Afghanistan: the United States chases tactical victories without linking the IW to the larger global strategic objective. Consider the United States' most recent attempt to extricate itself from Afghanistan.

Lessons from Afghanistan

In 2001, the United States launched a traditional war to compel the Taliban-controlled Afghanistan government to cease support for al Qaeda. By early 2002, the Taliban's main military forces were defeated and their war-making capability was annihilated, and the US military initiated stability operations in the newly held territory. Since 2003, the Taliban (with the Haqqani Network, Hezb-e-Islami Gulbuddin, among others) has launched an insurgency against the US coalitional partner, the Government of the Islamic Republic of Afghanistan (GIRoA). This insurgency features terrorist and criminal modes of fighting and has elicited a range of US responses, including traditional war operations featuring movements of large numbers of troops with close air combat support. After nearly twenty years, the consequences have been tragic: preservation and support for Phase IV (Stabilize) and Phase V (Enable Civil Authority) are proving ephemeral and could easily slip to Phase III (Dominate) or even Phase I (Shape) with lightning speed. Throughout operation ENDURING FREEDOM and its follow-on operation FREEDOM'S SENTINEL, establishing effective Afghan governance was a consistent line of effort. US and coalition forces sought primarily to enable the GIRoA to exercise sovereignty and ultimately negotiate with the Taliban for a peace that removed support for any international terror group.

After nineteen frustrating years, on February 29, 2020, the United States signed a conditional peace agreement with the Taliban. Ambassador Zalmay Khalilzad, the Special Representative for Afghanistan Reconciliation (SRAR), engaged in talks with the Taliban to achieve an agreement to safeguard the US homeland and reduce the number of US forces deployed in Afghanistan. As the agreed-upon joint declaration stated, any comprehensive peace agreement will be made up of four interconnected parts: (1) counterterrorism assurances; (2) troop withdrawal; (3) intra-Afghan negotiations that lead to a political settlement; and, (4) a comprehensive and permanent ceasefire.[23]

As of May 2020, the GIRoA and the Taliban have been at an impasse to facilitate prisoner exchange, impeding the first step in intra-Afghan negotiations. Still, US military troop levels rapidly declined from approximately 12,000–13,000 at the start of 2020 to an estimated 8,600 by mid-July 2020.[24] Also complicating matters, GIRoA recently overcame an internal political impasse between President Ashraf Ghani and First Vice President Abdullah Abdullah with Abdullah finally

recognizing Ghani's presidency in May in exchange for Abdullah heading the peace process and naming 50 percent of GIRoA cabinet posts. At the same time, the Taliban are pushing the limits of the agreement brokered between them and the United States.

As the US military engages less in direct action forms of IW (COIN and UW) and facilitates more indirect IW modes intended to consolidate GIRoA's legitimacy, a well-defined multinational, whole-of-government, Persistent Engagement approach is needed. In the meantime, negotiations have stalled. This should surprise no one. The conditional peace agreement was largely a product of direct-action tactical victories. SOF direct-action is important but it is not transformative. Rather, a negotiated peace with counterterror assurances keeping the US homeland safe will be possible only when the aims of the otherwise would-be insurgents align with US global objectives. When the inevitable political setbacks occur as part of the push and pull of the diplomatic process, the United States ought to reject the temptation of returning to an SOF direction action modality; SOF are incredibly effective for their purpose, but they, as Long shows, are strategically limited.

Persistent Engagement and Stability of the International System

Following the dissolution of the Soviet Union in 1991, the "West," the United States, and the other economically developed consolidated democracies attempted to extend the institutions that had served them so well—the peaceful resolution of disputes; liberal economic development; recognition of basic individual human integrity and political rights—to the former-Soviet sphere of influence, and through the rest of the world, thus bringing the so-called end of history.[25] The states that emerged from the Soviet European and Asian political community separately began to integrate Western political, economic, and cultural institutions into their newly reformed countries as these states attempted to integrate into the institutions, norms, and regimes articulated by the system leader, the hegemon, the United States.

Hegemonic Stability theory is attributed principally to the work of Robert Gilpin (see chapter 4), who asserts that hegemonic power is necessary to structure the international system, primarily for its own advantage but also to the advantage for most and, very commonly, for all in the system.[26] The hegemonic state has symbolic, economic, and military capabilities that can be used to entice or compel others to accept its leadership. The benefits derived by the hegemon are not necessarily what the system requires in terms of generalized benefits—it is frequently coercive but sometimes may appear munificent. A hegemonic state must also fulfill a functionally distinct security-related role that stabilizes international economic and politico-military relations.

This role is perhaps the most fundamental task associated with hegemonic governance. The hegemon creates a set of international interactions—a system—whereby its interests are maximized. The international system is specifically designed to advance the hegemon's own interest by creating international social, political, and economic arrangements.

Returning to the question of IW, the United States needs clearer doctrine and grand strategy to communicate the means and ends for IW to both those who execute these policies and the American people. Persistent Engagement gives the United States a narrative to integrate IW modalities (CT, UW, FID, COIN, and SO) to proactively maintain US equities in the international system. Persistent Engagement seeks a more integrated military and civilian leadership with a robust interagency process devoted to engaging threats to friendly regimes at the most proximate level with a capable, clearly intentioned IW force that fundamentally involves international and domestic partners in efforts to ultimately increase security and prosperity throughout the international system.

John Nagl's "The Hard Lesson of Insurgency" (chapter 9) points to the maintenance of the support of a broad swath of the operative population in any irregular campaign contesting or supporting state legitimacy as the primary and essential condition for victory. Nagl evokes Clausewitz's "fascinating trinity" of the people, army, and government and Clausewitz's view that just as nationalism serves as the basis for an effective army, nationalism (or subnationalism) may serve to resist the occupation and devour the rudiments of the enemy's capabilities.[27]

Clausewitz was speaking about resisting an occupation in guerilla war. Mao's revolutionary war theory would later incorporate the relevance of the masses in fomenting internal regime change, even revolution with Mao's inclusion of the triune: people, army, and government. Following the decline of the nation-state, the rise of nationalism, and the decline of imperial powers, Nagl reminds us of Mao's lessons, "the richest source of power to wage war lies in the masses of the people."[28] However, the people are useless if they don't believe in the cause or in maintaining the legitimacy of the state.

Persistent Engagement's IW focus is non-state armed groups as compared to cyberspace's sub-state actors. David Kilcullen's theory of competitive control follows from Nagl's deduction that the people, or the nation, are the key Clausewitzian "center of gravity" for IW.[29] According to Kilcullen, the armed group that best establishes "a normative system for resilient, full-spectrum control over violence, economic activity, and

human security[30]" is most likely to prevail in IW, a process that today is growing increasingly nuanced and complicated. Complicating factors, for Kilcullen, include (1) the proliferation of portable and effective killing machines; (2) the ubiquity of media and communication technology to spread different narratives—even fake news; (3) the growing disinclination of national publics to accept casualties, which has made for a more risk-adverse battlespace; and (4) the increase of urbanization. Urbanization's inexorable increase (10 percent in 1908, 50 percent in 2008, and 67 percent projected in 2050) underscores the rising complexity of the other IW ingredients,[31] leading to multidimensional non-state armed groups operating in a combination of cyber, sea, air, land, and space domains. "Competitive Control" meets "Persistent Engagement" on the key point that once again, it is the people, human security, who drive any such conflict-management system.

Conclusion

A key question of this essay is: What is the purpose of the use of force? It further asks, how should American defense policy be arrayed to "win" conflicts in the twenty-first century? To the extent that the United States seeks to maintain the US-led liberal system and exercise Persistent Engagement as articulated here, current US military contingency operations and other less kinetic modes of IW will continue. If the United States' "fascinating trinity" (government, military, and people) can accept the costs to further the stability of the international system, a longer peace is possible. For example, consider the fact that the US policy toward Korea has been a success even though it required resolve, commitment, and, most of all, patience. The traditional mode of war ended in 1953, yet US operations in the Republic of Korea (ROK) have incurred military casualties and required national wealth. In return, ROK has been secure and free (even if under the shadow of the Democratic People's Republic of Korea's regular threats), Northeast Asia has been stable for trade, Japan has not succumbed to a regional security dilemma, and the US military has not been forced into a long-term military engagement since 1953.

That type of massive cost has already been partly paid in Afghanistan. Continuing operations to oversee the destruction of ISIS, the protection of the nascent democratic (if struggling) Kabul regime, and a ceasefire with the Taliban will require high levels of resolve, commitment, and patience. The United States can demobilize and fully withdraw militarily when the political process has a chance to work. If the United States withdraws, it risks incentivizing ISIS in the short-term and undercutting the liberal world order in the long-term risks. Were the United States to immediately cease operations in Afghanistan, Iraq, North Africa, and everywhere else its representatives are at risk—shrink its footprint in the world—it would risk a type of leaderless systemic multipolarity not seen since the end of World War I.

USCYBERCOM's paradigm of Persistent Engagement illustrates a new way of thinking that considers the interconnectedness of the world and how the United States might affect change at a quickly evolving level. The United States should not be focused only on deterrence (punishment, denial, anti-access, or otherwise); rather it should more proactively, though not necessarily aggressively, punish or reward, not aggressively in accord with the threshold of US interests. Perpetual peace in the broadest sense is not at hand. However, to the extent that the United States recognizes the reality of forever war, or perpetual conflict, such low-level conflict—even if continuous—can be managed and minimized, provided the United States receives support from the American people.

Domestically, US policy-makers have not consistently communicated such a strategic vision to the American people. Kilcullen and Nagl emphasize the key role of popular support in foreign contexts; this point also plays domestically. Economically, we failed to teach free-trade benefits to the American public and then ameliorate the short-term dislocations occasionally (but predictably) resulting from free-trade regimes. Such is the case with the political aspects of the American-led liberal international system. There will be challenging situations, loss of life, and long-term expensive operations as a result of persistent engagement of US forces, but these challenges are nothing in comparison to the alternative of withdrawing and loosening the forces of chaos and anarchy in international politics.

Traditionally, wars were fought to some conclusion, be it a ceasefire with clearly identified conditions (Korean Conflict, Desert Storm, Yom Kippur War, and so on) or total victory and occupation (World War II). Wars of the twenty-first century, however, are not likely to be total wars or even "limited wars," as in the case of Korea and Vietnam, but rather perpetual wars of transformation or IW. We should not continue to use the concepts of victory created in those earlier eras to define "success" (not victory) when they no longer apply. This essay calls for the United States to incorporate concepts of Persistent Engagement to an asymmetric non-state opponent to positively affect friendly regimes as mal-actors seek control of the media, the economy, key administrative targets, military loyalty, and overall regime legitimacy.

This solution is very hard for the United States to accomplish. At this point, Persistent Engagement runs almost counter to the US political nature. A long-term effort to shape another nation's values and outlooks is not achieved with the "shock and awe," or overwhelming, use of force, that the United States employs in tra-ditional war to achieve a clear Clausewitzian culminating point of victory. Victory is farther over the horizon. Nagl reminds us of T. E. Lawrence's dictum that counterinsurgency victory is tantamount to "eating soup with a knife" (slow and messy); so, too, also are the terms of IW's broader strategic victory.

NOTES

1. Carl von Clausewitz, *On War*, ed. and trans. Michael Howard and Peter Paret (New York: Alfred A. Knopf, 1993).

2. Office of the Chairman of the Joint Chiefs of Staff, "JP 1, Doctrine for the Armed Forces of the United States," July 12, 2017.

3. Title 10—Armed Forces of 2010, 10 U.S.C. § 101 (2010).

4. Office of the Chairman of the Joint Chiefs of Staff, "Irregular Warfare: Countering Irregular Threats Joint Operating Concept," May 17, 2010.

5. Office of the Chairman of the Joint Chiefs of Staff, "Irregular Warfare."

6. Max Boot, *Invisible Armies* (London: W. W. Norton, 2014).

7. Clausewitz, *On War*.

8. Charles Edward Callwell, *Small Wars: Their Principles and Practice* (Lincoln, NE: Book Jungle, 2009).

9. Mao Zedong, *On Guerilla Warfare* (New York: Classic House Books, 2009).

10. US Marine Corps, *Small Wars Manual* (Washington, DC: Headquarters, US Marine Corps, 1990).

11. David Galula, *Counterinsurgency Warfare: Theory and Practice* (New Delhi: Pentagon Press; Praeger Security International, 2010).

12. John A. Nagl, *Learning to Eat Soup with a Knife: Counterinsurgency Lessons from Malaya and Vietnam* (Chicago: University of Chicago Press, 2009).

13. David Kilcullen, *Counterinsurgency* (Oxford: Oxford University Press, 2010).

14. Office of the Chairman of the Joint Chiefs of Staff, "JP 1, Doctrine for the Armed Forces of the United States," 25 March 2013.

15. Office of the Chairman of the Joint Chiefs of Staff, "Irregular Warfare."

16. Office of the Chairman of the Joint Chiefs of Staff, "Irregular Warfare."

17. Jason Healey and Stuart Caudill, "Success of Persistent Engagement in Cyberspace," *Strategic Studies Quarterly* 14, no. 1 (2020): 9–15.

18. Nagl, *Learning to Eat Soup with a Knife*.

19. US Department of the Air Force and Curtis E. LeMay Center for Doctrine Development and Education, "Irregular Warfare," July 12, 2016.

20. US Department of the Air Force and Curtis E. LeMay Center for Doctrine Development and Education, "Irregular Warfare."

21. Eitan Shamir and Eyal Ben-Ari, "The Rise of Special Operations Forces: Generalized Specialization, Boundary Spanning and Military Autonomy," *Journal of Strategic Studies* 41, no. 3 (April 16, 2018): 337–38.

22. Austin Long, "The Limits of Special Operations Forces," *Prism* 6, no. 3 (2016): 34–47.

23. US Special Representative for Afghanistan Reconciliation, "Joint Declaration between the Islamic Republic of Afghanistan and the United States of America for Bringing Peace to Afghanistan," US Department of State, accessed May 26, 2020, https://www.state.gov/wp-content/uploads/2020/02/02.29.20 -US-Afghanistan-Joint-Declaration.pdf.

24. Ben Wolfgang, "U.S. Troop Withdrawal Advances Despite Political, Health Strains, in Afghanistan," *Washington Times*, May 4, 2020, www.washingtontimes.com/news/2020 /may/4/us-troop-withdraw-afghanistan-advances-despite-tal/.

25. Francis Fukuyama, "The End of History?" *National Interest* no. 16 (1989): 3–18.

26. Robert G. Gilpin, *War and Change in World Politics* (New York: Cambridge University Press, 1981).

27. Nagl, *Learning to Eat Soup with a Knife.*

28. Mao Tse-Tung, *Selected Military Writings of Mao Tse-Tung* (Peking: Foreign Language Press, 1966), 266, quoted in Nagl, *Learning to Eat Soup with a Knife*, 21.

29. Kilcullen, *Counterinsurgency.*

30. Kilcullen, *Counterinsurgency.*

31. David Kilcullen, *Out of the Mountains: The Coming Age of the Urban Guerrilla* (Oxford: Oxford University Press, 2015).

Chapter 10

The Near Possible

Artificial Intelligence, International Competition, and the Balance of Power

MICHAEL C. HOROWITZ

In early September 2017, Russian President Vladimir Putin brought artificial intelligence from the labs of Silicon Valley, academia, and the basement of the Pentagon to the forefront of international politics. "Artificial intelligence is the future, not only for Russia, but for all humankind," he said. "It comes with colossal opportunities, but also threats that are difficult to predict. Whoever becomes the leader in this sphere will become the ruler of the world."[1]

Putin's remarks reflect a belief, growing in sectors and regions across the world, that advances in artificial intelligence will be critical for the future—in areas as varied as work, society, and military power. Artificial intelligence is a critical element of what Klaus Schwab, head of the World Economic Forum, calls the Fourth Industrial Revolution.[2] Eric Schmidt, the former CEO of Google, argues that artificial intelligence is so important to the future of power that the United States needs a national strategy on artificial intelligence, just as it had one for the development of space technology during the Cold War.[3] Elon Musk, the head of Tesla and SpaceX, has even said that growth in artificial intelligence technology, left unchecked, could risk sparking World War III.[4] These statements suggest that artificial intelligence will have a large and potentially deterministic influence on global politics and the balance of power.[5]

Whether artificial intelligence has revolutionary consequences or merely incremental effects, it is critical to grasp how and why it could matter in the national security arena. Despite a wave of articles about artificial intelligence in the popular press and trade journals, there has been less in the way of systematic academic work on the national security consequences of such developments. This article attempts to fill that gap by examining the effects on national security of narrow artificial intelligence, or systems designed to do deliberately constrained tasks, such as the Jeopardy-playing version of IBM's Watson or AlphaGo, designed to play the board game Go. Specifically, it assesses the issues AI stands to raise for the balance of power and international competition through the lens of academic research on military innovation, technological change, and international politics.

Popular writing on AI tends to focus almost exclusively on technology development. Technology has played a vital role in shaping global politics throughout history.[6] Hundreds of years ago, technologies such as the printing press allowed the written word to flourish. These set the stage for new forms of political protest and activity.[7] In the 20th century, nuclear weapons significantly increased the destructive capabilities of numerous countries.[8]

Yet the relative impact of technological change often depends as much or more on how people, organizations, and societies adopt and utilize technologies as it does on the raw characteristics of the technology.[9] Consider the aircraft carrier, which the British Navy invented in 1918. As the best in the world at using battleships, the Royal Navy initially imagined the utility of aircraft carriers as providing airplanes to serve as spotters for the battleship. The Japanese and US navies, however, innovated by using the aircraft carrier as a mobile airfield, fundamentally transforming naval warfare in the 20th century.[10] Or, consider the printing press again: Its role in accelerating nationalist political movements depended on the incentives that originally motivated those movements and the movements' ability to take advantage of the new technology's capability to spread information.[11]

What role will artificial intelligence play? In many ways it is too soon to tell, given uncertainty about the development of the technology. But AI seems much more akin to the internal combustion engine or electricity than a weapon. It is an enabler, a general-purpose technology with a multitude of applications. That makes AI different from, and broader than, a missile, a submarine, or a tank.

Advances in narrow AI could create challenges as well as opportunities for governments and military organizations. For example, narrow AI applications such as image recognition would help those militaries that are already wealthy and powerful and that can afford to keep up. It is harder to predict how AI applications could affect the heart of military organizations, influencing planning as well as questions of recruiting, retention, and force structure. What happens as militaries increasingly need soldiers who have training in coding and who understand how algorithms work? Or if swarming, uninhabited systems make large conventional military platforms seem costly and obsolete?

Michael Horowitz, "Artificial Intelligence, International Competition, and the Balance of Power," *Texas National Security Review* 1, no. 3 (May 15, 2018): 37–57.

Leading militaries often struggle in the face of organizationally disruptive innovations because it is hard to make the bureaucratic case for change when a military perceives itself as already leading.

What countries benefit from AI will depend in part on where militarily relevant innovations come from. Nonmilitary institutions, such as private companies and academic departments, are pushing the boundaries of what is possible in the realm of artificial intelligence. While some AI and robotics companies, such as Boston Dynamics, receive military research and development funding, others, such as DeepMind, do not, and actively reject engaging with military organizations.[12] Unlike stealth technology, which has a fundamentally military purpose, artificial intelligence has uses as varied as shopping, agriculture, and stock trading.

If commercially driven AI continues to fuel innovation, and the types of algorithms militaries might one day use are closely related to civilian applications, advances in AI are likely to diffuse more rapidly to militaries around the world. AI competition could feature actors across the globe developing AI capabilities, much like late-19th-century competition in steel and chemicals. The potential for diffusion would make it more difficult to maintain "first-mover advantages" in applications of narrow AI. This could change the balance of power, narrowing the gap in military capabilities not only between the United States and China but between others as well.

Experts disagree about the potential trajectory of the technology, however, which means that forecasts of the consequences of AI developments for the international security environment are necessarily tentative.[13] While the basic science underlying AI is applicable to both civilian and military purposes, it is plausible that the most important specific military uses of AI will not be dual use. Technological advances that are more exclusively based in military research are generally harder to mimic. It follows that military applications of AI based more exclusively in defense research will then generate larger first-mover advantages for early adopters. Moreover, if the computational power necessary to generate new, powerful algorithms prices out all but the wealthiest companies and countries, higher-end AI capabilities could help the rich get richer from a balance-of-power perspective. On the other hand, if leading militaries fail to effectively incorporate AI, the potential for disruption would also be larger.

This article defines artificial intelligence and examines what kind of technology AI is. It then turns to key questions and assumptions about the trajectory of narrow AI development that will influence potential adoption requirements for military applications of AI, a factor critical to shaping AI's influence on the balance of power. The paper then assesses how narrow artificial intelligence will affect the balance of power

in a world where dual-use AI has great military relevance and diffuses rapidly as well as a scenario in which military AI developments are more "excludable," limiting diffusion and generating more first-mover advantages.

How all this will play out over the next decade or more is unclear. Already, China, Russia, and others are investing significantly in AI to increase their relative military capabilities with an eye toward reshaping the balance of power. As the field of AI matures, and more implementations become plausible in arenas such as logistics, personnel, and even deployable units, countries will need to figure out how to use AI in practical ways that improve their ability to generate military power. The risk for the United States in terms of balance of power thus lies in taking its military superiority for granted and ending up like Great Britain's Royal Navy with the aircraft carrier in the mid-20th century—a technological innovator that is surpassed when it comes to organizational adoption and use of the technology.

What Is Artificial Intelligence?

What is artificial intelligence? There is no broad consensus on the specific meanings of terms such as "artificial intelligence," "autonomy," and "automation." For the purposes of this article, "artificial intelligence" refers to the use of computers to simulate the behavior of humans that requires intelligence.[14] Put another way, AI can be thought of as the ability of an artificial agent to achieve goals in a "wide range of environments."[15] A system with artificial intelligence is distinct from a robot or robotic system, which can be remotely piloted or autonomous.[16] For example, the Boston Dynamics SpotMini, which can open a door, is remotely piloted by a human operator and so would not qualify as AI.[17] *Automatic* systems, such as a toaster in the civilian world or, to use a military example, an explosive triggered by a tripwire, respond mechanistically to environmental inputs.[18] *Automated* systems, by contrast, operate based on multiple preprogrammed logic steps as opposed to the simplicity of a tripwire.[19] *Autonomous* systems have more latitude and are programmed, within constraints, to achieve goals, optimizing along a set of parameters.[20]

There are two main approaches to AI, broadly conceived. The first is symbolic artificial intelligence—the creation of expert systems and production rules to allow a machine to deduce behavioral pathways. IBM's Deep Blue, which defeated Garry Kasparov in chess in 1997, used a symbolic approach.[21] Computational, or connectionist, approaches to artificial intelligence, in contrast, typically attempt to allow for problem recognition and action by machines through calculations rather than symbolic representation.[22] Machine learning represents a key computational approach to artificial intelligence. Multiple computational techniques are used to create machine-learning algorithms, including Bayesian networks, decision trees, and deep learning. Deep learning, now popularly associated with artificial intelligence, is a technique that harnesses neural networks to train algorithms to do specified tasks, such as image recognition.[23] Some researchers are pursuing hybrid approaches that integrate both symbolic and computational approaches to AI. The hope behind hybrid approaches is that creating common languages will enable algorithms that can employ multiple pathways to learn how to do particular tasks, making them more effective.[24]

For the purposes of this article, the specific methods of AI that generate particular capabilities are less critical than understanding the general trajectory of the technology. In many cases, it is too soon to tell which methods will generate which capabilities.

AI Is an Enabler, Not a Weapon

The impact of the invention of a new technology depends, in part, on its potential basic uses.[25] Some communication technologies, such as the telegraph or telephone, were designed to more rapidly connect people in different locations. Munition technologies, such as missiles and bullets, are designed to inflict damage on a target. Railroads are a transportation technology, as is a bicycle. These broad categories of technologies have subcomponents that draw on various technologies themselves. For example, more than 300,000 parts go into an F-35.[26] Another category might then be called "enabling technologies," which are designed not specifically for a single purpose like the examples above but, instead, are general-purpose, with broad applications across many other types of technologies. Electricity is an enabling technology.

So what kind of technology is artificial intelligence? While the rhetoric of the "Third Offset"[27] and other discussions in the defense community sometimes make artificial intelligence seem like a munition, AI is actually the ultimate enabler. AI can be part of many specific technologies, analogous to the internal combustion engine as well as electricity.[28] Andrew Ng of Stanford University argues that, like the invention of electricity, AI could enable specific technologies in fields as diverse as agriculture, manufacturing, and health care.[29]

Artificial intelligence can operate in several dimensions. First, it can be used to direct physical objects, such as robotic systems, to act without human supervision. Whether in tanks, planes, or ships, AI can help reduce the need to use humans, even remotely, or as part of human-machine teams.[30] Swarm techniques, for example, generally involve the creation of supervised algorithms that direct platforms such as drones.

Second, artificial intelligence can assist in processing and interpreting information. Image-recognition algorithms can be used for tagging vacation photos and identifying products in stores as well as in Project Maven, a US military program that seeks to develop algorithms to automate the process of analyzing video feeds captured by drones.[31] While the applications in each case are different, the underlying algorithmic task—rapid image identification and tagging—is consistent. Third, overlapping narrow AI systems could be used for new forms of command and control—operational systems, including battle management, that analyze large sets of data and make forecasts to direct human action—or action by algorithms.[32]

What Type of Artificial Intelligence?

It is useful to think about the degree of artificial intelligence as a continuum. On one end are narrow AI applications such as AlphaGo, able to beat the best human Go players in the world. These are machine-learning algorithms designed to do one specific task, with no prospect of doing anything beyond that task. One can imagine narrow AI as relatively advanced forms of autonomous systems, or machines that, once activated, are designed to complete specific tasks or functions.[33]

On the other end of the spectrum is a "superintelligent" artificial general intelligence. This kind of AI would consist of an algorithm, or series of algorithms, that could do not only narrow tasks but also could functionally think for itself and design solutions to a broader class of problems. Describing an extreme version of this, Nick Bostrom writes about the risk of a superintelligent AI that could plausibly take over the world and perhaps even decide to eliminate humans as an inadvertent consequence of its programming.[34] In the middle of this spectrum, though perhaps leaning toward artificial general intelligence, is "transformative AI," or AI that can go beyond a narrow task such as playing a video game but falls short of achieving superintelligence.[35]

This article focuses on the potential effect that narrow applications of artificial intelligence could have on the balance of power and international competition. Among current AI technologies and advances, narrow applications are most likely to affect militaries—and with them the balance of power—over the next two decades. Moreover, even experts disagree about whether artificial general intelligence of the type that could outpace human capabilities will emerge in the short to medium term or whether it is still hundreds of years away. AI experts also disagree about the overall trajectory of advances in AI.[36] Surveys have found that only 50 percent of AI researchers believe that an AI system will be capable of writing a best-selling book by 2049. About 75 percent of AI researchers thought it could be 2090 before an AI system could write a best-selling book. That even highly trained experts disagree about these development issues illustrates a high degree of uncertainty in the field.

Given these questions about which AI technologies will be developed, this article focuses on the capabilities that are most likely to emerge in the next generation.

Technology and the Balance of Power

Emerging technologies primarily shape the balance of power through military and economic means.[37] Technologies can directly influence countries' abilities to fight and win wars. They can also indirectly affect the balance of power by impacting a country's economic power. After all, countries cannot maintain military superiority over the medium to long term without an underlying economic basis for that power.[38] Recall the decline of the Ottoman Empire or Imperial China.

However, it is not yet clear how the invention of specific AI applications will translate into military power. Despite continuing investment, efforts to integrate AI technologies into militaries have been limited.[39] Project Maven is the first activity of an "Algorithmic Warfare" initiative in the US military designed to harness the potential of AI and translate it into usable military capabilities. Still, many investments in the United States and elsewhere are in early stages. As Missy L. Cummings writes:

> Autonomous ground vehicles such as tanks and transport vehicles are in development worldwide, as are autonomous underwater vehicles. In almost all cases, however, the agencies developing these technologies are struggling to make the leap from development to operational implementation.[40]

It is important to distinguish these potential technological innovations from military innovations. While military innovations are often linked to changes in technology,[41] it is not always the case. Military innovations are significant changes in organizational behavior and ways that a military fights that are designed to increase its ability to effectively translate capabilities into power.[42] The use of aircraft carriers as mobile airfields by the United States and Japan is a prototypical example. While AI could potentially enable a number of military innovations, it is not a military innovation itself, and no applications of AI have been used in ways that would count as a military innovation at this point.

Because AI research and technology are still in their early stages, usage of AI in warfare is not even yet analogous to the first use of the tank in World War I, let alone effective use of combined arms warfare by the Germans in World War II (the military innovation now known as blitzkrieg). This limits analyses about how narrow AI might one day affect the balance of power

and international politics. Most research on technology and international politics focuses on specific, mature technologies, such as nuclear weapons, or on military innovations.[43] Since AI is at an early stage, examining it requires adapting existing theories about military technology and military innovation.[44]

My adoption capacity theory provides insight into how developments in AI will affect the balance of power.[45] This theory argues that the relative financial and organizational requirements for adopting a military innovation influence the rate of diffusion of that innovation and its impact on the balance of power. Financial considerations include calculating the unit costs of the hardware involved and determining whether the underlying capability is based on commercial or militarily exclusive technology. Other considerations include assessing the extent to which adopting the innovation requires disrupting the critical task of the military (i.e., what an organization views itself as attempting to achieve) or the status of key organizational elites (for example, fighter pilots in an air force). Given that adoption capacity theory focuses on major military innovations, however, it requires adaptation to be applied to artificial intelligence at present.

To determine how technological changes will shape the balance of power, adoption capacity theory suggests that three questions must be answered. First, while technology itself is rarely, if ever, determinative, how might use of a technology influence the character of warfare? Consider the machine gun. When deployed asymmetrically, it proved useful for the offense. But in combination with barbed wire, when possessed symmetrically, this technological advance helped create the trench-warfare stalemate of World War I.[46] More broadly, the Industrial Revolution and the shift in manufacturing to factories and mass production were behind the rifle's evolution from a niche, craft weapon possessed by a small number of forces to a widely available capability. This change influenced the relative lethality of battles as well as how militaries organized themselves and developed tactics.[47]

Second, how might different actors implement a given technology or be bureaucratically constrained from implementation, and what possibilities for military innovation will that generate? This question is particularly relevant because the challenges of organizational adoption and implementation of a technological innovation are closely linked with effectiveness. Those challenges are critical to determining how an innovation will impact international politics.

Decades of research demonstrates that the impact of technological change on global politics—whether it is change in economics, society at large, diplomacy, or military power—depends much more on how governments and organizations make choices about the adoption and use of new capabilities than on the technologies themselves.[48] Scholarship on military innovation by Barry Posen, Stephen P. Rosen, and others shows that technological innovation alone rarely shapes the balance of power.[49] Instead, it is how militaries use a technology that makes a difference.[50] A military's ability to employ a technology depends in part on the complexity of the technology, how difficult it is to use, and whether it operates in predictable and explainable ways. These factors influence the trust that senior military leaders have in the technology and whether they use it.[51] Additionally, the more bureaucratically disruptive it is to adopt a technology, the more challenging it can be for older, more established organizations to do so—particularly if the organization is underinvested in research and development designed to integrate new technologies and ideas.[52]

Consider that every country in Europe in the mid-19th century had access to railroads, rifles, and the telegraph around the same time. But it was the Prussian military that first figured out how to exploit these technologies, in combination, to rapidly project power. After that, other militaries adapted their organizations to take similar advantage.[53]

The example of the British Navy and the aircraft carrier further illustrates how organizational processes determine the impact of technology on military power.[54] As referenced above, despite having invented the aircraft carrier, the Royal Navy's institutional commitment to the battleship meant that it initially saw the value of this new technology almost exclusively in its ability to facilitate the use of airplanes to act as "spotters" for battleships. The United States and Japan, as rising naval powers with less invested in the importance of the battleship, thought more creatively about this innovation and realized that the aircraft carrier's real value lay in the independent striking power it offered.[55] Since battleships—and admirals with experience and comfort operating them—dominated the navies of many countries, thinking about the aircraft carrier as a mobile airfield required a difficult conceptual shift.[56]

Even after it became clear that the optimal use of aircraft carriers was as a mobile airfield, adopting carrier warfare proved challenging. The Chinese navy has been working on carrier operations for two decades and is only just starting to build real competency. The Soviet Union attempted to adopt carrier warfare for decades and failed. Simply put, the systems integration tasks required to operate the ship, launch and recover airplanes from the ship, and coordinate with other naval assets are very difficult to execute.[57] The larger the change within the organization required for a military to effectively utilize new technologies, the greater the bureaucratic challenges and, with them, the likelihood that powerful countries will not have the organizational capability to adopt. This is a key mechanism through which the balance of power can change.

Third, how will a new technology spread? The answer to this question will help determine relative first-mover advantages gained from adopting the technology.[58] While Kenneth Waltz initially suggested that emulation of military technologies happens quickly, subsequent research demonstrates that it is far more complicated.[59] The rate of diffusion matters: In the case of technologies that diffuse slowly, the country that first implements will have a sustainable edge over its competitors. But when other countries can rapidly adopt a new technology, the relative advantages of being first diminish.[60]

The diffusion of military technology occurs through multiple mechanisms, just like the diffusion of technologies in general.[61] Adoption capacity theory suggests a few factors that will be key in influencing the diffusion of narrow AI. The first is the unit cost of creating AI systems. The greater the hardware and compute costs associated with creating militarily relevant algorithms, the higher the barrier to entry will be. Alternatively, once the algorithms have been created, they become software and can more easily diffuse.

Moreover, technologies that have only military purposes tend to spread more slowly than technologies where commercial incentives drive their development. If a technology has only military uses—such as stealth technology—and it has a high unit cost and level of complexity, the number of actors who can emulate or mimic that technology is minimized.[62]

On the other hand, technologies with commercial incentives for development generally spread much faster. In the 19th century, the railroad, used as a "military technology," enabled rapid power projection and the massing of military forces to a greater degree than had previously been possible. Yet it was the commercial incentives for the fast shipping of goods that helped speed the construction of dense railroad networks around the world, making it difficult for countries to gain sustainable advantages in railroad capabilities.[63]

The Impact of AI on the Balance of Power

If Eric Schmidt, Vladimir Putin, Elon Musk, and others are correct that AI is a competitive battleground, what will be the character of that competition?[64] The United States and China seem to be furthest ahead in the development of AI. As the two most powerful countries in the world, the competition for global leadership in AI technology evokes, for many, 20th-century competitions such as the space race. Retired Marine Corps Gen. John Allen and SparkCognition CEO Amir Husain have argued that the United States therefore needs to do more to get and stay ahead.[65]

Global investments in artificial intelligence for economic and national security purposes are increasingly described as an arms race.[66] China published a national strategy on artificial intelligence in 2017 that said AI represents a "major strategic opportunity" and proposed a coordinated strategy to "build China's first mover advantage" and lead the world in AI technology.[67] Russia is investing heavily as well, especially in the military domain. Reports suggest that the Russian military is designing autonomous vehicles to guard its ballistic missile bases as well as an autonomous submarine that could carry nuclear weapons. In robotics, Russia is deploying remotely piloted tanks, such as the Uran-9 and Vehar, on the battlefield.[68]

China and Russia are not the only actors outside the United States interested in national security applications of AI. The character of AI technology, like robotics, makes many countries well positioned to design and deploy it for military purposes.[69] Commercial incentives for AI developments and the dual-use character of many AI applications mean that countries with advanced information economies are poised to be leaders in AI or at least fast followers.[70] In Southeast Asia, Singapore is on the cutting edge of AI investments (both military and nonmilitary). Other Southeast Asian nations are making advances in AI research as well.[71] In the military domain, South Korea has developed the SGR-A1, a semiautonomous weapon system designed to protect the demilitarized zone from attack by North Korea.[72]

AI also provides opportunities for capital-rich countries, which creates incentives to develop the technology. Wealthy, advanced economies that have high levels of capital but also have high labor costs or small populations—middle powers such as Australia, Canada, and many European countries—often face challenges in military recruiting. For these countries, technologies that allow them to substitute capital for labor are highly attractive. Indeed, Gen. Mick Ryan, commander of Australia's Defence College, argues that countries can take advantage of the intersection of AI and robotics to overcome the problems caused by a small population.[73] France's 2017 defense strategy review points to the development and incorporation of artificial intelligence as critical to the French military's ability to maintain "operational superiority."[74] Israel, a classic example of an advanced economy with more capital than labor, also funds military AI investments that would predict rocket launches and analyze video footage.[75] Lt. Col. Nurit Cohen Inger, who heads the unit of the Israeli Defense Forces (IDF) in charge of assessing the military relevance of AI, said in 2017 that, for the IDF, AI "can influence every step and small decision in a conflict, and the entire conflict itself."[76]

Given these investments, how might developments in AI affect military organizations and the character of war, and how might they diffuse?

AI and the Character of War

The "character of warfare" in a period can be defined as the dominant way to fight and win conflicts given existing technologies, organizations, and polities. The character of warfare changes in concert with the tools that become available and how they influence the ways militaries organize themselves to fight wars.[77] The shift to mass mobilization in the Napoleonic era exemplifies a nontechnological development that changed the character of warfare.

Applications of AI have the potential to shape how countries fight in several macro ways. On the broadest level, autonomous systems, or narrow AI systems, have the potential to increase the speed with which countries can fight, yet another similarity between AI and the combustion engine. Even if humans are still making final decisions about the use of lethal force, fighting at machine speed can dramatically increase the pace of operations.[78]

There are several military applications of AI currently in development or under discussion that can be considered, though many are at early stages. For example, some research shows that the way that neural networks can utilize imagery databases and classify particular scenes (such as a mountain) allows for a more accurate assessment of specific locations.[79] Additionally, the processing power that is possible with narrow AI systems has the potential to increase the speed of data analysis, as Project Maven in the United States aims to do. Investments in image recognition offer the hope of achieving faster, more accurate results than humans can achieve today, and is a likely avenue for continued investment and application (setting aside the questions of accidents, hacking, and other ways that systems could go awry[80]).

Successful implementation of AI beyond areas such as image recognition might lead to new concepts of operation that could influence force structure and force employment, or how militaries organize themselves and plan operations. One possibility is the use of large numbers of smaller platforms, known as swarms, for military operations. Algorithms and control systems designed to enable "swarming" already exist in the private sector and in academia.[81] Military-grade algorithms would require coordination with other military systems, including early-warning aircraft, inhabited aircraft, satellites, and other sensors. Deployed swarms in a combat environment would have to be capable of real-time adaptation to optimize operations if some elements of the swarm were shot down—a challenge that commercial applications would not necessarily face. Methods for developing swarming algorithms could include behavior trees or deep learning.[82]

Another potential application for narrow AI that could shape the character of war is coordination through layers of algorithms that work together to help manage complex operations. These algorithms could be expert systems that generate decision trees. Or they could involve algorithms developed through generative adversarial networks. In this approach, algorithms compete against each other to teach each other how to do various tasks. Some algorithms will need to be trained to assist in coordinating multiple military assets, both human and machine. In that case, adversarial learning could help compensate for the unique character of decision-making in individual battles and the problem of learning to adapt beyond the available training data.[83]

The ability to operate faster through algorithms that assist human commanders in optimizing battle plans, including real-time operations, could shift force employment and force structure, especially in the air and at sea. Since World War II, modern militaries have been engaged in a shift from quantity to quality in military systems. The thinking is that smaller numbers of expensive, high-quality systems are more likely to lead to victory in battles. AI could accelerate trends that challenge these long-running force-structure imperatives, such as the need to defeat adversaries with advanced anti-access, area-denial (A2/AD) networks with tolerable costs.

If algorithms and coordination at machine speed become critical to success on the battlefield, expensive, high-quality platforms could become vulnerable to swarms of sensors and lower-cost weapons platforms that are effectively networked together. AI could thus help bring quantity back into the equation in the form of large numbers of robotic systems. In the near to mid-term, however, optimal use of AI may lie in leveraging machine learning to improve the performance of existing platforms.

Incentives exist for nearly all types of political regimes to develop AI applications for military purposes. For democracies, AI can decrease the relative burden of warfare on the population and reduce the risk to soldiers, even more so than with remotely piloted systems, by reducing the use of personnel. For autocracies, which do not trust their people in the first place, the ability to outsource some elements of military decision-making to algorithms, reducing reliance on humans to fight wars, is inherently attractive.[84]

Organizational Politics and Artificial Intelligence

Despite uncertainty about specific military applications of AI, the examples of how AI can be used in a military context described above reveal that these capabilities have the potential to significantly disrupt organizational structures. Take the example of battle management coordination (whether in human-machine teams or not):

Successfully operating even semiautonomous battle management systems is likely to require new occupational specialties and shifts in recruiting, training, and promotion to empower individuals who understand both military operations and how particular AI systems function. Rosen shows that altering the promotion of military personnel to empower those with expertise in new areas is critical to adopting military innovations in general. AI should be no exception.[85]

As described above, the use of AI systems at the operational level could generate options for how militaries organize and plan to use force, due to the potential to use larger numbers of networked systems operating at machine speed instead of relying exclusively on small numbers of high-quality inhabited aircraft. Implementing such concepts, however, could require disruptive organizational shifts that could threaten to change which military occupations provide the highest status and are gateways to leadership roles. Already, this can be seen with the Air Force, dominated by fighter pilots, which has been relatively hesitant when it comes to investments in uninhabited aerial vehicles. It would also challenge entrenched bureaucratic notions about how to weigh quantity versus quality. Adopting narrow AI in the most optimal way could prove challenging for leading militaries, which will need trained personnel who can do quality and reliability assurance for AI applications to ensure their appropriate and effective use.

Other applications, such as Project Maven in the US Department of Defense, are easier to implement because they are sustaining technologies from the perspective of literature on organizational innovation.[86] Autonomous systems that can rapidly and accurately process drone footage do not disrupt high-status military occupational specialties, nor do they disrupt how military services operate as a whole. It is when optimal uses of narrow AI would require large shifts to force structure that the adoption requirements, and bureaucratic antibodies, ramp up. One example of bureaucratic resistance preventing the production of a new technology that could have proved disruptive is the US military's failure to fund the X-47B drone, a next-generation system that could take off from and land on aircraft carriers autonomously. This illustrates the way bureaucratic politics and organizational competition can hinder the adoption of innovative technologies.[87]

The strategic or organizational culture of a military or society can also indicate which will be best positioned to exploit potential advances in AI,[88] specifically, how open those cultures are to innovation. There is a risk of tautology, of course, in cultural arguments at times since it can be hard to measure whether an organization is capable of adopting a technology until it has tried to do so or done it. However, Emily Goldman's work on the Ottoman Empire suggests the value of developing metrics of cultural openness when it comes to predicting willingness to experiment and adopt AI systems.[89]

Interestingly, norms regarding force structure could also play a role in inhibiting the use of AI for certain military tasks. As Theo Farrell's research on the Irish Army after independence shows, militaries often mimic the functional form of more powerful actors even when doing so is not in their interest. Applying his insight in the case of artificial intelligence, some militaries may be less likely to use AI in ways that are organizationally disruptive, especially if doing so would involve shifts in visible force structure, such as a move from small numbers of advanced inhabited aircraft to swarming concepts that use cheaper, more disposable aircraft.[90]

Arguments about organizational and strategic culture are generally consistent with adoption capacity theory, since both focus on the challenges that innovations present when they disrupt the identity of an organization.[91] After all, militaries that already spend a lot on research and development, that are younger, and that have broad conceptions of their critical task are more likely to be culturally "open" and able to adopt new technologies or full innovations further down the development line.

The Diffusion of Militarily Relevant AI: Two Scenarios

There is a fundamental question about the extent to which militarily relevant uses of narrow AI will diffuse easily. Answering this question is necessary for predicting the first-mover advantages associated with a technological innovation, which in turn helps to determine its relative impact on the balance of power and warfare. To determine how easily a new technology will diffuse, adoption capacity theory suggests looking at the unit cost of the technology, especially the physical hardware.

Designing AI capabilities requires both software and hardware. This influences how to think about the "unit cost" of AI. Military capabilities based in hardware often spread more slowly than those based in software, generating more sustainable advantage for the first adopter of a given capability, especially when the unit costs of that capability are relatively high. The high unit cost of flattop aircraft carriers, for example, means that only wealthy and powerful countries adopt them.[92]

When it comes to platforms, algorithms are software rather than hardware. Take the example of the MQ-9 Reaper, a current-generation US military armed drone. The MQ-9 is remotely piloted, meaning that a pilot at another location directs the airframe and makes decisions about firing weapons against potential targets. The difference between this and an autonomous version that is piloted and operated by an algorithm is software. From the outside, the platform would look the same.

But, if narrow AI is software from the perspective of military technology, it is software that requires substantial hardware for its creation. The associated hardware costs—especially for advanced narrow AI applications—are potentially significant.[93] The more complex the algorithm, the more up-front computational hardware is required to "train" that algorithm.[94] Thus, corporate and academic AI research leaders have to invest in teraflops of computing power. This is a different kind of hardware than a tank or a cruise missile, but it is hardware all the same. Rapid advances in AI through deep learning and neural networks over the last decade have thus required advances in computing hardware. Joel Emer, an electrical engineering and computer science professor at MIT, states it plainly: "Many AI accomplishments were made possible because of advances in hardware."[95] After an algorithm has been trained, however, it can be applied without access to that computing environment, and the power necessary to run completed algorithms is dramatically reduced.

How rapidly AI capabilities will diffuse via simultaneous invention or mimicry will depend, in part, on the availability of computing power. If the cost of computing power continues to decline as chips become more efficient, then countries that are already home to advanced technology companies will have more access to AI capabilities faster than other countries without those kinds of technology companies.

If, on the other hand, the hardware costs of developing complex algorithms remain beyond the capacity of companies in most countries, diffusion will happen only deliberately, such as through trade or bilateral agreements at the nation-state level, or via espionage (i.e., hacking). This would likely slow the diffusion of most AI advances, increasing the advantages for innovators.

Determining the extent to which militarily relevant applications of AI are based on commercial technology versus exclusively military research is also a critical question raised by adoption capacity theory. While it is hard to know the answer at present, examining both scenarios will illustrate how that answer might shape the way AI affects the balance of power and the structure of international competition.

Dual-Use AI

Research on the future of work suggests that strong commercial drivers are incentivizing the development of AI around the world. A 2017 McKinsey Global

Institute report found a midpoint estimate of 400 million people, or 15 percent of the workforce, that are likely to be disrupted by automation before 2030.[96] Widely cited research by Carl B. Frey and Michael A. Osborne estimates that 47 percent of jobs in the United States are at risk of being replaced by automation. That includes lawyers, stock traders, and accountants, not just blue-collar jobs.[97] Companies across the economy have incentives to develop and use algorithms.

Commercial interest in AI is so high that some argue it—and the finite number of talented AI engineers—is holding back military developments.[98] What's more, the higher salaries and benefits that commercial companies can offer mean that militaries may have to turn to civilian companies to develop advanced AI capabilities. Google's decision to partner with the US Defense Department on Project Maven illustrates how the same talent and knowledge that will drive commercial innovation in AI may also be necessary for military technology innovation.[99]

When technology advances derive primarily from the civilian sector, rapid adoption of new technologies around the world becomes more likely. Commercial companies may spread the technology themselves, and the profit motive incentivizes rapid mimicry by related companies in different countries.[100] Companies in Brazil, Germany, Japan, and Singapore could become AI leaders or at least fast followers.

A commitment to open-source development by many of the major players in AI could also increase the rate of diffusion. In 2015, for example, Google opened up TensorFlow, its artificial intelligence engine, to the public.[101] Elsewhere, researchers committed to the open development of AI to help reduce the safety risk of algorithms that "break" in high-leverage situations publish their findings in ways that advance their cause—and make it easier for their algorithms to be copied.[102]

Even though advanced applications of commercial AI would require significant hardware and expertise, adoption capacity theory suggests that as the underlying basis of a technology gets more commercially oriented, it spreads relatively faster, as explained above. Companies like DeepMind have an edge today. But in such a scenario, there would be more companies around the world with relevant technological capacity. It is also easier for governments to leverage private-sector companies when those private-sector actors have nongovernmental market incentives for developing or copying technology.

So how would dual-use AI being critical to military applications of AI shape global power? As noted above, the period in which a technological innovator enjoys a market advantage shrinks when countries and companies can acquire or copy others' advances relatively easily. This makes it hard to stay ahead qualitatively.[103] In the AI and robotics realms, it is possible that this

will create yet another incentive for countries to focus on quantity in military systems. If leads in AI development prove difficult to sustain, advanced militaries are likely to have systems of approximately the same quality level, presuming they all reach the same conclusion about the general potential of integrating AI into military operations. In that case, countries may be more likely to try to gain advantage by emphasizing quantity again—this is in addition to the inherent incentives for mass that narrow AI might create.

If dual-use AI is critical to military applications of AI, the ability to design forces, training, and operational plans to take advantage of those dual-use applications will be a differentiating factor for leadership in AI among the great powers. The 1940 Battle of France illustrates what could ultimately be at stake in the most extreme case. Both the Germans on one side and the British and French on the other had tanks, trucks, radios, and airplanes that they could, in theory, have used for close air support. What gave the Germans such a large edge was blitzkrieg—a new concept of operations that could overwhelm even another advanced adversary.[104]

Let's return to the comparison between AI and the space race. If AI technology diffuses more rapidly because it has both commercial and military purposes, making first-mover advantages more difficult to sustain, comparisons to the space race may be limited. The space race was a bilateral challenge between the United States and the Soviet Union designed to put a person on the moon, which included both developments in rockets and technologies designed to keep humans alive in space, land on the moon, and return safely. The rocket development itself was also part of the creation of intercontinental ballistic missiles (ICBMs). And critical economic spillovers from the space race included development of the satellites that led to GPS and other key enablers of the Information Age. Yet overall, the race to the moon was run by two governments for national purposes—not primarily for dual-use economic gain.

The commercial drivers of AI technology, and the speed with which new algorithms diffuse, would make competition much broader than it was during the bilateral space race. Competition is much more likely to be multilateral, featuring countries and companies around the world. A better analogy might be to the competition surrounding the development of second industrial revolution technologies in the late 19th and early 20th centuries. France, Germany, Britain, Japan, the United States, and others vied for supremacy in steel production, chemicals, petroleum, electricity, and other areas.

For military applications of AI where the underlying technology is driven by commercial developments, the impact of a country getting ahead in AI technology, over time, would have unclear implications for relative power if a rival country was close enough to be a fast follower. Advances in commercially driven AI technology are about building new industries, changing the character of existing industries, and ensuring that the leading corporations in the global economy that emerges are based in one's own country.

Militarily Exclusive AI

The alternative to military applications of AI that are based in commercial developments is a world where military applications of AI are driven instead by research that is applicable only to militaries. Copying technological innovations of "excludable" technologies—those not based on widely available commercial technology—requires espionage to steal the technology (as the Soviets did with the atomic bomb) or mimicry based on observable principles of the technology.[105] There are several reasons, however, to think that many military applications of narrow AI will be unique in ways that will make them more difficult to copy.

First, the complexity of advanced military systems can make emulation costly and difficult. This is especially true when a number of components are not available on the commercial market and the ability to build them depends, in part, on classified information.[106] The same can also be said for some advanced commercial technology, of course, but this is not the norm. The inability to adapt commercial algorithms for some military purposes could limit the capacity of most states to produce relevant AI-based military capabilities, even if they have advanced commercial AI sectors. It could also mean that systems integration challenges for using militarily relevant algorithms are large enough to deter many militaries from investing heavily.[107]

Whatever the uncertainty about how specific AI advances will translate into military capabilities, some of the most important military applications of narrow AI—those with a potentially substantial impact on larger-scale military operations—may not have obvious civilian counterparts. Battle management algorithms that coordinate a military operation at machine speed do not necessarily have commercial analogues—even if supervised by a human with command authority—excluding the development of a narrow AI designed, say, to run a factory or operational system from top to bottom. In these arenas, military-grade algorithms may require conceptual breakthroughs that other countries may find hard to rapidly mimic.

Second, some military AI applications, such as image recognition, do have obvious commercial counterparts. Even in those cases, however, the cybersecurity concerns and reliability associated with military-grade technology can differ from those for civilian applications. Military AI systems deployed in the field may re-

quire hardening for electronic warfare and extra protections from spoofing and hacking that would be of relatively less concern in the civilian world. In military environments, adversaries' efforts to hack and spoof increase the need for security.

The potential for countries to have strong commercial AI research sectors may mean that even narrow AI developments with applications geared toward military use may be easier to mimic than, say, stealth technology has been over the last generation. But stealth is an outlier: It has proven uniquely difficult to copy relative to other military technologies over the past few hundred years.

For AI developments that do not have clear commercial analogues, there could be substantial first-mover advantages for militaries that swiftly adopt AI technologies, particularly if they can achieve computer-driven breakthroughs that are difficult to copy. What would this mean for AI competition? As described above, China's AI strategy highlights the way many countries increasingly view AI as a global competition that involves nation-states, rather than as a market in which companies can invest.[108] As Elsa Kania writes, the People's Liberation Army (PLA)

is funding a wide range of projects involving AI, and the Chinese defense industry and PLA research institutes are pursuing extensive research and development, in some cases partnering with private enterprises.[109]

Adopting militarily exclusive AI technologies could also generate significant organizational pressure on militaries. Even if it would be hard for most countries to be fast followers or mimic the advances of other militaries, great-power competition in AI would generate risk for those powers that are unable to adapt in order to organizationally exploit advances in AI, even if they are able to make technical advances. Traditionally, this risk is highest for the world's leading military power, in this case the United States. Leading military powers often struggle to envision how to use new technologies in ways that are organizationally disruptive. They can also be blind to that fact, believing they are in the lead right up to the point when their failure of creativity matters.[110]

From a balance-of-power perspective, this scenario would be more likely to feature disruption among emerging and great powers but not a broader leveling of the military playing field. The ability to exclude many countries from advances in AI would concentrate military competition among current leading militaries, such as the United States, China, and Russia. There could be significant disruption within those categories, though. A Chinese military that more rapidly developed critical algorithms for broader battle management, or that was more willing to use them than the United States, might gain advantages that shifted power in the Asia-Pacific. This assumes that these algorithms operate as they are designed to operate. All militarily useful AI will have to be hardened against hacking and spoofing. Operators will use narrow AI applications only if they are as or more effective or reliable as existing inhabited or remotely piloted options.[111]

While this discussion has focused on narrow AI applications, the notion of bilateral competition in AI may be most pressing when thinking about artificial general intelligence.[112] Although artificial general intelligence is beyond the scope of this paper, it would matter as a discrete competitive point only if there is a clear reward to being first, as opposed to being a fast, follower. For example, developing artificial general intelligence first could lock in economic or military leadership. Then others would not have the ability to adopt it themselves, or their adoptions would be somehow less relevant, and that could be a discrete "end point" to competition. It seems unlikely, however, that such development would be that discrete or that one country would get a lead in this technology that is so large that it can consolidate the impact of being a first mover before others catch up.

Conclusion

Technological innovations, whether the machine gun, the railroad, or the longbow, can influence the balance of power and international conflict. Yet their impact is generally determined by how people and organizations use the technology rather than by the technology itself.[113] It is too early to tell what the impact of narrow AI will be, but technology development suggests it will have at least some effect.

As an "enabling" technology that is more like electricity or the combustion engine than a weapon system, narrow AI is likely to have an impact that extends beyond specific questions of military superiority to influence economic power and societies around the world. This article demonstrates that technological innovation in AI could have large-scale consequences for the global balance of power. Whatever the mix of dual-use AI or militarily exclusive AI that ends up shaping modern militaries over the next few decades, the organizational adoption requirements are likely to be significant. Militaries around the world will have to grapple with how to change recruiting and promotion policies to empower soldiers who understand algorithms and coding, as well as potential shifts in force structure to take advantage of AI-based coordination on the battlefield.

Military and economic history suggests that the effect of narrow AI could be quite large, even if sugges-

tions of AI triggering a new industrial revolution are overstated. Adoption capacity theory shows that changes in relative military power become more likely in cases of military innovations that require large organizational changes and the adoption of new operational concepts. Even if the United States, China, and Russia were to end up with similar levels of basic AI capacity over the next decade, the history of military innovations from the phalanx to blitzkrieg suggests it is *how* they and others use AI that will matter most for the future of military power.

Whether AI capabilities diffuse relatively slowly or quickly, major military powers will likely face security dilemmas having to do with AI development and deployment. In a slow-diffusion scenario, if countries fear that adversaries could get ahead in ways that are hard to rapidly mimic—and small differences in capabilities will matter on the battlefield—that will foster incentives for quick development and deployment. In a rapid-diffusion scenario, competitive incentives will also exist, as countries feel like they have to race just to keep up.[114] Moreover, it will be inherently difficult to measure competitors' progress with AI (unlike, say, observing the construction of an aircraft carrier), causing countries to assume the worst of their potential rivals.

Competition in developing AI is underway. Countries around the world are investing heavily in AI, though the United States and China seem to be ahead. Yet even if the space-race analogy is not precise, understanding AI as a competition can still be useful. Such frameworks help people and organizations understand the world around them, from how to evaluate international threats to the potential trajectory of wars.[115] If likening competition in AI to the space race clarifies the stakes in ways that generate incentives for bureaucratic action at the government level, and raises corporate and public awareness, the analogy stands to have utility for the United States.

From a research perspective, one limitation of this article is its focus on the balance of power and international competition, as opposed to specific uses of AI. Future research could investigate particular implementations of AI for military purposes or other critical questions. Specific implementations could include the use of autonomous weapon systems able to select and engage targets on their own. These systems could raise ethical and moral questions about human control,[116] as well as practical issues surrounding war that is fought at "machine speed."[117] The integration of AI into early-warning systems and its ability to aid in rapid targeting could also affect crisis stability and nuclear weapons.[118] In the broader security realm, AI will affect human security missions.[119] By laying out an initial framework for how military applications of narrow AI could structure international competition and the balance of power, this article lays the groundwork for thinking through these questions in the future.

This article also raises a series of policy questions. When thinking about AI as an arena for international competition, one question is whether, in response to China's AI strategy, the United States should launch its own comprehensive AI strategy. In 2016, the Obama White House released an AI policy road map. It acknowledged the importance of US leadership in AI but focused mostly on regulatory policy questions.[120] The transition from Barack Obama to Donald Trump led to a pause in these efforts, though the White House recently announced the creation of a new committee of AI experts to advise it on policy choices.[121]

Some might argue that it is necessary for the United States to develop and announce a formal AI strategy similar to China's.[122] While there are plenty of private-sector incentives for the development of AI technology, only the government can coordinate AI investments and ensure the development of particular implementations that it considers critical for AI leadership.[123]

On the other hand, it is the free market in the United States, and its connections to the global economy, that have made the United States an engine of global innovation. More centrally planned economies have often struggled with innovation. During the Cold War, the Soviet defense-industrial base and military proved effective at perfecting existing technologies or adopting technologies. The centralized Soviet system, however, made true innovation more difficult.[124]

China is spending much more than the United States on AI research, and Chinese AI researchers are producing more papers on topics such as deep learning than US researchers.[125] How that translates into tangible advances in AI technology is unclear. From a balance-of-power perspective, one could argue that the optimal approach would involve a mixed strategy between market and government development of AI. In the economic arena, central planning can stifle innovation, meaning the role of government should be to fund basic research and then let market incentives do the rest.

The defense sector may be different, however. For the United States, it will be up to the Department of Defense to clearly outline what types of AI technologies are most useful and to seed research and development to turn those technologies into a reality. For any strategy, for both the United States and China, a principal challenge will be translating basic research in programs of record into actual capabilities. As Cummings writes about government agencies working on AI systems around the world, "The agencies developing these technologies are struggling to make the leap from development to operational implementation."[126]

More broadly, if investing in and appropriately utilizing AI is critical to military power in the 21st century, the US approach is a mixed bag. Optimists can point to investments in connecting cutting-edge research to US military forces through institutions such as the Defense Innovation Unit–Experimental (DIUx), the Strategic Capabilities Office, and the Defense Advanced Research Projects Agency (DARPA). From discussions of the "Third Offset" to "Multi-Domain Battle," senior military and civilian leaders are also taking the challenge of AI seriously.[127]

Meanwhile, a great deal of bottom-up innovation is happening in the US military, both in terms of developing technologies and experimenting with novel concepts of operation. It is possible that the research and smaller, experimental programs that the United States is funding will become part of mainstream US military programs, enabling the United States to stay ahead and sustain its military superiority. If narrow AI continues to develop, adopting the technology will require sustained attention by senior leaders.

Pessimists, however, can point to a gap between rhetoric and unit-level experimentation on the one hand and budgetary realities on the other.[128] There is a lot of discussion about the importance of artificial intelligence and robotics, as well as a clear desire among senior uniformed leadership to make the US military more networked, distributed, and lethal by taking advantage of AI, among other technologies.[129] This rhetoric has not yet caught up to reality in terms of US military spending on AI. When faced with a choice of investing in a next-generation drone, for example, the US Navy used its available programmatic dollars for the MQ-25 air-to-air refueling platform, which will support inhabited aircraft such as the F-35. The MQ-25 program was chosen over an advanced armed system—based on the X-47B demonstrator—with stealthy potential that could operate in dangerous conflict environments.[130] The MQ-25 decision may be seen as the canary in the coal mine if the US military falls behind in the coming decades—especially if a failure to appropriately adopt advances in AI and robotics turns out to be a key reason for that relative military decline.

At the end of the day, however, AI's effect on international politics will depend on much more than choices about one particular military program. The challenge for the United States will be in calibrating, based on trends in AI developments, how fast to move in incorporating narrow AI applications. This will be true whether those applications are dual-use or based in exclusively military research. And that challenge to leadership in AI in general, as well as in military power, is complicated by the movements of China and other competitors, all of which seem interested in leveraging AI to challenge US military superiority.

NOTES

1. James Vincent, "Putin Says the Nation That Leads in AI 'Will Be the Ruler of the World,'" *Verge*, Sept. 4, 2017, https://www.theverge.com/2017/9/4/16251226/russia-ai-putin-rule-the-world.

2. Klaus Schwab, *The Fourth Industrial Revolution* (New York: Crown Business, 2017).

3. Colin Clark, "Our Artificial Intelligence 'Sputnik Moment' Is Now: Eric Schmidt & Bob Work," *Breaking Defense*, Nov. 1, 2017, https://breakingdefense.com/2017/2011/our-artificial-intelligence-sputnik-moment-is-now-eric-schmidt-bob-work/.

4. Seth Fiegerman, "Elon Musk Predicts World War III," CNN, Sept. 4, 2017, http://money.cnn.com/2017/09/04/technology/culture/elon-musk-ai-world-war/index.html.

5. On technological determinism, see Merritt R. Smith and Leo Marx, *Does Technology Drive History? The Dilemma of Technological Determinism* (Cambridge, MA: MIT Press, 1994).

6. William H. McNeill, *The Pursuit of Power: Technology, Armed Force, and Society Since A.D. 1000* (Chicago: University of Chicago Press, 1982).

7. Jeremiah E. Dittmar, "Information Technology and Economic Change: The Impact of the Printing Press," *Quarterly Journal of Economics* 126, no. 3 (Aug. 2011): 1133–1172, https://doi.org/10.1093/qje/qjr035.

8. Robert Jervis, *The Meaning of the Nuclear Revolution: Statecraft and the Prospect of Armageddon* (Ithaca, NY: Cornell University Press, 1989).

9. In the military dimension, see Michael C. Horowitz, *The Diffusion of Military Power: Causes and Consequences for International Politics* (Princeton, NJ: Princeton University Press, 2010). For a critique of technology-focused thinking about the future of war, see Paul K. Van Riper and Frank G. Hoffman, "Pursuing the Real Revolution in Military Affairs: Exploiting Knowledge-Based Warfare," *National Security Studies Quarterly* 4, no. 3 (1998): 4; H. R. McMaster, "Continuity and Change: The Army Operating Concept and Clear Thinking About Future War," *Military Review* (2015), https://www.westpoint.edu/scusa/SiteAssets/SitePages/Keynote Speakers/Continuity and Change by LTG McMaster.pdf.

10. Clark G. Reynolds, *The Fast Carriers; The Forging of an Air Navy*, 1st ed. (New York: McGraw-Hill, 1968); Mark R. Peattie, *Sunburst: The Rise of Japanese Naval Air Power, 1909–1941* (Annapolis, MD: Naval Institute Press, 2001).

11. Marshall McLuhan, *The Gutenberg Galaxy: The Making of Typographic Man* (Toronto: University of Toronto Press, 1962).

12. Clemency Burton-Hill, "The Superhero of Artificial Intelligence: Can This Genius Keep It in Check?" *Guardian*, Feb. 16, 2016, https://www. theguardian.com/technology/2016/feb/16/demis-hassabis-artificial-intelligence-deepmind-alphago.

13. Katja Grace et al., "When Will AI Exceed Human Performance? Evidence from AI Experts," *arXiv* (May 2017), https://arxiv.org/abs/1705.08807.

14. This is based on the Russell and Norvig definition that artificial intelligence is about the construction of artificial rational agents that can perceive and act. See Stuart Russell and Peter Norvig, *Artificial Intelligence: A Modern Approach*, 3rd ed.

(Englewood Cliffs, NJ: Prentice Hall, 2009). Also see Calum McClelland, "The Difference Between Artificial Intelligence, Machine Learning, and Deep Learning," *Medium*, Dec. 4, 2017, https://medium.com/iotforall/the-difference-between-artificial-intelligence-machine-learning-and-deep-learning-3aa67bff5991.

15. Shane Legg and Marcus Hutter, "Universal Intelligence: A Definition of Machine Intelligence," *arXiv* (Dec. 2007): 12, https://arxiv.org/abs/0712.3329.

16. Michael C. Horowitz, "Military Robotics, Autonomous Systems, and the Future of Military Effectiveness," in *The Sword's Other Edge: Tradeoffs in the Pursuit of Military Effectiveness*, ed. Dan Reiter (New York: Cambridge University Press, 2017).

17. Matt Simon, "Watch Boston Dynamics' SpotMini Robot Open a Door," *Wired*, Feb. 12, 2018, https://www.wired.com/story/watch-boston-dynamics-spotmini-robot-open-a-door/.

18. This is based on the discussion in Paul Scharre and Michael C. Horowitz, "An Introduction to Autonomy in Weapon Systems," *Center for a New American Security Working Paper* (Feb. 2015): 5, https://www.cnas.org/publications/reports/an-introduction-to-autonomy-in-weapon-systems.

19. Michael C. Horowitz, Paul Scharre, and Alex Velez-Green, "A Stable Nuclear Future? The Impact of Automation, Autonomy, and Artificial Intelligence" (Philadelphia: University of Pennsylvania Press, 2017).

20. Scharre and Horowitz, "Autonomy in Weapon Systems," 6.

21. Murray Campbell, A. Joseph Hoane Jr., and Feng-hsiung Hsu, "Deep Blue," *Artificial Intelligence* 134, nos. 1–2 (2002): 57–83, https://doi.org/10.1016/S0004-3702(01)00129-1.

22. Ryszard S. Michalski, Jaime G. Carbonell, and Tom M. Mitchell, eds., *Machine Learning: An Artificial Intelligence Approach* (New York: Springer, 2013); Allen Newell and Herbert Alexander Simon, *Human Problem Solving* (Englewood Cliffs, NJ: Prentice Hall, 1972).

23. Robert D. Hof, "Deep Learning," *MIT Technology Review* (2013), https://www.technologyreview.com/s/513696/deep-learning/; Anh Nguyen, Jason Yosinski, and Jeff Clune, "Deep Neural Networks Are Easily Fooled: High Confidence Predictions for Unrecognizable Images," Paper presented at the Institute of Electrical and Electronics Engineers conference on computer vision and pattern recognition, 2015, https://arxiv.org/abs/1412.1897.

24. Antonio Lieto, Antonio Chella, and Marcello Frixione, "Conceptual Spaces for Cognitive Architectures: A Lingua Franca for Different Levels of Representation," *Biologically Inspired Cognitive Architectures* 19 (Jan. 2017), https://doi.org/10.1016/j.bica.2016.10.005.

25. Calestous Juma, *Innovation and Its Enemies: Why People Resist New Technologies* (Oxford: Oxford University Press, 2016).

26. Lockheed Martin, "Building the F-35: Combining Teamwork and Technology," accessed May 8, 2018, https://www.f35.com/about/life-cycle/production.

27. The "Third Offset" was a Department of Defense initiative led by Deputy Secretary of Defense Robert Work that was designed to preserve US military superiority through exploiting a generation of emerging technologies. Robert O. Work, *Deputy Secretary of Defense Remarks to the Association of the U.S. Army Annual Convention*, Oct. 4, 2016, https://www.defense

.gov/News/Speeches/Speech-View/Article/974075/remarks -to-the-association-of-the-us-army-annual-convention/.

28. Walter Frick, "Why AI Can't Write This Article (Yet)," *Harvard Business Review*, July 24, 2017, https://hbr.org/cover -story/2017/07/the-business-of-artificial-intelligence#/2017/07 /why-ai-cant-write-this-article-yet.

29. Andrew Ng, "Artificial Intelligence Is the New Electricity," *Medium*, Apr. 28, 2017, https://medium.com/@Synced/ artificial-intelligence-is-the-new-electricity-andrew-ng-cc132 ea6264.

30. Mick Ryan, "Building a Future: Integrated Human-Machine Military Organization," *Strategy Bridge*, Dec. 11, 2017, https://thestrategybridge.org/the-bridge/2017/12/11/building-a -future-integrated-human-machine-military-organization; Paul Scharre, *Army of None: Autonomous Weapons and the Future of War* (New York: W. W. Norton, 2018).

31. Gregory C. Allen, "Project Maven Brings AI to the Fight Against ISIS," *Bulletin of the Atomic Scientists*, Dec. 21, 2017, https://thebulletin.org/project-maven-brings-ai-fight-against -isis11374.

32. Note that this illustrates the importance of data in training algorithms. While there is some promise to synthetic data for training algorithms, there is not currently a substitute for data based on real-world experience. Thus, access to large quantities of useful data will be critical to designing successful algorithms in particular arenas. For an example of basic defense research on using AI to increase situational awareness, see Heather Roff, "COMPASS: A New AI-Driven Situational Awareness Tool for the Pentagon?" *Bulletin of the Atomic Scientists*, May 10, 2018, https://thebulletin.org/compass-new-ai -driven-situational-awareness-tool-pentagon11816.

33. Scharre and Horowitz, "Autonomy in Weapon Systems," 5.

34. Nick Bostrom, *Superintelligence: Paths, Dangers, Strategies* (Oxford: Oxford University Press, 2014).

35. Allan Dafoe, "Governing the AI Revolution: The Research Landscape" (New Haven, CT: Yale University, 2018), https://machine-learning-and-security.github.io/slides/Allan -Dafoe-NIPS-s.pdf.

36. Grace et al., "When Will AI Exceed Human Performance?"

37. McNeill, *The Pursuit of Power*.

38. David A. Baldwin, "Power Analysis and World Politics: New Trends versus Old Tendencies," *World Politics* 31, no. 2 (Jan. 1979): 161–194, https://www.jstor.org/stable/2009941; Robert Gilpin, *War and Change in World Politics* (New York: Cambridge University Press, 1981).

39. Scharre and Horowitz, "Autonomy in Weapon Systems."

40. Missy L. Cummings, "Artificial Intelligence and the Future of Warfare," Chatham House, Jan. 2017, https://www .chathamhouse.org/publication/artificial-intelligence-and -future-warfare.

41. Napoleonic warfare, or *levée en masse*, is an example of a military innovation not considered tied to technological innovations.

42. On military innovation in general, see Adam Grissom, "The Future of Military Innovation Studies," *Journal of Strategic Studies* 29, no. 5 (2006): 905–934, https://doi.org/10 .1080/01402390600901067.

43. Bernard Brodie et al., eds., *The Absolute Weapon: Atomic Power and World Order* (New York: Harcourt Brace, 1946); Stephen P. Rosen, *Winning the Next War: Innovation and the Modern Military* (Ithaca, NY: Cornell University Press, 1991); Barry R. Posen, *The Sources of Military Doctrine: France, Britain, and Germany Between the World Wars* (Ithaca, NY: Cornell University Press, 1984).

44. Posen, *Sources of Military Doctrine*; Rosen, *Winning the Next War*; Dima Adamsky, *The Culture of Military Innovation: The Impact of Cultural Factors on the Revolution in Military Affairs in Russia, the U.S., and Israel* (Stanford, CA: Stanford University Press, 2010); Theo Farrell, "World Culture and Military Power," *Security Studies* 14, no. 3 (2005): 448–488, https:// doi.org/10.1080/09636410500323187; Emily O. Goldman and Leslie C. Eliason eds., *The Diffusion of Military Technology and Ideas* (Stanford, CA: Stanford University Press, 2003).

45. Horowitz, *Diffusion of Military Power*, 10–11.

46. This relates to questions about the offense/defense implications of technology, though technology itself is rarely predictive. See Keir A. Lieber, *War and the Engineers: The Primacy of Politics Over Technology* (Ithaca, NY: Cornell University Press, 2005).

47. Stephen D. Biddle, *Military Power: Explaining Victory and Defeat in Modern Battle* (Princeton, NJ: Princeton University Press, 2004).

48. This is not meant to endorse or reject the notion of technology as a social construction. On that point, see Trevor J. Pinch and Wiebe E. Bijker, "The Social Construction of Facts and Artefacts: Or How the Sociology of Science and the Sociology of Technology Might Benefit Each Other," *Social Studies of Science* 14, no. 3 (1984): 399–441, http://www.jstor .org/stable/285355. What is key is that it is in the context of organizational behavior that the impact of technological change becomes clearest.

49. Posen, *Sources of Military Doctrine*; Rosen, *Winning the Next War*; Adamsky, *The Culture of Military Innovation*.

50. Nuclear weapons are arguably an exception to this pattern, given their unique destructive power. But they may be the exception that proves the rule.

51. Andrea Gilli and Mauro Gilli, "Military-Technological Superiority: Systems Integration and the Challenges of Imitation, Reverse Engineering, and Cyber-Espionage," *International Security* (forthcoming).

52. Mancur Olson, *The Rise and Decline of Nations: Economic Growth, Stagflation, and Social Rigidities* (New Haven, CT: Yale University Press, 1982); Horowitz, *Diffusion of Military Power*.

53. Dennis E. Showalter, *Railroads and Rifles: Soldiers, Technology, and the Unification of Germany* (Hamden, CT: Archon Books, 1975); Geoffrey L. Herrera and Thomas G. Mahnken, "Military Diffusion in Nineteenth-Century Europe: The Napoleonic and Prussian Military Systems," in *The Diffusion of Military Technology and Ideas*, ed. Emily O. Goldman and Leslie C. Eliason (Stanford, CA: Stanford University Press, 2003).

54. Another example is the tank. Applied to AI and drones, see Ulrike E. Franke, "A European Approach to Military Drones and Artificial Intelligence," European Council on Foreign Relations, June 23, 2017, http://www.ecfr.eu/article/ess ay_a_european_approach_to_military_drones_and_artificial _intelligence. In general, see David E. Johnson, *Fast Tanks and Heavy Bombers: Innovation in the U.S. Army, 1917–1945* (Ithaca, NY: Cornell University Press, 1998).

55. Horowitz, *Diffusion of Military Power.*

56. Horowitz, *Diffusion of Military Power.*

57. Horowitz, *Diffusion of Military Power.*

58. See Gilpin, *War and Change in World Politics*; Daniel R. Headrick, *The Tools of Empire: Technology and European Imperialism in the Nineteenth Century* (New York: Oxford University Press, 1981); Horowitz, *Diffusion of Military Power.*

59. Kenneth N. Waltz, *Theory of International Politics* (New York: McGraw-Hill, 1979).

60. Marvin B. Lieberman and David B. Montgomery, "First-Mover Advantages," *Strategic Management* Journal 9, no. 1 (1988): 41–58, https://doi. org/10.1002/smj.4250090706; Marvin B. Lieberman and David B. Montgomery, "First-Mover (Dis)Advantages: Retrospective and Link with the Resource-Based View," *Strategic Management Journal* 19, no. 12 (1998): 1111–1125, https://doi.org/10.1002/(SICI)1097 -0266(1998120)19:12<1111::AID-SMJ21>3.0.CO;2-W; Gerard J. Tellis and Peter N. Golder, *Will and Vision: How Latecomers Grow to Dominate Markets* (New York: McGraw-Hill, 2002).

61. Everett M. Rogers, *Diffusion of Innovations*, 5th ed. (New York: Free Press, 2003).

62. Horowitz, *Diffusion of Military Power.* For a recent argument about the complexity of stealth and the challenges of adoption, see Gilli and Gilli, "Military-Technological Superiority."

63. Showalter, *Railroads and Rifles*; Geoffrey L. Herrera, *Technology and International Transformation: The Railroad, the Atom Bomb, and the Politics of Technological Change* (Albany: State University of New York Press, 2006).

64. Eric Schmidt, "Keynote Address at the Center for a New American Security Artificial Intelligence and Global Security Summit," Center for a New American Security, Nov. 13, 2017, https:// www.cnas.org/publications/transcript/eric-schmidt-keynote-addre ss-at-the-center-for-a-new-american-security-artificial-intelligence -and-global-security-summit.

65. John R. Allen and Amir Husain, "The Next Space Race Is Artificial Intelligence," *Foreign Policy*, Nov. 3, 2017, http://foreignpolicy.com/2017/2011/2003/the-next-space-rac e-is-artificial-intelligence-and-america-is-losing-to-china/.

66. Tom Simonite, "For Superpowers, Artificial Intelligence Fuels New Global Arms Race," *Wired*, Sept. 8, 2017, https:// www.wired.com/story/for-superpowers-artificial-intelligence-fuels-new-global-arms-race/; Zachary Cohen, "US Risks Losing Artificial Intelligence Arms Race to China and Russia," CNN, Nov. 29, 2017, https://www.cnn.com/2017/11/29/politics/us -military-artificial-intelligence-russia-china/index.html; Julian E. Barnes and Josh Chin, "The New Arms Race in AI," *Wall Street Journal*, Mar. 2, 2018, https://www.wsj.com/articles/the-new -arms-race-in-ai-1520009261.

67. Graham Webster et al., "China's Plan to 'Lead' in AI: Purpose, Prospects, and Problems," New America Foundation, Aug. 1, 2017, https://www.newamerica.org/cybersecurity-initi ative/blog/chinas-plan-lead-ai-purpose-prospects-and-prob lems/.

68. Samuel Bendett, "Russia Is Poised to Surprise the US in Battlefield Robotics," *Defense One*, Jan. 25 2018, https://www .defenseone.com/ideas/2018/01/russia-poised-surprise-us -battlefield-robotics/145439/; Barnes and Chin, "The New Arms

Race in AI"; Samuel Bendett, "Red Robots Rising," *Strategy Bridge*, Dec. 12, 2017, https://thestrategybridge.org/the-bridge /2017/12/12/red-robots-rising-behind-the-rapid-development-of -russian-unmanned-military-systems; Valerie Insinna, "Russia's Nuclear Underwater Drone Is Real and in the Nuclear Posture Review," *Defense News*, Jan. 12, 2018, https://www.defense news.com/space/2018/01/12/russias-nuclear-underwater-drone -is-real-and-in-the-nuclear-posture-review/.

69. For an overview of AI and national security, see Daniel S. Hoadley and Nathan J. Lucas, "Artificial Intelligence and National Security," Congressional Research Service, Apr. 26, 2018, https://fas.org/sgp/crs/natsec/R45178.pdf. Also see Benjamin Jensen, Chris Whyte, and Scott Cuomo, *Algorithms at War: The Promise, Peril, and Limits of Artificial Intelligence*, working paper (2018).

70. This is similar to what is going on in robotics. See Horowitz, "Military Robotics, Autonomous Systems, and the Future of Military Effectiveness."

71. Sachin Chitturu et al., "Artificial Intelligence and Southeast Asia's Future," McKinsey Global Institute, Sept. 2017, 1, https://www.mckinsey. com/~/media/McKinsey/Global Themes /Artificial Intelligence/Artificial-intelligence-and-Southeast-Asias -future.ashx; Ng Eng Hen, "Speech at Committee of Supply Debate," Ministry of Defense, Singapore, Mar. 7, 2014, https://www. mindef.gov.sg/web/portal/mindef/news-and-events/latest-releases /article-detail/2014/march/2014mar06-speeches-00341/!ut/p/z0 /fY07D4IwFIV_iwNjcy-IMKMOalQWNNjFVLxKFcqjDei _t8hq3M53c h7AIQWuRCfvwshKicLyiQfnMF4uVuh7-3iWuBg dk2Q7m-_XhzCADfD_Abs.

72. Mark Prigg, "Who Goes There? Samsung Unveils Robot Sentry That Can Kill from Two Miles Away," *Daily Mail* (UK), Sept. 15, 2014, http://www. dailymail.co.uk/sciencetech /article-2756847/Who-goes-Samsung-reveals-robot-sentry-set -eye-North-Korea.html.

73. Ryan, "Building a Future: Integrated Human-Machine Military Organization."

74. "Strategic Review of Defence and National Security: 2017," French Ministry of Defense, Dec. 22, 2017, 3, https:// www.defense.gouv.fr/dgris/politique-de-defense/revue-strate gique/revue-strategique. On the European approach to drones and AI, also see Franke, "A European Approach to Military Drones and Artificial Intelligence."

75. Eliran Rubin, "Tiny IDF Unit Is Brains Behind Israeli Army Artificial Intelligence," *Haaretz*, Aug. 15, 2017, https:// www.haaretz.com/israel-news/tiny-idf-unit-is-brains-behind -israeli-army-artificial-intelligence-1.5442911; Yaakov Lappin, "Artificial Intelligence Shapes the IDF in Ways Never Imagined," *Aglemeiner*, Oct. 16, 2017, https://www.algemeiner.com/2017 /10/16/artificial-intelligence-shapes-the-idf-in-ways-never -imagined/.

76. Lappin, "Artificial Intelligence Shapes the IDF in Ways Never Imagined."

77. One could also argue AI has the potential to go beyond shaping the character of war and change the nature of war itself. From a Clausewitzian perspective, that war is human fundamentally defines its nature. Carl von Clausewitz, *On War*, trans. Michael Howard and Peter Paret (Princeton, NJ: Princeton University Press, 1989). Thus, the nature of war is unchanging. In theory, could AI alter the nature of war itself because wars will be fought by robotic systems, not people, and because

of AI's potential to engage in planning and decision-making that were previously human endeavors? U.S. Defense Secretary James Mattis speculated in February 2018 that AI is "fundamentally different" in ways that raise questions about the nature of war. See "Press Gaggle by Secretary Mattis en Route to Washington, D.C.," Department of Defense, Feb. 17, 2018, https://www.defense.gov/News/Transcripts/Transcript-View /Article/1444921/press-gaggle-by-secretary-mattis-en-route-to-washington-dc/. This is an important debate but one beyond the scope of this paper. For elements of this debate, see Kareem Ayoub and Kenneth Payne, "Strategy in the Age of Artificial Intelligence," *Journal of Strategic Studies* 39, nos. 5–6 (2016): 793–819, https://doi.org/10.1080/01402390.2015.1088838. Frank G. Hoffman, "Will War's Nature Change in the Seventh Military Revolution?" *Parameters* 47, no. 4, (2018): 19–31, https://ssi.armywarcollege.edu/pubs/parameters/issues/Winter _2017-18/5_Hoffman.pdf. Also see Kenneth Payne, *Strategy, Evolution, and War: From Apes to Artificial Intelligence* (Washington, DC: Georgetown University Press, 2018).

78. Robert O. Work, Deputy Secretary of Defense Speech at Center for a New American Security Defense Forum, Dec. 14, 2015, http://www. defense.gov/News/Speeches/Speech -View/Article/634214/cnas-defense-forum; John R. Allen and Amir Husain, "On Hyperwar," *Proceedings of the United States Naval Institute* 143, no. 7 (July 2017), https://www .usni.org/magazines/proceedings/2017-07/hyperwar.

79. Bolei Zhou et al., "Places: A 10 Million Image Database for Scene Recognition," *IEEE Transactions on Pattern Analysis and Machine Intelligence* (July 2017), https://doi.org /10.1109/TPAMI.2017.2723009.

80. Miles Brundage et al., "The Malicious Use of Artificial Intelligence: Forecasting, Prevention, and Mitigation," working paper (2018), https://arxiv.org/abs/1802.07228. Stephanie Carvin, "Normal Autonomous Accidents," *Social Science Research Network* (2018), http://dx.doi.org/10.2139 /ssrn.3161446.

81. For example, see Vijay Kumar, Aleksandr Kushleyev, and Daniel Mellinger, "Three-Dimensional Manipulation of Teams of Quadrotors," Google Patents, 2017, https://patents .google.com/patent/US20150105946.

82. Simon Jones et al., "Evolving Behaviour Trees for Swarm Robotics," in *Distributed Autonomous Robotic Systems*, ed. Roderich Grob et al. (Boulder, CO: Springer, 2018).

83. Tero Karras et al., "Progressive Growing of GANs for Improved Quality, Stability, and Variation," published as a conference paper in *International Conference on Learning Representations 2018* (2018), https://arxiv.org/abs/1710.10196.

84. Michael C. Horowitz, "The Promise and Peril of Military Applications of Artificial Intelligence," *Bulletin of the Atomic Scientists*, Apr. 23, 2018, https://thebulletin.org/military -applications-artificial-intelligence/promise-and-peril-military -applications-artificial-intelligence.

85. Rosen, *Winning the Next War*.

86. Clayton M. Christensen, *The Innovator's Dilemma* (Boston, MA: Harvard Business School Press, 1997). This also relates to strategies for innovating within militaries. See Peter Dombrowski and Eugene Gholz, *Buying Military Transformation* (New York: Columbia University Press, 2006).

87. Cummings, "Artificial Intelligence and the Future of Warfare," 9. Also see Lawrence Spinetta and Missy L. Cum-

mings, "Unloved Aerial Vehicles: Gutting Its UAV Plan, the Air Force Sets a Course for Irrelevance," *Armed Forces Journal* (Nov. 2012): 8–12.

88. Adamsky, *Culture of Military Innovation*.

89. Emily O. Goldman, "Cultural Foundations of Military Diffusion," *Review of International Studies* 32, no. 1 (2006): 69–91, https://doi.org/10.1017/S0260210506006930.

90. Farrell, "World Culture and Military Power."

91. Horowitz, *Diffusion of Military Power*.

92. Horowitz, *Diffusion of Military Power*.

93. Tim Hwang, "Computational Power and the Social Impact of Artificial Intelligence," Mar. 23, 2018, https://ssrn.com /abstract=3147971.

94. Hof, "Deep Learning."

95. Meg Murphy, "Building the Hardware for the Next Generation of Artificial Intelligence," *MIT News*, Nov. 30 2017, http://news.mit.edu/2017/building-hardware-next-generation-ar tificial-intelligence-1201.

96. James Manyika et al., "What the Future of Work Will Mean for Jobs, Skills, and Wages," McKinsey Global Institute report, Nov. 2017, https://www.mckinsey.com/global-themes /future-of-organizations-and-work/what-the-future-of-work-will -mean-for-jobs-skills-and-wages.

97. Carl B. Frey and Michael A. Osborne, "The Future of Employment: How Susceptible Are Jobs to Computerisation?" *Technological Forecasting and Social Change* 114 (Jan. 2017): 254–280, https://doi.org/10.1016/j.techfore.2016.08.019.

98. Cummings, "Artificial Intelligence and the Future of Warfare," 10.

99. Kate Conger and Dell Cameron, "Google Is Helping the Pentagon Build AI for Drones," *Gizmodo*, Mar. 6, 2018, https:// gizmodo.com/google-is-helping-the-pentagon-build-ai-for -drones-1823464533.

100. Horowitz, *Diffusion of Military Power*.

101. Cade Metz, "Google Just Open Sourced TensorFlow, Its Artificial Intelligence Engine," *Wired*, Nov. 9, 2015, https:// www.wired.com/2015/11/google-open-sources-its-artificial-inte lligence-engine/.

102. Dario Amodei et al., "Concrete Problems in AI Safety," *arXiv*, July 25, 2016, https://arxiv.org/abs/1606.06565. This commitment to openness has limits. Google has many proprietary algorithms, and Microsoft's Watson (which first came to fame when it defeated Ken Jennings, the greatest living human Jeopardy player) is also proprietary.

103. In extreme examples where first-mover advantages are difficult to generate, there can be advantages for rapid followers that do not have to pay initial R&D costs. Alexander Gerschenkron, *Economic Backwardness in Historical Perspective: A Book of Essays* (Cambridge, MA: Harvard University Press, 1962).

104. The Germans did not call it "blitzkrieg," explicitly. Ernest R. May, *Strange Victory: Hitler's Conquest of France* (New York: Hill and Wang, 2000); Posen, *Sources of Military Doctrine*.

105. The issue of algorithm theft raises questions of cybersecurity. This differs from more common questions about whether cyberweapons are autonomous weapons. On cyber in general, see Thomas Rid, *Rise of the Machines: A Cybernetic History* (New York: W. W. Norton, 2016); Rebecca Slayton, "What Is the Cyber Offense-Defense Balance? Conceptions,

Causes, and Assessment," *International Security* 41, no. 3 (2017): 72–109, https://doi.org/10.1162/ISEC_a_00267; Ben Buchanan, *The Cybersecurity Dilemma: Hacking, Trust, and Fear Between Nations* (Oxford: Oxford University Press, 2017); Nina Kollars, "The Rise of Smart Machines," in *The Palgrave Handbook of Security, Risk, and Intelligence*, ed. Robert Dover, Huw Dylan, and Michael Goodmans (London: Palgrave Mac-Millan, 2016), 195–211.

106. Stephen G. Brooks, *Producing Security: Multinational Corporations, Globalization, and the Changing Calculus of Conflict* (Princeton, NJ: Princeton University Press, 2005); Andrea Gilli and Mauro Gilli, "The Diffusion of Drone Warfare? Industrial, Organizational and Infrastructural Constraints," *Security Studies* 25, no. 1 (2016): 50–84, https://doi.org/10.1080 /09636412.2016.1134189.

107. Gilli and Gilli, "Military-Technological Superiority." Note this extends the argument to AI.

108. Elsa B. Kania, "Battlefield Singularity: Artificial Intelligence, Military Revolution, and China's Future Military Power," Center for a New American Security, Nov. 28, 2017, https://www.cnas.org/publications/reports/battlefield-singular ity-artificial-intelligence-military-revolution-and-chinas-future -military-power.

109. Kania, "Battlefield Singularity," 4.

110. Gilpin, *War and Change in World Politics.*

111. Paul Scharre, "Autonomous Weapons and Operational Risk," Center for a New American Security, working paper, (Feb. 2016), https://www. cnas.org/publications/reports/auto nomous-weapons-and-operational-risk.

112. Thanks to Heather Roff for making this point clear.

113. H. R. McMaster, "Continuity and Change: The Army Operating Concept and Clear Thinking About Future War."

114. On the security dilemma, see Robert Jervis, "Cooperation Under the Security Dilemma," *World Politics* 30, no. 2 (1978): 167–214, http://www. jstor.org/stable/2009958. This would also make arms control more difficult.

115. Yuen Foong Khong, *Analogies at War: Korea, Munich, Dien Bien Phu, and the Vietnam Decisions of 1965* (Princeton, NJ: Princeton University Press, 1992).

116. Michael C. Horowitz, "The Ethics and Morality of Robotic Warfare: Assessing the Debate Over Autonomous Weapons," *Daedalus* 145, no. 4 (2016): 25–36, https://doi.org /10.1162/DAED_a_00409.

117. On warfare at machine speed, see Work, Deputy Secretary of Defense Remarks. On AI and the speed of war, see Allen and Husain, "On Hyperwar."

118. Horowitz, Scharre, and Velez-Green, "A Stable Nuclear Future?"

119. Heather Roff, "Advancing Human Security Through Artificial Intelligence," Chatham House, May 2017, https://www .chathamhouse.org/publication/advancing-human-security-throug h-artificial-intelligence.

120. Ed Felten and Terah Lyons, "The Administration's Report on the Future of Artificial Intelligence," White House, Oct. 12, 2016, https://obamawhitehouse.archives.gov/blog/2016 /10/12/administrations-report-future-artificial-intelligence.

121. Aaron Boyd, "White House Announces Select Committee of Federal AI Experts," *Nextgov*, May 10, 2018, https:// www.nextgov.com/emerging-tech/2018/05/white-house-annou nces-select-committee-federal-ai-experts/148123/.

122. For a recent example, see William A. Carter, Emma Kinnucan, and Josh Elliot, "A National Machine Intelligence Strategy for the United States," Center for Strategic and International Studies and Booz Allen Hamilton, Mar. 2018, https:// www.csis.org/analysis/national-machine-intelligence-strategy -united-states.

123. Allen and Husain, "The Next Space Race Is Artificial Intelligence."

124. Matthew Evangelista, *Innovation and the Arms Race: How the United States and the Soviet Union Develop New Military Technologies* (Ithaca, NY: Cornell University Press, 1988).

125. Cade Metz, "As China Marches Forward on A.I., the White House Is Silent," *New York Times*, Feb. 12, 2018, https://www.nytimes.com/2018/02/12/technology/china-trump -artificial-intelligence.html.

126. Cummings, "Artificial Intelligence and the Future of Warfare," 9.

127. Tom Simonite, "Defense Secretary James Mattis Envies Silicon Valley's AI Ascent," *Wired*, Aug. 11, 2017, https://www .wired.com/story/james-mattis-artificial-intelligence-diux/; Gopal Ratnam, "DARPA Chief Touts Artificial Intelligence Efforts," *Roll Call*, Mar. 1, 2018, https://www.rollcall.com/news/politics /darpa-chief-touts-artificial-intelligence-efforts.

128. On bottom-up innovation, see Grissom, "The Future of Military Innovation Studies." On innovation inhibitors, see Adam M. Jungdahl and Julia M. Macdonald, "Innovation Inhibitors in War: Overcoming Obstacles in the Pursuit of Military Effectiveness," *Journal of Strategic Studies* 38, no. 4 (2015): 467–499, https://doi.org/10.1080/01402390.2014.917628.

129. Adm. Harry B. Harris Jr. et al., "The Integrated Joint Force: A Lethal Solution for Ensuring Military Preeminence," *Strategy Bridge*, Mar. 2, 2018, https://thestrategybridge.org /the-bridge/2018/3/2/the-integrated-joint-force-a-lethal-solu tion-for-ensuring-military-preeminence.

130. Sam LaGrone, "Navy Releases Final MQ-25 Stingray RFP; General Atomics Bid Revealed," *USNI News*, Oct. 10, 2017, https://news.usni.org/2017/10/10/navy-releases-final-mq -25-stingray-rfp-general-atomics-bid-revealed.

Why China Has Not Caught Up Yet

Military-Technological Superiority and the Limits of Imitation, Reverse Engineering, and Cyber Espionage

MAURO GILLI

Can adversaries of the United States easily imitate its most advanced weapon systems and thus erode its military-technological superiority? Do reverse engineering, industrial espionage, and, in particular, cyber espionage facilitate and accelerate this process? China's decades-long economic boom, military modernization program, massive reliance on cyber espionage, and assertive foreign policy have made these questions increasingly salient. Yet, almost everything known about this topic draws from the past. As explained in this article, the conclusions that the existing literature has reached by studying prior eras have no applicability to the current day.

Scholarship in international relations theory generally assumes that rising states benefit from the "advantage of backwardness," as described by Alexander Gerschenkron.[1] By free-riding on the research and technology of the most advanced countries, less developed states can allegedly close the military-technological gap with their rivals relatively easily and quickly.[2] More recent works maintain that globalization, the emergence of dual-use components, and advances in communications (including the opportunity for cyber espionage) have facilitated this process.[3] This literature is built on shaky theoretical foundations, and its claims lack empirical support.

The international relations literature largely ignores one of the most important changes to have occurred in the realm of weapons development since the second industrial revolution (1870–1914): the exponential increase in the complexity of military technology. This article argues that this increase in complexity has promoted a change in the system of production that has made the imitation and replication of the performance of state-of-the-art weapon systems harder—so much so as to offset the diffusing effects of globalization and advances in communications. On the one hand, the increase in complexity has significantly raised the entry barriers for the production of advanced weapon sys-

tems: countries must now possess an extremely advanced industrial, scientific, and technological base in weapons production before they can copy foreign military technology. On the other hand, the knowledge to design, develop, and produce advanced weapon systems is less likely to diffuse, given its increasingly tacit and organizational nature. As a result, the advantage of backwardness has shrunk significantly, and know-how and experience in the production of advanced weapon systems have become an important source of power for those who master them. This article employs two case studies to test this argument: Imperial Germany's rapid success in closing the technological gap with the British *Dreadnought* battleship, despite significant inhibiting factors; and China's struggle to imitate the US F-22/A Raptor jet fighter, despite several facilitating conditions.

Our research contributes to key theoretical and policy debates. First, the ability to imitate state-of-the-art military hardware plays a central role in theories that seek to explain patterns of internal balancing and the rise and fall of great powers. Yet, the mainstream international relations literature has not investigated this process.[4] Because imitating military technology was relatively easy in the past, scholars and policymakers assume that it also is today, as frequent analogies between Wilhelmine Germany and contemporary China epitomize.[5] This article investigates the conditions under which the imitation of state-of-the-art weapon systems such as attack submarines and combat aircraft is more or less likely to succeed.

Second, this article develops the first systematic theoretical explanation of why US superiority in military technology remains largely unrivaled almost thirty years after the end of the Cold War, despite globalization and the information and communication technology revolution. Some scholars have argued that developing modern weapon systems has become dramatically more demanding, which in turn has made internal

Mauro Gilli, "Why China Has Not Caught Up Yet: Military-Technological Superiority and the Limits of Imitation, Reverse Engineering, and Cyber Espionage," *International Security* 43, no. 3 (2019): 141–189. © 2019 by the President and Fellows of Harvard College and the Massachusetts Institute of Technology; published under a Creative Commons Attribution 4.0 International (CC BY 4.0) license.

This article was edited for length.

balancing against the United States more difficult.[6] This literature, however, cannot explain why in the age of globalization and instant communications—with cyber espionage permitting the theft of massive amount of digital data—US know-how in advanced weapon systems has not already diffused to other states. Other contributors to the debate on unipolarity have either pointed to the relative inferiority of Chinese military technology without providing a theoretical explanation, or they have argued that developing the military capabilities to challenge the status quo is, in the long run, a function of political will—an argument that cannot account for the failure of the Soviet Union to cope with US military technology from the late 1970s onward.[7] This article argues that in the transition from the second industrial revolution to the information age, the imitation of state-of-the-art military technology has become more difficult, so much so that today rising powers or even peer competitors cannot easily copy foreign weapon systems.[8] Our findings address existing concerns that China's use of cyber espionage and the increasing globalization of arms production will allow Beijing to rapidly close the military-technological gap with the United States.[9]

Third, the international relations literature accepts the claim that globalization and advances in communications have made the imitation of military technology easier; yet no one has empirically tested this proposition.[10] This failing is particularly concerning in light of the opportunities opened by cyber espionage—a practice that, according to many observers, could erode the US advantage in military technology. Richard Clark, a former US senior government official, believes that Chinese cyber espionage could result in the United States "hav[ing] all of [its] research and development stolen"; Gen. Keith Alexander, a former director of the National Security Agency, worries that cyber espionage could lead to "the greatest transfer of wealth in history."[11] With a few notable exceptions, however, international relations scholars have paid little attention to the advantages and limits of cyber espionage for copying foreign military technology.[12] Our research fills this gap and tests the conventional wisdom using the case of China, one of the states that has benefited the most from globalization and that has employed cyber espionage more extensively than any other country. [. . .]

Military-Technological Superiority

Military-technological superiority is a central theme in both international politics and international relations theory. Yet, the discipline has not studied the conditions under which states can close the military-technological gap with their rivals.

Military-Technological Competition

States compete to develop, field, and maintain the most advanced military platforms possible.[13] When a country develops a new military technology, its competitors will devise countermeasures and counter-innovations to limit, and possibly eliminate, the advantage their enemy derives from its innovation. Counter-innovations such as anti-air defense systems force innovators to further improve the performance of their technology.[14] The history of military innovation is, in the end, the history of innovation, counter-innovation, and further innovation.[15]

Although countermeasures and counter-innovations can be very effective, they permit countries only to negate the benefits an enemy gains from its innovations.[16] When countries seek to remain or become regional or global powers, or when they aim to deploy certain capabilities, however, they have to acquire specific military platforms, such as aircraft carriers for long-range power projection, jet fighters for air superiority, or submarines for sea denial. Some countries lagging behind in these capabilities will try to copy others' military innovations and, ideally, to outperform them.[17] Under the right conditions, imitation will facilitate and accelerate the ability of some states to catch up technologically.[18] First, by free-riding on the research and technology of innovators, imitators can save the resources they would otherwise need to invest to develop indigenously state-of-the-art technology.[19] Second, imitators can avoid making the mistakes of the innovators or, worse, embarking on technically unfeasible projects—a strong possibility when dealing with cutting-edge technologies.[20] Third, imitators can use their unused resources to improve existing technology and possibly outperform innovators.[21] In sum, imitators will derive an advantage when imitation is cheaper and faster than innovation.[22]

These conditions were present in the late nineteenth and early twentieth centuries, when rising powers such as Wilhelmine Germany, Imperial Japan, and the Soviet Union under Joseph Stalin could easily imitate foreign military technology and catch up with their rivals in a relatively short period of time.[23] Implicitly or explicitly, these and similar cases have informed the literature on the balance of power and on the rise and fall of great powers—a literature that largely has accepted the assumption that copying foreign military technology is relatively easy.[24]

Literature Review

The imitation of military technology plays a central but unappreciated role in the literature on international relations theory.[25] Internal balancing, for instance, often entails imitating foreign technology. Yet, international relations scholars have not investigated when and why efforts to imitate foreign weapon systems are successful.[26] Instead, they have assumed that states' intentions or incentives to imitate will ipso facto lead to success.[27]

According to Kenneth Waltz, for example, because of competition and socialization dynamics in international politics, the "weapons of the major contenders . . . come to . . . look much the same all over the world."[28] Similarly, Robert Gilpin argues that "there is a historical tendency for the military . . . techniques of the dominant state or empire to be diffused to other states in the system."[29] For P. W. Singer, "The problem for 'first movers' . . . is that they have to pay heavily" when developing military technology. In comparison, imitating countries "can 'free ride' on the early cost, copy what works and focus all their energy and resources solely on improving upon what the first mover does."[30] Interestingly, even some of the scholars who have questioned the literature's conventional wisdom agree with the proposition that the imitation of military hardware is relatively easy. In the words of Emily Goldman, "Hardware is often easy to acquire."[31] Similarly, Michael Horowitz writes that "it is [not] difficult to copy . . . specific technologies."[32]

Many scholars further argue that globalization and information technologies have facilitated and accelerated the diffusion of technology in the military realm.[33] Joseph Nye observes that, in the age of globalization, "technology . . . eventually spreads and becomes available to adversaries."[34] Some scholars claim that countries with advanced commercial industrial and technological capabilities can exploit their industrial and scientific base to develop state-of-the-art military technology.[35] Other scholars have stressed that, since the early 1990s, commercial research and development (R&D) has supplanted military R&D as the main driver of innovation.[36] As a result, many advanced technologies are now accessible on the global market at moderate cost, including those required for producing first-class military capabilities.[37] [. . .]

Problems with International Relations Theory

There are three problems with the conventional wisdom in international relations theory regarding the ability of states to copy foreign military technology. First, if imitation is easy, why do states invest in military innovation at all? Why not simply wait for others to develop innovations and then copy them?[38] Second, the assumption that imitation is easy is at odds with the literatures in economic history, economics, history of technology, management, science and technology studies, and sociology, which have sought to explain why some innovators retain a first-mover advantage, what the sources of industrial leadership are, and why very advanced companies sometimes fail to replicate an

innovation, even with full access to original blueprints and designs.[39] Third, imitating foreign technology also seems to be difficult in the commercial realm, where, according to international relations theory, it should be particularly easy. For instance, Google and Microsoft, two of the most advanced companies in the world, have struggled to cope with Apple's smartphone and tablet technology.[40] In the following section, this article explains why these trends are even more pronounced in weapons production.[41]

Complexity and Military-Technological Superiority

Since the second industrial revolution, the complexity of military technology has increased exponentially. This dramatic increase has changed the nature of innovation and of imitation, making the latter much more difficult to implement.

Complexity and the Integration Challenge

Complexity generates incompatibilities and vulnerabilities.[42] As complexity increases, the number and significance of incompatibilities and vulnerabilities also increase—exponentially.[43] Anticipating, detecting, identifying, understanding, and addressing all possible technical problems when designing, developing, and manufacturing an advanced weapon system pose major challenges.[44] Addressing them without creating new problems is an even greater challenge.[45] More challenging still is the need for weapons producers to design platforms that can incorporate cutting-edge and yet-to-be-developed technologies, and to limit their vulnerability to subtle and effective enemy countermeasures and counter-systems.[46]

Three developments help account for the increase in the complexity of military technology since the second industrial revolution. First, the number of components in military platforms has risen dramatically: in the 1930s, a combat aircraft consisted of hundreds of components, a figure that surged into the tens of thousands in the 1950s and to 300,000 in the 2010s.[47] As the number of components expands, the number of potential incompatibilities and vulnerabilities increases geometrically. Ensuring the proper functioning and mutual compatibility of all the components and of the whole system thus becomes increasingly difficult.[48]

Second, advancements in electronics, engineering, and material sciences have resulted in the components of major weapon systems becoming dramatically more sophisticated, leading military platforms to become "systems of systems."[49] Integrating large numbers of extremely advanced components, subsystems, and systems poses a daunting challenge. More sophisticated components have extremely low tolerances, which in turn require a degree of accuracy and precision in design, development, and manufacturing that was unthinkable a century ago.[50] For instance, aircraft engines in the 1900s and 1910s were "crude" mechanical devices that self-taught individuals could design, assemble, and install in their own repair shops.[51] In contrast, the production of today's aircraft engines is so technologically demanding that only a handful of producers around the world possesses the necessary technical expertise.[52] Consider that in turbofan engines, a "close clearance between [a rotary] part and its surroundings can be critical. One-tenth of 1 millimeter [i.e., 0.00393 inch] variation in dimension can have a significant impact on system compatibility."[53] The same is true of materials, electronics, and software, where minor imprecisions can have dramatic consequences.[54] For example, in modern jet fighters, software controls everything, from the operation of radars to the supply of oxygen. The expansion of onboard software functions is reflected in the increase in the number of software code lines from 1,000 in the F-4 Phantom II (1958), to 1.7 million in the F-22 (2006), and to 5.6 million in the F-35 Joint Strike Fighter/ Lightning II (2015).[55] Even a minor problem in those millions of lines of code could ground the aircraft or prove fatal.[56] This level of sophistication explains why software engineering is responsible for most of the delays and of the problems seen in advanced weapon systems.[57]

Third, modern weapon systems can now perform in extraordinarily demanding environmental and operational conditions, thanks to improvements in all metrics (e.g., speed, altitude ceiling for aircraft, and collapse depth for submarines).[58] These improvements, however, have increased the likelihood of technical problems.[59] The more sophisticated a component is, the more likely minor environmental changes will affect its performance.[60] In addition, as technological advances permit weapon systems to operate in once unfamiliar environmental conditions, designers and engineers are forced to deal with previously unknown physical phenomena.[61]

Change in the Nature of Innovation and Imitation

The increase in complexity and the resulting integration challenges have brought about a change in the very nature of innovation. In the late nineteenth and early twentieth centuries, innovation was primarily the product of conjecture, creativity, ingenuity, and intuition, as was the case with two of the most revolutionary military technologies of the twentieth century: submarines (1900) and aircraft (1903).[62] [. . .]

During the second industrial revolution, imitating countries could exploit the know-how and experience of their most advanced peers to develop state-of-the-

art military technology.[63] In fact, intuition and conjecture could be transferred from country to country with relative ease.[64] The main challenge these countries faced was to mobilize the necessary capital to launch production and to achieve the necessary economies of scale.[65] For industrialized countries, this challenge was not insurmountable.[66] Consider the naval rise of Imperial Japan. Because of its qualitatively modest domestic shipbuilding industry, in 1905 the Japanese navy mostly deployed British-made warships.[67] Yet, through a policy based on "copy, improve and innovate,"[68] involving the "purchase of specific foreign examples, the exhaustive analysis and testing of those models [and] their subsequent improvement,"[69] by 1912–13, Japan was able to commission two super Dreadnoughts that surpassed their British counterparts in both speed and tonnage.[70] And by the 1920s, "the skills available at both naval and commercial dockyards made Japan capable of turning out a range of warships that in design and construction were equal or superior to those of any navy in the world."[71]

Over time, however, the increase in complexity of military technology has made the process of imitation much more difficult. Economies of scale and exorbitant capital investments still represent major barriers for most countries seeking to enter the defense sector. Yet, simply extracting and investing resources is no longer sufficient to close the technological gap with the most advanced countries. Lacking the necessary know-how for weapon systems production has, in fact, become a major obstacle for actors trying to imitate foreign technology—wealthy countries included.[72] Japan's experience in the 1980s and 1990s offers a useful comparison to the Imperial era discussed above. As Stephen Brooks notes, despite Japan's then-primacy in high-technology and despite several decades of collaboration on weapons production with the United States, its F-2 fighter proved to be "a white elephant: no better than the F-16C [Japan built upon and] at least twice as expensive to produce."[73]

In the next two sections, this article explains why the increase in complexity has steadily eroded the advantages of imitation that some countries once enjoyed.

Absorptive Capacity

The increase in technological complexity over the past 150 years has exponentially raised the requirements to assimilate and imitate foreign military technology, thus canceling the first necessary condition for states to enjoy the advantage of imitation—relatively low entry barriers for the imitation of state-of-the-art weapon systems.

To free ride on the R&D of a foreign country, a country must be able "to identify, assimilate, and exploit knowledge from the environment."[74] But as scholarship from other disciplines shows, knowledge and experience are not public goods that can be easily and cheaply appropriated.[75] An imitator must possess an adequate absorptive capacity: material and nonmaterial capabilities such as laboratories, research centers, testing and production facilities, a skilled workforce, and a cumulative technological knowledge base (the stock of knowledge acquired through previous projects).[76] Without such absorptive capacity, the imitator will have to develop an advanced industrial, technological, and scientific base before it can copy foreign technologies. In the next two sections, this article explains how the increase in complexity has created massive and highly specific requirements for those seeking to imitate advanced weapon systems.

From Limited to Massive Absorptive Capacity Requirements

Whereas in the past, the requirements to imitate foreign military technology were limited, today, states need to master, to an unprecedented level, a much broader range of disciplines and activities.

Limited Capacity

In the aftermath of the second industrial revolution, the absorptive capacity required to imitate cutting-edge technologies was comparatively low for great powers. For industrialized countries, capital investments and sufficient economies of scale were essentially the only constraints, as entering weapons production required relatively little accumulated knowledge or experience.[77] During this period, "within many economic sectors, the knowledge required for moving out of the technological frontier was rather elementary scientific knowledge of a kind that had been available for a long time."[78] Even sectors such as metallurgy, which "placed a premium on basic chemical knowledge . . . drew primarily on elementary science when they drew on science at all."[79] This was also true for emerging fields such as aviation, which owed "practically nothing to the relatively mature state of the science of fluid dynamics."[80] In addition, the number of disciplines required in a given field was limited. For example, aviation design well into the late 1930s essentially required knowledge about "efficient aerodynamic structure and hydraulic controls."[81] Similarly, until World War II, submarine development required only reliable and powerful diesel engines, welding of metals, and efficient designs.[82]

In these circumstances, it is clear why "the period before 1914 . . . was unlikely to produce asymmetrical [revolutions in military affairs] that conferred enduring advantages." Technology moved swiftly across borders, and great powers were able to exploit it with relative ease—to the point that it "was indeed often

most convenient and cheapest to make use of another country's research and development."[83] For this reason, Germany in the 1930s could move from "possess[ing] no significant aircraft industry" to being "in the forefront of aviation technology" in just three years.[84]

Massive Capacity

The increase in the complexity of weapon systems has exponentially raised the absorptive capacity requirements to assimilate foreign know-how and experience and to imitate foreign military platforms.[85] The stock of accumulated knowledge has, in fact, expanded to the point of becoming a "burden" for those seeking to assimilate it.[86] The number of disciplines involved has increased dramatically, going well beyond those necessary for weapon systems development, and reaching into new, unexplored fields related both to the environmental conditions where the platform is expected to operate and to interactions between human beings and technology (e.g., ergonomics, human physiology, and cognitive sciences).[87] Moreover, imitators must master all of these disciplines, because the margins for error and imprecision have shrunk enormously. Infinitesimally small mistakes can have potentially catastrophic effects, given the low tolerances and vulnerability of many key components, as well as the demanding environmental and operational conditions in which military platforms are employed.[88]

The evolution of aircraft production illustrates this trend. Originally an empirical field, aircraft design in the 1920s and 1930s started to incorporate scientific discoveries from aerodynamics theory and engineering science as wooden strut-and-wire biplanes began giving way to streamlined all-metal monoplanes.[89] After World War II, the advent of rocket engines, radio communications, automatic guidance and control, and high-speed aerodynamics created new challenges. In response, aircraft manufacturers had to broaden and deepen their knowledge base to include fields such as weapons design, avionics, and material structures, as well as the training of aircrews, combat tactics, and, most importantly, human physiology and atmospheric sciences.[90] With supersonic speed and subsequent advances, the number and sophistication of disciplines required for aircraft development expanded to the point of being well ahead of scientific knowledge and understanding.[91] Work on the SR-71 Blackbird exemplifies these trends. Because of the friction resulting from flying at three times the speed of sound, the body of the Blackbird was exposed to temperatures above 600°F. To address the resulting problems, Lockheed had to develop "special fuels, structural materials, manufacturing tools and techniques, hydraulic fluid, fuel-tank sealants, paints, plastic, wiring and connecting plugs, as well as basic aircraft and engine design."[92] With the transition to fly-by-wire, the absorptive capacity requirements grew by an order of magnitude, as aircraft production expanded to a broad set of highly demanding fields such as electronics, computer science, and communications, with "software construction [being] the most difficult problem in engineering."[93] Moreover, given the nature of these disciplines, the margin for error has continued to shrink: a minor glitch in the software or the exposure of the hardware to unforgiving conditions (e.g., extreme heat, cold, or humidity) can be fatal.[94] With the increase in autonomy in military aviation, the number of disciplines required for weapons production has expanded to "unmanned systems, human factors, psychology, cognitive science, communication, human-computer interaction, computer-supporter work groups and sociology."[95]

From Generic to Specific Requirements

Since the second industrial revolution, the absorptive capacity required to imitate foreign technology has become so specific that countries can no longer exploit their civilian industries to catch up technologically in the military realm. This change has further raised the entry barriers for imitating advanced weapon systems.

Generic Requirements

In the second half of the nineteenth and early twentieth centuries, manufacturing benefited from unprecedented and possibly unique synergies and economies of scope.[96] The relatively low level of technological complexity imposed fairly loose requirements, permitting the adoption across different industries of the same machine tools, the same industrial processes, and the same know-how.[97] For instance, problems related to automobile production were "not fundamentally different from those which had already been developed for products such as bicycles and sewing machines."[98] As a result, "the skills acquired in producing sewing machines and bicycles greatly facilitated the production of the automobile."[99] With mass production, the opportunities for synergies and economies of scope among different industries expanded even further.[100] [. . .]

Specific Requirements

Opportunities for synergies and economies of scope, however, have diminished dramatically.[101] Weapon systems increasingly rely on extremely advanced technologies, such as data fusion or stealth, that in many cases have no application in the commercial sector. At the same time, they operate under uniquely demanding environmental and operational conditions (e.g., flying at Mach 2). The resulting large number of subtle and challenging technical problems has led to an exponential increase in the required degree of accuracy.[102] Consequently, imitators can no longer exploit their existing technological and industrial capabilities to assimilate foreign military technology: the absorptive capacity requirements have become progressively more specific.[103] "Specific" requirements refers to the fact that the laboratories, research centers, testing and production facilities, skilled workforce, and the cumulative technological knowledge base developed for a particular type of production cannot be easily redeployed for assimilating and exploiting foreign know-how and experience in weapon systems.[104]

For instance, the design of modern weapon systems requires advanced knowledge of enemies' countersystems, tactics, and doctrines, as well as of the environmental conditions of operations.[105] When copying foreign technology, countries need this knowledge to translate foreign information into actual designs.[106] Design capabilities are also extremely important when seeking to integrate foreign component technologies into a competitive military platform. As John Alic writes, "Early design choices largely determine ultimate performance and costs." Once a design has been chosen, "no amount of analysis, modification, and refinement can salvage a deficient concept."[107] Understandably, commercial enterprises do not possess the necessary design capabilities for military production and cannot develop them overnight.[108] In submarine design, for example, "the most challenging competencies . . . require at least ten years of experience and a Ph.D."[109] [. . .]

One could argue that through reverse engineering, industrial espionage, or cyber espionage, an imitating country could skip the design and development stages and manufacture a foreign weapon system using its existing industrial base. This argument ignores a key constraint: the increase in complexity has also made manufacturing processes more specific and possibly unique. Because of the requirements that military platforms need to meet, today's production processes must achieve stringent levels of precision that are alien to most industries.[110] For instance, the low observability to radar of stealth aircraft will be compromised if "the heads of [just] three screws [are] not quite tight and extend . . . above the surface by less than an eighth of an inch."[111] In the words of the F-117 Nighthawk's program manager, "In building the stealth fighter, we had to tightrope walk between extreme care and Swiss-watch perfection to match the low radar observability of our original computerized shape."[112] In turn, developing, updating, and preserving this type of manufacturing skill calls for highly specific training, practices, and processes. In the shipbuilding industry, workers across all technical skills require "6–8 years to reach at least 90 percent of optimum productivity."[113]

The unique requirements of manufacturing weapon systems go well beyond skills and processes. Take, for example, machine tools. In the early twentieth century, as discussed earlier, disparate fields such as the auto-mobile and sewing machine industries used the same machine tools. In contrast, since the end of World War II, the production of military aircraft engines has re-lied on machine tools with a degree of precision that no commercial company possesses or needs.[114] For its part, the US Navy has developed propellers that dra-matically reduce the acoustic signature of its subma-rines.[115] With help from the John Walker spy ring, the Soviet Union obtained information about how to man-ufacture US propellers.[116] Their production, however, required computer-controlled milling machines with a degree of accuracy that Soviet machines could not achieve.[117] In short, the Soviets could not rely on their existing capabilities to exploit the information they had obtained through industrial espionage.[118]

Technological Knowledge

The second condition for the advantage of imitation requires that imitating countries acquire, relatively eas-ily and quickly, the technological knowledge of how to design, develop, and/or manufacture a given military platform, so that they can take advantage of the inno-vator's advances before the platform becomes obso-lete.[119] The increase in the complexity of military tech-nology, however, has made technological knowledge increasingly tacit and organizational in nature, which means that it does not diffuse to other countries either easily or quickly.

Regardless of how advanced a country's industrial, scientific, and technological base is, the production of new military platforms requires work at the design, de-velopment, and manufacturing stages aimed at antici-pating, identifying, and addressing inherent idiosyncra-sies. These idiosyncrasies stem from the challenges related to the integration of state-of-the-art compo-nents, subsystems, and systems, as well as from hav-ing the platform operate under previously unexplored environmental conditions. As the director of Lock-heed's Skunk Works division, Chief Engineer Clarence "Kelly" Johnson, recalled when discussing the SR-71, "Everything about the aircraft had to be invented. Everything."[120] This article argues that the technologi-cal knowledge related to the production of advanced military platforms such as the SR-71 does not diffuse easily, because such knowledge is embedded in the organizational memory of the defense company that produced it.

From Codified to Tacit Knowledge

Over the past century and a half, weapons production has changed dramatically, as indicated by the increase in the development time of weapon systems from a few months to several years and even decades.[121] As noted

previously, in the late nineteenth and early twentieth centuries, innovations were the results of conjecture, creativity, ingenuity, and intuition (and sometimes of just plain luck or accidents).[122] This meant that the knowledge of how to produce a given technology was relatively simple; it could be written down in terms of principles and rules—it was codifiable. Codifiability permitted the spread of knowledge. Because of the growing complexity of weapons systems, however, in-novations have become the product of extensive pro-totyping, testing, experimentation, and refinement: as a result of this change, knowledge related to a given weapon system has become increasingly less codifi-able—it has become tacit. As former Secretary of De-fense Ashton Carter and coauthors have noted, "Tacit knowledge is a route for maintaining a technological edge in military systems: what cannot be written down can hardly be stolen."[123]

Codifiable Knowledge

During the immediate aftermath of the second indus-trial revolution, the knowledge behind most innova-tions was relatively simple: their logic and functioning were directly observable and understandable.[124] As such, an innovation generally carried within itself the very know-how related to its production process.[125] The simplicity of such know-how, in turn, allowed for the innovation's codification, and hence promoted its diffusion. This is what happened, for example, in manufacturing.

In the mid-nineteenth century, the implicit knowl-edge of skilled craftsmen was partially codified, allow-ing semiskilled workers to perform the manual tasks associated with the emergence of mechanized, stan-dardized manufacturing of interchangeable parts.[126] This trend was later reinforced with the development of the assembly line, which relied on the simplicity of the processes involved, and thus "the worker's implicit knowledge had to be made explicit."[127] Implicit knowl-edge was "gathered and analyzed" to permit the frag-mentation of work into a multitude of extremely simple tasks.[128] Beginning in the 1910s, the orga-nizational and technical principles of the assembly line and mass production were codified in articles and books.[129] The Ford Motor Company, the pioneer of the assembly line, also contributed to the codification of such knowledge when it decided to "have any part of its commercial, managerial or mechanical practice given full and unrestricted publicity in print."[130] Ford's transparency facilitated the diffusion of mass produc-tion processes to other industries.[131] [. . .]

Tacit Knowledge

Because of the increase in the complexity of military technology, the technological knowledge of how to de-sign, develop, and produce a given weapon system has become increasingly tacit. Tacit knowledge cannot be codified.[132] It entails knowledge derived mostly from experience and hence is retained by people and organizations: for this reason, it does not diffuse either easily or quickly.[133] Indeed, "the most effective way of [transferring tacit knowledge], despite telephone, video and other remote methods, is face-to-face interaction."[134] To replicate a given weapon system, an imitator needs direct access to the innovator's tacit knowledge—that is, access to the very people who worked on the system.[135] Otherwise, it will struggle to figure out what each part does, the requirements it is intended to meet, how to produce it, and how it is connected to other components—in other words, its design, development, and production know-how.[136] Moreover, disassembling a military platform into smaller components to observe and understand its functioning has become significantly more challenging. Today many weapon systems, such as jet fighters, "comprise highly integrated subsystems that are extremely difficult (if not impossible) to decompose into independent modules."[137] The introduction of electronics has reinforced this trend, as the functioning of software is governed not by observable physical laws (in contrast, for example, to aerodynamics), but by the software's internal correctness and its perfect integration with the weapon system's hardware.[138] [. . .]

Empirical Investigation

In this section, this article employs two cases to test our theory. First, it explains the rationale behind our case selection. Second, the article examines Imperial Germany's naval rearmament in the context of its naval rivalry with Great Britain from 1890 to 1916. Third, the article considers China's aerospace modernization program in the context of its competition with the United States from 1991 to 2018.

Research Design

The cases of Imperial Germany and contemporary China allow us to put our theory to a hard test and existing international relations theories to an easy test. In other words, if the conventional wisdom fails here, one should be skeptical of its validity under less favorable circumstances. Conversely, if our empirical investigation supports our argument, one should be confident about its success under more favorable conditions. [. . .]

Wilhelmine Germany and the All-Big-Gun Battleship, 1890–1916

In 1906, at the apex of the Anglo-German naval rivalry, the Royal Navy commissioned *Dreadnought*, an all-big-gun battleship that delivered higher speed, more stability, better armor protection, and, possibly more important, the firepower of two to three pre-Dreadnought battleships.[139] As such, *Dreadnought* made all existing battleships suddenly obsolete, thus canceling the capital investments that Britain's competitors had made during the past decade, including those of Imperial Germany.[140] Dreadnought battleships incorporated newly available component technologies and translated into practice British Adm. Jackie Fisher's maxim to "hit first, hit hard, and keep hitting."[141] First, Dreadnought battleships employed turbines rather than boilers: their lower weight, increased horsepower, and superior fuel efficiency resulted in greater speed (from 12 knots to a high of around 20 knots) without compromising range.[142] Second, because of developments in mechanics, electrical systems, and metallurgy, Dreadnought battleships carried longer-range quick-firing guns that, thanks to the first fire-control systems, extended the range of naval combat from a few thousand yards in 1905 to 12,000–20,000 yards in 1916.[143] Third, progress in metallurgy enabled the production of lighter but more resistant armor that, combined with developments in naval science, led to a doubling of battleship tonnage (from 15,000 to 30,000 tons).[144]

Absorptive Capacity

For Germany, the challenge appeared daunting; now it had to confront "by far the strongest shipbuilding industry in the world" with unrivaled experience in warship production.[145] In comparison, Germany's absorptive capacity in naval shipbuilding was relatively low in 1906. Until 1876, Germany was still purchasing most of its warships from Britain, and well into the 1880s, it still had no significant defense shipbuilding capability.[146] With the launch, in 1890, of its imperialist foreign policy (Weltpolitik), and the resulting increase in budget allocations to the navy, Germany began to learn important lessons both in weapons procurement and in warship design.[147] Yet, on the eve of the Dreadnought revolution, Germany had only slightly more than a decade of experience in warship production, and its industry was still struggling to produce advanced battleships, which were significantly inferior to their British counterparts.[148]

Second, Germany had a late start in reproducing Britain's *Dreadnought* design and several component technologies. This is because the very factors driving Germany's naval rise—domestic politics and bureaucratic ambitions—paradoxically were also responsible for slowing down, and possibly even harming, its naval modernization.[149] On the one hand, civil-military relations were unstable: Kaiser Wilhelm II, the great sponsor of German naval rearmament, constantly intervened in navy policy, inadvertently delaying "warship design and construction."[150] On the other hand,

Adm. Alfred von Tirpitz, appointed to lead the German Imperial Navy and fulfill the emperor's aspirations, was strenuously opposed to any increase in the capabilities of German battleships, because their additional costs risked undermining the domestic coalition supporting his naval plans.[151] As a result, the German Imperial Navy systematically ignored incoming intelligence about the development of *Dreadnought* and halted research in the technological domains underlying the new battleship's design, including turbines, fire-control systems, and long-range guns.[152] For instance, German naval yards continued to develop obsolete designs until late 1905, even though they had been aware since 1903 of the emerging all-big-gun battleship concept.[153] Similarly, until 1910 the German Imperial Navy designed its fire-control system for short-range naval engagements (around 6,000 yards).[154] Still, on the eve of World War I, no one in the German Imperial Navy "had thought it possible to fight effectively at a range of over . . . 16,250 yards."[155]

As a result, German investments in fire-control equipment initially remained limited, and the device Germany adopted in 1897 to measure bearing and bearing rate (the StandGerät) was much "clumsier" than its British counterpart (the Dumaresq).[156] Analogous considerations applied to German naval firepower: Tirpitz had long preferred "smaller-caliber guns firing relatively lightweight high-velocity shells." These shells, however, were ineffective at longer ranges, because they "lost velocity more quickly than heavier ones" and thus were unfit for the engagements that took place during World War I.[157] Finally, and paradoxically, Tirpitz's defense industrial strategy explicitly obstructed domestic research on turbines, thus failing to promote the development of an indigenous industry in this domain.[158]

Access to Foreign Technology and Know-How

The German Imperial Navy had relatively limited access to British *Dreadnought*-related technologies and technological knowledge—and, when it did, it did not use them.[159] Even though German naval yards had previous access to the all-big-gun battleship design, they did not immediately employ this information to improve either the warship designs they were working on or their design capabilities.[160] In the case of turbines, after having obstructed research in this realm, Tirpitz realized that German industry was lagging. Although he managed to have a British company establish a turbine production plant on German soil, he did not promote the transfer of technological know-how to German companies.[161]

Outcome

In line with our theory, within a few years, Germany was able to pose a serious challenge to Britain's naval dominance.[162] It made remarkable improvements in ship design and construction as well as in other key component technologies and, in some realms, it even managed to outperform the new British all-big-gun battleships.[163]

First, the German turbine industry caught up quickly, enabling the navy's battleships to match Britain's in terms of speed: by 1910–11, even the German companies that did not cooperate with foreign partners succeeded in indigenously producing modern turbines, which, in some cases, proved superior to their British counterparts.[164]

Second, with respect to light-but-resistant armor steel plates for fire protection, German technology outperformed British technology, as the thinner, and hence lighter, 6-inch armor plating produced by Krupp foundries in Germany "was approximately as effective as" the 8-inch steel armor plating manufactured by the Harvey United Steel Company in Britain.[165] German gun technology also caught up quickly: the transition to larger calibers proved unproblematic, and according to some accounts, by the start of World War I Germany possessed the most advanced naval guns in the world.[166] Behind Germany's success was its capacity to transfer Krupp's know-how in steel-plating to warship-building and to exploit the superiority of its chemical industry for the development of more advanced propellant charges. In fact, Germany's shells enjoyed "greater penetrative power" than the Royal Navy's.[167]

Third, Germany succeeded in leveraging its domestic civilian industry to catch up quickly in the realm of fire-control equipment, which it had initially neglected.[168] After the introduction of the British *Dreadnought*, the German navy recognized the inadequacy of its own long-range gunnery capabilities, and therefore started working on a rangefinder (the EU/SV-Anzeiger) more advanced than the StandGerät, which it had acquired in 1897.[169] To assess its new system, the navy acquired a rangefinder from a British company that, by mid-1907, "had recaptured the lead in fire-control instruments," and whose equipment (the Mark II) was considered the best available at the time.[170] The tests revealed similar performances between the British and German systems.[171] From 1908 until World War I, the Royal Navy continued upgrading its fire-control systems (introducing Mark III and Mark IV equipment), but Germany managed to keep pace. By the eve of the 1915 Battle of Dogger Bank, not only was the German fire-control system "similar in principle" to those of British warships,[172] but "at 20,000 yards," it was also "as accurate as the [British] 9-foot coincidence rangefinders at 15,000–16,000 yards,"[173] while its "spotting procedures could straddle more quickly."[174] In other words, Germany managed to get a lead in fire-control systems.[175]

Combat performance during the most important naval engagement of World War I, the 1916 Battle of Jutland, further supports our conclusions.[176] Despite some material and operational disadvantages that affected the mobility of German warships,[177] the two fleets performed very similarly in terms of accuracy: "117 British hits (2.45 percent) versus 83 German hits (2.3 percent)," thus suggesting that in terms of overall technology the two fleets were generally on par.[178] Interestingly, "German fire started excellently, but got worse as the day wore on, whereas British gunnery improved over time."[179] This indicates that the two sides enjoyed similar technology, but that over the duration of the battle, the Royal Navy could leverage its superior drilling, tactics, and experience.

In sum, despite all the countervailing pressures discussed earlier,[180] Germany managed in just a few years to imitate British Dreadnought battleships and to develop "superior North Sea fighting ships to their British contemporaries."[181] German ships had in fact "better range-finding equipment, superior fire-control, and improved compartmentalization . . . and better shells."[182] Moreover, German equipment "functioned excellently" during the war,[183] because some of its key components were "apparently better and more plentiful than in Great Britain."[184]

China and Fifth-Generation Fighter Aircraft, 1991–2018

The United States commissioned its fifth-generation stealth fighter, the F-22/A Raptor, in 2005. Like *Dreadnought*, the F-22 had no match when it was fielded, specifically because of its "first-look, first-shoot, first-kill" capabilities.[185] To begin, the application of stealth technology reduces by several orders of magnitude the observability of the F-22 to enemy sensors.[186] In addition, with its supercruising thrust-vectoring engines, the F-22 can achieve fuel-efficient supersonic speed and high maneuverability, enhancing its performance against enemy fighters.[187] Finally, the F-22 possesses superior and longer-range situational awareness thanks to its advanced onboard computer systems, software, and data-fusion capabilities: these attributes enable the collection, rapid processing, and exploitation of large amounts of different types of data that ultimately increase the F-22's battlefield performance.[188]

Absorptive Capacity

When in the late 1990s China started work to develop a fifth-generation fighter, its absorptive capacity in the military aviation domain was relatively limited.[189] China could assemble modern foreign weapon systems, but its experience with combat aircraft production was restricted to Soviet designs from the 1950s and

1960s.[190] The reasons for China's delay in combat aircraft production include economic backwardness, a command economy, and its international isolation, as well as some particular political choices, such as limiting the amount of attention paid to military aviation during the Cold War, especially when compared to missiles or warships.[191] China did not start from scratch, however. During the 1970s and 1980s, the Chinese defense industry worked on several programs, accruing some experience in military aviation.[192] Moreover, since the 1970s and in particular since the 1990s, China's industrial base has benefited tremendously from FDI, R&D joint ventures, and mergers and acquisitions with Western aerospace companies.[193] Most of the world's major jet engine producers, airline manufacturers, and companies specializing in avionics and aerospace component technologies have established a presence in China.[194] Chinese companies have also purchased machinery to "manufacture sophisticated weapon systems and related components."[195]

Access to Foreign Technological Knowledge

Unlike Imperial Germany and its efforts to imitate the Dreadnought battleship, China has benefited from massive access to foreign technological knowledge in its attempt to imitate US advanced jet fighters.

China has engaged more extensively in cyber espionage than any other country.[196] In 2007, 2009, and 2011, Chinese hackers entered the servers of the Pentagon and gained access to some fifty terabytes of data containing the designs and blueprints of US stealth fighters, as well as other critical information.[197] China has also relied extensively on traditional industrial espionage, including the recruitment of former engineers and scientists who worked for Western aerospace organizations.[198] Together, industrial and cyber espionage have given China extensive access to American know-how. Moreover, China managed to obtain an F-117 that crashed in Serbia in 1999, allowing it to inspect, analyze, and possibly reverse engineer the aircraft's stealth features.[199]

Further, since the 1960s, China has benefited from significant transfers of technology from more advanced countries.[200] In the 1970s, it had access to turbofan engines developed by Rolls-Royce.[201] In the 1980s, Israel provided extensive "weapon-making know-how" useful in the design, fire-control, avionics, and radar capabilities of China's fourth-generation aircraft.[202] Through Pakistan, China gained access to US F-16 Fighting Falcon jet fighters.[203] After the end of the Cold War, China signed an agreement with Pakistan to co-produce Pakistan's fourth-generation fighter, itself the result of a co-production project with the American Grumman Aerospace Corporation (the F-7P Sabre II "Super 7");[204] it also reached a licensing agreement with Russia for the production of its fourth-generation aircraft (the Sukhoi Su-27).[205] Russian experts have also provided Chinese workers and engineers "with the know-how to assemble Su-27 fighter aircraft using imported materials and equipment," and have trained them to "domestically manufacture key materials."[206] China has also been purchasing engines, radars, and other systems and subsystems from abroad in order to analyze and possibly replicate them.[207]

Outcome

Nevertheless, China's aerospace industry has struggled enormously to imitate US technology. In 2017, China commissioned the J-20 Black Eagle, a step that many analysts viewed as the end of the US monopoly on fifth-generation fighters.[208] Yet, serious doubts persist about whether the performance of the J-20 comes even close to that of the F-22. In fact, anonymous Chinese sources have admitted that China rushed the J-20 into service in response to increasing tensions in the South China Sea, despite capability gaps that make it inferior to the F-22.[209]

First, because of design similarities between the US F-22 and the Chinese J-20, many observers have concluded that China has been able to quickly replicate US technology.[210] A closer examination suggests otherwise. The J-20 displays several design flaws and nonstealthy features on the sides and in the rear of the fighter that dramatically increase its detectability to both radar and thermal sensors.[211] These limitations would represent a critical liability in air-to-air engagements with US fifth-generation jet fighters.[212] Moreover, the J-20 displays two small wing projections (canards) forward of the main wings. Generally intended to help the longitudinal equilibrium, and static and dynamic stability, of an aircraft, the canards also increase its frontal radar cross section, thus limiting its overall capabilities.[213] From an industrial perspective, that the J-20 carries canards suggests poor design.[214] As noted, little can be done about poor designs, which, once adopted, can be improved only marginally.[215] These flaws and features convey a more important message: China has been unable to fully copy US stealth designs and technology. Instead, it has had to engage in extensive experimentation, prototyping, and refinement, inevitably encountering problems in the process.[216]

Second, China has faced enormous challenges in developing one of the most important systems of modern jet fighters—powerful and reliable thrust-vectoring turbofan engines capable of supercruise. According to experts, this failing represents probably "the most glaring weakness of China's aviation industry."[217] For this reason, China has so far relied on compromises. For its early prototypes, from 2010 to 2017, it relied on

Russian underpowered engines that provide neither supercruise nor thrust-vectoring capabilities and that left a visible trail.[218] Subsequently, China decided to commission the J-20 into service by mounting indigenous but older and underpowered engines that also lack supercruise and thrust-vectoring capabilities.[219] This solution was intended to be temporary while work on the engines originally intended for the J-20 continued. These more advanced engines have experienced "critical problems," however, including an explosion during a ground test in 2015.[220] According to an anonymous source, as of 2018, "engineers ha[d] failed to find the key reason for the[se] problems,"[221] and apparently "there [was] no fundamental solution to overcome [them]."[222] In November 2018, China switched back to Russian engines for three of the four J-20s that performed at the biannual Airshow China in Zhuhai—an event China uses to showcase its aerospace accomplishments. This decision suggests that the "temporary" indigenous engines are not deemed very reliable.[223]

China's struggle to indigenously develop aircraft engines thus throws into question the growing belief among observers that China has closed the military-technological gap with the United States with respect to fifth-generation fighters.[224] Possibly more important, it also illustrates that the advantages of imitation that China has enjoyed have inevitably been limited. As mentioned earlier, several factors significantly facilitated China's efforts to develop turbofan engines; and from 2010 to 2015, it spent some $22 billion to develop an indigenous engine for its combat aircraft.[225] Yet, as of 2019, it continues to struggle.[226] According to an executive with a Chinese engine manufacturer, "The road to success is filled with setbacks and failures," and far from being able to take a shortcut, China has experienced the same problems of "each of the world's engine powers."[227] It is unknown how Chinese engines will perform and when they will be operational.[228] According to defense industry experts Tai Ming Cheung, Thomas Mahnken, and Andrew Ross, they "lag one to two generations behind leading international competitors, and the near-term prospects of narrowing this gap are poor."[229] In fact, the engine China is developing might not be sufficiently powerful to make the J-20 a "viable . . . air combat fighter."[230]

Third, military experts agree that China is also lagging in another key realm of fifth-generation fighters—avionics.[231] China's difficulties in this realm stem from the fact that aerospace sensors and software development currently pose some of the most daunting engineering challenges.[232] Software problems, in fact, are very difficult to anticipate: testing and refining must continue until the software is perfected, given that when the aerospace software fails, it fails "catastrophically."[233]

Because China has thus far been unable to copy US aircraft design and engines, there is little reason to believe that it has been more successful in this much more challenging realm. An additional consideration supports this assessment. The complexity of modern aerospace software is unprecedented.[234] Flight control software has become exponentially more complex, eliminating trade-offs in design—for example, between observability to radar and aerodynamic efficiency. In other words, complexity has moved from hardware to software.[235] In addition, software has taken over an increasing number of more complex functions—most prominently, automatic long-range enemy detection, geolocation, high-confidence identification, and accurate target tracking.[236] Little information is available on Chinese radar operation and data-fusion capabilities, but we can use available evidence on Chinese flight control as a proxy. This proxy is valid, because developing flight control software is far less demanding than software for radar operation and data fusion.[237] According to Chinese media, the J-20 still faces problems with its flight control software. There is thus little reason to believe that China has been able to develop the most challenging part of the J-20's onboard software.[238]

Fourth, the difficulties that China has encountered with the development of less advanced fourth-generation fighters further corroborate our argument. Despite the significant transfer of technology and support that China has received from Russia, Israel, and various European countries, its industry has struggled in this domain.[239] For instance, in 2004 China suddenly broke a licensing agreement with Russia on the Sukhoi Su-27, with the aim of exploiting the experience it had already gained to produce independently an indigenous version, the Shenyang J-11.[240] The production process did not go smoothly, however. For example, at "one point the [Chinese engines] were reportedly requiring overhauls every thirty hours of flight time, compared to four hundred hours for . . . the Su-27."[241] Similarly, according to US sources, some variants of this aircraft have been "in big trouble," as technical malfunctions have led to several crash landings.[242] Additionally, in 2016 China bought twenty-four new, heavily upgraded derivatives of the very aircraft it had copied from Russia (the Sukhoi Su-35).[243] Although the reasons for this purchase are unknown, it is further indicative of China's inability to produce a copy of this aircraft—or even a more advanced one such as fifth-generation jet fighters.[244] China has experienced similar problems with its carrier-based fighter aircraft, the Shenyang J-15 Flying Shark, a reverse-engineered version of a Russian fighter (the Sukhoi Su-33) that is more than thirty years old and that China purchased from Ukraine.[245] Because of the thrust constraints of its engine, the J-15 can take off from an aircraft carrier ski-jump with only half a fuel load or

with only four missiles, thus limiting either its range or its capabilities.[246] Even the Chinese media criticized it as a "flopping fish."[247] Because of recurrent fatal accidents and crashes, China recently decided to look for a replacement for this aircraft.[248]

Fifth, China has derived only limited cost and time advantages from its imitation efforts. According to Gabe Collins and Andrew Erickson, it is "reasonable to assume the J-20 has a unit cost of somewhere from US$100-to-$120 million. . . . By contrast, the F-22 costs around US$143 million per plane."[249] These estimates show that China has derived a cost advantage of just 14 to 20 percent, which is hardly impressive given that China is the country that has relied most extensively on both industrial and cyber espionage, and that has benefited massively from the transfer of technology through FDI, mergers and acquisitions, and the purchase of foreign components. Such a cost advantage is even less impressive given that the F-22 is now twelve years old, that the J-20 has significant deficiencies, and that its costs will inevitably increase further as China attempts to fix its problems and improve its performance. The latter point is critical, because "the final 10 percent striving towards maximum perfection costs 40% of the total expenditure on most projects."[250] The same is true with regard to time. The F-22 became operational in 2005—about twenty years after the project started.[251] Launched in the late 1990s and tested in 2010, the J-20 was officially commissioned in the fall of 2017.[252] Still, it is not yet fully operational and remains inferior to the F-22 on several dimensions: in other words, after more than twenty years, China has not yet closed the gap with the United States.[253]

A skeptical reader might wonder whether a more advanced country would have accomplished better results than China in imitating the F-22. The hardest case for our theory would be if the imitating country had the same aerospace capabilities as the United States and if it had access to all the technological knowledge related to the F-22. This case exists. In 2011, the US government interrupted production of the F-22. In 2017, the US Air Force commissioned a study to understand how much it would cost to restart production. In other words, the United States wanted to know what it would take to copy its own technology from just six years before. The findings are sobering: the same country that created the F-22 would have to spend $10 billion to restart the production of its fifth-generation fighter—equivalent to 25 percent of the total procurement cost for 194 aircraft.[254]

In sum, over the past twenty years, China has made impressive accomplishments in modernizing its aerospace industry. Given the extent to which it has benefited from globalization and cyber espionage, however, the evidence casts serious doubt on the claim that these two factors have brought about a revolutionary transformation that makes the imitation of foreign weapon systems much easier than it used to be.[255]

Conclusion

In his seminal article "Command of the Commons," Barry Posen argued that the unrivaled military-technological superiority of the United States gives it a key advantage over other countries.[256] According to the literature in international relations theory, however, such advantages should be temporary, especially in an era of globalization, real-time communications, and dual-use technologies: knowledge allegedly diffuses quickly, thus undermining one of the sources of US hegemony—superiority in military technology. This article has provided a theoretical explanation for why, three decades after the fall of the Berlin Wall and more than fifteen years after the publication of Posen's article, US weapon systems largely remain unrivaled.

This article has argued that the dramatic increase in the complexity of military technology observed over the twentieth century has significantly shrunk the advantage of backwardness described by Gerschenkron. On the one hand, the requirements for imitating modern weapon systems have become harder to meet. On the other, the technological knowledge of how to design, develop, and produce modern weapon systems has become less likely to diffuse. As a result, compared to the pre–World War I period, today imitating foreign weapon systems is more difficult. Countries cannot simply free ride on the research and development of the most advanced states: they first have to develop the industrial, scientific, and technological capabilities required for becoming first-tier weapons manufacturers; then, they must go through extensive trial and error to address the multitude of extremely small but challenging problems that weapons development entails.

The evidence presented shows that in comparison to the early twentieth century, when Germany could quickly catch up with Great Britain in all-big-gun battleships, in recent years China has faced enormous hurdles in closing the military-technological gap both with the United States in fifth-generation aircraft and even with Russia in fourth-generation jet fighters. China has struggled to achieve success despite its massive cyber-theft activities, the benefits it has derived from globalization, its acquisition of foreign companies and technology, and an unprecedented inflow of foreign direct investments.

This research provides a unified theory that helps explain why the imitation of advanced weapon systems has become more difficult with the transition from the industrial to the information age. Our theory holds also in other cases. For example, it helps account for the Soviet Union's incapacity to catch up with the

United States in the later phases of the Cold War.[257] Our theory thus challenges the view among international relations scholars that catching up technologically is about will—which, for states, ultimately means mobilizing the necessary capital. Although warranted in the past, this view is no longer valid, because simply pouring money into a project cannot generate the necessary defense-industrial base and experience with the technology being pursued.[258]

More important, by explaining the enduring military-technological superiority the United States currently enjoys, our research contributes to one of the most significant debates in the field of international relations theory: the potential for the United States to maintain its unrivaled power. Many observers and practitioners believe that US primacy in military technology is coming to an end, because of the diffusion of cheap counter-systems and because of opportunities to exploit both dual-use technologies and cyber espionage to free ride on more advanced countries' research. Chinese military strategists themselves "subscribe to the arguments [of] Alexander Gerschenkron" about the advantage of imitation, and their technology and industrial policies have tried as much as possible to rely on the acquisition, assimilation, and replication of foreign technology.[259] Our theory indicates that under the current technological paradigm, the entry barriers for modern military platforms will remain massive, even for the most advanced countries. Meanwhile, the tacit and organizational know-how related to the production of modern weapon systems will force aspiring great powers to engage in extensive and expensive experimentation and testing before they can deliver state-of-the-art technology. This article is not claiming that China or other countries are destined to fail in their attempts to close the military-technological gap with the United States. Rather, this article argues that rising great powers cannot easily copy foreign technology and thus catch up militarily at a fraction of the cost and at a fraction of the time of their competitors.

Indirectly, our research also addresses existing concerns about future counter-systems that China could deploy to contest the Western Pacific. Although some of these systems are comparatively cheap and unsophisticated (e.g., missiles), key platforms such as submarines and jet fighters are extremely complex, while other emerging technologies such as remotely piloted and autonomous vehicles are becoming increasingly sophisticated and costly, and are expected "to converge rapidly with those of manned aircraft."[260] Similarly, exploiting emerging technologies (e.g., robotics or artificial intelligence) for military purposes will not be easy: to integrate them into their weapon systems, countries will have to invest massively in a broad range of disciplines and gain experience through trial and error. The key question for the future is whether the fourth industrial revolution will bring about a paradigmatic transformation in production, and if so, how this transformation will change the dynamics of innovation and imitation. Given that "as the capabilities of autonomy increase . . . considerable system complexity will be created as the software and hardware is expanded,"[261] our research suggests that the difficulty of imitation will continue to increase. Further research should focus on this topic.[262]

NOTES

1. Alexander Gerschenkron, *Economic Backwardness in Historical Perspective: A Book of Essays* (Cambridge, Mass.: Belknap, 1962), pp. 5–30.

2. Kenneth N. Waltz, *Theory of International Politics* (New York: McGraw-Hill, 1979), pp. 74, 127; Robert Gilpin, *War and Change in World Politics* (Cambridge: Cambridge University Press, 1981), pp. 176–177; and Michael C. Horowitz, *The Diffusion of Military Power: Causes and Consequences for International Politics* (Princeton, N.J.: Princeton University Press, 2010), p. 34.

3. Wayne Sandholtz et al., eds., *The Highest Stakes: The Economic Foundations of the Next Security System* (New York: Oxford University Press, 1991); Richard A. Bitzinger, "The Globalization of the Arms Industry: The Next Proliferation Challenge," *International Security*, Vol. 19, No. 2 (Fall 1994), pp. 170–198, doi.org/10.2307/2539199; and Emily O. Goldman and Richard B. Andres, "Systemic Effects of Military Innovation and Diffusion," *Security Studies*, Vol. 8, No. 4 (Summer 1999), pp. 79–125, doi.org/10.1080/0963641990842 9387.

4. For a summary of the literature, see Goldman and Andres, "Systemic Effects of Military Innovation and Diffusion."

5. See, for example, Jean-Christophe Defraigne, "Is China on the Verge of a Weltpolitik? A Comparison of the Current Shift in the Balance of Power between China and the West and the Shift between Great Britain and Wilhelmine Germany," in Bart Dessein, ed., *Interpreting China as a Regional and Global Power: Nationalism and Historical Consciousness in World Politics* (New York: Palgrave Macmillan, 2014), pp. 293–323.

6. Stephen G. Brooks, *Producing Security: Multinational Corporations, Globalization, and the Changing Calculus of Conflict* (Princeton, N.J.: Princeton University Press, 2006); Jonathan D. Caverley, "United States Hegemony and the New Economics of Defense," *Security Studies*, Vol. 16, No. 4 (October–December 2007), pp. 598–614, doi.org/10.1080/0963 6410701740825; Eugene Gholz, "Globalization, Systems Integration, and the Future of Great Power War," *Security Studies*, Vol. 16, No. 4 (October–December 2007), pp. 615–636, doi .org/10.1080/09636410701740908; and Stephen G. Brooks and William C. Wohlforth, "The Rise and Fall of the Great Powers in the Twenty-first Century: China's Rise and the Fate of America's Global Position," *International Security*, Vol. 40, No. 3 (Winter 2015/16), pp. 7–53, doi.org/10.1162/ISEC_a _00225.

7. See Michael Beckley, *Unrivaled: Why America Will Remain the World's Sole Superpower* (Ithaca, N.Y.: Cornell University Press, 2018), pp. 69–71; and Nuno P. Monteiro, *Theory*

8. For a discussion of late nineteenth- and early twentieth-century innovations with features no longer seen, see, for example, Vaclav Smil, *Creating the Twentieth Century: Technical Innovations of 1867–1914 and Their Lasting Impact* (New York: Oxford University Press, 2005); and Vaclav Smil, *Transforming the Twentieth Century: Technical Innovations and Their Consequences* (New York: Oxford University Press, 2006).

9. Tai Ming Cheung, ed., *The Chinese Defense Economy Takes Off: Sector by Sector Assessments and the Role of Military End Users* (San Diego: Institute on Global Conflict and Cooperation, University of California, 2013).

10. A previous work of ours in part addresses this topic. See Andrea Gilli and Mauro Gilli, "The Diffusion of Drone Warfare? Industrial, Infrastructural, and Organizational Constraints," *Security Studies*, Vol. 25, No. 1 (Winter 2016), pp. 50–84, doi.org/10.1080/09636412.2016.1134189. More generally, however, few works have studied qualitative competition in military technology. An exception is Owen R. Coté Jr., *The Third Battle: Innovation in the U.S. Navy's Silent Cold War Struggle with Soviet Submarines* (Newport, R.I.: Naval War College, 2009).

11. Ron Rosenbaum, "Richard Clarke on Who Was behind the Stuxnet Attack," *Smithsonian Magazine*, April 2012, p. 12; and Gen. Keith Alexander, "Cybersecurity and American Power," keynote address, American Enterprise Institute, Washington, D.C., July 9, 2012.

12. Jon R. Lindsay, Tai Ming Cheung, and Derek S. Reveron, eds., *China and Cybersecurity: Espionage, Strategy, and Politics in the Digital Domain* (Oxford: Oxford University Press, 2015); and Robert Farley, "Intellectual Property, Cyber Espionage, and Military Diffusion," *Global Security and Intelligence Studies*, Vol. 1, No. 2 (Spring 2016), pp. 2–20, doi.org /10.18278/gsis.1.2.2.

13. Bernard Brodie and Fawn M. Brodie, *From the Crossbow to H-Bomb: The Evolution of the Weapons and Tactics of Warfare* (Bloomington: Indiana University Press, 1973), pp. 6, 137, 178; and Trevor N. Dupuy, *The Evolution of Weapons and Warfare* (New York: Da Capo, 1984), p. 199.

14. Andrea Gilli and Mauro Gilli, "The Dynamics of Military Innovations and Counter-Innovations," paper presented at the "Bridging the Straits" conference, Naval War College, Newport, Rhode Island, December 11–13, 2018.

15. Geoffrey Parker, *The Military Revolution: Military Innovation and the Rise of the West, 1500–1800* (New York: Cambridge University Press, 1996); and Kenneth Macksey, *Technology in War: The Impact of Science on Weapon Development and Modern Battle* (London: Guild, 1986), pp. 34–35.

16. See Andrea Gilli and Mauro Gilli, "The Spread of Military Innovations: Adoption Capacity Theory, Tactical Incentives, and the Case of Suicide Terrorism," *Security Studies*, Vol. 23, No. 3 (July–September 2014), pp. 513–547, doi.org /10.1080/09636412.2014.935233.

17. Martin van Creveld, *Technology and War: From 2000 B.C. to the Present* (New York: Touchstone, 1989), p. 229. Not coincidentally, the Soviet big-fleet program in the 1930s was driven by the slogan "Catch up and overtake." See Milan L. Hauner, "Stalin's Big-Fleet Program," *Naval War College Review*, Vol. 57, No. 2 (Spring 2004), p. 114, https://digital -commons.usnwc.edu/nwc-review/vol57/iss2/6.

18. See Yu-Ming Liou, Paul Musgrave, and J. Furman Daniel III, "The Imitation Game: Why Don't Rising Powers Innovate Their Militaries More?" *Washington Quarterly*, Vol. 38, No. 3 (Fall 2015), pp. 157–174, doi.org/10.1080/0163660X.2015.1099030.

19. Marvin B. Lieberman and Sigheru Asaba, "Why Do Firms Imitate Each Other?" *Academy of Management Review*, Vol. 31, No. 2 (April 2006), pp. 366–385, doi.org/10.2307/20159207; and Walter G. Vincenti, *What Engineers Know and How They Know It: Analytical Studies from Aeronautical History* (Baltimore, Md.: Johns Hopkins University Press, 1990), pp. 7–8.

20. David J. Teece, "Capturing Value from Knowledge Assets: The New Economy, Markets for Know-How, and Intangible Assets," *California Management Review*, Vol. 40, No. 3 (Spring 1998), pp. 55–79, doi.org/10.2307/41165943.

21. Michael L. Tushman and Philip Anderson, "Technological Discontinuities and Organizational Environments," *Administrative Science Quarterly*, Vol. 31, No. 3 (September 1996), pp. 439–465, doi.org/10.2307/2392832.

22. Marvin B. Lieberman and David B. Montgomery, "First-Mover Advantages," *Strategic Management Journal*, Vol. 9, No. 5 (Summer 1988), pp. 41–58, https://www.jstor.org/stable/2486211; and Marvin B. Lieberman and David B. Montgomery, "First-Mover (Dis)Advantages: Retrospective and Link with the Resource-Based View," *Strategic Management Journal*, Vol. 19, No. 12 (December 1998), pp. 1111–1125, https://www.jstor.org/stable/3094199.

23. Brooks and Wohlforth, "The Rise and Fall of the Great Powers in the Twenty-first Century," p. 9.

24. This is also true for the literature on offense-defense balance, which treats technology as a systemic variable. See Sean M. Lynn-Jones, "Offense-Defense Theory and Its Critics," *Security Studies*, Vol. 4, No. 4 (Summer 1995), pp. 660–691, in particular pp. 666–667, doi.org/10.1080/09636419509347600.

25. John A. Alic, "Managing U.S. Defense Acquisition," *Enterprise & Society*, Vol. 14, No. 2 (March 2013), p. 4, doi.org/10.1093/es/khs051; and Peter Dombrowski and Eugene Gholz, *Buying Military Transformation: Technological Innovation and the Defense Industry* (New York: Columbia University Press, 2006), pp. 12–14.

26. See Daniel H. Nexon, "The Balance of Power in the Balance," *World Politics*, Vol. 61, No. 2 (April 2009), pp. 330–359, in particular p. 351, doi.org/10.1017/S0043887109000124.

27. For an exception, see Alexander H. Montgomery, "Ringing in Proliferation: How to Dismantle an Atomic Bomb Network," *International Security*, Vol. 30, No. 2 (Fall 2005), pp. 153–187, doi.org/10.1162/016228805775124543.

28. Waltz, *Theory of International Politics*, pp. 74, 127.

29. Gilpin, *War and Change in World Politics*, pp. 176–177; see also pp. 1–3, 175–185, 227.

30. P. W. Singer, *Wired for War: The Robotics Revolution and Conflict in the 21st Century* (New York: Penguin, 2009), p. 239.

31. Emily O. Goldman, "Introduction," in Goldman and Thomas G. Mahnken, eds., *The Information Revolution in Military Affairs in Asia* (New York: Palgrave Macmillan, 2004), p. 7.

32. Horowitz, *The Diffusion of Military Power*, pp. 27–28; see also p. 34.

33. Bitzinger, "The Globalization of the Arms Industry"; Dennis M. Gormley, "Dealing with the Threat of Cruise Missiles," Adelphi Paper, No. 339 (London: International Institute for Strategic Studies, 2001); and Christopher Layne, "This Time It's Real: The End of Unipolarity and the *Pax Americana*," *International Studies Quarterly*, Vol. 56, No. 1 (March 2012), pp. 203–213, doi.org/ 10.1111/j.1468-2478.2011.00704.x.

34. Joseph S. Nye Jr., *The Future of Power* (New York: PublicAffairs, 2011), p. 36.

35. Sandholtz et al., *The Highest Stakes*.

36. See John A. Alic et al., *Beyond Spinoff: Military and Commercial Technologies in a Changing World* (Boston: Harvard Business School Press, 1992).

37. Aaron L. Friedberg, "The United States and the Cold War Arms Race," in Odd Arne Westad, ed., *Reviewing the Cold War: Approaches, Interpretations, Theory* (Portland, Ore.: Frank Cass, 2000), p. 215.

38. The same problem exists in economics. See Jess Benhabib and Mark M. Spiegel, "Human Capital and Technology Diffusion," in Philippe Anghion and Stephen N. Durlauf, eds., *Handbook of Economic Growth*, Vol. 1A (Amsterdam: Elsevier, 2005), p. 937, doi.org/10.1016/S1574-0684(05)01013-0.

39. Lieberman and Montgomery, "First-Mover Advantages"; Lieberman and Montgomery, "First-Mover (Dis)Advantages"; Alfred. D. Chandler Jr., *Inventing the Electronic Century: The Epic Story of Consumer Electronics and Computer Industries* (New York: Free Press, 2001); David C. Mowery and Richard R. Nelson, eds., *Sources of Industrial Leadership: Studies of Seven Industries* (New York: Cambridge University Press, 1999); and Harry M. Collins, "The TEA Set: Tacit Knowledge and Scientific Networks," *Science Studies*, Vol. 4, No. 2 (April 1974), pp. 165–185, doi.org/10.1177/030631277400400203.

40. Andrew McAfee and Erik Brynjolfsson, *Machine, Platform, Crowd: Harnessing Our Digital Future* (New York: W.W. Norton, 2017), p. 204.

41. Gilli and Gilli, "The Diffusion of Drone Warfare?" pp. 67–80.

42. Alic, "Managing U.S. Defense Acquisition"; Rebecca M. Henderson and Kim B. Clark, "Architectural Innovation: The Reconfiguration of Existing Product Technologies and the Failure of Established Firms," *Administrative Science Quarterly*, Vol. 35, No. 1 (March 1990), pp. 9–30, doi.org/ 10.2307/2393549; Eugene Gholz, "Systems Integration in the U.S. Defense Industry," in Andrea Prencipe, Andrew Davies, and Michael Hobday, eds., *The Business of Systems Integration* (New York: Oxford University Press, 2003), pp. 279–306; Eugene Gholz, "Systems Integration for Complex Defense Projects," in Guy Ben-Ari and Pierre A. Chao, eds., *Organizing a Complex World: Developing Tomorrow's Defense and Net-Centric Systems* (Washington, D.C.: Center for Security and International Studies, 2009), pp. 50–65; and Mike Hobday, "Product Complexity, Innovation, and Industrial Organization," *Research Policy*, Vol. 26, No. 6 (February 1998), pp. 689–710, doi.org/ 10.1016/S0048-7333(97)00044-9.

43. The curse of dimensionality in statistics provides a useful analogy of the exponential increase resulting from the arithmetic growth of the number of parameters and constraints.

44. Harvey M. Sapolsky, "Inventing Systems Integration," in Prencipe, Davies, and Hobday, *The Business of Systems Integration*, pp. 15–34; and Stephen B. Johnson, "Systems Integration and the Social Solutions of Technical Problems in Complex

Systems," in Prencipe, Davies, and Hobday, *The Business of Systems Integration*, pp. 35–55.

45. See Marco Iansiti, *Technology Integration: Making Critical Choices in a Dynamic World* (Boston: Harvard Business Review Press, 1997), pp. 104–106, 133.

46. Alic, "Managing U.S. Defense Acquisition," pp. 16–19; and David J. Berteau, "Foreword," in Ben-Ari and Chao, *Organizing a Complex World*, pp. vii–viii.

47. Alan S. Milward, *War, Economy, and Society, 1939–1945* (Berkeley: University of California Press, 1977), p. 185; Johnson, "Systems Integration and the Social Solutions of Technical Problems in Complex Systems," p. 40; and Jeremiah Gertler, "F-35 Joint Strike Fighter (JSF) Program" (Washington, D.C.: Congressional Research Service, April 29 2014).

48. Qing Wang and Nick von Tunzelmann, "Complexity and the Functions of the Firm: Breadth and Depth," *Policy Research*, Vol. 29, Nos. 7–8 (August 2000), pp. 805–818, doi .org/10.1016/S0048-7333(00)00106-2; and Carliss Y. Baldwin and Kim B. Clark, *Design Rules: The Power of Modularity*, Vol. 1 (Cambridge, Mass.: MIT Press, 2000), pp. 63–70.

49. Eugene Gholz, "Systems Integration in the U.S. Defense Industry," p. 281.

50. Guy Ben-Ari and Matthew Zlatnik, "Introduction: Framing the Complexity Challenge," in Ben-Ari and Chao, *Organizing a Complex World*, p.2.

51. Bill Gunston, *The Development of Piston Aero Engines: From the Wrights to Microlights: A Century of Evolution and Still a Power to Be Reckoned With* (Somerset, U.K.: Haynes, 1993), p. 105.

52. Vaclav Smil, *Prime Movers of Globalization: The History and Impact of Diesel Engines and Gas Turbines* (Cambridge, Mass: MIT Press, 2013), pp. 79–108.

53. Wedo Wang, *Reverse Engineering: Technology of Reinvention* (Boca Raton, Fla.: CRC, 2010), p. 266.

54. See Gholz, "Systems Integration for Complex Defense Projects," p. 50. See also Clarence L. "Kelly" Johnson with Maggie Smith, *Kelly: More than My Share of It All* (Washington, D.C.: Smithsonian Institute, 1985), p. 142.

55. Between the F-4 and the F-22, software has moved from controlling 8 percent to 80 percent of operations. Ali Mili and Fairouz Tchier, *Software Testing: Concepts and Operations* (Hoboken, N.J.: John Wiley and Sons, 2015), p. 6.

56. See Jeffrey J. Harris and G. Thomas Black, "F-22 Control Law Development and Flying Qualities," Conference Paper 96-3379 (Reston, Va.: American Institute of Aeronautics and Astronautics, July 1996), pp. 155–158.

57. Joe W. Heil, "Addressing the Challenges of Software Growth and Rapidly Evolving Software Technologies," *Naval Engineers Journal*, Vol. 122, No. 4 (December 2010), pp. 45–58, doi.org/ 10.1111/j.1559-3584.2010.00279.x.

58. Johnson, "Systems Integration and the Social Solutions of Technical Problems in Complex Systems."

59. Iansiti, *Technology Integration*, pp. 10–12, 110–116.

60. W. Brian Arthur, *The Nature of Technology: What It Is and How It Evolves* (New York: Free Press, 2009), pp. 45–67. See also Ben R. Rich and Leo Janos, *Skunk Works: A Personal Memoir of My Years at Lockheed* (New York: Little, Brown and Company, 1994), p. 82.

61. See David Miller and John Jordan, *Modern Submarine Warfare* (London: Salamander, 1987), pp. 44–45.

62. Alic, "Managing U.S. Defense Acquisition," pp. 1–36; and Barton C. Hacker, "The Machines of War: Western Military Technology, 1850–2000," *History and Technology*, Vol. 21, No. 3 (September 2005), pp. 255–300.

63. Holger H. Herwig, "The Battlefleet Revolution, 1885–1914," in MacGregor Knox and Williamson Murray, eds., *The Dynamics of Military Revolution, 1300–2050* (New York: Cambridge University Press, 2001), p. 126.

64. Paul Kennedy, *The Rise and Fall of the Great Powers: Economic Change and Military Conflict from 1500 to 2000* (New York: Random House, 1987), p. 198.

65. William H. McNeill, *The Pursuit of Power: Technology, Armed Force, and Society since A.D. 1000* (Chicago, Ill.: University of Chicago Press, 1982), pp. 262–264.

66. Gerschenkron, *Economic Backwardness in Historical Perspective*, pp. 31–51.

67. See, respectively, John Roberts, "The Pre-Dreadnought Age, 1890–1905," in Robert Gardiner, ed., *Steam, Steel, and Shellfire: The Steam Warship, 1805–1905* (London: Conway Maritime, 1992), p. 123; and Mark R. Peattie, "Japanese Naval Construction, 1919–41," in Phillips Payson O'Brien, ed., *Technology and Naval Combat in the Twentieth Century and Beyond* (London: Frank Cass, 2001), p. 97.

68. Peattie, "Japanese Naval Construction, 1919–41," p. 97.

69. Peattie, "Japanese Naval Construction, 1919–41," p. 94.

70. Spencer C. Tucker, *Handbook of 19th Century Naval Warfare* (Phoenix Mill, U.K.: Sutton, 2000), p. 225.

71. Peattie, "Japanese Naval Construction, 1919–41," p. 95.

72. Michael H. Best, "The Geography of Systems Integration," in Prencipe, Davies, and Hobday, *The Business of Systems Integration*, pp. 201–228.

73. Brooks, *Producing Security*, pp. 235–236. F-16s produced in Europe by license were consistently about 20 percent more expensive than those assembled in the United States. See Michael Rich et al., *Multinational Coproduction of Military Aerospace Systems* (Santa Monica, Calif.: RAND Corporation, 1981), pp. 79–120.

74. Wesley M. Cohen and Daniel A. Levinthal, "Innovation and Learning: The Two Faces of R&D," *Economic Journal*, September 1989, pp. 569–570, doi.org/10.2307/2233763.

75. That knowledge is a public good was a popular conception among economists, stemming from Kenneth J. Arrow, "Economic Welfare and the Allocation of Resources for Invention," in *The Rate and Direction of Inventive Activity: Economic and Social Factors* (Princeton, N.J.: Princeton University Press, 1962).

76. Wesley M. Cohen and Daniel A. Levinthal, "Absorptive Capacity: A New Perspective on Learning and Innovation," *Administrative Science Quarterly*, Vol. 35, No. 1 (March 1990), pp. 128–152, doi.org/10.2307/2393553.

77. Gerschenkron, *Economic Backwardness in Historical Perspective*, pp. 31–51.

78. Mowery and Rosenberg, *Technology and the Pursuit of Economic Growth*, p. 28.

79. See Mowery and Rosenberg, *Technology and the Pursuit of Economic Growth*, p. 31.

80. See John D. Anderson Jr., *The Airplane: A History of Its Technology* (Reston, Va.: American Institute of Aeronautics and Astronautics, 2002), p. 45.

81. Johnson, "Systems Integration and the Social Solutions of Technical Problems in Complex Systems," p. 40.

82. See Eberhard Rössler, *The U-Boat: The Evolution and Technical History of German Submarines*, trans. Harold Erenberg (Annapolis: Naval Institute Press, 1981), p. 50.

83. Herwig, "The Battlefleet Revolution, 1885–1914," p. 126.

84. Richard J. Overy, *War and Economy in the Third Reich* (Oxford: Clarendon, 1994), p. 181.

85. Richard C. Levin et al., "Appropriating the Returns from Industrial Research and Development," *Brookings Papers on Economic Activity*, Vol. 1987, No. 3 (1987), pp. 783–831, doi.org/ 10.2307/2534454.

86. Benjamin F. Jones, "The Burden of Knowledge and the 'Death of the Renaissance Man': Is Innovation Getting Harder?" *Review of Economic Studies*, Vol. 76, No. 1 (January 2009), pp. 283–317, doi.org/10.1111/j.1467-937X.2008.00531.x.

87. See Patricia Hamburger, David Miskimens, and Scott Truver, "It Is Not Just Hardware and Software, Anymore! Human Systems Integration in U.S. Submarines," *Naval Engineers Journal*, Vol. 123, No. 4 (December 2011), pp. 41–50, doi.org/10.1111/j.1559-3584.2009.00198.x.

88. Even minor problems can pose serious threats to military platforms given the presence of onboard ordnance and explosives, as well as the need to hide from enemy sensors. See, for example, Sherry Sontag and Christopher Drew with Annette Lawrence Drew, *Blind Man's Bluff: The Untold Story of American Submarine Espionage* (New York: PublicAffairs, 1998), pp. 109–120, 133–134.

89. Vernon Ruttan, *Is War Necessary for Economic Growth? Military Procurement and Technology Development* (Oxford: Oxford University Press, 2006), p. 44.

90. See Stephen B. Johnson, *The Secret of Apollo: Systems Management in American and European Space Programs* (Baltimore, Md.: Johns Hopkins University Press, 2006), pp. 1–80.

91. Mowery and Rosenberg, *Technology and the Pursuit of Economic Growth*, pp. 81–82; Alic et al., *Beyond Spinoff*, pp. 20–22; and Alic, "Managing U.S. Defense Acquisition," p. 17.

92. Johnson and Smith, *Kelly*, p. 137.

93. Winston Royce, "Current Problems," in Christine Anderson and Merlin Dorfman, eds., *Aerospace Software Engineering: A Collection of Concepts* (Washington, D.C.: American Institute of Aeronautics and Astronautics, 1991), p. 6.

94. Johnson and Smith, *Kelly*, p. 143.

95. U.S. Department of Defense, "Task Force Report: The Role of Autonomy in DoD Systems" (Washington, D.C.: U.S. Department of Defense, July 2012), pp. 46–49.

96. Will Mitchell, "Whether and When? Probability and Timing of Incumbents' Entry into Emerging Industrial Subfields," *Administrative Science Quarterly*, Vol. 34, No. 2 (June 1989), pp. 208–230, doi.org/10.2307/2989896.

97. David A. Hounshell, *From the American System to Mass Production, 1800–1932: The Development of Manufacturing Technology in the United States* (Baltimore, Md.: Johns Hopkins University Press, 1985).

98. Nathan Rosenberg, *Perspectives on Technology* (New York: Cambridge University Press, 1976), pp. 18–19, 26; and Hounshell, *From the American System to Mass Production, 1800–1932*, pp. 218–223, 227.

99. Rosenberg, *Perspectives on Technology*, p. 30. See also Glenn R. Carroll et al., "The Fates of *De Novo* and *De Alio* Producers in the American Automobile Industry, 1885–1981,"

Strategic Management Journal, Vol. 17, No. S1 (Summer 1996), pp. 117–137, doi.org/10.1002/smj.4250171009.

100. Rosenberg, *Perspective on Technology*, pp. 9–31.

101. Ruttan, *Is War Necessary for Economic Growth?* p. 58.

102. Eric von Hippel, "Task Partitioning: An Innovation Process Variable," *Research Policy*, Vol. 19, No. 5 (October 1990), pp. 407–418, doi.org/10.1016/0048-7333(90)90049-C.

103. Edward W. Steinmueller, "Industry Structure and Government Policies in the U.S. and Japanese Integrated Circuit Industries," in John B. Shoven, ed., *Government Policies toward Industries in the U.S. and Japan* (New York: Cambridge University Press, 1988), p. 344.

104. William Walker, Mac Graham, and Bernard Harbor, "From Components to Integrated Systems: Technological Diversity and Interactions between the Military and Civilian Sectors," in Philip Gummet and Judith Reppy, eds., *The Relations between Defense and Civil Technologies*, NATO ASI Series, Vol. 46 (Dordrecht: Springer Netherlands, 1988), pp. 17–37.

105. Dombrowski and Gholz, *Buying Military Transformation*, pp. 17–18; and Gholz, "Systems Integration for Complex Defense Projects," p. 54.

106. Shaker A. Zahra and Gerard George, "Absorptive Capacity: A Review, Reconceptualization, and Extension," *Academy of Management Review*, Vol. 27, No. 2 (April 2002), pp. 185–202, doi.org/ 10.2307/4134351.

107. Alic, "Managing U.S. Defense Acquisition," pp. 14–15.

108. Gholz, "Systems Integration for Complex Defense Projects," p. 54; and Brooks, *Producing Security*, pp. 235–238.

109. John F. Schank et al., *Sustaining U.S. Nuclear Submarine Design Capabilities* (Santa Monica, Calif.: RAND Corporation, 2007), pp. 92–94.

110. Rich and Janos, *Skunk Works*, pp. 76–78, 89–90. See also Howard Moon, *Soviet SST: The Technopolitics of the Tupolev-144* (New York: Orion, 1989), pp. 5–6.

111. Rich and Janos, *Skunk Works*, p. 69.

112. Alan Brown, quoted in Rich and Janos, *Skunk Works*, p. 81.

113. See Hans Pung et al., *Sustaining Key Skills in the UK Naval Industry* (Santa Monica, Calif.: RAND Corporation, 2008), p. 35.

114. Tom Lilley et al., *Problems of Accelerating Aircraft Production during World War II: A Report* (Boston: Division of Research, Graduate School of Business Administration, Harvard University, 1947); and Roberto Mazzoleni, "Innovation in the Machine Tool Industry," in Mowery and Nelson, *Sources of Industrial Leadership*, p. 189.

115. Quietness has become the key parameter of competition in submarine warfare since the end of World War II. See Coté, *The Third Battle*, pp. 20–35.

116. Coté, *The Third Battle*, p. 73.

117. Coté, *The Third Battle*, p. 69.

118. In the end, the Soviets managed to copy the propellers, but only after having acquired two pieces of equipment that had been subjected to an embargo: high-precision "nine-axes milling machinery tools" from the Japanese company Toshiba; and a computer device that could be used with them from a Norwegian defense company, Kongsberg. See Coté, *The Third Battle*; and Wende A. Wrubel, "The Toshiba-Kongsberg Incident: Shortcomings of Cocom, and Recommendations for Increased Effectiveness of Export Controls to the

East Bloc," *American University Journal of International Law and Policy*, Vol. 4, No. 1 (Winter 1989), p. 254.

119. Fernando F. Suarez and Gianvito Lanzolla, "The Role of Environmental Dynamics in Building a First Mover Advantage Theory," *Academy of Management Review*, Vol. 32, No. 2 (2007), pp. 377–392, doi.org/10.5465/amr.2007.243 49587.

120. Johnson and Smith, *Kelly*, p. 137.

121. Alic, "Managing U.S. Defense Acquisition," p. 3. See also Laurence K. Loftin Jr., *Quest for Performance: The Evolution of Modern Aircraft* (Washington, D.C.: NASA Scientific and Technical Information Branch, 1985), p. 7.

122. Hacker, "The Machines of War," p. 257.

123. Alic et al., *Beyond Spinoff*, p. 33.

124. Teece, "Capturing Value from Knowledge Assets," p. 64; Arthur, *The Nature of Technology*, pp. 45–67; and Alic, "Managing U.S. Defense Acquisition," pp. 1–36.

125. This, for example, is how the Soviet Union acquired the technological knowledge necessary to produce long-range heavy bombers after World War II. Yefim Gordon and Vladimir Rigmant, *Tupolev Tu-4: Soviet Superfortress* (Hinckley, U.K.: Midland, 2002).

126. Yasunori Baba, Shoichi Kuroda, and Hiroshi Yoshiki, "Diffusion of the Systemic Approach in Japan: Gauge and Industrial Standards," in Akira Goto and Hiroyuki Odagiri, eds., *Innovation in Japan* (New York: Oxford University Press, 1997), pp. 40–42.

127. Shoshana Zuboff, *In the Age of the Smart Machine: The Future of Work and Power* (New York: Basic Books, 1988), pp. 41–44.

128. Zuboff, *In the Age of the Smart Machine*, p. 44.

129. Hounshell, *From the American System to Mass Production, 1800–1932*, pp. 258–260.

130. Quoted in Hounshell, *From the American System to Mass Production, 1800–1932*, p. 260.

131. Hounshell, *From the American System to Mass Production, 1800–1932*, pp. 260–261.

132. Donald MacKenzie and Graham Spinardi, "Tacit Knowledge, Weapons Design, and the Uninvention of Nuclear Weapons," *American Journal of Sociology*, Vol. 101, No. 1 (July 1995), p. 63, doi.org/10.1086/230699.

133. Friedrich A. Hayek, "The Use of Knowledge in Society," *American Economic Review*, Vol. 35, No. 4 (September 1945), pp. 519–530, https://www.jstor.org/stable/1809376; and Michael Polanyi, *Personal Knowledge: Towards a Post-Critical Philosophy* (Chicago, Ill.: University of Chicago Press, 1958).

134. Wolfgang Keller, "International Technology Diffusion," *Journal of Economic Literature*, Vol. 42, No. 3 (September 2004), p. 756, doi.org/10.1257/0022051042177685.

135. See Collins, "The TEA Set," pp. 165–185; and MacKenzie and Spinardi, "Tacit Knowledge, Weapons Design, and the Uninvention of Nuclear Weapons," pp. 44–99.

136. Wesley M. Cohen and Richard C. Levin, "Empirical Studies of Innovation and Market Structure," in Richard Schmalensee and Robert Willig, eds., *Handbook of Industrial Organization*, Vol. 2 (Amsterdam: North Holland, 2007), p. 1093.

137. Charles H. Fine, *Clockspeed: Winning Industry Control in the Age of Temporary Advantage* (Reading, Mass.: Perseus, 1998), p. 141.

138. Dennis D. Doe, "Current Practices," in Anderson and Dorfman, *Aerospace Software Engineering*, p. 164; and James E. Tomayko, *Computers Take Flight: A History of NASA's Pioneering Digital Fly-By-Wire Project* (Washington, D.C.: National Aeronautics and Space Administration, 2000), pp. 24–25, 30.

139. Herwig, "The Battlefleet Revolution, 1885–1914," p. 120.

140. Macksey, *Technology in War*, p.57.

141. Barry Gough, *Churchill and Fisher: The Titans at the Admiralty Who Fought the First World War* (Toronto: James Lorimer, 2017), p. 3.

142. David K. Brown, *Warrior to Dreadnought: Warship Development, 1860–1905* (London: Chatham, 1997), pp. 180–187, 189–191.

143. Norman Friedman, *Battleship: Design and Development, 1905–1945* (New York: Mayflower, 1978), pp. 98–104.

144. See John Beeler, *Birth of the Battleships: British Capital Ship Design, 1870–1881* (Annapolis: Naval Institute Press, 2001).

145. Norman Friedman, *Fighting the Great War at Sea: Strategy, Tactic and Technology* (Yorkshire, England: Seaforth Publishing, 2014), p. 44; Philip Pugh, *The Cost of Seapower: The Influence of Money on Naval Affairs from 1815 to the Present Day* (London: Conway Maritime Press, 1986), pp. 139–151. Friedman, *Fighting the Great War at Sea*, p. 44; and Pugh, *The Cost of Seapower*, pp. 139–151.

146. Aidan Dodson, *The Kaiser's Battlefleet: German Capital Ships, 1871–1918* (Annapolis, Md.: Naval Institute Press, 2016), pp. 23–24.

147. Robert Gardiner, ed., *Conway's: All the World's Fighting Ships, 1860–1905* (Annapolis, Md.: Naval Institute Press, 1985), p. 32.

148. Dodson, *The Kaiser's Battlefleet*, pp. 25, 40, and, more generally, pp. 23–71.

149. Friedman, *Fighting the Great War at Sea*, pp. 73–101, 195–213; and Weir, *Building the Kaiser's Navy*, pp. 33–34.

150. Friedman, *Fighting the Great War at Sea*, p. 195; and Norman Friedman, *Naval Weapons of World War One: Guns, Torpedoes, Mines, and ASW Weapons of All Nations, An Illustrated History* (Barnsley, U.K.: Seaforth, 2011), pp. 121–123.

151. See Holger H. Herwig, "Imperial Germany," in Ernest R. May, ed., *Knowing One's Enemies: Intelligence Assessment before the Two World Wars* (Princeton, N.J.: Princeton University Press, 1986), pp. 62–97.

152. Weir, *Building the Kaiser's Navy*, pp. 30, 33, 47.

153. The two best examples are an open-access article anticipating the all-big-gun battleship design and reports from the German naval attaché in London. See, respectively, Vittorio Cuniberti, "An Ideal Battleship for the British Fleet," in Fred T. Jane, ed., *All The World's Fighting Ships* (London: Samson and Low, 1903), pp. 407–409; and Friedman, *Fighting the Great War at Sea*, p. 197. The idea was discussed, however, in 1901 "by navy gunnery experts in the US Naval Institute Proceedings" a magazine avidly read by members of the German Imperial Navy; see Tucker, *Handbook of 19th Century Naval Warfare*, p. 219.

154. Friedman, *Fighting the Great War at Sea*, p. 80; and Nicolas Wolz, *From Imperial Splendour to Internment: The German Navy in the First World War* (Yorkshire, England: Seaforth Publishing, 2015), pp. 98–118.

155. John Brooks, *Dreadnought Gunnery and the Battle of Jutland: The Question of Fire Control* (Abingdon, U.K.: Routledge, 2006), p. 218.

156. Norman Friedman, *Naval Firepower: Battleship Guns and Gunnery in the Dreadnought Era* (Barnsley, U.K.: Seaforth, 2008), pp. 158–163.

157. Friedman, *Naval Firepower*, p. 158.

158. See Friedman, *Naval Firepower*; and Friedman, *Fighting the Great War at Sea*, pp. 188–213.

159. Friedman, *Fighting the Great War at Sea*, p. 197.

160. Weir, *Building the Kaiser's Navy*, pp. 30, 33, 47; and Friedman, *Fighting the Great War at Sea*, pp. 122–123.

161. Weir, *Building the Kaiser's Navy*, pp. 29, 96–98.

162. Weir, *Building the Kaiser's Navy*, pp. 86–91.

163. Robert Gardiner, ed., *Conway's: All the World's Fighting Ships, 1906–1921* (Annapolis, Md.: Naval Institute Press, 1985), p. 145.

164. Gary E. Weir, "Tirpitz and Technology," *Naval History*, Vol. 4, No. 1 (Winter 1990), p. 41.

165. Gardiner, *Conway's: All the World's Fighting Ships, 1860–1905*, p. 36.

166. Friedman, *Naval Weapons of World War One*, p. 127.

167. Gardiner, *Conway's: All the World's Fighting Ships, 1906–1921*, p. 145.

168. See, respectively, Friedman, *Fighting the Great War at Sea*, p. 123; and Brooks, *Dreadnought Gunnery and the Battle of Jutland*, p.4.

169. Friedman, *Naval Firepower*, pp. 158–163; and Friedman, *Fighting the Great War at Sea*, p. 197.

170. Brooks, *Dreadnought Gunnery and the Battle of Jutland*, p.44.

171. Friedman, *Naval Weapons of World War One*, pp. 23–26; Brooks, *Dreadnought Gunnery and the Battle of Jutland*, pp. 78–210; and Friedman, *Naval Firepower*, pp. 68–81, 160.

172. Brooks, *Dreadnought Gunnery and the Battle of Jutland*, p. 502.

173. This is the Zeiss 3-meter system produced by Siemens & Halske. See Brooks, *Dreadnought Gunnery and the Battle of Jutland*, p. 216.

174. Brooks, *Dreadnought Gunnery and the Battle of Jutland*, p. 218.

175. Arthur Hezlet, *Electronics and Sea Power* (New York: Stein and Day, 1975), p. 121.

176. For the most recent and exhaustive scholarly investigation, see Brooks, *Dreadnought Gunnery and the Battle of Jutland*.

177. Brooks, *Dreadnought Gunnery and the Battle of Jutland*, p. 473; Wolz, *From Imperial Splendor to Internment*, pp. 98–118; and Friedman, *Fighting the Great War at Sea*, pp. 104–187.

178. Friedman, *Naval Firepower*, p. 166.

179. Friedman, *Naval Firepower*, p. 166.

180. Friedman, *Fighting the Great War at Sea*, pp. 73–101, 195–213; and Weir, *Building the Kaiser's Navy*, pp. 33–34.

181. See Friedman, *Fighting the Great War at Sea*, pp. 189–213. See also Gardiner, *Conway's: All the World's Fighting Ships, 1906–1921*, p. 145.

182. Tucker, *Handbook of 19th Century Naval Warfare*, p. 229.

183. Brooks, *Dreadnaught Gunnery and the Battle of Jutland*, p. 504.

184. The quotation refers to synchros, whose availability also enabled different design choices. See Friedman, *Naval Weapons of World War One*, p. 123.

185. See Ronald W. Brower, "Lockheed F-22 Raptor," in Cary R. Spitzer, ed., *The Avionics Handbook* (Williamsburg, Va.: CRC, 2001).

186. Doug Richardson, *Stealth: Deception, Evasion, and Concealment in the Air* (New York: Orion, 1989), pp. 24–57.

187. "Supercruise" means achieving supersonic speed without relying on afterburners. Afterburners increase the thrust of the engines by injecting fuel into the gas exhaust. This procedure significantly increases fuel consumption. Moreover, afterburners also expose the aircraft to enemy infrared search and track systems because of the enhanced heat.

188. Brower, "Lockheed F-22 Raptor."

189. Evan S. Medeiros, Roger Cliff, Keith Crane, and James C. Mulvenon, *A New Direction for China's Defense Industry* (Santa Monica, Calif.: Rand Corporation, 2005); Kenneth W. Allen, Glenn Krumel, and Jonathan D. Pollack, *China's Air Force Enters the 21st Century* (Santa Monica, Calif.: Rand Corporation, 1995), pp. 160–166.

190. Allen, Krumel, and Pollack, *China's Air Force Enters the 21st Century*, p. 159.

191. Shen Pin-Luenin, "China's Aviation Industry: Past, Present, and Future," in Richard P. Hallion, Roger Cliff, and Phillip C. Saunders, eds., *The Chinese Air Force: Evolving Concepts, Roles, and Capabilities* (Washington, D.C.: National University Press, 2012), pp. 251, 266–268.

192. These are the F-8 Finback, the F-8–2, the B-7/FB-7, and the K-8/L-8. See Allen, Krumel, and Pollack, *China's Air Force Enters the 21st Century*, pp. 150–153.

193. Roger Cliff et al., *Ready for Takeoff: China's Advancing Aerospace Industry* (Santa Monica, Calif.: RAND Corporation, 2011), pp. 35–87; and Chad J.R. Ohlandt et al., *Chinese Investment in U.S. Aviation* (Santa Monica, Calif.: RAND Corporation, 2017).

194. Cliff et al., *Ready for Takeoff*, pp. 35–88.

195. Cliff et al., *Ready for Takeoff*, p. 37.

196. William C. Hannas, James Mulvenon, and Anna B. Puglisi, *Chinese Industrial Espionage: Technology Acquisition and Military Modernization* (New York: Routledge, 2013).

197. David Axe, "Was China's Stealth Tech Made in America?" *Wired*, January 24, 2011.

198. Entities that have been victims of Chinese industrial espionage include Boeing, Pratt & Whitney, Rockwell, Rolls-Royce, and Wright-Patterson Air Base. Office of the National Counter-Intelligence Executive, *Foreign Spies Stealing US Economic Secrets in Cyberspace: Annual Report to Congress on Foreign Economic Collection and Industrial Espionage, 2009–11* (Washington, D.C.: U.S. Government Publishing Office 2011), p. 2; Stephen Chen, "America's Hidden Role in Chinese Weapons Research," *South China Morning Post*, March 29, 2017; and Stephen Chen, "China in Talks for Sale of Jet Engine Technology to Germany," *South China Morning Post*, January 18, 2018.

199. David Eimer, "China's Stealth Fighter 'Based on U.S. Technology'" *Telegraph*, January 23, 2011. It is important to emphasize that the theoretical explanation of how to reduce the radar cross section of an object has been known since 1962, when a Soviet physicist published an article in a scientific journal. Moreover, since the 1980s, several publications

have provided technical insights behind stealth technology—most prominently, the lecture notes of Allen Fuhs of the US Naval Postgraduate School and a textbook by Eugene Knott, John Schaeffer, and Michael Tuley of the Georgia Institute of Technology. See Rich and Janos, *Skunk Works*, pp. 19–20; and Richardson, *Stealth*, pp. 11–12.

200. Bates Gill, "Chinese Military-Technical Development: The Record for Western Assessment, 1979–1999," in James C. Mulvenon and Andrew N. Yang, *Seeking Truth from Facts: A Retrospective on Chinese Military Studies in the Post-Mao Era*. No. RAND-CF-160-CAPP (Santa Monica, Calif.: Rand Corporation, 2001), pp. 141–172; and Allen, Krumel, and Pollack, *China's Air Force Enters the 21st Century*, p. 155.

201. Medeiros et al., *A New Direction for China's Defense Industry*, p. 170.

202. Allen, Krumel, and Pollack, *China's Air Force Enters the 21st Century*, p. 155.

203. Phillip C. Saunders and Joshua K. Wiseman, *Buy, Build, or Steal: China's Quest for Advanced Military Aviation Technologies* (Washington, DC: National Defense University, 2011), p. 10.

204. Allen, Krumel and Pollack, *China's Air Force Enters the 21st Century*, p. 149.

205. Allen, Krumel and Pollack, *China's Air Force Enters the 21st Century*, p. 156.

206. Medeiros et al., *A New Direction for China's Defense Industry*, p. 27.

207. Siemon T. Wezeman, "Impact of Shifts in Arms Trade and Exercises on South Asia and Europe," in Lora Saalman, ed., *China-Russia Relations and Regional Dynamics: From Pivots to Peripheral Diplomacy* (Stockholm: SIPRI, 2017), pp. 85–88.

208. See, for example, Jeffrey Lin and P. W. Singer, "China's Stealth Fighter May Be Getting a New Engine," *Eastern Arsenal* blog, *Popular Science*, September 8, 2017; and "No Longer Just Catch-Up: China Will Soon Have Air Power Rivalling the West's," *Economist*, February 15, 2018.

209. See Minnie Chan, "China's J-20 Stealth Fighter Joins the People's Liberation Army Air Force," *South China Morning Post*, March 10, 2017; and Minnie Chan, "Why China's First Stealth Fighter Was Rushed into Service with Inferior Engines," *South China Morning Post*, February 10, 2018.

210. Eloise Lee and Robert Johnson, "China's J-20 and the American F-22 Raptor—You Are Not Seeing Double," *Business Insider*, June 4, 2012; and Jeffrey Lin and P. W. Singer, China's J-20 Stealth Fighter Jet Has Officially Entered Service, *Eastern Arsenal* blog, *Popular Science*, February 18, 2018, https://www.popsci.com/chinas-j-20-stealth-fighter-officially-enters-service.

211. Michael J. Pelosi and Carlo Kopp, "A Preliminary Assessment of Specular Radar Cross Section Performance in the Chengdu J-20 Prototype," *Air Power Australia Analysis*, July 4, 2011, http://www.ausairpower.net/APA-2011-03.html.

212. Some observers have downplayed these problems by arguing that the J-20 is allegedly not intended to be an air-superiority fighter. This conclusion is unwarranted. For a summary and a rebuttal of this argument, see Rick Joe, "J-20: Striker or Interceptor," *PLA Real Talk* blog, December 27, 2015, http://plarealtalk.com/2015/12/27/j-20-striker-interceptor/.

213. By adding edges to the design of an aircraft, canards increase the reflection of radar beams, and hence the radar cross section. Pelosi and Kopp, "A Preliminary Assessment of Specular Radar Cross Section Performance in the Chengdu J-20 Prototype."

214. Richard Aboulafia, "Monthly Newsletter" (Fairfax, Va.: Richard Aboulafia personal website, October 2012), http://www.richardaboulafia.com/shownote.asp?id=366.

215. David Axe, "Seven Secret Ways America's Stealth Armada Stays off the Radar," *Wired*, December 13, 2012.

216. Since the J-20 first appeared in late 2010, observers have noted several changes (primarily in the fuselage, tailbooms, vertical tails, and canards), suggesting that China has relied on trial and error to fix possible design problems. Bill Sweetman, "J-20 Stealth Fighter Design Balances Speed and Agility," *Aviation Week & Space Technology*, November 10, 2014, p. 57.

217. Medeiros et al., *A New Direction for China's Defense Industry*, p. 169.

218. The engine is the NPO Saturn AL-31. The exhaust inevitably compromises the aircraft's low observability. See Andrew Erickson and Gabe Collins, "The 'Long Pole in the Tent': China's Military Jet Engines," *Diplomat*, December 9, 2012; and Bill Sweetman, "China's Radar and Missile Work Means More Than Fighters," *Aviation Week & Space Technology*, December 1, 2014, p. 16.

219. The engine is the Shenyang WS-10.

220. Anonymous military sources, cited in Chan, "Why China's First Stealth Fighter Was Rushed into Service with Inferior Engines." The name of this engine is Xian WS-15.

221. Anonymous military source, cited in Minnie Chan, "China Reveals J-20 Stealth Fighter's Missile Carrying Capability at Zhuhai Air Show," *South China Morning Post*, November 14, 2018.

222. Anonymous military source, cited in Chan, "Why China's First Stealth Fighter Was Rushed into Service with Inferior Engines."

223. Minnie Chan, "China's New J-20 Stealth Fighter Engine a No-Show at Zhuhai Air Show after It Fails Reliability Tests," *South China Morning Post*, November 7, 2018.

224. The J-20 does not possess supercruise capabilities, so it is not a fifth-generation fighter.

225. Minnie Chan, "China Powers Up Military Jet Engine Tech to Wean Itself off Russian Imports," *South China Morning Post*, December 12, 2016. The amount is 168 billion yuan, equivalent to $21–$24 billion.

226. Chan, "Why China's First Stealth Fighter Was Rushed into Service with Inferior Engines." See also Chan, "China Reveals J-20 Stealth Fighter's Missile Carrying Capability."

227. Quoted in Greg Waldrom, "China's J-20 Set to Receive Indigenous Engine," *Flight Global*, March 13, 2017.

228. According some experts, this will happen soon. See, for example, Lin and Singer, "China's Stealth Fighter May Be Getting a New Engine."

229. Tai Ming Cheung, Thomas G. Mahnken, and Andrew L. Ross, "Frameworks for Analyzing Chinese Defense and Military Innovation," in Cheung, ed., *Forging China's Military Might: A New Framework for Assessing Innovation* (Baltimore, Md.: Johns Hopkins University Press, 2014), p. 35.

230. Carlo Kopp, "An Initial Assessment of China's J-20 Stealth Fighter," *China Brief*, May 6, 2011, p. 10.

231. Cheung, Mahnken, and Ross, "Frameworks for Analyzing Chinese Defense and Military Innovation," p. 35.

232. Royce, "Current Problems," p. 6.

233. Royce, "Current Problems," pp. 8–11.

234. See Mili and Tchier, *Software Testing*, p. 6.

235. For example, the low radar cross section of the F-117 was attainable by compromising its aerodynamics—a problem that was addressed by software. See Rich and Janos, *Skunk Works*, pp. 30–32, 46, 108.

236. Steve A. Fino, *Tiger Check: Automating the U.S. Air Force Fighter Pilot in Air-to-Air Combat, 1950–1980* (Baltimore, Md.: Johns Hopkins University Press, 2017).

237. Ninety percent of the 1.7 million lines of the F-22's code is "devoted" to radar operation and data fusion. See Mili and Tchier, *Software Testing*, p. 6.

238. Chan, "China's J-20 Stealth Fighter Joins the People's Liberation Army Air Force."

239. Medeiros et al., *A New Direction for China's Defense Industry*, p. 162.

240. Sebastien Roblin, "China Stole This Fighter from Russia—And It's Coming to the South China Sea," *National Interest*, July 24, 2016.

241. Roblin, "China Stole This Fighter from Russia."

242. David Axe, "China's Testing Woes Remind That Developing Carrier Planes Is Hard," *Wired*, March 21, 2013.

243. International Institute for Strategic Studies, *The Military Balance, 2015* (London: Routledge, 2015), p. 215.

244. Some observers even speculate that China bought these aircraft in order to copy, among other things, its thrust-vectoring engine. See, for example, Bradley Perrett, "China Has 11 Flanker Versions, with More Possible," *Aviation Week & Space Technology*, February 17, 2017, p. 50.

245. Dillon Zhou, "China J-15 Fighter Jet: Chinese Officials Defend New Fighter As Chinese Original, but Questions Remain," *Mic*, December 16, 2012.

246. David Cenciotti, "No Match for a U.S. Hornet: 'China's Navy J-15 More a Flopping Fish than a Flying Shark' Chinese Media Say," *Aviationist* blog, September 30, 2013, https://theaviationist.com/2013/09/30/j-15-critics/.

247. Cenciotti, "No Match for a U.S. Hornet."

248. Dave Majumdar, "China's Aircraft Carriers Have a Big Problem: Fatally Flawed Fighter Planes," *National Interest*, July 5, 2018.

249. Gabe Collins and Andrew Erickson, "China's New Project 718/J-20 Fighter: Development Outlook and Strategic Implications," *China SignPost*, January 17, 2011.

250. Rich and Janos, *Skunk Works*, p. 325.

251. See Jay Miller, *Lockheed Martin's Skunk Works: The Official History* (Leicester, U.K.: Midland, 1995), p. 175; and

Dennis R. Jenkins and Tony R. Landis, *Experimental and Prototype U.S. Air Force Jet Fighters* (North Branch, Minn.: Specialty Press, 2008), p. 234.

252. Richardson, *Stealth*, p. 93.

253. The advantages China derived from imitation also look quite modest in comparison to the first US stealth fighter, F-117: it entered service in 1987; its development took six years; and it cost $155 million. See David C. Aronstein and Albert C. Piccirillo, *Have Blue and the F-117A: Evolution of the Stealth Fighter* (Reston, Va.: American Institute of Aeronautics and Astronautics, 1997), p. 267.

254. United States Air Force, *F-22A Production Restart Assessment* (Washington, D.C.: United States Air Force, February 2017).

255. Saunders and Wiseman, "Buy, Build, or Steal," p. 48.

256. Barry R. Posen, "Command of the Commons: The Military Foundation of U.S. Hegemony," *International Security*, Vol. 28, No. 1 (Summer 2003), p. 10, doi.org/10.1162/016228803322427965.

257. See Stephen G. Brooks and William C. Wohlforth, "Power, Globalization, and the End of the Cold War: Reevaluating a Landmark Case for Ideas," *International Security*, Vol. 25, No. 3 (Winter 2000/01), pp. 5–53, doi.org/10.1162/016228800560516.

258. See Mark R. Brawley, "The Political Economy of Balance of Power Theory," in T. V. Paul, James Wirtz, and Michel Fortmann, eds., *Balance of Power: Theory and Practice in the 21st Century* (Palo Alto, Calif.: Stanford University Press, 2004), p. 80.

259. Tai Ming Cheung, *Fortifying China: The Struggle to Build a Modern Defense Economy* (Ithaca, N.Y.: Cornell University Press, 2008), p. 243.

260. Ministry of Defence, "Joint Doctrine Note 2/22: The U.K. Approach to Unmanned Aircraft Systems" (Shrivenham, U.K.: British Ministry of Defence, March 30, 2011), pp. 1–2.

261. Office of the Chief Scientist, *Autonomous Horizons: System Autonomy in the Air Force—A Path to the Future, Vol. 1: Human-Autonomy Teaming* (Washington, D.C.: United States Air Force, 2015), p. 6.

262. Andrea Gilli and Mauro Gilli, "Seapower and the Second Machine Age: The Robotics Revolution and the U.S. Command of the Commons," paper presented at the International Studies Association annual convention, Baltimore, Maryland, February 22–25, 2017.

The New Era of Nuclear Weapons, Deterrence, and Conflict

KEIR A. LIEBER AND DARYL G. PRESS

We have published a series of articles in recent years about the role of nuclear weapons in international politics.[1] Taken together, these articles advance two main arguments: First, technological innovation has dramatically improved the ability of states to launch "counterforce" attacks—that is, military strikes aimed at disarming an adversary by destroying its nuclear weapons. Second, in the coming decades, deterring the use of nuclear weapons during conventional wars will be much harder than most analysts believe. Both of these arguments have important implications for the US nuclear weapons modernization effort currently underway, and both have generated discussion and criticism in the nuclear analytical community. Thus, we offer here a brief summary of our main points and rebuttal to several of the criticisms.

The Counterforce Revolution and US Nuclear Primacy

The first set of arguments is about an important, yet virtually unnoticed, consequence of changes in military technology and the balance of power. In a nutshell, the same revolution in accuracy that has transformed conventional warfare has had equally momentous consequences for nuclear weapons and deterrence.[2] Very accurate delivery systems, new reconnaissance technologies, and the downsizing of arsenals from Cold War levels have made both conventional and nuclear counterforce strikes against nuclear arsenals much more feasible than ever before. Perhaps most surprising, pairing highly accurate delivery systems with nuclear weapons permits target strategies that would create virtually no radioactive fallout, hence, vastly reduced fatalities.

For nuclear analysts weaned on two seeming truths of the Cold War era—that nuclear arsenals reliably deter attacks via the threat of retaliation and that nuclear weapons use is tantamount to mass slaughter—the implications of the counterforce revolution should be jarring.

The conventional view linking nuclear weapons to stalemate and slaughter was correct during the latter decades of the Cold War. By the mid-1960s, a truly effective nuclear counterforce strike by either side—that is, a disarming blow by one superpower against the nuclear arsenal of the other—had become impossible.[3] Each of the superpowers wielded an enormous arsenal, which was deployed on a diverse set of delivery systems. The sheer number of targets that would have to be destroyed, combined with the limitations of contemporary guidance systems, virtually guaranteed that any disarming attack would fail, leaving the enemy with a large number of surviving weapons with which to retaliate. Furthermore, any significant counterforce strike would have produced enormous quantities of lethal radioactive fallout and hence caused millions of civilian casualties.[4] Most Cold War strategists—many of whom are still active in the nuclear analytical community today—came to instinctively associate nuclear weapons with stalemate and nuclear use with Armageddon.

But nuclear weapons—like virtually all other weapons—have changed dramatically over the past four decades. Modern guidance systems permit nuclear planners to achieve "probabilities of damage" against hardened nuclear targets that were unheard of during the Cold War. And heightened accuracy also permits nontraditional targeting strategies that would further increase the effectiveness of counterforce strikes and greatly reduce casualties.[5] The revolution in accuracy and sensors, and the relatively small contemporary arsenals, mean that nuclear balances around the world—for example, between the United States and China, the United States and North Korea, and perhaps in the future between Iran and Israel—bear little resemblance to the Cold War superpower standoff.

To illustrate the revolution in accuracy, in 2006 we modeled the hardest case for our claim: a hypothetical US first strike on the next largest nuclear arsenal in the world, that of Russia. The same models that were used during the Cold War to demonstrate the inescapability of stalemate—the condition of "mutual assured destruction," or MAD—now suggested that even the large Russian arsenal could be destroyed in a disarming strike.[6] Furthermore, the dramatic leap in accuracy—which is the foundation for effective counterforce—is based on widely available technologies within reach of other nuclear-armed states, including Russia, China, Pakistan, and others. Our overriding message is not about the US-Russian nuclear balance per se. Rather, our point is that key beliefs about nuclear weapons have been overturned; scholars and analysts need to reexamine their underlying assumptions about nuclear stalemate and deterrence.

Since 2006, we have discussed these issues with many nuclear analysts, US government officials, and military officers involved with the nuclear mission. Almost everything we learned reinforced our views about the counterforce revolution and suggests our earlier work understated the leap in US counterforce capabilities—with one exception. We previously argued that US "nuclear primacy"—the ability to use nuclear weapons to destroy the strategic forces of any other country—appeared to be an intentional goal of US policy-makers. We noted that even as the United States greatly reduced its nuclear arsenal, it retained, and in some cases improved, those nuclear forces that were ideally suited to the counterforce mission. Based on what we have subsequently learned, we would recast and sharpen this part of our argument to contend that the United States is intentionally pursuing "strategic primacy"—meaning that Washington seeks the ability to defeat enemy nuclear forces (as well as other WMD)—but that US nuclear weapons are but one dimension of that effort. In fact, the effort to neutralize adversary strategic forces—that is, achieve strategic primacy—spans nearly every realm of warfare: for example, ballistic missile defense, antisubmarine warfare, intelligence-surveillance-and-reconnaissance systems, offensive cyber warfare, conventional precision strike, and long-range precision strike, in addition to nuclear strike capabilities.

In sum, two fundamental "truths" about nuclear weapons—they reliably produce stalemate and their use would necessarily create mass casualties—have been quietly overturned by changes in technology and dramatic force reductions. Unfortunately, many contemporary analyses of nuclear politics seem to rest on the assumption that nuclear deterrence still functions as it did in the 1970s. The stipulation of mass slaughter under MAD conditions may be true for some nuclear relationships in the world but not for others. And new conditions generate new questions: for example, how is deterrence likely to work when nuclear use does not automatically imply suicide and mass slaughter? In particular, what are the implications for US nuclear policy?

The Problem of Coercive Escalation and US Nuclear Modernization

A second set of arguments stems from the problem of nuclear escalation and the future of the US nuclear arsenal. Our main claim is that deterring nuclear conflict will be much more difficult in the coming decades than many analysts realize. As nuclear weapons proliferate, it becomes increasingly likely that the United States will find itself in conventional conflicts with nuclear-armed adversaries. Those adversaries understand the consequences of losing a war to the United States—prison or death typically awaits enemy leaders.[7] Coercive nuclear escalation as a means of creating stalemate and remaining in power is one of the only trump cards available to countries fighting the United States.

Some analysts might scoff at the notion that a rational leader would use nuclear weapons against a superpower like the United States. But that retort conflates the logic of peacetime deterrence with the logic of war, and it ignores history. During peacetime, almost any course of action is better than starting a nuclear war against a superpower. But during war—when that superpower's planes are bombing command and leadership sites, and when its tanks are seizing territory—the greatest danger may be to refrain from escalation and let the war run its course. Leaders of weaker states—those unlikely to prevail on the conventional battlefield—face life-and-death pressures to compel a stalemate. And nuclear weapons provide a better means of coercive escalation than virtually any other.

The notion of countries escalating conflict to avoid conventional defeat may sound far-fetched, but it is well grounded in history. When nuclear-armed states face overwhelming conventional threats—or worry about the possibility of catastrophic conventional defeat—they often adopt coercive escalatory doctrines to deter war or stalemate a conflict that erupts. Pakistan openly intends to use nuclear weapons to counter an overwhelming conventional Indian invasion. Russia claims it needs theater nuclear weapons to counter NATO's conventional advantages. Israel expects to win its conventional wars but retains the capability for nuclear escalation to prevent conquest in case its conventional forces suffer a catastrophic defeat.

The discussion of coercive nuclear escalation should sound familiar to Western analysts, as it was NATO's strategy for three decades. From the mid-1960s until the end of the Cold War, NATO planned to deter war, and stalemate it if necessary, through coercive nuclear escalation. NATO understood that—by the mid-1960s—it could no longer win a nuclear war against the Soviet Union, but it still based its national security strategy on coercive escalation because it believed Warsaw Pact conventional forces were overwhelming.

In short, the escalatory dynamics that existed during the Cold War exist today—and they are just as powerful. States still face the same critical national security problem they faced during the Cold War and throughout history: namely, how to prevent stronger countries from conquering them. The high-stakes poker game of international politics has not ended; the players and the cards dealt have merely changed. Those who were weak during the Cold War are now strong, and another set of militarily "weak" countries—such as North Korea, Iran, Pakistan, and even China and Russia—now clutch or seek nuclear weapons to defend themselves from overwhelming military might, just as NATO once did.

What can the United States do to mitigate the problem of escalation? Ideally, it should avoid wars against nuclear-armed enemies. But that option may not be possible given current US foreign policy and alliances. War may erupt on the Korean Peninsula, ensnaring the United States in a battle against a desperate nuclear-armed foe. In the future, Washington may fight a nuclear-armed Iran over sea lanes in the Persian Gulf. And the United States could someday be dragged into war by a clash between Chinese and Japanese naval forces near disputed islands.

Alternatively, the United States could seek to develop conventional war plans designed to wage limited war without triggering enemy escalation. Development of alternative plans is sensible, but history shows that wars are difficult to contain, and modern conventional warfare is inherently escalatory.

A third option to mitigate these dangers is to retain, and improve, US nuclear and nonnuclear counterforce capabilities. Fielding powerful counterforce weapons may help deter adversary escalation during war—by convincing enemy leaders to choose a "golden parachute" rather than escalation—and would give US leaders better response options if deterrence failed. In particular, the United States should retain and develop nuclear weapons that bring together three key characteristics of counterforce: high accuracy, flexible yield, and prompt delivery.

To be clear, sharpening US counterforce capabilities is not a "solution" to the problem of adversary nuclear weapons. Although, ceteris paribus, it would be better to have excellent counterforce capabilities than to lack them, given enough time and motivation, many countries could greatly increase the survivability of their forces. But given the plausible prospect that the United States will find itself waging war against nuclear-armed states, and given the powerful incentives of US adversaries to brandish or use nuclear weapons, it would be reckless to proceed without a full suite of modern nuclear and nonnuclear counterforce capabilities.

Response to Our Critics

A recent conference panel devoted to our work raised several criticisms, some familiar and others new.[8] Be-

low we summarize the main objections and offer our response.

"The United States is not seeking to neutralize adversary deterrent forces."

Some critics argue that the United States is not seeking strategic primacy. They reject any intent behind the emergence of US nuclear primacy and downplay the effort to neutralize adversary deterrent forces in US military strategy. Instead of the United States bolstering its counterforce capabilities, critics emphasize how it is minimizing the role of nuclear weapons in national security strategy—as only this is consistent with international arms control and nonproliferation efforts aimed at convincing other states to forego strategic weapons, reduce existing arsenals, or cancel modernization programs. The implication is that we have mistakenly imputed sinister motives to US defense programs and planning.

Disavowal of the US pursuit of strategic primacy comes most frequently from those who work inside or outside the government on arms control and nonproliferation policy. Yet, those who work on US regional war plans and counterproliferation policy typically see nothing controversial in our claim that the United States seeks the ability to neutralize adversary strategic weapons. In fact, this effort appears to be official US policy. As a simple internet search shows, the US government does not hide the wide range of research and planning efforts underway that fall under the rubric of "defeat WMD" or "combatting WMD." And the underlying logic behind those efforts is simple: deterrence may fail, especially during conventional wars, and therefore the United States needs the ability to defend US forces, allies, and the US homeland from enemy WMD using, depending on the circumstances, conventional strikes, missile defenses, special operations, offensive cyberattacks, and in extreme cases nuclear strikes. In short, "defeating WMD" and "seeking strategic primacy" are essentially synonymous: protecting oneself from others' strategic weapons (which sounds reasonable) and neutralizing others' strategic deterrent forces (which sounds more malicious) are simply two phrases describing the same behavior.

Current US grand strategy—which takes an expansive definition of national interests and is committed to a global network of alliances—means that the United States may be drawn into wars with WMD-armed adversaries. We agree with many US government officials that the ability to neutralize those adversary capabilities in such a conflict may be critical. Others are free to disagree. But all analysts should recognize that current US efforts to neutralize adversaries' deterrent forces are inherently threatening to those states, and few should be surprised when those adversaries treat US pleas for greater arms reductions with considerable skepticism.[9]

"Nuclear weapons are unnecessary; conventional weapons can do the job."

A second criticism is that retaining (or improving) specific US nuclear weapons for the counterforce mission is unnecessary. The idea is that modern delivery systems are now so accurate that even conventional weapons can reliably destroy hardened targets. The key, according to this argument, is simply knowing the location of the target: if you know where it is, you can kill it with conventional weapons; if you do not, even nuclear weapons will not help. The implication is that even though counterforce capabilities are crucial, nuclear weapons are not needed for this mission.

This criticism is wrong, because there is a substantial difference between the expected effectiveness of conventional strikes and the expected effectiveness of nuclear strikes against a range of plausible counterforce targets. Even the most powerful conventional weapons—for example, the GBU-57 "Massive Ordnance Penetrator"—have an explosive power comparable to "only" 3–5 tons of TNT. By comparison, the least powerful (according to open sources) nuclear weapon in the US arsenal explodes with the equivalent power of roughly 300 tons of TNT.[10] The higher yield of nuclear weapons translates to greater destructive radius and higher likelihood of target destruction.[11] Against ordinary targets, the accuracy and destructive power of conventional weapons is sufficient. Against nuclear targets—if success is defined by the ability to destroy every weapon targeted—the much greater destructive radius of nuclear weapons provides a critical margin of error.

Furthermore, in real-world circumstances delivery systems may not achieve their usual levels of accuracy. Jammers that degrade the effectiveness of guidance systems and active defenses that impede aircraft crews or deflect incoming missiles can undermine accuracy. Even mundane things like bad weather can degrade wartime accuracy. Against hardened targets, conventional weapons must score a direct hit, whereas close is good enough when it comes to nuclear weapons. Lastly, many key counterforce targets are mobile. In those cases, nuclear weapons allow for greater "target location uncertainty" (when the target has moved since being observed) compared to their conventional counterparts.[12]

It is true that modern guidance systems have given conventional weapons far greater counterforce capabilities than ever before, but there is still a sizable gap between what nuclear and conventional weapons can accomplish.

"These arguments undermine US arms control and nonproliferation policy."

Finally, some critics suggest that whatever the truth of our claims, an open discussion of these issues is counterproductive because it undermines US arms control and nonproliferation objectives. They worry that our analysis emboldens defense hawks in other countries (particularly in Russia and China), undermines informal "Track II" diplomacy, and may catalyze foreign nuclear arms modernization. More broadly, by drawing too much attention to the leap in US nuclear capabilities and the utility of nuclear weapons for relatively weaker states, we undermine US efforts to delegitimize and prevent the spread of the nuclear weapons.

This critique is misguided for three reasons. First, other countries understand that the United States wields enormous counterforce capabilities and seeks to enhance them. For example, defense analysts in Russia and China closely watch and frequently comment on changes in US military capability. Moreover, potential US adversaries understand that nuclear weapons are uniquely suitable tools to deter a superior adversary or prevent catastrophic conventional defeat. This is why Pakistan relies on nuclear weapons to deter India; why Russia says it needs theater nuclear weapons; why Israel will not abandon the "Samson Option"; and why North Korea clings at such great expense to its nuclear weapons.

Second, stifling discussion of these issues is detrimental to US national security. For example, some defense analysts seem to have adopted the assumption that no country would deliberately use nuclear weapons against the United States, even though deliberate escalation was US policy when NATO felt it was too weak to defend itself against a Soviet invasion of Europe. If analysts continue to hold a false sense of the irrelevance of nuclear weapons even as US adversaries cling to them to try to keep the United States at bay—and if analysts convince enough policy-makers to do the same—there is a real danger the United States could stumble into a nuclear war. The lack of open discussion about the role of nuclear weapons is compounded by the constraints of security classification, which further limits the ability of policy-makers to explain important issues. In short, ignoring these issues—not discussing them—is the real danger.

Finally, unless they recognize the strategic incentives faced by countries like North Korea, Pakistan, Iran, and China, US leaders are susceptible to misattributing malign and aggressive intentions from those countries' efforts to acquire nuclear weapons or modernize delivery systems and arsenals. Unless US leaders understand that other countries rely on nuclear systems to keep more powerful potential adversaries in check—and unless they acknowledge to themselves that the United States is working steadily to neutralize adversary deterrent forces—they are more likely to misperceive enemy efforts to develop a robust deterrent force as a clear sign of hostility and as evidence that the other country is out of step with international standards of behavior. Simply put, the United States may prefer that its adversaries disarm or remain unarmed and thus leave themselves vulnerable to US power, but the fact that they often do not should not be misperceived as a sign of aggression.

Conclusion

The arguments we advance here raise new puzzles for scholars and pressing issues for policy-makers. Scholars need to reexamine much of the established wisdom about nuclear deterrence. From Schelling's early works to the present, many scholars have explored nuclear deterrence dynamics by modeling coercion under conditions of mutual vulnerability. Those models suggest that deterrence success depends principally upon resolve rather than capabilities (because the capability of each side to inflict unacceptable damage is an assumption of the model). Schelling's formulation made sense when he developed it—to explore the challenges of Cold War deterrence under conditions of MAD—but the same analytic framework is still used today even though many nuclear dyads are not characterized by nuclear stalemate. The counterforce revolution means that nuclear exchanges may not lead to mutual devastation—one party may suffer far less or even be spared entirely. Analytical models and conclusions derived from them (for example, about the importance of resolve over capabilities for deterrence success) need to be reexamined and updated.

The challenges facing US policy-makers, given the changes in the nuclear landscape, are profound. They must find a way to build sufficient counterforce capabilities to protect the United States and its allies from quite plausible adversary escalatory strategies—all the while avoiding building so much capability that it triggers a Cold War–style arms race with Russia and China. They must direct the US military to develop concepts for waging conventional war against nuclear-armed adversaries that would permit the United States to achieve its military objectives yet reduce the incentives for adversary escalation.

Perhaps most fundamentally, US leaders must encourage a more transparent and public debate about the roles and missions of US nuclear forces—and the capabilities that must be retained in the arsenal to execute those missions. Unfortunately, many contemporary nuclear analysts, policy advocates, and policy-makers seek to minimize discussion about nuclear weapons and simply assert that nuclear weapons are not particularly useful in the twenty-first century. That is a dangerous approach. The very reason the United States relied on nuclear weapons in the past is the reason potential US adversaries will rely on them now and in the future: nuclear weapons are a powerful deterrent against conventionally superior adversaries. In short, we need to be honest about why states rely on nuclear weapons, as we once did, and the dangers this poses for the United States and its allies.

NOTES

1. See Keir A. Lieber and Daryl G. Press, "The Rise of U.S. Nuclear Primacy," *Foreign Affairs* 85, no. 2 (March/April 2006): 42–54; Lieber and Press, "The End of MAD? The Nuclear Dimension of U.S. Primacy," *International Security* 30, no. 4 (Spring 2006): 7–44; Peter C. W. Flory, Keith Payne, Pavel Podvig, Alexei Arbatov, Lieber, and Press, "Nuclear Exchange: Does Washington Really Have (Or Want) Nuclear Primacy?" *Foreign Affairs* 85, no. 5 (September/October 2006): 149–57; Jeffrey S. Lantis, Tom Sauer, James J. Wirtz, Lieber, and Press, "The Short Shadow of U.S. Primacy?" *International Security* 31, no. 3 (Winter 2006/07): 174–93; Lieber and Press, "U.S. Nuclear Primacy and the Future of the Chinese Nuclear Deterrent," *China Security Quarterly*, no. 5 (Winter 2006/07): 66–89; Lieber and Press, "Superiority Complex: Why America's Growing Nuclear Supremacy May Make War with China More Likely," *Atlantic Monthly* 300, no. 1 (July/August 2007) 86–92; Lieber and Press, "The Nukes We Need: Preserving the American Deterrent," *Foreign Affairs* 88, no. 6 (November/December 2009): 39–51; Jan Lodal, James M. Acton, Hans M. Kristensen, Matthew McKinzie, Ivan Oelrich, Lieber, and Press, "Second Strike: Is the U.S. Nuclear Arsenal Outmoded?" *Foreign Affairs* 89, no. 2 (March/April 2010): 145–52; and Lieber and Press, "Obama's Nuclear Upgrade: The Case for Modernizing America's Nukes," *Foreign Affairs* (July 2011, Postscript).

2. We use "revolution in accuracy" as shorthand for a broad set of changes (still underway) that stem from the integration of computers into warfare. Among other things this has led to vastly improved guidance, surveillance, and command and control systems. Each of these improvements has greatly increased the ability to locate targets and precisely deliver munitions.

3. It is essential to differentiate the 1950s—during which the United States possessed a potent disarming capability against the Soviet Union—from the subsequent era of Cold War stalemate. During the 1950s, the US nuclear force far outmatched the meager Soviet arsenal. Until 1956, the Soviet Union had no weapons with the range to reach the United States, and even in the latter parts of the decade Moscow's rudimentary long-range nuclear arsenal was highly vulnerable to a nuclear disarming strike. The United States recognized its huge advantage and planned to fight and win World War III—if it occurred—by launching a massive nuclear disarming strike on the Soviet Union. Ironically, the era that spawned the term "mutual assured destruction (MAD)" was not characterized by the condition of MAD; nuclear stalemate only emerged later. See Lieber and Press, "Nuclear Weapons and International Politics," unpublished book manuscript.

4. See, for example, the fallout models in William Daugherty, Barbara G. Levi, and Frank von Hippel, "The Consequences of 'Limited' Nuclear Attacks on the United States," *International Security* 10, no. 4 (Spring 1986): 3–45; and Levi, von Hippel, and Daugherty, "Civilian Casualties from 'Limited' Nuclear Attacks on the USSR," *International Security* 12, no. 3 (Winter 1987/88): 168–89.

5. The accuracy revolution has greatly increased the probability that a given warhead will destroy a hardened target, but the full range of consequences is much broader. For example, high accuracy allows targeteers to assign many weapons to a given target, greatly increasing the odds of a successful strike. In the past, "many-on-one" targeting was difficult because weapons that missed their targets—but which detonated nearby—might create dust clouds that would shield the target from additional incoming warheads. This problem of "fratricide" has been essentially eliminated by the leap in accuracy. See discussion in Lieber and Press, "End of MAD?" 20–22. Additionally, the revolution in accuracy permits planners to target an enemy's hardened nuclear sites using low-yield weapons, set to detonate as airbursts, thereby vastly reducing fallout and collateral damage. See Lieber and Press, "The Nukes We Need," including the "Technical Appendix." We have subsequently redone the calculations underpinning our models of hypothetical counterforce strikes using the US Department of Defense VNTK (Vulnerability Number for Thermonuclear Kill) damage assessment system, and the core results are confirmed. (Contact authors for information on those results.)

6. Our analysis turned out to be a highly provocative exercise for some, including many Russian policy-makers and analysts. See, for example, "Russian Media See Article on U.S. Nuclear Primacy as Provocation," *OSC Analysis*, 3 April 2006; "Replying to Foreign Affairs Article, Expert Mulls Nuclear Arms Programs," *Krasnaya Zvezda*, 12 April 2006, translated in OSC, Doc ID: CEP20060411330004; Pavel K. Baev, "Moscow Puts PR Spin on its Shrinking Nuclear Arsenal," *Eurasia Daily Monitor*, 17 April 2006; "Moscow Rejects U.S. Authors' Claims of U.S. First-Strike Capability, as Putin Protects Nuclear Weapons Infrastructure," *WMD Insights*, issue 5 (May 2006): 17–21; and "Chinese Media Discusses U.S. Nuclear Superiority," *WMD Insights*, issue 5 (May 2006): 15–17.

7. The experience of leaders who recently lost wars to the United States is enlightening. In 1989 the United States conquered Panama and arrested its leader, Manuel Noriega; he has so far spent 23 years in prison. Saddam Hussein lost power, his sons were killed, and he was humiliated and hung in front of cheering enemies. Muammar Qaddafi spent his last days hiding

from US-supported rebels, who eventually found him and beat him to death on the side of a road. Even leaders whose countries were never conquered—i.e., they only suffered "limited" military defeats—often paid a high price. The Bosnian Serb leaders Radovan Karadzic and Ratko Mladic are in prison in The Hague, where Serbia's former leader, Slobodon Milosevic, died in detention.

8. "Roundtable on U.S. Nuclear Posture: Assessing the Lieber-Press Series in *Foreign Affairs*," Annual Conference of the International Security Studies Section (ISSS) of the International Studies Association and the International Security and Arms Control Section (ISAC) of the American Political Science Association, in conjunction with the Triangle Institute of Security Studies, 5 October 2012, Chapel Hill, North Carolina.

9. During the 2011 military intervention in Libya, the North Korean government proclaimed that NATO's action "teaches the international community a serious lesson" about the consequences of "nuclear dismantlement"—namely, it meant for Libya that the United States "swallowed it up by force." "Foreign Ministry Spokesman Denounces U.S. Military Attack on Libya," *Korea News Service*, 22 March 2011. The US State Department response—that NATO's action in Libya "has absolutely no connection with [Libya] renouncing their nuclear program or nuclear weapons"—obfuscates the issue because the North Korean claim was that the lack of Libyan nuclear weapons *permitted* (not triggered) NATO's attack; *New York Times*, 24 March 2011. That the North Korean regime's statement was more frank than the US one indicates the deep contradictions in US policy between the lofty proposals for nuclear disarmament and the desire to be able to use military force effectively against adversaries around the globe.

10. According to open sources, the lowest-yield setting of the B61 bomb is 0.3 kilotons, which means the equivalent of 300 tons of TNT. The GBU-57 explodes with roughly 1 percent of the B61's explosive power.

11. As a rule of thumb, destructive radius typically varies as a function of "yield" to the one-third power, so the B61 would have roughly 4.5 times the destructive radius of the most powerful conventional weapon.

12. Low-yield nuclear weapons could be detonated at altitudes that would create a sufficiently large lethal area on the ground against mobile missile systems to account for the target location uncertainty that is often created by lags between "sensor," "shooter," and "munition arrival" without subjecting large areas of enemy territory to destruction and without creating fallout.

Thermonuclear Cyberwar

ERIK GARTZKE AND JON R. LINDSAY

Introduction

In the 1983 movie *WarGames*, a teenager hacks into the North American Air Defense Command (NORAD) and almost triggers World War III. After a screening of the film, President Ronald Reagan allegedly asked his staff, "Could something like this really happen?" The Chairman of the Joint Chiefs of Staff replied, "Mr. President, the problem is much worse than you think." The National Security Agency (NSA) had been hacking Russian and Chinese communications for years, but the burgeoning personal computer revolution was creating serious vulnerabilities for the United States too. Reagan directed a series of reviews that culminated in a classified national security decision directive (NSDD-145) entitled "National Policy on Telecommunications and Automated Information Systems Security." More alarmist studies, and potential remedies, emerged in the ensuing decades as technicians and policy-makers came to appreciate the evolving threat.[1]

Cyber warfare is routinely overhyped as a new weapon of mass destruction, but when used in conjunction with actual weapons of mass destruction, severe, and underappreciated, dangers emerge. One side of a stylized debate about cybersecurity in international relations argues that offensive advantages in cyberspace empower weaker nations, terrorist cells, or even lone rogue operators to paralyze vital infrastructure.[2] The other side argues that operational difficulties and effective deterrence restrain the severity of cyberattack, while governments and cybersecurity firms have a pecuniary interest in exaggerating the threat.[3] Although we have contributed to the skeptical side of this debate,[4] the same strategic logic that leads us to view cyberwar as a limited political instrument in most situations also leads us to view it as incredibly destabilizing in rare situations. In a recent Israeli wargame of a regional scenario involving the United States and Russia, one participant remarked on "how quickly localized cyber events can turn dangerously kinetic when leaders are ill-prepared to deal in the cyber domain."[5] Importantly, this sort of catalytic instability arises not from the cyber domain itself but through its interaction with forces and characteristics in other domains (land, sea, air, etc.). Further, it arises only in situations where actors possess, and are willing to use, robust traditional military forces to defend their interests.

Classical deterrence theory developed to explain nuclear deterrence with nuclear weapons, but different types of weapons or combinations of operations in different domains can have differential effects on deterrence and defense.[6] Nuclear weapons and cyber operations are particularly complementary (i.e., nearly complete opposites) with respect to their strategic characteristics. Theorists and practitioners have stressed the unprecedented destructiveness of nuclear weapons in explaining how nuclear deterrence works, but it is equally, if not more, important for deterrence that capabilities and intentions are clearly communicated. As quickly became apparent, public displays of a nation's nuclear arsenals improved deterrence. At the same time, disclosing details of a nation's nuclear capabilities did not much degrade the ability to strike or retaliate, given that defense against nuclear attack remains extremely difficult. Knowledge of nuclear capabilities is necessary to achieve a deterrent effect.[7] Cyber operations, in contrast, rely on undisclosed vulnerabilities, social engineering, and creative guile to generate indirect effects in the information systems that coordinate military, economic, and social behavior. Revelation enables crippling countermeasures, while the imperative to conceal capabilities constrains both the scope of cyber operations and their utility for coercive signaling.[8] The diversity of cyber operations and confusion about their effects also contrast with the obvious destructiveness of nuclear weapons.

The problem is that transparency and deception do not mix well. An attacker who hacks an adversary's nuclear command and control apparatus, or the weapons themselves, will gain an advantage in warfighting that the attacker cannot reveal, while the adversary will continue to believe it wields a deterrent that may no longer exist. Most analyses of inadvertent escalation from cyber or conventional to nuclear war focus on "use it or lose it" pressures and fog of war created by attacks that become visible to the target.[9] In a US-China conflict scenario, for example, conventional military strikes in conjunction with cyberattacks that blind sensors and confuse decision-making could generate incentives for both sides to rush to preempt or

Eric Gartzke and Jon R. Lindsay, "Thermonuclear Cyberwar," *Journal of Cybersecurity* 3, no. 1 (2017): 37–48; reprinted by permission of Oxford University Press.

escalate.[10] These are plausible concerns, but the revelation of information about a newly unfavorable balance of power might also cause hesitation and lead to compromise. Cyber blinding could potentially make traditional offensive operations more difficult, shifting the advantage to defenders and making conflict less likely.

Clandestine attacks that remain invisible to the target potentially present a more insidious threat to crisis stability. There are empirical and theoretical reasons for taking seriously the effects of offensive cyber operations on nuclear deterrence, and we should expect the dangers to vary with the relative cyber capabilities of the actors in a crisis interaction.

Nuclear Command and Control Vulnerability

General Robert Kehler, commander of US Strategic Command (STRATCOM) in 2013, stated in testimony before the Senate Armed Services Committee, "We are very concerned with the potential of a cyber-related attack on our nuclear command and control and on the weapons systems themselves."[11] Nuclear command, control, and communications (NC3) form the nervous system of the nuclear enterprise spanning intelligence and early warning sensors located in orbit and on Earth, fixed and mobile command and control centers through which national leadership can order a launch, operational nuclear forces including strategic bombers, land-based intercontinental missiles (ICBMs), submarine-launched ballistic missiles (SLBMs), and the communication and transportation networks that tie the whole apparatus together.[12] NC3 should ideally ensure that nuclear forces will always be available if authorized by the National Command Authority (to enhance deterrence) and never used without authorization (to enhance safety and reassurance). Friendly errors or enemy interference in NC3 can undermine the "always-never" criterion, weakening deterrence.[13]

NC3 has long been recognized as the weakest link in the US nuclear enterprise. According to a declassified official history, a Strategic Air Command (SAC) task group in 1979 "reported that tactical warning and communications systems . . . were 'fragile' and susceptible to electronic countermeasures, electromagnetic pulse, and sabotage, which could deny necessary warning and assessment to the National Command Authorities."[14] Two years later, the Principal Deputy Under Secretary of Defense for Research and Engineering released a broad-based, multiservice report that doubled down on SAC's findings: "The United States could not assure survivability, endurability, or connectivity of the national command authority function" due to

major command, control, and communications deficiencies: in tactical warning and attack assessment where existing systems were vulnerable to disruption and destruction from electromagnetic pulse, other high altitude nuclear effects, electronic warfare, sabotage, or physical attack; in decision making where there was inability to assure national command authority survival and connection with the nuclear forces, especially under surprise conditions; and in communications systems, which were susceptible to the same threats above and which could not guarantee availability of even minimum-essential capability during a protracted war.[15]

The nuclear weapons safety literature likewise provides a number of troubling examples of NC3 glitches that illustrate some of the vulnerabilities attackers could, in principle, exploit.[16] The SAC history noted that NORAD has received numerous false launch indications from faulty computer components, loose circuits, and even a nuclear war training tape loaded by mistake into a live system that produced erroneous Soviet launch indications.[17] In a 1991 briefing to the STRATCOM commander, a Defense Intelligence Agency targeteer confessed, "Sir, I apologize, but we have found a problem with this target. There is a mistake in the computer code. . . . Sir, the error has been there for at least the life of this eighteen month planning cycle. The nature of the error is such that the target would not have been struck."[18] It would be a difficult operation to intentionally plant undetected errors like this, but the presence of bugs does reveal that such a hack is possible.

Following many near-misses and self-audits during and after the Cold War, American NC3 improved with the addition of new safeguards and redundancies. As General Kehler pointed out in 2013, "The nuclear deterrent force was designed to operate through the most extreme circumstances we could possibly imagine."[19] Yet vulnerabilities remain. In 2010, the US Air Force lost contact with 50 Minuteman III ICBMs for an hour because of a faulty hardware circuit at a launch control center.[20] If the accident had occurred during a crisis, or the component had been sabotaged, the USAF would have been unable to launch and unable to detect and cancel unauthorized launch attempts. As Bruce Blair, a former Minuteman missileer, points out, during a control center blackout the antennas at unmanned silos and the cables between them provide potential surreptitious access vectors.[21]

The unclassified summary of a 2015 audit of US NC3 stated that "known capability gaps or deficiencies remain."[22] Perhaps more worrisome are the unknown deficiencies. A 2013 Defense Science Board report on military cyber vulnerabilities found that while the

nuclear deterrent is regularly evaluated for reliability and readiness . . . , most of the systems have not been assessed (end-to-end) against a [sophisticated state] cyber attack to understand possible weak spots. A 2007 Air Force study addressed portions of this issue for the ICBM leg of the U.S. triad but was still not a complete assessment against a high-tier threat.[23]

If NC3 vulnerabilities are unknown, it is also unknown whether an advanced cyber actor would be able to exploit them. As Kehler notes, "We don't know what we don't know."[24]

Even if NC3 of nuclear forces narrowly conceived is a hard target, cyberattacks on other critical infrastructure in preparation to or during a nuclear crisis could complicate or confuse government decision-making. General Keith Alexander, Director of the NSA in the same Senate hearing with General Kehler, testified that

> our infrastructure that we ride on, the power and the communications grid, are one of the things that is a source of concern. . . . We can go to backup generators and we can have independent routes, but . . . our ability to communicate would be significantly reduced and it would complicate our governance. . . . I think what General Kehler has would be intact . . . [but] the cascading effect . . . in that kind of environment . . . concerns us.[25]

Kehler further emphasized that "there's a continuing need to make sure that we are protected against electromagnetic pulse and any kind of electromagnetic interference."[26]

Many NC3 components are antiquated and hard to upgrade, which is a mixed blessing. Kehler points out, "Much of the nuclear command and control system today is the legacy system that we've had. In some ways that helps us in terms of the cyber threat. In some cases it's point to point, hardwired, which makes it very difficult for an external cyber threat to emerge."[27] The Government Accountability Office notes that the "Department of Defense uses 8-inch floppy disks in a legacy system that coordinates the operational functions of the nation's nuclear forces."[28] While this may limit some forms of remote access, it is also indicative of reliance on an earlier generation of software when security engineering standards were less mature. Upgrades to the digital Strategic Automated Command and Control System planned for 2017 have the potential to correct some problems, but these changes may also introduce new access vectors and vulnerabilities.[29] Admiral Cecil Haney, Kehler's successor at STRATCOM, highlighted the challenges of NC3 modernization in 2015:

> Assured and reliable NC3 is fundamental to the credibility of our nuclear deterrent. The aging NC3 systems continue to meet their intended purpose, but risk to mission success is increasing as key elements of the system age. The unpredictable challenges posed by today's complex security environment make it increasingly important to optimize our NC3 architecture while leveraging new technologies so that NC3 systems operate together as a core set of survivable and endurable capabilities that underpin a broader, national command and control system.[30]

In no small irony, the internet itself owes its intellectual origin, in part, to the threat to NC3 from large-scale physical attack. A 1962 RAND report by Paul Baran considered "the problem of building digital communication networks using links with less than perfect reliability" to enable "stations surviving a physical attack and remaining in electrical connection . . . to operate together as a coherent entity after attack."[31] Baran advocated as a solution decentralized packet switching protocols, not unlike those realized in the ARPANET program. The emergence of the internet was the result of many other factors that had nothing to do with managing nuclear operations, notably the meritocratic ideals of 1960s counterculture that contributed to the neglect of security in the internet's founding architecture.[32] Fears of NC3 vulnerability helped to create the internet, which then helped to create the present-day cybersecurity epidemic, which has come full circle to create new fears about NC3 vulnerability.

NC3 vulnerability is not unique to the United States. The NC3 of other nuclear powers may even be easier to compromise, especially in the case of new entrants to the nuclear club like North Korea. Moreover, the United States has already demonstrated both the ability and willingness to infiltrate sensitive foreign nuclear infrastructure through operations such as Olympic Games (Stuxnet), albeit targeting Iran's nuclear fuel cycle rather than NC3. It would be surprising to learn that the United States has failed to upgrade its Cold War NC3 attack plans to include offensive cyber operations against a wide variety of national targets.

Hacking the Deterrent

The United States included NC3 attacks in its Cold War counterforce and damage limitation war plans, even as contemporary critics perceived these options to be destabilizing for deterrence.[33] The best known example of these activities and capabilities is a Special Access Program named Canopy Wing. East German intelligence obtained the highly classified plans from a US Army spy in Berlin, and the details began to emerge publicly after the Cold War. An East German intelligence officer, Markus Wolf, writes in his memoir that Canopy Wing "listed the types of electronic warfare that would be used to neutralize the Soviet Union and Warsaw Pact's command centers in case of all-out war. It detailed the precise method of depriving the Soviet High Command of its high-frequency communications used to give orders to its armed forces."[34]

It is easy to see why NC3 is such an attractive target in the unlikely event of a nuclear war. If for whatever reason deterrence fails and the enemy decides to push the nuclear button, it would obviously be better to disable or destroy missiles before they launch than to rely on possibly futile efforts to shoot them down, or to accept the loss of millions of lives. American plans to disable Soviet NC3 with electronic warfare, furthermore, would have been intended to complement plans for decapitating strikes against Soviet nuclear forces. Temporary disabling of information networks in isolation would have failed to achieve any important strategic objective. A blinded adversary would eventually see again and would scramble to reconstitute its ability to launch its weapons, expecting that preemption was inevitable in any case. Reconstitution, moreover, would invalidate much of the intelligence and some of the tradecraft on which the blinding attack relied. Capabilities fielded through Canopy Wing were presumably intended to facilitate a preemptive military strike on Soviet NC3 to disable the ability to retaliate and limit the damage of any retaliatory force that survived, given credible indications that war was imminent. Canopy Wing included

- "Measures for short-circuiting . . . communications and weapons systems using, among other things, microscopic carbon-fiber particles and chemical weapons."
- "Electronic blocking of communications immediately prior to an attack, thereby rendering a counterattack impossible."
- "Deployment of various weapons systems for instantaneous destruction of command centers, including pin-point targeting with precision-guided weapons to destroy 'hardened bunkers.'"
- "Use of deception measures, including the use of computer simulated voices to override and substitute false commands from ground-control stations to aircraft and from regional command centers to the Soviet submarine fleet."
- "Us[e of] the technical installations of 'Radio Free Europe/Radio Liberty' and 'Voice of America,' as well as the radio communications installations of the U.S. Armed Forces for creating interference and other electronic effects."[35]

Wolf also ran a spy in the US Air Force who disclosed that

the Americans had managed to penetrate the [Soviet air base at Eberswalde]'s ground-air communi-

cations and were working on a method of blocking orders before they reached the Russian pilots and substituting their own from West Berlin. Had this succeeded, the MiG pilots would have received commands from their American enemy. It sounded like science fiction, but, our experts concluded, it was in no way impossible that they could have pulled off such a trick, given the enormous spending and technical power of U.S. military air research.[36]

One East German source claimed that Canopy Wing had a $14.5 billion budget for research and operational costs and a staff of 1570 people, while another claimed that it would take over 4 years and $65 million to develop "a prototype of a sophisticated electronic system for paralyzing Soviet radio traffic in the high-frequency range."[37] Canopy Wing was not cheap, and even so, it was only a research and prototyping program. Operationalization of its capabilities and integration into NATO war plans would have been even more expensive. This is suggestive of the level of effort required to craft effective offensive cyber operations against NC3.

Preparation comes to naught when a sensitive program is compromised. Canopy Wing was caught in what we describe below as the cyber commitment problem, the inability to disclose a warfighting capability for the sake of deterrence without losing it in the process. According to *New York Times* reporting on the counterintelligence investigation of the East German spy in the Army, Warrant Officer James Hall, "officials said that one program rendered useless cost hundreds of millions of dollars and was designed to exploit a Soviet communications vulnerability uncovered in the late 1970's."[38] This program was probably Canopy Wing. Wolf writes, "Once we passed [Hall's documents about Canopy Wing] on to the Soviets, they were able to install scrambling devices and other countermeasures."[39] It is tempting to speculate that the Soviet deployment of a new NC3 system known as Signal-A to replace Signal-M (which was most likely the one targeted by Canopy Wing) was motivated in part by Hall's betrayal.[40]

Canopy Wing underscores the potential and limitations of NC3 subversion. Modern cyber methods can potentially perform many of the missions Canopy Wing addressed with electronic warfare and other means, but with even greater stealth and precision. Cyber operations might, in principle, compromise any part of the NC3 system (early warning, command centers, data transport, operational forces, etc.) by blinding sensors, injecting bogus commands or suppressing legitimate ones, monitoring or corrupting data transmissions, or interfering with the reliable launch and guidance of missiles. In practice, the operational feasibility of cyberattack against NC3 or any other target depends on the software and hardware configuration and organizational processes of the target, the intelligence and planning capacity of the attacker, and the ability and willingness to take advantage of the effects created by cyberattack.[41] Cyber compromise of NC3 is technically plausible though operationally difficult, a point to which we return in a later section.

To understand which threats are not only technically possible but also probable under some circumstance, we further need a political logic of cost and benefit.[42] In particular, how is it possible for a crisis to escalate to levels of destruction more costly than any conceivable political reward? Canopy Wing highlights some of the strategic dangers of NC3 exploitation. Warsaw Pact observers appear to have been deeply concerned that the program reflected an American willingness to undertake a surprise decapitation attack: they said that it "sent ice-cold shivers down our spines."[43] The Soviets designed a system called Perimeter that, not unlike the Doomsday Device in *Dr. Strangelove*, was designed to detect a nuclear attack and retaliate automatically, even if cut off from Soviet high command, through an elaborate system of sensors, underground computers, and command missiles to transmit launch codes.[44] Both Canopy Wing and Perimeter show that the United States and the Soviet Union took nuclear warfighting seriously and were willing to develop secret advantages for such an event. By the same token, they were not able to reveal such capabilities to improve deterrence and avoid having to fight a nuclear war in the first place.

Nuclear Deterrence and Credible Communication

Nuclear weapons have some salient political properties. They are singularly and obviously destructive. They kill in more, and more ghastly, ways than conventional munitions through electromagnetic radiation, blast, firestorms, radioactive fallout, and health effects that linger for years. Bombers, ICBMs, and SLBMs can project warheads globally without significantly mitigating their lethality, steeply attenuating the conventional loss-of-strength gradient.[45] Defense against nuclear attack is very difficult, even with modern ballistic missile defenses, given the speed of incoming warheads and use of decoys; multiple warheads and missile volleys further reduce the probability of perfect interception. If one cannot preemptively destroy all of an enemy's missiles, then there is a nontrivial chance of getting hit by some of them. When one missed missile can incinerate millions of people, the notion of winning a nuclear war starts to seem meaningless for many politicians.

As defense seemed increasingly impractical, early Cold War strategists championed the threat of assured

retaliation as the chief mechanism for avoiding war.[46] Political actors have issued threats for millennia, but the advent of nuclear weapons brought deterrence as a strategy to center stage. The Cold War was an intense learning experience for both practitioners and students of international security, rewriting well-worn realities more than once.[47] A key conundrum was the practice of brinkmanship. Adversaries who could not compete by "winning" a nuclear war could still compete by manipulating the "risk" of nuclear annihilation, gambling that an opponent would have the good judgment to back down at some point short of the nuclear brink. Brinkmanship crises—conceptualized as games of chicken where one cannot heighten tensions without increasing the hazard of the mutually undesired outcome—require that decision-makers behave irrationally, or possibly that they act randomly, which is difficult to conceptualize in practical terms.[48] The chief concern in historical episodes of chicken, such as the Berlin Crisis and Cuban Missile Crisis, was not whether a certain level of harm was possible, but whether an adversary was resolved enough, possibly, to risk nuclear suicide. The logical inconsistency of the need for illogic to win led almost from the beginning of the nuclear era to elaborate deductive contortions.[49]

Both mutually assured destruction (MAD) and successful brinksmanship depend on a less appreciated, but no less fundamental, feature of nuclear weapons: political transparency. Most elements of military power are weakened by disclosure.[50] Military plans are considerably less effective if shared with an enemy. Conventional weapons become less lethal as adversaries learn what different systems can and cannot do, where they are located, how they are operated, and how to devise countermeasures and array defenses to blunt or disarm an attack. In contrast, relatively little reduction in destruction follows from enemy knowledge of nuclear capabilities. For most of the nuclear era, no effective defense existed against a nuclear attack. Even today, with evolving ABM systems, one ICBM still might get through and annihilate the capital city. Nuclear forces are more robust to revelation than other weapons, enabling nuclear nations better to advertise the harm they can inflict.

The need for transparency to achieve an effective deterrent is driven home by the satirical Cold War film *Dr. Strangelove*: "The whole point of a Doomsday Machine is lost, if you keep it a secret! Why didn't you tell the world, eh?" During the real Cold War, fortunately, Soviet leaders paraded their nuclear weapons through Red Square for the benefit of foreign military attachés and the international press corps. Satellites photographed missile, bomber, and submarine bases. While other aspects of military affairs on both sides of the Iron Curtain remained closely guarded secrets, the United States and the Soviet Union permitted observers to evaluate their nuclear capabilities. This is especially remarkable given the secrecy that pervaded Soviet society. The relative transparency of nuclear arsenals ensured that the superpowers could calculate risks and consequences within a first-order approximation, which led to a reduction in severe conflict and instability even as political competition in other arenas was fierce.[51]

Recent insights about the causes of war suggest that divergent expectations about the costs and consequences of war are necessary for contests to occur.[52] These insights are associated with rationalist theories, such as deterrence theory itself. Empirical studies and psychological critiques of the rationality assumption have helped to refine models and bring some circumspection into their application, but the formulation of sound strategy (if not the execution) still requires the articulation of some rational linkage between cause and effect.[53] Many supposedly nonrational factors, moreover, simply manifest as uncertainty in strategic interaction. Our focus here is on the effect of uncertainty and ignorance on the ability of states and other actors to bargain in lieu of fighting. Many wars are a product of what adversaries do not know or what they misperceive, whether as a result of bluffing, secrecy, or intrinsic uncertainty.[54] If knowledge of capabilities or resolve is a prerequisite for deterrence, then one reason for deterrence failure is the inability or unwillingness to credibly communicate details of the genuine balance of power, threat, or interests. Fighting, conversely, can be understood as a costly process of discovery that informs adversaries of their actual relative strength and resolve. From this perspective, successful deterrence involves instilling in an adversary perceptions like those that result from fighting, but before fighting actually begins. Agreement about the balance of power can enable states to bargain (tacitly or overtly) effectively without needing to fight, forging compromises that each prefers to military confrontation or even to the bulk of possible risky brinkmanship crises.

Despite other deficits, nuclear weapons have long been considered to be stabilizing with respect to rational incentives for war (the risk of nuclear accidents is another matter).[55] If each side has a secure second strike—or even a minimal deterrent with some non-zero chance of launching a few missiles—then each side can expect to gain little and lose much by fighting a nuclear war. Whereas the costs of conventional war can be more mysterious because each side might decide to hold something back and mete out its punishment due to some internal constraint or a theory of graduated escalation, even a modest initial nuclear exchange is recognized to be extremely costly. As long as both sides understand this and understand (or believe) that the adversary understands this as well, then the relationship is stable. Countries engage nuclear powers with considerable def-

erence, especially over issues of fundamental national or international importance. At the same time, nuclear weapons appear to be of limited value in prosecuting aggressive action, especially over issues of secondary or tertiary importance, or in response to aggression from others at lower levels of dispute intensity. Nuclear weapons are best used for signaling a willingness to run serious risks to protect or extort some issue that is considered of vital national interest.

As mentioned previously, both superpowers in the Cold War considered the warfighting advantages of nuclear weapons quite apart from any deterrent effect, and the United States and Russia still do. High-altitude bursts for air defense, electromagnetic pulse for frying electronics, underwater detonations for anti-submarine warfare, hardened target penetration, area denial, and so on, have some battlefield utility. Transparency *per se* is less important than weapon effects for warfighting uses, and can even be deleterious for tactics that depend on stealth and mobility. Even a single tactical nuke, however, would inevitably be a political event. Survivability of the second strike deterrent can also militate against transparency, as in the case of the Soviet Perimeter system, as mobility, concealment, and deception can make it harder for an observer to track and count respective forces from space. Counterforce strategies, platform diversity and mobility, ballistic missile defense systems, and force employment doctrine can all make it more difficult for one or both sides in a crisis to know whether an attack is likely to succeed or fail. The resulting uncertainty affects not only estimates of relative capabilities but also the degree of confidence in retaliation. At the same time, there is reason to believe that platform diversity lowers the risk of nuclear or conventional contests, because increasing the number of types of delivery platforms heightens second strike survivability without increasing the lethality of an initial strike.[56] While transparency is not itself a requirement for nuclear use, stable deterrence benefits to the degree to which retaliation can be anticipated, as well as the likelihood that the consequences of a first strike are more costly than any benefit. Cyber operations, in contrast, are neither robust to revelation nor as obviously destructive.

The Cyber Commitment Problem

Deterrence (and compellence) uses force or threats of force to "warn" an adversary about consequences if it takes or fails to take an action. In contrast, defense (and conquest) uses force to "win" a contest of strength and change the material distribution of power. Sometimes militaries can change the distribution of information and power at the same time. Military mobilization in a crisis signifies resolve and displays a credible warning, but it also makes it easier to attack or defend if the warning fails. Persistence in a battle of attrition not only bleeds an adversary but also reveals a willingness to pay a higher price for victory. More often, however, the informational requirements of winning and warning are in tension. Combat performance often hinges on well-kept secrets, feints, and diversions. Many military plans and capabilities degrade when revealed. National security involves trade-offs between the goals of preventing war, by advertising capabilities or interests, and improving fighting power should war break out, by concealing capabilities and surprising the enemy.

The need to conceal details of the true balance of power to preserve battlefield effectiveness gives rise to the military commitment problem.[57] Japan could not coerce the United States by revealing its plan to attack Pearl Harbor because the United States could not credibly promise to refrain from reorienting defenses and dispersing the Pacific Fleet. War resulted not just because of what opponents did not know but because of what they could not tell each other without paying a severe price in military advantage. The military benefits of surprise (winning) trumped the diplomatic benefits of coercion (warning).

Cyber operations, whether for disruption and intelligence, are extremely constrained by the military commitment problem. Revelation of a cyber threat in advance that is specific enough to convince a target of the validity of the threat also provides enough information potentially to neutralize it. Stuxnet took years and hundreds of millions of dollars to develop but was patched within weeks of its discovery. The Snowden leaks negated a whole swath of tradecraft that the NSA took years to develop. States may use other forms of covert action, such as publicly disavowed lethal aid or aerial bombing (e.g., Nixon's Cambodia campaign), to discretely signal their interests, but such cases can only work to the extent that revelation of operational details fails to disarm rebels or prevent airstrikes.[58]

Cyber operations, especially against NC3, must be conducted in extreme secrecy as a condition of the efficacy of the attack. Cyber tradecraft relies on stealth, stratagem, and deception.[59] Operations tailored to compromise complex remote targets require extensive intelligence, planning and preparation, and testing to be effective. Actions that alert a target of an exploit allow the target to patch, reconfigure, or adopt countermeasures that invalidate the plan. As the Defense Science Board points out, competent network defenders

> can also be expected to employ highly-trained system and network administrators, and this operational staff will be equipped with continuously improving network defensive tools and techniques (the same tools we advocate to improve our de-

fenses). Should an adversary discover an implant, it is usually relatively simple to remove or disable. For this reason, offensive cyber will always be a fragile capability.[60]

The world's most advanced cyber powers, the United States, Russia, Israel, China, France, and the United Kingdom, are also nuclear states, while India, Pakistan, and North Korea also have cyber warfare programs. NC3 is likely to be an especially well defended part of their cyber infrastructures. NC3 is a hard target for offensive operations, which thus requires careful planning, detailed intelligence, and long lead-times to avoid compromise.

Cyberspace is further ill-suited for signaling because cyber operations are complex, esoteric, and hard for commanders and policy-makers to understand. Most targeted cyber operations have to be tailored for each unique target (a complex organization not simply a machine), quite unlike a general purpose munition tested on a range. Malware can fail in many ways and produce unintended side effects, as when the Stuxnet code was accidentally released to the public. The category of "cyber" includes tremendous diversity: irritant scams, hacktivist and propaganda operations, intelligence collection, critical infrastructure disruption, etc. Few intrusions create consequences that rise to the level of attacks such as Stuxnet or BlackEnergy, and even they pale beside the harm imposed by a small war.

Vague threats are less credible because they are indistinguishable from casual bluffing. Ambiguity can be useful for concealing a lack of capability or resolve, allowing an actor to pool with more capable or resolved states and acquiring some deterrence success by association. But this works by discounting the costliness of the threat. Nuclear threats, for example, are usually somewhat veiled because one cannot credibly threaten nuclear suicide. The consistently ambiguous phrasing of US cyber declaratory policy (e.g. "We will respond to cyber-attacks in a manner and at a time and place of our choosing using appropriate instruments of U.S. power."[61]) seeks to operate across domains to mobilize credibility in one area to compensate for a lack of credibility elsewhere, specifically by leveraging the greater robustness to revelation of military capabilities other than cyber.

This does not mean that cyberspace is categorically useless for signaling, just as nuclear weapons are not categorically useless for warfighting. Ransomware attacks work when the money extorted to unlock the compromised host is priced below the cost of an investigation or replacing the system. The United States probably gained some benefits in general deterrence (i.e., discouraging the emergence of challenges as opposed to immediate deterrence in response to a challenge) through the disclosure of Stuxnet and the

Snowden leaks. Both revelations compromised tradecraft, but they also advertised that the NSA probably had more exploits and tradecraft where they came from. Some cyber operations may actually be hard to mitigate within tactically meaningful timelines (e.g., hardware implants installed in hard-to-reach locations). Such operations might be revealed to coerce concessions within the tactical window created by a given operation, if the attacker can coordinate the window with the application of coercion in other domains. As a general rule, however, the cyber domain on its own is better suited for winning than warning.[62] Cyber and nuclear weapons fall on extreme opposite sides of this spectrum.

Dangerous Complements

Nuclear weapons have been used in anger twice—against the Japanese cities Hiroshima and Nagasaki—but cyberspace is abused daily. Considered separately, the nuclear domain is stable and the cyber domain is unstable. In combination, the results are ambiguous.

The nuclear domain can bound the intensity of destruction that a cyberattacker is willing to inflict on an adversary. US declaratory policy states that unacceptable cyberattacks may prompt a military response; while nuclear weapons are not explicitly threatened, neither are they withheld. Nuclear threats have no credibility at the low end, where the bulk of cyberattacks occur. This produces a cross domain version of the stability-instability paradox, where deterrence works at the high end but is not credible, and thus encourages provocation, at low intensities. Nuclear weapons, and military power generally, create an upper bound on cyber aggression to the degree that retaliation is anticipated and feared.[63]

In the other direction, the unstable cyber domain can undermine the stability of nuclear deterrence. Most analysts who argue that the cyber-nuclear combination is a recipe for danger focus on the fog of crisis decision-making.[64] Stephen Cimbala points out that today's relatively smaller nuclear arsenals may perversely magnify the attractiveness of NC3 exploitation in a crisis: "Ironically, the downsizing of U.S. and post-Soviet Russian strategic nuclear arsenals since the end of the Cold War, while a positive development from the perspectives of nuclear arms control and nonproliferation, makes the concurrence of cyber and nuclear attack capabilities more alarming."[65] Cimbala focuses mainly on the risks of misperception and miscalculation that emerge when a cyberattack muddies the transparent communication required for opponents to understand one another's interests, redlines, and willingness to use force, and to ensure reliable control over subordinate commanders. Thus a nuclear actor "faced with a sudden burst of holes in its vital warning and response systems might, for example, press the preemption button instead of waiting to ride out the attack and then retaliate."[66]

The outcome of fog of decision scenarios such as these depend on how humans react to risk and uncertainty, which in turn depends on bounded rationality and organizational frameworks that might confuse rational decision-making.[67] These factors exacerbate a hard problem. Yet within a rationalist framework, cyberattacks that have already created their effects need not trigger an escalatory spiral. While being handed a fait accompli may trigger an aggressive reaction, it is also plausible that the target's awareness that its NC3 has been compromised in some way would help to convey new information that the balance of power is not as favorable as previously thought. This in turn could encourage the target to accommodate, rather than escalate. While defects in rational decision-making are a serious concern in any cyber-nuclear scenario, the situation becomes even more hazardous when there are rational incentives to escalate. Although "known unknowns" can create confusion, to paraphrase Donald Rumsfeld, the "unknown unknowns" are perhaps more dangerous.

A successful clandestine penetration of NC3 can defeat the informational symmetry that stabilizes nuclear relationships. Nuclear weapons are useful for deterrence because they impose a degree of consensus about the distribution of power; each side knows the other can inflict prohibitive levels of damage, even if they may disagree about the precise extent of this damage. Cyber operations are attractive precisely because they can secretly revise the distribution of power. NC3 neutralization may be an expensive and rarified capability in the reach of only a few states with mature signals intelligence agencies, but it is much cheaper than nuclear attack. Yet the very usefulness of cyber operations for nuclear warfighting ensure that deterrence failure during brinksmanship crises is more likely.

Nuclear states may initiate crises of risk and resolve to see who will back down first, which is not always clear in advance. Chicken appears viable, ironically, because each player understands that a nuclear war would be a disaster for all, and thus all can agree that someone can be expected to swerve. Nuclear deterrence should ultimately make dealing with an adversary diplomatically more attractive than fighting, provided that fighting is costly—as would seem evident for the prospect of nuclear war—and assuming that bargains are available to states willing to accept compromise rather than annihilation. If, however, one side knows, but the other does not, that the attacker has disabled the target's ability to perceive an impending military attack, or to react to one when it is underway, then they will not have a shared understanding of the probable outcome of war, even in broad terms.

Consider a brinksmanship crisis between two nuclear states where only one has realized a successful penetration of the rival's NC3. The cyberattacker knows that it has a military advantage, but it cannot reveal the advantage to the target, lest the advantage be lost. The target does not know that it is at a disadvantage, and it cannot be told by the attacker for the same reason. The attacker perceives an imbalance of power while the target perceives a balance. A dangerous competition in risk-taking ensues. The first side knows that it does not need to back down. The second side feels confident that it can stand fast and raise the stakes far beyond what it would be willing to if it understood the true balance of power. Each side is willing to escalate to create more risk for the other side, making it more likely that one or the other will conclude that deterrence has failed and move into warfighting mode to attempt to limit the damage the other can inflict.

The targeted nature and uncertain effects of offensive cyber operations put additional pressure on decision-makers. An intrusion will probably disable only part of the enemy's NC3 architecture, not all of it (which is not only operationally formidable to achieve but also more likely to be noticed by the target). Thus the target may retain control over some nuclear forces, or conventional forces. The target may be tempted to use some of them piecemeal to signal a willingness to escalate further, even though it cannot actually escalate because of the cyber operation. The cyberattacker knows that it has escalation dominance, but when even a minor demonstration by the target can cause great damage, it is tempting to preempt this move or others like it. This situation would be especially unstable if only second strike but not primary strike NC3 was incapacitated. Uncertainty in the efficacy of the clandestine penetration would discount the attacker's confidence in its escalation dominance, with a range of possible outcomes. Enough uncertainty would discount the cyberattack to nothing, which would have a stabilizing effect by returning the crisis to the pure nuclear domain. A little bit of uncertainty about cyber effectiveness would heighten risk acceptance while also raising the incentives to preempt as an insurance measure.

Adding allies into the mix introduces additional instability. An ally emboldened by its nuclear umbrella might run provocative risks that it would be much more reluctant to embrace if it was aware that the umbrella was actually full of holes. Conversely, if the clandestine advantage is held by the state extending the umbrella, allies could become unnerved by the willingness of their defender to run what appear to be outsize risks, oblivious of the reasons for the defender's confidence, creating discord in the alliance and incentives for self-protective action, leading to greater uncertainty about alliance solidarity.

The direction of influence between the cyber and nuclear realms depends to large degree on which domain is the main arena of action. Planning and conducting cyber operations will be bounded by the ability of aggressors to convince themselves that attacks will remain secret, and by the confidence of nuclear nations in their invulnerability. Fears of cross-domain escalation will tend to keep instability in cyberspace bounded. However, if a crisis has risen to the point where nuclear threats are being seriously considered or made, then NC3 exploitation will be destabilizing. Brinksmanship crises seem to have receded in frequency since the Cuban Missile Crisis but may be more likely than is generally believed. President Vladimir Putin of Russia has insinuated more than once in recent years that his government is willing to use tactical nuclear weapons if necessary to support his policies.

Cyber Power and Nuclear Stability

Not all crises are the same. Indeed, their very idiosyncrasies create the uncertainties that make bargaining failure more likely.[68] So far our analysis would be at home in the Cold War, with the technological novelty of cyber operations. Yet not every state has the same cyber capabilities or vulnerabilities. Variation in cyber power relations across dyads should be expected to affect the strategic stability of nuclear states.

The so-called second nuclear age differs from superpower rivalry in important ways.[69] There are fewer absolute numbers of warheads in the world, down from a peak of over 70,000 in the 1980s to about 15,000 today (less than 5,000 deployed), but they are distributed very unevenly.[70] The United States and Russia have comparably sized arsenals, each with a fully diversified triad of delivery platforms, while North Korea only has a dozen or so bombs and no meaningful delivery system (for now). China, India, Pakistan, Britain, France, and Israel have modest arsenals in the range of several dozen to a couple hundred weapons, but they have very different doctrines, conventional force complements, domestic political institutions, and alliance relationships. The recent nuclear powers lack the hard-won experience and shared norms of the Cold War to guide them through crises, and even the United States and Russia have much to relearn.

Cyber warfare capacity also varies considerably across contemporary nuclear nations. The United States, Russia, Israel, and Britain are in the top tier, able to run sophisticated, persistent, clandestine penetrations. China is a uniquely active cyber power with ambitious cyber warfare doctrine, but its operational focus is on economic espionage and political censorship, resulting in less refined tradecraft and more porous defenses for military purposes.[71] France, India, and Pakistan also have active cyber warfare programs, while North Korea is the least developed cyber nation, depending on China for its expertise.[72]

It is beyond the scope of this article to assess crisis dyads in detail, and data on nuclear and cyber power for these countries are shrouded in secrecy. Here, as a way of summing up the arguments above, we offer a few conjectures about how stylized aspects of cyber power affect crisis stability through incentives and key aspects of decision-making. We do not stress relative nuclear weapon capabilities on the admittedly strong (and contestable) assumption that nuclear transparency in the absence of cyber operations would render nuclear asymmetry irrelevant for crisis bargaining because both sides would agree about the terrible consequences of conflict.[73] We also omit domestic or psychological variables that affect relative power assessments, although these are obviously important. Even if neither India nor Pakistan has viable cyber-nuclear capabilities, brinksmanship between them is dangerous for many other reasons, notably compressed decision timelines, Pakistan's willingness to shoot first, and domestic regime instability. Our focus is on the impact of offensive and defensive cyber power on nuclear deterrence above and beyond the other factors that certainly play a role in real-world outcomes.

First, does the cyberattacker have the organizational capacity, technical expertise, and intelligence support to "compromise" the target's NC3? Can hackers access critical networks, exploit technical vulnerabilities, and confidently execute a payload to disrupt or exploit strategic sensing, command, forces, or transport capacity? The result would be some tangible advantage for warfighting, such as tactical warning or control paralysis, but one that cannot be exercised in bargaining.

Second, is the target able to "detect" the compromise of its NC3? The more complicated and sensitive the target, the more likely cyberattackers are to make a mistake that undermines the intrusion. Attribution is not likely to be difficult given the constricted pool of potential attackers, but at the same time the consequences of misattributing "false flag" operations could be severe.[74] At a minimum, detection is assumed to provide information to the target that the balance of power is perhaps not as favorable as imagined previously. We assume that detection without an actual compromise is possible because of false positives or deceptive information operations designed to create pessimism or paranoia.

Third, is the target able to "mitigate" the compromise it detects? Revelation can prompt patching or network reconfiguration to block an attack, but this assumption is not always realistic. The attacker may have multiple pathways open or may have implanted malware that is difficult to remove in tactically meaningful timelines. In such cases the cyber commitment problem is not absolute, since the discovery of the power to hurt does not automatically disarm it. Successful mitigation here is assumed to restore mutual assessments of the balance of power to what they would be absent the cyberattack.

Table 1 shows how these factors combine to produce different deterrence outcomes in a brinksmanship (chicken) crisis. If there is no cyber compromise and the target detects nothing (no false positives) then we have the optimistic ideal case where nuclear transparency affords stable "deterrence." Transparency about the nuclear balance, including the viability of secure second strike forces, provides strategic stability. We also expect this box to describe situations where the target has excellent network defense capabilities and thus the prospect of defense, denial, or deception successfully deters any attempts to penetrate NC3. This may resemble the Cold War situation (with electronic warfare in lieu of cyber), or even the present day US-Russia dyad, where the odds of either side pulling off a successful compromise against a highly capable defender are not favorable. Alternately the attack may be deemed risky enough to encourage serious circumspection. However, the existence of Canopy Wing does not encourage optimism in this regard.

Conversely, if there is a compromise that goes undetected, then there is a heightened risk of "war" because of the cyber commitment problem. This box may be particularly relevant for asymmetric dyads such as the United States and North Korea, where one side has real cyber power but the other side is willing to go to the brink where it believes, falsely, that it has the capability to compel its counterpart to back down. Cyber disruption of NC3 is attractive for damage limitation should deterrence fail, given that the weaker state's diminutive arsenal makes damage limitation by the stronger state more likely to succeed. The dilemma for the stronger state is that the clandestine counterforce hedge, which makes warfighting success more likely, is precisely what makes deterrence more likely to fail.

The United States would face similar counterforce dilemmas with other dyads like China or even Russia, although even a strong cyber power should be more circumspect when confronted with an adversary with a larger/more capable nuclear and conventional arsenal. More complex and cyber savvy targets, moreover, are more likely to detect a breach in NC3, leading to more ambiguous outcomes depending on how actors cope with risk and uncertainty. Paradoxically, confidence in cyber security may be a major contributor to failure; believing one is safe from attack increases the chance that an attack is successful.

If the successful compromise is detected but not mitigated, then the target learns that the balance of power is not as favorable as thought. This possibility suggests fleeting opportunities for "coercion" by revealing the

Table 1. Cyber Operations and Crisis Stability

	Not compromised	Compromised
Not detected	Deterrence	War
Detected but not mitigated	Bluff (or use-lose)	Coercion (or use-lose)
Detected and mitigated	Spiral	Spiral

cyber coup to the target in the midst of a crisis while the cyberattacker maintains or develops a favorable military advantage before the target has the opportunity to reverse or compensate the NC3 disruption. Recognizing the newly transparent costs of war, a risk neutral or risk averse target should prefer compromise. The coercive advantages (deterrence or compellence) of a detected but unmitigated NC3 compromise will likely be fleeting. This suggests a logical possibility for creating a window of opportunity for using particular cyber operations that are more robust to revelation as a credible signal of superior capability in the midst of a crisis. It would be important to exploit this fleeting advantage via other credible military threats (e.g., forces mobilized on visible alert or deployed into the crisis area) before the window closes.

One side may be able gain an unearned advantage, an opportunity for coercion via a "bluff," by the same window-of-opportunity logic. A target concerned about NC3 compromise will probably have some network monitoring system and other protections in place. Defensive systems can produce false positives as a result of internal errors or a deception operation by the attacker to encourage paranoia. It is logically possible that some false positives would appear to the target to be difficult to mitigate. In this situation, the target could believe it is at a disadvantage, even though this is not in fact the case. This gambit would be operationally very difficult to pull off with any reliability in a real nuclear crisis.

Cyber-nuclear coercion and bluffing strategies are fraught with danger. Detection without mitigation might put a risk-acceptant or loss-averse target into a "use-lose" situation, creating pressures to preempt or escalate. The muddling of decision-making heightens the risk of accidents or irrational choices in a crisis scenario. Worry about preemption or accident then heightens the likelihood that the initiator will exercise counterforce options while they remain available. These pressures can be expected to be particularly intense if the target's detection is only partial or has not revealed the true extent of damage to its NC3 (i.e., the target does not realize it has already lost some or all of what it hopes to use). These types of scenarios are most usually invoked in analyses of inadvertent esca-

lation.[75] The essential distinction between "use-lose" risks and "war" in this typology is the target's knowledge of some degree of NC3 compromise. Use-lose and other cognitive pressures can certainly result in nuclear war, since the breakdown of deterrence leads to the release of nuclear weapons, but we distinguish these outcomes to highlight the different decision-making processes or rational incentives at work.

A "spiral" of mistrust may emerge if one side attempts a compromise but the defender detects and mitigates it. Both sides again have common mutual estimates of the relative balance of power, which superficially resembles the "deterrence" case because the NC3 compromise is negated. Unfortunately, the detection of the compromise will provide the target with information about the hostile intentions of the cyberattacker. This in turn is likely to exacerbate other political or psychological factors in the crisis itself or in the crisis-proneness of the broader relationship. The strange logical case where there is no compromise but one is detected and mitigated could result from a false positive misperception (including a third party false flag operation) that could [cause] conflict spiraling.[76] The bluff and coercion outcomes are also likely to encourage spiraling behavior once the fleeting bargaining advantage dissipates or is dispelled (provided anyone survives the interaction).

The risk of crisis instability is not the same for all dyads. It is harder to compromise the NC3 of strong states because of the redundancy and active defenses in their arsenal. Likewise, strong states are better able to compromise the NC3 of any states but especially of weaker states, because of strong states' greater organizational capacity and expertise in cyber operations. Stable deterrence or MAD is most likely to hold in mutually strong dyads (e.g. the United States and the Soviet Union in the Cold War or Russia today to a lesser extent). Deterrence is slightly less likely in other equally matched dyads (India and Pakistan) where defensive vulnerabilities create temptations but offensive capabilities may not be sufficient to exploit them. Most states can be expected to refrain from targeting American NC3 given a US reputation for cyber power (a general deterrence benefit enhanced by Stuxnet and Snowden). The situation is less stable if the United States is the attacker. The most dangerous dyad is a stronger and a weaker state (United States and North Korea or Israel and Iran). Dyads involving strong and middle powers are also dangerous (United States and China). The stronger side is tempted to disrupt NC3 as a warfighting hedge in case deterrence breaks down, while the weaker but still formidable side has a reasonable chance at detection. The marginally weaker may also be tempted to subvert NC3, particularly for reconnaissance; the stronger side is more likely to detect and correct the intrusion but will be alarmed by the ambiguity in distinguishing intelligence collection from attack planning.[77] In a brinksmanship crisis between them, windows for coercion may be available yet fleeting, with real risks of spiral and war.

Policy Implications

Skeptics are right to challenge the hype about cyberwar. The term is confusing, and hacking rarely amounts to anything approaching a weapon of mass destruction. Cyberspace is most usefully exploited on the lower end of the conflict spectrum for intelligence and subversion, i.e., not as a substitute for military or economic power but a complement to it. Yet the logic of complementarity has at least one exception regarding conflict severity, and it is a big one.

Offensive cyber operations against NC3 raise the risk of nuclear war. They do so because cyber operations and nuclear weapons are extreme complements regarding their informational properties. Cyber operations rely on deception. Nuclear deterrence relies on clear communication. In a brinksmanship crisis, the former undermines the latter. Nuclear crises were rare events in Cold War history, thankfully. Today, the proliferation and modernization of nuclear weapons may raise the risk slightly. Subversion of NC3 raises the danger of nuclear war slightly more. Cyberwar is not war per se, but in rare circumstances it may make escalation to thermonuclear war more likely.

NC3 is a particularly attractive counterforce target because disruption can render the enemy's arsenal less effective without having to destroy individual platforms. US nuclear strategy in practice has long relied on counterforce capabilities (including Canopy Wing).[78] Deterrence theorists expect this to undermine the credibility of the adversary's deterrent and create pressures to move first in a conflict.[79] If for some reason deterrence fails, however, countervalue strikes on civilian population centers would be militarily useless and morally odious. Counterforce strikes, in contrast, aim at preemptive disarmament or damage limitation by attacking the enemy's nuclear enterprise. Counterforce capabilities are designed for "winning" a nuclear war once over the brink, but their strategic purpose may still include warning if they can somehow be made robust to revelation. During the Cold War, the United States found ways to inform the Soviet Union of its counterforce ability to sink SSBNs, hit mobile ICBMs, and show off some electronic warfare capabilities without giving away precise details.[80] This improved mutual recognition of US advantages and thus clearer assessment of the consequences of conflict, but the military commitment problem was real nonetheless. The problem is particularly pronounced for cyber disruption of NC3. As one side builds more sophisticated NC3 to improve the credibility of its nuclear "warning," the other side engages in cyber operations to improve its capacity for nuclear "winning," thereby undermining the warning.

The prohibitive cost of nuclear war and the relative transparency of the nuclear balance has contributed to seven decades of nuclear peace. If this is to continue, it will be necessary to find ways to maintain transparency. If knowledge of a shift in relative power is concealed, then the deterrent effect of nuclear capabilities is undermined. This will tend to occur in periods where concern over nuclear attack is heightened, such as in the midst of a militarized crises. Yet there is no reason to believe that states will wait for a crisis before seeking to establish advantageous positions in cyberspace. Indeed, given the intricate intelligence and planning required, offensive cyber preparations must precede overt aggression by months or even years. It is this erosion of the bulwark of deterrence that is most troubling.

What can be done? Arms control agreements to ban cyberattacks on NC3 might seem attractive, but the cyber commitment problem also undermines institutional monitoring and enforcement. Even where the United States would benefit from such an agreement by keeping this asymmetric capability out of the hands of other states, it would still have strong incentives to prepare its own damage limitation options should deterrence fail. Nevertheless, diplomatic initiatives to discuss the dangers of cyber-nuclear interactions with potential opponents should be pursued. Even if cyber-nuclear dangers cannot be eliminated, states should be encouraged to review their NC3 and ensure strict lines of control over any offensive cyber operations at that level.

Classified studies of the details of NC3, not just the technical infrastructure but also their human organizations, together with war games of the scenarios above, may help nuclear war planners to think carefully about subverting NC3. Unfortunately, the same reconnaissance operations used to better understand the opponent's NC3 can be misinterpreted as attempts to compromise it.[81] More insidiously, private knowledge can become a source of instability insofar as knowing something about an adversary that improves one's prospects in war increases the incentive to act through force or to exploit windows of opportunity in a crisis that could inadvertently escalate.

Anything that can be done to protect NC3 against cyber intrusion will make the most dangerous possibility of successful but undetected compromises less likely. The Defense Science Board in 2013 recommended "immediate action to assess and assure national leadership that the current U.S. nuclear deterrent is also survivable against the full-spectrum cyber . . . threat."[82] Defense in depth should include redundant communications pathways, error correction channels, isolation of the most critical systems, component heterogeneity rather than a vulnerable software monoculture, and network security monitoring with active defenses (i.e., a counterintelligence mindset). Older technologies, ironically, may provide some protection by foiling access of modern cyber techniques (Russia reportedly still uses punch-cards for parts of its NC3[83]); yet vulnerabilities from an earlier era of inadequate safeguards are also a problem. For defense in depth to translate into deterrence by denial requires the additional step of somehow advertising NC3 redundancy and resilience even in a cyber-degraded environment.

Cyber disruption of NC3 is a cross-domain deterrence problem. CDD might also be part of the solution. As noted above, CDD can help to bound the severity of instability in the cyber domain by threatening, implicitly or explicitly, the prospect of military, economic, law-enforcement, or diplomatic consequences. Cyberattacks flourish below some credible threshold of deterrence and rapidly tail off above it. CDD may also help in nuclear crises. CDD provides policy-makers with options other than nuclear weapons, and perhaps options when NC3 is compromised. A diversity of options provides a variation on Schelling's classic "threat that leaves something to chance." In some dyads, particularly with highly asymmetric nuclear arsenals and technical capabilities, CDD may provide options for "war" and "coercion" outcomes (in the language of our typology) short of actual nuclear war. CDD does not necessarily improve deterrence and in many ways is predicated on the failure of deterrence, but the broadening of options may lessen the consequences of that failure (i.e., if a machine asks, "Do you want to play a game?" it would be helpful to have options available other than "global thermonuclear war"). The implications of choice among an expanded palette of coercive options in an open-ended bargaining scenario is a topic for future research.

Finally, every effort should be made to ensure that senior leaders—the President and the Secretary of Defense in the United States, the Central Military Commission in China, etc.—understand and authorize any cyber operations against any country's NC3 for any reason. Even intrusions focused only on intelligence collection should be reviewed and approved at the highest level. Education is easier said than done given the esoteric technical details involved. Ignorance at the senior level of the implications of compromised NC3 is a major risk factor in a crisis contributing to false optimism or other bad decisions. New technologies of information are, ironically, undermining clear communication.

NOTES

We thank Scott Sagan, William J. Perry, the participants of the Stanford Cyber Policy Program (SCPP) Workshop on Strategic Dimensions of Offensive Cyber Operations, and the anonymous reviewers for their comments. This research was supported by SCPP and the Department of Defense Minerva Initiative through an Office of Naval Research Grant [N00014-14-1-0071].

1. F. Kaplan, "WarGames" and cybersecurity's debt to a Hollywood hack, *The New York Times*, February 19, 2016; S. R. Schulte, "The WarGames Scenario": regulating teenagers and teenaged technology (1980–1984), *Television & New Media*, August 19, 2008; and Warner M. Cybersecurity: a pre-history, *Intell Natl Security* 2012, 27:781–99.

2. S. Borg, Economically complex cyberattacks, *IEEE Security and Privacy Magazine* 2005, 3:64–67; R. A. Clarke and R. K. Knake, *Cyber War: The Next Threat to National Security and What to Do About It* (New York: Ecco, 2010); J. Brenner, *America the Vulnerable: Inside the New Threat Matrix of Digital Espionage, Crime, and Warfare* (New York: Penguin Press, 2011); L. Kello, The meaning of the cyber revolution: perils to theory and statecraft, *Int Security* 2013, 38:7–40; and D. Peterson, Offensive cyber weapons: construction, development, and employment, *J Strat Stud* 2013, 36:120–24.

3. M. Dunn Cavelty, Cyber-terror—looming threat or phantom menace? The framing of the US cyber-threat debate, *J Informat Technol & Polit* 2008, 4:19–36; T. Rid, Cyber war will not take place, *J Strat Stud* 2012, 35:5–32; S. Lawson, Beyond cyber-doom: assessing the limits of hypothetical scenarios in the framing of cyber-threats, *J Informat Technol & Polit* 2013, 10:86–103; D. C. Benson, Why the internet is not increasing terrorism, *Security Stud* 2014, 23:293–328; and B. Valeriano and R. C. Maness, *Cyber War Versus Cyber Realities: Cyber Conflict in the International System* (New York: Oxford University Press, 2015).

4. E. Gartzke, The myth of cyberwar: bringing war in cyberspace back down to earth. *Int Security* 2013, 38:41–73; J. R. Lindsay, Stuxnet and the limits of cyber warfare, *Security Stud* 2013, 22:365–404; and J. R. Lindsay, The impact of China on cybersecurity: fiction and friction, *Int Security* 2014, 39:7–47.

5. B. Opall-Rome, Israeli cyber game drags US, Russia to brink of Mideast war, *Defense News*, November 14, 2013, http://www.defensenews.com/article/20131115/C4ISRNET07/311150020/Israeli-Cyber-Game-Drags-US-Russia-Brink-Mideast-War.

6. J. R. Lindsay and E. Gartzke, Cross-domain deterrence as a practical problem and a theoretical concept, in *Cross-Domain Deterrence: Strategy in an Era of Complexity*, E. Gartzke and J. R. Lindsay (eds.) (La Jolla, CA: Manuscript, 2016); and S. Carcelli and E. Gartzke, Blast from the past: revitalizing and diversifying deterrence theory, working paper (La Jolla, CA, 2016).

7. R. Powell, *Nuclear Deterrence Theory: The Search for Credibility* (New York: Cambridge University Press, 1990).

8. E. Gartzke and J. R. Lindsay, Weaving tangled webs: offense, defense, and deception in cyberspace, *Security Stud* 2015, 24:316–48; and J. R. Lindsay, Tipping the scales: the attribution problem and the feasibility of deterrence against cyber attack, *J Cybersecurity* 2015, 1:53–67.

9. B. R. Posen, *Inadvertent Escalation: Conventional War and Nuclear Risks* (Ithaca, NY: Cornell University Press, 1991); and S. J. Cimbala, Nuclear crisis management and "Cyberwar": phishing for trouble? *Strat Stud Quart* 2011, 5(1):117–31.

10. A. Goldstein, First things first: the pressing danger of crisis instability in U.S.-China relations, *Int Security* 2013, 37:49–89; D. C. Gompert and M. Libicki, Cyber warfare and Sino-American crisis instability, *Survival* 2014, 56:7–22; and C. Talmadge, Assessing the risk of Chinese nuclear escalation

in a conventional war with the United States, *Int Security* (forthcoming).

11. Hearing to Receive Testimony on U.S. Strategic Command and U.S. Cyber Command in Review of the Defense Authorization Request for Fiscal Year 2014 and the Future Years Defense Program, 2013.

12. A. D. Carter, J. B. Steinbruner, and C. A. Zracket, *Managing Nuclear Operations* (Washington, DC: Brookings Institution Press, 1987); and Office of the Deputy Assistant Secretary of Defense for Nuclear Matters, Nuclear command and control system, in *Nuclear Matters Handbook 2015* (Washington, DC: Government Printing Office, 2015), 73–81.

13. P. J. Bracken, *The Command and Control of Nuclear Forces* (New Haven, CT: Yale University Press, 1985); and B. Blair, *Strategic Command and Control* (Washington, DC: Brookings Institution Press, 1985).

14. U.S. Joint Chiefs of Staff. *A Historical Study of Strategic Connectivity, 1950–1981*, Special Historical Study (Washington, DC: Joint Chiefs of Staff, Joint Secretariat, Historical Division, July 1982).

15. U.S. Joint Chiefs of Staff. *A Historical Study of Strategic Connectivity*.

16. S. Gregory, *The Hidden Cost of Deterrence: Nuclear Weapons Accidents* (London: Brassey's, 1990); S. D. Sagan, *The Limits of Safety: Organizations, Accidents, and Nuclear Weapons* (Princeton, NJ: Princeton University Press, 1995); and S. Eric, *Command and Control: Nuclear Weapons, the Damascus Accident, and the Illusion of Safety* (New York: Penguin, 2014).

17. U.S. Joint Chiefs of Staff. *A Historical Study of Strategic Connectivity*.

18. Lee B. George, *Uncommon Cause: A Life at Odds with Convention, Volume II: The Transformative Years* (Denver, CO: Outskirts Press, 2016).

19. Hearing to Receive Testimony on U.S. Strategic Command.

20. M. Ambinder, Failure shuts down squadron of nuclear missiles, *The Atlantic*, October 26, 2010.

21. B. Blair, Could terrorists launch America's nuclear missiles? *Time*, November 11, 2010.

22. Government Accountability Office, *Nuclear Command, Control, and Communications: Update on DOD's Modernization*, GAO-15-584R (Washington, DC, June 15, 2015), http://www.gao.gov/products/GAO-15-584R.

23. Defense Science Board Task Force on Resilient Military Systems, *Resilient Military Systems and the Advanced Cyber Threat* (Washington, DC: Defense Science Board, 2013).

24. Hearing to Receive Testimony on U.S. Strategic Command.

25. Hearing to Receive Testimony on U.S. Strategic Command.

26. Hearing to Receive Testimony on U.S. Strategic Command.

27. Hearing to Receive Testimony on U.S. Strategic Command.

28. Government Accountability Office, *Information Technology: Federal Agencies Need to Address Aging Legacy Systems* (Washington, DC: Government Accountability Office, 2016).

29. A. Futter, The double-edged sword: US nuclear command and control modernization, *Bull Atomic Scientists*, June 29, 2016, http://thebulletin. org/double-edged-sword-us -nuclear-command-and-control-modernization9593.

30. C. Haney, Department of Defense press briefing by Adm. Haney in the Pentagon briefing room (U.S. Department of Defense, March 24, 2015). http://www.defense.gov/News/News -Transcripts/Transcript-View/Article/ 607027.

31. P. Baran, *On Distributed Communications Networks* (Santa Monica, CA: RAND Corporation, 1962).

32. D. D. Clark, A cloudy crystal ball: visions of the future, plenary presentation presented at the 24th meeting of the Internet Engineering Task Force, Cambridge, MA, July 17, 1992; J. Abbate, *Inventing the Internet* (Cambridge, MA: MIT Press, 1999).

33. A. Long and B. R. Green, Stalking the secure second strike: intelligence, counterforce, and nuclear strategy, *J Strat Stud* 2014, 38:38–73.

34. M. Wolf and A. McElvoy, *Man Without a Face: The Autobiography of Communism's Greatest Spymaster* (New York: Public Affairs, 1997).

35. B. B. Fischer, CANOPY WING: the U.S. war plan that gave the East Germans goose bumps, *Int J Intell CounterIntell* 2014, 27:431–64.

36. Wolf and McElvoy, *Man Without a Face*.

37. Fischer, CANOPY WING, 431–64.

38. S. Engelberg and M. Wines, U.S. says soldier crippled spy post set up in Berlin. *The New York Times*, May 7, 1989.

39. Wolf and McElvoy, *Man Without a Face*.

40. Fischer, CANOPY WING, 431–64.

41. W. A. Owens, K. M. Dam, and H. S. Lin, *Technology, Policy, Law, and Ethics Regarding U.S. Acquisition and Use of Cyberattack Capabilities* (Washington, DC: National Academies Press, 2009), 53; and D. Herrick and T. Herr, Combating complexity: offensive cyber capabilities and integrated warfighting, SSRN Electronic Journal, February 2016.

42. Lindsay, Stuxnet and the limits of cyber warfare, 365–404.

43. Lindsay, Stuxnet and the limits of cyber warfare, 365–404.

44. D. Hoffman, *The Dead Hand: The Untold Story of the Cold War Arms Race and Its Dangerous Legacy* (New York: Random House, 2009).

45. K. E. Boulding, *Conflict and Defense: A General Theory* (New York: Harper & Row, 1962).

46. B. Brodie, F. S. Dunn, A. Wolfers, et al., *The Absolute Weapon: Atomic Power and World Order* (New York: Harcourt, Brace and Co., 1946); A. Wohlstetter, The delicate balance of terror, *Foreign Affairs* 1959, 37:211–34; H. Kahn, *On Thermonuclear War* (Princeton, NJ: Princeton University Press, 1960); and G. H. Snyder, *Deterrence and Defense: Toward a Theory of National Security* (Princeton, NJ: Princeton University Press, 1961).

47. M. Trachtenberg, *History and Strategy* (Princeton, NJ: Princeton University Press, 1991); F. J. Gavin, *Nuclear Statecraft: History and Strategy in America's Atomic Age* (Ithaca, NY: Cornell University Press, 2012); and E. Gartzke and M. Kroenig, Nukes with numbers: empirical research on the consequences of nuclear weapons for international conflict. *Ann Rev Polit Sci* 2016, 19:397–412.

48. R. Powell, Nuclear brinkmanship with two-sided incomplete information, *Am Polit Sci Rev* 1988, 82:155–78.

49. T. C. Schelling, *The Strategy of Conflict* (Cambridge, MA: Harvard University Press, 1960); F. Zagare, Rationality and deterrence, *World Politics* 1990, 42:238–60; and T. C. Schelling, *Arms and Influence*, with a new preface and afterword (New Haven, CT: Yale University Press, 2008).

50. B. L. Slantchev, Feigning weakness, *Int Organ* 2010, 64:357–88.

51. Gavin, *Nuclear Statecraft*; and R. Powell, Nuclear brinkmanship, limited war, and military power, *Int Organ* 2015, 69:589–626.

52. G. Blainey, *Causes of War*, 3rd ed. (New York: Simon and Schuster, 1988); J. D. Fearon, Rationalist explanations for war, *Int Organ* 1995, 49:379–414; R. Powell, *In the Shadow of Power: States and Strategies in International Politics* (Princeton, NJ: Princeton University Press, 1999); D. Reiter, Exploring the bargaining model of war, *Perspect Polit* 2003, 1:27–43; and R. H. Wagner, *War and the State: The Theory of International Politics* (Ann Arbor: University of Michigan Press, 2010).

53. Carcelli and Gartzke, Blast from the past; Gartzke and Kroenig, Nukes with numbers, 397–412; and R. K. Betts, Is strategy an illusion? *Int Security* 2000, 25:5–50.

54. E. Gartzke, War is in the error term, *Int Organ* 1999, 53:567–87; and J. M. Kaplow and E. Gartzke, Knowing unknowns: the effect of uncertainty in interstate conflict, *2015 ISA Annual Convention* (New Orleans, 2015).

55. S. D. Sagan and K. N. Waltz, *The Spread of Nuclear Weapons: An Enduring Debate*, 3rd ed. (New York: W. W. Norton & Company, 2012).

56. E. Gartzke, J. M. Kaplow, and R. N. Mehta, Offense, defense and the structure of nuclear forces: the role of nuclear platform diversification in securing second strike, working paper, 2015.

57. E. Gartzke, *War bargaining and the military commitment problem* (New Haven, CT: Yale University Press, 2001); and R. Powell, War as a commitment problem, *Int Organ* 2006, 60:169–203.

58. A. Carson and K. Yarhi-Milo, Covert communication: the intelligibility and credibility of signaling in secret, *Security Stud*, forthcoming.

59. Gartzke and Lindsay, Weaving tangled webs, 316–48.

60. Defense Science Board Task Force on Resilient Military Systems, *Resilient military systems*.

61. C. Ash, Remarks by Secretary Carter at the Drell Lecture Cemex Auditorium (Stanford, CA: Stanford Graduate School of Business, 2015).

62. J. R. Lindsay and E. Gartzke, Coercion through cyberspace: the stability-instability paradox revisited, in *The Power to Hurt: Coercion in Theory and in Practice*, K. M. Greenhill and P. J. P. Krause (eds.) (New York: Oxford University Press, forthcoming).

63. Lindsay, Tipping the scales, 53–67; Lindsay and Gartzke, Coercion through cyberspace; and E. Colby, Cyberwar and the nuclear option, *The National Interest*, June 24, 2013.

64. S. J. Cimbala, *Nuclear Weapons in the Information Age* (New York: Continuum International Publishing, 2012); J. Fritz, *Hacking Nuclear Command and Control* (International Commission on Nuclear Non-proliferation and Disarmament, 2009); and A. Futter, Hacking the bomb: nuclear weapons in the cyber age, 2015 ISA Annual Conference (New Orleans, February 2015).

65. S. J. Cimbala, Nuclear deterrence and cyber: the quest for concept, *Air Space Power J* 2014, 87–107.

66. Cimbala, *Nuclear Weapons in the Information Age*.

67. R. Jervis, R. N. Lebow, and J. G. Stein, *Psychology and Deterrence* (Baltimore, MD: Johns Hopkins University Press, 1985); and J. M. Goldgeier and P. E. Tetlock, Psychology and international relations theory, *Ann Rev Polit Sci* 2001, 4:67–92.

68. Gartzke, War is in the error term, 567–87.

69. T. Yoshihara and J. R. Holmes, eds., *Strategy in the Second Nuclear Age: Power, Ambition, and the Ultimate Weapon* (Washington, DC: Georgetown University Press, 2012).

70. H. M. Kristensen and R. S. Norris, Status of world nuclear forces, Federation of American Scientists, 2016, http://fas.org/issues/nuclear-weapons/status-world-nuclear-forces.

71. Lindsay, The impact of China on cybersecurity, 7–47.

72. HP Security Research, *Profiling an Enigma: The Mystery of North Korea's Cyber Threat Landscape*, HP Security Briefing. Hewlett-Packard Development Company, August 2014, http://h30499.www3.hp.com/hpeb/attachments/hpeb/off-by-on-software-security-blog/388/2/HPSR%20SecurityBriefing_Episode16_NorthKorea.pdf.

73. R. Jervis, *The Meaning of the Nuclear Revolution: Statecraft and the Prospect of Armageddon* (Ithaca, NY: Cornell University Press, 1989).

74. T. Rid and B. Buchanan, Attributing cyber attacks, *J Strat Stud* 2015, 38:4–37.

75. Posen, *Inadvertent Escalation*; Cimbala, Nuclear crisis management, 117–31; Goldstein, First things first, 49–89; Gompert and Libicki, Cyber warfare, 7–22; and Talmadge, Assessing the risk.

76. R. Jervis, *Perception and Misperception in International Politics* (Princeton, NJ: Princeton University Press, 1976); and S. Tang, The security dilemma: a conceptual analysis. *Security Stud* 2009, 18:587–623.

77. B. Buchanan, *The Cybersecurity Dilemma* (London: Hurst, 2016).

78. Long and Green, Stalking the secure second strike, 38–73; and A. Long, *Deterrence—From Cold War to Long War: Lessons from Six Decades of RAND Research* (Santa Monica, CA: RAND Corporation, 2008).

79. R. Jervis, *The Illogic of American Nuclear Strategy* (Ithaca, NY: Cornell University Press, 1984); and S. Van Evera, *Causes of War: Power and the Roots of Conflict* (Ithaca, NY: Cornell University Press, 1999).

80. B. R. Green and A. G. Long, Signaling with secrets—Evidence on Soviet perceptions and counterforce developments in the late Cold War, in *Cross-Domain Deterrence: Strategy in an Era of Complexity*, E. Gartzke and J. R. Lindsay (eds.) (La Jolla, CA: Manuscript, 2016).

81. Buchanan, *The Cybersecurity Dilemma*.

82. Defense Science Board Task Force on Resilient Military Systems, *Resilient military systems*.

83. S. Peterson, Old weapons, new terror worries, *Christian Science Monitor*, April 15, 2004, http://www.csmonitor.com/2004/0415/p06s02-woeu.html.

The Security Implications of Climate Change
Charting Major Dimensions of the Challenge

JOHN R. ALLEN AND BRUCE JONES

At the time of writing, the 2019 Novel Coronavirus, or COVID-19, has been declared a pandemic by the World Health Organization and has infected citizens of almost every country in the world, with every sign that the consequences of the pandemic will deepen. At the upper end of projections, it is well within the range of the feasible that in some countries, COVID-19 will claim more lives than some recent wars. This is a stark reminder that natural phenomena, as well as manmade crises, can pose grave threats to state and society. The consequence of failing to respond early and aggressively to COVID-19 are plain to see, and they stand as a harbinger for what will happen if the United States refuses to take a leading role in preventing other natural threats to state and society.

Climate change poses just such a threat. As we gain ever greater understanding about the imminent, medium- and long-term effects of a rise in the average global temperature, so too do we understand that climate change will likely be a defining, if not the defining, existential challenge of our time. No country, and no sector of the economy or society, will be unaffected by these changes. In some areas, the impact will be severe; and in some instances, acute security challenges will surely follow. This essay charts some of those security consequences, both for the United States and for the international community as a whole.

Backdrop

For countries that are well governed and have diverse economies and robust social and political institutions, including the United States, moving to limit the rise in average global temperatures, while simultaneously navigating the impacts of changing weather patterns, will be a mammoth, but in principle, a manageable exercise. That of course assumes that policy is informed by science and driven by an effective combination of private-sector innovation and effective public policy measures, and that the political leadership of the country and of key institutions—at federal, state, and local levels—understands the gravity and scale of the challenge.[1] That such leadership is currently lacking at the federal level in the United States poses a serious challenge; however, such is the nature of the United States that state, local, civic, corporate, and academic leadership is making up a substantial portion of the gap in the meantime.[2]

For years, there have been detailed plans for how to control emissions, and for decades those plans have not been followed. Thus, the world is now locked into significant warming, and probably soon it will be locked into more. That is a huge problem that merits a serious response.

For advanced industrial societies, the major costs associated with warming temperatures will arise from erosion of agricultural productivity; costs imposed by adverse weather effects and changes in the biological stock; health effects of warming temperatures, including the effects of extensive forest fires and migration of tropical diseases into temperate regions that previously kept them at bay; and the direct cost of expending resources to adapt the industrial base and the physical stock of the country, such as transportation infrastructure and urban infrastructure, in ways that limit carbon emissions. Some of the costs may be unexpected—as when Hurricane Sandy caused power outages as far west as Michigan, or when Hurricane Irene caused substantial damage from inland flooding in New England, in additional to the damage to more traditional storm-hit parts of the southern East Coast of the United States. The costs to the United States of just one of these super-storms has been estimated at $70 billion.[3]

For countries with less developed political and economic institutions, navigating climate change may prove a more challenging task. Particularly hard hit will be large, populous countries at the lower- to middle-income range, which will have to simultaneously manage weather shocks and the process of engaging in economic development with lower-carbon technologies. Countries such as Nigeria and Ethiopia, with populations in excess of 100 million and the aspiration to develop further, may face particularly acute challenges—though they are also best placed to absorb and make effective use of well-targeted sustainable development assistance.

Were a warming planet the only change in front of us, it would already impose substantial burdens on policy-making to effectively handle the coming economic and social changes. However, changing weather patterns intersect with ongoing changes in socioeconomic development, existing dynamics of conflict, and a shifting power structure in the international order as a whole. The interplay across those set of changes are where we will find the most challenging dynamics.

Climate and Conflict

This trend is best mapped, so far, in the domain of internal conflict. Internal conflict is where most of the research on conflict dynamics has been concentrated in the past decade, and it has been by far the dominant form of warfare in the post–Cold War era. Consequently, there is a robust set of experiences and data from which to draw and against which to test models of change. Across the domain of internal conflict, substantial work has been undertaken to map the effect of climate-related impacts, such as changing patterns of rainfall and weather shocks.

Now, conflict in all its forms is a complex human endeavor and rarely attributable to a single dynamic or cause. That complexity is reflected in the research literature, which highlights multiple recurrent sources of conflict. Most prevalent are low levels of economic development; low capabilities of the state; and intergroup inequality.[4] Another factor, highlighted by the World Bank among others, is a recent history of conflict. States and societies that have recently experienced conflict are far more likely than others to experience another bout of conflict and becoming trapped in some cases in a cycle of conflict and underdevelopment, often for decades.[5]

Across these multiple sources of pressure on states, shocks associated with changing weather patterns—especially changing patterns of rainfall—can be mapped. Looking to the past, the best science suggests that climate impacts add to the risk of conflict in low-income societies by around 5 percent.[6] But that is looking to the past, when temperature rises and attendant weather effects have been limited. A recent major study published in *Nature*, which brings together more than a dozen of the leading social and physical scientists tracking the effect of changing weather patterns on conflict, produces a sobering picture of what lies ahead. With an anticipated 2-degree Celsius rise in average global temperatures, we see an increase in the risk and lethality of conflict of around 13 percent; with a possible 4-degree rise, that risk spikes further upward to over 25 percent.[7]

Internal conflicts can also be shaped by external shocks. Over the past three decades, internal conflicts have arisen when major regional and global changes have driven shifts in resource flows and/or external political support. The collapse of the Soviet Union led to substantial conflict in eastern Europe. The end of the Cold War, ironically, led to a surge in conflicts in Latin America and Sub-Saharan Africa—though that was quickly followed by a surge in peacemaking and peacekeeping efforts by the United Nations, regional organizations, and Western powers, resulting in a gradual but steady decline in levels of violence.[8] A deep change in the geopolitical and economic landscape in the Middle East and North Africa (initially encapsulated in the phrase "Arab Spring") led to a surge in conflict and violence both within states and across the region, which at the time of writing, accounts for roughly 90 percent of all battle deaths in conflict. And, indeed, the ongoing global COVID-19 crisis may very well amount to a similar shock to areas most heavily affected by the virus.

Across those waves of conflict, irrespective of region, the countries most at risk of conflict are those at the lowest end of the income scale. Those countries in turn are most likely to rely heavily on agriculture for substantial shares of their GDP. And the agriculture industry is of course most directly affected by changing weather patterns, and in particular by shifts in patterns of rainfall or loss of ground water, as well as by related consequences of warming average temperatures.

Hardest hit will be Sub-Saharan Africa. Using the same models and same metrics that predict a nearly 25 percent rise in levels and lethality of conflict globally under a 4-degree temperature rise, a recent study suggests a 54 percent increase in conflict in Sub-Saharan Africa alone.[9] This would result in several hundred thousand additional battle deaths and the displacement of millions. And the patterns of war tell us that the effects of this will not be limited to the individual countries affected but will spread both within Africa and beyond by the vectors of transnational terrorism and by mass migration.

Rising temperatures also have an effect on interpersonal violence and on crime, including the attendant loss of life and potential security consequences from those two forms of human violence.[10] Anyone who has experienced civil conflict in Iraq or North Africa has witnessed first-hand the ways in which extreme heat can seriously exacerbate social tensions, amplifying preexisting cleavages or sources of conflict and hampering efforts to restore the peace.

Wider Security Issues

As we range out to other forms of conflict and insecurity, the pattern of causality is less certain because the incidences are rarer, the effects are less direct, and the timeframes are longer. At the very least, though, we need to be mapping and considering the following sets of issues from both an American and an international security perspective. As we do so, we also need to be cognizant of the fact that we are seeing real-time effects play out in ways that show bigger and bigger impacts and growing tail risks. Preparing for the tail risks of large-scale, severe impacts from climate change must become a standard part of risk assessment for American and international security institutions.

Migration

The effects of conflict are not limited to the country in question; they spread, subregionally and beyond. The most important vector of this spread is through refugee flows and related forms of migration. Consider the manner in which the flow of more than 3 million refugees from genocide in Rwanda in the mid-1990s proceeded to help to destabilize the whole of Central Africa. Again, low state capability is a key issue here: states with greater levels of wealth and more robust institutions are better able to handle the sudden inflow of large numbers of refugees. Even there, however, social stresses can be substantial, as we saw with the very sudden flow of more than 1 million refugees from Syria and other conflict-affected parts of West Asia into Europe in the summer and fall of 2015.

Already, Turkey is straining with the effects of hosting nearly 3 million Syrian refugees. As conflict levels increase due to changing climate, among other reasons, so too will refugee flows and related forms of migration, such as climate migration. Under some estimates, Latin America, Sub-Saharan Africa, and Southeast Asia will generate as many as 143 million climate migrants by 2050, with many of these individuals fleeing directly into Europe.[11] This would have substantial, even severe, consequences for political stability in southern Europe in particular.

Sea-Level Rise

Perhaps the most extensive, though not the most immediate, security consequences from a warming climate will come from sea-level rise. This will have several major impacts.

First, we are likely to see substantial migration from low-level island states, whose populations may migrate to coastal areas in Southeast Asia to escape the effects of climate change. This can have destabilizing effects similar to those just described for Europe. Second, sea-level rise is already putting economic pressure on important states in the coastal areas of the Indian Ocean, notably Bangladesh and Myanmar—both of which have large populations and large parts of their agricultural land in low-lying areas heavily exposed to rising sea levels. Perhaps Bangladesh, which has weaker state capacity, is the threshold indicator of what's to come: Bangladesh lost as many as 250,000 people during Cyclone Nargis in 1998. So far, we have not seen as severe loss of life in Myanmar, but if sea-level rise increases along with average temperature, we may see similar consequences. Myanmar, of course, plays a highly consequential role in Asian security politics, given its geographical location between India and China and its potential to serve as an alternative route for China into the Indian Ocean bypassing the Malacca Straits.[12]

Sea-level rise is very likely to directly affect the physical survival of several small island states. This is a security risk in its own right for those countries, but it could also have wider implications, especially in the Western Pacific where US naval installations and US naval defense are highly dependent on a series of small island installations across the region. This is already a topic of concern for US Indo-Pacific Command (USINDOPACOM) leadership. And beyond the simple rise of sea levels, as the seas continue to warm, the resulting cyclones and hurricanes will be fed more energy from the warmer surfaces; this will make them more destructive both in an absolute sense and because these storms will drive surges of higher sea levels farther and farther inland—creating greater human misery, destruction, and economic stress. These intersecting climate effects will be devastating.

Great-Power Relations

Changing climate patterns and industrial countries' collective response to climate change could also have substantial geopolitical implications. Two countries whose posture matters a great deal to both American and international security are Saudi Arabia and Russia—one a putative US security partner, albeit a troubled one, the other a US adversary. Both rely immensely on the sale of fossil fuels (oil and gas) for their GDP and for state income. Saudi Arabia, for its part, has begun to think through what it means for them as a society that we will see a transition away from fossil fuel consumption over the next twenty years—but it has not done much to act on this. Russia, to be sure, has not. How these two countries cope with that change will likely have substantial implications for the stability and security of their regions and, in the case of Russia, for international security as a whole. We have only begun to think through this potentially challenging issue.

A very different question is India, an indispensable partner to the United States in the management of the Indo-Pacific region. India has 400 million people who have little or no access to modern energy. As a democratic society, it has no choice but to attempt to industrialize to provide greater access to energy for its poor. But should India industrialize through the same carbon intensive pathways as both the West and China, then we will likely be locking in at least 4 degrees of temperature rise—an intolerable risk.

How do we square this circle? Substantial transfer of both technology and resources is likely to be necessary if India is going to be able to maintain an effective strategy for development while navigating much tighter restrictions on carbon emissions.[13] This is an area where American leadership—from the federal government, to be sure, but also from states, cities, companies, and think tanks—can make a critical difference. And if the United States is not part of the solution for India, what should be the most important bilateral partnership of the twenty-first century will suffer.

The Arctic

A fourth, and already consequential impact of changing weather patterns, is occurring in the Arctic. Warmer temperatures and the attendant melt of sea ice are changing the patterns of flow across a once-frozen north. The Arctic is now providing new routes for trade during the summer months and could soon see year-round travel with ice-hardened ships and convoys of container ships. Certainly within twenty years, the northern sea route will open up a new shipping lane from the major container ports on China's eastern shore to the markets of the eastern United States and across the Atlantic to Europe. The implications of this could be wide ranging.

More immediately, changing weather patterns have opened up major new areas for deep-sea energy exploration, especially in the Barents Sea and the adjacent Norwegian Sea. Virtually every major energy company in the world is engaged in one or more projects of exploration in the Barents. As of now, there are still challenges to recovery, and at low energy prices it seems unlikely that firms will invest the resources to fully develop these fields. But as other resources become constrained, substantial development will take place. And some of this is driven not by markets, but by geopolitics. Already we are seeing the development of major new gas fields in the Yamal Peninsula by a Russian state-owned gas firm and the flow of large quantities of natural gas from these fields to China. The flow of fossil fuels from the Russian high north to China is emerging as a central pillar in the evolving, and dangerous, relationship between these two most important non-Western powers.

American Leadership

In all of the above—in its economic effects, its effects on development, its effects on conflict, and its effects on geopolitics—climate change rebounds to the question of the effects on American leadership.

Since 1940, the United States has led the free world in defense against a series of fundamental threats. A critical feature of American leadership in the wake of World War II was that it combined security responses with economic opportunity—the United States was the great advocate and the great protector of liberalization, free trade, and later globalization. This allowed societies to participate in win-win economics while gaining security support through an alliance or friendship with the United States. And since the end of the Cold War, the United States has been the unquestioned leader of the international security architecture, the international order as a whole, and global governance.

However, there are now several challenges to American leadership. Much of the security community is seized with these, most of all the challenge posed by the rise of China as an economic and increasingly a strategic actor. But the security community has not yet adequately seized the implications of climate change for American leadership.

This has two essential dimensions. First, more fully understanding and preparing for the impacts laid out above—from increased conflict and migration to sea-level rise to changing patterns of stability and instability in great-power relations, climate change will affect multiple dimensions of international security in a direct sense. But there is also a second, consequential feature of the issue.

Whatever it is that the American population and US leadership think of climate change, much of the rest of the world, including core American allies, treat climate change as a top-tier issue, one requiring seriousness of purpose and extensive global cooperation. If the United States fails to lead the world in mitigating climate change and in preparing to adapt to the consequences of the changes already baked into natural systems, this will contribute to the already diminishing confidence in American standing and American leadership. The consequences of this would rebound across every aspect of the American alliance dynamic and include America's viability as a leader of the international order. In fact, these consequences are already becoming apparent.

Serious American leadership requires not just reengaging at the federal level, but also putting into place institutions and incentives that play to America's great strengths—our decentralized capacity to act at the state, city, and local level and our ability to mobilize enormous civic, academic, and commercial innovation. American leaders will also have to balance the following challenge—namely, the fact that across the international system there is a growing need to mobilize the community of democracies to rally in defense of the multilateral order and to tackle shared global challenges. Climate change, however, is a problem that will also require extensive cooperation with China (as well as the other major growing economies, especially in Asia). That need not be premised on warm relations between ourselves and the Chinese, and we certainly cannot take such relations as a given, or even likely. Rather, we have to invest in understanding how to drive cooperation under conditions of competition, even rivalry. In some areas, climate change may have to proceed like arms control, with a shared sense on both sides of the consequences of unchecked emissions, parallel commitments, and some form of verification.[14]

Climate change will affect every industry and every sector in every society of the world. It is already seen in enraged weather patterns battering the East Coast, the changing water table in the Great Plains, forest fires in California, energy productivity in the once frozen North, and industrial development. Managing those changes and generating the kinds of international structure and cooperation needed to flow resources to the most necessary areas and build resilience, and manage the change, will be a fundamental test for the international order in the coming years. If the United States fails to lead, it risks squandering its moral standing and its leadership at a critical time in the international order—with serious, perhaps severe, costs.

NOTES

The authors would like to thank Dr. David Victor, professor of international relations at the School of Global Policy and Strategy and director of the Laboratory on International Law and Regulation, and Samantha Gross, fellow in the Cross-Brookings Initiative on Energy and Climate, for their thoughtful comments and intellectual input in support of this essay.

1. David Victor, Frank W. Geels, and Simon Sharpe, "Accelerating the Low Carbon Transition: The Case for Stronger, More Targeted and Coordinated International Action" (Washington, DC: The Brookings Institution, November 2019).

2. Mark Muro, D.G. Victor, and Jacob Whiton, "How the Geography of Climate Damage Could Make the Politics Less Polarizing" (Washington, DC: The Brookings Institution, January 2019).

3. Eric S. Blake, Todd B. Kimberlain, Robert J. Berg, John P. Cangialosi, and John L. Beven II, "Tropical Cyclone Report Hurricane Sandy" (University Park, FL: National Hurricane Center, February 12, 2013).

4. Katherine J. Mach, Caroline M. Kraan, W. Neil Adger, Halvard Buhaug, Marshall Burke, James D. Fearon, Christopher B. Field, Cullen Hendrix, Jean-Francois Maystadt, John O'Loughlin, Philip Roessler, Jürgen Scheffran, Kenneth Schultz, and Nina von Uexkull, "Climate as a Risk Factor for Armed Conflict," *Nature* 571 (June 2019): 193–197.

5. World Bank, *World Development Report 2011: Conflict, Security, and Development—Overview (English)* (Washington, DC: World Bank Group, 2011).

6. Solomon M. Hsiang, Marshall Burke, Edward Miguel, "Quantifying the Influence of Climate on Human Conflict," *Science* 321 (September 13, 2013): 1–14.

7. Mach et al., "Climate as a Risk Factor for Armed Conflict."

8. Virginia Page Fortna, *Does Peacekeeping Work? Shaping Belligerents' Choices After Civil War* (Princeton, NJ: Princeton University Press, 2008).

9. Marshall B. Burke, Edward Miguel, Shanker Satyanath, John A. Dykema, and David B. Lobell, "Warming Increases the Risk of Civil War in Africa," *Proceedings of the National Academy of Sciences of the United States of America* 106 (December 6, 2009): 20670–20674.

10. Michael J. Lynch, Paul B. Stretesky, and Michael A. Long, "Climate Change, Temperature, and Homicide: A Tale of Two Cities, 1895–2015," *Weather, Climate, and Society* 12, no. 1 (December 13, 2019): 171–81.

11. Kanta Kumari Rigaud, Alex de Sherbinin, Byran Jones, Jonas Bergmann, Viviane Clement, Kayly Ober, Jacob Schewe, Susana Adamo, Brent McCusker, Silke Heuser, and Amelia Midgley, "Groundswell: Preparing for Internal Climate Migration" (Washington, DC: The World Bank, 2018).

12. Thant Myint-U, *Where China Meets India: Burma and the New Crossroads of Asia* (New York: Farrar, Straus and Giroux, 2018).

13. Bruce Jones and Samir Saran, An *"India Exception" and India-U.S. Partnership on Climate Change* (Washington, DC: The Brookings Institution, January 12, 2015).

14. This is an area where Brookings scholars have begun to innovate and explore alternative models. See forthcoming work by Thomas Wright, by David Victor, and by Bruce Jones and Nils Gilman.

Epilogue

Defense Policy Resilience in the Face of Black Swans and Grey Rhinos

WILL ATKINS

To paraphrase Winston Churchill, we are not even at the end of the beginning of the coronavirus crisis. At the time of this writing, the United States alone faces more than 8.1 million known cases and more than 500,000 deaths as a result of the novel coronavirus, SARS-CoV-2, which has given rise to the COVID-19 disease.[1] The authors of this volume certainly hope that by the time this text is published the pandemic has been contained—if not eliminated. Even with such a conclusion, however, the effects on American society and the challenges to our approach to strategic thinking will have only begun.

For many, this global pandemic is a "Black Swan"— a term popularized by Nassim Nicholas Taleb in 2007, to refer to something that is highly improbable, or even unimaginable.[2] For those who consider the pandemic to be a Black Swan event, "Nobody could have seen it coming."[3] Others, such as Michele Wucker, consider the pandemic to be a "Grey Rhino"—a massive, two-ton event that everyone can see on the horizon, even if they are unsure of when (or if) the charge might occur, thereby making avoidance inherently difficult.[4] Both Grey Rhinos and Black Swans have useful, albeit different, explanatory value when analyzing defense policy.

Grey Rhinos tend to be those events that current defense policy is well aware of but unwilling or ill-equipped to deal with. These type of events include potential threats such as climate change, artificial intelligence, cyberwarfare, hypersonics, and quantum computing. Each of these threats constitutes a Grey Rhino—stomping the ground and getting ready to charge—that policy-makers are aware of, but forecasting when or if these events will occur can make Grey Rhinos just as unpredictable as Black Swans. Since Grey Rhino events are foreseeable—that is, policy-makers know that they *may* occur at some point— aggressive and forward-looking defense policy can allow for educated guesses as to what risks the event entails and how to go about minimizing that risk. Most importantly, Grey Rhinos give the chance to act, even if it is impossible to determine if or when the event might occur. As a result, defense policy aimed at Grey Rhinos must be well-equipped to dodge or deflect the adverse effects of a charge when the timing might catch policy-makers by surprise.

Black Swans, on the other hand, are inherently unforeseeable and therefore require policy that is much more resilient to unknown threats. In these cases, there is less probability of dodging or deflecting a threat that no one saw coming. Here, defense policy must be well equipped to absorb and recover from the adverse effects of a Black Swan event.

The sudden and unexpected COVID-19 pandemic provides ample opportunity to analyze the challenges facing American defense policy in an increasingly complex and interconnected global environment. COVID-19 illustrates the changing nature of what constitutes a national security threat to the United States. It also highlights the need for resilient defense policy—one that adequately prepares to dodge or deflect the unexpected charge of a Grey Rhino, while improving the United States' ability to absorb and recover from adverse Black Swans.

To do so, modern defense policy must move beyond ineffective analyses of the component parts, must include all domains present within a complex system, and must be evaluated against tangible resiliency metrics to ensure such policies are adaptable and flexible to counter the threat from a world of unknown unknowns. Unlike most defense regulations that provide ample direction on *what* to perform, this essay attempts to provide guidance on *how* to go about achieving such a change in defense policy-making. As national security threats become more diverse, frequent, and costly, failures in predicting their occurrence are to be expected—both Black Swans and Grey Rhinos are inherently unpredictable—though this should not preclude the development of effective responses to such unforeseen events.

Changing Nature of National Security Threats

More than a year and a half before the COVID-19 outbreak, former Obama administration homeland security advisor Lisa Monaco used the 100th anniversary of the 1918 Spanish flu pandemic to warn that "pandemic disease poses one of the greatest threats to global stability and security."[5] Microsoft founder Bill Gates used the same anniversary to argue that "a global flu epidemic could kill more people in the short-term than terrorism or climate change."[6] He continued: "We need to think through how to handle quarantines, make sure supply chains will reach affected areas, decide how to involve the military, and so on."[7] Even the Director of National Intelligence ranked vulnerability to a large-scale outbreak of contagious disease as one of the top threats facing the country.[8]

Despite these warnings, little action was taken to avoid being crushed by the impending Grey Rhino. While defense professionals in the United States were focused on great-power competition with China and Russia, funds were diverted from the Defense Threat Reduction Agency's budget for biosecurity threats and instead used to research hypersonic weapons and artificial intelligence.[9] Additionally, while funding for renovation of the nuclear stockpile was increased 20 percent, the National Security Council's Pandemic Preparedness and Response Directorate was disbanded, leaving the nation without a dedicated team for such contagions.[10]

These dichotomies highlight the need for a renewed analysis of what constitutes a national security threat to the United States and which resources should be allocated to combat these challenges. To date, COVID-19 has killed more people than Vietnam, Korea, and the War on Terror—combined.[11] Early in the crisis, the pandemic was able to achieve something no adversary had been able to accomplish since World War II: it knocked a US Navy aircraft carrier out of service.[12]

To make matters worse, the effects of COVID-19 are also likely to exacerbate the threats emanating from already-fragile countries. For those nations previously facing severe conflict or natural disasters, the shock is going to be more acute and the impact more devastating in terms of deaths and disruption of basic services. For many of these nations, their ability to provide water, sanitation, health care, and hygiene services were limited to begin with, and vulnerable groups such as refugees and the elderly are often those most likely to lack such basic services.[13] As an example, at the time of this writing in May 2020, Burkina Faso faced 796 known cases and 51 deaths as a direct result of the coronavirus.[14] At least another 850 people had been killed due to COVID-related unrest.[15] Despite a nation in lockdown, their health care system was overwhelmed, displacement was spiraling, and terrorist and insurgent groups had already taken root. "So far more than 760,000 people have been displaced and almost a million are in need. Many of these people have been displaced over the past three months, as the security situation has deteriorated rapidly."[16] Such power vacuums may well lead to similar conflicts as

recently illustrated in Iraq, Afghanistan, and Syria—conflicts that the US military would do well to avoid.

The US military certainly possesses unique capabilities that are well suited for some aspects of pandemic response. This alone would require appropriate defense policy to implement. However, this is not to argue that the Defense Department needs to add "pandemic response" to its already long list of tangential missions. The simple act of naming global pandemics a national security threat would result in the organization of a whole-of-government response to these types of Grey Rhinos. According to Monaco, "An appropriate strategy should be tailored to the multifaceted nature of the threat pandemics pose and should include diplomacy and foreign aid along with public health preparedness."[17]

In truth, some have argued that Americans may look at national security differently from now on and may no longer be willing to give the Department of Defense such a large budget to defend against foreign threats that few see coming.[18] In theory, that largesse was unable to prevent the coronavirus from killing sixty times more Americans than 9/11, with more fatalities reported every day. As a result, the funding for an expansion of the nation's pandemic response may very well be reallocated from within the Defense Department's budget—already the single largest discretionary spending item for the nation. Some have even warned that the coming defense cuts would need to be very deep and disruptive, requiring defense leaders to make extremely hard choices.[19] Defense priorities such as equipment modernization, increased force end-strength, and procurement plans may all need to be reduced or eliminated. Service rivalries might even intensify as the nascent Space Force joins the clamor for shares in a shrinking defense budget. However, naming pandemics a national security threat and developing a whole-of-government response may actually "free the Defense Department to focus on the kinds of adversaries it is best designed to deter and defeat: the ones we can see."[20]

As David Barno and Nora Bensahel argue, "The United States that eventually emerges after [this] crisis will be deeply transformed and will have new and different priorities. We in the national security community must ready ourselves for this new era, where economic recovery and preparing for domestic threats like pandemics will be far greater concerns for most Americans than threats from foreign adversaries."[21] Shifting priorities, shrinking budgets, and increasing global complexities are all likely to produce a fundamentally different US military posture than previously known.

As Lawrence Freedman describes (chapter 8), eventually a nation's existing political, economic, and social structures can respond to initial attacks, preventing the event from resulting in system collapse. Conversely, systems that lack such resilience may be unable to successfully meet these challenges. This resilience can only be achieved by anticipating (or at least hedging against) not only the initial Black Swan, but the subsequent second- and third-order effects of such an event. Failure to do so can prove costly in terms of military lives and strategic advantages lost.

Slow-burning and complex crises have revealed the need for the United States to generate more innovative and effective public policies and governance practices for a wider range of national security challenges. These crises might include the opioid epidemic, pandemics, migration, climate change, and financial markets—to name a few. Each of these complex systems is an integral part of our lives, and each has the potential to fail in ways that separate them from traditional understandings of security challenges. "As the world becomes more connected—the culmination of the promise of globalization—it becomes more complex. That complexity carries with it benefits for some and a hidden cost for all: fragility."[22] This fragility is introduced by a series of pressures not previously understood as national security threats and can only be adequately addressed with resilient defense policy.

Risk versus Resilience

In order to develop such resilient defense policy, one must move beyond the buzzword to understand exactly what resilient defense policies would look like. Much of the confusion surrounding the overarching concept of resilience is due to the varying definitions in use by different industries. As a result, our understanding of resilience changes depending on the context in use.

The Office of the Secretary of Defense for Policy (OSD-P) definition of resilience provides some insight into how defense policy-makers view resilience: it is "the ability of an architecture to support the functions necessary for mission success with higher probability, shorter periods of reduced capability, and across a wider range of scenarios, conditions, and threats, in spite of hostile action or adverse conditions."[23] The problem is that this definition of resilience tends to focus narrowly on battle-damage characteristics that the military is well conditioned to address.

In the military, systems are often described as resilient if they are robust or impenetrable (e.g., a resilient information network), though as the OSD-P definition illustrates, it is also used to describe a military force with the ability to provide operational capacity despite disruption, whether natural or man-made, inadvertent or deliberate.[24] This is very similar to the physical sciences, where materials and objects are deemed resilient if they resume their original shape upon being bent or stretched. In human psychology, this concept is described as the ability to "bounce back" after encountering difficulty or trauma.

In each of these contexts, resilient systems are required in order to respond effectively in the face of a challenge or an adverse effect. In engineering terms, this ability to "bounce back," or overcome challenge, depends on how well a policy or piece of infrastructure is engineered to absorb and recover from damages caused by adverse events. In the context of engineering resilience, principles such as robustness, redundancy, and modularity are relied upon. This is the type of resilience being referred to when describing a resilient piece of military infrastructure. However, this is but one aspect of what resilience means. In an ecological sense, resilience also deals with how close a system is to collapse. In the context of *ecological* resilience, concepts such as flexibility, adaptability, and resourcefulness are utilized—concepts that are largely absent from the military's definition above. By combining both aspects of resilience, a resilient defense policy would anticipate a multitude of unknown threats and would be nimble enough to respond quickly and adapt to lessons learned.[25]

These two facets of resilience need not be compartmentalized, however, as each model "brings with it a set of conceptual guidelines that are complementary and desirable."[26] In fact, such hybrid resilience is necessary to create a system that is resilient to a wider range of threats. Defense policy should be robust, redundant, and modular (engineering resilience), as well as flexible, adaptable, and resourceful (ecological resilience). When combined, resilience is simply "the ability to plan and prepare for, absorb, recover from, and more successfully adapt to adverse events."[27]

Often, discussions of defense policy resilience distill to debates about how much "risk" the Defense Department or the United States is willing to accept. Unfortunately, this distinction hinders the development of resilient defense policy. Compared to resilience, risk "quantifies known hazards and expected damages" in a way that assumes advance knowledge of the effect of a known event. Such knowledge may occur when dealing with Grey Rhino events, but here, the effects of such an event may still be relatively unquantifiable since the potential timing of the event is unknown.

Additionally, this type of risk calculation is simply not possible when dealing with emerging and unforeseen threats, such as true Black Swan events. For these types of unimaginable threats, the effects are entirely unknown. As a result, "using risk assessment to measure system resilience only offers solutions to incremental, known risks, and does little to manage unforeseen events or perform under the stress of catastrophe."[28] Resilient defense policy therefore "depends upon specific qualities that risk assessment cannot quantify, such as system flexibility and interconnectedness."[29]

Two examples serve to illustrate the fallacy of basing defense policies on the concept of risk as opposed to a more appropriate discussion of policy resilience. First, the creation of the Transportation Security Administration and the installation of armored cockpit doors were actions taken to reduce the *risk* of another 9/11-type terrorist attack. However, these changes did nothing to create a more *resilient* aviation system, capable of absorbing and recovering capabilities in the event that another such event were to occur. Similarly, the Trump administration's current emphasis on building a wall along the southern border of the United States may reduce the *risk* of illegal immigration. However, the wall is a perfect example of planning for one specific type of threat. Even if this wall is built along the entire southern border, it will do nothing to increase the resilience of the American economic, health care, and social welfare systems—the second- and third-order effects of illegal immigration. If and when immigrants find another way into the country, the system will be just as unlikely to absorb the adverse effects of illegal immigration; nor will recovery time be lessened.

Understanding this difference between risk and resilience is vital for the development of effective defense policy. These two examples illustrate how current defense policy frequently addresses specific, identifiable risks, without making the underlying system more resilient against a multitude of threats. When faced with future Black Swans or Grey Rhinos, current defense policies will be found lacking. To avoid such miscalculations, we need to learn from our failures to prepare for, absorb, recover from, and adapt to the sudden outbreak of COVID-19. This requires an investigation into how we might use systemic thinking to develop resilient defense policies for future Black Swan or Grey Rhino events.

Systemic Thinking

These miscalculations are due, in part, to a critical shortfall in the art of strategic thinking (see chapter 6). As noted by Daniel McCauley, today's leaders have "lost the ability to look and plan ahead."[30] However, in order to deal with an increasingly complex and uncertain world, a new developmental paradigm must be constructed. As global interdependencies increase, changes in the economic, social, religious, or military realms demand strategic consideration. Global health concerns are no different.

Benjamin Jensen notes that as the world becomes a more interconnected system, "systems tend to be resilient and adaptive, reorganizing and mutating in response to change."[31] The failure of such systems is therefore rarely the result of a single shocking event. Rather, fragility in the system develops from "a combination of factors that interact in unpredictable

ways."[32] Therefore, strategic foresight is not intended to avoid or prevent Black Swan or Grey Rhino events from happening, but rather to prepare for the inevitable second- and third-order effects that such a shock would bring about.

Traditionally, it isn't the initial shock of a large population falling ill that leads to a national security breakdown, but rather the failure of a public health system, the resulting economic decline due to large numbers of quarantined workers, and the strain on global supply chains for everything from personal protective equipment (PPE) to foodstuffs. As a result, "Failure in one part of the system can cascade into other parts—such as how the current pandemic stresses public health—and, through our response, ripples into the economy, causing mass layoffs and a collapse in consumer confidence, trade, and industrial production."[33]

Black Swans are, by their very nature, unpredictable. And since planners cannot prepare for every unimaginable scenario, defense policy must anticipate the second- and third-order effects that are inevitable—even if we cannot predict their cause. That is, the inability to predict Black Swans requires the capability to react more efficiently to the repercussions of such events. For example, any number of Black Swan events might cause mass migration, mass unemployment, or health care system collapse. The goal is not to predict the *cause* of these effects. The goal of resilient policy is the ability to address these challenges regardless of what caused them.

Likewise, while defense planners can see Grey Rhinos on the horizon (which allows for a better approximation of the event's second- and third-order effects), these events' unpredictable timing leads to similar challenges ensuring adequate preparedness. Resilient defense policy ensures that the system is ready to absorb and recover from these adverse effects, regardless of when they might occur.

Such is the case for complex, interconnected systems. Foreseeing these developments and establishing our response to them rely heavily on the art of strategic thinking. Traditional military planning efforts utilize various frameworks to analyze the operational environment, taking into account the political, military, economic, social, infrastructure, and informational (PMESII) factors that may affect potential courses of action in response to various crises.[34] Too often, this is where the analysis ends, resulting in missed complex interactions between various PMESII nodes. That is, without a more complete picture of the operating environment, potential courses of action cannot be adequately analyzed, and second- and third-order effects may be missed—the exact effects that must be planned for when we cannot predict the initial events.

It is just these kind of staggering second- and third-order effects of the COVID-19 pandemic that have the potential to cause systemic failure. In a single week early in the crisis, almost 3.3 million Americans applied for unemployment benefits—five times more than in the previous record-setting week in 1982.[35] More than 36 million people have filed for unemployment, and economists estimate that more another 5 to 10 million Americans could be unemployed before this crisis ends.[36] Small businesses have already begun shuttering, and tax revenues for 2020 will inherently be depressed—providing the government far less money to spend on recovery efforts.[37] Homelessness, hunger, and extreme poverty could all reach catastrophic levels. "The severity of this sudden economic crisis will profoundly shape the lives and spending patterns of Americans for years (and perhaps even decades) to come, as they grapple with these disastrous consequences."[38]

Though these effects may not be avoidable, planners and policy-makers need a way to understand (and plan for) the relationships between seemingly disparate nodes of the operating environment. Such strategic thinking "is a cognitive process used to design and sustain an organization's competitive advantage. It is a holistic method that leverages hindsight, insight, and foresight and precedes strategy or plan development. Strategic thinking relies on an intuitive, visual, and creative process that explores the global security environment to synthesize emerging patterns, issues, connections, and opportunities."[39]

This type of thinking is essentially the opposite of the traditional analyses taught throughout professional military education. Joint doctrine currently employs "systematic" thinking, which emphasizes separating the individual pieces of what is being studied into manageable parts. This emphasis is why PMESII frameworks are so widely utilized throughout military planning. By contrast, *systemic* thinking focuses on the interaction between the various nodes being studied. Instead of breaking the system down into smaller chunks, it actually *expands* to include all actors, factors, and forces working upon a system—often resulting in a complex systems map of the operating environment. For this reason, systemic thinking is frequently more effective in solving the most difficult problems—complex issues involving numerous, interdependent variables.[40]

By utilizing systemic thinking, defense policy can also be analyzed according to how resilient it is within each of the various domains that encompass all large, complex systems:

- Physical Domain (P): analyzing resilience in the physical domain often entails a measurement of the level of robustness, redundancy, and modularity of a particular system;
- Information Domain (I): resilience in the information domain consists of what we know about the

physical domain and includes data use, transfer, analysis, and storage;
- Cognitive Domain (C): this has to do with human processes—i.e., translating, sharing, and acting upon knowledge to make, communicate, and implement decisions throughout the system; and
- Social Domain (S): this involves interactions and entities that influence how decisions are made, including government regulations, religions, cultures, and languages.[41]

Continuing the use of the coronavirus pandemic as a case study, defense policy that attempts to meet this challenge would be analyzed according to the physical, information, cognitive, and social (PICS) domains listed above. For example, current methods of thinking about individual nodes of a system result in large warehouses of PPE on hand in the event of a global pandemic. This worldwide staging of emergency equipment would meet the requirements of a resilient policy in the physical domain—which is where most resilience analyses stop. Systemic thinking, on the other hand, might allow decision-makers to foresee the PPE supply chain and equipment-tracking challenges in the information domain due to large portions of the population under quarantine. Today, countries around the globe are struggling with critical shortages in medical supplies and equipment, and "these shortages threaten to leave curable patients untreated and health professionals exposed, with potentially grave consequences."[42] Similarly, resilience analyses in the cognitive and social domains might have prepared policy-makers for the challenges associated with a population that does not want to abide by quarantine regulations or differences in how political parties might approach the crisis.

This is not to say that defense leaders should have predicted when this Grey Rhino might have charged, but in today's global security environment, where defense professionals cannot claim expertise in every conceivable challenge, planners must develop policy that is resilient in the face of unknown unknowns. That is, knowing that a global pandemic was certainly possible, resilient defense policy should have been developed to mitigate the second- and third-order effects certain to be caused—whenever the event might occur. This mitigation is best achieved by ensuring policy resilience within all of the domains present in complex, interconnected systems.

Policy resilience is based on the recognition that the strategic environment has changed and that civil structures, resources, and services are the first line of defense for modern societies. Resilient policies involve the whole of government with an integrated private sector and act as a deterrent against adversaries, while cushioning the blow from non-actor threats (e.g., global pandemics). "Resilient societies also have a greater propensity to bounce back after crises: they tend to recover more rapidly and are able to return to pre-crisis functional levels with greater ease than less resilient societies."[43]

To assist in the creation of such resilient defense policy, table 1 combines the various aspects of resilience across the top (prepare, absorb, recover, and adapt—PARA), and the domains that encompass all large, complex systems (physical, information, cognitive, and social—PICS) down the left side.[44] This table provides a measure of policy resilience for defense policy planners to consider.

Returning to the discussion of Black Swan and Grey Rhino events, the PARA-PICS framework allows for defense policy to be focused on the type of events it is meant to address. For example, policies intended to address Grey Rhinos—pandemics, climate change, and artificial intelligence—would have more of an empha-

sis in the "Prepare" and "Absorb" aspects of policy resilience, as policy-makers attempt to dodge and deflect an unanticipated charge from a known threat. However, since Black Swan events are inherently unknown, very little can be done to prepare for such an event. Instead, resilient defense policy here would emphasize the absorption and recovery from the unavoidable adverse effects to come.

Conclusion

The final effects of the coronavirus are as of yet unknown. What is known, however, is that American defense policy should undergo a significant evolution in response to the second- and third-order effects of an enemy that cannot be seen or addressed with traditional military might.

To meet the various challenges of a period of uncertainty, including those posed by Black Swans and

Table 1. **Defense Policy Resilience Considerations (PARA-PICS)**

Prepare	Absorb	Recover	Adapt
Physical			
Can the policy be used to prepare for numerous potential adverse events?	Does the policy reduce the time needed to reverse adverse effects?	Does the policy reduce the time needed until full functionality is restored?	Can the policy be adapted following an event to allow for improvement?
Which potential events will cause the greatest effect on the population?			Does the policy help the population to adapt to a "new normal?"
Information			
How well does the policy detect the emergence of a range of potential threats?	How well does the policy detect when and what damage has occurred?	Does the policy minimize the time required to gather and disseminate damage info?	Does the policy allow for the detection of trends, or changing threats and vulnerability levels?
Cognitive			
Has an adequate range of scenarios been considered for this policy?	Can the policy be implemented quickly in the event of an adverse event?	Do specific contingency plans exist?	What is the flexibility of policy-makers to update governing regulations to address changes?
Does the policy help prepare individuals to disseminate information about potential threats?		Does the policy address the second- and third-order effects of a range of potential threats?	
Social			
Have adequate resources been allocated to preparing for a range of events?	Does the policy address adverse effects on population due to indirect effects in addition to primary threat?	What resources will be required to restore full functionality?	What is the anticipated willingness of the populace to accept changes to standard procedures?

Grey Rhinos, forward-thinking military planners need to develop defense policy that is resilient enough to prepare, absorb, recover, and adapt to a myriad of adverse events in all of the domains present in large, complex systems (physical, information, cognitive, and social). Consequently, some aspects of defense policy should remain in place—such as the current focus on capabilities-based planning and an emphasis on jointness. Military planning should not be directed at avoiding specific Black Swan events, as they are by definition, unpredictable. Nor should policies rely on the ability to forecast when a Grey Rhino might occur. However, this analysis suggests that defense policy needs increased emphasis on second- and third-order effects, which can be identified by expanding the aperture to include all actors, factors, and forces present within the system. "Much of what we have to learn is not about the science of prediction but the art of timely response."[45]

As professional football player turned MIT mathematics professor John Urschel argues, although Black Swans and Grey Rhinos are difficult to predict, "improbable things happen all the time in life. It's just extremely hard to predict which improbable things will occur."[46]

NOTES

1. "Coronavirus Disease 2019 (COVID-19)," Centers for Disease Control and Prevention, https://www.cdc.gov/coronavirus/2019-ncov/cases-updates/cases-in-us.html.

2. N. N. Taleb, *The Black Swan: The Impact of the Highly Improbable*, vol. 2 (New York: Random House, 2007).

3. Michele Wucker, "No, the Coronavirus Pandemic Wasn't an 'Unforeseen Problem,'" *Washington Post*, March 17, 2020, https://www.washingtonpost.com/outlook/2020/03/17/no-coronavirus-pandemic-wasnt-an-unforseen-problem/.

4. Wucker, "No, the Coronavirus Pandemic Wasn't an 'Unforeseen Problem.'"

5. Lisa Monaco, "The Coronavirus Shows Why the U.S. Must Make Pandemic Disease a National Security Priority," *Lawfare Blog*, February 7, 2020, https://www.lawfareblog.com/coronavirus-shows-why-us-must-make-pandemic-disease-national-security-priority.

6. Leah Rocketto, "Bill Gates Says a Deadly Flu Epidemic Is One of the Biggest Threats to Humanity," *Insider*, December 30, 2018, https://www.insider.com/deadly-flu-epidemic-biggest-threat-bill-gates-2018-learnings-2018-12.

7. Rocketto, "Bill Gates Says."

8. Daniel R. Coats, "Worldwide Threat Assessment of the US Intelligence Community," Director of National Intelligence, January 29, 2019, https://www.dni.gov/files/ODNI/documents/2019-ATA-SFR---SSCI.pdf.

9. Gregory D. Koblentz and Michael Hunzeker, "National Security in the Age of Pandemics," *Defense One*, April 3, 2020, "https://www.defenseone.com/ideas/2020/04/national-security-age-pandemics/164365/.

10. Monaco, "The Coronavirus Shows Why."

11. "Coronavirus Disease 2019 (COVID-19)."

12. "Coronavirus Disease 2019 (COVID-19)."

13. James Blake, "Covid-19 and Conflict Zones: Prepare Now or Face Catastrophe," *New Security Beat* (The Woodrow Wilson International Center for Scholars, April 6, 2020), https://www.newsecuritybeat.org/2020/04/covid-19-conflict-zones-prepare-face-catastrophe/.

14. "Coronavirus Disease (COVID-19) Pandemic," World Health Organization, May 15, 2020, https://www.who.int/emergencies/diseases/novel-coronavirus-2019.

15. Henry Wilkins Henry and Danielle Paquette, "Terror in the Countryside, Coronavirus in the City: In Burkina Faso, There's No Safe Haven," *Washington Post*, April 15, 2020, https://www.washingtonpost.com/world/africa/terror-in-the-countryside-coronavirus-in-the-city-in-burkina-faso-theres-no-safe-haven/2020/04/14/12979bda-783f-11ea-a311-adb1344719a9_story.html.

16. Blake, "Covid-19 and Conflict Zones."

17. Lisa Monaco, "Pandemic Disease Is a Threat to National Security," *Foreign Affairs*, March 3, 2020, https://www.foreignaffairs.com/articles/2020-03-03/pandemic-disease-threat-national-security.

18. David Barno and Nora Bensahel, "After the Pandemic: America and National Security in a Changed World." *War on the Rocks*, March 31, 2020, https://warontherocks.com/2020/03/after-the-pandemic-america-and-national-security-in-a-changed-world/.

19. Barno and Bensahe, "After the Pandemic."

20. Koblentz and Hunzeker, "National Security in the Age of Pandemics."

21. Barno and Bensahel, "After the Pandemic."

22. Benjamin Jensen, "When Systems Fail: What Pandemics and Cyberspace Tell Us about the Future of National Security," *War on the Rocks*, April 9, 2020, https://warontherocks.com/2020/04/when-systems-fail-what-pandemics-and-cyberspace-tell-us-about-the-future-of-national-security/.

23. Department of Defense, *Space Policy (DoDD 3100.10)* (Washington, DC: Office of the Secretary of Defense, Policy, 2012), 12.

24. Defense Science Board, *Task Force Report: Resilient Military Systems and the Advanced Cyber Threat* (Washington, DC: Office of the Under Secretary of Defense for Acquisition, Technology and Logistics, 2013), 2.

25. D. A. Eisenberg, I. Linkov, J. Park, M. Bates, C. Fox-Lent, and T. Seager, "Resilience Metrics: Lessons from Military Doctrines," *Solutions* 5, no. 5 (2014): 76–87.

26. Eisenberg et al., "Resilience Metrics."

27. "Resilient America," The National Academies of Science, Engineering, and Medicine, n.d., https://www.nationalacademies.org/resilient-america/about.

28. Eisenberg et al., "Resilience Metrics."

29. Eisenberg et al., "Resilience Metrics."

30. Tony Zinni and Tony Koltz, *Leading the Charge: Leadership Lessons from the Battlefield to the Boardroom* (New York: Palgrave Macmillan, 2009), 28.

31. Jensen, "When Systems Fail."

32. Jensen, "When Systems Fail."

33. Jensen, "When Systems Fail."

34. J. D. Lawrence and J. L. Murdock, *Political, Military, Economic, Social, Infrastructure, Information (PMESII) Effects Forecasting for Course of Action (COA) Evaluation* (Menlo Park, CA: SRI International, 2009).

35. Barno and Bensahel, "After the Pandemic."

36. Paul Davidson, "Another 3 Million Americans File Jobless Claims as Layoffs Continue to Ravage Economy," *USA Today*, May 14, 2020, https://www.usatoday.com/story/money/2020/05/14/coronavirus-3-million-workers-file-jobless-claims-layoffs-continue/5188141002/.

37. Barno and Bensahel, "After the Pandemic."

38. Barno and Bensahel, "After the Pandemic."

39. Daniel H. McCauley, "Rediscovering the Art of Strategic Thinking," *Joint Force Quarterly* 81 (April 2016): 29.

40. Will Atkins, Sean Yarroll, and Dong Hyung Cho, "More Cowbell: A Case Study in System Dynamics for Information Operations," *Air and Space Power Journal* (Summer 2020): 20–35.

41. Eisenberg et al., "Resilience Metrics."

42. Stephen Biddle and Tami Davis Biddle, "Wartime Lessons for Industrial Mobilization in a Time of Pandemic," *War on the Rocks*, April 3, 2020, Retrieved from https://warontherocks.com/2020/04/wartime-lessons-for-industrial-mobilization-in-a-time-of-pandemic/.

43. Wolf-Diether Roepke, "Resilience: The First Line of Defence," *NATO Review*, February 27, 2019, https://www.nato.int/docu/review/articles/2019/02/27/resilience-the-first-line-of-defence/index.html.

44. This chart pulls heavily from previous work developing resilience metrics for military use. See Eisenberg et al., "Resilience Metrics."

45. D. Gouré, "Hunting for Black Swans: Military Power in a Time of Strategic Uncertainty" (Lexington Institute, Air Force Strategy Conference, June 2008), 8.

46. John Urschel and Louisa Thomas, *Mind and Matter: A Life in Math and Football* (New York: Penguin Press, 2019), 67.

Afterword

EDITORS OF *AMERICAN DEFENSE POLICY* (9TH ED.)

In June 2019, we, the editors of this volume, assembled in the McDermott Library at the US Air Force Academy to plan the ninth edition of *American Defense Policy*. It had been fourteen years since *American Defense Policy, 8th ed.* was published and much had changed for American security studies. While the eighth edition responded to the September 11 attacks and the ongoing counterinsurgency wars in Iraq and Afghanistan, the landscape in 2019 was decidedly different.

The threats from non-state actors had not diminished; indeed, the United States was entering its eighteenth year in Afghanistan while an unspecified number of troops remained in Iraq. The Islamic State, al-Qaeda, and Hezbollah continued as major threats to security in hotspots across Africa, the Middle East, and Asia. At the same time the United States remained embroiled in operations to subdue non-state actors, great-power politics was again a pressing issue. Balance-of-power competition reminiscent of the Cold War was on the rise. Russia was perfecting grey-zone operations, instigating trouble with invasions of Ukraine, and siding with President Bashar al-Assad in the Syrian civil war. Meanwhile, China was steadily building its military forces and making aggressive moves in the South China Sea, not to mention enacting assertive economic policies that threatened US primacy. And while the rise of Russia and China threatened the status of the United States as a global hegemon, smaller states such as North Korea, now part of the nuclear club of nations, and Iran continued to agitate global security with increasingly sophisticated weapons programs.

Beyond these more "traditional" threats were new issues that strained the existing international system. Cyberwarfare joined the traditional warfighting domains and threatened to turn power grids and economic systems into new avenues of warfare. Influence warfare went to new heights as adversaries used social media and artificial intelligence to target civil society itself, creating false information and undermining democratic institutions, such as elections. The effects of climate change created conditions for conflict over scare resources and produced unmanageable refugee crises. All the while, a new administration pursued a significant departure from traditional American engagement, tearing up nuclear, economic, and climate accords, and threatening to withdraw the United States from NATO. With the announcement in the midst of a pandemic that the United States would cease funding and leave the World Health Organization, the administration appeared to be willing to have the United States "go it alone." The future of the liberal world order was in peril.

As editors, we wrestled with how to encapsulate the enormity of the expanding mission facing US defense policy. Each of these global issues was pressing, but the US capacity to counter each was nearly impossible. It was questionable if the United States possessed the resources, manpower, and political will to counter all the myriad pressures. As one of our editors remarked, it was as if the United States was playing a game of Twister—the classic Milton Bradley game where players stretch themselves into seemingly impossible contortions to keep their hands and feet on their assigned circles. Left foot red: the United States deploys troops to Syria to support operations against the Islamic State; right hand green: the US State Department declared that the Chinese government is committing genocide against the Uyghur people. The number and complexity of the moves across the board threatened to topple the United States.

As we imagined Uncle Sam contorted across the Twister mat, we considered the role of the United States in the world. The unipolar moment seemed to be gone or at least fading, but what was next? In this time of uncertainty, what was the role of the United States? Was it to be the world's defender of democracy or the global police officer? Should the United States prioritize protecting its homeland and invigorating the American economy? It seemed as though the United States may have been going through an identity crisis.

Adding to this crisis, technological and societal changes were sending shock waves through the American defense system. Although it could persist in the near term, the defense system had become so large and cumbersome that it struggled to adapt to and incorporate urgently needed revolutionary changes. Under this pressure, policy was desperately lagging, and there existed a largely unspoken recognition that the United States was still trying to adapt mid-twentieth-century solutions to twenty-first-century questions.

In this game of Twister, the United States was desperately trying to reach down to tamp out crises across the globe and to reach up to integrate the next ground-breaking technology, all the while bending over to conceal problems, such as shortfalls in the defense budget or an armed force exhausted by nearly two decades of continuous conflict. These types of maneuvers could only be sustained for a short time before everyone in the game collapsed. We worried that if policy-makers did not change the game, or play it differently, the United States would lose the next war or fade away as China ascended to a global hegemonic status.

With this analogy in mind, our editorial team designed the scope of the book to capture the complexity of the situation and the competing goals of defense policy. To provide insight into the fundamental drivers of defense policy, we sought classic works that have provided the theories and values that have influenced how the United States envisions its place within an ever-changing international environment. To shed light on the complexity of the policy-making process, we looked for innovative articles that described the multiplicity of players, challenges to the profession of arms, and the tensions that arise as smaller budgets must straddle larger mission sets. Finally, we wanted to portray how the United States adapts to the rapidly changing security environment and the disruptive technologies that typify the emerging battlefield.

These were important matters, and it was a lofty goal to capture all of this in one volume. We debated which works best capture the United States' values and grand strategies. We discussed how to include the innumerable impacts of the American defense policy-making process, ranging from women in combat, the politicization of the military, and the use of contractors and the National Guard to supplement active duty armed forces. Lastly, we struggled to include all the technological innovations of the past fifteen years that revolutionized the battlefield while making space for the traditional military missions. The gap was vast and widening: nuclear weapons remained a bedrock function of the US military while the Space Force was just standing up.

We were well into the book when a Grey Rhino trampled across the globe in the form of COVID-19 (see the Epilogue). As the virus brought the world to its knees, we pondered what this pandemic would mean for defense policy. It could change everything—how the United States conceptualized both allies and enemies, how it deployed troops and utilized resources, and how it utilized technologies. On the other hand, COVID-19 might not change anything, and defense policy would continue on the same trajectory.

For the editing team, the pandemic confirmed at least one thing: there was no way we could cover every important topic in this one volume. Although we wanted to delve into theories of great-power rivalries, rising powers, and continuing non-state threats, we would need to carefully cull the literature for pieces that gave an overview of the complex environment. We wanted to cover the conventional battlespace, weapons of mass destruction, and the emerging space domain, but we would need to choose selections that provided a more general sense of the multifaceted military theaters. While we dreamed of articles covering a vast array of emerging technology, such as hypersonic weapons, quantum computing, or biotechnology, we realized we would need to be content with articles that provided a taste of innovations in the conduct of war while leaving the reader eager to do more research.

This volume, in sum, is an attempt to do all of the above. We hope it conveys the complexity of defense policy as the United States twists and bends to meet myriad expectations. It is meant to portray the vast goals and strategies that underlie policy, the competing missions that vie for the attention of the US Armed Forces, and the constraints that limit what is possible to achieve in foreign policy. Finally, it is designed to give students of defense policy a taste of the intricacies of the process and a hunger to be part of shaping future outcomes.

About the Contributors

GORDON ADAMS

Gordon Adams is a Distinguished Fellow at the Stimson Center and professor in the US Foreign Policy program at the School of International Service, American University. He has published widely on defense and national security policy, the defense policy process, and national security budgets. For five years he was associate Director for National Security and International Affairs at the Office of Management and Budget, the senior White House budget official for national security.

JOHN R. ALLEN

General John R. Allen (Ret) currently serves as the eighth president of the Brookings Institution. He is a retired US Marine Corps four-star general and former commander of the NATO International Security Assistance Force and US Forces in Afghanistan. Prior to his role at Brookings, Allen served as senior advisor to the secretary of defense on Middle East Security and as special presidential envoy to the Global Coalition to Counter ISIL. Allen is the first Marine to command a theater of war, as well as the first Marine to be named commandant of midshipmen for the US Naval Academy.

WILL ATKINS

Lieutenant Colonel Will Atkins currently serves as an instructor of Political Science at the United States Air Force Academy. He began his career as a C-130 Navigator and Weapons Officer, serving six operational deployments to Iraq and Afghanistan as both an aircrew member and political-military strategist. In this capacity, he advised the Afghan president and national security advisor during the development of that nation's first National Security Strategy. Additionally, he previously served as a nonresident fellow at the Center for Strategic and International Studies (CSIS)–Pacific Forum, and an adjunct fellow at the American Security Project.

DEBORAH D. AVANT

Deborah Avant is the Sié Chéou-Kang Chair for International Security and Diplomacy and Director of the Sié Chéou-Kang Center for International Security and Diplomacy at the Josef Korbel School of International Studies, University of Denver. Her research (funded by the Institute for Global Conflict and Cooperation, the John D. and Catherine T. MacArthur Foundation, and the Smith Richardson Foundation, among others) has focused on civil-military relations, military change, and the politics of controlling violence. Avant serves on numerous governing and editorial boards and has testified before congressional committees and the Commission for Wartime Contracting.

MICHAEL BARNETT

Michael Barnett is University Professor of International Affairs and Political Science at George Washington University. His research interests include the Middle East, humanitarian action, global governance, global ethics, and the United Nations. His current research projects range from international paternalism, to the changing architecture of global governance, to the relationship between human rights and humanitarianism. Barnett is a member of the Council on Foreign Relations and the recipient of many grants and awards for his research.

SALLY BARON

Sally Baron currently holds the Philip J. Erdle Endowed Chair in Engineering Science at the United States Air Force Academy. She previously held the Holland Coors Distinguished Professor position, in which she taught both management and astronautics and published frequently on evolving acquisitions-related defense policy, including commercial-off-the-shelf product management. She received her PhD in Industrial Engineering from Stanford University in 2002, and her career includes time with the Central Intelligence Agency and National Reconnaissance Office. She is widely published and is the recipient of multiple awards, including the CIA's Exceptional Performance Award and the Carl Janssen Award for Teaching Excellence.

JEFF J. S. BLACK

Jeff J. S. Black received his PhD in Political Theory and International Relations from Boston College, and he teaches at St. John's College in Annapolis, Maryland. He has served as a Resident Fellow in Civil-Military Relations at the Stockdale Center for Ethical Leadership of the US Naval Academy and as a subject-matter expert for Coming Home: Dialogues on the Moral, Psychological, and Spiritual Impacts of War. He also served as Associate Dean for the Graduate Program at St. John's from 2011 to 2015.

JESSICA BLANKSHAIN

Jessica Blankshain is Assistant Professor of National Security Affairs at the US Naval War College in Newport, Rhode Island. She has a PhD in Political Economy and Government from Harvard University, and her research interests include civil-military relations, bureaucratic politics, and organizational economics. She teaches the Leadership Concepts and Policy Analysis subcourses, as well as electives on Central Challenges of American National Security and Civil-Military Relations. Blankshain is a former graduate fellow of the Rumsfeld Foundation and a former research fellow at the Belfer Center for Science and International Affairs.

HAL BRANDS

Hal Brands is a resident scholar at the American Enterprise Institute, where he studies US foreign policy and defense strategy. Concurrently, Brands is the Henry A. Kissinger Distinguished Professor of Global Affairs at the Johns Hopkins School of Advanced International Studies. Brands has previously worked as special assistant to the secretary of defense for strategic planning and lead writer for the National Defense Strategy Commission. He was a Council on Foreign Relations International Affairs Fellow from 2015 to 2016. He has also consulted with a range of government offices and agencies in the intelligence and national security communities.

BEN BUCHANAN

Ben Buchanan is Assistant Teaching Professor at Georgetown University's School of Foreign Service, where he conducts research on the intersection of cybersecurity and statecraft. He also serves as a Senior Faculty Fellow at Georgetown's Center for Security and Emerging Technology. In addition, he has written journal articles and peer-reviewed papers on artificial intelligence, attributing cyber attacks, deterrence in cyber operations, cryptography, election cybersecurity, and the spread of malicious code between nations and non-state actors.

DALE C. COPELAND

Dale Copeland is Professor of International Relations, with a focus on security studies and international political economy. His research interests include the origins of economic interdependence between great powers; the logic of reputation-building; bargaining and coercion theory; the interconnection between trade, finance, and militarized behavior; and the impact of the rise and decline of economic and military power on state behavior. He has been the recipient of numerous awards, including MacArthur and Mellon Fellowships and a postdoctoral fellowship at the Belfer Center for Science and International Affairs at Harvard University.

EVERETT CARL DOLMAN

Everett Dolman is Professor of Comparative Military Studies at the US Air Force School of Advanced Air and Space Studies, where he has been identified as Air University's first space theorist. Dolman began his career as an intelligence analyst for the National Security Agency, and moved to the US Space Command in 1986. In 1991, he received the Director of Central Intelligence's Outstanding Intelligence Analyst award. Dolman is also co-founder and managing editor of *Astropolitics: The International Journal of Space Power and Policy*.

JEFFREY DONNITHORNE

Colonel Jeffrey W. Donnithorne is the Commandant of the Air Force's School of Advanced Air and Space Studies as well as a professor of Strategy and Security Studies. He began his career as an F-15E Strike Eagle WSO, serving two operational tours with four combat deployments and over 300 combat hours in Iraq and Afghanistan. During his time at Air University, Donnithorne has served as the Commander of the 31st Student Squadron at Squadron Officer

School, the Director of the Center for Strategy and Technology and its Blue Horizons program, and most recently as Air University's Chief Academic Officer. He received his PhD from Georgetown University.

DANIEL W. DREZNER

Daniel Drezner is Professor of International Politics at the Fletcher School of Law and Diplomacy at Tufts University. He is also a nonresident senior fellow at the Brookings Institution and a contributing editor at the *Washington Post*. He specializes in international politics, international finance and monetary policy, and globalization and trade. He has previously held positions with the Civic Education Project, the RAND Corporation, and the US Department of the Treasury.

JOSEPH F. DUNFORD, JR.

General Joseph F. Dunford, Jr., (Ret) is a resident Senior Fellow with Harvard Kennedy School's Belfer Center for Science and International Affairs. Dunford served as the 19th Chairman of the Joint Chiefs of Staff, the nation's highest-ranking military officer, and the principal military advisor to the president, secretary of defense, and National Security Council from October 1, 2015, through September 30, 2019. Previously, he was the 36th Commandant of the United States Marine Corps and Commander of the International Security Assistance Force and US Forces in Afghanistan. A graduate of the US Army Ranger School and US Army War College, Dunford earned master's degrees in Government from Georgetown University and in International Relations from the Fletcher School of Law and Diplomacy at Tufts University.

COLIN DUECK

Colin Dueck is a Professor in the Schar School of Policy and Government at George Mason University, and a nonresident fellow at the American Enterprise Institute. His current research focus is on the relationship between party politics, presidential leadership, American conservatism, and US foreign policy strategies. He has worked as a foreign policy adviser on several Republican presidential campaigns and acted as a consultant for the Department of State, the Department of Defense, and the National Security Council.

ERIC EDELMAN

Ambassador Eric Edelman is a counselor at the Center for Strategic and Budgetary Assessments and the Roger Hertog Distinguished Practitioner-in-Residence at the Philip Merrill Center for Strategic Studies at Johns Hopkins School of Advanced International Studies. He has led organizations providing analysis, strategy, policy development, security services, trade advocacy, public outreach, citizen services, and congressional relations. Edelman was twice an ambassador and was formerly an undersecretary of defense for policy.

MARTHA FINNEMORE

Martha Finnemore is University Professor of Political Science and International Affairs at George Washington University in Washington, DC. Her research focuses on global governance, international organizations, ethics, and social theory. She is a Fellow of the American Academy of Arts and Sciences, has been a visiting research fellow at the Brookings Institution and Stanford University.

LAWRENCE FREEDMAN

Lawrence Freedman is a visiting professor at the Blavatnik School of Government, University of Oxford. He was Professor of War Studies at King's College London from 1982 to 2014, and was Vice-Principal from 2003 to 2013. Freedman has written extensively on nuclear strategy and the Cold War, as well as commenting regularly on contemporary security issues. Elected a Fellow of the British Academy in 1995 and awarded the Commander of Order the British Empire in 1996, he was appointed Official Historian of the Falklands Campaign in 1997.

FRANCIS FUKUYAMA

Francis Fukuyama is Olivier Nomellini Senior Fellow at Stanford University, where he also serves as Mosbacher Director of the Center on Democracy, Development, and the Rule of Law and Director of the Ford Dorsey Master's in International Public Policy.

MICHAEL D. GAMBONE

Michael D. Gambone received his doctorate from the University of Chicago in 1993. His books include *Long Journeys Home: American Veterans of World War II, Korea, and Vietnam* (2017). He has also published articles in the *Journal of Military Ethics*, *Armed Forces & Society*, the *Journal of Third World Studies*, and the *Yale Journal of International Studies*. Gambone served as a site security specialist in Mosul, Iraq, in 2006 and as an officer in the 82nd Airborne Division from 1985 to 1988. He is Professor of History at Kutztown University of Pennsylvania.

LYNNE CHANDLER GARCIA

Lynne Chandler Garcia is Associate Professor of Political Science at the US Air Force Academy. Her areas of research include civil discourse, empathy and efficacy in political behavior, foreign policy, military operations, and the art of pedagogy for underprivileged learners. Before coming to the Air Force Academy, she served as a military analyst at the Combat Studies Institute, Fort Leavenworth, Kansas, where she co-authored a series of eleven books covering US Army operations in Afghanistan and Iraq. She received her PhD at the University of Maryland, College Park.

BISHOP GARRISON

Bishop Garrison is co-founder and president of the Rainey Center, a public policy research organization in Washington, DC. He also serves as Director of National Security Outreach at Human Rights First. He previously served as interim executive director of the Truman National Security Project and Truman Center for National Policy. Garrison graduated from West Point in 2002 and served two US Army deployments in Iraq, earning two Bronze Stars, a Combat Action Badge, and a Meritorious Service Medal. He served in national security positions in the Obama administration and as a deputy foreign policy adviser on Hillary Clinton's presidential campaign. He is a graduate of the College of William and Mary Law School.

ERIK GARTZKE

Erik Gartzke is Professor of Political Science and Director of the Center for Peace and Security Studies at the University of California, San Diego. Gartzke's research focuses on war, peace, and international institutions. He has written on cyberwar, trade and conflict, and the effects of economic development, system structure and climate change on war. Gartzke's research has been published in numerous academic journals and edited volumes.

MAURO GILLI

Mauro Gilli is Senior Researcher in Military Technology and International Security at the Center for Security Studies at the Swiss Federal Institute of Technology, Zurich. His research interests include military technology, diffusion of military innovations, political economy of national security, rise and fall of great powers, and more generally security studies. He has been a consultant for a leading aerospace defense company and for the department of defense of a NATO country.

ROBERT GILPIN

Robert Gilpin was a scholar of international political economy and the Professor Emeritus of Politics and International Affairs at the Woodrow Wilson School of Public and International Affairs at Princeton University. He additionally held the Eisenhower Professorship, also at Princeton. Gilpin specialized in political economy and international relations, especially the effect of multinational corporations on state autonomy.

T. X. HAMMES

T. X. Hammes is Distinguished Research Fellow at the Institute for National Strategic Studies at the National Defense University. He specializes in future strategic concepts, humanitarian assistance and disaster relief, and insurgency and irregular warfare. Prior to his retirement from active duty, Hammes served for thirty years in the US Marine Corps and commanded an intelligence battalion, an infantry battalion, and the Chemical Biological Incident Response Force.

MICHAEL C. HOROWITZ

Michael C. Horowitz is Professor of Political Science and the Interim Director of Perry World House at the University of Pennsylvania. His research interests include technology and global politics, military innovation, the role of leaders in international politics, and forecasting. Horowitz previously worked for the Office of the Undersecretary of Defense for Policy in the Department of Defense. He is affiliated with the Foreign Policy Research Institute, the Center for Strategic and International Studies, and the Center for a New American Security.

G. JOHN IKENBERRY

G. John Ikenberry is the Albert G. Milbank Professor of Politics and International Affairs at Princeton University in the Department of Politics and the Woodrow Wilson School of Public and International Affairs. He is also Co-Director of Princeton's Center for International Security Studies. Ikenberry served as a member of the Policy Planning Staff in 1991–1992, as a member of an advisory group at the State Department in 2003–2004, and as a member of the Council on Foreign Relations Task Force on US-European relations, the so-called Kissinger-Summers commission.

BRUCE JONES

Bruce Jones is Senior Fellow and Director of the Project on International Order and Strategy at Brookings. Between 2014 and 2019 he served as Deputy Director and then Vice President and Director of the Foreign Policy Program, and earlier as Director of the New York University Center on International Cooperation. His scholarship examines the evolution of the multilateral order, including changing great-power relations and global governance. He served with the UN in field assignments in Kosovo and the Middle East, and as the Deputy Director for the UN's High-Level Panel on Threats, Challenges, and Change.

TIM KANE

Tim Kane is the JP Conte Fellow in Immigration at the Hoover Institution at Stanford University. He specializes in economic growth, immigration, and national security. Kane's latest book is *Total Volunteer Force: Lessons from the US Military on Leadership Culture and Talent Management*. Kane served twice as a senior economist at the Joint Economic Committee of the United States Congress. A graduate of the US Air Force Academy, he served as an intelligence officer in the US Air Force with two tours of duty overseas.

CHERYL A. KEARNEY

Brigadier General Cheryl Kearney, US Air Force (Ret), was the Permanent Professor and Department Head of the Political Science Department at the United States Air Force Academy from 2007 to 2019. She was a career intelligence officer serving at the Supreme Headquarters Allied Powers Europe, Belgium; Misawa Air Base, Japan; Torrejon Air Base, Spain; and Baghdad, Iraq. She is a Reserve Officer Training Corps graduate from the University of Pittsburgh; earned her master's degrees from the Naval Postgraduate School and National War College, and earned her PhD in Government from Georgetown University. In 2016, she was a Supreme Court Fellow and continues to serve as a Commissioner for the Supreme Court Fellows Program.

DAVID KILCULLEN

David Kilcullen is Professor of International and Political Studies, School of Humanities and Social Sciences, University of New South Wales, Canberra, and Professor of Practice in Global Security, Arizona State University. He is a renowned counterinsurgency expert and the author of the bestselling books *The Dragons and the Snakes: How the Rest Learned to Fight the West*, *The Accidental Guerrilla*, and *Counterinsurgency*, in addition to a number of other publications.

MICHAEL P. KREUZER

Lieutenant Colonel Michael P. Kreuzer is Assistant Professor of Airpower Strategy at Air University, Maxwell Air Force Base, Alabama. He is a career intelligence officer who has served as the Director of Intelligence of the Kapisa Provincial Reconstruction Team in Afghanistan (Operation ENDURING FREEDOM 2010), the Director of Intelligence for Task Force Air (Operation INHERENT RESOLVE 2020), as well as serving as the Director of Operations for Distributed Ground Station 1 and the Director of US Air Force Intelligence Officer Formal Training.

MIRIAM KRIEGER

Colonel Miriam Krieger is Permanent Professor and Department Head of the Department of Political Science at the US Air Force Academy. She received her PhD from Georgetown University in 2018 with a focus on civil-military relations and international security and has published on military diplomacy, foreign military assistance, and military coups. Before coming to the Academy, she served as Chief of the Strategic Initiatives Division for the Chairman of the Joint Chiefs and flew F-16s in the Republic of Korea, Florida, and Arizona. She was both a Truman and Marshall Scholar, and was the winner of both the Chief of Staff of the Air Force's Prestigious PhD and the Wilma Vaught Visionary Leadership Award.

SETH LAZAR

Seth Lazar is a philosopher at the Australian National University. He has worked on the ethics of war and moral decision-making under risk, and now on the moral and political philosophy of artificial intelligence, publishing papers and books with the world's leading philosophy journals and presses. He is Head of the School of Philosophy at the Australian National University and Project Lead of the recently launched Humanising Machine Intelligence Grand Challenge project (hmi.anu.edu.au), which unites philosophers, computer scientists, and social scientists in the goal of developing moral machine intelligence, grounded in democratically legitimate values.

KEIR A. LIEBER

Keir A. Lieber is Associate Professor in the Edmund A. Walsh School of Foreign Service and Director of the Center for Security Studies and Security Studies Program. He also holds a joint appointment in the Department of Government. As a member of the inaugural class of Andrew Carnegie Fellows, Lieber received a major research grant from the Carnegie Corporation of New York to support his project, "Nuclear Weapons and the New Era of Strategic Instability."

CONWAY LIN

Lieutenant Colonel Conway Lin is a 2000 graduate of the United States Military Academy and is an officer in the US Army Signal Corps. He has contributed to various publications related to economics and national defense. He has a Master of Public Policy from the Harvard Kennedy School and served as an assistant professor in the Department of Social Sciences at West Point. He is currently assigned to the National Security Agency at Fort Meade, Maryland.

JON R. LINDSAY

Jon Lindsay is Assistant Professor of Digital Media and Global Affairs at the Munk School of Global Affairs and Public Policy and Department of Political Science at the University of Toronto. He specializes in information technology and military power, cybersecurity, and cross-domain deterrence. He has also served in the US Navy with assignments in Europe, Latin America, and the Middle East.

AUSTIN LONG

Austin Long, a nonresident Foreign Policy Research Institute Senior Fellow, is a senior political scientist at the nonprofit, nonpartisan RAND Corporation. His research interests include low-intensity conflict, intelligence, military operations, nuclear forces, military innovation, and the political economy of national security. Long previously was an assistant professor at Columbia University's School of International and Public Affairs. Long has also served as a consultant to the Massachusetts Institute of Technology's Lincoln Laboratory, Science Applications International Corporation, the Department of Defense's Office of Net Assessment, and the International Crisis Group.

JOSEPH S. LUPA

Lieutenant Colonel Joseph S. Lupa, Jr., is an operations analyst in the Air Force. He has master's degrees in Operations Research from the Air Force Institute of Technology and in Statistics from Ohio State University. He has held positions in Personnel and Operational Test and on the Joint Staff in Global Force Management. He is currently assigned to the Combined Air Operations Center at Al Udeid Air Base as the Operations Assessment Team Chief and leads a team of five operations analysts who assess and guide the employment of air power in the CENTCOM theater of operations.

MEGAN H. MACKENZIE

Megan MacKenzie is Professor of Gender and War in the Department of Government and International Relations at the University of Sydney. Her research is broadly aimed at reducing war; it bridges feminist theory, critical security studies, and critical/post-development studies. MacKenzie has contributed research on topics including sexual violence in war, truth and reconciliation commissions, military culture, images and international relations, and women in combat.

MICHAEL J. MAZARR

Michael J. Mazarr is a senior political scientist at the RAND Corporation. He came to RAND in November 2014 from the US National War College, where he was a professor and associate dean. He has worked at research institutes, including a decade at the Center for Strategic and International Studies and a period as President of the Henry Stimson Center; as a senior staffer on Capitol Hill; and as Special Assistant to the Chairman of the Joint Chiefs. He is a former Naval Reserve intelligence officer. He has worked on US defense policy, conventional force posture, nuclear weapons and deterrence, East Asia (especially the Korean peninsula), counterinsurgency, and counterterrorism.

JOHN MCCAIN

John McCain was a Vietnam War veteran and a six-term US senator from the state of Arizona, who served as ranking member and Chair of the Senate Armed Service Committee. He was also the Republican nominee for the 2008 presidential election. McCain graduated from the Naval Academy in 1958. He served as an aviator in the US Navy until 1981, fighting in the Vietnam War and spending more than five years as a prisoner of war. McCain earned the Silver Star, Bronze Star, Purple Heart, and Distinguished Flying Cross.

DANIEL H. MCCAULEY

Daniel H. McCauley is currently serving as a faculty member at National Defense University's Joint and Combined Warfighting School in Norfolk, Virginia. McCauley is a recognized expert in strategic foresight, design, and strategy and is a frequent presenter and guest panelist. McCauley spent twenty-five years in the US Air Force flying various aircraft as well as serving in US and NATO staff positions.

MICHAEL E. MCINERNEY

Lieutenant Colonel Michael E. McInerney commissioned from the United States Military Academy in 1999 as an armor officer. His operational assignments include deployments to the Balkans, Iraq, and Afghanistan. Following command of a tank company, he transitioned to the Force Management functional area. He has a master's degree in Public Policy from Duke University and served as an assistant professor in the Department of Social Sciences at West Point. He is currently attending the Air War College at Maxwell Air Force Base.

CHRISTOPHER D. MILLER

Lieutenant General Christopher D. Miller, US Air Force (Ret), is the Helen and Arthur E. Johnson Chair for the Study of the Profession of Arms at the US Air Force Academy Center for Character and Leadership Development. His active service included leadership as the Air Force's Deputy Chief of Staff for Strategic Plans and Programs, US Northern Command and NORAD's Director of Strategy, Plans, and Policy, and as deployed Commander for all Air Force operations in Afghanistan. He also commanded the Air Force's B-2 wing and B-1 bomber units and held a wide variety of positions in policy analysis, international relations, human resources, aviation, and academia. He was a 1980 distinguished graduate of the Air Force Academy and earned graduate degrees from the US Naval War College and Oxford University.

JAMES N. MILLER

James N. Miller is a senior fellow at the Harvard Kennedy School's Belfer Center for Science and International Affairs, where he leads a project on preventing war among great powers. Prior to his appointment at the Belfer Center, he worked as Under Secretary of Defense for Policy advising Secretaries Leon Panetta and Chuck Hagel, Principal Deputy Under Secretary of Defense for Policy under Secretary Robert Gates, and as senior staff for the House Armed Services Committee. He was awarded the Department of Defense's highest civilian award, the Medal for Distinguished

Public Service, four times. Miller received his PhD in public policy from the Harvard Kennedy School and was an assistant professor at Duke University.

JOHN A. NAGL

John Nagl is the ninth Headmaster of The Haverford School in Haverford, Pennsylvania, and a member of the Board of Advisors at the Center for a New American Security, of which he was previously president. Nagl has testified before the Senate Foreign Relations Committee and the Commission on Wartime Contracting and served on the 2010 Quadrennial Defense Review Independent Panel (the Hadley/Perry Commission). Nagl was a Distinguished Graduate of the US Military Academy Class of 1988 and served as an armor officer in the US Army for twenty years.

HENRY R. NAU

Henry R. Nau is Professor of Political Science and International Affairs at the Elliott School of International Affairs, George Washington University. Nau focuses on economic policy, foreign affairs and national security, and US politics. From January 1981 to July 1983, he served on President Reagan's National Security Council as Senior Director for International Economic Affairs.

RENÉE DE NEVERS

Renée de Nevers is Associate Professor in the Department of Public Administration and International Affairs at The Maxwell School at Syracuse University. Her current research focuses on great-power efforts to protect or manipulate sovereignty when confronted by new security challenges and the regulation and accountability of private military and security companies. She has been a research fellow at the Belfer Center for Science and International Affairs, Stanford University's Center for International Security and Cooperation, the Hoover Institution, and the International Institute for Strategic Studies, and was a Fulbright Scholar in Russia in 2011.

JOSEPH S. NYE, JR.

Joseph S. Nye is a Harvard University Distinguished Service Professor, Emeritus, and former Dean of the Harvard's Kennedy School of Government. His expertise resides in international relations and security, public leadership and management, and politics. He has served as Assistant Secretary of Defense for International Security Affairs, Chair of the National Intelligence Council, and Deputy Under Secretary of State for Security Assistance, Science, and Technology.

MICHAEL E. O'HANLON

Michael O'Hanlon is a senior fellow and Director of Research in Foreign Policy at the Brookings Institution, where he specializes in US defense strategy, the use of military force, and American national security policy. He co-directs the Security and Strategy team, the Defense Industrial Base working group, and the Africa Security Initiative within the Foreign Policy program. He is an adjunct professor at Columbia, Georgetown, and Syracuse Universities and a member of the International Institute for Strate-

gic Studies. O'Hanlon was also a member of the external advisory board at the Central Intelligence Agency from 2011 to 2012. He holds a doctorate from Princeton University in Public and International Affairs and has published extensively on defense strategy and policy.

MANCUR OLSON, JR.

Mancur Olson, Jr., was an American economist and social scientist who taught economics at the University of Maryland, College Park. His most influential contributions were in institutional economics and in the role that private property, taxation, public goods, collective action, and contract rights play in economic development. To help bring his ideas to the attention of policy-makers, Olson founded the Center for Institutional Reform in the Informal Sector, which was funded by the United States Agency for International Development.

SUE PAYTON

Sue Payton was United States Assistant Secretary of the Air Force (Acquisition) from 2006 to 2009. The owner and Chief Executive Officer of SCI Aerospace, Inc., she has more than thirty-seven years of experience working in senior industry and government positions in military services, defense agencies, coalition partners, the Joint Chiefs of Staff, the Office of the Secretary of Defense, the intelligence community, Congress, and universities. Her positions included Manager of Advanced Technology at Lockheed Martin, Director of the National Center for Applied Technology, and Deputy Under Secretary of Defense for Advanced Systems and Concepts. She is a frequent writer and innovator in the defense acquisition space.

DARYL G. PRESS

Daryl Press is Associate Professor of Government and the Dartmouth College Coordinator of War and Peace Studies at the John Sloan Dickey Center. His research and teaching focus on US national security policy, in particular the changing global balance of power, the evolution of technology and warfare, and the future of deterrence. Press has consulted for the US Defense Department for more than two decades, and he is a member of the US State Department's historical advisory committee.

THOMAS RID

Thomas Rid is Professor of Strategic Studies at Johns Hopkins University's School of Advanced International Studies. He is a recognized expert in cybersecurity, information security, and strategic and security issues. Rid testified on information security in front of the US Senate Select Committee on Intelligence as well as in the German Bundestag and the UK Parliament.

JOHN RILEY

John Riley is Professor of Political Science at the US Air Force Academy. He received his PhD in Political Science from George Washington University. His more recent research interests have focused on disengagement of rebel groups, prevention of radicalization among refugees, and the use of private military contractors. His work has been published in such venues as *Armed Forces & Society*, the

Wisconsin Journal of International Law, and the *Yale Journal of International Affairs*.

DAVID SACKO

David Sacko is Professor of Political Science at the US Air Force Academy, where he currently serves as Division Chief and Research Director. Since joining the Academy in June 2002, he has been Fulbright Scholar to the University of Warsaw and a Minerva Initiative funded scholar. Recent research interests include Russian and Central European security affairs, irregular warfare, and the effect of hegemonic governance on interstate conflict. He currently serves as Chair of the Advisory Board for the International Security section of the American Political Science Association.

BRANDON D. SMITH

Commander Brandon D. Smith is a 2002 graduate of the US Naval Academy and a Naval aviator, flying the MH-60S Seahawk through multiple squadron assignments. His shore assignments include the Navy Office of Legislative Affairs and the Joint Staff, J-3 directorate. He is a graduate of the Joint Combined Warfare School at the Joint Forces Staff College and has a Master of Public Administration from Old Dominion University. He currently serves as the Executive Officer for Navy Talent Acquisition Group Pittsburgh, where he oversees the recruitment of highly qualified men and women from Pennsylvania, New York, Maryland, and West Virginia for Naval service.

JAMES M. SMITH

James M. Smith is Director of the Air Force Institute for National Security Studies housed within the Department of Political Science at the US Air Force Academy. On active duty he served as an Air Force pilot and operational planner. He also served academic assignments at the Air Force Special Operations School, the Air Command and Staff College, and West Point's Department of Social Sciences, where he was also Associate Dean for Academic Research. Smith holds a bachelor's degree from the Air Force Academy, a master's degree from the University of Southern California, and a doctorate from the University of Alabama.

DON M. SNIDER

Don M. Snider is Professor of Political Science, Emeritus, US Military Academy at West Point, and currently serves as an adjunct research professor, Strategic Studies Institute, US Army War College. While teaching and mentoring future leaders for the Army, he led the Academy's effort, and more recently those of other services, to renew the study of military professions, their ethics, and their civil-military relations. He publishes and lectures extensively and in 2015 received the Morris J. Janowitz Lifetime Achievement Award from the Inter-University Seminar on Armed Forces and Society.

HEW STRACHAN

Sir Hew Strachan is the Bishop Wardlaw Professor at the St. Andrews School of International Relations. *Foreign Policy* magazine named him one of its global thinkers of 2012, he was knighted in the 2013 New Year's Honours, and he won the Pritzker Prize for Lifetime Achievement in Military Writing in 2016. He serves on the Chief of the Defence Staff's Strategic Advisory Panel and on the Defence Academy Advisory Board and is a specialist advisor to the Joint Parliamentary Committee on the National Security Strategy.

MICHAEL WESLEY

Michael Wesley is Director of the Griffith Asia Institute at Griffith University, Queensland. Wesley has published widely on the subjects of Asia-Pacific politics and security and Australian foreign policy. Formerly, he was Senior Lecturer in Political Science at the University of New South Wales and Assistant Director-General, Transnational Issues Branch, Office of National Assessments for the Australian government.

RICHARD ZECKHAUSER

Richard Zeckhauser is the Frank P. Ramsey Professor of Political Economy, Kennedy School, Harvard University. His contributions to decision theory and behavioral economics include the concepts of quality-adjusted life years, status quo bias, betrayal aversion, and ignorance (states of the world unknown) as a complement to the categories of risk and uncertainty. Apart from academics, Zeckhauser is a senior principal at Equity Resource Investments, a real estate private equity firm.

Index

Page references in *italics* indicate a figure; page references in **bold** indicate a table.